52

A-Z OF THE
GRAND NATIONAL

Th
s

Re

A-Z OF THE GRAND NATIONAL

The Official Guide to the World's Most Famous Steeplechase

John Cottrell and Marcus Armytage

highdown

A Racing Post company

Published in 2008 by Highdown,
an imprint of Raceform Ltd
Compton, Newbury, Berkshire, RG20 6NL

A catalogue record for this book is available from the British Library.

ISBN 978-1-905156-43-6

Designed by Adrian Morrish
Printed and bound in Great Britain by William Clowes Ltd, Beccles, Suffolk

Dedicated to the Memory of
Arthur 'Skerry' Butler and Arthur 'Jim' Pollard

THE AUTHOR

Born in Weston-super-Mare, John Cottrell entered journalism as a reporter with the *Bristol Evening Post* and later became a sports editor with Beaverbrook Newspapers. His 'obsessive interest' in the Grand National dates back to 1961 when he first wrote about the race for *Sports Illustrated*, and subsequently his many articles on racing have been syndicated worldwide. Besides ghost-written works for international sportsmen, his sports books include *Man of Destiny*, a biography of Muhammad Ali; *A Century of Great Soccer Drama*; and *The Punters' Guide to the Grand National*. His non-sporting works include *The World Stood Still*, a best-selling account of the assassination of President John F. Kennedy, biographies of Richard Burton, Laurence Olivier and Julie Andrews, plus various travel books.

THE EDITOR

Marcus Armytage has written a number of racing books including *Generous*, *Hell For Leather*, *Hands And Heels* and *Hot Cherry*. His work with the pen began with a racing column for the *Newbury Weekly News* and progressed to the *Racing Post*, spending a season and a half as Newmarket correspondent. Since 1993 he has worked as racing correspondent for the *Daily Telegraph* and, latterly, also for the *Horse & Hound*.

PREFACE

Here at last is a comprehensive and indispensable guide to the Grand National; a monumental work of reference designed to settle all questions relating to the world's most famous steeplechase, while at the same time capturing the race's extraordinary wealth of drama and romance, of heroic triumphs and heart-breaking failures.

With more than 600 entries, *The Official A-Z of the Grand National* records every aspect of the race, from its beginnings in 1839 until the present time. It provides portraits of all its leading protagonists – horses, riders, trainers, owners and officials. At the same time, by way of statistical analysis and noted changes in the course and handicapping, it contains valuable information to guide the would-be punter.

Which horse and which jockey have most often competed in the Grand National; and which have been most successful? Who have been the unluckiest losers? What have been the greatest gambles on the race? When were there instances of foul play? What tactics are most favoured by jockeys?

Which owner correctly foresaw his horse winning in a dream? Which lady owner attacked her jockey with an umbrella after he had remounted her horse three times to finish fourth and last? Which jockey, dubbed 'the kamikaze pilot', sustained more than a hundred fractures in falls at Aintree? Which winner followed his victory by appearing nightly on stage in a melodrama performed at London's Drury Lane Theatre? Which two horses won the National when making their first-ever public appearance over fences? Which horse and jockey have completed the National course in the second fastest-ever time but have never had it officially recorded?

What is the truth about *Moifaa*, the New Zealand 'starved elephant' who won in 1904 after reputedly being shipwrecked in the Irish Sea? Which jockey was correctly told, 'You'll only win if all the others fall down'? Which trainer, when asked by his jockey for advice, said, 'Keep remounting'? Which well-known tipster wrote in *The Sporting Life* that *Lord Gyllene* (the easy winner) "has as much chance of success as Ginger Spice joining a convent," and said of *Camelot Knight* (third-placed) that 'there is more chance of Anneka Rice finding the Holy Grail than this horse has finishing in the first dozen'?

The answers to all Grand National questions are to be found in this A-Z guide that is crammed with anecdotes, facts and figures to form the most complete record of the race which every year, uniquely for a single sporting event, commands an audience of more than 600 million television viewers around the globe.

AUTHOR'S NOTE

For nearly 150 years, a majority of racing historians recognised the Grand Liverpool Steeplechase, run on Tuesday, February 26, 1839, as being the first Aintree Grand National. More recently, however, research has presented evidence that the inaugural Grand Liverpool Steeplechase was held on February 29, 1836, at Aintree, and not at nearby Maghull as previously recorded.

Nevertheless, in this comprehensive record, we choose to continue to recognise the 1839 race as the year of the first Grand National – not because this conforms with traditional thought but because the earlier steeplechases held at Aintree were unworthy of being regarded as either 'grand' or 'national'. The 1836 steeplechase was a mere selling race and those held at Aintree in 1837 and 1838 involved only four and three runners respectively. In 1839, when Jem Mason won on *Lottery*, there were 53 entries, 17 starters and an estimated 40,000 attendance – a truly grand beginning.

FOOTNOTE

The following abbreviations appear:

a = aged
bd = brought down
F = fell
f = firm
gf = good to firm
g = good
gs = good to soft
hy = heavy
ko = knocked over
nq = not quoted
oh = out of handicap
ow = overweight
pu = pulled up
ref = refused
s = soft
ur = unseated rider

ABANDONED

Five times in the Second World War the Aintree Grand National was suspended, and three times in the First World War it was transferred to Gatwick. In the early years it was twice switched to a different day for bad weather. Yet remarkably – in the face of torrential rain, blinding snowstorms, thick fogs, animal rights demonstrations and bomb threats – the most famous steeplechase has only once been completely abandoned: in 1993 when the race was declared void after seven horses had covered the full course following a second false start.

However, abandonment for 49 hours (officially defined as a postponement) was necessary on Saturday, April 5, 1997, following telephone calls (received at 2.49 p.m. and 2.52 p.m.) warning that there was a bomb on the racecourse and that it would be detonated at 4.p.m. The Irish voice, speaking from a public phone-box and claiming to represent the IRA, gave no details of the bomb's location. But he used a recognised codeword, and the warning came only two days after IRA bomb threats had forced the closure of three motorways. It had to be taken seriously.

After the running of the 2.55 race, Aintree was placed on full security alert; and at 3.16 p.m. it was announced that everyone – more than 60,000 racegoers, plus officials, trainers, jockeys, press, catering staff etc. – had to leave the racecourse at once. The result was organised chaos – not least because some 6,000 cars and coaches had to be left on the course overnight and then properly searched before owners could collect them the following day.

So immediate was the order to exit that many jockeys on this bitterly cold afternoon had to leave still wearing their racing silks and breeches. Only one jockey, Jonathan Lower, was allowed back in the weighing room; he needed to recover his medication for diabetes. Meanwhile, the press and broadcasters had to abandon their valuable equipment. J.P. McManus, the legendary gambler, did not even have time to collect his betting cash left in a private box. The Tote was forced to leave a reported half-million pounds in cash inside the course, the money being removed under police escort the next day. One Tote girl, however, enterprisingly walked out on the Saturday with £7,000 in her knickers rather than leave the cash unguarded in her booth.

At this time more than 50 horses remained in the stables. They should have been left unattended. However, Phil Sharp, the lad responsible for *Suny*

Bay, defiantly and dutifully stayed behind with a colleague. They not only took charge of feeding and watering until stable staff were allowed back just before 6 p.m.; more importantly they freed some horses from their tack which might otherwise have led to a serious injury (one horse, for example, was found to have already got his legs hopelessly entangled in his reins). Of the 38 Grand National runners, a few remained at Aintree overnight, seven were ferried to stables at Haydock Park and others faced a long drive home.

The 150th Grand National was now rescheduled for 5 pm. on Monday. It would be the only race of the day and entrance would be free. The postponement put the horses under greater stress and, indeed, two horses – *Belmont King* and *Over The Stream* – would be withdrawn from the race. (The former, happily, won the Scottish National two weeks later).

Meanwhile, Saturday had seen a mad scramble for taxis and hotel rooms. Sports halls, schools and churches provided overnight shelter for more than 2,000 people. Everton Sports Centre alone took 500 who were given bedding and fed on burger and chips; and most admirably many hundreds of warmhearted Liverpudlians opened their homes to stranded racegoers and jockeys. Later a plaque would be put up by Aintree Racecourse Company Ltd to express gratitude for the generous hospitality of local residents on the night of April 5, 1997.

In this respect, there was justification for talk of how 'the Dunkirk spirit' had prevailed. But there was a darker side: a mindless minority of racegoers pulling fences apart and littering the course with debris, including glass from broken bottles; angry scenes as people scrambled for taxis and – with a mobile-phone blackout over the area – hammered on the few available telephone boxes; and more chaos on the Sunday when there was a long, unexpected delay in allowing drivers to retrieve 7,000 stranded cars and coaches.

The reorganisaton of the race set the biggest challenge for Charles Barnett, managing director of Aintree racecourse, and his staff. By Monday mountains of litter had to be cleared, vandalised fences and running rails repaired. And much work remained in the aftermath. Thousands of items of lost property were to be claimed. Some £320,000 had to be paid out as Saturday tickets were returned for a 50 per cent refund.

One on-course bookmaker would later claim that

his bag, containing £2,000, had disappeared over the lost weekend. However, for the betting industry in general, the rescheduling came as a huge relief since an estimated £70 million had been laid out on the race with the bookies expected to take a £5 million profit. Moreover, on the Monday, many betting shops enjoyed a greater volume of business than on the Saturday.

Some 20,000 racegoers turned up for the Monday race, all being subject to a body search before being allowed to enter. This time no cars were allowed into the racecourse car parks. The Princess Royal returned for the race. Prime Minister John Major now also attended, and TV coverage, beginning at 4 p.m., commanded an audience of some 12 million. A few minutes before the race two more bomb warnings were received, but this time the caller stated where the bombs had been placed, and nothing was found there.

Thirty-six horses made the line-up. A few had had their prospects marginally improved by a delay which had seen the course trampled by thousands of racegoers and the ground made still firmer by drying conditions. But some, most notably the strongly fancied *Suny Bay*, were positively disadvantaged by the faster going. The grey would finish runner-up, albeit beaten a full 25 lengths by *Lord Gyllene* who, faced with a less than two-hour journey to his home stable, had been relatively untroubled by the postponement.

Remarkably, unlike the Cheltenham Gold Cup, the Grand National has never surrendered completely to severe weather – not even in 1901 when, faced with a raging snowstorm, all the jockeys unsuccessfully petitioned for a postponement. In 1955, it was generally expected that it would be abandoned since much of the course resembled a quagmire. Controversially, after an 11 a.m. inspection, the stewards elected to go ahead but with the elimination of the Water Jump at the heart of the most waterlogged area. Thirteen of the 30 starters completed the course and there were no serious injuries.

Similar conditions threatened in 1994 when Aintree took heavy snow and 27mm of rain on the eve of the race. An early morning inspection was called and the decision to go ahead was vindicated when, shortly before the race, the skies cleared and the course was bathed in brilliant sunshine. Again, in 2001, at a time when much racing had been lost in the battle to avert the spread of foot-and-mouth dis-

ease, the race was threatened by the fall of 17mm of rain in the preceding 24 hours. This time a few critics – trainers and jockeys not among them – argued passionately that the race should have been abandoned. Yet this was never officially considered and, though there were only four finishers, two of them remounted, the extremely soft ground ensured a slow pace and a cushion for fallers; and again there were no noteworthy injuries to horse or rider.

Certainly, any run-of-the-mill meeting would have been abandoned with such boggy conditions. But such drastic action, purely because of the state of the ground is not to be lightly taken when, as in 2001, you have 52,000 people at the course and some 500 million viewers eagerly anticipating the race. *See also:* Void National; Postponements.

ABBOT, Terence

Irish professional jockey who rode *Abd-El-Kader* to Grand National victory – by just 'half a neck' – in 1851. It was Terry Abbot's good fortune to get the ride in place of the relatively inexperienced Chris Green who, on his Aintree debut in 1850, had ridden the bay gelding to win in record time. Judging his forward move to perfection, Abbot drove his diminutive horse into the lead at the last fence, then held on to gain the verdict in the closest of National finishes so far.

Altogether Abbot rode in seven Nationals, starting with three outsiders who failed to finish: *Frederick* (1847), *Saucepan* (1848) and *The Iron Duke* (1849). In 1850 he had a more sporting chance – on six year old *Farnham*, a 15-1 shot. Completing the course for the first time, he was the fifth of only seven finishers in a National that had the then record number of 32 starters.

In 1853 when *Abd-El-Kader* was bidding for a hat-trick, there was again a jockey change – Denis Wynne taking the ride and having to pull up after one circuit. The following year, reunited with the dual winner, Abbot brought him home the fifth of seven finishers. On his last National appearance, in 1854, he failed to finish on the 50-1 outsider, *La Gazza Ladra*.
See also: Abd-El-Kader.

ABD-EL-KADER

The first horse to win the National twice – in successive years (1850-51) – and the first to break ten minutes for the race. On his Aintree debut, the eight year old bay gelding was rated a 'no-hoper', not even quoted in the betting. For all his successes in Ireland, he was judged too small (just under 15.2 hands) to cope with the National fences; also he was opposed by the last two winners, *Chandler* (1848) and the bay *Peter Simple* (1849), and he had a rider – Chris Green, son of a Norfolk farmer – who was a newcomer to the race.

It was a National in which only seven of 32 starters (then a record number) managed to finish. But 'Little Ab', as he came to be popularly known, jumped like a stag throughout, made relentless progress from the second Becher's onwards, and – in a pulsating finish – won at his first attempt in record time (9min 57.5sec), by one length and three from *The Knight of Gwynne* and *Sir John* respectively. The former was the first to be runner-up in successive Nationals.

The following year, raised only 6lb by the handicapper (from 9st 12lb to 10st 4lb) 'Little Ab' started as the 7-1 joint second favourite with *Sir John*, also from Ireland, and a point behind *Rat-Trap*, the mount of Jem Mason, the celebrated jockey who had won the first-ever National on *Lottery*. Ridden by a more experienced jockey, Irishman Terry Abbot, he was held up on the first circuit and then progressed to figure in an even closer finish, prevailing by just 'half a neck' from the mare *Maria Day*, with *Sir John*, two lengths back, again third.

This unprecedented success represented a triumph of talent-spotting on the part of Henry Osborne, of Dardistown Castle, Co. Meath. In 1827, when travelling on the Shrewsbury to Holyhead mailcoach, he occupied the box-seat and was attracted by the action of a handsome brown mare in the team. He bought her for 40 guineas, named her *English Lass*, and trained her very successfully for racing in Ireland. Subsequently, she produced nine foals, the eighth and only useful one being the diminutive *Abd-El-Kader*, by the club-footed stallion *Ishmael*.

Abd-El-Kader was trained and eventually owned by Osborne's son, Joseph. Editor of *The Horsebreeder's Handbook* and a noted gambler, Osborne Jnr won plenty of races with him in Ireland. But, despite a success at Worcester, the little chaser made little impression in England prior to his Aintree debut. In contrast, when he was seeking a National hat-trick in 1852, he was so respected that he was anchored by a full stone increase in the weights.

Yet again having a change of jockey (Denis Wynne), 'Little Ab' was this time pulled up after one circuit. In 1853, dropped 8lb and reunited with jockey Abbot, he was leading by some 100 yards at the Water. But there was nothing left in the tank and the eleven year old finished fifth, with only seven of 21 starters completing the course.

The following year 'Little Ab' was a nonrunner, having been injured on the journey from Dublin. Finally, in 1858, after a four-year gap, he was brought back by a new owner for one more appearance – at the ripe old age of 16. As on his first triumph, he was ridden by Chris Green. Racing over treacherous ground in a snowstorm, he fell at the second. Remarkably, though his National days were over, the old boy went on to win several more races in Ireland before being retired.

See also: Abbot, Terence; Osborne, Joseph; Gambles.

ADELPHI HOTEL, The

The history of the Grand National is inextricably linked with that of Liverpool's Adelphi Hotel, a great Victorian pile rebuilt in luxurious splendour in 1912 to cater for passengers from large cruise liners, and more recently nominated by novelist Beryl Bainbridge as her favourite building – 'magnificently grand like an ocean liner'. (A not inappropriate description since its magnificent Sefton Suite is a replica of the first class smoking lounge of the steamship *Titanic*).

From the very beginning the hotel profited greatly from the introduction of steeplechasing to Liverpool; and for many years the hotel was to be the scene of riotous post-National celebrations. Here, in pre-Second World War days, the huge lounge would be decked out in a recreation of the Aintree course, with alcoves decorated to resemble the fences; and, in the dining room, each table was provided with chocolate horses carrying the colours of the first three finishers. Then, towards the end of the celebration dinner, young bloods would leap, whooping, over the jumps. And by three in the morning the high jinks were known to climax with drunken revellers commandeering the waiters' large silver trays and tobogganing down the main staircase (the 'Adelphi Cresta') into the hotel lobby.

In its heyday, as many as 1,850 guests would gather for the traditional Grand National Dinner followed by a gala ball. At times celebrations got

A

seriously out of hand. One year the younger set used upturned six-foot-long tables as well as trays for a succession of toboggan runs, and subsequently the son of a famous lord was presented with a 300 guineas bill for damages.

For the staff a most memorable night came on the Friday of March 23, 1934, when the eccentric 28 year old millionairess Dorothy Paget (wearing an evening dress reputedly made out of surplus curtain material) celebrated the record-breaking run of her wonder horse, *Golden Miller*. She had reserved the top table overlooking the ballroom for her 50-odd guests, and her arrival was greeted by Joe Orlando's band striking up a version of 'Here Comes The Bride' – an ironic choice for such a dedicated spinster. Her frail father, Lord Queensborough, made a long speech before proposing a toast to 'My daughter, her horse *Golden Miller* – and the British Empire'. Meanwhile, behind the scenes, her secretaries were preparing to hand out a £5 note to each and every one of the Adelphi's employees. A fiver was as much as some 500 revellers had each paid to attend the dinner-dance.

In the 1950s, in the wake of post-war austerity, the hotel again became the scene of riotous parties. Revellers swung on chandeliers and one year they seized on shoes left outside 84 rooms and threw them out of upstairs windows. A special National night dinner is still held at the Adelphi, and it remains the custom for the head chef to create a display of chocolate horses and riders, with the placed jockeys given their correct colours. But nowadays a mere 350 guests attend the dinner which is an infinitely more staid affair; and no longer are there riotous celebrations.

The demise of Adelphi celebrations on the grand scale came in 1947 as a result of Mrs Mirabel Topham's decision to switch the Grand National from Friday to Saturday. Since the National was now held on the last day of the Aintree meeting, there was no longer an inducement for racegoers to stay on for the night after the big race. Furthermore, from the 1980s onwards, the hotel's association with the Grand National was strongly challenged by the Holiday Inn built near the racecourse. However, in 1988, following an extensive refurbishment, the Adelphi's post-race ball was revived with the aid of sponsorship by the Variety Club of Great Britain.

In modern times the most chaotic night in the history of the hotel, now named the Britannia Adelphi, came on Saturday, April 5, 1997, when IRA bomb threats caused the postponement of the National for 49 hours. Like all hotels in Liverpool, it was besieged by stranded racegoers. Every vacant room was taken, plus floor space in the function rooms. Jockeys came, too, some – still in their silks – abandoning their starvation diets to booze, dancing at the disco, and then crowding into the hotel's basement sauna in the middle of the night. It was not, however, the Adelphi's finest hour, with as much as £45 being charged for a mattress on the floor.

For the record, only one horse is known to have stayed at the Adelphi. Three weeks before the 1954 Grand National a 21 year old golden palomino stallion checked in – registering with a pencil clutched between his teeth. It was 'Trigger' of Roy Rogers film fame.

See also: Trudgill, Robert

AGE (Horses)

Youngest

Five horses – all five year olds – tie for the honour of youngest Grand National winner: *Alcibiade* (1865), *Regal* (1876), *Austerlitz* (1877), *Empress* (1880) and *Lutteur III* (1909). Their record will not be equalled. The last five year old to run in the National was *Grakle* in 1927, and from 1931 the race was restricted to horses of six years and over. In turn, six year olds were banned from 1987 but then readmitted from 1999 onwards. Since 1940 all winners have been at least eight years old.

Oldest

The oldest winner is *Peter Simple* (1853) who was 15 years of age when he triumphed for the second time. He competed again at 16 but, being cruelly burdened with top weight of 12st, he failed to finish. Only one other 15 year old has even managed a place: the great *Manifesto*, who finished third in 1903 despite carrying 12st 3lb. The following year, at 16, *Manifesto* became the oldest of all finishers – tenth under Ernie Piggott, grandfather of Lester.

Since the Second World War the Grand National has most often been won by nine year olds – 22 wins compared with 12 by ten year olds, 11 by eight year olds, and eight by horses aged 11 and 12.

Following modifications to the fences in 1990 no one age-group has clearly dominated, though this period has produced only one 12 year old winner (*Royal Athlete*, 1995) and none under eight years old. Overall, modern history is strongly against National contenders under eight and over eleven.

Six year olds

Whereas six year olds won 13 Grand Nationals in the 19th century, they were only twice successful in the 20th century. This reduction may be partly attributed to the fact that they have been entered in progressively fewer numbers; also there was a period (1987 to 1998) when the race was only open to horses of seven years or more. Nevertheless, it remains significant that one has to go back as far as 1915 to find the last six year old winner (*Ally Sloper*).

In 1999, when the race was reopened to six year olds, Martin Pipe entered three: *Cyfor Malta*, *Farfadet V* and *Tamarindo*. Only the latter, a French product, made it to the line-up. He had been pulled up on his last four runs and now he fell at the first Becher's. Again, in 2000, Pipe had the only six year old runner: *Royal Predica*. He fell at the first fence.

Pipe's other six year old entry in 2000 was the supremely promising *Gloria Victis* who had impressed so greatly in winning the Racing Post Chase that the handicapper had lumbered him with a massive 11st 10lb for the National. But tragically he was doomed never to make it to Aintree, having suffered a fatal fall when challenging strongly two out in the Cheltenham Gold Cup.

Even now, after thousands of rides, Tony McCoy remembers the loss of *Gloria Victis* as the saddest moment in his career. Moreover, at the time his despair soon turned to anger as he received letters suggesting that it was cruel to subject such a young novice to the rigours of the supreme championship of steeplechasing in which there was no weight allowance for age. He countered: 'To me it didn't matter if he was a five year old or a ten year old, he was that good.'

But are six year olds really mature enough for such stern challenges as the Gold Cup and the National? True, French imports like *Gloria Victis* have experience of fences from an earlier age than chasers prepared in other countries. And since they tend not to sustain their standard of performance over so many years it is logical to strike early while they are in outstanding form. The fact remains that six year olds continue to disappoint in the National.

In 2001 Pipe ran two: *Kaki Crazy* and *Exit Swinger*. The former fell at the third fence, the latter was brought down at the sixth, Becher's Brook.

In 2002 he had five six year olds among his 16 National entries. Two made it to the 40-strong field: *Majed* falling at the 22nd, *Iris Bleu* falling at the fifth. None appeared in 2003 and the following year there was only one among 122 entries: the French-bred *Kelami* who, in December, had won for Francois Doumen over three miles at Kempton and was now in the handicap proper on 10st 7lb. He was in the rear when brought down at the first. In 2005, the sole six year old starter, French-bred *L'Aventure*, finished 15th. It was the first time in 65 years that a six year old had even completed the course, the last having been *Luxborough*, 11th in 1940.

Seven year olds

Seven year olds have won at least 22 Grand Nationals, nine of their successes being recorded in the 20th century. But despite this reasonable score, the fact remains that they have never been successful since *Bogskar*'s victory in 1940. True, seven year olds have finished second on six occasions since that only wartime National but it is noteworthy that one has not even gained a first-four place since 1971 when *Black Secret* was beaten a neck by nine year old *Specify*.

This modest record can be partly explained by the fact that they have been hugely outnumbered. Between 1960 and 1999 there were only 34 seven year olds among 1,443 National runners. Whereas a record ten had appeared in the 1947 National (the best finishing tenth), only four ran in the whole of the 1980s and just seven in the 1990s. So far 11 have appeared in this century, but there was not even one in 2002 and 2007.

More pointedly, however, the decline may be attributed to an advance in training methods and wider recognition of the fact that, in general, seven year olds are not quite mature enough for a marathon test over the National fences. John Lawrence (now Lord Oaksey) was inclined to that view as long ago as 1963 following his experience on seven year old *Carrickbeg*, who went down by just three-quarters of a length as runner-up to the 66-1 outsider *Ayala*. He noted that *Carrickbeg* was a much improved horse as an eight year old and he genuinely believed that he would have been capable of winning the 1964 National but for sustaining an injury at Sandown two months before the race.

The evidence of results elsewhere suggests that it is the special demands of the Aintree National that finds seven year olds out. Elsewhere they seem to cope much more easily. For example, they have an outstanding strike-rate in the Irish Grand National run over a mile less in distance and they have run creditably in the Cheltenham Gold Cup, competing with older horses on equal terms. But Aintree is another matter. In 1977, after winning the Gold Cup by six lengths, seven year old *Davy Lad* crashed out at the first open ditch and was retired after breaking down the following season. In 1994 *Young Hustler* finished a good third in the Gold Cup only to fall at the eleventh at Aintree, albeit being unluckily brought down when the riderless *Ushers Island* fell directly in front of him.

It is perhaps noteworthy that the First Lady of Aintree, trainer Jenny Pitman, who always made the welfare of her horses the top priority, was reluctant to subject seven year olds to the hurly-burly of the National. She was only once tempted to do so: running *Team Challenget* in the 1989 National after he had finished third in Cheltenham's three-mile Kim Muir Memorial Handicap Chase. He ran so creditably that, coming to the 27th fence, his rider Mike Bowlby thought he was in with a chance. But then, under heavy going, the seven year old began to fade and finished ninth. Bowlby commented: 'He will be better next year'.

From 1997 onwards, no one challenged with seven year olds more often than the champion trainer Martin Pipe. But they all failed: in 1997, *Evangelica*, the last of 17 finishers; 1998, *Damas*, ref. 11th, and *Decyborg*, pu. 27th; 1999, *Eudipe*, fell fatally at the second Becher's; 2001, *Tresor de Mai*, fell 2nd; 2003, *Majed*, a distant 12th; *Iris Bleu*, pu. 16th; 2004, *Jurancon II*, fell 4th, *Montreal*, fell 6th; 2006, *Whispered Secret*, ur. 1st.

To be sure, these runners included several no-hopers; *Damas*, *Decyborg* and *Majed* were 200-1 shots and *Whispered Secret* a 100-1 outsider. On the other hand, three – *Eudipe*, *Iris Bleu* and *Jurancon II* – were leading fancies and one had the benefit of the most successful of all jump jockeys. A.P. McCoy had high hopes on *Jurancon II*, one of four 10-1 co-favourites. But, like three other seven year olds in the race, he failed to get round. Indeed, since 1997 only one of 16 (*Majed*) has managed to finish.

Eight year olds
With 19 victories, eight year olds have the third best record in the Grand National. Fourteen of those wins came in the 20th century, but in the past three decades their successes have been few and far between – two wins in the 1970s, just one in the 1980s, and one again in the 1990s. However, in 1992, eight year olds most unusually filled the first three places with *Party Politics*, *Romany King* and *Laura's Beau*. And ten years later they provided the winner (*Bindaree*) and the runner-up (*What's Up Boys*).

Nine year olds
The first-ever Grand National of 1839 was won by a nine year old (*Lottery*) and in later years this age group began to achieve the highest strike-rate, providing at least 43 winners, with 33 coming in the 20th century. Nine year olds scored a hat-trick (1910-12) and won four successive Nationals (1948-51). *Lord Gyllene's* success in 1997 ended an unusual eight-year run without a nine year old winner. Then, in 1999, nine year olds truly reasserted themselves, taking the first three places by way of *Bobbyjo*, *Blue Charm* and *Call It A Day*. The following year they again provided the winner (*Papillon*) and the runner-up (*Mely Moss*), and they had another winner with *Hedgehunter* in 2005.

Ten year olds
Nineteen Grand Nationals have been won by a ten year old. From 1861 to 1879 the age group went through 19 years without providing a winner, and none figured in the nine Nationals between 1909 and 1920. However, it is perhaps noteworthy that since 1990, when fence modifications made the course less challenging, there have been five ten year old winners, three of them – *Monty's Pass* (2003), *Numbersixvalverde* (2006) and *Silver Birch* (2007) – coming within a five-year period.

Eleven year olds
In the early history of the National 11 year olds had a dismal record – no more than four known wins in the 19th century, and just four more successes in the first seven decades of the 20th century. But then came three wins in the 1980s; and, since the easing of fences (notably Becher's) in 1990, the age group has provided four winners, including the fastest of them all, *Mr Frisk*.

Twelve year olds
Just ten Grand Nationals are known to have been won by 12 year olds, and when Fred Winter tri-

umphed by ten lengths on *Kilmore* in 1962, the race had its oldest winner since 1923 and the first recorded success by a 12 year old since *Chandler* 114 years earlier. Remarkably, 12 year olds have scored eight times since then (most famously with *Red Rum*'s third victory in 1977) and have gained six other places. In 1989 they provided the winner and runner-up (*Little Polveir* and *West Tip* respectively) and the following year *Durham Edition* finished second. Subsequently there have been two winners of that age: *Royal Athlete* (1995) and *Amberleigh House* (2004), with one (*Royal Highlander*, fourth in 2000) running into a place.

Thirteen year olds
Only two 13 year olds are recorded as Grand National winners: *Why Not* (1894) and *Sergeant Murphy* (1923). Moreover, since 1923, only three have ever been placed: *Overshadow* (third, 1953), *Eternal* (fourth, 1964) and *Rondetto* (third, 1969). Subsequently, the best performance by a 13 year old has been the fifth place gained in 1994 by the 100-1 outsider *Fiddlers Pike*, brilliantly ridden by the extraordinary 51 year old Mrs Rosemary Henderson.

In the light of this record it is a wonder that any 13 year olds are still entered. Yet three appeared in 1999 and four in 2001. All failed to finish. In 2005, when three out of four failed to get round, the exception was the defending champion, *Amberleigh House*, who laboured home in tenth place. It was the same story the following year with a trio of 13 year olds – *First Gold*, *Prince Ri* and *Native Upmanship* – being 100-1 non-finishers.

Fourteen year olds
A 14 year old has never won the Grand National. Indeed, throughout the history of race, only seven have ever completed the course – the best results being achieved by past winners: the great *Manifesto* (third in 1902), *Why Not* (fifth, 1895) and *Sergeant Murphy* (fifth, 1924). The last to complete the course were *Schubert* (1948) and *Clyduffe* (1949), finishing 13th and 10th respectively. In fairness, it should be noted that very few 14 year olds have run in the race. Only one appeared in the 1950s, three in the 1960s, and since then just four have competed: *Rondetto* (1970), unseated rider at the third; *Go-Pontinental* (1974), a faller; *Into The Red* (1998), pulled up at the 17th; and *Amberleigh House* (2006),

pulled up before the 21st. No runner over fourteen has been recorded since 1929 when 15 year old *Hawker*, a 200-1 outsider, was pulled up in a record 66-strong field.

AGE (Jockeys)
Youngest
The youngest jockey to ride a winner of the Grand National is Bruce Hobbs who was 17 years and three months old in 1938 when he triumphed by a mere head on *Battleship*, the diminutive American chaser trained by his father Reg. Joe Tizzard was also 17 – just one week older than Hobbs – when he rode in the 1997 Grand National. Having ridden fewer than 15 winners under Rules he was granted a special licence by the Jockey Club to take part, riding *Straight Talk*, who had unseated the great Tony McCoy at Aintree the previous November. Following postponement of the National forced by IRA bomb scares, the luckless teenager had a five-hour journey home in the back of a horsebox, sitting on an upturned bucket. Remarkably, on the Sunday he rode three point-to-point winners in Dorset. Then he went all the way back to Aintree for what was to be a tragic National debut. *Straight Talk* broke a leg in falling at the 14th fence and had to be put down.

Oldest
The oldest jockey to ride a winner of the Grand National was Dick Saunders, aged 48 when he scored on *Grittar* (1982), so eclipsing the previous benchmark belonging to Tommy Pickernell, who had been 41 when winning on *Pathfinder* in 1875. The oldest rider to appear in the Grand National is Tim Durant, a 68 year old American grandfather when he finished 15th (remounted) on *Highlandie* in 1968. Another grandfather – amateur John Thorne – was 54 years old when he finished four-lengths second on his own *Spartan Missile* in 1981. The Duke of Alberquerque was 56 when he suffered serious injuries in falling off his *Nereo* in the 1976 National. To his fury, he was debarred the following year by a new ruling that amateur riders over 50 must pass a pre-race medical examination. Amateur David Pitcher, having been unseated in two previous Nationals, was 53 years old in 1989 when he rode his own *Brown Trix*, one of two horses to suffer a fatal fall at the first Becher's. Mrs Rosemary Henderson set the ladies' record in 1994 when, aged 51, she came home fifth on her own *Fiddlers Pike*.

A

AGED

A blanket expression – no longer applied – to denote racehorses that are more than six years old. In the 19th century many Grand National runners, including a few winners, were simply listed as 'aged'.

AINTREE RACECOURSE

The home of the Grand National is located on the A59 at Ormskirk Road, Aintree, in the northern suburbs of Liverpool, some six miles from the city centre. The racecourse, occupying some 250 acres, has two distinct, left-handed chasing circuits. The Mildmay Course, opened in 1953, is almost rectangular, nearly one and a half miles round with sharp turns, a 260-yard run-in and steeplechase fences constructed in orthodox style from birch. The roughly pear-shaped Grand National course – less sharp but far more demanding – is the longest in Britain: almost two and a quarter miles round, completely flat, with fences built from thick hawthorn and dressed with spruce, fir or gorse, and most of them involving a drop with the landing side marginally lower than the take-off-side.

In the 19th century many steeplechases were initiated by publicans and tradesmen seeking to draw crowds and promote business in their vicinity. William Lynn, the landlord of the Waterloo Hotel in Liverpool, was responsible for introducing racing to the village of Aintree (Anglo-Saxon for 'one tree') on land which he had leased from the Earl of Sefton. The foundation stone of a grandstand was laid on February 7, 1829, by Lord Molyneux, and five months later the first meeting – for Flat races only – was held. Experiments with hurdle racing followed, and on February 29, 1836, the first Liverpool Grand Steeplechase was staged there.

Contrary to most record books and the writings of many leading historians, this steeplechase – won by The Duke, ridden by Captain Martin Becher – arguably merits recognition as the inaugural Grand National. However, that distinction has been popularly awarded to the more well-documented Liverpool Grand Steeplechase held at Aintree on February 26, 1839, and won by Lottery, ridden by Jem Mason.

In 1839, the race was over 'four miles across country', much of it run over ploughed fields and with the ruling that 'no rider to open a gate or ride through a gateway, or more than 100 yards along any road, footpath or driftway'. There were 29 jumps, the only severe tests being two formidable fences with brooks and a 4ft 8in high stone wall that had to be negotiated only once. From 1885 onwards the course was fully turfed and largely railed. Today the race covers four miles 856 yards over an oval circuit, with 16 fences, all to be jumped twice with the exception of The Chair (15th) and Water Jump (16th) which are missed out on the second circuit. After the 30th fence there is a gruelling 494-yard run-in to the finish.

In 1915 the racecourse was handed over to the War Office for the duration of hostilities. Similarly, after the 1940 National, it was requisitioned by the military, serving as a depot for Army trucks and eventually housing as many as 16,000 troops, mainly Americans, in the build-up to the D-Day invasion of mainland Europe. Racing was resumed in 1946 and three years later Aintree came under new ownership when Messrs Topham Ltd, the lessees for almost a century, purchased the land for a reputed £275,000 from the Earl of Sefton. As managing director, following the death of her husband, the forceful Mrs Mirabel Topham was responsible for many innovations – among them the addition of the Mildmay Course in 1953, soon followed by the introduction of a motor-racing circuit of such quality that it was to host a European Grand Prix and five British Grands Prix, the first of which was won by Stirling Moss in 1955.

In December, 1973, the racecourse was sold for £3 million to Liverpool property developer Mr Bill Davies. In danger of extinction, the Grand National was saved in 1975 when Ladbrokes undertook to manage and administer Aintree for seven years at a rent of £250,000 a year. Course facilities were much improved and eventually, after years of grave uncertainty, Aintree's future was secured in 1983 when it came under the ownership of the Jockey Club, being administered by its subsidiary, Racecourse Holdings Trust.

From 1972 until 1992 the three-day Spring Festival was the only meeting staged at Liverpool all season. But then the November meeting was revived, its highlight being the Becher Handicap Chase over three miles three furlongs of the National course. At the Spring meeting National fences, including Becher's, Valentine's and The Chair, are tackled in the John Hughes Memorial Chase (formerly the Topham) and the amateurs' Fox Hunters' Chase, both over two and three-quarter miles.

A

In the early years Aintree racecourse was reached by railway and by paddleboat via a nearby canal. It is still accessible by rail with a station just one minute from the main entrance. But the vast majority of racegoers now arrive by car or coach while a privileged minority journey by air, either disembarking from helicopters on a special six-acre enclosure or landing at John Lennon Airport, 20 minutes drive away. In recent years huge improvements to the racecourse have included the building of the Queen Mother Stand (opened, 1991) and the Princess Royal Stand (1998). Giant Star Vision screens in some public enclosures provide a full view of the Grand National, and numerous tents, boxes, chalets and hospitality suites are available for the more affluent.

Shortly before the 2006 National, phase one of Aintree's two-year £35 million redevelopment programme – including a magnificent new press room, a new winner's enclosure and new weighing room – was completed; and in 2007 the second phase saw the opening of two new, five-tier, interlinked grandstands, named Derby and Sefton, with upper floors overlooking the National start and giving unprecedented views over the entire course.
See also: Lynn, William; Topham, Mirabel; Davies, William; Fences; Course Changes.

ALBERQUERQUE, Duque de

No amateur rider has exemplified the courage and determination of National Hunt jockeys more dramatically than Beltran de Osorio y Diez de Rivera, the 18th Duque de Alberquerque, a Spanish nobleman who dreamed of Grand National glory from the age of eight when he first saw the race on a cinema newsreel. Seven times, as a rider-owner, he appeared in the National line-up, suffering an appalling catalogue of injuries but returning again and again with a stubborn resolve that some critics thought to be bordering on madness. He had his last Aintree ride at the age of 57, and even then only new medical regulations prevented him coming back for more.

Born in 1919, the Duke of Alberquerque bore a title dating back to 1464 and among his ancestors was an ambassador to the court of King Henry VIII. He was 33 when he began the pursuit of his magnificent obsession. Having ridden in French steeplechases, the tall Spaniard made his Aintree debut in the 1952 Grand National, putting up 10lb overweight on his own eight year old *Brown Jack III*,

trained by Peter Cazalet. Avoiding the mayhem that saw ten fallers at the first, he remained close up until the sixth where a heavy fall left him concussed and hospitalised with cracked vertebrae. It was 11 years before he was seen at Aintree again, this time on a horse with proven ability to get round the course.

Irish-bred *Jonjo*, originally a 370-guineas yearling named after his owners, John O'Hagen and Joe Thompson, had fallen in the 1960 National. The following year, as the 7-1 favourite, again ridden by Pat Taaffe, he had finished seventh. The duke had then bought the 11 year old to make a serious bid for National glory in 1962. Unfortunately, his strong contender was ruled out that year by serious leg trouble.

A major operation, performed by the French vet Esouard Pourot, saved *Jonjo* for racing. But he was 13 when he finally returned to Aintree in 1963 and now went off as a 66-1 outsider. Steering an outside course, the Spanish nobleman completed the first circuit in fine style and was well up with the leaders before being unluckily brought down at the 21st. For once he escaped with only cuts and bruises.

In 1965 the duke took a nasty fall at Valentine's first time round when riding his *Groomsman*, a 100-1 shot who had failed in the National one year before. This time he was taken to Walton General Hospital with a broken leg – the 22nd fracture of his race-riding career. Yet, undeterred, he came back in 1966 with his 12 year old *L'Empereur*, trained by Toby Balding. Again he was on a 100-1 outsider and, though prominent early on, his horse was short on stamina and had to be pulled up at the 26th.

Seemingly, as six years passed by, Aintree had seen the last of the indomitable Spaniard who by now had sustained more than 30 fractures on European racecourses. But then, in 1973, aged 54, he came back on his latest purchase, seven year old Spanish-bred *Nereo*, prepared by the great Fred Winter. Again his horse had to be pulled up, this time at the Canal Turn but only because he had unluckily broken a stirrup leather eight fences earlier.

One year later *Nereo* was a 100-1 chance, with a derisory 66-1 on offer just for completing the National course. The bookies were hardly being generous. Two weeks before the race the duke had had 16 screws removed from a patched-up leg; and just one week before, he had broken his collarbone. Under present-day regulations, with every jockey being required to produce his medical record book at a race

17

A

meeting, he would never have been allowed to ride at Aintree.

Yet the duke amazed everyone, not only completing the course for the first time but also finishing eighth behind *Red Rum* in a 42-strong field. He was overjoyed and could reflect that they might have done even better if he had been as fit as his horse. Thus his hopes were high for a fresh challenge in 1975. But again, just one week before the National, he suffered a bad fall. It was another broken leg and this time he had to accept the view of trainer Fred Winter that it would be madness to ride.

Still he would not abandon his dream of National glory. In 1976 he returned on his *Nereo*, again priced at 100-1. He rode brilliantly to stay on board when sandwiched between horses at the seventh, and was heading the field when they came back on to the racecourse. But then, at the 13th, he was thrown, landing so heavily and amid flying hooves that he had to be rushed, still unconscious, to the intensive care unit of Walton Hospital. His horrendous injuries included a fractured right thigh bone, fractured vertebrae and seven broken ribs. By his own reckoning, he had now sustained 107 fractures at Aintree.

Unbelievably, this most persistent of owner-riders prepared to compete in the 1977 Grand National. But now the authorities decided it was time to draw the line. The Jockey Club had ruled that no amateur over 50 could ride without first passing a medical examination. Despite having trained hard to achieve peak fitness, the 58 year old Spaniard found himself banned from race-riding in Britain. 'I couldn't understand it,' he said later. 'It was my body, my horse and my responsibility.'

Outraged and despondent, he was a mere spectator from Fred Winter's box when his replacement, Robert Kington, figured prominently on *Nereo* before falling at the second Becher's; and in 1978 he saw his 12 year old *Nereo* complete the course under Mark Floyd to be the 14th of 15 finishers. The daredevil duke's extraordinary association with the National was finally over. But he continued to be remarkably active and, at the age of 72, he completed the 721-mile pilgrimage to Santiago da Compostella – on foot. He died two years later in Madrid. *See also:* Balding, Gerald Barnard 'Toby'.

ALCIBIADE

The first five year old and the first French-bred horse to win the Grand National. Moreover, aston-ishingly, this brave chestnut achieved his greatest steeplechase triumph in 1865 when having his first-ever race over fences.

Alcibiade – by *The Cossack* out of *Aunt Phillis* – had originally been brought over from France by Count Lagrange. Unimpressive on the Flat, he was eventually claimed for £400 after winning a selling race as a three year old. His new owner was a famed sportsman of the day: Old Etonian Benjamin John ('Cherry') Angell, soon to be a founder member of the National Hunt Committee.

Ostensibly, Mr Angell was taking a wild gamble in choosing the Grand National for his five year old's first appearance in a steeplechase. But he was a shrewd operator; and, as reflected by *Alcibiade*'s 100-7 place in the market, his young novice had been heavily backed by connections. Indeed, unknown to the general public, the newcomer had taken readily to the jumps and in private trials he had easily outclassed stablemate *Bridegroom* who had finished fourth and second in the Grand Nationals of 1861 and 1862 respectively.

But there was nothing to commend him to punters. Immaturity and inexperience seemed against him; furthermore he was to be ridden by an amateur – Captain Henry Coventry of the Grenadier Guards – who was likewise making his Grand National debut. For many spectators, their unfounded doubts about the captain's riding ability were reinforced by the way he took *Alcibiade* on the long, wide way round the first circuit.

Positions, however, changed dramatically on the second circuit as a string of runners were pulled up and *Merrimac*, far out in front, began to fade. By the last fence it had become a two-horse race between *Alcibiade* and *Hall Court*, a six year old, also ridden by an Army captain. In an extraordinary neck-and-neck duel, they were inseparable all the way up the straight; and, to all but those standing alongside, they were still inseparable at the finish. The judge proclaimed *Alcibiade* the winner by a head. Emblematic, the 1864 winner and now favourite, was 50 yards back in third place.

The victorious Capt. Coventry never raced in the National again. But *Alcibiade* was brought back five more times. In 1866, raised 12lb to an anchor weight of 12st 2lb, he threatened to be a contender when falling at the second Becher's. He did not compete in 1867 but came back in the next three years to finish third, fourth and eighth respectively, on the first

18

two occasions being ridden by the colourful Colonel 'Curly' Knox of the Scots Guards. Finally, in 1871, the first-time National winner went off as a 100-I outsider and failed to finish.

See also: Coventry, Captain Henry; Tempest, Captain Arthur Cecil.

ALDANITI

The 11 year old chestnut gelding who, in 1981, scored the most emotive victory in Grand National history. The fact that this success provided a fairy-tale ending to rider Bob Champion's heroic conquest of cancer was enough to ensure its place among the most moving and unforgettable of all sporting triumphs. It was made even more miraculous by virtue of the fact that the horse, as well as the jockey, was making a comeback against all the odds.

Bred by Mr Thomas Barron at the Harrogate Stud in Co. Durham, *Aldaniti* was by *Derek H*, a tough handicapper on the Flat, out of the undistinguished mare *Renardeau*. His name had been created by Mr Barron out of the first two letters of each of his grandchildren's names: Alastair, David, Nicola and Timothy. He was still unraced when, in May, 1974, he was sent to the Ascot Bloodstock Sales as a four year old and bought by trainer Josh Gifford for 4,100 guineas. Eight months later, much to the surprise of everyone, *Aldaniti* started his racing career by easily winning an Ascot novices' hurdle at 33-1 with Champion in the saddle. Immediately he was sold by the Giffords to their neighbouring clients, Nick and Valda Embiricos. But there were no more wins over hurdles and, early in 1976, the gelding finished a race lame. He needed to be fired on his forelegs and was off the racecourse for more than a year.

Reintroduced as a chaser, *Aldaniti* made a most promising start over fences, scoring three wins and finishing third in the 1977 Hennessy Cognac Gold Cup. Already Champion was predicting that he would one day win the Grand National. But then again he was found to be lame, this time with two pieces of bone chipped off his pastern near the fetlock joint on his right hind leg. Now he was out of action for seven months.

After a preliminary race in December, 1978, *Aldaniti* again showed considerable promise when he finished a distant third in a snowswept Cheltenham Gold Cup, followed by a close-up second in the Scottish Grand National. Meanwhile, however,

Champion had learned that he had cancer which required immediate courses of chemotherapy treatment. In fighting to survive, his one great motivation was the cherished dream of riding *Aldaniti* in the 1980 Grand National.

It was not to be. In November, while still undergoing treatment, Champion went to Sandown to see *Aldaniti* being ridden by Richard Rowe in his first run of the season. To his dismay, the horse was pulled up lame near the finish. Yet again he had broken down – and on the same off-fore leg as before. This time he was so badly crippled that Josh Gifford believed he would never race again.

As in 1978, *Aldaniti* was restricted to his box at the Embiricoses' Barkfold Manor Stud where for many months he was patiently nursed by the head lady groom, Beryl Millam, and her assistants. By December, 1980, he had recovered sufficiently to be returned to Findon for serious training; and providentially, that same month saw Champion so restored to professional fitness that he was voted by racing journalists the Amoco National Hunt Jockey of the Month.

In February, the two ex-invalids were reunited for the Whitbread Trial Handicap Chase at Ascot. It was intended to be a gentle warm-up in preparation for the Grand National; and *Aldaniti*, at 14-1, was the outsider of eight runners. But after being settled at the rear of the field, the 11 year old, showed such irrestistible form that, without being hard ridden, he went on to win by four lenghts.

Aldaniti came out of that race so well that a challenge for the Cheltenham Gold Cup was now clearly within his compass. To Champion's huge relief, owner Nick Embiricos, ever supportive of his jockey's ambition, ruled against it. The Grand National would remain the one big objective – a decision soon vindicated when he was allotted 10st 13lb by the handicapper, a sporting weight and one that would not commit his jockey to drastic fasting.

In December, the owner had backed *Aldaniti* in the National to the tune of £250 each-way at 66-1. Now, on the great day, his horse was backed down to 10-1, second only to *Spartan Missile*, the 8-1 favourite, and ahead of 11-1 *Rubstic*, the 1979 winner. Over-eager at the start, *Aldaniti* gave Champion his most anxious moment when he stood off too far at the first and nosed the turf on landing. He scraped untidily over the second, but thereafter got his act together and by the 11th – sooner than the jockey

A

would have wished – he had surged to the front. Early on the second circuit he had challengers for the lead; each time he jumped superbly and was quicker away from his fences.

When second placed *Royal Mail* bungled his jump at the penultimate fence, it seemed that the one serious threat was out of contention. *Aldaniti* safely fiddled the last, but so often leaders had been outpaced over the long, testing run-in; and now, out of the blue, the favourite was finishing with an extraordinary flourish. *Spartan Missile*, owned, trained and ridden by John Thorne, a 54 year old grandfather, was closing on him with every stride until, over the last 100 yards, driven with all the strength that Champion could muster, *Aldaniti* proved the stronger. To tumultuous applause, with strong men weeping with joy, the courageous, champion duo achieved their epic victory by four lengths, with *Royal Mail* a further two lengths back in third.

Aldaniti was brought back for one more Grand National challenge, only to fall at the first fence. He was then immediately retired – but only from racing. For years to come he was to help raise millions on behalf of the Bob Champion Cancer Trust by way of special public appearances and not least, in 1987, by walking from Buckingham Palace to Liverpool. On that long walk, which netted some £820,000, the 17 year old gelding had 250 different riders (one for each mile), including many celebrities, all of whom had guaranteed a minimum of £1,000 in sponsorship. It climaxed on Grand National day, with Bob Champion riding the last mile on to Aintree racecourse. Stabled at Barkfold Manor, home of the Embiricos family at Kirdford in Sussex, *Aldaniti* died peacefully in 1997, just over a week before he was due to lead a parade of ten past winners as part of the 150th Grand National celebrations. He was aged 27 and was buried in the stables' grounds.
See also: Champion, Bob; Gifford, Josh.

ALLY SLOPER

Six year old winner, in 1915, of the only wartime Aintree Grand National. His victory gave both rider Jack Anthony and trainer Aubrey Hastings their second success in the race. It also marked the first time that there had been a National winner owned by a woman: Lady Nelson, widow of Sir William Nelson who had won the Ascot Gold Cup with *Tangiers*.

Ally Sloper – Lincolnshire-bred, by *Travelling Lad* out of *Sally In Our Alley* – had fetched a mere 25 guineas at Doncaster yearling sales. The buyer, Mr Sugden E. Armitage, then sold him on to his neighbour at Wantage: Herbert Randall, the former jockey who had won three of the 1902 Classics on the immortal *Sceptre*; and in turn Randall sold the gelding to Lady Nelson for £700. Results quickly proved it to be a bargain price. On the eve of the 1914 National, *Ally Sloper* won the Stanley Steeplechase at Aintree; and as a five year old he also won the Becher and Valentine chases over the great Liverpool fences.

In the 1915 National, however, his jumping was far from secure. A too early take-off landed him atop the second fence and Jack Anthony only kept his seat with the aid of his brother Ivor who reached out from aboard his own mount, *Ilston*, to give him a steadying hand. Then, at the Canal Turn, he stumbled on landing, leaving Jack hanging desperately around his neck.

By the end of the first circuit, *Ally Sloper* was well behind the leaders. But his jumping was now improving and he made steady progress through a greatly reduced field. Only *Balscadden* was going better, but he fell two fences out, enabling *Ally Sloper* to take the lead at the last and hold it to win by two lengths from *Jacobus*.

In 1916, with Aintree requisitioned by the Army, the first of three wartime substitute steeplechases was held at Gatwick over a course of four miles 856 yards. But here the fences were undemanding, and, with jumping ability of minor value, *Ally Sloper*, a 9-2 favourite who had been raised 21lb in the weights, could finish only eighth. One year later, he achieved third place at 20-1, and in 1918 he was a faller. The gelding was ten years old when the Grand National returned to Aintree in 1919. There, ridden by Ivor Anthony, he failed to finish.
See also: Anthony, Jack.

ALVERTON

The Grand National has witnessed many great triumphs and tragedies; and in the latter category none is more poignant than the sad fate of the nine year old chestnut geldng *Alverton*. When he made his Aintree debut in 1979 he was a winner of 22 races – as many on the Flat as over jumps – and was strongly fancied to become the first horse to achieve the Cheltenham Gold Cup-Grand National double since the great *Golden Miller* in 1934.

Trained by Peter Easterby, *Alverton* had won the

Gold Cup in a snowstorm by 25 and 20 lengths from *Royal Mail* and *Aldaniti*, who two years later were to finish third and first respectively in the National. However, despite the big winning margin, he had had a hard-fought race – strongly contested by *Tied Cottage*, a last fence faller – and was going on to Aintree only 16 days later.

After long deliberations, it had been decided to run him because he was seemingly so well recovered from Cheltenham. Also, on 10st. 13lb., he could never be more generously handicapped. Indeed, he looked thrown-in at the weights; and, again partnered by champion jockey Jonjo O'Neill, he went off the 13-2 favourite.

Being up with the leaders, *Alverton* escaped the chaos at The Chair where two loose horses veered across the fence putting out nine contenders in the ensuing pile-up. The favourite continued to make smooth progress and by the time he approached Becher's for the second time he was still cantering and looking like a certain winner. But then, after jumping so immaculately, he had a fatal, inexplicable lapse, ploughing straight into the fence and breaking his neck on hitting the ground beyond. Very possibly he had suffered a heart attack when trying to take off.

See also: O'Neill, Jonjo.

AMATEUR RIDERS

The Grand National is one of the few major sporting events in which amateurs have proved capable of competing against professionals with some chance of winning. In this, they have been successful on 40 occasions, though only five times since the 1946 resumption of the race after the Second World War.

Three riders share the record for the most wins (three) by an amateur: Thomas Pickernell, alias 'Mr Thomas' (on *Anatis*, 1860, *The Lamb*, 1871, and *Pathfinder*, 1875); Tommy Beasley (*Empress,* 1880, *Woodbrook*, 1881, and *Frigate*, 1889) and Jack Anthony (*Glenside*, 1911, *Ally Sloper*, 1915, and *Troytown*, 1920).

Three amateurs have scored two wins apiece: Alec Goodman (*Miss Mowbray*, 1852 and *Salamander*, 1866); John Maunsell Richardson (*Disturbance*, 1873, and *Reugny*, 1874) and Ted Wilson (*Voluptuary*, 1884, and *Roquefort*, 1885).

From 1839 to 1842 the Aintree Grand National was officially declared as being for 'gentlemen riders'. In fact, on its first running, no more than seven or eight of the 17 riders were true amateurs, and both the winner and runner-up were ridden by professionals. In 1843, when the steeplechase was made a handicap, the reference to 'gentleman riders' was dropped. But, as always, a clear distinction continued to be made between amateurs and professionals, the former being named with the prefix 'Mr' or whatever higher title they held.

During the 19th century, the honours were fairly even, the paid riders winning 35 Grand Nationals to 26 by the amateurs, four of whom were serving Army officers. Since then the professionals have increasingly asserted their dominance, winning all but 14 of the Nationals in the 20th century. The only amateur winners since 1946 are: Captain Bobby Petre on *Lovely Cottage* (1946), Tommy Smith on *Jay Trump* (1965), Charlie Fenwick on *Ben Nevis* (1980), Dick Saunders on *Grittar* (1982) and Marcus Armytage on *Mr Frisk* (1990). However, in this post-war period, another five amateurs have finished second: A.S. ('Phonsie') O-Brien on *Royal Tan* (1951); John Lawrence (later Lord Oaksey), beaten by three-quarters of a length on *Carrickbeg* (1963); Jim Dreaper, beaten only a neck on *Black Secret* (1971); John Thorne on *Spartan Missile* (1981); and Colin Magnier, three-quarters of a length second on *Greasepaint* (1983).

Remarkably, amateur-ridden horses have achieved the fastest and third fastest Grand National winning times: *Mr Frisk* with Marcus Armytage, and *Grittar* with Dick Saunders respectively. In more recent years another amateur (Chris Bonner) has most notably managed to finish twice in a place: in 1995 winning a hard-fought battle for third place on *Over The Deel* at 100-1 and the following year finishing fourth on 33-1 chance *Sir Peter Lely*, only a short head behind third-placed *Superior Finish*.

Three times the Grand National has been won by an amateur making his one and only appearance in the race: Fred Hobson on *Austerlitz* (1877), Lord Manners on *Seaman* (1882) and Dick Saunders on *Grittar* (1982).

AMATEUR TRAINERS

While many amateur jockeys have competed in the Grand National, amateur trainers are now few and far between. They are called permit-holders and can train only horses belonging to themselves or their immediate family. Most notably, in the modern era,

A

Frank Gilman, a Leicestershire-based farmer, was responsible for *Grittar*, the 1982 winner. The 2001 victory of *Red Marauder* is officially credited to permit-holder and owner Norman Mason. In reality, however, preparation of the winner was essentially the work of Mason's stable jockey and assistant, Richard Guest.

AMBERLEIGH HOUSE

Grand National winner in 2004 when, as a 12 year old veteran, he provided classic vindication of the old cliché 'horses for courses' and demonstrated to perfection the merits of the old tactical maxim: 'hunt round on the first circuit and ride a race on the second'. Having won and twice finished second in the Becher Chase, no horse in the 39-strong field had a finer record over the big Aintree fences; and, patiently ridden on the day, he made relentless progress from Becher's second time around, then stayed on strongly to take the lead in the last 100 yards and win by three lengths and two from *Clan Royal* and *Lord Atterbury* respectively.

With this victory – coming 27 years after *Red Rum*'s third and final triumph – 73 year old Donald 'Ginger' McCain joined the great Fred Rimell as the only trainer to have sent out four Grand National winners. And Irish-born jockey Graham Lee achieved the enviable record of having finished third and first in just two National appearances.

It was way back in 1983 that McCain had a few drinks in a Southport wine bar with Liverpool-born John Halewood and then joined him in watching a video of *Red Rum* winning the National. Afterwards Halewood said that one day they would find another winner. Indeed, this had been his ambition ever since 1977 when, as a young boy accompanied by his father, he had visited Aintree for the first time. On that occasion they did not have enough money to gain admission to the main enclosures and viewed *Red Rum*'s third victory from the embankment at the Canal Turn. Times had changed. Halewood Jnr was now a hugely successful businessman.

The first McCain-Halewood challenge for the National gave no hint of their success to come. In 1986, shortly before the race, they acquired eight year old *Dudie* who, one year earlier had bowled along in front before falling at the 19th. Now, as a 100-chance, he unseated Kevin Doolan at the third and, after being remounted, he fell at Becher's. Years passed and, while McCain was unsuccessful with

seven more National outsiders, multi-millionaire Halewood prospered greatly by way of Halewood International, one of the major British independent producers and importers of speciality drinks.

Then, in 2000, McCain saw *Amberleigh House* win a race at Punchestown. Bred in Ireland – by *Buckskin* out of *Chancy Gal* – the gelding was scoring his fifth victory in three years; and he had never won over more than two and a half miles. Yet the canny trainer judged him to be a National horse in the making. On Halewood's behalf, he bought the eight year old out of Michael Hourigan's yard in Limerick for £75,000.

When *Amberleigh House* arrived from Ireland at three o'clock in the morning, he looked so meek and bedraggled that McCain thought they had delivered the wrong horse. Subsequently, he showed nothing special when tried over three miles, finishing a remote seventh at Haydock and being pulled up at Uttoxeter. Thus, with strong doubts about his stamina, he went off as a 150-1 outsider in the 2001 Grand National.

As it happened, *Amberleigh House*'s National debut was totally inconclusive since this was the year of near-unraceable conditions, when only four horses finished, two of them remounted. He was hit broadsides by *Paddy's Return*, the blinkered, riderless rogue who also put out eight other runners when veering across the Canal Turn; and he suffered a deep cut to his off-hind, with such persistent bleeding that he needed to be transferred to the Leahurst Equine Hospital at Neston, Cheshire.

The following November, again ridden by Warren Marston, he proclaimed his real potential when he jumped 22 of the National fences in winning the Tote Becher Chase at 33-1. But then, much to the trainer's chagrin, he was allotted only 9st 6lb for the 2002 National, meaning that 34 withdrawals were needed to guarantee him a run. McCain had expected a higher weight in view of *Amberleigh House*'s proven form over the Aintree fences. He bitterly deplored the presence of 'a string of no hopers' among the National's record 144 entries and argued that any horse that had won over the course should be given 10st. The result was that his big hope missed the cut as the fourth of four reserves. Instead he ran in the Topham Chase and finished ninth.

Two weeks later *Amberleigh House* won a chase over an extended three miles at Bangor. Then, in November, 2002, after a warm-up hurdle race at Haydock and third place in a chase at Ascot, he returned to Aintree where he finished a distant but gallant second in the 15-runner Becher Chase, giving 8lb to the winner *Ardent Scout*. Significantly, he was 17 lengths ahead of third-placed *Blowing Wind,* who had been third in two Grand Nationals, and fallers in the race included the last National winner *Bindaree* and the much-lauded *Moor Lane*.

'He will be even better with the extra mile in the National,' said McCain. And so it proved. This time *Amberleigh House* made the line-up on 10st 4lb. Going off unfancied at 33-1, he galloped into contention at the 24th, the Canal Turn, and was going so well three out that for a moment the trainer thought he might win on the 30th anniversary of *Red Rum's* first victory. He was second coming to the last but, unfortunately, though admirably ridden by newcomer Lee, he could not remotely match the finishing pace of *Monty's Pass*, and in the last few strides he was overhauled by *Supreme Glory*, the 12 lengths runner-up. With admirably absurd modesty, McCain remarked, 'If he had had a proper trainer he would have won.'

Owner John Halewood felt that *Amberleigh House's* Grand National chance had come just two years too late. But after a long layoff the 11 year old came back as strong as ever in November, 2003. That month he finished fourth in a chase at Ascot, then returned to Aintree where, after leading at the last in the Becher Chase, he was beaten only a short head by *Clan Royal* who had a 7lb advantage. This time McCain was to be well satisfied when the National weights were framed. *Amberleigh House*, allotted 10st 7lb, was generally 25-1 ante-post but in the trainer's view he should have really been 'a very short-priced favourite'. A further 3lb rise in the weights did not diminish his chances. He was now conceding only 5lb to *Clan Royal*, one of the National's four 10-1 co-favourites.

The race began discouragingly for Mr Halewood. His other runner, the six year old French-bred *Kelami*, trained by Francois Doumen, was brought down at the first. Then *Amberleigh House* was badly baulked, meeting so much interference that he virtually had to jump Becher's from a standstill. 'I promise you,' said Lee, 'eight out of ten horses wouldn't have been able to do it.' From that point on, wisely as it proved, the jockey resigned himself to riding a patient, waiting race. Clawing his way back on the second circuit, *Amberleigh House* was lying fourth

at the last. There, the long-time front-runner *Hedgehunter* fell, and then the leading *Clan Royal*, whose jockey had lost his whip four out, gave away vital ground in wandering to the left and having to be hauled back to negotiate the Elbow.

Racing, as always, with a strand of *Red Rum's* mane stitched into his browband, *Amberleigh House* became only the third 12 year old to win the National since Rummy's triumph in 1977. It was essentially a family triumph with all the McCains playing a part – Ginger being ably supported by his wife Beryl, by son and assistant trainer Donald riding the gelding in all his work, and daughter-in-law Sian as the dedicated groom.

Following his victory there was hopeful talk of bringing *Amberleigh House* back for one more tilt at the National which, if successful, would have made him only the third teenage winner in the history of the race and McCain the only trainer ever to have taken the prize five times. Once again, he first returned to Aintree for the Becher Chase in November, 2004, and this time, on a top weight of 11st 10lb, conceding 24lb to winner *Silver Birch*, he finished running on strongly, a most respectable fifth. The following February he had a useful warm-up, finishing fourth over an extended two and a half miles at Wetherby; and three days later, when the National weights were announced, McCain declared himself well pleased with the allotted 11st, a rise of just 4lb. 'We've got a winning weight,' he boomed.

Early in March, in his last prep race, *Amberleigh House* did no more than finish in his own time over an inadequate three miles at Doncaster. Yet still he remained as short as 10-1 for the National despite the facts that no winner had carried as much as 11st since 1988 and no 13 year old had won since 1923. Furthermore, no runner had scored back-to-back victories since *Red Rum* in 1974. The stats proved a fair guide. The old boy drifted out to 16-1 on the day and, never in contention, finished tenth.

In October, 2005, after a half-year rest, he began his last campaign with two runs over inadequate distances, being outpaced in a three-mile handicap chase at Chepstow and in a two-and-a-half-mile listed chase at Wetherby. As usual he then ran well in the Becher Chase over the Aintree fences, being in with every chance coming to the last. But thereafter the 13 year old was outpaced, finishing a respectable seventh – 22 lengths ahead of another and much younger former National winner, *Bindaree*.

A

Although a 14 year old has never won the National, the irrepressible McCain was still saying that *Amberleigh House* would 'take a lot of beating' in the 2006 race. But, in reality, his 50-1 odds were more than generous. Never in real contention, he was pulled up before the 21st fence and so began his well-earned retirement.
See also: McCain, Donald; Lee, Graham.

AMBUSH II

In 1900, six year old *Ambush II* became the first horse to carry the royal colours to victory in the Grand National. He was owned by Edward, Prince of Wales and his success marked the beginning of an extraordinary royal racing year as the prince went on to Triple Crown glory with his *Diamond Jubilee*'s winning of the 2,000 Guineas, the Derby and St Leger.

Ambush II was bred in Ireland, from the 1874 Irish Derby winner *Ben Battle* (the sire of *Bendigo* and grandsire of the great *Manifesto*) out of *Miss Plant*. Remarkably, as a two year old, he failed at auction to reach the reserve of a mere 50 guineas. But later his potential was recognised by Mr G.W. 'Tommy' Lushington, a prominent amateur rider-turned-trainer, who picked him out when asked by Lord Marcus Beresford to find a chaser fit to race for the prince. The purchase price had risen to 500 guineas.

As a four year old, *Ambush II* began his royal racing career by winning a four-mile maiden plate in Ireland; then made such progress as a chaser that he was entered for the National in the following year. The big jump in class appeared merited when, in February, 1899, the youngster was a comfortable winner of the Prince of Wales Steeplechase at Sandown – beating, among others, *The Soarer* and *Drogheda*, both former Grand National winners. On his Aintree debut he went off the third favourite, behind *Gentle Ida* and the 1897 winner *Manifesto*.

It was a most promising National debut by the five year old, finishing seventh in the race won for the second time by *Manifesto*. The following year, though raised more than a stone in the weights, the royal runner was made the 4-1 second favourite to win the first National of the 20th century – marginally behind *Hidden Mystery* and two points ahead of *Manifesto*, now 12 years old and set to carry a seemingly impossible 12st 13lb. Again he was to be ridden by the versatile Algy Anthony, who had won the 1899 Irish Derby.

There were only 16 starters and this field was quickly reduced at the first fence where an outsider bolted off the course and the Irish six year old *Covert Hack* was a faller, Significantly, the latter, a stablemate of *Ambush II*, ran on riderless, harassing the leaders and causing the favourite to fall when they met that same fence a second time. Briefly, beyond Valentine's, *Ambush II* lost the lead to *Manifesto*, but from two fences out he asserted his 24lb advantage and held on comfortably to win by four lengths and a neck from *Barsac* and *Manifesto* respectively.

It was three years before *Ambush II* reappeared in the National, now as the first runner owned by a reigning monarch, King Edward VII. But this time it was his turn to be burdened with the top weight of 12st 7lb. In the circumstances, he ran brilliantly to be in contention approaching the last; and when the Duke of Westminster's strong running *Drumree* collapsed on the flat – seemingly seized with a fit of staggers – another royal victory looked very possible. But then, uncharacteristically, *Ambush II* blundered at the final fence and fell, leaving the race at the mercy of *Drumcree*, a three-lengths winner from *Detail* with *Manifesto* staying on for a distant third place.

Ambush II was made the 7-2 favourite the following year, even though he was again on top weight, dropped only a pound. This time he fell at the third fence. It was his fourth and final National. Early in 1905 he trailed home last in a chase at Kempton Park and then, while being galloped in preparation for Aintree, he burst a blood vessel and died. Desperate to have a runner in the forthcoming National, the King bought the 1904 winner, *Moifaa*, as a replacement.
See also: Anthony, Algernon.

AMERICANS

Two Americans have ridden winners of the Grand National: Tommy Smith on *Jay Trump* (1965) and Charlie Fenwick on *Ben Nevis* (1980). There have been three American-bred winners: *Rubio* (1908), *Battleship* (1938) and *Jay Trump*.

Americans who have owned winners of the Grand National: Stephen Sandford (*Sergeant Murphy*, 1923); Charles Schwartz (*Jack Horner*, 1926); Mrs Florence Ambrose Clark (*Kellsboro' Jack*, 1933); Mrs Marion du Pont Scott (*Battleship*, 1938); John K. Goodman and Ronald B. Woodard

(*Team Spirit*, 1964); Mrs Mary Stephenson (*Jay Trump*, 1965); Thomas McCoy (*Highland Wedding*, 1969); Raymond Guest (*L'Escargot*, 1975); Redmond C. Stewart, Jnr (*Ben Nevis*, 1980); Mrs Lois Duffey (*Mr Frisk*, 1990); and Betty Maxwell Moran (*Papillon*, 2000).

In 1968 the 68 year old American Tim Durant became the oldest rider to appear in the race. The only American lady to ride in the National: Mrs Joy Carrier on her husband's *King Spruce* in 1983. At 28-1 *King Spruce* was then the shortest-ever priced National runner to be ridden by a woman. The nine year old fell at the first Becher's.

See also: United States; Maryland Hunt Cup.

ANATIS

In winning the 1860 Grand National by half a length, ten year old *Anatis* provided a second success for owner Mr Christopher Capel of Prestbury House, near the Cheltenham course, who had scored only two years earlier with his *Little Charley*. It was also a first victory for the extraordinary amateur rider Thomas Pickernell who, under the pseudonym of 'Mr Thomas', was destined to ride in 17 Nationals, winning three and three times finishing in a place.

Anatis – a bay mare by *King Dan* out of *Johnstown Lass* – made her National debut, along with 'Mr Thomas', in 1859 when she finished fifth at 25-1. One year later, having been raised only 6lb to a mere 9st 10lb, she was backed down to 7-2 favouritism. Like *Little Charley*, she was trained by William Holman, and the fact that she had not raced once in the interim prompted many punters to regard her as 'a good thing' who had been specially laid out for the race.

In fact, Holman had chosen not to to risk *Anatis* over fences for a full year because she suffered from a weakness in her forelegs. Back at Aintree, 'Mr Thomas' carefully nursed the mare round in mid-division for much of the first circuit, then made rapid progress to take second place behind *Xanthus* at the Water Jump. Two fences out they moved into the lead but now came a breathtaking late challenge from the entire *Huntsman* who had made a remarkable late run since his blunder at the second Becher's.

From the last fence *Anatis* and *Huntsman* were locked in a neck-and-neck duel that was only resolved near the end of the run-in when Pickernell flourished his whip for the first time, spurring the

mare home to a half-length victory, with *Xanthus* six lengths back in third.

The rider of *Huntsman* was Captain Thomas Manners Townley, not long since returned from the Crimea where he had seen action with the 10th Hussars at the siege of Sebastopol. After the race, and for years to come, he insisted that he would have won the National but for his misfortune in losing both stirrup irons at the second Becher's. 'Mr Thomas', for his part, was equally adamant that *Anatis* was a worthy winner.

Raised a further 8lb, *Anatis* at 4-1 was again the National favourite in 1861. She was well placed when, late on the first circuit, she was brought down by a faller. The following year, under the new ownership of Sir E. Hutchinson, but still ridden as always by 'Mr Thomas', she came back for her fourth and last National. There were only 13 starters, the smallest field since 1841. But again, most harshly, the handicapper had raised the 12 year old 8lb. Never able to go the pace, *Anatis* had to be pulled up, the race being won her old rival *Huntsman*, 3-1 favourite and now ridden by a most experienced professional, Harry Lamplugh.

See also: Pickernell, Thomas; Townley, Captain Thomas Manners.

ANCHOR BRIDGE CROSSING

The intersection made by the Melling Road between fences 12 and 13.

See also: Melling Road.

ANGELL, Benjamin John

A founder member of the Grand National Hunt Committee, which in 1866 became officially responsible for administering and governing steeplechasing. Behind the scenes he had worked tirelessly towards the creation of an efficient ruling body, and as a leading light on the new committee he played a major role in improving the image and organisation of National Hunt racing.

Mr Angell, popularly known as 'Cherry', adapted from his nickname of 'Cherubim' at Eton College, was a prominent raceowner who had a runner in nine of the 11 Grand Nationals between 1861 and 1871. His first entry, *Bridegroom*, was fourth and runner-up in 1861 and 1862 respectively. Three years later, most remarkably, he won the National with the French-bred *Alcibiade*, a £400 bargain buy who was a five year old having his first-ever run in

A

a steeplechase. His prize chaser fell in 1866 but was third in 1868, fourth in 1869 and eighth in 1870. *See also:* Alcibiade; National Hunt Committee.

ANGLO

Shock 50-1 winner of the 1966 Grand National – astonishingly by 20 lengths from the Scottish hope *Freddie* who, following his narrow defeat the previous year, went off at 11-4, the shortest-price favourite since *Golden Miller* 31 years before. Both horse and rider (Tim Norman) were making their first appearance in the race, and their victory gave Fred Winter his second successive National winner in just two years as a trainer.

Like Winter's 1965 winner, *Jay Trump*, *Anglo* – an Irish-bred chestnut by *Greek Star* out of *Miss Alligator* – had raced without distinction on the Flat as a two year old. Originally he was named *Flag of Convenience* and ran in the colours of Major-General Sir Randle Feilden, who became Senior Steward of the Jockey Club. The general eventually let him go, bought out of a seller by a farmer for a mere 110 guineas. However, within two years *Anglo* had greatly improved in conformation, so much so that he fetched 2,500 guineas when purchased by trainer Ryan Price on behalf of Mr Stuart Levy. His new owner was a partner with Nat Cohen (owner of the 1962 National winner *Kilmore*) in Anglo-Amalgamated Films – hence the choice of his new name.

Under the tutelage of Ryan Price, *Anglo* won over hurdles and the following season scored four successive wins in novice chases. But then, in 1964, having been disqualified from training, Price passed the six year old gelding on to his long-time friend Winter, the man who had ridden his 1962 National winner, *Kilmore*.

Anglo raced creditably in his first season with Winter, but then went off the boil with a long losing run. Indeed, apart from winning a very ordinary three-mile chase at Windsor, he did nothing to command respect on his way to Aintree in 1966. Thus, out of the handicap proper, he was one of 25 runners in a 47-strong National field to race off the minimum 10st. However, as Winter rightly judged, his unfancied runner was to prove well suited by a marathon trip.

Unusually, possibly uniquely, no fewer than 42 runners survived as far as The Chair. Thereafter, the number of fallers readily mounted; and, after lying inconspicuously in mid-division, *Anglo* moved re-lentlessly through the field, finally catching the long-time leader *Forest Prince* at the second last. From then on, his superior stamina told to devastating effect. *Freddie*, the hot favourite, moved into second place on the run-in but, with an extra stone and a half to carry, he was engaged in a hopeless pursuit.

Having won comfortably on his National debut, *Anglo* came back in 1967 with an extra 15lb to carry, and with a new owner (Mr J.R. Gaines) and a new jockey (Harry Beasley). He was pulled up in the chaos created by the riderless *Popham Down*. It was his last National, the race being won the following year by his half-brother, *Red Alligator*.

See also: Norman, Tim; Winter, Fred; Red Alligator.

ANIMAL RIGHTS

Since Aintree was once the scene of bear-baiting and cock-fighting, it was only to be expected that animal rights activists would turn their attention to the Grand National. Indeed, concern over the welfare of horses in the National was voiced from the race's very beginning in 1839 when one Liverpool newspaper savaged the marathon chase as 'an affront to humanitarian principles'. In 1870, after *The Colonel* had beaten *The Doctor* by a neck in the most thrilling finish yet seen, the RSPCA took out a writ against jockey George Holman for the excessive whipping and spurring of the runner-up. But it was not until 1911 that an Act of Parliament was passed to protect animals from cruelty; and only in the 1920s did the National begin to become the subject of serious criticism.

Until that time there had only twice been a National field of 30 or more runners – 30 in 1866 and 32 in 1909. Now, with the lure of increased prize money, fields of 30-plus became the norm, rising to a record 42 in 1928 (when only two managed to finish) and then to a staggering 66 runners in 1929. Remarkably, this decade did not see a marked increase in the number of fatalities. But the sight of many horses suffering distressing falls resulted in the RSPCA making formal protests from 1922 onwards. That year had seen the fatal falls of *Awbeg* and *The Inca II*, and the horrific dive of *Wavertree* who ended up trapped in Becher's Brook. As a result, there were calls for less demanding jumps and more demanding conditions of entry.

These calls were especially strident following the

demise of four runners in the 1954 National. In response, Aintree supremo Mrs Mirabel Topham said: 'There are just as many accidents in hurdle races but they do not seem to get the publicity.' There would be no question of making modifications before the next National. In 1959, after only four horses had finished in the National, the League Against Cruel Sports sent to Home Secretary Rab Butler suggestions to prevent casualties: more stringent entry qualifications; raising the steep drop on the landing side of Becher's; and limiting the number of runners to 25. Mrs Topham dimissed them as 'tripe'.

Meanwhile searching questions were asked in both Houses of Parliament. In reply, Mr Butler contended that allegations of cruelty were not borne out by the senior vet who had examined all the horses after the finish of the 1959 race. But he agreed to have talks with the National Hunt Committee and the following year he attended the National, the first to be televised. There were no serious casualties and afterwards he congratulated the Aintree executive on its efficient organisation.

Nevertheless the pressure for change was now significantly mounting. It had become the custom for RSPCA representatives to attend every Grand National and work amicably with the Aintree management, making constructive observations and suggesting changes. Most notable among these changes were the introduction of sloping 'aprons' on the take-off side of fences in 1961 and, at long last, the filling-in of the treacherous V-shaped ditch on the landing side of Becher's Brook in 1990. At the 1995 Grand National meeting, after three horses had perished in Aintree's John Hughes Memorial Handicap Chase, Bernard Donigan, the RSPCA's equine consultant, condemned the 'ill-informed' criticism of the National course from animal rights activists. He concluded that the racing surface at Aintree was 'the finest in Britain' and stressed the safety and welfare improvements made over the last ten years and the reduction of fatalities. But still the protests continued.

In 1997 the biggest ever security operation – 500 policemen in addition to 300 security staff – was mounted amid heightened fears of a major animal rights protest. As it happened, it was the IRA, with bomb scares, who caused chaos, though during the confused evacuation some protesters reportedly threw broken bottles on to the course. Two horses perished in the postponed Grand National. However, the race was thoroughly monitored by RSPCA inspectors, present at every fence, and Mr Donigan judged that the pace of the race rather than the stiff fences were crucial to the fatal falls. He felt the course was well within the capacity of the runners but suggested that the field maximum should be lowered from 40 to 30.

The 1998 National saw three fatalities. As a result qualifications for horses and riders were tightened, and every runner was subjected to an on-track veterinary check. Other changes included having a trough of water and oxygen masks near the finishing line for exhausted horses, a widening of the first fence by two metres, and a slight raising of the landing level over Becher's and The Chair.

The following year, when seven year old *Eudipe* was the one fatality, the RSPCA inspectors were satisfied that his back-breaking fall at Becher's was an unpredictable accident. This was the first National in 32 years not to be monitored by their consultant Donigan. At 73, he was recovering from major heart surgery and was soon to retire. By his campaigning he had played a key role in bringing about numerous safety improvements.

In 2000 welfare groups were especially active after five horses had been killed in the first two days of the Aintree meeting – albeit only two of them over National fences. This time an organisation called Animal Aid Society took to picketing betting shops. David Muir, Mr Donigan's successor in 1998, now announced a major research programme to analyse horse racing and examine the causes of fatalities and injuries. In conjunction with the Animal Health Trust, the RSPCA was already investigating every horse fatality over a two-year period.

This year, in the traditional pre-race address by the chairman of the stewards' panel, jockeys were reminded that, under the rules concerning improper riding, they faced disciplinary action if it was felt that they had attempted to complete the course on a tired horse who should have been pulled up. As usual, too, jockeys were advised of the importance of going a sensible gallop to the first fence. Five horses, in fact, fell at the first, but happily none of the 19 fallers in the race suffered serious injury.

In 2006 a big advance in horses' welfare came with the building of a state-of-the-art veterinary amenity. No longer would stables be used for administering first aid; and henceforth most injuries could be treated on site with only the most serious cases being transported by horse ambulance 15 miles to Leahurst Equine Hospital, a part of Liverpool University based on the Wirral. The new Aintree facility had a padded floor, bright lighting to aid stitching wounds, a television and video-recorder to show how horses had fallen, a digital X-ray unit and a computer-point enabling images to be sent directly to specialists around the world.

It is a measure of the racecourse executive's consideration for horses' welfare that in 2007 Aintree did not hestitate to put aside commercial considerations and abandon the final race of the Grand National day so that vets could give on-the-spot treatment to a National runner (*Graphic Approach*) who had run loose after falling at the second Becher's and now lay concussed on the course in front of the grandstand.

Meanwhile, it still remains the practice, after every Grand National, for the Aintree management to hold discussions with the Jockey Club and the RSPCA to see if anything further can be done to improve safety for horses and riders. However, while some traditionalists argue that the course is no longer challenging enough, there will always be more demands and demonstrations by animal activists, some of whom are opposed to all horse racing. *See also:* Course Changes.

ANNE, Duchess of Westminster

Owner of *Last Suspect*, the shock 50-1 winner of the 1985 Grand National, and far more famously of *Arkle*, the greatest steeplechaser of all time. *Arkle*'s 25 victories included three successive Cheltenham Gold Cups (1964-66), the Irish Grand National and every other major National Hunt race except the Aintree Grand National. Staunchly the duchess refused to risk her beloved superstar in the Liverpool marathon and later offered the classic riposte: 'Anyway, I knew he could win it, so what's the point in running.'

Born April 13, 1915, the only daughter of Brigadier-General Edward Sullivan of Glanmire House, Co. Cork, Anne grew up in an equine environment, and by her teens she had developed into an outstanding horsewoman, regularly riding to hounds and taking part in horse shows. At the age of 31 she became the fourth wife of the 2nd Duke of Westminster, the richest man in England, who was nicknamed 'Bend Or' after the first of his grandfather's four Derby winners. Two years after the Duke's death in 1953 she became increasingly involved in racing, with Tom Dreaper as her trainer; and in 1958 she had

her first major success with *Sentina,* who won the Champion Chase before going on to the National and being brought down at Becher's. Ten more Cheltenham Festival victories would follow, giving her a total only three less that the record of Dorothy Paget, the leading post-war owner.

Besides *Arkle*, notable horses to carry her famed yellow and black colours included *Ben Stack*, the 1964 Champion Chase winner; *Kinloch Brae*, the 1969 Cathcart Challenge Cup winner who one year later, as favourite in the Cheltenham Gold Cup, was jumping brilliantly until falling at the third last; and not least, the prolific *Ten Up*, winner of the 1974 Sun Alliance Chase and the 1975 Gold Cup. Her one great sadness at Cheltenham came in 1993 when the promising *Cherrykino*, whom she had bred, fell fatally at the seventh fence in the Gold Cup.

Ever concerned for the well-being of her horses, the duchess steered clear of the National for many years and in 1985 it was only as a result of the persuasive powers of jockey Hywel Davies that she and trainer Tim Forster agreed to let *Last Suspect* take his chance. The following year her unlikely winner was brought out of retirement to appear at Aintree again, this time being pulled up at the 18th. Late in her life the duchess had two more representatives in the National: the Forster-trained *River Mandate*, who was pulled up four out in 1997, and finally *Carbury Cross*, the first National runner to be saddled by Jonjo O'Neill, who finished seventh in 2003.

Hugely popular with racegoers, the duchess was also much involved with breeding, having kept up her family's famous Eaton Stud near Chester, and she actively supported many charities including the RSPCA, the Save the Children Fund and the Riding for the Disabled Association. She died in August, 2003, aged 88.

See also: Last Suspect; Forster, Tim; Davies, Hywel; Arkle.

ANTE-POST BETTING

The great attraction of ante-post betting is the lure of far more favourable odds than are likely to be available on the day of the race. But in respect of the Grand National it is especially fraught with dangers. The chances of a horse being withdrawn in the two months between the announcing of the weights and the race day are high. Preparation may have gone badly, or perhaps an injury occurred. An especially sad example was in 2007.

When the Cheltenham Festival saw the demise of *Little Brick* who had been backed to win £1 million at Aintree. Soon afterwards, at Uttoxeter, the 10-1 National favourite *Nil Desperandum* suffered a fatal injury; and just one week before the big race *Far From Trouble*, who had been as short as 10-1, had to be put down following a leg infection.

Whatever the reason for an accepted entry failing to make the line-up, the stake on a non-runner is lost unless the bookmaker has made a special 'with a run' declaration. Futhermore, an equally strong argument against ante-post betting on the National lies in the fact that the ante-post punter cannot know the state of the going on the day of the race. Thus, there is added risk in backing any horse that needs a specific type of ground.

In any event, ante-post favourites have an appalling record, and the horse made favourite on publication of the weights invariably fails. In 1991 *Rinus* and *Twin Oaks* were shortest in the initial ante-post betting. The former fell; the latter did not run. In 1992 *Carvill's Hill* and *Twin Oaks* led the market. The former did not run; the latter finished fifth. In 1994 *Double Silk* and *Moorcroft Boy* were joint favourites. The former fell; the latter finished third. In 1995 ante-post favourite *Master Oats* finished seventh.

In 1996 three horses headed the ante-post betting: *Master Oats* and *Smith's Band*, who did not run, and *Deep Bramble* who was pulled up. In 1997 only one of four joint favourites went on to take part and that one (*Lo Stregone*) was pulled up. In 1998 the market leaders were *Suny Bay*, *Rough Quest* and *Time For A Run*. This time, more encouragingly, *Suny Bay* was second. But *Rough Quest* was pulled up and *Time For A Run* did not run. In 1999 *Double Thriller* and *Teeton Mill* were the early ante-post favourites. The latter was subsequently withdrawn; the former 7-1 on the day.

Remarkably in 2000 *Young Kenny* was the clear market leader despite being burdened with 12st top weight. Mostly 10-1, when the weights were announced, he went off at 14-1 and fell at the tenth. However, this was a freakishly good year for ante-post punters who followed a tipster in form. The *Racing Post*'s 'Pricewise' (then Melvyn Collier) had recommended taking the 33-1 about *Papillon* on the day of the race. He won at 10-1.

In 2001 *Papillon* was the popular choice to win the race again. When the weights were announced

he was promptly cut from 16-1 to 10-1 favouritism. He was later judged to be an unlikely runner, along with all other Irish horses, following the great outbreak of foot-and-mouth disease. But, five days before the National, Irish horses were given the green light to travel. *Papillon* faced unfavourable heavy ground and, after being remounted, he was the last of four finishers at 14-1. In 2002 the initial ante-post favourites were *Supreme Glory* (withdrawn with tendon damage) and *Moor Lane* (failed to make the cut).

In 2003 ante-post leader *Ad Hoc* fell at the 19th. On the other hand, 'Pricewise' (now Tom Segal) rightly picked out *Monty's Pass* at 40-1 when the weights were announced – and importantly, as he noted, his selection was one who 'goes on any ground'. In 2004 he opted for *Joss Naylor*, a 25-1 chance who would 'ideally want a bit of give underfoot'. Luckily he got the ground but, going off at 10-1, he was always well behind and was pulled up before the 19th.

Obviously, when long-price ante-post odds are successfully taken, the rewards can be spectacular – witness the most long-range punt of Nigel Payne who, as a part-owner of *Earth Summit*, backed his young gelding, £100 each-way at 33-1, to win the National in any year up to and including 2000. He placed the bet in 1993 and collected five years later when *Earth Summit*'s starting price was 7-1. Moreover, the winner had also been tipped by 'Pricewise' (Melvyn Collier) when he was 25-1.

More recently, in 2005, *Hedgehunter* was a most inviting 25-1 ante-post before going off as 7-1 favourite; and the following year 'Pricewise' hit the bullseye yet again when picking out *Numbersixvalverde* as a good 25-1 bet. Overall, however, the evidence is against heavy ante-post betting on the Grand National.

See also: Betting; Tipsters.

ANTHONY, Algernon

England-born but Ireland-domiciled, Algy Anthony – no relation of his famous namesakes in racing – was that rarest of riders: one who starred over jumps and on the Flat. In 1900 he had the distinction of riding the first royal winner of the Grand National: Edward, the Prince of Wales's six year old *Ambush II*, on whom he had finished seventh the year before. Remarkably, that victory over Aintree's fences was sandwiched between his winning of the 1899 Irish

A

Derby on *Oppressor* and the 1900 Irish Oaks on *May Race*.

Anthony was born in Cheltenham in 1872 and migrated to Ireland after gaining valuable experience with Sam Darling, the Master of Beckhampton in Wiltshire. In addition to riding, he became an assistant to Mr G.W. 'Tommy' Lushington who trained at Eyrefield Lodge near the Curragh, formerly the famed base of Henry Eyre Linde. There, in 1897, he was introduced to *Ambush II*, a four year old that Mr Lushington had bought on behalf of the Prince of Wales.

Before riding in the royal colours at Aintree, Anthony had appeared in three Grand Nationals – falling on *Swanshot* (1896), pulling up on *Chevy Chase* (1897) and finishing fifth on *Dead Level* (1898). Though *Ambush II* was only seventh on his National debut, his performance as a five year old was impressive enough to raise high hopes of a royal victory the following year; and these were fulfilled when Anthony timed his late challenge to perfection, finishing four lengths ahead of *Barsac*, with the incredible, 12 year old *Manifesto*, giving 24lb to the winner, just a neck back in third.

There was no chance of *Ambush II* reappearing in the 1901 Grand National since, two months after the death of Queen Victoria, the Court was then still in official mourning. Consequently, Anthony rode *Covert Hack*, the stablemate who one year earlier had fallen at the first fence where, after completing a circuit riderless, he had crucially brought down the favourite, *Hidden Mystery*. This time *Covert Hack* finished seventh. Switching back to the Flat, Algy partnered *Carrigavalla* for a second Irish Derby success. The following year, in the National, he was on the 6-1 joint favourite, the Duke of Westminster's *Drumree*. They were knocked over at the fourth.

After the prince had become King Edward VII, Anthony wore the royal colours in three more Nationals. In 1903, he was back on *Ambush II* – the first time that a reigning monarch had been represented in the race. Though raised 18lb. to the huge top weight of 12st 7lb, the brown gelding was still very much in contention as the leaders approached the last. And when the most threatening *Drumree* inexplicably collapsed on the flat, the crowd roared in anticipation of another royal victory. But then, seconds later, *Ambush II* made his first mistake, hitting the final fence hard and crashing with Anthony to the ground.

When *Ambush II* returned one year later he went off the 7-2 favourite. But he had been dropped only one pound in the weights and this time, watched by the King, he fell at the third, the first open ditch. After a two-year gap, Anthony was back on a rank outsider, *Roman Love* who never went the pace and had to be pulled up. Then, in 1908, he was on King Edward's *Flaxman*. Unluckily, when well up with the leaders, he broke a stirrup leather early on the second circuit; and he did well to bring the eight year old bay gelding home in fourth place at 33-1.

In 1910, Algy had his 12th and last Grand National ride – on *Judas*, the second favourite who had been the runner-up the previous year. Now he was an early faller, one of many victims of an early pileup. But, happily, his long association with the Grand National ended in triumph – in 1920 when he trained the 6-1 winner *Troytown*.

See also: Ambush II; Troytown.

ANTHONY, Ivor

Although he was the leading amateur jumps jockey at the age of 21 and the champion National Hunt jockey in 1912, Ivor Anthony was rather overshadowed as a rider by his brilliant younger brother Jack, a triple winner of the Grand National. He himself rode in nine Nationals, only twice completing the course, his best efforts being a third place on Lord Derby's *Axle Pin* in 1912 and a fourth place when making his debut on *Crautacaun* in 1906. Moreover, another brother, Owen, riding in only two Nationals, went one better with a second place on *Irish Mail* in 1913.

As a trainer, however, Ivor asserted his seniority. He gained invaluable experience, serving as assistant at the famous Wroughton stable near Swindon in Wiltshire, where Aubrey Hastings had turned out two National winners: *Ally Sloper* (1915) and *Master Robert* (1924). Following the death of her husband in May, 1929, Mrs Hastings kept the operation going, with Ivor in charge.

A stern authoritarian and confirmed bachelor, Anthony had many successes as the Master of Wroughton. These included two National winners: *Kellsboro'Jack* (1933), the seven year old who won in a new record time of 9min 28sec, and *Royal Mail* (1937). He also turned out two winners of the Cheltenham Gold Cup, *Morse Code* (1938) and *Poet Prince* (1941), won the 1934 Champion Hurdle with *Chenango*, and took charge of the extraordinary *Brown Jack* who, having been switched from

30

hurdling to the Flat, went on to win the Queen Alexandra Stakes (six times), the Goodwood and Doncaster Cups (1930), and the Chester Cup and Ebor Handicap (1931).

Ivor always rated American-owned *Kellsboro' Jack* the greatest Aintree jumper he had ever known; and every summer after the Second World War, when attending Saratoga races, he would make time to visit the horse's grave in the Adirondack foothills and join his host, Mr F. Ambrose Clark, in a celebratory drink of champagne.

See also: Kellsboro' Jack; Royal Mail; Anthony, John; Brothers.

ANTHONY, John Randolph

Born in Carmarthenshire, 1890, the youngest of three Welsh brothers to ride in the Grand National, 'Jack' Anthony is a member of that select group of jockeys – 'the magnificent seven' – who have achieved three victories in the great Aintree steeplechase. His strike-rate as an amateur in the National was extraordinary: three wins in his first five rides. Curiously, as a professional, he did not have the same impact: seven rides without victory, though he ended his spectacular National record with a flourish, finishing on the runner-up in successive years and then coming third.

Anthony's first appearance in the National (1911) was a chance ride on *Glenside* after the booked jockey, 'Titch' Mason, had broken a leg shortly before the race. Trainer Captain R.H. Collis chose him as the substitute because he had ridden the one-eyed gelding in minor chases in Wales. At Aintree, on atrociously heavy ground, *Glenside*, a faller the previous year, won by 20 lengths by virtue of the fact that he was the only one of 26 starters to complete the course without being remounted.

The following year Jack did not appear in the National, the family being represented by brother Ivor who finished third on Lord Derby's *Axle Pin*. He was a faller on *Regent* in 1913 when another brother, Owen, was a distant second on *Irish Mail*. And in 1914, the year he won the National Hunt jockey championship with 60 successes, he failed to finish on *Couvrefeu II*. Then, in the only Aintree National of the First World War years, he drove home six year old *Ally Sloper* to win by two lengths from *Jacobus* and make Lady Nelson the first woman to own a National winner.

Anthony's second National success was a most improbable one since *Ally Sloper* had blundered his way round the first circuit. Most alarmingly, he had landed atop the second fence. There, Jack was sliding off when his brother Ivor, alongside on *Ilston*, reached out to haul him back into the saddle. Next, at the Canal Turn, *Ally Sloper* had stumbled badly on landing, and this time, grasping him round the neck, Jack managed to heave himself back in place.

Five years later, when Anthony returned to Aintree, the course was a glue-pot, as it had been for his first winning ride. But this time there could be no carefully coaxing round his horse, as he had done on *Glenside*. He was on a giant Irish gelding – *Troytown*, the 6-1 second favourite – who not even he could restrain. The tearaway had only one style of running. Jack surrendered and gave him his head.

Troytown duly made all the running, powering ahead like a steam train with a host of fallers left in his wake. He slipped up only once, at the plain fence after the second Valentine's, where sheer strength carried him through rather than over the obstacle; and he stormed on to win by a comfortable 12 lengths, having led from start to finish. Only four others completed the course.

With three victories behind him, Jack Anthony was now recognised as the supreme Aintree specialist. But, having turned professional, he failed to finish in his next four Nationals. In 1921 and 1922 he fell on *Daydawn* and *Clashing Arms* respectively, the latter being owned by Colonel W.S. Anthony, a fourth horse-loving brother, who would rise to the rank of Major-General in the Royal Veterinary Corps. In 1923, surprisingly, he fell on 11-2 favourite *Forewarned*; and in 1924 he pulled up on *Music Hall*, a former winner anchored on 12st 7lb.

In 1925, again on the favourite, *Old Tay Bridge*, he took the lead after the last only to be denied on the run-in by the sprint-like finish of *Double Chance*. And, 12 months later, the same combination went down in similar circumstances, relegated to second place by the fast-finishing *Jack Horner*. Jack's twelfth and last National ride, in 1927, was on Mr Stephen Sanford's *Bright's Boy*, the seven year old who had finished one length behind him a year before. Though raised almost a stone to a top weight of 12st 7lb, *Bright's Boy* raised his rider's hopes of a fourth National win when he hit the front at the final open ditch. But again his mount was to be outpaced in a pulsating finish, beaten one length and the same by the favourite *Sprig* and a 100-1 rank

A

outsider, the one-eyed *Bovril III*.

Twice champion jockey, Anthony retired from the saddle in 1928 to concentrate on a career as a trainer at Letcombe in Oxfordshire, where his most notable National contender was *Easter Hero* who, in 1929, so gallantly finished second in a 66-strong field while trying to defy top weight and the added handicap of spreading a plate halfway round the second circuit. The following year Jack prepared *Easter Hero* to win a second successive Cheltenham Gold Cup and he saddled *Brown Tony* to win the Champion Hurdle. But he continued to be dogged by ill-luck when turning out horses for the National. In 1930 he sent out *Sir Lindsay* who finished third – beaten only a neck and one and a half lengths after jockey Dudley Williams had lost both stirrup irons. Then, in 1934 and 1935, he gained third place with *Thomond II* who, in the opinion of many, would have won in the latter year but for the hard race he had had 15 days before when going down by a mere three-quarters of a length after an epic duel with *Golden Miller*.

If his riding career had not been interrupted at its peak by the First World War, it is entirely possible that Jack Anthony would have challenged the record number of five Grand National wins achieved by George Stevens. Ironically, like the great Stevens, he sustained his most serious injury when falling from a hack – the accident occurring on a visit to the United States. He never fully recovered and died in 1954.
See also: Glenside; Ally Sloper; Troytown; Brothers.

ANTHONY, Owen

Though Owen Anthony rode in only two Grand Nationals – far fewer than brothers Jack and Ivor – he made a notable debut, finishing second on six year old *Irish Mail* in 1913 when there were only three finishers, with the third being remounted. The following year he was on the rank outsider *Great Cross* and, like his brothers who also appeared in the race, he failed to complete the course.

Born in 1886, the son of a Welsh farmer, Owen rode 110 winners as a jump jockey. Then, after taking out a trainer's licence, he had almost immediate success with the 1922 National victory of *Music Hall*. Based at Lambourn in Berkshire, his many later successes included three Cheltenham Gold Cup winners – *Thrown In* (1927), *Golden Miller* (1936) and *Roman Hackle* (1940) – and a winner of the Champion Hurdle, *Solford* (1940).

A bluff, straight-speaking Welshman, he was the one trainer who successfully stood no nonsense from the tyrannical owner, Dorothy Paget. In 1935, when he replaced Basil Briscoe as the trainer of *Golden Miller*, he told her straight that she could forget her custom of telephoning her serfs in the middle of the night. He usually liked to be in bed by 10 p.m., 'at which time I take the phone off the hook'. But even he was unable to persuade Miss Paget to stop running her wonder horse over the Aintree fences which, despite that historic 1935 victory, he so obviously hated.

Owen ended his training career with two spectacular triumphs at the 1940 Cheltenham Festival – taking his third Gold Cup plus the Champion Hurdle with *Solford*. He died the following year.
See also: Music Hall; Golden Miller; Paget, Dorothy; Brothers.

APPEARANCES
Horses
Most Grand National appearances
8 – *Manifesto* (1895-1904), winning twice, finishing third three times and fourth once.
7 – *Hall Court* (1865-72), twice runner-up.
 Frigate (1884-90), one win and three times runner-up.
 Gamecock (1885-91), one win, one third place.
 Why Not (1889-96), one win, one second and one third place.
 All White (1919-27), best: a third place when remounted.
Most consecutive appearances
7 – *Frigate* (1884-9), one win, three second places.
 Gamecock (1885-91), one win, one third place.
6 – *Peter Simple*, grey (1841-46), once runner-up, twice third.
 Peter Simple, bay (1849-54), two wins.
 Hall Court (1865-70), twice runner up.
 Grakle (1927-32), one win.
 Gregalach (1929-34), one win, one second place.
 Cloncarrig (1948-53), fell in all.
 Wyndburgh (1957-62), three times runner-up, once fourth.
 Mr What (1958-63), one win, twice placed third.
 West Tip (1985-90), one win, one second and two fourth places.

Jockeys

Most appearances (excluding 1993 void National)

19 – Tom Olliver (1839-1859), 3 wins, 3 times runner-up, once third.

17 – Tommy Pickernell as 'Mr Thomas' (1859-77), 3 wins, 2 thirds, 1 fourth.
Pat Taaffe (1951-70), 2 wins, 1 fourth.

16 – Ted Wilson (1873-1890), 2 wins, 1 second.
Michael Scudamore (1951-66), 1 win, 1 second, 1 third.

15 – George Stevens (1852-71), 5 wins, 1 third, 1 fourth.
Arthur Nightingall (1886-1904), 3 wins, 1 second, 4 thirds, 1 fourth.
Jeff King (1964-80), 1 third, 1 fourth.
Carl Llewellyn (1988-2006), 2 wins, 1 third.

14 – Charles Boyce (1851-66), 1 win, 1 second.
Richard Dunwoody (1975-99), 2 wins, 1 second, 3 thirds, 2 fourths.

Most consecutive appearances

17 – Tom Olliver (1839-55).

16 – Michael Scudamore (1951-66).

14 – Richard Dunwoody (1975-99).

13 – Peter Scudamore (1981-93) 1 third, 1 fourth.

12 – Harry Beasley (1879-90).
Ted Leader (1922-33).
Tim Hamey (1926-37).
Carl Llewellyn (1995-2006).

ARCHER, Frederick

Trainer of *Double Chance*, the 1925 Grand National winner, Fred Archer was a grandson of William Archer who had won the 1858 National on *Little Charley* and a nephew of the immortal Flat jockey whose name he shared. He had been gifted *Double Chance* by Captain Anthony de Rothschild under whom he had served as a trooper in a squadron of the Royal Bucks Hussars during the First World War.

De Rothschild had regarded the chestnut gelding as being unsound. But Archer, now setting up as a trainer at Malton, hacked and hunted him, and finally saddled him to win a modest chase at Wetherby. Soon after *Double Chance* broke down. Archer resorted to 'firing' to treat his strained tendons and following a move to Newmarket he revitalised him sufficiently to win five small races. He then sold a half-share in the horse to Liverpool cotton broker David Goold, in whose colours he made his debut at Aintree. It was *Double Chance*'s sole

run in the Grand National and, with an amateur rider, Major J.P.Wilson, he won by four lengths from *Old Tay Bridge*, a favourite giving him 17lb. *See also:* Double Chance.

ARCHER, William

One of 13 children, William Archer was only 11 years old when he ran away from home to find work as an apprentice Flat jockey. He made his mark so quickly that within six years he had been hired by the Emperor of Russia as a rider and as manager of his stud near St Petersburg. However, his health suffered so greatly in the harsh Russian winters that he returned to England two years later, and was now compelled by weight problems to turn to jump riding.

Ironically, it was in extreme cold, 13 years later, that he rode to his greatest victory – winning the 1858 Grand National in a blinding snowstorm on board *Little Charley*, with *Weathercock*, four lengths back, finishing runner-up for the second successive year. Archer was then 32, married with four children, the youngest being one year old Frederick James, who would become the most famed Flat jockey in the land: the immortal Fred Archer.

Like Christopher Capel, the owner of *Little Charley*, Archer lived at Prestbury near the Cheltenham racecourse. After failing to finish in his first three Grand Nationals – on *Tramp* (1847), Lord Strathmore's *Naworth* (1848) and *Napoleon* (1849) – he was seventh on *Vengeance* (1850) and sixth on *Warner* (1852). He did not complete on *View Halloo* (1853) but the following year was runner-up on six year old *Spring*, beaten fifteen lengths by the hotshot favourite *Bourton* who was giving away a colossal 30lb.

Having failed to finish on the rank outsider *Dan O'Connell* in 1856, Archer triumphed on his last appearance in the National. He lived on to see all the great victories of his precocious youngest son who was to become 13 times champion jockey, riding the winners of 2,748 races including the Derby five times and sixteen other Classics. Then, in 1886, came Fred Archer's tragic suicide at the age of 29. His grief-striken father died three years later. *See also;* Little Charley; Holman, William.

ARKLE

By common consent, the greatest steeplechaser never to run in the Aintree Grand National. Indeed, *Arkle*

A

was the supreme chaser of the second half of the 20th century, if not of all time. His long list of triumphs between 1963 and 1966 includes the Cheltenham Gold Cup (three times); The King George VI Chase; the Irish Grand National; the Hennessy Cognac Gold Cup (twice); the Whitbread Gold Cup; and the Leopardstown Chase (three times). In 1965 he defied 12st 7lb to become the only horse to win the Cheltenham and Whitbread Gold Cups in the same season. Altogether, he won 27 of 35 races and was second or third in five others. His achievements in handicaps separated him from all other steeplechasers since regularly he gave two to three stones and a beating to high-class opponents – becoming so dominant that in Ireland two handicaps were framed: one to be implemented if he ran, the other if he did not. Only four times in 26 chases was he beaten over fences. When defeated half a length by *Stalbridge Colonist* in the 1966 Hennessy Cognac Gold Cup he was conceding two and a half stone to the winner who would go down by only three-quarters of a length to *Woodland Venture* in the 1967 Gold Cup.

Irish-bred – unprepossessingly by *Archive* out of *Bright Cherry* – *Arkle* was bought as a three year old for 1,150 guineas by Anne, Duchess of Westminster, who named him after the mountain facing her home in Sutherland. Ironically, his arrival in 1961 at Tom Dreaper's stables was not greeted with universal enthusiasm. His future rider, Tom Taaffe, sneered: 'He moves so terribly you could drive a wheelbarrow between his hind legs.' But, as it proved, Arkle was not only a chaser of supreme courage and intelligence but he was endowed with an unusually low heartbeat, a greyhound-like style of overlapping his forelegs with his hind-legs, and such secure jumping ability that he never fell in a race. So marked was his superiority (he could comfortably win handicaps when carrying 12st 7lb) that it prompted the introduction in England of 'extended' handicaps, allowing weights to be greatly increased if *Arkle* was a non-runner.

Arkle had an outstanding trainer, a brilliant rider and a caring owner for whom the welfare of her horses was the paramount consideration. The Duchess of Westminster was adamant that her beloved wonder horse would never be subjected to the rough-and-tumble of the Aintree National. But when – 15 years after *Arkle*'s demise – she did agree to having a contender, the result was a most unexpected victory for her 50-1 shot, *Last Suspect*.

See also: Anne, Duchess of Westminster; Dreaper, Tom.

ARMYTAGE, Marcus David

A throwback to the Corinthian days of the 1870s and 1880s, 25 year old Marcus Armytage was, in 1990, an Old Etonian amateur winning the Grand National at the second attempt. On *Mr Frisk*, he triumphed by three-quarters of a length in the fastest-ever time of 8min 47.8sec. Moreover, just three weeks later, the combination achieved a unique double in winning the Whitbread Gold Cup by a record margin of eight lengths.

Though Armytage was an amateur, combining race-riding with a journalistic career as Newmarket correspondent for the *Racing Post*, he was born on July 17, 1964 into a family steeped in the racing tradition. His parents – Roddy and Sue – were successful trainers at East Isley, Berkshire, their many National contenders including the Scottish National winner *Barona*, fourth under Paul Kelleway in 1976 after ousting *Red Rum* for favouritism; *Proud Tarquin* (1973) seventh; *Black Secret* (1973) tenth; *Lean Forward* (1978) 13th; and *Two Swallows* (1984) sixth. His mother (née Whithead) was an international show jumper. His younger sister, Gee, was a most accomplished jump jockey who would complete the first circuit on *Gee-A* in the 1988 National before a strained back muscle forced her to pull up.

Like his sister, Marcus started out in junior show-jumping. Later, at Eton, he would slip out of college to ride at nearby Windsor; and he rode his first chasing winner in 1982 at the age of 17. But his racing appearances were few and far between as he moved to the Royal Agricultural College, Cirencester, graduating with a diploma in Rural Estate Management, and eventually turning to journalism. In the 1984-85 season he had seven successes as an amateur, most notably winning well in a two-mile handicap hurdle at Aintree on Grand National day. His mount was *Seagram*, destined to win the National six years later.

The following season – opposed by his sister in the Fox Hunters' Chase – he had his first ride over National fences. He finished sixth on *Rocamist* while Gee was fourth on *Gala Prince*, both horses being trained by their father. At this stage, Gee was to enjoy considerably more success than Marcus; and in 1987 she had a spectacular double at the

Cheltenham Festival, winning the Kim Muir on *The Ellier* and the Mildmay of Flete on *Gee-A*.

That same year, but for bad luck, Marcus and Gee would have been the first brother and sister to compete in the same Grand National. However, a knee injury kept Gee out of the race while Marcus, making his National debut, did well to get as far as the 23rd fence before pulling up on *Brown Veil*, a 200-1 outsider trained by his father. A year later, in 1988, 22 year old Gee made an even more impressive National debut, well placed and going strong on *Gee-A*, when, at the second Becher's, she had to pull up.

Earlier in the 1987-88 season, Marcus had been at Doncaster to ride in a bumper when, with favoured jockeys committed elsewhere, he picked up a spare ride on *Mr Frisk*. Together, they won the Sheila's Cottage Chase; and the following season he was re-united with the chestnut gelding who opened his campaign with victory in an amateur riders' race at Ascot. Subsequently, Richard Dunwoody – trainer Kim Bailey's first choice – rode *Mr Frisk* to third place in the Hennessy Cognac Gold Cup, and stable jockey Ronnie Beggan was in the saddle when *Mr Frisk* won the Sheila's Cottage Chase again.

Beggan was scheduled to ride again in the 1989 National, but *Mr Frisk* was a late withdrawal because of the soft ground. Thereafter, Marcus regularly partnered the chestnut, winning the Punch Bowl Amateur Chase at Ascot, finishing a good third in the Hennessy, and then fourth under top weight in Cheltenham's 1990 Kim Muir Chase before going on to glory at Aintree.

Immediately after his sensational, record-breaking Grand National victory, Marcus had to tackle the demands of his new professional career – preparing a story for the *Racing Post*. Unfortunately, the fates denied him the pleasure of reporting a unique brother-and-sister appearance. While he had been riding to glory, Gee was in hospital after breaking a leg in a fall at Ludlow. Otherwise she would have been on her beloved *Gee-A,* who finished 18th.

In 1991, the winning partnership was back at Aintree but *Mr Frisk* was now 12 years old, without fast ground and with an extra stone on his back. Marcus had to pull him up at the second Becher's. The following year, he emulated his sister with a Cheltenham Festival double, in the Kim Muir and the National Hunt Challenge Cup. But he did not have a ride in the National and when he returned to Aintree in 1993 it was the year of the notorious void

race. His mount was the rank outsider *Travel Over* and no runner had greater misfortune. *Travel Over* badly twisted and bruised a tendon when he became tangled up in the starting tape and he was subsequently pulled up after the first fence.

In 1995 Marcus was on *Romany King*, a 40-1 shot who had not won since 1992, the year in which he was runner-up in the National. They did well to dead-heat for fifth place with *Into The Red*. Finally, in 1996, the celebrated amateur had a farewell reminder of the extreme vicissitudes to be experienced in the National. On his last appearance he went out at the first fence on *Bishops Hall*. The following year he was to have ridden top-weighted *Master Oats* in the National but, with the late withdrawal of *Time For A Run*, Norman Williamson was released to resume his partnership with the 1995 Cheltenham Gold Cup winner.

Armytage finally retired from racing in 2000 with a total of 100 winners, including three Cheltenham Festival successes; and today he is fully occupied as the racing correspondent of the *Daily Telegraph* whose staff he joined in 1993.

See also: Mr Frisk; Bailey, Kim; Dick, Dave; Durant, Tim; Brothers and Sisters.

ASCETIC'S SILVER

Bred by Patrick J. Dunne at his Carrollstown Stud at Trim, Co. Meath, *Ascetic's Silver* – a chestnut son of the super-sire *Ascetic* out of the thoroughbred mare *Silver Lady* – had the unusual distinction of finishing first (without a rider) in the 1905 Grand National and then winning in partnership with his rider the following year.

Remarkably, after falling at the third fence in 1905, this eight year old entire had got up to continue riderless for almost two circuits and finish ahead of the winning *Kirkland*. It was a solo performance that impressed the Honourable Aubrey Hastings who had fallen in the same race from Prince Franz Hatzfeldt's *Dearslayer*. Subsequently, following the death of Mr Dunne, he persuaded the German prince to let him buy the horse for 800 guineas.

Hastings had recently made his training base at Wroughton near Swindon, Wiltshire, where the great Tom Olliver had trained the 1874 Derby winner *George Frederick*. There he was destined to train four National winners; and in the case of *Ascetic's Silver* he chose to go on a drastic diet so that he could take the ride himself.

Prince Hatzfeldt had three runners in the 1906 National, none of them fancied in the betting which was headed by *John M.P.* a hot 7-2 favourite seeking his ninth chase win in a row. *Ascetic's Silver* went off at 20-1 despite the fact that he had won the 1904 Irish Grand National and was a half-brother of two Aintree National winners, *Drumcree* and *Cloister*. In a fast-run race, which saw *John M.P.* fall in the lead at the Canal Turn, he was held up for a late challenge, asserting his superiority at Valentine's on the second circuit and then powering on to win by ten lengths from the six year old *Red Lad*. His half-sister *Aunt May* finished third and and his 12 year old half-brother, *Drumcree*, came home in eighth place.

Although *Ascetic's Silver* was raised almost two stone in the weights for his return in 1907, he went off the co-favourite with *Red Lad* (a faller). Again ridden by his trainer, he did well to survive severe interference and finish sixth. The winner (*Eremon*) was a massive 34lb better off. Surprisingly the handicapper was no less harsh when the entire came back as a 12 year old in 1909. Allotted the top weight of 12st 7lb, he was going well when he broke down and had to be pulled up. It was the end of a career in which, owing to his tendency to break blood vessels, he had won only five races.

See also: Hastings, Aubrey; Hatzfeldt, Prince Franz; Sires.

ASSHETON-SMITH, Sir Charles Garden

Before changing his name by royal licence in 1905, Sir Charles Assheton-Smith was plain Charles Garden Duff, a wealthy quarry owner. It was under that name, in 1891, that he became the owner of a horse who looked a sure Grand National winner: Lord Dudley's brilliant *Cloister*, the unlucky runner-up at Aintree that year, just half a length behind *Come Away*. Running in the colours of Mr Duff, *Cloister*, the 11-2 favourite, was second again in 1892, beaten by 20 lengths when conceding almost two stone to the winner, *Father O'Flynn*. But in 1893 the nine year old bay gelding became the first horse to carry the maximum 12st 7lb to National victory.

In 1894 and 1895 *Cloister* was the short-priced ante-post favourite for the National, and in both years he was withdrawn with injury shortly before the race. Mr Duff shared the popular opinion that his horse had been the victim of foul play. His bitterness, however, was soon tempered by an upturn in his fortunes. He unexpectedly inherited a large estate on the Welsh border, and with a boosted fortune he successfully resumed his policy of buying horses with obvious National potential.

In 1910 – one year before gaining his knighthood – Mr Assheton-Smith challenged with *Jerry M*, a gelding so outstanding that he was given the maximum weight on his National debut. *Jerry M* finished second to *Jenkinstown*, but came back two years later to become only the third horse ever to win with 12st 7lb. And one year later Sir Charles had his third National winner: *Covertcoat*, a half-brother to *Jenkinstown*.

Sir Charles would have had a fourth National winner – and his third in three years – if owner-trainer Mr Tom Tyler had accepted his offer for a young gelding called *Sunloch*. But it was only after *Sunloch* had won the 1914 race that debt-ridden Tyler agreed to sell; and this time Sir Charles had made a rare bad investment. *Sunloch* scored no more victories of note. It was, however, of no consequence to his owner. He died in Camarthenshire in September at the age of 63, six months before the running of the only wartime National. Returned to Mr Tyler, *Sunloch* ran again when the National was resumed in 1919, but he was now 13 years old and had to be pulled up on the first circuit.

See also: Cloister; Jerry M; Covertcoat; Gore, Robert.

ATTENDANCE

As stated earlier, steeplechases in the 19th century were primarily initiated by innkeepers and tradesmen seeking to draw crowds and promote business in their vicinity. Such was the case with the Aintree Grand National; and to this end it was hugely successful from the start. Though Aintree's inaugural Grand Liverpool Steeplechase of 1839 was held on a Tuesday, it was reported that vast horses arrived in Liverpool 'by steamers, railways, coaches, chaises, gigs and wagons', and that at Aintree 'a greater crowd was never before seen on any racecourse.' The crowd was an estimated 40,000, filling the Grandstand and packing the minor stands. And attendance was no less great in 1843 when the chase became a handicap and racecards were provided for the first time.

By the 1860s crowds were more conservatively estimated at 30,000, though the turnout was probably greater in 1863 when the Grand National fell on the eve of a national holiday declared for the wedding of Edward, Prince of Wales and Princess Alexandra. In the early 1870s estimates rose to more than 40,000, and at the turn of the century the crowds swelled still further, spurred by the popularity of the great *Manifesto* – the *Red Rum* of his day – and by the presence of the Prince of Wales, the 1900 winning owner with his *Ambush II*.

The new millennium brought more record crowds following the high of 1903 when for the first time the National had a runner in the colours of a reigning monarch, King Edward VII. A sharp decline began in 1912 when a coal miners' strike played havoc with the railways, and three years later the course was to be abandoned to the War Department. But in 1919, following war's end, the crowds flocked back in greater numbers than ever; and the attraction of the National was sustained – interest being boosted in the 1920s by American involvement and by the introduction of radio coverage in 1927. From 1933 to 1937, the great *Golden Miller* was a major draw; and in the latter year there was the added bonus of a first visit by King George VI and Queen Elizabeth.

No one, however, did more indirectly to boost attendance than Adolf Hitler. Hungry for great sporting entertainment after the Second World War, British citizens turned out in phenomenal numbers for the Grand National revival in 1946. Estimates of the racecourse crowd have varied wildly from 300,000 to 400,000. Certainly, that year saw the largest ever attendance, and, despite the rain and the mist, there was also a huge crowd in 1947 when the race-day was switched from the traditional Friday to Saturday so that British industry would not suffer.

In the following years attendances steadily fell and in the hope of halting the decline, the Aintree management returned in 1957 to staging the race on the Friday. It was not a success and thereafter Saturday was the norm. The beginning of television coverage in 1960 was not designed to encourage journeying to Aintree but later in that decade attendance rose in the light of reports that the Grand National was doomed to extinction. It then fell away alarmingly in the 1970s, the attraction of *Red Rum* being offset in 1974 and 1975 by huge rises in admission charges. In the latter year it slumped to an all-time low of 9,000.

But now, for seven years, the race was to be efficiently managed by Ladbrokes. John Hughes was appointed clerk of the course and the progress was extraordinary. In 1976 the attendance leapt to

42,000. By 1982, partly through cutting gate prices and intensive marketing by Nigel Payne, it was near 50,000. At the same time, through valuable sponsorship and TV rights negotiated by Hughes, the racecourse facilities were hugely improved. In the 1990s, the Saturday crowds ranged from some 46,000 to 59,000, and the figures increased still further in the new century, rising to more than 59,000 in 2000 and – after a small dip in 2001 due to bad weather and the foot-and-mouth crisis – to 63,500 in 2002, the latter increase remarkable since this was the first tax-free National of modern times without the need to be on course to avoid tax.

Since then the Saturday crowds have continued to rise, topping 70,000 every year since 2003. Similarly attendance for the three-day meeting has steadily risen, approaching the 150,000 mark, more than treble the total of 20 years earlier.

AUSTERLITZ

In common with his owner and amateur rider, the extraordinary Freddy Hobson, *Austerlitz* won the Grand National (1877) at his first and only attempt. Bred by Lord Scarborough (by *Rataplan* out of the mare *Lufra*), this big, five year old chestnut entire had shown useless form when running for two seasons on the Flat. But he immediately took to jumps, winning two hurdles and a Sandown chase before making his youthful Aintree debut. There he dominated a 16-strong field for much of the race, holding a lead from the second Becher's onwards and forging ahead from the last to win by four lengths and a neck from *Congress* and *The Liberator* respectively. The 11 year old *Congress*, runner-up for the second successive year, was almost two stone worse off at the weights and was ridden by Joe Cannon, who had beaten him by a neck on *Regal* the previous year.

At that time there had been serious doubts about Mr Hobson's unique and eccentric jumping technique which comprised holding on to the cantle of his saddle after take-off, this in the belief that by leaning back he would distribute weight to the horse's advantage. As a result, *Austerlitz* had gone off eighth in the betting, at 15-1. The following year, with the experienced professional Robert I'Anson booked to take the ride, he was made the hot 9-2 favourite. But on the morning of the race – to the vocal outrage of many punters – he was withdrawn, reportedly with heat in a leg. Like the unorthodox Hobson, he was not to appear in the National again. Indeed, following his Ain-

A

tree victory, he had only one more race (unplaced) before being retired and taking up Stud duties without any noteworthy success.
See also: Hobson, Frederick.

AUSTRALIA

While Australians have sent over racehorses to achieve spectacular success on the Flat in England, they have made just one great challenge for the Grand National prize: with ten year old *Crisp* who went off as 9-1 joint favourite in 1973. Owned by Sir Chester Manifold, he did all the right things in advance: arriving early to become acclimatised, to be made familiar with English fences, and to run in the minimum three races to qualify for handicapping purposes. Unfortunately, he qualified too well, revealing such jumping ability that the handicapper allotted him a mighty 12st for the National, equal top weight with *L'Escargot* who had twice won the Cheltenham Gold Cup (1970 and 1971) and the Whitbread Gold Cup of 1972. Unfortunately, too, his challenge coincided with the National debut of an exceptional eight year old called *Red Rum*. *Crisp* was beaten three-quarters of a length in record time by 'Rummy' who had a colossal 23lb advantage in the weights. Judged on that race alone, *Crisp* was seen by trainer Fred Winter and many cognoscenti as the greatest National horse of all time.

Two Australian jockeys, both tragically short-lived, have ridden a Grand National winner. The first was Tasmanian-born William Watkinson, who rode *Jack Horner* to victory in 1926 and three weeks later died from injuries sustained in a fall at Bogside. Three years later, making his second appearance in the race, Robert Everett triumphed on *Gregalach*, a 100-1 shot in a record field of 66 runners. A former Royal Navy officer who had gained most of his riding experience in South Africa, Everett rode in five Nationals before joining the Fleet Air Arm and losing his life in Second World War action.
See also: Crisp; Everett, Robert; Watkinson, William.

AYALA

Shock winner of the 1963 National when he was one of 18 66-1 outsiders in a 47-strong field that included past winners *Kilmore*, *Nicolaus Silver* and *Mr What*. His victory – by just three-quarters of a length from *Carrickbeg* – fulfilled a lifetime's ambition for his trainer and half-owner Keith

Piggott, who, three years earlier, had bought the chestnut gelding at Epsom for 250 guineas.

Bred by Mr J.P. Philipps at the Dalham Hall Stud, near Newmarket, *Ayala* was never well regarded. However, having been sired (out of *Admiral's Bliss*) by the 1950 Ascot Gold Cup winner *Supertello*, he originally fetched 400 guineas at the 1954 Newmarket December sales. Then, having been a flop on the Flat, he was knocked down at the sales for a mere 40 guineas.

Next, as a three year old, *Ayala* was picked up for a song to be used as a hunter in Dorset by the family of Mr John Chapman, a patron of Piggott. Again he disappointed, was briefly tried over hurdles, then sent to the Epsom sales where he was bought by Piggott, who subsequently offered a half-share to the celebrated London hairstylist, Mr P.B. 'Teasy-Weasy' Raymond.

Piggott rightly judged that *Ayala* might make a chaser, and in the 1960-61 season, the strapping chestnut won three chases in reasonable style. But the next season he had leg trouble and had to be pin-fired. Thus, as a nine year old, he came to his first Aintree National with relatively little racing experience, and with judgment of his prospects reflected in his Tote starting price of 141-1.

However, although *Ayala* had fallen in his penultimate race before Aintree, he was not seen as a no-hoper by his connections. He had won a three-mile chase at Worcester only 11 days earlier and had bottomless stamina. Lester Piggott, the trainer's son, later wrote in his autobiography: 'He was a very safe jumper for whom the Liverpool fences would hold no terrors. I had schooled the horse myself at home and knew that he had just come to himself. In Pat Buckley my father had booked a very good light-weight jockey, and we judged that he might just have a squeak.'

From the start, John Gifford and *Out And About* predictably made all the running, threatening to steal the race until, towards Becher's second time around, the pack at last began to close. Beyond the Canal Turn, *French Lawyer* took the lead; then, four fences from home, *Out And About* was a faller, in the process briefly – but crucially in retrospect – interfering with *Carrickbeg*.

Meanwhile *Ayala* had made only one mistake: hitting the Canal Turn first time round. On coming to it a second time he was steered though a huge hole which he himself had mainly created. He was now well in contention and, as the leaders came on to the racecourse, he was close up – with *French Lawyer*, *Hawa's Song* and *Carrickbeg* – behind 10-1 favourite *Springbok*, the narrow leader,

Two fences out, *Carrickbeg* inched ahead; and he took the final fence nearly a length in front of *Ayala*, doubling that lead as they came to the Elbow. At this point he looked all over the winner. But then, some 50 yards from home, the seven year old changed his legs and visibly began to weaken. The rhythm was gone and, despite having the advantage of the rails, he was just pipped at the post by *Ayala*, with *Hawa's Song* five lengths back in third.

Ayala, the longest-priced winner since *Russian Hero* (1949), broke a small bone in a foot in his next race and never won again. Raised 7lb and now ridden by David Nicholson, he was a 33-1 faller in the 1964 National. The following year, with Stan Mellor up, he was the only one of 47 runners to fall at the first fence. Elsewhere he fared no better, failing to make the frame in eight other races.

See also: Buckley, Pat; Piggott, Keith; Oaksey, Lord; Raymond, P.B.

B

BAILEY, Kim Charles

Trainer of *Mr Frisk*, the 11 year old chestnut gelding who won the 1990 Grand National by three-quarters of a length in the record time of 8min 47.8sec, and three weeks later became the first horse to complete the National-Whitbread Gold Cup double in the same season. Two years later Kim Bailey saddled the 15-2 National favourite, *Docklands Express* who finished fourth; and he again had the clear favourite in 1995: *Master Oats* who finished seventh at 5-1.

Born May 25, 1953, educated at Radley, Kim Bailey had his appetite for racing whetted when, as a schoolboy, he won £20 by drawing 100-1 shot *Foinavon* in a 1967 Grand National sweepstake. Subsequently he gained valuable experience working with Humphrey Cottrell and, in turn, two trainers with outstanding Grand National records, Tim Forster and Fred Rimell.

In January, 1978, he took over from his father, trainer Ken Bailey. Only 24 years old and having held his licence for just one week, he sent out *Shifting Gold* (John Francome up) to win the Mildmay Cazalet Memorial Chase at Sandown. For the National, however, following three successive wins and one fall, this promising nine year old was carrying top weight of 11st 6lb and, under Bob Champion, he fell at the tenth.

Kim's next National challengers were pulled-up long-shots: *Menford*, a 100-1 chance ridden by Mark Perrett in 1983, and *Late Night Extra*, a 500-1 outsider ridden by the top amateur Mr Tim Thomson Jones in 1986. But three years later he bought his own yard in Lambourn, and in his first season there he saddled the National winner.

Again using an amateur rider, Mr Marcus Armytage, he had won spectacularly with a 16-1 shot. The dramatic turnaround owed much to his then wife Tracey. Opposing her husband's judgment, she had pressured him into buying *Mr Frisk* at the 1986 Doncaster sales with a final bid of 15,500 guineas. The gelding was then sold on to Mrs Lois Duffey, an American lady in her late seventies.

Subsequently, Tracey played a key role in *Mr Frisk*'s training. Since the horse suffered badly from a sore back, he was always exercised without a saddle in his first racing season with the Baileys. Tracey regularly led him off the reins while riding her former three-day eventer *Barnaby*. Moreover, a week before the 1990 National, she was still exercising

him even though she was seven months pregnant with her second child.

When *Mr Frisk* followed up his National success with victory in the Whitbread it was by a record winning margin of eight lengths. And the next year Bailey won the Whitbread again, with *Docklands Express*, who went on to win the Racing Post Chase for the second time in 1992 and then to be beaten only by a short head and a length when finishing third in the 1992 Cheltenham Gold Cup.

His next outstanding chaser was *Master Oats* who, following a dominating run in the Greenalls Gold Cup, was the subject of a massive gamble for the 1994 Grand National. Backed down to 9-1, the eight year old jumped immaculately and was in contention until inexperience told with his fall at the 13th. The following year, despite having an extra 24lb to carry, the chestnut gelding was even more strongly fancied since he had won the Welsh National, and the Cheltenham Gold Cup by 15 lengths. Bailey was hugely optimistic in his belief that *Master Oats* ('the most exciting horse I've trained') could succeed where ten other Gold Cup winners had failed: attempting to emulate the great double achieved by *Golden Miller* 61 years before.

When winning at Cheltenham, the nine year old gelding had jumped indifferently on the first circuit. Therefore, prior to the National, Bailey turned to Yogi Breisner, the former Swedish international eventer who had won fame as a horse psychologist. To make *Master Oats* concentrate more on jumping they put him over show-jumping poles set at varying heights and distances apart. At Aintree they were delighted with his fitness and jumping, and he went off the 5-1 clear favourite. Unfortunately, the meticulous preparation counted for little as *Master Oats*, burdened with a top weight of 11st 10lb, was denied his favoured soft ground. Outpaced, he faded over the last half-mile to finish seventh. In the view of his rider, Norman Williamson, he would have won on soft going. Kim Bailey's other National runner, *Romany King*, deaded-heated for fifth place at 40-1.

By now Bailey had established himself as a leading jumps trainer, renowned for his attention to detail and headed only by Martin Pipe and David Nicholson in the trainers' table. In 1995, besides his success in the Gold Cup and the Welsh National, his remarkable achievement had been the transformation of *Alderbrook* from a failed novice to Cheltenham Champion Hurdler winner. Other career wins would include the 1996 Scottish Champion Hurdle with *Alderbrook*; a second Mildmay/Cazalet Memorial Chase with *Mr Frisk*; the Racing Post Chase twice with *Docklands Express*; and valuable races with *Man O'Magic*, *Kings Fountain* and *Positive*.

All the while he longed for a second Grand National triumph. As he had told Martin Pipe after *Miinnehoma*'s 1994 win, 'the hardest thing about winning the National is giving the trophy back'. In 1996 his National runner was *Over The Stream*, a first ride in the race for Andrew Thornton. They finished 13th at 50-1. The following year he had a more realistic chance with the return of his classy *Master Oats*. But somewhat harshly the Gold Cup winner was still saddled with 11st 10lb, conceding more than a stone to all other runners; and he was further handicapped by the two-day postponement caused by the IRA bomb threat. In the interim, the going became faster and, in the circumstances, the mud-lover did remarkably well to finish fifth. Bailey's other contender, outsider *Glemot*, unseated his rider at the seventh fence.

In 1998 he entered three horses – *Cariboo Gold*, *Linden's Lotto* and *Parsons Boy* – but none made it to the National line-up. Similarly, in 1999, his three entries were to be withdrawn, one of them being *Betty's Boy*, who had won the William Hill National Hunt Handicap Chase at the Cheltenham Festival. By now, despite having a loyal, hard-working staff, Bailey's fortunes had taken a depressingly downward turn. Gone were the glory days of the mid-1990s. He had two dreadful seasons with horses suffering from a persistent lung infection and, worst of all, there was the sad break-up of his marriage.

Late in 1999 he sought to make a new determined start: moving with 74 horses from Lambourn to the remote village of Preston Capes, near Daventry, Northamptonshire. There he had built a new, state-of-the-art base, including a seven-furlong, all-weather gallop. Still he was cruelly dogged by misfortune. The first season was blighted by the foot-and-mouth epidemic. And one week before the 2000 Grand National he suffered a heartbreaking blow: *Betty's Boy*, the 12-1 third favourite for the big race, had to be put down after breaking a hind leg while having his last pre-Aintree gallop. It reduced Bailey's National team to two: *Cariboo Gold* and *Druid's Brook*. The former missed the 40-runner cut, being made the third reserve. The latter, a 66-1

chance, unseated his rider at the 12th.

Williamson, who was to have ridden *Betty's Boy*, appeared instead on the Charles Egerton-trained *Mely Moss*, who was having his first race for almost a year. The nine year old gave him a brilliant ride, going down by only a length and a quarter to the victorious *Papillon*. It was a big disappointment for trainer and jockey but nothing compared with that of Bailey whose long run of ill-luck would continue in a year which saw his all-weather gallop washed away by floods and a losing streak that brought only one winner from 73 runners sent out. Then, in November, came some relief at last when Williamson rode *Supreme Charm* to victory in the Sporting Index Chase over Cheltenham's cross-country course. The nine year old went on to run in the 2001 National, falling at the 15th, The Chair.

In 2002 *Supreme Charm* again just made the cut for the National line-up. Though two pounds of the handicap, he was the main market-mover two days before the race, being cut to 25-1 from 50-1. Given ideal fastish ground, he had a tremendous run under Robert Thornton before weakening at the 26th and finishing fifth. Bailey ended the season with 36 winners and was 12th in the trainers' numerical table. In 2003 and 2004 his National runner was the outsider *Wonder Weasel*, who fell at the third fence on his first appearance and then, as a 200-1 shot, was pulled up before the 28th.

The following season, Bailey's fortunes went from bad to worse as his yard was cruelly hit by a virus. His hopes rested almost entirely on one horse: *Longshanks* who had finished runner-up in the 2004 Topham Trophy. The eight year old was aimed all season at the 2005 National and, given a promising weight of 10st 1lb, he was backed down to as short as 16-1. But cruelly he was to narrowly miss the cut in a year when, uniquely, all 40 runners were in the handicap proper. With *Longshanks* made the third reserve, Bailey sought a consolation prize by running him in the eve-of-National Topham Chase. He finished fourth as 9-2 favourite.

In September, 2006, after so many disappointing seasons, Bailey moved to Thorndale Farm, Andoversford, near Cheltenham – setting up a most attractive new base with 36 stables, a testing all-weather gallop, five schooling fences including an open ditch and 30 acres of paddocks. It marked a new beginning for a trainer who had saddled more than 1,000 winners and who remained the only current licence-holder to have trained the winners of the Gold Cup, the Champion Hurdle and the Grand National.

On Boxing Day he ended a barren 30-day spell by landing a 525-1 treble at Huntingdon and subsequently he was delighted when his *Longshanks* was allotted a sure qualifying weight of 10st 7lb for the 2007 National. Unfortunately, the ten year old bruised a foot in early April. He was fit to run after being sent to an equine spa to recover and being fitted with a special racing plate with a groove cut out of the front to give the foot extra protection. But the interrupted preparation did not help and at Aintree, under Tony Dobbin, he ran strongly for a long way before fading to finish a distant seventh.
See also: Mr Frisk.

BALDING, Andrew Matthew
The son of the great Flat trainer Ian Balding, Andrew was born on December 29, 1972 into a multi-talented extended family that lived and breathed racing. After working for his uncle Toby, trainer of two Grand National winners, he rode as an amateur over the jumps and gained two years' experience with Jack and Lynda Ramsden. Then, in the 1998-99 season, he became his father's assistant with responsibility for half of the Kingsclere string. Successes achieved in his father's name included two Cesarewitch winners (*Top Cees* and *Distant Prospect*) and the winner (*Pentecost*) of the 2002 Britannia Handicap at Royal Ascot.

In July, 2002, Ian announced that he was to retire at the end of his 38th season, handing over the licence at Kingsclere to Andrew. The following New Year's Day his son took charge of 110 horses being primed for the Flat season – and only three jumpers, *Moor Lane*, *Gunner Welburn* and *Logician*. However, the first two were of such quality that Ian said he would be jealous if Andrew went on to saddle a Grand National winner.

Their big hope was *Gunner Welburn*, a high-class hunter chaser formerly with Caroline Bailey, daughter of Dick Saunders, winner of the 1982 National on *Grittar*. He had been first and second in the past two runnings of the Martell Fox Hunters' Chase over the National fences. Now, in the 2003 Grand National, he led from the 19th until two out where he weakened to finish in fourth place.

It was a promising enough start for 30 year old Andrew in only his fourth month as a licensed trainer. And subsequently he enjoyed spectacular success on the Flat – most notably on June 6, 2003, an amazing Oaks day, when he won the Classic with *Casual Look* and completed a four-timer with victories in Princess Elizabeth Stakes (*Aldora*), the Vodafone Surrey Stakes (*Rimrod*) and the Vodafone Corporate Handicap (*Passing Glance*). Brilliantly, he finished his first full season with 54 winners and prize money of £1.18 milion.

His hopes were high for the 2004 National since the preparation of *Gunner Welburn* had been even better this year. But the 12 year old gelding, though prominent on the first circuit and lying sixth at the halfway stage, was again found lacking in stamina. Tony Dobbin pulled him up at the 20th fence. The following year *Gunner Welburn* was too lowly rated to make the cut for the National, and it was on the Flat that Andrew had his most spectacular succeses. He went into 2005 with a wealth of equine talent, including *Free To Air*, a two year old son of Derby winner *Generous*, due to run in the colours of his sister Clare; and most sensationally the globetrotting *Phoenix Reach* who, after winning in Toronto and Hong Kong, took the £500,000 Dubai Sheema Classic at Nad Al Sheba in 2005 and went on to boost his winnings to nearly £2 million in a 14-race career. In 2007 he had his first Royal Ascot winner with *Dark Missile* taking the Wokingham.
See also: Balding, Ian Anthony.

BALDING, Clare Victoria
Born January 29, 1971, the elder sister of Andrew Balding, Clare was riding almost as soon as she could walk, being not quite three years old when she broke her collarbone in a fall from her Shetland pony. By her teens she had become a highly accomplished horsewoman: the leading amateur Flat jockey in 1989 and 1990 and champion lady rider in 1990.

She went on to read English at Cambridge University where she was president of the Union, subsequently joined Radio Five and then undertook the full BBC training course, inevitably becoming a racing reporter before switching to television and emerging as a formidable all-round presenter. In 2003 she was voted the Sports Reporter of the Year and the Racing Journalist of the Year.

Among her early memories of the Grand National was the day in 1989 that her uncle, trainer Toby Balding, landed his second victory with *Little*

Polveir. That day, as an 18 year old, she was with other members of her family supporting her brother at a point-to-point meeting. She recalled: 'We had this tiny little telly plugged into a cigarette lighter in the horsebox. We all crammed in and we could barely see a thing. But luckily *Little Polveir* led pretty much the whole of the second circuit, so we could just about tell that he won.'

Eleven years later Clare was to join Sue Barker in taking over from Des Lynam at the Aintree meeting and has brilliantly served as the key anchor presenter of Grand National television coverage ever since.

BALDING, Gerald Barnard 'Toby'

An outstanding dual-purpose trainer, Toby Balding won the Grand National in 1969 with *Highland Wedding*, and 20 years later chalked up a second victory with *Little Polveir*. Altogether he trained some 2,000 winners. Over the jumps his successes included the 1992 Cheltenham Gold Cup with *Cool Ground*; the Champion Hurdle twice, with *Beech Road* (1989) and *Morley Street* (1991); the Martell Aintree Hurdle five times in succession (1989-93); the Mildmay of Flete Chase twice; the Irish Sweeps Hurdle; the Eider Chase four times, the Topham Trophy twice, the Coronation Hurdle, and not least two Breeders' Cup Chases in a row which resulted in him becoming the first English-based trainer to receive (twice) the Eclipse Award, America's highest accoldate from the nation's racing media. As late as 2004 he sent out a winner at the Grand National meeting: *Accipiter* in the Sefton Novices' Hurdle; and on the Flat his many wins included the John Porter Stakes, the Stewards' Cup, the Portland Handicap, the Ayr Gold Cup and the November Handicap.

Born September 23, 1936, Hampshire-based Toby hailed from a family steeped in racing tradition. His grandfather, Bert Balding, was a successful horse dealer and fine horseman. His uncle Barnie, as an amateur rider, had finished fourth on *Drinmond*, a 66-1 chance, in the 1927 Grand National. But above all – like his younger brother Ian who won over 70 races as an amateur jumps jockey and went on to become a champion Flat trainer – he was strongly influenced by his father Gerald, a great all-round sportsman and England polo captain for two decades.

Gerald, too, had ridden at Liverpool and he was a trainer for more than 35 years. The best horse he trained was *Arctic Gold,* whom he had bought for

his great friend, American millionaire 'Jock' Whitney. Having won the Great Yorkshire Chase and being unbeaten in his last three races, the six year old chestnut went off as 8-1 favourite in the 1951 National but fell when leading at the Canal Turn first time round.

Marlborough-educated, Toby Balding turned to training in 1956 after completing his National Service in the Queen's Life Guards and having had several years experience as a point-to-point jockey. Aged 20, he was the youngest person ever to receive a trainer's licence. Almost immediately he ventured into the Grand National minefield with two Colonel W.H. Whitbread-owned long-shots – *Athenian* and *Carey's Cottage* – who failed to finish in 1957; and nearly a decade went by before he began to apply himself regularly to the Aintree challenge.

In 1966 he had two contrasting challengers – nine year old *Highland Wedding*, third in the betting, and *L'Empereur*, a 100-1 outsider owned and ridden by the Duque de Alberquerque whom the trainer described as 'a total kamikaze pilot and brave as a lion'. The Spanish duke pulled up four fences from home. *Highland Wedding* finished eighth, as did Toby's next National candidate, 100-1 shot *Scottish Final*, in 1967.

In 1968, *Highland Wedding* went one place better, finishing seventh, and the following year, under Eddie Harty, he gave Balding his first National success at a time when the stable was bang in form. Returning to Aintree on the back of three successive wins, the 12 year old held the lead from the Canal Turn second time around and won by a comfortable 12 lengths. At the same meeting the trainer saddled *Dozo* to win the Topham Trophy.

One year later Harty rode *Dozo* into fourth place in the National, while Toby's other runner, *Game Purston*, a 100-1 outsider with an amateur rider-owner, failed to finish – as did the stable's *Country Wedding*, under Bob Champion, in 1971 and 1972. Subsequent National runners included *Mr Vimy*, a 100-1 no-hoper pulled up in 1973; *Vulgan Town*, sixth in 1974; *Carroll Street*, eighth in 1977; the big bay Eider Chase winner *Lucky Vane*, fourth in 1984; and *Blackrath Prince*, tenth in 1985.

Four years later Balding's second Grand National success – again with an experienced 12 year old – was, to say the least, highly fortuitous. Only six weeks before the 1989 race he had bought *Little Polveir* on behalf of his old friend Mr Edward

Harvey who was looking for a horse to be ridden by his soldier-son in the Grand Military Gold Cup at Sandown. As Toby himself acknowledged, the most valuable work had been done by the previous trainer, John Edwards, who had already turned out *Little Polveir* to run in three Aintree Nationals and had been preparing him for a fourth.

With heavy going much in his favour, the proven stayer jumped safely throughout and held off all rivals on the run-in to win by seven lengths from another 12 year old, *West Tip*. It was just one of three triumphs for Balding on an extraordinary day. He had already turned out the Champion Hurdler, *Beech Road*, to win the opening Sandeman Aintree Hurdle; and he was to take the last race, the Mumm Prize Novices' Hurdle, with top-weighted *Morley Street*, his 54th winner of the season. In doing so, he set a new world record for National Hunt prize money won on a single day.

There was just one major blot on his otherwise perfect day. In the Grand National he was also responsible for *Brown Trix*, ridden by his 53 year old owner, Mr David Pitcher. The bay gelding, a 300-1 outsider, fell fatally at Becher's, so deep in the ditch that he needed to be winched out before his winning stablemate led the field over the brook on the second circuit.

Balding did not have a runner in the 1990 National. That year, however, he achieved a unique training success as *Morley Street* became the first horse to be voted National Hunt Horse of the Year in both the U.K. and the U.S.A. Then, in 1992, he came close to scoring a third Grand National success when his eight year old *Romany King* hit the front at the Canal Turn, only to be overhauled by the long-striding *Party Politics*, who held on to win by two and a half lengths. In the same race Balding also saddled Gold Cup winner *Cool Ground* and the outsider *Sirrah Jay* who were the tenth and last respectively of 22 finishers.

After the race Balding criticised jockey Richard Guest for having made too much use of *Romany King*, but later he modified that view, expressing doubts as to whether the horse was an out-and-out stayer. A broken leg prevented Guest from trying to go one better in 1993 when *Romany King*, now the joint second favourite, was more mature and very well handicapped with only an extra four pounds. Adrian Maguire took the ride for his National debut and completed the course in third place only to find that the race was void. Toby's other runner, the

outsider *Farm Week*, fell at the fourth fence.

In 1994, again favourably weighted and with Guest back on board, *Romany King* fell in the National. The following year, on his third and last appearance, he dead-heated for fifth place under Mr Marcus Armytage, but by then the brown gelding had been moved to the stable of trainer Kim Bailey. Subsequently, Balding had one more Grand National runner – in 2000 when he took charge of *Kendal Cavalier*, a most definite stayer who, in the previous season, had won the Welsh National and finished seventh in the Aintree National. This time the grey finished 12th.

Toby Balding finally retired in November, 2004, handing over his licence to his son-in-law, Jonathan Geake. In 48 years as a trainer, he had made a contribution to racing that far transcended his brilliance in turning out winners. He served on numerous committees (including chairmanship of the National Hunt Committee from its inception in the 1960s); and he was the guiding light of the National Trainers' Federation. Now he was elected an Honorary Member of the Jockey Club and was one of the first to be named as a director sitting on the British Horseracing Authority, which took over as the sport's governing and regulatory body in 2007.

Many trainers had their grounding under his guidance, including David Elsworth, Jim Old and John Edwards. Moreover, he helped to bring on many top jockeys including Bob Champion, Richard Linley, Richard Guest, Adrian Maguire and Barry Fenton. Most shrewdly, when scouting for a 7lb claimer in 1994, he signed up at Wexford races a young man who had only once raced over fences. His name: Tony McCoy, who in his first season (1994-95) would become the top conditional jockey with a record 74 winners, then go on to break all records while stable jockey to Martin Pipe.

See also: Highland Wedding; Little Polveir; Harty, Eddie; Frost, Jimmy.

BALDING, Ian Anthony

Although his racing involvement was originally as an amateur rider in National Hunt (he won over 70 races including Cheltenham's 1963 National Hunt Chase on *Time*), Ian Balding – unlike his older brother Toby – primarily achieved great distinction as a trainer for the Flat, most famously saddling the incomparable *Mill Reef* in 1971 to win the Derby, the Eclipse Stakes, the Prix de l'Arc de Triomphe and the King George VI and Queen Elizabeth Stakes.

Born on November 7, 1938 in Long Branch, New Jersey, U.S.A., educated at Marlborough, Millfield and Christ's College, Cambridge, Balding was an all-round sportsman par excellence. Besides race-riding, he played rugby union for Cambridge, Bath and Dorset and Wilts, boxed for his university, and in later years continued to pursue skiing, squash, tennis, cricket and golf. On one occasion he rode a winner in the first at Huntingdon and that same afternoon played at full-back for Cambridge.

Ian's first winner over jumps was trained by his brother for whom he rode 89 more winners. Then he made an extraordinary start as a trainer, winning the 1964 Dewhurst with *Silly Season* and being the second leading Flat trainer in his first full year of 1965. For 37 years (until 1999) he served as one of the Queen's trainers. In 1971 he became champion trainer, and with such superstars as *Selkirk* and *Lochsong* he went on to take numerous Group 1 prizes in England, Ireland, France, Italy and Germany, and to become three times the leading international trainer. His successes over hurdles included *Insular* whom he trained to win the 1986 Imperial Cup for the Queen Mother, and *Crystal Spirit*, winner of the 1991 Sun Alliance Novices' Hurdle.

As assistant to the Queen's trainer, Captain Peter Hastings-Bass, he had taken over the Kingsclere (Berkshire) stables when his mentor tragically died of cancer at the age of 42. Five years later, in 1969, he married the captain's daughter Emma – a partnership that reinforced his family connections with the Grand National. Emma's grandfather, Aubrey Hastings, had trained and ridden the 1906 winner *Ascetic's Silver* and had turned out two other National winners: *Ally Sloper* (1915) and *Master Robert* (1924).

On March 29, 1969, when his brother saddled the National winner *Highland Wedding*, Ian was playing rugby for Newbury. Once the race had started he took every opportunity to kick the ball far into touch so that he could momentarily hear the commentary on a spectator's radio. Then, at the final whistle, he dashed to the changing rooms and as soon as possible drove hell-bent for Aintree to join in the family's victory celebrations.

Yet it was not until 1995 that Ian himself turned his attention to the Grand National as a result of his long association with the 87 year old American billionaire Paul Mellon. That year his National runner was Mellon's *Crystal Spirit* who had won well over two and a half miles at Cheltenham and Ascot. Bred at Balding's Kingsclere Stud, *Crystal Spirit* was out of Mellon's broodmare, *Crown Treasure* and sired by the champion miler *Kris*. In the mating, they had been looking for speed but now they were asking the eight year old to race over nearly four and a half miles. Under Jamie Osborne, he got the distance but finished 14th.

In 2002, at the age of 63, Balding was still dreaming of joining the elite, four-strong group of trainers who had won both a Derby and a National. And this year he at last had an outstanding contender in ten year old *Moor Lane*, so impressive in the Great Yorkshire Chase that he was made the 14-1 market leader when the weights for a 144-strong National entry were announced. However, with an allotted 9st 7lb, he needed 31 defectors to get a run. He missed the cut by two and so ran in the Topham Chase, finishing way down the field. Ian still had a runner in the National: the 11 year old New Zealand import, *Logician*. But this 80-1 long-shot was brought down, one of nine casualties, at the first fence.

By now a new generation of horse-mad Baldings was making a mark in the racing world. Ian's daughter Clare was emerging as an outstanding racing reporter; and in July, 2002, Ian announced that he would retire at the end of the season, to be succeeded by his son and assistant trainer, Andrew. He ended his career with more than 2,000 winners. *See also:* Mellon, Paul; Balding, Andrew.

BALLOT

Controversially, after the Grand National had been limited to 40 runners in 1984, a ballot system was introduced to choose between horses who straddled the cut on equal weight. Wisely this flawed random method of selection was abandoned in 2003 following bitter complaints the previous year when Ginger McCain (*Amberleigh House*) and Mark Pitman (*Browjoshy*) saw their horses balloted out in favour of entries who were inferior on ratings that had been revised since the weights were framed. Thereafter, the disputed place or places in the line-up would be awarded to the horse with the highest rating at the 48-hour declaration stage.

BARNES, Maurice Allen

Winning jockey on ten year old *Rubstic* – Scotland's first success – in the 1979 Grand National. He was making his debut in the race, a relatively obscure rider compared with the jockeys who joined him in a three-way battle to the finishing line. The runner-up *Zongalero*, beaten one and a half lengths, was ridden by three times champion Bob Davies who had won the previous year on *Lucius*. In third place was *Rough and Tumble*, the mount of the brilliant John Francome.

Though lacking National experience, Maurice at least had the benefit of expert advice on how to run his race. His father, Tommy Barnes, also making his National debut, had finished second on *Wyndburgh* in 1962. Moreover, Maurice was on a horse of proven stamina over four miles-plus and one that had never fallen in a race. Keeping *Rubstic* up with the pace throughout, Barnes was clear of The Chair when two riderless horses caused a pile-up there. On the second circuit, no runner was travelling more easily than *Alverton*, the lightly weighted favourite and recent 25-length winner of the Cheltenham Gold Cup. But then, tragically, he crashed into the Becher's fence and broke his neck in the fall. The safe-jumping *Rubstic* was the first of only seven to complete the course.

Born on February 18, 1951, in Cumbria, Maurice Barnes was eighteen when he rode his first winner as an apprentice jockey to his father. Later, having been retained by trainer Charlie Bell at Hawick in Roxburghshire, he rode almost exclusively in Scotland and the north of England. Though his strike-rate was modest, his riding skill was considerable – as most plainly demonstrated in 1972 when sensationally, after losing his irons at the final fence, he managed to resist two strong challengers on the run-in to win the Scottish Grand National on Mr Bell's *Quick Reply*.

In the 1977-78 season Barnes regularly partnered *Rubstic*, together winning the Durham National Chase over three and a half miles at Sedgefield and finishing second in the Scottish Grand National over four miles one furlong. *Rubstic*'s jumping ability and stamina were well proven and yet, at Aintree, he went off at 25-1, punters doubtless influenced by the fact that Scotland had never produced a Grand National winner.

Barnes made three appearances in the National, all of them on *Rubstic*. In 1980, though raised 11lb in the handicap, his mount started as 8-1 favourite. The gelding was well placed to make a challenge when he suffered his first-ever fall at The Chair.

Finally, in 1981, Maurice safely steered the 12 year old round to be the seventh of twelve finishers in the 1981 National, so famously won by the courageous duo, Bob Champion and *Aldaniti*.

Although he was soon advised to retire from the saddle after a bad fall at Cartmel, Maurice did, in fact, ride in one more race at Aintree. On the day of the 1995 Grand National he was one of ten former National winning jockeys to take part in a six furlong Flat race on behalf of the Bob Champion Cancer Trust. And once again, riding *Chinour*, he was first past the post, followed home by Champion, Tommy Stack and Tommy Carberry.

Meanwhile, with the support of the Injured Jockeys' Fund, Maurice had initially gained his HGV licence to work as a lorry driver. He and his wife Anne then developed a bed and breakfast business at their six-bedroomed farmhouse near Penrith and renovated two old buildings to provide self-catering holiday accommodation. In 1999 the Barnes family moved to a 180-acre sheep farm on Tarnside, Cumbria, where they would run self-catering lodges and a training yard for up to 25 horses.

Here, Maurice successfully established himself as a trainer, investing £50,000 in a half-mile-long, all-weather gallop and showing that he still had a shrewd eye for equine potential when, in 2004 at Ascot sales, he paid 1,200 guineas for a gelding (named *Torkin King*) who, as a hurdler, would become the money-spinning star of his stable. *See also:* Rubstic.

BARNETT, Charles Henry

As an amateur jockey, Charles Barnett completed the National course in the Fox Hunters' Chase of 1973. Two decades later he took overall charge at Aintree, his appointment as managing director unhappily coinciding with the only Grand National to be declared void following the failure of the antiquated recall system after a false start. Then, in 1997, following IRA bomb threats, he had the unenviable task of announcing that everyone must leave the racecourse – 'And I mean everyone' – and faced the daunting challenge of getting a vandalised, litter-strewn course fit for a rearranged National just 49 hours later.

Born July 15, 1948, Barnett was educated at Eton and Christ Church, Oxford. A qualified solicitor, he spent eight years in marine insurance in London, then moved to Merseyside, working in shipping before taking the post of chief executive of Haydock Park racecourse in 1984. He moved to Aintree following the death of John Parrett in December, 1992, and then, for seven years, he tackled the additional role of chief executive at Chester racecourse. He officiated at his 15th and final Grand National in April, 2007, after which he took up a new appointment – as successor to Douglas Erskine-Crum in the role of Ascot's chief executive.

In his reign at Aintree, Barnett proved himself an outstanding administrator and was the driving force behind major improvements. The last of these was the construction of two new grandstands, named Derby and Sefton, and an equestrian centre completed on time and budget shortly before his departure. 'I absolutely love Aintree and will miss it terribly,' he declared following his appointment to Britain's premier racecourse. 'The Grand National is etched into my heart, but Ascot has its own unique attraction.'

Shortly before the 2007 Grand National, trainer Ginger McCain, never lost for words, suggested that one of the new grandstands should have been named the Charles Barnett stand. 'I have nothing but complete and utter admiration for the man, but he's a dirty, rotten windy bastard for going down south to Ascot.'

Then, ironically, Barnett's days at Aintree ended as they had begun – with a false start (happily not disastrous) and later a difficult decision: rightly abandoning the final race so that vets could give on-the-spot treatment to a distressed National faller lying on the track.

BARONS, David

West Country trainer and part-owner of New Zealand-bred *Seagram*, the aptly named winner of the 1991 Seagram Grand National. Shrewdly, David Barons twice gave the sponsors the chance of buying the horse to run in their name. But the offers were declined since, irrespective of ownership, any success by the eponymous runner would afford excellent publicity for the company. Artfully, when Martell Cognac took over sponsorship of the National in 1992, the trainer came up with another eponymous New Zealand-bred challenger. But his *Martell Boy* – also offered unsuccessfully to the sponsors – was not in the *Seagram* class and never made it to the National.

Barons made a number of visits to New Zealand in search of potential steeplechasers, and it was his wife Jennifer who bought *Seagram* on his behalf as a three year old. Initially the chestnut gelding raced in the colours of Maincrest Limited, performing well over hurdles. But then, after his first win over fences, he broke down badly, and subsequently, when the Liverpool company went out of racing, the trainer took over ownership. At that stage he did not regard the little horse as anything special.

Seagram now had his forelegs treated with carbon-fibre tendon implants and, during a one-year layoff, the Barons gradually nursed him back to full fitness. After two of his four chase wins in the 1988-89 season, David sold a half-share to Sir Eric Parker. The gelding followed up with three wins in the next season and struck top form in the build-up to the 1991 National which he won by five lengths from *Garrison Savannah*, the Cheltenham Gold Cup winner. The trainer's other runner, outsider *Bumbles Folly*, was pulled up before the 21st.

Born December 6, 1936, Barons successfully trained a large string of racehorses on his 600-acre farm at Kingsbridge in Devon. He rarely challenged for the National, a notable early exception being in 1973 when he sent out *Prophecy* to finish eighth and *Green Plover* 14th in the *Red Rum-Crisp* classic. But he soon proved the value to be had in New Zealand shopping – especially with *Playschool*, a winner of the Welsh National and the Hennessy in 1987. That year brought the trainer's second successive Hennessy victory, having scored the previous year with *Broadheath*, also ridden by Paul Nicholls who would later gain invaluable experience as assistant trainer to Barons before going on to succeed Martin Pipe as Britain's champion jumps trainer.

After an impressive eight-lengths beating of *Forgive 'N Forget* in the Vincent O'Brien Gold Cup at Leopardstown, *Playschool* was made 100-30 favourite for the 1988 Cheltenham Gold Cup. Unhappily, the tough import was pulled up three out, having run so abysmally that the trainer believed he must have been got at. A dope test failed to support his belief, though for some reason the horse never again recaptured his form of old.

In 1990 Barons scored a remarkable one-two in the National Hunt Chase Challenge Cup when *Topsham Bay* and *Royal Battery* finished first and second at 40-1 and 25-1 respectively. Two years later he challenged for the Grand National with two New Zealand-bred runners: *Seagram*, now 12 years old and with an extra 12lb to carry, and *Royal Battery*, an 80-1 shot who had the same granddam as *Playschool*. Both struggled off the pace and were pulled up before three out. In 1994 the trainer again had a National runner in partnership with Sir Eric Parker: 11 year old *Topsham Bay*, his dual Whitbread Gold Cup winner, who had been unplaced three weeks earlier in the Cheltenham Gold Cup. A 25-1 shot, the bay gelding unseated his rider (Jimmy Frost) after being hampered at the 13th.

Barons emigrated to New Zealand in 2001. Five years later, when *Playschool* died, he said that he was probably a better horse than his Grand National winner, and he still contended that he would have won the Cheltenham Gold Cup 'if he hadn't been doped'.

See also: Seagram; Nicholls, Paul.

BARRY, Ronald

Twice the National Hunt champion jockey, initially in 1972-73 with a then record total of 125 wins, Ron Barry could count himself exceptionally unlucky never to have won a Grand National. For so many years – 1967-75 and 1978-83 – he was stable jockey to trainer Gordon Richards. But he was never at the Greystoke yard at the right time, specifically in 1978 and 1984 when Richards saddled National winners, *Lucius* and *Hallo Dandy* respectively.

Even so, in 1978 Barry was offered the National ride on *Lucius* after stable jockey David Goulding had been ruled out with a minor injury. But cruelly circumstances were against him. He could not take up the offer because he was already booked to partner *Forest King* for trainer Ken Hogg. So Bob Davies got the winning ride. Meanwhile, salt was rubbed into the wound when Barry found himself without a mount as *Forest King* was a late withdrawal.

Born on February 28, 1943, in Co. Limerick, Barry – popularly known as 'Big Ron' – left his native Ireland after serving a five-year apprenticeship with Tommy Shaw. Intially, he rode for the small East Lothian stable of Wilfred Crawford, the former Scotttish rugby union international. Then, in 1967, he was offered the chance to ride Richards's first jumper, *Playlord*, who had been winning over hurdles. Thereafter he partnered *Playlord* in all his eight wins over fences, including the Great Yorkshire Chase and the Scotttish National in 1969.

During his first spell with Richards, Barry won the jockey championship in successive years, 1973 and 1974. But ironically his greatest success came in the one major chase that his boss never managed to win: the Cheltenham Gold Cup. In 1973 Ron took the ride on *The Dikler*, trained by Fulke Walwyn. Under present-day medical controls, this would not have been allowed since only ten days earlier he had broken his collarbone. Nonetheless, the tough, irrepressible jockey chose to defy the pain, and brilliantly he weaved through the field and caught the odds-on favourite *Pendil* on the uphill run-in to snatch victory by a short head.

In the National he was on well-supported *Princess Camilla*, an out-and-out stayer whose last run had been a winning one over four miles one furlong at Warwick. The mare was never up with the blistering pace set by *Crisp* and eventually refused. However, Barry went on to ride the Walwyn-trained *Charlie Potheen* to victory in the Whitbread Gold Cup, a race he had first won for Richards on *Titus Oates* in 1971. The following year he won it a third time on *The Dikler*.

After a break to ride as a freelance, when his wins included the 1976 Schweppes Gold Trophy on Irish Fashion, Barry rejoined Richards in mid-1978 and most notably gave *Man Alive* a brilliant ride to win the 1979 Mackeson Gold Cup.

When 'Big Ron' retired in October, 1983, the Grand National and the Champion Hurdle were the only notable omissions on his career record. He had ridden seven times in the National, starting with a fifth place on *Sandy Sprite* in 1971. The following year he looked likely to have a great chance on Richards-trained *Red Sweeney*, the ante-post favourite. But this most talented chaser had to be withdrawn with a bruised foot two days before the race. Instead, Barry rode the stable substitute, *Gyleburn*. They fell at the first fence.

Princess Camilla, his 1973 mount, was a difficult mare who predictably refused, and in 1974 he was on *Straight Vulcan*, a faller. The following year he finished fifth on his old friend *The Dikler*. Incredibly, when *The Dikler* came back in 1976 as a 13 year old he was set to carry a weight exceeded only by that of *Red Rum*. Ron gave him a remarkable ride to finish sixth. Six years later the Irishman had his last National ride on another 13 year old, *Coolishall*, who was a faller. On quitting the saddle, he ran his own company constructing timber-framed boxes and horse shelters, and became the Jockey Club's

Inspector of Courses for the north, serving for 19 years until his retirement in 2006.
See also: Richards, Gordon; Doughty, Neale; Humour.

BATTLESHIP

They dubbed him 'the American Pony' – at 15.2 hands high, the smallest horse to run in the National since *The Lamb*, dual winner of 1868 and 1871. Even his trainer (Reg Hobbs) judged him too small to cope with Aintree's high fences. Yet *Battleship*, a blinkered, 11 year old, chestnut entire, triumphed in 1938 to become the first National winner both American-owned and -bred.

Battleship had outstandingly pedigree, having been bred in Kentucky from the legendary *Man O'War* out of the French Oaks winner *Quarantine*. He was so versatile that during his career he won over distances ranging from four and a half furlongs on the Flat to four and a half miles over fences. Trainer Hobbs used to say that if he had had him as a four year old on the Flat he could have won the Ascot Gold Cup.

As it happened, *Battleship* broke down as a four year old in the States, and he was sold by Walter J. Salmon for a mere $6,000 with the promise of another $6,000 if he ever proved fit for steeplechasing. The buyer was millionairess Mrs Marion Du Pont Scott, wife of Hollywood film star Randolph Scott, and three years later she reaped a huge reward when the little horse won the 1934 American Grand National.

Following that famous victory at Belmont Park, *Battleship* broke down again. But after being 'fired' (treatment with red-hot irons for recurrent tendon strain) he regained form sufficiently to induce Mrs Scott to send him to England in the autumn of 1936. The aim was to give him experience over English fences and gain qualification for the 1937 National. That year Hobbs persuaded the owner not to run her diminutive horse at Aintree. He tried to do so again in 1938 but Mrs Scott would not agree. By now, after all, *Battleship* had won three races over English fences and, running for the first time in blinkers, he had gone down by only three-quarters of a length in the National Hunt Chase at the Cheltenham Festival.

On the morning of the 1938 National, even though his son Bruce was due to take the ride, Hobbs made one last attempt to persuade Mrs Scott to withdraw her stallion. His greatest fear was that the horse, so handicapped by his size, would hit the ground with his nose when descending steeply over the drop fences. In the hope of reducing this possibility he had the reins lengthened by 18 inches so that his son could slip them further at the big drop fences in familiar hunting style.

As it happened, *Battleship* jumped so superbly that it was not until the third last that he made a serious mistake, almost collapsing on landing and so losing four or five lengths to the only other leading contenders, *Royal Danieli* and *Workman*. Later Bruce would claim that this blunder was a crucial benefit since his horse had been running too freely and was best coming from behind.

Given a brief respite, *Battleship* now came back as strongly as ever, overhauling the weakening *Workman* and closing at the last fence to within three lengths of the contrastingly big, long-striding *Royal Danieli*. He took that fence at superior speed but soon afterwards his chances seemed reduced as a loose horse, the six year old French-trained *Takvor Pacha*, came between the two leaders, forcing Bruce to switch his mount over to the stands side.

On the long run-in *Battleship* steadily closed the gap but, with the leaders separated by the width of the course, it was never clear which one had the advantage. It was still uncertain at the finish, and only after a long, suspenseful delay, was the judges' verdict announced: victory for *Battleship* by a head. At 40-1, the entire was the first blinkered winner of the National; and at 17, Bruce Hobbs was the youngest winning jockey.

It was a bitter disappointment for rider Dan Moore, so narrowly beaten on the Irish runner-up; and – contrary to newsreel evidence – he would always insist that he would have won with the advantage of a photo-finish. Happily, 37 years later, he would enter the Grand National roll of honour as the trainer of the victorious *L'Escargot*. And *Workman*, who had finished a bad third to *Battleship*, would win the following year.

Meanwhile a close-up view of *Battleship* showed how nearly the trainer's worst fears had been realised. Smears of blood around the nose – not evidence of a broken blood vessel as first supposed – were found to have come from a cut opened up through contact with the ground. Mercifully, in the light of an inevitable rise in the weights, *Battleship* was not asked to face Aintree's fences again.

B

Accompanied by his young rider, he was shipped home on the *S.S. Manhattan*, arriving to a tumultuous welcome in New York. Thereafter he enjoyed a long retirement on Mrs Scott's Montpelier Farm in Virginia. At stud, he served as a hugely successful stallion, siring eleven stakes winners on the Flat and three winners of the American Grand National. Eventually blind in one eye, he lived on to the ripe old age of 31.

See also: Hobbs, Reginald; Hobbs, Bruce; Americans; United States.

BEASLEY, Bobby

Historic memories were truly revived in the Grand National of 1961 when the grey *Nicolaus Silver* was ridden by Bobby Beasley to a five lengths victory. It was 90 years since a grey (*The Lamb*) had last won the National; and 70 years since Bobby's grandfather, Harry Beasley, had ridden and trained *Come Away* to win the greatest steeplechase prize by half a length.

Ostensibly, it followed the familiar pattern of a young jockey maintaining a great family tradition; and no dynasty had produced more renowned riders than the Beasleys of Co. Kildare. But this time it was different. Though Bobby (née Henry Robert, August 26, 1935) had grown up in an equestrian environment, he was 14 years old before he even sat on a horse. His father, Harry (junior), had been a leading jockey on the Flat, winner in 1929 of the 2,000 Guineas on *Mr Jinks*, and was now a prominent trainer. But he made no effort to get his son into the saddle; rather he encouraged him to pursue a more stable, academic career.

For his part, initially, Bobby had no burning desire to ride. Then he was persuaded by his grandmother to give it a try; and once in the saddle the teenager quickly caught the family 'bug'. Riding was in his blood, after all. At 16, he rode his first winner as an amateur on the Flat, soon turned professional, and was only 19 when he made his Grand National debut. The year was 1957, and on the diminutive mare, *Sandy Jane II*, a 40-1 chance, he did well to complete the course, the tenth of 11 finishers.

His first famous victory came two years later, and ironically it was on a bay named after Captain Roderick Owen, the amateur jockey who had almost come to blows with Bobby's grandfather after being so narrowly beaten in the 1891 Grand National. 'Bunny' Cox was the regular rider of Lord Fingall's

Roddy Owen, but generously he suggested that the horse might have a better chance in the 1959 Cheltenham Gold Cup with young Beasley on board. The new partnership duly won – albeit greatly aided by the last fence blunder of *Pas Seul* which, in turn, hampered two other strong contenders. And the following year Bobby won another big one: the Champion Hurdle on *Another Flash*.

Above all else, it remained his declared ambition to maintain family tradition by winning the Grand National – as achieved by his grandfather Harry, by his uncle Tommy three times, and his new father-in-law, Arthur Thompson, twice. However, it was with a large measure of luck that Bobby came to have *Nicolaus Silver* for his second National appearance in 1961. Irish trainer Paddy Sleator, who retained him, agreed that he should accept an offer to ride for Fred Rimell. But then, in preparatory races, the jockey was not greatly impressed with the grey. As Mercy Rimell has recalled, he was reluctant to ride him in the National, but she and her husband insisted that he honour his commitment. In fact, the Rimells had wanted Stan Mellor as their stable jockey. But by the time he finally agreed, they had already engaged Beasley.

As it happened, *Nicolaus Silver* gave his rider only one anxious moment, when pecking on landing over Becher's the second time round. Otherwise, he jumped superbly well, took the lead at the second last, and won strictly on merit at 28-1. Bobby had become only the second rider (following Fred Winter) to have achieved the Grand National-Cheltenham Gold Cup-Champion Hurdle treble. And now, with his savings boosted by a £2,500 share of the prize money, he was able to safeguard his future by buying a farm in Ireland.

Twice more Bobby rode *Nicolaus Silver* in the National, finishing seventh in 1962 and tenth in 1963. The following year he was knocked off his mount, *Lizawake*, who went on to complete the full course alone; and in 1966 he pulled up on *Stirling* in the race which *Anglo* won by 20 lengths to give trainer Fred Winter his second successive National victory.

Having joined Winter at Uplands, Beasley took over on *Anglo* for the 1967 National. But the horse had been raised more than a stone, and he had to be pulled up in the race which saw the entire field brought to a standstill in the pile-up created by the riderless *Popham Down*. It would be five years before he rode in the National again. For by now

Bobby was fighting a seemingly losing battle – a long, despairng battle against alcoholism. It was an illness that contributed to the break-up of his marriage and eventually landed him in hospital. Though the Master of Uplands had sympathetically kept his old stable jockey job open, Bobby chose to return to Ireland and try to rebuild his life away from the limelight. He did so with magnificent resolve and, after a spell as an insurance salesman, he returned to the work he did with supreme style and strength: riding winners. In 1972 he made his eighth and last appearance in the Aintree National, only to be brought down on the seven year old longshot *Alaska Fort*. Then, with the 'old enemy' truly beaten, he teamed up with his friend, Pat Taaffe, now a trainer, to seal a most sensational come-back. First came major triumphs over hurdles on the headstrong, unpredictable *Captain Christy* who had previously put three work-riders in hospital. Bobby not only controlled the 'rogue' over hurdles but went on, in 1974, to give him a masterful ride to win – after a fifteen year gap – a second Cheltenham Gold Cup. It was the first time that the race had been won by a novice chaser since *Mont Tremblant* in 1952.

It was a fairy-tale climax to a tempestous career which has seen him take virtually all of jump racing's greatest prizes. Totally weaned off the booze, Bobby now remarried and established a more stable life as a family man and trainer. Based in Ireland, he saddled his first winner in 1976, then moved back to England. He eventually abandoned training and, as a supremely confident and defiant teetotaller, he spent eight years running a public house and later helping to run a vineyard in Kent. In January 2008 he died of cancer, aged 72.

See also: Nicolaus Silver.

BEASLEY, Harry

Though he achieved only one Grand National victory – compared with the three of his eldest brother Tommy – it may be argued that Harry was the most remarkable rider in racing's most remarkable family. Certainly, of the four Beasley brothers who competed in 19th century Nationals, he had the most prolonged and prolific career. With only one break, he rode in 13 Nationals between 1879 and 1892; and after finishing third on *Mohican* in 1883 he was second three years in a row. Away from Aintree, his many successes included two victories in the Grand Steeplechase de Paris. He was 73 years old when he rode in his last chase at Punchestown; an incredible, record-setting 83 when he made his final race appearance, partnering his own filly *Mollie* in Baldoyle's Corinthian Plate.

Ironically, two of brother Tommy's National victories were on horses – *Woodbrook* (1881) and *Frigate* (1889) – that Harry had previously ridden into fifth and second place respectively. Harry's one success came late – at his 12th and penultimate attempt – on *Come Away* (1891), an Irish gelding that he himself had trained. And it was achieved by just half a length and after an unsustained objection.

Harry made his National debut in 1879 when he finished ninth on *Turco* – behind brothers Tommy (third) and Willie (eighth), with another brother, John, failing to finish. Similarly, for the next three years, he was to be overshadowed by Tommy – fifth on *Woodbrook* in 1880 while Tommy won on *Empress*; a faller in 1881 while Tommy won on *Woodbrook*; a faller on *Mohican*, the short-priced favourite in 1882, when Tommy finished second on *Cyrus*.

In 1883 he at last finished ahead of Tommy – third to his fifth. Then came the unprecedented frustration of coming second in three successive Nationals – on *Frigate* (1884 and 1885) and *Too Good* (1886). And another big disappointment was to come in 1888. That year Harry was looking a sure winner as he sailed over the second Becher's on the joint favourite *Usna*. Only one rival was getting near him: brother Willie on the Aintree regular, *Frigate*. But then, at the Canal Turn, *Usna* dislocated a shoulder on landing, veered off to the right and in the process took *Frigate* with him. Willie managed to get his mare back on course, but critically she had lost a huge amount of ground and ultimately finished ten lengths behind the winner, *Playfair*.

So often the Beasley brothers exchanged their mounts. The Irish gelding *Come Away* was a notable exception. Harry was the only jockey ever to ride him. He was also the trainer. *Come Away*'s legs were not designed to withstand jarring on hard ground; and legend has it that, in the hard winter prior to the 1891 National, Harry would gallop him on The Curragh after dark, and by the light of storm lanterns, before the going was too firm with frost.

Whatever, his training methods certainly got results. *Come Away* arrived at Aintree with seven wins out of nine starts behind him, and he went off as 4-1 favourite. He won by half a length, though

B

arguably he would have been beaten if Captain E.R. 'Roddy' Owen, on the second placed *Cloister*, had not made the fatal error of going for a non-existent gap between the leader and the rails.

Racing days were now over for *Come Away* who was pulled up lame after his National win. Harry came back one more time but he never had a real run. In 1892 his mount, *Billie Taylor*, bolted and carried him off the racecourse. Brother Willie, also making his swansong, finished fifth on *Flying Column*. It marked the end of the Beasley era at Aintree.

Elsewhere Harry rode in many more races. He was still riding in 1929, the year his son Harry won the 2,000 Guineas on *Mr Jinks*; and he lived on to the age of 89, dying peacefully in 1939, three years after his son Patrick (Rufus) Beasley had won the St Leger and the Eclipse Stakes on *Boswell*, and four years after the birth of his grandson Bobby – the boy who would grow up to win the 1961 Grand National on *Nicolaus Silver*.
See also: Owen, Captain E.R.; Come Away.

BEASLEY, Thomas

The extraordinary record of Tommy Beasley speaks for itself. In twelve rides he won the National three times – on *Empress* (1880), *Woodbrook* (1881) and *Frigate* (1889); twice finished second – once by only a head; scored one third place and two times was fifth. But no less he is to be remembered as the man who blazed the trail for a unique and almost incredible family assault on steeplechasing's greatest prize.

It began so obscurely: in 1877, when Tommy, as a young Irish amateur, made his National debut on *Sultana*, a 50-1 outsider who had to be pulled up. One year later he commanded attention, riding a mare called *Martha* who looked all over the winner at the last, only to be beaten two lengths on the run-in by *Shifnal*. But it was on his third appearance, in 1879, that Aintree had the first hint of the shape of things to come. That year he headed a veritable Beasley invasion, as the eldest of four brothers – Tommy, Harry, Willie and Johnny – who were seeking National glory. Between them they would have 34 rides in the race.

Though Harry was arguably the best of the bunch, Tommy – mainly in partnership with the renowned Irish trainer Henry Eyre Linde – had by far the superior National record. In 1879 he overshadowed his three brothers, finishing third on *Martha*, with Willie and Harry eighth and ninth respectively. The next year, despite losing a stirrup early on, he gained his first win on *Empress*, with Harry fifth and John eighth. And he followed up with another Linde-trained winner, *Woodbrook*, while Harry was on a faller.

It was merely by a head, in 1882, that Tommy failed on *Cyrus* to become the only rider to achieve a unique hat-trick of National victories. By 1883 he had been at least placed in six successive Nationals. And it was not until his ninth National that he experienced a fall – in 1887 when he was riding six year old, Linde-trained *Spahi*, strangely a hot 9-2 favourite despite the fact that he had never been raced over hurdles let alone fences.

Tommy's third win came after an eight-year gap when he won by just a length from *Why Not* on the brave mare *Frigate*, who was running in her sixth National after three times being runner-up. Two years later, in 1891, Tommy had his last National ride, finishing fifth on the Linde-trained *Cruiser* while brother Harry achieved his long overdue success on *Come Away*.

Remarkably, this outstanding National record had been preceded by no less notable achievements on the Flat. Before turning to 'chasing, Tommy had won the Irish Derby three times and numerous races on the Continent. His jump successes abroad included the 1882 Grand Steeplechase de Paris.
See also: Empress; Woodbrook; Frigate.

BEASLEY, William

Willie was the unluckiest of the great Beasley brothers. Only once in six Grand Nationals did he have a well-supported horse to ride and on that occasion, in 1888, he finished second on *Frigate*, the mare his brother Tommy would ride to victory the following year. Arguably, Willie might have won that day but for a cruel twist of fate. He was sharing the lead with brother Harry (on the joint favourite *Usna*) soon after they had cleared Becher's the second time around. Then, at the Canal Turn, *Usna* dislocated his shoulder on landing and veered far to the right, carrying *Frigate* with him. Willie rode brilliantly to get his mare back into the race. But far too much ground had been lost and *Frigate* finished ten-lengths second to *Playfair*.

Joining his three brothers in the race, Willie had made his National debut in 1879, finishing eighth on the outsider *Lord Marcus*. Seven years passed before he revisited Aintree and again he came home eighth, on *Lady Tempest*. The following year, 1887, he fell on Lord Cholmondeley's 100-1 shot, *The Hunter*, and in 1889, riding for the same owner, he was seventh on *The Fawn*.

Willie was the last of the Beasley brothers to be a finisher in the race, taking fifth place in 1892 on *Flying Column*, a 50-1 chance. For the fifth time in six appearances he had completed the course. But just six weeks later he would be dead, having failed to recover from injuries suffered in the Kildare Hunt Plate at Punchestown.

BECHER, Captain Martin Wiliam

As England's most celebrated cross-country rider, Captain Becher competed in the first hurdle meeting to be held at Aintree in 1835, winning two of the races. In February of the following year he rode *The Duke* to a one-length victory in the first Aintree steeplechase; and in 1839 he rode a bay horse called *Conrad* in the Grand Liverpool Steeplechase that came to be regarded, controversially, as the first Grand National.

At that time, there were only three really formidable obstacles: a stone wall, 4ft 8in high, and two treacherous jumps over brooks. *Conrad*, a relative outsider at 20-1, was close up in second place, when he hit the timbered top of the fence guarding the first brook. The captain was propelled into the chilly waters beyond, and there, taking shelter as the field thundered over him, he reputedly remarked dryly, 'Water should never be taken without brandy.'

Some say it was the absence of whisky, not brandy, that he deplored. Whatever – as he had done in many chases before, Becher stubbornly remounted and set off in pursuit. He caught up with the leaders but only to take another cold bath in the equally hazardous second brook. Although this obstacle (now known as Valentine's) ended his challenge, it was the first brook that was to bear his name ever after: the notorious Becher's Brook.

Born in 1797, the son of an ex-soldier who had become a Norfolk farmer and horse-dealer, Becher was in Brussels at the time of the Battle of Waterloo, serving in the storekeeper's department of the War Office. He was later given the courtesy title of 'captain', while serving with the Duke of Buckingham's yeomanry regiment and parading with his unit at the coronation of King George 1V.

Ostensibly a professional rider in all but name, Becher succeeded Dick Christian as the dominant rider of English steeplechasing in the 1830s. Sporting distinctively thick side-whiskers, he was hugely popular with the public because he was so reliably determined and competitive, and at the same time renowned for his sportsmanship and good-natured antics out of the saddle. Crucially, he was a very close friend of innkeeper and trainer Thomas Coleman, the so-called 'Father of Steeplechasing', who had devised the great St Albans Steeplechase over four miles in 1830.

Becher regularly rode horses for Coleman and for long periods lodged at his home. Most famously he was associated with *Vivian*, the great gelding on whom he had won the marathon Vale of Aylesbury Chase in 1834 and 1836. In the latter year he also won the St Albans but in most distressing circumstances – his mount, the much-loved grey *Grimaldi*, dropping dead after passing the winning post.

In 1835 Becher had encouraged innkeeper William Lynn to do for Liverpool what Coleman had done for St Albans – greatly boosting local trade with the attraction of a steeplechase. The captain duly won the first Aintree chase (a seller) on *The Duke* in 1836. The following year the event was promoted more ambitiously, arguably being the forerunner of the Grand National; and again *The Duke* was the winner, but this time the rider was a Mr Henry Potts, Becher missing the race because he had been engaged at St Albans the day before. One year later, at Aintree, he was back on *The Duke*, the 2-1 favourite, and finished third.

Though it was a financially unrewarding occupation, Becher continued to race in public until 1847 when he was 50 years old. However, after his immortalised fall into the Aintree brook, he never rode in the National again; and within a few years he would be overshadowed by two outstanding riders, Jem Mason and Tom Olliver.

In his later years, he worked as an 'inspector of sacks' for the Great Northern Railway, and on retirement he settled with his family in Maida Vale, north London. He died there, aged 67, on October 11, 1864, and was buried at Paddington cemetery, Willesden.

See also: Lynn, William.

BECHER'S BROOK
Named after Captain Martin Becher following his

B

fall in the first (1839) Aintree Grand National, Becher's Brook is the sixth fence on the first circuit and the 22nd the next time around. It marks the beginning of a gradual left U-turn which is completed, two fences later, by the sharp bend at the Canal Turn. Before it was modified in 1990, jockeys said that tackling this obstacle felt like jumping off the edge of the world.

Fear of the unknown made it regarded as the most formidable challenge on the course. Until 1990, the horse on approach could only see a wall of spectators beyond the towering spruce; and then, as now, he could be caught out by the inordinate size of the drop on the landing side. The height of the fence is 4ft 10in on take-off but as much as 6ft 4in on the landing side, the drop being slightly greater for riders opting for the shorter inside route.

Most ominously, before 1990, the ground immediately beyond the fence used to slope back into the ditch, thus creating a V-shape void. On average, horses would land 9ft 5in beyond the fence. But those who touched down short were liable to roll back down the slope – as happened in 1989 when *Brown Trix* fell fatally, so deep in the ditch that he had to be winched out frantically before the field arrived there a second time.

Becher's Brook was originally 8ft wide and guarded, a further three and a half feet back, by a stout timber fence. The jump was sited on the most heavily ploughed section of the course and confusingly the landing ground was three feet below the take-off level. If Captain Becher had not famously fallen there in 1839 it might conceivably have been named Barker's Brook after the jockey who was left severely concussed when his horse, *Weathercock*, fell there in the second Grand National.

By 1885, when the National course took on the completely railed and turfed appearance of today, Becher's was 7ft 6in wide and 6ft deep. Other fences involved unexpected drops but at least the ground on their landing side was flat. Becher's was already seen as the most challenging because, in addition, it had landing ground that was cruelly sloped backwards at 45 degrees.

In response to protests after four horses had perished (not at Becher's) in the 1954 National, the Aintree management announced changes to ease the hazards of the course. But the changes were minor and seemingly made no marked difference to the most notorious jump. Many great jockeys would continue to come to grief at this point – not least, among them, the master horseman John Francome. He was knocked out and broke a bone in his right hand in 1976 when leading *Golden Rapper* made his first error, nose-diving at Becher's second time around; and here, in 1982, riding *Rough and Tumble*, he was thrown into the ditch when another horse pulled up in front of them.

Criticism of Becher's really took off in 1987 when, via television, millions of viewers saw the second favourite, an attractive grey called *Dark Ivy*, take an especially horrific fall there after being impeded by *Attitude Adjuster* at the moment of take-off. He hit the top of the fence and plunged to his death in the sloping ditch beyond. Two years later criticism of the National was so intense that the subject reached the floor of the House of Commons. In the 1989 race, a five-horse pile-up at Becher's had seen two killed: the Irish runner *Seeandem* who broke his neck when failing to clear the brook, and the amateur-ridden *Brown Trix*, a 300-1 outsider who plunged headlong into the ditch. Over the past 20 years six horses had perished at Becher's.

This time the Aintree authorities felt compelled to take positive action. Most controversially their changes to the course included filling in the ditch on the landing side of Becher's to make level ground and so ensure that never again could a horse be trapped in its sharp 'V' shaped ditch. It provided an extra five feet of landing space. In addition, the right-hand outside running rail beside Becher's was re-sited further back and guarded by a newly planted hedge – a measure arguably no less important since it stopped horses being distracted at a critical stage by the sudden sight of photographers and spectators. It was hoped, too, that these changes would encourage more horses to jump straight, whereas previously some had tended to skew to the left in mid-air, so adding to the risk of collisions.

Surprising as it might seem, many jockeys strongly disapproved of the softening of Becher's. None was more critical than Peter Scudamore, then champion jockey, who observed that the race was no longer the same as it was when his father, Michael, won on *Oxo*. 'The National was unique; it was a test and now they've spoiled it,' he said. Moreover, he expressed the fear that Becher's might become even more dangerous because there was no longer a marked difference in the drop – formerly 23in as opposed to 17in – on the inside and outside respectively.

His suggestion was that jockeys might no longer be inclined to favour the outer side of Becher's and that a stampede down the inner could lead to a horrible pile-up.

On the other hand, Mr John Parrett, Aintree's manager and clerk of the course, was hopeful that jockeys would now use the whole of the fence rather than favour one side. *'Last Suspect, Rhyme 'N' Reason* and *Hallo Dandy* all won the National jumping Becher's on the outside, and I hope jockeys will take advantage of the new option offered.'

Following the changes to the course, plus the advent of unusually fast ground, it was not surprising that, in 1990, the course record was broken by both the winner *Mr Frisk* and the runner-up *Durham Edition*. The fast ground inevitably increased the risks and, sadly, there were two fatalities: *Roll-A-Joint* who broke his neck in falling at the Canal Turn, and *Hungary Hur* who was pulled up at the 20th fence with a broken leg. But there were only two fallers at Becher's, and both were unharmed.

In 1998, after the National had seen three fatalities (again not at Becher's), further changes included widening the first fence and raising the landing level slightly at Becher's and The Chair. Though its steep drop is still a considerable challenge, all the evidence indicates that Becher's is now much less hazardous. Since the major changes prior to the 1990 race 15 horses have been killed in the Grand National. But not one of them came to grief at Becher's; and though nine horses exited there in 2004 this was due more to congestion and interference rather than the difficulty of the obstacle. Nevertheless, it remains the most famous steeplechase jump in the world, so respected that people have even chosen to get married in its shadow.
See also: Becher, Captain Martin; Fences; Tactics.

BELPER, Lord
Long before succeeding to his father's title in 1956, Lord Belper was popularly known as Ronnie Strutt, a highly proficient amateur rider on the Flat and over fences. Born Alexander Ronald George Strutt, and educated at Harrow and Sandhurst, he was only 21 when he won Cheltenham's four-mile National Hunt Chase on *Crown Prince*, owned by his stepfather Lord Rosebery. Two years later, as owner-rider, he made his Aintree debut on the same gelding, a 66-1 chance in the 1936 Grand National. They

finished fourth to *Reynoldstown*, and returned the following year to come fifth at 50-1 to *Royal Mail*.

Though he had a runner in the 1939 National (*Sporting Piper*, a faller under Mr John Hislop) Strutt did not ride in the race again. Following wartime service (wounded in action with the Coldsream Guards) he became a keen huntsman (a Master of the Quorn) and later served as racing manager to the shipping tycoon Stavros Niarchos. As a racehorse owner, he was most famously associated with *Persian Lancer,* who had been written of with serious leg trouble when Belper took him over from Niarchos. *Persian Lancer* ran only twice in five years; then, in 1966, revitalised by trainer Ryan Price, the eight year old became the oldest winner of the Cesarewitch.

In his later years Lord Belper had horses in the Yorkshire stable of Mick Easterby, among them the chaser *Mick's Star* and the prolific sprint winner *Master Pokey*. In 1988, more than half a century after his debut in the race, he aspired to win the Grand National with the former. *Mick Star*, an eight year old, lightly weighted and to be ridden by Phil Tuck, became the ante-post favourite. But in the end he was a non-runner. His disappointed owner died in 1999, aged 87.

BENNET, Captain Geoffrey Harbord
Aintree has never seen a more stubbornly determined rider than Captain 'Tuppy' Bennet. Born in 1895, at East Barton, Bury St Edmunds, the son of a National Hunt trainer, he served during the First World War in France and Egypt; and following demob he set his heart on winning the Grand National. His 1920 debut ended in a fall on a rank outsider, *Picture Saint*. But never again – come what may – would this indomitable amateur rider fail to complete the course.

In the 1921 National, which saw more casualties than ever before, he fell three times on eight year old *Turkey Buzzard*. And three times he climbed back into the saddle, finally riding him into fourth place – the last of the finishers in a 35-strong field. The horse's loving owner, Mrs H.M. Hollins, was not impressed. Wielding an umbrella, she chased the captain round the paddock, cursing him for subjecting her beloved gelding to such an ordeal.

One year later, Bennet again landed on the turf, unseated at the fence after the second Valentine's. Again he remounted, and on the aptly named *A*

Double Escape, a 40-1 shot, he battled back to be the last of five finishers in a field of 32, one place behind *Sergeant Murphy* (also remounted).

By now the captain was fast establishing himself as the leading amateur rider; and arguably – as a veterinary surgeon by profession – he was well qualified to judge a horse's fitness after a fall. He rode many winners for his trainer-brother, Sam Bennet, and he ended the 1922 season by taking over on *Sergeant Murphy* and riding him to victory in the Scottish Grand National.

He kept the ride in the 1923 National, and for the first time he got round unscathed. On his fourth appearance in the race, 13 year old *Sergeant Murphy* jumped securely, never being passed after leaping into the lead at the second Becher's. He won by three lengths, the oldest winner since *Why Not* in 1894 and the first ever to be American owned. Afterwards the captain was personally congratulated by King George V.

One day later, over the same course, Bennet was triumphant again, in the inaugural Liverpool Foxhunters' Chase. He went on to end the season as the top amateur rider with 62 winners, only two less than the professional champion, Fred Rees. And that same year, in July, the captain was married in a fashionable wedding at St. George's, Hanover Square, London.

But sadly, his glorious run of good fortune was to end abruptly in tragedy. On December 27, after falling on *Ardeen* in the minor Oteley Chase at Wolverhampton, he received a fatal kick to the head from a passing horse. A blood clot formed and he died 17 days later, having never regained consciousness. He was aged 29. It was this tragedy, following other serious skull injuries to jump jockeys, that finally persuaded the National Hunt Committee to make compulsory the wearing of crash helmets in steeplechases.

See also: Sergeant Murphy; Blackwell, George; Sanford, Stephen.

BEN NEVIS

American-owned and American-ridden winner of the 1980 Grand National when 30 runners faced quagmire conditions and only four finished. Having been brought down at Aintree the previous year, and still without a single win after a dozen races in Britain, 12 year old *Ben Nevis* was an unfancied 40-1 shot; and yet he won by 20 lengths and a further ten lengths from *Rough and Tumble* and *The Pilgarlic* respectively.

Bred in England – by *Camiri* out of *Ben Trumiss* – *Ben Nevis* was an unbroken five year old when he was first bought by civil servant Mrs Jane Porter to ride in Yorkshire point-to-points. Relatively small, nervous and excitable, he fell in his first two races and won his third. At that stage, even without chasing experience, he attracted the eye of Redmond C. Stewart Jnr, a visiting American. Always on the lookout for horses suitable to race over timber, he bought him over the dinner-table after joining a shooting party in Yorkshire.

When the somewhat frail-looking six year old arrived in the United States in 1974, Baltimore banker Charlie Fenwick, the buyer's son-in-law and a leading amateur rider, was unimpressed. But the judgment of Mr Stewart proved remarkably sound. Having twice owned a winner of the prestigious Maryland Hunt Cup, he would double that total with *Ben Nevis*, ridden by Fenwick to victory in the Hunt Cups of 1977 and 1978. In all, *Ben Nevis* was to win 12 successive races, seven over timber, before, as an unbeaten chaser, he was sent back to England to bid for Grand National glory.

A complete reversal of form – 12 races without a win – was to follow the arrival of *Ben Nevis* at Wantage, Oxfordshire, to be trained by Captain Tim Forster. His defeats were attributed to the hated soft or heavy going that he regularly encountered. But when he arrived at Aintree for the 1979 National, good going was in his favour, and consequently he was well backed, joint fourth in the betting at 14-1. Only bad luck in running put paid to his chances. At The Chair he ran into a pile-up created by two riderless horses veering across the course. Nine runners were put out of the race and though Mr Fenwick remounted to clear the ditch he abandoned the hopeless chase at the next fence.

One year later everything seemed to be against *Ben Nevis* in his second National bid. He was 12 years old, had been lowered only 4lb in the handicap, and was still without a win after a year in England. He had been coughing four days before the race; and, worst of all, he faced desperately heavy going. As Forster later explained, he would never have run the horse but for the fact that connections and so many supporters had travelled all the way from the States. His instructions to the jockey before the race were simple: 'Keep remounting,' he said.

But seemingly *Ben Nevis* had now adapted to heavy conditions. He led the field from the second Becher's onwards and powered away from his challengers on the run-in to win comfortably from *Rough and Tumble* ridden by John Francome. Only two others of 30 starters completed the course. Back in the United States, *Ben Nevis* was retired to Mr Stewart's Maryland estate, and following the death of his owner in 1986, he spent the rest of his days in the care of Mr Fenwick, the second American to have ridden a winner of the Aintree Grand National. *See also:* Forster, Captain Tim; Fenwick, Charles.

BERRY, Frank

Born in 1952, Frank Berry was a remarkably versatile and stylish jockey who first made his mark on the Flat, springing to fame when he rode *Giolla Mear* to win the 1968 Irish St Leger for the President of Ireland. Increasing weight soon forced him to turn to jumps and he proceeded to become ten times champion jockey in Ireland and winner of the 1972 Cheltenham Gold Cup on *Glencaraig Lady*. Altogether he won six races at the Cheltenham Festival including the 1981 Queen Mother Champion Chase (*Drumgoran*) and the 1985 Sun Alliance Chase (*Antarctic Bay*).

In his first Aintree Grand National Berry finished eighth on *Money Boat* (1972). But in seven subsequent rides he only twice completed the course, being 12th on *Tacroy* (1984) and seventh on *The Ellier* (1987). Since retiring from the saddle, however, he has regularly been involved with outstanding Grand National contenders in his capacity as the racing manager for J.P. McManus, owner of more than 100 racehorses.

Berry's son Fran began race-riding in 1996 and at one time it seemed that he would emulate his father by switching from the Flat to jump racing. Most notably the Kilcullen-based jockey won the 2000 Ladbroke Handicap Hurdle on *Mantles Prince*. But unlike his father he had no rising weight problems and, being able to make 8st 8lb, he later reverted successfully to concentrating on the Flat. *See also:* McManus, John Patrick.

BETTING

In the early years of the Grand National the biggest bets usually took the form of private wagers struck between wealthy rival owners. Nevertheless, bookmakers – having first appeared on English race-courses in the late 18th century – were in attendance at Aintree from the beginning. The race soon became hugely popular with on-course punters, though for many decades it remained a relatively modest gambling event compared with the Epsom Derby.

Today, however, the National generates at least six times as much betting as that on the Derby. Money gambled on the race may be surpassed by betting on some collective events: the World Cup, the Cheltenham Festival, Royal Ascot and Glorious Goodwood. But, as a single sporting event, the National attracts the biggest turnover of all – lately an estimated £250 million-plus.

The first major innovation in Grand National betting came in 1930 following the establishment of the Horserace Totalisator Board which operated a new pool system commonly known as the Tote, and more disrespectfully as the Nanny (nanny goat). Now, for the first time, punters had an alternative to betting against bookmakers. Under the Tote system they were, in effect, betting against one another, their bets going into a pool with the odds continually fluctuating in response to the pattern of betting and the total sum finally being shared out among successful punters.

Since no fixed odds are offered at the time of placing a bet on the Tote, there can be major differences between the Tote return and the SP returns from bookmakers. In 1946, for example, *Lovely Cottage* won the National at 25-1 but was a miserable 11-1 on the Tote. Conversely, in 1948, *Russian Hero*, the 66-1 winner, was a colossal 202-1 on the Tote. And best of all, when *Foinavon* was the 100-1 winner in 1967, the Tote paid 444-1.

Although bettting flourished illegally off-course, the Grand National only really took off as the biggest betting event of all from 1961 onwards, following the legalisation of off-course betting shops, which mushroomed in a couple of years to a peak of almost 20,000 throughout Britain. Betting continued to advance apace despite the 1966 re-introduction of a betting tax (initially 2.5 per cent) which had previously been tried unsuccessfully for three years in the 1920s. From 1987 the tax was confined to off-course betting only, and within two years betting on the National had hit the £50 million mark – a figure that would be doubled after 2001 when the tax (then nine per cent) was abolished completely.

In 1993 the betting industry had suffered a major blow when the Grand National was declared void.

B

However, in 1995, betting on the race rose to £80 million, an increase of £5 million on the previous year. The bookies were then hit by the introduction of the National Lottery, costing them an estimated £120 million a year in turnover, and by Frankie Dettori's 1996 'magnificent seven' at Ascot, costing them around £30 million. In the light of this background, the industry was hugely relieved in 1997 when, following bomb scares, it was decided to reschedule the National rather than abandon it altogether. Remarkably, betting shops reported more business with the National run on Monday instead of the Saturday.

Over the years bookies have enjoyed a number of great escapes on the National – most notably in 1986 when an estimated £1 million was staked on 13-2 favourite *Mr Snugfit* who had been runner-up the year before. Carrying the colours of famed speculator Terry Ramsden, he made a late challenge to finish fourth. Scandalously, however, some layers did not pay on fourth place in those days. Only after 1990 did it become universal practice to recognise the fourth in all handicaps with 16 runners or more. But fortune still favoured the bookies in the 1991 Grand National. There were huge bets on *Bonanza Boy* after he had been leased to a national newspaper. Off as 13-2 favourite, he narrowly missed fourth place to the loss of myriad each-way backers.

In keeping with the name of its first winner, the Grand National continued to be commonly regarded as a gigantic lottery. However, it did not always work out heavily in the bookmakers' favour. In 1996 they took quite a pasting when the winner was *Rough Quest*, a long-time favourite eased from 5-1 to 7-1, and third place was taken by a huge each-way fancy, *Superior Finish*. The latter had attracted a flood of money after being leased to a tabloid for the day, with a late jockey booking combining the talents of trainer Jenny Pitman and Richard Dunwoody, both twice previously successful in the race. The flood reduced *Superior Finish*'s odds from 25-1 to 9-1, and it was calculated that if he had won the bookies would have had to pay out £75 million – including £107,000 to a Mr Peter McGrane of Melksham, Wilts, who had 'won' the horse in a newspaper competition.

In 1999, more than ever before, one horse threatened to cripple the bookies: the long-time ante-post favourite *Double Thriller*. On the eve of the race William Hill claimed that they were facing a near

£5 million payout if the nine year old won. Hill's liabilities had been swollen by more than £2 million as a result of their offer of a £20 free bet on the *Spring Double* to potential shareholders in their abandoned stock market flotation. This consolation bet on the Lincoln and National was offered to 90,000 disappointed share applicants; and an estimated 10,000 of the 50,000 bets struck on the first leg were placed successfully on the 9-1 favourite *Right Wing*. Thus, over £1.1 million in winnings automatically went on to the leading National contenders – especially *Double Thriller* whose price was cut from 5-1 to 7-2 after the Lincoln.

History favoured the bookies: it was 102 years since favourites – *Winkfields Pride*, 7-2, and *Manifesto*, 6-1 – had won the Lincoln and the National respectively. As it happened, on race day *Double Thriller* went out to 7-1, with *Fiddling The Facts* made the 6-1 favourite. Providentially for William Hill they did not suffer for long. *Double Thriller* crashed out at the first fence. On-course bookies, however, had a very bad day indeed because there had been so much late money for *Bobbyjo*, the 10-1 winner, and for *Call It A Day*, third at 7-1, and *Addington Boy*, fourth at 10-1.

This year the Tote recorded an on-course turnover of more than £1 million, a rise of almost 12 per cent on the 1998 record; and in Hong Kong (where *Double Thriller* started the 9-2 favourite) punters staked some £2 million on the race. Betting on the National was increasing year by year, and by now a variety of novelty bets was being introduced – on the age of the winner, the number of finishers, and even, in the case of Sporting Index, a wager revolving around how many times Jenny Pitman would kiss Des Lynam on BBC Grandstand and whether she would cry on camera.

Meanwhile, in 2000, for the first time, hundreds of thousands of punters were having their Grand National flutter via the internet, taking advantage of tax-free betting available from offshore operatives. It was not a smooth beginning since many would-be punters ran into traffic jams. This was probably just as well for the layers since the National was a near-disaster for them as punters in their tens of thousands plunged on the widely tipped *Papillon* whose odds on the day shortened from 33-1 to 10-1. Hills had laid one bet of £33,000 to £1,000.

This time there was no escape for the bookies. It was estimated that overall *Papillon*'s victory cost them at least £10 million – the result of what was described as the greatest public gamble in the history of the National. Ladbrokes alone escaped heavy punishment, having artfully priced *Papillon* at 16-1 from the start of the day. Their PR director Mike Dillon had long thought *Papillon* an ideal National type and his view had been strengthened early on when he took a bet from trainer Ted Walsh – 'just a few quid' – to win at special odds of 40-1.

However, no tears needed be shed for the bookies on this occasion. They gained valuable compensation by way of the third fence fall of *Dark Stranger*, the 9-1 favourite and the greatest liability for Ladbrokes. In addition results of other Aintree races went heavily in their favour. Moreover, while this was one of the worst-ever Nationals for the layers, their losses were more than counter-balanced the following year when 36 of 40 starters failed to finish in quagmire conditions and the winner was *Red Marauder* at 33-1.

The most popular punter was Steve Thoburn, a market trader who at the time was on trial for – contrary to European law – selling bananas by the pound rather than by metric measure. He had won £2,400 by backing *Red Marauder*. But overall the National of 2001 was a bookies' benefit of epic proportions. It was estimated that they had made up to a £20 million profit on the race in a year when betting reached new heights for a variety of reasons. Internet betting was now efficiently organised, available to punters from more than 200 countries. Three internet bookmakers – unlike the Big Three (William Hill, Ladbrokes and Coral) – enterprisingly offered to pay out on the first five finishers. And punters were all the more keen to have a flutter at a time when the foot-and-mouth epidemic had caused so many race meetings to be cancelled.

Furthermore, for the first time, the National was shown live on TV in mainland China with its 200 million potential viewers. Though some citizens there were able to bet via registered internet accounts, betting was still illegal in China – and fortunately so for the bookies since many Chinese punters were inclined to back any horse with the 'lucky colour' red in its name.

In 2002 betting rose to still greater heights with the staging of the first tax-free National of modern times. An estimated £100 million was gambled on the race and one year later this estimate rose to £110 million. Having suffered a disastrous Chel-tenham Festival in 2003, the bookmakers now gained huge relief from a Grand National in which none of the leading fancies figured in the frame. However, this bonanza was lessened for Hills and the Tote who had laid huge bets at 33-1 by the owners of *Monty's Pass*.

The next big 'bookies' benefit' came in 2007 when the winner was *Silver Birch* at 33-1, followed home by *McKelvey* (12-1), *Slim Pickings* (33-1) and *Philson Run* (100-1). That year the industry estimates put the turnover for the day between £250m and £275m.

See also: Ante-Post Betting; Gambles; Tipsters; Spring Double.

BIBBY, Frank

The old cliché about 'safety in numbers' was blown sky high in the 1910 National when owner Frank Bibby sought to increase his chances by having three runners – *Caubeen*, *Wickham* and *Glenside* – in a 25-strong field. Remarkably, *Wickham*, a 66-1 outsider, put his two other horses out of the race – knocking over *Caubeen*, the 8-1 third favourite, in a collision, and then bringing down *Glenside*, a 25-1 chance, as he himself fell at the fence before Becher's.

Nevertheless, Mr Bibby, a Liverpool manufacturer, remained a fanatical supporter of his great local chase. For more than two decades horses ran in his familiar colours, beginning with *Zodiac II* in 1901 and ending with *Wavertree* in 1922. His persistence was rewarded with two National winners: *Kirkland* (1905) and *Glenside* (1911). In addition, he had the runner-up with *Kirkland* (1904) and third place with *Kirkland* (1903) and *Caubeen* (1909).

The key to his success was the hugely popular partnership he formed with Frank 'Tich' Mason, the Liverpool-born jockey who rode *Kirkland* in four Nationals, always completing the course. In 1905, when *Kirkland* was the 6-1 second favourite, Bibby paid Mason not to ride for two weeks prior to the Aintree meeting. He did not trouble to take the same precaution when his one-eyed *Glenside* was a 20-1 chance in 1911 and, sure enough, a broken leg cost Mason the ride. But no matter. The choice of substitute rider was positively inspired: John Randolph Anthony, a newcomer who would gain the first of his three National victories.

Altogether Bibby had 21 runners in 16 Nationals, and the family tradition was carried on by his

daughter. As Mrs D. Thompson, she was the owner of *Forest Prince* who, in a 47-strong field, finished third, behind *Anglo* and *Freddie*, in the 1966 National.
See also: Mason, Frank; Kirkland; Glenside.

BICESTER, Lord

With millionaires Mr J.V. Rank and Mr 'Jock' Hay Whitney, financier Lord Bicester was an unwilling member of the triumvirate of owners who, before and after the Second World War, most persistently pursued without success their great ambition to have a Grand National winner. Between 1939 and 1956 17 horses ran in his colours in the National, but only once did he gain a place – with his eight year old *Roimond*, beaten eight lengths into second by *Russian Hero* in 1949. Nothing, however, could dampen this Old Etonian's enthusiasm; even beyond the age of 80 he was still flying to Ireland to look for likely jumpers.

After failing twice with his first contender *Rockquilla* (a faller in 1939 and 13th in 1940), Lord Bicester launched his post-war challenge with a most promising prospect, seven year old *Silver Fame*, a half-brother to *Bogskar*, the 1940 National winner. Trained by George Beeby, *Silver Fame* was to develop into a truly outstanding chaser. By 1951, when he became the first 12 year old to triumph in the Cheltenham Gold Cup (by a disputed short head from Mr Rank's *Greenogue*), he had won more than half of his 49 races, nine of them at Cheltenham. Yet he fell in three successive Nationals, the last being the 1948 race when he was the 9-1 favourite.

That year Lord Bicester had two other runners in the National: *Parthenon*, who had fallen in 1947, and *Roimond*, a highly regarded seven year old. The former finished seventh at 100-1, and though *Roimond* fell on his Aintree debut, he was strong enough in 1949 to be given top weight of 11st 12lb. Superbly ridden by a newcomer named Dick Francis, he was bettered only by one of 42 rivals, *Russian Hero*, with an 18lb advantage.

In 1950, when joint top in the weights and the betting, *Roimond* was a faller; and he met the same fate in 1951 and 1952. Failure in the 1951 National was especially hard for Lord Bicester to bear since he had another formidable contender in the race: ten year old *Finnure*, runner-up in the 1950 Cheltenham Gold Cup. His rider, Francis, was full of confidence, having had five wins on the big, gutsy chestnut,

including the Champion Chase at Liverpool and the 1949 King George VI Chase when, by half a length, he became the first horse to beat the great *Cottage Rake* over fences in England. But in the National, through absolutely no fault of his own, *Finnure* was one of 11 fallers at the first, having jumped it perfectly only to land amid a great pile-up of horses and jockeys.

In 1953, Lord Bicester's *Senlac Hill*, a 66-1 outsider, finished fifth in the Grand National won comfortably by *Early Mist*. The owner was both delighted and amazed that his horse, a notoriously erratic jumper, had done so well. Nevertheless, the result was especially galling for the luckless lord since, in the previous year, he had been outbid for *Early Mist* at the dispersal sale of horses owned by the late Mr Rank.

Lord Bicester had some consolation when winning the Irish National with his *Royal Approach* in 1954. But his last Aintree contender, *Mariner's Log*, was a faller in 1955 and 1956. In the latter race, as a special tribute, the horse ran in the colours of a renowned owner who had died one month earlier.

BIDDLECOMBE, Terence Walter

A rider of extraordinary courage and balance, the flamboyant Terry Biddlecombe rode 908 winners and was champion jockey three times (once jointly) despite suffering an appalling catalogue of injuries: scores of concussions; fractures of collarbone (eight times), arms (five times), shoulder blades, vertebrae, ribs, wrists, fingers, thumbs and a leg, plus kidneys severely bruised when, with a foot caught in the stirrup, he was dragged 200 yards by a runaway horse. But he was fated to ride in 11 Grand Nationals without success, his best being a second place in 1972.

Unluckily, injury had cost him the ride on *Gay Trip* when the little bay gelding won the 1970 National under Pat Taaffe. One year later horse and rider were reunited in the race, but *Gay Trip*, the 8-1 favourite, was now penalised with top weight, and he was one of five fallers at the first fence. Then, in 1972, Biddlecombe had high hopes of victory: again with *Gay Trip*, and this time he had only one rival to beat towards the end of the long run-in. At that stage, it seemed a hopeless task, having to concede a whopping 22lb to *Well To Do*, ridden by champion jockey Graham Thorner. Yet he finished only two lengths behind the winner; and, in the view of trainer Fred Rimell, Biddlecombe would have

B

had his National win if he had not chosen to race so wide in search of faster ground, so giving away far more than the distance by which *Gay Trip* was beaten.

Even 35 years later, the trainer's widow, Mercy Rimell, would echo that view. Recalling Fred's all-time record of saddling four National winners, she told Marcus Armytage: 'It would have been five if Terry Biddlecombe hadn't gone five miles instead of four and a half on *Gay Trip* in 1972.'

Born on February 2, 1941, the younger of two brothers in a Gloucestershire farming family, Terry grew up in his father's world of gymkhana. He won 22 races as an amateur before turning professional in the 1959-60 season; and four years later he began to have great success as first jockey to the Rimells, gaining the jockeys' championship in 1964-65 and retaining the title the following season when he became the first jump rider to have more than 100 winners in successive seasons. His third title, gained in 1968-69 with 77 winners, was shared with his one-time brother-in-law Bob Davies.

Most notably, in 1967, Terry superbly drove home *Woodland Venture* to win the Cheltenham Gold Cup by just three-quarters of a length. In the 1969 Gold Cup he was only narrowly beaten on *Domacorn* after losing his whip, and three other times he finished third in the race. Other successes included two Mackeson Gold Cups on *Gay Trip*, the Triumph Hurdle on *Coral Diver* and the first Irish Sweeps Hurdle on Normandy. His Grand National rides were: *Aliform* (fell, 1960); *Blonde Warrior* (11th, 1962); *Loyal Tan* (17th, 1963); *Red Thorn* (pulled up, 1964); *Culleenhouse* (12th, 1965); *The Fossa* (fourth, 1966); *Greek Scholar* (fourth, 1967); *Vultrix* (fell, 1968); *Fearless Fred* (fell, 1969); *Gay Trip* (fell, 1971); and *Gay Trip* (second, 1972).

A hugely popular personality, the charismatic and cavalier Biddlecombe remained the 'cheekie chappie' of National Hunt racing despite his countless injuries and a constant and tedious battle against the scales. The battle was finally lost in 1974. In his last big race, the Cheltenham Gold Cup, he finished third on the Queen Mother's *Game Spirit*. After the Festival he retired from race-riding and had his colourful career recounted on TV in 'This Is Your Life'. In 1995, after two failed marriages and a long-overdue conquest of alcohol, the ever-cheerful ex-carouser hit life's jackpot with his marriage to trainer Henrietta Knight – a heaven-made partner-

ship that proved hugely successful in every way.

Together, 'Hen' and Terry had many big-race successes – most famously with *Best Mate* who won the 2002 King George VI Chase and one year later became the first horse to win back-to-back Cheltenham Gold Cups since *L'Escargot* 32 years before. In 2003 they enjoyed a sensational shock victory in the King George with *Edredon Bleu* at 25-1 and in 2004 completed an Arkle-equalling hat-trick of Gold Cup wins with *Best Mate*. In contrast, they had no success with their few Grand National runners: *Full Of Oats* in 1997 and *Chives, Maximize* and *Southern Star* in 2003. However, in 2002 Terry had played an important part in the Grand National victory of *Bindaree* by virtue of the fact that he had been responsible for greatly improving the riding style of the winning jockey, Jim Culloty.

Meanwhile, the family riding tradition had been carried on by Terry's son Robert who, in January, 2000, had scored the first of a series of point-to-point wins on *Rectory Garden*. He rode eight winners under Rules as an amateur and in 2002 became a conditional rider with trainer Nigel Twiston-Davies before being forced to retire prematurely by increasing weight.

See also: Knight, Henrietta; Rimell, Fred; Culloty, Jim.

BINDAREE
Winner of the 2002 Grand National, by one and three-quarters of a length, after a hard-fought duel with *What's Up Boys* on the run-in. The 20-1 victory represented a second success for trainer Nigel Twiston-Davies (four years after scoring with *Earth Summit*) and made Jim Culloty the first jockey to achieve the Cheltenham Gold Cup-National double since John Burke 26 years before.

On breeding, *Bindaree* was fully entitled to triumph in a Grand National. His sire was *Roselier* whose progeny included *Royal Athlete*, the 1995 winner; *Suny Bay*, the runner-up of 1997 and 1998; and *Moorcroft Boy* and *Ebony Jane*, third and fourth respectively in 1994. And for good measure he was out of the mare *Flowing Tide*, granddam of the 1980 Oaks winner, *Bireme*.

Bindaree was bought as a yearling for a mere Ir2000 guineas by Jimmy Mangan, a renowned horse dealer of Co. Cork (destined to train the 2003 National winner *Monty's Pass*) and sold on the following year. He came to Britain in 1999 as a successful Irish point-to-pointer, now owned by the property tycoon Raymond Mould and his wife Jenny whose many high-class jumpers had included the Cheltenham Gold Cup hero *Charter Party* and the King George VI Chase winner *Barton Bank*, both trained by David Nicholson.

The Moulds had been the first owners to put horses with Nigel Twiston-Davies, their next-door neighbour in Naunton, Gloucestershire, and with that trainer *Bindaree* immediately made his mark in National Hunt racing with four wins including the Grade 1 Challow Novices' Hurdle at Cheltenham. Subsequently, at the Festival, he was a useful fourth to *Monsignor* in the Royal and SunAlliance Novices' Hurdle, but he was then was well beaten at Aintree in the Sefton Novices' Hurdle.

In the 2000-01 season, the gelding took well to fences, scoring three wins and showing his ability to tackle the most formidable obstacles when, on the eve of the Grand National, he finished fourth in Aintree's John Hughes Memorial Trophy over an extended two miles five furlongs, a race which saw a mass of fallers and only seven finishers. The following season, prior to his National debut, he was campaigned hard, his six races including the Thomas Pink Gold Cup, the Hennessy Cognac Gold Cup, the Welsh National and the National Hunt Handicap Chase at the Cheltenham Festival. Though reasonably consistent, he never finished better than third.

Tragically, Jenny Mould had died of cancer in 2000; and ironically it was acknowledged that, if she had been alive, *Bindaree* would probably not have been entered for the National, a race that she strongly disliked. Previously her husband had had only one runner in the race: *Grange Brake* (pulled up in 1997) who had been leased to him by Jenny as a Christmas present. Now *Bindaree* was to be one of three runners trained by Twiston-Davies in the National, the others being *Beau*, an unlucky contender in 2001, and *Frantic Tan*. Stable jockey Carl Llewellyn opted to ride *Beau*. Jamie Goldstein was to ride *Bindaree*, but three days before the race, he was desperately unlucky to break his right leg in a novice chase. Culloty was the supersub.

In striking contrast to the quagmire of 2001, this year's National was run on fastish ground which had needed to be watered the day before. As an eight year old newcomer, *Bindaree* was less fancied than his more experienced stablemate *Beau*, an 11-1

chance. Both avoided the bunching which saw nine horses, including the heavily backed *Paris Pike*, eliminated at the first fence. *Beau*, however, unseated his rider when lying in second place at the 14th. One fence later *Bindaree* joined the leaders, and coming to the second Becher's he went to the front, ahead of the long-time pace-setter *The Last Fling*. Meanwhile the grey *What's Up Boys*, winner of the Hennessy Cognac Gold Cup, was making relentless headway and he jumped into the lead at the final fence.

At the Elbow, when *Bindaree* was some two lengths adrift, Culloty sought to challenge on the outside. Then, as his rival wandered across, he vitally switched to the inside and galvanised the chestnut gelding into the decisive finishing burst up the rail. Far behind the impressive duellists were *Blowing Wind* (third) and *Kingsmark*, another son of Roselier, in fourth place. That one victory prompted Twiston-Davies to abandon his plans to retire from training.

In November, 2002, reunited with Llewellyn, *Bindaree* tried to emulate *Earth Summit* who had won the Becher Chase after the National. But this time at Aintree he came to grief at the second fence. Getting up quickly, he galloped on riderless before barging into the running rail near the racecourse stables. One week later, at Newbury, he unseated Llewellyn in a handicap chase at Newbury, but another week on, he finished a seven lengths second behind *See More Business* over an extended three miles two furlongs at Chepstow. His next runs, fourth and eighth, prompted intensive schooling to try to restore his confidence for another National bid.

This time *Bindaree* was saddled with 10st 11lb at Aintree, 7lb more than his winning weight of the year before. Under Llewellyn he made mistakes at Becher's both times but made sufficient late headway to finish a respectable sixth, albeit 40 lengths behind *Monty's Pass*. Back at Aintree the following November he fell in the Becher Chase but showed improvement in December when finishing second to *Sir Rembrandt* in the John Hughes Rehearsal Chase at Chepstow; and three weeks later, in slogging conditions and teeming rain, he narrowly reversed those places to win the Welsh National and become the general ante-post favourite to win a second Aintree National.

When the weights were announced for the 2004

National, *Bindaree* was allotted 11st 1lb and Twiston-Davies declared that 'we can't possibly beat W*hat's Up Boys* again at this year's weights.' With the weights raised a further 3lb, *Bindaree*, one of four co-favourites, was hampered and unseated at the first Becher's. However, at the end of the year, he was still showing fine form. Returning to Chepstow for the Welsh National, with an extra 11lb to carry, he led the field round the first circuit and finished a close-up fifth.

Remarkably, Twiston-Davies judged *Bindaree* to have every chance of winning again when making his fourth National appearance in 2005. But the 11 year old, high in the weights on 11st 3lb, faded on the second circuit to finish 11th.

The following November, on his seasonal debut, he was again severely handicapped, carrying the second highest weight in the Becher Chase over the Aintree fences. Surprisingly, after taking an early lead, he made several mistakes and finished well behind in eighth place.

It had been hoped to race him next in the Welsh National which he had won in 2003. But, on discovery that he had damaged a hind leg, it was decided to retire him. He had won almost £500,000 in prize money and ironically, in 40 races, he had been ridden by Carl Llewellyn with the single exception of the Grand National.
See also: Culloty, Jim; Llewellyn, Carl; Twiston-Davies, Nigel.

BIRCH, Arthur
In 1904 Arthur Birch was an obscure, little known jockey, whose only big race experience had been the ride on *Padishah*, a 66-1 outsider who had failed to finish in the 1901 Grand National. Then, suddenly and unexpectedly, he found himself propelled into the limelight. His second National ride was on New Zealand's much maligned *Moifaa*. The huge brown gelding had been likened in appearance to a starved elephant, but now he was to score a sensational victory on his Aintree debut.

One week earlier Birch had been amazed by *Moifaa*'s pace and power in an Epsom gallop of four miles over fences. He knew what to expect but for much of his extraordinary Aintree ride he was struggling in vain to restrain the hard-pulling giant who powered through and over fences while the majority of runners in the 26-strong field were falling in his wake. Unchallenged on the run-in, *Moifaa* came

home the 25-1 winner by a comfortable eight lengths, finishing so full of running that the jockey was still struggling to restrain him after passing the post.

Birch never knew such fame again. He did not retain the ride in 1905 when *Moifaa* returned to Aintree under the new ownership of King Edward VII – the honour going instead to the veteran Bill Dollery who had won the National by 40 lengths on *Cloister* (1893) and had finished third on *Van Der Berg* (1895). Though he was the hot 4-1 favourite, *Moifaa* laboured on his reappearance, falling at the second Becher's. He never won another race in Britain. Similarly, Birch appeared only once more at the scene of his single triumph: in 1906 when his National mount, *Dathi*, another 25-1 shot, was a faller. The following December he broke his back in a fall at Gatwick. Confined to a wheelchair, he died in 1911, aged 36.
See also: Moifaa.

BLACKSHAW, Martin
Between 1973 and 1979 Martin Blackshaw rode in seven successive Grand Nationals, starting and ending on 100-1 outsiders (*Swan Shot* and *Oskard* respectively) that failed to finish. On his second appearance, in 1974, his mount, *Princess Camilla* was so fractious at the line-up that the start had to be delayed. She was the last of 17 finishers.

But one year later Martin enjoyed the ride of a lifetime over the first circuit as 20-1 chance *Glanford Brigg* stormed ahead from the first Becher's and brilliantly swerved around loose horses who threatened to cause chaos where the course funnelled into The Chair. He still headed affairs on the second circuit but then visibly began to tire, finally surrendering the lead at the 19th fence. He finished eighth.

In contrast, the combination made an early exit in 1976, one of three to fall at the first Becher's. Then, in 1977, Blackshaw – now a highly successful French-based jockey – had his best National chance, being a late booking to ride *Churchtown Boy*, a ten year old gelding who, only two days before the big race, had comfortably won the Topham Trophy over two miles and six furlongs of the National course. However, this was the year when all performances would be eclipsed by the success of *Red Rum* in seeking his record-breaking third win.

In a 42-strong field, *Churchtown Boy*, a 20-1 chance, was to be the only threat to *Red Rum*. Coming to the second last he was just two lengths behind the leader. But then he bungled his jump and, though receiving 22lb, he could not make an impresssion on 'Rummy' who pulled away to win by 25 lengths. The following year *Churchtown Boy* was again going well when he crashed out at The Chair; and the jockey hurled his whip to the ground in his disgust at seeing another winning chance slip away. Subsequently he turned to training in France only to have his life tragically cut short by a car accident.

BLACKWELL, George

On a misty Friday in March, 1923, George Blackwell became only the second trainer to have turned out the winner of the Derby and the Grand National. His famous double – the first in the 20th century – was achieved when *Sergeant Murphy*, at the fourth attempt, triumphed by four lengths from past winner *Shaun Spadah*. It was the first National to have an American winning owner (Stephen Sanford) and the last to be won by a 13 year old horse.

Unusually, Newmarket-based Blackwell was a trainer famed for his achievements in Flat racing long before he made his mark in National Hunt. He was renowned as the man who, in 1900, introduced to English racing the 18 year old American jockey Danny Maher. Subsequently, in a tragically short-lived career, Maher went on to win the Derby three times, the St Leger twice, the 2,000 Guineas twice, and the 1,000 Guineas once. He was also the champion Flat rider of 1908 and 1913. Most notably, in 1903, Blackwell trained the Triple Crown winner *Rock Sand*, with Maher taking the winning rides in the Derby and the St Leger.

Strangely, tragedy stalked those who shared in Blackwell's major victories. Maher died in a London nursing home in 1916. Captain G.H. Bennet, the winning amateur rider on *Sergeant Murphy*, died ten months after his famous victory following a fatal fall. And the long-serving *Sergeant Murphy* had to be put down in 1926 after breaking a leg in a minor handicap chase at Bogside. In contrast, Blackwell lived on until 1942. He was 81 when he died and, until one year before, he was to be seen out walking almost every day at Newmarket.
See also: Sergeant Murphy.

BLETSOE, Bernard

Head of a large, long-established Northamptonshire farming family (six sons and three daughters),

Bernard Bletsoe bred, owned and trained the 1901 Grand National winner, *Grudon* – a success attributed, in large part, to his ingenuity in coating *Grudon*'s hooves with two pounds of butter to prevent snow 'balling' within the horse's shoes and causing him to slip.

One year before this entire had been ridden by Bletsoe's son, Morgan, appearing in his second National after being eighth on *Barsac* (1898). *Grudon* then finished sixth and the owner-trainer felt that he would have won if his son had not got a foot caught in the bridle. Thus in 1901, when the racecourse was blanketed in snow, he entrusted the ride to Aintree specialist, Arthur Nightingall, seeking his third National win. *Grudon*'s victory was especially fortuitous for Bletsoe since earlier he had offered the horse for £500 to Mr J.G. Bulteel on condition that they would share the £1,975 prize if he went on to win at Aintree. The offer had been declined – a rare misjudgment by Mr Bulteel, famed for his £4,000 bargain buy of the great *Manifesto*.

Mr Bletsoe was not so fortunate as the trainer of an American-bred five year old called *Rubio* who broke down badly. *Rubio* eventually recovered and, with a new trainer, won the 1908 Grand National at 66-1. But there was one huge consolation: the winner was ridden that day by Bletsoe's son, Bryan, making his debut in the race.
See also: Grudon; Bletsoe, Henry Bryan.

BLETSOE, Henry Bryan

In six out of seven Grand National rides, spanning 14 years, Bryan Bletsoe failed to complete the course. Remarkably, the one exception came at his first attempt – in 1908 when, by a stroke of good fortune, he picked up the ride on 66-1 outsider *Rubio*, the first American-bred winner of the race.

Shortly before that National, stable jockey William Bissill had the choice of two horses – *Rubio* and *Mattie Macgregor* – trained by Fred Withington. After they had been paired in a four-mile trial gallop near Bernard Bletsoe's training centre at Denton, Northamptonshire, Bissill opted for the latter. Bletsoe's son, Bryan, though relatively inexperienced, promptly jumped at the chance to ride the former and won by ten lengths – from *Mattie Macgregor!*

Subsequently, after falling in three Nationals – on *Young Buck* (1909), *Viz* (1911) and *Blow Pipe* (1914) – Bryan went off to war, serving in Egypt as an officer in the Northamptonshire Yeomanry.

On his return he rode in three more Nationals – on *Irish Dragon* (1919), *Glencorrig* (1921) and *Wavertree* (1922), each time failing to complete the course. However, his achievements elsewhere included wins in the Irish, Scottish, Welsh and South African Nationals.

After retiring from the saddle he turned to training, and during the Second World War he worked for the BBC. Though he died without children, the family tradition was to be carried on by his nephew, another Bernard, whose wife had a 100-1 outsider – *Odye Hills* (failed to finish) in the 1988 National. *See also:* Rubio; Bletsoe, Bernard.

BLINKERS

In the past 70 years only four horses wearing blinkers have won the Grand National: *Battleship* (1938), *Foinavon* (1967), *L'Escargot* (1975) and *Earth Summit* (1998). However, this statistic does not strongly support the belief that horses are somehow disadvantaged by having headgear, either blinkers or visor, which limits their vision in a race so fraught with the threat of interference. In reality, it has little relevance since so few blinkered horses line up for the race.

In the 2001 National no fewer than ten of the 40 runners were fitted with headgear. But this was exceptional. On average, roughly only one in ten starters appear in blinkers. Furthermore, a number of National contenders – most memorably the close 2002 runner-up, *What's Up Boys* – have run well in blinkers without actually winning.

Conversely, there is every reason for believing that, once they are without a rider to steer them away from trouble, blinkered horses are liable to be a major threat to their rivals. Thus, most notoriously, in 1967, the riderless, blinkered *Popham Down* veered from the inside right across the front of the 23rd fence, so causing the biggest pile-up in Grand National history. In much the same way, the blinkered *Paddy's Return* fell at the third in 2001 and, spurning the escape gaps in the running rail before and after every fence, he continued riderless as far as the Canal Turn where unpredictably he careered across the fence, eliminating ten other horses in the process.

As a result, a number of racing pundits – most notably three times champion jockey Stan Mellor – have suggested that National runners should be banned from wearing blinkers. Although this idea has been officially rejected, the Jockey Club has agreed that the matter should be kept 'under review'.

Certainly trainers in general are strongly opposed to any such move. As shown in the performances of *Earth Summit* and *What's Up Boys*, the fitting of blinkers can lead to considerable improvement by way of helping a horse to concentrate more. On the other hand, there is no guarantee that blinkers will sustain improvement. As Tony McCoy prophetically observed before his bruising third fence fall on the 2000 National favourite, *Dark Stranger*: 'Often horses shine in blinkers on their debut and then disappoint if they get used to their effect.'

BOBBYJO

On April 10, 1999, just 24 days after winning a two-mile hurdle race, *Bobbyjo* became the first Irish-trained winner of the Grand National since Tommy Carberry rode *L'Escargot* to victory 24 years before; and by neat coincidence the winner was trained by Tommy and ridden by his son Paul – the first ever father-and-son combination to take the prize.

It was a success story in the finest Irish tradition. *Bobbyjo* was not only Irish-bred, trained and ridden, but owned by a son of Galway, one of nine children, who had left home at 16 to find work in a Tottenham pub. Twenty four years later, now owner of a string of north London pubs, Robert (Bobby) Burke, was back in Galway, seated at an alehouse bar, when a friend, Liam Mulryan, casually mentioned that he was planning to sell his 20 horses to give more time to his building business. Without asking to see them, Burke offered to buy half a dozen. They included a six-month-old foal which he later named *Bobbyjo*, combining his own first name with that of his wife, Jo.

Bred by Liam Skehan, *Bobbyjo* was by *Bustineto* out of *Markup*. His sire, though by *Bustino*, so strong on stamina, had been best over seven furlongs on the Flat. However, there was plenty of staying power on his dam's side to compensate. He was reared on the Galway farm of the owner's brother, Eugene, then sent to Tommy Carberry's yard in Co. Meath.

Initially unimpressive in his races, *Bobbyjo* registered his first win in April, 1996, when ridden by Paul's younger brother Philip over hurdles at Down Royal. The following season he scored three times over fences but was judged too novicey to run in the 1997 Irish National. Then, in November, he revealed his potential in jumping brilliantly to win the Porterstown Handicap Chase at Fairyhouse. The following Easter, in the Irish Grand National, he was tried for the first time beyond three miles one furlong. Under Paul Carberry, he handled the extra four furlongs well, winning by half a length from *Papillon*. In addition to the £78,350 first prize, he collected a £50,000 bonus on the strength of his earlier course win.

Though *Bobbyjo* had enjoyed an 11lb advantage over *Papillon*, connections were convinced that he was an outstanding chaser. But, on the face of it, his subsequent form was hardly encouraging. Between October and February of the 1998-99 season, he was never better than fourth in five chases. In these races, however, he carried big weights on unsuitably soft or heavy ground. He was a different proposition on good going. Moreover, in March, on his last outing before the National, this out-and-out stayer had sufficient speed to win a two-mile handicap hurdle at Down Royal. Following the example of the great Vincent O'Brien, trainer Carberry had chosen this unusual route to Aintree rather than give him a hard warm-up over fences on testing ground. Over hurdles *Bobbyjo* had been ridden by seven-pound claimer Philip Carberry. Now brother Paul took over for the marathon challenge.

Owner Burke brought to Aintree ten coachloads of customers from his London pubs; and the race conditions raised their hopes high. The nine year old gelding, who had never won on heavy going, had his favoured good ground; and the weather was perfect. A week earlier he had been as long as 33-1. Now a late plunge saw his odds cut from 16-1 to 10-1.

Three of the other 31 runners were more strongly fancied. From the moment the weights were announced the hot favourite had been *Double Thriller*; and following his fourth in the Cheltenham Gold Cup, he was regarded as a blot on the handicap with only 10st 8lb to carry. On the day, he went off the joint second favourite, 7-1 with *Call It A Day*, behind 6-1 *Fiddling The Facts*. But to the dismay of myriad punters, he jumped too big and was the sole faller at the first.

With Carberry clinging to the inside route, *Bobbyjo* was towards the rear in the early stages. He then made rapid progress but not sufficient to get involved in the bunching at the second Becher's where five casualties included *Fiddling The Facts* and *Eudipe*, a fatal faller under Tony McCoy. Valuable ground was gained when cutting the corner at the Canal Turn and at this stage he was one of ten horses

headed by *Blue Charm* that remained in with a chance.

Coming to the second last *Bobbyjo* narrowly avoided the fall of the Irish long-shot *Merry People* and touched down just behind *Brave Highlander* and *Call It A Day*. With the former now fading, three horses – *Bobbyjo*, *Call It A Day* (Richard Dunwoody) and *Addington Boy* (Adrian Maguire) – were left in close pursuit of the Scottish hope *Blue Charm*, a late spare ride for veteran Lorcan Wyer replacing the trainer's son Mark Bradburne who had broken his collarbone 24 hours earlier in the Aintree Fox Hunters'.

Blue Charm led over the last. Then, just after the Elbow, Carberry found he was squeezed for room as Maguire rode across him to grab the inner. Later he judged that this may have been to his advantage as it helped him to give his horse a momentary breather. Switched to the outside, *Bobbyjo* revealed hidden reserves, surging past the long-time leader and pulling clear to win by ten lengths, the first of 18 to finish. *Blue Charm*, trained by Sue Bradburne, was second at 25-1.

On Sunday *Bobbyjo* arrived home to wild, extended celebrations in the Co. Meath village of Ratoath near the Carberry yard at Ballybin. Two weeks later, without incurring a penalty, he started as hot favourite to win the Whitbread Gold Cup, plus a £50,000 bonus. This time Paul Carberry was unavailable for the ride, being in hospital for an emergency operation on his spleen following a fall on the gallops. Ridden by Adrian Maguire, *Bobbyjo* took the sixth prize of £900.

The following season, trainer Carberry gave *Bobbyjo* a light campaign, restricting him in 2000 to three hurdle races over two and a half miles, with son Philip back on board. They finished ninth, then fourth, and finally – 20 days before the National – fifth at Leopardstown, ten lengths behind the third placed *Papillon*. With this low-key build-up, Carberry had been hoping *Bobbyjo* would be allotted a weight between 10st 5lb and 10st 10lb. The strategy failed because this year senior handicapper Phil Smith chose to reintroduce the 'Aintree factor'. Taking last year's performances into consideration, he put *Bobbyjo* on 11st 6lb – 20lb more than he had carried when winning (uniquely in modern times) from a stone out of the handicap.

The omens were not good. *Bobbyjo* had not jumped a fence in public since the Whitbread almost a year ago. He was attempting to win back-to-back Nationals, a feat not achieved since *Red Rum*'s success in 1974. More significantly, he was now giving 8lb to *Papillon* from whom he had received weight when beating him half a length in the 1998 Irish National. Yet, such was his high reputation, that he went off a well-supported 12-1.

Excuses could be made for *Bobbyjo* in the 2000 National. Most especially he lost a lot of ground at the second Becher's when he was almost brought down as *Esprit de Cotte* fell directly in front of him. But, in truth, he was now much less sure in his jumping and Paul Carberry did well even to get him round, finishing ten places behind *Papillon* who had been backed down on the day from 33-1 to 10-1.

It was to be his Aintree swansong. A third National bid was planned but, in February, 2001, *Bobbyjo* was retired after suffering a shattered carpal bone behind his near-fore knee when running in the Grand National Trial Handicap Chase at Fairyhouse. A few days before the National, he was at a veterinary hospital at the Curragh when he incurred complications following an operation for the injury. The 11 year old, a winner of eight races and more than £350,000 in prize money, had to be put down. He was buried on a farm in the Co. Galway village of Mullaghmore, the childhood home of his owner. *See also:* Carberry, Thomas; Carberry, Paul.

BOGSKAR

Winner in 1940 of the only Grand National to be run during the Second World War. Before a diminished crowd, with many spectators in uniform, the seven year old *Bogskar* was fittingly ridden by one of several jockeys on leave from the Services: Flight Sergeant Mervyn Jones, a nephew of the renowned Anthony brothers. The gelding was both owned and trained by Lord Stalbridge at Eastbury in Berkshire.

Bred in Co. Dublin – by *Werewolf* out of *Irish Spring* – *Bogskar* was bought by Lord Stalbridge as a three year old. He went through three seasons without a win, finally losing his maiden tag in Gatwick's 1940 National Trial Chase. A faller in his last race before the National, he made his Aintree debut as a 25-1 chance.

Making steady progress, *Bogskar* moved into fourth place at the end of the first circuit, but now, going ominously well, were two former National runners-up: the favourite *Royal Danieli* and the great Scottish hope, *MacMoffat*. When the former

fell at the second last, the latter was left in the lead and seemed to have the race at his mercy. *MacMoffat*, however, was being harassed by *National Night* who had lost his rider (Mervyn Jones's brother, Hywel) on falling at the 14th fence. *Bogskar* drew level at the last, stumbled on landing, but then showed the greater turn of speed over the run-in to win by three lengths from *MacMoffat*, with *Gold Arrow*, a 50-1 shot, a further six lengths behind.

When the National was resumed six years later, *Bogskar* and *MacMoffat* returned to the fray, even though they were 13 and 14 years old respectively. Both were fallers. Sadly, *Bogskar* now had a different jockey. Two years after his National triumph, Mervyn Jones had been killed in his Spitfire on a photo-reconnaissance mission over the fjords of Norway. In 1947, the veteran *Bogskar* made a third and final appearance in the National, now a 100-1 outsider and again a faller.

See also: Stalbridge, Lord; Jones, Mervyn Anthony.

BOURTON

Formerly named *Upton*, the bay *Bourton* – by *Drayton* out of an unrecorded dam – became in 1854 the first clear favourite to win the Grand National. Remarkably that year, following the controversial late withdrawal of long-time market-leader *Miss Mowbray*, *Bourton* was sent off at 4-1 despite the fact he had fallen on his two previous appearances, had since been raised 10lb in the weights, and was now ridden by a relatively obscure jockey named John Tasker.

Clearly both the handicapper and plenty of punters had got it right. By the time they reached Becher's second time around, more than half the 20-strong field had fallen by the wayside and Mr William Mosley's *Bourton* was moving up fast on the leaders. Coming to the last he overook *Crabbs,* who was ridden by the highly experienced Denis Wynne and had a colossal 38lb advantage in the weights. Thereafter he stormed further and further ahead to win with ease by 15 lengths from *Spring*, a light-weighted six year old, with *Crabbs* a further ten lengths back in third.

Sadly, in the following year, triumph turned to tragedy – for both horse and rider. On the understanding that *Bourton* would now be retired, owner Moseley sold his National winner for a mere £50. But the new owner, a Leamington man, chose to race the old horse (his age is not recorded). The following season the bay gelding broke his fetlock-joint when falling at the Water Jump in a chase at Warwick and later had to be put down. Six weeks earlier, by a macabre coincidence, his National winning rider had also been killed in a fall on the same racecourse.

See also: Tasker, John.

BOYCE, Charles

Fourteen times in 16 years (1851 to 1866) Charlie Boyce rode in the Grand National; and he used his familiarity with Aintree to such effect that the management was prompted to change the staking out of the course. It happened in 1857 when, in riding *Emigrant* to victory, he gained valuable advantage by running wide on a strip of firm ground outside the ploughed land between the Canal Turn and Valentine's. Thereafter, flags were erected in line with the outer limits of fences to prevent a repeat of his manoeuvre.

It was a measure of Boyce's fine horsemanship and strategy that, despite often being on rank outsiders, his finishes comprised a first, second, fifth, sixth and seventh place. In 1852 his second National ride, *Maurice Daley*, was not even quoted in the market, and yet was runner-up by just one length to *Miss Mowbray*. Two years later he had his first booking on a renowned chaser, *Peter Simple*, but by then the dual National winner was 16 years old and cruelly lumbered with 12st top weight. He failed to finish.

Boyce's best chance came in 1857 when 11 year old *Emigrant* was fourth in the betting at 10-1. Together they had finished sixth the previous year and now they enjoyed a 6lb drop in the weights. After no fewer than seven false starts in pouring rain, *Emigrant* was fast away with Boyce soon pushing him into the lead. He was mindful that the big gambling owners, George Hodgman and his bookmaker partner Mr Green, had not only backed *Emigrant* heavily to win but had also struck a private wager that their horse would lead at the end of the first circuit.

Having secured the one-circuit bet, Boyce eased up slightly on the second, surrendering a big lead from Becher's onwards. Again he steered a wide course to avoid the worst of the bog-like ground, and once over the last flight he held off the late challenge of six year old *Weathercock* to win fairly cosily by three lengths. His achievement was all the more remarkable since he had ridden with the upper part of one arm strapped to his side, having severely injured it when out hunting one week earlier. In seven subsequent Nationals his best effort was fifth place on *Xanthus*, a 50-1 shot in 1861. Four years later he was looking an almost certain winner on *Arbury* when they came down at the second Becher's.

The victory of *Emigrant* had netted a small fortune for Messrs Hodgman and Green, especially the latter who reportedly won some £25,000. Duly grateful they presented Boyce with £1,000, and later Mr Hodgman wrote in his memoirs: 'Of Boyce as a man or a rider I do not know how to write too eulogistically. To my mind, over a country he was so far the best of his contemporaries that I should not care to select a second. He was a splendid specimen of physical development, and singularly handsome. His manners were charming.'

See also: Emigrant.

BRABAZON, Aubrey

Born in 1920, Aubrey Brabazon was a remarkably versatile jockey, winning two Irish Classics, the 1948 Oaks on *Masaka* and the 1950 2,000 Guineas on *Mighty Ocean*, and at the same time achieving greatness over the jumps – most notably on *Cottage Rake* whom he first rode to a 20 lengths victory at Leopardstown on Boxing Day, 1946.

On *Cottage Rake* (1948-50) 'The Brab' became the first jockey to score a hat-trick in the Cheltenham Gold Cup. (*Golden Miller*'s incredible five wins had involved four different riders). He also won the 1948 King George V1 Chase on *Cottage Rake* and successive Champion Hurdles on *Hatton's Grace* (1949-50), all these victories being achieved for trainer Vincent O'Brien.

The combination of Brabazon and *Cottage Rake* was so formidable that it gave rise to a popular Irish verse:

Aubrey's up, the money's down,
The frightened bookies quake.
Come on, my lads, and give a cheer,
Begad, 'tis Cottage Rake.

But the treasured *Rake* was never risked in the Grand National and 'The Brab' himself only twice appeared in the race: in 1946 when he finished fourth on Miss Dorothy Paget's *Housewarmer*, and in 1947 when he fell at the first Becher's on *Luan*

Casca. As a trainer, he made three successive National challenges with *Quintin Bay* (pulled up by Pat Taaffe in 1965, sixth at 100-1 in 1966 and eleventh in 1967). He died in 1996.
See also: Dempsey, Edward.

BRADLEY, Graham John
National Hunt racing inevitably subjects jockeys to many ups and downs, and arguably – by way of clashes with authority rather than falls and injuries – none has experienced a wild rollercoaster ride to compare with that of Graham Bradley, the hedonistic Yorkshireman who, most fittingly, entitled his autobiography '*The Wayward Lad*'.

The 'ups' in Bradley's tempestuous 23-year riding career are clearly defined. In his heyday he was regarded as the one of the most popular and artistic of all jump jockeys. He rode more than 730 winners, his big race successes including the Cheltenham Gold Cup (on *Bregawn*, 1983), the King George VI Chase (*Wayward Lad*, 1985); the Martell Hurdle (*Morley Street*, 1993); the Champion Hurdle (*Collier Bay*, 1996); the Hennessy Cognac Gold Cup (*Bregawn*, 1982, and *Suny Bay*, 1997), the Welsh National (*Righthand Man*, 1984, and *Stearsby*, 1986); the Irish Grand National (*Rhyme 'N' Reason*, 1985); the Grand Annual Chase (*Pearlyman*, 1986, *My Young Man*, 1992, *Sound Reveille*, 1995, and *Uncle Ermie*, 1997); the Sun Alliance Novice Chase (*Kildimo*, 1987); the Tripleprint Gold Cup (*Senor El Betrutti*, 1997) and the Supreme Novices' Hurdle (*French Ballerina*, 1998).

The much-publicised 'downs' in his career have revolved around his brushes with the law and the many times he has incurred the wrath of the Jockey Club. These, however, have tended to overshadow the biggest disappointment of his career: that he rode in 13 Aintree Grand Nationals without ever winning. Ironically, when he was on a National winner (*Hallo Dandy* in 1985), the victor of the previous year fell at the very first fence.

Bradley's father had once been travelling head lad to Arthur Thompson who rode two National winners – *Sheila's Cottage* (1948) and *Teal* (1952). As a boy, Graham idolised Lester Piggott and dreamed of becoming a Flat jockey. But having weighed into the world (September 8, 1960) at 9lb 3oz he was never going to achieve that ambition. His first winning ride, in 1980, was on *Talon* in a two-and-a-half-mile hurdle at Sedgefield. The trainer was Tony Dickin-

son, soon to be succeeded by his son Michael, the racing genius who now became the key mentor in shaping Bradley's riding style and advancing his career. With Michael, Graham had all his early big race victories – most notably in 1983 when the first five home in the Cheltenham Gold Cup were Dickinson-trained. And with him he had his first two Grand National rides. In 1983 he finished seventh on *Political Pop*. In 1984, *Ashley House*, second in the weights, went brilliantly round the first circuit, then buried him at the Chair.

At the end of that season, Michael Dickinson left to become private trainer to the leading Flat owner, Robert Sangster. His mother, Monica, took over the licence and provided Bradley with many more big-race winners before he went on to be stable jockey to Toby Balding and later to Charlie Brooks. But the one constant in his changing fortunes was his ill-luck in seeking Grand National success. In 1985, he was a last minute replacement for injured Neale Doughty on *Hallo Dandy*. The 1984 winner, raised 10lb in the weights, soared over the first, then inexplicably nose-dived. In 1986 he was on the Martin Pipe-trained *Ballinacurra Lad*, a faller at the 26th.

In 1987 Bradley at last had high hopes of Grand National success. He was convinced that in *By The Way*, winner of the 1985 Whitbread Gold Cup, Mrs Dickinson had an ideal jumper for Aintree; so convinced that he personally wrote to the owner, Mrs Chris Feather, seeking to persuade her to let her nine year old run. The lady relented and subsequently *By The Way* became second favourite in the ante-post betting behind the 1986 winner *West Tip*. Then came a bitter blow: the gelding suffered a split pastern on the gallops and was out of the race.

One year on and fates were crueller still. *By The Way* was third favourite for the National, just a month away, when he broke a leg in a chase at Sedgefield and had to be put down immediately. Bradley walked away in tears.

Though he had triumphed in Welsh and Irish Nationals, Bradley's Aintree hoodoo was to be unrelenting. He pulled up at the 25th on *Barthes* (1989), finished 15th on *Course Hunter* (1990), pulled up on *Solidasarock* (1991), was unseated at The Chair on *Rowlandsons Jewels* (1992), fell on Lady Lloyd Webber's *Black Humour* (1994). Worst of all, in 1995, he smashed the bones in his left ear and was unconscious for 45 minutes when falling at

B

the third on *Zeta's Lad* (1995).

Next, in 1997, Bradley made the costliest error in respect of his Grand National dream: he chose to ride *Couldnt Be Better* in the Greenalls Gold Cup in preference to Charlie Brooks' other runner, *Suny Bay*. The reject won and the owner Andrew Cohen duly chose to let Jamie Osborne keep the ride in the National. Bradley was so depressed that he came close to quitting. He had come to regard *Suny Bay* as a streering job at Aintree.

As it happened, the brilliant grey finished second in the postponed 1997 National. Meanwhile Bradley had pulled up four out on *Lo Stregone*, otherwise known by his critics as 'Slow Stregone'. After 11 rides in the race he had still not bettered his first effort and he had only twice completed the course.

Bradley's hopes soared anew when he had the ride on *Suny Bay* in the 1998 National. But now he paid the price for having ridden the grey to a convincing win in the Hennessy Cognac Gold Cup. The handicapper was duly impressed and thus, like the great *Crisp*, *Suny Bay* was to be cruelly denied National victory by a prohibitive weight, raised from 10st 3lb to a top weight of 12st. Bradley gave him a brilliantly ride on unsuitably heavy ground and briefly, approaching the second last, he thought he would win. But in the end there was no resisting his sole challenger, *Earth Summit*, who powered ahead on the run-in to win by 11 lengths. Like *Crisp*, *Suny Bay* had been beaten by a horse with a 23lb advantage.

The following year, just six days after taking a very heavy fall in the Irish Grand National, Bradley was back at Aintree to make another challenge on *Suny Bay*. But again the grey was on top weight, conceding 12lb to his nearest rival. It was Brad's 13th Grand National ride – and he finished 13th. His luck had truly run out. Three days later he had to report to Charing Cross police station from which he had been freed on bail since his arrest in early January by a force investigating illegal doping and race-fixing. Furthermore he now had his licence temporarily suspended by the Jockey Club pending the police investigation.

In June 1999, the long-drawn-out nightmare ended with all charges being dropped and his licence being restored. But by now all the fun had gone out of racing and he retired in November immediately after riding *Ontheboil* to victory at Haydock. Happily he made a success of his new career as a bloodstock agent. But then, in 2002, he suffered a surprisingly severe blow – being warned off by the Jockey Club for eight years after being found guilty on various corruption charges, the most serious being that of passing on privileged information for money. On appeal, his suspension from all racing-related activities was reduced to five years. But it meant that, at 42, this most charismatic and stylish horseman was banned from racecourses and licensed training stables, and no longer permitted to have any dealing with racehorses until 2007. *See also:* Suny Bay.

BRASSIL, Martin

Trainer of *Numbersixvalverde*, the 2006 Grand National winner. Operating a small yard at Dunmurray in Co. Kildare, Martin Brassil succeeded with his first-ever runner in the race and on only his second visit to Aintree where, 26 years earlier, he had appeared as an amateur rider in a race for claiming jockeys.

Born in Newmarket-on-Fergus, Co. Clare in 1957, Brassil was once a trainee hotel manager at the Shelbourne, Dublin's most famous hotel. But horse racing was always his first love and, following a bad, ankle-smashing fall as an amateur rider at Punchestown, his thoughts turned to a training career. He gained experience working with Mick O'Toole and Neil McGrath; then, in 1995, set up as a trainer with the support of property developer Bernard Carroll.

For 11 years Brassil operated with no more than a dozen horses – none of them out of the ordinary until, in 2001, he bought an unraced brown gelding on behalf of Carroll who named him after the address of his villa on the Algarve in Portugal. The trainer rode *Numbersixvalverde* in all his work-outs and recognised the gelding's long-term potential after he had broken his maiden over hurdles at the third attempt in December, 2002.

The trainer's judgment was finally endorsed in 2005 when *Numbersixvalverde* achieved the rare double of winning the Thyestes Chase and then the Irish Grand National in only his second season as a chaser. Following those successes, Brassil saw his string more than double in number; and immediately after the victory at Aintree his yard at Dunmurray was greatly strengthened by the transfer to him of the six year old France-based hurdler *Ambobo*, owned by Irishman Sean Mulryan.

The year 2007 started well for Brassil, most notably when he sent out *Nickname* for an impressive win in the Ladbrokes Normans Grove Chase at Fairyhouse. Meanwhile, as 12 months before, he again campaigned *Numbersixvalverde* over hurdles in the build-up to the National. But this time there was no hiding the chaser's potential from the handicapper who duly raised him 9lb for the Aintree return. Subsequently, *Numbersixvalverde* stayed on well into fourth place behind *Homer Wells* in the Bobbyjo Chase over three miles one furlong. In contrast, though a well-backed 14-1 chance, he weakened four out over the National trip and finished a distant sixth.

See also: Numbersixvalverde; Madden, Niall.

BRAYLEY, Edward

Originally a 'Punch and Judy' man, Edward Brayley made his fortune in the theatre and invested heavily in relentlessly pursuing his dream of owning a Grand National winner. He contended for every National from 1866 to 1874, sometimes having two runners in the same race, once as many as three; and for years he seemed doomed to disappointment.

His first runners – *Ibex* (1866) and *Sea King* (1867) – failed to finish; then, in 1868, he had two serious challengers: *Moose*, the 8-1 second favourite, and *Pearl Diver*, 10-1. Brayley declared the latter his main hope and indeed the bay gelding had impressed only 24 hours before the race by easily winning a handicap hurdle. But it was *Pearl Diver*'s great misfortune that year to come up against an outstanding six year old, *The Lamb*. Brilliantly ridden by George Ede, the little grey prevailed by two lengths from *Pearl Diver* with the third horse, former winner *Alcibiade*, ten lengths behind. Mr Brayley's other contender was pulled up.

In 1869 Brayley again had a strong double hand: six year old *Fortunatus*, the 7-2 clear favourite, and *Pearl Diver*, now raised 23lb to a top weight of 12st 7lb. Under Johnny Page, the former was contesting the lead three out when he had to be pulled up through sheer exhaustion. Meanwhile *Pearl Diver* had fallen, and again the National had an outstanding winner in *The Colonel*.

Remarkably, the handicapper chose to keep *Pearl Diver* on the same top weight for the 1870 National, 9lb more than *The Colonel* who was to win again. The burden was decisive, *Pearl Diver* lying in third place when he came to the end of his tether just two fences from the finish. Like Brayley's other run-

ners, *Moose* and five year old *Casse Tete*, he failed to finish.

When the handicapper finally relented, dropping him 16lb in 1871, *Pearl Diver* was past his best. He was made the 4-1 favourite and did well enough to finish fourth, only six lengths behind the winner, again *The Lamb*. As before, *Casse Tete*, a 66-1 chance, failed to complete the course.

Despite so much frustration, Mr Brayley, nicknamed 'Old Boots', stubbornly refused to abandon his dream; and ironically his persistence was finally rewarded when least expected – in 1872 when his seven year old *Casse Tete*, on the minimum weight, won the National at her third attempt. He had gained the coveted prize with a little chestnut mare, a failure on the Flat, that he had bought out of a seller for little more than £200.

To be sure, *Casse Tete* had enjoyed a fair measure of luck in a National which saw a number of horses brought down and two falling fatally. At the penultimate fence the lead was being disputed by *Casse Tete* and *The Lamb*, with *Harvester*, owned and ridden by Mr Arthur Yates, beginning to make a threatening late challenge. But *Harvester* broke down on clearing the fence and *The Lamb* – giving a colossal 35lb to *Casse Tete* – could no longer go the pace. The only danger at the end was *Scarrington* and he twisted a plate, cutting a foot badly, before finishing six lengths behind the winner. *Despatch*, the 100-30 favourite, was a further six lengths back in third, with *The Lamb* a most worthy fourth. With his dream achieved, it was no matter to the owner that *Casse Tete* failed to finish in two subsequent Nationals and never won another race.

See also: Casse Tete.

BREEDING

Though conformation can be an important factor, the value of an unraced thoroughbred will largely be determined by its pedigree; and similarly experts will examine the pedigree to assess its likely strengths in terms of speed, stamina and distance. But the importance of breeding, so critical on the Flat, counts for much less over the jumps. Thus, on pedigree, no one could have predicted that the most famous Grand National horse would be *Red Rum*, sired by a champion miler out of a rogue mare. And by the same token, analysis of National winners shows no common factors in terms of shape or size. They may be deformed like the ungainly *Tipperary*

Tim, gigantic (over 17 hands) like *Party Politics* and the elephantine *Moifaa*, or diminutive (just over 15 hands) like *The Lamb* and *Abd-El-Kader*.

At the same time, it can sometimes be hugely profitable to follow certain bloodlines. In the 1930s, for example, the flour-milling millionaire Mr J.V. Rank was on the right track when he told his agents to look out for yearlings by *My Prince*, sire of the 1929 Grand National winner *Gregalach*. It would have paid off if only he had not been badly advised against buying *Reynoldstown*, who was to win the National in 1935 and 1936. Then, in 1937, salt was rubbed into the wound when he saw his *Cooleen* beaten into second place by *Royal Mail* – another son of *My Prince*.

Besides three winners *My Prince* sired two horses placed in the National: *Easter Hero* (second, 1929) and *Thomond II* (third, 1934 and 1935). Mr Rank at last hit the jackpot when he bought *Prince Regent*, by *My Prince* out of *Nemaea*. *Prince Regent* became Ireland's champion chaser and won the 1946 Cheltenham Gold Cup. But the Second World War denied him experience over the Aintree fences, and when he finally went there it was arguably too late. Under top weight he finished third in 1946 and fourth in 1947, and was carried out when running as a 13 year old in 1948.

Notably, breeding has also proved a valuable guide in respect of *Ascetic*, *Cottage* and *Vulgan*, all of whom sired three Grand National winners; *Jackdaw* and *Menelek*, sires of two winners; and, most especially, *Roselier*, responsible for 17 National runners including winners *Royal Athlete* and *Bindaree*, dual runner-up *Suny Bay*, and placed horses *Moorcroft Boy*, *Ebony Jane* and *Kingsmark*.

The Grand National has twice been won by half-brothers: *Vanguard* (1843) and *Pioneer* (1846), and *Anglo* (1966) and *Red Alligator* (1968); and in 1929 half-brothers *Gregalach* and *Easter Hero* finished first and second in a 66-strong field. Full sisters, *Emblem* and *Emblematic*, won in successive years, 1863 and 1864.

See also: Sires.

BRETHERTON, Bartholomew

Amateur rider of *Jerry*, 12-1 winner of the second Grand National in 1840. His success owed much to a pile-up at the old stone wall at the end of the first circuit. There, four front-runners – including *The Nun*, the 4-1 favourite, and *Lottery*, the first National winner – came to grief; and only three of the 13

starters completed the course without falling. Jumping cleanly throughout, *Jerry* won by four lengths from *Arthur* who had been remounted after falling heavily at Becher's Brook second time around. Another four lengths back in third place was *Valentine*, who had made such a sensational twisting jump at the second brook that it was subsequently named after him.

Though he had missed the 1839 National, Bretherton was familiar with the course, having ridden in the first Liverpool Steeplechase held at Aintree in 1836. That year, on 9-1 chance *Cockahoop*, he had finished third behind *The Duke* and *Polyanthus*. Some controversy surrounded his riding at the time. The 2-1 favourite *Laurie Todd* had been unlucky to fall on the second circuit, and there was a suggestion, unproven, that *Bretherton* had deliberately borne down on the favourite's rider to thwart his attempt to remount.

Following his victory in the 1840 National, Bretherton rode five more times in the race without any degree of success. In 1841, when there was the smallest-ever field of just 11 starters, he fell at the first Becher's on Lord Villiers' *Goblin* but remounted to become the last of seven finishers. The following year he failed to complete the course on Lord Maidstone's *Satirist*, and in 1843 he came home fifth on *Goblin*.

At that stage, Bretherton took a break from racing to take over his father's coach business at Yardley, Birmingham. Then, after a four-year gap, at the age of 42, he returned to the National fray to ride *Wolverhampton*, a rank outsider who, in a record 29-strong field, shared top weight with two leading challengers, *Chandler*, 12-1, and *The Curate*, 6-1 favourite. In the closest finish yet seen, *Chandler* won by half a length and one and a half lengths from *The Curate* and *British Yeoman* respectively.

Wolverhampton failed to get round, and yet Bretherton was sufficiently impressed to buy the horse to make another challenge in 1849. This time *Wolverhampton* was a well-supported 12-1 chance. But the race was run in treacherously heavy conditions, and after a blatant false start without the runners being recalled. Three horses fell fatally and *Wolverhampton* came down in a six-horse pile-up on the second circuit. It was Bretherton's last National ride. As an owner, he had only one more runner in the race: the outsider *Chatterbox* who was pulled up in 1853. Having retired to Liverpool, the

National's second winning jockey died, aged 68, three days after the running of the 1874 race.
See also: Jerry.

BREW, Charlotte

The 'Essex girl' who, in 1977, at the age of 21, became the first woman to ride in the Grand National. In a 42-strong field, she appeared on her own horse, *Barony Fort*, a 12 year old and one of four starters priced at 200-1. Most creditably, they cleared 26 of the 30 fences before the big (17.1 hands) chestnut gelding finally refused.

Ungallantly, her participation was preceded with an avalanche of derision and disapproval from prejudiced individuals in the media and racing who argued that females riding in the National belonged strictly to the realms of Velvet Brown fiction. The fact remained that Charlotte had already become the first woman to ride over one circuit of the National course, having finished fourth on *Barony Fort* in the 1976 Greenall Whitley Foxhunters Chase. And with that run, her horse had fully qualified for the 1977 National.

Born June 14, 1955, and educated – like Olympic horsewoman Princess Anne – at Benenden in Kent, Charlotte Brew (later Mrs Jeremy Budd) graduated from Pony Club events to hunting, eventing and riding in more than 200 point-to-point races. Even before reaching her teens, inspired by Elizabeth Taylor's success in *National Velvet*, she had dreamed of riding in the Grand National. Finally, after years of humouring their daughter, Richard and Judith Brew relented. In support of her burning ambition they bought *Barony Fort*, a well-bred Irish gelding who, though lacking in speed, was an excellent jumper and had proven his stamina in a four-mile chase at Cheltenham.

Besides regularly riding *Barony Fort* in point-to-points, usually finishing second, the tall (5ft 10in) Charlotte prepared for the National by building up her strength with a rigorous training programme – working out with a personal trainer in the gym, swimming and road running. And all the while she was under relentless pressure from reporters and photographers. Though she received hundreds of letters from well-wishers, the media was never so supportive. It was a measure of how her chances were rated that Ladbrokes, who had taken over management of the race, generously gave her a free £20 bet with guaranteed odds of 500-1 against her

completing the course. By race day, however, she was more realistically priced at 8-1 for finishing in the race.

On the eve of the National, to ease pre-race tension, Charlotte went out dancing and on to a casino, escorted by jockey Ian Watkinson who was to ride *Sage Merlin*, a 20-1 chance. The following morning they walked the course together. Already the tactics were clear in her mind. Her sole objective was get round safely; to that aim she would maintain a moderate pace and steer a wide course to avoid fallers and the bigger drops on the inside.

The plan worked well. Charlotte held back at the start, not joining in the stampede that saw seven horses eliminated at the first and another four at the first open ditch. Though always one-paced in the rear, *Barony Fort* jumped immaculately throughout the first circuit. Thereafter, cheers greeted the completion of his every jump and especially when – unlike three horses directly ahead – he safely cleared the second Becher's.

By now her mount had been tailed off, but still Charlotte was resolved to finish, and, ever more slowly, *Barony Fort* plodded on as far as the 26th fence. Then they came to the last open ditch and there, with nothing left, her 12 year old firmly refused, not once but four times. Charlotte was hugely disappointed, felt that she had failed miserably. But to put her ride in proper perspective it may be noted that, among 31 horses failing to finish, *Barony Fort* had travelled farthest of all.

Inevitably, her historic ride in the 1977 National was eclipsed by the extraordinary performance of 12 year old *Red Rum* in achieving his record third victory. (The winner's trainer, Ginger McCain, was incidentally among those who very strongly disapproved of a woman taking part). But six months later the intrepid Charlotte blazed another trail for her sex – by tackling that most daunting cross-country challenge: Czechoslovakia's perilous Velka Pardubicka, over four miles and 2.5 furlongs. There, on *Barony Fort*, she safely negotiated all the big fences, including the awesome Taxis hedge, and looked a likely winner until being brought down at the final river crossing.

With a precedent firmly established, more women followed Charlotte in the National. She herself reappeared five years later, riding her mother's ten year old *Martinstown*, a 100-1 outsider. Sadly she got no further than the third fence where she landed on top

of jockey Ron Barry. But at least that year her sex had plenty to celebrate – as Geraldine Rees, the last of eight finishers on *Cheers*, became the first woman to complete the full course.
See also: Lady Riders.

BRISCOE, Basil

Basil Briscoe was responsible for bringing *Golden Miller* to England, and for training the brilliant bay gelding to win four successive Cheltenham Gold Cups, the third of which was immediately followed by victory in the 1934 Grand National in record-breaking time – an unprecedented double. Yet sadly, after so much sterling work, his association with the so-called 'horse of the century' was doomed to end in acrimony and disillusionment.

It had all gone so well in his early years, even though his family had been totally opposed to his interest in horses. His father, the head of a hardware empire, was determined that his son should study estate management following an education at Eton and Clare College, Cambridge. But young Briscoe soon rebelled, and in 1926 he gained invaluable experience as pupil assistant to Harvey Leader, uncle of the leading jockey Ted Leader. It was the year that the trainer turned out *Jack Horner* to win the Grand National.

Aided by a large inheritance from his parents' sheep-farming enterprises in Australia, Briscoe was now able to indulge his enthusiasms: riding regularly with hunts and setting up as a trainer at Longstowe Hall, near Cambridge. At the same time, he gained election to White's club in London and mixed with the West End's smart set.

In 1930 a winning streak at a chemin-de-fer party prompted Basil to push his luck further: taking up the telegraphed offer of a three year old gelding in Ireland. He was buying 'blind', but he had already heard good reports of this horse. And now, for £500, he was the owner of *Golden Miller*. At first sight, he was unimpressed by the physical appearance of *Golden Miller*. Subsequently, the gelding was un-placed in a minor hurdle race at Southwell, and six weeks later Briscoe offered to sell him, without profit, to his friend and patron, Philip Carr. Sportingly, Carr insisted on paying a 'proper price' of £1,000.

With the continued backing of Carr, Briscoe might well have enjoyed a gloriously untroubled career. But it was not to be. Together, they saw *Golden Miller* develop into a brilliant four year old; they also had an outstanding hurdler called *Insurance* and a useful jumper, *Solanum*. Then came tragic news: Mr Carr was terminally ill. He instructed Briscoe to sell all his horses and, if necessary, accept a lower price in return for the privilege of keeping those he wished to continue to train.

It was at another chemin-de-fer party that Basil made a fateful transaction: selling *Golden Miller* and *Insurance* for some £12,000 the pair, and *Solanum* for £3,500. The new owner, for whom he would train them, was the young millionairess, Miss Dorothy Paget. Still, his future looked bright. He moved to superior new training premises at Beechwood House, Exning, on the fringe of Newmarket Heath. *Insurance* went on to become the first horse to win the Champion Hurdle twice (1932-33). *Golden Miller* won the Cheltenham Gold Cup four times (1932-35) and became the first horse to achieve the Gold Cup-Grand National double. But, for all this success, the difficult Miss Paget was never content to leave the racing programme of her horses to her trainer's judgment. She was liable to telephone after midnight to discuss plans and, after a race, was known to engage her trainer for several hours in conducting a post-mortem.

The breaking point came following the 1935 National, in which *Golden Miller*, going off the 2-1 favourite, had been backed by Briscoe to win him £10,000. Doubtless, this big gamble added to the trainer's stress on seeing his superstar unseat Gerry Wilson at the 11th fence. Soon after, his short fuse truly snapped when the ever-dictatorial Miss Paget insisted on racing *Golden Miller* in the Champion Chase, just 24 hours later. Above all, he objected to her continued use of Wilson, a jockey who had recently been critical of his training methods. *Golden Miller* again unseated his rider, and a bitter row between trainer and owner ended with the exasperated Briscoe ordering Miss Paget to remove all her horses from his stables. The Miller went on to win a fifth Cheltenham Gold Cup in 1936 with Owen Anthony as trainer.

Meanwhile, Briscoe's fortunes cruelly faded. He moved to smaller training quarters. A succession of gambles failed. He was officially declared bankrupt and a few months later his young wife died of tuberculosis. Then, while serving as a driver for the Royal Army Service Corps in Egypt, he too contracted tuberculosis. No longer the breezy optimist

of his youth, he ended his days as a lorry driver, collecting manure from Newmarket stables. He died in August, 1951, after suffering serious injuries in a fall at the Crown Inn, Swaffham Prior, Cambridgeshire, where he had been living. He was aged 48, and his beloved *Golden Miller* would outlive him by six years.
See also: Golden Miller; Paget, Dorothy; Wilson, Gerry.

BROADCASTING

In 1927, for the first time, countless millions shared in the excitement of the Grand National courtesy of BBC radio coverage. Enthralled, they gathered at home round the wireless to hear events described by commentators Meyrick Good and George Allison. The former, a journalist on *The Sporting Life*, called home *Sprig*, a supremely popular winner not only because he was the 8-1 favourite but also because he had been bred by Captain Richard Partridge before returning to the First World War trenches where he was killed in action shortly before the 1918 Armistice. Allison, a newspaper reporter, was responsible for describing the scenes before and after the race. Subsequently he became a regular BBC anchorman until, in 1934, he succeeded the late and great Herbert Chapman as manager of Arsenal Football Club.

At this time there was no commentator's box at Aintree. Manning a microphone, with a second mike hanging in front of him to record the crowd reaction, Meyrick Good had to operate from the stands where, to add to his nervousness, he was seated next to King George V. From his position, on a misty afternoon, he was unable to identify all the 24 fallers in a then record field of 37. Nevertheless, he effectively captured the thrills and spills, and was unable to contain his personal excitement when Ted Leader on *Sprig* jumped the last fence ahead of Jack Anthony on *Bright's Boy*.

'Come on, Ted', cried the commentator, 'You'll win!' Then, as the second microphone picked up the deafening roar of the crowd, his words were lost. But doubtless he was overjoyed to see *Sprig* win by one length from a fast-finishing, 100-1 shot called *Bovril III*. Good had backed *Sprig* to win and was a lifelong friend of Ted Leader.

While the BBC had dabbled, somewhat ineptly, at covering the 1926 Derby, this was the first hugely popular broadcast of an English horse race. It occu-

pied just over an hour of air-time. And ever since then the B.B.C. has covered the National – with one lamentable exception: in 1952, when Tophams Ltd, who had purchased the Aintree racecourse from the Earl of Sefton in 1949, became deadlocked in negotiations with the BBC over copyright of the race commentary.

Mrs Mirabel Topham, widow of the former head of Tophams Ltd, stood firm in the face of a huge public outcry. Finally, she sought an 11th-hour compromise – by recruiting her own scratch team of commentators headed by racing journalist Bob Butchers. But this was a hopelessly amateurish affair, all the more confused by the misty conditions, a large field of 47 starters, and a huge number of fallers. To the amazement of listeners the race was won by *Teal* who, so they had been told, was one of ten fallers at the very first fence!

It was not until 1960, after years of negotiations, that the BBC secured the rights to televise the Grand National. The first television commentators were Peter O'Sullevan, Clive Graham and Peter Bromley; and that year, by coincidence, the race was won by the clear favourite (*Merryman II*) for the first time since 1927, the year of the first radio commentary.

O'Sullevan, who had made his National debut on radio in 1947, continued to be the TV commentator until his retirement in 1997 when he covered the race for the 50th and last time. Bromley, having been switched to radio, covered his 42nd and last National in 2001.
See also: Television; O'Sullevan, Sir Peter; Bromley, Peter.

BROMLEY, Peter

Although Peter Bromley became the famed and so distinctive radio voice of racing throughout four decades, he also took part – along with Peter O'Sullevan and Clive Graham – in the first televised coverage of the Grand National in 1960. It was an unnerving experience since he was required to climb a huge scaffolding tower in order to cover the far side of the course. Having no head for heights, he was initially terrified. But there was – in retrospect – one amusing moment. When midway through his commentary, he was distracted by a tap on the shoulder and a chirpy cry of 'Wotcha, cock'. It was the champion jump jockey Fred Winter who, following an early fall on *Dandy Scot*, had climbed the tower for a clear view of the race.

Born on April 30, 1929, the son of a dentist, Bromley was educated at Cheltenham College and Sandhurst. He was an excellent shot as well as a fine horseman, and in 1952 he narrowly missed selection for Britain's modern pentathlon Olympic team. Following three years' service as an officer in the 14/20th King's Hussars, he became an assistant trainer and an amateur rider. A broken leg soon forced him to quit the saddle; then, after gaining valuable experience as a pioneer racecourse commentator, he joined the BBC, being appointed their first specialist sports correspondent in 1959.

As BBC radio's racing correspondent and commentator, Bromley covered 42 consecutive Grand Nationals; and, like O'Sullevan, he rated the 1973 *Red Rum-Crisp* duel the greatest of them all. He also enjoyed a modest degree of success as a racehorse owner – most notably with *Treasury Bond*, unbeaten in four races as a two year old in 1975 before being sold to the United States. The horse was trained by his close friend, Ryan Price, and later Bromley wrote the trainer's biography, *The Price of Success*.

Bromley's last Aintree assignment, in 2001, was to be one one of the toughest – trying to account for so many fallers in a mud-bath National which saw only four of 40 starters complete the course. He retired two months later following a final commentary on the Derby. An outstanding broadcaster and great champion of racing, he died after a year-long battle with pancreatic cancer in June, 2003.

See also: Broadcasting; Television.

BROOKSHAW, Stephen

Trainer of the runaway 1997 Grand National winner, *Lord Gyllene*, Steve Brookshaw hailed from a great racing dynasty. His father, Peter, had won the 1950 Aintree Fox Hunters' on *Hilmere*. Elder brother, Peter Jnr, had trained *Fealty* to win the 1984 Sun Alliance Hurdle. Most famously, his late uncle, Tim, had been champion jockey of 1958-59, the season in which he rode *Wyndburgh*, runner-up by only one and a half lengths in the National. Steve was just eight years old at the time of that National. Subsequently, he would watch a video of the race over and over again, and he came to own the broken stirrup which arguably had cost his uncle victory.

Born on November 18, 1950, Steve rode in point-to-points from the age of 14, then went on to become a leading amateur jump jockey. Most importantly, his career was influenced by millionaire owner Stan Clarke, an old family friend. On Mrs Clarke's *Mount Argus*, he won 23 point-to-points and hunter chases; and on being persuaded by Mr Clarke to train under permit, he proceeded to send out 43 pointing and hunter chase winners for him in eight years. In 1995 he took out a full licence and the following year he underlined his training talent by bringing back Mr Clarke's rejuvenated *Rolling Ball* to win Aintree's Fox Hunters' Chase at the ripe old age of 13.

By 1997 Brookshaw had nearly 30 horses in his charge at Preston Farm stables, at Uffington, near Shrewsbury. The great star there was the big New Zealand-bred *Lord Gyllene* who was ridden out most days by Steve's wife, Zena.

In the 1996-97 seasson he struck irresistible form, scoring a hat-trick of wins at Uttoxeter and then, three weeks before the Grand National, finishing second in Uttoxeter's Midlands National over four and a quarter miles.

After IRA bomb scares had forced a 49-hour postponement, *Lord Gyllene* led the 36-strong National field from start to finish, with the grey *Suny Bay* 25 lengths back in second place. Thus, Brookshaw had saddled the Grand National winner in only his second full season as a trainer. Thoughts immediately turned to a repeat victory in 1998. Unfortunately, *Lord Gyllene* suffered a series of injuries that limited him to only two races in the next three years. He was never the same force again, and after 2000 Brookshaw no longer enjoyed Mr (soon to be Sir) Stanley Clarke's patronage.

In 2001 Brookshaw again had an Aintree runner: *No Retreat*, formerly owned by Clarke and a first National ride for Jason Maguire. But this was the year of quagmire conditions with only four finishers, two of them remounted. *No Retreat*, an eight year old who had not won beyond two miles five furlongs, fell at the Water Jump. The following season was a dismal one for the trainer, but in February, 2003, he ended a 303-day drought in style when sending out *Valleymore* to win the £20,000 final of the Red Square Vodka 'Fixed Brush' Novices' Hurdle series at Haydock.

He now hoped to challenge for the 2004 National with *Cassia Heights*, but the nine year old was too lowly rated to make the cut. Instead he was entered for the £40,600 Topham Chase, a race the trainer had previously won in 1999 with *Listen Timmy*. Under Jim Culloty, in a 29-strong field, *Cassia Heights* won at 33-1, so maintaining Brookshaw's outstand-

ing strike-rate for races over National fences.
See also: Lord Gyllene; Dobbin, Tony; Clarke,
Sir Stanley.

BROOKSHAW, Tim

No jockey deserved to win an Aintree Grand
National more than the genial, highly talented Tim
Brookshaw. Six times, between 1950 and 1958, he
rode in the race. But usually he was on long-priced
outsiders, and he completed the course only once,
finishing ninth on *Merry Throw*, a 40-1 shot in 1957.
Then at last, in 1959, he was given a real opportunity.
As the leading National Hunt rider, he was booked to
ride *Wyndburgh*, the reliable nine year old who had
been placed second in 1957 and fourth in 1958, and
who was now fourth in the betting at 10-1.

Brookshaw seized the opportunity superbly well.
Riding at first towards the rear, he steadily moved up
the field until, at the second Becher's, he was battling with *Oxo* for the lead. But there, on landing
steeply, his off-side stirrup-iron broke. For the sake
of balance, he freed his foot from the on-side iron
and rode on determinedly but at a considerable disadvantage. 'Look, no feet', he shouted across to his
great friend Michael Scudamore on *Oxo* – and a few
unprintable expletives besides.

Very probably that one unlucky mishap –
leaving him to ride without stirrups over eight fences
and a mile and a half – cost him the race. In a masterful exhibition of horsemanship, he managed to finish with a flourish, *Wyndburgh* closing rapidly on
Oxo towards the end of the long run-in, only to be
denied by a mere one and a half lengths. The previous year's winner *Mr What* was a further eight
lengths back in third.

Brookshaw, who became champion jockey that
season with 83 wins, rode twice more in the National. In 1961 he was sixth on *Wyndburgh*, the race
being won by *Nicolaus Silver*, a horse he had previously ridden and had judged to be too cautious a
jumper for Liverpool. Finally, in 1963, he was 11th
on *Eternal*, a 12 year old safe jumper who had won
a dozen chases.

That year he won the Scottish National on
Pappageno's Cottage, but then, in December, this
brave and most unlucky rider had his career ended
by an horrific fall – fatal for his mount *Lucky Dora*
– in a handicap hurdle at Aintree. He had already
broken his collarbone six times, his legs, nose and
ankles twice. Now his back was broken and, aged

34, he was left paralysed from the waist down. Yet
he refused to let the disability end his riding. He
devised a pulley to hoist himself aboard a horse
and actually went on to take part in jockeys' show-
jumping competitions and to ride in a 'veterans'
charity Flat race in Ireland.

Tim's tragic fate in 1963 highlighted the disgrace-
ful lack of financial provisions for jockeys who had
their livelihood suddenly ended; and that lack was
further underlined three months later when jockey
Paddy Farrell, a father of four, suffered the same fate
in falling on *Border Flight* in the National. These
tragedies resulted in the setting up of the Farrell/
Brookshaw Fund, and most importantly they
spurred the belated establishment of the Injured
Jockeys' Fund. Tim died in 1981 as the result of another fall, one possibly caused by a stroke or a heart
attack.
See also: Wyndburgh; Injuries; Injured Jockeys'
Fund.

BROTHERS

*Brothers who have ridden to victory in the Grand
National*
Tommy Beasley (1880, 1881, 1889) and Harry
 Beasley (1891)
Fred Rees (1921) and Lewis Rees (1922)

Brothers who have trained Grand National winners
Joe Cannon – Regal (1876)
Tom Cannon – Playfair (1888)

The most phenomenal brothers in the history of the
race are the Beasleys: Tommy, Harry, William and
John. In 1879 all four rode in the Aintree race. Three
of the brothers rode in the Nationals of 1880, 1884,
1887 and 1889; and two appeared in the Nationals of
1881, 1882, 1883, 1885, 1888, 1891 and 1892.

Two Irish brothers, Alan and William McDonough, rode in five of the first nine Grand Nationals,
those of 1839, 1841, 1844, 1846 and 1847. While
the latter never completed the course, the former finished fifth in the first National of 1839 and was on
the runner-up in the next two years. George Holman,
who competed in 11 Nationals, was joined by his
younger brother John in 1864, 1867 and 1869; and
in 1872 finished sixth with another younger brother,
Alfred, one place behind.

William and Arthur Nightingall both rode in the
Nationals of 1886, 1888, 1889 and 1891. In 1888,

for the first time, two pairs of brothers rode in the National – the Nightingalls being joined by William and Harry Beasley. Coming to the final Canal Turn, Harry on *Usna* and brother William on *Frigate* were sharing the lead when *Usna*, the Irish favourite, dislocated his shoulder on landing and carried *Frigate* far out to the right. It probably cost *Frigate* the race. Having to make up a mass of lost ground, she finished second to *Playfair*. Willie and Arthur Nightingall were third and ninth respectively.

In 1896 the brothers Tom and Joe Widger rode in the National, the former falling on *Wild Man From Borneo*, owned by his brother John and ridden to victory by Joe the previous year. Next came three brothers, Jack, Ivor and Owen Anthony, all failing to finish in the 1914 National. Jack and Ivor also rode in the Nationals of 1915, 1921 and 1922. The 1915 race was a triumph for brotherly teamwork as Ivor, riding *Ilston*, leaned over to help Jack into the saddle when he was sliding off *Ally Sloper* after a blunder at the second fence. Subsequently, *Ilston* fell and *Ally Sloper* went on to win.

In the 1920s Harry Brown rode in four Nationals, once finishing second, while his brother Frank failed to finish on his only appearance, in 1923. The stars of that decade were Fred and Lewis Rees. They both rode in eight Nationals; and remarkably their victories came in successive years: Fred on *Shaun Spadah* (1921) and Lewis on *Music Hall* (1922). Frank and Robert Lyall, the eldest and youngest respectively of five jump jockey brothers, both rode in the National, but in different decades. Frank's best was second place on *Bloodstone* in 1912, beaten six lengths by *Jerry M*. Bob won on *Grakle* in 1931, by one and a half lengths from *Gregalach*.

In 1940 when Flight Sergeant Mervyn Jones won on *Bogskar*, he was cheered home by his brother Hywel – also on leave from the RAF – who was near the finishing line after falling at the 14th fence on Mr 'Jock' Whitney's *National Night*. Tim and Martin Molony rode in the Nationals of 1947 and 1948 without finishing. In 1958 Tim Brookshaw fell on *Pippykin* while his brother Peter, an amateur rider, finished seventh on *Holly Bank*, a 50-1 chance.

The outstanding brothers of this period, however, were Ireland's Pat and 'Tosse' Taaffe. The former was to ride in seventeen Nationals, winning two; the latter riding in eight and four times finishing in the frame. On six occasions they both appeared in the race, most notably in 1955 when Pat won on *Quare Times* and his younger brother took third place on *Carey's Cottage*.

Most ironic was the first Grand National (1967) in which both brothers Josh and Macer Gifford appeared. The latter was on *Popham Down*, the 66-1 outsider brought down by the fall of *Meon Valley* at the first. And it was the riderless *Popham Down* who would be responsible for the mass pile-up at the 23rd which only the straggler *Foinavon* cleared at the first attempt. Arguably it cost Josh a National victory on the 15-2 clear favourite. Taking *Honey End* back a full 50 yards to make a second approach to the decimated fence, he finished the 15 lengths runner-up to 100-1 *Foinavon*.

The following year both brothers failed to complete the course, and in 1969, the last time they appeared together, Josh finished fifth on *Bassnet* while Macer was ninth on *Furore II*. That same year two American brothers, both amateurs, were among the 30 riders: George Sloan on his grey *Peccard* and Paul Sloan on *Terossian*, both 50-1 chances. The former fell at the first Becher's and the latter refused.

In 2004, the year after he had won the National on *Monty's Pass*, Barry Geraghty was joined for the first time by his elder brother, Ross. Both completed the course: Barry fourth on *Monty's Pass* and Ross tenth on *The Bunny Boiler*. In 2007, Paul Carberry, who had ridden the 1999 National winner *Bobbyjo*, was joined by his brother Philip. The latter fell at the first on the 8-1 co-favourite *Point Barrow*, while the former, on *Dun Doire*, continued towards the rear and finally pulled up four out.

BROTHER AND SISTER

In 2006 Paul and Nina Carberry achieved the distinction of being the only brother and sister to have ridden in the same Grand National. Both were on 33-1 shots. Nina was the last of nine finishers on *Forest Gunner* while her brother, a National-winning jockey, fell on *Sir OJ* at the second Becher's.

There is only one other instance of a brother and sister having appeared in the National. Gee Armytage pulled up on *Gee-A* at the second Becher's (22nd) in 1988, one year after her brother Marcus had made his National debut, pulling up on *Brown Veil*, a 200-1 outsider at the 23rd. Marcus also became a National-winning jockey (in 1990 on record-breaking *Mr Frisk*). But, solely because of injuries, he and his sister were twice denied the chance to appear in the National at the same time.

In 2007 there was the unprecedented possibility of two brothers and their sister competing in an Aintree National. It occurred when Nina Carberry, Ireland's champion amateur jump jockey, was booked to ride *A New Story* against her brothers Paul (on *Dun Doire*) and Philip (on *Point Barrow*). If all three had ridden at Aintree it would have been the first time that three siblings had competed in one National since 1889 when three Beasley brothers appeared.

Unfortunately, Nina's mount (allotted 10st) was unlikely to make the cut, and so he was switched to the Irish National where Nina did indeed compete against her brothers. She was unseated three out after *A New Story* had been badly hampered. Philip finished ninth on *Well Tutored*, and Paul pulled up on *Mac Three* before the 16th.

See also: Armytage, Marcus; Lady Riders.

BROWN, Harry Atherton

A strong contender for the title of the Grand National's unluckiest rider, Old Etonian Harry Atherton Brown was an extraordinary cavalier character who rode his first winner in 1907 at the age of 18, quickly established himself as leading amateur jump jockey, and in 1919 won the National Hunt jockey championship – a feat never since achieved by a non-professional.

Brown made four attempts to realise his cherished ambition to win the Grand National. The first was in 1920 on his own nine year old bay gelding, *The Bore*. For much of the second circuit he maintained the chief challenge to the ultimate winner, *Troytown*, before fading into third place a few fences from home. The following year, *The Bore* was 9-1 favourite and looking the likely winner as he led a decimated field with *Shaun Spadah*. But then he crashed out at the penultimate fence. Harry broke his collarbone in the fall, but such was his determination (all the greater since he had backed himself £500 each-way) that he remounted and rode on in agony, with his right arm hanging limply at his side. He was rewarded with a distant second place.

As the leading amateur rider, Brown was again on the favourite in the 1922 National, this time Lord Woolavington's *Southampton*, who came to Aintree on the back of six successive wins. But the six year old gelding was second highest in the weights and he fell at the very first fence. The following year Harry was a spectator at the National, the family being represented by his brother Frank, a highly accomplished rider in his own right, who now had to pull up on a rank outsider, *Cinzano*.

That year the National was attended by King George V, together with the Prince of Wales. Before the race Harry was chosen to conduct the prince on a guided tour of the course. The story goes that, along the way, the prince asked about the prospects of the various runners and said that he himself rather fancied having a bet on *Sergeant Murphy*. Ever forceful in his opinions, Brown declared: 'Good God! Don't do that. He's as old as I am. He's not a horse at all!' At his fourth attempt, 13 year old *Sergeant Murphy* won by three lengths.

In 1924, for the third time, the indefatigable jockey found himself on the National favourite. His mount was 12 year old *Conjuror II*, who had finished third the previous year when ridden by an inexperienced Oxford undergraduate, son of the owner, Major C. Dewhurst. Significantly, Brown had recently given the horse a tremendous ride in the inaugural Cheltenham Gold Cup, going down by a mere head to champion jockey Fred Rees on *Red Splash*, with *Gerald L* a neck back in third. Now *Conjuror II* – trained by Tom Coulthwaite, seeking his third National winner – was popularly thought to be unbeatable. He went off at 5-2, the shortest priced favourite since *Regal* (remounted to finish sixth) in 1879. And he had 29 rivals compared with *Regal's* 17.

Conjuror II started well, jumping perfectly and being close up behind the leaders as he came to Becher's Brook. But then, as he took off, a loose horse barged into him. By the time Brown rose from the turf he found that his horse had galloped on. *Conjuror II* was subsequently caught by another jockey, Bill O'Neill, who had been thrown. O'Neill mounted and used him to catch up with his original charge, *Libretto*. Brown did not ride in the National again.

A prolific shot, an expert stalker and a fisherman, Brown was caricatured as 'Charlie Peppercorn' in Siegfried Sassoon's *Memoirs of a Fox-hunting Man*. So often an unlucky loser on horseback, he had considerable success in his more leisurely activities; and it was typical of the passionate sportsman that one day, on arriving early at Hereford races, he decided to put his unexpected free time to good use. He went on to the banks of the Wye and landed a record 44-pound salmon.

In his riding career Harry suffered fractures of the

B

pelvis, both arms and a leg, plus a number of broken ribs and collarbones. But these were minor compared with those of his brother Frank whose multiple injuries included a fractured skull, a score of concussions and finally a broken back. Harry himself kept riding for 22 years, being finally put out of the saddle by a severely broken wrist.

BUCKINGHAM, John Anthony

Three days before the 1967 Grand National, 26 year old John Buckingham was preparing to attend an uncle's funeral when he received a most unexpected phone call. It was an invitation to ride a nine year old called *Foinavon* in the big race. The brown gelding was regarded as a fairly ordinary chaser and three jockeys had already declined the ride because the owner would only pay the basic riding fee of £5. 10s. But Buckingham eagerly grabbed his first chance to compete in the National. And on April 8, having spent the previous night sleeping on two armchairs pushed together in a boarding house, he set off in a 44-strong field on a 100-1 yellow-blinkered no-hoper.

Just under nine minutes and 50 seconds later, Buckingham was dismounting from one of the most improbable winners in Grand National history. *Foinavon* had triumphed by a full 15 lengths and suddenly the jockey found himself propelled into brilliant, unfamiliar limelight – besieged by would-be interviewers and booked the following evening for a West End appearance on *Sunday Night At The London Palladium* with Bob Monkhouse.

Buckingham won on *Foinavon* because, coming from a hundred yards in the rear, he was the only rider who successfully steered his horse clear of the carnage created at the 23rd fence by the riderless *Popham Down*. Much emphasis was placed on his good fortune. The fact remains that to a degree he made his own luck. He sensibly took a wide course, kept his mount running strongly to the end, and won in a respectable time. It is a measure of his horsemanship that he went on to complete the course in four Grand Nationals out of four.

Unusually for a jump jockey, Buckingham (born July 10, 1940) never sat on a horse before leaving school at 15. At that stage he was offered work on the Oxfordshire estate of Mr Edward Courage for whom his mother was employed as a dairymaid. He was given the choice of three jobs: assisting the shepherd or the gamekeeper, or working as a stable

lad. He opted for stable lad, and it was in that capacity that he first went to the National – accompanying Mr Courage's great mare, *Tiberetta*, who finished third, second and fourth in the years 1957 to 1959.

In the latter year Buckingham rode his first winner, *Sahagun*, in a hurdle race at Southwell. But it was another eight years before he scored his first major success: victory on Mr Courage's *San Angelo* in Cheltenham's Grand Annual Challenge Cup, The following day, in the Cheltenham Gold Cup, a horse called *Foinavon*, ridden by his trainer John Kempton, finished a distant last at 500-1.

If Kempton was to ride *Foinavon* at Aintree three weeks later, it would have entailed putting up 10lb overweight. So it was that the trainer offered the ride to Buckingham, a jockey who, in eight years, had ridden only 44 winners – ten of them, however, in the current 1966-67 season. His first Grand National ride was on such a seeming no-hoper that neither trainer nor owner, Cyril Watkins, troubled to attend the race.

After the sensational success at Aintree (his minute racing fee was boosted by ten per cent of the £17,630 first prize), Buckingham hoped for a major upturn in his fortunes as a jockey; and indeed, for a while, he was in much greater demand. He had his best season with 21 winners and was to ride in three more Grand Nationals. To his great regret, however, a broken arm kept him out of the 1968 National when he eagerly looked forward to challenging on *San Angelo*, a 25-1 chance. Bill Rees took the ride, finishing 12th. *Foinavon*, now 66-1 and partnered by Phil Harvey, was brought down at the Water Jump.

The following year Buckingham finished 12th on 66-1 shot *Limeburner*. In 1970 he was the sixth of seven finishers on Mr Courage's *Pride of Kentucky*, and in 1971, he remounted *Limeburner* to come home in 12th place. That last year he had seriously threatened to ride another 100-1 winner, leading at the Canal Turn second time around, but then falling at the second last when going strong in third place.

It was just four years since his most famous victory. Now, after his greatest disappointment as a rider, and discouraged by a season that brought him a broken knee and only one winner in 81 rides, he exchanged his silks and breeches for the blue apron of a jockey's valet. Long after, he was to be the subject of hugely sympathetic stories about the fickleness of fame and how the mighty have fallen. But the violins were unduly plaintive. In reality, the ex-jockey, who had ridden 89 winners, was now content to have a steady income from a job that enabled him to remain so close to the sport that he loved. For 30 years he was to be employed at the heart of racing – a master valet who was hugely popular and respected in race dressing rooms up and down the country. In those three decades he 'looked after' 14 Grand National winners including Graham Thorner, Charlie Fenwick, Carl Llewellyn, Richard Dunwoody, Hywel Davies and Marcus Armytage.

'Buck', as he was always known in racing circles, sold his valeting business to jockey Chris Maude in 2001 following the death of Tom, his brother and long-time partner. Life in retirement was not easy. In 2002 he was diagnosed with diabetes and then he underwent surgery on his spine to repair damage from his riding days. But, despite failing eyesight, he continued to play golf, and in 2002 a testimonial golf day, thanking him for his work on behalf of the Injured Jockeys' Fund, was held in his honour. It was attended by many great jockeys, past and present, including Josh Gifford who, on *Honey End*, had finished second behind *Foinavon* so many years before. *See also:* Foinavon; Kempton, John.

BUCKLEY, Pat

Born (July, 1943) near Naas in Co. Kildare, Pat Buckley learned to ride under the tuition of Mrs O'Brien Butler whose ponies he used to ride in the show ring. He was only 13 years old when he joined Neville Crump's stable high up on Middlesham Moor in Yorkshire. Six years later the teenager won the 1963 Grand National by three-quarters of a length on the 66-1 outsider, *Ayala*. It was only his second appearance in the race. Moreover, he had only been approached to ride *Ayala* one week before going to Aintree, being first introduced to the horse on the Monday.

The late offer of the ride on *Ayala* came as a most welcome consolation since this year he had been replaced by Gerry Scott on *Springbok*, now the National's 10-1 clear favourite to give Crump his fourth success in the race. The previous year Buckley – standing in for the injured Scott – had made his National debut on the well-supported *Springbok*, coming to grief at the first fence when the eight year old jumped far too big.

Now the young jockey rode a remarkably mature race, with *Ayala* making only one serious mistake when carving a great hole through the Canal Turn first

time around. Timing his challenge to perfection, Buckley drove *Ayala* into a narrow lead before the second last, but almost immediately he was passed by John Lawrence (now Lord Oaksey) on *Carrickbeg*. Being on a mount more noted for stamina than speed, he called out 'Go on, John, you'll win'.

To his everlasting credit, Buckley never relaxed in his effort; and, to his surprise, his resolution paid off as *Carrickbeg*, having led over the final fence, began to weaken in the last 100 yards. *Ayala* caught the leader just 20 yards from home and snatched victory. *Springbok*, who had surprisingly faded two fences out, was the fifth of 22 finishers.

Remarkably, Buckley's first major success was quickly followed by another, as the following month he won the Whitbread Gold Cup on the Crump-trained *Hoodwinked*, a victory he repeated one year later on the same stable's *Dormant*.

A series of injuries was now limiting his rides, but altogether he was to compete in ten Grand Nationals, his post-winning rides being on *Rough Tweed* (1966, fell at the third); *Limeking* (1967, brought down at the 23rd fence); *Rutherfords* (1968, finished fourth), *Arcturus* (1969, finished sixth); *Permit* (1970, brought down at the third), *Just A Gamble* (1972, fell at the 17th); *Canharis* (1973, brought down at The Chair); and *San Feliu* (1974, finished ninth).

He was especially unlucky in the notorious Foinavon National, being well poised at the second Becher's to make a challenge on *Limeking*, a 33-1 shot, only to have his hopes dashed at the next fence when the riderless *Popham Down* caused a gigantic pile-up. The following year, on eight year old *Rutherfords*, the second favourite, he was up with the leaders almost throughout before, like all others, being decisively outpaced by *Red Alligator*. But shortly afterwards he had the big consolation of winning the Scottish Grand National on Lady Hay's *Arcturus*. Forced to retire in 1976 as a result of injury, he went on to train horses for the Sultan of Oman before becoming a racecourse commentator in Dubai. *See also:* Ayala.

BUDD, Mrs Jeremy
See: Brew, Charlotte.

BULLOCK, John Arthur
An ex-paratrooper and prisoner-of-war, Johnnie Bullock first appeared in the Grand National as a

professional rider in 1950 when he fell at the first Becher's on *Cavaliero*, a 66-1 outsider. One year later, he returned on the unfancied mare *Nickel Coin*, a 40-1 shot, and triumphed by six lengths in a chaotic race – the so-called 'Grand Crashional' – that saw only three of 36 starters complete the course, with the third having been remounted.

Certainly, Bullock's success was aided by an outrageous, undeclared false start that resulted in 12 horses being eliminated at the first fence in the mad scramble to make up lost ground. No one, however, took better advantage of the circumstances. And this was in a year when riders who came to grief included Dick Francis, Bryan Marshall and Tim Brookshaw; and four interesting newcomers: Pat Taaffe, Fred Winter, Dave Dick and Michael Scudamore.

Riding patiently and steering clear of trouble, Bullock kept his out-and-out stayer reasonably well-placed throughout the first circuit, and by then only four rivals remained. Three of these had fallen out of the running by the fence after the second Becher's, and when the leader *Royal Tan* blundered at the last, *Nickel Coin* had only to be ridden out to win by six lengths.

Born in 1917 in Walsall, Bullock was 19 year old when he first rode as a professional jump jockey, only to have his career soon curtailed by the Second World War. In September, 1944, he was taken prisoner during the distastrous bid of the First British Airborne Division to capture the farthest bridge over the Rhine at Arnhem. But late in the following year he was back in the saddle, struggling to make progress as a jockey until 1949-50 when he began riding regularly for trainer Fred Rimell. Ironically, his winners that season included a horse named *Arnhem*, over hurdles at Ludlow.

Another winner, in 1950, was *Mighty Fine* whom he rode for Rimell in a four-mile chase at Cheltenham. In that same race was the bay mare *Nickel Coin*. She finished way back among the also-rans but afterwards her rider, one Dick Francis, declared that she was an ideal Grand National type and he would love to ride her at Aintree. But he could not, being claimed to ride *Finnure* for Lord Bicester.

Much earlier, Bullock had ridden *Land Fort*, a hugely promising young chaser with National potential. Subsequently this gelding was to be partnered regularly by the champion jockey Tim Molony. But when it came to the Grand National,

Molony was not available, having been booked for Mr J.H. Whitney's 8-1 favourite *Arctic Gold*. Rimell approached Bullock to take the ride but advised him, before accepting, to check first that he was not required by trainer Jack O'Donoghue for *Nickel Coin*. Bullock duly rang O'Donoghue who replied: 'Oh, yes, I suppose you had better ride her.'

Thus, somewhat fortuitously, Bullock was re-united with *Nickel Coin*, a mare he had twice ridden before, winning a chase at Lingfield and finishing second in another at Sandown Park. In the National, *Finnure* and *Land Fort* (now ridden by Bryan Marshall) were among the 12 casualties at the first fence, and the much-vaunted *Arctic Gold*, a six year old, was one of five fallers at the Canal Turn.

Despite his triumph on *Nickel Coin*, one of 32 winning rides in the 1950-51 season, it was another four years before Bullock rode in the National again. Then, on the rank outsider *Steel Lock*, he led the field over Becher's and was going well until being knocked over at the last open ditch. In 1956, again on a 66-1 outsider, *Clearing*, he was the eighth of nine finishers. He was a faller at the fourth on *Armorial III* (1957) and at the fifth on *Rendezvous III* (1958). His sixth and last National, on *Eagle Lodge* (1959), ended in a refusal three out. Having retired four years later, he died in his native Walsall in 1988.

See also: Nickel Coin

BULTEEL, Major Sir John Crocker DSO, MC

As Aintree's clerk of the course (1936 to 1946) Sir John played a key role in improvements to the Grand National course. His interest in the race was deep-rooted, fostered in childhood when his father, Mr J.G. Bulteel, became the owner of the great *Manifesto*, bought for the bargain price of £4,000 and then backed to huge profit to win the National a second time. In addition, his uncle Walter was a leading amateur rider who rode in five successive Nationals (1906-10), beginning with a best finish of eighth on the top-weighted, 33-1 chance, *Drumcree*.

John Crocker Bulteel was eight years old when *Manifesto* won for his father in 1899. Educated at Eton, he served with great distinction in the First World War and made his own first bid to win the National in 1922 with his nine year old bay gelding *Taffytus*. It was a hugely encouraging Aintree debut by *Taffytus* who finished third at 66-1 under a brilliant newcomer named Ted Leader. But, though he was third and second favourite in the Nationals of 1923 and 1924 respectively, he never completed the course again in three successive attempts.

Starting at Windsor, Sir John went on to serve as clerk of the course at Liverpool, Lingfield and Hurst Park; and, long after he had left Liverpool, Aintree supremo Mrs Topham continued to seek his advice. He was Secretary to the Ascot Authority when he died suddenly in 1956, aged 65.

BURIALS

Famously the great *Red Rum* has his grave opposite the Grand National winning post; and his irrepressible trainer, Ginger McCain, has said that he wants to be buried alongside him. Less well-known is the fact that every year Aintree receives about 50 requests from people with a deceased relative who had expressed a wish to have their ashes scattered on or beside the Grand National course. The most popular sites are next to *Red Rum* and on the landing side of Becher's Brook. The former is not always acceptable because, so it has been officially said, 'too many ashes tend to kill off the grass'.

BURKE, John Martin

When 23-year-old John Burke on *Rag Trade* scored by two lengths over *Red Rum* in the 1976 Grand National he became the fifth jockey to have achieved the Cheltenham Gold Cup-National double in the same season and he gave trainer Fred Rimell his fourth success in the race. Significantly, he was judged by the Rimells to be the best horseman of the many jockeys they had employed, supremely stylish 'with the most beautiful hands'.

Born in February, 1953, the son of a schoolmaster in Co. Meath, Burke left Ireland at 17 to ride for the Rimells. It was a measure of his promise that, while still an amateur, he was given his first National ride, in 1974, on eight year old *Rough House*, fourth in the betting on 14-1. The combination fell at the eighth, the Canal Turn; and one year later, after

Burke had turned professional and had won the Great Yorkshire Chase on *Rough House*, they disappointingly fell at the fifth. But now the young jockey was to enjoy a meteoric rise to fame.

He won the 1975 Midlands National on *Rag Trade*, a big clumsy jumper that had been rejected by John Francome after they had finished tenth at Aintree. The following season, having taken over as Rimell's stable jockey from the retired Ken White, he had an extraordinary purple patch – winning the Cheltenham Gold Cup on *Royal Frolic* and both the Welsh and Aintree Grand Nationals on *Rag Trade*.

In 1977, just 24 hours after winning Aintree's Maghull Novices' Hurdle on *Samuel Pepys*, Burke was on the 15-2 Grand National favourite *Andy Pandy*, and the Rimells were hopeful of scoring a record fifth win. The eight year old indeed jumped brilliantly round the first circuit but then, 12 lengths in the lead, he fell when landing badly over the second Becher's, so leaving the way clear for *Red Rum* to go on to his record third victory. Some consolation came later in the month when Burke rode *Andy Pandy* to victory in the Whitbread Gold Cup.

Altogether, Burke competed in 11 Grand Nationals. His other rides were *Brown Admiral* (tenth in 1978); *Royal Frolic* (sixth, 1979); *Royal Frolic* (refused four out, 1980); *Senator Maclacury* (fifth, 1981); 100-1 shot *Hot Tomato* (fell at the last, 1983); *Lucky Vane* (fourth of a record 23 finishers, 1984) and *Lucky Vane* (pulled up lame, 1985). His many successes for the Rimells included the 1978 Triumph Hurdle on *Connaught Ranger*.

Lightly built, Burke was luckier than so many jump jockeys in never having a real weight problem. Unfortunately, however, the quiet Irishman had difficulty in handling success when so young. He returned to Ireland for a while and, after struggling with a drink problem, he settled back in England as a freelance, finally retiring from the saddle in 1985. Ten years later, working as an assistant trainer, he suffered a fatal heart attack. He was only 41.
See also: Rag Trade.

C

CAMPBELL, General Sir David

The first serving cavalry officer to triumph in the Grand National – on a 40-1 outsider, *The Soarer* in 1896. For both horse and rider (then a subaltern in the 9th Lancers) it was their first appearance in the race, and they won by just a length and a half from past winner *Father O'Flynn*, also 40-1, with the mare *Biscuit* the same distance back in third. Having recently won the Grand Military Gold Cup on *Nelly Gray*, David Campbell thus completed the double achieved by Lord John Manners, a Grenadier Guards officer, in 1882.

Campbell could claim more than a rider's share in the National victory. He had bought *The Soarer* unbroken, out of a field, while serving in Ireland, and had introduced him to chasing as a four year old, finishing second in the 1893 Irish Grand Military. The following year he scored seven wins on the bay gelding and he rode him out for most of his pre-National runs on the gallops of trainer Willie Moore at Weyhill, near Andover, Hampshire.

As a six year old *The Soarer* had suffered eight defeats before winning his last race of the season, a three-and-a-half-mile chase at Kempton on Boxing Day. Then, after two unsuccessful runs in 1896, Campbell had sold him for £600 to Colonel William Hall Walker (later Lord Wavertree) on condition that he would ride the horse in the forthcoming Grand National and, if successful, would keep the Cup and half the £1,975 stake.

Campbell prepared for his first National with military precision, studying past reports of the race and familiarising himself with every part of the course. He concluded that the best route was down the middle and, sticking to that route, he avoided trouble in a race that saw 14 fallers (half the field), including, at the first fence, the future superstar *Manifesto*. The *Soarer* struck the front two out and only just held on to resist the fast-finishing *Father O'Flynn*, who had unluckily met with interference at a crucial late stage.

Campbell came all the way from India to ride *The Soarer* again in the 1897 National. But he broke his collarbone when his horse crashed at Valentine's and did not return for the gelding's final run (fell at the Water Jump) the following year. In the First World War he commanded the 9th Lancers in France and by the time of his retirement he was General Sir David Campbell, in command at Aldershot. He died, aged 67, in 1936, the year when Fulke Walwyn, on

Reynoldstown, became the third officer of the 9th Lancers to win the National – following after Campbell and Frank Furlong on *Reynoldstown* (1935). *See also:* Soarer,The; Wavertree, Lord.

CANAL TURN, The

The eighth and 24th fence, 5ft high with foundations consisting of formidable hawthorn stakes covered with Norwegian spruce. Sited where the course approaches the Leeds-Liverpool Canal that runs parallel with the far side of the track, the Canal Turn vies with The Chair in being regarded as the toughest fence on the course – tricky because it needs to be met and jumped at an angle.

The Canal Turn requires an immediate 90-degree pivot to the left on landing to get in line for Valentine's Brook, the first in a straight line of four fences, all 5ft high. The recognised tactic is to drift out to the right on approach and then cut back left at take-off, making a crab-like manoeuvre to minimize the corner and save precious ground. The main danger is of being brought down or carried far wide – losing as much as ten lengths – by horses on the inside jumping straight and across one's path. Second time round, however, when there is less congestion, jockeys tend to get in as tight as possible as every yard saved at this point could be the difference between success and failure.

The greatest chaos occurred here in 1928 when *Easter Hero* landed on top of the fence first time round, preventing most of the 42-strong field from getting over and causing many to fall back into the open ditch which, until 1929, preceded the jump. That year only two horses completed the course. Subsequently the ditch was filled in but the Canal Turn continued to claim many victims.

In the early years it was not unusual for loose horses to miss this sharp left-hand bend and career straight on into the canal. This has long since been prevented by the erection of railings at the corner. Nonetheless, the nature of the turn makes it remain a major hazard, especially when horses are bunched on the inside; and this was well illustrated in 2001 when the riderless *Paddy's Return*, having fallen five fences earlier, galloped on wide before veering sharp left only yards from the Canal Turn. In the process he took eight horses out of the race on the first circuit. This time just four finished, two of them remounted.
See also: Loose horses.

84

CANNON, Joseph

Belonging to a long line of distinguished horsemen, Joe Cannon was only 27 years old when he had the distinction of both training and riding a Grand National winner: Captain James Machell's *Regal* in 1876. That year the hot 3-1 favourite was Machell's other runner *Chandos* who, under Joe's brother Tom, had come fourth in the 1873 Epsom Derby. Yet Joe still thought he had the better chance on five year old *Regal*, a 25-1 shot; and no one was more qualified to judge. After all, as the captain's recently appointed private trainer, he had prepared both of them for Aintree and he knew his mount to be much the more reliable jumper.

So it proved, with *Chandos*, a six year old entire, narrowly surviving a blunder at the Water Jump and then falling at the fence after Valentine's the second time around. In contrast, *Regal* had a smooth passage, one of three in a line coming to the last, and then, over the long straight, being matched stride for stride by another 25-1 chance, *Congress*. In one of the finest finishes ever seen, Cannon powered home *Regal* to win by a neck. It gave Machell his third National winner in four years.

The following year Cannon took the ride on *Congress*, who, now owned by Lord Lonsdale, was making his fifth consecutive appearance in the race. The 11 year old brown gelding again finished second, this time by four lengths, but it was nonetheless a truly remarkable effort since he had been raised 13lb to a top weight of 12st 7lb, and was conceding almost two stone to the winner, *Austerlitz*.

Altogether Cannon rode in seven Nationals, beginning with Machell's *Franc Luron*, a faller in 1872. He failed to finish on Lord Aylesford's five year old *Reugny* in 1873, came home sixth on Machell's *Disturbance* (1874) and fell on *Bacchus*, another five year old, in 1879. His last National, in 1880, saw him reunited with *Regal*, now owned by Lord Aylesford and made the 5-1 favourite. The former winning pair fell at the second fence.

See also: Regal; Cannon, Tom.

CANNON, Tom

Between 1866 and 1889 Tom Cannon was an outstanding jockey on the Flat, winning no fewer than 13 Classics, comprising the 2,000 Guineas and the Oaks (both four times), the 1,000 Guineas (three times), plus the 1880 St Leger on *Robert The Devil* and the 1882 Derby on *Shotover*. Remarkably, in the

evening of his great riding career, he also contrived to train a Grand National winner: the seven year old *Playfair*, a 40-1 outsider who won by ten lengths from *Frigate* in 1888. Thus he emulated the achievement of his brother Joe who had trained *Regal*, the winner of the 1876 National.

Based at Danebury, Hampshire, near the old Stockbridge racecourse, Tom was married to Kate Day, a niece of Sam Day who rode three Epsom Derby winners. They had four children, including Mornington ('Morny') Cannon, six times champion jockey in the 1890s; Kempton Cannon who won the 1904 Derby on *St. Amant*; and Margaret Cannon, who married Ernest Piggott, grandfather of the incomparable Lester.

It was with his father-in-law, at Danebury, that Ernest served his riding apprenticeship before going on to ride in 11 Grand Nationals and winning two, on *Jerry M* (1912) and *Poethlyn* (1919).

See also: Playfair; Cannon, Joe,

CARBERRY, Paul

Irishman Paul Carberry (born February 9, 1974) was 14 months old when his father, Tommy, triumphed at Aintree on *L'Escargot*. Twenty-four years later, on *Bobbyjo*, he became the first son of a Grand National-winning jockey to emulate his father in the race. At the same time he was scoring the first Irish success since his father's victory.

For good measure, Paul also had a maternal grandfather (Dan Moore) was had missed Grand National victory by a mere head when going down on *Royal Danieli* to the 1938 winner *Battleship*. Race-riding was in his blood, the National in his psyche. Thus the boy – three years old when riding his first pony on the family farm outside Dublin – never deviated in his ambition to become a jockey, not even after his brother Thomas had suffered a fall that knocked him unconscious and caused him to suffer periodic fits afterwards.

Still a schoolboy when winning his first point-to-point by a short head, Paul developed a style – riding as short as many Flat jockeys – that was totally different from that of his father who favoured the traditional deep seat and long reins. As an amateur, he was only 16 when he had a nightmarish introduction to Aintree's fences. Riding *Joseph Knibb* in the Fox Hunters' Chase, he had such an horrendous fall at the seventh fence that it was decided that he should give Aintree a miss for a few years. Meanwhile, he

C

became a champion apprentice under Jim Bolger and, at 18, joined the burgeoning Co. Meath stable of Noel Meade. Like his father, he won on his first ride at Cheltenham.

In 1993, when 19 years old, he rode his first Cheltenham Festival winner (*Rhythm Section*) and finished a creditable seventh in the Irish Grand National. The following year, after being third on *Shirley's Delight* in Cheltenham's Triumph Hurdle, he first rode in the Aintree Grand National, being unseated at the 27th from his father's 66-1 chance *Rust Never Sleeps*. Two years later he won the Tote Gold Trophy Hurdle on *Squire Silk* and scored his first win over the Aintree fences when giving 33-1 shot *Joe White* a brilliant ride in the John Hughes Memorial Chase. Then, back in the National, he showed exceptional skill in coaxing the 100-1 outsider *Three Brownies*, a renowned slowcoach, into sixth place.

Early in the 1996-97 season, when commuting to England as retained jockey for the Yorkshire-based industrialist-owner Sir Robert Ogden, Carberry was put out of racing for three months with a broken arm. But he came back to ride dozens of winners and in 1997 he recovered from a knee injury just in time to ride in the National, gaining fourth place on *Buckboard Bounce* (40-1).

One year later, having returned to racing in Ireland, he came back to ride 200-1 no-hoper *Decyborg*, trained by Martin Pipe. He did well to keep the seven year old prominent for more than a circuit. But it was always a lost cause (along the way he was seen to be casually chatting with Simon McNeill on another outsider, (*Greenhil Tare Away*) and he finally pulled up three out.

A courageous, supremely stylish rider, with a very fine sense of pace and exceptional balance and patience, Paul chose to stay in Ireland because of his passion for regular hunting there. At the same time he gained a reputation as something of a hellraiser given to spur-of-the-moment high jinks. One of his many exploits was to unload a hunter from a trailer he saw parked in a Cashel street and then ride into the bar of a nearby pub, McCarthy's.

His fondness for alcohol was such that J.P. McManus reputedly bet him £50,000 that he could not stop drinking for a year. He won the bet but declined an offer of double that sum for another year's abstinence. Thereafter, the occasional tipple certainly did not diminish his skill in the saddle. Though suffering his full share of injuries – including breaking the same leg three times – he continued to maintain outstanding form, scoring many major victories in Ireland on such top chasers as *Florida Pearl*, *Imperial Call* and *Looks Like Trouble*.

In the 1999 National, Carberry was at last on a serious contender; and he was brimful of confidence. He had won the 1998 Irish Grand National on *Bobbyjo*, so emulating the feat of his father on *Brown Lad* in 1975 and 1976. Now, at Aintree, the nine year old had his favoured good ground and was a popular 10-1 chance. He gave his rider a great feel going down to the start. Moreover, for once in his life, the party-loving jockey (nicknamed 'Alice' because the song '*Living Next Door To Alice*' was his party piece) had had an early night, in bed at 9 p.m.

Carberry's plan was to stay handy throughout and make a late challenge, and it worked like a dream. He took the lead only after clearing the last and then surged ahead on the run-in. When he passed the winning post, ten lengths clear of *Blue Charm*, he stood tall in his stirrups, flourishing his whip overhead, and then made a unique dismount – seizing a wooden beam above the winner's enclosure and hoisting himself aloft.

Dreaming of a repeat Grand National win, Carberry now stayed teetotal for six months prior to returning to Aintree. In 2000 he gave Noel Meade his first Cheltenham winner, riding *Sausalito Bay* who beat *Best Mate* in the Supreme Novices' Hurdle, But then, after finishing second on *Florida Pearl* in the Gold Cup, he was out of action with a recurring back injury, and only at the eleventh hour was he pronounced fit to ride in the National. That day he had the pleasure of seeing brother Philip score his first success in England, winning the opening race, the Cordon Bleu Handicap Hurdle, on *Sharpaten*. But he himself was out of luck. *Bobbyjo* was no longer the same force in the National; and, with an extra 20lb to carry, he finished 11th.

Tragically, one year later, an injury had fatal results for *Bobbyjo*; and, with only a few days to go, Carberry was left without a ride in the National. The following season, unlike so many of his countrymen, he continued to resist offers to ride regularly in Britain, and early in 2002 he was leading the Irish jump jockeys' table with 75 winners, 21 more than his nearest rival Barry Geraghty. Coming over for the Cheltenham Festival, he rode at his masterful best to win the National Hunt Handicap Chase on

Frenchman's Creek. But the next day a minor injury to his hand when falling in the Royal and Sun-Alliance Chase cost him the ride on *Marlborough* in the Gold Cup.

Carberry resumed riding only six days before the 2002 Grand National but his hopes of a second victory were sky high. He was set to partner the hugely fancied market leader, Sir Robert Ogden's *Ad Hoc*, who had been an impressive, runaway winner of the 2001 Whitbread Gold Cup, well clear of runner-up *What's Up Boys*. At Aintree, however, *Ad Hoc* was to be arguably the unluckiest horse in the race. A 10-1 chance, he was jumping brilliantly and travelling well when brought down four from home by the faller *David's Lad*. Meanwhile *What's Up Boys* ran on strongly to finish a close second to *Bindaree*. Afterwards, Carberry said he 'felt sick', convinced that he could have won on a horse who had been going as strongly as his winner *Bobbyjo* three years before. Though poised to win the Irish jump jockeys' championship for the first time, he said he would have exchanged all his 92 winners for another National success.

Two days before the 2003 National, Carberry returned to riding, having missed more than a week since being 'head-butted in the stomach by a stag' while out hunting. He came back to Aintree sporting orange-dyed hair, and this time his mount was even more strongly supported, *Ad Hoc* going off at 9-1. But they started badly and, having survived a blunder at the first, they parted company at the 19th. Three weeks later, with Ruby Walsh in the saddle, *Ad Hoc* gained huge compensation by winning the Whitbread a second time.

At the 2004 National meeting, Carberry gave 12 year old *Lord Of The River* a masterful ride to win the Martell Ember Inns Handicap Chase, and the following day he was judged to have a major chance in the National on *Joss Naylor*, trained by Jonjo O'Neill and one of four co-favourites. He took the ride despite a fall two races earlier that required stitches in his lower lip, but disappointingly *Joss Naylor* was always in the rear and was pulled up before the 19th.

The opening day of the 2005 Cheltenham Festival brought remarkably mixed fortunes for the Carberry family. In the Champion Hurdle, Paul was rather harshly criticised for waiting too long on *Harchibald*, beaten a neck by joint-favourite *Hardy Eustace*. Later, in the Fred Winter Juvenile Handicap Hurdle,

he was unplaced on *Rolling Home*, the race being comfortably won by 20-1 shot *Dabiroun* – given a copybook ride by Paul's 20 year old sister, Nina. Conversely, Nina – the first woman jockey to win a professional race at the Festival since Gee Armytage in 1987 – was thrown before the start of her next race, while Paul later opened his account with victory in the Pertemps Handicap Hurdle Final on *Oulart* and scored again on *Fota Island* in the Grand Annual Handicap Chase. Then, one day later, he took Uttoxeter's Midlands National on *Philson Run*.

The week before the 2005 Aintree meeting Carberry was out of action, having burst a leg blood vessel in a fall. After one race at the meeting, he was forced to rest for another day. But he came back on National day to win the opening hurdle race on *Definate Spectacle*. Then, riding the giant (17.3 hands), parrot-mouthed, Irish contender *Colnel Rayburn* in the main event, he was well in contention as far as the second Becher's where his tenth National mount began to weaken, subsequently being pulled up before the 27th. He ended the season as the champion Irish jockey.

The following season Carberry made his mark at Cheltenham in December, storming up the hill to snatch victory on *Sir OJ* in the Robin Cook Memorial Gold Cup Handicap Chase, and immediately afterwards taking the Bula Hurdle on *Harchibald*. That same month, at Leopardstown, he won the prestigious Lexus Chase on *Beef Or Salmon*.

At the Cheltenham Festival he won the Royal and SunAlliance Novices' Hurdle on *Nicanor* and the Champion Bumper on *Hairy Molly*, giving him a career total of nine Festival winners. But thereafter it was his sister Nina and brother Philip who made the headlines. In the Grand National Nina was the last of nine finishers on *Forest Gunner* while Paul was left with a sprained ankle after falling on *Sir OJ* at the second Becher's. Nine days later Philip scored the biggest success of his career, winning the Irish National on 20-1 shot *Point Barrow*, while Nina – soon to be crowned as Ireland's champion amateur jumps jockey – was unplaced in the race on *Star Clipper*. And the following month, no less sensationally, Philip rode 16-1 chance *Princess d'Anjou* to become the first foreign jockey to win the Grande Steeple-Chase de Paris since Fred Winter on *Mandarin* in 1962.

In 2007 a foot injury kept Paul out of the Cheltenham Festival, and there it was left to brother Philip and sister Nina to carry the Carberry flag. The former rode 16-1 shot *Sublimity* to victory in the Champion Hurdle and ended the Festival with a win on *Pedrobob* in the County Hurdle. The latter won the Cross Country Handicap Chase on *Heads Onthe Ground* – beating *Silver Birch* by three and a half lengths.

Though still sidelined, Paul was now scheduled to ride *Dun Doire*, one of the joint ante-post 10-1 favourites for the Grand National. The other favourite at the time, *Point Barrow*, was to be ridden by brother Philip. And confusingly yet another P. Carberry was emerging on the racing scene: Peter John, the youngest of five brothers, who at 16 had just had his first ride in a bumper.

As so often in the past, Paul went to Aintree on the back of injury, this time having returned to racing only eight days before the National. It was his 12th appearance and his mount, shrewdly campaigned by trainer Tony Martin, was most favourably weighted. But *Dun Doire*, deprived of the soft going he so badly needed, was always towards the rear and had to be pulled up four out. By Paul's high standards, it had been a disappointing season in which he rode 63 winners to finish fourth in Ireland's jump jockeys' championship.

Philip Carberry, too, had had huge disappointment in the National where 8-1 co-favourite *Point Barrow*, who had never fallen in a race before, made his exit at the first fence. But overall he could look back on a hugely successful 12 months. This season he had had 37 rides in France and many more were likely to follow after his signing of a contract with leading owner Jean-Paul Senechal. Meanwhile sister Nina was again Ireland's top amateur jumps jockey, finishing tenth in the championship table with 30 wins.

See also: Bobbyjo; Carberry, Thomas; Brothers and Sisters.

CARBERRY, Thomas

In successive Grand Nationals (1973-75), Tommy Carberry finished third, second and first on *L'Escargot*; and when his son Paul won on *Bobbyjo* in 1999 he joined the elite group of men who have both ridden and trained Grand National winners, a double last achieved by Fred Winter 34 years earlier. His famous 'double' crowned a family connection with the race that had begun tenuously in 1970 when, as stable jockey, he had married his boss's daughter, née Pamela Moore. His father-in-law was

Dan Moore, the jockey-turned-trainer who, on *Royal Danieli*, had been beaten just a head by *Battleship* in the 1938 National.

Born on September 16, 1941, at Garristown, Co. Dublin, Tommy was a schoolboy when he learned to ride on mounts from the Fairyhouse yard of Dan Moore. As a teenager, he rode in races for Curragh trainer Jimmy Lenehan, and he twice became champion apprentice on the Flat (1958 and 1959) before his riding weight prompted him to return to Moore and switch to jump racing. His first Grand National mount (in 1963) was a distinguished one: *Mr What*, the 1958 winner who had since twice finished in third place. But this most consistent campaigner, making his sixth appearance in the race, was now 13 years old and a 66-1 outsider. He was brought down four fences from the finish.

Having moved to England to join trainer Fulke Walwyn, Carberry had his first notable success when winning the 1964 Massey-Ferguson Chase at Cheltenham on *Flying Wild*. The following year, in his second Grand National, he pulled up on the seven year old, French-owned long-shot *Vulcano*. Then came the first of eight National rides on horses owned by Mr Raymond Guest, the millionaire U.S. ambassador to Ireland. His *Packed Home*, trained by Dan Moore, was a faller at the first Becher's in 1966, and one year later finished fifth at 100-1 after being brought to a standstill in the mass 23rd fence pile up caused by the riderless *Popham Down*.

Tommy Carberry's Aintree disappointments continued with *Great Lark* (refused at the ninth in 1968) and *Kilburn* (a faller at the second Becher's in 1969). Meanwhile, however, he had been united with the chestnut gelding whom he would later rate as the best horse he ever rode. On Mr Guest's *L'Escargot* he had won the Gloucester Hurdle at the 1968 Cheltenham Festival, and two years later they were to achieve their most surprising success, winning the Cheltenham Gold Cup at 33-1.

In 1971, after a second Gold Cup win on *L'Escargot*, Tommy was brought down to earth in the National with a fall at the tenth on Mr Guest's *Cnoc Dubh*. A year later, for the first time, he was on the National favourite: *L'Escargot*. But the nine year old gelding had had a hard race three weeks earlier when finishing fourth in the Gold Cup. Now, carrying 12st top weight on his Aintree debut, he was baulked and knocked over at the third fence.

Again, in 1973, *L'Escargot* was sent to the

National after finishing fourth in the Gold Cup; and again he was burdened with the 12st. maximum. This time, outpaced on ground faster than he would have liked, he finished third, 25 lengths behind *Red Rum* and *Crisp* who both shattered the course record.

Carberry's hopes of National success seemed highest in 1974 when *L'Escargot* was the second favourite, ahead of *Red Rum* who had been raised 23lb. in the handicap. But the extraordinary 'Rummy' dominated from the second Becher's onwards. Finishing the seven lengths runner-up, *L'Escargot* had seemingly missed his chance of National glory.

That was never Tommy's view, however. In 1975, having recently won his third Cheltenham Gold Cup on *Ten Up*, he went to Aintree brimful of confidence. *L'Escargot* was now 12 years old while *Red Rum* was a ten year old favourite seeking a hat-trick of wins. On the other hand, allowing for his poor seasonal form and his age, *L'Escargot* had been dropped 10lb in the weights; and the soft going was in his favour. On race day, to the bemusement of his colleagues, the ever good-humoured Tommy declared categorically that he would win.

And so he did, achieving his most cherished ambition at the 11th attempt. Apart from a fright at the small seventh fence, when a bungled jump had the jockey clinging to his neck, *L'Escargot* thrived in the conditions; and, with an 11lb advantage, he drew away from 'Rummy' after the last to win by 15 lengths. Amazingly, within a five-week period, Carberry had come first in the Gold Cup, the Irish Grand National, the Topham Trophy and the Aintree National.

In the next three years Tommy made a most spirited effort to equal Pat Taaffe's record of four Cheltenham Gold Cup wins, each time finishing runner-up – on *Brown Lad* (1976), *Tied Cottage* (1977) and *Brown Lad* (1978). His 1978 attempt would very probably have succeeded if the Gold Cup had not been abandoned in the face of a freak snowstorm and re-scheduled for one month later. The switch gave the winner, *Midnight Court*, the fastish ground that he needed and veteran *Brown Lad*, beaten seven lengths, conditions that he hated.

In the meantime Tommy had had only one more ride in the National, being a first fence faller on Jim Dreaper's *War Bonnet* in 1977. Now, following his disappointment at Cheltenham, he went on to Aintree for his 13th and, as it proved, final appearance.

Unhappily, and most surprisingly in the light of his proven skill and experience, his National swansong was to be marred by a huge error in judgment. He was on ten year old *Tied Cottage*, the 9-1 second favourite. Predictably, this most headstrong of front-runners set off like a scalded cat to lead over the first fence and go well clear of the field by the fifth. All the while, however, he had been jumping awkwardly to the left. With Becher's Brook looming some 30 yards ahead, the gelding continually pulled left, to such a degree that he was almost sideways-on when coming to his take-off. His fall on landing was inevitable, and providentially he was far enough ahead not to cause a major pile-up.

Still greater disappointments were to follow. In the 1979 Gold Cup, *Tied Cottage* crumbled at the last when fractionally in the lead. Then, in 1980, it seemed that Carberry had achieved his fourth win at last when *Tied Cottage* led the Gold Cup field from start to finish. But three weeks later – at the time of the Grand National meeting – the Moores were told that their horse had been disqualified following a positive drug test. Inadvertently, as it transpired, his feed had been contaminated by contact in transit with cocoa.

Tommy Carberry retired from the saddle with a most enviable record which included 13 victories at the Cheltenham Festival and at home two wins in the Irish Grand National on *Brown Lad*. He then switched to training at Ballybin in Co. Meath and for many years his winners were few and far between.

His first Grand National runner, *Royal Appointment* (1985), unseated his rider at the 19th. Nine years later he saddled the first National ride for his son Paul: *Rust Never Sleeps*. The ten year old, a 66-1 chance, had previously finished second in the Irish National, but he had never won beyond two and three-quarter miles and now he unseated his rider at the 27th. At his next attempt Carberry was third time lucky, triumphing with *Bobbyjo*, winner of the 1998 Irish Grand National.

It was essentially a family achievement. *Bobbyjo*, the 1999 winner, was ridden at home by Tommy's wife Pamela, in many prep races by their son Philip, and at Aintree by their older son Paul. Their jubilation was so great that the trainer received a reprimand from the stewards after Philip, together with daughter Nina and a friend, had rushed on to the course to congratulate Paul, in the process forcing

C

Richard Dunwoody to snatch up on third-placed *Call It A Day*, and then fall off.

Tommy rated that success 'more special than winning on *L'Escargot*', and generously this outstanding horseman insisted that his son Paul was 'a better jockey than I was'. He returned *Bobbyjo* to Aintree in 2000 but, with an extra 20lb to carry, he could finish only 11th. And one year later, shortly before he was due to reappear in the National, *Bobbyjo* tragically had to be put down following complications when undergoing an operation for an injury.

See also: Moore, Dan; Carberry, Paul; L'Escargot; Bobbyjo.

CASEY, William Terence

Trainer near Dorking in Surrey of ten year old *Rough Quest*, the winner as 7-1 favourite of the 1996 Martell Grand National by a length and a quarter from *Encore Un Peu*. The victory – only declared after a stewards' enquiry – was the highest point in the switchback career of a quiet, unassuming Irishman who, with great courage and dignity, fought to overcome so many vicissitudes and cruel twists of fate.

From a non-racing background, Terry Casey (born June 2, 1945, in Co. Donegal) played truant as a child to indulge his passion for riding. He began his racing career on The Curragh as a 15 year old apprentice with Aubrey Brabazon. The former leading jump jockey later remembered him as a 'very well mannered and trustworthy' boy who 'never really looked like making it as a jockey'.

In the 1960s Terry rode six winners for Richard Dunwoody's father, George, who was based near Belfast. He spent three years as head lad to Paddy Mullins. Then, at the age of 30, he moved to England to become head lad at the Leicestershire stable of permit-holder Frank Gilman for whom he was to win hurdle races on, among others, the future Grand National winner *Grittar*. There, however, he was to suffer a heartbreaking tragedy: the death, only six months after their marriage, of his young wife who choked fatally on a piece of meat.

By 1982, the year of *Grittar*'s National victory, Terry was back in Ireland serving for three years as head lad to his principal mentor Paddy Mullins in Co. Kilkenny. Having ridden a career total of 46 winners, he then left to establish his own yard at The Curragh and turned out his first winner, *Town Special*, at Clonmel in September, 1983. Two years later he returned to England to help John Upson set up as a trainer at Towcester; and he quickly made his mark, having his first big success with *Glenrue*, the 20-1 winner of the 1986 Whitbread (later John Hughes Memorial) Trophy at Liverpool. Other notable winners with Upson included hurdlers *Nick The Brief* and *Fred The Tread*; *Over The Road*, successful in the 1988 National Hunt Chase at Cheltenham; and the prolific Flat race sprinter *Aughfad*.

In 1989, Casey again set up on his own, and that year, with *Celtic Barle*, he won the Sidney Banks Memorial Novices' Hurdle for the second time. Three years later he moved from Banbury into Malt House stables at Lambourn. By 1994 he had to sell his yard for a big loss, relinquishing his licence following a dreaded virus in his stable and ensuing financial difficulties at a time of recession. Yet two months later he bounced back. Successfully answering an advertisement which attracted more than a hundred applicants, he became a salaried trainer, taking over from Tim Etherington at the Beare Green (Surrey) yard of Andrew Wates, Jockey Club member and chairman of Kempton Park. Among his new charges in the Henfold House Stables was the out-of-form *Rough Quest*.

Casey possessed a natural affinity with horses. He personally rode out *Rough Quest* every day, and now he came to recognise that the bay gelding had some disability that caused his muscles to tie up under pressure. The vet diagnosed a muscle enzyme problem that caused lactic acid to build up in the hindquarters and brought on a form of cramp. After much trial and error, Casey adopted a special feeding regime, with vitamin E a vital ingedient, plus a rigid exercise schedule.

Improvement swiftly followed. In March, 1995, the nine year old won the Ritz Club Handicap Chase at the Cheltenham Festival – his first success since his novice days. Next month he won at Punchestown. The following year he won the Racing Post Chase at Kempton, and three weeks later an impressive runner-up to *Imperial Call* in the Cheltenham Gold Cup – a performance that resulted in his promotion to National favouritism.

At first Casey and Wates judged it unwise to send *Rough Quest* to Aintree so soon after his hard Gold Cup race. But the 50 year old trainer now found that the gelding gave him an even better feel than before going to Cheltenham. Connections had a late change of heart, much to the relief of jockey Mick Fitzgerald who was to ride the winner in only his second Grand National.

Casey went on to enjoy his numerically most successful season, 20 winners in 1996-97. *Rough Quest*, who missed the 1997 National through injury, returned the following year and Casey had high hopes of him becoming the first horse since *Red Rum* to regain his National crown. His star, now 12 years old and second in the weights, jumped superbly but struggled to go the pace in the clinging mud and was pulled up at the penultimate fence.

Casey's last notable winner was *Splendid Thyne* in the Spa Hurdle of 1999. Late that year the trainer was diagnosed with throat cancer. Determinedly he fought back, and the following autumn, when his treatment was declared successful, he was out riding again. But cruelly, a few months later, the dreaded disease re-emerged and his long, courageous battle was finally lost in the summer of 2001. He was 56 years old.
See also: Rough Quest; Fitzgerald, Mick.

CASSE TETE

Bred by the Duke of Newcastle – by *Trumpeter* out of *Constance* – *Casse Tete* failed to make any impression on the Flat and was subsequently bought out of a seller for little more than £200 by Mr Edward Brayley. On her 1870 Grand National debut, as a five year old, she failed to finish at 100-1 and fared no better the following year when she went off at 66-1. Subsequently, *The Times* correspondent was to observe that '*Casse Tete* looked as though she were in training for an anatomical museum instead of the Grand National'.

But the little chestnut mare (just 15h 3in) was improving with experience, as shown by her third place behind *Harvester* in Croydon's Great Metropolitan Chase. Again ridden by Johnny Page, she was well backed by connections for the 1872 National and came to the front, alongside dual winner *The Lamb*, at the penultimate jump. *Harvester*, strongly closing on the pair, was now the major threat. But when looking a certain winner, he wrenched off a plate on over-jumping the last and broke down. Thereafter, with *The Lamb* conceding a full two and a half stone to his rival, the outcome was never in doubt. *Casse Tete*, on the minimum weight, won at 20-1 by a comfortable six lengths from *Scarrington*, with *Despatch*, the favourite, and

The Lamb another six lengths and two behind respectively.

It was a second National success for Page who had won on *Cortolvin* in 1867, and great recompense for Mr Brayley who had seen his *Pearl Diver* finish second in 1868 and fourth in 1871. But *Casse Tete* never won another race. She was knocked over in the 1873 National and the following year, when second favourite, she was a faller.
See also: Brayley, Edward; Page, John.

CAUGHOO

The second of only three outsiders to win the Grand National at 100-1. Remarkably, in 1947, when there was a 57-strong field, the second largest in the history of the race, the eight year old won by 20 lengths, the greatest margin since the 1920s when *Tipperary Tim* (1928) and *Shaun Spadah* (1921) won by a distance. Those horses, however, scored in chaotic Nationals which saw only two and four finishers respectively. *Caughoo* was followed home by 20 rivals.

Though *Caughoo* had won Downpatrick Ulster Nationals in 1945 and 1946, he looked an unlikely prospect for Aintree. Bred by Mr Patrick Power of Fethard-on-Sea, County Wexford, he was by *Within-The-Law* out of *Silverdale*, neither of whom had ever raced over the jumps. At yearling sales, he had been bought for a mere 50 guineas by two Dublin brothers, Herbert McDowell, a veterinary surgeon, and John McDowell, a jeweller. Herbert took charge of training the unbroken two year old at Malahide, Co. Dublin.

In 1947, the McDowells had toyed with the idea of going for a third successive Ulster National. Instead, despite *Caughoo*'s poor seasonal form, they opted to send him to Aintree since there he would have one huge advantage over most other National runners: he was fully fit. This was the year of the three-month long Big Freeze, with record snowfalls and then, with the thaw in mid-March, horrendous floods. For almost eight weeks no racing was possible. In consequence, few trainers had been able to prepare their horses adequately. *Caughoo* was a notable exception, having been worked regularly over the snow-free foreshore of Sutton Strand near Dublin.

The long break in racing had one other major influence on the 1947 National. It sparked off a stampede of entries as owners eagerly grabbed at a

C

rare chance to bid for much-needed prize money. On March 29, a huge field included the classy *Prince Regent*, a top-weighted 8-1 favourite after finishing third in the race last year; *Jack Finlay*, the 100-1 runner-up in 1946, now 33-1; and Dorothy Paget's fourth-placed *Housewarmer*, 25-1. But in general it looked an undistinguished line-up, with no fewer than 26 runners priced at 100-1 and 20, including *Caughoo*, on the minimum weight of 10st.

When the field set off on the cavalry charge to the first fence, conditions suggested a perfect recipe for disaster: so many horses below race fitness; a fog greatly limiting visibility; and rain falling on ground already so boggy that the first day of the meeting had seen all 16 runners fall in the Stanley Chase. As far as could be seen, there was not a major pile-up at any one point, but certainly there were at least 26 fallers, and three of the 21 finishers were remounted.

At Becher's, Irish challenger *Lough Conn* led from Miss Paget's second-string, the grey *Kilnaglory*, with *Caughoo* well behind in a spread-out field. *Lough Conn* was still leading a full circuit later, with four riderless horses close by. But by then, as the runners disappeared out of sight, *Caughoo* had moved up into second place. When the survivors were next seen, coming on to the racecourse proper, *Caughoo* had a clear lead over *Lough Conn*, now struggling on the heavy going. The former blundered at the last fence but, once jockey Eddie Dempsey had steadied him, he was never in danger as superior stamina enabled him to stretch out his lead. Thus, his success completed an astonishing 'Spring Double' since only three days earlier *Jockey Treble* had won the Lincoln, also at 100-1.

Daniel McCann, the rider on *Lough Conn*, would much later allege, sensationally and unreasonably, that fellow Irishman Dempsey had cheated by loitering somewhere around the 12th in the fog and so missing out at least 15 fences before making his winning run. An ensuing lawsuit resulted in magistrates dismissing the claim and upholding Dempsey's honour. As shown by newsreel film, he had legitimately won by 20 lengths, with Mr John Hislop on *Kami*, a further four lengths back in third.

Caughoo, however, would never again have conditions so much in his favour. In 1948, with an extra 15lb to carry, on faster ground and against fitter rivals, he had to be pulled up at the Canal Turn second time around. In 1949, as a 66-1 outsider, ironically with McCann in the saddle, he ran out at the fifth fence after losing his bridle; and later that year he suffered a fatal injury. In macabre fashion, *Caughoo*'s stuffed head is now preserved in Drogheda, and it once had an owner who liked to place it on a seat before the television on each Grand National day.

See also: Dempsey, Edward; Fitness.

CAZALET, Peter Victor Ferdinand

When the Queen Mother's *Devon Loch* collapsed so memorably with the 1956 Grand National at his mercy, royal trainer Peter Cazalet was inevitably reminded of another day of heartbreaking disappointment at Aintree – the day, 20 years earlier, when his closest friend, Lord (then plain Mr Anthony) Mildmay had been robbed of victory on the 100-1 outsider *Davy Jones*.

Back in the 1930s the racing careers of Cazalet and Mildmay had been inexorably entwined. Together with London stockbroker Edward Paget, they gathered a few jumpers at Fairlawne, the Cazalets' imposing family estate at Shipbourne, near Tonbridge, Kent. Much encouraged by Paget's experience in the 1932 Grand National (he finished three lengths second on *Egremont*), they both made their National debut as promising young amateurs the following year. Cazalet – on *Shaun Goilin*, the 1930 winner, now 13 years old and a 40-1 chance – completed the course in an unrecorded position. Mildmay fell at the first on the Cazalet-owned *Youtell*, 100-1 outsider.

In the 1934 National, Cazalet fell on *Master Orange*, a 66-1 outsider. The following year Mildmay took over that mount while his friend rode his own, seven year old *Emancipator*. Both were fallers; and in 1936 Cazalet again failed to finish on *Emancipator* while Mildmay, on the much longer-priced *Davy Jones*, only failed to win when, with broken reins, his horse ran out at the last.

Cazalet had his last National ride in 1937 when his *Emancipator* had to be pulled up; then he soon gave up race-riding after breaking his wrist in a fall at Sandown. Two years later, with the outbreak of the Second World War, he and Mildmay – both Old Etonians – followed the same course again: serving with distinction as officers in the 2nd (Armoured) Battalion of the Welsh Guards. Then, on demob, they formed a successful partnership – Cazalet becoming a prominent trainer at Fairlawne, and Mildmay soon establishing himself as a successful owner

C

and the leading National Hunt amateur rider.

In 1948 they believed that they had an outstanding National candidate in *Cromwell*, a seven year old, owned and ridden by Lord Mildmay. This time they both experienced the cruel twist of fate, *Cromwell* becoming another unlucky loser as his rider, suddenly seized by crippling cramp in the neck, could finish no better than third. One year later, as 6-1 favourite, *Cromwell* was beaten on merit into fourth place.

On that National day, Cazalet's stable jockey, Tony Grantham, had been recruited at the last minute to replace an injured jockey on a 50-1 chance called *Monaveen*. Afterwards he reported to his 'guv'nor' that the eight year old had jumped brilliantly until falling at the 19th, the open ditch. As a result, *Monaveen* was the choice a few months later when, at Mildmay's suggestion, Queen Elizabeth agreed to have a horse in training for National Hunt racing.

Peter Cazalet, born in 1907, had known the Queen since childhood through Her Majesty's friendship with his elder sister Thelma, later Mrs Cazalet-Kier, MP. Following the purchase of *Monaveen*, owned jointly by the Queen and Princess Elizabeth, he became the Queen's first National Hunt trainer, holding the position until his death from cancer in 1973 at the age of 66. During those years he saddled 262 winners for the Queen Mother but oddly there was only one Cheltenham Festival winner – *Antiar* in the 1965 Spa (now Stayers') Hurdle. David Mould, who rode 106 of Her Majesty's winners, once explained: 'He was a very good trainer but very hard on his horses. All our horses were good up to January, then they were gone. He could never save one for Cheltenham.' On the other hand, he had certainly saved *Devon Loch* well enough for the 1956 Grand National.

His other National runners for the Queen Mother were *Monaveen* (fifth, 1950), *M'As-Tu-Vu* (fell, 1955 and 1956), *Laffy* (fell, 1964) and *The Rip* (seventh, 1965). And he saddled her first winner over the big Aintree fences: *Silver Dome* in the 1964 Becher Chase. His best result in the National was with Mr Gregory Peck's *Different Class* who finished third under David Mould as the 17-2 favourite in 1968, after being brought down in the chaos of the previous year. In 1961 he saddled fourth-placed *Scottish Flight II* for regular patron Mrs A.T. Hodgson; and his many runners for Colonel W.H.

Whitbread included *Athenian* (1958, fell); *Kapeno* (1966, fell, 1967, tenth); *Beau Bob* (1971, unseated rider) and *Cloudsmere* (1972, fell).

Over the years Cazalet was an extraordinarily successful sportsman. He represented Oxford University at cricket, lawn tennis and rackets; scored centuries for Eton at Lord's and for Kent in the county championship; rode winners in point-to-points and under Rules; and was the champion National Hunt trainer of 1949-50, 1959-60 and 1964-65 when he had a then record 82 winners. He won the King George VI Chase four times in the 1950s and the Champion Chase and Mackeson Gold Cup with *Dunkirk*; saddled his 1,000th winner before the age of 60; sent out the Queen Mother's 250th winner in 1972, and, two months before his death, had his last big winner – at Aintree, with *Inch Arran* in the Topham Trophy. But, throughout 41 years as a trainer, the most longed-for success – in the Grand National – always eluded him, just as it had done for his ill-fated friend, Lord Mildmay.

See also: Mildmay, Lord; Monaveen; Devon Loch; Royal Runners.

CHADWICK, Robert

Although he was 26 when making his Grand National debut (knocked over on *Hill of Bree* in 1906) doughty, Yorkshire-born Robert Chadwick had a remarkably long association with the race. In a career spanning the gap of the First World War, he rode in ten Nationals, winning on *Jenkinstown* (1910), achieving two second places and one third, and making his last appearance at the age of 42.

In extraordinary circumstances, and in Nationals ten years apart, he achieved a unique double: twice remounting his horse to run into a place. In 1911, the joint second favourites, *Rathnally* and *Caubeen*, collided at the fence after the second Becher's, leaving *Glenside* far ahead in the lead. But Chadwick remounted the former, a six year old, and fought back to finish runner-up by 20 lengths. Only two others finished, and they, too, were remounted.

Similarly, in 1921, Chadwick remounted *All White*, owned by Colonel Hall Walker (later Lord Wavertree), to finish a distant third in the National. And again, by an astonishing coincidence, only four completed the course, with the second, third and fourth being remounted.

His one National success came on the well-handicapped *Jenkinstown*, who scored by three lengths

93

C

from *Jerry M*, who was conceding 30lb, with the rank outsider *Odor*, the third of only five finishers, a further three lengths behind. Previously he had finished eighth on the outsider *Chorus* in 1908, and the following year had given *Judas*, a 33-1 chance, a brilliant ride in a 32-strong field to finish two lengths second to *Lutteur III*, the favourite, with the third far away.

In 1912 he fell at the third on *Rathnally*, his runner-up of the previous year, and in 1915 he pulled up on outsider *The Babe*. When the National was resumed after the war, injury cost him the ride on five year old *All White*. Making the first of his seven appearances, the ill-named brown gelding finished fifth at 66-1 and would certainly have done better if the substitute French jockey had not stopped after the second Becher's in order to bring up his pre-race snack. Reunited with *All White*, Chadwick rode him in his last three Nationals – falling in 1920, finishing third in 1921, and being brought down at the Canal Turn in 1922.

See also: Jenkinstown; Wavertree, Lord.

CHAIR, The

The Chair is the 15th and biggest fence, at 5ft 2in, on the course with a 6ft wide open ditch on the take-off side. It was so named because of its position adjacent to a small, iron-railed enclosure atop a stone pillar where, in early years, a so-called 'Distance Judge' sat on a chair. There the 'judge' was in full view of the run-in to the finish, and it was his duty to signal the retirement of any horses – said to be 'distanced' – which had not reached his position by the time the first finisher had passed the winning post.

Sited in front of the stands, The Chair is a most daunting fence, one that looks all the bigger because it is relatively narrow, just 15 yards wide. Here, until 1862, there was simply a plain gorse fence leading on to the Water Jump. But then, following the one jockey fatality in National history, it was decided to slow the pace at this point by introducing an open ditch on the approach side – a move that certainly made it no less precarious.

Subsequently, a number of jockeys have rated it as the most difficult of them all. Amateur rider John Hislop described it as 'the obstacle that makes my heart beat faster. It stands up against the skyline, grim, tall and formidable ... seeming as impenetrable as a prison wall'. Significantly, when the 1999 Grand

National was being screened at Hong Kong's Happy Valley racecourse, it was a replica of The Chair that they chose to construct to give racegoers an idea of how awesome Aintree's fences could appear.

Most tragically it was here in 1964 that Paddy Farrell, four times northern champion jockey, fell on *Border Flight*, suffering a back-breaking injury that would leave him unable to walk again. In 1979 it was the scene of the biggest pile-up since the chaos of the 1967 Foinavon National – two riderless horses veering across the fence and in the process eliminating nine contenders. And the difficulty of the fence was further underlined in 1980 when it saw the exit of *Rubstic,* who had won the National the previous year and had never before suffered a fall.

Loose horses can be especially threatening here as runners funnel on the approach to the narrow obstacle. On the other hand, The Chair does not account for an unduly high number of fallers since those horses reaching it will by then have covered two miles and have become accustomed to Aintree's big fences. Though demanding extra effort in the jumping, it does not present an inordinate drop to complicate the landing. Furthermore, it is not met by horses nearing the end of their tether because, mercifully, along with the following Water Jump, it is one of just two out of 32 obstacles that are jumped only on the first circuit.

See also: Fences; Tactics; Loose horses.

CHAMPION, Robert OBE

The history of the Grand National has so many stories of triumph over tragedy, but none more uplifting than the inspirational victory of Bob Champion on *Aldaniti* in 1981. It was greeted with tumultuous applause unequalled even by the rapturous reception that marked *Red Rum*'s record-breaking third success in 1977. It brought congratulatory messages from all over the world; was followed by a best-selling biography and a major movie starring John Hurt; and, most imporantly it led to the foundation of the Bob Champion Cancer Trust that would raise millions to fight the disease that the winning jockey had conquered against all odds.

Champion was born (on June 4, 1948) to ride. For more than two centuries members of his family had been professional huntsmen; and thus he was put on a pony almost as soon as he could walk. Disenchanted by a first-jump fall into stinging nettles, he did not take up riding regularly until he was nine.

Thereafter his enthusiasm grew apace. At ten, he was riding to hounds. At 15, while studying for an engineering diploma at Trowbridge College in Wiltshire, he was frequently riding in point-to-points and already determined to become a jockey.

But nothing came easily for Champion. In August, 1967, as an amateur rider, he joined the large team of trainer Toby Balding at Fyfield, near Andover in Hampshire. On only his second day he was put in hospital when the chaser *Dozo* reared up on him and left him with a broken left ankle and several fractured bones that had to be pinned. Nearly three months passed before he was fit to have his first ride and then came the abandonment of racing during the foot-and-mouth epidemic. In January, 1968, he rode his first winner: novice chaser *Altercation*, a 20-1 chance at Plumpton. Two weeks later, having fallen on *Altercation*, Bob was stretchered off unconscious, back to hospital for stitches to his head wounds.

In 1968-69, his first professional season, Bob rode just 15 winners. Most notably, in February, he rode *Highland Wedding* to the gelding's third success in Newcastle's Eider Chase. The following month the 12 year old chaser won the Grand National – but with the more experienced Eddie Harty on board. Discouragingly Bob had few rides, and only ten wins, in the 1969-70 season; and then his left ankle was broken again when being thrown by another unruly novice chaser.

His first Grand National ride came in 1971: on *Country Wedding*, a small mare who had the same sire as *Highland Wedding* but not the same jumping ability. On this 50-1 long-shot, Bob decided to track Terry Biddlecombe on *Gay Trip*, the previous year's winner. An unfortunate choice. *Gay Trip* fell at the first and brought down *Country Wedding* in the process.

In the 1972 National, again on *Country Wedding*, Champion went down at the 11th. He ended the season with only ten wins, and then, with so many jockeys competing for rides at the Balding yard, he decided to go freelance. The next season brought him 227 rides and 29 wins. In the 1973 National he had a most creditable ride on *Hurricane Rock*, a 100-1 chance who was placed third at the last before fading to be the sixth of 17 finishers.

His career steadily progressed after 1974 when he gained a retainer from Josh Gifford at Findon in Sussex. In 1975 his successes included a four-timer for Gifford at Huntingdon. In the 1977-78 season he

had 56 wins, a total exceeded only by Jonjo O'Neill and John Francome. In the summer of 1978 he had several winning rides in the United States, and in November he had his biggest success at that point: a five lengths victory when puttting up 4lb overweight on *Approaching* in the Hennessy Cognac Gold Cup. But during these years he sustained plenty of broken bones, cuts, bruises and concussions, and all the while he was having to take the most drastic measures to keep down his weight.

In 1974 he had again finished sixth in the Grand National, this time on *Manicou Bay*, a 40-1 chance. But four subsequent Nationals had brought no improvement. His rides: Lord Chelsea's well-backed *Money Market* (1976) who finished 14th; *Spittin' Image* (1977), fell at the first; top-weighted *Shifting Gold* (1978), fell at the tenth; and *Purdo* (1979), fell when leading at the first Becher's. Meanwhile, however, he had been greatly heartened by his ride on *Aldaniti* who had finished a distant third to the ill-fated *Alverton* in the 1979 Cheltenham Gold Cup. That performance, in appalling weather, sparked his dream of winning the National on *Aldaniti* in 1980.

Then, in the summer of 1979, came the shattering diagnosis that initially made him feel suicidal. A malignant testicle was removed but a subsequent, exploratory chest operation confirmed that his only hope of survival was to begin immediate chemotherapy treatment to combat the spread of cancerous cells. In those early years of its development, the side-effects of chemotherapy were more severe; and now, throughout the cycles of treatment, only one incentive sustained Bob's fighting spirits: the dream of recovering to ride *Aldaniti* at Aintree in March.

In November, after four courses of treatment, he prematurely started riding out for Paul Cole at Lambourn. But he was too weak to carry on. More courses were necessary. Then, to add to his despair, he saw *Aldaniti* pulled up at Sandown on his first outing of the season. The Gifford-trained gelding needed to be pin-fired for a damaged tendon and would certainly not be fit to race again for another year.

In January, 1980, after his fifth and final course of chemotherapy, an emaciated Champion left the Royal Marsden Hospital in Sutton, Surrey; and at once he began to push himself to the limits in a fanatical bid to rebuild his wasted muscles. In three months he gained four stone in weight. Retained by the BBC at the Grand National meeting, he walked the course for a recording with Derek Thompson, his friend since childhood. Then came a series of trips to the United States where he rode his first winners on the Flat.

Still exercising relentlessly (riding out, running, and playing tennis and squash) he began his National Hunt comeback at the end of August, and some three weeks later, he rode *Physicist* to a hard won victory over three and a quarter miles at Fontwell Park, his first success over fences for more than 16 months. Three days later, at Stratford, he was severely bruised in a somersaulting fall, and yet stubbornly he took another ride two hours later – and won.

Champion was back with a vengeance. In December, after he had had winning doubles at Ascot and Towcester, racing journalists voted him the Amoco National Hunt Jockey of the Month, an award he gained again in February, 1981. Most importantly, that month, his wins included the Whitbread Trial Handicap Chase at Ascot on the 14-1 outsider of eight. The winning chaser, also now fully recovered, was *Aldaniti*. The Grand National dream was alive again.

To Bob's immense relief, owner Nick Embiricos chose not to have *Aldaniti* run in the Cheltenham Gold Cup. Instead the jockey rode *Approaching*, finishing well down in the field. Two weeks later, the Grand National meeting started disastrously for *Aldaniti*'s connections. On the opening day Mrs Embiricos's *Stonepark*, ridden by Richard Rowe, suffered a fatal first fence fall in the Topham Trophy. Then, in the last race, Bob suffered a heavy fall on *Kilbroney* and was kicked in the back by an oncoming runner. For once, however, Bob's luck was good. He had a hoof-sized bruise on the back but no broken bones. He rode the next day in a novice hurdle and was pronounced fit for the National.

Despite all the intense media pressure, Champion had no qualms when mounting up for his ninth Grand National bid. Indeed, as he would recall 20 years later, 'I had never been so confident of winning in my life. I thought it was a formality.' With *Aldaniti* set to carrry 10st 13lb he had no difficulty making the weight. He was on the 10-1 second favourite; and he had complete faith in the ability of the 11 year old gelding. 'My only worry was getting over the first fence because he goes off so fresh.'

And so, seemingly predestined, as though following a Hollywood script written in heaven, the heart-rending drama climaxed with a gloriously happy, fairy-tale ending. *Aldaniti* overjumped the first fence, dangerously nosing the ground on landing, but then steadily advanced through the field to take the lead after the 11th. Still ahead when fiddling the last, he then held on to resist, by four lengths, a fast and furious late challenge from the 8-1 favourite, *Spartan Missile*.

There was anti-climax one year later when *Aldaniti* – now a 12 year old with an extra 10lb to carry – was one of many fallers at the first fence. But no matter. The greatest-ever horse-and-rider comeback had been achieved, and it prompted so many unsolicited donations to the Royal Marsden Hospital that the Bob Champion Cancer Trust was established in 1983. Though retired from the saddle (he had ridden more than 400 winners in his relatively short professional career), Bob now found himself committed to a no less exhausting routine as he toiled to maintain an over-demanding schedule of special appearances, after-dinner speeches and lectures to raise millions of pounds for the cause.

His charity-raising efforts included a whirlwind world tour and, most notably, the biggest fund-raiser was a 250-mile walk by *Aldaniti* from Buckingham Palace to Aintree, with 250 people, including many celebrities, each riding one mile and guaranteeing at least £1,000 in sponsorship. Bob himself rode the last mile which ended with the great duo cantering down the course before the start of the 1987 Grand National.

Meanwhile, taking out a licence in mid-1982, Bob had set up as a trainer near Bury St Edmunds. At first he had some 30 horses and his owners included the Queen Mother who sent him *Army Council*. There were some memorable successes, most notably with the chaser *Pat's Minstrel*. But always it was a struggle financially with ever-diminishing returns. By late 1998 he had only five horses and he announced his retirement from racing.

Still he drove himself unsparingly on behalf of charity, with his trust eventually raising some £13 million for cancer research. In addition he was undertaking tours of schools on behalf of the Northern Racing College, promoting riding as a career for youngsters. Finally, in March, 2001, he suffered a heart attack and was compelled to ease up. The following month, for the first time in 20 years, he was conspicuous by his absence at the Grand National. *See also:* Aldaniti; Giffford, Josh; Thorne, John.

CHAMPION JOCKEYS

It is generally accepted by National Hunt jockeys

that, however talented a rider may be, he can only win the Grand National if he is on the right horse – the 'right horse' being the one that performs best on the day without inadvertently suffering a mishap. Quite simply, the National is no respecter of reputations, with luck in running a prerequisite of great and moderate riders alike.

Thus, since 1900, Grand National winners have been ridden by only fourteen jockeys who have, at some time, held Britain's National Hunt jockey championship: Percy Woodland, Frank Mason, Ernie Piggott, Mr Jack Anthony, Bill Smith, Fred Rees, Ted Leader, Gerry Wilson, Bryan Marshall, Fred Winter, Graham Thorner, Bob Davies, Tommy Stack and Richard Dunwoody. Of these Wilson won the most titles (seven) but only one National, on *Golden Miller*, 1934. Similarly, Frank Mason was six times champion jockey, winning one National, on *Kirkland*, 1905.

Champions who have been denied Grand National victory include Peter Scudamore (eight titles) John Francome (seven), Billy Stott and Tim Molony (five), Fred Rimell and Josh Gifford (four), Stan Mellor and Terry Biddlecombe (three), Ron Barry and Jonjo O'Neill (two) and one-time champions Jack Dowdeswell, Dick Francis and Tim Brookshaw. Most famously, the winningmost jump jockey of all time, Tony McCoy, champion every season since 1995-96, continues to pursue his first Grand National win.

Seven jump jockeys have ridden 1,000 or more winners in British National Hunt racing: Tony McCoy, Richard Dunwoody, Peter Scudamore, John Francome, Stan Mellor, Peter Niven and Adrian Maguire. Of these only one had been successful in the Grand National: Dunwoody, on *West Tip*, 1986, and *Miinnehoma*, 1994.

In recent years leading jockeys in Ireland have had a good record in the Grand National. However, Frank Berry, ten times the champion rider in Ireland and winner of the 1972 Cheltenham Gold Cup on *Glencaraig Lady*, rode in eight Nationals and never finished better than in seventh place, on *The Ellier* (1987).
See also: Dowdeswell, Jack.

CHAMPION TRAINERS

Since the Second World War, just six champion trainers have saddled a winner of the Grand National. Both Neville Crump and Vincent O'Brien were twice winners of the National Hunt Trainers' Championship, and both were successful three times in the National. Fred Winter (eight times champion) and Fred Rimell (four times) both turned out two National winners. Fulke Walwyn (five times champion) had only one winner. Most remarkably, Martin Pipe, 15 times champion, had more Grand National runners (81) than any trainer in history, but just one winner, *Miinnehoma* in 1994.

Champion trainers denied Grand National victory include Ryan Price (five times the title-holder), Peter Cazalet, Michael Dickinson and Peter Easterby (all three times champion), and Paul Nicholls, Nicky Henderson and David Nicholson (twice leading trainer).
See also: Trainers.

CHANDLER

The first recorded 12 year old to win the Grand National – in 1848, by just half a length from *The Curate*, the 6-1 favourite, with *British Yeoman* one and a half lengths back in third. It was the closest finish yet seen and it marked a brilliant Aintree debut by both horse and Captain Joseph Lockhart Little, his rider and half-owner.

Few National winners have had a more humble background than *Chandler*. A brown gelding by *Doctor Faustus* out of an unknown dam, he was despised by his owner-breeder (Sir Edward Scott), who called him a 'fiddle-headed brute'; and he gained his name after being passed on to a chandler of Sutton Coldfield in settlement of a bill. He was now used to pull the chandler's cart. Then, after being traded, he was used by his third owner, a Mr Garnett, to pull his gig whenever he went out to the Bonehill harriers meet.

Chandler's future was changed entirely by chance. One day a leading amateur rider, Captain William Peel, found that his hunter had not arrived in time for him to join in the meet. Desperate, he borrowed 'the brute' who was unhitched from Mr Garnett's gig, and subsequently he was so impressed with the ride that he bought the horse for 20 guineas with his own hunter, now arrived, thrown in for good measure. It was a bargain beyond belief since Mr Garnett soon chose to return the hunter; and a few days later Captain Peel sold the same horse for 60 guineas. *Chandler* had cost him nothing.

Captain Peel was an outstanding horseman. He rode in five Grand Nationals, most notably finishing fifth on *Eagle* (1846) and fourth on *Pioneer* (1847) and winning the Paris Steeplechase on *Culverthorpe*, the runner-up to *Pioneer* in the 1846 National. But he was slow to introduce *Chandler* to racing. For five years the gelding was used as a hunter. When at last he made his mark as a steeplechaser he was ridden by Peel's close friend, Captain 'Josey' Little. By gambling and winning on *Chandler*, Little – popularly known as 'The Captivating Captain' – recovered from threatened bankruptcy and made so mucb profit that he was able to buy a half-share in the horse.

Renowned for his prodigious leaps, *Chandler* was one of three runners allotted a top weight of 11st 12lb for the 1848 National. He went off a well-supported 12-1 chance, third in a market headed by *The Curate*. The favourite was the mount of the great Tom Olliver who had been Captain Little's riding coach and now, as it emerged, he had trained his pupil rather too well. *The Curate* struck the front, ahead of *British Yeoman*, on landing over the last, but on the long run-in Little galvanised *Chandler* into an electrifying finish to pass them both and so become the first Army officer to ride a National winner.

Meanwhile, Captain Peel had been brought down on eight year old *Pioneer*. Still, the victory of *Chandler* brought him ample compensation. With his co-owner he shared some £7,000 in winning bets. The following year, in his last National, Peel failed to finish on his own *Proceed*, a 9-1 chance. *Chandler*, with a top weight of 12st 2lb, was not even quoted in the betting. But creditably, in very heavy going, Little brought him home the fifth of only six finishers in a 24-strong field.

In 1850, in his last National, *Chandler* was 14 years old, the oldest of 32 starters. Again ridden by Captain Little, he collided with Lord Strathmore's well-fancied *Rat-Trap* near the Canal Turn and failed to finish.

See also: Little, Captain Joseph Lockhart.

CHARITY

In the first Aintree Grand National of 1839, *Charity*, a 20-1 chance, was well in contention until, near the end of the first circuit, she refused to tackle the 4ft. 8in. high stone wall in front of the stands. Two years later, however, the infamous stone wall was replaced by an artificial Water Jump, and now she returned to become the first mare to win the National. In one of the closest of all finishes, she

triumphed by one length and half a length from *Cigar* and *Peter Simple* respectively.

Charity – a bay mare by *Woodman* out of an unknown dam – had her first success as a five year old in a hunters' flat race in 1835 and was then sold to Mr William Vevers of Donnington Court, Hertfordshire. Mr Vevers was not only a prominent trainer but also an exceptional horseman in his own right. He was 67 years old when he had his last winning ride, in an 1849 Ledbury steeplechase on his own *Vengeance*. The following year *Vengeance* finished seventh in the National and in 1851 his *Vain Hope* was fifth. But he himself never rode in the race, and for the most part he recruited the leading professional Tom Olliver to ride *Charity*, primarily over hurdles.

Following her refusal in 1839, and having run up a string of defeats in the interim, *Charity* was not well fancied for the 1841 National. At 14-1 she was sixth in the betting on a race that had only 11 runners, all of them on 12st except for *Lottery*, the first National winner, now the 5-2 favourite and burdened with an impossible 13st 4lb.

On the plus side, *Charity* was partnered by Mr A. Powell, a highly experienced cross-country rider who had ridden in the two previous Nationals. He kept her well placed throughout and then timed his challenge to perfection, taking the last in third place before producing a storming late run to snatch victory from the two greys, *Cigar* and *Peter Simple*. Officially the mare had won in the colours of Lord Craven, but almost certainly she was still at least part-owned by Mr Vevers.

Charity did not reappear in 1842; nor in 1843 when the race became a handicap and, for one year only, the dreaded stone wall was re-introduced to disastrous effect. The following year she was re-united with Powell and lightly handicapped, but in this, her third and last National, she fell halfway at the Water Jump. She was then retired to Mr Vevers' estate after finishing second in a Swindon chase to the 1843 National winner *Vanguard*.

CHEATING

As already recorded, the most outrageous allegation of cheating in the Grand National occurred when Daniel McCann, beaten 20 lengths on *Lough Conn* in 1947, falsely accused Eddie Dempsey, the winning rider of *Caughoo*, of having hidden in the fog and missed out at least half of the 30 fences. In the early history of the race rumours abounded of horses having been 'nobbled' by outsiders before the race, and in a few cases they were seemingly well-founded. But there is no evidence to suggest that connections of a runner have been involved in skull-duggery.

However, one amateur rider has actually confessed to bending the rules in the National. In his 1999 book, *Crossing The Line: The World of Racing Revealed*, Mr Charles Brooks revealed how he 'cheated' – though to no real advantage – when weighing out on the 45-1 chance *Insure* in the 1987 National. Being hopelessly over-weight, he carried 'a tiny saddle a good ten pounds lighter than the one on which I ended up riding in the race.' He had had no expectation of getting round and having to weigh in. As it happened, *Insure* was the last of 22 finishers, but it was all inconsequential since the clerk of the scales allowed the jockey to weigh in minus his saddle.
See also: Foul Play.

CHELTENHAM GOLD CUP

A non-handicap race run over three miles two and a half furlongs with a stamina-sapping 237-yard uphill finish, the Cheltenham Gold Cup is now recognised as the supreme championship of steeple-chasing. However, when it was inaugurated in 1924, it was viewed primarily as a useful form guide and trial for the then infinitely more important Grand National, which was worth £8,240 to the winner compared with the Gold Cup's £685.

From the beginning, it was not unusual to see horses prominent in the Gold Cup going on to Aintree. But does Cheltenham really provide a guide to how a Gold Cup horse may run when handicapped in the National? More pointedly, does the National come too soon after the testing Cheltenham challenge – the great chases usually being about three weeks apart, and very occasionally, because of the moveable feast of Easter, as few as 15 days apart? More and more these questions would come to be asked, the issue being complicated by the fact that the National weights are framed before Cheltenham, so denying the handicapper the opportunity of taking Gold Cup form into account.

In 1924, after he had been a head second in the first Gold Cup, *Conjuror II* became the 5-2 favourite for the National, the shortest priced starter since *Regal* in 1879. It made sense since he had been

an unlucky third in the 1923 National and, because he was now 12 years old, the handicapper had chosen not to raise him in the weights. He was still on 11st for Aintree despite having carried 12st so well at Cheltenham. However, his performance at Aintree gave no conclusive answer to the above questions since he was well up with the leaders when he was an unlucky faller after being baulked by a riderless horse at the first Becher's.

On the other hand, subsequent events strongly suggested that it was unwise to run a horse in both the Gold Cup and National of the same year. Three successive Gold Cup winners – *Ballinode* (1925), *Koko* (1926) and *Thrown In* (1927) – were all well-fancied fallers at Aintree following victory in the Cheltenham Gold Cup. To be sure, *Easter Hero*, the 20-length Gold Cup winner of 1929, ran spectacularly well at Aintree where, in the biggest-ever field of 66 runners, he finished second under a top weight of 12st 7lb. But most telling was the record of *Grakle* who ran in six successive Nationals (1927 to 1932), being the second favourite in 1927, favourite in 1930 and co-favourite in 1932. He failed to finish on four occasions, and when he won it was in the one year (1931) that he had not run at Cheltenham beforehand.

Confusingly, in 1933, *Golden Miller*, the dual Gold Cup winner, was a faller at Aintree while the race was won by *Kellsboro' Jack* who had been a mere also ran at Cheltenham. Then, in 1934, the Cheltenham hoodoo was at last overcome as the extraordinary Miller put in a devastating finishing burst to win at Aintree only 16 days after gaining his third Gold Cup. But that 'double' was unique – as was *Golden Miller* who went on to win five successive Gold Cups.

In 1937 it was generally accepted that third-placed *Thomond II* would have won the National if only he had not been subjected 15 days earlier to an exceptionally hard race in the Gold Cup where he went down by just three-quarters of a length to *Golden Miller*. Thereafter, for many years, horses were far less often entered for both races – rare exceptions including *Prince Regent* who, in 1946, won the Gold Cup and finished second in the National, and *Mont Tremblant* who was the 1953 runner-up at Aintree after being unplaced at Cheltenham.

In 1967, just over three weeks after finishing a distant last at Cheltenham, the blinkered *Foinavon* won the National at 100-1. But that, of course, was

C

a freak result – only made possible by the riderless *Popham Down* who brought all but the winner to a standstill at the 23rd fence. It did nothing to weaken the argument that history was against National contenders who had so recently run in the testing Gold Cup.

Nevertheless, in 1972, the first and second in the National betting were horses who had been unplaced in the big Cheltenham race. The former, *L'Escargot*, was knocked over; the latter, *Gay Trip*, finished two lengths runner-up in a 42-strong field. Then, in 1973, most unusually, the National field included three runners – *L'Escargot*, *Crisp* and *Spanish Steps* – who sixteen days earlier had finished fourth, fifth and sixth respectively in the Gold Cup. At Aintree, remarkably, they finished third, second and fourth respectively, with *Crisp* beaten only three-quarters of a length by *Red Rum*, enjoying a 23lb advantage in the weights.

While third-placed *L'Escargot*, the dual Gold Cup (1970, 1971) winner, had been the knocked over favourite in the 1972 National, it is perhaps significant that – like *Grakle* – he had his best Aintree runs when not previously turning out at Cheltenham. Thus, when less frequently tested, he was runner-up to *Red Rum* in 1974 and, as a 12 year old, beat the great 'Rummy' by 15 lengths in 1975.

There was now some encouragement for National contenders who had previously run in the Gold Cup without having had too hard a race. For example, *The Dikler* finished fifth and sixth at Aintree after being unplaced at Cheltenham in 1975 and 1976. Other also rans would soon do considerably better. But it remained bad news for Gold Cup stars. In 1977, following a six lengths win at Cheltenham, *Davy Lad* seemed to be thrown in at the National weights with a mere 10st 13lb. But it was a bridge too far for the seven year old who had only 16 days to recover from his Gold Cup success; he fell at the first open ditch and was retired the following season after breaking down.

Then, in 1979, came the tragedy of nine year old *Alverton* who had won the Gold Cup by a staggering 25 lengths. He, too, looked most generously treated on 10st 13lb as opposed to 12st at Cheltenham, and he was backed accordingly to 13-2 favouritism. As a much-depleted field began the second circuit, he was moving so easily that he looked almost certain to emulate *Golden Miller*'s 'double'. But, unpredictably, he altered his stride pattern on approaching

the second Becher's, crashed chest-on into the top of the fence and broke his neck on the hitting the ground. His was such a weak take-off that it was surmised that he had suffered a heart attack.

In 1981, nine year old *Spartan Missile* was made the 8-1 National favourite after an eye-catching run in the Gold Cup. He put in a tremendous late challenge to finish second behind *Aldaniti*. Similarly, the following year, punters latched on to a National contender who had run reasonably well at Cheltenham. They were rewarded when, just 16 days after finishing sixth in the Gold Cup, the 7-1 favourite *Grittar* won at Aintree by 15 lengths.

1987 was another year with only a 16-day gap between Cheltenham and Aintree. And this time there was encouraging National form by horses that had run in various races at the Festival meeting. *The Tsarevich* (12th in the Mildmay of Flete) finished second; *Lean Ar Aghaidh* (second in the Kim Muir) was third; *West Tip* (fourth in the Gold Cup) was fourth; *The Ellier* (first in the Kim Muir), was seventh; and *Attitude Adjuster* (fourth in the Foxhunters') finished eighth.

In 1988 *Rhyme 'N' Reason* went to the National with outstanding seasonal form and was arguably the best handicapped horse in the race. Yet he did not go off as a favourite, largely because he had fallen at the fourth fence from home in the Gold Cup. But that was more a slip than a proper fall; and at Aintree he went from last to first to win by four lengths.

In 1989 the class horse in the race was 11 year old *The Thinker*, winner of the 1987 Gold Cup. Like *Rhyme 'N' Reason*, he went to Aintree following a fall in the Gold Cup, but unlike that winner he was severely handicapped on 11st 10lb, giving 9lb to *Bonanza Boy* and more than a stone to most others. Finishing strongly, he did remarkably well to come home third behind *Little Polveir* and *West Tip*. The runner-up had finished fifth in the Gold Cup. *Dixton House*, the light-weighted favourite, who had won the Ritz Club Handicap Chase at Cheltenham, fell at the first Becher's.

In the 1990s, after Aintree's fences had been made less unforgiving, there was growing evidence that owners and trainers were more amenable to the idea of running a horse in both the Gold Cup and National. Moreover, during the running of the 1991 race, it appeared almost certain that *Golden Miller*'s 'double' was to be equalled at last. Just 23 days after his short-head Gold Cup victory, *Garrison Savannah* set off at Aintree as the 7-1 second favourite. He was lightly handicapped on 11st 1lb, jumped superbly and led by about eight lengths when coming to the Elbow. But now, cruelly, the slogging run-in found him out. He began to falter and just 100 yards out *Seagram* swept past to win by five lengths.

Like the disappointing *Dixton House* two years earlier, *Seagram* had raced at the Cheltenham Festival, winning the Ritz Club. He was now the first horse to win the National after winning at the Festival since 1961 when *Nicolaus Silver* followed up his victory in the amateur riders' Kim Muir Memorial Challenge Cup.

Coincidentally, in 1992, *Cool Ground* was in the same situation as *Garrison Savannah* had been – carrying 11st 1lb at Aintree 23 days after a short-head win (over *The Fellow*) in the Gold Cup. He was 14lb well in at the weights but was outpaced as the leaders rounded the turn for home and finished a distant tenth. *Docklands Express*, third in the Gold Cup, was fourth as the 15-2 favourite.

Twelve months later four of the first five horses to complete the course had run at the Cheltenham Festival. This, however, was the year of the void National. Next, in 1994, Gold Cup winner *The Fellow* (10lb well in) was sent on to Aintree and backed down to 9-1. But this so popular French horse, a winner of two King George VI Chases and the Grand Steeplechase de Paris, was never at home with soft conditions and now, faced with heavy going, he was soon struggling on the second circuit, almost falling at Becher's and then, thoroughly exhausted, crashing out at the Canal Turn.

Young Hustler, a good third at Cheltenham, was also inconvenienced by the going. Only seven years old, he was lying fourth when brought down at the 11th. Nevertheless, the winner did come out of the Gold Cup field. *Miinnehoma*, who had not had a hard race in finishing a poor seventh, triumphed by one and a quarter lengths from the mudlark *Just So*. Significantly, also, he had been very lightly raced, at Aintree having only his third outing of the season.

Gold Cup form was never more popular than in 1995 when the first three home at Cheltenham – *Master Oats*, *Dubacilla* and *Miinnehoma* – were all short in the Grand National betting, with *Master Oats* the hot 5-1 favourite. Although *Master Oats* had fallen at Aintree the previous year, trainer Kim

Bailey was bullish about his chances. 'He's got a lot of weight (11st 10lb) but he's the best horse in the race and he can do it.' Thus the nine year old chestnut gelding was hugely fancied as the 11th horse attempting to emulate *Golden Miller*'s double.

At Cheltenham he had won by an impressive 15 lengths. However, he had jumped indifferently round the first circuit, and that day two of the 22 fences had been omitted because of the state of the ground. Now, significantly, he was not to have his favoured soft ground in the National; outpaced, he faded over the last half-mile to finish seventh. But at least *Dubacilla*, the Gold Cup runner-up, stayed on well to finish fourth. *Miinnehoma* was pulled up at the second Valentine's. Most noteworthy was the fact that the 40-1 winner *Royal Athlete* was a 12 year old who had been third in the 1993 Gold Cup one month before falling in the void National but who, this year, had been a late withdrawal from Cheltenham.

1996 was another year with a mere 16 days between the Gold Cup and the National. *Rough Quest*, the four lengths runner-up at Cheltenham, was seen as a handicap 'good thing', being due to race off a 19lb higher mark in future handicaps. But it had been much the same with *The Fellow*, *Cool Ground* and *Garrison Savannah*, all defeated at Aintree; and the fact remained that no placed horse in the Gold Cup had come good at Aintree since 1934. In a signed statement featured in full-page Coral advertisements, ex-champion jockey John Francome declared: 'Even in what looks a substandard National, one horse I cannot see winning is the Cheltenham Gold Cup runner-up *Rough Quest*. He has had a hard race and has had only two weeks to recover from it.'

Francome was not alone in that view. But this year Gold Cup form at last came up trumps at Aintree. *Rough Quest*, as 7-1 favourite, triumphed by one and a quarter lengths. *Young Hustler*, as in the Gold Cup, finished fifth. Moreover, the narrowly beaten runner-up was *Encore Un Peu*, who had also run at Cheltenham, being just pipped at the post in the Kim Muir over three miles one furlong.

In 1997, *Go Ballistic*, fourth in the Gold Cup, was pulled up in the National. Then, in 1998, just 16 days after being fifth in the Gold Cup, the grey *Suny Bay* put in a staggering performance at Aintree to finish runner-up for the second year in succession, this time conceding 23lb to the winner *Earth Summit*.

In 1999 *Double Thriller* was made a hot National favourite after finishing fourth in the Gold Cup. It was clear that if the handicapper could have taken into account that Cheltenham run he would have allotted him at least a stone more than his 10st. 8lb. But 23 days after Cheltenham the bold-jumping former hunter fell at the first Aintree fence. *Go Balllistic*, the Gold Cup runner-up, was as short as 8-1 for the National but was withdrawn. *Addington Boy*, fifth at Cheltenham, finished fourth at Aintree.

The 9-1 favourite for the 2000 National was *Dark Stranger*, trained by Martin Pipe and ridden by champion jockey A.P. McCoy. At Cheltenham, 24 days before, he had hacked up impressively to win the Mildmay of Flete Chase over an extended two and a half miles. But at Aintree he fell at the first open ditch (the third).

Once again, in 2002, the National field included three horses who had run in the Gold Cup: *Marlborough*, fourth at Cheltenham, followed home by *What's Up Boys* and *Alexander Banquet*. All three were among the top four in the weights at Aintree; *and Marlborough*, on 11st 12lb, fell at the first and *Alexander Banquet*, 11st 11lb, at the sixth. But the grey *What's Up Boys*, on 11st 6lb, finished runner-up by just one length and three quarters – truly remarkable considering that no horse had carried more than 11st to victory since *Corbiere* (11st 4lb) 20 years before. The 20-1 winner, *Bindaree*, had run at Cheltenham (an unpromising seventh in the William Hill National Hunt Handicap Chase) and was on a mere 10st 4lb.

The weight factor was even more strongly emphasised the following year when the most competitive of Nationals saw no fewer than 35 of 40 starters running out of the handicap proper. Four of them had raced at the Cheltenham Festival – *Chives*, *You're Agoodun* and *Behrajan*, seventh, ninth and tenth respectively in the Gold Cup, and *Ad Hoc*, a decent third in the William Hill National Hunt Handicap Chase. *Ad Hoc* and *Chives* were leading fancies, but the former (on 11st 1lb) unseated his rider at the 19th and the latter (11st 5lb) was pulled up before the 12th. *Behrajan* on top weight (11st 12lb) finished tenth while *You're Agoodun* (10st 9lb) fell at the 19th. Significantly, the first nine home were carrying less than 11st.

Long gone now are the days when the Cheltenham Gold Cup was regarded as a warm-up for the much more prestigious National. Today it is the ultimate target, the greatest measure of steeplechasing talent, a race won by horses of such quality that they are rarely to be risked in the hurly-burly at Aintree. Still *Golden Miller*'s Gold Cup-National double remains unique; and overall horses placed in other races at the Cheltenham Festival have a bad record in the National. Most pointedly, in 2003, the first six finishers in the National had purposefully missed out Cheltenham in being specially targeted for Aintree. Results certainly support such caution: *Seagram* remains the only Cheltenham Festival winner to have prevailed in the National since 1961 when *Nicolaus Silver* scored 17 days after his success in the Kim Muir Memorial Challenge Cup.

In the past decade only two horses have won the National after running at Cheltenham: the aforementioned *Bindaree* (2002) and *Silver Birch* (2007) who, most unusually, had a four-week break after running second in the Cross-Country Handicap Chase. Of those who have tackled the Gold Cup and National in the same year, the greatest hero of modern times must surely be *Hedgehunter*, the 2005 National winner. The following year, he was runner-up at both Cheltenham and Aintree, in the latter case when carrying top weight of 11st 12lb and when arguably only ground-deadening overnight rain denied him success by working in favour of *Numbersixvalverde* who, with an 18lb advantage, won by six lengths.

Though only one horse has won the Gold Cup and National in the same season, six jockeys have done so: *Tommy Cullinan* (1930) on *Easter Hero* and *Shaun Goilin*; Gerry Wilson (1934) on *Golden Miller*; Fred Winter (1962) on *Mandarin* and *Kilmore*; Tommy Carberry (1975) on *Ten Up* and *L'Escargot*; John Burke (1976) on *Royal Frolic* and *Rag Trade*; and Jim Culloty (2002) on *Best Mate* and *Bindaree*.

CLARKE, Sir Stanley William CBE

Owner of *Lord Gyllene*, the runaway winner of the 150th Grand National which was postponed following IRA bomb scares. Born on June 7, 1933, the son of a brewery labourer and a maid, Stanley Clarke began work at the age of nine years old, as a butcher's errand boy, and at 16 became a plumber's apprentice in Burton upon Trent. Starting his own plumbing business at the age of 21, he later switched to property development – with such success that in 1987 he sold his construction company for £51 million. By 2004, following further real estate ventures, the *Sunday Times* Rich List judged that he had increased his worth to at least £148 million.

Clarke traced his love of horses back to his days as a delivery boy, and his National ambitions were fired especially on seeing the victory of *Grittar* in 1982. It became his custom to choose his own horses, many of them imported from New Zealand on the recommendation of his antipodean 'talent spotter', Jim Mellow; and on seeing a video of *Lord Gyllene* he was reminded of the legendary *Red Rum*. His many other shrewd buys included the prolific winner *Barton* who captured Cheltenham's Royal and SunAlliance Novices' Hurdle in 1999, and *Rolling Ball*, winner of the Festival's 1991 Sun Alliance Novices' Chase. The former was named after the village of Barton-under-Needwood, Staffordshire, where the owner had lived for most of his life.

Clarke became a member of the Jockey Club and chairman of the British Bloodstock Agency. But his most valuable and lasting contribution to racing was made by his acquiring and revitalising ailing racecourses. It led to the foundation of Northern Racing Ltd. which came to own and operate nine racecourses; and most notably he was responsible for the transformation of Uttoxeter into one of the finest courses in the land. It was there, in the Midlands National, that his *Lord Gyllene* finished runner-up prior to his triumph at Aintree.

While that 1997 National victory was a dream-come-true for the owner and his wife, Hilda, the same year ended with a veritable nightmare when they were brutalised by masked burglars who invaded their home and robbed them of £500 and jewellery. Similarly, the year 2000 brought cruelly contrasting events. Having raised millions of pounds for various charities, Clarke was informed in November that he was to be knighted for his work on behalf of the community in Staffordshire. Then, almost at the same time, he received the most distressing news of his life: he had cancer. Typically, he reacted with determination, contacting a top specialist and eventually having an operation that involved taking away three-quarters of his liver.

Though cutting down on his previous workaholic lifestyle, Sir Stanley continued to remain a major player as an owner and breeder of racehorses. He was represented in the 2001 National by *Listen Timmy* who, like *Lord Gyllene*, was ridden by Tony Dobbin. He fell at the Water Jump. The following year Lady Clarke ran the grey *Gun'N Roses II* who unseated his rider at the seventh.

Sir Stanley now had a dozen horses in training and, as the owner of Dunstall Hall in Staffordshire, he was restoring to its former glory the great mansion where his mother had once worked as a maid. But finally, in 2004, his brave three-year battle against cancer was lost. He was 71. He had made millions but he and his wife had also given millions in their support of charities, among them the Lichfield Cathedral Trust, Animal Health Trust and various racing welfare organisations. Lady Hilda Clarke continued to be involved in racing, and in the 2005 National her colours were carried by the Martin Pipe-trained *Polar Red* who finished 13th at 100-1.

See also: Lord Gyllene; Brookshaw, Stephen.

CLOISTER

Bred in Ireland by Lord Fingall, *Cloister* won the Grand National only once but in a style that places him firmly in the race's pantheon of all-time greats. Only *Red Rum* has commanded more superlatives in victory, and rightly so since *Cloister* raised steeplechasing to an entirely new level of excellence. He did not merely outclass all his rivals in the 1893 National; he pulverised them with a breathtaking exhibition of jumping and galloping that was hailed as the greatest ever seen.

The records from that run speak for themselves. *Cloister*, a nine year old dark bay, was the first horse ever to carry the maximum weight of 12st 7lb to National glory – an achievement only three others – *Manifesto* (1899), *Jerry M* (1912) and *Poethlyn* (1919) – would ever equal. He was the first horse to win the race by 40 lengths. And he won in a time, a fraction over 9min 32sec, that would not be surpassed for 40 years.

Strength, speed, stamina. The only thing that *Cloister* really lacked was luck. Given luck he would have won on his National debut in 1891 instead of finishing half a length second to *Come Away* after his rider had erred in going for a non-existent gap between his rival and the rails. With luck, he would not have been so harshly raised in the weights that he was condemned to be runner-up again in 1892 – to a horse (*Father O'Flynn*) with an almost two-stone advantage. Again, with luck, he would not have gone mysteriously lame shortly before the Nationals of 1894 and 1895 for which he was the strong ante-post favourite.

C

Originally, on breeding, there was nothing to commend *Cloister*. Neither his dam, *Grace II*, nor his sire, *Ascetic*, was highly regarded; indeed, the former was at one time used daily for deliveries by a village postman. *Ascetic*, however, had unsuspected talents as a stallion. He would sire not only *Cloister* but also two more National winners: *Drumcree* (1903) and *Ascetic's Silver* (1906).

From the beginning *Cloister* showed exceptional promise, being only four years old when, most significantly, his three wins over fences included the Aintree Hunt Chase. He had several different owners before his first National in 1891. Then, as a seven year old, he carried the colours of Lord Dudley and was trained by Richard Marsh who would later prepare horses for King Edward VII and King George V. His rider, who ignored Marsh's advice and lodged an objection to the 1891 winner, was Captain Roddy Owen, an amateur horseman renowned for his courage and determination.

After that unlucky run, *Cloister* changed hands again. He had a new owner, Mr Charles Garden Duff (later Sir Charles Assheton-Smith); a new rider, Mr J.C. Dormer; and a new trainer, the highly experienced Arthur Yates. Unfortunately, however, he had revealed in defeat his full potential. For the 1892 National the handicapper gave him the highest weight (12st 3lb), and, whereas he had gone off at 20-1 the previous year, he was now made the 11-1 favourite.

That weight sealed *Cloister's* fate and after leading for most of the second circuit he was beaten by a full 20 lengths. Yet still the handicapper was unrelenting. For his third National, the twice runner-up was saddled with 12st 7lb. At the time no horse had won the race with more than 12st and not even 12st had been successfully carried since 1842 when the National was not yet a handicap. But it was a measure of *Cloister's* extraordinary reputation that these hugely adverse statistics did not deter the public from supporting him to the tune of 9-2 favouritism. The message had been made clear by the way he had made light of 12st 7lb in winning his one prep race, Aintree's Grand Sefton over three miles. Physically, *Cloister* was now at his peak.

This year a jockey change was forced by a fall at Sandown that had cost Mr Dormer his sight in one eye. *Cloister's* new rider, stable jockey William Dollery, had the experience of seven previous Nationals. But he had never before encountered a horse remotely giving him the feel of supercharged power that was conveyed by *Cloister*. On going unusually firm and fast, and with a field of only 15 starters, *Cloister* took the lead approaching the second fence and never surrendered it, all the while jumping faultlessly and galloping relentlessly in a smooth, long-striding style that left all others floundering in his wake.

Astonishingly, his huge weight was never a factor; and nor was the lack of any competition to spur him along. This was a horse totally at ease with himself, physically and mentally in full command over every yard of the National's four and a half miles. At the second last, his nearest rival, *Aesop*, was 12 lengths behind, and now he increased his lead at every stride to romp home the winner by a full 40 lengths – the biggest-ever winning margin. Curiously, just three months later, Harry Barker, the versatile rider of *Aesop*, was to finish on the runner-up in another big race – the Epsom Derby!

In 1862 *Huntsman* had been credited with a record winning time of 9min 30sec, just over two seconds faster than *Cloister's*. Yet that does not compare with *Cloister's* performance. Also a nine year old, *Huntsman* was carrying a mere 11st. More to the point, he was racing one year before the course was extended by about two furlongs and Becher's and Valentine's were made more difficult. Facing an infinitely sterner test, *Cloister* won in a time that was unsurpassed until 1933 when *Kellsboro' Lad*, carrying 12lb less, achieved a record 9min 28sec.

A few weeks after that most famous National win, *Cloister* was beaten at Sandown by *Horizon*. But the following year he was expected to return fresh and strong for a new challenge. He was allotted 12st 12lb for the National and immediately emerged as the ante-post favourite, his odds shortening to an unprecedented 6-4. Then, inexplicably, as the race day drew near, the odds went out to 6-1. And at that point, as though foreseen in the market moves, *Cloister* was reported to have finished slightly lame after his final gallop at Sandown. He was subsequently passed fit only for the lameness to recur when he was tried again over jumps. The vet diagnosed pain in the sciatic nerve and he was withdrawn from the National.

Was *Cloister* the victim of some skullduggery? Rumours abounded; and, contrary to the view of trainer Yates, owner Duff strongly suspected foul play. Consequently, he adopted high security measures before the 1895 National. *Cloister* was moved to Harry Escott's yard near Lewes and plain-clothes detectives were hired to watch over his wonder horse.

In November, 1894, *Cloister* had carried 13st 3lb in winning the Grand Sefton Chase at Liverpool by 20 lengths, so rather rebutting the suggestion that he had might have been permanently weakened by the effort of his epic National run. Now he was reported to be working well, and so once again he was made the ante-post favourite. And then, once again, after the odds had lengthened for no obvious reason, *Cloister*'s preparation went horribly wrong.

Six days before the race, on a warm-up gallop over fences at Lewes, he performed well for a mile; and then, suddenly, for no apparent reason, he collapsed and rolled over, clearly in pain. Again, he was withdrawn from the National to a huge outcry of 'foul play' with which Mr Duff fully concurred.

It was indeed extraordinary that, in successive years, market moves seem to have anticipated training setbacks. But the evidence was entirely circumstantial and the possibility remains that the horse, under the strain of his great deeds, had developed some unidentified internal weakness that could manifest itself at any time. The mystery will always remain. *Cloister* retired with a National record of second, second and first, and a career record of 35 races, winning 19 and being placed in 11 others.

See also: Dollery, William; Yates, Arthur; Assheton-Smith, Sir Charles.

COLLIS, Captain Robert

As an amateur, Captain Robert Collis twice rode in the Grand National. In 1907 he was on the last of eight finishers, *Napper Tandy*, owned by an Army colleague. In 1909 he was a faller on Mr Frank Bibby's *Wickham*, the roguish gelding who, the following year, would bring down his two stablemates, *Caubeen* and *Glenside* before falling himself. Then, by a very considerable measure of good luck, he joined the National's honours list – not as a jockey but as the trainer of *Glenside*, the improbable, one-eyed winner of 1911.

Taking over the training of both *Caubeen* and *Glenside* at Kinlet in Worcestershire, Captain Collis achieved his success when the National was run on atrociously heavy ground and for the first time saw only one horse complete the course without having fallen. Coming to the undemanding 23rd fence, now known as the Foinavon, *Caubeen* and *Rathnally*, the joint second favourites, were far in the lead when they collided going for the same gap in the fence. It left *Glenside*, a 20-1 chance, in the clear, and though visibly distressed he struggled home to victory by 20 lengths, ahead of three other finishers who had been remounted.

Good luck aside, Captain Collis could take some credit for this victory. Most importantly, when *Glenside*'s jockey, Frank 'Titch' Mason, broke a leg shortly before the 1911 National, he had been shrewd enough to choose as substitute a young amateur who had ridden *Glenside* in a few minor chases in Wales. The amateur, making his Aintree debut, was John Randolph Anthony who would go on to win the National three times from his first five appearances.

Unfortunately, *Glenside* did not have the benefit of Anthony when Collis sent him back to Aintree in 1912. Reputed to have a wind problem, he was such a lowly regarded National winner that he went off as a 40-1 outsider. He fell at the third fence. *See also:* Glenside.

COLONEL, The

Remarkably, *The Colonel* achieved his first Grand National victory (1869) when he was a six year old entire who had had only one previous experience of running in a steeplechase. One year later he became the second horse – following *Abd-El-Kader* 19 years earlier – to win successive Nationals; and in the process he provided jockey George Stevens with a record – still unequalled – of five victories in the race.

By *Knight of Kars* out of *Boadicea*, *The Colonel* had Exmoor ponies in his pedigree, but he was nevertheless a handsome black horse, bred and owned by Mr John Weyman of Brampton, Shropshire. In his early years he had no formal training, his jumping education simply comprising being ridden across country by local farm boys. Thereafter he was campaigned hard and almost exclusively over hurdles; and only six days before his first appearance at Aintree he won a Nottingham hurdle race in the name of Mr Matthew Evans, who possibly had an equal share in the entire.

Although he was a novice chaser, *The Colonel* was well supported for his National debut simply because he was the mount of the greatest of jump jockeys. George Stevens was married to Mr Evans' niece but he had accepted the ride strictly on his own judgment of the hurdler's potential over fences.

C

Riding one of his brilliant waiting races, he held back on the first circuit, then made relentless progress to join *Gardener*, the surprise leader, three out. Once over the last, *The Colonel* drew steadily away to win by a comfortable three lengths from the 100-1 outsider *Hall Court*, with *Gardener*, another long-shot, one length back in third. Thus Stevens broke Tom Olliver's record of three National wins.

The punters have never excelled the appraisal they made of the runners in the 1870 National. *The Colonel* was made the 7-2 hot favourite, followed in the betting by *The Doctor* (5-1), *Primrose* (10-1) and *Surney* (100-8) – and they finished precisely in that order. But it was an exceedingly close run thing. *The Colonel* had been raised 19lb to 11st 12lb, and he went to Aintree without having had a single race in the past 12 months. Thus there were doubts about his ability to make up the huge leeway as Stevens stuck to his usual strategy of patiently riding from the rear.

Again Stevens began his challenging move after Valentine's second time around. But *The Doctor*, under George Holman, was closing equally fast on the leaders and, after landing over the last, the two were locked side by side in the long battle to the line. It was virtually a sprint finish in which *The Colonel* prevailed by just a neck over *The Doctor*, with *Primrose* five lengths behind.

The Colonel's first win had been in Mr Weyman's name, his second in Mr Evans'. Now they agreed to sell their champion chaser to Baron Oppenheim for £2,600. The great jumper failed to produce the same form in Germany and was duly sent back to England to be prepared for the 1871 National. He was made the 8-1 third favourite – behind *Pearl Diver* and *The Lamb* – and again he had the supreme Stevens on board. But this time he was anchored by a decisive top weight of 12st 8lb and Stevens played his usual waiting game in vain. Never able to catch the leaders, *The Colonel* came home as the sixth of eight finishers.

Baron Oppenheim had duplicated his mistake of buying a dual National winner (*The Lamb*) who would be hit too hard by the handicapper to score a third success. However, *The Colonel* became a most successful stallion on being put out to stud in Beberbeck, East Prussia, and reportedly he was also loaned out several times to serve at ceremonial occasions as a charger for Kaiser Wilhelm I.
See also: Stevens, George.

COME AWAY

The winner, following an objection, of the 1891 Grand National – by half a length from Lord Dudley's magnificently consistent *Cloister*. A seven year old bay gelding, *Come Away* was both trained and ridden by Harry Beasley, who was achieving long overdue success on his 12th of 13 appearances in the race. In contrast, *Come Away* was making his National debut and, finishing lame, was destined never to race again.

Irish-bred, *Come Away* was out of the mare *Larkaway*, with some uncertainty in the records as to whether his sire was *Umpire* or *Cambuslang*. But there was never any doubt about his huge potential. As a four year old he was the shock winner of the Conyngham Cup and two years later, under the new ownership of Mr W.G. Jameson, he won the Conyngham Cup again and, more significantly, the Valentine Chase at Aintree.

His form prior to the 1891 National was irresistible. Having won seven of nine races and being partnered, as always, by the popular Harry Beasley, he was made the 4-1 clear favourite, ahead of the previous year's winner *Ilex* and *Cruiser*, a six year old ridden by Harry's eldest brother Tommy, seeking his fourth National win. Three other past winners were in the high quality field: *Voluptuary*, now 13, and the 12 year olds, *Gamecock* and *Roquefort*.

Never prominent on the first circuit, *Come Away* made his forward move on the second and assumed command at Valentine's, albeit strongly pressed by three rivals. After the top-weighted *Why Not* had fallen two from home, it became strictly a two-horse race, a neck-and-neck duel on the run-in between *Come Away* and *Cloister*. Then Captain Roddy Owen, on the latter, made a fatal error in going for a non-existent gap on the rails. As Beasley held his position, *Cloister* lost momentum in being switched to the outside and was beaten by just half a length with *Ilex* far back in third.

An objection was immediately lodged by Owen on the grounds of having been 'jostled' on the run-in. To the delight of favourite backers, it was swiftly overruled by the stewards; and, after three times finishing second, Harry Beasley at last had his first National win. *Come Away*'s winning time of 9min. 58sec. was the fastest recorded since *The Lamb*'s run of 20 years before.
See also: Beasley, Harry; Owen, Captain Edward Roderick.

CONGRESS

First appearing as a seven year old in 1873, *Congress* rates high among the most gallant losers in Grand National history. In 1876, on his fourth bid, he figured in one of the most exciting of all finishes, going down by a neck to the five year old *Regal*. The following year he was equally unlucky. He met with interference from a fallen horse that cost him many lengths and briefly his rider lost his irons; and yet he again finished second – this time beaten four lengths by a five year old (*Austerlitz*) who had almost a two stone advantage in the weights.

A brown gelding – by *Compromise* out of *Countess* – *Congress* was ridden in four successive Nationals (1873-76) by Ted Wilson, the brilliant amateur who was destined to win back-to-back Nationals on *Voluptuary* and *Roquefort* in the mid-1880s. He failed to get round on his first two appearances at Aintree, but was so impressive during the following season that he was raised a stone to a top weight of 12st 4lb for the 1875 National. Going off the 7-1 joint second favourite, he led over the first Becher's but faded in the late stages to be the last of eight finishers.

In 1876 *Congress* was 10lb lower in the weights. Coming to the last, he shared the lead with *Regal* and *Shifnal*, and over the last 200 yards he matched the former stride for stride all the way to the line. Though they finished on opposite sides of the course, it was judged that Captain James Machell's *Regal*, trained and ridden by Joe Cannon, had prevailed by a neck, with *Shifnal* three lengths back in third.

Machell, who had enjoyed his third National win in four years, now bought *Congress* and the following November ran him successfully in Aintree's Grand Sefton Chase. Then, for a handsome profit, he shrewdly sold *Congress* and *Regal* to Lord Lonsdale, who aimed to run both in the 1877 National.

Though he would not have a National runner in his name until 1884, it is understood that Edward, Prince of Wales, had a half share in *Congress* in 1877; and last year's winning jockey, Joe Cannon, was booked for the ride. But, with *Congress* raised 13lb to top weight, it was to prove a lost cause. On his one and only Aintree appearance, the entire *Austerlitz*, owned and ridden by Mr Fred Hobson, powered away on the run-in to win by a comfortable four lengths. By a neck *Congress* snatched the runner-up spot from *The Liberator* (receiving 23lb). On his fifth and last run he had become the first horse to finish as high as second in the National with a top burden of 12st 7lb.

See also: Wilson, Edward; Regal; Austerlitz.

COOK, John Dennis

Winning jockey on nine year old *Specify*, a 28-1 chance in the 1971 Grand National. Prevailing by a neck in one of the tightest of finishes, he pulled off an unprecedented double for Epsom-based trainer John Sutcliffe and owner Fred Pontin, having two months earlier won the Schweppes Gold Trophy Hurdle by a head on their 33-1 long-shot *Cala Mesquida*.

At the age of 33, John Cook was having only his third ride in the race. His introduction had come in the chaotic 1967 National when only *Foinavon* cleared the 23rd fence at the first attempt. He finished a distant 15th on *Ross Sea*, a 66-1 outsider. Three years later he was going well on *Specify*, still in touch with the leaders, when he comfortably cleared the second Becher's only to be brought down by *The Otter* falling directly in his path.

Born in June, 1937, Cook was naturally drawn to a racing career since his parents were employed at the Kingsclere stables, near Newbury. But for years it was an uphill struggle making the grade as a rider. He served an apprenticeship at Kingsclere with Evan Williams and Peter Hastings-Bass before being called up for National Service in the Royal Navy. Subsequently, being overweight for riding on the Flat, he turned to National Hunt racing. Rides remained few and far between until 1962 when, by advertising for work, he gained employment with Frank Cundell, the Oxfordshire trainer. Gradually the winners came, and in the 1965-66 season he achieved 36 victories and 11th place in the jockeys' championship.

It was in 1969 that Cook truly established his reputation as a leading jockey. At the Cheltenham Festival he won the Champion Novices' Chase on Mr Edward Courage's *Spanish Steps*; and eight months later, on the same chaser, he scored his biggest success to date, winning the Hennessy Cognac Gold Cup by 15 lengths.

After his unlucky ride in the 1970 National, he feared the worst as *Specify* passed into the ownership of the holiday camp magnate Fred Pontin and joined the stable of John Sutcliffe. Other jockeys were booked to ride the highly promising chaser in the

C

new season. But then came Cook's brilliant ride for the stable in the Schweppes Gold Trophy. He was the obvious choice to partner *Specify* at Aintree again.

Gay Trip, last year's winner, was the 8-1 favourite in the 1971 National. But he had been raised to 12st top weight and now, under Terry Biddlecombe, he was one of five fallers at the first fence. *Specify* made his forward move on the second circuit, and coming to the last he was one of five horses with an equal chance of victory. Luckily a gap opened up at the Elbow, allowing him to squeeze between the leading pair. Then, once again, Cook proved his strength and flair in an all-out duel to the line. Taking the inside rail, working frantically with hands and heels, he spurred his horse on to snatch victory in the last strides from *Black Secret*, ridden by amateur Jim Dreaper. Just two and a half lengths separated the first three home.

Sadly, Cook's greatest triumph was also his last. A fractured leg prevented him from riding *Specify* when he finished sixth in the 1972 National; and the break proved to be so severe that it ended his race-riding career. Compelled to retire, he later emigrated with his family to Australia and there, after a long, brave battle against illness, he died in 1999. He was only 62.

See also: Specify; Sutcliffe, John.

CORBIERE

Following *Red Rum* in the 1970s, the Jenny Pitman-trained *Corbiere* stands out with *West Tip* as being one of the two great Aintree specialists of the 1980s – his record in five successive Grand Nationals being first, third, third, fell and 12th. His narrow victory in 1983 most memorably marked the first time that the winner had been saddled by a lady trainer, a woman who would be a dominant force in National Hunt racing for years to come. And it may be argued – certainly by Mrs Pitman – that only the harshness of the handicapper prevented the gallant chestnut gelding from joining the National's all-time greats.

By the stallion *Harwell* out of the mare *Ballycashin*, *Corbiere* was named by his owners, the Burrough brewing family, after a lighthouse near their home in the Channel Islands. He was trained by Mrs Pitman from the age of three, and she recognised that he had exceptional courage when, early on, he was the one horse on the gallops to battle on in a hailstorm, holding his head high into the wind and sleet. The surprise winner of a Nottingham

bumper in 1979, he developed into a top-class hurdler before being gifted to Mr Bryan Burrough by his father as a 21st birthday present, then rapidly made his mark over fences. In 1983, as an eight year old, he became a leading contender for the Grand National following his impressive winning of the Welsh National at Chepstow.

At Aintree, in a 41-strong field, *Corbiere* went off at 13-1, fifth in the betting behind last year's winner *Grittar*, made 7-1 favourite despite a half-stone rise in the weights. Ridden by 23 year old Ben de Haan, he led over the first fence alongside the notorious, tearaway front-runner *Delmoss*. As in the previous year *Delmoss* proceeded to make all the running on the first circuit; then both he and *Corbiere* were headed by a 60-1 shot, *Hallo Dandy*. Never far off the lead, *Corbiere* outpaced *Hallo Dandy* from Valentine's and, after the last, he had a four lengths advantage over the fast finishing *Greasepaint*.

Ridden by an amateur, Mr Colin Magnier, the Irish hope *Greasepaint* rallied superbly on the long run-in, steadily closing the gap and going down by only three-quarters of a length with *Yer Man* 20 lengths back in third. *Corbiere* had held on bravely in giving away 11lb to his eight year old challenger. But who knows – might it have been a dead-heat if Magnier had not been putting up 2lb overweight?

Logically, in the light of that close finish, *Corbiere* and *Greasepaint* were raised 10lb and 9lb respectively for the 1984 National, with the latter, now ridden by Tommy Carmody, made the 9-1 favourite. But for smart students of form, the handicap 'snip' was *Hallo Dandy*, the outsider who had jumped so surely to finish fourth in 1983 on unfavourably soft going. Now, raised only 1lb to a mere 10st 2lb, he had the top of the ground he required and was a well-backed 13-1 chance, ahead of *Corbiere*, 16-1.

In a National that saw a record number of 23 finishers, *Corbiere*, on a top weight of 12st, made a great forward surge in the later stages to come home third, one and a half lengths behind *Greasepaint*, with *Hallo Dandy* the winner by four lengths. The trainers of both the second and third felt their horse had been harshly treated by the handicapper, a view unchanged before the 1985 National when *Greasepaint* and *Corbiere* carried just three pounds and four pounds less respectively. Moreover, on a top weight of 11st 10lb, *Corbiere* was one of only two horses carrying 11st or more in a 40-strong field.

With Peter Scudamore taking over from the injured Ben de Haan, *Corbiere* jumped immaculately, again showing that he reserved his best performances for Aintree. Indeed, two out he was looking a likely winner as he led from a tiring *Greasepaint*. Bravely he resisted the strong challenge of *Mr Snugfit*, but then his 25lb disadvantage told. *Mr Snugfit* landed in the lead at the last; then out of the blue, from eight lengths back, came the 50-1 chance *Last Suspect* to wear down the leaders and snatch victory by one and a half lengths. *Corbiere* was another three lengths back in third, with *Greasepaint* fourth.

In February, 1986, *Corbiere* returned to form with a win at Warwick, followed by a 15 lengths second to *Last Suspect* at Chepstow. For the National he was allotted 11st. 7lb., a weight exceeded only by that of the 100-1 Czech no-hoper *Essex* who, without British form, was automatically on top weight. On analysis he was not so badly handicapped, being on 14lb. and 10lb. better terms with *Last Suspect* and *Mr Snugfit* respectively. Unfortunately, and most uncharacteristically, he fell at the fourth fence. As a 12 year old, making his fifth and final National appearance, he finished 12th. Then, on retirement from racing, Jenny Pitman's brave and beloved 'Corky' had a useful spell in the show-jumping ring and gave valuable service in helping to tutor over fences a remarkable quartet of unbroken three year olds from Ireland – the four to be named *Royal Athlete*, *Garrison Savannah*, *Esha Ness* and *Willsford*. With the passing years *Corbiere*'s stature has been enhanced by the fact that in over two decades no other horse has carried as much as 11st 4lb to victory in the National.

See also: Pitman, Jenny; Haan, Benjamin de.

CORTOLVIN

Lord Poulett had three runners in the 1866 Grand National, but only one of them finished in that roughhouse race: seven year old *Cortolvin*, the 8-1 second favourite, who ran strongly over the second circuit to chase home the unchallenged ten-length winner, *Salamander*. Yet the owner of the brown gelding – Irish-bred (by *Chicken* or, more probably *Cheerful Horn*, out of *Dairymaid*) – was unimpressed. He believed *Cortolvin* was deficient in courage and stamina, and so he sold him to the Duke of Hamilton.

Cortolvin was duly sent to France to be schooled by Yorkshire-born Harry Lamplugh who had trained and ridden the 1862 National winner, *Huntsman*. One year later, he reappeared at Aintree as a 16-1 chance, having been raised 7lb to 11st 13lb, a weight that had never been carried to victory since the race became a handicap in 1843. Again he was ridden by Johnny Page, and they led the field from the second fence to Becher's. Then, most astutely judging the pace to be too frantic, Page held up his horse and so avoided the confusion at the Canal Turn where three contenders for the lead were knocked over. There, one circuit later, he moved to the front and by a comfortable five lengths held off the late challenge of the five year old mare *Fan*, who had a 24lb advantage in the weights.

The well-backed *Fan* would doubtless have been much closer if he had not lost many lengths in being caught up in the mayhem at the Canal Turn. He was to appear in three more Nationals but with the same dismal outcome. Each time, curiously, he refused at the second fence, and consequently for many years that modest obstacle was named after him.

Having watched his reject win the 1867 National, Lord Poulett then saw his only runner, *Genievre*, trail home the last of ten finishers in the 23-strong field. However, he would gain ample consolation when winning one year later, and again in 1871, with *The Lamb*. As for the big-gambling Duke of Hamilton, *Cortolvin*'s success got him out of serious financial difficulties. In addition to £1,600 prize money he reputedly picked up at least £10,000 in winning bets. Furthermore, it was said that he collected another £10,000 in bets when *Cortolvin*, making his last big race appearance, went on win the Scottish National at Bogside.

See also: Page, John; Lamplugh, Harry.

COULTHWAITE, Tom

Born at Pendleton, near Manchester, in 1861, Tom Coulthwaite was the most unusual of all successful National Hunt trainers: a man who had never ridden a horse in his life and yet was responsible for turning out three Grand National winners – *Eremon* (1907), *Jenkinstown* (1910) and *Grakle* (1931).

To be precise, Coulthwaite did make one attempt to ride a horse. But he was immediately thrown and vowed never to try it again. Yet, in his youth, he was tough enough to scrum down for the Swinton Rugby XV and athletic enough to run for Salford Harriers.

C

Before turning to National Hunt training, he worked as a bookmaker's clerk, a provision merchant and a butcher.

It was experience as an athletics coach that led Coulthwaite to the Turf. A bookmaker friend suggested that he might profitably apply his successful stamina-building techniques to training runners of the four-legged variety. He began by purchasing one mare, *Kendale*, whom he trained on the New Barnes course. Then, after winning a race at Carlisle, he decided in 1899 to set up his own stables at Hazelslade, near Hednesford in Staffordshire.

The Hazelslade establishment had a grim history. Some 40 years earlier it had been occupied by the serial poisoner William Palmer. There, after losing heavily in backing his mare, *Nettle*, to win the 1853 Oaks, he had poisoned his wife for £13,000 insurance money, and had then plotted more killings for profit. In striking contrast, this was the happiest of homes for the Coulthwaites, a well-matched couple with so many friends that they needed to hire Rugeley Town Hall when they came to celebrate their golden wedding. And here, to the amazement of the professional racing world, Tom began to achieve wonders as a trainer. In 1902 came the first of his six winnings of the Lancashire Handicap Chase, and the following year, at the Manchester Easter meeting, he saddled eight winners in two days.

The leading NH trainer of his day, Tom had a masterly knack of getting his horses to peak at the right time. Nothing was left to chance. At Hednesford he had replicas of all the major Aintree fences, and of especially testing jumps in France and at other English courses. He was also a firm believer in individual diet for his horses, personally preparing their food and having a diet sheet displayed in each horse's box.

Coulthwaite truly demonstrated his brilliance by turning two lowly rated horses into Grand National winners: *Eremon* and *Jenkinstown*, both bargain buys at £400 and £600 respectively. He got the former so fit for Aintree that, ten days after winning the National, *Eremon* romped home, from pillar to post, in the Lancashire Chase, with an extra 12lb on his back.

In 1913 he suffered a devastating blow, being warned off following an investigation by the National Hunt Committee into the running of two of his horses. But after the First World War, with his licence restored, it was business as usual. Indeed, in 1924, Tom looked set to have a third National winner. His representative was 12 year old *Conjuror II*, recently beaten by only a head in the Cheltenham Gold Cup. Third at Aintree the previous year, *Conjuror II* was still on 11st. Considered to be thrown in at the weights, he went off at 5-2, the shortest priced favourite for 45 years. Unluckily, when well in contention, he was knocked over by a loose horse at the first Becher's.

In 1927, after he had moved to Rugeley in Staffordshire, Coulthwaite's stable included two young chasers, *Gregalach* and *Grakle*. Both were sold that year, the former being moved to Newmarket where Tom Leader trained him to win the 1929 National. Coulthwaite, however, always contended that *Grakle* was the better prospect. The horse remained in his charge and, sure enough, the trainer's opinion was arguably vindicated in 1931 when *Grakle*, at his fifth attempt, got up to win the National, just one and a half lengths ahead of *Gregalach*, who was giving him half a stone. Thus, 21 years after his last success, Old Tom became the fourth man – along with William Holman, W.H. Moore and Aubrey Hastings – to have trained three National winners. A lifelong teetotaller and non-smoker, he retired in 1932 and lived on to see a dozen more Nationals. He died in 1948 at the age of 87.

See also: Eremon; Jenkinstown; Grakle.

COURAGE, Edward Raymond CBE

Following in the frustrated footsteps of Mr J.V. Rank, 'Jock' Hay Whitney and Lord Bicester, brewery magnate Edward Courage was an owner whose persistent pursuit of a Grand National winner was doomed to failure. With 14 runners spanning two decades, this Old Etonian, who bred and trained many fine jumpers near Banbury, Oxfordshire, had to be satisfied with having one runner-up, two horses placed third and three finishing fourth.

Rarely has an owner-trainer set out for National glory in such promising style. Confined to a wheelchair since being struck down with poliomyelitis in 1938, he was 50 years old when he began his long campaign in 1957 with a nine year old mare called *Tiberetta*. His 66-1 outsider, a truly outstanding jumper, finished third. The following year, after winning the Becher Chase, *Tiberetta* went one better – albeit well beaten by *Mr What* – and in 1959 achieved a hat-trick of places as the fourth of only four finishers.

Five years passed before Mr Courage had another strong contender: the well-supported *Border Flight*. But now came tragedy when, as horses bunched up at The Chair, the gelding took an horrendous fall that left jockey Paddy Farrell lying motionless with a broken back. The accident, involving a professional jockey with a wife and four young children to support, highlighted the appalling lack of adequate compensation for such an eventuality. Subsequently, as a leading campaigner for change, Mr Courage was to play a major role in promoting the establishment of the Injured Jockeys' Fund.

Back in the mid-1950s, Mr Courage had employed as a stable lad the 15 year old son of a dairymaid on his Oxfordshire estate. The boy, John Buckingham, rode his first winner in his boss's maroon and yellow colours in 1959 and had his first big success on the stable's *San Angelo* in Cheltenham's Grand Annual Challenge Cup in March 1967. A few weeks later – to the astonishment of both jockey and Mr Courage – he rode the 100-1 outsider *Foinavon* to National victory.

The following year – for the first time since the 1964 tragedy – Mr Courage resumed his bid for National success. His entry, *San Angelo*, finished 12th under Bill Rees, deputising for the injured Buckingham. In 1970, with Buckingham booked for the ride, his *Pride of Kentucky* came home in sixth place; and in 1971 the gelding unseated his rider. Two years later Mr Courage at last had another truly strong contender: *Spanish Steps*, a son of his great *Tiberetta*, and winner of the 1969 Hennessy. Trained by the owner, he finished fourth in the year of *Red Rum*'s brilliant debut.

Mr Courage made his most determined bid in 1974, saddling three runners, *Spanish Steps*, *Royal Relief* and *Quintus*. But none had a chance against the incomparable 'Rummy'. *Royal Relief*, twice a winner of Cheltenham's two-mile Champion Chase, crashed out with Lord Oaksey at the first fence. *Quintus* finished 12th. Meanwhile, just like his dam two decades before, *Spanish Steps* proved remarkably consistent in the National: again fourth in 1974, then third in 1975 and finally ninth as a 13 year old in 1976. But victory was never to be; and Mr Courage died six years later, aged 76.
See also: Injuries.

COURSE CHANGES
It is popularly believed that reforms to the Grand National course are a relatively recent development, reflecting a more humane society and more vigorous campaigning by animal rights activists. In reality, demands for a less hazardous National have been going on intermittently ever since the race began at Aintree in 1839 with eight of 17 starters being fallers, including one fatality.

After the first running, the *Liverpool Mercury* carried an editorial condemning the extreme hazards of the race. 'It was no doubt a very exciting spectacle, but we no more be reconciled to it on that account than we are to cockfighting, bullbaiting or any other popular pastime which is attended with the infliction of wanton torture to any living being.'

Remarkably, this adverse reaction came at a time when the majority of the fences (then 29 jumps in all) were much less daunting than those of today; and when the distance was shorter (two circuits totalling roughly four miles). In 1839 most fences comprised no more than a gorse-topped, 2ft high bank with a ditch on the near side. Certainly, it was a severe test of stamina since the race was mainly run over ploughed farmland. But there were only three really formidable obstacles: a stone wall, 4ft 8in high, towards the end of the first circuit and in front of the stands, and two treacherous jumps over brooks. And such was the ill-defined nature of the course that, from 1839 to 1849, the rules stipulated: 'No rider to open a gate or ride through a gateway, or more than 100 yards along any road, footpath or driftway.'

Since then the Grand National course has undergone many modifications. Today it is an oval circuit covering two miles and two furlongs, with 16 fences, 14 of which must be jumped twice. Over the years the most important changes have been as follows:

1841 The Stone Wall, responsible the previous year for eliminating four of twelve starters, including the **1839** Winner *Lottery*, is replaced by an artificial Water Jump, 10ft wide and 3ft deep, with a thorn fence on the take-off side.

1843 Disregarding the views of owners and riders, the racecourse executive chooses to re-introduce the Stone Wall – presumably for the sake of dramatic spectacle. Two horses crash out here amid shattered masonry; and *Lottery* only escapes disaster by putting in a quite extraordinary leap.

1844 The Stone Wall is eliminated once and for all, and the Water Jump becomes a permanent feature.

C

1845 Two sections of the course are laid with turf for the first time but for the most part the race continues to be run over deep ploughed fields.

1858 Flags are erected in line with the outer limits of fences to prevent a reccurrence of the advantage stolen by the 1857 winner (*Emigrant*) who was taken wide of the ploughed land between the Canal Turn and Valentine's to run on firmish ground.

1862 This year, tragically, a jockey suffers a fatal fall in a pile-up at the plain fence before the Water Jump. Consequently, to slow the pace at this point, an open ditch is introduced on the approach side to the fence now known as The Chair. At the same time the race is made more testing. The overall distance is increased by about two furlongs, making a trip of almost four and a half miles; and the erection of posts and rails at Becher's and Valentine's make these fences still more challenging.

1885 At last the entire Grand National course is turfed and fully marked out on the inside by running rails, so giving it its present-day appearance. Although it did not form part of the course proper, a preliminary hurdle is now introduced and, as a loosening-up procedure, it was a compulsory jump on the way down to the start.

1888 By marginally cutting off the final turn leading back towards the finish the course is shortened by about 25 yards, bringing it closer to its present distance of four miles 856 yards. However, any advantage gained by the change is offset by the introduction of two plain fences to replace the easier hurdles before the run-in. Indeed, from this time, all remaining hurdles gave way to proper fences.

1907 The preliminary hurdle, introduced in 1885, is now dispensed with.

1929 Following the huge pile-up caused by *Easter Hero* the previous year, the great ditch on the take-off side of the Canal Turn is filled in.

1955 Following four fatalities in the 1954 National the landing ground over Becher's is marginally raised and the following fence (No. 7) is lowered six inches to bring it to the minimum 4ft 6in allowed under National Hunt rules.

1961 From this year, the fences, though still formidable, are no longer so uninvitingly upright on approach. In response to fierce criticism in recent years, they are furnished with sloping 'aprons' on the take-off side.

1980 Following the previous year's huge pile-up at The Chair, gaps are left in the inner running rail so that riderless horses approaching The Chair have a convenient way out. Unfortunately, as the race shows, horses cannot be relied upon to make their way to the nearest exit.

1990 The death of the handsome grey *Dark Ivy* in 1987 and two more horses in 1989 (all falling at Becher's) leads to a public outcry that cannot be ignored. Most notably, the treacherous V-shaped ditch on the landing side of Becher's is filled in to provide level ground. Spectators are no longer allowed to stand next to the rail on the approach to the fence. More importantly, the outside running rail besides Becher's is moved back from the course and guarded by a newly planted hedge – measures which eliminate the danger of horses being suddenly distracted by the sight of a wall of photographers and spectators beyond the brook. Plastic rails – replacing wooden ones – are also introduced.

1999 The previous year, when only six horses completed the course, five had fallen at the first fence and three had fallen fatally by the fifth. Now, in an attempt to reduce the chances of an early pile-up, the first fence is widened by two metres, making it the widest on any steeplechase course in the country. In addition the landing level over Becher's and The Chair is marginally raised.

2001 In November, 2000, a number of jockeys riding in the Becher Chase had commented that the National fences are still too upright. The authorities now respond by introducing a more prominent guard rail and a deeper toe board to fences, with extra spruce above the guard rail to make an improved slope on the apron. Jockeys find the fences more inviting, with horses less likely to back off them.

See also: Fences; Becher's; Canal Turn; Foinavon; The Chair; Water Jump; Valentine's.

COVENTRY, Captain Henry

An officer in the Grenadier Guards, Captain Henry Coventry established a 100 per cent record as a Grand National rider. He appeared only once in the race, at the age of 23, and he won by a head – in 1865 on the five year old chestnut entire *Alcibiade*.

That year his cousin, Lord Coventry, had two former winners in the National: the sisters *Emblem* and *Emblematic*. But in the end the only serious challenge to *Alcibiade* came from six year old *Hall Court*, a 50-1 outsider ridden by another Army officer, Captain A.C. Tempest of the 11th Light Dragoons. Barely half a length divided them when

Hall Court landed first over the 30th fence, and throughout the long run-in they were inseparable, with both officers making frantic use of the whip. They finished a full 50 yards ahead of the 5-1 favourite, last year's winner *Emblematic*; and the result was uncertain until called by the judge.

This narrowest of victories was extraordinary on a number of counts. It was a first National for both horse and rider. *Alcibiade*, the first French-bred horse to win the race, had never run in a steeplechase before; and Coventry had little experience of riding in public. A five year old horse had never previously won the National; and for much of the race Coventry took his mount wide, on the longest way round. The captain was much criticised by spectators for taking the outside route; however, it crucially kept him out of trouble in a race that saw only six of 23 starters complete the course.

Though *Alcibiade* never won another race, he was to appear in five more Nationals, finishing third, fourth and eighth in 1868-1870. His great rival, *Hall Court*, contested six more Nationals, finishing runner-up with Captain Tempest again in 1869. In contrast, Captain Coventry – popularly known as 'Bee' and renowned for his strong Anglo-Saxon language when meeting trouble in a race – never rode in the National again. The following year, along with his lordly cousin and Mr B.J. Angell, the owner of *Alcibiade*, he was one of 13 members of the newly formed Grand National Hunt Committee which now took responsibility for administering and governing steeplechasing. His last notable win, on Mr Henry Chaplin's *Emperor III*, was achieved in the 1867 National Hunt Steeplechase run at Clapham Park, near Bedford.

See also: Alciabiade; Tempest, Captain Arthur Cecil.

COVENTRY, Lord (George William, 9th Earl)

A founder member of the Grand National Hunt Committee in 1866, Lord Coventry became a key figure in the development of steeplechasing and in particular he helped to restore and advance the prestige of the Grand National. At the age of 25, he made a sensational start as the owner of National runners, beginning with two successive winners – seven year old *Emblem* (1863) and that mare's six year old sister *Emblematic* (1864). He had bought them for only 300 guineas and 250 guineas respectively, and most importantly he had the services of his close friend George Stevens, who would go on to ride National winners a record five times.

London-born (May 9, 1838), educated at Eton and Christ Church, Oxford, Lord Coventry was an expert in breeding and an owner with many horses trained at his family seat at Earl's Croome, near Kinnersley, Worcestershire. But his National challengers were few and far between. In 1865, he ran his two former winners in a hat-trick bid. Both were heavily clobbered by the handicapper – *Emblematic*, with Stevens, finishing a distant third, and *Emblem* being pulled up. Two years later his five year old *Tennyson*, a 50-1 outsider, finished eighth with Stevens. Then, in 1868, his quest for a third National win ended in tragedy. His top-weighted six year old *Chimney Sweep* went off as the 7-1 favourite but never even reached the first fence. Clipping one of the boulders that then marked the way across the Melling Road, he broke a foreleg and had to be put down.

It was to be 19 years before Lord Coventry again had a runner in the National – *Mediator*, a 100-1 no-hoper who was a faller in 1897. More seriously, he next challenged with *Inquistor*, the 6-1 joint favourite in 1902. Disappointingly, the seven year old black gelding fell after having led midway on the first circuit. The following year he fell at the second, and in 1904, though a well-supported 9-1 chance, he fell at the fourth.

Lord Coventry did not contest the National again, though he might well have achieved a third success but for an error in judgment. In 1905 he had seen an Irish-bred entire, *Ascetic's Silver*, fall at the third and then continue riderless to complete the full National course ahead of the winner *Kirkland*. Following the death of his owner-breeder, the entire came up for sale and Lord Coventry, ignoring expert advice, was the underbidder when Aubrey Hastings went to 800 guineas on behalf of Prince Franz Hatzfeldt. Trained and ridden by Hastings, *Ascetic's Silver* duly won the 1906 National by a comfortable ten lengths.

Elsewhere, however, Lord Coventry continued to have racing successes until well into his eighties. Most famously the story is told of how he entered a bookmaker's office in 1923, removed his hat and gloves, and then declared: 'I would like £100 each-way on my mare *Verdict* in the Cambridgeshire.' He was leaving the office when, on impulse, he turned back and said, 'No, I think I'll have £200 each-way.' The inspired last-minute change earned him an extra

C

£2,000 as *Verdict*, dam of the 1935 Oaks and 1936 Ascot Gold Cup winner *Quashed*, won by a neck from the powerful French horse *Epinard*. Lord Coventry died seven years later, aged 91.
See also: Emblem; Emblematic.

COVERTCOAT

Seven year old winner of the 1913 Grand National, scoring by a distance from the only other finishers, *Irish Mail* and the remounted *Carsey*. Only once before, in 1882, had so few horses completed the course. But then there were only 12 starters. This time a field of 22 had been reduced to just three by the second Becher's. At that stage, *Carsey* was the strong-looking leader. However, he came to grief at the final fence, leaving *Covertcoat* to gallop home in his own good time. The victory gave 31 year old jockey Percy Woodland his second National win, ten years after his first success on *Drumcree*. It also provided a third winner for owner Sir Charles Assheton-Smith, and the second in successive years for Sir Charles and trainer Robert Gore.

Irish-bred – by *Hackler* out of *Cinnamon* – *Covertcoat* was a half-brother to the 1910 National winner *Jenkinstown*. After being hunted for a while, he won the Maiden Plate at Punchestown and was then sent to Goffs Sales in Dublin when his owner-trainer-breeder, Mr James Maher, decided to give up training. There, like the 1912 Aintree hero, *Jerry M*, he was bought (for £1,075) by the shrewd Bob Gore on Sir Charles's behalf. Thus, they had picked up two National winners for a mere £2,275.

In the 1912 National *Covertcoat* was a 33-1 shot who, like his half-brother, failed to finish. The following year, on the strength of one promising win over three and a half miles at Sandown in December, he was made one of four joint second favourites for his Aintree return. Ernie Piggott, last year's winning jockey on *Jerry M*, was booked to ride. But then a late injury led to his replacement by Woodland, who came in for a winning ride just as he had done as a last minute substitute on *Drumcree*.

In 1914 the winning combination challenged again, this time as the clear 7-1 favourite. But *Covertcoat* had been unsuccessful in his three prior races and he had been raised more than a stone to 12st 7lb. Unsurprisingly, he failed to finish in a race won *Sunloch*, who was receiving a full three stone from the 1913 winner. Though only eight years old, he was now retired.

See also: Assheton-Smith, Sir Charles; Gore, Robert; Woodland, Percy.

CRICKMERE, John

As an amateur rider, during the first decade of the Grand National, Mr John Crickmere established a remarkable record of consistency. Making just three appearances in the race, he never failed to complete the course, finishing third, first and fourth. And but for a freak stroke of bad luck he would have won the National at his first attempt.

On his Aintree debut in 1843, when the National was a handicap race for the first time, Mr Crickmere was riding the Cheltenham-trained *Dragsman*, a 10-1 chance, fourth in the betting, Heading the market in a 16-strong field was *Peter Simple*, third in the two previous years, former winner *Lottery*, and last year's fourth, *The Returned*.

Patiently ridden on the first circuit, *Dragsman* avoided the bunching that saw two horses crash out at the notorious Stone Wall, which was never again to be included among the obstacles. Crickmere then spurred him on in pursuit of *Peter Simple*, finally taking over the lead after the second Becher's. With the top-weighted favourite visibly tiring, *Dragsman* pulled away from the field and looked a certain winner coming to the last. But then, inexplicably, he suddenly swerved off course, jumping a gate and bolting down a side lane.

Vanguard and *Nimrod* were now left to fight out the finish, with the former prevailing by three lengths. Meanwhile Crickmere had managed to regain control of *Dragsman* and take him back to tackle the last fence. Incredibly, despite the long detour, they finished third – only half a length behind the runner-up.

One year later Crickmere had a more obvious chance. His mount, *Discount*, was a six year old entire who had been such a total flop on the Flat that he had changed hands many times, being sold at an ever-increasing discount – hence his name. But now he had proved such a natural jumper that he was made the 5-1 joint favourite in his first National.

Carrying a moderate weight in a field of only 15 runners, *Discount* was the least inconvenienced by the quagmire conditions. Crickmere delayed his challenge until approaching the final fence and then, once over, they powered away for an easy win by 20 lengths from *The Returned*, with *Tom Tug* one length back in third. *Discount*, the first six year old winner, did not run in the National again; and Crickmere made his last appearance the following year when taking over on *Tom Tug* and finishing fourth. *See also:* Discount.

CRISP

Arguably, the greatest chaser to run in the Grand National without actually winning; and certainly the most impressive runner-up in the history of the race. Admittedly, 1961 modifications had made Aintree's most daunting fences more horse-friendly. Nevertheless, the jumping performance of ten-year-old *Crisp* in 1973 was extraordinary, breathtaking, unforgettable. On his Aintree debut, he opened up a lead of at least 25 lengths and shattered the course record by more than 18 seconds. Yet, caught in the last strides, he cruelly went down by three-quarters of a length to an eight year old gelding with a massive 23lb advantage in the weights – a horse called *Red Rum*.

A bay gelding – by *Rose Argent* out of *Wheat Germ* – *Crisp* was bred in Australia by his owner Sir Chester Manifold and had won twice on the Flat and five times over hurdles before emerging as a champion chaser, most notably with his winning of the Melbourne Cup Chase. He arrived in England in November, 1970, having triumphed en route in America's Carolina Hunt Cup; and he was to be trained at Uplands, Lambourn, by the masterful Fred Winter who had already saddled two National winners, the American *Jay Trump* (1965) and *Anglo* (1966).

Since eight year old *Crisp* had not had the requisite three runs in Britain to guide the handicapper, he was automatically burdened with top weight of 12st 7lb for his first race in England. It was a two-mile handicap chase at Wincanton, and astonishingly he made light of the weight, storming round under Paul Kelleway to win by 15 lengths. The following month, at Cheltenham, he was even more dominant over two miles, winning the Queen Mother Champion Chase by 25 lengths. At this point, however, it was never dreamed that the free-running *Crisp* might become a contender over the Grand National's marathon distance. His target was the Cheltenham Gold Cup and there were even doubts about such a speedy two-miler staying that trip over three and a quarter miles.

Winter gradually built him up for three-mile racing, and to such good effect that in 1972 – following a weight-giving Kempton victory over *The Dikler* and *Kinloch Brae* – he was made the Gold Cup antepost favourite. But then, with unfavoured soft going encountered at Cheltenham, the trainer judged that *Crisp* would need to be held up to get the trip. It was an error. The big Aussie liked to bowl along in front; now, resentful of being restrained, he lacked his usual zest and from two fences out ran sluggishly to finish only fifth.

The following year saw a dramatic change in tactics. *Crisp* was to be put back to two miles at the Cheltenham Festival and, 18 days later, sent over more than double the distance in the Grand National. Again held up, he finished third in the Champion Chase. Yet he was by no means underrated for his National debut. Along with *L'Escargot*, the former dual Gold Cup winner, he was allotted the top-weight of 12st and went off with *Red Rum* as the joint 9-1 favourite in a 38-strong field.

This time, it was decided, *Crisp* was not to be restrained in the early stages; and the outcome was sensational. Never had a chaser tackled the National fences with such seemingly contemptuous ease. *Grey Sombrero*, the Whitbread Gold Cup winner, led approaching the first Becher's. But there the Australian champion put in a huge jump to begin the most exhilarating display of front-running ever seen at Aintree. Thriving on the fast going, taking the Winter-favoured inside route, he was ten lengths clear after the 12th fence, 15 lengths approaching The Chair, and a staggering 25 lengths ahead by the 19th. Thereafter, only one horse – the lightly weighted *Red Rum* – could make any impression on the runaway leader.

Two fences out, *Crisp* gave the first signs of tiring, but coming to the last he was still some 15 lengths ahead of his nearest rival. Now, however, that punishing, 494-yard run-in on the flat took its terrible toll. Having enjoyed a dream ride for more than four miles, jockey Richard Pitman felt his mount losing his smooth action, and for the first time he decided to pick up his stick just to wake him up.

His own harshest critic, Pitman subsequently judged it to be 'a fatal and basic riding error' that cost him three lengths – and the race. When he took his right hand off the reins, *Crisp* drifted further to the left – only fractionally off-line approaching the Elbow but enough to make a crucial difference as *Red Rum* steadily closed the gap and nosed ahead just two strides before the winning post. Both horses

C

had smashed *Golden Miller's* 39 year old course record, finishing 25 lengths ahead of third placed *L'Escargot*. As radio commentator Peter Bromley fairly observed: 'We will never see another race like that in a hundred years.'

Eight months later the two record-breakers met again, at Doncaster in a match at level weights of 11st 10lb. *Crisp's* victory by eight lengths was taken as confirmation of his superiority. But it was *Red Rum* – not *Crisp* – whose exploits would bring him the most enduring fame. Having scored two wins after his great National run, *Crisp* ran six more times without success, ending his career with a fourth place in the 1975 Whitbread Gold Cup. Having developed leg trouble, he was now retired to the hunting field in Yorkshire. Aged 22, Australia's classiest chaser died of a heart attack out hunting in 1985, while his more celebrated rival would enjoy public adulation for another decade.

See also: Red Rum; Winter, Frederick; Pitman, Richard.

CRUMP, Neville Franklin

A leading National Hunt figure for more than half century, Neville Crump stands out as one of the greatest trainers in the history of steeplechasing. His Grand National record rates alongside the best: three wins – with *Sheila's Cottage* (1948), *Teal* (1952) and *Merryman II* (1960) – and five places. In addition he trained the winners of five Scottish Nationals, three Whitbread Gold Cups, two Welsh Nationals, a Hennessy, the Massey-Ferguson and Mackeson Gold Cups, the Grand Sefton Chase, the Topham Trophy, the Mildmay of Flete and Cathcart Challenge Cup.

Born on December 27, 1910, in Beckenham, Kent, the son of an outstanding horseman and one-time rancher in Australia, Crump was educated at Marlborough and Balliol, Oxford, where he joined the cavalry squadron before going on to take a commission in the 4th Hussars. He became a prominent rider in point-to-points, rode as an amateur under Rules, and after four years' service he resigned from the Army in 1935, mainly because he felt cavalry regiments should be involved with horses not tanks.

His training career, begun in 1937 on a small scale at Upavon on Salisbury Plain, was soon interrupted by the Second World War. Initially he served with the North Somerset Yeomanry in Palestine and later, with the rank of captain, became responsible for tank training at Barnard Castle, Co. Durham. On demob, he settled in Middleham, Yorkshire, where he rapidly built up one of the most powerful stables in the land – one so formidable that he would have strong contenders in most of the Grand Nationals held over the next quarter of a century.

The great upturn in Crump's fortunes followed his success in the 1948 Grand National with the 50-1 victory of *Sheila's Cottage*, an ill-tempered mare that only his stable jockey Arthur Thompson could control. Two years later he saddled *Wot No Sun*, the runner-up to *Freebooter*; and in 1952 he took first and third place with *Teal* and *Wot No Sun* respectively, while his two other runners – *Skyreholme*, ridden by Dick Francis, and 100-1 outsider *Travellers' Pride* – were fallers. That year he finished as the National Hunt champion trainer with 41 wins.

In 1953 the brilliant *Teal* was made the ante-post favourite for the National, but sadly he never returned to Aintree. He fatally ruptured a gut during the Cheltenham Gold Cup, a race which Crump had confidently expected him to win. In 1957, his 5-1 clear National favourite, *Goosander*, finished a disappointing sixth, but at least the captain had the consolation of winning the first Whitbread Gold Cup with *Much Obliged* and ending that season as champion trainer with 39 wins.

Crump enjoyed his most rewarding victory three years later – when nine year old *Merryman II*, the 13-2 favourite, romped home to win the first televised Grand National by 15 lengths. It was his third success in the race – equalling the triple triumphs of trainers William Holman and Vincent O'Brien – and a training feat all the more creditable since Crump had struggled to get *Merryman II* ready in time after suffering an inflamed bone in a foot.

The captain rated *Merryman II* 'the best Liverpool horse I have trained – one of the few greats', a judgment fully merited on the strength of his running in the 1961 National. That year, the ten year old returned to Aintree with an extra stone on his back and still managed to finish second – behind *Nicolaus Silver* who had a 25lb advantage. In 1963 the Crump-trained *Springbok*, a first fence faller the previous year, went off as the 10-1 favourite. He finished fifth and was sixth the following year.

In 1966, the captain had yet another strong challenger in *Forest Prince*, owned by Mrs D. Thompson whose father Frank Bibby had won with *Kirkland* (1905) and *Glenside* (1911). Ridden by

Gerry Scott, who had triumphed on *Merryman II*, he finished third in a 47-strong field. Two years later, the super-consistent trainer took fourth place with *Rutherfords*, ridden by his now regular rider Pat Buckley. His other runners, 50-1 chances *Phemus* and *Forecastle*, were both pulled up.

For the 1969 National he saddled Lady Hay's *Arcturus* who finished sixth under top weight. Then he ran *Permit* (1970), brought down; *Canharis* (1973), brought down; *San Feliu* (1974), ninth; *Glen Owen* (1975), fell; *Collingwood* (1977), ninth; *Irish Tony* (1978), fell; *Salkeld* (1980), fell; and *Imperial Black* who, after falling in 1984, finished sixth at 66-1 in 1985.

Captain Crump was renowned for his scrupulousness and honesty, a trainer whose horses were reliably well prepared and ran on their merits. He was 72 when he saddled *Canton*, his fifth Scottish National winner; 77 when he sent out his last Grand National runner: *Repington* who refused at the 18th in 1988. Having retired the following year, he died in 1997 at the age of 86.

See also: Sheila's Cottage; Teal; Merryman II; Thompson, Arthur Patrick; Scott, Gerald; Buckley, Pat.

CULLINAN, Thomas Brady

Having just turned professional, the Irish ex-amateur Tommy Cullinan had the most extraordinary introduction to the Grand National. On his 1928 debut – aboard the champion American chaser, *Billy Barton*, a 33-1 chance – he found himself coming to the final fence with only one of the 41 other starters left in the race. But then his mount hit the last and sunk to the ground on landing. At the same time, the 100-1 shot *Tipperary Tim* put in a clean jump and went on to win by a distance. Remounting with difficulty, Tommy rode on to finish second – and last.

Cullinan was again on *Billy Barton* (raised 10lb in the weights) in 1929 when the National had an all-time record 66 starters. This time, being among a vast number of fallers, he was unable to remount. But now he was entering the golden period of his strangely mixed racing career. In 1930 he returned to Aintree as the great hero of Cheltenham, having recently won both the Gold Cup (on *Easter Hero*) and the Champion Hurdle (on *Brown Tony*) – a big race double never before achieved by the same jockey and trainer (Jack Anthony) combination.

When *Easter Hero*, owned by American millionaire 'Jock' Hay Whitney, was found unfit for the National, Tommy took the ride on second favourite *Shaun Goilin*. It was a case of third time lucky. At the second last, when close-up behind the mare *Melleray's Belle* and Mr Whitney's full-of-running *Sir Lindsay*, Cullinan lost his stirrups; and he was still narrowly behind coming to the last. But *Sir Lindsay* hit that fence hard and crucially his jockey Dudley Williams also lost his irons on landing.

In the circumstances it was incredible that the riders were able to join in the closest finish seen for 48 years. Cullinan drove home his pale chestnut to score by just a neck from Scottish-owned *Melleray's Belle*, with the somewhat unfortunate *Sir Lindsay* just one and a half lengths back in third. Thus, he became the first man to have won the National, Gold Cup and Champion Hurdle in the same year.

Sadly, Cullinan's luck now began to run out. He had four more National rides – *South Hill* (1931), *Evolution* (1932), *Kilbuck* (1934) and *Trocadero* (1935) – but all were long-shots that fell. Year by year he had found bookings increasingly scarce, and in 1935 he retired from the saddle to turn to training, first as a permit-holder, then as a Didcot-based licensed jumps trainer. It was not a success. Then came the war and a tragic ending. Having enlisted as a private, he was serving with an Anti-Aircraft unit when he suffered an overwhelming fit of depression and used his rifle to take his own life.

See also: Shaun Goilin; Tipperary Tim.

CULLOTY, James Hugh

In 2002 Jim Culloty became only the sixth jockey to win the Cheltenham Gold Cup and the Grand National in the same season. The former success was achieved with *Best Mate*, whom he gave a copybook ride as stable jockey to Henrietta Knight and Terry Biddlecombe. The latter was with *Bindaree*, a ride he only picked up three days before the race – after Jamie Goldstein as third choice had suffered a broken leg in a fall at Ludlow and Tom Scudamore had declined the ride to stay loyal to Mark Pitman's *Smarty*.

It was a glorious, unforgettable double for a 28 year old Irishman who had taken a long, hard and tortuous path to develop into a highly professional jockey. Born in Killarney on December 18, 1973, the son of an accountant, he showed no natural talent for riding in his early years. Yet he always

C

loved horses, so much so that in his early teens he worked as a part-time hotel porter to save the money to buy a pony. At 18, he found work at a point-to-point yard in Cornwall – not expecting to make a career as a jockey but just for the sake of working with horses.

In his year with David and Lyn Broomfield, he rode four point-to-point winners. More importantly, he gained invaluable experience and strengthened up mentally and physically. Then, after two years with another small stable, he joined Knight's yard at West Lockinge Farm, near Wantage, Oxfordshire, riding his first winner (*Karicleigh Boy*) at Exeter in January, 1994. There, as he subsequently acknowledged, he owed a huge debt to former champion jockey Biddlecombe who 'more or less changed my riding style'. In the 1995-96 season he was the champion amateur rider with 40 wins.

His first notable wins came in 1996: on *Stompin* (Cordon Bleu Hurdle); *Morceli* (Peregrine Chase); and *Proud Sun* (Horse and Hound Cup). But it was four years before he had a truly major ride: on Jim Lewis's *Best Mate* in the Supreme Novices' Hurdle at the Cheltenham Festival. After getting boxed in, he was devastated to finish in second place. It was the key point in his career. Despite criticism of his ride, trainer and owner crucially remained supportive. He went on to ride his first Festival winner: *Lord Noelie* in the Royal and SunAlliance Novices' Chase.

Subsequently, he feared for the worst when a broken right arm cost him the ride on *Lord Noelie* in the Hennessy Cognac Gold Cup and on *Best Mate* in the King George VI Chase. Champion jockey Tony McCoy took over on the latter, but unsuccessfully; and, to Culloty's great relief, he was promised that he could resume on *Best Mate* in the Gold Cup. Following his impressive victory at Cheltenham, he was without a ride in the National. Mark Pitman then offered him the ride on *Browjoshy* but to his dismay that horse became the first reserve for Aintree after missing the 40-runner cut. Happily, Pitman now agreed to release him to be a late substitute on *Bindaree*.

At that time Culloty – nicknamed 'Snoze' by his colleagues because of his big nose – had a Grand National record of three rides and three falls. On his National debut in 1997 he had fallen at the first fence after landing too steeply on *Full Of Oats*. In 2000 and 2001 he was on *Village King* for Philip Hobbs, going down at the 20th and the eighth re-

spectively. Now he proved himself to be a hugely improved horseman, avoiding the first fence chaos that saw nine horses eliminated, hunting round in mid-field for much of the way, taking the lead at the second Becher's and then, after surrendering it to *What's Up Boys* at the last, switching *Bindaree* at the Elbow to produce a brillliant finishing burst up the rail to win by three-quarters of a length.

The following December he again suffered the huge disappointment of losing the King George VI ride on *Best Mate* – this time as a result of a three-day suspension for dropping his hands and losing third place in a Doncaster bumper. McCoy took over and won. But no matter. More glory lay ahead with his masterful handling of *Best Mate* to triumph by ten lengths at Cheltenham for the first back-to-back Gold Cup success since *L'Escargot* 32 years before.

On to the Grand National, this time aboard *Maximize*, trained by Henrietta Knight and owned by her sister, Lady Vestey. He was now biddng for a unique 'double-double' – back-to-back winners of the Gold Cup and the National. Hopes were high since the nine year old gelding was a 16-1 chance who had never fallen and had recently been a useful fourth in the William Hill Handicap Chase at Cheltenham. But after chasing the leaders to The Chair, *Maximize* visibly weakened and then was one of five fallers at the 19th.

Nevertheless this was Culloty's best season so far – 51 wins, 31 of them on Knight-trained horses, including *Midland Flame* in the Martell Cognac Novices' Handicap Chase at the Grand National meeting. It climaxed with victory in the Irish National when he was making his first appearance in the race and riding for the first time the Dessie Hughes-trained *Timbera*, whom he judged to be 'a brilliant jumper, just the type for the Aintree National'.

The 2003-4 season brought the perfect and most unexpected consolation for his previous loss of the winning ride on *Best Mate* in the King George VI. To the absolute delight of Henrietta Knight – and the bookies – he won the great race on *Edredon Bleu* at 25-1. Two days later he rode *Best Mate* to victory in the valuable Ericsson Chase at Leopardstown. Then at the Cheltenham Festival, came wild celebrations of an all-Kerry win in the Champion Bumper on *Total Enjoyment* followed by an unforgettable third successive victory on *Best Mate* in the Gold Cup.

The Grand National, however, brought a huge disappointment when he lost a ride on the favourite

Timbera, withdrawn after being found to have mucus in his lungs. There was some consolation when he scored a notable shock win on the eve of the National: bringing home *Cassia Heights* in a chaotic, 29-runner Topham Chase at 33-1 (74-1 on the Tote!). But in the big race he was now on a 33-1 chance, *Just In Debt*, who survived several blunders before being hampered by a loose horse and unseating his rider at the Foinavon (23rd). He finished the season with a total of 58 wins that had earned more than £1 million in prize money.

Unluckily the new season brought a major setback when a fall at Exeter resulted in him needing surgery for serious damage to his right thumb. Returning to the saddle after a six-week layoff, he said that he intended to ride for another five years – to pay for the future home he was building in Co. Cork.

His great disappointment in 2005 was the withdrawal of *Best Mate* from the Cheltenham Gold Cup. Henrietta Knight was also without a runner in the National. However, he was booked for a strong Irish contender in *Nil Desperandum*, a 16-1 chance, and they advanced well on the second circuit to take the £10,500 prize money for sixth place. Four months later, having been left feeling dazed whenever suffering a fall, he retired for health reasons at the relatively tender age of 31 and bought a farm in Co. Cork. Subsequently, he started a family with his wife Susie, took out a training licence and had 30 boxes built at his new home in Churchtown, the village where the great Vincent O'Brien began his training career.

See also: Bindaree; Twiston-Davies, Nigel.

CUNNINGHAM, Thomas

Run on desperately heavy ground, the 1849 Grand National developed into a two-horse race between the bay *Peter Simple* and *The Knight of Gwynne*. Captain D'Arcy, owner and rider of the latter, had staked a substantial sum on his horse, a well-fancied 8-1 chance. And so, on the run-in, when they could make no impression on *Peter Simple*, he shouted out offers, rising from £1,000 to £4,000, for his rival to surrender the lead. But Tom Cunningham, on *Peter Simple*, was not to be bought. He drove the bay home to win by three lengths with the 5-1 favourite, *Prince George*, a distance back in third.

Like the 11 year old *Peter Simple* (not to be confused with the grey entire of the same name that had been runner-up in 1845) amateur rider Cunningham was making his first appearance in the race. Fortuitously, they profited from a false start which resulted in a *fait accompli* as starter Lord Sefton's efforts to recall the 24 runners were drowned by the roar of the crowd. *Peter Simple* stole an early lead and held it while so many floundered behind, three falling fatally and only six completing the course.

Cunningham was so encouraged that he bought the 20-1 winner before challenging again the following year. This time the combination went off as 5-1 favourites in a record field of 32 starters. *But Peter Simple* had been raised 16lb to top weight of 12st 2lb and he never got into the race after colliding with another runner at the first. Little *Abd-El-Kader*, carrying a mere 9st 12st and unquoted in the betting, won by a length; and again, with a new owner and rider, *The Knight Of Gwynne* was runner-up.

In the 1851 National, with a professional booked for the ride, *Peter Simple* again failed to finish. Presuming him to be past his best, Cunningham now sold the 13 year old. But *Peter Simple* proved everyone wrong. After falling in 1852 and again being sold, the veteran came back in 1853 with the great Tom Olliver to win a second National, scoring by three lengths at the ripe old age of 15 – an all-time record that will never be equalled.

See also: Peter Simple (Bay).

CURE-ALL

The first big shock winner of a Grand National, by two lengths in 1845 when he was a newcomer and outsider not even quoted in the official betting. It was a fairy-tale ending for his owner-rider, Lincolnshire farmer Mr William Loft. He had bought *Cure-All* for £60 after the horse, with a £260 reserve price, had fallen and crippled himself when giving a demonstration of his jumping at the Horncastle Fair sales.

Yorkshire-bred – by *Physician* out of an unrecorded mare – *Cure-All* was owned by a horse-dealer and then by a Northampton tailor before being sent to the sales in 1843. After the lame brown gelding had been nursed back to fitness by his devoted groom Kitty Crisp, farmer Loft rode him regularly to the Brocklesby Hounds, then decided to try him in a chase at Lincoln. *Cure-All* fell at the last but, after being remounted, was beaten only a neck by a well-proven chaser called *Crocus*.

Cure-All now became a late entry for the 1845 National, but only by a chance occurrence. The

C

nominated runner of Mr W. Sterling Crawford had suffered an injury, and so it was agreed that the nomination could be transferred to *Cure-All* provided that the horse ran in Mr Crawford's name. Though he had little experience of steeplechasing, Mr Loft, the true owner, was allowed to take the ride.

According to contemporary reports, the dutiful Kitty Crisp walked all the way – well over a hundred miles – in leading *Cure-All* to Liverpool from the farm at Healing near Grimsby. At Aintree they encountered such icy conditions (the Leeds and Liverpool Canal was completely frozen over) that Mr Loft and another owner protested to the stewards. The race, delayed until nearly five o'clock, was only run after they had been out-voted by other owners.

Following the controversial last-minute withdrawal of the 5-1 favourite *The Knight Templar* – said to have met with an accident – the 1843 winner *Vanguard*, again ridden by the great Tom Olliver, led the betting at 4-1. Briefly *Cure-All* was quoted at 15-1 but he was not sufficiently backed to gain an official starting price.

The ground was indeed treacherous, 11 of the 15 runners failing to finish and one of them being destroyed. Though *Vanguard* led from the start, he could not handle the going and had to be pulled up after completing one circuit. Making a late challenge, *Cure-All* scored by two lengths and two over the grey *Peter Simple* and *The Exquisite* respectively – a success made possible by Loft who had artfully found a strip of better ground on the second circuit.

The following day, *Cure-All* and Kitty made the long walk back home, being greeted on arrival by the ringing out of the Healing church bells. One year later, with Mr Loft officially recognised as the rider-owner, the brown gelding returned to Aintree, this time being priced at 16-1. But now his weight had been raised 13lb to a top weight of 12st 4lb and he faced a much stronger field of 22 runners. In this, his last National, he soon had to be pulled up. Meanwhile, Mr Crawford's bid to be the winning owner in successive years was denied when his six year old *Veluti*, the 11-2 clear favourite, broke down in the lead at the second last.
See also: Loft, William.

CZECH REPUBLIC AND SLOVAKIA
Horse racing, especially over jumps, has a long tradition founded in the days of the old Czechoslovakia – Slovakia broke away peacefully on January 1,

1993 – and surviving throughout the years of Communist rule. Most famously, the Czech Republic stages – usually on the second Sunday in October – the Velka Pardubicka, a cross-country race over four miles and two and a half furlongs and 32 obstacles which vies with the Grand National for the title of 'most demanding steeplechase in the world'.

The old Czechoslovakia was first represented in the Grand National in 1931 when *Gyi Lovam* (on 11st 3lb) went off as a 100-1 outsider. A winner of the marathon Pardubicka, he was going well when, along with the 5-1 favourite *Easter Hero*, he was one of several victims of a pile-up caused by a riderless horse at Becher's. His rider-owner, Captain Rudi Popler, gamely remounted and fought hard to catch the leaders before falling at the last open ditch.

It was not until 1986 that another Czech runner, again a 100-1 outsider, appeared at Aintree. A talented staying chaser named *Essex*, he was an eight year old finely muscled black stallion, bred in Hungary, with Russian and Venezuelan blood lines, and a winner of six races over fences. Frozen ground had prevented him having a run in the six months since he had fallen towards the end of the marathon Pardubicka when 300 metres clear of the field. Nevertheless, he was reputedly in prime condition and coachloads of Czech supporters travelled over to cheer him on.

Unfortunately, the bold jumping entire – owned by the Workers Co-operative and ridden by his trainer, 37 year old Mr Valcav Chaloupka – paid the penalty for being without the necessary British race form to guide the handicapper. *Essex* was therefore automatically burdened with top weight of 12st. He made a promising enough start, successfully negotiating Becher's and the Canal Turn, but had to be pulled up at the 15th because of a broken girth buckle.

The following year, 1987, Czechoslovakia was represented by the ten year old brown gelding *Valencio*, who had won the Pardubicka. He had at least been given one preliminary run at Newton Abbot. But it made no difference. As usual, the Czech challenger was burdened with 12st, his chances being reflected by the longest of odds, 500-1. He jumped well enough under Roger Rowell and, in a year which saw a record 22 finishers, he would probably have completed the course if he had not been brought to a complete

120

standstill by a loose horse before the 25th fence.
In 1991, Chaloupka was back on another 100-1
Czech runner: the eight year old mare *Fraze*, who
had been a neck second in the Pardubicka. But
again, without any qualifying races, the foreign
runner went off under top weight of 11st 10lb. She
spread a plate after Becher's and was pulled up before the 17th. Similarly, in 1993, a Slovak-bred runner (*Quirinus*) appeared as the top-weighted rank
outsider. His rider, Jaroslav 'Cheeko' Brecka,
worked wonders to stay in the saddle after a blunder
at Becher's. But all to no avail. This was the void
National; and *Quirinus*, winner of the 1992 Pardubicka, was pulled up after completing one circuit.

Three coachloads of supporters had had a wasted
30-hour journey to see their champion chaser race.

Quirinus returned in 1994, and harshly he was
still carrying top weight despite being 12 years old.
He went off as a 250-1 outsider and unseated Brecka
at The Chair. In 2002 two Czech horses – *Sankt
Moritz* and *Decent Fellow*, both trained by the legendary Josef Vana – were entered for the National.
But they were way out of the handicap, having no
hope of a run with a record 144 entered for 40
places. The former, who had twice run in cross-
country races at Cheltenham, suffered a fatal fall in
that year's Pardubicka.
See also: Velka Pardubicka; Foreign Horses.

D

DANIELS, William

Although *Gamecock* appeared in seven successive Grand Nationals (1885-91), professional jockey William Daniels was only once booked for the ride and that was the winning one – in 1887 when the eight year old gelding, a 20-1 chance, joined the more fancied *Savoyard* at the last and stayed on to beat him by three lengths with *Johnny Longtail* a distant third.

In a chequered career, Daniels gained only two rides in the National despite having enjoyed victory at the first attempt. His one success was unusual in two respects. *Gamecock* was his first ride following the restoration of his licence after a period of suspension; and 24 hours after winning the National he rode *Gamecock*, carrying an extra two stone, to victory in Aintree's Champion Steeplechase, which was run over one circuit of the National course.

One year later, when *Gamecock* had been raised 20lb in the weights, amateur Captain E.R. Owen took the ride in the National and came home seventh. Daniels, making his second and last appearance, failed to finish on *Old Joe*, the 1886 winner who had been a faller the previous year.
See also: Gamecock.

DAVIES, Bertram Robert

Winning jockey in the 1978 Grand National when he prevailed on nine year old *Lucius* in one of the tightest of all finishes, by half a length and a neck from *Sebastian V* and *Drumroan* respectively. His well-deserved success was remarkable in that it came so late in his career. Bob Davies had begun race-riding in 1964, had shared the National Hunt jockeys' championship with Terry Biddlecombe in 1968-69 and had won the title outright in 1970 and in 1972. Yet, in all those years, he had only three Grand National rides, two of them on virtual no-hopers. The first came in 1968 when he quickly departed on the 100-1 outsider *Beecham*; the second in 1973 when he finished eighth on *Prophecy*; and the third in 1977 when he fell on another 100-1 shot, *Duffle Coat*.

Born on May 14, 1946, the son of a Shropshire farmer who was a highly skilled horseman, Davies began riding as a toddler, graduating from pony club events to winning point-to-points from the age of 14. Having won his first chase in 1966, he turned professional the following year and made remarkably rapid progress. In successive seasons his number of winners rose from 40 to 77, a total that tied him with

Biddlecombe for the title. And the latter score was achieved despite a fall that put him out of the saddle for a month with two broken vertebrae.

That fall, two days before the 1969 National, cost him a ride in the race on Mrs Robert Sangster's newly purchased *The Inventor*. It was arguably no great loss since *The Inventor* was to fail to complete the course in three attempts. But oddly, in view of Davies's great success elsewhere, further rides in the National were to be few and far between. Indeed, it was not until 1978 that he at last found himself on a worthy contender. The chance came six years after he had won his third championship, and at a time when the 31 year old jockey was no longer competing for major honours and had thought all hopes of National glory had passed him by.

Even then it was only by fortuitous circumstances that he gained his first winning chance. On the weekend before the National, David Goulding, the regular rider of *Lucius*, badly bruised his coccyx in a Wetherby race. As a replacement, trainer Gordon Richards sought the services of Ron Barry. But that jockey was already booked to partner *Forest King* in the National; and so Davies was the 11th hour substitute.

Ironically, a minor injury caused the late withdrawal of *Forest King*. But by now the booking had been made. Fortified by a bottle of Guinness, Bob mounted *Lucius*, a 14-1 chance, for the first time in the Aintree paddock and, following race instructions to the letter, he successfully delayed his challenge for the lead as long as possible. He had won the National in his 14th season, and just to show it was no fluke he came back the following year to finish runner-up on *Zongalero*, beaten only one and a half lengths by *Rubstic* even though he was found to have finished lame. Again he had made the most of an opportunity arising only because trainer Nicky Henderson had chosen him as a last-minute substitute for an injured jockey.

In the twilight of his career he was to have two more National rides. In 1980, when only four horses finished in quagmire conditions, he had to pull up on *The Vintner* after the 17th. Finally in 1982 – for the third time deputising for an injured jockey (Steve Smith Eccles) – he picked up another dream ride: on *Royal Mail*, the top-weighted second favourite, who had finished third to *Aldaniti* the previous year. But this time the New Zealand-bred 12 year old, a namesake of the 1937 National winner, fell at the first

Becher's. Shortly afterwards Davies announced his retirement and then took up duties with the Jockey Club, officiating at Hereford and then as clerk of the course at Bangor-on-Dee and Ludlow. *See also:* Lucius.

DAVIES, Hywel James
In winning the 1985 Grand National on the 50-1 chance *Last Suspect*, Welshman Hywel Davies provided the history of the race with yet another extraordinary triumph against all the odds. Thirteen months earlier he had suffered an horrendous fall, and en route to hospital the unconscious jockey stopped breathing several times but each time was revived. Months of rest followed and, having missed the 1984 National, he looked forward all the more to returning to Aintree in 1985. Then came the depressing news: both owner and trainer were agreed that his mount should be withdrawn from the race.

Owner Anne, Duchess of Westminster had never favoured subjecting her horses (most notably *Arkle*) to the hurly-burly of the National. Her reluctance to run *Last Suspect* was strengthened when, in his last pre-Aintree run, the notoriously moody, tail-swishing gelding resorted to his familiar habit of pulling himself up when he felt he had done enough. Only Davies still had faith in the horse and, in the end, after much eloquent pleading, the 28-year-old jockey persuaded the duchess and trainer Captain Tim Forster to let the 'rogue' take his chance.

In three previous appearances, Hywel had failed to finish in the National. On his 1981 debut, most unluckily, his leathers had broken, resulting in him being unseated from *Royal Stuart* at the 20th. *Tiepolino*, his long-shot mount in 1982, had to be pulled up; and the following year, when on the very useful *Spartan Missile*, he was unseated at the second Becher's. Now, after hunting round patiently on the first circuit, he produced *Last Suspect* for a devastating late challenge, making up some eight lengths from behind *Mr Snugfit* at the last, and snatching victory by one and a half lengths.

Davies was born in Cardigan on December 4, 1956; and in graduating from point-to-points to National Hunt racing, he followed in the footsteps of his elder brother Geraint (Taffy) who was runner-up to John Francome in the conditional jockeys' championship, rode 38 winners and finished second on *Barona* in the 1973 Whitbread Gold Cup. Sadly, Geraint was forced to retire in 1974 after sustaining head injuries in a fall at Kempton, and then, with support from the Injured Jockeys' Fund, became a blacksmith. (He was only 52 when he died of a heart attack in 2002).

Resolutely, Hywel remained determined to pursue a racing career, and as an amateur in January, 1977, he rode his first winner, *Mr Know All* at Fontwell Park. And there, four months later, as a 7lb claimer, he scored his first double for trainer Josh Gifford. Having turned professional, he went on, like his brother, to join trainer Roddy Armytage near Newbury, Berkshire, and next he moved to Letcombe Bassett, Oxfordshire, where he became first stable jockey to Captain Tim Forster, with Richard Dunwoody as his understudy. Thereafter, his strike-rate steadily improved, peaking with 85 wins in the 1982-83 season.

Last Suspect gave Forster his third Grand National winner. But, having won at the third attempt, Davies only once in six subsequent rides completed the National course again. In 1986, he had to pull up *Last Suspect* early on the second circuit. In 1988, he was on 50-1 *Northern Bay*, pulled up at the 19th, and in 1989 on 66-1 *Friendly Henry*, who fell at the 11th. Meanwhile, his career had continued to be interrupted by all too frequent injuries.

In 1990 Hywel had his best Cheltenham Festival, winning the Grand Annual Chase on *Katabatic* and the Queen Mother Champion Chase on *Barnbrook Again*. Then came his great chance of a second National success. Once more he was on a Forster-trained runner: *Uncle Merlin*, an American-bred winner of the Maryland Hunt Cup. The nine year old bay gelding, a 16-1 chance, was jumping superbly and looking a likely winner when he came to the second Becher's with a three lengths lead. But there he hit the top of the fence, landed awkwardly with his unlucky rider hanging around his neck in a vain attempt to remain in the saddle. It left the race at the mercy of the record-breaking *Mr Frisk*.

In the 1991 National, Davies, putting up 2lb overweight, was unseated at the second Becher's from the 80-1 chance *Blue Dart*; and in 1992, this time 3lb overweight, he finished 11th on *Ghofar*. That year, with a splendid career total of more than 700 winners, the courageous Welshman retired from the saddle. He subsequently ran a thriving horse feed business near Swindon and served as a part-time racing correspondent for BBC Wales. His one contribution to English television was a comic one.

123

D

On April Fool's Day, 2000, he fooled John McCrir-ick on Channel 4's *The Morning Line* by posing as 'Howard Davies', a winner of the 'Monkey Business' £500 free bet, who could speak only in Welsh.

Since then Hywel's son James – a godson of Peter Scudamore – has begun to follow in his father's footsteps. In 2004, 19 years after his father's famous victory, he gained an 11th-hour ride in the National when reserve *Bramblehill Duke* replaced the withdrawn *Red Striker*. Unfortunately his 12 year old mount was a 200-1 rank outsider who refused at the first Becher's. Unseated, James was taken to hospital to be treated for neck injuries.

See also: Last Suspect; Forster, Captain Tim.

DAVIES, William

In November, 1973, property developer Bill Davies completed a deal with Mrs Mirabel Topham whereby his company, Walton Group, bought Aintree racecourse for £3 million. The company undertook to run the Grand National for at least five years, though at the same time the aim was to develop the land, hopefully gaining planning permission for a 40-acre shopping centre.

The world's most famous steeplechase was now under the control of a 39 year old, bearded Liverpudlian who had first glimpsed the race as a small boy peering through railings bordering the course and who, on leaving school at 15, had begun his working life as a £4 a week plasterer. Encouragingly, his first term of ownership saw a doubling of the Levy Board's £10,000 contribution towards the prize money, and the self-made millionaire showed a direct personal interest in the race by buying the seven year old chaser *Wolverhampton* to represent him in the 1974 National.

But it was a false dawn. While Davies talked of bringing back Grand Prix racing to Aintree and introducing various new attractions including a £100,000 Aintree Derby, his approach only led him into ever-growing conflict with the Jockey Club who would reject his request for a £75,000 grant and his proposal for an Aintree Derby. At the same time, further increases in the price of admission in 1975 saw attendance figures slump to a new low for the National in modern times. To add to Davies's misfortunes, his National contender *Wolverhampton* (pulled up in 1974) dropped dead on the gallops in preparation for the 1975 race.

All the while the financial problems of Aintree's new owner were steadily mounting in the face of rising interest rates. (Reportedly he had borrowed some £2,750,000 from the banks to secure his Aintree deal). Following the 1975 National he revealed that he was selling the racecourse to Mr Patrick McCrea, an Irish property developer. But this new deal soon fell through; and with all offers for the racecourse failing to meet Davies's asking price, the Jockey Club was threatening to have the Grand National switched from Aintree to Doncaster.

At the 11th hour, the Aintree Grand National was saved – temporarily at least – by the intervention of Ladbrokes who, in December, 1975, entered into a seven-year contract with Davies to lease the course at a rent of £250,000 a year. Under their highly professional management, the Grand National flourished anew, with the racing programme greatly strengthened and course facilities immeasurably improved.

But what would become of the National when the arrangement with Ladbrokes expired in 1982? As the deadline approached, negotiations to save the National became increasingly desperate and convoluted. All Davies's efforts to secure planning permission for development on the racecourse had come to nought and by now his asking price had risen from £4 million to £7 million, far more than the Levy Board was prepared to pay. And the crisis-point now loomed large again as the Aintree Grand National Appeal, launched by the Jockey Club, failed to raise the required sum.

The 1983 National went ahead after the Jockey Club's subsidiary, Racecourse Holdings Trust, had paid £250,000 for the right to run the race. Under the new deal the Club was to pay a further £250,000 for an option to buy the course for £4 million. But still the future of the race was not secure. Then once again, at the 11th hour, the Fifth Cavalry came to the rescue – this time in the form of the Canadian whisky firm Seagram who, in 1984, undertook to sponsor the National for five years for a total sum of £700,000, with an option for another five years. As a result of this deal, Davies and his bankers reluctantly bowed to the inevitable and accepted £3.4 million for Aintree racecourse, now owned by the Jockey Club and under the management of its Racecourse Holdings Trust.

See also: Topham, Mirabel.

DAWSON, Richard Cecil

The first trainer to turn out winners of both the

Epsom Derby and the Grand National. Irish-born (November 27, 1865), Dick Dawson followed in the footsteps of his father, a prominent Irish trainer and breeder, immediately after graduating at Dublin University. He had his first winner at Waterford in 1888 and for several years ran a stud farm near Dublin. In 1897 he was the underbidder for Eyrefield Lodge, The Curragh, famed base of the late Henry Linde, who had trained the winners of successive Grand Nationals – *Empress* (1880) and *Woodbrook* (1881). Nevertheless, Dawson's own success, as trainer of a National contender, was immediate. That same year he moved to Whatcombe, near Newbury in Berkshire, from where Paul Cole subsequently sent out the 1991 Derby winner *Generous*, and as co-owner, he took with him a five year old bay gelding named *Drogheda*. Going off in a snowstorm at 25-1, *Drogheda* duly won the 1898 National at his first and last attempt.

After such an auspicious start as a trainer, Dawson turned to the Flat with even greater success. He began by winning the 1902 Royal Hunt Cup with *The Solicitor*, and the Stewards' Cup with *Mauvezin*. Both horses, like so many of his winners, were owned by Lord Carnarvon. Having moved to Newmarket in 1914, Dawson became the champion Flat trainer two years later when he sent out *Fifinella* to win both the Derby and Oaks. Subsequently, after parting company with his leading patron, Edward Hulton, he returned to Whatcombe and in 1922 became the Aga Khan's first trainer in England. Spectacular victories followed. In 1924 he took the 2,000 Guineas with *Diophon* and the St Leger with *Salmon Trout*, and finished champion trainer again. His third title came in 1929 when he sent out *Trigo* to win both the Derby and the St Leger. One year later he gained his third Derby with the Aga Khan's *Blenheim*.

Dawson nearly crowned his career with an extraordinary double. In 1944 his *Giraud* and *Misty Morning* finished second in the Cambridgeshire and the Cesarewitch respectively. He retired the following year and died one decade later, at his home at Newbury, aged 89.
See also: Drogheda; Derby, The.

DEAD-HEATS

Remarkably, in a race over nearly four and a half miles, three horses (*Alcibiade*, 1865, *Seaman*, 1882, and *Battleship*, 1938) have won the Grand National

by just a head. *Half Caste*, 1859, was judged the winner by 'a short neck' and *Abd-El-Kader*, 1851, by 'half a neck'. Five others have won by a neck. Yet never – despite the introduction of the photo-finish camera in 1947 – has the judge called a dead-heat for first place; and it was not until 1972 that horses were declared to have dead-heated in a place. That year, *Black Secret* and *General Symons* were placed equal third – three lengths behind *Gay Trip*, the two lengths runner-up to winner *Well To Do*. In 1995 *Romany King* and *Into The Red* dead-heated for the fifth spot.

DEBUTS

More than 80 horses have won the Grand National when making their first appearance in the race. And only a handful of these had previously gained experience over the National fences by running in one-circuit Aintree races. In the 1990s eight of the nine winners were making their National debut; and only *Rough Quest*, a faller in the John Hughes Trophy, had encountered the big fences before. Seven of them had previously run in at least 14 chases elsewhere, whereas *Lord Gyllene* (1997) had been a novice the previous season.

This century four of eight winners have scored on their National debut: *Papillon* (2000), *Bindaree* (2002), *Monty's Pass* (2003) and *Numbersixvalverde* (2006). Two of them – *Bindaree* (John Hughes) and *Monty's Pass* (Topham Trophy) – had seen the fences before. And, most unusually, like *Lord Gyllene*, *Bindaree* and *Numbersixvalverde* were successful in only their second season as chasers. The last horse to win while still a novice was *Mr What* (1958).

In recent years it has not been unusual to see winners who have been tuned up for Aintree in hurdle races. However, such is the competition that it is now totally inconceivable that a horse might win the National without previous experience of steeplechasing. Yet it was not always so. In 1859 the winner, *Half Caste*, was a six year old who had only once before run (and fallen) in a steeplechase. More unusually, in 1865, five year old *Alcibiade* won by a head when making his first public appearance over fences. And in 1884 that feat was equalled by six year old *Voluptuary* whose previous experience of jumping had been confined to two hurdle races.

The oddest debutant of all was six year old *Spahi* who, in 1887, lined up in a 16-strong National field

D

as the 9-2 clear favourite even though he had never before raced over jumps, neither hurdles nor fences. His reputation rested entirely on his smart form on the Flat; also, his reckless support owed much to the fact that he was trained by Henry Linde and to be ridden by Tommy Beasley – the formidable Irish combination that had already won two Nationals with *Empress* (1880) and *Woodbrook* (1881). Absurdly described by an Irish racing informant as a 'steeplechasing certainty', the complete novice crashed out at the first open ditch. One day later *Spahi* was again running impressively on the Flat but, back at Aintree the following year, the chestnut, now more realistically priced at 30-1, went out with an early refusal.

How times have changed. More than a hundred Nationals have now been run without a single case of a horse even winning on its seasonal debut. The last to achieve that feat was the Irish mare *Frigate*, a three times runner-up, who finally scored in 1889 when having her first race for 11 months.

However, *Mely Moss*, trained by Charles Egerton and ridden by Norman Williamson, came mighty close to equalling it in 2000 when he was beaten only a length and a quarter by *Papillon*. The nine year old – rarely raced because of his fragile legs and a tendency to break blood vessels – was having his first run for 346 days and only his sixth race in four seasons since being imported from France.

Following a wind operation, *Mely Moss* was once again making his seasonal debut when he reappeared for the 2001 National. But this time, after a 364-day layoff, he was to be one of eight horses unluckily put out of the race on the first circuit when the riderless *Paddy's Return* veered across the fence at the Canal Turn.

Thus, history remains strongly against a horse winning the National on its seasonal debut. Indeed, it is even against a horse winning without having had a race in the same year. The last to do so was the six year old bay gelding *Drogheda* who made his first and only appearance at Aintree in 1898.

Nowadays one finds that almost all National winners have had a prep run within at least six weeks, and usually less, of going to Aintree. The one exception in recent years has been *Hedgehunter* who successfully appeared in 2005 after a 49-day layoff. In the entire 20th century no winner scored following a break longer than the 84 days of *Specify* (1971), though *Durham Edition* came close to

breaking that record when he finished runner-up in 1990 after a break of 102 days.

These figures, however, pale into insignificance when compared with the record of *The Lamb* who was having his first race for two years when winning his second National in 1871. And, more remarkably, the great *Manifesto* was 14 years old in 1902 when – after a break of nearly two years – he carried a colossal 12st 8lb into third place.

Just as scores of horses have won the National at their first attempt, so scores of jockeys have been successful on their National debut. Those who have most recently scored at the first attempt are Paul Carberry on *Bobbyjo* (1999), Ruby Walsh on *Papillon* (2000) and Niall Madden on *Numbersixvalverde* (2006). In 2003 National debutants Leighton Aspell and Graham Lee finished second and third on *Supreme Glory* and *Amberleigh House* respectively. Most unusually, in 1965, 50-1 chance *Mr Jones* was brought home in third place by Christopher Collins, an amateur who had never ridden a winner under Rules.

DE HAAN, Benjamin

The successful rider in 1983 of *Corbiere*, the first Grand National winner to be trained by a woman and the last to carry more than 11st 1lb to victory. As stable jockey to Jenny Pitman, Ben de Haan was on the best of her three runners and gave the chestnut gelding a copybook ride, holding off the late challenge of *Greasepaint* by three-quarters of a length. One year later they came back to finish a most creditable third, while giving 26lb to the winner *Hallo Dandy* and 12lb to runner-up *Greasepaint*.

At the age of 23, Ben de Haan was winning the Grand National at the third attempt, having previously ridden *Royal Exile* (sixth in 1981) and the Pitman-trained *Monty Python* (refused at the first Becher's, 1982). Injury kept him out of the 1985 National when *Corbiere*, under Peter Scudamore, again finished third. The partnership was resumed in the next two years but by then *Corbiere* was past his best and, still in the grip of the handicapper, he fell at the fourth in 1986 and finished 12th in 1987.

Subsequently, de Haan was on National longshots. In 1988, riding *Insure*, an 80-1 outsider trained by Fred Winter, he was unseated at the 23rd. Then, in three successive Nationals, he was on Mrs Pitman's unfancied *Team Challenge*. In 1990, they finished 11th. In 1981, they were up with the leaders

126

D

when *Team Challenge* hit the 18th; and in 1992 they finished 21st at 100-1.

Born on July 9, 1959, Ben grew up with horses since his mother was housekeeper to trainer Charlie Smith. He was 15 years old when he joined the famous Uplands yard of Fred Winter as a stable boy. Five years later he rode his first winner and went on to enjoy a big race success at his first Cheltenham Festival, winning the Grand Annual Chase on the Winter-trained *Stopped*.

Since champion jockey John Francome had the pick of rides as Winter's number one, de Haan welcomed the opportunity to be retained by Mrs Pitman and it led to his hugely successful partnership with *Corbiere*. The partnership advertised their prospects for Aintree when winning the Welsh National by a head in December, 1982. On his Grand National debut, *Corbiere* won at 13-1 and came back in the next four years.

In 1993 Ben at last appeared to have a sporting chance of a second Grand National victory. He was on ten year old *Royal Athlete* who, with *Garrison Savannah*, was one of two fancied Pitman-trained runners. But this was the void, improperly started National. *Royal Athlete* fell at the tenth and ironically it was Mrs Pitman's third-string *Esha Ness* who went on to complete the course, finishing first to no purpose. Two years later *Royal Athlete* would come back to win at 40-1. But the void National was Ben's last before going on to become a trainer at Lambourn.

See also: Corbiere.

DELAYED STARTS

The first Grand National of 1839 began two hours late (shortly after three o'clock) owing to a mix-up in weighing out the riders and then a series of false starts under the supervision of Lord Sefton. Again, the following year, there was confusion in weighing out jockeys and the scheduled 1.30 p.m. start was delayed until after three.

In the early years brief delays from false starts were commonplace, the worst being in 1857 when the starter only got the 28 runners off at the eighth attempt. The longest single delay came on March 5, 1845, following protests that the frozen ploughed fields were unfit for racing. The 15 owners were assembled to vote on the issue. The race finally went ahead at five o'clock and was ironically won by *Cure-All* whose owner was one of

two who had protested against going ahead.

In 1858, when heavy snow caused the National to be postponed from Wednesday to Saturday, there was a unique delay as runners were called back from the start because they had neglected to parade before going down. In 1865 an outsider, aptly named *Acrobat*, held up proceedings with a display worthy of a bucking bronco at a rodeo and finally the race went off without him. In 1898 and 1901, the runners waited at the start for ten and 16 minutes respectively to allow a snow blizzard to abate.

In modern times, following the introduction of a starting tape in 1925, there have been few delays. In 1952, after a number of horses had broken the tape, it took another 12 minutes to get the runners under way. In 1974 there was a prolonged delay as Martin Blackshaw struggled to bring the moody mare *Princess Camilla* under control. The following year the field went off almost 20 minutes late because *Junior Partner*, having spread a plate, had to be re-shod at the start.

In 1977 there was a brief delay as police removed a handful of demonstrators protesting at the conviction of an armed robber; and in 1991 the start was held up as *Ten of Spades* spread a plate and then further delayed by banner-waving animal rights demonstrators invading the course. In 2005 the race began 25 minutes later than originally scheduled but that was a pre-arranged postponement to allow for TV coverage of the wedding of Prince Charles and Camilla Parker Bowles.

See also: False Starts.

DEMPSEY, Edward

In 1947, on his first ever visit to England, Irish jockey Eddie Dempsey won the Grand National on *Caughoo*, the second of only three horses ever to win the race as 100-1 outsiders. His success – achieved in fog and rain and on heavy going – owed much to the superior fitness of his mount in a year when the Big Freeze had confined English horses to their yards for nearly two months. It was nonetheless an astonishing success for a rider virtually unknown outside of Ireland and of no great repute at home.

Born in Co. Meath in 1911, Dempsey first appeared in races in 1933 but for many years his riding was largely confined to working horses on the gallops, and he was almost 30 before he got the leg-up on a really serious horse: a six year old superbly bred gelding called *Prince Regent* and trained by

127

Tom Dreaper. In 1941 he rode him to a neck victory in the Enniskerry Hurdle at Phoenix Park, Dublin, and there, later that same year, they won the Webster Champion Cup Chase.

That season *Prince Regent* went on to win four more races, including the 1942 Irish Grand National under 12st 7lb. But by now this budding superstar was being ridden by more well-established jockeys. For Dempsey it was back to business as usual – scraping a living from riding-out work and picking up the occasional booking. One such ride, in December, 1945, was on a six year old gelding called *Caughoo*, who had been bought as a yearling for 50 guineas by veterinary surgeon Herbert McDowell, and his brother John, a jeweller. Trained by the former, *Caughoo* was being aimed at the 1946 Ulster National which he had won at Downpatrick the year before.

With Dempsey as his regular partner, *Caughoo* performed promisingly in his prep races, but as the big one drew near the luckless Eddie was injured in a bad fall. Having to rest for several months, he was replaced by the renowned Aubrey Brabazon who rode *Caughoo* to a comfortable victory. Subsequently, Dempsey was the regular rider again, but in the remainder of his 1946 races and early in 1947 *Caughoo* was dismally sluggish. His poor form prompted the McDowell brothers to abandon their plan of bidding for a third Ulster National success. Instead, without any high expectations, they opted for the Aintree Grand National. At least their outsider would be fully fit, having had the benefit of regular workouts on the snow-free beach of Sutton Strand near Dublin.

On March 29, 1947, no fewer than 57 horses, most of them ill-prepared, lined up for the Grand National. It was the second largest field in the history of the race, and the 8-1 clear favourite was Dempsey's long-lost partner *Prince Regent*, winner in 1946 of the Cheltenham Gold Cup and, over National fences, Aintree's Champion Chase. One year before, in the National, he had finished third as the 3-1 favourite under a top weight of 12st 5lb. But now he was 12 years old and with a top weight of 12st 7lb. His opponents included 20 horses on the minimum 10st and no fewer than 26 who were rated 100-1 no-hopers.

At the first Becher's, the leader was the 33-1 Irish hope *Lough Conn*, with *Caughoo* well behind. Thereafter, and for much of the race, the runners were out of vision in the fog. When they came back into full view of the stands, *Lough Conn* was still at the head of affairs and then perhaps ten lengths in the lead coming to Becher's again. But *Caughoo* was now making relentless progress and on the home stretch it emerged that he was well in front. He blundered the last fence but Dempsey steadied him and they went on to score by 20 lengths from *Lough Conn* – the biggest winning margin since 1928 when *Tipperary Tim* was the first 100-1 winner. In fourth place was the harshly weighted *Prince Regent* whose career total of 18 victories over fences would surely have been much greater but for being restricted in his prime by the Second World War.

Later Dempsey was the subject of the most outrageous allegation in Grand National history – accused to his face by Daniel McCann, the Irish rider of *Lough Conn*, of having cheated by taking a short cut in the fog. They promptly came to blows, and the dispute was then carried on in court where McCann repeated his astonishing claim that Dempsey had taken *Caughoo* over the plough on approaching Becher's (the sixth), and had then lingered somewhere around the 12th fence until the runners came round again. The magistrates dismissed the charge, which was not backed up by newsreel evidence, and seemingly attributable to too much Irish liquor.

There was, however, another side to the story. According to Peter O'Sullevan, who in 1947 was covering his first Grand National, 'Eddie Dempsey compounded the rumours. He had hit skid row and was trying to get a few quid from some distinguished journal like *The People*. He allowed it to be inferred from them that he'd been extremely clever and hidden behind a haystack. Anybody who could find a haystack at Aintree deserved to get away with it.'

In 1948 Dempsey returned to Aintree on *Caughoo*, now a 28-1 chance, but with an extra 15lb to carry and ground too fast for his liking, the former winner, like *Lough Conn*, had to be pulled up. In 1950, making his third and last National appearance, Eddie was a faller at the seventh fence on *Cadamstown*, a 66-1 chance. He retired at the end of that season and died 39 years later, aged 77. As for McCann, he failed to finish on his four other National rides. And ironically, in 1949, he was aboard *Caughoo*, when the 66-1 chance ran out at the fifth fence after losing his bridle.
See also: Caughoo.

DERBY, The

Only one horse has run in the Epsom Derby and gone on to win the Grand National. The distinction belongs to *Voluptuary*, the six year old who won at Aintree by four lengths on his debut over fences in 1884. Three years earlier he had finished sixth to *Iroquois* in the Derby, having briefly led the field as they rounded Tattenham Corner.

Voluptuary ran in three more Grand Nationals, each time failing to complete the course. Among other Derby runners to have appeared in the National, the most notable were Mr John Elmore's *A British Yeoman* and Mr Henry Chaplin's *Ryshworth*. The former, unplaced at Epsom in 1843, was third and sixth in the Nationals of 1848 and 1849 respectively. He failed to finish in 1850 and was then brought down in 1856 when, under new ownership, he was turned out at the ripe old age of 16. *Ryshworth*, fourth in the 1869 Derby, was six lengths runner-up in the 1873 National.

Donzelon, unimpressive in the 1924 Derby, went on to win the Scottish Grand National five years later. But he flopped as the 50-1 outsider of four in the 1930 Cheltenham Gold Cup and 17 days later, at 66-1, he fell on his only appearance in the Aintree Grand National. In contrast, *Brienz* was very useful on the Flat, winning the 1928 Dewhurst Stakes and finishing third to *Trigo* in the 1929 Derby. His victories over fences included the Coventry Cup Chase at the 1933 Cheltenham Festival and he finished fourth in the 1936 Gold Cup behind *Golden Miller*, *Royal Mail* and *Kellsboro' Jack*. But unlike that famous trio he failed at Aintree, falling in the Nationals of 1935 and 1936.

The last Derby horse to run in the National was *Permit*. Tailed off at Epsom in 1966, he never scored on the Flat but showed considerable promse over fences, finishing third in the 1969 Haydock National Trial and the 1971 Greenall Whitley National Trial. The chestnut gelding failed in his two Grand Nationals – brought down in a pile-up at the first open ditch in 1970 and falling as a 100-1 outsider in 1972.

Four trainers have saddled winners of the Derby and the Grand National. Dick Dawson led the way with *Drogheda* (1898) at Aintree followed by three Derby winners: *Fifinella* (1916), *Trigo* (1929) and *Blenheim* (1930). George Blackwell emulated his feat in 1923 when he won the National with *Sergeant Murphy* 20 years after his Epsom success with *Rock Sand*. Willie Stephenson achieved the

double with *Arctic Prince* (1951) and *Oxo* (1959); and outscoring them all was Vincent O'Brien with a hat-trick of National winners – *Early Mist* (1953), *Royal Tan* (1954) and *Quare Times* (1955) – and six Derby winners between 1962 and 1982.

See also: Voluptuary; Entires.

DEVON LOCH

The Queen Mother's brilliant chaser, destined to be forever remembered as the unluckiest and most mysterious loser in Grand National history. Mysterious because – though theories abound – no one has been able to explain conclusively why the ten year old bay, after safely clearing all thirty fences, collapsed in a heap with the 1956 race at his mercy.

As a son of *Devonian*, out of *Coolaleen*, *Devon Loch* was descended from Lord Derby's *Hyperion*, the 1933 Derby winner who sired the winners of 752 races. Bred by Mr William Moloney in Co. Cork, he was sold as a yearling for 550 guineas to Colonel Stephen Hill-Dillon, who initially raced him as a five year old on the Flat. It was already evident that *Devon Loch* looked more suitable for chasing, and in 1951 he was sold to the royal trainer, Mr Peter Cazalet, with the proviso that a further £1,000 would be paid if he won the Cheltenham Gold Cup and £2,000 if winning the Grand National.

In England, *Devon Loch* began his National Hunt career by finishing runner-up in two hurdle races and – in his first novice chase – second to *Mount Tremblant*, who was soon to win the Cheltenham Gold Cup. Leg trouble then led to him being fired and rested for two years. Meanwhile he showed great promise in training and had time on his side.

Returning to racing as an eight year old, he scored two wins; and in the next season, prior to his National debut, he won at Lingfield and Sandown, finished fifth in the three-mile King George VI at Kempton, and second in the National Hunt Chase at Cheltenham. Long before, jockey Bryan Marshall had forecast that *Devon Loch* would one day win the Aintree National. Now, well backed by stable connections on his Aintree debut, the ten year old went off at 100-7, joint fourth in the National betting with *E.S.B.* and *Pippykin*. There were only 29 runners, including two former winners, *Early Mist* and *Royal Tan*, and last year's third-placed *Carey's Cottage*. For the first time the Queen Mother had two runners, her second string being *M'as Tu Vu* who, having fallen the previous year, was made a 40-1 chance.

D

Four horses went at the first fence. They included *Early Mist* and *Must*, the eight year old 7-1 favourite. *M'as Tu Vu* was prominent throughout the first circuit, but three fences later he fell with two others; and the second favourite, *Sundew*, came down at Becher's. Meanwhile, *Devon Loch* was jumping superbly, having been threatened only once – at the first Valentine's where he had to twist in mid-air to avoid the fallen *Domata*. He now cruised up into contention, taking second place at the Canal Turn; and after the front-running *Armorial III* had fallen at the fence after Valentine's, he took over the lead, closely followed by *Eagle Lodge*, *Ontray*, *E.S.B.* and *Gentle Moya*.

While all his rivals were now being hard-ridden, *Devon Loch* was still full of running. As Dick Francis later wrote in his autobiography, 'Never had I felt such power in reserve, such confidence in my mount, such calm in my mind'. And that confidence was fully justified; his horse continued to jump and gallop strongly, clearing the last fence a length and a half ahead of *E.S.B.*, then powering ahead on the run-in to establish such a lead – all of ten lengths – that, with no more than 60 yards to go, he needed only to canter home to win.

The crowd now sustained almighty cheers in anticipation of an assured royal victory (the first for 56 years); and many hats were already being raised in salute. Then it happened, the most astonishing fall in Grand National history. For no apparent reason, *Devon Loch* raised his forelegs as though taking off for a jump, then suddenly belly-flopped on to the turf, his legs splayed out on the ground in a style reminiscent of Bambi's first venture on to ice in the 1942 movie.

Hanging on, his arms around the horse's neck, Dick Francis managed to remain on board. But when *Devon Loch* regained his feet he stood stock-still, apparently unable to restart after having sensationally stalled. A stunned Francis dismounted and threw down his whip in despair. Nearby, in the stands, his wife fainted. Meanwhile, a disbelieving Dave Dick, previously reconciled to being a distant second, sailed by on *E.S.B.* to win by ten lengths from *Gentle Moya*, with *Royal Tan* a further ten lengths back in third.

There was a stunned silence as Francis was given a lift by a passing ambulance and *Devon Loch* was led away to the stables. Subsequently, bearing her disappointment with supreme dignity, the Queen Mother consoled her jockey, congratulated Mrs Leonard Carver, the winning owner, and not least checked on the welfare of her horse. To her great relief, the vet pronounced *Devon Loch* to be perfectly sound.

Why then had he collapsed when galloping alone on the flat? At the time, Francis's first thought was that his horse had broken a hind leg. Later, reviewing the many theories, he concluded that the deafening cheers, raised by nearly a quarter of a million spectators, had totally unnerved and confused his horse. 'I have never in my life heard such a noise,' he later wrote. 'The tremendous noise was growing in volume with every second, and was being almost funnelled down from the stands on to the course.'

Another much-favoured theory – one certainly fitting in with the style of his fall – was that *Devon Loch* had attempted to jump an imagined obstacle, perhaps having glimpsed the edge of the Water Jump beyond the guard-rail to his left; or mistaking the shadow of a fence for the real thing. Certainly, it was not unknown for a National runner to take off unnecessarily; *Grudon* had jumped a footpath on his way to winning in 1901.

But such notions were dismissed by the jockey; and, similarly, he was not impressed by suggestions that *Devon Loch* had been seized by sudden cramp, had suffered a mild 'heart attack', had experienced a small blood clot in the hind legs causing temporary paralysis, or perhaps had slipped on a patch of wet ground created by a leaking stopcock near the Water Jump.

Dick, the winning jockey, described the roar-of-the-crowd theory as 'a load of rubbish'; he suggested that *Devon Loch* had a breathing problem and was momentarily starved of oxygen – a view that was shared by the Rimells who had turned out the winner. Whatever the explanation, the belly-flop fall cost *Devon Loch* not only victory but also a new Grand National record. The winning time of *E.S.B* was 9min 21 $\frac{2}{5}$sec, just fractionally more than a second outside the record set by *Reynoldstown* in 1935 – and by staying on his feet the Queen Mother's horse would surely have bettered that.

After a six-month break, *Devon Loch*, reunited with Francis, won two races: a two-and-a-half miles hurdle and a match against *Early Mist* at Sandown. Then he was second to stablemate *Rose Park* in the King George VI at Kempton. But, like his luckless jockey, he was never to compete in the National again. In January, 1957, he looked a likely winner when carrying top weight of 12st 1lb in the Mildmay Memorial Chase at Sandown. At the second last, however, his rider Arthur Freeman sensed his mount was in discomfort, and he eased up to finish fourth. The bay, found to be lame with a recurrence of tendon trouble, was retired. Besides several hurdles, he had won eight steeplechases.

Devon Loch was now gifted to Sir Noel Murless to serve as a hack, being mainly ridden by his teenage daughter Julie, later the first Mrs Henry Cecil. He ended his days in the royal stables at Sandringham, having to be put down in 1963, aged 17. *See also:* Francis, Richard; Cazalet, Peter; Royal Runners.

DICK, David Victor

Winning rider on *E.S.B.*, the horse that profited from *Devon Loch*'s extraordinary collapse in the 1956 Grand National. Four years later, on the occasion of being presented to the Queen Mother at the Cheltenham Festival, the jockey – grinning broadly as usual – confessed ashamedly that, after his Aintree victory, Her Majesty had asked him what he thought when he saw that strange fall – 'and, without thinking, I blurted out: 'I was delighted, ma'am.' I shouldn't have said it.'

Dave Dick, a jockey renowned for his good humour and sportsmanship, greatly sympathised with Dick Francis's cruel departure on *Devon Loch*. Nevertheless he was entitled to rejoice at his own good fortune that day. Over the years he had had his fair share of bad luck in the saddle; and no rider had worked harder for success, with weight being his constant problem – almost as many hours spent in Turkish baths as in the saddle. To ride *E.S.B.* at 11st 3lb, he had had to waste nearly 10lb.

Born on March 8, 1924 at Epsom, Dick was educated at Ewell Castle School, along with Fred Winter who would become his close friend. He was initially apprenticed to his father as a Flat jockey and rode his first winner – *Carton*, trained by Winter's father – at Brighton in 1938. Three years later, having begun to ride for George Lambton, he immediately showed enormous promise – most notably when, aged 17, he won the 1941 Lincoln on *Gloaming*. Then came wartime service – working with pack mules in Scotland and finally in Palestine – and by the time the Second World War ended his weight had ballooned from well under 8st to over 11st.

In 1945, having despaired of getting rides, the 6ft tall, long-legged ex-Serviceman tried his hand at pig farming. But he missed race-riding too much. Determinedly, he sought to make his mark as a National Hunt rider, and in 1951 – along with Fred Winter and Michael Scudamore – he made his Grand National debut. Riding *Rowland Roy*, a 50-1 chance, he survived the first fence chaos arising from an undeclared false start, then got beyond Becher's before becoming one of many more fallers in a race that saw only three finish.

One year later he returned to Aintree on the crest of a wave. Booked by the eccentric Dorothy Paget, who so often changed her jockeys, he had ridden her six year old *Mont Tremblant* to a ten-lengths victory in the Cheltenham Gold Cup – a race in which *E.S.B.* was a faller at the final fence. Now, in his second National, he finished third in a 47-strong field on *Wot No Sun*, behind *Teal* and Miss Paget's much fancied *Legal Joy*, ridden by Scudamore because Dick had been unable to make the weight.

In 1953, after being partnered by Dick Francis in four races, *Mont Tremblant* returned to Cheltenham with Dick back on board. This time, after finishing fourth in the Gold Cup, they were to move on to Aintree. The omens were not good, the seven year old being harshly burdened with top weight of 12st 5lb, a full stone more than any of the other 30 runners. In the circumstances, Dick did extraordinarily well to bring the chestnut gelding home in second place, albeit 20 lengths behind *Early Mist*, who was receiving 17lb.

Disaster followed. In 1954 Miss Paget's *Legal Joy* returned to the National fray, now raised 13lb in the weights. With Dick on board, he was one of four horses to suffer a fatal fall. In 1955, Dave again found himself on a horse unfavoured by the weights: Prince Aly Khan's newly acquired *Royal Tan*, raised 11lb for his victory the previous year. They came home in 12th place.

Such were Dick's mixed fortunes before his gifted victory in the 1956 National. Hopelessly outpaced on the long run-in, he had resigned himself to defeat when, 50 yards from the winning post, *Devon Loch* pancaked on the ground. But once the incredible had happened, he galvanised his mount afresh and went on to win in the fourth fastest time yet achieved becoming the only jockey ever to have won both legs of the 'Spring Double', Lincoln and National. Reasonably, he explained that he felt no

D

guilt in profitting from *Devon Loch*'s misfortune because *E.S.B.* had been brought to a standstill at the first fence after the Canal Turn and might otherwise have been a contender in his own right.

As it happened, there was one person in the Royal Box that day who could take some pleasure from *E.S.B.*'s win: Sue Whitehead, an international showjumper who, at the time, was stepping out with Dave Dick. Thirty-four years later she would have far more reason to rejoice at Aintree. Then, as Mrs Roddy Armytage, she would see her son Marcus win the Grand National in record time on *Mr Frisk*.

Twice more Dick rode *E.S.B.* in the National, each time figuring prominently before his mount tired under a considerably higher weight. They finished eighth in 1957, sixth in 1958. His next ride in the race came in 1961, on *Mr What*, the 1958 winner. But again a huge weight increase counted against them. They finished 11th.

It was the same story in the next three Nationals. In 1962, he was 13th on *Merryman II*, who was anchored on top weight following his first and second places in 1960 and 1961. In 1963 he was 20th on top-weighted *Frenchman's Cove*, and in 1964 he was yet again on the most penalised horse: *Pas Seul*, on whom he had achieved an extraordinary victory in the 1961 Whitbread Gold Cup after their second place in the Cheltenham Gold Cup. This time he was a faller at the 12th.

Dick had his last National ride in 1965, going well on *Kapeno*, the third joint favourite, until being brought down at the second Becher's. That day he put up 7lb overweight. The long battle with the scales was being seriously lost, but it was a severe knee injury – incurred from a fall the following year – that finally forced his retirement. Briefly he worked as a bloodstock agent in London, and went on to become manager of the Wyld Court Stud near Newbury, Berkshire, and then racing manager to Sheikh Fahd al-Sabah of Kuwait. Married, with two children, he retired in 1986 and his daughter, Daisey, kept up the family association with horses by representing Britain at three-day eventing.

Dick was too heavy to contend for the jump jockeys' championship. However, it was a measure of his fine horsemanship that, in 13 National appearances, he only three times failed to complete the course. He was distinguished most by his immense body strength and supreme power in a tight finish; also as one of the last jockeys to ride almost hunting length. In all, he won 348 races over jumps; and most famously he was associated with the great two-miler *Dunkirk* on whom he won his second Champion Chase in 1965 and then beat *Mill House* at level weights at Ascot. His winners included many trained by Fulke Walwyn for Dorothy Paget; also some horses owned by the Queen Mother. Indeed, when he rode *Antiar* to victory in the 1965 Spa (now Stayers') Hurdle he became the only jockey ever to win for Her Majesty at the Cheltenham Festival. He died in February, 2001, aged 76.

See also: E.S.B.; Paget, Dorothy; Humour.

DICTATOR

The first Grand National fatality. In 1839, on the second circuit of the inaugural race, *Dictator* burst a blood vessel at the second of two brooks (later named Valentine's) when he hit the fence hard and fell. He was remounted by Mr J.S. Oswell, but the damage had already been done. He dropped dead at the next fence.

See also: Fatalities.

DISCOUNT

The chestnut entire who in 1844 – on his only Aintree appearance – became the first six year old to win the Grand National, scoring by 20 lengths and one length over *The Returned* and *Tom Tug* respectively.

Discount, sired by *Sir Hercules* out of *Mininkin*, was originally called *Magnum Bonum*, under which name he was a dismal failure on the Flat. He was resold many times, being so despised that it is recorded that, having finally sold him for £80, a dealer called Payne was actually offered £50 to take him back. Eventually he was sold for a pittance to another dealer, Mr Quartermaine of Piccadilly, who wittily renamed the horse in recognition of the fact that he had been offered him again and again at an increasing discount.

Once put over fences, *Discount* showed considerable jumping flair – to such a degree that, on his Grand National debut, he was made the 5-1 joint favourite with *Marengo*. There were only 15 runners but these included *Charity*, the 1841 winner; *Nimrod*, the 1843 runner-up; and, on top weight, *Peter Simple* who had twice finished third.

This was the first National to be run on boggy ground in torrential rain, providing such an exceptional test of stamina that most of the nine finishers came home greatly distressed. Only *Discount* thrived in these conditions, challenging for the lead at the last fence and powering away from all rivals over the run-in to win by a then record distance of 20 lengths from *The Returned*, who was conceding 16lb to the winner. One length behind in third was the outsider *Tom Tug* whose rider was so totally exhausted that he had to be lifted off his mount.

For the third time in its six years, the National winner was ridden by an amateur: Mr John Crickmere who had been unlucky not to win the previous year when finishing a close-up third on *Dragsman* after his horse had bolted off course. The following year, in the absence of *Discount*, he took over on *Tom Tug* and finished fourth.

See also: Crickmere, John.

DISTANCE, A

When a horse has won a race by more than 30 lengths the margin is officially recorded as 'a distance'. Six times the Grand National has been won by a distance, beginning in 1893 when *Cloister* was judged to have won by 40 lengths from *Aesop*. Twice a distance has divided first and second, plus the runner-up and the third – in 1913 when there were only three finishers, *Covertcoat*, *Irish Mail* and *Carsey* (remounted); and in 2001 when four finished, with distances dividing *Red Marauder*, *Smarty* and *Blowing Wind* (remounted). Other distance winners are *Shaun Spadah* (1921), *Tipperary Tim* (1928) and *Mr What* (1958).

See also: Finishes.

DISTANCE, Grand National

The first Grand National of 1839 was officially 'four miles across country', but the course was so vaguely defined with scattered posts and rails that the seven finishers certainly covered more than four miles. By accident, in 1846, the course was incorrectly flagged; as a result the five of 22 runners to finish covered almost five miles and the winner was a six year old gelding, *Pioneer*, not even quoted in the betting.

In 1863, the distance was officially extended to four and a half miles. Five years later, following questions about the exact distance run, the course was officially re-measured and found to be 30 yards short of four and a half miles. The distance is now recognised as four miles 856 yards – the longest race run in Britain under Jockey Club Rules.

For many years it was presumed that horses with proven form over such a marathon distance were most likely to win the National. But then, in 1970, the race was won by 20 lengths by *Gay Trip* whose successes had previously been confined to races over less than three miles. His trainer, Fred Rimell, subsequently suggested that, in reality, a classy two-and-a-half miler was ideally suited to the National, and this view gained added credence the following year when the race was narrowly won by *Specify*, whose principal success had been in the 1969 Mildmay of Flete Challenge Cup over two miles four and a half furlongs.

Two years later Rimell's theory truly took hold when, 18 days after finishing third in Cheltenham's two-mile Champion Chase (the race he had won by 25 lengths in 1971), the extraordinary *Crisp* ran over more than double the distance, finishing three-quarters of a length behind the record-breaking *Red Rum* to whom he was conceding a massive 23lb. And it was to gain renewed support when *Classified* and *The Tsarevich* – both recognised two-and-a-half-mile specialists – finished third and second in 1986 and 1987 respectively.

Since then, however, there has been scant evidence that middle-distance runners are well suited to the National. Why? In 1990 Mercy Rimell, who had helped her husband train *Gay Trip*, suggested that recent modifications to the fences had made all the difference. She wrote in her book, *Reflections on Racing*, that it had previously been harder to win a National. 'Jumping was the name of the game. Today you've got to have a horse that stays a lot better because the fences are that much easier, so it's more of a race. Years ago it was a jumping competition. That's the way I look at it. Today your moderate two-and-a-half-mile horse wouldn't have the speed. I'm sure I'm right about that.'

On the other hand, there was nothing 'moderate' about *Gay Trip* and *Crisp*. Endowed with speed and stamina, they had sufficient class to make their mark over widely ranging distances. Arguably they were exceptions to the rule. For overall, results no longer speak in favour of two-and-a-half-milers. In fact, since 1970 the National has never been won by a horse who had not previously raced over three miles or more.

During the 1990s all the leading players in the National had winning form over at least three miles one furlong. Moreover, in that whole decade, the finishers included only two horses that had previously

D

not won beyond two miles five furlongs: *Sure Metal*, 17th in 1996, and *Back Bar*, 14th in 1999. In 1998 a strongly fancied 12-1 starter, ridden by champion Tony McCoy, was *Challenger Du Luc*, who had won six times over an extended two and a half miles but was unproven over three miles. He fell at the first fence. Two years later the luckless McCoy again put his faith in a horse that had never won over three miles plus but had been so impressive when winning the Mildmay of Flete. *Dark Stranger* went off as the 9-1 favourite and duly unseated the champion at the first open ditch.

In that same National there was no great surprise when *Red Marauder* fell at the first Becher's. After all, he had dubious stamina at this time, having never won beyond two miles four and a half furlongs. But there was near astonishment when he came back in 2001 to win at 33-1. Moreover third place went to *Blowing Wind*, another McCoy mount that had never won beyond a near two and a half miles.

However, these results were not to renew belief in the National potential of middle-distance chasers. Rather it was a freak outcome in a year of such quagmire conditions and so many fallers that only two horses completed the course without being re-mounted. Moreover, though he was the clumsiest of jumpers, *Red Marauder* had stamina influence through his sire's dam *Precipe Wood*, as he had proven seven months earlier in gaining a three-mile win at Market Rasen.

In the circumstances it was extremely surprising that, in 2002, *Blowing Wind* went off as the 8-1 National favourite. Surprising, too, that McCoy should see him as 'an ideal National type' when the nine year old had scored all his nine wins over distances ranging from two miles to the two miles four and a half furlongs of his latest success in the Mildmay of Flete.

Ostensibly, *Blowing Wind* performed most creditably to be the third of 11 finishers. But the harsh truth of the matter is that, on good going, he did not see out the trip. He ran out of steam from three out and thereafter was hopelessly outpaced by *Bindaree* and *What's Up Boys*. The latter, a close-up second, finished 27 lengths ahead of him. Since then no results have challenged the strong evidence that, barring some freak pile-up of near *Foinavon* proportions, it takes a proven three-miler to win the Grand National.

DISTURBANCE

A handsome, bay entire, *Disturbance* won the 1873 Grand National even though he was only six years old and burdened with a top weight of 11st 11lb on his first appearance in the race. His success marked the beginning of a great purple patch for both rider and owner. The former, Old Harrovian John Maunsell Richardson, would win the National again the following year on the six year old, 5-1 favourite *Reugny*. The latter, Captain James Machell, would, in the space of four years, become the first owner to have three National winners.

Disturbance – by *Commotion* out of *Polly Peacham* – was bred and initially raced by Mr James Barber, owner of *Fan*, the five year old runner-up in the 1867 National. He was not highly regarded by Barber and, after riding the horse to victory in the Corinthian Handicap at Ayr, Richardson was able to buy him cheaply on behalf of the great gambler, Captain Machell.

Trained by Richardson, *Disturbance* fell at the second fence when making his Aintree debut in the Sefton Chase. But thereafter he proved reliable over both hurdles and fences, and he comfortably won the Croydon Steeplechase on his way to the Grand National. However, in the light of his youth and big weight, he was priced at 20-1 in a market headed by *Footman* and *Ryshworth* who had been fourth in the 1869 Derby. The 28-strong field also included the previous year's winner, *Casse Tete*.

In a fast-run race, *Disturbance* was steered clear of the many fallers, his challenge being delayed until approaching the last behind the second favourite *Ryshworth*. Richardson was now confident. Having once trained the race leader for Mr Henry Chaplin, he knew that, for all his superior speed, the ex-Derby runner lacked resolution under pressure. And so it proved, *Ryshworth* began to fade when *Disturbance* drew alongside, and the latter powered away to win by six lengths with the mare *Columbine* a further ten lengths back in third. Only six runners completed the course.

Unfortunately it could not be established whether *Disturbance* had won in record time since the time-keeper's watch had stopped during the race. However, a considerable compliment was paid to the winner on the following day when *Ryshworth* carried 12st 7lb to a comfortable victory in the Sefton Chase.

Having had his first National winner after five

attempts, Captain Machell entered three horses in 1874. Again Richardson won for him on a six year old and by six lengths, but this time he had chosen to ride *Reugny* who had failed to finish the year before. *Disturbance*, ridden by Joe Cannon, had no chance on a colossal 12st 9lb and did well to finish sixth at 25-1. He was now retired and, under the ownership of Lord Hastings, performed as a stallion at the Melton Constable stud in Norfolk. He lived on to the age of 29.
See also: Richardson, John Maunsell; Machell, Captain James.

DOBBIN, Anthony

In 1997, after an IRA bomb scare had caused the Grand National to be postponed for 49 hours, Tony Dobbin, still in his riding silks, was left tramping the streets for several hours before managing to contact a friend and a get a lift home. But he was luckier than many other jockeys. Living only one hour from the course, he was home by 10.30 p.m. and had an undisturbed weekend: playing golf on the Sunday, and then returning to Aintree for what he likened to an armchair ride on *Lord Gylenne*. The New Zealand-bred bay gelding led from the first fence to the finish, winning by 25 lengths from Suny Bay. As the rider modestly expressed it, 'I was just a passenger, my horse was so good.'

Victory brought Dobbin overnight celebrity and two days later he was pressing the button to start the televised National Lottery draw. But regrettably, what should have been the greatest day in the young jockey's life was clouded by the senseless action that had ruined the Saturday staging of the 150th Grand National. After his emphatic win, the Catholic Ulsterman spoke of his embarrassment at the IRA's threatened bombing; how he was ashamed to say he was from 'over there'. Moreover, three months later it was reported that, in response, hardline republican sympathisers had subjected his elder sister, Patrica Perry, to a campaign of intimidation in the jockey's home town of Downpatrick, Co. Down.

Born on May 1, 1972 in Downpatrick, Tony was inspired to become a jockey by his father, Paddy, who used to take him hunting with the Eastdown Foxhounds. He rode in pony races from the age of ten; was only 15 when – in pursuit of his riding ambition – he left Northern Ireland to work in the Newmarket stables of trainer Neville Callaghan. After just three days

he surrendered to homesickness. But he was soon crossing the Irish Sea again, this time to join the Cumbrian yard of Jonjo O'Neill. Three weeks after celebrating his 18th birthday, he rode his first winner, romping home four lengths clear on *Stay Awake* in an 18-runner Flat race at Hamilton.

In 1993 Dobbin moved only a dozen or so miles to the Little Salkeld yard of trainer Maurice Barnes who had won the 1979 Grand National on *Rubstic*. There, in just one full season, given more outside rides, his career progressed apace: 45 wins including, most notably, victory with his first ride at the Cheltenham Festival – on *Dizzy* in the County Handicap Hurdle. That year, 1994, also saw his Grand National debut. It ended at the first open ditch where he was unseated from the 66-1 chance *Ushers Island*.

Dobbin's horsemanship now earned him the job of stable jockey at the famed Greystoke yard of Gordon Richards. He promptly became the leading conditional jockey of the 1993-94 season. In November his winning streak included a four-timer at Hexham and a treble at Ayr; and then came his biggest success to date – victory on the brilliant grey *One Man* in the Hennessy Cognac Gold Cup.

In 1995 he missed a Grand Natonal ride on *General Pershing* (a faller at the third fence) through a back injury which he aggravated by exercising on his first day out of hospital. A much bigger disappointment came when, having only recently recovered from a broken collarbone, he lost to Richard Dunwoody the winning King George VI ride on *One Man*. Dunwoody kept the ride in the Cheltenham Gold Cup, but there *One Man* faded badly after the second last.

It was a cruel stage in Dobbin's career. The owner of *One Man* had demanded a jockey change; and similarly he was replaced by Dunwoody on *Unguided Missile*. He had lost rides on the two best horses in his stable, and to his further dismay, Robert Ogden, one of Richards' principal owners, chose to employ his own jockey in Paul Carberry. For a time rumours of Dobbin's imminent departure from Greystoke were rife.

Meanwhile, however, he enjoyed his share of major wins on such as *The Grey Monk*, *Addington Boy* and *Better Times Ahead*; and in 1996 he had his first Aintree success when winning the Crowther Homes Becher Chase on *Into The Red*. And then, ironically, the Ogden-Carberry partnership worked in his favour. Richards was training Mr Ogden's *Buckboard Bounce* for the 1997 Grand National and, with Carberry booked, Dobbin was free to take the ride on the Steve Brookshaw-trained *Lord Gyllene*. Dobbin knew the New Zealand-bred bay gelding well. In January they had won together at Uttoxeter, and in March – only three weeks before the great Aintree challenge – they had finished second in the Midlands National, again over four miles two furlongs. Now they were to dominate at Aintree where the only threat came from the riderless *Glemot* who ran across *Lord Gyllene* at the Water Jump. There, only the jockey's instant response in checking his horse on the approach, avoided a collision. Otherwise he had a dream ride in winning the Grand National on his second appearance. *Buckboard Bounce*, the horse he would have ridden but for contractual obligations, finished fourth.

Dobbin, popularly known as 'Dobbs', ended the season with a tally of 73 winners. The following year he was out with a broken thumb at the time of the National. Then, in September, 1998, his boss Gordon Richards died, being succeeded at Greystoke by his son Nicky. Tony stayed on as first jockey, and in the 1999 National he was the 17th of 18 finishers on *Avro Anson*. That year he had Aintree victories in the John Hughes Memorial Trophy Chase and the Becher Chase; and remarkably, riding the 66-1 chance *Go Ballistic* in the Cheltenham Gold Cup, he was beaten only a length by *See More Business*. But he was again disappointed when returning for the 2000 National. Riding in the *Lord Gyllene* colours on *Listen Timmy*, a 50-1 shot, he narrowly escaped being brought down at the first fence and finally pulled up after the Water Jump.

He finished that season with a tally of 72 winners, taking fifth place in the jockeys' championship. Then, in the summer of 2000, he was out of the saddle for three months following surgery on his shoulder; and in the 2001 Grand National he again had to pull up after one circuit on *Listen Timmy* who hated the heavy ground. However, he was now firmly established as a leading jump jockey; and in 2002 he started his Cheltenham Festival with a 20-1 winner, *Freetown*, in the Pertemps Final Handicap Hurdle. He missed a Gold Cup ride on *Cyfor Malta*, having suffered minor head injuries when falling in an earlier race. But this disappointment paled into insignificance following the tragic loss of his brother, Barney, who had been killed in a car accident the

previous week. As he expressed it: 'People don't understand that this is just a game. There are better things in life.'

In December, 2002, Dobbin won the Welsh National for owner J.P. McManus and trainer Jonjo O'Neill on *Mini Sensation*. But he was left without a ride in the Aintree Grand National when *Gunner Welburn* just missed the cut, running instead in the Martell Fox Hunters' Chase and finishing runner-up. His one consolation was victory in the Martell Novices' Hurdle on *Quazar* at 16-1. In addition he finished the season fourth in the jockeys' championship, having reached a century of winners for the first time.

Again, in 2003, he was deprived of his scheduled National ride when the well-supported *Kingsmark* was withdrawn two days before the race with heat in a leg. But it was still a rewarding Aintree meeting. On the Friday he had a 35-1 double, winning the Martell Cognac Handicap Chase on *Master Tern* and a novices' hurdle on *Limerick Boy*. Then, at the expense of the injured Norman Williamson, he had the good fortune to pick up a great spare ride in the National: Lady Lloyd Webber's *Killusty*, a 12-1 chance. They were making good headway in the race when *Killusty* blundered the 20th and fell two fences later at Becher's. Dobbin finished the season with an excellent strike-rate of 109 wins from 482 rides.

The following year his National ride was on *Gunner Welburn* who had finished fourth in 2003. Lying sixth at the end of the first circuit, the 12 year old gelding then weakened and was pulled up before the 20th. This time Dobbin ended the season with only 89 wins from 499 rides but it was sufficient to secure him fourth place in the jockeys' championship.

In contrast, in 2005, he had passed his century of winners before going to the National meeting where he scored a sensational first-day treble, winning the three hurdles races on *Monet's Garden*, *Faasel* and *Turpin Green*, all trained by Nicky Richards. Having survived a very nasty fall in the Topham Chase, he came back the next day to finish ninth in the National on *Just In Debt*, a 33-1 shot who had been runner-up over the Aintree fences in the Becher Chase of the previous November.

In the 2005-6 season, Dobbin finished fourth in the jockeys' championship with 91 wins and joined the distinguished group of jump jockeys who have ridden 1,000 winners. But he had a disappointing ride in the National, having to pull up on the Nicky Richards-trained *Direct Access* before the 19th.

One year later, only five days before the National, Tony suffered a heavy fall in the Irish version, being seriously hampered and unseated three out on *Cloudy Lane*. His lower right arm was trodden on and it was expected that he would have to miss Aintree. But luckily, there was no fracture, just soft-tissue damage that necessitated wearing a cast for two days. He bounced back at Aintree to score in the Melling Chase on *Monet's Garden*, his 63rd win of the season; and the following day, in the National, he figured prominently on the Kim Bailey-trained *Longshanks* until the ten year old – only recently recovered from a bruised foot – weakened two out , finishing seventh, more than 40 lengths off the winner.

See also: Lord Gyllene; Richards, Gordon.

DOCKERAY, George

George Dockeray is renowned as the Flat-race jockey who rode a 50-1 winner of the Epsom Derby (Lord Egremont's *Lapdog*) in 1826, and three years later won the Oaks on Lord Exeter's *Green Mantle*. However, he also merits distinction in the annals of jump racing: as the unsung trainer of the three Grand National winners: *Lottery* (1839), *Jerry* (1840) and *Miss Mowbray* (1852).

During the early years of steeplechasing there were no establishments to compare with the great training centres so familiar today. Most Grand National runners were owned by members of the landed gentry who developed their horses as hunters and left any race preparation to an uncredited employee or perhaps to a professional jockey.

In the case of the National's first winner, however, it is known that Mr John Elmore's *Lottery* was originally schooled by jump jockey Jem Mason and then, early in 1839, sent to Epsom to be tuned up for Aintree by Dockeray who worked him with his Flat thoroughbreds. Following his retirement from racing, the famed *Lottery* was to serve as Dockeray's hack.

In 1840 the classic winning jockey was also responsible for the preparation of *Jerry* in whom Mr Elmore very probably had an undeclared financial interest. And twelve years later he played a part in preparing *Miss Mowbray*, a rank outsider who was not even quoted in the betting in a year when *Royal Blue* was the first 100-1 runner in Grand National

history. The following year *Miss Mowbray* finished runner-up and then, in the 1855 National, suffered a fatal fall.

See also: Lottery; Jerry; Miss Mowbray.

DOLLERY, William

The professional jockey who, after seven unsuccessful rides in the Grand National, shared in the most astonishing and conclusive performance ever seen at Aintree: the 1893 victory by 40 lengths of the top-weighted, 9-2 favourite *Cloister*. He was on the first horse to carry 12st 7lb to victory in the National and they won in a time, a fraction over 9min 32sec, that would remain unsurpassed for 40 years.

As stable jockey with trainer Arthur Yates, Bill Dollery picked up the ride after *Cloister*'s previous rider, amateur Mr J.C. Dormer, had lost an eye in a horrendous fall at Sandown. He was a most worthy replacement, having shown his mettle on long-priced outsiders – finishing seventh on *Cortolvin* (50-1) in 1886, fifth on *Chancery* (100-1) in 1887, and sixth on *Gamecock* (66-1) in 1891. Now, in contrast, he was on an outstanding staying chaser who had been beaten only half a length in the 1891 National, and had been runner-up again the following year.

There were only 15 runners in the 1893 National, ten less than in the previous year. It was, however, regarded as a quality field; one including *Father O'Flynn* who had beaten *Cloister* by 20 lengths in 1892, and *Why Not*, the one length runner-up of 1889, who now had the assistance of top jockey Arthur Nightingall. But, as it happened, it was no contest. Early on, Dollery abandoned his efforts to hold up his mount, allowing the eager *Cloister* to set his own pace; and that pace on the fast going was a blistering one throughout.

From the second fence onwards, *Cloister* relentlessly increased his lead. Towards the end of the first circuit Dollery briefly restrained him but soon, recognising that he was still full of running, he gave him his head. Over the last three-quarters of a mile *Cloister* extended his lead with every stride. He not only beat seven year old *Aesop* by 40 lengths but gave him 31lb in the process, with *Why Not*, the 5-1 second favourite, a bad third.

Bill Dollery had originally worked as a shepherd before joining Yates as a stable lad. Altogether he appeared in 13 Nationals, an astonishing total since his rides were spread over 20 years. Following his

D

Aintree debut on *Cortolvin* and his creditable fifth on *Chancery*, he failed to finish on *Johnny Longtail* in 1888, then rode in three successive Nationals on *Gamecock*, the 1887 winner, finishing tenth and sixth with one fall in between. In 1895 he was third on *Van Der Berg* and in 1898 he pulled up on *Nepcote*.

After a four-year gap the veteran jockey came back for three more National rides. He was a faller on *The Pride of Mabestown* (1903) and pulled up on *May King* (1904). His last appearance was in the royal colours – in 1905 when he was aboard the giant *Moifaa* who had been bought by King Edward VII following his famous victory the previous year. They fell at the second Becher's.
See also: Cloister.

DOUBLE CHANCE

Winner of the 1925 Grand National, on his first and last appearance in the race, *Double Chance* was a nine year old chestnut gelding who had first raced without distinction on the Flat. Regarding him to be of little value, his owner, Captain Anthony de Rothschild, had made a gift of the horse to an ex-trooper who had served in his squadron of the Royal Bucks Hussars during the First World War. That ex-trooper, just starting out as a trainer, was Fred Archer, nephew of the immortal Flat-racing jockey, and grandson of William Archer, who had won the 1858 National on *Little Charley*.

Bred at the Rothschilds' Southcourt Stud, *Double Chance* was out of the mare *Kelibia* with his uncertain sire being either *Roi Herode* or *Day Comet*. At first only hunted, Archer's gift-horse revealed a surprising flair for jumping and went on to win two minor chases before breaking down and needing firing treatment for strained tendons. Eventually, following Archer's move to Newmarket, he won five more races – three of them on the run-up to the 1925 National.

Shortly before the National, Archer sold a half-share in the horse to a Liverpool cotton broker, Mr David Goold. At Aintree, the newcomer ran in Mr Goold's colours and was ridden by amateur Major 'Jack' Wilson, a dare devil First World War airman whose famous exploits included shooting down a German Zeppelin over Hull and surviving a parachute jump so hazardous that his hair literally turned white overnight. Wilson was now returning to the National despite a painful debut in 1923 when he

was thrown headlong over Becher's by the outsider *Trentino*.

In a race of many fallers, *Double Chance* was prominent throughout. A big leap took him into a narrow lead at Valentine's and he was still just in front at Becher's the second time around. But then the order changed and after the Canal Turn it appeared more and more to be a straightforward duel between two leaders: *Fly Mask*, last year's runner-up, and *Old Tay Bridge*, the 9-1 favourite ridden by Jack Anthony, seeking his fourth National win.

The two were still well ahead at the last when suddenly the ex-Flat horse seemed to sprout wings. Receiving more than a stone from his rivals, *Double Chance* rapidly closed the gap, outpaced them on the long run-in, and was still going away when he won by four lengths from *Old Tay Bridge*, with *Fly Mask* a further six lengths back.
See also: Archer, Frederick; Wilson, Major John Philip.

DOUGHTY, David Neale

Doughty by name and by nature, Welsh-born Neale won the 1984 Grand National on the 13-1 chance *Hallo Dandy* and went on to establish an extraordinary record of consistency in the race. Only once in ten runnings did he fail to complete the course. Before winning, he had finished fifth and then fourth; and subsequently he came home 12th, sixth, seventh, third and fifth. Even in the void National of 1993, he stubbornly got round, being the sixth of seven finishers on *On The Other Hand*.

Born October 20, 1957, the son of a steel worker, Neale was so horse-mad as a boy that he sneaked rides on pit ponies that had been put out to pasture near Pyle in Glamorgan. Finally his father was induced to buy him a pony of his own. On leaving school he found work in the Lambourn stable of Fulke Walwyn; then he began riding for trainer Wilfred Crawford at Haddington, East Lothian, and scored his first win at the age of 19 in a novice hurdle race at Perth. Next came a move south to join trainer Bill Marshall at Newmarket; and his career properly took off in 1979, when Crawford recommended him to Gordon Richards who was seeking a second jockey to Ron Barry. Since Barry had also ridden for Crawford before moving to Greystoke, Richards took notice. He studied Doughty in action at Warwick and, impressed by style and strength, immediately offered him a job.

At the time Neale was reluctant to leave Newmarket where he greatly enjoyed working with Marshall. The trainer, however, advised him that the job would give him a far better chance of riding class horses. Doughty compromised by riding for both trainers but soon found the travelling too exhausting and settled at Greystoke full time. That first season he started off by riding a 2,199-1 five-timer for Richards at Carlisle, and the following season he gave his boss an elusive first winner at the Cheltenham Festival, scoring comfortably on *Current Gold* in the 1981 National Hunt Champion Chase. Moreover, within an hour, he had made it a double by riding *Lord Greystoke* to a seven lengths victory in the Cathcart Challenge Cup.

Neale had hoped to ride *Current Gold* in the 1980 Grand National. But, despite being placed in the Scottish and Welsh National, it was not until his success at Cheltenham that the horse finally qualified for Aintree. By then, in 1982, he was 11 years old and past his best. Making his Grand National debut, Doughty did well to ride him into fifth place after narrowly escaping a fall at the second Becher's. He finished that season with 33 winners, five more than former champion jockey Barry.

In the 1983 National Neale went one place better on *Hallo Dandy* who jumped spectacularly well throughout to finish fourth at 60-1 on ground too soft for his liking. The following year he starved himself to get down to 10st 2lb, and with *Hallo Dandy* well handicapped and on favourable going, the combination triumphed by four lengths, the first of a record 24 finishers.

Having taken over from the retired Ron Barry as stable jockey, Doughty finished the 1983-84 season with 48 winners. The following season his tally of 45 would have been much higher but for layoffs with injuries, one of which kept him out of the 1985 National. At Aintree, he was a mere spectator, watching in horror as deputy Graham Bradley and *Hallo Dandy* crashed out at the first fence. Neale and *Hallo Dandy* were reunited for the 1986 National but the former winner, now 12 years old, had lost his pace and finished a distant 12th.

For Doughty this was also a bad year for injuries and, unhappily, he was harshly criticised after being unseated on the mare *Another City* in the Scottish National. The suggestion was that he might have stayed on board if he had been fully recovered from an earlier injury. The controversy resulted in Doughty taking a two-year break from Greystoke. In the 1988 National he was riding the Jimmy Fox-trained *Friendly Henry*, a 100-1 shot, but still managed to get home in sixth place. The following year he was seventh for Mercy Rimell on *Gala's Image*. Then, in 1990, back with Gordon Richards, he had high hopes of scoring a second victory on nine year old *Rinus*. But these hopes were to be killed by the unusually firm going. On ground welcomed by connections of the record-breaking winner *Mr Frisk* and runner-up *Durham Edition*, he did remarkably well to finish third, albeit beaten by 20 lengths.

In 1991 *Rinus* was back, going off – behind 13-2 *Bonanza Boy* – as 7-1 joint second favourite with *Garrison Savannah*, the Cheltenham Gold Cup winner. But, unlike *Hallo Dandy*, he was raised 7lb for his second National bid. He moved up into second place on the second circuit and was still going well in third place when he muddled the 19th and then unseated his rider at the next. After eight Nationals, Neale's 100 per cent finishing record was ended. However, this was to be his best-ever season, with 96 winners.

Rinus did not survive to make a hoped-for third National bid. But Doughty still had a powerful contender from the Greystoke yard: 12 year old *Twin Oaks*. On this relentless galloper he had won the 1991 Greenall Whitley Gold Cup, scooping the £50,000 bonus offered for the chaser scoring most points in Haydock races that season. Neale held the horse in such high regard that he named his house in Windermere after him.

In the 1992 National, *Twin Oaks* was third in the betting at 9-1. But the gelding was now 12 years old and in Richards' view too harshly handicapped with a top weight of 11st 7lb. So it proved. He was unsuited by the fast pace on drying ground, blundered over the 17th and, though rallying strongly, weakened in the final stages to come home the fifth of 22 finishers.

Doughty's last National ride – prior to his retirement and a new career developing and renovating old properties – was his most bitterly disappointing one. For three weeks in 1993 he had lived on lettuce to make ten stone on the Richards-trained *On The Other Hand* who, three weeks before Aintree, had carried 12st 7lb to victory in the Grand Military Gold Cup over an extended three miles at Sandown. Then he found that all his wasting efforts were in vain because of a bungled start. Ever determined, he

D

completed the course for the ninth time, being the sixth of seven finishers in a race declared void.

In 2005 he completed a circuit at Aintree one more time – on foot. He was walking the course with Carrie Ford prior to her much-vaunted bid to become the first lady rider of a National winner. *See also:* Hallo Dandy.

DOWDESWELL, Jack

Of all the champion jump jockeys who have been denied success in the Grand National, none met with more misfortune than Jack Dowdeswell, Britain's leading rider of the 1946-47 season. In eight appearances at Aintree he never completed the course. His record: *Second Act* (1939), fell; *Second Act* (1940), broke down; *Good Date* (1947), fell; *Limestone Cottage* (1950), fell; *Cadamstown* (1951) fell; *Ordnance* (1954), fell; *Roman Fire* (1955), brought down; *Armorial III* (1956), fell.

In truth, however, Dowdeswell was rarely given a National mount worthy of his talents. His first four rides at Aintree were on 100-1 no-hopers. Then, when riding a 50-1 chance in 1951, he was one of 12 riders (including such luminaries as Bryan Marshall, Dick Francis, Michael Scudamore and Pat Taaffe) eliminated in a record first fence pile-up.

In 1955, riding a 66-1 outsider, he miraculously escaped serious injury at the first Becher's where he landed amid thrashing hooves after his horse had been unluckily brought down by the falling *E.S.B.* The following year he was at last on a strong contender in Mme K. Hennessy's *Armorial III*, a 20-1 chance. But this was the National now remembered solely for the extraordinary collapse of the Queen Mother's *Devon Loch* that gifted the race to *E.S.B.* Soon forgotten was Jack's bold bid on a seven year old who led the field for so long – all the way from the first fence until the 26th where he clipped the fence with his hind legs and fell.

It was Dowdeswell's National swansong. Born on May 27, 1917, he had started riding as a 14 year old apprentice on just two shillings a week. Now, in 1956, with a total of some 350 winners, he retired at the age of 38. It was remarkable that his career had lasted so long since he was often described as 'the jockey who has broken every bone in his body'. He himself remembered having broken 52 different bones; and eventually he had his collarbones removed, explaining, 'It seemed the sensible thing to do; it was a waste of good riding time mending them

purely so that I could go out and break them.'

Happily, against all odds, so many injuries had no long-term ill effects. He rode out in Lambourn well into his seventies. Indeed, Jack went on to become the oldest living champion jump jockey. In 2007, as a 90 year old, he returned to Newbury as a special guest on the 75th anniversary of his first winner at the Berkshire track in 1932; and a few days later, with Betty, his wife of 67 years, he celebrated the 60th anniversary of his being crowned Britain's champion jump jockey.

DREAMS

Great races – not least the Grand National and the Derby – can so concentrate the mind in advance that inevitably some enthusiasts will dream in their subconscious of the outcome; and the odds are that someone, somewhere, will happen to foresee the true result. All too often stories of such prescience have to be taken on trust. One major exception is the well-documented case of Lord Poulett who foresaw the 1871 National victory of his little Irish-bred grey *The Lamb*. It is beyond dispute because, three months before the race, he put it on record in a letter to the celebrated amateur jockey Mr Thomas Pickernell. He wrote:

> *My dear Tommy,*
> *Let me know for certain whether you can ride for me at Liverpool on The Lamb. I dreamt twice last night I saw the race run. The first dream he was last and finished amongst the carriages. The second dream I again saw the Liverpool run. He won by four lengths, and you rode him, and I stood close to the winning post ... I saw the cerise and blue sleeves and you ... Let me know as soon as you can, saying nothing to anyone.*

Only the distance was wrong in Lord Poulett's second dream. With his new jockey and a new trainer, and raised 12lb in the weights, *The Lamb* won his second National by two lengths. Despite the owner's wish for secrecy, news of his dream spread like wildfire before the race and the grey was heavily backed to go off the 11-2 second favourite.

Curiously, another well-recorded case also involved two dreams with the second proving accurate. It happened in 1935 when Mr W.H. Harrison, a racehorse owner of Wychnor, Staffordshire, planned to join a group of friends in attending the National for the first time. Long before the race he said he had had a vision of the finish. But this dream made no sense since the winner, only identified by the No. 4, was ridden by a woman. Moreover its number did not tie-in with the colours of the rider.

But then, in a later dream, on the eve of the final acceptances, he again saw the race won by horse No. 4; and this time the colours correctly matched those to be carried by *Reynoldstown*. More remarkably, as it came to pass, he saw the colours to be carried by *Golden Miller*, the 2-1 favourite, fall at the fence after Valentine's and just six horses reach the finish. Told of the dreams, Mr Harrison's friends decided that a lady on the winner simply signified success for an amateur. They duly backed No. 4, *Reynoldstown*, who went off at 22-1 under amateur rider Frank Furlong.

See also: Lamb, The; Poulett, Lord.

DREAPER, Thomas William

One of the greatest of Irish National Hunt trainers destined never to saddle a winner of the Aintree Grand National. Following a successful career as an amateur jockey (1922-1940), he enjoyed even greater success as a trainer, saddling ten winners of the Irish Grand National, a record five of the Cheltenham Gold Cup, plus winners, at least once, of all other Gold Cup chases in England. But, cruelly, circumstances conspired to deny him success in the race he most wanted to win.

Born in 1898, Tom Dreaper was for many years a full-time farmer and an outstanding, part-time amateur rider until his career was ended by a fall at Naas that resulted in a triple leg fracture and a fortnight of unconsciousness. Relatively late he turned to training on a small scale at his Greenogue farm, Kilsallaghan, near Dublin; and he was 40 years old when his career really took off with the arrival of four horses owned by the flour-milling tycoon J.V. Rank.

To his amazement, Dreaper found that he had been selected to succeed Rank's trainer, Bobbie Power, who had died in a road accident. And among the horses sent to him was a truly outstanding prospect: *Prince Regent*, on whom he had had his last winning ride in a 'bumper' at Naas. *Prince Regent* proved his greatness in 1942 when he won the Irish National while carrying 12st 7lb and conceding 12lb to the runner-up, Miss Dorothy Paget's

Golden Jack. But owing to the Second World War, it was not until 1946 that he finally got to Aintree. By then he was an 11 year old and following victory in the Cheltenham Gold Cup he was lumbered with top weight of 12st 5lb. Giving at least two stone to most other runners, and with unfavoured heavy ground, he finished third after leading at the last fence. In the 1947 Grand National, raised still higher in the weights, he finished fourth.

In 1952 Dreaper had another strong contender in his stable: Mr Rank's *Early Mist*. In the National, the seven year old was one of ten casualties at the first fence. He was young enough to have more chances at Aintree. But that year, following the death of Mr Rank, most of his bloodstock was put up for sale. Dreaper then saw *Early Mist* win the 1953 National – with Vincent O'Brien as his trainer.

It was on Dreaper's advice, in 1960, that Anne, Duchess of Westminster paid 1,150 guineas at the Goffs sales in Dublin for an unraced three year old. The horse was duly named *Arkle*; and, under Tom's regular schooling methods, he emerged as the greatest chaser of all time, winner of 27 of his 35 races, including three successive Cheltenham Gold Cups, the King George VI Chase, the Irish Grand National, the Hennessy Gold Cup (twice) and the Whitbread Gold Cup. But the owner would never allow him to compete in the Aintree National.

Meanwhile, Tom challenged for the National with *Double Crest* (1961, ref.) and *Kerforo* (1962, fell); and finally his last bid was to prove his best. It came in 1971 when he saddled seven year old *Black Secret*, by the St Leger winner *Black Tarquin*. The bay gelding, ridden by his son Jim, a 20 year old amateur new to the race, miraculously survived a major blunder at the fence after Becher's, and he was one of five leaders almost in a line coming to the last. Then, on the run-in, *Specify* threaded through a gap to take the inside rail and went on to grab victory from *Black Secret* in his last strides. After a quarter of a century of trying, Dreaper had been denied a Grand National winner by a neck.

In January, 1972, having won almost all the big steeplechases except the Aintree National, and having completed yet another season as the leading National Hunt trainer in Ireland, Dreaper was prompted by failing health to hand over his Greenogue stable to his son. Jim continued the run of family success but, like his father, he was denied success at Aintree. His first National runner as a trainer was *Black*

141

Secret who dead-heated for third place in 1972. His subsequent challengers were: *Black Secret* (tenth in 1973); *War Bonnet* (fell in 1977 and 1978); *Barney Maclyvie* (fell, 1981); *Kilkilowen* (13th in 1986); *Hard Case* (fell, 1988).

In 1975 Jim had his second of four Irish Nationals winners, and that same year Tom proudly saw his son follow in his footsteps by winning the Cheltenham Gold Cup with the Duchess of Westminster's *Ten Up*, a gelding he himself had bought five years earlier. One month later, he died, aged 76, at his home in Kilsallaghan; and the name of Tom Dreaper in racing is now carried on by his grandson, riding for trainer Ferdy Murphy.
See also: Arkle; Early Mist; Prince Regent.

DROGHEDA
Winner of the 1898 Grand National which was controversially run – and barely seen – in a blinding snowstorm. In a 25-strong field, the six year old *Drogheda* took the lead at the end of the first circuit and was still leading at the final fence where he held off the late challenge of the 7-1 second favourite *Cathal* and went on to win by three lengths with *Gauntlet* four lengths back in third.

Sired by *Cherry Ripe* out of *Eglantine*, the 1887 Irish Grand National winner, *Drogheda* was a 25-1 chance making his first and last appearance in the race. Ironically, in a year when a freak mishap led to the withdrawal of much-fancied *Manifesto*, *Drogheda* was ridden by John Gourley whose National experience was limited to riding *Manifesto* in 1896, the year he fell in a collision at the first fence.

Drogheda, born near the town that gave him his name, was bred by Mr G.F. Gradwell, a leading official in Irish National Hunt racing. After winning the 1897 Galway Plate he was sold as a five year old to Mr R.C. Dawson and Mr G.C.M. Adam, an ex-officer of the 14th Hussars – the price reportedly being £1,500, plus a further £300 if he won the Grand National. He was subsequently taken to England following Dick Dawson's decision to quit his homeland and set up as a trainer at Whatcombe near Newbury in Berkshire.

Drogheda won two races for his co-owners before going to Aintree. However, when winning the National in the colours of Mr Adam, the bay gelding was having his first run of the year – a not unprecedented feat, but one that has not been emulated since. He never raced at Aintree again as his trainer

began to concentrate on Flat racing with almost immediate and extraordinary success which would include turning out no fewer than three Epsom Derby winners.
See also: Gourley, John; Dawson, Richard Cecil.

DRUMCREE
Winner of the 1903 Grand National when he was ridden by a late substitute: Percy Woodland, a 21 year old professional, who was destined to enjoy a brilliant career both over jumps and on the Flat. The jockey who missed the ride because of a broken collarbone was Hugh Nugent, a talented amateur and the son of Sir Charles Nugent who trained *Drumcree* at Cranborne in Dorset. He had ridden the bay gelding when runner-up in the 1901 National and again when finishing seventh in 1902.

Drumcree was extremely well-bred, being by the great steeplechasing sire *Ascetic* out of *Witching Hour*, a useful point-to-pointer; and he was named after the home of his dam in County Westmeath. He was originally bought by trainer Sir Charles on behalf of Messrs. Owen Williams and C.S. Newton, and it was in the colours of the former co-owner that he made his National debut in 1901.

That year, when the National was controversially run in a blinding snowstorm, seven year old *Drumcree* finished four lengths behind the entire *Grudon*. He could perhaps be regarded as an unlucky loser since, during the race, he had lost one plate and twisted another. In contrast, the winner – a sure-footed leader throughout – was artfully aided by having had butter spread into his hooves to prevent snow from 'balling' into hard lumps inside his shoes and making him more liable to slip.

Before the 1902 National *Drumcree* was sold for a reported £2,500 to Mr J.S. Morrison, a wealthy businessman with large interests in South Africa. Still trained by Sir Charles and ridden by his son, he now had an extra 12lb to carry and, after taking an early lead, he laboured on the heavy going and finished seventh. The following season, however, *Drumcree* showed consistent form, returning to Aintree on the back of three successive wins under Hugh Nugent. As a result, despite a further 7lb rise in the weights, he was made the 13-2 favourite in a 23-strong field that included King Edward VII's 1900 winner *Ambush II* and the great dual winner *Manifesto* making his seventh appearance at the age of 15.

It was the first National to be attended by the

reigning monarch. The weather was fine and the going good. But with *Ambush II* setting a furious pace from the start horses fell in rapid succession, ten of them failing to complete the first circuit. As the leaders approached the last fence *Drumcree* had a marginal lead from the similarly named *Drumree*, *Ambush II* and the second favourite *Detail*. Then, seemingly seized with a fit of the staggers, the Duke of Westminister's *Drumree* slumped – *Devon Loch*-like – on the flat. Now a great roar went up as the King's horse moved into second place. But *Ambush II*, weighed down with a massive 12st 7lb, blundered the last and fell; and *Drumcree* ran on strongly to win by three lengths from *Detail*, with gallant old *Manifesto*, giving 32lb to the runner-up, well back in third.

Tragically, having lost through injury his great chance of National glory, Hugh Nugent was never able to resume his partnership with *Drumcree*. Later that year he fell fatally in a hurdle race at Ostend; and it was not until 1906 that his grieving father returned *Drumcree* to Aintree. The handsome gelding was now a 33-1 chance, most unreasonably burdened with 12st top weight. Ridden by amateur Walter Bulteel, brother of *Manifesto*'s privileged owner, he finished eighth in the race won by his half- brother, *Ascetic's Silver*. The following year, as a 13 year old, he fell on his final appearance. *See also:* Woodland, Percy.

DUFF, Charles Garden
Owner of three Grand National winners.
See also: Assheton-Smith, Sir Charles.

DUNWOODY, Thomas Richard MBE
Of all champion jockeys in modern times, Richard Dunwoody achieved the most outstanding record in the Grand National. Between 1975 and 1999 he competed in 14 consecutive Nationals and was placed in eight. Besides winning twice – on *West Tip* (1986) and *Miinnehoma* (1994) – he was second on *West Tip* (1989); third on *Superior Finish* (1996), *Samlee* (1998) and *Call It A Day* (1999); fourth on *West Tip* (1987 and 1988) and sixth on *Bigsun* (1990).

Dunwoody was born (January 18, 1964) into a racing family in Co. Antrim. His father, George, a jockey-turned-trainer, had run away from home as a teenager to find work with horses. His mother was the daughter of Epsom trainer Dick Thrale who had ridden (and fallen) in the chaotic 66-runner National

of 1929. Thus, their Irish-born son was riding a pony at the age of two, hunting with the hounds when only six. Two years later the family moved from Ireland to Gloucestershire, then to Newmarket; and subsequently, at boarding school, Richard was so set upon becoming a jockey that he starved himself to the point of collapse and hospitalisation.

Most appropriately, at the end of his riding career, Dunwoody would entitle his autobiography *Obsessed*. As he frankly revealed, he was totally obsessed with riding winners – an obsession pursued at alarming emotional expense, not least eventually in respect of his long-suffering, supportive wife, and involving a most punishing routine of running, gym work, dieting and saunas as he fought a constant battle with the scales. Beyond that, he never lost his appetite for riding despite experiencing nearly 700 bruising falls.

In December, 1981, after brief spells working for Paul Kelleway and John Bosley, he joined Captain Tim Forster's yard in Letcombe Bassett where he learned much from stable jockey Hywel Davies. The following year he had his first ride: finishing second on *Mallard Song*, a 33-1 chance, in a two-mile Flat race at Chepstow. His first winner came in May, 1983: on *Game Trust* in Cheltenham's hunter chase meeting. The number of rides increased in 1984 when Davies was sidelined through injury, and in 1984-85, his first professional season, he rode 46 winners and almost as many seconds and thirds. Most importantly, that season, he had two winners at the Cheltenham Festival when riding for Michael Oliver. One was *Von Trappe* in the Coral Golden Handicap Hurdle Final. The other, most significantly, was *West Tip* in the Ritz Club Chase.

Dunwoody had already won with *West Tip* in the Mildmay-Cazalet Chase at Sandown. Now, 16 days after Cheltenham, they moved on to Aintree for their first appearance in the Grand National. *West Tip*, the joint 13-2 favourite, was leading the race but fell after getting in too close at the second Becher's, and the race was won by 50-1 *Last Suspect*, ridden by Hywel Davies, to give Captain Forster his third National success.

But valuable lessons had been learned – he vowed never again to lead the field over Becher's second time, reasoning that many others besides himself had come to grief in similar circumstances – to such an extent that 21-year-old Richard, the youngest rider in the race, boldly declared afterwards: 'We'll come back next year and win.' And so they did. Again the youngest rider on parade, Dunwoody rode a fine tactical race, only striking the front on the run-in when *West Tip* overhauled *Young Driver* and stayed on to win by two lengths. Three more times this famous partnership would compete in the National, each time finishing in a place. In 1987, carrying 10lb extra, *West Tip* finished fourth, outpaced, like all others on the run-in, by *Maori Venture*, winning in the then third fastest time. In 1988, they were again fourth (to *Rhyme 'N' Reason*) and in 1989 seven lengths second to *Little Polveir*.

Remarkably, the brave *West Tip* came back for a sixth consecutive National in 1990 and, as a 13 year old, finished tenth. But this time Dunwoody was on *Bigsun*. They came home a distant sixth behind the record-breaking *Mr Frisk*. The following year they pulled up before the second Canal Turn, and in 1992 Richard came to grief at Becher's where his mount, second favourite *Brown Windsor*, collided with another horse and was brought down.

Next came the fiasco of the 1993 National that was declared void. At the chaotic false start Dunwoody had the tape wrapped around his neck. But he was not too disappointed because his mount, *Wont Be Gone Long*, had recently shown poor jumping form. And soon afterwards came the news that his great hero and rival, Peter Scudamore, had retired. It left the way open for him to gain his first jockeys' championship (with 173 winners) after three times being runner-up.

In the 1985-86 season, Dunwoody had joined David Nicholson's yard to be second jockey to Scudamore, who later became first jockey to Fred Winter and then to Martin Pipe. In the process 'Scu' had smashed all records – winning the jockeys' championship in seven consecutive seasons, reaching a career total of 1,678 winners, and achieving an unprecedented 211 winners in one season (1988-89).

By this time Pipe had become such a dominant trainer that his stable jockey was – barring accidents – almost assured of becoming the champion. And so, in 1993, Richard succeeded 'Scu' in the job. But it was not the anticipated smooth ride to success. A brilliant new talent had suddenly emerged, and Dunwoody would only retain his title after an exhausting, nerve-racking, neck and neck, ten-month duel with Adrian Maguire that went all the way to the wire. Their titanic battle was resolved on the last day of the season, the final score of their winners, 197 to 194.

The highlight of that hardest of seasons came at Aintree when no fewer than five of the 36 Grand National runners were trained by Martin Pipe. Dunwoody chose 11 year old *Miinnehoma*, who had won Cheltenham's 1992 Sun Alliance Chase under Scudamore. As when winning on *West Tip* in 1986, he was on horse number eight and racing on slush-heavy ground; and the omens proved right. *Miinnehoma*, a 16-1 chance, gave him only one moment of anxiety when pecking on landing over Becher's second time around. Slowing only when left in the lead, he responded to the late challenge of the mudlark *Just So* to win by one and a half lengths.

Richard had five more rides in the National. In 1995, with 10lb extra, *Miinnehoma* had to be pulled up before the 21st. Then, following his break from the Pipe stable, came Jenny Pitman's *Superior Finish*, third to *Rough Quest* (1996), and her *Smith's Band* (1997), tragically killed after a fall at the 20th. In 1998 he had an excellent chance on the Philip Hobbs-trained *Samlee*, an out-and-out stayer who had won the Becher Chase at Aintree in November and went off the 8-1 second favourite. But, as in the Welsh National, *Samlee* again finished third behind *Earth Summit*, Dunwoody's own tip to win the race.

His last National (1999) came just five days after he had broken Scudamore's record of 1,678 domestic wins by a jump jockey. Putting up 2lb overweight, he was on Nicholson's *Call It A Day*, winner (with Maguire) of the 1998 Whitbread Gold Cup. They were beaten on the run-in, going down by ten lengths and a neck to *Bobbyjo* and *Blue Charm*. Unrevealed at the time was the full extent of muscular damage to Dunwoody's right arm. For many months he had been stubbornly riding with an arm injury that prevented him from raising the whip in his right hand.

In December, 1999, after consulting numerous specialists in Europe and the United States, Dunwoody finally accepted their unanimous opinion: at 35, while still a leading National jockey, he had to retire. He had been three times champion jockey. He had ridden more than 100 winners in ten consecutive seasons (beating Scudamore's eight). He had finished first in 1,699 of 9,399 races – at the time of his retirement the most wins ever achieved in Britain by a jump jockey, ahead of Scudamore (1,678), John Francome (1,138) and Stan Mellor (1,035). His record as the winningmost jump jockey stood until

2002, when it was overtaken by the irrepressible Tony McCoy.

Over 17 seasons, this most fiercely competitive of jockeys had won most of the major races in the NH racing calendar, including the Cheltenham Gold Cup on *Charter Party* (1988), the Champion Hurdle on *Kribensis* (1990), the Irish Grand National on *Desert Orchid* (1990), the King George VI Chase four times, the Mackeson Gold Cup three times and the Breeders' Cup Chase twice plus the Whitbread Gold Cup on *Cache Fleur* (1995). Along with Fred Winter, Willie Robinson and Bobby Beasley, he was one of only four jockeys since the Second World War to have won the 'Big Three' – Champion Hurdle, Cheltenham Gold Cup and Grand National. Besides *West Tip* in the National, he had most famously partnered the beloved grey 'Dessie' to win seven races, including the King George VI Chase in 1989 and 1990.

Unlike so many champion jockeys Dunwoody did not maintain a connection with racing once his riding days were over. As he admitted in his autobiography: 'Retired, I am trying to live a normal life and, to be honest, I don't think I am very good at being normal.' Not content with running his own sports marketing company, he now took up an extraordinary range of activities, most of them on behalf of charities.

In April, 2000, he drove his Porsche 911 in a supporting Cup race to the British Grand Prix. One year later, when the Grand National was being run, he was away on a four-month flying-and-backpacking tour of the world. He took up road running, achieving a most worthy 1 hr. 26 min. in the Great North Run and competing in the London and New York marathon and the London Triathlon; in addition, he went into sports management and took a BBC media course. But he dearly missed big-time racing, as indicated in 2002 when he sounded out the Jockey Club about returning from retirement to take over from the injured Adrian Maguire on *Florida Pearl* in the Cheltenham Gold Cup. He was politely advised that he could not expect to prove himself fit enough to resume a licence at only a few days' notice.

Yet soon afterwards he was fit enough to run the London Marathon in just over 3 hrs 10min, finishing ahead of his old race rivals Marcus and Gee Armytage; and then he set off on a 150-mile sleigh-pulling trek across the frozen wastes of Baffin Island in the Arctic Circle, with all the proceeds going to the Motor Neurone Disease Association which works to combat the disease that claimed trainer Colin Nash for whom he had ridden his first winner so many years ago. Similarly, in 2003, at Grand National time, he was travelling on skis and pulling a sled as he competed in a 330-mile team race to the magnetic North Pole. Enduring severe hardships, and twice dislocating his right shoulder in falls, he and his partner, Tony Martin, finished second in the Polar Race – again raising funds for the MNDA.

Having recovered from reconstruction surgery on his shoulder, he was still relentlessly seeking to fill the void left by the lost thrill of race-riding. He went on to drive the Sahara Desert in the World Cup Rally; to take part in the Gumball 3000 Rally; and to climb Aconcagua, the highest peak in the Andes, on behalf of the International Spinal Research Trust.

Feeling so much fitter than when he 'retired', Dunwoody was still dreaming of a return to the saddle at the age of 41. But that dream was finally abandoned in 2005 after a series of X-rays and MRI scans on his neck. Though a spinal root operation had been successful, his neck had become more arthritic over the years and the chances of breaking it in a fall were judged to have increased.

But nothing was allowed to stop his charity work. In 2008 he successfully tackled his toughest ever challenge – following the hazardous route to the South Pole that Sir Ernest Shackleton had proposed taking in 1914.

See also: West Tip; Miinnehoma; Tactics.

DURANT, Tim

Dubbed 'The Galloping Grandad', American Tim Durant became the oldest rider to complete the Grand National course when, in 1968, he remounted his own *Highlandie*, a 100-1 chance, at the second Becher's, and came home the 15th of 17 finishers in a 44-strong field. He was making his third and last attempt to get round at the age of 68. Durant's stubborn determination to finish in the National epitomised the nature of a colourful character whose ambition led him on a rollercoaster ride through life.

Having graduated from Yale University, where he read Russian literature, he aimed first to become a millionaire by the age of 30. He married into a most wealthy family, prospered as a New York stockbroker, then lost both his fortune and his wife in the wake of the 1929 Wall Street crash.

The young man now went west to make a new career in Hollywood. As a teenager he had been a

D

keen huntsman in Connecticut, and his riding skills and rangy ruggedness ensured him regular work in cowboy movies. He became a good friend of director John Huston who used him in several pictures, most notably his Civil War movie, *The Red Badge of Courage*; also of Charles Chaplin who employed him as press agent and investment adviser.

Though never more than a bit-player in Hollywood, six foot tall Durant became a prominent figure in the movie colony, not least as the founder of the West Hunt Club in Los Angeles. He escorted such megastars as Greta Garbo and Paulette Goddard; and when he eventually re-married, it was in Ireland, from the country home of Huston who, as a regular rider to foxhounds, turned out in full hunting gear for the wedding.

After turning 60, Durant became obsessed with a new ambition: to ride in the Grand National. To counter arguments that he was 'too old', he demonstrated his fitness by riding in a marathon race over the Sierra Nevada mountains. Then, having gained the financial support of his married daughter, Mrs Marjorie Dye, he flew to England and acquired a ten year old chestnut gelding, *Aerial III* in the Oxfordshire stable of trainer Roddy Armytage. As a past winner of the Liverpool Fox Hunters Chase, *Ariel III* was regarded as a worthy challenger for the 1966 National.

The 66-year old American now began an intensive fitness training programme, and he became familiar with the Aintree fences by completing the course in the Becher Chase. Then, to his utter dismay, *Aerial III* was ruled out of the National by tendon trouble. Mrs Dye promptly came to rescue. After consulting the Armytages, she bought another experienced chaser, ten year old *King Pin*, as a substitute. Her father first rode him in a Kempton chase, finishing runner-up. Then, accompanied by massive publicity, and with huge support from Americans who had formed a Tim Durant Preservation Society, he made his bid to become the oldest winner of the National. The bid ended with an exhausted *King Pin* having to be pulled up, but not before the 'galloping grandad' had successfully nursed his 100-1 mount over two-thirds of the course.

It was an honourable attempt but seemingly the old man's last as one setback followed another. Firstly, *King Pin* had to be put down after falling with Durant in a race in Sweden. Then the American

was diagnosed with having bone cancer in an ankle. His lower leg, he was told, would need to be amputated. Durant, however, refused to accept the initial prognosis. He flew from Los Angeles to seek a second opinion in New York, and there he underwent an operation to remove the diseased lump. It was so successful that he went back into training for a second National bid. This time, *Aerial III* was race-fit, but again the American was on a 100-1 outsider, one of 13 in the 44-strong field.

It was the year of the sensational pile-up caused at the small 23rd fence by the riderless *Popham Down*, a melée avoided only by *Foinavon* who came from far behind to win at 100-1. But that was no excuse for Durant's failure. His National had ended at the 19th – largely, in the trainer's opinion, because the American, stubbornly refusing to carry a stick, had hunted round in such an amateurish style.

Back in North America, Durant rode much more effectively to win a major chase in Toronto, and the following year, aged 68, he was again bidding for National glory. His mount – bought a few weeks before the race – was an 11 year old Irish-trained gelding named *Highlandie*. For the third time he was riding a 100-1 outsider, and this time bookies confidently laid a bet of £500 and a case of champagne against the American veteran completing the course.

Their expectations were seemingly met when they saw Durant tumble out of the saddle on landing over Becher's second time around. But they had not allowed for his stubborn streak. The American never released his grip on the reins. Both horse and rider got up from the turf and, having remounted, the 'galloping grandad' set off in pursuit of the field – to such effect that he came home in 15th place with just two other finishers behind him, the last, *Quintin Bay*, being ridden by Willie Robinson, who had won the 1964 National on *Team Spirit*.

His ambition satisfied, Durant donated his £500 winnings to the Injured Jockeys' Fund and flew home to a great hero's welcome. Though he would not compete at Aintree again, he continued riding in America for several more years and undertook coast-to-coast lecture tours recalling his great Grand National adventure. The tough old campaigner was 85 years old when he finally lost a renewed battle with his cancerous enemy.

See also: United States.

DURHAM EDITION

One of the greatest of Aintree specialists to be denied a deserved Grand National victory. In four attempts – the last as a 13 year old – *Durham Edition* finished second (1988), fifth (1989), second (1990), and sixth (1991), each time in partnership with the equally unlucky Chris Grant, who had also been on a runner-up, *Young Driver*, in 1986.

A chestnut gelding – by *Politico* out of *Level Stakes* – *Durham Edition* was a careful jumper and the most reliable of the many National contenders to be trained by Arthur Stephenson. He opened his account over hurdles in the 1983-84 season and he won three chases in each of the next four seasons. Prior to his 1988 National debut he showed his best form when third in the Hennessy Gold Cup behind *Playschool*.

At Aintree, going off at 20-1 in a 40-strong field, he had a three lengths lead over the last fence only to be outpaced by *Rhyme 'N' Reason*. In 1989 the heavy ground stretched his stamina beyond its limit. Then, in 1990, he at last had his favoured fast ground, and as a 12 year old, he broke *Red Rum's* course record. But *Mr Frisk* broke it marginally better to win by three-quarters of a length.

In his final National, the veteran *Durham Edition* was harshly burdened with his highest weight and went off at his longest price of 25-1. Steadily moving up on the second circuit, he finished a most honourable sixth.

DUTTON, William Parker

Rider of the Grand National's most improbable winner: *Tipperary Tim*, the tubed, parrot-mouthed plodder who became the first 100-1 success in 1928 when only two of 42 starters completed the course, with the distant second having been remounted.

Son of a Cheshire farmer, Billy Dutton originally chose the law as a career. When he was articled to his uncle, a Cheshire solicitor, he was already earning the reputation of being one of the best amateur National Hunt riders in the country, most notably having won Liverpool's 1925 Foxhunters Chase on ten year old *Upton Lad*. On the same bay gelding, however, he was a faller when making his National debut in 1926, and again the following year.

Having recently passed his final law examination with honours, Dutton returned for his third National with no hope whatsoever of victory. His only ambition was to complete the course. Thus, trailing the field almost from the start, he chose to take the widest route because 'I found the going was soundest on the far side where there was not even a footprint'. The tactic ensured that he kept out of trouble – most notably avoiding the horrendous pile-up at the Canal Turn that decimated the field on the first circuit. To his amazement, when approaching the last, only one other horse and rider were left in contention; and there his lone rival, the American champion chaser *Billy Barton*, fell. *Tipperary Tim* plodded on to win by a distance.

Dutton was so thrilled by his success that he quit his law career to concentrate on riding. But he was never to experience such a triumph again. In 1929, *Tipperary Tim*, raised 10lb for his freak win, was again a 100-1 shot. This time he was a faller, one of 56 who failed to finish in a National with 66 starters, the biggest field of all time. In 1930 Dutton fell on *Blennerhasset*, a 66-1 chance, and in 1931, on his last appearance, he was brought down on *Mallard*, another 100-1 outsider.

The following year Dutton started training at Hednesford, Staffordshire, later moving to Malton, North Yorkshire. Such was his versatility as a trainer that at one time the horses in his yard ranged from the giant *Limber Hill*, an outstanding marathon chaser, to two top-rated sprinters *Pappa Fourway* and *Bright Boy*. The former sprinter won 12 races including the July Cup, the King's Stand Stakes, Diadem Stakes and Gosforth Park Cup. *Bright Boy's* 16 wins included the Nunthorpe Stakes (twice), the July Cup, King George Stakes, Cork and Orrery Stakes and the King's Stand.

Dutton's most notable National Hunt success came in 1956 when, after an impressive King George VI Chase victory, *Limber Hill* went on to win the Cheltenham Gold Cup under the former National-winning jockey, Jimmy Power.

In 1957 he was represented in the National by the little eight year old mare *Red Menace* (a faller), but that same year also brought a major success on the Flat when he won the 1957 Cesarewitch with *Sandiacre*. He died one year later – he was only 57. *See also:* Tipperary Tim.

E

EARLY MIST

Winner of the 1953 Coronation Year Grand National, registering the first victory in an unprecedented hat-trick for trainer Vincent O'Brien and the first of two successive triumphs for jockey Bryan Marshall and owner Mr Joe Griffin. One year before – on his National debut as a seven year old under Pat Taaffe – *Early Mist* had been one of ten fallers at the first fence.

It was an ironic turnaround since *Early Mist* – a big chestnut gelding by *Brumeux* out of *Sudden Dawn* – had previously been owned by Mr J.V. Rank, the flour-milling magnate who, with fourteen runners over two decades, had spent a fortune in vain pursuit of owning a National winner. Sadly he died three months before seven year old *Early Mist* made his National debut in the colours of Mrs Rank; and subsequently the chaser was sold for 5,300 guineas at a dispersal sale of Mr Rank's horses. The buyer was the canny O'Brien, acting on behalf of Mr Griffin, a young Dublin businessman who had prospered in the post-war canning industry, becoming known in the trade as 'Mincemeat Joe'.

O'Brien found *Early Mist* a difficult horse to train. He had to be fired and was never a natural jumper. Essentially he needed his rider to make up his mind for him and, realising this, the trainer decided that Marshall would be the ideal jockey for him. Marshall had only one opportunity to ride him before going to Aintree – on St Patrick's Day when they jumped just two fences at Ballydoyle. But it was enough to convince the jockey that he had to gather the hesitant horse very purposefully before every jump.

In 1953 there were no past winners in a relatively small National field of 31; and injury had prevented O'Brien from running *Royal Tan,* who had finished second in both the Irish and Aintree Nationals of 1951. With the advantage of hindsight it now seems remarkable that *Early Mist*, at 20-1, should have gone off eighth in the betting – this for the representative of an Irish wizard who, only three weeks earlier, had turned out *Knock Hard* to become his fourth winner of the Cheltenham Gold Cup in six years.

Right from the start Michael Scudamore led the way on seven year old *Ordnance*. They were narrowly ahead of *Early Mist* at Becher's, then accelerated to establish a ten-length lead by the Canal Turn. *Ordnance* still headed the field at the end of the first circuit but he could no longer sustain such a blistering pace. Two fences before Becher's he fell, leaving *Early Mist* in front, closely followed by Miss Dorothy Paget's top-weighted *Mont Tremblant.* Losing concentration, *Early Mist* brushed through the top of the last fence but thereafter, with a 17lb advantage, he powered away from his main rival, and he looked unextended as he passed the winning post 20 lengths clear of *Mont Tremblant,* with Lord Sefton's *Irish Lizard* a further four lengths back in third. It was a dazzling performance and yet O'Brien would say of his winner: 'He had a bit of speed. He wasn't a jumper as such.'

Mr Griffin performed a celebratory jig beside *Early Mist* in the unsaddling enclosure; and he had the winner again in 1954, with *Royal Tan,* also trained by O'Brien. But that year his frail-founded business empire collapsed in ruins and his horses had to be sold – *Early Mist* to Mr John Dunlop and *Royal Tan* to Prince Aly Khan. Both winners reappeared for the 1955 National, along with two other O'Brien-trained runners, *Quare Times* and *Oriental Way.* Bryan Marshall opted to ride *Early Mist,* the 9-1 second favourite following a useful fourth-placed run in the Cheltenham Gold Cup. But this year, raised 15lb in the weights, the champion chaser struggled on the extremely heavy ground, as did the top-weighted *Royal Tan.* They finished ninth and 12th respectively behind O'Brien's third National winner, *Quare Times.*

In his fourth and last Grand National, in 1956, *Early Mist* was both trained and ridden by Bryan Marshall. Now an 11 year old, burdened with top weight, he ended his National career as it had begun – one of four runners to fall at the very first fence. *See also:* O'Brien, Vincent; Marshall, Bryan.

EARTH SUMMIT

Winner of the 1998 Grand National, when, as 7-1 favourite and an out-and-out stayer favoured by the heavy ground, he triumphed by eleven lengths from his only serious challenger, the gallant *Suny Bay* who was giving him 23lb. It was a second Grand National success for jockey Carl Llewellyn and the first of two for trainer Nigel Twiston-Davies. It made the ten year old bay gelding the first horse to have won the Scottish, Welsh and Aintree Nationals; also the first since *L'Escargot* (1975) to win the Grand National wearing blinkers.

Foaled on April Fool's Day, 1988, *Earth Summit*

was by the leading National Hunt sire *Celtic Cone* out of *Win Green Hill*. Though his dam, a chase winner over an extended two miles, was not highly regarded, stamina aplenty was promised by way of an outstanding stallion who, before becoming a useful jumper, had won the Ascot Stakes, the Queen Alexandra Stakes and the Yorkshire Cup, and had been runner-up in the Ascot Gold Cup.

Originally sold as a two year old for £4,000, *Earth Summit* was a four year old gelding when sent by Peter Scudamore Bloodstock Ltd to the Doncaster sales. There, he was bought for a mere 5,800 guineas on behalf of a six-man syndicate put together by Nigel Payne, Aintree's PRO, and including Ricky George, the goalscoring hero of non-League Hereford's famous 1972 FA Cup defeat of Newcastle. They chose his name because it was the time of the Earth Summit in Brazil and because of the 'green' connection through his dam. Later they nicknamed him 'Digger' because he so often clawed up his bedding into a heap.

As recalled by Payne, when *Earth Summit* was first paraded at the Twiston-Davies yard, jockey Steve Smith Eccles remarked: 'Plain little thing, isn't he? Still, he might win you a seller one day.' How soon this view was proved wrong. On his racing debut, a National Hunt Flat race over an extended two miles at Cheltenham, the four year old finished second of 25 runners. The following year, 1993, he had 11 outings, winning a novice hurdle and novices' chases at Haydock and Chepstow. From the beginning he showed huge potential whenever running on soft or heavy ground over three miles or more. He was a supremely accurate jumper, and it was now discovered that he greatly improved with blinkers.

The thought that he was 'an ideal Grand National type' was first expressed by Llewellyn early in 1994 when, in his first run as a six year old, he won over an extended two and a half miles at Cheltenham. Back there in March, as a 66-1 chance, he finished seventh in a very high quality Sun Alliance Chase. One month later he proved his true staying power by romping home to a 14 lengths victory in the four miles one furlong Scottish National at 16-1. Eased up by David Bridgwater ahead of the joint favourites *Bishop's Island* and *Superior Finish*, he was the youngest ever winner of the race.

That victory brought prize money of £29,700 and the following season the syndicate's 'Gold Digger'

brought in another £38,269 by winning the Young Chaser Championship Final at Cheltenham and the Peter Marsh Chase at Haydock, and finishing second in the Welsh National, held at Newbury that year. As a result, he was made the 10-1 co-favourite for the 1995 Grand National. Then everything started to go wrong.

Minor tendon trouble caused him to miss the Aintree National, and a nine-month break followed. Then, in February, 1996, after two comeback runs, he was cruising at the front in the Greenalls National Trial at Haydock when he slipped on the flat, falling so badly that his fetlock lay horizontal to the ground. He had a suspensory ligament damaged so severely that it was feared he would never race again. As it was, he had to be rested a full year before gradually being brought back into work under the care of his dedicated lass Marcella Bayliss.

Twenty-one months after his injury *Earth Summit* finally returned to racing. finishing fifth in two loosening-up chases. Then, in December, 1997, he revealed his supreme staying power of old. As a 25-1 chance, ridden by Tom Jenks, he held on in deep mud to resist the late surge of *Dom Samourai* in the £30,846 Welsh National. The great money-spinner was back.

One month later 'Digger' struggled to finish a remote sixth in the Peter Marsh Chase at Haydock; and so, when the Grand National weights were announced, the ten year old was a best priced 25-1 while his longer-priced stablemate *Young Hustler* became all the rage, being regarded as a handicap snip on 10st 2lb. All that changed, however, on the run-up to the race. *Young Hustler* was subsequently withdrawn; and, with the promise of heavy going, the mud-loving *Earth Summit*, on a sporting 10st 5lb, was a late market mover, being made the 7-1 favourite by punters and the most napped runner by the tipsters. Close behind in the betting were *Samlee*, *Rough Quest* and *Him of Praise*, followed by the top-weighted *Suny Bay*, an 11-1 chance who was conceding a colossal two stone to 30 of the runners in the 37-strong field.

Through the injury of Jenks (broken leg), *Earth Summit's* former regular partner, Carl Llewellyn, picked up the ride; and after hunting round the first circuit he was surprised how easily his horse then moved up through the field. Many were pulled up or fell, and when the French challenger *Ciel de Brion* and *Greenhil Tare Away* went at the 26th and

E

27th respectively, *Earth Summit* was left with only one serious rival: *Suny Bay*. As they crossed the Melling Road and headed back towards the stands, Graham Bradley on *Suny Bay* shouted across to say that they were so far ahead (about 30 lengths) of the rest that perhaps they should steady up. At that stage he thought he would win.

But Llewellyn had no need to steady up. Still full of running, *Earth Summit* was two to three lengths ahead at The Elbow and, though the grey gallantly fought back, his 23lb disadvantage on deep ground soon proved decisive. Only four others completed the course, with *Samlee* (Richard Dunwoody) and *St Mellion Fairway* (Andrew Thornton) fighting out a close battle for the other places. Such was the bottomless ground that the winning time, 10min 51.4sec, was the slowest since 1883 when *Zoedone* won in 11min 39sec.

Seven months later *Earth Summit* returned to Aintree for his seasonal debut. He was now burdened with 12st top weight, giving a stone to his nearest rival, two stone to the majority, and yet he won the Becher Chase by 11 lengths from *Samlee*, now 18lb better off, with only one other runner completing the course. The following month he was a fine second to *Suny Bay* off level weights at Haydock but then came two disappointing runs prior to the Grand National, in which he was set to carry 9lb more than last year.

Jenks had partnered *Earth Summit* in his four previous races. Now he was jocked off in favour of Llewellyn and instead took the ride on 13 year old outsider *Commercial Artist*. But it proved no great loss. Though *Earth Summit*, a 16-1 chance, was impeded by a pile-up at the second Becher's, he was never going the pace on ground faster than he liked. Weakening three out, he finished eighth. However, his jumping was as immaculate as ever; and the Aintree specialist had now jumped 81 National fences without falling,

That number was boosted to 102 when, after another seven-month break, *Earth Summit* finished a distant fifth under 12st in Aintree's Tote Becher Chase. But while his jumping remained safe the old relentless galloping was missing. The handicapper had clearly got his measure as was shown one month later when he plodded home ninth in the Welsh National. It was his last race. He was retired in January, 2000, after heat had been discovered in a foreleg, and then presented to his lass, Marcella Bayliss, who continued to care for him at Naunton, just outside Cheltenham.

In his seven-year career *Earth Summit* had run in 41 races, winning ten and being placed in eight, and he had earned a staggering £372,565 in prize money. Diagnosed with cancer of the liver, he died in 2005, aged 17.

See also: Twiston-Davies, Nigel; Scudamore, Peter; Llewellyn, Carl; Payne, Nigel; Fixes; Gambles.

EASTER HERO

One of the greatest of the chasers to run in the Grand National without winning. Irish-bred – by *My Prince* out of *Easter Week* – *Easter Hero* first appeared in the race in 1928 as an eight year old with a hugely promising record. He had won the 1926 Molyneux Chase at Liverpool and the 1927 Becher Chase, and recently, after six successive wins, he had been purchased by Belgian financier Captain A. Lowenstein for the then colossal sum of £7,000.

Such was *Easter Hero*'s reputation that, on his National debut, he was heavily handicapped with 12st 5lb and went off joint fourth in the betting. It seemed well justified in the early stages; he set a fast pace from the start and, despite the boggy ground, was jumping superbly. But then he came to the notorious open ditch at the Canal Turn, misjudged his take-off and landed squarely on top of the fence, with the rest of the field bearing down upon him. The result was the worst pile-up yet seen, with only two of 42 starters going on to finish, and only one – the 100-1 *Tipperary Tim* – doing so without having fallen.

Despite that costly misjudgment, *Easter Hero* was given the top weight of 12st 7lb for the 1929 National, and made the 9-1 favourite. After all, he had won his last five races, including, most recently, the Cheltenham Gold Cup by an impressive 20 lengths. He had a new trainer, the masterful Jack Anthony; also a new owner, U.S. millionaire 'Jock' Hay Whitney, following the presumed suicide of Captain Lowenstein who had vanished when flying in his private plane over the North Sea.

This year the dreaded ditch at the Canal Turn had been filled in to prevent a repeat of the 1928 fiasco. But now there was a new kind of hazard: a record field of 66 starters, including many of inferior quality. Again, *Easter Hero* was front-running and jumping in brilliant style. And he dominated as far as

Valentine's the second time around. But thereafter he began to labour, having most unluckily twisted a plate. Bravely he ran on in discomfort, trying to preserve his lead. But finally he was overhauled after the second last by his half-brother *Gregalach*, a 66-1 chance with a 17lb weight advantage. He was beaten six lengths, with *Richmond II* a distant third.

In 1930 *Easter Hero* again won the Cheltenham Gold Cup by 20 lengths – the first horse to succeed twice in the race – but he was kept out of the National by a tendon sprain. Nevertheless, when he returned to Aintree the following year, he was again burdened with 12st 7lb and made the 5-1 favourite. This year he arrived fresh, the Gold Cup having been cancelled, and he was ridden by Fred Rees, the winning rider in the 1921 National.

Yet again, *Easter Hero*, now 11 years old, was hugely impressive; and he was well placed to mount a challenge as the leaders came to Becher's the second time around. But there *Solanum* was brought down by a riderless horse. The favourite, directly behind them, had no escape route and, along with several others, was brought crashing down.

It was the brilliant chestnut's last National bid. One day later he dead-heated with a fairly ordinary chaser in the two-mile Champion Chase Cup, and he was immediately retired to serve his American owner as a hunter. A winner of 20 steeplechases and the first dual Cheltenham Gold Cup victor, he died in Virginia at the age of 28.

See also: Whitney 'Jock' Hay; Tipperary Tim; Gregalach.

EDE, George Matthew

It was under the pseudonym of 'Mr Edwards' that the tall, elegant George Ede chose to ride in nine Grand Nationals. On his debut in 1858 he finished second on the 25-1 shot *Weathercock*. One decade later he rode at his brilliant best to triumph on Lord Poulett's *The Lamb*, driving the diminutive grey home to win by two lengths after a neck-and-neck duel with *Pearl Diver*.

Born 1834, the son of a wealthy Southampton landowner, Ede was strictly an amateur rider, and an outstanding one, having been tutored in horsemanship by Ben Land Snr. He and his twin brother Edward were educated at Eton, both emerging as prominent cricketers. Later, with his close friend and patron Lord Poulett, George founded the Hampshire Cricket Club for whom he batted with distinction,

scoring 1,200 runs for the county in 1863.

Between his promising debut and his victory, Ede's National rides were undistinguished – *Master Bagot* (1861) fell; outsider *The Freshman* (1863), fell; 9-2 favourite *Jerusalem* (1864) remounted and later pulled up; outsider *Ace Of Hearts* (1866) fell; *Genierve* (1867) last of ten finishers. In 1869 he was sixth on *Despatch* and the following year he failed to finish on *Guy of Warwick*. But elsewhere he had now ridden more than 300 winners.

Ede regarded the 1870 National as his farewell appearance; he was soon to be married and had already decided to retire from serious racing. But just as he was about to leave Aintree, a trainer, Mr Carew, begged him to stay on to ride *Chippenham* the next day in the Grand Sefton Chase. His friend and companion Arthur Yates strongly advised him against it. 'Don't ride the brute, George, He'll kill you.' But George was not one to duck a challenge. He did ride the temperamental *Chippenham*, and the horse did kill him. After a nose-diving fall at the fence before the Water, the rider, with one leg trapped in the iron, was dragged a hundred yards and trampled upon. He never regained consciousness.

It was the same fence that had claimed the life of James Wynne eight years before. And the loss of so popular an amateur rider, at the age of 36, was to be followed one year later by the loss of the most popular professional rider, George Stevens, who suffered a fatal off-course riding fall.

See also: The Lamb; Poulett, Lord.

EDWARDS, Mr

The pseudonym of the winner of the 1868 Grand National on *The Lamb*.

See also: Ede, George Matthew.

EGERTON, Charles

In 2000 trainer Charles Egerton saddled the first horse since the great *Manifesto* (1902) to be placed in the Grand National on his seasonal debut. More remarkably, his fragile nine year old *Mely Moss*, having his first race for 346 days, was beaten only a length and a quarter in bidding to emulate a first-time-out victory last achieved by the Irish mare *Frigate* in 1889.

For a moment, as *Mely Moss* showed briefly ahead of *Papillon* over the second last, Egerton thought he was going to win. But then he realised that his horse, being spurred on with maximum

E

energy by 'Stormin' Norman' Williamson, was only helping a rival who was prone to idle when left in front without a challenge. His runner-up, a 25-1 chance, narrowly lost the duel to the line but finished 12 lengths ahead of third-placed *Niki Dee*.

It was a brilliant achievement on the part of a trainer who had fine-tuned his first National runner after problems that had limited *Mely Moss* to just five races since the start of 1997. He sought to do even better in the 2001 National when his chaser, raised 6lb in the weights, came out after a layoff of 364 days. But this was the year of the great quagmire when only two finished without falling. *Mely Moss* was jumping brilliantly when he landed amid the pile-up that saw eight runners exiting at the Canal Turn first time round.

Born September 25, 1963, Egerton had been fascinated by horse racing since his schooldays at Eton where he was a member of the Equestrian Society and visited racecourses whenever the opportunity arose. After two years with trainer Nick Gaselee and a brief spell as coffee boy at the British Bloodstock Agency, he learned most about horses while working in Australia for trainer Colin Hayes. Back in England he became a partner in a bloodstock company and, setting up as a trainer in 1991, had a winner with his very first runner, *Torrent Bay*, at Windsor. Though operating on a small scale at Chaddleworth in Berkshire, and being hit especially hard by a virus in 1998, he was to achieve a remarkably high strike-rate, turning out such high-class hurdlers as *Mysilv*, *Teaatral*, *Shadow Leader* and *Decoupage*.

In 2001, when preparing *Mely Moss* for his second National bid, Egerton amazed his friends by his determination in preparing himself for no less a challenge: shedding more than three stones from his 18-stone frame to run in the London Marathon on behalf of the Countryside Alliance. The following year he ran *Mely Moss* in the National again. This time his horse was appearing after one seasonal outing – a three-mile chase at Sandown, and it was noteworthy that Williamson chose him in preference to the long-time ante-post favourite *Moor Lane*. Unluckily he was brought down at the 27th when going well and, remounted, was the last of 11 finishers.

In 2003 Egerton was represented by *Killusty*, a hugely promising nine year old with five wins in his last five races but only just out of the novice stage as

a chaser. With Tony Dobbin replacing the injured Williamson, he was making good headway until falling at the second Becher's.

It was four years before Egerton again made a National bid, and this time – not long after some of his horses had suffered from a viral infection – he had two runners: *Gallant Approach* and *Graphic Approach*. The former was tailed off after blundering at The Chair but plodded on to trail in the far distant last of 12 finishers. The latter, a 100-1 shot, fell at the second Becher's, subsequently jumped a rail and ran loose before collapsing concussed in front of the grandstands, where his need for on-the-spot treatment caused the last race of the meeting to be abandoned. Sadly, nearly four weeks later, the long battle to save *Graphic Approach* was finally lost when he developed pneumonia.

ELBOW, The

The point of the Grand National course, halfway along the 494-yard run-in, where horses need to tack right on approach to bypass The Chair and Water Jump, and then run straight to the finish. Failure to do so results in the loss of valuable ground, a classic example being the run of second-placed *Clan Royal* who wandered left in 2004 after clearing the last. A whipless Liam Cooper had to drag him back to negotiate The Elbow and was beaten by three lengths.

ELDER, Tommy

At the end of the 20th century, Tommy Elder was, at 91, the oldest living Grand National jockey. He recalled that he was paid ten guineas to ride in the race in the 1930s. His National rides were: Lord Rosebery's *Keen Blade* (1936) fell; *Lucky Patch* (1939) refused; and *Red Eagle* (1940), the 16th of 17 finishers. Hailing from Coxwold near Thirsk in Yorkshire, Elder rode more than 400 winners including victories in the Scottish National and the Welsh National. He also scored an out-of-the-saddle victory at the Grand National meeting when he successfully led a threatened strike in protest at Mirabel Topham's proposed plan to charge jockeys for parking on the Aintree racecourse.

ELLIOTT, Gordon

The glorious impartiality of the Grand National – granting no favours on grounds of age, experience or reputation – was admirably illustrated on the sun-drenched afternoon of April 14, 2007, when a boyish-looking 29 year old Irishman led in the winner of the near £400,000 first prize. Gordon Elliott, a novice trainer who had not yet turned out a single winner in his native Ireland, had landed the world's most famous steeplechase with 33-1 shot *Silver Birch* whom he had only bought as 'a fun horse for cross-country races'.

Triumphant with his first National runner, the fresh-faced Elliott had once spent a year valuably working for the all-conquering Martin Pipe who was to have just one National winner from 81 runners; and, ironically, he had acquired the rejected *Silver Birch* out of the yard of Paul Nicholls, the champion trainer who had now saddled 37 National contenders without one success.

Gordon Elliott was still a schoolboy when he began working with horses at Tony Martin's stable in Co. Meath. He went on to become one of Ireland's most successful point-to-point jockeys, riding 200 winners and a further 50 under Rules.

Having moved in 2002 to the Pipe yard in Somerset as an amateur jockey, he twice had hopes of riding in the National, and twice they were dashed – firstly because his licence failed to come through in time, and secondly because a more experienced rider had become available. Then, after he had rejoined Martin in Ireland, rising weight and a shoulder injury led to his retirement from race-riding in January, 2006.

It was not until the following July that he began training at Capranny Stables in Co. Meath – a yard he rented from Barry Callaghan, who happened to be a part-owner of *Dun Doire*, the ante-post favourite for the 2007 National. Jokingly, Elliott later remarked that he might be in danger of eviction if he were to win the National at his landlord's expense.

Initially, such a result seemed beyond the realms of possibility. After all, Elliott had trained only three winners in Britain, and none in his homeland; and his only Aintree qualifier was a reject that had been picked up for a mere 20,000 guineas at the 2006 Doncaster Spring sales with plans to run him in point-to-points and cross-country races on behalf of his owner, 26 year old Brian Walsh.

But Elliott was to work wonders with *Silver Birch*. Riding him out with the Ward Union Hunt, he rekindled the horse's enthusiasm, had him jumping with all the zest that had seen him win the Becher Chase and then the Welsh National back in 2004.

Rejuvenated, the 10 year old gelding proved his well-being at the Cheltenham Festival with a fine run over three miles seven furlongs in the cross-country chase, finishing second and well ahead of Nicholls' National entries *Le Duc* and *Royal Auclair*.

The rookie trainer had been thinking of saving *Silver Birch* for the La Touche race at Punchestown in late April and then perhaps the marathon Pardubicka in the Czech Republic. But now he and Walsh favoured going for the National – encouraged not least by a handicap mark of 10st 6lb, 6lb less than the weight *Silver Birch* had carried when unluckily falling at The Chair in the 2006 National.

At Aintree Elliott was the youngest and least experienced of trainers involved with the National. The day after saddling the winner, he had two runners at Worcester, both unsuccessful. But no matter. That Sunday he was parading his first big-race winner at the Curragh, and then in Trim, a few miles from where *Bobbyjo* had been trained. For the sixth time in nine years the Irish were hailing a conquering Grand National hero. Just three weeks later, at Kilbeggan, Elliott turned out *Toran Road* in a handicap chase to score his first win under Rules in his native Ireland. At 29, he was now clearly marked out as a trainer with a bright future ahead.

See also: Silver Birch; Power, Robbie.

ELMORE, John

Owner of *Lottery*, the first Grand National winner; also of the 1842 winner, *Gay Lad*. John Elmore was such an active and artful horse dealer – buying and then selling or leasing animals to a wealthy clientele – that he may, as rumoured, have also been at least part-owner of the 1840 winner, *Jerry*, who ran in the colours of one of his clients, Mr Henry Villebois.

Certainly, Elmore had owned *Jerry* not long before the National, having won the Leamington Steeplechase with him. One theory is that the true ownership was concealed at Aintree because Elmore already had a runner (*Lottery* again) and did not wish market moves to indicate which horse was favoured by his stable. In a field of only 12, *Lottery* went off the 4-1 second favourite while *Jerry* was an outsider at 12-1.

Based near Harrow, North London, Elmore was one of the shrewdest operators in the land. At the 1836 Horncastle Horse Fair in Lincolnshire, he paid only £120 for his most famous chaser *Lottery*. And typical of his astute dealings was his purchase of

E

Sir William, winner of the 1838 Grand Steeplechase at Maghull near Aintree. Having bought the unruly chaser for £350, he promptly resold him to Lord Cranstoun for £1,000.

Following his victory in the 1839 National, *Lottery* went on win the 1840 Cheltenham Steeplechase but the result was an 18lb penalty for his reappearance at Aintree. In both 1841 and 1842 he was made the favourite despite a monstrous 13st 4lb on his back. By the latter year Elmore recognized that it was an impossible burden to carry, and so he successfully entered another runner, eight year old *Gay Lad*, with the renowned Tom Olliver booked for the ride.

Spread over the first sixteen years of the Grand National, his runners comprised: *Lottery* (1839, first); *Lottery* (1840, fell); *Lottery* (1841, pulled up); *Lottery* (1842, pulled up); *Gay Lad* (1842, first); *Lottery* (1843, seventh); *British Yeoman* (1848, third); *British Yeoman* (1849, sixth); *Mulligan* (1851, seventh) *Everton* (1852, fell); and *Janus* (fourth in 1855).

See also: Lottery; Jerry; McDonough, Alan; Mason, Jem.

ELSWORTH, David Raymond Cecil

Trainer of *Rhyme 'N' Reason* who, on his one and only appearance in the race, made an extraordinary recovery to come from last to first in the 1988 Grand National. Equally, David Elsworth is renowned as the trainer of the wonderful, long-serving, long-staying *Persian Punch*, winner of 20 races and more than £1 million in prize money on the Flat, and, above all, of *Desert Orchid*, the most beloved grey of modern times and, along with *Arkle*, the greatest chaser never to be risked in the Aintree National.

Born December 12, 1939, three months after the outbreak of the Second World War, Elsworth started out as a National Hunt jockey at the age of 18. He rode for 15 years and appeared in the Grand National of 1968 when, going well, he was unlucky to be brought down at the 23rd fence on eight year old *Chamoretta*, a 100-1 outsider. Ten years later he set up as a trainer at Whitsbury, near Fordingbridge in Hampshire, and very rapidly emerged as a master of his art whether preparing horses for the Flat or over jumps. As many experts observed, he had an intuitive racing brain, a rare gift for understanding how a horse thinks and how it needs to run.

On the Flat, he was especially famed and feared for his ability to bring horses to peak form for big handicaps. Though his Whitsbury operation was not in the league of the big-time stables, he turned out *Mighty Flutter* to take third place in the Epsom Derby (1984) and *Norse Dancer* to finish third at 100-1 in the 2,000 Guineas (2003). His outstanding winners included *In The Groove* who won the Irish 1000 Guineas, International Stakes and Champion Stakes in 1990, and the Coronation Cup in 1991; and *Seattle Rhyme* who scored in the 1991 Racing Post Trophy at Doncaster. Moreover, he trained and half-owned *Island Sands* before he was sold to Godolphin and went on to win the 2,000 Guineas of 1999.

All the while he was also making great strides as a jumps trainer. In 1983 his National runner, *Canford Ginger*, was pulled up, and on his return in 1984 he was a 100-1 shot who came home the last of 23 finishers. But four years later, in complete contrast, he returned to Aintree to take first place and, with the victory of *Rhyme 'N' Reason*, seal his bid for the 1987-88 National Hunt trainers' championship. It confirmed his standing as the most versatile trainer in the land. His other jump triumphs include the Triumph Hurdle with *Heighlin*; (1980) and *Oh So Risky* (1991); the Queen Mother Champion Chase (1989 and 1990) with *Barnbrook Again*; the Tote Gold Trophy Hurdle with *Jamesmead* (1988); and – with the great *Desert Orchid* – the 1989 Cheltenham Gold Cup, the King George V1 Chase a record four times, the 1988 Whitbread Gold Cup and the 1990 Jameson Irish Grand National.

Such are the vagaries of the jumping game that, in 1989, one year after winning the National, Elsworth saw his only Aintree runner – 80-1 shot *Cerimau* – fall at the first fence. In 1990 he ran the Hennessy Cognac Gold Cup winner *Ghofar*, attempting to be the first seven year old winner for 50 years. He finished a far distant 14th. Again, in 1992, he sent out a seven year old, *Mighty Falcon*, together with his more favoured *Ghofar*. They finished 11th and 18th respectively. In the void National of 1993 his well-supported *Givus A Buck* was the fifth of seven to complete the course. Then came his *Mighty Falcon*, a 250-1 outsider, brought down at the 13th in 1994; and *Cool Ground*, a 13 year old finishing 11th in 1995.

In 1999 Elsworth announced that he was to give up National Hunt racing to concentrate on the Flat. After more than 20 years in the jumping game, he was no longer enjoying it because he so often had to deal with injury problems. But he still had a fine and burgeoning stable of horses to run on the Flat with his son taking a leading role in the new century.

In the 2005-6 season, he moved his yard of around 100 horses from Whitsbury to Newmarket, taking over David Loder's former base at Egerton House Stables. At the age of 66, with never a thought of retiring, he was delighted with his new improved facilities and as ambitious and enthusiastic as ever.

His only sadness at this time came with the loss of *Desert Orchid* who had been retired in December, 1991 after falling in his attempt to win the King George VI Chase for a fifth time. The beloved 'Dessie' died at Egerton House in November, 2006, at the age of 27.

Reflecting on the super-grey's career, Elsworth said one regret was that his most beautiful chaser had never had a crack at the Grand National. 'It would have been the wrong way for him (left-handed) but they are very long straights on the National course, with rows of fences. He is one horse who would not have been intimidated. In fact, I think he would have loved it.'

See also: Rhyme 'N' Reason; Powell, Brendan; Greys.

EMBLEM

The winner by 20 lengths of the 1863 Grand National, *Emblem* was a seven year old chestnut mare, sired (out of *Miss Batty*) by *Teddington*, who in 1851 had been the first of Sir Joseph Hawley's four Derby winners. Owned by 25 year old Lord Coventry, she was ridden by his close friend George Stevens and, as the 4-1 second favourite, triumphed at the first attempt.

Bred in Wales, *Emblem* was bought as a three year old by a Mr Halford, who later sold her on to Lord Coventry for 300 guineas. Shortly afterwards she ran so appallingly in a Flat race that Halford offered to call off the sale. The young peer not only declined the offer but later, with inspired good judgment, paid him a further 250 guineas for the mare's full sister, *Emblematic*.

Though described as a 'weedy mare', *Emblem* had won seven races on the Flat before moving to Lord Coventry's Earl's Croome estate near Kinnersley, Worcestershire, and then being sent for schooling over fences – first by Tom Golby at Northleach, Gloucestershire, and later by Cotswold trainer

Edwin Weever. Initially a most reluctant jumper, she suddenly came good after being hunted with the North Cotswold Hounds and proved herself to be a natural steeplechaser.

In the National, the masterful Stevens followed his customary tactic, holding up his mount on the first circuit, then making his forward move to launch a late challenge. *Emblem* was still full of running when they struck the front after the penultimate fence. Muddling over the last, she frightened her many backers as she stumbled badly on landing. But Stevens brilliantly got her balanced before powering away on the run-in to win easily from *Arbury*. It was the jockey's second National success.

That same year *Emblem* won the Cheltenham Steeplechase, but she missed the next National which was won by her six year old sister *Emblematic*. When she did come back, in 1865, it was with a top weight of 12st 4lb, the largest penalty seen for many years. Her connections were not surprised to see her pulled up while her preferred sister, the chosen mount of Stevens, finished third. She was duly sent to stud, having four foals, and died in 1871.

See also: Coventry, Lord; Stevens, George

EMBLEMATIC

Though physically most unimposing, *Emblematic* – like her two years older sister *Emblem* – won the Grand National at the first attempt. In a year, 1864, when only five of 25 starters managed to finish, her success owed much to the wily George Stevens who took so much care to keep the frail-looking six year old out of trouble.

True, they struggled awkwardly over the Water, but thereafter they steadily closed on the leaders. At the last, *Emblematic* and *Arbury* were together, far out in front; and on the run-in the former pulled ahead to win by three lengths with the third (*Chester*) a distance behind. It was a third National win for Stevens and, like Lord Coventry, he had heavily backed his mount to win.

It could be reasoned that *Emblematic*'s performance did not compare favourably with that of her sister. She had won in a slower time, albeit in a field with nine more runners; and, while *Emblem* had scored by 20 lengths when receiving 6lb from *Arbury*, she had won by only three when receiving 20lb from the same runner-up. However, when both of Lord Coventry's winning mares were entered for the 1865 National, *Emblematic* was the declared

E

preference of both owner and rider, despite having been raised 18lb in the weights to 11st 10lb.

Key factors were the booking of Stevens for *Emblematic* and the massive 12st 4lb allotted to *Emblem*, a top weight that had never been carried to victory in the race (and would not be carried until *Cloister*'s win in 1893). As a result, *Emblematic* was backed down to 5-1 favouritism, and punters thunderously roared when they saw Stevens, in typical style, moving steadily up the field on the second circuit. But this time the leaders were too strong. Thoroughly outpaced on the run-in, *Emblematic* finished third, some 50 yards behind *Alcibiade* and *Hall Court*, the former winning by a head with Lord Coventry's cousin, Captain Henry Coventry, in the saddle.

Like her sister, *Emblematic* was sent to stud after her two National appearances. Unlike *Emblem*, she ended her days in Prussia, where she was further employed for breeding.
See also: Coventry, Lord; Stevens, George; Emblem.

EMIGRANT

In 1857 the 11 year old *Emigrant* won the Grand National by three lengths from six year old *Weathercock*, a 25-1 chance owned by trainer Ben Land Snr. The great irony was that Land had reluctantly sold the 10-1 winner to bookmaker George Hodgman as the result of a losing run of cards when attending the Shrewsbury races. Hodgman then sold a half-share in the bay gelding to a fellow bookmaker; and, encouraged by *Emigrant*'s sixth place in the 1856 National, the co-owners backed him to win a small fortune the following year.

Above all, they owed their bonanza to the brilliance of jockey Charlie Boyce who, following a recent hunting injury, was riding *Emigrant* with the upper part of one arm strapped to his side. On both circuits, after clearing the Canal Turn, Boyce shrewdly and crucially switched his horse to the wide outside to pick out a strip of firm ground beyond the heavy ploughed land bordering the canal. It gave him such an advantage that the Aintree management subsequently delineated the outer limits of the course with flags lined up with the far sides of fences.

From his earliest runs over fences, *Emigrant* – by *Melbourne* out of *Pandora* – had impressed jockey-turned-trainer Land as an outstanding prospect for the National. Thus it was only in desperation that he sold him for £590 with the promise of an extra £100 if the horse won at Shrewsbury. He did win and he followed up with two more successes before being the last of six finishers under Boyce in the 1856 National.

At Aintree the following year *Emigrant* had been dropped 6lb in the weights and his big-gambling owners were confident of success, not only hitting the bookies but also striking a private wager, betting Mr. T. Hughes, who had four runners in the race, that their horse would be first over the Water Jump. After seven false starts *Emigrant* took an early lead and held on to it throughout. He did not appear in the race again, and the unlucky Ben Land never did achieve his dream of owning a National winner.
See also: Land, Ben Snr; Boyce, Charlie.

EMPRESS

The victory of *Empress*, a five year old mare in the 1880 Grand National, proclaimed the arrival of a dominant new force in European steeplechasing: an Irish force spearheaded by the amazing Beasley brothers in alliance with a new super-trainer, Henry Eyre Linde. Four Beasleys had ridden in the 1879 National. Now three of them returned with Tommy, the eldest, winning on *Empress*, and brothers Harry and John finishing fifth and eighth on *Woodbrook* and *Victoria* respectively.

Empress, a big (over 16 hands) chestnut mare by *Blood Royal* out of *Jeu des Mots*, had recently been sold to Mr P. Ducrot. But she was essentially the product of Henry Linde, a farmer in County Kildare, who would become the foremost trainer of the 1880s. He had bought her as a three year old and had named her after Empress Elizabeth of Austria who regularly visited his Eyrefield Lodge home near the Curragh when she hunted in Ireland. After running her a few times on the Flat he began schooling her as a four year old over the near-replica of the National course that he had laid out at Eyrefield.

Though she had shown excellent form over fences in Ireland, *Empress* was fifth in the betting on her Aintree debut, 8-1 in a field of only 14. Opposing her were three former National winners - *The Liberator* (1879), *Shifnal* (1878) and *Regal* (1876). However, the age allowance gave her a huge advantage – a full two stone in respect of *The Liberator*, and 18lb over *Shifnal* and the favourite *Regal*.

Patiently nursed round the first circuit, *Empress*

lost several lengths when Beasley was seeking to recover a lost stirrup. But it made no difference. She moved steadily through the field and showed her superior strength with a colossal leap at the last. Gallantly, *The Liberator* put in a determined late challenge but she had no real chance at the weights and was beaten by two lengths, with the grey *Downpatrick* a head back in third.

A criticism of Linde's harsh training methods were that they sometimes took too great a toll on young horses, weakening their legs and making them more liable to break down. This was the case with *Empress* who never raced again and was retired to stud. Nonetheless, a formidable Irish invasion had been launched. Linde and Tommy Beasley would repeat their National success next year with *Woodbrook* and then, with *Cyrus* in 1882, miss their hat-trick by only a head.

See also: Linde, Henry Eyre; Beasley, Thomas

ENTIRES

Nowadays an entire – an ungelded male horse – is rarely to be seen in steeplechases, the last one of note being *Fortina*, six year old winner of the 1947 Cheltenham Gold Cup. But they were relatively common in the 19th century when nine were successful in the Grand National: *Discount* (1844), *Wanderer* (1855), *Freetrader* (1856), *Half Caste* (1859), *Alcibiade* (1865), *Disturbance* (1873), *Reugny* (1874), *Austerlitz* (1877) and *Shifnal* (1878). Just three were winners in the 20th century: *Grudon* (1901), *Ascetic's Silver* (1906) and *Battleship* (1938) who, at 40-1, was the longest priced of them all.

The youngest entires to win the National were *Alcibiade* and *Austerlitz*, both five years old; the oldest, *Grudon* and *Battleship*, aged 11. *Battleship* won in the fastest recorded time (9min 27sec) for a full horse. *Discount* scored by the greatest distance (20 lengths) and yet in the slowest time, just under 14 minutes.

In 1876 an imposing six year old chestnut entire called *Chandos* started as the 3-1 favourite in the National. Three years earlier he had finished fourth in the Epsom Derby, and he had shown brilliant form over hurdles. Alas, he was not the same force over the great Aintree jumps. He narrowly survived a major blunder on the first circuit but crashed out on landing at the fence after Valentine's second time around.

It is generally believed that *Davy Jones*, a seven year old tubed entire, would have won the 1936 National if the buckle of his reins had not been jolted open when he was leading at the penultimate fence. Without means of steering, his rider, Lord Mildmay, could not prevent him veering off the course at the final fence. He was a 100-1 outsider.

In 1986 Czechoslovakia was represented in the National by *Essex*, an eight year old entire with an excellent record at home: three wins and two seconds in his last six races. True, he had fallen in his most recent race but that was in the supremely testing, four and a quarter mile Velka Pardubicka when he had cleared all the major obstacles to establish a huge lead only to trip up at a small fence towards the end. However, without British form to guide the handicapper, he was automatically saddled with a prohibitive 12st top weight. The bold-jumping black stallion was pulled up at the 15th because of a broken girth buckle.

Why are the overwhelming majority of chasers now gelded? The obvious answer is that a fully equipped horse has so much more to fear in jumping his gear over a fence packed with menacing birch. In addition, there is the consideration that the entire is liable to have more on his mind than just jumping, and especially so when mares are on parade. Since the obstacles are so much easier, entires may more readily be risked over hurdles. But even there they are few and far between – the most notable exception being the great *Monksfield*, winner of the Champion Hurdle in 1978 and 1979.

ENTRIES

Although, since 1984, the Grand National has been restricted to a maximum of 40 runners, the most famous steeplechase has seen the number of entries steadily rise – from an average of around 100 in the late 1990s to a record 152 in 2005 – and then fall back to 117 in 2007. Entry (each now costing £450) closes in January and the following month the allotted weights are announced, with those farthest out of the handicap having little or no hope of qualifying.

Conditions of Grand National entry have been subject to various changes over the years. During the first nine decades, however, they could afford to be lax. In the 19th century, the race only once (in 1850) had as many as 32 runners and fields were usually much smaller – as few as ten runners in 1883, 11 in 1841 and 12 in 1840. The need for tighter rules of entry only began to arise in the 1920s when 90-plus

E

entries became the norm and the number of runners rose to a record 37 in 1927 and then 42 in 1928. The latter year saw for the first time the freakish emergence of a 100-1 winner, *Tipperary Tim*, one of only two finishers. As a result, owners were encouraged to believe that quite ordinary chasers were not without a chance in the great National lottery; and the outcome was the biggest field of all time – 66 horses lined up at the start in 1929.

Fortunately, despite producing another 100-1 winner (*Gregalach*) that year, the race had a reasonable field of 41 starters in 1930. But the need to restrict the number of entries was now recognised; and in 1931 five year olds were no longer eligible and entry was limited to horses that had been placed in chases over at least three miles or had won a race worth £500 or more. In the next ten Nationals, fields ranged from 27 runners to 37.

It was not until 1947 that the number of runners again reached alarming proportions. The great winter freeze of that year had resulted in all British racing being abandoned for nearly two full months. As a result owners were desperate to have their horses run and inevitably the National, held two weeks after the resumption of racing, was a powerful magnet. It attracted the second largest number of runners: 57.

This was an exceptional circumstance and in the 1950s the number of runners fell to a more acceptable level. At the same time, however, there was growing concern about the safety factor – an issue highlighted especially in 1959 when only four of 34 starters completed the course and one fell fatally. It led to demands not only for an easing of the fences but of tighter conditions of entry to keep out horses totally unsuited by the demands of Aintree's obstacles. Thus, in 1960, a minimum rating for would-be contenders was introduced. That year there were only 26 runners.

On the other hand, the modification of fences – made to look more inviting with a sloping 'apron' on the take-off-side – encouraged connections of the best chasers to target the race and, in turn, this resulted in more and more horses competing from out of the handicap. It raised the quality but also the number of runners – 47 in 1963 and the same again in 1965 and 1966 when there were 109 entries.

Although those totals were never achieved again, the new Aintree management decided in 1984 that, in the interests of safety, the National should in future be limited to a maximum field of 40. At the same time they greatly encouraged more entries by widening eligibility to any horse of seven years of age or more who had won any steeplechase in the past two and a half years. The result was a record 141 entries.

Forty runners now became the norm until 1995 when only 35 horses made it to the line-up, and the following year, when there were 82 entries, the field shrank to 27, the lowest figure since 1960. While this was partly due to a winter that had interrupted training schedules, it was nevertheless so disappointing that the British Horseracing Board lowered the minimum rating qualification from 120 to 110 for 1997 and increased the burden carried by the top weight. The best horse was to be allocated 12st as opposed to 11st 10lb in the previous four years. At the other end of the handicap the minimum qualification was reduced by 10lb to include horses officially assessed at 110.

The greater weight assigned to the highest rated horses allowed more horses to run off their proper handicap rating, in the process making the race more competitive. At the same time the lowering of the minimum standard made many more horses eligible for entry, the dual aim being to attract class horses while producing a field as close as possible to the safety factor of 40.

In 1997 there were 102 entries, with only 21 being in the handicap proper. The following year there were 103 entries, the highest number since 1986 when 109 were nominated. Nevertheless, in 1999, when 95 qualified for entry, the new official senior handicapper, Phil Smith, was given three briefs: to get more entries, to get more horses in the handicap proper, and to get horses of the highest quality. He achieved the second of those aims in 2000, when remarkably 66 of the 99 entries were in the handicap proper (allotted 10st or more). It thus provided for a highly competitive Grand National, with only seven of 40 horses running from out of the handicap.

The handicapper went on to achieve his other objectives in 2001. That year there were 133 entries and his discretionary framing of the weights encouraged keeping in high-class horses. Fourteen of these entries came from one trainer (Martin Pipe) and ten of them made it to the line-up – constituting a world record for the most horses run by one trainer in one race. In 2002 Pipe provided 16 of the 144 entries; and in 2003 19 of 149.

The pattern was much the same in 2004 when Pipe had 17 of 122 entries; and, as four years before, Mr Smith artfully compressed the handicap to get 66 horses carrying their allotted weight. In 2005, when a record purse of £700,000 attracted a record 152 entries, Pipe was for once outgunned at that stage, his 13 entries being surpassed by 14 from trainer Jonjo O'Neill. That year a record 19 were nominated by one owner, J.P. McManus; and in 2006 Pipe raised the bar to a new height with a staggering 22 entries out of the 148 total.

The following year there were 117 entries, the lowest total since 108 in 2000, a fall seen as evidence that owners and trainers were recognising the greater emphasis on quality in the National and the fact that a horse now needed to be rated around 130 to get the chance of a run. Champion trainer Paul Nicholls now had the biggest individual stable entry (eight) and J.P. McManus was the owner with the most entries (nine).

However, contrary to expectation, 2008 brought a major resurgence. No fewer than 150 horses were entered, with trainers David Pipe and Peter Bowen leading the way with 11 entries each, followed by Nigel Twiston-Davies (eight) and Paul Nicholls and Willie Mullins (seven). And as usual J.P. McManus was the owner with most entries (11).
See also: Rules of Entry; Ratings; Handicapping.

EREMON

Seven year old winner of the 1907 National, on his first and last appearance in the race. A bay gelding – by *Thurles* out of *Daisy* – *Eremon* was bred by James Cleary in Ireland and was judged to suffer from thick-windedness, a condition that greatly diminished his value. As a result, he fetched only £400 on being sold to Mr Stanley Howard. Subsequently, he was sent to Hednesford in Staffordshire, to be trained by Tom Coulthwaite, formerly an athletics coach.

Coulthwaite's stamina-building methods eventually developed *Eremon* into a powerful chaser. In 1906 he won the first steeplechase ever to be staged at Newbury, and the following year, with two recent victories behind him, he went to Aintree with an obvious chance under a generous 10st 1lb He was made 8-1 third favourite in a 23-strong field of moderate quality if one disregarded the 1903 winner *Drumcree*, now 13, and last year's winner, *Ascetic's Silver*, who had been raised a massive 26lb to the top weight of 12st 7lb.

Eremon led the dash to the first fence, but at the second his rider, Alfred Newey, suffered a broken stirrup leather. He gamely rode the rest of the race without one of his irons. Furthermore, for much of the race *Eremon* was seriously harassed by a riderless horse, and again and again Newey used his whip to keep the offender at bay. With many contenders falling behind him, he held the lead from the Canal Turn to win by six lengths from *Tom West*, with outsider *Patlander* a neck back in third.

The fact that *Eremon* had been too lightly handicapped was made clear ten days later when, with an added 12lb, he romped home in the Lancashire Chase. On that showing, a second National win – even on top weight – did not seem beyond him. But, sadly, it was never to be put to the test. A few weeks after his victory in Manchester, he needed to be put down, having suffered an injury after bolting on the gallops. For owner Stanley Howard, however, huge consolation was close at hand. He acquired a replacement in *Jenkinstown*, another bargain buy whom Coulthwaite would train to win the National. *See also:* Newey, Alfred; Coulthwaite, Tom.

E.S.B.

Like Joe McGhee, winner of the sensational 1954 Empire Games marathon, *E.S.B.* triumphed in a race where an incredibly unlucky loser gained more lasting fame than the victor. McGhee's success was eclipsed by the unforgettable sight of the gallant, dehydrated Jim Peters staggering to agonising defeat in the searing heat of Vancouver. Similarly, two years later, *E.S.B.*'s success was overshadowed by the belly-flopping failure of *Devon Loch* in the Aintree Grand National.

E.S.B. (not, as a visiting New Yorker supposed, named after the Empire State Building) took the initials of his parents, having been bred in County Kildare – out of the mare *English Summer* by *Bidar*. As an unbroken three year old he was bought by trainers Fred and Mercy Rimell on behalf of Mr Rolie Oliver whose son, Michael, would later win the National with *West Tip*. That same year they sent him out to win a hurdle race at Wincanton, enabling the big-gambling Olivers to make a killing.

E.S.B. then really showed his potential when, under Martin Molony, he won a four year old Juvenile Chase at Cheltenham by 20 lengths. The following season, he won two of nine races and was in the frame six others. Now, however, a bad run

E

in gambling forced Mr Oliver to sell his horse. He was bought jointly by Mr Geoffrey Kohn, who was to win the 1957 National with *Sundew*, and by huntswoman Mrs Leonard Carver, wife of a Birmingham auctioneer. Still with the Rimells, *E.S.B.* won four of his next six races, was runner-up once, and fell at the last fence in the 1953 Cheltenham Gold Cup when lying second to *Mont Tremblant*.

The owning partnership, however, did not work out since both owners wanted *E.S.B.* to run in their name. So the big, brown gelding was sent to the Newmarket sales, and there Mrs Carver went to a then massive 7.500 guineas to retain the horse outright. Trained by his owner, *E.S.B.* won seven races in his next three seasons. He first appeared in the National in 1955 and, as a 66-1 outsider, fell at Becher's first time round. Then he was sent back to Fred Rimell, whose wife Mercy was a close friend of Mrs Carver, formerly the champion lady showjumper, Stella Pierce. Like three past National winners – *Emblem*, *Emblematic* and *Forbra* – he was to be trained at the picturesque yard of Kinnersley in Worcestershire.

Improvement quickly followed. *E.S.B.* returned to Aintree in 1956 with wins at Haydock and Manchester immediately behind him; and with the highly experienced Dave Dick in the saddle, he was backed down to 100-7, joint fourth in the betting with the Queen Mother's *Devon Loch* and *Pippykin*. Prominent throughout, *E.S.B.* lost perhaps ten lengths when he was badly hampered by *Armorial III* at the second Valentine's. Yet he was only fractionally behind *Devon Loch* when they came to the last. Outstanding jumping had kept him in contention. But now, on the long run-in, the tiring ten year old was hopelessly outpaced by the royal runner, and as a huge gap opened up Dick resigned himself to taking second place. Indeed, he was surprised that his doubtful stayer had kept going as long as he had.

What followed is now the most vividly remembered calamity in Grand National history: the mysterious collapse of *Devon Loch* within 50 yards of the winning post. Revitalised by his rider, *E.S.B.* was driven past his stationary rival to take the prize by ten lengths from *Gentle Moya*, with *Royal Tan* a further ten lengths back in third.

For all his good fortune, *E.S.B.* deserves to be remembered as more than just a lucky winner. Though the Rimells believed he was really a two-and-a-half-

mile horse, the fact remains that his winning time of 9min 21²/₅ sec was only fractionally more than a second outside the record set by *Reynoldstown* in 1935, and only narrowly bettered by the times of *Golden Miller* (1934) and *Bogskar* (1940). His was the fourth fastest run yet seen in the National and that victory brought his career record to an impressive 19 wins in chases and one over hurdles.

E.S.B. was a doughty chaser in his own right, as proved by his subsequent performances. He won the Grand Sefton Trial Chase at Hurst Park, and was beaten only half a length in the Whitbread, then called the Queen Elizabeth Chase. Returning to Aintree in 1957, with an extra 10lb on his back, the gelding was leading at the second Becher's before the weight finally told. He finished eighth. One year later, as a 12 year old with only 1lb less to carry, it was the same story. He was the sixth of seven finishers – a creditable end to a most worthy racing career. The classy jumper then enjoyed a long and comfortable retirement on the Carvers' estate at Lapworth in Warwickshire, where he died in his 30th year.
See also: Devon Loch; Dick, Dave; Rimell, Fred.

ESCOTT, Harry

At his yard on the South Downs at Lewes, Harry Escott trained two Grand National winners. He took over responsiblity for the preparation of five year old *Lutteur III*, French-owned, -bred and -ridden, in the few months prior to his 1909 victory. One decade later he turned out *Poethlyn*, the successful hot favourite in the first post-First World War National.

Escott was also an accomplished rider and in November, 1894, he rode the great *Cloister* – burdened with a colossal 13st 3lb following his runaway 1893 National victory – to a 20-length success in the Grand Sefton Chase at Liverpool. Subsequently, he took charge of *Cloister*'s preparation for another National. His yard was guarded by private detectives following the horse's suspicious late withdrawal in 1894. But again *Cloister* had to be scratched after a mysterious collapse on the gallops.

For Harry there was very nearly a huge consolation. On six year old *Cathal*, his substitute ride, he finished second in the 1895 National – beaten just a length and a half by *Wild Man From Borneo*, with the third horse far behind. It was his fourth and last ride in the race. Previously he had failed to complete the course, his mounts being outsider *Conscript*

E

(fell, 1886), *Roman Oak* (knocked over, 1891) and 5-1 joint favourite *Nelly Gray* (bolted, 1894).

Now the family tradition was to be carried on by his son Anthony who competed in six Nationals. He began by finishing third on *Pollen* in 1919, then fell on the outsider *Irish Dragon* (1920), *White Surrey* (1921) and *Vaulx* (1922). His last two Aintree rides were on former Nationals winners: 15 year old *Sergeant Murphy* who finished tenth (remounted) in 1925; and *Sprig*, a 50-1 faller in 1929.

See also: Cloister; Poethlyn; Lutteur III; Parfrement, Georges.

ESHA NESS

The 50-1 'winner' of the Grand National That Never Was, being the first of seven horses to complete the course in the 1993 race declared void after two false starts. That day *Esha Ness* was the least fancied of Jenny Pitman's three runners, his stablemates being *Garrison Savannah*, pulled up after one circuit, and *Royal Athlete*, a faller at the tenth. His performance in this greatest steeplechase farce would be insignificant except for one most noteworthy fact. He covered the course in 9min 1.4 sec, the second fastest time in the history of the race.

A bay gelding – by *Crash Course* out of *Beeston* – *Esha Ness* was one of four unbroken three year olds bought by Mrs Pitman in Ireland in 1986. With truly remarkable vision, she had picked out future winners of the Cheltenham Gold Cup (*Garrison Savannah*), the Grand National (*Royal Athlete*), the Midlands and Scottish Nationals (*Willsford*), and the so deserving *Esha Ness*.

Scoring his first win over two miles at Sandown in the 1986-87 season, *Esha Ness* was gradually upped in distance and looked a Grand National prospect in January, 1993, when finishing a good second to *Jodami* in the Mandarin Chase over an extended three miles two furlongs at Newbury. Two months later he went off the 5-1 favourite in the Kim Muir at Cheltenham but did not jump fluently in finishing a distant fifth.

At Aintree, however, he was on top jumping form and, ridden by John White, successfully held off the fast-finishing challenge of *Cahervillahow*. All to no avail. The rider buried his face in his hands, the trainer was sobbing in the weighing room, and the

owner, Mr Patrick Bancroft, was disconsolate, having dreamed for years of winning a Grand National. As for *Esha Ness*, he was never the same force again. He was 12 years old when he finally reappeared with White in the 1995 National, and he had not won a race since 1992. Now he fell at the 12th fence while stablemate *Royal Athlete* – one of six Mrs Pitman-trained contenders – ran on to win at 40-1.

See also: Void National; Pitman, Jenny; White, John.

EVERETT, Robert

The Australian jockey who won the 1929 Grand National on 100-1 outsider *Gregalach*, the first of ten finishers in a record field of 66 starters. Formerly in the Royal Navy, Bob Everett had been a professional rider for less than a year after serving an apprenticeship in South Africa and riding *Rossieny*, one of 40 non-finishers in the chaotic 1928 National.

One year after their sensational victory Everett was a faller on *Gregalach*, now raised 10lb to 12st top weight in the National. But his mount was then semi-fit after an interrupted preparation. When *Gregalach*, still on 12st, returned fully fit in 1931 he finished runner-up, beaten only one and a half lengths by the more fancied *Grakle*. Unluckily, however, the Aussie had been replaced as rider by Jack Moloney. He himself fell again, this time on *Kakushin*.

After a five-year gap, Everett had three more National rides – on *Sunspot* (1937), a 100-1 faller; and on *Dominick's Cross*, who fell in 1938 and finished sixth at 33-1 in 1939. Then, with the outbreak of war, he promptly returned to the Navy. In the summer of 1941, as an officer in the Fleet Air Arm, he took on the most hazardous role: flying fighter planes that could be catapulted from the bows of Atlantic merchant ships.

As a pilot defending convoys, Everett fended off German bombers and accounted for several U-boats. Unfortunately, once launched, a cata-fighter could not return to its ship, and if not in range of land the pilot could only bail out or ditch his aircraft close to a friendly ship in the hope of being picked up. Bob Everett, like so many of his heroic compatriots, met death by drowning.

See also: Gregalach.

F

FALLERS

The worst Grand National in terms of the number of fallers was in 1929 when a record field of 66 runners saw only ten complete the course. While some horses were pulled up, at least 40 were fallers. One year earlier only two of the 42 starters had finished the race with the runner-up having been remounted. But at least 20 of these non-finishers were put out of the race without actually falling.

In percentage terms, the worst year was 1951 when the so-called 'Grand Crashional' saw 33 of 36 starters falling or being brought down, with the last of three finishers being remounted. Other high falling rates occurred in 1921 (31 of 35); 1922 (27 of 33); 1911 (21 of 26); 1913 (16 of 22); and 2001 (31 of 40). At the other end of the scale only eight of 40 fell or were knocked over in 1987 when Aintree celebrated the 150th anniversary of the birth of the Grand Liverpool Steeplechase.

In 2001 the marsh-like conditions were so bad that one bookmaking company offered odds of 6-1 against the entire field of 40 getting over the first fence. Two went there, followed by three fallers at the second and three at the third, and two at the fourth. Only four horses (two remounted) completed the course.

The unenviable record for falling in the Grand National belongs to the brown gelding *Cloncarrig* who appeared in six successive years (1948-53) and fell every time. Yet he was not a complete no-hoper. In 1950, ridden by Bob Turnell, he actually led the field, narrowly ahead of the eventual 15-length winner *Freebooter*, when he fell at the penultimate fence. The following year he went off as 10-1 second joint second favourite but this time he was one of many fallers resulting from the stampede caused by the failure to call a false start. On his last falling appearance he was 13 years old and a rank outsider at 66-1.

It is one of the myths of the National that a previous fall in the race is a permanently scarring experience likely to preclude a later success. It does not stand up to analysis, as shown by a number of comeback wins, among them those of *Manifesto* (1897), *Early Mist* (1953), *Sundew* (1957), *Team Spirit* (1964), *West Tip* (1986) and *Red Marauder* (2001). However, history is against any horse that has fallen in a race immediately prior to running in the National, the great exception being the 1988 winner *Rhyme 'N' Reason* who had merely slipped on landing over the fourth last in the Cheltenham Gold Cup. In the 1990s only one of nine winners (*Rough Quest*) had fallen in the season of his victory. *See also:* Finishers; Fences; Pile-Ups; Casualties; Riderless Horses.

FALSE STARTS

From its very beginning the Grand National was troubled with false starts. In 1839 there were a number of recalls before the 3rd Earl of Sefton officially set the 17 runners on their way in the inaugural race at Aintree. Moreover, this had followed much longer delays caused by bungled weighing -out formalities, and so the first National went off two hours late.

Amazingly, in 1857, the race only began in driving rain after no fewer than seven false starts. In 1869 there were three false starts. But it was not until 1951 that the National was seriously affected by a bungled start. On this occasion the 'false start' was undeclared and the outcome was a mad stampede to make up lost ground, with 11 horses falling at the first fence. Only three of 36 runners finished: the 40-1 winning mare *Nickel Coin*, runner-up *Royal Tan*, and the remounted *Derrinstown*. Inevitably, there was bitter criticism of the starter (Mr Leslie Firth) who inexplicably had set the field off when some 20 horses were still milling around in preparation to take their place in the line-up.

One year later, despite stern warnings to jockeys, a number of horses broke the starting tape. This time they were properly recalled, the starter being so demanding that a full 12 minutes passed before they were off and running. But there was still a mad scramble to the first fence where no fewer than ten runners came to grief. Then, in 1993, came a complete and disastrous breakdown in the starting procedure, with so many horses charging on after a second false start that the race had to be declared void.

The year 2000 saw the introduction of starters being empowered to issue 'yellow card' warnings to jockeys who failed to obey orders at the start. In the event of reoffending a jockey would be dealt with by the stewards. At Ascot, a week before the National, senior starter Simon Morant reported all nine jockeys in a novice chase for taking up a position before they had been called in to line up. They were fined a total of £1,065 for anticipating the start.

It was not until 2006 that the National experienced another false start. This time it was quickly corrected. Starter Peter Haynes raised his yellow flag after *Ross Comm* had broken the starting tape

F

and the runners were successfully waved back by the flagman stationed in the centre of the track well before the first fence. However, it still seemed a most antiquated system: the re-start being delayed by more than five minutes while the broken ends of the orange elastic were being tied together.

Again, in 2007, there was a false start with the tape being broken by headstrong horses. More seriously, there was an eight-minute delay; and subsequently starter Haynes, a former jockey, blamed the jockeys for failing to obey his instructions.

Apparently too many were involved to have them punished with fines. Haynes later explained: 'There are marker poles two metres behind the line and the starter has to be confident that the horses are behind it before he can let the field go.' Whatever, the starting procedure remained unsatisfactory and yet another review was promised. One proposal was the reintroduction of a line, ten metres back from the tape, with penalties for jockeys whose horses transgress.

See also: Void National.

FAN, The

In 1869 the second fence of the National course was named The Fan after the bay mare which – for the second successive year – had persistently refused to tackle the obstacle. At the time it was arguably harsh derision of a horse that had not only cleared the second as a five year old in 1867 but had gone on to finish runner-up to *Cortolvin*. But it was to be proved fully justified. In 1870, *Fan* scored a hat-trick of refusals, stubbornly bracing himself as soon as he came to the second.

FATALITIES

Only one jockey (James Wynne in 1862) has suffered a fatal fall in the Grand National. In this respect, the race is no more dangerous than other steeplechases; and certainly its dangers pale into insignifance when compared with the perils of the cross-country phase of three-day eventing. In 1999 five riders perished in eventing on British courses – an extraordinary total even allowing for the fact that an enormous number of men and women compete in the sport.

For jump jockeys extreme injuries are more liable to occur in races run at a faster sustained pace than the Grand National allows. Tragically, a number of riders have competed in the National with distinc-

tion only to fall fatally elsewhere. In 1855, one year after winning the National on *Bourton*, jockey John Tasker was killed in a chase at Warwick. Three weeks after winning the 1926 National on *Jack Horner,* Bill Watkinson fell fatally in a £100 chase at Bogside in Scotland; and soon after finishing third in the 1935 National on *Thomond II*, Billy Speck was killed by a fall in the first race of the Cheltenham spring meeting.

Inevitably, over the years, many horses have been killed in the Grand National. But again, in this respect, the Liverpool course has a record no worse than that of other major jump courses; and the three-day Aintree meeting has never known a death-toll to compare with the ten fatalities of the 1996 Cheltenham Festival. The fact is that when equine fatalities do occur in the National they always gain far more publicity than those happening elsewhere.

The worst year for National fatalities was 1954 when there were only 29 starters, the smallest field since the war. One horse dropped dead in the running and three more had to be destroyed – a tragic outcome that gave rise to a huge outcry for the fences to be made less demanding. As a result, the landing ground at Becher's was marginally raised and the following fence (No. 7) was lowered six inches to the minimum 4ft 6in allowed under National Hunt rules. There were no fatalities in the next five years and it was not until 1961 that a noteworthy change was made: fences being furnished with sloping 'aprons' on the take-off side to make them less uninviting.

It was the demise of the handsome grey *Dark Ivy* in 1987 and of *Brown Trix* and *Seeandem* in 1989 (all victims of Becher's Brook) that led to more significant modifications in 1990. Most importantly, these included the filling in of the treacherous V-shaped ditch on the landing side of Becher's. But despite the changes two horses perished in the 1990 National when exceptionally firm going enabled *Mr Frisk* to break the course record. There were five other fatalities in the three days of the Aintree meeting, and these occurred not over the formidable National fences but during the fast and furious pace over hurdles.

Three horses were lost in the 1998 National run on heavy ground, all of them falling in the early stages when neither the bigger obstacles nor exhaustion could have become a factor. A two-month investigation by the Jockey Club concluded that the fatalities were unrelated, unfortunate accidents, and that no casual link was established between any of them and heavy going, the condition of the course, the height of the fences, the speed to the first fence or the number of runners (37).

The RSPCA representative concurred and welcomed the safety measures subsequently taken. These included encouraging more high-rated horses to run; pre-race veterinary inspections for all declared runners; widening of the first fence by two metres; and the introduction of a Jockey Club panel with the power to veto entries.

Despite the tragedies on heavy ground in 1998, the overall evidence suggests that the hazards of the Grand National are greatest when the going is fastest; and so, by judicious watering, the Aintree management ensures that the National is never again run on such fast going as occurred in 1990. In 2001 there were many complaints that the ground was unfit for racing, and indeed only two horses completed the course without falling. But, significantly, the boggy ground ensured such a slow pace and a cushioning of falls that no horses or jockeys were seriously injured.

Recorded fatalities (possibly not comprehensive) in the Grand National are as follows
Dictator (1839); *Clansman* (1845); *Counsellor*, *The Sailor* and *Blue Pill* (1848); *Eatwell* (1854); *Miss Mowbray* (1855); *Banstead* (1856); *The Conductor* (1861); *Telegraph* (1863); *Chimney Sweep* (1868); *Lord Raglan* (1871); *Primrose and Nuage* (1872); *Wild Monarch* (1882); *Carrollstown* (1894); *True Blue* (1901); *Awbeg* and *The Inca II* (1922); *Lone Hand* (1926); *Stort* (1929); *Derby Day II* (1930); *Swift Rowland* (1931); *Avenger* (1936); *Symbole* (1946); *Legal Joy, Coneyburrow, Dominick's Bar* and *Paris New York* (1954); *Henry Purcell* (1959); *Avenue Neuilly* (1963); *Grey Sombrero* (1973); *Land Lark* and *Beau Bob* (1975); *Winter Rain* (1977); *Alverton* and *Kintai* (1979); *Earthstopper* (1984); *Dark Ivy* (1987); *Brown Trix* and *Seeandem* (1989); *Roll-A-Joint* and *Hungary Hur* (1990); *Ballyhane* (1991); *Rust Never Sleeps* (1996); *Smith's Band* and *Straight Talk* (1997); *Pashto, Do Rightly* and *Griffins Bar* (1998); *Eudipe* (1999); *Manx Magic* and *The Last Fling* (2002); *Goguenard* (2003); *Tyneandthyneagain* (2006); *Graphic Approach* (2007).

Three of these died after completing the race. In 1894, Lord Shaftesbury's seven year old *Carrollstown* finished seventh but then collapsed fatally with exhaustion in the paddock. In 1984 *Earthstopper*, making his National debut, passed the finishing post in fifth place and then immediately dropped dead. *Ballyhane* died from a haemorrhage ten minutes after finishing 11th.

See also: Animal Rights; Becher's Brook; Course Changes; Wynne, James; Injuries.

FATHER O'FLYNN
Seven year old winner on his Grand National debut in 1892. A small (15.2 hands) Shropshire-bred bay gelding, *Father O'Flynn* surged ahead on the run-in to win by 20 lengths from the favourite *Cloister* who was conceding 26lb to the leader. And ironically he was ridden by Captain Roddy Owen who had been half a length runner-up on *Cloister* the previous year when he unsuccessfully lodged an objection to the winner.

Bred near Shifnal by Mr E. C. Wadlow, *Father O'Flynn* was by *Retreat* out of *Kathleen*, being related through his sire to the Derby-winning *Hermit*. Under the ownership of the Marquess of Cholmondeley, he was raced nine times on the Flat as a two year old, opening his account by winning a seller at Liverpool. Then, after a year's rest, he was heavily campaigned on the Flat, over hurdles and mostly in hunter-chases. In three years he had 41 races and he was sent to the sales after he had won six of 13 relatively minor events as a six year old.

Sold for 470 guineas, *Father O'Flynn* was now trained at Melton Mowbray by his new owner, Australian-born Old Etonian Gordon Wilson, a subaltern in the Household Cavalry. Though he went to Aintree on the back of two chase wins, he was lightly weighted on 10st 5lb and went off at 20-1, equal in the betting with the 1890 National winner *Ilex* who was at a 30lb disadvantage.

In a race much obscured by a heavy mist, *Cloister* was looking a certain winner as he led the field turning for home beyond the 28th fence. But gradually *Father O'Flynn* narrowed the huge gap and once over the last his enormous weight advantage truly told. He powered away to win comfortably from *Cloister* and third-placed *Ilex*; and, having achieved his great sporting ambition, Captain Owen promptly quit racing and applied for active military service abroad.

The following year *Father O'Flynn*, raised 20lb in the weights, finished a far distant sixth in the

F

15-runner National which *Cloister* won by an incredible forty lengths under 12st 7lb. Then, after
being beaten in the Lancashire Chase, the seven year
old was sold by Mr Wilson who, like Capt. Owen,
would give priority to a military career. He was a
Lieut.-Colonel when, in 1914, he was killed in command of his regiment at Ypres.

Ridden by his new owner, Mr Cecil Grenfell,
Father O'Flynn was a faller in the 1894 National
and finished seventh in 1895. Remarkably, one year
later, he came late to launch a tremendous challenge
to *The Soarer*, failing to win a second National by
only a length and a half, with third placed *Biscuit*
the same distance behind. On this, his fifth and last
National, the eleven year old was the runner-up out
of 28 starters – the largest field for 23 years – and at
odds of 40-1.
See also: Owen, Captain Edward Roderic.

FATHERS AND DAUGHTERS
There are two instances of a father and daughter
having appeared in the Grand National. Mr John
Alder was ninth on his *Tant Pis* in 1965 and his
daughter, Valerie, fell at the Canal Turn on her *Bush
Guide* in 1984. Tommy Carberry rode in 13 Nationals, winning on *L'Escargot* in 1975, and his daughter, Nina, finished ninth on *Forest Gunner* in 2006.

FATHERS AND SONS
Seven times fathers and sons have combined to win
the Grand National together as trainer and jockey
respectively
  John and Garrett Moore – with *The Liberator*
    (1879)
  John and Arthur Nightingall – with *Ilex* (1890)
  Tom and Ted Leader – with *Sprig* (1927)
  Noel and Frank Furlong – with *Reynoldstown*
    (1935)
  Reg and Bruce Hobbs – with *Battleship* (1938)
  Tommy and Paul Carberry – with *Bobbyjo*
    (1999)
  Ted and Ruby Walsh – with *Papillon* (2000)
In 2000, Ted and Ruby Walsh became the first
father-and-son team to win the Aintree and Irish
Grand Nationals in the same season.

Father and son who individually trained National
winners:
  Tom Rimell – *Forbra* (1932)
  Fred Rimell – *E.S.B.* (1956), *Gay Trip* (1970),
    Rag Trade (1976).

Father and son who both rode a National winner:
  Tommy Carberry on *L'Escargot* (1975)
  Paul Carberry on *Bobbyjo* (1999)

Other fathers and sons who rode in the National:
  Denis Wynne, 12 rides (won, *Matthew*, 1847;
    fourth, *Alfred*, 1849; second, *The Knight of
    Gwynne*, 1850; third, *Crabbs*, 1854)
  James Wynne, one ride, 1862, (fatally brought
    down on *O'Connell*)

Harry Escott, four rides (second, Cathal, 1895)
Anthony Escott, six rides (third, Pollen, 1919)

Tommy Barnes, one ride (second, *Wyndburgh*,
    1962)
Maurice Barnes, three rides (won, *Rubstic*,
    1979)

Bob Turnell, seven rides (third, *Irish Lizard*,
    1953)
Andy Turnell, 13 rides (third, *Charles Dickens*,
    1974)

Richard Pitman, six rides (second, Steel Bridge,
    1969; second, *Crisp*, 1973)
Mark Pitman, three rides (second, *Garrison
    Savannah*, 1991)

Michael Scudamore, 16 rides (won, *Oxo* 1959;
    seeond, *Legal Joy*, 1952; third, *Irish Lizard*,
    1954)
Peter Scudamore, 12 rides (third, *Corbiere*
    1985; fourth, *Docklands Express*, 1992)

Ray Goldstein, one ride, 1989
Jamie Goldstein, one ride, 2001

Peter Scudamore, 12 rides
Tom Scudamore, five rides (eighth, *Blowing
    Wind*, 2003)

Hywel Davies, ten rides (won, *Last Suspect*,
    1985)
James Davies, one ride, 2004

Ted Walsh, one ride, 1975
Ruby Walsh, five rides (won, *Papillon*, 2000;
    fourth, *Papillon*, 2001; fourth, *Kingsmark*,
    2002; won, *Hedgehunter*, 2005)

Lord Daresbury (as Mr Peter Greenall), one
    ride, 1975
Mr Tom Greenall, one ride, 2005

Colin Tinkler, four rides, 1976-79

Andrew Tinkler, two rides (sixth, *Smarty*, 2004)

Niall Madden Snr, six rides, between 1978 and 1989

Niall Madden Jnr, two rides (won, *Numbersixvalverde* (2006)

Tommy Carberry, 13 rides (won, *L'Escargot*, 1975; second, *L'Escargot*, 1979; third, *L'Escargot*, 1973)

Philip Carberry, one ride, 2007

If the Second World War had not dashed Geoffrey Scudamore's plans to ride in the Grand National (an ambition achieved by his son, grandson and great-grandson) the family would have set a record of four generations as National riders.

FAVOURITES

Favourite backers got off to a good start when the first Grand National of 1839 was won by *Lottery* at 5-1. But it was 14 years before a clear favourite won the race again and thereafter they became progressively more rare. Whereas ten clear favourites won in the second half of the 19th century, only three won in the first half of the 20th century and only four in the second half. Altogether 160 Grand Nationals have produced just 19 clear winning favourites and eight successful joint favourites. Only three clear favourites have won in the past quarter of a century.

Of all losing favourites the most unusual was the Scottish hope *Freddie* who, despite being saddled with top weight, went off as short as 7-2 in 1965 and then 11-4 the following year. On both occasions he finished runner-up, in the latter beaten only three-quarters of a length by the American *Jay Trump*.

Winning clear favourites
Lottery (1839) 5-1; *Bourton* (1854) 4-1; *Anatis* (1860) 7-2; *Huntsman* (1862) 3-1; *The Colonel* (1870) 7-2; *Reugny* (1874) 5-1; *Roquefort* (1885) 100-30; *Ilex* (1890) 4-1; *Come Away* (1891) 4-1; *Cloister* (1893) 9-2; *Manifesto* (1897) 6-1; *Drumcree* (1903) 13-2; *Poethlyn* (1919) 11-4; *Sprig* (1927) 8-1; *Merryman II* (1960) 13-2; *Grittar* (1982) 7-1; *Rough Quest* (1996) 7-1; *Earth Summit* (1998) 7-1; *Hedgehunter* (2005) 7-1.

Winning joint favourites
Discount (1844) 5-1; *Matthew* (1847) 10-1; *Woodbrook* (1881) 11-2; *Why Not* (1894) 5-1;

Lutteur III (1909) 100-9; *Jerry M* (1912) 4-1; *Freebooter* (1950) 10-1; *Red Rum* (1973) 9-1.

FENCES

There are 16 fences, all of which have to be jumped twice with the exception of the 15th (The Chair) and the 16th (the Water Jump); and all, except the Water Jump, must be at least 4ft 6in high. While fences at other racecourses are constructed from bundles of coppiced birch sticks, those at Aintree are built up of hawthorn branches 'dressed' with fir, gorse or distinctive green branches of spruce that are cut, sorted and transported from conifer plantations in the Lake District during the month before the race. It is the thorn that gives the fences their special character. A horse can brush through a birch fence but cannot get away with it so easily when hitting the National fences.

Prior to 1961 the Aintree fences were perpendicular, so forbidding that they were described as 'bloody great green stone walls'. But that year they were furnished with sloping 'aprons' on the take-off side. It made them no smaller but much less uninvitingly upright; and it induced horses to take off two feet further back rather than getting in too close and being unable to gain sufficient height. Thereafter, it has been suggested, strong jumping ability was no longer to be an absolute prerequisite for success in the race, as illustrated by the victories of *Maori Venture* (1987) and *Red Marauder* (2001).

In 2001 the fences were made even more 'horse friendly', being given a more pronounced slope. The most significant change, however, had been made in 1990 when the treacherous V-shaped ditch on the landing side of Becher's Brook was filled in to provide level ground.

Fence one (and 17)

Only 4ft 6in high (excluding water jumps the minimum height allowed in steeplechasing), this is one of the smallest fences on the course and yet it represents a perilous challenge, often claiming a disproportionate number of fallers as runners dash, all too eagerly, over the 420 yards from the start to the first obstacle. In 2004, a team of researchers – veterinary surgeons at Liverpool University – studied the fate of all 560 horses in the past 15 Nationals and concluded that this fence was the one to be feared most, with horses being seven times more likely to fall here than at other plain jumps with no ditch.

Every year, in the weighing room, the Senior Steward goes through the formality of warning jockeys about making a mad stampede to the first. But statistics indicate that it has no marked effect. Moreover, experience can count for little when there is congestion at this fence. Over the years it has not merely sorted out the weaker jumpers but has also accounted for such heavily backed runners as *Challenger Du Luc* (1998), *Double Thriller* (1999), *Micko's Dream* (2000) and *Paris Pike* (2002). Moreover, it has brought to grief many past winners – among them *Russian Hero*, *Early Mist*, *Ayala*, *Gay Trip*, *Aldaniti*, *Hallo Dandy* and the great *Golden Miller*.

Similarly, jockeys have had reverses of fortune here. Bob Champion, brought down at the first on his 1971 National debut, fell there again when making his 1982 swansong on *Aldaniti*, his winner of one year before. In 1996 Jason Titley also went down there on *Bavard Dieu* one year after winning the National on *Royal Athlete*. Conversely, Mick Fitzgerald fell there on *Tinryland* in 1995, one year before winning on *Rough Quest*; and he went down there again, on *Marlborough* in 2002.

The worst stampede from 'the off' was seen in 1951 when the race was started with many horses still facing the wrong way. A false start should have been declared. Instead, jockeys engaged in a reckless effort to make up lost ground with the result that 12 horses – precisely one third of the entire field – crashed out at the first. The unlucky riders included three who would return to win the race in that same decade – Bryan Marshall (twice), Pat Taaffe and Michael Scudamore.

All 66 runners (the biggest ever field) cleared this fence in 1929 – remarkably so since, even with small fields, it is usual for at least one horse to exit here. In 1982 ten horses – more than a quarter of the field – failed to survive the first fence. In 1995 seven horses – a fifth of the field – went out there. In 1998 and 2000 there were five casualties. In 2001, a year of quagmire conditions, a novelty bet was 6-1 against the entire field safely clearing the first. There were few takers. As it happened there were only two fallers there – surprisingly few since just two of 40 starters would complete the course without falling.

However, it was business as usual the following year. In the competition to attract customers, one small bookmaking group broke new ground by offering to refund stakes to punters who saw their selection exit at the first fence. The offer was well worth taking. No fewer than nine horses – almost a quarter of the field – fell when bunching up at the first.

In 1998 the Jockey Club rightly rejected the idea of reducing the height of the first fence, already at the regulation minimum. But one year later, in the hope of reducing congestion, the Aintree management decided to widen the first fence by two metres, making it the widest on any steeplechase course in the country. Several leading figures in National Hunt racing argued that this change would make no significant difference. They saw speed not space as the problem, the long run to the fence resulting in some horses running too free and over-jumping.

One counter-measure, repeatedly suggested, is to move the fence back – perhaps as much as half the distance from the start and so reducing the build-up of pace on the approach. The Aintree management were encouraged by the results of a similar measure which had been applied in 2003 to the Topham Chase and the Foxhunters' Chase. Such a drastic change to the Grand National will surely be strongly resisted by traditionalists.

Fence two (and 18)

A plain 4ft 7in high fence of no special difficulty. The most notable casualty here was *Freebooter*, the 1950 National winner. The following year he avoided the mass pile-up at the first only to be brought down at the second by the falling, riderless *Gallery*.
See also: Fan, The

Fence three (and 19)

A more serious obstacle, 5ft high, preceded by a yawning six-foot wide open ditch and with the ground sloping away on the far side. Here the horse needs to have plenty of momentum before catching sight of the ditch. It is the first real test of jumping and clearing it well can give a confidence boost. Stand off too far and you will not clear it. Get in too close and you risk being knocked over in the rush. It has often caused wholesale trouble, most notably in 1970 when it eliminated no fewer than eight of the 28 starters, including the 13-2 favourite *Two Springs*. In 1977 this first open ditch claimed four runners, including the Cheltenham Gold Cup winner *Davy Lad*. In 1996 it accounted for the former winner *Party Politics* and in 2000 the strongly fancied *Dark Stranger*, ridden by champion Tony McCoy. John Francome has said that, if he was still riding today, only two Aintree fences would give him concern: the third and The Chair.

F

Fence four (and 20)

A relatively straight-forward plain obstacle, 4ft 10in high. Yet it was here – second time around – that Neale Doughty, who completed the course in nine of his ten Grand National rides, had the only blot on his copybook, falling on *Rinus* when disputing the lead in 1991. Still more surprisingly, it was at the fourth in 1986 that *Corbiere*, after winning and twice finishing third, uncharacteristically hit the top of the fence and fell.

Fence five (and 21)

Another plain fence, 5ft high, and one that sees relatively few fallers. However, it was here – second time round – that 14 year old *Kilmore*, the 1962 winner, fell in 1964, so ending the 11th and last National ride of the great Fred Winter who had twice won the race and who would come back to win it in the next two years as a trainer.

Fence six (and 22)

This, too, is a plain fence, but on approach a hedge on either side is a warning that something special lies in store. Ahead stands the most famous (and infamous) steeplechase obstacle in the world: Becher's Brook, only 4ft 10in high on the take-off side but with a confusing drop on the landing side liable to catch out any horse that lands too steeply. In 1989 it was the scene of such horrendous falls that it was modified to make landing much less perilous.
See also: Becher's Brook

Fence seven (and 23)

Set at a slight angle, this fence is a mere 4ft 6in high, but so easy after Becher's that it can be taken too casually and possibly surprise any horse anticipating another drop. It was here, on the second circuit in 1967, that a mass pile-up caused by a loose horse brought all runners except one to a standstill and handed the race to 100-1 shot *Foinavon* after whom the fence was subsequently named. One year later *Rondetto* fell at the same innocuous fence and brought down *Chamoretta* ridden by David Elsworth.
See also: Foinavon, The.

Fence eight (and 24)

A 5ft-high fence presenting a major challenge and being fraught with dangers since many riders meet it an angle, jumping sharply to the left to minimize the 90-degree turn in the course and so save precious

ground. It was the scene of its biggest pile-up in 1928 when the dual Cheltenham Gold Cup winner *Easter Hero* landed on top of the eighth. Again, in 2002, it was here on the first circuit that the riderless *Paddy's Return* veered across to take out eight runners.
See also: Canal Turn.

Fence nine (and 25)

No sooner has the sharp Canal Turn been negotiated than one must get a horse properly balanced in time to tackle the first of four fences, all 5ft high, in a straight line on the way to the Melling Road. This one bounds a 5ft 6in wide brook but, despite a drop on the landing side, it is less formidable than Becher's Brook and has claimed far fewer scalps. In 2006 *Ballycassidy*, an 80-1 shot, ran a blinder to lead from the ninth fence and was still ahead, six lengths clear and going well, when he fell at the same fence (25th) on the second circuit.
See also: Valentine's Brook.

Fence ten (and 26)

A 5ft-high plain fence in front of the Sefton Stand. Not very challenging. However, in 1965, second time around, it caught out the well-backed *Rondetto* who was leading when he clipped the top of the fence and fell. Similarly, in 1988, one year before he won the National, *Little Polveir* had a narrow lead when he took off much too soon at the 26th and landed smack on the fence, hurling Tom Morgan skywards.

Fence 11 (and 27)

Another 5ft-high fence, more imposing and slightly more threatening since it is bordered on the take-off side by the second 6ft wide open ditch and has a bigger drop than its third fence counterpart. Here, on the first circuit, the great *Golden Miller* three times dug in his heels and ended his bid for a second National win; and here, in 1932, the riderless *Pelorus Jack* ran across the front of the ditch, putting two thirds of the runners out of the race. In 1977 Charlotte Brew, the first lady rider in the National, had her historic appearance ended when her *Barony Fort* refused at the 27th.

Fence 12 (and 28)

Similarly, a 5ft-high fence followed by a 5ft 6in-wide ditch but with less of a drop on the landing side. In 1947, one year after winning the National on *Lovely*

Cottage, Capt. Bobby Petre's reappearance ended at the 28th when the outsider *Tulyra* ran across his mount *Silver Fame*, a future Cheltenham Gold Cup winner. And it was here, on the first circuit in 1964, that top-weighted Gold Cup winner *Pas Seul* fell with Dave Dick. Following this fence is a long run of about half a mile, back over the Melling Road before runners begin to swing left towards the penultimate obstacle on the way to the finish.

Fence 13 (and 29)

This is only 4ft 7in high and usually it is not a case of unlucky 13. However, it was here, on the first circuit in 1994, that a mini pile-up saw five horses come down, including the strongly fancied *Double Silk* and *Master Oats*, a future Gold Cup winner. Most sensationally, in 1936, the 100-1 shot *Davy Jones* led the field when he pecked on landing over the 29th, causing the reins to break and making it impossible for amateur rider Anthony (later Lord) Mildmay to prevent his seemingly certain winner from running out at the last.

Fence 14 (and 30)

The last obstacle second time around, just 4ft 6in high and fairly straightforward. On the first circuit it precedes the biggest obstacle on the course (The Chair), and on the second circuit it marks the beginning of the so crucial, stamina-testing 494-yard run-in to the finish. No horse has ever fallen at the last when having a clear lead. But two – *Billy Barton* (1928) and *Pelorus Jack* (1933) – have fallen at the 30th when disputing the lead. Though he won the National in 1954 *Royal Tan* twice had trouble with the last fence, blundering crucially when having a narrow lead in 1951 and crashing out there when lying third in 1952. An exhausted *Hedgehunter* fell at the last when lying third in 2002. The strongly fancied *Beau* cleared the 14th well in 2002 only to stumble and unseat his rider in his first stride after landing.

Fence 15

The most formidable-looking obstacle on the course: a fence 5ft 2in high preceded by the third open ditch, 6ft wide, but with a narrow approach that makes it appear all the more daunting, and confusingly with ground higher on landing than on the take-off side. Over the years it has claimed many victims, most notably in 1979 with a pile-up that put nine runners out of the race. *Russian Hero* (when leading in 1951), *Ayala* (1964) and *Rubstic* (having his first-ever fall in 1980) are past winners who have been eliminated at the challenging 15th; and tragically it was here in 1964, with so many runners funnelling into the take-off area, that Paddy Farrell suffered his paralysing, back-breaking fall on *Border Flight*. Mercifully, like the obstacle to follow, this fence has only to be jumped once.
See also: Chair, The.

Fence 16

The last obstacle on the first circuit and one rarely causing problems, being the smallest. It comprises a fence of a mere 2ft 6in but requires a big enough leap to clear the 12ft 6in expanse of water beyond. A left-hand turn past the winning post follows, leading on to the start of the second circuit. Most unusually, the Water Jump was the scene of a mini-pile-up in 1968 when the previous year's lucky winner *Foinavon* was one of four horses to be brought down.
See also: Water Jump.

FENWICK, Charles Jnr

Fifteen years after the success of Tommy Crompton Smith on *Jay Trump* (1965), Charlie Fenwick, on 12 year old *Ben Nevis*, became the second American to win the Grand National. Like his predecessor he was an amateur rider who triumphed on a gelding trained in England after twice winning the Maryland Hunt Cup. But, unlike *Jay Trump*, who squeaked home by three-quarters of a length, his mount scored by a comfortable 20 lengths, albeit in a much slower time on heavy ground.

In winning the 1980 Grand National, merchant banker Charlie Fenwick was turning a childhood dream into reality. Just like Crompton Smith before him, he came from a long line of Americans with a fanatical interest in racing and hunting. He was raised on a farm bordering the Maryland Hunt Cup course; and he was a grandson of Howard Bruce, the Baltimore industrialist who had failed so sensationally to win the 1928 Grand National with his champion gelding *Billy Barton*.

With English-bred *Ben Nevis*, owned by his father-in-law, Redmond C. Stewart, Fenwick enjoyed 12 successive wins in America. Then, in 1978, the unbeaten chaser was sent back to England to be trained for the 1979 National by Captain Tim

F

Forster. Later that year Charlie followed with his wife and three children and spent more than four months preparing for the big challenge. But all his high hopes were to be dashed when he ran into Aintree's worst pile-up since the 1967 *Foinavon* fiasco.

It happened at The Chair where two pilotless horses veered across the course, leaving the oncoming pack with nowhere to go. Nine horses were duly eliminated. Brought down by one of the loose horses, the American stubbornly remounted *Ben Nevis* and tried to give chase. Then, correctly accepting the hopelessness of his position, he pulled up at the next fence.

While *Ben Nevis* remained in England to be prepared for a second National bid, Fenwick needed to return home to attend his business interests. Thereafter, he only rode the chestnut gelding by commuting across the Atlantic for one race at a time; and on gong back to Aintree *Ben Nevis* had still not scored a single win in a dozen outings in Britain. As a twelve year old, he was dropped four pounds in the weights and he went off unfancied at 40-1.

The subsequent performance exceeded Charlie's wildest dreams. *Ben Nevis*'s previous defeats were attributed to soft going that he hated. Yet now he triumphed in quagmire conditions, destroying his challengers with his far superior stamina on the run-in and being the first of only four finishers in a 30-strong field. Six years later, following the death of Mr Stewart, the Grand National winner was retired to Fenwick's farm. By now Charlie had established himself as a leading trainer of steeplechasers; and still riding in his fortieth year, he won both the Maryland Hunt Cup and the American Grand National Timber Stakes in 1987.

Altogether Charlie had won the Hunt Cup five times and the American National a record eight times. Greatly encouraged by the 1982 victory of a 48 year old amateur (Dick Saunders on *Grittar* in 1982) the American still harboured hopes of making another Aintree challenge. But though he prepared *Sugar Bee*, his 1987 Maryland Hunt Cup winner, for the 1988 National, he never quite managed it. However, he did have a very tenuous connection with the record-breaking 1990 National success of *Mr Frisk*, trained by Kim Bailey and owned by Mrs Lois Duffey. The elderly American lady had several horses in Charlie's Maryland stable and she consulted him before agreeing that *Mr Frisk* could run at Aintree. Seven years passed and once again Fenwick had

fresh hopes of another American winner of the National. He had trained a big (17.2 hands) grey called *Buck Jakes* to win two Maryland Hunt Cups and two American Grand Nationals. Moreover, the initial Maryland win in 1995 had smashed *Ben Nevis*'s course record. Accordingly, he arranged to send *Buck Jakes* to Forster to be prepared for an Aintree bid. But this was one dual Maryland winner who did not adapt well to English fences. Though qualifying for a National handicap with three runs in Britain, his record read 4PP and he was subsequently withdrawn and then retired.

See also: Ben Nevis, Forster, Captain Timothy; Thorner, Graham; Maryland Hunt Cup; United States.

FIELDS

The smallest Grand National fields

10 starters in 1883 when six year old *Zoedone* was the first of seven finishers

11 runners in 1841 when the mare *Charity* won by a length, again with seven finishers (one remounted)

12 starters in 1878 and 1882

13 runners in 1840, 1862 and 1881

Largest fields

66 runners in 1929 when seven year old *Gregalach*, a 100-1 chance, was the first of ten finishers

57 in 1947 when another 100-1 winner (*Caughoo*) emerged out of the heavy mist.

49 in 1950, won by 10-1 joint favourite *Freebooter*

47 in 1952, 1963, 1965 and 1966

In 1959 the rules were amended to allow no more than 50 runners; and since 1984, for the sake of improved safety, the field has been restricted to a maximum of 40. Subsequently the field has only once fallen well below the maximum – in 1996 after a harsh winter had interrupted training schedules and a change in entry rules had demanded a higher level of minimum ability, That year, despite a record £250,000 guaranteed total prize money, only 27 of the 82 original entries made it to the line-up. It was the smallest field since 26 ran in 1960.

In 2001 Martin Pipe set a record for the number of runners sent out by one trainer in the National. His ten starters represented a quarter of the field.

Previously the record had been held by Jenny Pitman with six runners in 1995 when she won with *Royal Athlete*. Pipe saddled five runners in 1994 when he won with *Miinnehoma*. *See also:* Entries.

FILMS

See: National Velvet; Champion, Bob.

FINISHERS

The highest number of finishers in a Grand National occurred in 1984 when *Hallo Dandy* led home 23 of 40 runners who completed the course. The next best is 22 finishers: in 1963 when *Ayala* won with 47 starters, and in 1987 and 1992 when *Maori Venture* and *Party Politics* respectively won with 40 starters. In 2005 *Hedgehunter* led home 21 finishers from a field of 40. That number had been matched in 1947, when it was unremarkable since there was a 57-strong field, the second largest in the history of the race.

The fewest finishers in a Grand National

Two (one remounted) in 1928, the year of 100-1 winner, *Tipperary Tim* – 42 ran

Three in 1882.Winner, *Seaman* – 12 ran

Three (one remounted) in 1913. Winner, *Covertcoat* – 22 ran

Three (one remounted) in 1951. Winner, *Nickel Coin* – 36 ran.

Four (three remounted) in 1911. Winner, *Glenside* – 26 ran

Four (three remounted) in 1921. Winner, *Shaun Spadah* – 35 ran

Four in 1959. Winner, *Oxo* – 34 ran.

Four in 1980. Winner, *Ben Nevis* – 30 ran

Four (two remounted) in 2001. Winner, *Red Marauder* – 40 ran

The percentage of finishers rose after the fences were sloped in 1961 but even after modifications in 1990 – most notably levelling out the landing side of Becher's – there were still some years when few completed. This usually occurs when there is heavy ground, as in 1994 and 1998 with just six finishers, and in 2001 with only four.

FINISHES

The photo-finish camera was first used at a British racecourse (Epsom) in April, 1947. It has never been needed to decide the result of the Grand National, though if it had been available it would certainly have been useful at the Nationals of 1865, 1883 and 1938. Winners of the closest finishes in the history of the race:

1865 *Alcibiade* (100-7) by a head from *Hall Court* (50-1)

1938 Battleship (40-1) by a head from *Royal Danieli* (18-1)

1883 *Seaman* (10-1) by a head from *Cyrus* (9-2)

1859 *Half Caste* (7-1) by 'a short neck' from *Jean du Quesne* (10-1)

1870 *The Colonel* (7-2) by a neck from *The Doctor* (5-1)

1876 *Regal* (25-1) by a neck from *Congress* (25-1)

1930 *Shaun Goilin* (100-8) by a neck from *Melleray's Belle* (20-1)

1954 *Royal Tan* (8-1) by a neck from *Tudor Line* (10-1)

1971 *Specify* (28-1) by a neck from *Black Secret* (20-1)

1848 *Chandler* (12-1) by half a length from *The Curate* (6-1)

1860 *Anatis* (7-2) by half a length from *Huntsman* (33-1)

1875 *Pathfinder* (100-6) by half a length from *Dainty* (25-1)

1891 *Come Away* (4-1) by half a length from *Cloister* (20-1)

1964 *Team Spirit* (18-1) by half a length from *Purple Silk* (100-6)

1978 *Lucius* (14-1) by half a length from *Sebastian V* (25-1)

Most overwhelming finishes

1893 *Cloister* (9-2 fav) won by 40 lengths

1913 *Covertcoat* (100-9) by a distance

1921 *Shaun Spadah* (100-9) by a distance

1928 *Tipperary Tim* (100-1) by a distance

2001 *Red Marauder* (33-1) by a distance

1958 *Mr What* (18-1) by 30 lengths

1977 *Red Rum* (9-1) by 25 lengths

FITZGERALD, Michael Anthony

Winner of the 1996 Grand National on *Rough Quest*, after which success he famously declared: 'I have never enjoyed 12 minutes so much. Sex is an anticlimax after that.' But Mick Fitzgerald did not enjoy

F

the 12 minutes or so that followed his orgasmic experience. During that agonising time he was the first National jockey to await the outcome of a stewards' inquiry before being declared the winner of the world's greatest steeplechase.

Riding for his fellow countryman, trainer Terry Casey, the amiable, articulate Irishman had triumphed on his second attempt. In contrast, his National debut, one year before, had seen him catapulted out of the saddle at the first fence. Moreover, on landing, he had then suffered the agony of being kicked in the privates by his tumbling mount, the Nicky Henderson-trained *Tinryland*, a 50-1 chance.

Born in Cork on May 10, 1970, Fitzgerald had humble beginnings. His father was a mechanic, his mother a cleaning lady in a pub, but both gave him unwavering support when he first showed his natural riding skills as a junior show-jumper on the pony circuit. He was still at school when he started riding out for trainer Richard Lister in Co. Wexford; and his parents continued to back him even though the school principal called round to urge them to continue with their son's education.

Set on a riding career, 15 year old Fitzgerald joined the Lister yard full-time and had his first race-ride (on *Being Bold*) at Gowran Park in April, 1986. It was not an encouraging start. As a Flat jockey, with rides few and far between, he was still without his first winner when he moved to the stables of John Hayden at Kilcullen, near the Curragh. And there he fared no better, facing a losing battle against the scales that ruled out any future on the Flat.

In pursuit of a career in National Hunt, Mick moved to England in 1988, joining trainer John Jenkins at Royston, Hertfordshire, and then soon moving on to the small yard of permit-holder Richard Tucker at Blackborough, Devon. One month later, in December, 1988, he at last had his elusive first success: a win by six lengths on *Lover's Secret* in a selling hurdle at Ludlow. Another winner soon followed. But then came a bleak losing run, a year and a half passing before he rode his third winner – *Sunset Sam* trained by permit-holder Ray Callow – again in a selling hurdle.

Until that point, in the spring of 1990, Fitzgerald had been planning to seek a riding future with trainer John Nicholson in New Zealand. Now, just in time, his career took an upward turn, firstly when riding for Somerset trainer Gerald Ham, and then, more especially, having a string of winners for an Exeter-based trainer, Mrs Jackie Retter.

In the 1991-92 season – having dieted drastically after peaking at an alarming 12st 3lb – Fitzgerald had 38 wins, but disappointingly his introduction to the Grand National was long delayed. In 1992, when he was due to make his debut on *Bumbles Folly*, the New Zealand-bred gelding missed the 40-limit cut by one. The next year he came to Aintree with justifiably high hopes. Aged 22, he had ridden 41 winners to take an unassailable lead in the race for the conditional jockeys' title; and now he was on one of the best outsiders, the remorseless stayer *Just So* who – belying his nickname 'Just Slow' – had finished fast to take sixth place in the National of the previous year. This time, alas, his mount was withdrawn shortly before the race – not a great loss as it happened since this falsely started National would be declared void.

By now Fitzgerald was establishing himself as a leading jumps jockey, sixth in the table with 68 wins in the 1993-94 season. He had his first Cheltenham Festival success on Lady Lloyd Webber's *Raymylette* in the Cathcart Challenge Cup and he was soon getting plenty of class rides as the retained jockey of top trainer Nicky Henderson. But in 1994 he again missed the National, this time through the late withdrawal of *Windy Ways*; and that year, ironically, *Just So* finished runner-up under Simon Burrough, beaten only a length and a quarter by *Miinnehoma*.

In November, 1995, the year of his painful National debut on *Tinryland*, Mick had been due to ride *Rough Quest* for trainer Terry Casey in the Hennessy Cognac Gold Cup. But he missed the ride through a rare suspension and was replaced by Jamie Osborne. The in-form gelding finished runner-up, well beaten by *Couldnt Be Better*. One month later Mick rode *Rough Quest* at Ascot, being beaten only a neck by *Unguided Missile*.

Unfortunately, his stable commitments prevented him riding *Rough Quest* in the Leopardstown Chase in January, 1996, and the Racing Post Chase in February. Ridden by Richard Dunwoody, the horse fell four out in the former and won the latter. But happily Mick was free to be reunited with *Rough Quest* in the Cheltenham Gold Cup and they finished an excellent second to *Imperial Call*. Immediately, the runner-up became all the rage for the Grand National 16 days later, seeming to be a handicap snip on a mere 10st 7lb.

Rough Quest was made the 7-1 clear favourite. However, it did not augur well when, on the Thursday before the 1996 Grand National, Mick fell on *Tudor Fable* in the John Hughes Memorial Trophy. This, following his first fence fall on *Tinryland*, meant that he had now started out over the National fences seven times and had only once got round – on *Skinnhill*, tenth in the 1992 John Hughes. Nonetheless, the jockey was brimful of confidence, having survived the threat of losing yet another National ride.

Only two weeks earlier Fitzgerald had been shocked by the news that *Rough Quest* was to be withdrawn from Aintree and aimed at the later Irish National. The disappointed jockey was booked instead to ride the Nick Gaselee-trained *Bavard Dieu*. But then, providentially, trainer Casey and owner Andrew Wates had second thoughts. Gaselee gracefully accepted the change of plans and found a rather useful replacement in Jason Titley, rider of the 1995 National winner *Royal Athlete*.

In an ironic reversal of fortunes, it was now Titley who was unseated at the first fence in the National, suffering two fractured ribs in the process. Meanwhile *Rough Quest*, so far unproven beyond three miles two furlongs, never made the semblance of a mistake. Familiar with his habit of idling in front, Fitzgerald held him up over the first circuit; then, moving up on the second, he delayed his challenge for as long as he dared. Coming to the last, he was still five lengths adrift of the leading *Encore Un Peu*. By The Elbow *Rough Quest* had drawn level. As he edged ahead he veered to the left, coming perilously close to his rival, then held on to win by a length and a quarter.

Fitzgerald went on to many more big race victories with rides on such top-class horses as *Remittance Man*, *Marlborough*, *Bacchanal*, *Travado* and *Tiutchev*. In February, 1998, he again proved his masterful judgment of pace in bringing *Sharpical* from way-back last to first in winning Newbury's Tote Gold Trophy. Above all, he rode a brilliant race in winning the 1999 Cheltenham Gold Cup – his fourth success of the meeting – on the blinkered *See More Business*, trained by his West Country brother-in-law Paul Nicholls. Coming to the last they had been level with *Go Ballistic*, an outsider Mick had ridden in six of his wins. Knowing the challenger so well, he confidently held on to triumph, albeit by only one length. And that year he

also rode *See More Business* to victory in the King George VI Chase.

Yet the Irishman had a bad run in the Grand National following his 1996 victory. In 1997, when the two-day delay following an IRA bomb scare brought drying ground, his mount *Go Ballistic* was promoted to 7-1 favouritism. Like *Rough Quest*, *Go Ballistic* had reportedly come out well from the Cheltenham Gold Cup in which he had finished fourth. He was also the best handicapped horse according to the official ratings. But this was his seventh race in a hard season and, with Mick putting up 3lb overweight, the eight year old gelding was always behind at Aintree, finally being pulled up at the penultimate fence and found to have a broken blood vessel.

In 1998, having missed the previous National through injury, *Rough Quest* was strongly fancied to regain his Aintree crown, despite having fallen in the Gold Cup 16 days earlier. But he was now 12 years old, high in the weights, and though jumping superbly was unable to go the pace in the clinging mud. Fitzgerald pulled him up at the penultimate fence. In 1999 he was on the Henderson-trained *Fiddling The Facts*, the 6-1 favourite who was trying to become the first mare to win since 1951. She was travelling well, just behind the leaders, when she over-jumped and landed head-first over the second Becher's.

In 2000, after collecting injuries to ankle, ribs and hand, Mick was resolved to ride in the National again and he just won the battle for fitness in time. But again he went out at the second Becher's, this time falling when well-placed on eight year old *Esprit De Cotte*, a 50-1 chance. At the end of the season he was fourth in the jump jockeys' table with 107 wins from 551 rides.

Prior to the 2001 National, champion jockey Tony McCoy remarked: 'Look at Mick Fitzgerald. Everyone remembers him for winning on *Rough Quest* but he's had five other rides and never got around. It's all about the horse.' But it is also about luck in making it to the start and having luck in running. That year Mick did not make it to the start. On National day he fell in the second race, bruising his shoulder so badly that he had to give up his ride on *Esprit De Cotte* (a faller at the 11th). Mick recovered in time to finish second on *Ad Hoc* in the Scottish National.

In March, 2002, at Sandown, he rode *First Love*, the last of 461 winners owned by the Queen Mother.

Then came another disappointment in the National. His mount, *Marlborough*, reminded him of *Rough Quest*, both having overcome jumping problems in their early days and both needing to be held up for a late run. But the big difference was that *Marlborough* was burdened with top weight of 11st 12lb following the late withdrawal of *Florida Pearl*. Now he was one of nine fallers at the first.

Such was the gutsy character of Fitzgerald that it was only after he had won a race on *Fadalko* that an X-ray revealed that he had been riding with a fracture of the left wrist incurred in the National. It put him out for the rest of the jumps season. Nonetheless he finished third in the jockeys' championship with 109 winners; and early in the following season he joined the top ten in the all-time jump jockeys' list by passing Fred Winter's total of 923 jump winners.

In February, 2003, after a layoff with a cracked ankle bone, Mick rode his first winner for nearly four weeks: the novice chaser *First Love*, so giving the Queen her first jumps success in 53 years. The following April, in the National, he fell at The Chair on the unfancied eight year old *Katarino*; and then the new season brought a four month layoff as his shattered ankle required surgery. But again the tough Irishman bounced back, riding as strongly as ever with the Henderson stable in irresistible form.

The year 2003 closed with his powerful finish on *Iris Royal* to win Cheltenham's Tripleprint Gold Cup Handicap Chase for the second successive year and a four-timer at the Kempton post-Christmas meeting. At the start of 2004 he remained in brilliant form, his wins including the £52,000 Victor Chandler Chase at Ascot on *Isio*. But then came another setback: in early February he broke his left arm in a fall at Sandown and depressingly missed rides on a remarkable run of big-race winners from the Henderson stable. He recovered just in time to ride the heavily-weighted *Kingsmark* in the National, but the ground was not soft enough for his 66-1 mount who completed in his own time to be the ninth of 11 finishers.

At 34 the jockey was still insisting that retirement was 'the furthest thing from my mind'. His big remaining ambition was to win a Champion Hurdle, so completing a 'full house' with his Gold Cup, Champion Chase, Grand National and King George VI Chase. Instead, at the 2005 Cheltenham Festival, he added the Royal and SunAlliance Chase to his bow, with victory for Henderson and owner Trevor

Hemmings on *Trabolgan*. One month later his tenth National ride ended three fences out when he had to pull up on the classy two-and-a-half-miler *Fondmort*.

The following season the Irishman faced the biggest setback of his career: in July a fall at Market Rasen resulted in a broken neck necessitating a bone-graft with inserted rods. He spent nine weeks in a surgical collar; and yet, true to form, he once again determinedly returned to the saddle, resuming just in time to ride top-weighted *Trabolgan* to victory in the Hennessy Cognac Gold Cup and, one week later, *Kauto Star*, winner of the Tingle Creek Trophy Chase.

At the Cheltenham Festival he was seen riding at his strongest to bring home *Fondmort* in the Ryanair Chase; and he quickly followed up with victory on *Non So* in the Racing Post Handicap Chase. But his misfortune in the National continued. Riding French-bred *Juveigneur*, he was one of five fallers at the first – the third time he had made such an early exit.

The following September he announced that he would retire at the end of the 2006-7 season and become director of racing for Club ISM (International Sports Management). But would he? Because now he faced a welcome new circumstance: he was enjoying riding as much as ever before, with the winners coming thick and fast.

In November, 2006, he narrowly missed a second successive win in the Hennessy, finishing runner-up on *Juveigneur*. But thereafter he was regularly visiting the winner's enclosure: a rare hurdle success for the Queen on her *Barbers Shop*; a big Haydock double on hurdlers *Afsoun* and *Amaretto Rose*; a four-timer at Fakenham; a runaway victory on *Punjabi* in the Adonis Juvenile Novices' Hurdle at Kempton. Though he was approaching his 37th birthday, his horsemanship was undiminished. He had huge prospects of adding to his portfolio of 14 Cheltenham Festival winners; and with some 1,200 winners under his belt, he still hoped to round off his career with a flourish.

At Cheltenham, he was disappointed with a hat-trick of successive third places followed by a second place in a photo-finish on *Juveigneur* in the William Hill Trophy Handicap Chase. But at Aintree, after being second on *Punjabi* in a novice hurdle, he pulled off a huge upset by winning the Sefton Novices' Hurdle on 20-1 shot *Chief Dan George* at the expense of odds-on favourite *Wichita Lineman*. In the National, he never threatened on the French-bred *Kelami* and needed to pull up at the last. Nevertheless, his 60 winners for the season were sufficient to persuade him to compromise on the question of retirement. He would continue his 17-year partnership with Henderson but would ride much less in the summer months when he would work as ambassador for the prestigious Club ISM, a partnership run by Chubby Chandler whose clients included Lee Westwood, Darren Clarke and Andrew Flintoff.

See also: Rough Quest; Henderson, Nicky; Stewards' Inquiry; Humour.

FLETCHER, Brian

When Brian Fletcher retired from the saddle on medical advice in 1976 it was with a Grand National record surpassed in the 20th century only by Jack Anthony who, in 12 rides, had scored three wins, two seconds and one third place. Fletcher, in nine appearances, had achieved three wins, one second, and two third places.

Born May 18, 1947, Fletcher was such a riding fanatic that even before leaving school (Barnard Castle Grammar) he was competing at 'flapping meetings' – that is, races held without the sanction of a recognised turf authority. Then, as a 16 year old, he seized the chance to go legitimate, being apprenticed to Denys Smith, a newly licensed National Hunt trainer with a yard at Bishop Auckland, Co. Durham. In his first season of 1964-65 he rode three winners from 20 outings and then progressed so rapidly that, at the age of 19, he was entrusted with the 1967 Grand National ride on *Red Alligator* while Terry Biddlecombe took over on Smith's more favoured *Greek Scholar*.

It was a baptism of fire and Fletcher, who had already scored two wins on *Red Alligator*, came through with flying colours. While only John Buckingham on *Foinavon* had a run uninterrupted by the mass pile-up at the 23rd fence, young Brian had sufficient determination and presence of mind to renew his challenge. Three times he put *Red Alligator* at the fence, finally getting over and pressing on so hard that they finished third behind the runaway *Foinavon* and the favourite *Honey End*, and ahead of *Greek Scholar* in fourth.

One year later, having lost his claim to a weight allowance, Fletcher was again showing remarkable maturity, skillfully avoiding fallers at Becher's and otherwise enjoying a trouble-free ride on *Red Alligator* who struck the front at the last open ditch and then drew remorselessly away from all rivals to win by 20 lengths. *Moidore's Token* was runner-up, a neck ahead of Gregory Peck's clear favourite *Different Class*. Remarkably, young Brian ended the season as the second most successful jockey with 70 wins.

Made 13-2 favourite despite his 13lb rise in the weights, *Red Alligator* fell in the 1969 National, and again on his fourth and final appearance in 1970. The following year Fletcher again failed to finish – on Mrs R.E. Sangster's *The Inventor* who refused at the last open ditch. Meanwhile he had continued to be one of the most successful northern-based jockeys. But then came a horrendous fall that prevented him riding in the 1972 National. It was in a novices' chase at Teesside Park racecourse, and as he lay unconscious for ten days with severe head injuries and a broken arm it seemed likely that his racing career had ended.

Defying medical advice, Fletcher stubbornly returned to racing after seven months of struggling to regain fitness. In October he rode his first winner since his fall in February; and now he was rewarded with a huge, well-earned stroke of good fortune. When jockey Tommy Stack was unavailable, trainer Donald 'Ginger' McCain invited Brian to ride a most promising seven year old gelding that had won four successive chases. Now, over 3 miles 3 furlongs at Ayr, came a fifth win; and he kept the ride for the build-up to Aintree. The gelding was *Red Rum*.

With good reason, connoisseurs will remember the epic 1973 Grand National, above all, for the extraordinary performance of the courageous *Crisp* who, with a 23lb disadvantage, went down by only three-quarters of a length to a joint favourite winning in a record time of 9min 1.9 sec. The fact remains that *Red Rum* would not have snatched victory without masterful judgment on the part of Fletcher in choosing the right moment to begin trying to cut down *Crisp*'s seemingly unassailable lead.

Red Rum's true greatness was only proven the following year when, given that extra 23lb to carry, he triumphed by seven lengths from *L'Escargot*, so making Fletcher the first jockey to ride three National winners since Jack Anthony's success on *Troytown* 54 years before. Then, just three weeks later, Brian rode a clever waiting race to bring *Red Rum* home first in the Scottish Grand National.

F

In 1975, the famous partnership went off as 7-2 favourites to achieve a unique hat-trick of Aintree Grand National wins. But this time top-weighted *Red Rum* was running on unfavourably soft ground and giving an extra 10lb to the dual Cheltenham Gold Cup winner, *L'Escargot*. Though the old rivals were side by side in the lead at the last, Brian had already recognised that *L'Escargot* was going more easily, shouting out to jockey Carberry, 'Go on, Tommy, you've got it won'. Hopelessly outpaced on the run-in, he had to settle for second place, 15 lengths behind the winner and eight ahead of the consistent *Spanish Steps*.

Red Rum would go on to endorse his reputation as the supreme Aintree specialist by finishing second again in the National of 1976 and winning a third time in 1977. But this was without the rider who had partnered him in 28 races. Following a disagreement between trainer and jockey (there had been calls for *Red Rum*'s retirement after Brian had independently told the Press that the great horse had not given him 'the old feel'), Tommy Stack eventually took over on 'Rummy' while Brian concluded his great National record in 1976 by finishing a most worthy third – behind *Rag Trade* and *Red Rum* – on the mare *Eyecatcher*, a 28-1 chance.

Fletcher had been heartbroken by the loss of his partnership with *Red Rum*; and his appetite for National Hunt racing had been further blunted by so many years of enduring the legacy of that skull-fracturing fall at Teesside Park: black-outs, acute headaches and fading memory. And now, following a fall at Uttoxeter, he had a narrow escape when blacking-out on the motorway on his homeward drive. This time he heeded medical advice, retiring from the saddle in 1976. In later years he settled in Wales, breeding and dealing in Welsh cobs. He donated his National trophies to the Aintree museum, along with the saddle he had used when achieving his unforgettable triumphs on *Red Rum*.

See also: Red Alligator; Red Rum; McCain, Donald; Le Mare, Noel.

FOINAVON

Shock winner of the 1967 Grand National when, as a 100-1 outsider, he was the sole beneficiary of a mass pile-up at the relatively innocuous 23rd fence. The day before the race *Foinavon* was a 500-1 chance, and such a no-hoper that neither his trainer nor owner were at Aintree to see him run. Charles Benson, the renowned tipster of the *Daily Express*, expressed the general view when he advised, 'Not the boldest of jumpers; he can be safely ignored, even in a race noted for shocks.' Yet the nine year old won by a clear 15 lengths, a success that paid out a record 444-1 on the Tote.

It was the most extraordinary upset in National history because it came about so suddenly, so improbably, and so late. As many as 30 of the 44 runners had safely negotiated the notorious Becher's the second time around. Then, at the next fence, the smallest on the course, all the horses except one were brought to a standstill as the result of the chaos created by *Popham Down*, a blinkered ten year old who had been running riderless since being knocked over at the very first fence.

Unaided, *Popham Down* had successfully negotiated 21 fences, including Becher's twice. Yet, inexplicably, on approaching the easiest obstacle, just 4ft 6in high and a mere formality for the remaining contenders, he suddenly veered across the field from left to right, and – in the words of Lord Oaksey (then riding as Mr John Lawrence) – 'cut down the leaders like a row of thistles'.

The only horse to keep running was the yellow-blinkered *Foinavon*, ridden by John Buckingham who, approaching the 23rd, saw the most ghastly bedlam ahead: a riotous jumble of horses writhing amid shattered broom and gorse, and jockeys scrambling to safety or trying to recapture their mounts. Steered to the wide outside and through a gap between loose horses, *Foinavon* alone cleared the mini-fence at the first attempt, albeit almost from a standstill, in show-jumping fashion.

At Becher's, the 22nd fence, *Foinavon* had been trailing a hundred yards behind the leaders. After being steered clear of the carnage at the next fence, he was soon a hundred yards ahead. Seventeen horses – some remounted, some making a second or third attempt at the fence – came away from the debris of the 23rd to remain in pursuit. But too late. *Foinavon* galloped on to win comfortably from *Honey End*, the 15-2 favourite whom Josh Gifford had taken back 50 yards to make a second run at the 23rd. *Red Alligator* (30-1), destined to win with Brian Fletcher next year, was a further three lengths back in third place.

In effect, the outcome of the 1967 National had been decided by a horse acting entirely on his own. Though some critics would condemn the race as 'a farce', its sensational nature – and the fact that it was injury-free – at least had one most welcome effect. It stimulated demands to 'save the National' which at the time was threatened by negotiations to sell the Aintree site for building development.

Bred in Co. Limerick, *Foinavon* was sired by *Vulgan*, out of *Ecilace*, and therefore a half-brother to the 1964 Grand National winner *Team Spirit*. As a yearling he was sold for 400 guineas, and soon after, on the strength of his pedigree, he was bought by trainer Tom Dreaper on behalf of Anne, Duchess of Westminster, who had him named – like her *Arkle* and *Ben Stack* – after a Scottish mountain. He eventually won three minor chases in Ireland, but was all too often a faller. Re-sold, he disappointed another owner and was sent over to the Doncaster sales as a seven year old. There he was snapped up for 2,000 guineas by trainer John Kempton on behalf of two owners – Messrs Cyril Watkins and Mac Bennellick – who had asked him to find a horse to run in the National.

Kempton regularly rode the brown gelding with the Old Berkshire Hunt and improved his jumping to such good effect that he finished a creditable fourth in the King George VI Chase on Boxing Day. But mainly the horse gained publicity because of his great attachment to the white goat called Susie who was to accompany him to Aintree. The pair were inseparable at Kempton's small yard at Compton in Berkshire. *Foinavon* shared his box with the goat, twice daily lapped up his still warm milk, and travelled with him to race meetings.

Despite his promising showing in the King George, *Foinavon* was one of 13 runners priced at 100-1 for the National, his prospects dismissed because he had failed to win in 15 outings that season and, under Kempton, he had finished a poor seventh and last at 500-1 in the Cheltenham Gold Cup. John Buckingham, a newcomer to the race, was the late jockey booking since the trainer-rider would have put up about 10lb overweight.

With John Kempton busy riding at Worcester, it was left to the trainer's father, Jack, to saddle *Foinavon* at Aintree. Meanwhile, Mr Watkins, now the sole owner, chose to watch the race on TV at his home in Finchampstead, Berkshire. When he saw his no-hoper survive the great pile-up to take the lead, he could not bear the suspense and went out into the garden until it was all over. He returned to find his wife weeping with tears of joy. Besides

£17,630 prize money, they would collect several thousands of pounds in winning bets.

Somewhat harshly, *Foinavon* was dubbed 'the National's luckiest winner'. Moreover, despite having won in a time three seconds faster than *Anglo* the previous year, he continued to be held in such low esteem that he carried only 5lb more on his return to Aintree in 1968 and was again a long shot, now 66-1. This time, when well up with the field, he was brought down at the Water. He did not compete in the National again, but he scored several more successes following his Aintree victory including, in October, 1968, another freak result: at Uttoxeter where, after being tailed off in a three-mile chase, he trailed home alone after a loose horse had brought down the runaway leader and caused the only other contender to be carried out. He was put out to grass after finishing distressed at Kempton Park; and after a long life in retirement he was buried at Compton.

See also: Kempton, John; Buckingham, John.

FOINAVON, The

The small, 4ft 6in fence, coming after Becher's Brook, that it is the seventh to be jumped on the first circuit and the 23rd on the second. It is so named because it was here, second time around in 1967, that the riderless *Popham Down* cut right across the course, causing a pile-up that brought almost the entire field to a standstill and so enabled *Foinavon*, a 100-1 chance, to gain his most improbable victory. Unusually, the 23rd also proved troublesome the following year. There, when well in contention, the Jeff King-ridden *Rondetto* fell, bringing down in the process *Chamoretta*, the 100-1 mount of David Elsworth.

On the first circuit, when horses are relatively fresh, it very rarely causes problems. The main exception was in the quagmire conditions of 2001, when it accounted for three fallers including the blinkered *Paddy's Return*, who ran on riderless and eliminated a fifth of the field at the Canal Turn.

See also: Fences.

FORBRA

Owned by a retired bookmaker (Mr William Parsonage of Ludlow), *Forbra* was a seriously underrated chaser. In 1932, as a seven year old making his first Grand National appearance, he was a 50-1 chance, and on his return he went off at 33-1. Yet he

F

achieved a most impressive record at Aintree: three runs in the National, finishing first on his debut, sixth in 1933 and fourth in 1934.

A brown gelding – by *Foresight* out of *Thymbra* – *Forbra* was originally raced unsuccessfully on the Flat, then sold to Mr Harry Hunt of Uppingham, Leicestershire, who ran him over hurdles. His real strength only showed when he was sent to Kinnersley, Worcestershire, to be schooled over fences by trainer Tom Rimell. He was an outstanding jumper, so safe that he was to be labelled 'the horse that could not fall'. At that point, Mr Parsonage bought him for 1,500 guineas.

Forbra first qualified for the Grand National in unusual circumstances. In December, 1931, he had finished five-lengths runner-up to the great *Golden Miller* in a chase at Newbury. But he was then declared the winner following a successful objection on the grounds that 'the Miller' had carried an incorrect weight. The value of the race was sufficient to make *Forbra* eligible for the National.

As it happened, however, *Forbra* was only entered for the race – one year earlier than planned – because he had disqualified himself for Aintree's Stanley Steeplechase (his intended target) by winning a chase at Taunton. Now, as a seven year old newcomer to the National, he was facing powerful opposition that included *Grakle*, *Gregalach* and *Annandale* (the first three in 1931), plus a third former winner, *Shaun Goilin*, and a worthy favourite in the outstanding Irish mare, *Heartbreak Hotel*.

On his Aintree debut, *Forbra* was up with the leaders throughout the first circuit. Ridden by the experienced professional, James 'Tim' Hamey, he had the good fortune to avoid a pile-up created by the riderless *Pelorus Jack* who ran across the 11th fence, putting out two-thirds of the runners, including *Gregalach*, and halting the challenge of *Heartbreak Hotel*. Then, following the fall of *KCB* at the Water Jump, the race began to develop into a straightforward battle between *Forbra* and *Egremont*, both light-weighted on 10st 7lb.

From the 18th fence onwards, the two horses pulled well clear of the rest, running on neck and neck until, at the fence after Valentine's, *Forbra* was fractionally ahead. *Egremont*, a 33-1 chance ridden by amateur Mr Edward Paget, was barely a length behind when they came to the last, but on the run-in *Forbra* asserted his superior speed, pulling away to win by three lengths with *Shaun Goilin* a distant third. Only eight of 36 starters finished, two of them after being remounted.

Forbra was the third Grand National winner to have be sent out from Kinnersley – following *Emblem* (1863) and *Emblematic* (1864); and, under Tom's son Fred, four more would emerge from that famous base: *E.S.B.* (1956), *Nicolaus Silver* (1961), *Gay Trip* (1970) and *Rag Trade* (1976). On his National reappearance he maintained his reputation as the safest of jumpers. But, having taken a 16lb hike in the weights, he was unable to go the pace; and it was the same in 1934. That year, with a new rider, Gerry Hardy, he was in a quartet of leaders at Valentine's second time. Thereafter he was outpaced by the other three and finished a well-beaten fourth to *Golden Miller* who was winning in record time.

It was his last National. The following January, not long after the death of his owner, the consistent ten year old broke a leg when racing at Newbury and had to be put down.

See also: Hamey, 'Tim' James; Gambles.

FOREIGN RUNNERS

From the very beginning in 1839 the Irish have sent over horses in numbers to challenge for Grand National glory. They first did so successfully with *Matthew* in 1847 and they have been a major force at Aintree ever since. Indeed, with the addition of their mass participation in the Cheltenham Festival, the Irish have become such an integral part of the British racing scene that they are no longer seen as truly foreign challengers.

Thus, excluding Irish runners, it may be said that the first overseas Grand National challenge came in 1856 when *Jean du Quesne* and *Franc Picard* were sent over from France. Both were trained by Harry Lamplugh, the son of a Yorkshire jump jockey, and both failed to finish, the former as the 9-2 favourite.

The first non-Irish winner from overseas was *Huntsman* (1862), a 3-1 favourite ridden by French-based Lamplugh and owned by a French nobleman. But this hardly qualifies as a foreign triumph since *Huntsman* was English-bred, and had been English-owned when previously finishing third and second in the National. By the same token, we may discount the victories scored by *Alcibiade* (1865) and *Reugny* (1874), both French-bred horses but both English-owned and -trained. In 1883 the winner, *Zoedone*, was owned and ridden by a foreigner, Austrian diplomat Count Charles Kinsky. But this six year old mare was English-bred and -trained.

It was not until 1904, after 65 years of British and Irish dominance, that the Grand National had a truly foreign winner. This was the giant *Moifaa*, New Zealand-bred and -owned. Why did he succeed where others had travelled from overseas and failed? The key factor was the weight he carried: a modest 10st 7lb compared with the 12st 6lb borne by the 7-2 favourite, King Edward VII's *Ambush II*, and the 12st 1lb allotted to the incomparable *Manifesto*, now 16 years old.

On his New Zealand record, *Moifaa* might have been expected to carry much more. At home he had won nine of 13 races; and, giving three stone to his nearest rival, he had carried a massive 13st to victory over three and a half miles. But crucially *Moifaa* was not judged on that record alone. Prior to the 1904 National he had run in three English races, each time without distinction, and the handicapper assessed him accordingly.

Over and over again, before *Moifaa*'s success and since, foreign challengers have been hopelessly handicapped in the National because, lacking previous runs in Britain to serve as a guide, many have automatically been anchored on top weight. It happened in 1866 when the French contender, *L'Africaine*, reputed to be the best jumper in all Europe, was saddled with 13st 2lb; in 1867 when the French mare *Astrolabe* was burdened with the most weight; and again in 1868 when *Astrolabe* and *Buszke*, Hungary's first challenger, shared top weight.

Nearly a century later overseas entries were still making their mission impossible by failing to provide British form to guide the handicapper. Thus, in 1961, *Reljef* and *Grifel*, the first-ever Russian entries, went off as top-weighted, 100-1 no-hopers. A smiliar fate befell seven year old *Fujino-o* from Japan in 1966; the most worthy *Essex*, a Russian-bred, Czech-ridden and -owned entire, in 1986; American *Bewley's Hill* and the 500-1 Czech entry *Valencio* in 1987; Czech star *Fraze* in 1991; and yet another Czech 500-1 shot *Quirinus* in 1994.

On the other hand, following *Moifaa*'s example, a few foreign challengers have triumphed after taking the trouble to qualify for proper handicapping by running in Britain before going to Aintree. Disregarding the first American-bred winner *Rubio* (1908), who was both English-owned and -trained,

France led the way in 1909 with five year old *Lutteur III*, French-bred, -trained and -ridden. The young gelding, given time to acclimatise in England and gain experience over English drop fences, won off a reasonable weight of 10st 11lb.

In the 1920s and 1930s American millionaires maintained a massive 'cheque book' campaign to become owners of a Grand National winner, and they succeeded with *Sergeant Murphy* (1923), *Jack Horner* (1926) and *Kellsboro' Jack* (1933). But these winners had Irish or English backgrounds. The great American breakthrough – with a horse shipped across the Atlantic – finally came in 1938 with the victory of *Battleship*, a Kentucky-bred chestnut entire owned by Mrs Marion du Pont Scott, wife of Hollywood film star Randolph Scott.

Significantly, *Battleship* had been sent over to England far in advance of his challenge, being given a year and a half to experience English fences and qualify as a handicapper for the National. This formula for success was to be repeated by *Jay Trump* (1965), American-bred, -owned and -ridden, and by *Ben Nevis* (1980) who, though bred in England, had been brought over from the United States and was also American-owned and -ridden.

In more recent times, two New Zealand-bred horses have won the National: *Seagram* (1991) and *Lord Gyllene* (1997). However, the former had an English owner and had been raced in Britain since being purchased as a three year old. The latter, son of a New Zealand Derby winner, was not a strictly British-made chaser, having established himself as the second best novice chaser in his native land. But for two years before his Aintree success he had been English-owned, -trained and -raced.

Thus, history clearly shows that foreign (non-Irish) horses are not a serious threat unless they have been brought over well in advance and have qualified for handicapping purposes by running in three races. Even then – as shown in 1973 – the most brilliant of overseas challengers can still be beaten by the handicapper. That year the Australian chaser *Crisp* seemed to have all the necessary credentials to win the National. He came over three years in advance, qualified for handicapping, and like winners *Jay Trump* and *Anglo* (1966) he was trained by the great Fred Winter. The only trouble with *Crisp* was that he was really too good. Arguably, he came over too soon and qualified too well.

Crisp oozed so much class that the handicapper

F

allotted him a mighty 12st for his National debut, a top weight equalled that year only by *L'Escargot* who had twice won the Cheltenham Gold Cup. The greatest of all foreign invaders was beaten by just three-quarters of a length in the then fastest National ever run, and by an exceptional newcomer who had a 23lb weight advantage: *Red Rum.*

See also: Australia; Czech Republic; France; Japan; New Zealand; Norway; Russia; Spain; United States.

FORSTER, Timothy Arthur OBE

With two notable exceptions (the Cheltenham and Whitbread Gold Cups) Captain Tim Forster trained winners of almost all the major English steeplechases. His successes included the 1974 Hennessy Cognac Gold Cup and the 1976 King George VI Chase with *Royal Marshal II*; two Mackeson Gold Cups with *Pegwell Bay* (1988) and *Dublin Flyer* (1995); and no fewer than 13 Cheltenham Festival winners. But, above all, he is renowned for three Grand National triumphs – with his own horse *Well To Do* (1972); the American-owned, 40-1 chance *Ben Nevis* (1980); and the 50-1 shot *Last Suspect* (1985).

Born in London on February 27, 1934, Old Etonian Forster grew up with a racing background, his father Douglas owning a number of Flat horses including *Light Harvest*, winner of the 1956 Wokingham at Royal Ascot. He was only 28 when, after six years' service with the 11th Hussars and two years' experience in racing, he set up as a trainer based at Letcombe Bassett, Oxfordshire. His first success came at Cheltenham in 1963 when *Baulking Green* scored in the United Hunts Chase, a race he would win three more times.

Nine years later, with extremely mixed emotions, Forster became the first owner-trainer to saddle the National winner since Major Furlong's second success with *Reynoldstown* in 1936. Mixed because he felt great sadness that *Well To Do*'s original owner had not lived to see the victory she had predicted one year before.

In 1966 Forster had purchased the unbroken three year old *Well To Do* for 750 guineas on behalf of Mrs Heather Sumner. Five years later, when the trainer's first National runner, *Bowgeeno*, finished in fourth place at 66-1, Mrs Sumner told him: 'Never mind, we'll win it next year.' But within two months she had died of cancer, leaving her trainer

the choice of any one of her five horses. He opted for her favourite, *Well To Do*.

In 1972, Forster was so doubtful about running his gift-horse in the National that he met the confirmation deadline for entries with only 15 minutes to spare. As race day approached, however, *Well To Do* was in such peak form that the trainer was uncharacteristically optimistic. And rightly so. With a light weight of 10st 1lb and champion jockey Graham Thorner on board, the chestnut gelding triumphed by two lengths over former winner *Gay Trip*, burdened with 22lb more.

Seven years later Forster had a doubly strong hand in the National: Lord Leverhulme's so consistent *Mr Snowman*, a 10-1 second favourite who had never fallen, and *Ben Nevis*, a 14-1 chance who was strongly tipped to win by Lord Oaksey. The latter, American-owned, had outstanding credentials as a dual winner of the Maryland Hunt Cup. But he had been handicapped accordingly – one of only two runners in a 34-strong field to carry 11st-plus – and he was to be ridden by an American amateur, Charlie Fenwick, who had never won a race over English fences.

The outcome reinforced Forster's natural pessimism. Stable jockey Thorner was a faller on *Mr Snowman* and *Ben Nevis* was one of nine runners to be put out of the race in a mêlée created by loose horses at The Chair. So hopeful in 1979, the trainer was now gloomy about the prospects of running *Ben Nevis* again the following year. Indeed, if it had not been for the pressure of American connections, he would have been inclined to withdraw their entry. The Maryland champion was now 12 years old, had a dismal record for the season, and, worst of all, had been coughing four days before the race.

When the National going turned to heavy, it was seen as the knock-out blow to *Ben Nevis*'s chances. Known to hate the mud, he went out to 40-1, 19th in the betting. And the outlook of Forster was nicely reflected in his memorable parting advice to jockey Fenwick: 'Keep remounting.' But now, in just 10 min 17.4 sec, all of Forster's hard work – 12 months of schooling, planning and often having to race *Ben Nevis* on unfavoured soft – came to fruition. From the second Becher's onwards, *Ben Nevis* dominated the race, powering ahead to win by an astonishing 20 lengths, with only three other starters completing the course.

It was the same familiar story of triumph against

180

all expectation when Forster had his third National winner in 1985. *Last Suspect* was so moodily difficult that only most persuasive pleading by stable jockey Hywel Davies talked Forster and owner Anne, Duchess of Westminster into agreeing to let the 'rogue' run. Before the race the trainer was asked about using the owner's colours on another horse in the following race. Gloomily he replied that it would not be possible. '*Last Suspect* won't be back in time.'

To the amazement of owner and trainer, *Last Suspect* got up in the last strides to win by a length and a half from *Mr Snugfit*. In that same race the joint favourite, *West Tip*, was a faller at the second Becher's. His rider – second jockey to Forster – was another future champion who had learned his trade at the academy so effectively run by the master of Letcombe Bassett: Richard Dunwoody, destined to win two Grand Nationals and finish placed in six others.

In 1986 *Last Suspect* ran again in the National but he reverted to his moody old ways and had to be pulled up at the 18th. Forster's other runner, Lord Chelsea's *Port Askaig*, fell at the first. It was 1990 before the captain was represented again and this time he had a real chance of saddling a fourth Grand National winner. Nine year old *Uncle Merlin*, like *Jay Trump* and *Ben Nevis*, was an American winner of the Maryland Hunt Cup; and remarkably, unlike his successful predecessors, he was well out of the handicap proper and so running on the 10st minimum.

For once the normally pessimistic trainer quietly fancied his contender. Alas, after jumping superbly and leading the ultimate, record-breaking winner *Mr Frisk* for 22 fences, he was three lengths clear when he made a mistake at the second Becher's and left Hywel Davies slowly slipping sideways out of the saddle.

In 1994 Forster moved from Letcombe Bassett, Oxforshire, to Downton Hall, near Ludlow, Shropshire. His big race winners continued to flow, most notably with *Dublin Flyer*, *Martha's Son* and *Maamur*. And of all his training successes he valued most highly the success of *Martha's Son*, so long plagued with serious leg injury but brought back to win the Queen Mother Champion Chase in 1997. That same year, even though he was bravely fighting multiple sclerosis, cancer and heart trouble, he made his most determined bid to equal Fred Rimell's record of four National triumphs. He had no fewer than four entries: *Dublin Flyer*, *Maamur*, *General Wolfe* and Anne Duchess of Westminster's *River Mandate*.

Dublin Flyer was allotted top weight of 12st and made 10-1 favourite 'with a run'. But after a disappointing showing in the Gold Cup he was withdrawn; and so was *Maamur*. 'The Captain' was relatively bullish about *General Wolfe* who had finished second in the 1996 Scottish National. However, this was the year when horses suffered extra stress with a second journey to Aintree after the National had been postponed two days by IRA bomb threats. Moreover both *General Wolfe* and *River Mandate* had their chances lessened by the drying ground. The former was the 16th of seventeen finishers, the latter pulled up at the 21st.

Finally, in 1998, Forster had three National entries: *General Wolfe*, *River Mandate* and, most interestingly, *Buck Jakes*, a dual Maryland Hunt Cup victor, reviving memories of his success with *Ben Nevis*. Sadly, none of them made it to the line-up; and later that year, soon after winning Cheltenham's National Hunt Chase with *Wandering Light*, the great trainer retired with a total of 1,346 winners. The following year, aged 65, the extraordinarily courageous captain finally lost his battle with crippling illness.

He would be forever remembered as a hugely popular figure in racing circles – a man renowned for his modesty and dry, self-effacing wit. And it is a rare measure of his Grand National record that anyone backing all of his runners each-way would have made a considerable profit.

See also: Well To Do; Ben Nevis; Last Suspect; Thorner, Graham; Fenwick, Charles; Davies, Hywel.

FOUL PLAY

The first instance of foul play came in the first Grand National of 1839 when *Rust*, a well-backed Irish challenger ridden by William McDonough, was running so well that an unsporting, mercenary mob invaded the course and deliberately hemmed in the horse until all other runners had long since passed by. This action was made possible because the course layout then included a narrow stretch of lane – optional for riders – where it was possible for *Rust* to be completely blocked.

Again, in 1842, though with less obvious intent, some hooligans ventured on to the course and

F

baulked *Peter Simple* after he had taken the lead beyond Valentine's second time around. The hard-pulling grey was so alarmed that he threw his amateur rider out of the saddle. Remounted, he finished third, 19 lengths behind the winner *Gay Lad*. Four years later McDonough was again a victim of interference. This time, when going well on *Lancet*, a 10-1 chance, he was knocked out of the saddle by a spectator who invaded the course on horseback.

In 1847 there were unsubstantiated rumours that the brilliant Irish mare, *Brunette*, had been nobbled before the race. However, ridden by William's brother, Alan McDonough, she ran creditably to finish sixth when conceding two stone to the winner *Matthew*. More certainly, in 1854, some person or persons unknown 'got at' the hot favourite, *Miss Mowbray*, by applying a blister to her near fore-leg. To the bitter disgust of racegoers, and the great disappointment of veteran rider Jem Mason, the heavily backed mare was withdrawn only one hour before the off.

In 1885, former winner *Zoedone* was the 5-1 second favourite, having been heavily backed in spring doubles with the Lincoln Handicap winner, *Bendigo*. On the first day of the Aintree meeting, the course was rife with rumours that she would be 'stopped' from winning. Indeed, her rider-owner, Count Charles Kinsky, had received a number of anonymous letters, warning him that an attempt would be made on his mare. Consequently, he had hired detectives to watch over her night and day, and all her feed and drinking water were carefully checked.

On the race day, *Zoedone*, looking in fine fettle, was led down to the course where she was to be mounted by her rider. However, owing to the pressure of racegoers who had scrambled over the rails for a better view of runners, it was some time before the count could join his horse on the course. It would later be suggested that she had been 'got at' in this interval. Whatever, when Kinsky prepared to mount, he noticed that a smear of blood had appeared on his white jacket. The mare had rubbed her nose against his sleeve; and now, on examining *Zoedone*, he observed a small puncture mark near a nostril. This was hardly conclusive evidence but the belief that she had been doped was lent the strongest support by her subsequent running.

At this time it was customary for all runners to jump a preliminary 'practice hurdle' on their way to the start. *Zoedone*, incredibly, fell at this trivial obstacle. Then, remounted, she started lethargically in the race proper, trailed the field thereafter and somehow struggled on before finally crashing into the fence before Becher's second time around. Rolling over, she lay motionless for several minutes, and a quarter of an hour elapsed before she was fit enough to be led back. Though only eight years old, the gallant mare never raced again.

In 1894 there was a huge outcry when *Cloister*, the ante-post favourite, was withdrawn shortly before the National. Curiously, the wonder horse of the time had drifted out in the market shortly before his injury in training was reported. When exactly the same coincidence occurred before the 1895 National the allegations of skulduggery were positively thunderous. Owner Charles Duff was convinced that his horse had been nobbled. But the evidence was entirely circumstantial.

In 1910 the National Hunt Committee followed the example, set on the Flat by the Jockey Club in 1903, by officially declaring the doping of horses to be illegal. Happily, there has so far never been an instance of a Grand National runner being found to have been given illegal drugs. But rumours of foul play continued to arise from time to time.

In 1935, after *Golden Miller* had won his fourth successive Cheltenham Gold Cup, jockey Gerry Wilson reported to trainer Basil Briscoe that he had been offered £3,000 to stop the hot favourite in the National. He said he had rejected the offer but was unwilling to name the person who had approached him. Subsequently, security guards watched over the wonder horse night and day, and Briscoe slept with a 12-bore shotgun at his side. Top-weighted *Golden Miller* duly went off in the National at 2-1 – the shortest price ever. He unseated his rider at the 11th fence.

As already recorded, the most outrageous allegation of foul play came years after Eddie Dempsey had won the 1947 National on *Caughoo*, a 100-1 chance, by 20 lengths from *Lough Conn*. Daniel McCann, the rider of the runner-up, accused his fellow Irishman of having taken a short cut in the thick Aintree fog, in the process missing out at least 15 of the 30 fences. A punch-up ensued, then a law-suit with McCann repeating his accusation in court. The magistrates dismissed his claim which seemed to be largely the product of too much Irish liquor.

In 1961 the National was preceded by a riot of rumours about a major doping scam being plotted. Most improbably, one rumour had it that crooks planned to nobble a third of the 35-strong field. After the race had been won by *Nicolaus Silver*, it was suggested that the gang had slipped up by doping the wrong grey when breaking into the Rimells' Kinnersley yard. The Rimells had indeed taken the precaution of moving another grey (*High Spot*) into *Nicolaus Silver*'s box, and the story was lent some credence by the fact that *High Spot* never raced again. But there was nothing in the running of the race, or in the pattern of betting, to support the belief that any horses had been 'got at'.

Again, in 1962, maximum security was in force at Kinnersley after jockey Bobby Beasley had received letters threatening him with dire consequences if he were to win again on *Nicolaus Silver*. But the anonymous writers need not have bothered. As it happened, the grey had no chance of winning on unfavourably heavy going, and he did well to finish seventh.

In 1999, one year after the event, jockey Carl Llewellyn revealed that on the morning of the 1998 National, he had received an anonymous call on his mobile. The caller, he said, offered to make him 'a very rich man' if he did not win on *Earth Summit* who had been backed down from 50-1 to 7-1 favouritism. Dismissing it as just a crank call, he did not report the bribe at the time; just disregarded it and won.

See also: Cheating; Dempsey, Edward; McDonough, Alan; Miss Mowbray; Zoedone.

FRANCE

French horses first contested the Grand National in 1856 when leading owner Baron de la Motte sent over two challengers: *Franc Picard* and *Jean du Quesne*. Both were trained by Yorkshire-born Harry Lamplugh who also rode the latter, the 9-2 favourite. They both failed to finish, but Lamplugh and *Jean du Quesne* (now owned by the Vicomte de Quinchy) returned to finish sixth in 1857 and second (by only 'a short neck') in 1859.

The first French-owned winner was *Huntsman* (1862), ridden and trained by Lamplugh. True, he was prepared in France, but he was essentially an English product who had finished third and second in the National before being sold to the French nobleman, Vicomte de Namur. In 1865 *Alcibiade* became the first French-bred winner and the first successful five year old. But again, this young chestnut entire had raced only in England, and had been English-owned and -trained ever since being claimed out of a selling race at Epsom.

One year later there were two prominent French contenders: *Laura*, a five year old mare, and *L'Africaine*, reputed to be the best jumper in Europe. The former, the 7-1 favourite ridden by Lamplugh, fell at the second in a pile-up that also put an end to the challenge of *L'Africaine* who was absurdly burdened with a monstrous 13st 2lb In 1867 the winner, *Cortolvin*, had been trained by Lamplugh in France, but he was Irish-bred, owned by the Duke of Hamilton and ridden by an Englishman, Johnny Page. Meanwhile the true French challenger – Baron Finot's mare *Astrolabe* – had been knocked over when carrying a top weight of 12st 7lb; and she was still on the top weight when finishing fifth in 1868.

In 1874 there was a French-bred winner, Captain James Machell's six year old entire *Reugny*. But he was English-owned, -trained and -based; and, having been campaigned only in England, he had gained a relatively light weight. In contrast, horses sent across the Channel without English form to guide the handicapper continued to be at a huge weight disadvantage. In 1875 Baron Finot's chestnut mare *La Veine*, winner of the Grand Steeplechase de Paris, went off the 6-1 favourite but, under 11st 12lb, a big weight for a five year old, she finished a close-up third, conceding 15lb to the eight year old winner *Pathfinder*. Similarly, the Marquis de St Sauveur's *Wild Monarch* was anchored under top weight when finishing fourth in the 1879 National.

At last, in 1909, one Frenchman got the message. M. James Hennessy gave his five year old entire *Lutteur III* time to acclimatise in England and gain experience of English fences in a warm-up steeplechase at Hurst Park, which he won most impressively, just 16 days before going to Aintree. By then, with some allowance for his tender age, he was already reasonably handicapped on 10st 11lb In a National which had 32 runners, equalling the 1850 record, *Lutteur III* duly won by two lengths to become the first winner to be French-owned and -bred, and ridden by a Frenchman, Georges Parfrement.

The handicapper, of course, did not give him a second chance. On his return in 1911 *Lutteur III* was burdened with an extra 20lb. Absurdly, in view of his weight and the very heavy going, the entire went off as 7-2 favourite; and he ended his run see-

F

sawing atop the fence after Becher's. But such was his class that three years later the handicapper was even more severe. In his third and last National, *Lutteur III* was allotted 12st 6lb, conceding no less than 41lb to the ultimate winner, *Sunloch*. Most creditably he achieved third place, with another French contender, *Trianon III*, the runner-up on his third appearance in the race.

Thereafter, however, the Grand National was to be without serious French challengers for decades to come, with foreign interest increasingly focused on American invaders. In 1931 France's 50-1 shot *Rhyticere* finished fourth. Otherwise, the country's few entries were woefully weak – as evinced in 1936 by the Marquis de San-Miguel's *Oeil De Boeuf*, a 100-1 outsider who fell at the first fence and in the process brought down the great *Golden Miller*; and again, in 1938, when the Marquis's six year old *Takvor Pacha*, having soon lost his rider, ran on to come between leaders *Battleship* and *Royal Danieli* in their neck-and-neck duel to the winning post.

In 1946 there were two 33-1 French challengers – *Kami* and *Symbole*. The former was going particularly well until he fell at the second Becher's. The latter, sadly, fell fatally at the same fence. Then, in 1953, there at last came a French-bred National runner of distinction: Dorothy Paget's *Mont Tremblant* who, the previous year, had won the Cheltenham Gold Cup as a six year old. Unfortunately, at Aintree he was burdened with a savage top weight of 12st 5lb and had to settle for second place behind *Early Mist* who was carrying 17lb less.

It was not until the 1980s that French steeplechasing flourished anew with the emergence of a supremely formidable new talent: M. Francois Doumen, trainer extraordinaire. He burst on to the British racing scene in sensational style in 1987 when he brought over *Nupsala* who, as a 25-1 outsider, won the King George VI Chase – 15 lengths ahead of the great *Desert Orchid*.

Combining a powerful string of jumpers with a Flat-racing team, Doumen ran a family operation with his wife and sons Xavier and Thierry; and now he became the most feared foreign invader. He won the King George four more times – with *The Fellow* (1991 and 1992), *Algan* (1994) and *First Gold* (2000). With *The Fellow* he missed the Cheltenham Gold Cup by only a short head in 1991 and 1992, and finally won the cherished prize in 1994. Other

successes included the 2000 Triumph Hurdle with *Snow Drop* and major prizes on the Flat in Hong Kong and Dubai with his *Jim and Tonic*. Yet remarkably he was to know only disappointment in the Grand National.

His most obvious great hope lay with *The Fellow*. Following his narrow miss in the 1991 Gold Cup this six year old bay gelding had become the youngest King George winner since *Mandarin* 18 years earlier. But it was another three years before he was at last entered for the National. He was then allotted a fair weight of 11st 4lb and having won the Gold Cup on the mandatory 12st, he was backed down to 9-1 at Aintree. However, he had only three weeks to recover from his hard-earned, one-length victory at Cheltenham, and now the heavy going was hopelessly against him. Totally exhausted, *The Fellow* crashed out at the Canal Turn second time around, and he was deservedly retired the following year.

In 1996 Doumen's nine year old *Val D'Alene* was one of three strictly French horses entered for the National, the others being *As de Carres* and *Sylver Dargent*. The last of these was a seven year old who had no rating in England and so was automatically given a prohibitive top weight (with *Master Oats*) of 11st 10lb. On the other hand, *As de Carres*, quoted at 40-1, looked an absolute handicap snip. He had beaten some of France's best chasers in December, 1995, and had then been artfully transferred to Josh Gifford to be prepared for Aintree with two hurdle races and one chase. Thus he gained a long handicap assesment of 9st 6lb, a full 22lb less than *Val D'Alene* whom he had beaten seven and a half lengths in a £60,000 chase at Auteuil when receiving 12lb.

At the entry stage, it seemed an ideal set-up for a second truly French victory. Unfortunately, all three French challengers were to be withdrawn before the final declaration. But still there was to be huge consolation when *Encore Un Peu* – a 14-1 chance trained by Martin Pipe – came closest to being the first French-bred winner since *Lutteur III*. Ridden by David Bridgwater and running 9lb out the handicap, he was beaten just a length and a quarter by *Rough Quest* and then only after a stewards' inquiry.

By now another major training force had emerged in French jump racing: Guillaume Macaire who won the 1996 Grand Steeplechase de Paris with *Arenice* and became champion trainer in 1997 and 1998. But it was still left to Doumen to saddle France's Grand National challengers. In 1998 his runner – and a first

National ride for his 18 year old son, Thierry – was *Ciel de Brion*. The eight year old chaser had won over the big fences of Auteuil, had finished fourth in the Hennessy Cognac Gold Cup and was now running from out of the handicap proper. But he had never won over a distance beyond two miles six furlongs; and though prominent for a long time at Aintree he eventually struggled in the heavy going and fell at the 26th in a race that saw only six finishers.

Two years later Doumen had high hopes for his nine year old *Djeddah* who, on his last run, had finished fifth in a high-class renewal of the Racing Post Chase at Kempton. But to his dismay the gelding was harshly allotted 11st 8lb and, as feared, it proved a decisive factor. Under Thierry, *Djeddah* finished an honourable ninth, two places ahead of the last year's winner *Bobbyjo*. In three more appearances, though progressively dropped in the weights, he would not improve on that position. In 2001 he was one of eight casualties at the Canal Turn first time round, a pile-up having been caused by the riderless *Paddy's Return*. He was unlucky again in 2002 when, like the much-fancied *Ad Hoc*, he was brought down at the 27th; and in 2003, now a 12 year old, he finished a distant eleventh. The following year Doumen ran six year old *Kelami*, brought down at the first; and in 2005 he gained seventh place with *Innox*.

Since the turn of the century there had been a significant upsurge in the number of French-bred horses being imported by Britain; and it has been reflected by the many entered for the Grand National. Their overall record at Aintree, however, has been fairly disappointing. In 2003 not one of 12 French imports in the line-up managed a place. In 2004 and again in 2006, only one of 12 completed the course. In 2007, just one of ten made any impression: *Liberthine*, finishing fifth, more than 20 lengths off the winner.

However, a few have greatly impressed. *Mely Moss* was runner-up in 2000 – beaten only a length and a half by *Papillon* – when having his first race for 364 days. *Clan Royal* was a good second in 2004 and third in 2006. In the year between he was desperately unlucky to be carried out by a loose horse when leading at the approach to the second Becher's, and that day six of fourteen French-bred runners completed the course, the most notable being *Royal Auclair*, the 40-1 runner-up.

Jump racing in France has always been distinctively different in that horses are schooled over fences at a very early age, often as two years olds in November and December; and then, as three years olds, they will begin hurdling in March and perhaps chasing in September. In contrast, their British and Irish counterparts tend not to be schooled until they are four or five and usually only develop into mature chasers from the age of seven or eight.

Times were now changing as British buyers became more adept at spotting young French horses that had had few races and were less liable to an early burn-out. Anthony Bromley, a partner in the Newmarket bloodstock agency Highflyer, led the way, having bought about 150 French jumpers in 2000-01. Martin Pipe also set the trend for acquiring French jumpers – among them *Cyfor Malta*, *Champleve*, *Lady Cricket*, *Or Royal*, and not least, *Magnus*, bought for an auction record of near £340,000. Moreover, his leading rival Paul Nicholls strongly supported this trend. In consequence, many French-bred horses now appear at the Cheltenham Festival and at Aintree.

So far, however, six and seven year old French imports have fared badly in the National. Indeed, in modern times the only French-bred horses to run with distinction have been *Encore Un Peu*, *Mely Moss* and *Clan Royal*, all runners-up at the age of nine; *Blowing Wind*, third as an eight year old and again when aged nine; and *Royal Auclair*, finishing second as an eight year old. There has still not been a French-bred winner since *Lutteur III* in 1909. *See also:* Foreign Runners.

FRANCIS, Richard OBE, MBE

As a consistently best-selling author, Dick Francis wrote 39 thrillers and won numerous international awards. Yet he never conclusively solved the greatest mystery of his life: why he failed to win the 1956 Grand National after clearing all 30 jumps on the Queen Mother's *Devon Loch* and having a ten-length lead with no more than 60 yards to go to the finishing post.

His explanation of *Devon Loch*'s collapse – the best remembered fall in National history – is that his mount was confused by the unprecedented roar of the crowd in anticipation of a royal victory. But other theories abound, most popularly that the ten year old bay had belly-flopped after attempting to leap an imagined jump. Whatever, it was a heartbreaking end to participation in Nationals for both horse and rider.

While *Devon Loch* was making his first and last

appearance in the National, Francis was competing for the eighth time. Curiously, his first ride had been his most successful. In 1949, on Lord Bicester's top-weighted *Roimond*, a 22-1 chance, he finished second, beaten eight lengths by *Russian Hero* who outstayed his gelding on the run-in. By huge irony, the winner, a 66-1 outsider with an 18lb advantage, was a horse that Francis had often ridden successfully for trainer George Owen and a few months earlier had helped to recover from a life-threatening bout of colic.

Born on October 31, 1920 at Tenby in Pembrokeshire, Francis was riding at the age of five and left school at 15 to pursue his ambition to be a jockey, so following in the footsteps of both his father and grandfather. The former, Vincent Francis, was now managing the hunting stables of W.J. Smith at Holyport, near Maidenhead in Berkshire; and in those pre-war days Dick was responsible for schooling the ponies on which the royal princesses, Elizabeth and Margaret, were taught to ride.

Francis had still to make his mark as a jockey when he joined the RAF to serve as a young fighter and bomber pilot in the Second World War. On demob, he became a National Hunt jockey, having his first ride in October, 1946, on *Russian Hero*, trained by George Owen in Cheshire. It was a tough initiation, his first winner (*Wrenbury Tiger* in a hunter-chase at Bangor-on-Dee) not coming until May, 1947; and on his wedding day that year he had his arm in a sling, the result of breaking a collarbone in a fall at Newport the previous week. But he progressed apace. In 1948, when he turned professional, he was invited to ride regularly for Lord Bicester; and in the 1953-54 season, riding for Peter Cazalet and Frank Cundell, he took the jockeys' championship with 76 winners.

The chance to ride for Lord Bicester's powerful stable – accepted with Owen's approval – had been the key break in Francis's career. It brought him some famous big-race victories. But also, as no one could have imagined, it led to that outstanding Grand National debut in which he finished second on the conker-coloured *Roimond*. This was the only time in four Nationals that the temperamental *Roimond* completed the course, and Francis followed up with a comfortable win in the Welsh National on *Fighting Line*.

Overall, however, his luck in the Aintree National was mostly bad. In 1950, he was again on *Roimond*,

raised three pounds and now 10-1 joint favourite with the eventual winner, *Freebooter*. The unpredictable dark chestnut had one of his off- jumping days and fell at the seventh fence. (*Russian Hero*, incidentally, went at the first). In 1951, following the chaos of an undeclared false start, Francis's mount – Lord Bicester's *Finnure* – was one of 12 fallers at the first fence. He had jumped it perfectly only to land amid a mad mêlée of jockeys and horses rolling about on the ground. It was an especially severe disappointment since Francis had great expectations of the horse on which he had had five wins, including the Champion Chase at Liverpool and, most brilliantly, victory over the great *Cottage Rake* in the 1949 King George VI Chase. Now, having twisted his hock in the Aintree fall, *Finnure* was never to be quite the same horse again.

In 1952, with *Skyreholme*, Francis was again on one of a huge number of early fallers, this time going out at the seventh.The following year he was on Lord Bicester's *Senlac Hill*, a notoriously unreliable jumper who had twice put him in hospital. The chestnut gelding went off as a 66-1 outsider, with 50-1 on offer against him even completing the course. Miraculously Francis nursed him round to be the fifth of five finishers.

In the 1954 National, he pulled up at the 19th on the no-hoper *Icy Calm*, and in 1955 he was a first fence faller on Lord Bicester's *Mariner's Log*. Though his owner had recently died, *Mariner's Log* (again a faller) still ran in Lord Bicester's name in the 1956 National. But Francis, now stable jockey to Peter Cazalet, was on *Devon Loch*, who jumped immaculately throughout, in difficulty only at Valentine's, first time round, where he had to twist in mid-air to avoid landing on the fallen *Domata*.

After that most famous of National defeats, Francis rode *Devon Loch* in three more races – winning one and finishing second in the other two, which included the King George VI Chase. Altogether he had partnered 11 winners in the royal colours, including five on *Devon Loch*. In 1956 the Welsh-born jockey had the consolation of winning the Welsh National on *Crudwell*. But then, in January, 1957, injury caused him to miss the ride on *Devon Loch* in the Mildmay Memorial at Sandown; and in that race the royal chaser broke down. He had to be retired; and Francis, weakened by so many falls, decided that he, too, had passed his racing sell-by date. Then, following a decade in which he had ridden 345 winners, he developed a writing career by way of his work on weekly articles for the *Sunday Express* and on his life story, *The Sport of Queens*.

In that hugely successful autobiography, Francis wrote: 'In all my life I have never experienced a greater joy than the knowledge that I was going to win the National.' Incredibly, his joy had been misplaced, but how quickly he turned that tragedy to triumph! His first novel, set against a racing background and published in 1962, was appropriately entitled *Dead Cert*. Thereafter, in collaboration with his highly literate wife Mary, he produced roughly one best-selling thriller a year, their 38 works selling more than 60 million copies in 35 languages. Mary died in 2000; and two years later, from his Caribbean home in the Cayman Islands, Dick announced his retirement.

In 2006 Francis returned to Aintree to open the course's new weighing-room complex. The following year, at the time of the National, he was recuperating following an operation for a quadruple heart by-pass, plus a valve replacement. But he watched the race on television; and it was a measure of exactly how much the Grand National meant to him that he said would gladly exchange all the wealth and fame and decades of good living that he had earned as a writer for the joy of winning that 1956 National.

Later in 2007 he had his right leg amputated after suffering circulatory problems related to his open heart surgery. He accepted it with the same indomitable spirit that has served him well as a wartime Spitfire pilot, as a jump jockey who had broken most body parts, including his nose (five times), his skull (twice), his arm, wrists, three vertebrae, countless ribs and his collarbone (12 times) and who had fought a long-running battle with prostate cancer. Never complaining he remarked of his amputation: 'My only regret is not winning the Grand National.' Subsequently he saw the publication of his 40th novel – *Dead Heat* – written in collaboration with his 45 year old son Felix.
See also: Devon Loch; Cazalet, Peter; Royal Runners.

FRANCOME, John MBE

Until the arrival of the phenomenal Tony McCoy, John Francome was invariably addressed by TV racing pundit John McCririck as 'Greatest Jockey' and judged by many to be the finest jump jockey never to have won the Grand National. In a 16-year National Hunt career, he was seven times champion jockey and rode 1,138 winners, more than half of them for the renowned Fred Winter. He won a Cheltenham Gold Cup, two King George VI Chases and two Hennessy Gold Cups, the Champion Hurdle, the Tote Gold Trophy and the Welsh National; and he scored a hat-trick in a single afternoon of the Cheltenham Festival. But success in the greatest steeplechase narrowly eluded him, a second and a third place being his best from nine National bids.

Francome was to call his autobiography *Born Lucky*. But there was really no luck about his phenomenal success, both on and off the racecourse. He was a supremely stylish horseman, strong in body and mind, and a masterful tactician with the shrewdest judgment of pace. Equally he was naturally well-equipped for a television career with a likeable personality, razor-sharp wit and the self-confidence of an ex-jockey who had once brazenly dared to describe stewards as 'Cabbage Patch dolls'.

Unlike Winter, his career-long master, Francome had no family links with horse riding. Born on December 13, 1952, the son of a Swindon builder, his introduction to riding came via seaside donkeys, a milkman's horse and then a pony (without saddle) which his father bought for him at the age of six. As a junior show-jumper he won international honours and then, in 1969, having left school with just two CSEs, he was hired as a stable lad for Winter at Uplands, Lambourn. He had his first ride, a winning one, in a 1970 three-mile hurdle at Worcester, and five years later, on the retirement of Richard Pitman, he took over as Winter's number one jockey. His first jockey championship came with 96 winners in 1975-76, and between 1980 and 1985 he rode more than 100 winners in five successive seasons.

His Grand National debut, in 1972, ended when *Cardinal Error*, the 12-1 joint second favourite, refused after being baulked at the third. In 1975, he finished tenth on the Arthur Pitt-trained *Rag Trade*. But the following year, when *Rag Trade* reappeared, Francome missed the ride. The gelding had been sent to trainer Fred Rimell and was now to be ridden by Irish jockey John Burke. However, it hardly seemed a loss at the time. Mercy Rimell has recalled that, after an earlier ride on *Rag Trade*, Francome had declared: 'That's the most horrible horse I've

F

ever ridden, and I'll never ride him again in anything.'

What irony! In the 1976 National, 'Born Lucky' John suffered an almighty fall when leading on *Golden Rapper,* who plunged head first into the ground over Becher's the second time around. He woke up in Walton hospital with a sore head and a broken bone in his right hand. Meanwhile the clumsy *Rag Trade* – despite crashing through rather than over several fences – had managed to win by two lengths from *Red Rum.*

In 1978, Francome finished seventh on *Lord Browndodd;* and in 1979, when only seven of 34 starters finished, he came home six-and-a-half lengths third on the aptly named *Rough and Tumble,* beaten for stamina on the run-in by *Rubstic* and *Zongalero.* Francome and *Rough and Tumble* renewed their challenge in 1980, this time finishing 20-lengths second to *Ben Nevis* in atrociously heavy conditions that saw only four of 30 runners complete the course.

In 1981 he finished tenth on 12 year old *So,* trained by Michael Oliver. ('It looked terrible in the paddock, went to the post like a crab, and I wouldn't have backed him to jump over sixpences, never mind 30 Aintree fences'). Then, back on *Rough And Tumble* for a third time in 1982, he unusually lost his cool when Hywel Davies pulled up a tired *Tiepolino* just in front of Becher's, causing his own mount to dig in his heels, leaving the jockey dangling over the fence, still clinging on to the reins. Out with a broken collarbone in 1983, his subsequent rides were former winner *Grittar* (10th, 1984) and *Drumlargan* (pulled-up, 1985).

One month later, having achieved his seventh jockey championship with 101 winners, Francome ended his riding career being trampled into the ground by *The Reject* at Chepstow's open ditch. Just the day before he had ridden four winners. Now he shrewdly chose to retire while still at the top, briefly pursuing an ambition to be a trainer on the Flat, then settling instead for a permanent place on the Channel 4 Racing team and later successfully adding novel-writing to his bow.

Despite his Midas touch, 'Lucky John' still lacked good fortune with the Grand National. In 1987 William Hill offered him a £500 bet for charity. Inspired, he picked *Maori Venture* at 50-1 – but chose another horse for his own bet!
See also: Tipsters.

FREDDIE

Scottish-owned and -trained *Freddie* never won a Grand National. However, he stands out as one of the race's greatest losers. Having won his past two races, plus the 1964 Foxhunters' Challenge Cup at Cheltenham, the eight year old brown gelding was allotted the top weight of 11st 10lb for the 1965 National, and yet, despite that handicap mark, he was so highly regarded that he went off as the 7-2 favourite of 47 runners.

Ridden by Pat McCarron, *Freddie* was prominent from the start to finish. Coming to the last he had only one challenger: the American champion *Jay Trump.* They met it together but *Jay Trump,* despite a clumsy jump, now began to pull away. *Freddie,* giving 5lb, nevertheless fought back strongly, finally going down by only three-quarters of a length, with *Mr Jones* 20 lengths back in third. One year later, with only a Japanese no-hoper carrying a greater weight, *Freddie* was again the runner-up in the 47-strong field, this time an 11-4 favourite beaten 20 lengths by *Anglo* who was receiving a stone and a half.

Scotland's outstanding National challenger was bred and trained by his owners Reg and Betty Tweedie on their farm near Kelso. At one time ridden in the rounding-up of sheep, he developed via hunting and point-to-points into a hugely successful steeplechaser. In the 1964 Scottish Grand National he was beaten only half a length by *Popham Down,* who had a 22lb weight advantage. The following year he finished runner-up to the supreme *Arkle* in the Hennessy Gold Cup.

In 1967, after winning the Gallagher Gold Cup at Sandown, *Freddie* returned to Aintree for his third consecutive National appearance. Harshly he was lumbered with a greater burden than ever, 11st 13lb, the second highest weight in a 44-strong field. He was well placed when, like so many others, he was caught up in the 23rd fence chaos which, created by the riderless *Popham Down,* allowed *Foinavon* to come home a comfortable winner at 100-1. He completed the course in 17th place. Seven months later, after showing signs of a heart murmur, he was retired to the Tweedies' farm and lived on until 1985.
See also: Scotland; Unlucky Losers.

FREEBOOTER

A brilliant winner of the 1950 Grand National (many rated him the best since *Golden Miller* in 1934),

Freebooter was a supremely powerful jumper who, again and again, proved his special liking for Liverpool races. When making his National debut, the nine year old bay gelding did make one near-disastrous error at The Chair. But once steadied by jockey Jimmy Power he stormed back to win impressively by 15 lengths from *Wot No Sun*, with *Acthon Major* a further ten lengths back in third.

An Irish-bred son of *Steel Point* out of *Proud Fury*, *Freebooter* was first recognised as a horse of possible potential by trainer Dan Moore who had ridden in five Aintree Nationals, being beaten by only a head on *Royal Danieli* in 1938. He spotted him in 1944 as an unbroken three year old, running loose in a field in Co. Waterford, and eventually bought him for 620 guineas at the Dublin sales. Two years later, he recommended the gelding to Yorkshire trainer Bobby Renton, who bought him on behalf of Mrs Lurline Brotherton for 3,000 guineas.

Freebooter was to be rated by Ripon-based Renton as the best horse he ever trained. It was in March, 1949, that he first showed real promise in winning the Champion Chase at Liverpool. Looking every inch a Grand National winner in the making, he came back in the autumn and again proved his liking for Aintree when carrying 12st 4lb to victory over Princess Elizabeth's *Monaveen* in the Grand Sefton Chase. Though the royal runner reversed those placings in the Queen Elizabeth Steeplechase at Hurst Park, *Freebooter* went on to win the Great Yorkshire Chase and was subsequently made the 10-1 joint favourite for the 1950 National, along with Lord Bicester's *Roimond*, who had finished runner-up the previous year. *Monaveen*, receiving 12lb from *Freebooter*, was next in the betting, together with *Wot No Sun*.

On a glorious spring day, *Russian Hero*, the 1949 shock winner, was first in a field of 49 to fall. He went down at the first, and thereafter the lively pace saw more fallers come at an alarming rate. On landing over Becher's, *Freebooter* narrowly led from *Monaveen* and *Roimond*. The former cleared it clumsily but came back to head the field, only to weaken following a mistake at the 14th. At the next jump, The Chair, *Freebooter* made his one major error. Taking off too soon, he hit the obstacle hard, pitching Jimmy Power out of the saddle and leaving him desperately clinging on to his mount's neck. Remarkably, Power contrived to regain his seat, then patiently gave *Freebooter* a

breather before seeking to make up lost ground.

On the second circuit, *Freebooter* made relentless progress and after a brilliant jump at Becher's moved up to take second place behind Mr J.V. Rank's *Shagreen*, closely followed by *Cloncarrig* and then *Monaveen*. *Shagreen* fell at the next; and when, after a hard-fought duel, *Cloncarrig* fell at the penultimate fence, *Freebooter* was left on his own, to power home in impressive style. Only seven finished.

When the victor returned to Liverpool he was narrowly beaten by *Shagreen* in the Sefton, but that was after a long layoff and with a top weight of 12st 7lb. It was the only occasion, in eight appearances at Aintree, that *Freebooter* would complete the course without winning. Naturally, when he lined up for the 1951 National, he was strongly supported, a joint second in the betting despite a huge top weight of 12st 7lb. But luck was against him. After what should have been declared a false start, there was a mad stampede to the first fence, and in the ensuing chaos he was brought down by a faller at the second.

In 1952, Bryan Marshall took over the ride; and though again carrying the maximum weight, *Freebooter* went off as the 10-1 favourite on the strength of four wins that season. He had previously fallen when favourite in the Cheltenham Gold Cup and now, after taking the lead at Becher's second time round, he fell at the Canal Turn when duelling with the eventual winner *Teal*.

Freebooter now had 18 months off with a badly strained hock. Then, in November, 1953, the 12 year old came back one more time in spectacular style – winning the Becher Chase by three lengths with a 12st 7lb handicap and so confirming his reputation as a truly great Aintree specialist. He retired with a record of 17 steeplechase wins, his other big-race successes being the Great Yorkshire Chase (1950) and the Grand Sefton for a second time in 1951, again under 12st 7lb.

Though *Freebooter* was her only Grand National winner, owner Lurline Brotherton had phenomenal success with other jumpers, notching up no fewer than 250 winners between 1946 and 1975. But she sold one useful prospect before he made his indelible mark. Sent in 1972 to the Doncaster sales where he fetched 6,000 guineas, this seven year old gelding would win the National the following year. His name was *Red Rum*.

See also: Power, James Joseph; Renton, Robert.

F

FREEMAN, Arthur Robert

On March 29, 1958, Arthur Freeman mounted eight year old *Mr What* for the first time and took him down to the start of the Grand National. Just under ten minutes later, the bay gelding, who had never raced outside Ireland before, came home the winner by 30 lengths – the greatest winning distance for three decades. For Freeman, booked only one week before the race, it was his greatest triumph – and, some cynics might say, a costly error. Though the prize for the owner was a record £13,719, it was a winning distance too far. The handicapper reacted accordingly. Heavily penalised, *Mr What* would never win another chase in more than 30 attempts, five of them being reappearances in the Grand National.

Born January 7, 1926, the son of Zetland huntsman Bill Freeman, Arthur began racing as a Flat jockey in 1939 when he was apprenticed to George Lambton, the Newmarket trainer of so many great Classic winners. He was following in the footsteps of his elder brother Bill who, 12 years earlier, had ridden *Cap-a-Pie* to win the Ebor for Lord Derby. But then came active wartime service as an infantryman, and he would not ride again until 1945 when taking part in a BAOR race meeting at Hanover racecourse.

Soon after his demob, Freeman was too heavy to ride on the Flat. Turning to National Hunt in 1950, he later joined trainer George Archibald who provided him with his first Grand National ride, 50-1 chance *Wait and See* in 1953. In a race with only five finishers his horse was brought down at the first open ditch. But the following season he was riding so well that he was booked by royal trainer Major Peter Cazalet, who subsequently employed him as second stable jockey to Dick Francis at Fairlawne, near Tonbridge in Kent. As such, on his second National appearance in 1955, he rode French-bred *M'As-Tu-Vu*, the Queen Mother's first runner in the race after a break of five years. Close to the lead after one circuit, the gelding then began to tire, blundering the second Becher's and falling four from the finish.

In the 1956 National – forever remembered for the mysterious collapse of the Queen Mother's *Devon Loch* – Freeman was again on *M'As-Tu-Vu*. For the second time the combination won at Lingfield on the way to Aintree, but there *M'As-Tu-Vu* was 40-1, the much less fancied of Her Majesty's two runners. He fell at the 19th. And one year later Arthur fared much worse in the National – being brought down on *Rendezvous III* at the very first fence.

Five days before the 1958 National Freeman was still without a mount. Then came a surprise approach by Irish trainer Tom Taaffe. With his sons Pat and 'Tosse' already booked for other rides, he urgently needed a jockey for *Mr What*. There was only one problem. The lowly rated gelding had such a light weight that Freeman would need to go on to a crash diet. He did, but on the race day he still had to put up 6lb overweight.

Despite this considerable handicap, Irish punters plunged at Aintree on *Mr What*, the gelding shortening from 33-1 to 18-1, one of five at that price behind *Goosander* and last year's runner-up *Wyndburgh* who was the 6-1 clear favourite. If backers thought that mudlark *Mr What* would benefit from the heavy going, they judged rightly. He thrived in these conditions, lying always handy on the first circuit, hitting the front at the second Becher's and then pulling further and further away from all others.

Between the last two fences *Mr What* was comfortably in the lead when Freeman had a violent attack of cramp that was attributed to his 'wasting' in trying to make the weight. Though in considerable pain, he managed to stay on board as the clear leader made his one and only error, blundering his way through the last. After passing the winning post, he doubled up in pain and on reaching the unsaddling enclosure staggered off to weigh in. As he later explained, '*Mr What* was so far in front that he was merely cantering. He hit the obstacle so hard that, if he had been travelling at racing speed or if he had been tired, he would certainly have fallen.'

In 1959 Freeman rode two winners at the Cheltenham Festival and finished third on *Lochroe* in the Gold Cup. But he was without a ride in the National since 'Tosse' Taaffe was available for *Mr What* who, now 6-1 favourite and carrying an extra 17lb, finished third. He ended that season with 49 winners and for the second successive year he was third in the National Hunt jockeys' championship.

He was reunited with *Mr What* for the 1960 National, but the ten year old gelding was on the top weight, with 19lb more than when winning two years before; also he was racing on unfavourable fast ground. He was well placed when falling at the second Becher's. *Mr What* would run in three more Nationals but this was Arthur's sixth and last. Tough and brave, so long working hard to overcome his weight problem and many injuries, including a severe skull fracture, he retired that year on medical advice.

Away from Aintree, Freeman's most famous victory had been on the Cazalet-trained *Turpial* in Hurst Park's Triumph Hurdle; and he had ridden 22 winners for the Queen Mother, including ten successes on her *Double Star*. On retirement he set up as a trainer just outside Royston in Hertfordshire; and in 1962 he went shopping for a yearling colt to help build up his string. The price of the one he selected was too high. Then he spotted a little foal nearby and said, 'Tell you what, throw that one in for luck and we've got a deal.' The deal was done. The foal subsequently finished second as a two year old in the Lincoln Plate and after winning over hurdles was passed on to another Newmarket trainer, Denis Rayson. Ironically, Freeman had missed having another Grand National winner. The foal he had chosen was *Specify*, who would triumph at Aintree in 1971.

As a trainer he saddled several big-race winners but later had to be helped by the Injured Jockeys' Fund to combat alcoholism. Long dogged by ill-health, he died in 1988.
See also: Mr What.

FREETRADER
Winner of the 1856 Grand National when, in a pulsating finish, with three runners in a line over the last, he triumphed by half a length and four from *Minerva* and *Minos* respectively. A seven year old bay entire, *Freetrader* provided the first of five winning rides for the great George Stevens.

Sired by *The Sea*, who had been fourth in the 1840 Aintree National, *Freetrader* had raced on the Flat and over hurdles before being bought for 90 guineas by Mr W. Barnett, a Cheltenham ex-army captain. In the 1855 National, as a 50-1 outsider, he had shared the lead with *Maurice Daley* coming to the last. But both blundered there and were overhauled by *Wanderer*, the winner from *Freetrader* by two lengths, with *Maurice Daley* a further four lengths back in the fourth.

Remarkably, when the runner-up returned in 1856 with only a 2lb increase in the weights, he went off at 25-1. For the first time there was no past winner in the race. On the other hand, for the first time the 21-strong field included two French challengers: outsider *Franc Picard* and *Jean du Quesne* who was

the 9-2 favourite. Both French horses, however, failed to finish. And Mr Barnett's second, more favoured runner, top-weighted *Sir Peter Laurie*, bolted off the course at the Canal Turn.

From the start *The Forest Queen* set a fast and furious pace, and she was still leading when the field approached the 23rd fence. Then, incredibly, a demented, unidentified spectator ran towards the leader just as she was landing over the small obstacle. The mare instinctively swerved off the course and was out of the race. It left the French favourite in the lead but now, under his Yorkshire-born trainer Harry Lamplugh, he faded and was soon pulled up, leaving the aforementioned three light-weights to fight out a sprint-like finish.

Freetrader and George Stevens teamed up again in 1857, and again went off at 25-1. This time, raised just 8lb in the weights, they failed to finish. For the former it was his last National appearance; for the latter it was just the third of fifteen in an astonishing career.
See also: Stevens, George.

FRIGATE
A magnificent mare who deservedly triumphed in the 1889 Grand National at the sixth attempt after the frustration of three times finishing runner-up. Held up on the first circuit, she came late to jump into the lead at the last; then bravely resisted the strong challenge of *Why Not* by a length, so giving Tommy Beasley his third National win of the 1880s. Most remarkably, the mare had won on her seasonal debut – a feat never since equalled, although *Mely Moss* came close 111 years later when finishing runner-up by a length and a quarter to *Papillon*.

In other ways *Frigate*'s National record was unique. After finishing second on her first two appearances she was sold by her owner-breeder Matthew A. Maher of Ballinkeele, Ennisorthy, Co. Wexford. Then, after failing to finish in two Nationals for two different owners, she was bought back by Mr Maher and subsequently finished second and first. Furthermore, she only ran well at Aintree when ridden by one of the Beasley brothers.

Frigate had a most illustrious pedigree, being by *Gunboat* out of *Fair Maid of Kent*. The former was a son of the highly regarded chaser *Sir Hercules* and a relation of the first National winner *Lottery*. The latter was a granddaughter of the Triple Crown winner *Gladiateur*, (nicknamed 'Avenger of Waterloo' after becoming the first French-bred winner of the Epsom Derby in 1865) and she was related to *Stockwell* and *Touchstone*, both St Leger champions and prolific sires of Classic winners. Yet, regardless of her ancestry, *Frigate* never raced on the Flat. Instead she began hunting at four and the following year, in only her second race, she won the four-mile 1883 Conyngham Cup at Punchestown.

On her 1884 National debut, as a six year old ridden by Harry Beasley, the little (just over 15 hands high) mare finished four-lengths second to *Voluptuary*. In 1885, on her seasonal debut, she was again ridden by Harry, and again finished second, by two lengths to *Roquefort*. The following year, under new ownership, she was ridden by *Jack Jones* and fell before reaching Becher's. Then, owned and ridden by Mr F.E. Lawrence, a young Army officer, she was pulled up in the 1887 National.

It was Willie Beasley who now urged Mr Maher to buy back the mare; and immediately *Frigate* was again sparkling under members of the Beasley family. With Willie in the saddle she won the Manchester Handicap Chase and came second again in the National. Indeed, she might well have won that 1888 National but for an incident at the Canal Turn. There she was carried far out to the right as the favourite and leader *Usna* (ridden by Harry Beasley) swerved on landing. Though she made up an enormous amount of lost ground to regain the lead, she had nothing left to resist the challenge of *Playfair*, the winning outsider.

Just when it seemed that *Frigate* was doomed to remain always the bridesmaid, she bounced back – trained by her owner in Co. Wexford – to win the National as an 11 year old. It was her only race of the year and she ran only two more times. The following season, in her seventh and last National, she was burdened with top weight of 12st 7lb and ended a great racing career as a faller. On retirement, she was by general consent regarded as the best mare ever to win the National and she had a record that would not be surpassed until the emergence of the great *Manifesto*.
See also: Beasley, Tommy, Harry and Willie.

FROST, James Douglas
Winning jockey when making his Grand National debut in 1989 on *Little Polveir*, a 12 year old who had finished ninth in 1986 but had unseated his rider in the two following years. The bay gelding had

been purchased only six weeks earlier to give his new owner's son a ride in the Grand Military Gold Cup at Sandown. It was Jimmy Frost who, after studying a video of the 1988 National, had badgered trainer Toby Balding into trying to persuade the owner to let the old campaigner have a fourth bid for Aintree glory.

As Frost observed, *Little Polveir* had been going well in the 1988 National and was actually in the lead when he got the 26th fence all wrong and spectacularly threw off Tom Morgan. 'I thought he might be one of those old chasers who come alive in the supercharged atmosphere of National day, and I was proved right.' Though the jockey was putting up 3lb overweight, *Little Polveir* jumped well throughout and, favoured by the heavy going, outstayed all rivals to win a slow-run race by seven lengths from *West Tip*. Then, to round off his greatest day, 30 year old Frost won the last race – the Mumm Prize Novices' Hurdle – on *Morley Street*.

Devon-born (July 31, 1958), the son of a trainer and a lady point-to-points rider, Jimmy Frost was only 13 years old when he became the youngest ever winner of a point-to-point. Two years later, on *Mopsey* at Taunton, he scored the first of his 510 successes under Rules. Initially riding as an amateur on the Devon circuit while still living on the family farm in the Dartmoor National Park, he became noted for his ability to get home on most difficult mounts. In 1986 he first rode for Toby Balding when winning on *Lucky Vane* in a long-distance chase at Sandown, and so began a seven-year partnership with a trainer who liked to joke that his stable jockey was 'long legs and no brain – just the job'.

It was only after joining Balding's Fyfield Stables near Andover, Hants, that Jimmy made marked progress in his career. Having had his first National ride at the age of 30 he made only four more appearances in the race. In 1990 he was on the Martin Pipe-trained *Torside*, an outsider totally unsuited by the fast going. He pulled up at the sixth fence. In 1991, on 150-1 long-shot *Bumbles Folly*, trained by David Barons, he again had to pull up, this time after the 20th.

Three years went by without a National ride. Then he reappeared on *Topsham Bay*, a dual Whitbread winner who had recently run well in the Cheltenham Gold Cup and who, like the 1991 National winner *Seagram*, was owned by Sir Eric Parker and trained by Barons. Though faced with unfavourably heavy ground, the 25-1 chance was well in contention when a riderless horse ran across him at the 13th and Frost was unseated. Five years later Jimmy ended his Grand National record in respectable style, coming home ninth on the 200-1 shot *St Mellion Fairway*.

By 2001, following the retirement of Simon McNeill, Frost, at 42, was the oldest jump jockey still riding. His colleagues called him 'the Peter Pan of the weighing room'. In March, 2002, he completed 30 years in the saddle, then took over from his father as trainer at the family's Hawson Stables near Buckfastleigh in Devon. A few days later, immediately after riding *Bohill Lad* to victory at Exeter in a handicap hurdle, he announced his retirement from the saddle. His last outing as a jockey had also given him his first winner as a trainer.

Besides *Little Polveir*, his big-race winners had included *Morley Street* (Aintree Hurdle, 1990, 1991; Ascot Hurdle 1990, 1991; Breeders' Cup Chase 1990, 1991; and Champion Hurdle, 1991); *Forest Sun* (Supreme Novices' Hurdle. 1990); *Crystal Spirit* (Sun Alliance Novices' Hurdle, 1991); and *Spinning* (Swinton Hurdle, 1993). In a farewell tribute, Ian Balding, trainer of *Crystal Spirit* and *Spinning*, described Jimmy as 'the most superb horseman and the best rider of a novice our family have ever known'.

See also: Little Polveir.

FURLONG, Frank

As an amateur rider, then a subaltern in the 9th Lancers, Frank Furlong established a truly remarkable Grand National record. On his 1933 Aintree debut, riding his father's *Really True*, a 66-1 hope, he finished three-lengths second to the record-breaking *Kellsboro' Jack*. On his third and last appearance he won by three lengths on his father's second string, *Reynoldstown*. And but for a weight problem he might have been on *Reynoldstown* when the nine year old won a second successive National.

Frank's record is all the more noteworthy because he was a relative latecomer to riding. In the 1920s, after his parents had moved from Ireland to England, he was sent to the small preparatory school of St Neots, Eversley, in Hampshire, where he was a contemporary of Bob Petre, a future Scots Guards officer destined to win the 1946 National on *Lovely Cottage*. Frank went on to Harrow, and until the age of 18 he showed not the slightest interest in his father's love of riding.

His enthusiasm for equestrianism only really developed after he had joined a cavalry regiment. Then he struck up a lasting friendship with fellow officer Fulke Walwyn with whom he would later form a training partnership. Meanwhile, in 1932, he had made his mark at the Cheltenham Festival by winning the four-mile National Hunt Chase on his grandmother's hunter, *Robin O'Tiptoe*.

In 1933 he made his spectacular National debut on *Robin O'Tiptoe*'s half-brother, *Really True*. The following year he failed to finish on *Really True*, the 7-1 favourite; and, in 1935, he returned to the National seeking his fourth win of the season on his father's highly strung eight year old, *Reynoldstown*. There was a field of only 27, but these included the shortest price favourite in National history: *Golden Miller*, last year's record-breking National winner, and now 2-1 after achieving his fourth consecutive victory in the Cheltenham Gold Cup.

As reflected by the betting, *Really True* – now ridden by the professional Danny Morgan – was Major Noel Furlong's stronger challenger. But they fell at Becher's first time round, and at that point on the second circuit, it was the major's second string, *Reynoldstown*, who took the lead, fractionally ahead of the second favourite, *Thomond II*.

The pair battled all the way to the last fence. But *Thomond II*, who had had such a telling duel with *Golden Miller* in the Cheltenham Gold Cup, now began to fade, finally giving way to *Blue Prince* who finished in second place, three lengths behind the relentless, long-striding *Reynoldstown*. On his debut, *Reynoldstown* had broken the National record by one fifth of a second; and Frank had become the second Old Harrovian (following John Mansell Richardson in 1873 and 1874) to ride the National winner.

That evening the Furlongs, together with Fulke Walwyn, celebrated in riotous style at the Adelphi Hotel, and the major duly rewarded his son with a gift of £1,000. Though it was strictly a personal reward, Frank, as a matter of honour, felt duty-bound to relinquish his amateur status – setting an example that his friend Fulke would follow one year later after emulating Frank's National success on *Reynoldstown*.

Though he had turned professional, Furlong Jr. never rode in the National again. After his first success, he had rapidly put on too much weight. He now retired from the Army, and when war loomed in 1939 he promptly chose to join the Fleet Air Arm to train as a pilot and attained the rank of Lieutenant Commander.

F

In May 1941, Frank Furlong played a valuable role in one of the great actions of the Battle of the Atlantic: tracking Germany's most powerful battleship, the 45,000-ton *Bismark* after it had sunk Britain's mighty battlecruiser, *H.M.S. Hood*. Attacks by Swordfish aircraft launched from *H.M.S. Ark Royal* involved such long-range flying that on one raid he ran out of fuel and had to ditch in thick fog. For three days and nights he survived in a rubber dinghy, and then, by good fortune, was picked up by an off-course Allied ship.

Sadly, that good fortune did not last. Though he successfully flew many combat missions, he was finally killed when crash-landing his damaged aircraft on Salisbury Plain at the end of a reconnaissance flight. He left behind a widow, and a baby daughter, Griselda, who was raised by Major and Mrs Furlong. *See also:* Furlong, Major Noel; Reynoldstown.

FURLONG, Major Noel

In 1919, Major Noel Furlong was a keen huntsman and point-to-point rider living in Fermoy, Co. Cork. That year, as a Protestant married to a Catholic, he found it necessary to escape the Troubles by moving to England. With his wife and nine year old son he settled in Leicestershire, and a few months later he attended the Grand National for the first time. By chance, on the train journey to Liverpool, he met Jack and Algernon Anthony, trainer and rider respectively of the subsequent winner, *Troytown*. Their success sparked off the thought that perhaps one day his family might match that father-and-son victory.

Thirteen years later the Furlongs made a remarkable first attempt to win the National. On his father's *Really True*, a 66-1 chance, son Frank finished three-lengths second to a winner (*Kellsboro' Jack*) who had achieved a record time. The following year, *Really True*, now 7-1 favourite, fell at the fence after Valentine's second time around. But no matter. In the meantime, the major had returned to Ireland for the express purpose of finding a future National winner. The horse he bought – for £1,500 – was a well-bred but highly temperamental, jet-black gelding called *Reynoldstown*.

In the 1935 National eight year old *Reynoldstown* was a 22-1 shot, owned by Major Furlong, trained (at Skeffington, Leicestershire) by the major, and ridden by his son Frank. Thus, when he triumphed in the race, sub-editors could not resist the headline: 'National won by three Furlongs'. One year later, with Fulke Walwyn replacing an overweight Frank as rider, *Reynoldstown* became the first horse to win successive Grand Nationals since *The Colonel* in 1870.

Major Furlong refused to enter *Reynoldstown* for a hat-trick-seeking bid in 1937 – a decision largely made in protest at the new handicapping conditions which extended the weight range (formerly 12st 7lb to 10st 7lb) to 12st 7lb to 10st. He could not entertain the probability of his horse having to concede a massive 35lb to some of his rivals.

Instead, his dual winner was rewarded with a long and pampered retirement. The major made only one more foray into the National: with *Litigant*, a faller in 1940. By then his son Frank had joined the Fleet Air Arm, serving with distinction in the Second World War before tragically perishing in a crash landing. Noel himself lived on to the age of 85. *See also:* Furlong, Frank; Reynoldstown; Walwyn, Fulke.

GAMBLES

Initially big gambles on the Grand National were confined to private wagers between wealthy rival owners. It was a white-bearded Irishman – Mr Joseph Osborne of Dardinstown Castle, Co. Meath – who led the way in taking on a bookmaker in spectacular style. In 1850, as the owner and trainer of *Abd-El-Kader*, he backed his little bay gelding to pull off the double of the Lincolnshire Steeplechase and the National. The bet was £10,000 to a £150 stake.

The gamble failed because Osborne's horse swerved in the Lincolnshire, running outside a course boundary marker. But no matter. The owner still made a killing as *Abd-El-Kader* went on to become the first horse to win the National twice. At Aintree in 1850 'Little Ab' was not even quoted in the official betting. Nevertheless, shortly before the off Mr Osborne was able to get odds of 40-1 to a £100 win bet. The following year his horse went off as joint 7-1 second favourite. But reportedly he got on early at £10,000 to £500. It was a close run thing; *Abd-El-Kader* was declared the winner by 'half a neck'.

In 1866 Mr Edward Studd, a retired indigo planter, recognised that he had an outstanding chaser in *Salamander* and backed him to win £4,000 at 40-1. The unfancied seven year old romped home for an easy ten lengths victory. Another big gambling owner was Mr J.G. Bulteel, the wealthy financier who bought the 1897 Grand National winner *Manifesto* for £4,000. In 1899 he took a huge chance in plunging heavily on his horse to win a second National. *Manifesto* was burdened with 12st 7lb, a weight that had only once been carried to victory in the history of the race. Moreover, he was conceding a stone to the 4-1 favourite *Gentle Ida*; and Mr H.M. Dyas, the former owner of both contenders, was adamant that no horse could successfully give a stone to the mare. As it happened, *Gentle Ida* fell at Valentine's and *Manifesto* went on to win by five lengths. Bulteel took a fortune out of the ring, his various stakes said to have included one bet of £10,000 to £800.

When stockbroker Mr Edward Paget rode in the 1932 National he was bidding to win £4,000 to a £1 stake on the Spring Double. He had already pulled off the first half with the Lincolnshire Handicap victory of *Jerome Fandor* at 40-1. Now he made a tremendous effort to win on the unfancied new-

comer *Egremont*. There were 36 starters but by the end of the first circuit he had only one horse to beat: *Forbra*, a 50-1 shot ridden by the professional jockey Tim Hamey. After matching *Forbra* stride for stride for most of the second circuit, *Egremont* went down by just three lengths.

Another, more spectacular, gamble narrowly failed when Mr F.N. Gee staked £100 each-way on his eight year old bay mare *Zahia*, a 100-1 outsider in the 1948 National. Approaching the second last *Zahia* was challenging strongly for the lead and looking a likely winner. Then, inexplicably, her rider Eddie Reavy took the wrong route and missed out the final fence. A certain place had been squandered and another mare, 50-1 shot *Sheila's Cottage*, came from behind to snatch a one-length victory from *First Of The Dandies*.

It was a different story the following year when nine year old *Russian Hero* was a shock winner at 66-1. The bay gelding had been a faller in his previous three races and his trainer was reluctant to enter him in the National. But the owner, Mr W. F. Williamson, a tenant farmer of Aldford, Cheshire, had insisted that he should run. After all, he had staked £10 ante-post on his outsider at 300-1!

Unfortunately, Mr Williamson was a compulsive gambler who did not subscribe to the quit-when-you're-ahead school. His coup persuaded him that this was 'easy money' and, pushing his luck, he bought two more horses cheaply. The bookies welcomed his custom and his horses proved such costly failures that in the end he could only give them away. As for *Russian Hero*, he never won another race after his Aintree success and fell in three subsequent Nationals.

Much shrewder was Mr Harry Lane, a massive (22 stone) construction engineer of South Shields who bought *Teal* for £2,000 and then landed a six-figure gamble in backing his bay gelding to win the 1952 Grand National. But another keen gambler who pushed his luck too far was Mr Jeremy Vaughan, the young owner of *Nicolaus Silver* who, heeding the confidence of trainer Fred Rimell, backed his horse heavily from 40-1 down to 28-1. The grey he had bought for £2,600 gained him a £20,000 prize for winning the 1961 National, plus huge profits from the bookies. Later, after a losing run, Mr Vaughan needed to sell his beautiful grey. Nonetheless, he had greatly enjoyed his good fortune while it lasted, and most especially because

G

he had gone one better than his father who had owned the 1948 runner-up *First Of The Dandies*.

In 1952 the professional backer, Joe Sunlight, placed a bet that with hindsight seems positively foolhardy. He backed *Brown Jack III*, trained by Peter Cazalet, to win £10,000 at 40-1. The horse was to be ridden by a 32 year old Spanish amateur making his debut in the race. Moreover, the owner-rider, the Duke of Alberquerque, was putting up a colossal 10lb overweight. *Brown Jack III* duly came down at the sixth and his unconscious rider was taken to hospital with cracked vertebrae.

By and large, of course, true professional punters tend to avoid the Grand National like the plague. But there have been other exceptions, most notably Alex Bird whose first-ever noteworthy win came in 1938 from a £10 bet at 40-1 on *Battleship*. Then, after wartime service in the Royal Navy, he became a full-time punter. True, his vast wealth was subsequently founded on his development of a one-eyed, on-the-line technique that enabled him to bet on the outcome of photo-finishes with unrivalled success. Nevertheless, he loved the National so much that he had his own private dining-room at Aintree; and he made his interest pay big dividend – scooping £70,000 from *Freebooter's* win in 1950 and £50,000 from *Teal's* in 1952.

Two years later the shrewd Mr Bird was extremely unlucky to miss another killing on the National. Starting at ante-post odds of 40-1, he heaped bets on *Tudor Line* (10-1 at the off). Basically his judgment was sound, and almost certainly he would have reaped a profit of half a million pounds – except for one small but fatal error on the part of *Tudor Line's* trainer, Bobby Renton. Unfortunately, Renton chose to leave off the 'pricker', a small brush that was usually fitted on the right of the bridle to discourage *Tudor Line* from his pronounced tendency to jump to the right. Without it, the chestnut gelding jumped out to the right at the last two fences, lost crucial ground, and went down to *Royal Tan* – beaten by a neck!

In December, 1980, shipbroker Nick Embiricos, owner of 11 year old *Aldaniti*, daringly asked trainer Josh Gifford to place a bet of £500 each-way on his horse at 66-1. With good reason, Gifford judged it to be too extravagant so long before the National was to be run. Instead he invested £250 each-way. Still, it reaped a £20,000 pay-out, much of which was then lavished on a round of celebration parties.

Wisely, there was no attempt to repeat the coup when *Aldaniti* returned to Aintree for his last race, crashing out at the first fence.

A great gamble – pulled off in 1984 by City of London insurance broker Richard Shaw – was remarkable because he was betting on the first horse he had ever owned: *Hallo Dandy*, bought for £25,000 with the National strictly in mind. After the nine year old had jumped brilliantly to finish fourth on his 1983 debut, Mr Shaw immediately began backing him for the 1984 race – initially at 66-1 and continuing to spread his bets at diminishing prices without any big enough to alarm the various bookmakers. *Hallo Dandy* won at 13-1.

But this was small beer compared with the punt of Mr Terry Ramsden who, in 1986, placed a record £50,000 each-way bet at 8-1 on *Mr Snugfit*, the 1985 close runner-up he had bought only two weeks earlier for £100,000. If he won, the owner would make £600,000 on the bet; and since he had already backed his horse at 10-1, he reckoned he could win £1 million altogether. As it was, he had a narrow but profitable escape with *Mr Snugfit*, the 13-2 favourite, making up a huge distance from three out to snatch fourth place.

Arguably, the most wildly ambitious gamble was that of Mr Chris Liveras who, on December 7, 1983, backed his unraced four year old, *Mr Chris*, to win the 1989 Grand National. With a stake of £250 at 1,000-1, he stood to collect a quarter of a million pounds. Six years later *Mr Chris* just squeezed into the 40-maximum field as the worst handicapped horse in the race. Going off at 200-1, the chestnut gelding fell at the 16th, the Water Jump.

Jockeys are notoriously bad at picking winners but at least John Francome, then retired from the saddle, made an inspired choice in 1987. When William Hill offered him a £500 bet for charity he hit the jackpot by backing *Maori Venture* at 50-1. But, typically of Sod's Law, he put his own money on a different horse!

On March 18, 1997, an anonymous punter walked into a William Hill betting shop in the City of London and laid out £21,800 in cash on the Irish-trained *Time For A Run* to win the National two weeks later. His ante-post stakes: £10,000 at 25-1 and £10,000 at 20-1, with the then nine per cent tax paid. The worst possible happening ensued: *Time For A Run* was withdrawn through injury. The same punter then retaliated with £25,000 each-way at

16-1 on *Wylde Hide*, a horse also owned by the legendary Irish gambler, J.P. McManus. At the time this was reputed to be the biggest single bet ever struck with Hills on the National.

Furthermore, McManus himself had plunged heavily on *Wylde Hide*; unsubtantiated reports alleged that he had backed his horse to win £2 million. Certainly Hills stood to lose over half a million on his ante-post bets alone, and now they enjoyed the greatest of escapes. As it happened, the IRA not only sabotaged the National with their bomb scares but also diminished J.P.'s chances of a spectacular coup. The ensuing two-day postponement of the race saw drying ground that vitiated *Wylde Hide*'s chances. *Wylde Hide* unseated Charlie Swan at the 22nd.

The year 1997 also brought a spectacular near-miss when Stan Clarke, owner of *Lord Gyllene*, struck a £100,000 – £2,000 bet with Ladbrokes that his horse would win two big handicaps at Uttoxeter (the Singer and Friedlander National Trial and the Midlands Grand National) and finish in the first four of the Aintree National. *Lord Gyllene* won the first race and the last but was runner-up to *Seven Towers* in the Midlands. A trivial loss for the owner, however, since the Grand National now had a first prize of more than £178,000.

The following year saw another sad National day for a supporter of J.P. McManus horses. In London, on the preceding Tuesday, an unidentified Hills punter staked a cool £10,000 in cash each-way on *Gimme Five* at 66-1. A win would have netted him a world record £825,000, with a place only worth £155,000. Cruelly, Sod's Law struck again. The Irish hope finished fifth at 25-1.

In 1999 the most ambitious novelty bet went down before the National had begun. One decade earlier, Mr Ray Woodcock, a civil engineeer from Halifax, West Yorkshire, had placed a £400 bet with Ladbrokes in a combination of doubles and one treble. He was betting that by the end of the millennium Cliff Richard (4-1) would receive a knighthood, a British heavyweight (10-1) would win a world title, and a woman (33-1) would ride a National winner.

Fortunately, Ladbrokes had agreed to pay if any two happened before 2000, and indeed the first two came through, bringing the punter £11,000. But the best National result by a woman was Rosemary Henderson's fifth in 1994 and no lady rider even appeared in the remaining Nationals of the 20th

century, so denying Mr Woodcock any chance of netting a further £128,000.

A most fortuitous bet came off in 1999. Bobby Burke, who controlled a string of north London pubs, had been a bold and lucky gambler before pledging to quit punting in 1992. But now, as the owner of a runner in the National, he could not resist ending his self-imposed ban. His horse was *Bobbyjo* and he backed him £200 each-way at 40-1 with much of his £10,000 winnings going on a series of victory celebrations.

In 2002 a north London punter in his seventies entered a William Hill shop with £1,000 in cash in a Sainsbury's carrier bag. He staked the lot on *Celibate* to win at 100-1, seemingly unfazed by the fact that the National had seen only four 100-1 winners in 163 years. At least he got a fair run for his money. The outsider chased the leaders as far as the 17th, blundered at the 23rd, and was the sixth of 11 finishers.

However, all these gambles pale into insignificance compared with the killing made in 2003 when the most spectacular flutter was appropriately launched by a Mr Mike Futter. The 57 year old owner of a chain of bingo halls in Ireland, Blackpool-born Mr Futter was the head of the five-man Dee Racing Syndicate, owners of *Monty's Pass*. In September, 2002, he had collected £250,000 from their gelding's winning of the Kerry National. Now, 'playing with the bookies' money', he began backing *Monty's Pass* ante-post for the Grand National – first with modest bets each-way at 66-1, 50-1 and 40-1. Then, after the National weights were announced and the *Racing Post*'s ' Pricewise' had recommended *Monty's Pass*, he plunged in again – his bets including £3,000 each-way at 33-1 with William Hill and with the Tote, and later £9,000 each-way with Ladbrokes at 16-1. His total return, including a share of the first prize money, was well in excess of £800,000 – all this from a horse that had cost his syndicate 35,000 Irish pounds. And, unlike most big gamblers on the National, he never had to suffer any seriously anxious moments during the running of the race.

An owner of horses for some 20 years, Mr Futter – now renamed 'Mr Flutter' – had started betting at the age of 16 but had previously concentrated largely on point-to-points. Remarkably, it seems that the great *Monty's Pass* coup was not his biggest punt. He had stood to win £1.5 million after backing

G

each-way at 1,000-1 a point-to-pointer called *Tim French* to win the 2002 Cheltenham Gold Cup. The horse never made it to the race.

When *Monty's Pass* was raised a full stone for the 2004 National Mr Futter did not back his horse to win again. Instead he plunged ante-post on *Be My Manager*, £5000 each-way at 66-1, then backed *Hedgehunter*, £5,000 each-way at 16-1 and £10,000 each-way at 14-1 – bets that, if successful, would bring another near £1 million return. *Be My Manager* did not make it to the line-up and long-time leader *Hedgehunter* fell at the last. But no matter. Despite a further 3lb rise in the weights, this inspired gambler had also chosen to back *Monty's Pass* to the tune of £15,000 each-way at 20-1. His former winner was beaten more than 20 lengths but sneaked into fourth place to give a Mr Futter a £60,000 return. Furthermore, given a £1,000 charity bet with Paddy Power, who were paying out on the first five places, he had again backed *Monty's Pass* – £500 each-way on behalf of Sports Relief.

In contrast, a Coral punter suffered a huge disappointment in 2006 when he staked £4,500 on an accumulator comprising four football matches, *Electrocutionist* to win the Dubai World Cup and *Clan Royal* to win the National. Successful with the first five legs, he missed a pay-out of more than £230,000 when *Clan Royal* finished third.

See also: Betting; Systems; McManus, J.P.

GAMECOCK

The aptly named *Gamecock* – a gelding renowned for his alarmingly low head carriage – fell on his Grand National debut as a six year old in 1885. But he was to come back for the next six years, finishing third at 50-1 in 1886, then winning in 1887 by three lengths from *Savoyard*. Such was his gameness that, one day after his National win, he turned out to carry an extra two stone (12st 12lb) to victory in Aintree's Champion Chase.

It was a triumph for the rigorous training methods of Jimmy Gordon who ran him daily over four-mile gallops at Oulton Park, Cheshire. Bought as a three year old for a mere £150, *Gamecock* markedly improved in conformation and developed great stamina to become a regular National campaigner. He won the Grand International Chase at Sandown in 1886 and in the build-up to his third National he had been third at Aintree in the Grand Sefton Chase and second in the Great Sandown Chase.

Remarkably, the consistent *Gamecock* was a 20-1 chance in the 1887 National while the hot 9-2 clear favourite was *Spahi*, a six year old entire who had never raced in a steeplechase or even in a hurdle race. *Spahi* was regarded by many as 'a sure thing' simply because he had reportedly schooled brilliantly over fences, and because he was trained by the masterly Henry Linde and to be ridden by Tommy Beasley, a combination seeking their third National success.

There were only 16 starters and the novice favourite crashed out at the third fence. *Gamecock*, ridden by William Daniels, a jockey making his National debut and having his first ride following a suspension, remained in touch with the leaders throughout but only took the lead after clearing the last alongside the third favourite *Savoyard* whom he outstayed on the run-in.

For local racegoers it was a hugely popular victory since *Gamecock* was owned by a Liverpool man, a Mr Thornewill, who, following the example of some amateur riders, chose to use a pseudonym (Mr E. Jay) when involved with racing. After that success he sold his winner and the gelding was to have three different owners during the course of his subsequent appearances.

Unfortunately for them, the handicapper reacted to *Gamecock*'s win by always erring on the side of caution. For the 1888 National he was raised 18lb to 12st 4lb, and with a new rider (Capt. Roddy Owen) he finished seventh. In 1889, again with a change of jockey (Bill Dollery), he came home the last of ten finishers. Even as a 12 year old, making his seventh and last appearance, *Gamecock* was lumbered with 12st 4lb. He finished an honourable sixth at 66-1 and ended with a career record of 28 steeplechase wins.

See also: Daniels, William.

GARRISON SAVANNAH

Runner-up in the 1991 Grand National, so narrowly failing to emulate *Golden Miller*'s 1934 achievement of winning steeplechasing's two greatest prizes in the same year. *Garrison Savannah*, the Jenny Pitman-trained eight year old, went off the 7-1 second favourite, behind *Bonanza Boy*, and was judged by form students to be a handicap 'snip' on 11st 1lb, the weights having been set before his Cheltenham Gold Cup triumph. 'Gary' jumped the last better than his only two serious rivals, *Seagram* and *Auntie*

Dot. He went about six lengths ahead and looked home and hosed until, at the Elbow, he began to falter. *Seagram* stayed on doggedly and collared him about 100 yards out to win by five lengths.

For jockey Mark Pitman, it was a heartbreaking replay of the 1973 National when, as a seven year old, he had seen his father Richard, on *Crisp*, have the race cruelly snatched from him on the run-in by *Red Rum*. 'He just died on me,' said Mark afterwards. It may be fairly argued that this great chaser would have achieved that elusive 'double' but for the arrival of rain on Grand National morning, creating dead ground on which he did not quite get home.

A bay gelding – by *Random Shot* out of *Merry Coin* – he was an unbroken three year old when, in 1986, Mrs Pitman bought him in Ireland for £5,600. He passed into the ownership of three businessmen who ran the Autofour Engineering Company in Cheltenham and they named him *Garrison Savannah* after a racecourse they had visited in Barbados. On his racing debut in 1987 he won a Kempton bumper race at 25-1. He went on to success in his first novice hurdle and in December, 1988, won the three-mile Coral Golden Hurdle at Cheltenham.

One year later he made an impressive start over fences, winning a novice chase by 25 lengths and going on to win the 1990 Sun Alliance Chase at Cheltenham. His success under Mark Pitman in the 1991 Gold Cup was by the shortest of short heads from *The Fellow*. Back problems and spasmodic lameness then caused him to miss much of the following season, but he came back to finish seventh in the Gold Cup before going on to make another Grand National bid.

At Aintree *Garrison Savannah* was Mark Pitman's choice of three runners saddled by his mother. Alas, it was the year of the most infamous false start. He was pulled up after completing one circuit while his unfancied stablemate *Esha Ness* carried on to finish first in a race declared void. The next year he did not jump with his familiar fluency in the Gold Cup and was pulled up; and in the National, most uncharacteristically, he refused at the 17th. He made his last Aintree appearance in 1995, finishing ninth in the National won by his stablemate *Royal Athlete*. As a 13-year-old veteran, the gallant 'Gary' managed to win three races before being retired in November, 1996. He died in 2005 and has his grave overlooking Cheltenham racecourse.

See also: Pitman, Jenny; Pitman, Mark.

GASELEE, Nicholas Auriol Digby Charles
Trainer of *Party Politics*, the eight year old brown gelding who, in 1992, won the Grand National at the first attempt, by two and a half lengths from *Romany King*. Three years later, Nick Gaselee worked wonders to bring back his fragile giant to finish second to *Royal Athlete* in the National – this after his horse had had two wind operations and had incurred numerous ailments including a septic corn, lameness in his near-fore hock and recurring bruising to his near-fore and pedal bone.

Born January 30, 1939, the son of an Army colonel, Gaselee was educated at Charterhouse and served in the Life Guards from 1958 to 1963. His involvement with the National was initially as an amateur rider. Most creditably, on his 1966 debut, he rode *Jim's Tavern*, a 100-1 outsider, into fifth place. The following year, when *Foinavon* raced to victory after all other runners had been brought to a halt by a riderless horse, he finished tenth on Mr W.H. Whitbread's *Kapeno*, a faller on his two previous Aintree runs. Finally, in the 1968 National, he was brought down on *Chu-Teh*.

Gaselee gained valuable training experience as assistant to the great Fulke Walwyn who had both ridden and trained a Grand National winner. In 1979 he challenged for the National with the chestnut *Purdo* who, under Bob Champion, led from the start until crashing out at the first Becher's. The following year he saddled *So And So*, a faller at the second Becher's, and in 1983 he ran the well-fancied *Keengaddy* who, under Steve Smith Eccles, was leading after the first Becher's only to be carried wide at the Canal Turn and then falling at Valentine's.

Having taken over the Saxon House stables at Upper Lambourn, Gaselee was represented in the 1990 National by *Bob Tisdall*, the last of 20 finishers. Meanwhile he had taken charge of *Party Politics* who, starting as a five year old, showed huge potential in his first season over fences. Lightly raced, the superb jumper was brought to a perfectly timed peak for the 1992 National.

Yet the trainer judged his National winner to be a stone better horse in 1993, well able to defy a 9lb rise in the weights and become the first since *Red*

G

Rum to win the race twice. That year, however, because of the costliest false start in racing history, *Party Politics* had to be pulled up after completing one circuit. With his horse starting as 7-1 favourite, Gaselee had good reason to believe that the void race had robbed him of a famous double. But even more aggrieved that day was his neighbour at Upper Lambourn: Mrs Jenny Pitman who, in great distress, had seen her *Esha Ness* complete the full course in first place.

Fitted with a tube in his neck to aid breathing, *Party Politics* had only one race in the following season, being withdrawn from the 1994 National after cracking a pedal bone. He also had such soft soles that he needed to have a special leather piece inserted between his hoof and the racing plate. Yet Gaselee had him fit enough to run brilliantly in the 1995 National, finishing seven lengths runner-up to *Royal Athlete*. Then, ambitiously, he ran him in the 1996 National with only one previous race behind him in which he had been pulled up.

That year Gaselee had two runners at Aintree, the other being the former Michael Cunningham-trained *Bavard Dieu* who had been sent to Saxon House after being bought by a group of 14 Americans, including Jack Goodman who had had a share in Walwyn's 1964 winner *Team Spirit*. Jason Titley took the ride and, one year after his triumph on *Royal Athlete*, he was unseated at the first and suffered two broken ribs. In a similar change of fortunes, Carl Llwellyn fell on *Party Politics* at the third.

In 1998 Gaselee entered 12 year old *Christmas Gorse* for the National but the gelding did not make it to the line-up. Similarly, in 2002 his entry *Strong Paladin* was way out of the handicap and did not run. He retired the following year.

See also: Party-Politics.

GATWICK

When the Aintree Grand National was suspended during the First World War, three substitute races were held at Gatwick, on the site of the present-day airport. The distance was a stamina-testing four miles 856 yards, but this course was right-handed and much less demanding than Aintree. The birch fences were infinitely easier, the highest being the 11th (and 23rd) at 4ft 10 in; and the run to the first fence was shorter, so lessening the danger of building up too much speed on approach.

The first of these races, in March, 1916, was known as 'The Racecourse Association Steeplechase'and was won by six year old *Vermouth*, ridden by Jack Readron. Only one of the 21 starters was a faller. In 1917 and 1918 the race was given a new title: 'The War National Steeplechase'.

The second Gatwick 'National' brought a shock not entirely dissimilar to the bigger mishap that would befall *Devon Loch* in 1956. American-bred *Limerock* moved smoothly into the lead after the penultimate fence and impressively cleared the last, looking a certain winner. But then, on the run-in, the seven year old bay horse suddenly and inexplicably sank to his knees and rolled over. One popular explanation was that he had slipped on a patch of ground still treacherous following a snowfall earlier in the day. Whatever, it presented a comfortable eight lengths win to *Ballymacad*, trained by Aubrey Hastings, ridden by Edmund Driscoll, and owned by Sir George Bullough, who subsequently gifted his winnings (about £1,000) to the St Dunstan's Home for Blinded Soldiers.

In 1918 the 11 year old *Ballymacad* finished third under Ivor Anthony. The winner of this last 'Gatwick National' was *Poethlyn* who, again ridden by Ernie Piggott, would win the 1919 Aintree National under a top weight of 12st 7lb and at the record short price of 11-4. Gatwick staged its last official meeting in 1940.

See also: World War I.

GAY LAD

Winner of the 1842 Grand National, by four lengths and 15 from *Seventy Four* and *Peter Simple* respectively. An eight year old bay gelding, *Gay Lad* made John Elmore the winning owner for the second time in the four years of the race and provided professional jockey Tom Olliver with the first of his three National victories.

Of unrecorded provenance, *Gay Lad* was making his Aintree debut in the last National before it became a handicap race. There were only 15 starters and, at 7-1, he was fourth in the betting headed by Mr Elmore's 1839 winner *Lottery*. All runners carried 12st except *Lottery* who again had a devastating 18lb penalty for having won the 1840 Cheltenham Steeplechase.

As one year before, the favourite struggled under the huge burden of 13st 4lb and was pulled up by Jem Mason after Becher's on the second circuit. At that stage, the headstrong grey *Peter Simple* was moving into the lead, seemingly threatened only by *Gay Lad* and Lord Mostyn's *Seventy Four*, who had been runner-up under Olliver in the first 1839 National. Unfortunately, there was another unexpected threat. Some hooligans in the crowd ventured on to the course, baulking *Peter Simple* so badly that his amateur rider was thrown out of the saddle.

Jumping brilliantly, *Seventy Four* now opened up a substantial lead only to fade markedly on approaching the last. He had nothing left for the run-in and *Gay Lad* strode past him to win with plenty in hand. The luckless *Peter Simple*, having been re-mounted, gained third place, 19 lengths behind the winner, and only two others finished.

Just six days later *Gay Lad* turned out again and, with an extra 15lb to carry, won a major chase at Oxford. He ended the season with two more wins but never appeared at Aintree again.

See also: Olliver, Tom; Elmore, John.

GAY TRIP

A small (just 16 hands) bay gelding, strikingly similar in appearance to the 1964 National winner *Team Spirit*, eight year old *Gay Trip* triumphed by 20 lengths in the 1970 race – a victory most remarkable because he had never previously won over a distance of more than two and a half miles. Notably, too, it provided a third success for trainer Fred Rimell and a magnificent swansong for jockey Pat Taaffe who had won 15 years earlier on *Quare Times*.

Bred and first raced by Mr F.D. Farmer near Naas, *Gay Trip* – out of *Turkish Tourist* – was a son of *Vulgan*, sire of so many strong steeplechasers. After a single win on the Flat, he was put over hurdles as a five year old by trainer Dan Moore. Then, with two wins from eight outings, he was recommended by Taaffe to Rimell, who was seeking a horse on behalf of his close friend Anthony Chambers, a leading huntsman and one-time National Hunt rider. Visiting Ireland, the Rimells delayed a decision because the horse had a leg blister. One month later, on seeing *Gay Trip* fully recovered, they judged him to be an excellent jumping prospect.

On his England debut, in the autumn of 1967, *Gay Trip* fell at the water jump in a novice chase at Newbury. But thereafter he proved himself the safest of jumpers, winning his next race at Doncaster and following up with two more successes and a second

place in the Champion Novices' Chase at the Cheltenham Festival. In the next season, after his impressive winning of the Mackeson Gold Cup, it was decided to prepare him for the 1970 Grand National.

The pre-race omens, however, were far from good. Sixteen days before the National, *Gay Trip* had finished a distant sixth in the Cheltenham Gold Cup won by the Dan Moore-trained *L'Escargot*. He had never won when upped in distance to three miles or more; and yet, at Aintree, without previous experience in the race, he was set to carry the top weight of 11st 5lb. Furthermore, a recent fall had landed his regular rider, Terry Biddlecombe, in hospital.

Seeking a replacement jockey, the Rimells turned to the man who had found them the horse: 40 year old Taaffe, now in his last season but still strong enough to have been beaten by only a length and a half on *French Tan* in his tenth and last Cheltenham Gold Cup. Meanwhile they had booked Ken White to ride their other National contender, *French Excuse*, who was joint second favourite compared with *Gay Trip*, seventh in the betting at 15-1.

Following instructions to the letter, Taaffe patiently hunted *Gay Trip* round the first circuit. They cruised up to fourth place by the Canal Turn, took the lead at the second last, and then powered away from all others to win by 20 lengths from the American-owned *Vulture*, also a son of super-sire *Vulgan*. In a field of 28, the smallest for a decade, there were only seven finishers.

Gay Trip did not win another race before returning to the National in 1971. Nevertheless he was allotted the top weight of 12st and went off as the 8-1 clear favourite in a 38-strong field. This time, reunited with Biddlecombe, he was one of five to fall at the first fence. One year later, in his third National, he was on 11st 9lb, with only one of 42 starters set to carry more. But the Rimells believed he was sufficiently strong and athletic to cope with the weight, and their hopes were greatly raised when *L'Escargot*, the top-weighted favourite and dual Cheltenham Gold Cup winner, was knocked over at the third. Meanwhile, *Gay Trip* was cruising round on the inside and, as in 1970, he would make his move on the second circuit.

Looking for faster ground, Biddlecombe now chose to steer a course down the middle. By the second last he was up with the three leaders. Then, on the long run-in, as *Black Secret* and *General Symons*

G

began to weaken, *Gay Trip* had only one to beat. But that one was *Well To Do*, ridden by the current champion jockey Graham Thorner and with a 22lb weight advantage. In the end, the concession proved too great and gallant little *Gay Trip* went down by two lengths, with *Black Secret* and *General Symons* three lengths back in a dead-heated third place.

As a ten year old *Gay Trip* had run in his last National. It remained the firm belief of the Rimells that he would have won the race a second time in 1972 if only Biddlecombe had not ridden so wide on the second circuit, giving away perhaps 30 lengths to be beaten by only two. In any event, there can be no denying that *Gay Trip*, winner of eight chases, including two Mackeson Gold Cups and the Heinz Chase at Ascot, was a jumper of true class and versatility. The Rimells rated him the best of their four National winners.

See also: Rimell, Frederick; Taaffe, Pat; Biddlecombe, Terry.

GERAGHTY, Barry

Winning jockey on *Monty's Pass* in the 2003 Grand National, enjoying such a dream ride that he likened it to 'a schooling session'. Always in the first six, *Monty's Pass* went to the front two out and thereafter ran on so strongly that Geraghty could afford to look over his shoulder on the run-in before driving on to victory by 12 lengths and two from *Supreme Glory* and *Amberleigh House* respectively. It crowned the most spectacular spell in the jockey's six-year career.

Only three weeks earlier 23 year old Geraghty had been the leading jockey at the Cheltenham Festival with five wins, so equalling a record shared by Fred Winter, Jamie Osborne and Tony McCoy. Between Cheltenham and Aintree, he had shown his fine horsemanship when riding in the Midlands National at Uttoxeter. True, he was only fifth on *Silver Steel*, but that was after his saddle had slipped, leaving him to ride bareback over the last three fences. Then, on the eve of the Grand National, he had won the £46,400 Martell Cognac Sefton Novices' Hurdle on *Iris's Gift*, trained by Jonjo O'Neill.

Geraghty was the third Irish-based jockey in five years to ride the Grand National winner; and like the others – Paul Carberry and Ruby Walsh – he was born on September 16, 1979 into a family involved with racing for generations. His father was the renowned horse dealer 'Tucker' Geraghty, a former amateur jockey who trained a few horses, in-cluding the improving *What Odds* for the syndicate owners of *Monty's Pass*. His brothers Ross and Norman were also jockeys, the former having won the 2002 Irish Grand National on *The Bunny Boiler*. And notably his grandfather, Laurence, was the Co. Meath farmer responsible, in 1927, for breeding the incomparable *Golden Miller*, the only horse ever to win the Cheltenham Gold Cup and the Grand National in the same year.

After years of riding as a schoolboy in pony races, Barry became apprenticed to Noel Meade at Castletown in his home county of Meath; and at the age of 17 rode his first winner under Rules: *Stagalier* at Down Royal. The following year, 1998, he scored his first major success (the Midlands National on *Miss Orchestra*) and incredibly that was only his third ride over fences. Profiting from injuries to rivals Walsh and Carberry, he went on to become the Irish champion jump jockey of the 1999-2000 season. In the following two years, having his own share of injuries, he was runner-up for the championship.

It was as Irish champion-elect, in 2000, that Geraghty made his Grand National debut, picking up a late chance ride on *Call It A Day* who had finished third the previous year under Richard Dunwoody. The gelding's seasonal form was not encouraging and he went off at 50-1. In contrast, Barry's great friend and rival Ruby Walsh – also making his National debut – was on the hugely fancied *Papillon*, a 10-1 chance. Ruby won at the first attempt; Barry finished a respectable sixth.

Geraghty's second National ride, in 2001, was a hopeless cause – on 12 year old *Hanakham* who had been retired when with Martin Pipe, then re-launched with trainer Ginger McCain. His mount had fragile legs and had shown his best form on fast ground. Now, high in the weights, he faced an Aintree quagmire which would result in only four horses completing the course, two of them having been remounted. *Hanakham* fell at the second fence.

In 2002 Geraghty's career truly took off. That year his many big race wins included the Hennessy Cognac Gold Cup (on *Alexander Banquet*), the Queen Mother Celebration Chase (*Cenkos*), the Thomas Pink Gold Cup (*Cyfor Malta*), the Martell Cup and the Heineken Gold Cup (*Florida Pearl*), the Irish Independent Arkle Trophy Chase (*Moscow Flyer*) at the Cheltenham Festival; and the Guinness Kerry National on *Monty's Pass*.

202

Barry's National hopes positively soared after his success in a mud-slogging Hennessy. The classy Willie Mullins-trained *Alexander Banquet* was immediately made ante-post favourite for Aintree. Subsequently he finished sixth in the Cheltenham Gold Cup. But he was set to carry a massive 11st 11lb in the National and, worse, the drying ground turned against the proven mudlark. Drifting significantly in the market, he unseated his rider at the first Becher's.

At this stage Geraghty was best known for his partnership with *Moscow Flyer* ('the greatest horse I've ridden'). At Cheltenham 2003 they scored again, this time in the Queen Mother Champion Chase; and the latest Irish wunderkind also won the Pertemps Hurdle Final (*Inching Closer*), the JCB Triumph Hurdle (*Spectroscope*), the County Hurdle (*Spirit Leader*) and the William Hill National Hunt Handicap Chase (*Youlneverwalkalone*). With two more notable victories – the Singer and Friedlander National Trial on *Mini Sensation* and the Aon Chase on *Valley Henry* – his lead up to the Grand National could hardly have been more propitious.

J.P. McManus's much fancied *Youlneverwalkalone* was the obvious choice for Geraghty to ride in the National; and indeed the nine year old became a major market mover, being backed down to 8-1 joint second favouritism. Significantly, however, the jockey had already chosen to stay loyal to *Monty's Pass* on whom he had won the previous September. The chaser had proven his ability over the big Aintree fences when finishing second in the 2002 Topham Trophy; and now he jumped brilliantly again to win at 16-1. In contrast, *Youlneverwalkalone* soon went lame and was pulled up at the 12th.

Relatively tall (at 5ft 9in, he had wasted down to 10st 5lb to ride *Monty's Pass*), Geraghty had already had his share of injuries – crushed vertebrae on two occasions, and in the 2001-02 season a broken collarbone and a hairline facture of the elbow, But now, at the age of 23, he had firmly established himself, along with Carberry and Walsh, as one of the great triumvirate of Irish-based jockeys. After his Grand National win, the amiable, chubby-faced Irishman took over a pub called Archers in Kells, Co. Meath, and later bought a farm, choosing to remain in his native land rather than accept offers to become a leading stable jockey based in England.

In March, 2004, deputising for the injured Mick Fitzgerald on the Nicky Henderson-trained *Isio*,

Geraghty won the inaugural £100,000 Vodafone Gold Cup at Newbury. One month later he was back on form at Aintree, winning the first race of the Grand National meeting, an extended three-mile hurdle, on *Iris's Gift*, and the following day the £87,000 Melling Chase on *Moscow Flyer*. Then, in the big one, he did as well as could be expected: nursing round *Monty's Pass*, 17lb higher in the weights, to reward each-way backers with a fourth place at 20-1. At the same time his elder brother Ross, 27, was making his National debut on *The Bunny Boiler*, with whom he had won the 2002 Irish Grand National. He, too, completed the course, being the tenth of 11 finishers.

The year ended on a high note for Geraghty when he won the Tingle Creek Chase on *Moscow Flyer* and then survived a near-fall at the last to win the King George VI Chase on the Tom Taaffe-trained six year old *Kicking King*. Another hugely popular Champion Chase victory was secured on *Moscow Flyer* at the 2005 Cheltenham Festival, and then came the greatest prize of all: the Gold Cup won on *Kicking King*.

At the Aintree meeting he scored his usual win on *Moscow Flyer*. But again, in the National, he had no real chance at the weights on *Monty's Pass*. Burdened with 11st 6lb, and now an unfancied 33-1 shot, the 12 year old was the 16th of 21 finishers.

In the 2005-6 season he repeated his King George VI win on *Kicking King*, albeit at Sandown instead of Kempton Park. At the Cheltenham Festival, he made a bold challenge on *Macs Joy* before going down to *Brave Inca* in the Champion Hurdle. Then came a great winning double in the Royal and SunAlliance Chase (*Star De Mohaison*) and the Coral Cup (*Sky's The Limit*). At Aintree he won the Mildmay Novice Chase on *Star De Mohaison*, and then in the National he rode a fine race to finish in sixth place on 66-1 shot *Puntal*, who was having his first outing for 484 days. Meanwhile, in Ireland, his duel with Walsh for the jockeys' championship went into the final week of the season, finally being lost by 81 winners to Ruby's 90.

The following season started badly with a broken nose and cracked cheekbone suffered in a fall at Galway. But at the Cheltenham Festival he won the Champion Bumper on *Cork All Star* and went on to ride a great race in the 2007 National, bringing 33-1 shot *Slim Pickings* into late contention and leading at the 26th only to be headed when hitting

G

the last and then being outpaced on the run-in to finish third, two lengths off the winner. He ended the season third in Ireland's top jockeys' table with 67 wins and second only to champion Walsh in terms of prize money with more than 1.6 million euros. *See also:* Monty's Pass.

GERMANY

In Germany steeplechases and hurdle races only occur as occasional events staged at meetings primarily devoted to Flat racing. Attempts to popularise jump racing have failed, and so far there has been no Grand National challenge by German-bred and -trained chasers. However, with very mixed fortunes, several Germans have sought Grand National glory by buying and entering British and Irish horses.

The first and most extravagant bid was made by Baron E. Oppenheim who bought *The Colonel* after he had won the Nationals of 1869 and 1870, and then *The Lamb* after his second win in 1871. But his cheque-book challenges came all too late. When *The Colonel* ran in the Baron's colours in 1871 the eight year old was weighted with a massive 12st 8lb and did well to finish eighth under the expert handling of the great George Stevens, who had ridden five National winners and who three months later was to be killed by a fall. Similarly, in 1872, *The Lamb* was raised 16lb to a top weight of 12st 7lb and did well to finish fourth.

After the 1878 National, a German, Herr Oeschlaeger, bought the seven year old *Martha* who had finished a good second under Tommy Beasley. He retained the great Irish amateur rider for the 1879 race but this time the mare was a well-beaten third. Subsequently Oeschlaeger bought *Woodbrook* who had won the 1881 National with Beasley. But his hopes were cruelly and quickly dashed when *Woodbrook* suffered a fatal illness the following year. His last National runner, six year old American-bred *Idea*, failed to finish in 1884.

The next, more persistent, challenge came from German-born Prince Franz Hatzfeldt who had no fewer than 11 runners in six Nationals between 1904 and 1910. Having failed with *Dearslayer*, a faller in 1904 and 1905, he became a winning owner at the third attempt with *Ascetic's Silver*, one of his three runners in the 1906 National. Irish-bred, and trained and ridden by Aubrey Hastings, *Ascetic's Silver* won by a comfortable ten lengths. The prince's next best

was a fourth place with seven year old *Carsey* in 1910.

Having been bought by Baron Oppenheim, two dual Grand National winners ended their days in Germany. Put out to stud in Beberbeck, East Prussia, *The Colonel* became a most successful stallion and also served at ceremonial occasions as a charger for Kaiser Wilhelm I. Unhappily, *The Lamb* was denied a well-earned retirement, having to be put down after breaking a foreleg on treacherous ground in the Grosser Preis von Baden-Baden Chase. *See also:* Hatzfeldt, Prince Franz.

GIFFORD, Joshua Thomas MBE

Though four times the National Hunt champion jockey, and rider of some 700 winners (642 over jumps), Josh Gifford is now best remembered for his key role in the most moving of all Grand National results: the triumph of Bob Champion on *Aldaniti* in 1981. While rightly celebrated for the jockey's comeback after a courageous battle against cancer, that success also represented a remarkable feat on the part of the trainer in revitalising a horse that had been written-off after three long layoffs with injury.

Born in Huntingdon on August 3, 1941, Gifford belongs to that select group of champion National Hunt jockeys who have never triumphed in the Grand National; and, rarer still, he is one of the very few to have become a champion jump jockey following a racing career on the Flat. Having won over 50 races as a teenage apprentice on the Flat, he was forced by his rising weight to turn to National Hunt riding in 1958; and he rapidly progressed through the ranks to become champion jockey with 70 wins in the 1962-63 season. He retained that title with 94 wins, then broke his thigh in a fall at Nottingham and fractured it again in a car accident the following summer.

After an enforced 15-month break, Josh came back to recapture his crown in 1966-67 with 122 winners, one more than Fred Winter's record total of 14 years before; and he took the title again the following year. Primarily his success was achieved in partnership with trainer Ryan Price, based at Findon in West Sussex. His victories included the Triumph Hurdle (*Beaver II*) and the Welsh National (*Forty Secrets*) in 1962; the Schweppes Gold Trophy, which he won four times between 1963 and 1967; the 1967 Mackeson Gold Cup (*Charlie*

G

Worcester); and the 1969 Whitbread Gold Cup (*Larbawn*).

Gifford's first ride in the National came in 1962 when he was a faller at the 11th on *Siracusa*. One year later, in his first championship-winning season, he was on board the notorious tearaway *Out and About* who predictably set a cracking pace from the start and stretched out a lead so great that it seemed that he might steal the race. The Irish eight year old, making his debut in England, was still leading at the Canal Turn second time around but now, closely pressed by others, he was nearing the end of his tether, and four fences from home he crashed to the ground. In avoiding him on *Carrickbeg*, amateur John Lawrence (the future Lord Oaksey) lost five lengths – and arguably the race.

On his return from injury, Josh finished ninth on *Vulcano* in the 1966 National. The following year he at last had a real hope of winning the National for Ryan Price on *Honey End*, the 15-2 clear favourite. And very probably he would have done so but for the freak 23rd fence pile-up that brought to a standstill all of the field, with the exception of the trailing *Foinavon*.

Ironically, that pile-up was caused by the riderless *Popham Down*, a 66-1 outsider who had been ridden by Josh's brother, Macer, when he was brought down by the fall of *Meon Valley* at the first. As it was, Josh took *Honey End* back a full 50 yards to make a second approach to that decimated fence and still he managed to finish in second place, 15 lengths behind the freak 100-1 winner. His three subsequent rides in the National were on *Regal John* (refused, 1968), *Bassnet*, (fifth, 1969) and *Assad* (seventh, 1970).

Josh retired from the saddle in 1970, the year after his marriage to show jumper Althea Roger-Smith. Taking over as trainer of Ryan Price's jumpers at Findon, he was still only 28 years old and had a second distinguished career ahead of him. In 1973 his first National runner was *Fortune Bay II*, an unsurprising faller with his amateur rider-owner American George Sloan. However, each season brought an increasing number of winners, and in 1978, when he won the Hennessy Gold Cup with *Approaching*, he was close behind Fred Winter for the title of champion trainer. Two years later his National runner, *Mannyboy*, unseated Richard Rowe at the first. Nonetheless, that year brought his 500th winner as a National Hunt trainer; and appropriately

the horse (*Physicist*) was ridden by Bob Champion when having his first race in the U.K. for 16 and a half months.

Throughout his agonising struggle for survival, Champion had been given invaluable support by Josh and his wife, Althea; and his vital motivation was the dream of a winning Grand National ride on *Aldaniti* who, as an untried four year old, had been bought by Gifford in 1974 on the advice of his father-in-law, George Roger-Smith. When, against all odds, that dream was realised on April 4, 1981, Josh was left speechless, his cheeks soaked with tears of joy. As he expressed it many years later, reflecting on his many National rides and runners, 'the one I thought couldn't win was the one that did'.

In 1982, the veteran *Aldaniti* was one of ten starters who failed to survive the first fence in the National. Next, in 1985, Josh's challengers were *Shady Deal* (fell, third) and long-shot *Roman Bistro* (ref. 18th); and the following year he had another first fence faller: Mr Jim Joel's well-fancied *Door Latch*. In 1987 his two 50-1 runners were *You're Welcome* (owned, like *Aldaniti*, by his Sussex neighbour and long-time friend Nick Embiricos), and *Bright Dream*. They finished 5th and 18th respectively.

In 1988, when his long-awaited first Cheltenham Festival winner, *Golden Minstrel*, initiated a hat-trick, Gifford became the odds-on favourite to win his first National Hunt trainers' championship. But the longed-for title was snatched from his grasp when his great friend David Elsworth won the 1988 Grand National with *Rhyme 'N' Reason* and followed up with *Desert Orchid*'s victory in the Whitbread Gold Cup.

That season had brought his biggest tally of winners (91). But his two National contenders had failed to get round, *You're Welcome* being pulled up at the fifth, *Bright Dream* being brought down at the 22nd. He was not to have another runner in the Grand National until 1991 when he had no fewer than four: *Golden Minstrel* (finished seventh), *Foyle Fisherman* (tenth), *Ballyhane* (11th) and *Envopak Token* (pulled up before the fourth fence after spreading a plate). The following year *Golden Minstrel* finished 15th at 150-1. Then, in 1995, he ran 12 year old *Topsham Bay*, the dual Whitbread Gold Cup hero, who finished tenth, and the big, well-named *Jumbeau* (brought down at the first). Neither of his entries for the 1996 National – *As de*

205

G

Carres and *Topsham Bay* – made it to the line-up.

In 1997 his National runner was *Spuffington*, a complete outsider and, according to the handicapper, the worst horse in the race. Never in real contention, he unseated his rider at the 22nd. One year later, however, Gifford's hopes of a second National success were high; and indeed, *Brave Highlander*, owned by Nick Embiricos, was cruising at the start of the second circuit. But then, while looking a major threat, he unseated Philip Hide at the Canal Turn on the second circuit. A most courageous stayer, he went on with Hide to compete in four successive Nationals, most notably finishing sixth in 1999 and fourth in 2000, both times at odds of 50-1.

Finally, in 2001, Gifford dreamed of seeing *Brave Highlander* become the first teenage Grand National winner since *Sergeant Murphy* in 1923. Highly superstitious, he still followed exactly the pre-race arrangements he had made when *Aldaniti* had won – staying at the same Southport hotel and having his horse stabled at Haydock Park. But this year no amount of luck could help. It was a chaotic National run in quagmire conditions; and in the circumstances, his veteran Aintree specialist, 5lbs out of the handicap proper, did well to be one of only eight horses to get as far as the 19th where he fell.

Josh, approaching 60, was now in his 32nd season of training at Findon, his successes including the Grand National, the Hennessy Cognac Gold Cup, the Whitbread Gold Cup, the Tote Gold Trophy, the Mackeson Gold Cup (twice) and ten Cheltenham Festival races. His final National entry was *Skycab* in 2003, but this 11 year old was much too far out of the handicap to make the 40-horse line-up. Instead, three weeks later, he ran successfully in a handicap chase over an extended two and a half miles at Sandown, so giving Josh a victory with his very last runner before handing over his training licence to his 31 year old son Nick.

As a trainer he retired with a total of 1,587 winners. Almost to the day he had completed half a century in racing; and valuably, over the years, he had advanced the careers of many notable jockeys and had helped the development of an outstanding new trainer, Paul Nicholls. He had also well prepared Nick to take over at Findon, aided by sister Tina, an international event rider.

In 2004, Nick's first Grand National runner – *Skycab*, a 200-1 chance – had unseated his rider at the sixth. But the family still had high hopes of having another National winner, and those hopes rested especially on French-bred *Joly Bey* who, as a six year old, had been bought by Josh at the Doncaster sales for a staggering £240,000. The purchase was on behalf of multi-millionaire John Dunsdon and it was to be a 21st birthday present for his undergraduate son David.

Joly Bey fell in Aintree's 2004 Topham Chase, but in February of the following year David Dunsdon, a former winner of the Fegentri World Championship for amateur riders, rode him to an impressive handicap chase win over an extended three miles at Sandown. It was judged time for his eagerly awaited National debut and at Aintree he went off a well-supported 16-1 chance. The eight year old made strong headway on the second circuit as far as the second Becher's. But he failed to stay and, fading after three out, was the 14th of 21 finishers.

It was a season when Nick Gifford was dogged by ill-fortune, his plans being cruelly dashed by injuries and some unexpected departures. Subsequently, in 2005-6, he had some highly promising charges, not least J.P. McManus's *Straw Bear* who, at the Cheltenham Festival was only just pipped at the post by *Noland* in the opening Supreme Novices' Hurdle. But he was without a runner in the National as *Joly Bey*, whose breathing problem had been cured by surgery, now had to be withdrawn with a muscle problem. And in 2007 the stable's only National entry, *Latimer's Place*, missed the cut – instead running a good third in a roughhouse Topham Chase.

See also: Aldaniti; Champion, Bob; Foinavon; Honey End; Gambles; Brothers.

GILMAN, Frank

Breeder, owner and trainer of *Grittar*, the 15 lengths winner of the 1982 Grand National. A Leicestershire farmer, Frank Gilman bred *Grittar* out of his mare *Tarama* and first raced him over five furlongs at Nottingham as a two year old. Later, when put over hurdles, *Grittar* was ridden by stable jockey Terry Casey who would himself train a Grand National winner (*Rough Quest*) in 1996.

After Casey had returned to his native Ireland, Gilman entrusted *Grittar* to fellow farmer Dick Saunders who had long been riding his point-to-pointers and hunter chasers. In 1981 the partnership scored in the Foxhunter Chase at both Cheltenham and Liverpool; and when *Grittar* became favourite for the 1982 National following his promising sixth in the Cheltenham Gold Cup, Gilman remained loyal to his old friend even though the 48 year old amateur had no previous experience in the race. At Aintree he was rewarded with record prize money of £52,507, plus his winning bets – 'I had a bit at 8-1 and £100 at 10-1'.

Gilman entered *Grittar* in two more Nationals. In 1983, as the 6-1 favourite despite carrying top weight, he finished a distant fifth under Paul Barton; and in 1984, as joint second favourite, with champion jockey John Francome on board, he finished tenth.

See also: Grittar; Saunders, Dick.

GLENSIDE

The first horse to win the Grand National (1911) when all the others were fallers or pulled up. The previous year, in a National almost as chaotic, *Glenside* has been knocked over by his wildly veering stablemate *Wickham* at the fence before the second Becher's. This time he struggled home to win by 20 lengths, with only three others finishing after being remounted.

Like *Tipperary Tim*, the second horse to win the National (1928) when all others fell or dropped out, *Glenside* was physically a most improbable winner. He had only one eye and was reputed to have a wind problem. Irish-bred, by *St. Gris* out of *Kilwinnet*, he had been bought cheaply by Mr Frank Bibby of Liverpool after winning a £38 race at Tenby. His principal achievement before going back to Aintree had been second place in the 1910 Grand Sefton.

In 1905, when winning the National with his *Kirkland*, Mr Bibby had taken the precaution of paying jockey Frank Mason not to race-ride in the two weeks before the Aintree meeting. He did not adopt the same policy in 1911, and Mason duly broke a leg shortly before the National, so missing his booked ride on *Glenside*. But the trainer, Captain R.H. Collis, found a most able substitute: amateur John Randolph Anthony, one of two Welsh brothers who had ridden *Glenside* in minor chases.

Twenty-six starters lined up for the 1911 National to be run in torrential rain over atrociously heavy ground. Shortly before, having hobbled over part of the course, Mason predicted that none of them would get round without falling. And, even though the fences had been marginally lowered since last year's race, he was so very nearly right.

The pattern of the race was set from the first fence which claimed five casualties. Only eight survived the first circuit, and after the second Becher's the race seemed to be between the joint second favourites, *Rathnally* and Mr Bibby's other runner, *Caubeen*. But at the next fence – later to become known as the notorious 'Foinavon' – both horses headed for the gap which had been created first time round by the falling 7-2 favourite, *Lutteur III*. There they collided, leaving only two serious contenders, *Glenside* and *Shady Lady*. The latter fell at Valentine's, and it now only remained for Anthony to patiently nurse his distressed mount on to finish.

Near total exhaustion, his tongue hanging out, the nine year old *Glenside* plodded on to win by 20 lengths from *Rathnally*, with *Shady Lane* a further three lengths back. A distant fourth and last, also re-mounted, was *Fool-Hardy*, whose owner-rider, Mr W. Macniell, was determined to collect on a private bet that his 50-1 shot would complete the course.

For the brilliant newcomer Jack Anthony this was the first of three National victories; for *Glenside* his last big success. The bay gelding's win at odds of 20-1 clearly made no great impression, for when he returned the following year, raised 11lb in the weights, he went off at 40-1. Now ridden by the highly regarded Irish amateur Harry Ussher, he fell at the third fence.

See also: Bibby, Frank.

GOING, The

At all British meetings, whether races are on the Flat or over jumps, the 'going' – i.e. the prevailing state of the ground – is officially described as firm, good to firm, good, good to soft, soft or heavy. In the case of the Grand National, the least desirable of these conditions are the extremes of firm and heavy.

As might be expected, the fastest winning times in the National have been achieved on fastish ground. The going was good to firm when *Reynoldstown* set a new course record in 1935; firm when that record was lowered progressively by *Red Rum* (1973) and *Mr Frisk* (1990), and good to firm when *Esha Ness* set the then second fastest time in the void National of 1993. The downside is that horse and rider are seen to be at greatest risk under such conditions.

Although two horses fell fatally in the record-breaking 1990 race, there is no statistical evidence that equine fatalities in the National occur more often when the ground is on the fast side. However,

G

because of the greater pace and hardness of the ground, the potential for more serious injuries is certainly there; and, significantly, this fact gained official recognition after the National of 2002.

Since quagmire conditions had turned the 2001 National into a fiasco, there was great relief in 2002 when, at the start of racing, the ground was officially proclaimed as 'good'. But, in reality, it was rather more than good. Under brilliant sunshine, the ground was drying fast and by the time of the National 'off' it was very much on the fastish side of good. Consequently there was tremendous pace in the 40-runner cavalry charge to the first fence, a dash so fiercely competitive that the fence claimed nine starters, the second highest toll there in half a century, and including the joint second favourite, *Paris Pike*.

As a result, the Aintree management became much more alert to drying conditions. In 2003, when March was one of the driest non-summer months on record, the course was watered regularly; and even on the eve of National day (April 5), when the ground was declared 'good', the management was ready to water still further if there was any chance of it becoming faster. This is now standard procedure.

Fast ground has always been a rarity for the National. Throughout the history of the race the going has been firm on only seven occasions, and good to firm just ten times. But henceforth, with water hoses at the ready, it is unlikely that there will ever be fastish ground again; and as a result the record time of *Mr Frisk* may well stand for all eternity.

In contrast, groundstaff have yet to devise a means of combating heavy going which is liable to decimate the field to farcical numbers. There has been an average of eight finishers on the 28 occasions when the National has been run on heavy ground. In 1947, severely testing conditions saw 16 finishers but that year there were 57 starters, the second largest field in history. (Incidentally, earlier at that meeting, Aintree's Stanley Chase had seen all 16 runners fall).

With heavy going there were only three finishers in the 1882 National; four (three remounted) in 1911; five in 1920; two (one remounted) in 1928; four in 1980; six in 1994 and 1998; and four (two remounted) in 2001. Inevitably so many fallers on treacherous ground has led to shock results, most notably *Rubio* (66-1) in 1908; and *Tipperary Tim*

and *Caughoo* (both 100-1) in 1928 and 1947 respectively. It was heavy in 1980 when *Ben Nevis* won at 40-1; in 1989 when most unusually the race was won by a horse (*Little Polveir*) who was 7lb out of the handicap and with jockey Jimmy Frost putting up 3lb overweight; and in 2001 when the notoriously clumsy jumper *Red Marauder* prevailed at 33-1.

The one consolation is that heavy ground can help to cushion the falls of horse and rider and at the same time, by reducing the pace, make falls less dangerous. To be sure, there was heavy going in 1998 when three horses perished at the first fence but it was generally agreed that the gruelling conditions were not to blame. Indeed, of the 56 recorded fatalities in National history only nine occurred on heavy going.

Overall, statistics indicate that the National is most likely to see a large number of finishers when the going is good – as in 1984 and 1987 when there were 40 starters with a record 23 and 22 respectively completing; and in 1996 and 1997 which saw 17 finishers from fields of 27 and 36 respectively. Good to soft has also yielded plenty of finishers.

GOLDEN MILLER

Popularly known as 'the horse of the century', and generally rated alongside *Arkle* as one of the two greatest chasers ever seen, *Golden Miller* was the first to achieve the Cheltenham Gold Cup-Grand National double. That year, 1934, he won the National in record-breaking time despite carrying 12st 2lb, and he went on to complete an unequalled five successive Gold Cup victories.

Golden Miller ran in five successive Nationals but, for all his brilliance, only once completed the course. The fact was that he hated the Aintree fences and after winning over them once was too intelligent to tackle them again. Three times, carrying top weight, he was asked to repeat his success. Each time he dug in his heels and refused when coming to the open ditch that flanked the 11th fence.

Nonetheless, he truly merits his reputation as a wonder horse – and not merely on the strength of a Cheltenham record which would probably have been even more remarkable if the 1937 Gold Cup meeting had not been cancelled because of snow and frost. When breaking the 1933 National record set by *Kellsboro'Jack*, he was 7lb higher in the weights. And he was carrying 12lb more than *Reynoldstown*, who, in turn, broke his record by a mere one-fifth of a second in 1935.

His origins, however, were relatively humble. He had been bred in Co. Meath, by the five-guinea stallion *Goldcourt* out of *Miller's Pride*, a mare initially bought for hunting by a young Army officer on leave from the the the First World War trenches. When the soldier failed to survive a second tour of duty in France, *Miller's Pride* remained in the care of local farmer, Mr Laurence Geraghty. For a fee of £5 he mated her with *Goldcourt*, and the mare duly produced two moderate chasers, *May Court* and *May Crescent*, and then, in 1926, the remarkable *Golden Miller*.

As a yearling, 'the Miller' went for 100 guineas at the Dublin Sales. Then, as an unbroken three year old, he was bought for 500 guineas by Basil Briscoe, a young trainer based at Longstowe, near Cambridge. Briscoe had never seen the horse. But he had heard good reports about the gelding, and he took up the telegraphed offer immediately after enjoying a winning run at a London chemin-de-fer party.

Golden Miller, once seen, disappointed him greatly. He described the animal, so bedraggled on arrival by sea and rail, as having 'a wet bear-like coat sticking up in places like a porcupine and plastered in mud from head to tail'. And that unfavourable first impression was not improved when, on his debut run in England, 'the Miller' was unplaced in a minor two-mile race over hurdles at Southwell.

Nonetheless he caught the eye of Briscoe's close friend and patron, Philip Carr (father of England cricket captain Arthur Carr) – so much so that the well-to-do stockbroker and sportsman, on being offered the gelding for £500, insisted on paying double that sum. Still trained by Briscoe, *Golden Miller* immediately justified Carr's belief in his potential. Ridden by Bob Lyall (later to win the National on *Grakle*), he came second in a hurdle race at Newbury, then won over hurdles at Leicester and Nottingham. Lyall proclaimed him the best three year old he had ever ridden.

In February, 1931, as a four year old, *Golden Miller* made his chasing debut at Newbury and began his long partnership with jockey Gerry Wilson. Thoughtfully, Wilson was not too hard on the newcomer to fences. But Mr Carr, having backed his horse heavily to win, was not best pleased when they were beaten a short head by an experienced handicapper. Then, disappointingly,

Golden Miller was denied a first appearance at Cheltenham, the meeting being abandoned in the face of foul weather.

Tragically, Mr Carr never would see his *Golden Miller* run at Cheltenham. Struck down by a terminal illness, he instructed Briscoe to sell all his horses – 'and take a lower price if you can keep those you want to train.' Basil sold three jumpers on condition that they remained in his care: 'the Miller' and *Insurance* (£12,000 the pair) and *Solanum* (£3,500).

The deal was struck at another chemin-de-fer party, and the buyer was the young millionairess Dorothy Paget, daughter of Lord Queensborough. Subsequently, Briscoe moved his operations to Exning, near Newmarket and close to first-class training facilities afforded by the old steeplechase course. There, all three jumpers flourished. Most notably, in both 1932 and 1933, *Insurance* and *Golden Miller* won the Champion Hurdle and Cheltenham Gold Cup respectively.

As a five year old *Golden Miller* was not eligible for the 1932 National. But the following year he arrived at Aintree on the back of a run of five wins in five races, including a second Gold Cup won by ten lengths. Despite a big handicap weight of 12st 2lb, he went off as 9-1 favourite.

Throughout his unbeaten run, *Golden Miller* had been ridden by the champion jockey Billy Stott. Now Stott was discarded on the orders of the volatile Miss Paget, apparently because she had heard that he had privately expressed his opinion that 'the Miller' would not survive the National course. Ted Leader, who had also had his differences with Miss Paget, took over the ride – but only as a special favour to Briscoe.

Stott's doubts were, in fact, well-founded in view of *Golden Miller's* bold style of jumping and his tendency to veer to the right. True, use of the whip had kept him straight enough over the left-handed Cheltenham course. But would it be enough over Aintree's more testing circuit, also left-handed?

The challenge was indeed too much for a six year old without previous experience over those daunting jumps. Leader, who had ridden 'the Miller' to his first Gold Cup victory, only just contrived to stay on board when the gelding hit the top of Becher's second time around. Then, as they moved up on the leaders, they took the Canal Turn too sharply and stumbled to the ground. Leader never rode the gelding again.

G

Now came the extraordinary season of 1933-34. In November, on heavy going at Lingfield and under yet another new jockey (Gerry Wilson), *Golden Miller* scored a comfortable victory over his famous rivals, *Kellsboro' Jack* and *Thomond II*. Two defeats followed, but these were misleading. When *Thomond II*, in receipt of 7lb, beat him by a length and a half at Kempton Park on Boxing Day, it was over a mere two and a half miles and on unsuitable fast ground. And when *Southern Hero* beat him round the sharp bends of Hurst Park, the winner was receiving a massive 28lb.

Once again it was the Cheltenham Gold Cup, with runners on equal terms, that proved a true measure of his class. On soft ground, the Miller took the lead at the third last fence and romped home unchallenged to win the coveted prize for the third successive year.

Still nagging doubts remained about the suitability of his jumping style over National fences. These, plus his failure in 1933, explain why a triple Gold Cup winner went off as 8-1 second favourite in the 1934 National. One point ahead of him in the betting was ten year old *Really True*, who had finished three lengths second to record-breaking *Kellsboro' Jack* the previous year. The favourite seemed most generously weight on 11st 4lb, whereas *Gregalach* – for the third successive year – was carrying the top weight of 12st 7lb, with *Thomond II* on 12st 4lb and the *Miller* again on 12st 2lb.

As the 30 starters set off at a blistering pace, Wilson chose to keep *Golden Miller* to the rear of the field, delaying his move until late on the first circuit. Then, as they crossed the Melling Road a second time, he moved up to join *Delaneige* in the lead, with other fancied runners close behind. When *Really True* fell at the plain fence after Valentines's, just four serious contenders remained: *Delaneige*, *Golden Miller*, *Forbra* and *Thomond II*.

Still, Wilson sat patiently on 'the Miller', delaying an all-out challenge until the final fence. There he drew level with *Delaneige* and, once given his head, *Golden Miller* powered ahead on the flat to sprint home by five lengths from a nine year old with a 10lb advantage. His winning time – controversially clocked by two separate timekeepers as 9min 20.4sec and 9min 20.2sec – had broken the course record (9min. 28 sec.) set by *Kellsboro' Jack* (carrying half a stone less) just one year before. And it was the first time that a horse had achieved the Gold Cup and Grand National double.

In 1935 *Golden Miller*'s National bid came only 15 days after his record-breaking, hard-won fourth Gold Cup victory, by just three-quarters of a length from *Thomond II*. He was also on the top weight of 12st 7lb. Yet at one time the bookies had him as short as 6-4 against. He was considered unbeatable, and he was now guarded night and day after jockey Wilson's revelation that he had been offered £3,000 to pull up the hot-shot at Aintree.

Going off at 2-1, the shortest-ever priced National favourite, 'the Miller' now revealed his lack of appetite for Aintree's fences. At first he jumped well, despite the unfavoured firm ground. But then, suddenly, he dug in his toes on coming to the 6ft-wide open ditch after Valentine's. Remarkably, though he had come almost to a complete halt, he somehow contrived to jump the 5ft high fence beyond the ditch from a near-standstill position. In the process, however, he pitched his rider over his head.

Dorothy Paget, the most demanding of owners, now insisted that *Golden Miller* should race again, in the Champion Chase the following day. This time he unseated Wilson at the very first fence. Miss Paget's decision, strongly opposed by the trainer, prompted Briscoe to demand that she immediately remove all her horses from his stables. The Miller was now to be trained by Owen Anthony, the Welshman who had prepared the 1922 National winner, *Music Hall*.

With a new trainer and a new jockey (Evan Williams), *Golden Miller* won his fifth Cheltenham Gold Cup and then went to the National as 5-1 second favourite. This time, through no fault of his own, he was brought down at the first fence by the 100-1 French outsider *Oeil De Bouef*. Williams swiftly remounted and gave chase, but again 'the Miller' was reluctant to tackle the 11th fence and its open ditch on the take-off side. There he stubbornly dug in and refused to go one step further.

Even now Miss Paget would not recognise the obvious message. In 1937, after the cancellation of the Cheltenham meeting, she insisted on running her ten year old wonder horse in yet another National, again on top weight, again with a new jockey (Danny Morgan). The decision was all the more deplorable since this year the minimum weight was reduced from 10st 7lb to 10st. It meant that 'the Miller' would have to concede a massive 35lb to some of his rivals.

Going off the 8-1 favourite, *Golden Miller* again refused at that same open ditch beyond Valentine's. And now, at last, Miss Paget relented. Her greatest chaser would never race at Aintree again. In 1938 he finished two lengths second to *Morse Code* in the Cheltenham Gold Cup, and the following February he ended his career, unplaced in a chase at Newbury. In all, he had achieved 29 victories in 55 races and he had been ridden by 15 different jockeys. At Miss Paget's Elsenham Stud farm in Essex, with *Insurance* as his constant companion, he lived on in retirement until 1957 when, aged 30, he was put down following a heart attack.
See also: Paget, Dorothy; Briscoe, Basil; Wilson, Gerry; Stott, William; Leader, Ted.

GOLLAN, Spencer Herbert

Born in New Zealand on January 22, 1860, Spencer Gollan was a wealthy sheep farmer and bloodstock breeder, and his country's most extraordinary all-round sportsman, winning prizes for running, rowing, sculling, swimming, boxing, shooting, billiards, fives, golf and steeplechasing. He achieved his greatest sporting ambition when he sent over his giant, ungainly brown gelding, *Moifaa*, to win the 1904 Grand National.

Down under, Gollan became a legendary race-horse owner, his successes including New Zealand's Derby, Oaks, St Leger, Canterbury Cup and Grand National; and, in Australia, Sydney's Derby and Oaks and Melbourne's Oaks and St Leger. In England he won the Sandown Grand Prix, the City and Suburban and two Coronation Cups, and had numerous victories in chases with *Ebor* and *Norton* and over hurdles with *The Bimkin* and *Saxon*. He also took time off from racing to be a member of a triple-sculling crew that set an unusual record by rowing some 104 miles, from Oxford to Putney, in 13hrs 56sec.

Though fourth in the betting at 10-1, Gollan's first National challenger, *Norton,* was a never-prominent faller in 1897. His second and last contender was *Moifaa* who had won nine races in New Zealand before being transported to England and, as legend falsely had it, being shipwrecked en route. Following his victory, the owner sold *Moifaa* to King Edward VII. Thirty years later, just five days after his 74th birthday, Spencer Gollan died of his injuries after being run over by a London bus.
See also: Moifaa.

GOODMAN, Alec

Alec Goodman rates among the truly great amateurs in Grand National history. Though a jump jockey of proven ability, he did not compete in the race until he was 30 years old. He then won at the first attempt, on a rank outsider; came third the following year; later finished on the runner-up; and at the age of 44 achieved his second National success on another long-shot. Altogether he rode in the race 11 times.

Born in Cambridgeshire in 1822, Goodman gained useful experience working during school holidays at a horse breaker's yard in Peterborough. At 18 he began riding impressively in steeplechases and he continued to race and to hunt long after he had established himself as a hugely successful farmer. His brilliant and lengthy career owed much to supreme fitness – his strength never weakened by fasting since he could get down to as little as 9st 4lb without difficulty.

Goodman's first National mount, in 1852, was *Miss Mowbray*, also competing in the race for the first time. However, both had performed with distinction elsewhere, and the mare was entered by a most successful owner, Mr T. F. Mason. So it was strange that they were not even quoted in betting that, for the first time, had a starter (*Royal Blue*) priced at 100-1.

Goodman rode *Miss Mowbray* like an old campaigner, perfectly timing his challenge at the last and holding on gamely throughout the run-in to win by a length from *Maurice Daley*. The following year, the mare, raised by 8lb, went off as 5-1 favourite. But Goodman was on Mr Mason's preferred runner, *Oscar*, the 6-1 joint second favourite. This time the punters were nearer the mark. The stablemates came together at the last and thereafter *Miss Mowbray* proved the stronger. Neither, however, could compete with the ancient mudlark *Peter Simple*, who thrived on the extremely heavy going and strode home to win by three lengths from *Miss Mowbray*, with *Oscar* a further three lengths behind.

On his return to the National, Alec Goodman was brought down on the long-shot *British Yeoman* in 1856 and then failed to finish on the rank outsider *Minos* in 1857. But then, after a three-year gap, he achieved second place on *Arbury*, a 25-1 chance, in 1863. He fell on *Portland* (1864) and *The Czar* (1865), but on his ninth appearance, in 1866, he again triumphed on a long-shot, 40-1

G

chance *Salamander*, a seven year old whom he had never ridden before. In a race with many fallers, this newcomer only caught the eye in late stages, moving steadily forward over the second circuit, then turning on a blistering turn of speed to pass the leaders and hold on for a comfortable ten lengths win. The following week the combination won even more easily in the Grand Annual Chase at Warwick.

That same year, on *Shangarry*, Goodman won the National Hunt Steeplechase for the third time in four rides. He subsequently appeared in two more Grand Nationals – a seventh place on *Shakespeare* (1867) and a sixth place on *Helen* (1868). Then in 1871, following a winning ride in the Hunt Cup Chase at Warwick, he retired from the game. Remarkably, in more than 30 years of riding, he had suffered nothing more than a broken collarbone, and that was from a fall when hunting. He died in 1904 at the age of 82.
See also: Salamander; Miss Mowbray.

GORE, Robert George

A Dubliner by birth, and a descendant of the Earls of Arran, Bob Gore worked at one time with the master trainer Henry Eyre Linde at the Curragh. There, Linde was responsible for preparing Grand National winners – *Empress* (1880) and *Woodbrook* (1881) – in successive years. As it happened, two decades later, when based at Findon in Sussex, Gore would be the next man to equal that rare training feat, turning out the National winners *Jerry M* (1912) and *Covertcoat* (1913).

An inspired judge of equine potential, Gore was entirely responsible for selecting as well as training his two National winners. In the case of *Jerry M*, he defied an adverse vet's report in recommending the five year old Irish-bred bay gelding to Mr (later Sir) Charles Assheton-Smith, who had won the 1893 National with *Cloister*. Bearding his patron at Claridge's, the trainer was so persistent that Assheton-Smith finally volunteered to let the toss of a coin decide. He lost the toss and, for £1,200, he gained a truly great steeplechaser.

From that start *Jerry M* fully justified Gore's assessment, winning first time out in the £500 New Century Chase at Hurst Park and following up with such success in the Stanley and Becher chases at Aintree that he was allotted 12st 7lb for his 1910 National debut as a seven year old. Gallantly he went down by just three lengths to *Jenkinstown* to

whom he was conceding more than two stone; and that same year he won the 1910 Grand Steeplechase de Paris, then the world's richest chase with a £6,360 prize.

Two years later Gore brought *Jerry M* back to Aintree, and the nine year old, ridden by Ernie Piggott, became the third horse – after *Cloister* and *Manifesto* – to defy a top weight of 12st 7lb in the National. He was not only an outstanding jumper and stayer, but in the opinion of his trainer he had enough speed to have won a six furlong sprint on the Flat.

Similarly, Gore proved his sound judgment when recommending the £1,075 purchase of *Covertcoat* who gave Sir Charles his third National success when winning by a distance from the only two other finishers. But *Jerry M* was an infinitely superior chaser and when his owner died in 1914 the great National winner was bequeathed to his Findon trainer.
See also: Jerry M; Covertcoat; Assheton-Smith, Sir Charles.

GOURLEY, John

Jockey John Gourley rode in only two Grand Nationals and yet, with that limited involvement, he most unexpectedly encountered both of Kipling's two imposters. In 1896, on his National debut, he was privileged to ride a chaser of exceptional potential, the great *Manifesto*, only to have his dreams of glory shattered at the first fence where his mount fell in collision with the 100-1 outsider *Redhill*. The following year he was a frustrated bystander as *Manifesto* – reunited with his original rider, Terry Kavanagh – romped home the winner by 20 lengths.

In 1898 Gourley was booked to ride the six year old *Drogheda*, a 25-1 chance. But he feared that the race would again be dominated by the horse on which he had fallen. *Manifesto* was the strong antepost favourite to win a second successive National. Then, by a strange twist of fate, a freak mishap led to his withdrawal.

In a race run in a blinding snowstorm, *Drogheda* took the lead near the Water Jump and held on to it throughout the second circuit to win by three lengths from the second favourite *Cathal*. The winning owner, Mr C.G.M Adams, rewarded the rider with a life pension. And, like *Drogheda*, Gourley did not appear in the National again.
See also: Manifesto; Drogheda.

GRAKLE

In 1927, Tom Coulthwaite, trainer of two Grand National winners – *Eremon* (1907) and *Jenkinstown* (1910) – had two promising five year olds in his care: *Grakle* and *Gregalach*, both owned by the Rt. Hon Thomas Kennedy Laidlaw. He judged the former to be the better prospect for the National. But *Grakle*, though going off as second favourite following his two lengths second place in the Cheltenham Gold Cup, was a faller that year on his Aintree debut. And subsequently both five year olds were sold – *Gregalach* for 5,000 guineas to Mrs M.A. Gemmell and *Grakle* for 4,000 guineas to Liverpool cotton broker Mr Cecil R. Taylor.

Coulthwaite, however, continued as trainer of *Grakle*; and he still believed in his potential after he had failed to finish, along with 40 others, in the chaotic 1928 National. In the following year, the bay gelding – bred in Co. Carlow, by the impressive stallion *Jackdaw* out of *Lady Crank* – finished third in the Cheltenham Gold Cup, then went on to be sixth to the victorious *Gregalach* in the 1929 National. One year later, having again been runner-up in the Gold Cup, *Grakle* was made the clear favourite for the National. And again, ridden by Keith Piggott, he was a faller.

Then, in 1931 – at the fifth attempt – the faith of his trainer was finally rewarded. Most significantly, this was the first and only time that *Grakle* was not made to run in both the Gold Cup and the National, the former event having been abandoned due to frost. Following the loss of Cheltenham, there was an especially strong field of 43, headed by the brilliant *Easter Hero*, runner-up in 1929, and again the top-weighted favourite. The field also included former winner *Gregalach*, plus *Shaun Goilin*, *Melleray's Belle* and *Sir Lindsay* who had been divided by only a length and a half when finishing first, second and third respectively in the 1930 National.

At the end of the first circuit, covered on fast ground at a furious pace, *Gregalach* was leading by a length from *Great Span*. As expected, *Easter Hero* was close behind, jumping faultlessly alongside *Solanum*. But then, at Becher's, came unavoidable disaster. A riderless horse brought down *Solanum* directly in front of *Easter Hero*, and together they eliminated the favourite.

Grakle, always close-up, made his forward move after the Canal Turn; and when he landed over the final fence he was a length ahead of *Gregalach*, with no others in contention. Now, on the long run-in, the two former stablemates matched stride for stride – until, as they entered the last hundred yards, jockey Bob Lyall showed *Grakle* the whip.

Lyall was under orders to delay using the whip as long as possible since his horse had always tended to hang in response to the stick. This time two slaps were sufficient to spur him ahead, finishing just one and a half lengths ahead of *Gregalach*, with another ten lengths back to *Annandale*, a 100-1 shot in third place. The winning time was just two-fifths of a second short of the record 9min. 32⅖ sec. set by *Cloister* in 1893. At the age of 69, Coulthwaite had saddled his third Grand National winner. But clearly he had been wrong in his assessment of *Gregalach* and *Grakle*. The former, after all, had been giving the latter half a stone when going down so narrowly in the second fastest National. Furthermore, *Gregalach* had scored his 1929 National win in a record field of 66 runners and was so highly rated by the handicapper that he was saddled with the 12st 7lb top weight in three successive Nationals (1932-34).

Meanwhile, in 1932, *Grakle* had been entered for a fourth Gold Cup bid. Going to Cheltenham on the back of three wins, he was made the odds-on favourite. But he was unlucky again. He was moving well in the rear when he jinked in mid-air to avoid a faller, in the process throwing off his amateur rider, Jack Fawcus. Now a new superstar was born as the five year old *Golden Miller*, under Ted Leader, raced on to victory. Immediately after passing the winning post, Leader had the quickness of mind to grab the reins of the loose-running *Grakle* and lead him into the unsaddling enclosure.

Coulthwaite was so impressed by the thoughtful deed that he later presented Leader with a silver cigarette case inscribed 'Actions speak louder than words'. At the time it had seemed important to take quick control of *Grakle*, bearing in mind that he would soon be heading for his sixth Grand National. But once again the demands of running at both Cheltenham and Aintree would prove too much. Under the second highest weight of 12st 3lb, and with Fawcus in the saddle, *Grakle* was the joint favourite and yet failed to finish. Still only ten years old, he would not be entered in the National again.

Grakle retired with a record of 12 steeplechase wins and is now permanently remembered by way of the 'Grakle noseband', a device consisting of two

G

straps crossed over the horse's nose to help prevent excessive pulling.
See also: Gregalach; Coulthwaite, Tom; Lyall, Bob; Hamey, Tim.

GRAND NATIONAL

In 1937 the Liverpool Racecourse Executive officially celebrated the 'The Centenary Year of the Grand National'. Yet, confusingly, by popular consent, Tuesday, February 26, 1839, was accepted as being the date of the first Aintree Grand National, with the great steeplechase being won by a bay gelding named *Lottery*, owned by Mr John Elmore, trained by George Dockeray at Epsom and ridden by Jem Mason.

The discrepancy arose because racing historians still hotly disputed whether earlier steeplechases staged outside Liverpool were run at Maghull or nearby Aintree. In his 1937 history, *A Hundred Grand Nationals*, racing journalist Mr T.H. Bird had weighed up the evidence and found in favour of the chases of 1837 and 1838 having been run at Aintree. Thus Tophams Ltd, the racecourse lessees, chose to mark the centenary in 1937.

However, it has since become clear that racing on the marshy land at Maghull ceased in 1835, and that the first 'Liverpool Grand Steeplechase' was, in fact, staged at Aintree on February 29, 1836. That day, with the 2-1 favourite *Laurie Todd* unluckily falling on the second circuit, this race was won by *The Duke* (3-1), ridden by Captain Martin Becher, in the tortoise-like time of 20min 10sec and by one length from *Polyanthus*, the mount of Dick Christian, the famous rider nearing the end of his career. *The Duke* – a chestnut gelding owned by a Mr Sirdefield, landlord of the George Inn, Great Crosby – returned to win again in 1837 and finished third in 1838.

Undoubtedly, the 1836 event may be fairly viewed as being the inaugural Grand National. However, that was a mere selling race, with ten starters and the 'winner to be sold for 200 sovereigns, if demanded'. As for the Liverpool Steeplechases of 1837 and 1838, when the aldermen of the city donated 100 sovereigns in addition to the ten sovereign stake per entry, these races involved only four runners and three runners respectively – hardly contests worthy of Grand National status.

Moreover, further confusion surrounds the Liverpool Chase of 1838. The official record in the Racing Calendar (*Steeplechases Past*) gave the winner as *Sir Henry* ridden by Tom Olliver. But according to Mr Bird's research there was no such horse as *Sir Henry* at that time. Citing the result that appeared in the *Liverpool Standard* of that time, he correctly found that the winner was *Sir William*, a roguish chestnut owned and ridden by Alan McDonough.

What remains beyond dispute is the fact that the Grand Liverpool Chase was contested at Aintree in 1839 by 17 runners; and, being unrivalled that year by great chases elsewhere, it is the first to be worthy of 'national' status. Indeed, before and after, *Bell's Life of London* (later incorporated into *The Sporting Life*) carried headings referring to 'Grand National Steeple Chase' (sic) and called it 'the greatest steeple chase ever known in this or any other country'. Acceptance, albeit spurious, of 1839 as the year of the first Grand National took hold from the 1860s onwards.

The primary aim in instituting the race had been to boost local trade; and this it handsomely achieved from the start, drawing to Liverpool countless thousands of visitors who came by stagecoaches, horse-drawn carriages, canal boats and the new-fangled steam-train service. In 1839 an estimated 40,000 people flocked to Aintree for a steeplechase in which the 17 starters – surviving from an original entry of 55 – all carried 12st.

The race was officially declared as being for 'gentleman riders' and to be run 'four miles across country'. This description was not entirely accurate. At least nine of the riders were not truly amateurs, having been paid for racing in the past. Also the course, so vaguely defined, covered an uncertain distance of more than four miles. However, it was certainly 'across country' – being run over open farmland, much of it heavily ploughed and marked out only with the occasional post and rails. There were 29 obstacles, the most formidable being two fences with wide brooks and, near the end of the first circuit in front of the stands, a menacing 4ft 8in high stone wall which had to be jumped only once. The others were mostly ordinary banks and hedges, with the finish being over two hurdles.

The 1839 Aintree steeplechase, flag-started by the Earl of Sefton, certainly merited its 'Grand Liverpool' title. Four years later, however, the 'grand' was dropped. The race had been made a handicap and its far-reaching appeal was recognised by a new title, 'The Liverpool and National Handicap Steeplechase'. It was not until 1847 that the world's greatest steeplechase was officially given its present-day name: 'The Grand National Handicap Steeplechase'.

See also: Aintree; Lynn, William; Becher, Captain Martin; Potts, Henry; McDonough, Alan; Olliver, Tom; Course Changes; Fences.

GRANT, Christopher

Nicknamed 'Rambo' for his fearless style of riding, Chris Grant stands out as one of the Grand National's unluckiest losers, three times on the runner-up and twice having cleared the last fence in the lead only to have victory snatched from his grasp on the long, stamina-sapping run-in. In 1986 he landed over the last with a one length lead on *Young Driver*, a 66-1 chance, and finally went down by two lengths to the stronger finishing *West Tip*, with *Classified* 20 lengths back in third. It happened again in 1988, this time with a three lengths lead at the last on *Durham Edition* before being well outpaced by *Rhyme 'N' Reason*.

Most amazingly, in 1990, Grant broke the National course record on a 12 year old but was still denied victory. It was now his turn to try to snatch the race on the run-in after taking the last in second place. And it seemed that he might succeed as he gradually moved up on *Durham Edition* to draw level with the leader. He had timed his challenge to perfection, but yet again the last 200 yards or so found his mount out. On unusually firm going, *Mr Frisk* pulled out that little bit extra to get home by three-quarters of a length; and again, as in 1986, Grant finished 20 lengths ahead of the third. The winner had shattered *Red Rum*'s 1973 course record by 14 seconds.

Born on October 14, 1956, Grant had 13 Grand National rides. His early experiences in the race were not encouraging: on *Flashy Boy*, a faller in 1980; *The Vintner*, pulled up in 1981 and 1983; *Midnight Love*, a faller, 1984; and on *Captain Parkhill*, a 100-1 shot, who was the last of eleven finishers in 1985. But then came his magnificent near-miss on *Young Driver*, an unfancied newcomer to the race.

In 1987 he was the 19th of 22 finishers on *Why Forget* and in 1989, as Arthur Stephenson's retained jockey, he had the choice between his runner-up of the year before or the classy, top-weighted *The Thinker*, a former Cheltenham Gold Cup winner. He chose the reliable *Durham Edition* but on the eve of the race, faced with heavy going, he predicted that *West Tip* would nearly win and that his own horse would have difficulty staying in the ground. He was absolutely right. *West Tip* went down to the out-and-out stayer *Little Polveir*, with *The Thinker* third and *Durham Edition* finishing fifth.

With a natural weight of 12st, Grant had to battle against the scales throughout his career. In addition he fought back determinedly, again and again, to overcome severe injuries. In 1979 he broke his left leg in a fall at Market Rasen and again, in the 1988-89 season, he had a long enforced rest after breaking his right leg in two places. Following his own strict routine, mostly cycling and swimming, he got back in March, 1989, to ride six winners before going on to the National.

In 1991 Grant stayed loyal to *Durham Edition* even though the twice runner-up was now 13 years old. Remarkably they finished sixth, their worst position in four appearances. In 1992 he was ninth on *Stay On Track*s and finally, in 1994, at the age of 37, he pulled up on the 66-1 chance, *He Who Dares Wins*. He ended with the remarkable record of having finished runner-up eight times riding in races over the National fences. As a trainer, he was back at Aintree on Grand National day, 2006, when he saddled *Double Vodka* who finished third in the opening handicap hurdle race at 66-1.

GREASEPAINT

Though never a Grand National winner, Irish-bred *Greasepaint* stands out, like his more successful half-brother *West Tip*, as one of the great Aintree specialists. Sired by *Gala Performance* out of *Wind Swift*, the chestnut gelding made a most impressive National debut in 1983 when, with amateur rider Mr Colin Magnier, he finished strongly, closing a four-length gap on the run-in to go down by just three-quarters of a length to *Corbiere*, with the third placed *Yer Man* 20 lengths in arrears.

Having changed ownership, and now trained by Dermot Weld and ridden by Tommy Carmody, the nine year old went off as the 9-1 favourite in the 1984 National. Again, with an extra 10lb to carry, he was the runner-up. As before, he rallied well at the close but this time he was carrying 9lb more and conceding a full stone to the winner *Hallo Dandy*. He was beaten four lengths, with *Corbiere* a further one and a half lengths back in third.

In 1985, *Greasepaint* was the 13-2 joint favourite

with his half-brother. For the third successive year he finished in the frame, albeit in fourth place. His extraordinary liking for Aintree was underlined by the gelding's consistent failure elsewhere. Indeed, he did not win a single race between March, 1983, and January, 1986. Only by winning a minor race at Tramore did he qualify just in time for the 1986 National. Then, on his last appearance, when well past his best, he was the tenth of 17 finishers. *See also:* Runners-up.

GREEN, Christopher

Son of a Norfolk farmer, Chris Green had a remarkably consistent record in the Grand National. In the first six of his eight rides, he scored two wins, a second place and a sixth. Moreover, when he scored his first success in 1850 – by one length on an unquoted outsider, the tiny bay *Abd-El-Kader* – both horse and rider were making their debut in the race.

Green was not back on board when 'Little Ab' repeated his win the following year, and he did not reappear in the National until 1854 when he was the sixth of seven finishers on *Half-And-Half*. In 1856 he failed to finish on the rank outsider *Stamford*, but one year later showed that he had lost none of his riding flair when finishing three lengths runner-up on Ben Land's 25-1 shot *Weathercock*.

Eight years after their victory, Green and 'Little Ab' were reunited in 1858. The dual winner, appearing in his fifth National, was now 16 years old and he fell at the second. Then, after a nine year gap, Green bounced back with his second National win, on the 7-1 second favourite *Half Caste*. It was a triumph for experience. Judging his six year old mount to be pulling too hard, the jockey restrained *Half Caste* to surrender the lead approaching the second Becher's. Then, on the run-in, he forged back in front to hold on by just 'a short neck' from *Jean Du Quesne*.

Green failed to finish in his last two Nationals – on the outsider *Lefroy* (1860) and *Cockatoo* (1861), but ten years later he returned to Aintree as a winning trainer, having been chosen to take over from Ben Land in preparing *The Lamb* for his second victory. *See also:* Abd-El-Kader; Half Caste; The Lamb.

GREEN, Reginald

The most dedicated aficionado of the Grand National, having devoted his life to writing about it and collecting memorabilia and form books relating to the race. Such was his total commitment to the most

famous steeplechase that Reg Green scheduled his marriage on March 26, 1960, so that he was able to make a taxi-rush from the church to Aintree in time to see the favourite *Merryman II* win the National by 15 lengths.

Born in 1937, Green first saw Aintree when it was occupied by American forces in the Second World War. There was no racing then but already, for a boy barely six years old, interest in the National was beginning to take hold – fostered by his father's stories of the great race and how he had had a big winning bet on *Sprig*, the 8-1 winner of 1927. Seated on his father's shoulders near Becher's, he witnessed the first post-war National in 1946 and has been going back ever since, missing out only in 1982 when, dutifully visiting his wife Brenda in hospital, he watched the favourite *Grittar* win on her bedside television.

Today Reg Green's home, within a few miles of Aintree, houses the largest private collection of Grand National memorabilia. A prolific and official historian of the race, his books include, most notably, *A Race Apart* (1988) and *The Grand National: Aintree's Official Illustrated History* (2000).

GREGALACH

Sixty six! That was the incredible record number of runners in the 1929 Grand National which seven year old *Gregalach* won at 100-1. Ironically, for the specific purpose of avoiding such quantity at the expense of quality, two changes had been made to the conditions of entry: raising the starting fee to £100 and introducing a second forfeit stage at which horses could be withdrawn. Both served to no avail.

The moves had been prompted by the debacle of 1928 when a then record field of 42 had seen only two finishers. And as a further defensive measure, the authorities had chosen to fill in the great open ditch on the take-off side of the Canal Turn, the scene of the huge pile-up the previous year. But, as it happened, the 1928 disaster was no deterrent to owners. Quite the reverse. All too many took the view that, if the National could be won by a tubed plodder like the 100-1 outsider *Tipperary Tim*, then there was hope for any stable, however small. And a rise of prize money – £13,000 to the winning owner – was a further incentive.

As the betting reflected, no one took the 1928 result seriously. *Tipperary Tim*, the winner, was again 100-1, and *Billy Barton*, the remounted runner-up, was 20-1.

Although his erratic jumping had caused last year's chaos at the Canal Turn, *Easter Hero* was the 9-1 favourite, having won his last five races of the season, including the Cheltenham Gold Cup. *Sprig*, the 1927 winner, was 50-1 and, ominously, the field included 26 no hopers priced at 200-1.

Easter Hero was now the great American hope. Following the disappearance of his owner Captain A.Lowenstein (presumed killed when his private plane mysteriously vanished over the North Sea), the classy chestnut had been acquired by U.S. millionaire 'Jock' Hay Whitney. Other American-owned runners were *Mount Etna*, *Bright's Boy*, *Darracq*, *Ballyhanwood* and *Billy Barton*.

No fewer than five runners, including *Sprig*, were trained by Tom Leader; and the lowest rated of these was *Gregalach*, one of eight 100-1 shots. Irish-bred, out of the mare *St. Germanie*, this seven year old chestnut was a half-brother to *Easter Hero*, both having been sired by *My Prince*. He was superbly built, had been bought for 5,000 guineas by Mrs M.A. Gemmell, and was almost always accompanied by a rough-haired terrier.

Gregalach's record – four wins including the Stanley Chase and then a long series of seconds – had earned him a relatively high handicap weight of 11st 4lb. But he had run indifferently before falling at Sandown, only eight days before his first National; and he was also unfancied by punters since he had an unnoted rider: Australian Robert Everett, a former naval officer, who had gained most of his riding experience in South Africa.

Thoughts of the disastrous Charge of the Light Brigade sprang to mind as the 66 thundered off towards the first Aintree fence. Remarkably, every one cleared the obstacle unscathed. But ten runners fell or refused at the first open ditch; and two American hopes went out when *Mount Etna*, ridden by Ted Leader, collided in mid-air with *Darracq*.

Though *Easter Hero* was predictably setting the fierce pace, he surrendered the lead when jockey Jack Moloney deliberately held him back to approach the Canal Turn with special caution. This time, the brilliant chestnut sailed impressively over the fence, then powered back into the lead. Meanwhile the number of fallers, including *Tipperary Tim*, was mounting fast; and as the field completed the first circuit less than a third of the starters remained. Again Moloney eased back on nearing the Canal Turn, and two challengers – *Richmond II* and

Shady Hook – were allowed to move ahead. Then again he quickly reasserted his superiority.

After Valentine's, *Easter Hero* seemed to have the race at his mercy. But now, suddenly, the top-weighted favourite began to slow the pace. Unbeknown to the roaring crowd, he was battling on in agony after spreading a front plate; and all the while just one challenger was hard on his hooves: the rangy, white-starred *Gregalach*.

Long matching *Easter Hero* stride for stride, *Gregalach* finally accelerated past him after the penultimate fence. He then pulled steadily away to win by six lengths with *Richmond II* a far distant third and a 20-1 shot, *Melleray's Belle*, in fourth place. For the second successive year the National had a 100-1 winner. A record number of 56 horses had failed to complete the course, and three of the ten finishers were priced at 200-1.

Like the previous 100-1 winner, *Gregalach* (raised 10lb to the top weight of 12st) was a faller when he returned the following year for a National in which only six of 41 starters completed the course. But, unlike *Tipperary Tim*, he was no freakish one-race wonder. Indeed, though he never repeated his victory, he ranks among the National's all-time greats.

There was good reason for his failure in 1930. That year, when recovering from a bad splint, he had been declared a doubtful starter, and was only pronounced fit at the 11th hour. But it was different in 1931 when he was ninth in the betting at 25-1. Back to peak fitness, still on 12st and now ridden by Jack Moloney, he led narrowly after the first circuit, and, jumping immaculately, was still leading – from *Great Span* and *Grakle* – when they came to Becher's where, most unluckily, the 5-1 favourite *Easter Hero* was brought down.

Arguably, *Gregalach* would have gone on to win if he had not put in such a colossal leap at the Canal Turn. That extravagant jump propelled him so far forward that he had to run wide around the right-angled turn, so losing valuable ground and allowing three horses to challenge him on the inside.

Still, as they came to the last, only one horse could stay with him: his former stablemate *Grakle*, also a nine year old. On the long run-in, they were far in front, battling side by side to the line. But then, for the first time, jockey Bob Lyall showed *Grakle* the whip, and, with a half-stone advantage, the third favourite gradually inched ahead over the last hundred yards to win by just one and a half lengths, with

G

Gregalach ten lengths ahead of *Annandale*, a 100-1 shot back in third. *Shaun Goilin*, the 1930 winner, was the sixth of ten finishers in a field of 43. And, significantly, the winning time was 9min 32⅖secs – just two-fifths of a second off the record time set by *Cloister* in 1893.

It is an indication of *Gregalach*'s true greatness that the handicapper saw fit to lumber him with top weight of 12st 7lb for the next three Grand Nationals. This in a period which saw the emergence of such National Hunt giants as *Kellsboro' Jack* and *Golden Miller*.

In 1932 *Gregalach* was a most unlucky victim of the chaos created by the riderless *Pelorus Jack* who reduced the field by two-thirds when running across the front of the open ditch at the 11th. Knocked over just as he was taking off, he crashed into the fence and rolled over on top of his rider, Fred Thackray. The jockey, a highly promising amateur, was so severely injured that he could never ride in the National again.

In 1933 *Gregalach* went off as a second favourite, one point behind *Golden Miller*, the brilliant six year old who had just scored his second Cheltenham Gold Cup triumph. Now the huge weight handicap truly told, and he had to be pulled up in a race won in record time by *Kellsboro' Jack*.

In 1934, *Gregalach* ran in his fifth and final National. Though still, unreasonably, carrying 12st 7lb, the 12 year old was leading narrowly at the Water but was a spent force after the Canal Turn second time round, again having to be pulled up.
See also: Grakle; Everett, Robert; Fields.

GREYS

Only two greys have ever won the Grand National: *The Lamb* (1868 and 1871) and *Nicolaus Silver* (1961). Four have finished runner-up: *Cigar* (1841), *Peter Simple* (1845), *Suny Bay* (1997 and 1998) and *What's Up Boys* (2002). Three have gained a third place: *Peter Simple* (1841 and 1842), *Downpatrick* (1880) and *Loving Words* (1982); and four have been fourth: *Downpatrick* (1884), *Glangesia* (1930), *The Beeches* (1969) and *Kingsmark* (2002).

This modest record is hardly surprising in modern times when it is estimated that only around three per cent of racehorses are classified as greys. However, they appeared in greater numbers in the 19th century and early 20th century, and yet still went through nine decades without emulating the success of the dual winner *The Lamb*.

The 90-year drought was at last ended by the five-lengths victory of *Nicolaus Silver*, ridden by Bobby Beasley, in 1961. The grey finished seventh the following year and was tenth in 1963 when another grey, Mr Gregory Peck's *Owen's Sedge*, was seventh. In 1964, most unusually, a grey – Mr Raymond Guest's *Flying Wild* – had the distinction of starting as one of four joint favourites. Unfortunately, the handicapper had chosen to burden him with the second highest weight, and his fate was to be the only faller at the first fence.

Nine months later *Flying Wild*, albeit with a 32lb advantage, proved his courage when he fought tenaciously to win by a nose from the supreme *Arkle* in the Massey-Ferguson Gold Cup at Cheltenham. But when he returned to the National in 1966 he was again seriously handicapped with the third highest weight, and he needed to be pulled up.

In 1969 Paul Mellon's *The Beeches* finished fourth. But it was not until 1982 – 21 years after the success of *Nicolaus Silver* – that a grey came home in the first three. This was nine year old *Loving Words*, a 16-1 shot, who was the third of eight finishers in a race that saw ten of the 39-strong field fall at the first fence. Though he passed the post 15 lengths and a distance behind *Grittar* and *Hard Outlook* respectively, it was a notable run since he had been badly hampered by two fallers at the last open ditch. Rider Richard Hoare was unseated, but he remounted to put in a brave late challenge.

The following year, the grey *Tower Moss*, a 300-1 chance, was one of three fallers at the first. Then, in 1984, the grey *Two Swallows* finished sixth after losing a hard-fought battle with *Earthstopper* who tragically dropped dead after snatching fifth place.

It is a sad fact that most Grand National fatalities are briefly mourned, then soon forgotten. Significantly, however, the name of one fatal contender remains indelibly imprinted on the public's psyche and that is *Dark Ivy*, the 11 year old trained by Gordon Richards and ridden by Phil Tuck in 1987. He is best remembered because he was the most beautiful grey; also one strongly tipped to be the first of his colour to win the National for 26 years. He attracted such a late rush of support that he went off the 11-2 second favourite.

Certainly, *Dark Ivy*'s seasonal form was impressive and he was arguably the best handicapped horse in the race. Richards compared him more than favourably with his 1984 winner *Hallo Dandy*; and on the ice-cold afternoon of the National the grey was adjudged the best-looking horse in the parade. A quarter of an hour later he was dead, having taken a most hideous, neck-breaking fall into the then sloping ditch at Becher's after being severely impeded on take-off by *Attitude Adjuster* and then sandwiched in the air between that horse and *Why Forget*.

How ever illogical, there was now a mounting superstition that greys were somehow cursed in the National. This was given fresh support in 1988 when Jenny Pitman's *Smith's Man* pulled up lame after landing awkwardly over the second fence and the only other grey in the race, *Brass Change*, under Martin Kinane, fell at the third last.

More to the point, as highlighted by the tragedy of *Dark Ivy*, it was now clear that greys – purely by virtue of their attractive looks – aroused special popularity that sometimes transcended the merits of their racing form. Quite simply, a grey could be regarded by some aesthetes as being too beautiful to be subjected to the roughhouse of the Grand National.

For instance, one dared not contemplate the public reaction if such a cruel fate as *Dark Ivy*'s had later befallen the most famous and beloved of all greys, *Desert Orchid*. In looks he was worthy of Hollywood stardom, in the tradition of the mounts of Hopalong Cassidy and the Lone Ranger. At the end of 1989 a *Racing Post* poll elected 'Dessie' the top jumper of the 1980s. He had won the 1988 Whitbread Gold Cup, the 1989 Cheltenham Gold Cup (the only grey to do so) and the King George VI Chase three times, and he had reaped more prize money than any other horse in the history of steeplechasing.

Then, to the consternation of so many fans, trainer David Elsworth boldly announced that he was entering the grey for the National. However, one of the owners, Jimmy Burridge, was unhappy about the idea for a number of reasons: the Aintree course was left-handed (not in his favour), the race was a handicap and he seemed certain to be lumbered with more than 12st; also it would come only three weeks after the Cheltenham Gold Cup.

As numerous newspaper and telephone polls showed, public opinion was overwhelmingly opposed to their national treasure being risked in such a rough-and-tumble. Indeed, feelings ran so high that the police had to mount a special guard on the home of Mr Elsworth who had received threatening letters from fanatical Dessie-lovers.

When the weights were duly announced, *Desert Orchid* was given 12st 2lb, which some trainers judged to be over-generous. But it was of no consequence. It was never agreed that Dessie should run in the both the Gold Cup and National, and he was swiftly withdrawn from the latter. In February, he carried 12st 3lb to victory in the Racing Post Chase at Kempton. In the Gold Cup, as odds-on favourite, he finished third to *Norton's Coin* (100-1) and *Toby Tobias* (8-1). But the following month he won the Irish Grand National and ended the year with a record fourth victory in the King George.

Could *Desert Orchid* – rated by Richard Dunwoody as 'the finest horse I rode' – have won the National? Perhaps not. David Elsworth always reckoned that he was a stone better on a right-handed course. And Neville Crump, trainer of three Grand National winners, once expressed the opinion that he would have overjumped in the National. But we shall never know for certain. In 1991, just before his 13th birthday, his enthralling career ended with a rare fall in the King George. Providentially, he retired unscathed with a record of 34 wins in 72 races.

In the same way, another outstanding grey was never allowed to run in the National: *One Man*, winner of the 1995 and 1996 King George VI Chases with Dunwoody, and the 1994 Hennessy Cognac Gold Cup with Tony Dobbin. But there was good reason why he should have missed any chance to give his trainer Gordon Richards a third National success: he lacked the stamina for such a marathon. Tragically, Aintree was still his undoing. On the eve of the 1998 National, and one month after his brilliant victory in the two-mile Queen Mother Champion Chase, *One Man* broke a hind leg on taking a heavy fall when leading the field in the Mumm Melling Chase. He was immediately put down.

In the meantime there had been no change in the failure of greys to make their mark in the National. No fewer than three greys appeared in the disorganised line-up for the 1993 National: *Stay On Tracks*, *Farm Week* and *Howe Street*. But this was the National That Never Was. *Farm Week* (200-1) and *Howe Street* (66-1) fell at the fourth and 20th respectively, the latter when disputing the lead. *Stay On Tracks*, a 50-1 chance who had finished ninth the previous year, was among the dozen pulled up after one circuit.

G

In 1995, running on unsuitably fastish ground, the Irish grey *Desert Lord* fell at the 21st fence. And there was more talk of a 'grey jinx' the following year when the 1994 Irish National winner *Son Of War*, lying in tenth place, ran out of room at the Canal Turn second time around and unseated Conor O'Dwyer. It was a shattering blow for Irish supporters. All season the grey's campaign had been geared to peaking at Aintree. He was the most popular choice among leading tipsters and he had been backed down to 8-1 joint second favouristism.

For much of the 20th century it was usual, with a few notable exceptions, to associate the colour grey with sprinters or milers since so many greys could be traced back to 'The Spotted Grey Wonder', *The Tetrarch*, a lightning fast sprinter who won all seven of his races as a two year old in 1913. Subsequently he sired three St Leger winners but for the most part his progeny were noted for speed rather than stamina.

However, in relatively recent times, greys have emerged more frequently as excellent chasers – a development which owes much to the long and continuing influence of *Roselier*, the grey stallion who sired such notable grey chasers as *Suny Bay*, *Senor El Betrutti*, *Baronet* and *Kendal Cavalier*, plus many major, non-grey National players, among them winners *Royal Athlete* (1995) and *Bindaree* (2002), and *Moorcroft Boy* and *Ebony Jane*, third and fourth respectively in 1994.

Of the Roselier greys, by far the most outstanding was *Suny Bay*, trained by Charlie Brooks, an Old Etonian who had served as an assistant to the great Fred Winter and who had ridden *Insure*, the last of 22 finishers in the 1987 Grand National. True, he had a history of setbacks: bad lungs, bad legs and a broken jaw sustained in a 1996 spill at Sandown; and he had burst a blood vessel on his first run of the 1996-97 season. But as an eight year old he went to Aintree in 1997 with outstanding credentials; he was well handicapped on 10st 3lb, (over a stone well-in on the official ratings), was a classy jumper of proven stamina and had a record of six wins in nine chases. Now he was seeking a £100,000 bonus after a 19-lengths triumph in the Greenall Grand National Trial Chase at Haydock.

Sadly, however, he was to be a notable victim of the IRA bomb scare that resulted in a 49-hour postponement. The ground was drying in the interim and *Suny Bay* was at his best on soft going. It was a huge blow for Brooks who had been obsessed with the National since seeing it on television at the age of six and who always said that he would rather win this race than the Cheltenham Gold Cup. 'I don't think he'll win now,' said the trainer. 'But not to run would be a real empty feeling. We want to run to stick it up them (the IRA).'

On the Monday, *Lord Gyllene* led from start to finish. *Suny Bay*, under Jamie Osborne, emerged as his main rival but all hope was lost when he blundered through at the last open ditch (the 27th). Outpaced thereafter, he finished second – but 25 lengths in arrears. The other grey on parade, *Dextra Dove*, was pulled up at the 27th.

In 1998 there was a most interesting grey among the ten originally entered for the National: *Buck Jakes* who, like the 1980 winner *Ben Nevis*, was a dual Maryland Hunt Cup victor being sent over in advance to Captain Tim Forster. Unfortunately, he never took to English fences and was withdrawn. Nonetheless, this year was to see a truly great performance by one of two greys in the race. While *Diwali Dancer* fell at the first fence, the other, *Suny Bay*, qualified as the unluckiest grey not to win a National.

Suny Bay had been raised from 10st 3lb to a colossal 12st top weight. He had been hugely impressive when winning the Hennessy Cognac Gold Cup in November and now he had favourably soft ground at Aintree. But this was asking for a miracle. In contrast to his ideal preparation for the 1997 National, his build-up for 1998 had been a veritable disaster. In December, he had returned from the King George VI Chase with badly pulled muscles requiring much physiotherapy and, in desperation, the introduction of a faith healer with 'magic' hands' Then, after finishing fifth in the Cheltenham Gold Cup, he came home with hind legs spiked with gorse and was given painkillers for the soreness.

Now, only 16 days later, he was in the National, giving at least 10lb to all his rivals and two stone to 30 in the 37-strong field. On bottomless ground, he was attempting to carry 12st to victory – a feat only achieved by *Red Rum* in the past 52 years.

Suny Bay was nearly brought down by *Challenger Du Luc*, one of five fallers at the first. Thereafter, he was trouble-free, given a brilliant ride by Graham Bradley who hugged the inside to take the shortest route and moved him steadily through the field on the second circuit to take third place at the Canal

Turn. By the Melling Road he had only one rival, *Earth Summit*, and they took the last fence together. But now, on the long run-in, *Earth Summit*'s 23lb advantage proved cruelly decisive and he pulled away to win by 11 lengths, with *Samlee* far back in third place. The grey was the most gallant loser since *Crisp*, also conceding 23lb, went down to *Red Rum* in 1973. Timeform commented: 'In form terms this was the best performance in the race for over 20 years and one of the best in the race in the modern era.'

For the 1999 National, *Suny Bay* – now with Simon Sherwood in his first year of training as Charlie Brooks's successor at Uplands – was meanly dropped only 1lb, still on top weight and conceding 12lb to his nearest rival, *General Wolfe*. In his two previous races he had fallen in Ireland and had been pulled up in the Gold Cup. The majestic grey had never been quick enough for the challenge over Cheltenham's sharp, undulating and turning track. Aintree was ideal for him; but now, with the good ground against him, the two-times runner-up finished 13th at 12-1.

That year there had been no fewer than eight greys in the original entry of 103, six of them in the handicap proper. Only three made it to the line-up. In addition to *Suny Bay*, there was the David Nicholson-trained *Baronet* and the Welsh National winner *Kendal Cavalier*. The former fell at the fourth. The latter, trained by Nigel Hawke, who had ridden *Seagram* to victory in 1991, finished seventh under Barry Fenton, making his debut in the race.

In 2000 there were again three greys in the National field. *Senor El Betrutti*, a 100-1 outsider ridden by the twice National winning jockey Carl Llewellyn, was one of five fallers at the first fence. *Kendal Cavalier* finished 12th. To the misfortune of *Suny Bay*, the official handicapper had this year chosen to reintroduce the 'Aintree factor', taking into consideration the past course record of runners. Consequently, without impressive seasonal form, the extraordinary grey was lumbered with the second highest weight of 11st 12lb. His chance was fairly reflected in his starting price of 66-1, and he again finished 13th.

While seven greys were entered for the 2001 National, none made it to the line-up. The following year no fewer than five appeared in the 40-strong field: *Kingsmark*, *What's Up Boys*, *Carryonharry*, *Gun 'N' Roses* and *Birkdale*. Three were among the 11 who completed the course, with the outstand-

ing run being that of *What's Up Boys*, the Hennessy Cognac Gold Cup winner and the runner-up in the previous year's Whitbread Gold Cup.

Three weeks after finishing fifth in the Cheltenham Gold Cup, *What's Up Boys* went off in the National under a massive 11st 6lb. Rider Richard Johnson delayed his move until the Canal Turn and thereafter the grey made relentless progress to join *Bindaree* in a titanic duel from two out. He led on the run-in, but finally a 16lb concession to *Bindaree* proved too much. He was beaten a mere length and three-quarters, with champion Tony McCoy on *Blowing Wind* 27 lengths back in third.

Kingsmark, too, had been outstanding. The nine year old had fallen only once in 17 chases; and now, though anchored on a hefty 11st 9lb, he gave Ruby Walsh a brilliant ride, only weakening from two out to finish in fourth place. The other grey finisher was *Birkdale* in tenth.

In 2004 *What's Up Boys* and *Kingsmark* were again both high in the weights. The former, brought down, was one of nine horses eliminated at the first Becher's (ironically along with his old rival *Bindaree*); the latter was the ninth of 11 finishers, A third grey in the race, seven year old 100-1 shot *Royal Atalza*, was pulled up two out. Again, in 2005, three greys appeared: *Strong Resolve*, the 9-1 second favourite, who finished a poor 17th of 21 finishers; and *Double Honour* and *Marcus Du Berlais*, both 25-1 chances who unseated their riders on the second circuit. Well-supported *Ross Comm*, the only grey in the 2006 National, fell at the fourth fence; and in 2007 the two grey longshots, *Kandjar D'Allier* and *The Outlier*, both failed to finish.

See also: Lamb, The; Nicolaus Silver; Suny Bay; Elsworth, David.

GRITTAR

Comfortable winner of the 1982 Grand National when both horse and rider (48 year old amateur Dick Saunders) were appearing in the race for the first time. Bred, owned and trained by Leicestershire hunting farmer Frank Gilman, nine-year-old *Grittar* was the first clear favourite (7-1) to win since *Merryman II*, 22 years before.

A neat, well-proportioned bay with a distinctive white star, *Grittar* was by the grey *Grisaille*, a one-time sprinter, out of *Tarama*, a winner of two novice hurdles. As a two year old, he had two unplaced runs on the Flat; and later he showed useful form over hurdles, winning two well-contested novice events and being placed in six other races. Then, as a six year old, he was switched to point-to-points and hunter chases, being successfully ridden by Saunders and by his young daughter, Caroline.

His career over fences took off impressively in 1981 with wins in four of his first five races; and these included the Foxhunter Chases at Cheltenham and at Liverpool where he was covering a circuit of the National course for the first time. Alarm bells then rang when he damaged tendons in a run on firm ground at Southwell, but he recovered well and in 1982, 16 days before the National, he advertised his Aintree prospects by finishing a respectable sixth in the Cheltenham Gold Cup.

In one of his prep races *Grittar* had been ridden at Ascot by champion jockey John Francome who had experience of six Grand Nationals, finishing third and second in 1979 and 1980 respectively. Yet Gilman resisted the temptation to turn to a leading professional and insisted that *Grittar* should be partnered by his regular rider. Thus, for the first time, the National saw a clear favourite go off under an amateur who was 48 years old.

Saunders gave *Grittar* a copy-book ride, avoiding the chaos that saw ten horses eliminated at the first fence, staying well up with the pace and taking the lead at the second Becher's. Thereafter, with his proven stamina being fully exploited, *Grittar* was never headed; and he pulled steadily away on the run-in to win by 15 lengths from Lady Wates's *Hard Outlook* with a distance back to the grey *Loving Words* (remounted) in third.

Unlike his jockey, who retired immediately after the race, *Grittar* appeared in two more Grand Nationals. In 1983, despite being raised 7lb to the top weight of 11st 12lb, he went off the 6-1 clear favourite. Ridden by Paul Barton, he finished fifth; and the following year he was tenth under Francome. The safest of jumpers, he had always completed the National course, but he never won another race after his Aintree success.
See also: Saunders, Dick; Gilman, Frank.

GRUDON

Eleven year old winner of the 1901 Grand National, controversially run in a blinding blizzard over a snow-covered course. It was his third attempt, having previously finished seventh in a snowstorm in 1898 and sixth in 1900. And his victory was partly attributed to 2lb of butter!

Unusually, *Grudon* was an entire; also one of lowly breeding, having been sired – out of the mare *Avis* – by *Old Buck* who was being used as a plough horse. His success was a triumph for his owner Mr Bernard Bletsoe. He had bred and trained the horse at Denton, Northamptonshire. Furthermore, he was credited with a crucial masterstroke. On the day of the 1901 National, after inspecting the course, he sent out a stable boy to purchase 2lb of butter from a local shop. This he packed into *Grudon*'s hooves to eliminate the risk of snow 'balling' on his feet.

In the 1900 National, when he was a 40-1 chance in a field of only 16, the entire had been well ridden by Mr Bletsoe's son, Morgan. For his return, however, the owner-trainer recruited a rider of outstanding expertise: Arthur Nightingall. *Grudon* was now 9-1 third favourite. Even so, Nightingall agreed with all the other jockeys that the conditions were totally unfit for racing.

Despite a unanimously signed petition for a postponement, the stewards ruled that racing should go ahead. The runners set off after a 16-minute delay, and *Grudon* led from the start. He was still leading by two or three lengths when the runners came back into view at the end of the first circuit. Never headed, his only error was to jump a footpath on the run-in. While 15 of 24 starters failed to finish, he came home four lengths ahead of *Drumcree* and in the remarkably smart time of just under 9min 48sec.

It was Nightingall's third National victory. While he rode in three more Nationals, gaining a second and fourth place, *Grudon* would not appear at Aintree again. He had just two more races and after breaking down in Manchester's Lancashire Chase was retired to serve at stud.
See also: Bletsoe, Bernard; Nightingall, Arthur.

GUEST, Raymond

No racehorse owner has enjoyed more varied success on both sides of the Atlantic than the American millionaire Raymond Guest. Virginia-born in 1907, he swept all before him while serving as U.S. ambassador in Dublin during the 1960s and 1970s. In the States his outstanding horse was *Tom Rolfe*, winner in 1965 of the Preakness Stakes, Citation Handicap and American Derby. In England, he won two Cheltenham Gold Cups with *L'Escargot*, the Derby with *Larkspur* (1962) and the mighty *Sir Ivor* (1968). The latter also won the Washington DC International, the 2,000 Guineas and the Champion Stakes, and had the supreme distinction of being judged by Lester Piggott as the best horse he had ever ridden.

But Mr Guest's passionate pursuit of Grand National success came hardest of all; and it began in most discouraging style. His first runner, the amateur-ridden *Virginius*, was brought down in 1957. Next, in 1964, he saw his eight year old grey mare *Flying Wild* crash out at the very first fence. He was without a runner the following year but at least had the pleasure of seeing the prize go to *Jay Trump*, both American-bred and -owned. In 1966 he was double-handed, but again disappointed. *Flying Wild* was pulled up by Pat Taaffe and his *Packed Home* was a faller under Tommy Carberry.

Next came the chaotic Foinavon National. This time he at least had a finisher, his 12 year old *Packed Home* being put back in the race to come home fifth, like the winner, at 100-1. But in the following four years he had three more failures: *Great Lark*, a faller in 1968, and both his runners – *Cnoc Dubh* and *Smooth Dealer* – being non-finishers in 1971.

By now the great owner of the Flat at last had a truly outstanding chaser: *L'Escargot*, trained by Dan Moore and winner of the Cheltenham Gold Cup in 1970 and 1971. Again, however, Mr Guest's lifelong dream of National glory seemed doomed to frustration. In 1972, *L'Escargot*, as top-weighted favourite, was knocked over at the third fence. In 1973, he was a well-beaten third behind two exceptional contenders, *Red Rum* and *Crisp*, and in 1974 he was again outpaced by *Red Rum*, being runner-up by seven lengths with long-shot *Charles Dickens* only a short head back in third.

In 1975, it seemed to many that *L'Escargot*, now 12 years old, had missed his chance. Yet Mr Guest remained hugely optimistic. For the first time *Red Rum* had to contend with soft going in the National and now his great rival had an 11lb advantage in the weights. These factors proved crucial when they jumped the last side by side. *L'Escargot* powered ahead to win by 15 lengths, so fulfilling the ambition that his owner had pursued for 18 years.

An ecstatic Mr Guest led in the winner whom he promptly retired and gifted, as planned, to Joanie Moore, the trainer's wife. It was five years before he again had a Grand National entry, but it was no longer a serious challenge. His ten year old *Casamayor*, a 50-1 shot, fell in 1980 and failed to finish at 100-1 in 1981. Mr Guest died at his home in Virginia in December, 1991, aged 84.
See also: L'Escargot; Moore, Daniel; United States.

GUEST, Richard Charles
Winning rider of *Red Marauder* in the sensational 2001 Grand National, when, on bottomless ground, only seven of 40 runners completed the first circuit and only four finished, the third and fourth after being remounted. It was his eighth ride in the National, his previous best having been in 1992 when he rode *Romany King* into the lead at the 24th (Canal Turn) but finally went down by two and a half lengths to the stronger staying *Party Politics*.

Richard Guest was born on July 10, 1965 into a family steeped in racing tradition. His father, Charlie Guest, was a jockey for 17 years, riding under both codes before becoming a trainer in Belgium and Holland. Uncle Joe was a jump jockey for more than a quarter of a century, with about 300 winners. Uncle Nelson rode for Gordon Richards, Fulke Walwyn and Bill Payne before moving to Scandinavia where he trained the winners of five Classics. And Richard's older brother, Rae, rode some 600 winners before setting up as a Newmarket trainer.

Richard was only 11 years old, a mere five and a half stone, when he wrapped metal chains around his waist to persuade Newmarket trainer Jeremy Hindley that he was heavy enough to ride out; and he was still a schoolboy when he rode work on the ill-fated Derby winner, *Shergar*. Following a spell with Sir Michael Stoute, he moved on to National Hunt racing, beginning a six-year association with trainer Toby Balding, having his first winner at the age of 20 and two years later his first Cheltenham Festival success, on *Neblin* in the 1987 County Hurdle. He then joined trainers Sue and Harvey Smith as their stable jockey in West Yorkshire.

Before his National victory on *Red Marauder*, Richard's most sensational success had come in 1989 when he won the Champion Hurdle on the 50-1 outsider *Beech Road*. Later successes included the 1992 First National Chase on the Smiths' *Kildimo* and the 1994 Becher Chase on *Into The Red*. But, above all, he was remembered as the jockey who, in April, 1998, had thrown his riding licence at the Perth stewards when they judged him guilty of not trying. It was the third time in 12 months that he had been convicted of a breach of the non-triers' rule.

G

For Guest, now suspended for nearly three months, it was the last straw. He felt that his quiet riding style – sitting still, all the while gripping and squeezing with his long legs – was totally misunderstood by the officials. As he later expressed it: 'I had gone to the point of extremes at times to prove that my way of riding was the right way; that you can ride them quietly from the rear, holding them together on the bridle for a late run, without trying to cheat anyone. I have never stopped a horse for money.'

Having announced his retirement, Richard briefly considered starting a new career in the United States. But then came a timely offer from millionaire businessman Norman Mason to be his stable jockey and assistant trainer at the Brancepeth Manor Farm yard near Durham. The partnership blossomed, flourishing notably in November, 1998 when Guest scored a decisive win on *Red Marauder* in the valuable First National Bank Gold Cup at Ascot. And it would enable Mason – who described his assistant as a 'miracle worker' – to achieve his two declared ambitions: to be champion permit trainer and to win the Grand National.

When winning the 2001 National, Guest was, at 35, the oldest jockey in the race. He had made seven previous appearances, beginning with a great debut as runner-up on *Romany King* in 1992. After that race trainer Balding had criticised him for having come too soon on *Romany King*, but he later modified that view, recognising that the horse was probably not an out-and-out stayer. The following year Richard missed the National with a broken leg. But it was no loss. His friend Adrian Maguire took the ride on *Romany King* and, on his National debut, determinedly completed the course in third place only to find that the false-started race was declared void.

Guest's next National rides were *Romany King* (1994), fell at the fourth; *Into The Red* (1995), dead-heated fifth with *Romany King*; *Into The Red* (1996), the 15th of 17 finishers; *Yeoman Warrior* (1998), pulled up at the 19th; *Frazer Island* (1999), an outsider with a sequence of 13 defeats, who was cantering when he fell at the second Becher's; and *Red Marauder* (2000), a faller at Becher's first time round.

In 2000 Guest had boldly predicted that he would win the National on *Red Marauder*, winner of five of his six chases, all on softish ground. But that year the drying ground was not in his favour. In the

circumstances it was rather ironic that in 2001 he was one of many who argued that the race should be called off because of the quagmire conditions. However, he changed his mind after walking down to Becher's Brook. The previous day he had comfortably won the Heidsieck Diamant Blue Novices' Handicap Chase on *Red Striker*; and now he recognised that the going could again help his cause. Subsequently he employed his controversial riding style to perfection, riding patiently off the pace and producing *Red Marauder* for a decisive late challenge approaching the final fence.

One year later Guest experienced a complete reversal of fortune. Unable to make the 10st to ride *Red Ark*, he picked up – as a result of Maguire's neck-breaking fall – a far more promising ride: Major Ivan Straker's *Paris Pike*, a former winner of the Scottish National who was set to carry 10st 13lb and went off as a strongly fancied 10-1 shot. It made no difference. On good, relatively fast ground, both *Red Ark* and *Paris Pike* fell at the first fence, along with seven others.

In February, 2003, Guest made a tremendous start as a licensed trainer in full command of Mason's expanding yard, having six winners in his first week, Meanwhile, at a time when Jim Culloty was out injured, he had the good fortune to be united with a most promising Henrietta Knight chaser: *Chives*. In December, 2002, he had showed all his old skills when bringing home the seven year old to finish second in the Welsh National under a big weight and on very heavy ground; and horse and rider combined so well together that he kept the ride.

Now, after finishing seventh in the Cheltenham Gold Cup, *Chives* went into the National as a much-fancied 10-1 chance. And Guest was in the extraordinary position of riding him in opposition to two horses he himself had trained: *Red Striker* and *Red Ark*. Disappointingly, *Chives* blundered the 11th and was pulled up before the next with a broken blood vessel. *Red Ark* was well behind when pulled up at the 25th, *Red Striker* fell at the 27th.

Guest appeared to have hung up his boots after a second-placed ride at Market Rasen in July, 2003. But seven months later he was back in the saddle and hoping to have one more ride in the National on *Red Striker*. His stable's main challenger, however, was to be Mason's *Tyneandthyneagain* who, in January, had won the Great Yorkshire Handicap Chase over three miles at Doncaster.

At Cheltenham, he turned out his first Festival winner: *Our Armageddon* in the Cathcart Chase. Then his plan to make a riding comeback in the National was scuppered when the Jockey Club – partly in response to concerns expressed by the Racehorse Owners' Association – introduced a new integrity rule that no longer allowed trainers to ride against one or more of their own horses. As it happened this was of no consequence. Both *Tyneandthyneagain* and *Red Striker* were withdrawn for the lack of soft ground.

The former finally made it to the National line-up as a 100-1 shot in 2006 but by then he had a new owner and trainer. Tragically, when running loose after falling at the first, he crashed fatally into the last open ditch. Meanwhile, Guest had sent out 12 year old *Shotgun Willy* who led as far as the first Valentine's only to weaken later and be pulled up before the 18th. The following year he trained *European Dream* to win the William Hill Spring Mile Handicap at Newcastle on the first day of the Flat, but his one National entry, *Shannon's Pride*, was never within a chance of making the cut.

See also: Mason, Norman; Red Marauder.

H

HALF CASTE

A six year old brown entire, *Half Caste* had only once competed in a steeplechase prior to his Grand National debut in 1859, and he had then been a faller. Yet at Aintree he was made the 7-1 second favourite and he earned the distinction of prevailing in one of the closest finishes ever seen.

His strong support in the betting owed much to the fact that he was both trained and ridden by Chris Green who had won the 1850 National on *Abd-El-Kader* and had been runner-up on *Weathercock* in 1857. In the running, that jockey's experience proved crucial; recognising that the young newcomer was pulling too hard, he restrained him on the second circuit and purposefully surrendered the lead before Becher's.

When the new leader *Xanthus* fell at the Canal Turn, *Half Caste* was left back in front but only marginally ahead of six others; and at the final fence he was under pressure from *Anatis* and *Jean Du Quesne*, one of three French challengers. For half of the long run-in he kept a clear lead but thereafter *Jean Du Quesne*, ridden by Yorkshireman Harry Lamplugh, matched him stride for stride in a pulsating duel to the post. Though they seemed inseparable at the finish, *Half Caste* was declared the winner by 'a short neck' with the fast-finishing *Huntsman* just one length back in third.

Green was to ride in two more Nationals, boosting his total to eight. But *Half Caste* faded into obscurity, having won on his first and only appearance at Aintree.

See also: Green, Christopher.

HALL COURT

Owned and sometimes ridden by Captain J. M. Browne, *Hall Court* had the extraordinary distinction of finishing a head second in the Grand National as a 50-1 outsider, and second again at odds of 100-1. On the latter occasion, in 1869, he was the longest-price contender to come so close to winning.

On his 1865 National debut, as a six year old, *Hall Court* figured in the most drawn-out steeplechase duel ever seen – a neck-and-neck, stride-for-stride battle with the French-bred five year old *Alcibiade* all the way from the last fence to the finishing line. He went down by a mere head with last year's winner *Emblematic* 50 yards back in third. Four years later, he was beaten three lengths by *The Colonel*. On both occasions, he was ridden by

Captain A.C.Tempest, an Army friend of the owner.

Seven times *Hall Court* appeared in the National, his riders including Captain Browne, and the highly experienced 'Mr Thomas' and Ben Land Jnr But it was only under Tempest – albeit with a more favourable weight – that he performed with distinction. With other riders he was a faller in 1866 and 1867, seventh in 1868, and a non-finisher on his last two runs in 1870 and 1872.

See also: Tempest, Captain Arthur Cecil.

HALLO DANDY

Winner by four lengths of the 1984 Grand National which, newly limited to 40 runners, saw a record number of 23 horses completing the course. Ridden by Welshman Neale Doughty, the outstanding jumper gave northern trainer Gordon Richards his second National win in six years and sealed a considerable betting coup for his first-time owner, City of London insurance broker Richard Shaw.

A powerfully built bay gelding – by *Menelek* out of *Dandy Hall* – *Hallo Dandy* was an unbroken three year old when at Ballsbridge sales he went for £10,000 to Mr Jack Thompson, who duly sent him to be trained by Ginger McCain of *Red Rum* fame. He showed only moderate form over hurdles before the trainer, recognising his jumping potential, sent him out to win a Haydock novice handicap chase as a six year old. But then, after winning two more minor races, he developed leg trouble and needed to be fired. Subsequently, he was moved from Southport to the Greystoke yard of Gordon Richards in Cumbria.

Early in 1982 *Hallo Dandy* showed considerable promise when finishing third in a chase over Aintree's Mildmay course and Richards was beginning to see him as a useful National prospect. But there was a problem. It seems that the owner's wife objected to him having a runner in such a demanding race. Mr Thompson suggested that, in the circumstances, Richards could sell the gelding with the proviso that the gelding remained at Greystoke. He would not, however, accept an offer of less than £25,000.

Remarkably, Richards found a buyer who had never owned a horse before. Mr Shaw took up the offer strictly with the 1983 Grand National in mind. In the build-up to Aintree *Hallo Dandy* was placed in three of his four outings. But on the day, with soft going seemingly against him, he went off as an unfancied 60-1 chance.

Ridden by Doughty, he had a National debut exceeding all expectations. Jumping boldly and cleanly throughout, he took a narrow lead at the start of the second circuit and held it until being joined by *Corbiere* after Becher's. Their duel only ended when, approaching the penultimate fences, *Hallo Dandy* began to tire on the soft ground, fading so fast that he finished fourth, far behind the winning *Corbiere*.

Almost at once the shrewd Mr Shaw began backing his horse to win the 1984 National, originally getting odds of 66-1. Encouragingly, *Hallo Dandy* won his first chase of the next season, but he was then beaten at Kelso and pulled up in the Hennessy Cognac Gold Cup. He was not raced again until after the National weights had been declared. Controversially, in the light of his 1983 run, handicapper Captain Christopher Mordaunt had set him to carry just 1lb more compared with an extra 10lb for *Corbiere* and 9lb more for last year's runner-up *Greasepaint*.

At that point, odds of 33-1 were still available about *Hallo Dandy* but that price soon went after he had finished second in his one prepare at Ayr, and the odds shortened dramatically once it was seen that he would get the good ground that he favoured. Brought to a perfectly timed peak by the master of Greystoke, *Hallo Dandy* went off at 13-1. Doughty rode him patiently from the start, delaying his forward move until the second circuit. A mighty leap at Becher's saw him jump into a prominent position and by the 26th fence he was challenging *Greasepaint* for the lead. He took it at the second last, soon opening up a four lengths gap.

As in 1983, *Greasepaint* rallied bravely and for a moment looked like gaining an advantage as the leader veered to his right after clearing the last. But the light-weighted *Hallo Dandy* asserted his superior pace over the final half-furlong to win by four lengths, with the strong finishing *Corbiere* only a further one and a half lengths back in third.

When *Hallo Dandy* returned to the National in 1985 it was with an extra 10lb to carry and a new jockey, Graham Bradley, replacing the injured Doughty. Seventh in the betting at 14-1, he unseated his rider at the first fence. Doughty was back on board in 1986 but the still fine jumper was now 12 years old and, despite a recent win, was lacking in pace. Never in serious contention, he was the 12th of 17 finishers.

At the end of the season, 'Dan the Man' was retired in the care of Lord Onslow whom he served well as a hunter before being put out to grass eight years later. In 1994 he was found to be in such a deplorable condition that he was admitted to the Thoroughbred Rehabilitation Centre. There, happily, the 20 year old was restored to fitness and able to live in comfort for more than 12 years, being just 33 when having to be put down in January, 2007. At least his period of neglect was not without benefit. It highlighted the need for greater care of former racehorses and now, for every horse entered in a race, 50p goes to the charity, Retraining of Racehorses, and each trainer and jockey contributes as part of their annual licence renewal.

See also: Richards, Gordon; Doughty, Neale.

HAMEY, 'Tim' James Henry

Grand National winning jockey – at his seventh attempt – when riding seven year old *Forbra*, a 50-1 shot, to victory in 1932. Having escaped a mass pile-up at the 11th fence, Tim Hamey covered the entire second circuit with only one serious rival, amateur Mr Edward Paget on *Egremont*, and he prevailed by three lengths with former winner *Shaun Goilin* a remote third.

Born in Lincolnshire in 1906, James Hamey had been known as 'Tim' ever since he was first apprenticed to a stable which already had a confusing number of lads called Jimmy. He began as a jockey on the Flat, scoring his first win at the age of 16. His proud memories of those early racing years included narrow victories over two giants of the Turf, Steve Donoghue and Charlie Smirke, and riding four winners on one day in Guernsey.

Soon, however, he could no longer make the weight for the Flat. Turning to National Hunt riding, he almost immediately became noted for his skilful handling of headstrong jumpers and raw novice chasers; and in 1926, aged 21, he scored his first major triumph: winning the Cheltenham Gold Cup on Mr Frank Barbour's imposing, front-running bay, *Koko*. A delighted owner promptly booked Hamey to ride his eight year old *Koko* in the Grand National.

Usefully, on the opening day of the Aintree meeting, Tim picked up a spare ride on *Lotus Land*, an outsider in the Stanley Chase. He thus gained an introduction to the big drop fences; and, despite riding part of the race with a broken stirrup iron, he

H

managed to finish runner-up. On his National debut, however, Tim was dumped on the turf by the tearaway *Koko* at Becher's first time round. The following year he was a faller in the National with Lord Grimthorpe's *Lissettt III*, and in 1928, on Sir Keith Fraser's *Ardeen*, he was one of 40 out of 42 riders who failed to complete the course. The latter race was won by *Tipperary Tim*, a 100-1 chance, whom Tim had ridden earlier in the season.

Altogether, Hamey rode in 12 successive Nationals (1926 to 1937). He first completed the course in 1929 when, faced with 65 rivals, he skilfully rode *Grakle*, a most difficult ride, into sixth place. Two years later, when *Grakle* won the National at the fifth attempt, Tim was on board *Solanum*, who was unluckily brought down at Becher's by a riderless horse. The small consolation was a £50 gift from *Grakle's* owner 'for showing him how to get round two years ago', and a handwritten note of similar thanks from the winning jockey Bob Lyall.

The following year Tim was mourning the fact that he had been left without a National ride when, after racing at Newbury, he chanced to meet trainer Tom Rimell in a pub. As a result he was booked to partner *Forbra*. The gelding was the less fancied of Rimell's two runners in the National, but at least, said the trainer, he was 'a horse that cannot fall'. And so it proved, in a National in which only six of 36 starters completed the course.

In the 1933 National Hamey showed that his success on *Forbra* was no fluke by finishing sixth on the gelding, now 16lb higher in the weights. Subsequently, in four more Nationals, he failed to finish. Then, in 1938, one year after his last National ride on *Delaneige*, the race was won by *Battleship*. Tim had been the first jockey to ride the American entire in England in the 1936-37 season, but they had parted company after falling at Wolverhampton.

Early in his career, Tim had moved to the Cheltenham area and was indeed the first 'local boy' to star in the Gold Cup, winning it on his first and only appearance. Now, on retiring from the saddle, he set up as a trainer at Prestbury, so close to the scene of his triumph that, in 1958, his farmland was purchased to allow expansion of the racecourse. He retired from racing in the mid-1970s. Meanwhile the Hamey association with the National had been continued by his son Rex who rode seven times in the race, completing the course only once, with a seventh place on *Clearing* (1955). In 1954 he was brought down on

Hierba, an outsider trained by his father.

In 1985, Tim made a hugely nostalgic return to Aintree where, immediately before the National, Princess Anne was presenting Aynsley fine-bone china trophies to former winning jockeys. He was the oldest recipient to take part in the ceremony; and in his latter years he was also the oldest surviving winner of the Cheltenham Gold Cup. He died five years later, shortly after the running of the 1990 National.

See also: Forbra; Rimell, Tom.

HANDICAPPING

In the beginning all Grand National runners competed off a level weight of 12st. The first horse to be 'handicapped' in the race was the 1839 winner, *Lottery*. On his return to Aintree, in 1840, he had fallen at the Stone Wall. But, in 1841, the Wall had been removed; and now, while all others carried 12st, he was burdened with 13st 4lb under a special ruling that 'the winner of the 1840 Cheltenham Steeplechase will carry an extra 18lb.' Absurdly, *Lottery* went off the 5-2 favourite, and mercifully he was pulled up when nearing total exhaustion on the second circuit. He suffered the same discriminatory penalty with the same result in 1842, thus twice having the biggest weight ever to be carried in the race.

In 1843 the Grand National was made a handicap proper, with 'the top weight to be 12st 8lb and the bottom weight 11st, and any winner from the date of declaration to carry 5lb extra'. A highly experienced handicapper, Edward William ('The Wizard') Topham, was appointed, and he assessed the merits of the 16 runners, giving top weight to *Peter Simple* who had finished third in the two previous years and had scored several recent wins that saw him raised to 13st 1lb. *Peter Simple* finished eighth, one place behind *Lottery* on 12st 6lb. The first six finishers carried 11st 10lb or less. The winner, *Vanguard* under the great Tom Olliver, was raised a full stone when he reappeared, being pulled up, two years later.

Meanwhile the bottom weight was now being progressively reduced – to 10st 7lb in 1844, 10st 2lb in 1845 and 10st in 1846. Subsequently it went into free-fall with *The Pony* on as little as 8st 7lb in 1850 (receiving 51lb from the top weight!), and sinking to an all-time low in 1858 when *Conrad* (remounted) finished fifth on 8st 4lb. The highest weight carried during the 1850s was 12st 2lb.

In 1864, a more reasonable handicap range was introduced: 12st 2lb down to a 10st minimum. But it did not last. The following year, on his reappearance, the 1863 winner *Emblem* carried 12st 4lb; and in 1866 the handicapper – doubtless influenced by the 1865 win of French-bred *Alcibiade* – was so frightened by the reputation of the French star *L'Africaine* that he burdened him with a colossal 13st 2lb. With a weight never equalled since, *L'Africaine* was knocked over at the second fence and did not appear at Aintree again.

Since then, with the exception of the great *Manifesto*, third on 12st 13lb in 1900, no Grand National contender has carried more than 12st 8lb. *Freebooter*, a faller in 1952, was the last to carry the long-time top weight of 12st 7lb, and 12st has not been exceeded since 1956 when *Royal Tan* finished third on 12st 1lb. Over the years, however, the minimum weight continued to fluctuate – 9st 7lb from 1894 to 1921; 10st from 1922 to 1930; and 10st 7lb from 1931 to 1936. Finally, in 1937, it settled on 10st.

Thereafter, until 2005, in all years but one, it was usual to see the lowest rated runners carrying the 10st minimum. The one odd year in this period was 1965 when the handicapping was thrown into disarray by the withdrawal of the great *Mill House*. Such was the unusual shape of the handicap that the stipulated rise in the weights resulted in 36 of 47 starters carrying a bottom weight of 10st 13lb. The race was won by the American-bred *Jay Trump* on 11st 5lb with the top weight *Freddie* (11st 10lb) runner-up by three-quarters of a length.

Today the weights in all handicap races are determined by way of an official list of ratings (0 to 175) for all National Hunt horses that is maintained by the British Horseracing Authority (BHA) which, in 2007, took over from the British Horseracing Board (BHB) as the governing authority of British racing. These ratings are revised weekly to take into account latest performances.

For many years, however, the Grand National has been the one race in which the handicapper is not guided by ratings alone. At his own discretion, he may take into account the 'Aintree factor' – i.e. sometimes choosing to give extra weight to horses that had previously run well over the course. Often this has effectively killed off any chance of a National winner repeating his success in the race. Every year the allotted Grand National weights

are announced in February and no weight is added as a penalty for a horse scoring a subsequent win during the two-month run-up to the big race. Horses allotted less than the mandatory 10st minimum are described as being 'in the long handicap' or 'out of the handicap proper'. But all this can change if, at the five-day or overnight declaration stage, the horse with the minimum top weight allowed is withdrawn. When this happens, the next horse in the pecking order is raised to that top level and all others are raised by the same margin in the weights. Thus it becomes possible that a horse below the 10st mark may be drawn into the handicap proper.

Interestingly, only nine horses have won off the 10st minimum weight in the past 90 years and only four running from 'out of the handicap' in the past 30 years. However, the chances of out-of-the-handicap horses seemingly improved after 1990 when Aintree's most formidable fences were modified. In 1994 *Just So* was runner-up when running from 22lb out of the handicap; and in 1996 *Encore Un Peu* was a close second off a long handicap mark of 9st 5lb, with *Sir Peter Lely* (oh. 12lb) and *Three Brownies* (oh. 22lb) finishing fourth and sixth respectively.

In 1996, most unusually, there had been only 27 runners with 17 of them running from out of the handicap. It strengthened the view of some critics who had suggested that the race, with less demanding fences, had been relegated to being just another staying chase for handicapping purposes. The BHB responded by lowering the minimum rating qualification for entry from 120 to 110 and increasing the burden to be carried by the initial top weight from 11st 10lb to 12st.

Thus, in their efforts to produce a field as close as possible to the safety factor of 40, they made more horses eligible for entry and at the same time sought to attract more class horses running off their true handicap rating. It did not exactly work out. The 1997 entries rose from 82 to 102, but only 21 were in the handicap bracket, headed by *Dublin Flyer* on 12st. At the final declaration stage, following the withdrawal of *Dublin Flyer*, most unusual circumstances prevailed. The weights were now led by *Master Oats*, the 1995 Gold Cup winner, on 11st 10lb. *Nahthen Lad* came next on 10st 9lb and in a 40-strong field no fewer than 31 horses were in the long handicap.

If *Master Oats* was now withdrawn the weights

H

would have had to rise 15lb to achieve the mandatory top weight of 11st 10lb. But he was not and so, significantly, such leading fancies as *Lord Gyllene*, *Antonin*, *Wylde Hide* and *Dextra Dove* – all just 1lb out of the handicap – were left to run on the 10st minimum rather than 11st. *Lord Gyllene* dominated the race from start to finish, beating *Suny Bay* (10st 3lb) by 25 lengths, with third place taken by 100-1 chance *Camelot Knight* who was 22lb out of the handicap proper.

The following year, 1998, there was further ammunition for racing pundits who criticised the National for lack of quality: no fewer than 30 of 37 runners were in the long handicap, the lowest of them being a trio who, on their ratings, were 32lb off the 10st minimum.

In 1999, Mr Philip Smith, a former maths teacher, succeeded long-serving Mr Christopher Mordaunt as the BHB's senior jumps handicapper. That year there were 95 entries, ten less than in 1998, and only 32 starters as opposed to the previous 37. And, most unusually, the winner (*Bobbyjo*) and the runner-up (*Blue Charm*) were running from out of the handicap, by one stone and 16lb respectively.

But things were about to change. Smith had been given three briefs by the BHB in respect of the Grand National: to get more entries, to get more horses in the handicap, and to attract the best horses possible. Over the next few years he made steady progress towards achieving all three aims.

In 2000 he restored the 'Aintree factor', a move that saw *Bobbyjo* allotted 11st 6lb the following season; and remarkably 65 others of the 99 entries were allotted the 10st minimum or more. On the day 33 of the 40-strong field were in the handicap proper, making it the most competitive National for many years.

In 2001 there were 133 entries, including the first 12 finishers of the year before. Smith had encouraged the participation of the best horses by giving none more than 12st, the weight allotted to the former Cheltenham Gold Cup winner *See More Business*, who was 8lb better off than in a normal handicap. Moreover, as a result of his adjustments, 39 entries were in the handicap proper, instead of only a dozen if he had stuck to his official ratings.

But the five top-rated horses were always doubtful runners and, sure enough, they all came out eventually, leaving *Beau* (11st 1lb) at the head of the handicap. Since the stipulated minimum top weight

was 11st 10lb all the runners had to be raised 9lb. As a result, *Smarty* (originally on 9st 5lb) was brought into the handicap proper while 13 of the 40 runners remained in the long handicap. *Smarty* finished runner-up to *Red Marauder* (10st 11lb), the pair being only two of four to finish without being remounted.

In 2002 the handicapper dropped the maximum top weight from 12st to 11st 12lb, so attracting a record 144 entries, including no fewer than twelve Gold Cup horses. An unprecedented number (33) were in the handicap proper and the top nine in the weights were all set to race off marks as much as 7lb lower than they would have elsewhere. But following the withdrawal of *Florida Pearl* the weights were raised 5lb so that no fewer than 31 of the 40 runners were carrying more than the 10st minimum.

By 2003 a further milestone had been reached: an entry of 149 with only four of the 40 starters out of the handicap proper. Smith's three aims had been achieved and truly consolidated. There was quality and quantity, and the race was admirably competitive. This progress continued in 2004 when, as four years before, Smith artfully compressed the top of the handicap to have 66 of 122 entries set to run off their allotted weight. Such was the quality that he had 23 entries at 11st or more as opposed to just six when he first handicapped the race in 1999. His ambition was to have every runner in the handicap proper and this year he again came close with 36 out of 40 starters.

Finally that target was achieved in 2005, following a record entry of 152, and a record 92 in the handicap proper when the weights were framed. To compress the weights Smith had set the initial top weight *Grey Abbey* (rated 166) a mark of only 158, a move that resulted in other entries also being set marginally below their official marks.

On the day, following a 3lb rise in the weights through withdrawals, all 40 starters were running off 10st 5lb or more. To make the race even more competitive he had applied the 'Aintree factor' in assessing a number of horses; and, learning from the experience of recent years, he said he was no longer to be fooled by the successful Irish ploy of having horses 'naff around over hurdles' to gain a more favourable weight.

Thus, over a period of five years, Smith had admirably reshaped the race – most notably raising the quality by luring in top-class chasers with more generous marks than they could expect to receive in other handicap races. However, it remained to be seen whether he had truly got to grips with that 'Irish ploy'. In the 2004-5 season *Hedgehunter* ran in five hurdle races, only making his winning seasonal debut over fences after the National weights had been framed. He then won at Aintree by 14 lengths on 11st 1lb. Similarly, in 2006, the winner *Numbersixvalverde* had been campaigned over hurdles to protect his handicap mark.

Nonetheless, it was now clear that Smith had successfully raised the quality of Grand National fields to an unprecedented level. In 2007, no fewer than 87 of 117 qualified entries were in the handicap proper, a record proportion; and for the third year in succession all 40 runners carried more than the 10st minimum – i.e. were in the handicap proper.
See also: Ratings; Weights; Rules of Entry; Lottery.

HANLON, J

Winning jockey on *Wanderer*, a 25-1 chance, in the substandard 1855 Grand National which had been postponed from the previous week because of severe frost. It was one victory that did not please the winning owner, Mr Dennis. Believing that his bay entire had no hope of lasting out in the boggy conditions, he had plunged heavily on the other Irish runner, six year old *Boundaway*, at 50-1.

Hanlon's success, by two lengths from *Freetrader*, was a triumph for safety-first tactics. Though he was in the lead after the Canal Turn, second time around, he chose to take a pull at his free-running horse, so allowing two challengers, *Freetrader* and *Maurice Daley*, to pass by. Racing flat out, the two leading rivals blundered through the last fence; and as they completely lost their stride *Wanderer* moved smoothly ahead, winning by virtue of his stamina and secure jumping in atrociously heavy conditions.

Hanlon rode in three other Nationals – on rank outsider *The Iron Duke* (1850), *Jumpaway* (1856) and 50-1 chance *Sting* (1857). On all three occasions he failed to finish.
See also: Wanderer.

HARTIGAN, Frank

Trainer of *Shaun Goilin*, the ten year old chestnut gelding who, on his first appearance, won the 1930 Grand National in one of the tightest of all finishes, by a neck and one and a half lengths from *Melleray's Belle* and *Sir Lindsay* respectively. With this success

Irishman Frank Hartigan emulated the achievements of his uncles Garrett and Willie Moore. The former had won the National on his own horse, *The Liberator* (1879), and the latter had trained three National winners: *Why Not* (1894), *The Soarer* (1896) and *Manifesto* (1899).

Formerly an outstanding jockey in his homeland, Hartigan succeeded his uncle Willie as trainer at Weyhill, near Andover in Hampshire. Before his success with *Shaun Goilin* he had twice saddled the National runner-up: *Old Tay Bridge* in 1925 and 1926. A highly versatile trainer, he went on to become one of the first to turn out more than 2,000 winners.
See also: Shaun Goilin.

HARTY, Edward Patrick

Winning rider of *Highland Wedding* in the 1969 Grand National, having been a late booking after the gelding's regular jockey, Owen McNally, had broken his elbow in a fall. One year earlier he had finished tenth on the 100-1 chance, *Steel Bridge*. Now, on his seventh National appearance, he won by 12 lengths from *Steel Bridge*, ridden by Richard Pitman.

Dublin-born (June 10, 1937), Eddie Harty was the son of Captain Cyril Harty, an Irish Army officer who was a successful amateur rider and later the trainer of the 1944 Irish Grand National winner, *Knight's Crest*. After experience in junior show-jumping, he began competing in hurdle races at the age of 14, won numerous point-to-points, and scored his first steeplechase victory at 16.

At the end of his teenage years, restless Eddie went to the United States to find work as a cowboy. Two years later he returned to amateur riding in Ireland and sprang to prominence in 1960 when – after making his Grand National debut on *Knoxtown*, a faller at the first Becher's – he was selected to ride for Ireland in the three-day 'Military' event at the Olympic Games in Rome.

Having turned professional, he made a first fence exit in the 1961 National when he fell on *Floater*, a 50-1 chance trained by Fred Rimell. But thereafter Eddie consistently completed the course: eighth on *Cannobie Lee* (1962), seventh on *April Rose* (1964), sixth on *Solbina* (1967), tenth on *Steel Bridge* (1968). He recalled that his hopes soared especially high in the 1967 race when he saw the great pile-up at the 23rd fence. 'They went down like a pack of

H

cards in front of me and I thought 'I've won the National'. But you can't afford the luxury of excitement. My horse refused and I fell like a kid at a gymkhana.' Then, like so many others, he remounted and set off in vain pursuit of 100-1 *Foinavon*.

Following a victory on *Glenn* in the Welsh Grand National, Harty had his most notable wins in the 1968-69 season. In November, riding *Jupiter Boy* for Rimell, he scored a dramatic short-head success in the Mackeson Gold Cup. On the opening day of the Aintree National meeting, he won the Topham Trophy Chase for the second time on the Toby Balding-trained *Dozo*; and two days later, for the same trainer, he took the winning ride on *Highland Wedding*, who had finished eighth and seventh respectively in the Nationals of the two preceding years.

Eddie appeared in two more Grand Nationals, finishing fourth on *Dozo* in 1970 and being brought down on *Twigairy* at the first fence in 1971. The following year, now in his mid-forties, he became a trainer based at the Curragh. His one National challenger – *Sandpit*, ridden by Tommy Carmody – was a faller in 1979.
See also: Highland Wedding; Balding, Toby; Olympians.

HASTINGS, The Hon. Aubrey

Though he rode a faller (Prince Franz Hatzfeldt's *Dearslayer*) on his Grand National debut in 1905, Aubrey Hastings immediately turned the experience to his own advantage. That day he was impressed by another faller, *Ascetic's Silver*, who went on riderless to complete the course ahead of the winner. Outbidding Lord Coventry, he bought the eight year old chestnut entire for 800 guineas on behalf of his patron, the aforementioned prince; then trained him and, after going on a crash diet, rode him to a ten lengths victory the following year.

Hastings rode *Ascetic's Silver* in two more Nationals. In 1907, under the top weight of 12st 7lb, they finished sixth; and two years later, with no relief from the handicapper, they failed to finish. On the latter occasion he expressed his belief that the 12 year old would have won but for breaking down at the Canal Turn. 'I would ride in the Grand National every day if I could be on the back of a jumper like *Ascetic's Silver*.'

With the prince's support, Hastings established himself as trainer of a large stable at Wroughton near

Swindon in Wiltshire. There, Tom Olliver and Tom Leader had trained the 1874 Derby winner *George Frederick*, and the yard's fame continued as Hastings trained two more Aintree National winners, *Ally Sloper* (1915) and *Master Robert* (1924), plus *Ballymacad*, winner of the 1917 Gatwick wartime substitute, re-named the War National Steeplechase.

In May, 1929, Hastings dropped dead after playing polo. His widow continued to keep the Wroughton stable in operation, and there his former assistant, Ivor Anthony, would train more National winners: *Kellsboro' Jack* (1933) and *Royal Mail* (1937). His son, having later taken the name of his godfather, was the leading Flat trainer Peter Hastings-Bass, master of Kingsclere in Berkshire.
See also: Ascetic's Silver; Ally Sloper; Master Robert; Hatzfeldt, Prince Franz; Balding, Ian.

HATZFELDT, Prince Franz

Though born, on June 15, 1853, into German nobility and married to a wealthy American, Prince Hatzfeldt was a devoted Anglophile who rented a large estate in Wiltshire and launched a determined attack on the Grand National with the assistance of his long-time friend, Aubrey Hastings. Between 1904 and 1910 he had 11 runners in six Nationals.

After twice failing with his *Dearslayer*, a faller in 1904 and 1905, Prince Hatzfeldt had three horses – *Ascetic's Silver*, *Dearslayer* and *Hard To Find* – trained for the 1906 National by Hastings at Wroughton near Swindon. The best of these, the Irish-bred *Ascetic's Silver*, had fallen at the third fence in the 1905 National but had completed the course riderless to finish ahead of the winner *Kirkland*. Now, having been bought by Hastings on the prince's behalf, he was ridden by his trainer to a comfortable ten lengths victory. Meanwhile, *Hard To Find* was a faller, and in his third National *Dearslayer* (pulled up) was desperately unlucky, having been well in contention on the second circuit when a broken saddle-tree resulted in his rider losing his stirrup irons.

Not surprisingly, *Ascetic's Silver* was raised to a massive 12st 7lb for his return to Aintree in 1907. In finishing sixth he was conceding 26lb or more to all of those ahead of him. Two years later he came back as a 12 year old and, given no relief in the weights, failed to finish. The owner's other runner, *Rathvale*, finished 13th.

Prince Hatzfeldt made his last National challenge

232

in 1910 when *Rathvale* was a faller and his seven year old *Carsey* finished fourth. That same year the racing world was shocked by the news of the prince's sudden death from a heart attack while staying at Claridge's Hotel, London. He was aged 57.

In his lifetime, the prince had been an inveterate gambler. But he could never match the good fortune of his wife, Princess Clara. The daughter of an impoverished Sacramento grocer, she had been adopted by the Californian railway magnate Collis Potter Huntingdon who, on his death in 1900, left her $75 million. Like her husband, the princess died in London of a heart attack, in 1928 aged 66.

See also: Hastings, the Hon. Aubrey; Ascetic's Silver.

HAWKE, Nigel John

Winning rider of New Zealand-bred *Seagram* who, after being eight lengths adrift at the last, put in a storming finish to take the 1991 Grand National by five lengths from *Garrison Savannah*, the recent Cheltenham Gold Cup winner. Like *Seagram*, 25 year old Nigel Hawke had succeeded on his first appearance in the race – a remarkable achievement for a jockey only two months out of his claim.

Cornish-born on January 13, 1966, Hawke began his apprenticeship with trainer David Barons, based in Kingsbridge, Devon, and made a promising start with 12 wins in less than six months as a conditional jockey. The following season, 1988-89, he was introduced to *Seagram*, newly purchased by Barons and Sir Eric Parker. Together they made a big impression in 1990 when, after finishing third in the Racing Post Chase, they were beaten only a head by *Bigsun*, under Richard Dunwoody, in Cheltenham's Ritz Club National Hunt Handicap Chase.

The following season *Seagram* was ridden in four races by Roddi Greene but, from January, 1991, Hawke took over for the build-up to Aintree, winning the ASW Handicap Chase over four miles at Cheltenham and returning there to score impressively in the Ritz Club, a victory that resulted in *Seagram* being backed down to 12-1 for the Grand National three weeks later.

Though a newcomer to the National, Hawke gave the 11 year old gelding a masterful ride at Aintree, the only one serious blunder being at the 12th where the jockey did well to remain on board. Ridden patiently throughout the first circuit, *Seagram* then made steady progress, moving up on the leaders at

Valentine's and staying on well to take the lead about 100 yards out. Then it was on to Sandown where, in the jockey's estimation, *Seagram* performed brilliantly to finish a good fourth in the Whitbread Gold Cup. 'He ran a blinder but there were just too many miles on the clock.'

This was to be a striking example of Grand National success not bringing instant stardom for the winning jockey. Nigel's career hardly took off after the Aintree triumph; and one year later, back at Aintree, he had no chance on *Seagram* who was now 12 years old, out of form and weighted with 12lb more. Never going well, the gelding was pulled up before three out.

Both horse and rider were making their second and last National appearance. *Seagram* was retired at the end of the season. Then Nigel's riding career was cruelly ended by a fall at Newton Abbot. Treatment of his head injuries revealed a blood clot on the brain; and, after a long period of recuperation he bravely began in 1995 to make a new career as a trainer. His biggest success came in the virus-hit 1998-99 season, when he saddled the grey *Kendal Cavalier* to win the Welsh National by half a length from *Fiddling The Facts*.

An out-and-out stayer, *Kendal Cavalier* needed heavy ground to have a chance of making Nigel a member of the elite group who have both ridden and trained a Grand National winner. He did not get it in 1999 and, considering the good going, he ran well under Barry Fenton, being nearly brought down at the second Becher's, then staying on to finish seventh.

See also: Seagram.

HEDGEHUNTER

Impressive 14-length winner of the 2005 Grand National when he became the first horse in 17 years to carry 11st or more to victory. He gave jockey Ruby Walsh his second Aintree National win of the new millennium, and was a first for Irish trainer Willie Mullins and for the multi-millionaire owner Trevor Hemmings, who had until then failed with 14 contenders.

Hedgehunter – Irish-bred by *Montelimar* out of *Aberedw* – had originally been purchased by Mullins from dealer Tom Costello following a request from Archie O'Leary, owner of *Florida Pearl*, to find a likely chaser for his friend Niall Quaid, a Limerick man living in Canada. Quaid named the horse, but he subsequently found that he could not travel to Ireland and suggested that the trainer find a new owner. Mullins duly persuaded bloodstock agent David Minton to buy the gelding on behalf of Hemmings.

Early in his career *Hedgehunter* had a long spell of seconditis, registering just one win in 15 runs over hurdles before being tried over fences in the 2002-03 season. He proved a safe jumper best suited by a test of three miles or more and, after his first chase win – making all in heavy going at Punchestown in February, 2003 – his programme was carefully geared to a Grand National debut the following year.

Before going to Aintree he had only won two chases in nine starts. But all of his last three runs had been in major races. He had finished fourth in the Hennessy at Newbury, third (albeit 22 lengths behind *Bindaree*) in the Welsh National at Chepstow, and finally he had scored a runaway win in the Thyestes Chase at Gowran Park. That last performance, in January, 2004, showed him to be a genuine stayer who improved when reverting to front-running tactics.

Given a long break, and again ridden by David Casey, *Hedgehunter* was backed down to 11-1 for his National debut, one point behind four co-favourites. He took the lead at the tenth and held it until approaching the 29th when he was headed by *Clan Royal*. Lying a close-up third coming to the last, he seemed certain of a place. But there, through exhaustion, he fell for the first time in his career; and with *Clan Royal* wandering to the left on the run-in *Amberleigh House* stormed through for a three lengths win.

Following that fall *Hedgehunter*'s training and programme was totally geared to having him ripe for a second Grand National challenge. In February, 2005, when announcing the allotted weights, senior jumps handicapper Phil Smith declared that he was not going to be duped again by the tactic of having horses 'naff around in hurdles in Ireland'. But this hardly showed with *Hedgehunter*. Prior to the framing of the weights, he ran in five hurdle races to protect his handicap mark. Now he was allotted 10st 12lb, no more than he had carried so well the previous year.

Subsequently *Hedgehunter* made his seasonal debut over fences and won the Grade 3 Bobbyjo Chase over an extended three miles at Fairyhouse.

Following withdrawals, the National weights were raised 3lb, but this made no significant difference since all the runners were in the handicap proper. With Walsh taking over from the unluckily injured Casey, *Hedgehunter*, the 7-1 clear favourite, was foot-perfect except for hitting Valentine's.

After the 21st Walsh briefly lost an iron, perhaps costing him half a length or so. But this proved no disadvantage, giving him that much extra space to avoid the trouble at Becher's where his greatest rival, *Clan Royal*, was carried out by a loose horse. That incident left *Hedgehunter* in the lead and he never lost it, heading the field by a couple of lengths at the last and then pulling remorselessly away on the run-in to capture the record £406,000 first prize.

That victory – announced by the Queen at the Windsor Castle reception following the Charles-Camilla royal wedding – was rated by the *Racing Post* jumps handicapper Steve Mason as the best winning performance in the National in the past ten years. Moreover, trainer Mullins forecast that he would be a still stronger chaser next year. One thing was certain: he would never get in with such a sporting weight again.

True enough, he was raised to 11st 10lb for the 2006 National and following the withdrawal of *Monkerhostin* he was sharing top weight of 11st 12lb with last year's runner-up *Royal Auclair*. Yet three weeks before returning to Aintree he had run so brilliantly as runner-up in the Cheltenham Gold Cup that he had become as short as 4-1 favourite – this for a horse seeking to be the first to win successive Nationals since *Red Rum* 31 years before.

As it was, he went off as 5-1 joint favourite with *Clan Royal* and he ran magnificently to be left in the lead when *Ballycassidy* fell at the 25th and thereafter only to be headed at the last. Quite possibly he would have achieved an historic back-to-back double but for overnight rain that had deadened the ground, making his top weight tell against him all the more. In consequence, he was outpaced on the long run-in by *Numbersixvalverde* who had an 18lb advantage and was beaten six lengths, with *Clan Royal* one length and a quarter back in third.

He had proved himself to be a truly great Grand National performer; and after a troubled preparation which saw him compete in just two hurdle races during the 2006-07 season, he returned for a fourth attempt. Lumbered with a top weight of 11st 12lbs, he was never far off the pace but he was hampered at both Becher's and the Canal Turn before getting tired at the second last and fading to finish a nevertheless creditable ninth behind *Silver Birch*. *See also:* Mullins, William; Walsh, Ruby; Hemmings, Trevor.

HEMMINGS, Trevor

Over the years many racehorse owners have been relentless in seeking Grand National glory. In the 21st century none has pursued that aim with greater determination than Trevor Hemmings, the one-time apprentice bricklayer who went on to make a £980 million fortune, his many assets including the Blackpool Tower (bought for £74 million in 1998), the Winter Gardens and a large chunk of the town's Golden Mile. In the process he suffered an astonishing run of cruel misfortune and saw 11 of his 14 National runners fail to complete the course before finally being rewarded with the 14-length triumph of *Hedgehunter* in 2005.

London-born (in 1935) but Lancashire-bred after being a wartime evacuee, Hemmings made his first fortune in building, then moved into the leisure industry, leading a management buyout of Pontins holiday camps in 1987. Sixteen years earlier he had won the contract to build Fred Pontin's latest holiday village at Southport, and it was from that time – his ambition fired by Pontin's 1971 victory with *Specify*, costing a mere £12,000 – that he resolved one day to have a Grand National winner.

Hemmings became a racehorse owner in 1985, starting with *Northern Trust*, a winner on the Flat; and in 1992 he made his first Grand National challenge with the Stan Mellor-trained *Rubika* who finished in 14th place. But it was not until the turn of the century that he launched an all-out bid to win the National. In 2000, the year that he bought the Littlewoods pools business for £161 million, he had two contenders: *The Last Fling*, who finished seventh, and *Esprit De Cotte*, a faller at the 22nd. Then, to strengthen his hand, he bought the brilliant chaser *Young Kenny* who, under top weight, had been a tenth fence faller on his National debut.

Sadly, after winning the 2000 Becher Chase at Aintree and becoming ante-post favourite for the 2001 National, *Young Kenny* had to be put down following an injury in the De Vere Gold Cup at Haydock. Thus, in the 2001 National, Hemmings again had to rely on *The Last Fling* and *Esprit De Cotte*. Both failed to survive the first circuit.

In 2002, at the 11th hour, Hemmings bought the strongly fancied *Beau*, an unlucky loser in the previous National. He now had three runners carrying his colours at Aintree, all without success. *Beau* unseated Carl Llewellyn at the 14th. *Goguenard* fell at the first. *The Last Fling* was a long-time leader, only to fall fatally at the Canal Turn second time around.

Again, in 2003 Hemmings had three National runners. His well-supported *Chives* was pulled up after breaking a blood vessel at the 11th. *Southern Star* was the last of 14 finishers. And, for the second consecutive year, the owner's dream of National success ended in tragedy when *Goguenard* was killed in a freak, mid-air collision at the 19th. His one consolation at the meeting was winning the Martell Cognac Novices' Handicap Chase with *Midland Flame*.

The 68-year-old tycoon, who employed Michael Meagher as his racing manager and had various trainers ('to encourage competition') was still not to be deterred. In 2004 he had five National entries, representing so strong a challenge that in January four of them were quoted at 20-1 or lower in ante-post lists. The following month this classy quartet – *Artic Jack*, *Chives*, *Southern Star* and *Hedgehunter* – were in the handicap proper with the last-named, trained in Ireland by Willie Mullins, looking an especially strong challenger following his impressive winning of the Thyestes Chase at Gowran Park. He became the new ante-post favourite.

On the second day of the Grand National meeting Hemmings won the Mildmay Novices' Chase with *Simply Supreme*. But, alas, it did not mark a change of fortune for the owner in the big one. Three of his horses made it to the line-up. *Artic Jack* fell at the first. *Southern Star* was pulled up before the 18th. Then, in heartbreaking fashion, his strongly fancied *Hedgehunter* – a long-time leader and looking the likely winner two out – came down at the last when lying close-up in third place. It was the first time the eight year old had ever fallen.

Two weeks later Hemmings seemed to be making an equally strong three-handed challenge to win the Scottish National. Again there was huge disappointment. Though his well-fancied *Tipsy Mouse* gained fourth place, *Midland Flame* faded and his long-time favourite *Simply Supreme* fell at the first.

In 2005 he enjoyed a success at the Cheltenham Festival, with *Trabolgan* winning the Royal and SunAlliance Chase, and one month later his

H

Hedgehunter went off as the 7-1 clear favourite in the National. At Aintree, Hemmings watched on a giant TV screen as Ruby Walsh brought home the nine year old in dominating style. During the race, so the cloth-capped tycoon said, he was worried, happy and intense all at the same time. Finally he was over the moon – too euphoric to take an interest in his second runner, 150-1 shot *Europa*, plodding home the last but one of 21 finishers. 'Now,' he declared, 'my life is complete.'

In November, 2005, he took the Hennessy Cognac Gold Cup with *Trabolgan*, hugely impressive under top weight; and by now he had 66 horses in training with 14 different trainers. No fewer than 14 were engaged at the 2006 Grand National meeting; and of them all *Hedgehunter* remained his greatest pride and joy. Only three weeks earlier *Hedgehunter* had run a blinder to finish runner-up in the Cheltenham Gold Cup and now he was equally brilliant in finishing runner-up under top weight in the National. The owner's other runner, *Juveigneur*, fell at the first.

The day ended with Hemmings having a winner (*Pangbourne*) in the concluding bumper and two weeks later he was represented by seven year old *Our Ben* in the Irish Grand National. As at Aintree his runner was trained by Willie Mullins, ridden by Ruby Walsh and burdened with top weight of 11st 12lb; and ironically this time it was drying ground that counted against him and he was pulled up.

In 2007, the year he was made an Honorary Member of the Jockey Club, Hemmings had eight National entries, one less than J.P. McManus, the owner with the most; and he further boosted his chances by purchasing the well-fancied *Idle Talk* and moving him to Donald McCain's yard. Just three made it to the line-up: top-weighted *Hedgehunter* (finished ninth); *Billyvoddan* (pulled up before the 19th; and *Idle Talk* (unseated rider at the 19th). His successes that season included Cheltenham's Grand Annual Chase with *Andreas* and Ascot's BGC Silver Handicap Chase with 25-1 shot *Billyvoddan*.
See also: Hedgehunter.

HENDERSON, Nicky
Three times the leading National Hunt trainer, Nicky Henderson has so far been tantalisingly denied success in the Grand National. In his very first season of training he turned out *Zongalero*, runner-up to *Rubstic* by just one and a half lengths in the 1979

National. Subsequently, in 28 years of trying, he has never bettered that second place despite sending out 23 more challengers, among them *Classified* (1985, fifth, and 1986, third); *The Tsarevich* (1987, five lengths second); and *Brown Windsor* (1990, fourth).

Born in 1950, Henderson was originally expected to pursue a career in the City like his father, John, who, following wartime service as ADC to Field Marshal Lord Montgomery, was a stockbroker, a director of Barclays Bank and a Jockey Club member. But he never took to stockbroking and office life. Instead he was drawn inexorably to a career in racing even though his first ride in the Cheltenham Festival landed him in hospital for a fortnight after falling heavily on *Ballycowan*, a 33-1 outsider in the Kim Muir Chase. As a young amateur, he had 75 winning rides, including *Happy Warrior* in the 1977 Fox Hunters' Chase at Aintree. He had already had several years' experience working as an assistant to the great Fred Winter, and in July, 1978, he took out a training licence.

He quickly proved himself to be a most consistent trainer of top-class jumpers, and in 1985 he broke his Cheltenham Festival duck with a spectacular treble. His many stars from this time on included *See You Then* who scored a hat-trick of victories in the Champion Hurdle (1985-87); *First Bout* (1985), *Alone Success* (1987) and *Katarino* (1999), winners of the Triumph Hurdle; *Remittance Man* (1991 Arkle Chase and the 1992 Queen Mother Champion Chase); *Bacchanal* (the 2000 Stayers' Hurdle); *Marlborough* (the 2001 Tote Gold Trophy Chase); and *Sharpical*, *Geos* and *Landing Light*, all winners of the Tote Gold Trophy Hurdle, in 1998, 2000 and 2001 respectively. In January, 2000, he joined the select band of trainers to have scored 1,000 successes; and by 2002 he had mopped up all the principal Cheltenham prizes bar the Gold Cup, having trained 25 winners in 17 festivals, a record surpassed only by Martin Pipe.

Of all his National contenders none was more unlucky than the courageous *Zongalero*, ridden by Bob Davies who was seeking his second win in a row. After his so narrow defeat it was found that he had finished lame. He returned in 1980 and 1981 under Steve Smith Eccles but both times failed to finish. Subsequently Henderson challenged unsuccessfully with *Sun Lion* (1982, fell) and *Spartan Missile* (1983, unseated rider, and 1984, finished 16th). Then came his strongest bids between 1985 and

1990 with *Classified*, *The Tsarevich* and *Brown Windsor*.

In 1992 Henderson moved his base two miles – from Windsor House in Lambourn to Seven Barrows. It was a highly successful move – though not as far as the Grand National was concerned. That year *Brown Windsor*, the 8-1 second favourite, was up with the leaders when he jumped left under Richard Dunwoody, collided with a rival and fell at the first Becher's. Then, in an extraordinary run of ill-luck, he had four National starters who failed to get beyond the first fence.

In 1993 he saddled *Wont Be Gone Long*, who three years earlier had won the John Hughes Chase over National fences in record time. Now he saw his runner and rider (Richard Dunwoody) become entangled in the starting tape and never start in a farcical race that was declared void. Then came *Henry Mann* (1994), *Tinryland* (1995) and *Pashto* (1998), all fallers at the first, the last mentioned fatally so.

In 1999 the trainer had high hopes for *Fiddling The Facts*, owned by Jersey-based Mrs Bunny Roberts whose grandfather had owned and bred the 1926 Derby winner *Trigo*. The eight year old mare, ridden by Mick Fitzgerald, was backed down to 6-1 favouritism on race day. She was also the most strongly tipped runner, having been placed in many of the leading Grand National trials including the Hennessy Cognac Gold Cup, the Welsh National and the Greenalls. But she was not well suited by the good going and was one of five fallers at the second Becher's.

In 2000 his one runner *Esprit De Cotte* belied his 50-1 odds, travelling well until coming down at the 22nd, Becher's. The following year he fell at the 11th. In 2002 Henderson entered five for the National but only two ran: *Marlborough* and *Goguenard*. The former had been fourth in the Cheltenham Gold Cup and was favoured by the drying ground. But he was carrying the top weight of 11st 12lb, and along with his stablemate he was one of nine fallers at the first fence. Such was Henderson's Aintree hoodoo that he had had only one winner at the Grand National meeting in the past eight years, and he had gone ten years without having a runner complete the National. Yet such was his success elsewhere that he finished the season fifth in the trainers' championship with 93 winners and prize money of £850,544.

That year Henderson's most famous patron, the Queen Mother, died at the age of 101. The Queen decided to honour her mother's love of National Hunt by keeping her best young jumpers in training; and thus, in February, 2003, when the trainer sent out *First Love* to win a novice chase at Folkestone, he had saddled the first horse to win over fences in the Queen's colours.

In 2003 he entered six horses for the National: *Marlborough* (given joint top weight on 11st12lb); *Katarino*, *Heres III*, *Stormyfairweather* and 'out of the handicap' *Ceanannas Mor* and *Cimarrone Cove*. Only *Katarino* (10st 8lb) made it to the line-up, unseating Mick Fitzgerald at the 15th. Yet, as usual, the trainer continued to have major successes elsewhere. In October, he took the Cesarewitch with *Landing Light*, ridden by Pat Eddery who was winning the race for the first time just before his retirement. And the new jumps season saw an absolutely astonishing run of victories, including the Paddy Power Gold Cup with *Fondmort*, the Tripleprint Gold Cup (*Iris Royal*), a fourth Tote Gold Trophy Handicap Hurdle (*Geos*), a first Racing Post Chase (*Marlborough*), and the Vodafone Gold Cup Chase with *Isio*.

But then, as usual, the days of good fortune abruptly ended with the Grand National. None of his five entries – four in the handicap proper – made it to the line-up. The biggest disappointment was the withdrawal of *The Bushkeeper*, most favourably weighted on 10st 3lb. The ten year old, plagued with fragile front legs, had not run since winning at the Cheltenham Festival two years earlier. One week before the National, when the trainer looked to be winning the long battle to get him right, the old weakness returned. As a result, Henderson was left without a National runner for the first time in eight years. He ended the season fifth in the trainers' championship with prize money of £1,197,814 from 79 winners.

In 2005 Henderson increased his tally of Cheltenham Festival winners to 28 with *Trabolgan* (Royal and SunAlliance Novices' Chase), *Juveigneur* (Fulke Walwyn Kim Muir Amateurs Handicap Chase) and *Liberthine* (Mildmay of Flete Handicap Chase). He also came close in the inaugural Daily Telegraph Festival Trophy Chase run over two miles five furlongs. His French-bred *Fondmort* finished such a good second to *Thisthatandtother* that he eventually decided to send him on to the National. 'The old theory with two and a half milers is that you need class and a really good jumper, and he scores on both counts.' Unfortunately, he did not score on staying power; weakening after the second Becher's, he had to be pulled up before the 28th.

The first big win of the 2005-6 season came with *Trabolgan* becoming the first top-weighted horse to take the Hennessy Cognac Gold Cup since 1984. At the Cheltenham Festival, he took second and third place in the William Hill Handicap Chase with *Juveigneur* and *Irish Hussar* respectively. Then came a glorious winning double with Mick Fitzgerald scoring on the long-serving *Fondmort* in the Ryanair Chase and on *Non So* in the Racing Post Plate Handicap Chase.

But the final day brought the most emotional triumph of all: success with 20-1 shot *Greenhope* in the Grand Annual Chase which last year had been named posthumously after Nicky's father, Johnny Henderson, who had done so much to secure the future of Cheltenham racecourse when it was under threat from property developers in 1963. Accompanied by his brother Harry, Nicky received the trophy from his sister Josie and declared: 'You have to believe in fairy-tales now.'

But there was to be no fairy-tale in the National. Two of his five entries made it to the line-up: *Juveigneur*, one of the five fallers at the first, and 100-1 shot *Iris Royal*, pulled up before the 17th. The following season he was the sixth most successful jumps trainer in Britain with 74 winners and near £1million in prize money. At Aintree he won with *Scots Grey* making all in the 27-runner Fox Hunters' Chase. Then, in the 2007 National, his one runner, *Liberthine*, was the best of ten French-bred challengers, finishing fifth under her amateur rider, Sam Waley-Cohen.

HENNESSY COGNAC GOLD CUP
Run over three miles two and a half furlongs at Newbury in November, the Hennessy is a highly prestigious handicap test of staying chasers that can be a useful guide to Grand National prospects, though not so much in respect of the winner. After winning the 1962 Hennessy, *Springbok* finished fifth as the 10-1 favourite in the National. *Spanish Steps*, the 1969 winner, was a latecomer to the National, finishing fourth in 1973 and 1974 and third in 1975.

In more recent years two Hennessy winners have come close to winning the National. *Suny Bay* won at Newbury in 1997 after being runner-up in the Na-

tional and was second again at Aintree the following year. And in 2002, another grey, *What's Up Boys*, made a most gallant bid to achieve the Hennessy-National double, going down by only one and three-quarter lengths to *Bindaree*, fifth in the Hennessy and now with a 16lb advantage in the weights.

Horses placed in the Hennessy have been more successful. *Red Rum* was a short-head runner-up in the race before scoring his second National win in 1974; *Aldaniti* was third in the 1977 race, four years before winning at Aintree; *Mr Frisk* third at Newbury before winning the 1990 National. *Party Politics* was a good second ahead of *Docklands Express* in the Hennessy before his Aintree success in 1992, with *Docklands Express*, the favourite, finishing fourth; and *Rough Quest* was second before going on to win the 1996 National in which *Superior Finish* (third in the Hennessy) was third again.

Red Marauder, like *Bindaree*, had been fifth at Newbury before his National victory in 2001. Most unlucky was *Freddie*, second in the 1965 Hennessy to the mighty *Arkle*. He had been beaten by only three-quarters of a length in the 1965 National and in 1966 he was runner-up at Aintree again.

Staged at Newbury since 1960, the Hennessy was originally held at Cheltenham under the sponsorship of the celebrated family of brandy fame. Appropriately the first race in 1957 was won by Madame Kilian Hennessy's *Mandarin*; and it was a member of the same family, M. James Hennessy, who was the French owner of the last five year old to win the Grand National: *Lutteur III* in 1909.

HIGHLAND WEDDING
It was third time lucky for *Highland Wedding* when the 12 year old gelding won the 1969 Grand National after finishing eighth and seventh on his previous appearances. And especially lucky for former Olympic rider Eddie Harty who gained his seventh National ride when *Highland Wedding*'s regular jockey, Owen McNally, suffered a fractured elbow.

Bred by Mr John Caldwell at Prestwick, Ayrshire, *Highland Wedding* was a brown gelding by *Question* out of *Princess*, and owned in partnership by U.S. sportsman Thomas McKoy Jr. and Canadian Charles Burns. In the 1966 and 1967 Nationals he ran in the Burns colours of white with a green maple leaf, but his one victory was achieved in the American's colours.

Although trainer Toby Balding has had countless

big-race triumphs, he was most proud of *Highland Wedding*'s Aintree success – 'because he was a total product of the system'. He had first seen him in action on television and had subsequently bought him for a client from the point-to-point field of his great friend and near-neighbour Peter Calver who had ridden him putting up a stone overweight. Recognising his promise, he conspired to see that he only raced when the new amateur owner was not available to take the ride.

Sold on to the North Americans, *Highland Wedding* first advertised his Aintree prospects in February, 1966, when, under McNally, he romped away with the Eider Chase at Newcastle by 20 lengths. As a result he was made third favourite for the 47-runner National, and he was in strong contention at the second Becher's. But thereafter he was well outpaced, and he fared no better when he returned in 1968 with an extra stone on his back.

At that time it seemed that his best chance in the National had gone. But the following season, despite his age, *Highland Wedding* went off as the 100-9 third favourite. In a relatively small field of 30, he was well supported with good reason. He had proven form over the course, came to Aintree on the back of three successive wins, and represented an in-form Toby Balding stable which had just won the Topham Trophy with the Harty-ridden *Dozo*. Moreover, though his stamina had been endorsed by a third success in the four-mile Eider Chase at Newcastle, he was now running in the National on a 10lb lower weight.

Patiently ridden over the first circuit, *Highland Wedding* drew level with the leaders at the second Becher's. At that point the course commentator mistook him for a faller but, in fact, he was foot-perfect and was never threatened after hitting the front at the Canal Turn. He led over the last, then steadily drew further ahead to win by 12 lengths from *Steel Bridge*. Subsequently he was sent into retirement in Canada.

See also: Harty, Edward; Balding, Gerald 'Toby'.

HOBBS, Bruce Robertson

Superlatives abound in the action-packed life of Bruce Hobbs who, in 1938, at the age of 17, became the youngest-ever winning rider in the Grand National, on one of the smallest of horses (*Battleship*, 15.2 hands) and by the narrowest of margins (a head from *Royal Danieli*). He also had one of the shortest

professional riding careers, beginning on his 16th birthday, December 27, 1936, and ending on September 3, 1939 when – immediately following the declaration of war – he was signed on for the British Army.

Bruce was born to ride. He began life in the United States where his father, Reg Hobbs, was Master of the Horse to American millionaire F. Ambrose Clark, grandson of the founder of Singer Manufacturing. He was two years old when his family moved back to England in 1922, initially so that Reg could look after Mr Clark's hunters at Melton Mowbray, Leicestershire. Thereafter he grew up in an environment dominated by equestrianism – winning Pony Club prizes, riding regularly with the hunt from the age of nine, appearing in his first hurdle race at 14, and one year later winning his first race, over hurdles at Wolverhampton.

By this time, his father had taken out a trainer's licence and had moved to Lambourn, where he primarily represented Mr Clark and his wife Florence who had won the 1933 National with her *Kellsboro' Jack*. Through the Clarks, Reg had also acquired other American owners including, most notably, millionairess Mrs Marion Du Pont Scott, wife of film star Randolph Scott.

In 1937, as a 16 year old professional, Bruce had his first ride in the National – on Mrs Ambrose Clark's blinkered, seven year old *Flying Minutes*, a 66-1 chance. They went well, leading at the first fence of the second circuit but finally being separated four from home. That same year the combination was beaten only by a short head in the Sefton Chase over the National course.

One year later, as a much more experienced rider and now a towering six-footer, Bruce aimed to make another National bid on *Flying Minutes*. But the gelding broke down shortly before the race. In the end, Bruce was left with the choice of two horses in his father's yard: *Bagatelle* and *Battleship*, a diminutive entire owned by Mrs Scott. He opted for *Battleship* on whom he had won two races that season – a decision made simply because that choice offered him the larger riding fee.

For all his successes in the States, and some promising runs in England (he had been beaten by only three-quarters of a length and a head in the National Hunt Chase at the Cheltenham Festival, when a broken nose suffered in the Champion Hurdle had prevented Bruce taking the ride)

H

Battleship – dubbed 'the American pony' – was generally regarded as too small to cope with Aintree's daunting fences. Even his trainer took that view. He went off at 40-1.

Wisely, Reg Hobbs had the reins lengthened so that his son could slip them further at the big drop fences. Even then *Battleship* was to finish with a blooded nose through frequent contact with the ground. For the most part, however, he jumped the big fences magnificently; and in his horsemanship that day Bruce showed remarkable maturity for his years.

In fact, *Battleship* jumped almost too well. Having approached the plain fence after Becher's at the wrong angle, he took it perfectly, then had to switch direction to line up for the Canal Turn. The switch was so sudden that Bruce was caught off balance and he started to slide off. At that precise moment, Fred Rimell, riding alongside on *Provocative*, leaned over to push his rival back into the plate.

The only big jumping error came at the third last where, on landing, Bruce required all his skills to remain in the saddle. Four or five lengths were lost; yet, ironically, so the jockey believed, that blunder helped *Battleship* to win the race. 'He had to come from behind as he was running too freely at that stage. If he had gone clear he'd have given up, thinking his task was done, but the mistake stopped him in his tracks.'

Bruce gave his mount time to recover. Then they passed the tiring *Workman* and, by the last fence, came within two to three lengths of the leader, *Royal Danieli*.

The gap rapidly closed; thereafter, on the long run-in, it was impossible to separate the two leaders as they matched stride for stride, on opposite sides of the course. Spectators were none the wiser at the finish, and only after a long delay was the judges' verdict announced: victory for *Battleship* by a head.

Two weeks later Bruce won the Welsh Grand National on *Timber Wolf*, and he ended the season with 35 winners. But he never rode in the Aintree National again. He went to the United States where – by scoring in Long Island's Cedarhurst version of the National – he became the first jockey ever to win three Grand Nationals in one year. Then, late in 1938, he severely damaged his spine in a selling hurdle race at Cheltenham. Paralysed down the left side of his body, he was told that he would never ride again.

Defying medical opinion, Bruce returned to the saddle six months later, and in April, 1939, rode *Poor Duke*, the first winner trained by Fulke Walwyn. But again his career was immediately cut short – this time by the outbreak of war. He joined up on the first day.

To remain with horses, Hobbs chose to join the North Somerset Yeomanry; and in April, 1940, when the Grand National was being run, he had already left to serve in Palestine. He was then commissioned into the Queen's Own Yorkshire Dragoons; and in May, 1943, he so distinguished himself in action against a strongly defended German position near Tunis that he was awarded the Military Cross.

After demob, Bruce fought a losing battle to waste down from 14st 7lb to a race-riding weight. Subsequently he embarked on a long, often unrewarding, career as a trainer. He had his first major success at Aintree – winning the 1946 Grand Sefton Chase with *War Risk* who, two years later, was to finish 11th in the Grand National. Later, after a period of much hardship, he turned to work with Flat-racers at Newmarket.

For years Bruce did valuable service as stable lieutenant to the Queen's trainer Captain Cecil Boyd-Rochfort. He hoped eventually to succeed his boss on retirement, but the old Captain soldiered on so long that, in 1960, he briefly quit racing to become a travelling salesman for Gibson's, the Newmarket saddlers. It was not long, however, before he was back in racing, now working as assistant to Major Jack Clayton at Newmarket. Finally, in 1964, he had sufficient backing to strike out on his own as trainer with much deserved success.

During 20 years based at the Palace House stable in Newmarket, he had many major winners on the Flat – among them *Tyrnavos*, the 1980 Irish Derby winner; *Tromos* (Dewhurst Stakes); *Tachypous* (Middle Park Stakes); *Stilvi* (Duke of York Stakes and King George Stakes); *Tolmi* (Coronation Stakes); *Cry of Truth* (Cheveley Park Stakes); and *Jacinth* (the Cheveley and the Coronation Stakes). Eleven times he had horses placed in English classics; and in 1977 he landed his first across-the-card four-timer. Other successes came in the Nassau Stakes (three times), the Stewards' Cup, the Magnet Cup, the Northumberland Plate and the Gimcrack Stakes.

Though he retired in 1985, he continued to be very actively involved with racing – as a director of

the National Stud and as a member of the Jockey Club serving on the disciplinary committee. He died, aged 84, in 2005.
See also: Battleship; Hobbs, Reginald

HOBBS, Reginald
Descended from a long line of Leicestershire hunting folk, trainer Reg Hobbs established a large yard at Melton Mowbray in the early 1920s with the backing of the American sewing-machine millionaire F. Ambrose Clark whose major ambition was to own a Grand National winner. Ironically, it was another trainer (Ivor Anthony) who helped Mr Clark to realise that dream with the success, in his wife's name, of *Kellsboro' Jack* in 1933. But five years later Hobbs, now based at Upper Lambourn, turned out the National winner (*Battleship*) on behalf of another American, Mrs Marion Du Pont Scott, wife of the movie star Randolph Scott.

It was in 1936 that Mrs Scott sent over *Battleship*, winner of the 1934 American Grand National, to be prepared for the Aintree challenge. Hobbs eventually persuaded her not to run the diminutive chestnut in the 1937 National. He argued that the stallion was too small to cope with the huge Aintree fences, pointing out that 'the horse could not even see over The Chair, let alone Becher's'. He held the same view in 1938 but this time was over-ruled by the owner.

At the Adelphi Hotel, on the eve of the National, Reg remarked that *Battleship*'s chances were so slim that he could not bring himself to have even a small bet on the horse. 'That's ridiculous,' retorted London bookmaker Percy Thompson. 'I'll lay you 66-1. You must have £1,000 to £15, just in case you have to buy champagne.' Reg half-heartedly accepted the generous odds. *Battleship* won at 40-1.

It was a doubly great training feat by Reg. He had not only prepared *Battleship* well, but he had also played a major part in developing the fine horsemanship of his son Bruce, at 17 the youngest ever rider of a Grand National winner. In all, Hobbs Snr won six races with *Battleship* and he went on to become the National Hunt champion trainer in 1941 and 1942. In the latter year, before racing finally surrendered to the Second World War, he scored one more major triumph: winning the Cheltenham Gold Cup with Lord Sefton's French-bred *Medoc*.
See also: Hobbs, Bruce; Battleship.

HOBSON, Frederick
The expression 'Hobson's choice' was given new meaning by this extraordinary Old Etonian who became a winning rider and owner on his one and only appearance in the Grand National. His bizarre choice, when taking his horse over a fence, was to lean back and grip with one hand the rear of his saddle. He based the technique on his theory that, by putting his weight as far back as possible, he was lessening the strain on the horse's shoulders.

Now there was no doubting Freddy Hobson's horsemanship. In 1867 the man popularly known as 'The Squire' had topped the table of amateur riders, ahead of the great George Ede and his lifelong friend Arthur Yates. He was also a noted horse owner, most famously having won major Flat races with his *Hampton,* who went on to sire three Derby winners. But when, in 1877, he mooted the possibility of riding his own horse, *Austerlitz*, over the daunting National fences, friends told him that – in view of his racing style – it was madness.

The preferred choice of stable connections was professional jockey Robert I'Anson. He had been responsible for schooling *Austerlitz* and he had ridden in seven Nationals, finishing fourth on *Surney* (1870), second on *Scarrington* (1872) and third on *Shifnal* (1876). But Yates, who had the experience of three National rides, thought otherwise. He strongly urged his friend to go ahead. And so Hobson took the plunge, making his debut on a five year old chestnut entire, priced at 15-1, while I'Anson stayed with *Shifnal*, the 100-15 favourite.

Right from the off, *Austerlitz* forged to the front, and at each fence the spectators watched in wonder as the horse sailed over with a rider holding the reins one handed and leaning back like some cowboy on a bucking bronco. Sooner or later it seemed he must fall. But the technique worked remarkably well. Briefly *Austerlitz* lost the lead only to regain it late on the first circuit. He cleared the Water with a spectacular leap and thereafter held off all challengers until, at the penultimate fence, he was caught and then passed by *The Liberator* under the expert handling of 'Mr Thomas', riding in his 17th and last National.

Austerlitz, however, had the more in reserve. With another clean jump at the last he powered ahead to win by four lengths from the fast-finishing *Congress*, who was giving him almost two stone. *The Liberator*, just a neck behind, was third; and

H

Shifnal, who would win next year with a different owner and jockey, was a well-beaten sixth. Hobson had won the National on his first and final attempt.

Hobson's life was curiously bound up with his friend Yates. They often raced against one another; and, albeit separately, in 1869 they had both unsuccessfully entered their first runner in the National. Subsequently, Hobson married the granddaughter of John Gully, the celebrated prizefighter, racehorse owner and Member of Parliament. Ten years later, following a divorce, the ex-Mrs Hobson married no other than Arthur Yates.
See also: Austerlitz; Yates, Arthur.

HOLMAN, George
The second of six sons of William Holman, trainer of Grand National winners *Freetrader* (1856), *Little Charley* (1858) and *Anatis* (1860), George became a professional rider after making a fourth-placed National debut on his own *Fosco*, a 40-1 outsider, in 1863. Altogether he would ride in 11 Nationals and it was his great misfortune that, on his best hope, he came up against an outstanding horse that had won the previous year and a rider who already had a record four victories.

The year was 1870 and Holman on *The Doctor*, a 5-1 second favourite, was opposed by George Stevens on *The Colonel*, a seven year old who had been raised 19lb for his 1869 win. In a pulsating finish, arguably the best ever seen at Aintree, they battled side by side all the way to the line where *The Colonel* prevailed by a neck.

Holman had many successes elsewhere, most notably at Cheltenham where, like his father, he rode five winners of the Grand Annual. But, apart from *The Doctor*, he had only one outstanding mount in the National: the awesome jumper *L'Africaine* in 1866. Unfortunately, the French chaser arrived with such a huge reputation that he was burdened with a staggering 13st 2lb, a weight never equalled since. Unluckily, too, he was badly knocked about in a collision at the second fence and was eventually pulled up.

George's other National rides included a fourth place on *Globule* (1867) and on *Master Mowbray* (1873). Three times, in 1864, 1867 and 1869, he competed alongside his younger brother John who never completed the course. In 1872, when he finished sixth on *Master Mowbray*, he had another younger brother, Alfred, one place behind on

Ouragan II. In 1874 Alfred took over on *Master Mowbray* and finished fifth at 50-1. Two years later George came back for one last ride on *Master Mowbray* and was the last of seven finishers.

HOLMAN, William
Based at Cleeve Hill, overlooking Cheltenham racecourse, William Holman headed one of the most prominent families in mid-19th century racing. Three of his six sons rode in the Grand National while he himself had twice finished in a place on *Sir Peter Laurie* – third in 1852 and fourth in 1853. But it was as a trainer that he most greatly excelled, being the first in National history to saddle three winners: *Freetrader* (1856), *Little Charley* (1858) and *Anatis* (1860).

Throughout his career Holman worked almost exclusively with local associates. Mr W. Barnett, owner of *Sir Peter Laurie* and *Freetrader*, was a Cheltenham man – as was Mr Christopher Capel, the owner of *Little Charley* and *Anatis*. Furthermore, all Holman's National winners were ridden by local jockeys: George Stevens, William Archer and Tommy ('Mr Thomas') Pickernell.

It was not entirely coincidence that Stevens and Pickernell developed into giants of steeplechasing, the former scoring a record five Grand National wins. Both benefited from tutelage under Holman, an outstanding horseman who five times rode the winner of Cheltenham's Grand Annual. His fourth son, Alfred, also became a trainer, and later manager of Cheltenham racecourse; and in 1955 the family tradition was briefly revived when William's great-grandson, Lt. Col, W.R. Holman, finished eighth on rank outsider *Wild Wisdom* in the National.
See also: Freetrader; Little Charley, Anatis; Archer, William; Capel, Christopher.

HUDSON, Frank
By way of the 1957 triumph of *Sundew*, ex-jockey Frank Hudson became one of the most unusual trainers of a Grand National winner. Unusual because *Sundew* – a giant 11 year old chestnut who had suffered crashing falls on his two previous appearances in the race – was the only chaser in Hudson's small yard at Henley-in-Arden, Warwickshire.

It was a success that owed much to the brilliant riding of Fred Winter who that season won the third of his four jockeys' championships. But a key factor, too, was *Sundew*'s super fitness. As the only jumper in Hudson's 11-horse care, he had the benefit of exclusive attention, developing exceptional power and strength that showed especially in 1955 when he was runner-up in the Welsh Grand National and won the National Trial at Haydock.

Taking an early lead in the 1957 National, *Sundew* made a number of errors but each time his sheer strength powered him through rather than over fences. Never headed after the fourth fence, he stayed on to win by eight lengths from the seven year old *Wyndburgh* who was a stone better off in the weights. Two days later Hudson joined in a victory parade through the streets of Henley-in-Arden. It was the highlight of his training career. *Sundew* never won again and eight months later suffered a fatal fall in a pile-up at Haydock's Water Jump. *See also:* Sundew; Winter, Frederick Thomas.

HUMOUR

Humour – unlike courage, triumph and tragedy – is not a word that readily springs to mind in relation to the Grand National. Nonetheless, the world's toughest steeplechase has not been without its light-hearted moments, such has been the mischievous nature of a good many riders, including champion jump jockeys John Francome and Terry Biddlecombe.

The latter regarded Dave Dick, the 1956 winning rider on *E.S.B.*, as 'the funniest man in racing'. An exuberant playboy in his youth, Dick was once moving up to the start of a Grand National when he spotted a man with a banner that proclaimed: 'Repent or your sins will find you out.' He grinned at his nearest rival and quipped. 'If that's the case, I won't get as far as the first.'

But it is Francome's great friend and fellow prankster, Steve Smith Eccles, who has provided the most light relief in Grand National history. Even when making his 1980 debut in the race Steve acted in typically cavalier style. His mount, *Zongalero*, was the 11-1 third favourite, jointly with *Rough and Tumble*, ridden by Francome. Unfortunately, the bay gelding, raised 8lb since finishing runner-up the previous year, now knew what to expect and was a most reluctant jumper.

On the second circuit, Smith Eccles found himself at the back of the field, alongside Tommy McGivern on *Drumroan*. McGivern began telling him a joke, but then fell before he could finish it. The jockey was just getting up when Steve suddenly reappeared at his side. *Zongalero* had refused at the 20th and so the

clown prince of steeplechasing had ridden back to hear the punchline to McGivern's joke.

Most famously, the story is told of Smith Eccles's misadventure in 1986 when he had his best chance of National success, riding Nicky Henderson's *Classified*. The trouble began on the first day of the Aintree meeting when Steve was highly disappointed to be beaten on *River Ceiriog*, the horse he had ridden to a 15-length victory at 40-1 in the Supreme Novices' Hurdle at Cheltenham. He now sought consolation in the whisky bottle; and he was still in a dark mood when he arrived at the Royal Clifton Hotel, Southport, where he was staying with his long-time partner, Di Haine. A domestic row ensued with the consequence that the jockey stomped off to go out drinking with some mates. Afterwards, being *persona non grata*, he opted to sleep off the booze in the back of his street-parked Mercedes.

It was a disturbed night. Steve woke up to find himself being driven he knew not where by a teenage thief-cum-joyrider. The thief, even more shocked than his passenger, promptly jammed on the brakes, leaped out and ran off into the dark. Steve duly drove back to his hotel and resumed his sleep on the back seat, this time without leaving his car keys in the ignition.

Inevitably, next day, this natural comedian could not resist telling the story to friends at Aintree. In turn, the story came to the attention of the BBC TV team and on Grand National morning his 'kidnapping' was reported in national newspapers. The details of his late-night boozing were scarcely designed to inspire confidence in a jockey preparing for the most physically demanding of chases. Fortunately the jockey did much to redeem himself by his skillful riding. *Classified*, who had finished fifth under John White the previous year, jumped smoothly throughout and was leading after the second Becher's before being well outpaced by *West Tip* and *Young Driver*. Third place at 22-1 was no disgrace.

By 1999, Nicky Henderson had been trying to win the National for 21 years but had never come closer than his second place with *Zongalero* in his first season of training. This year, however, he seemingly had an outstanding chance with the mare *Fiddling The Facts* who was to be backed down to 6-1 favouritism.

But one week before the National the trainer received a most distressing fax on Aintree-headed

H

paper. It informed him that regrettably mares were to be banned from the National because they distracted geldings. Momentarily stunned, he then remembered the date. It was April Fools' Day. The hoaxer was not identified. *Fiddling The Facts* ran as planned but unfortunately was one of five fallers brought down in a melee at the second Becher's. Similarly, on another April 1, authorities were briefly fooled when ex-jockey Ron Barry, as the northern inspector of courses, reported to his Jockey Club bosses that the National start would have to be moved because of holes dug by badgers.

Another April Fools' hoax had taken place in 1991 when *Sporting Life* ran a lead article announcing that Tracey Bailey, wife of trainer Kim, was to take over the ride on *Mr Frisk*. Another trainer, John Webber, was so outraged by the 'jocking off' of the winning rider of the year before, Marcus Armytage, that he offered the amateur the ride on his runner, *Auntie Dot*. To this day it was always one of the jockey's regrets that he did not take up the offer. In unfavourable soft conditions he pulled *Mr Frisk* up while, under Mark Dwyer, *Auntie Dot* was a gallant third behind *Seagram*.

Such is the toughness of jump jockeys that they can even find humour in a moment of excruciating pain. Thus, Mick Fitzgerald, who won the National on *Rough Quest* in 1996, has chosen as his funniest sporting memory the time he fell at the first fence on *Tinryland*, a 50-1 shot, in the 1995 National. On landing, the horse stood on his rider's private parts and, lying on the floor in agony, the jockey started to panic in fear of internal damage.

But, as Fitzgerald recalled, he still saw the funny side when he suddenly found himself being attended by a St John's Ambulance man who was dressed in drag – 'stockings, a dress, lipstick, the whole Monty. Why he was dressed in women's clothes, I still do not know. When I finally reached the ambulance, I could not help laughing.'

HUNTSMAN

In terms of consistency, the entire *Huntsman* rates as one of the greatest of all Grand National runners. He appeared at Aintree only three times – each time under different ownership – and he came home third (by only a short neck and one length) in 1859; second (by just half a length) in 1860; and first (by a clear four lengths) in 1862.

Originally trained and owned by Ben Land Snr,

and ridden by his son, the six year old *Huntsman* came with a late rattle to finish a close third on his National debut. Though he continued as trainer, Land now bowed to financial pressures and reluctantly sold the entire to Captain George Warwick Hunt, a cavalry officer renowned for his good fortune. (It is recorded that, as a result of a late regimental transfer, Hunt missed sailing in 1852 on the ill-fated troopship *Birkenhead* which foundered off the coast of Africa with the loss of 446 lives in shark-infested waters. And two years later he had survived in the Charge of the Light Brigade at Balaclava.)

Captain Hunt was an accomplished horseman who often rode in races in Paris and Baden Baden. However, for his 1860 National bid, he chose to have *Huntsman* ridden by his friend Captain Thomas Manners Townley, now retired following service with the 10th Hussars in the Crimea. The plan was that *Huntsman* – raised 6lb and going off as a 33-1 outsider – should run as a pacemaker for his more fancied stablemate *Goldsmith*. But, as it happened, he was never required to fulfil that role since Land Jnr on *Goldsmith* irrationally chose to take an early lead which he held beyond Becher's before fading and failing to finish.

For once the owner's famous luck deserted him. *Huntsman* made relentless progress, moving into a challenging position on the second circuit. Unfortunately, and crucially, his rider lost both irons at the second Becher's, and then one iron when clumsily clearing the last. Thereafter, though his mount was to be beaten only half a length by the mare *Anatis*, Townley knew full well that he was losing the run-in duel – hence his shouting in vain of an offer of £1,000 for rival jockey Tommy ('Mr Thomas') Pickernell to give him the race.

Huntsman was now sold to the French nobleman Viscount de Namur and transferred to France to be trained and ridden by Yorkshire-born Harry Lamplugh, who had been on runner-up *Jean Du Quesne* in that so close 1859 finish. Curiously, after two narrow defeats, he was dropped 8lb in the weights for the 1862 National. Backers knew a good thing when they saw one. They made him a hot 3-1 favourite in a field of only 13 runners, and he duly obliged by a comfortable four lengths. He represented the first French success in the race. However, his victorious swansong met with little rejoicing, the occasion being grimly overshadowed

by the terrible fall – soon to prove fatal – of Irish jockey James Wynne.
See also: Lamplugh, Harry; Land, Ben Snr; Land Ben, Jnr; Townley, Captain Thomas Manners.

HYDE, Timothy

Born in 1908, and initially best known for his successes in the show-jumping ring, Irishman Timmy Hyde came relatively late to the Grand National, making his debut on seven year old *Cabin Fire*, a faller in 1938. But one year later he joined the National Hall of Fame, scoring an all-Irish three lengths victory on *Workman*, and but for the intervention of the Second World War it is odds-on that he would have triumphed at least once more as the regular partner of superstar *Prince Regent*.

Hyde sprang to racing prominence in 1938 when he won the Irish Grand National on *Clare County*. Ex-jockey Jack Ruttle, a trainer at Celbridge, Co. Dublin, persuaded him to turn professional, and he picked him out as the jockey best suited to take over the ride on Sir Alexander Maguire's *Workman*, the Irish gelding who had finished a bad third in the 1938 National.

It was an inspired choice. Timing his challenge to perfection, Hyde took his mount into the lead after Valentine's second time around, survived a last fence collision with *Black Hawk*, and held on to win by three lengths from the Scottish hope *MacMoffat* with Dorothy Paget's favourite *Kilstar* 15 lengths further back in third place. Backed by most everyone in the owner's hometown of Navan, Co. Meath, *Workman* was the first Irish winner of the race since *Troytown* in 1920.

In 1940, in the only Grand National held during the Second World War, Hyde had to pull up on Sir Alexander's *Sterling Duke*. When he returned to Aintree six years later it was to ride the hot 3-1 favourite, Mr J.V. Rank's *Prince Regent*, on whom he had recently triumphed in the Cheltenham Gold Cup. But it was all too late.

During the war *Prince Regent* had been a dominant force in Irish racing. His first major success had come in 1942 when Timmy rode him in the Irish Grand National, carrying 12st 7lb and winning by a length from Dorothy Paget's *Golden Jack*, who was receiving nearly a stone in weight. Altogether, Hyde was to ride him in 28 consecutive races, winning 12 times and, under a huge weight, twice finishing runner-up in the Irish Grand National. But in 1946, when *Prince Regent* finally made his long delayed debut at Aintree, he was 11 years old and lumbered with 12st 5lb, conceding more than two stone to 25 of his 33 rivals.

Unaided by heavy going and unfamiliar with Aintree's big drop fences, *Prince Regent* had some difficulty in jumping at first. In the circumstances Hyde did brilliantly to keep him up with the pace and then to take the lead after clearing Valentine's for the second time. But thereafter he was constantly harassed by loose horses, and, though still leading at the last, he now had nothing left and was overhauled on the run-in by 100-1 chance *Lovely Cottage* and 100-1 chance *Jack Finlay* to whom he was giving 25lb and 31lb, respectively. As winning jockey Capt. Bobby Petre would say afterwards: 'Tim Hyde was so hampered by those loose horses, he had to ride about three finishes in the last half-mile.'

Hyde rode in two more Nationals, each time on a *Prince Regent* severely handicapped despite his advancing years. In 1947, when the 12 year old was 8-1 favourite, he was carrying the maximum 12st 7lb, conceding 19lb to his nearest rival and giving two stone-plus to 45 runners in the record 57-strong National field. In appalling conditions, Hyde brought the gallant old chaser home in fourth place – behind a 100-1 winner, *Caughoo*, who had a two and half stone advantage in the weights. Incredibly, in 1948, 13 year old *Prince Regent* was still on top weight, and in this, his last National, Timmy could do nothing to prevent his horse being carried out by a loose horse at the fence after the second Becher's.

Cruelly, Tim's luck changed only for the worse. In 1951 a fall left him paralysed and permanently confined to a wheelchair. Doggedly he fought back and, assisted by son Tim (later a renowned bloodstock agent) he went on to train horses at his home in Cashel, County Tipperary. He died in 1967.
See also: Workman; Prince Regent.

I

ILEX

The Aintree bookmakers took one of their severest hammerings in 1890 when six year old *Ilex* won the Grand National at his first attempt. Owner Mr George Masterman, well-known as a serious betting man, had publicly declared that his entry, having been allotted a mere 10st 5lb, was a nailed-on certainty barring interference in the running. The punters got the message. Despite his modest credentials and bulky build, *Ilex* went off the 4-1 clear favourite and duly romped home by a comfortable twelve lengths.

Ilex – a chestnut gelding by *Rostrevor* out of *Vatonia* – had made his racing debut as a four year old, finishing last in a hunters' chase at Plumpton. Two years later, when entered for the National, he had only one success to his name: victory in a mere two-mile selling hunters' chase at Leicester after which he was bought in for 250 guineas. Significantly, however, in the meantime he had changed hands and had been sent to Epsom-based trainer John Nightingall.

Mr Masterman had bought *Ilex* on the recommendation of jockey Arthur Nightingall. Now, under the jockey's father, the gelding rapidly progressed, showing his real potential in December, 1889, when finishing runner-up in the Great Sandown Chase. Subsequently, on declaration of the National weights, the confident owner plunged in with heavy bets.

Ostensibly it was a dangerous gamble. There were only 16 runners but unusually they included the first three finishers in the previous year's National: *Frigate*, *Why Not* and *M.P. Frigate* had won after three times being runner-up in the race. And there was another past winner in the field: old *Voluptuary* who had been bred by Queen Victoria at Hampton Court. *Ilex*, however, was receiving at least a stone from all of them, and in the case of *Frigate* and *Why Not* at least two stone.

The weights proved decisive. *Why Not* fell at the fourth fence and, being remounted, would finish a far distant fifth. *Frigate*, ridden by three-times winner Tommy Beasley, went down at the fence before Valentine's. It was there, on the second circuit, that patiently ridden *Ilex* cruised into the lead and he was never seriously challenged thereafter. He won easily from *Pan*, a 100-1 outsider carrying the same light weight. A bad third was *M.P.*, on whom Arthur Nightingall had finished third the previous year.

Arthur had now scored what was to be the first of his three National wins as a jockey; and for his fa-ther it added success as a trainer to his win as an owner, with *Shifnal* in 1878.

Ilex confirmed his class one week later by winning the prestigious Lancashire Chase at Manchester. And the handicapper reacted predictably. *Ilex* was raised by 26lb for his second National. Going off as the 5-1 second favourite, he finished a distant third but was so respected that he went up still further, to a top-weight 12st 7lb, for his third and last appearance in 1892. Again he came home third, so ending his big-race career with a record of three Nationals without ever being out of the first three. Though he never won another race, it is noteworthy that the brilliant Arthur Nightingall judged him to be the best he had ever ridden. Appropriately, on retirement, he was gifted to the jockey who for some years rode him as a hunter in Surrey.

See also; Nightingall, John and Arthur.

INJURIES

When it comes to returning to the fray after suffering crippling injuries National Hunt jockeys are a breed apart. Their grittiness is exemplified by the record of Fred Winter, Grand National winner on *Sundew* (1957) and *Kilmore* (1962). In his career he had 319 falls, suffering a fractured skull and spine, a broken leg, a punctured lung, and various other broken bones. And he was one of the luckier ones. Fred Rimell, for example, twice broke his neck as a jockey before going on to become the only trainer of four Grand National winners. Others have been crippled for life.

However, for all Aintree's reputation as presenting the most formidable drop fences in jump racing, the fact remains that the Grand National is no more hazardous for jockeys than many other chases, and indeed less hazardous than some. Serious injuries are most likely to occur in chases and hurdle races run at great pace on fastish ground. But, by way of watering, the going for the National is now rarely, if ever, likely to be on the firm side of good; and the size of the fences is a discouragement to trying to take them at speed.

That said, the National certainly presented special hazards before course modifications were made in the 20th century – most notably the furnishing of fences with sloping 'aprons' on the take-off side in 1961, and in 1990 the filling in of the treacherous V-shaped ditch on the landing side of Becher's, plus the introduction of plastic rails instead of wooden ones. In addition, for more than a century, the dangers were all the greater because of lax rules that admitted horses of inferior quality and jockeys still handicapped by recent injuries; and it was not until 1984 that a safety limit of no more than 40 runners was introduced.

The first recorded injury came in the second National (1840) when a jockey called Barker was left severely concussed after falling at Becher's on *Weathercock*. A Press report deplored the fact that connections of the horse had not even troubled to enquire about the condition of their rider who had been carried to a nearby farmhouse and was still lying there more than two and a half days later. Such neglect reflected the casual attitude towards professional riders that was taken at the time by the racing elite. 'Non-gentlemen' riders were mere hired help; only the amateurs were to be accorded the title 'Mr', while many professionals were identified by surname alone.

Barker took two more horrendous falls in the National – on *Sam Weller* in 1842, and on *Marengo* in 1847 when he was again rendered unconscious. But he did survive the course once, finishing fourth on Lord Maidstone's *Caesar* in 1844.

The most tragic accident in National history came in 1862 when, with 11 of only 13 starters still in the field, *Playman* crashed into the fence before the Water, bringing down two others – *Willoughby* and *O'Connell*. In the process, James Wynne, the rider of the latter, was left lying on the turf when the riderless *Playman* fell and rolled over him. The crushed jockey was never to regain consciousness.

This remains the only instance of a jockey being fatally injured in the National; and the likelihood of a repetition was marginally diminished in 1924 when it became compulsory to wear crash helmets for protection. However, there were very real fears of a repeat in 1932, when former National winner *Gregalach* was knocked over by a riderless horse. Fred Thackray, his hugely promising amateur rider, was trapped beneath him and so severely injured that he could never ride in the race again.

In terms of the number of injuries suffered by one jockey in the Grand National the prize almost certainly belongs to the Duke of Alberquerque, the stubborn Spanish nobleman who three times was rushed to Walton General Hospital and who calculated that over the years he had suffered more than 100 fractures at Aintree. Finally it was only the Jockey Club that stopped him competing – by ruling in 1977 that no amateur over 50 could ride without first passing a medical examination.

Today such a restriction applies to jockeys of all ages. Every jockey must bring along a Medical Record Book from the Jockey Club in which his injuries are recorded, and then he has to be formally passed fit to ride. In addition, since 1990, stricter qualifications for jockeys in terms of experience have applied. Furthermore, back protectors as well as crash helmets have become mandatory; and now jockeys diagnosed with concussion are suspended for at least a week, after which their condition is to be re-assessed by neuro-psychological screening.

On average a National Hunt jockey is likely to suffer a fall once in every 13 rides. The commonest injury is a broken collarbone since shoulders most often make the first contact with the ground, and some of the worst injuries are the result of being kicked following a fall. There are many examples of a fall bringing a jockey's career to a premature end, sometimes leaving him in dire circumstances. Yet, deplorably, it was not until 1964 that steps were taken to provide some measure of compensation by the creation of the Injured Jockeys' Fund – and then it was only established as a result of campaigning by private individuals.

It was events in 1963 and 1964 that finally spurred action. In December, 1963, Tim Brookshaw, who had ridden in eight Grand Nationals, was deprived of his livelihood at the age of 34, having broken his back on falling in a handicap hurdle at Aintree. Three months later, in the National, another 34 year old jockey, Paddy Farrell, suffered an equally horrendous fall when *Border Flight* failed to take off and ploughed straight into The Chair. A father of four young children, he, too, had broken his back and was left paralysed from the waist down.

Farrell had ridden in six Grand Nationals, most notably finishing third on *O'Malley Point* in 1961, and he had been the North's top jockey for the past four seasons. Now, suddenly, he had no means of supporting his family. But then *Border Flight*'s owner-trainer, Mr Edward Courage – himself confined to a wheelchair after being struck down by polio in his early thirties – combined with Mr Clifford Nicholson, Paddy's employer, to launch a Brookshaw-Farrell Appeal. The response was enormous and it led – in no small part due to the tireless efforts of amateur jockey John Lawrence,

I

now Lord Oaksey – to the foundation of the Injured Jockeys' Fund in 1964, with the Queen Mother becoming its patron in 1970 and Lord Oaksey its president in 2002.

The IJF now provides invaluable assistance to all injured jockeys who have been licensed to ride under the Rules of Racing. At any one time it has as many as 800 former riders on its books and over the years it has paid out more than £8 million in helping jockeys, and their spouses and dependants. Further support has been provided by the Levy Board Accident Scheme which pays a weekly sum to any jockey unable to ride through injury. Into this fund every jockey pays a small proportion from every riding fee he receives.

See also: Fatalities; Rules of Entry.

IRELAND

Since two Irish fox-hunting gentleman, Edmund Blake and Cornelius O'Callaghan, gave birth to the word 'steeplechase' in 1752 by racing from steeple to steeple in Co. Cork, it is entirely appropriate that Ireland should have had the greatest overseas impact on the world's most famous steeplechase which is run over roughly the same distance as that original cross-country chase from St John's Church, Buttevant, to St. Mary's Church at Doneraile. Indeed, the Grand National, like the Cheltenham Festival, has long since become a distinctly Anglo-Irish celebration.

The Irish have been competing regularly in the National ever since it was first run in 1839. That year owner Mr Tom Ferguson brought over three contenders: *Daxon*, *Rust* and *Barkson*. Both *Daxon* (ridden by the owner) and *Barkson* were fallers, but *Rust* mounted such a serious challenge that opposing punters unsportingly invaded the course and brought him to a halt. The following year, half of the 12-strong field was made up of Irish runners and one of them, *Valentine*, ridden and owned by an Irish amateur (Alan Power), left an indelible mark on the National by clearing the second brook in such sensational style that it was named Valentine's.

However, it was not until 1847 that the Irish wildly celebrated their first success, narrowly winning with the lightly-weighted, Coolreagh-bred *Matthew*, the 10-1 joint favourite. Three years later they struck again with little Irish-bred *Abd-El-Kader* who went on to become the first horse to win successive Nationals. Since then, though many were English-owned and -trained, the majority of Grand

National winners have been bred in Ireland.

The roll of Irish-bred winners includes the most distinguished ones: *Red Rum*, the National's only triple champion; *Golden Miller*, the only horse to win the Cheltenham Gold Cup and the National in the same year; *Manifesto*, who ran in a record eight Nationals, scoring two wins, two thirds and a fourth place; *Cloister*, twice runner-up before winning by a record 40 lengths under a massive 12st 7lb; and dual Cheltenham Gold Cup winner *L'Escargot*.

Moreover, Ireland has been no less distinguished in producing trainers and riders of National winners. Spearheading the former group was the masterful Henry Eyre Linde, who had replicas of the big Aintree fences erected at the Curragh and, following Mr Garrett Moore's Irish victory on *The Liberator* (1879), saddled successive winners *Empress* and *Woodbrook*.

Garrett's younger brother Willie subsequently trained three National winners, *Why Not* (1894), *The Soarer* (1896) and *Manifesto* (1899), a triple that would be equalled by the greatest Irish wizard of them all, Michael Vincent O'Brien, who, having won three consecutive Cheltenham Gold Cups and three consecutive Champion Hurdles, duly became the only trainer to saddle three successive Grand National winners: *Early Mist* (1953), *Royal Tan* (1954) and *Quare Times* (1955).

As for Irish-born jockeys, the shape of things to come was most clearly defined by the great Beasley invasion of 1879 when, for the first and only time, four brothers were riding in the National. Though another Irishman would ride the winner that year, Beasleys would be back again and again, Tommy winning in 1880, 1881 and 1889, Harry scoring as rider and trainer in 1891, and Harry's grandson, Bobby, winning on *Nicolaus Silver* in 1961.

Ever after Irish-born jockeys would be prominent on the British racing scene, the successful contenders for National glory including such worthies as dual winners Bryan Marshall, Pat Taaffe and Richard Dunwoody, plus Willie Robinson, Eddie Harty, Tommy and Paul Carberry, Jason Titley, Mick Fitzgerald, Tony Dobbin, Ruby Walsh, Jim Culloty and Barry Geraghty. Remarkably, in 1970, the first five finishers in the National were brought home by Irishmen.

Since 1995 no fewer than ten of 13 National winners have been ridden by sons of the Emerald Isle. In National Hunt generally, Irish jockeys have become a dominant force in England – a situation that can be partly attributed to the fact that the dream of becoming a great jump jockey is a so much greater spur in Ireland where such status commands hero-worship akin to becoming a David Beckham across the water.

There were, however, a few lengthy gaps between Ireland's triumphs with horses. When *Workman* won at Aintree in 1939 it was the first success by an Irish-bred, -owned and -trained challenger since *Troytown* in 1920. And after the success of *Mr What* in 1958 there was not another Irish-trained National winner until *L'Escargot*, ridden by Tommy Carberry, beat *Red Rum* in 1975. Then came the longest period – almost a quarter of a century – without an Irish winner.

In 1996, Ireland appeared to have an especially good chance of ending the losing run. There were five Irish contenders in a small field of 27; and these included two leading fancies: *Son Of War* and *Life Of A Lord*. The former, winner of the 1994 Irish National, was ridden by Conor O'Dwyer, bidding for a Gold Cup-National double, and was a first Aintree runner for trainer Peter McCreery whose grandfather, Tom Taaffe, had turned out the 1958 winner *Mr What*. The latter, trained by A.P. O'Brien, was ridden by Charlie Swan, who had finished second on *Cahervillahow* in the void National of 1993.

There was good support, too, for *Wylde Hide*, owned owned J.P. McManus and trained by Arthur Moore whose father, Dan, had saddled the 1975 winner *L'Escargot*. Yet not one of them made the frame. *Wylde Hide* was in contention when he was slightly checked by the riderless *Son Of War* and his jockey was unseated at the Canal Turn on the second circuit. The best Irish performance came from the 100-1 outsider *Three Brownies*, ridden by Paul Carberry into sixth place, with two more Irish runners, *Life Of A Lord* and *Antonin*, seventh and eighth respectively.

In 1997, Ireland was again strongly represented with such leading fancies as *Feathered Gale*, *Antonin* and *Wylde Hide*. But again, in a year when the National was postponed 49 hours by IRA bomb threats, none finished in a place – the only consolation being that the winner, New Zealand-bred *Lord Gyllene*, was ridden by an Irishman, Tony Dobbin.

In 1998 there were two Irish runners: the J.P. McManus-owned *Gimme Five* who finished fifth and the mare *Dun Belle* who unseated her rider at the ninth. And then, hey presto, like a long wait for buses, along came two Irish winners in a row – the 24-year drought being ended in 1999 by the victory of *Bobbyjo*, trained by Tommy Carberry and ridden by his son, Paul, and followed in 2000 by another Irish father-and-son (the Walshes) win with *Papillon*.

In 2003, with the success of *Monty's Pass*, Ireland had had three National winners in five years – all of them from relatively small yards. That total was raised to four winners in seven years when no fewer than ten Irish horses contested the 2005 National, with one of them, *Hedgehunter*, winning.

Following this encouraging trend, 2006 saw a record number of Irish horses (38) entered for the National. Twenty-one made it to the 40-runner line-up and such was their dominance that they took first, second and fourth places while the third and fifth finishers, though England-based, were both owned and trained by Irishmen, J.P. McManus and Jonjo O'Neill respectively. Now it was five National wins in eight years for the Irish, and only by a short head had they failed to equal the 1-2-3 clean sweep they had scored in the Cheltenham Gold Cup and Champion Hurdle of the previous month.

In 2007 that score was advanced to six wins in nine years with the shock 33-1 success of *Silver Birch* who, in a rare reversal of the long-established trend, had been purchased in England to be owned, trained and ridden by Irishmen.

In recent years several of these Irish successes have been attributed to the canny Irish ploy of running contenders over hurdles to protect their handicap mark and only racing them over fences after the National weights have been framed. But primarily the great Irish revival is to be explained in economic terms. It coincides with an era of such booming prosperity that most Irish owners are now wealthy enough to reject offers from British trainers who had so often snapped up the best Irish-bred chasers. Furthermore, Irish racing has enjoyed the benefit of Government subsidies, assisting racecourse improvements, increasing prize money and providing tax exemptions for home-based jockeys and very generous tax concessions for stud owners.

Quite simply, with their unrivalled knack of breeding class jumpers and their passion for National Hunt racing (all but three of their 27 courses are used for jumping as well as Flat racing) the Irish can be expected to be a dominant force in the Grand National for years to come.

I

IRISH GRAND NATIONAL

The Irish Grand National, run over three miles five furlongs, is the main feature of the three-day Easter meeting at Fairyhouse, north-west of Dublin, and was first staged in 1870. In all those years, however, only four winners have also been successful in the Aintree Grand National – *Ascetic's Silver* (Irish 1904, Aintree 1906); *Rhyme 'N' Reason* (Irish 1985, Aintree 1988); *Bobbyjo* (Irish 1998, Aintree 1999); and *Numbersixvalverde* (Irish, 2005, Aintree 2006).

Conversely, in recent years, numerous Irish National winners have challenged unsuccessfully for Aintree glory: *Omerta* (1991 winner) pulled up lame before the seventh in 1992; *Ebony Jane* (1993) finished fourth in 1994 and 12th in 1995; *Son Of War* (1994), unseated rider at the 24th in 1996; *Feathered Gale* (1996), pulled up four out in 1997; *Mudahim* (1997) unseated rider at the sixth in 1999; *Davids Lad* (2001), fell at the 27th in 2002; and *The Bunny Boiler* (2002) finished tenth in 2004.

However, the brilliant *Prince Regent* (Irish winner in 1942 under 12st 7lb) would in all probability have triumphed at Aintree but for the five lost years of the Second World War which meant that he could only make his challenges when arguably past his prime. Always on top weight, he finished third as 3-1 favourite in 1946, fourth as 8-1 favourite in 1947, and was carried out when competing as a 13 year old in 1948. Subsequently, two of the great Irish National winners – *Arkle* (1964) and *Desert Orchid* (1990) – were never allowed to run in the Aintree National.

Since the turn of the century two Irish National losers have gone on to score at Aintree. *Papillon*, a close runner-up in the 1998 Irish National, won at Liverpool in 2000. *Red Marauder* was a distant tenth at Fairyhouse in 2000 before his shock victory in the 2001 Aintree National.

Unlike the horses, winning Irish National jockeys have enjoyed a good strike-rate in the Aintree National. Since 1990 six have scored in both Nationals: Richard Dunwoody, Jason Titley, Paul Carberry, Ruby Walsh, Barry Geraghty and Jim Culloty. Such success, however, was never a possibility for the winning rider in the 1964 Irish National. That year, for the first time, the winner (*Bentom Boy*) was ridden by a lady jockey, Mrs Ann Ferris, with her sister Rosemary Stewart finishing third on *Dawson Prince*! It would be another 12 years before lady riders were allowed to compete in National Hunt races in Britain.

Like the Aintree National, the Irish National remains a major gambling event, but no longer to such an extent as when it was the subject of the Irish Hospital Sweepstakes established in 1930 under supervisory legislation passed by the Dail. Tickets were then sold for £1 at home and abroad (especially North America) with a percentage of the proceeds funding hospitals. If your ticket was drawn it was attached to a runner in the National, and the ticket-holder with the winning horse won £50,000 (the equivalent of more than £1.5 million today) with lesser prizes for the placed horses. In 1961 sales peaked at £18 million, but thereafter they declined in the face of competition from state lotteries in North America, and the scheme was abandoned in 1987.

JACK HORNER

In 1926 the Yanks landed in hordes at Liverpool in the hope of witnessing a second victory by an American-owned horse. Young Stephen Sanford had fired their enthusiasm with the success of his *Sergeant Murphy* in 1923. Now he was double-handed with his latest purchases, *Bright's Boy* and *Mount Etna*. And there was a third U.S-owned challenger: nine year old *Jack Horner* who, just over two weeks earlier, had been snapped up for £4,000 by the wealthy, polo-playing American stockbroker, Charles Schwartz.

One year before, after three previous failures, American sportsman Morgan de Witt Blair had backed himself to get round the National course on his co-owned *Jack Horner*, a 40-1 chance. Only two weeks prior to the race he had undergone an operation for appendicitis, but still he won his bet, finishing a distant seventh. Now, under new ownership, the chestnut gelding was to have an Australian jockey: William Watkinson, who had been runner-up on *Drifter* in 1922.

Charlie Schwartz had no great confidence in his National challenger. He had come to England determined – no expense spared – to buy the best prospect available. At Claridge's in London, he had been introduced to trainer Harvey 'Jack' Leader, who expressed the opinion that *Bright's Boy* was the most likely winner of the race, with *Sprig* the next best bet. But neither horse was for sale; and only after eliminating other strong contenders did they arrive at *Jack Horner* who was being trained by Jack Leader on behalf of Mr Kenneth Mackay, the future Lord Inchcape.

Mr Mackay, who had taken over sole ownership from Morgan Blair, agreed to sell for £4,000, plus an extra £2,000 if the horse won the National. But *Jack Horner*'s chance of success was not highly rated. He was a 25-1 shot, and the nine horses ahead of him in the betting included *Sprig*, the 7-1 favourite; *Old Tay Bridge*, the 1925 runner-up; *Silvo*, third in 1924; *Koko*, the recent Cheltenham Gold Cup winner; and *Grecian Wave*, ridden by last year's winning jockey, Major J.P. Wilson.

Jack Horner had an unimpressive background. Bred at the Melton Stud, by *Cyllius* out of *Melton's Guide*, he had frequently been re-sold. As a plain-looking five year old, he had carried his then owner, Lord Barnby, over 15 miles cross-country in a marathon fox-hunt with the Blankney pack. He later

changed hands for 160 guineas before eventually passing into the ownership of Morgan Blair who sold a half-share to Kenneth Mackay. In his favour, however, he was lightly weighted for the 1926 National on 10st 5lb, had an experienced rider, and an excellent trainer. One of five Leader brothers belonging to the renowned Newmarket family, Jack had sought to boost the gelding's speed by working him with two year olds on his gallops at Exning in Suffolk.

In the National, *Jack Horner's* prospects were almost immediately improved by the falling of second favourite *Silvo* and *Grecian Wave* at the very first fence. Then, at Becher's, another leading fancy, *Koko*, was brought down. More fell on the second circuit and, coming to the last, *Bright's Boy* and *Old Tay Bridge* were competing for the lead. But *Jack Horner* had never been far off the pace and now, on the long run-in, he asserted his huge weight advantage, out-galloping them to win by three lengths.

For the second successive year, Jack Anthony, seeking his elusive fourth National win, was runner-up on *Old Tay Bridge*, one length ahead of Sanford's *Bright's Boy*. A flurry of Stars and Stripes hailed the finishing of American-owned horses in first and third place. And with a mighty congratulatory slap on the back, owner Charlie Schwartz knocked trainer Leader off his perch in the stands.

The rich American proposed rewarding the winning jockey with a gift of £4,000 and, after a discussion, he agreed to change this to four annual payments of £1,000. Tragically, the Tasmanian-born Bill Watkinson did not live to enjoy his new-won riches. Three weeks later he suffered a fatal fall in the Montgomerie Chase at Bogside in Scotland. That same year *Jack Horner* broke down when being trained for the 1927 National. He would not race again, but, happily, he lived on to enjoy a long and comfortable retirement in the U.S.A.
See also: Watkinson,William; United States.

JAPAN

In the past quarter of a century horseracing has grown apace in Japan, attracting gigantic crowds and generating a betting turnover rivalled only by Hong Kong. Although Flat racing predominates, jump racing is advancing in popularity, as evinced in April, 2000, with the staging in Tokyo of the Nakayama Grand Jump, Japan's first international steeplechase. An invitational event run over two miles and four

J

and a half furlongs, it had a then record first prize equating to nearly half a million pounds which was won by the home country's *Gokai*. M. Francois Doumen of France saddled the close runner-up, *Boca Boca*, and England's Venetia Williams secured the third place, worth some £119,000, with *The Outback Way*, ridden by Norman Williamson.

The Nakayama Grand Jump – a test of speed rather than stamina on a twisting, undulating circuit – remains Japan's toughest steeplechase, involving 20 fences and, most challengingly, a water jump, only 3ft high but 12ft in length. Moreover, until 2008, with prize money increased to £730,000, it has for the time being surpassed Aintree's great showpiece for the title of the world's richest steeplechase.

So far, however, Japan has not made a serious challenge for the Grand National. Their one contender appeared in 1966: *Fujino-o*, a seven year old chestnut gelding owned by Mr Kazuo Fujii. He was prepared for Aintree by Fulke Walwyn and ridden by the strong and fearless Jeff King, making the third of his 15 appearances in the National. Unfortunately, he lacked the necessary runs in Britain to guide the handicapper and was automatically awarded the top weight of 12st, so having to give two stone to 24 of the runners in a 47-strong field. Deservedly a 100-1 shot, he was never able to go the pace and his run soon ended with a refusal.

JAY TRUMP

The first Grand National winner (in 1965) to be American-bred, -owned and -ridden. Making his first and last appearance at Aintree, the eight year old *Jay Trump* triumphed by just three-quarters of a length from *Freddie*, the short-priced Scottish favourite; and, remarkably, his amateur jockey, Tommy Crompton Smith, was also making his debut in the race.

Bred in Pennsylvania – by *Tonga Prince* out of *Be Trump* – *Jay Trump* was first raced unsuccessfully on Flat dirt tracks, and as a two year old he survived a racing accident that left him with a 15-inch gash in his off-foreleg requiring 29 stitches. He had failed a number of different owners when Crompton Smith claimed him out of a seller for a mere $2,000 on behalf of Mrs Mary Stephenson (later LeBlond) of Cincinnati, Ohio, a one-time polo player and leading huntswoman. The lady had been seeking a horse to win the prestigious Maryland Hunt Cup, and, with Tommy as trainer and rider, *Jay Trump*

duly obliged – not once but twice (1963-64). Moreover, he won nine other lesser races.

As initially demonstrated by *Billy Barton*, the remounted runner-up in the 1928 National, a winner over Maryland's four miles of formidable, upright timber fences, was liable to prove a major player at Aintree. And in this instance the challenge by *Jay Trump* was plotted with supreme precision and care. Eight months before the 1965 National he was sent over to England to gain the necessary experience and qualify for handicapping purposes. Moreover, the choice of trainer was positively inspired. Responsible for his preparation would be a man who had only just set up as a trainer in a dilapidated Uplands yard at Upper Lambourn, Berkshire. He had no proven ability as a trainer. But his knowledge of English steeplechasing, and the National especially, was beyond compare. Four times champion jockey, Fred Winter had ridden 11 times in the National and had won in 1957 on *Sundew* and as recently as 1962 on *Kilmore*.

Most importantly, Winter was equipped to be a dual-purpose trainer, not only preparing *Jay Trump* but also giving meticulous coaching to Crompton Smith, a highly skilled amateur rider but totally lacking in experience over English fences. The American came over four months in advance to be instructed by the master.

Jay Trump was the first runner to be sent out by Winter and the bay gelding launched a brilliant training career by winning a three-mile chase with Tommy at Sandown. In four more preparatory races he won two, at Windsor and Newbury, and in between finished second to *Frenchman's Cove* in the 1964 King George VI Chase, albeit when only two runners were risked on the treacherous going.

Then, just three weeks before the National, the alarm bells sounded: Lambourn was hit by a coughing epidemic. Luckily, *Jay Trump* remained off the casualty list, but with every other horse in the yard eventually affected it was only a matter of time before he too succumbed. Emergency action was needed and taken. The champion chaser was isolated in a stable half a mile away, and thereafter Tommy literally lived with him.

Very probably *Jay Trump* was spared infection because – unlike English horses – he had had vaccinations prior to being shipped across the Atlantic. Also he only had fodder flown over from the States. In any event, he arrived at Aintree in fine fettle and, considering his record, was reasonably handicapped on 11st 5lb, the same figure as the second favourite, the Queen Mother's *The Rip*. However, only one of 47 runners was more heavily weighted: *Freddie*, the 7-2 favourite with 5lb more.

Freddie was one of the first to clear Becher's; and there, immediately behind the leaders, five horses came down in a pile-up. But *Jay Trump* avoided the chaos as Tommy, following instructions precisely, cruised round patiently on the inside. Jumping superbly, the American champion steadily advanced over the second circuit and was contesting *Freddie* for the lead as they came to the second last together.

No others were in contention as, matching stride for stride, they duelled to the last. Though failing to jump it cleanly, *Jay Trump* powered one length into the lead. Then, on the long run-in, being challenged all the way, an over-eager Crompton Smith made his one mistake: for the first time he used his whip. Hating it, the bay flashed his tail and momentarily faltered.

Fortunately, as the only man to ride *Jay Trump* over the jumps, Tommy instantly recognised his error. He put down the whip and, riding out with hands and heels, spurred his mount home to prevail by three-quarters of a length from a Scottish hope who was superbly ridden by Pat McCarron and beaten only by his 5lb disadvantage. In third place, 20 lengths back, was *Mr Jones*, a 50-1 chance ridden by amateur Christopher Collins, a National debutant who had never won a race under Rules.

Jay Trump emerged so well from the National that he was raced three months later in the French equivalent at Auteuil: the Grand Steeplechase de Paris which Winter had so spectacularly won on *Mandarin* in 1962. There, coming to the last, the great chaser was marginally in the lead. But this time, having wasted excessively to make the weight, Tommy lacked the strength to power his horse home. They finished a close-up third, beaten only two and a half lengths by the great mare *Hyeres III*. It was, arguably, his finest performance.

Back home, the American wonder horse now crowned his extraordinary racing career with a third triumph in the Maryland Hunt Cup. He was then promptly retired as a nine year old, being occasionally ridden to hounds by his owner and living on in cosseted retirement to a ripe old age.
See also: Winter Fred; Crompton Smith, Tommy; Maryland Hunt Cup.

JEALOUSY

As a five year old, on her Aintree debut, the brown mare *Jealousy* had failed to get round in the Grand National of 1859. Two years later, under new ownership, her promise was so outstanding that the shrewd George Stevens, winning rider in the 1856 National, turned down 13 offers in favour of the ride. Then, to his chagrin, an owner who retained his services refused to release him; and, more maddeningly still, the horse he was booked to ride was withdrawn at the 11th hour.

Jockey Joe Kendall was thus reunited with *Jealousy*, the 5-1 second favourite. Heading the market was another mare: *Anatis*, winner of the previous year and again ridden by Mr Thomas Pickernell. But *Anatis*, now an 11 year old, had been raised 8lb in the weights. In contrast, the improving *Jealousy* was reckoned to be thrown in on a mere 9st 12lb; and so it proved.

Throughout the first circuit *Jealousy* was ridden patiently while, from Becher's onwards, *Redwing* and the tearaway *Xanthus* duelled for the lead. The former was several lengths ahead at the second Valentine's when he fell on stumbling over *The Conductor*, a fatal faller first time round. With *Xanthus* fading and *Anatis* already brought down, only three horses remained in contention and the contest was virtually decided at the last when *Jealousy* stormed to the front and held on comfortably to win by two lengths and four from *The Dane* and *Old Ben Roe*.

Under new ownership for the third time, *Jealousy* returned in 1863 and went off as 3-1 favourite – remarkably so since she had an extra 26lb to carry and was racing over a course that had been extended by about a quarter of a mile to make a distance of near four and a half miles. In the circumstances, Kendall did well to bring the mare home the sixth of six finishers. Another mare, *Emblem*, was the 20 lengths winner, giving Stevens the second of his record five victories.
See also: Kendall, Joseph.

JENKINS, W.H.P.

Because he soon ballooned to a colossal weight, W.H.P. Jenkins only once rode in the Grand National – in 1869 when he was the eighth of nine finishers on the 100-1 outsider *The Robber*. At the time he was an undergraduate at Merton College, Oxford, and always rode as an amateur under the pseudonym

J

of 'Mr P. Merton'. Similarly, Mr J.J. Atkinson, the fellow undergraduate who owned *The Robber*, adopted the pseudonym of 'Mr Doncaster'.

Born at Caerleon, Monmouth, Jenkins went on to become one of the best-known characters in steeple-chasing. Operating a large stable at Upton in Warwickshire, he was recognised as an outstanding judge of equine potential and sent out a great many winners. Yet he had just one success in the National – in 1883 when he saddled the six year old mare *Zoedone*, who, owned and ridden by Count Charles Kinsky, won by a comfortable ten lengths.

Like his contemporary Arthur Yates, Jenkins was renowned as a trainer who worked both his horses and riders hard; and in this respect, by bringing both *Zoedone* and Count Kinsky to peak fitness, he played a key role in the latter winning the National on his debut.

See also: Zoedone; Pseudonyms.

JENKINSTOWN

Although nine year old *Jenkinstown* won the 1910 Grand National, it is inevitably recognised that the great hero of the race was the three lengths runner-up: *Jerry M*, a seven year old who was burdened on his debut with a top weight of 12st, 7lb and was conceding more than two stone to the winner.

Jenkinstown was lightly weighted (10st 5lb) on the strength of a poor record that boasted nothing more than victory in a minor two-mile chase at Wolverhampton. However, he had the same owner and trainer as *Eremon*, the 1907 National winner – Stanley Howard and Tom Coulthwaite respectively. Also he had a jockey, Yorkshireman Robert Chadwick, who had finished second on *Judas* the previous year.

An Irish-bred bay gelding, by *Hackler* out of *Playmate*, *Jenkinstown* had won two modest chases in Ireland before being bought by Mr Howard for £600. He was still without a single success in England before being entered for the 1908 National, and there he was soon pulled up while the race was won by another 66-1 outsider, *Rubio*. When he returned two years later, he was left on the same light weight and was fourth equal in the betting behind *Jerry M*, *Judas* and last year's third-placed *Caubeen*.

This time *Judas* was ridden by Algy Anthony, winner of the 1900 National on *Ambush II*. But he was to be a faller while the less fancied *Jenkinstown* was one of the few runners to keep out of trouble.

Remarkably, the 25-strong field was reduced by more than half before even the fourth fence was reached. Only six remained by the second Becher's, and then just five after the Canal Turn where the leading *Springbok* had to be pulled up when jockey Bill Payne's saddle slipped.

Jerry M, the classy 6-1 favourite, was now powering ahead, with only *Jenkinstown* in a position to mount a challenge. It came two fences out as they fought out a prolonged duel, stride by stride. Then, on the run-in, a 30lb concession proved too much for the gallant *Jerry M* and he went down by three lengths, with *Odor*, the complete outsider, a further three lengths behind.

The victory, worth £2,500 in prize money alone, represented a sizeable profit for Mr Howard. But *Jenkinstown* was never so effective once he had been raised in the weights. He was pulled up in the 1911 National when only four finished on the heavy going; and, having been sold for a rumoured £3,000, he was pulled up lame after the second Becher's in 1912 when *Jerry M*, ridden by Ernie Piggott, gained his deserved National success despite still carrying 12st 7lb. *Jenkinstown* died that same year.

See also: Coulthwaite,Tom; Chadwick, Robert.

JERRY

Winner of the second Grand National (1840) by four lengths and four from *Arthur* and *Valentine* respectively. The Lincolnshire-bred chaser, by *Catterick* out of *Sister To Jerry*, had had a bewildering number of dissatisfied owners – among them six different lords of the realm – before being bought by Mr John Elmore, the leading horse-dealer who had the distinction of owning the first National winner, *Lottery*.

While it is recorded that *Jerry*, under Mr Elmore's ownership, had won the 1837 Grand Leamington Steeplechase, considerable doubt surrounds his ownership when winning at Aintree. Officially, he ran in the colours of one of Mr Elmore's customers, a Mr Henry Villebois. But it has been suggested that the horse-dealer retained at least an interest in the newcomer and wished to disguise the fact lest he was required to state his preferred runner – *Jerry* or his declared entry, *Lottery* – and so prompt market moves in favour of the former.

As it was, *Jerry* went off at 12-1 while *Lottery* was the 4-1 second favourite, a point longer than Lord McDonald's *The Nun*. There were only 12 starters and six of these were Irish challengers, among them the outsider *Valentine*, owned and ridden by Mr Alan Power. Following Lord Sefton's flag-start, *Valentine* soon overhauled *Lottery* and led the field at a furious pace. His jockey had one primary aim: to win a hefty wager that he would be the first to reach the 4ft 8in high stone wall sited in front of the stands and near the end of the first circuit.

Power won his bet; and along the way his front-runner cleared the second brook in such extraordinary style that the jump was ever after to be known as Valentine's.

Coming to the wall he had been strongly challenged by *Lottery* but there the first National winner had blundered – hitting the fearful obstacle hard, falling amid demolished stonework, and in the process bringing down three horses close behind him. The casualties included the favourite and Sir George Mostyn's well-supported *Seventy Four*.

Valentine briefly threatened to win an even bigger prize as he led the way back into the country, but then he began to tire and gave way to *Arthur* and *Jerry*. The former fell when in the lead at the second Becher's and his rider, Mr Alan McDonough, quickly remounted, just as he had done in the first National. He then launched an astonishing late challenge to the weakening front-runner. But it was too late. *Jerry*, ridden by amateur newcomer Mr Bartholomew Bretherton, held on throughout the long run-in to be the first of only four finishers. For the second consecutive year the National winner had been trained by George Dockeray.

Confusingly, in 1847, a horse called *Jerry* finished a close-up third in the National and failed to get round in two more appearances. But this was not the 1840 winner. The victorious *Jerry*, of undetermined age, never appeared at Aintree again and was well beaten by *Lottery* in his one subsequent race, the Leamington Chase.

See also: Elmore, John; Bretherton, Bartholomew; Dockeray, George.

JERRY M

Never has a Grand National entry been more harshly complimented by the handicapper than *Jerry M*. On his first appearance, as a mere seven year old in 1910, he was allotted the top weight of 12st 7lb. And when he returned two years later, for his second and last appearance, he was treated exactly the same.

As it happened, the treatment was more or less justified. In 1910, the handicapper was rightly impressed with the outstanding form of *Jerry M*, first signalled by his commanding performance in the Becher Chase as a five year old. The punters agreed. The powerfully built gelding – under the same ownership as the great 1893 winner *Cloister* – was made 6-1 favourite on his debut.

It was a race which saw a dozen horses eliminated by the third fence and only nine still standing first time round. *Jerry M* ridden by Edmund Driscoll, took the lead at the second Valentine's, only to be joined two fences out in a long stride-for-stride duel by nine year old *Jenkinstown*. Then, on the run-in, the weight concession told. *Jerry M* gallantly went down by three lengths to a horse with a colossal 30lb advantage.

Three months later, again ridden by Driscoll, *Jerry M* confirmed his greatness with a three lengths victory in the Grand Steeplechase de Paris, then the world's most valuable chase. But he incurred leg trouble in the process and was not sound in time for the 1911 National. The following year, however, after an 18 months' break, he proved his well-being in winning at Hurst Park, and was duly made 4-1 joint favourite for his Aintree reappearance. He now had a new rider: Ernie Piggott, father of Keith, who would train the 1963 National winner *Ayala*, and grandfather of the incomparable Lester.

This time, on top weight, *Jerry M* was conceding 10lb to his nearest rival, *Rathnally*, runner-up the previous year and now the other joint favourite. It seemed a harsh penalty at the start, but not at the finish. Riding patiently as instructed, Piggott delayed his all-out challenge until clearing the last fence. Then *Jerry M* was given free rein and he strode past long-time leader *Bloodstone* to win by six lengths.

It was a victory greeted with thunderous applause by a crowd that recognised a truly great champion, one who had equalled the record weight-carrying feat of *Cloister* and *Manifesto*.

Jerry M – by *Walmsgate* out of an unnamed *Luminary* mare – had been bred in Co. Limerick and bought as a yearling by Joe Widger, the leading horse-dealer who had won the 1895 National with *Wild Man From Borneo*. Widger named the bay gelding after a horse-breeding friend Jerry Mulcair, and he was about to sell him to Sir Edward Hulton when the deal was scuppered by a veterinary report that found the horse to be thick-winded.

J

Findon (Sussex) trainer Robert Gore, however, remained convinced that the gelding, winner of four races in his first season, had considerable potential. On his recommendation, *Jerry M* was bought for £1,200 by Charles Assheton-Smith, formerly Mr Charles Duff, the wealthy quarry owner who had won the 1893 National with the legendary *Cloister*.

The transaction spoke volumes for Gore's expert judgment since Assheton-Smith had been most reluctant to buy. Twice his vet had been sent to Ireland to inspect *Jerry M*, and he had repeated his doubts about the horse's soundness of wind. Yet Gore persisted so forcefully that in the end his patron volunteered to toss a coin to decide the issue. The trainer won.

Irish by birth, Gore had become a highly successful trainer at Findon, and there he quickly brought *Jerry M* to peak form. In 1908, his first year in England, the five year old won the New Century Chase at Hurst Park and both the Stanley Chase and Becher Chase at Liverpool. The following summer, jumping consistently well, he finished second in the four-and-a-quarter mile Grand Steeplechase de Paris. Then, prior to his National debut, he won the Valentine Chase at Liverpool, and – in the rarest of hiccups – fell at Newbury when he was 1-20 – on in a two-horse race.

After his outstanding triumph in the 1912 National, it was thought that *Jerry M*, as a nine year old, could be capable of still more great deeds. But it was not to be. His supreme winning run at Aintree would be his last. Having won 14 of 20 races in four seasons, he was retired after suffering a back injury and recurring wind problems. In 1914, following the death of his owner, now Sir Charles, he was bequeathed to his brilliant trainer, but almost immediately afterwards he contracted a debilitating disease and had to be put down.

See also: Gore, Robert; Piggott, Ernie; Assheton-Smith, Sir Charles.

JOCKEYS

Most Grand National winning rides
Five – by George Stevens (1856, 1863, 1864, 1869 and 1870).
Three – by Tom Olliver, Tommy Pickernell, Tommy Beasley, Arthur Nightingall, Jack Anthony and Brian Fletcher.

Youngest winner
17-year-old Bruce Hobbs who, in 1938, rode *Battleship* to victory by a head over *Workman*.

Oldest winner
Farmer Dick Saunders, aged 48, when winning on *Grittar* in 1982.

Most appearances
Tom Olliver (1839-59) with 19 rides, including three wins, three times runner-up and once third.

Winning jockeys who also trained a Grand National winner
Algy Anthony (*Ambush*, 1900), trained *Troytown* 1920.
Fulke Walwyn (*Reynoldstown*, 1936), trained *Team Spirit* (1964).
Fred Winter (*Sundew*, 1957), trained *Jay Trump* (1965) and *Anglo* (1966).
Tommy Carberry (*L'Escargot*, 1975), trained *Bobbyjo* (1999).

JOEL, Henry Joel 'Jim'

When *Maori Venture* triumphed by five lengths in the 1987 Grand National, 92-year-old Mr Jim Joel became the oldest winning owner in the history of the race, having beaten by three years the previous record age of Noel le Mare whose colours were carried to a third National victory by *Red Rum* in 1977. At the same time he joined the small band of owners who have had success both in Aintree's big race and the English Derby.

Never was victory for an owner more long overdue. It was 30 years since Mr Joel had had his first runner placed in the National: the striking grey *Glorious Twelfth* who was third favourite when finishing fourth in the race. His next outstanding challenger was *The Laird* who had been beaten only a neck by *Fort Leney* in the 1968 Cheltenham Gold Cup. This classy chaser was a ten year old when, in 1971, he was finally entered for the National. Having won his three previous races, he was made the joint third favourite and the subject of major gambles. But *The Laird* fell at the third fence.

Yet again, in 1986, Mr Joel had the third favourite in the National: the widely tipped *Door Latch* from the Josh Gifford yard that had produced the famed 1981 winner *Aldaniti*. The previous year, having ridden the horse in the Cheltenham Gold Cup, John Francome predicted shortly before his retirement that *Door Latch* would win a Grand National. But the chestnut gelding's solitary appearance in the race proved a huge disappointment. The nonagenarian owner journeyed to Aintree only to see his great hope, a 9-1 chance, fall at the first fence.

One year later Mr Joel at last realised his dream of National success, and ironically it came with an unfancied runner. *Maori Venture* was 12 in the betting at 28-1; a useful enough chaser, strong on stamina but generally regarded as too erratic a jumper to cope with the great Aintree fences. As it happened, under jockey Steve Knight, he jumped safely throughout and finished strongest of all to overcome *The Tsarevich* and *Lean Ar Aghaidh* on the run-in. The victory came 20 years after the veteran owner had won the 2,000 Guineas and the Derby with his Noel Murless-trained *Royal Palace*.

Born in 1894, Jim Joel belonged to a family whose extraordinary rags-to-riches progress had been founded in the diamond fields of South Africa. His grandfather had barely scraped a living as the landlord of the *King of Prussia* public house in the East End of London. But his father Jack was a millionaire before the age of 30, having left England with his brother Solly to join an elder brother, Woolf, in the Kimberley mines. There they had prospered under the guidance of an uncle, Barnett ('Barney') Barnato, who had become with Cecil Rhodes one of the giants of the diamond industry.

The family extended their interests to many other enterprises in South Africa, including breweries and collieries. Its leading members, however, had very contrasting fates. Uncle Barney was drowned at sea in 1897 and two years later Woolf was murdered. At that point, Solly took over the running of their huge business interests while Jack returned to England to represent their companies' interests in the City and, eventually, to become a major pillar of the racing establishment.

As a breeder and owner Jack Joel had remarkable success, his wins including no fewer than 11 English Classics between 1911 and 1921. On his father's death in 1940, Jim inherited the Childwick Bury Stud near St Albans and continued to make the family's racing colours (black with scarlet cap) famed throughout the land. His first Classic success came in 1944 with *Picture Play*'s winning of the 1,000 Guineas. It was 23 years before the next came. Then his *Royal Palace* won not only the Derby and 2,000 Guineas but also the Coronation Cup, the Eclipse Stakes and the King George and Queen Elizabeth Stakes.

Over more than four decades, the unassuming Jim Joel had some 800 winners on the Flat. These included no fewer that 26 victories at Royal Ascot and, in 1980 and 1981, success in the 1,000 Guineas and the St Leger with *Fairy Footsteps* and *Light Cavalry* respectively. Unlike his father he did not achieve a full house of Classic wins, missing out with the Oaks in which his *West Side Story* was beaten by a whisker. On the other hand, he was an outstanding supporter of both racing codes, enjoying 353 wins over jumps between 1946 and 1992, including 12 at the Cheltenham Festival.

Mr Joel was not at Aintree to witness his surprise success in the Grand National. At the time he was flying back from a holiday in South Africa, and subsequently he received the news with joyful incredulity. He remained active for several more years and at the age of 93 was still commuting daily to the City of London from his home near St. Albans. In March, 1992, the chaser *Buck Willow* was the 50th winner to be sent out for him by Josh Gifford. But the owner died later that month, just two weeks before the Grand National, aged 97. In his will he bequeathed to the Queen Mother any horse of her choice and she opted for his National Hunt Chase winner *Keep Talking*.

See also: Maori Venture; Turnell, Andrew.

JOHNSON, Richard Evan

It was the great misfortune of Richard Johnson to emerge as the outstanding English jump jockey at the time when Irishman Tony McCoy was firmly establishing himself as the most prolific winning rider in National Hunt history. Season after season, from 1997-98 onwards, he was destined to finish runner-up in the jockeys' championship; and, though no one could compete with the mighty McCoy-Pipe combination, his challenge was not aided by untimely injuries.

In October, 2001, when he broke his right leg falling from *Ilicio II* at Exeter, he had already ridden 81 winners, well behind McCoy but still twice as many as any other rival. In late August, 2002, he was scoring even faster, with 73 winners, when he smashed the same leg in a novices' handicap chase, being thrown at the last fence at Newton Abbot from *Lincoln Place* who then rolled on top of him. At the time he was again the nearest challenger to McCoy who was about to pass Richard Dunwoody's record of 1,699 winners.

J

The son of a Herefordshire farmer, Johnson was born (July 21, 1977) into a racing environment. His father, Keith, was an accomplished amateur rider; his grandfather, Ivor, a permit-holder; and following Ivor's death Richard's mother, Sue, took over the permit to train. Riding almost as soon as he could walk, Richard progressed via pony club, gymkhanas and eventing; and then, on leaving school at Belmont Abbey in Hereford, the 16 year old began his most valuable education – like so many stars of jump racing profiting from experience at David Nicholson's yard near Temple Guiting in Gloucestershire.

His rise was meteoric. He rode his first winner, *Rusty Bridge*, at Hereford in April, 1994. After two more years he would be scoring a century of winners in every season – the first of his many big race successes being the 1997 Champion Novice Hurdle at Punchestown on *Midnight Legend*. That year, aged 19 years 309 days, he became the youngest-ever jump jockey to win 100 races in a season; and by April, 2003 he had achieved his 1,000th winner, joining the giants, McCoy, Richard Dunwoody, Peter Scudamore, John Francome and Stan Mellor, with only McCoy having reached that mark in faster time. In January, 2004, he passed Francome's total of 1,138 to go fourth in the all-time list of winning jump jockeys in Britain and reached his ninth consecutive century since turning professional ten years before.

As early as the year 2000 Johnson had declared: 'I would rather be champion than ride the winner of the Grand National, the Gold Cup or any other big race.' That year, with his greatest ambition once again denied by McCoy, he won his first Cheltenham Gold Cup on *Looks Like Trouble*; and two years later, he went one better than the mighty McCoy by finishing runner-up in the National on the Philip Hobbs-trained *What's Up Boys*.

Until that time Johnson had had a dismal record in the National. Though usually on a fancied runner, he had never completed the course in five rides and had only once got round the first circuit. Yet, given the opportunity he had expected, he might well have won the race at the first attempt. In 1997 he had suffered the double heartbreaking shock of losing the rides on *Mr Mulligan*, victorious under McCoy in the Cheltenham Gold Cup, and *Lord Gyllene*, the runaway winner of the National. Previously he had twice ridden *Lord Gyllene* to victory; now, instead,

he was fated to make his teenage National debut on the long-shot *Celtic Abbey* who was well placed when unseating him at the Chair. The following year he was on the Nicholson-trained *Banjo*, one of five fallers at the first; in 1999 on *Baronet* who fell at the fourth.

In 2000 – the year that he began a much-publicised romance with Zara Phillips, daughter of the Princess Royal – Johnson enjoyed a terrific National ride on *Star Traveller* until his horse went lame heading back from the Canal Turn for a second time. In 2001 his mount *Edmond* (on whom he had won the 1999 Welsh National) went well until blundering at The Chair.

Then, in 2002, came his greatest National ride. As instructed by Hobbs, he took the middle to outer route; and he struck the front on *What's Up Boys* at the penultimate fence and soared over the last to take a three lengths lead. But in a pulsating finish, with the lead changing three times, the gallant grey was just outstayed by *Bindaree* who had a 16lb advantage at the weights. He went down by just a length and three-quarters with McCoy, on the favourite *Blowing Wind*, finishing third for the second successive year.

It is noteworthy that *What's Up Boys*, on 11st 6lb, was burdened with a weight that had not been carried to National victory since *Red Rum's* success a quarter of a century before. One year later Johnson was on *Behrajan* who, like the grey, had finished fifth in the Cheltenham Gold Cup. But this time the challenge was even greater. Anchored on a top weight of the 11st 12lb, *Behrajan* finished tenth, the only one of seven horses carrying more than 11st to complete the course.

At the end of that season Johnson was second to McCoy in the jockeys' championship with 147 wins from 725 rides and prize money of £1,714,671. Subsequently, in the next title race, he poached an early lead of 18 as McCoy lost 65 days after sustaining a broken arm in June, 2003. But nothing had really changed. Hard man McCoy stormed back to regain the lead. In February, 2004, following his absence with a triple fracture of the left cheekbone, that lead was reduced to just two wins. But within only nine days, McCoy was back in the saddle, widening the gap once again. Both men made an early exit in the Grand National (Johnson brought down on *What's Up Boys* at the first Becher's); and McCoy went on to retain his title with 209 wins from 800 rides compared with Johnson's 186 from 891 rides.

In the 2005 National, Johnson was always behind on the Henry Daly-trained *Jakari* and finally pulled up before the 20th. The season ended with McCoy reaching a remarkable double century and winning his tenth successive title despite having left champion trainer Pipe to join Jonjo O'Neill. And for once Johnson was relegated to third place. Having remained loyal to trainer Hobbs, he saw his runner-up spot taken by Timmy Murphy who, retained by Pipe, had scored eight more wins.

In 2006 it was business as usual with Johnson (167 wins) a close-up second to McCoy (178 wins). In the National he pulled up before the 27th on the Pipe-trained 50-1 chance *Therealbandit*. One year later he won Aintree's opening hurdle race well on *Mighty Man*; and on the Saturday, following an extraordinary late move in the National market, he found himself on the 8-1 co-favourite, *Monkerhostin*. But his 11th National ride soon ended with a refusal at the seventh, the little Foinavon. And yet again he finished the season second to the mighty McCoy.

JONES, John

Winning rider on *Shifnal* in a Grand National (1878) with only 12 starters. 'Jack' Jones was most notable for his consistency, failing only once to finish in nine appearances in the race. Besides his one victory, he was second on Lord Marcus Beresford's *Chimney Sweep* (1874), fourth on the same horse in both 1876 and 1877, and second again for Lord Beresford on *Jackal* in 1879.

The one time he failed to finish was not without distinction. In 1884 he was the first National jockey to ride in royal colours, being aboard *The Scot*, the 6-1 favourite owned by the Prince of Wales, later King Edward VII. The horse jumped brilliantly round the first circuit only to fall at the second Becher's. Five years later Jones came back to Aintree for one more ride – taking fifth place on the prince's *Magic*.

In 1878 *Shifnal*, owned and trained by John Nightingall, was making his third successive appearance in the National, having previously finished third and sixth. But this was the first time he had Jones on board, and the experienced jockey had his 7-1 chance in front at the end of the first circuit. The Irish mare *Martha*, ridden by Tommy Beasley, then took over the lead, and she was still ahead coming to the last. But *Shifnal* finished the stronger, winning a

shade cosily by two lengths with the more fancied Irish mare, *Pride of Kildare*, a further ten lengths back in third. Beasley frivolously lodged an objection on the grounds of foul riding by Jones but this was summarily dismissed.

Besides his previous first in royal colours, Jones was also the first trainer to be employed by the Prince of Wales. That royal connection was to be most dramatically renewed in 1900 when the prince had a racehorse so wayward and downright vicious that he would only behave for the stable lad who 'did' him. The horse was *Diamond Jubilee* who won the Triple Crown – the 2,000 Guineas, the Derby and the St Leger – and the Newmarket Stakes. And the 'lad' who rode him was Jones's son, Herbert, who would remain the royal jockey for many years – long enough to be on the King's horse, *Amner*, when he was brought down in the sensational 1913 Derby by the suicidal suffragette, Miss Emily Wilding Davison.

See also: Shifnal.

JONES, Mervyn Anthony

Welsh-born winning rider in the 1940 Grand National when both he and his mount – seven year old *Bogskar*, owned and trained by Lord Stalbridge – were making their debut in the event. In this, the only National held during the Second World War, Flight Sergeant Mervyn Jones had been granted special leave from the RAF Appearing with him in the race, on Mr J. H. Whitney's *National Night*, was his brother Hywel, a more experienced jockey who also held the rank of flight-sergeant.

The scene at Aintree was unlike any other: a National day when the majority of spectators were in uniform and spectators were advised where to take shelter if air raid sirens sounded. The 4-1 favourite of 30 runners was top-weighted *Royal Danieli* who had been beaten by only a head in 1938. Strongly fancied, too, was the Scottish hope *MacMoffat*, last year's runner-up. *Bogskar*, having fallen in his last race, was a 25-1 chance, while *National Night* was a 100-1 outsider.

National Night was first past the finishing post. Unfortunately, he had lost his rider when falling at the 14th plain fence. Subsequently, the loose horse played his part by continually harassing *MacMoffat* who was leading two fences out following the fall of the favourite. *Bogskar*, never prominent on the first circuit, was now well in contention. Mervyn brought

J

him level with the leader at the last, then powered him ahead to win by four lengths, with 50-1 shot *Gold Arrow* a further six lengths back in third.

Brother Hywel was beside the finishing line to cheer home Mervyn who was scoring a victory that had been achieved three times by their celebrated uncle, Jack Anthony. '*Bogskar* gave me a wonderful ride,' said the winning jockey. 'He never put a foot wrong.' Indeed, his time of 9min. 20⅗sec. was only two-fifths of a second outside the record, and he had

won in a year when there was a near-record number of 17 finishers.

After the war *Bogskar*, now 13 years old, raced one more time in the National. But Mervyn Jones was not there to take the ride. Tragically, only two years after his Aintree triumph, he had disappeared when flying a Spitfire on a photo-reconnaissance mission over the fjords of Norway. He was just 22 years old.

See also: *Bogskar*.

KAVANAGH, Terry

Rider of the legendary *Manifesto* when he scored the first of his two Grand National victories in 1897. Having finished fourth and been unluckily knocked over on his two previous appearances, *Manifesto* went off the 6-1 favourite and made nearly all the running together with the six year old newcomer *Timon*. When the latter blundered two fences out, he was left unchallenged and romped home to win by 20 lengths from 100-1 outsider *Filbert*.

Irish-born Terry Kavanagh was first introduced to the National in 1888 by the famed Curragh-based trainer Henry Eyre Linde who had won the race in successive years with *Empress* (1880) and *Woodbrook* (1881). For his Aintree debut he was chosen to take over from the great Tommy Beasley on *Spahi* who, one year earlier, had absurdly started as the 9-2 favourite when having his first ever race over fences. An entire at his best on the Flat, *Spahi* had fallen at the third in 1887 and now, as a 30-1 chance, he soon refused to jump.

It was three years before Kavanagh returned to Aintree, beginning a run of eight successive appearances with a fall on Lord Zetland's five year old *Choufleur*. He first completed the course in 1892, finishing a well-beaten fourth on *Ardcarn.The* following year he pulled up on *Choufleur*, now a 100-1 shot; and in 1894 he rode a brilliant finish on six year old *Lady Ellen II* to be runner-up – beaten just a length and a half by joint favourite *Why Not* and pipping third-placed *Wild Man From Borneo* by a head.

Manifesto was still maturing when he made his National debut in 1895. Though Kavanagh brought him home in fourth place, he lost the ride to John Gourley in 1896. That year he fell on the 66-1 chance *Miss Baron* while *Manifesto* was the unlucky victim of a collision at the first fence. Then, with the partnership restored, they achieved their famous victory. The jockey's one great regret was that his mentor, Henry Linde, had not lived to witness the triumph. One week earlier the renowned trainer had died of Bright's disease.

In 1898, just over a week before the National, *Manifesto* escaped from his box, suffering an injury that put him out of the race. Instead Kavanagh rode *Cruiskeen II*, a 100-1 rank outsider who had to be pulled up. It was his ninth and last appearance in the race while the extraordinary *Manifesto* would come back five more times, winning again in 1899, and three times finishing in third place. *See also:* Manifesto.

KELLEWAY, Paul

Renowned for his strength and gritty determination, Paul Kelleway was destined to score his greatest victory on a big chestnut that he had previously ridden without reward in three successive Grand Nationals. The horse, revitalised as a 12 year old by trainer Ryan Price, was Lady Weir's mud-loving *What A Myth* on when he won the 1969 Cheltenham Gold Cup by a length and a half from *Domacorn* ridden by Terry Biddlecombe.

In the 1966 National, as the second favourite, *What A Myth* had unluckily fallen with five others in a pile-up at the second Becher's. Thereafter, he was to be lumbered with 12st top weight on his reappearances at Aintree. In 1967, just three weeks after he had finished a close-up third in the Gold Cup, Kelleway brought him home ninth in the chaotic Foinavon National; and in 1968 he was a faller.

Born in 1940, Kelleway began his career on the Flat, being just 15 when he rode his first winner, *Golovine*, at Haydock Park. Almost a decade later he made his National debut, finishing 11th on *John O'Groats* in 1964. Immediately after his triumph at Cheltenham in 1969, Kelleway had no hope in the National, being a faller on 100-1 outsider *Ballinbointra*. The following year he made his exit at the first fence on *Perry Hill* and he did not return until 1974 when he was unluckily carried out on Mr W.H. Whitbread's *Cloudsmere*, another 100-1 long shot.

Meanwhile, however, his big-race wins had included successive Champion Hurdles on the brilliant *Bula* (1971-72) and the 1971 Two Mile Champion Chase on the mighty *Crisp*. Finally, in 1975, he was united in the National with a truly promising chaser: Mr Whitbread's nine year old *Barona*; and again he suffered the most outrageous misfortune at Aintree.

The official record simply states that *Barona*, an unfancied 40-1 chance, was a faller. But it was not that clear-cut. Before the bay gelding fell, he was alongside *April Seventh* who was unluckily brought down at the first Becher's. As he was propelled backwards on *April Seventh*, Andy Turnell reached out desperately for the nearest thing at hand. That happened to be an arm of Paul Kellaway who was promptly pulled off his mount. When he told the extraordinary story of what had happened to Roddy

K

Armytage, *Barona*'s handler, the trainer advised the racecourse doctor that he stand the jockey down with concussion.

The only consolation for Paul was that he went on to ride *Barona* to victory in the Scottish National. When they returned to Aintree the following year, *Barona* went off as the 7-1 favourite and came with a late challenge to finish fourth with Kelleway reporting this time that the only time the horse had caught hold of the bridle was when a dog had chased him across the Melling Road. But again they went on to win the Scottish National.

It was Kelleway's last Grand National ride. In 1977, having ridden 392 winners, he successfully set up as a Newmarket trainer, quickly making his mark with *Swiss Maid* in the 1978 Champion Stakes; and three years later winning the Prix de Diane with *Madam Gay*, named after his daughter Gay Kelleway who in 1987 would become the first lady jockey to ride a winner at Royal Ascot. The lion-hearted Paul died of cancer in 1999 at the age of 58.

See also: Turnell, Andrew.

KELLSBORO' JACK

Relishing the fast going, seven year old *Kellsboro' Jack* made his only Grand National appearance a winning one of truly great distinction. In 1933, when he came home three lengths ahead of *Really True*, he set a new record time for the race: 9min 28sec. And, to the vociferous delight of a large U.S. contingent, he became the third American-owned winner – following *Sergeant Murphy* (1923) and *Jack Horner* (1926).

Bred at Kellsboro', near Kells in Co. Kilkenny, *Kellsboro' Jack* was logically named, being by *Jackdaw* out of *Kellsboro' Lass*. He was originally bought by Mr F. Ambrose Clark, the American sewing-machine millionaire, and placed in the care of Ivor Anthony who trained at Wroughton, near Swindon, Wiltshire – over the same gallops that been used by National winners *Ascetic's Silver* (1906), *Ally Sloper* (1915) and *Master Robert* (1924)

As a six year old the gelding was so often unlucky in his races that Anthony could only suggest that perhaps a change of ownership might also bring a change of fortune. Clark agreed to give it a try. He 'sold' the horse for just £1. The new owner was his wife, Florence, and sure enough the change worked. *Kellsboro' Jack* won three of his next four races, including a 20 lengths success in the 1932 Stanley Chase, run over one circuit of the Grand National course. Despite that success, he went off in the National at 25-1, with ten runners preferred in the betting. These included top-weighted, past winner *Gregalach*; the brilliant Irish mare *Heartbreak Hill*; and, first and foremost, *Golden Miller*, hailed as a 'wonder horse' after gaining his second successive Cheltenham Gold Cup and now coming to Aintree with a seasonal record of five wins in five races.

For all his achievements, the fact remained that *Golden Miller* was a favourite severely handicapped (on 12st 2lb) for a six year old. Also he was unfamiliar with Aintree's daunting fences, and that inexperience showed when he clumsily cleared Becher's the second time around. He narrowly escaped a fall there, but then he tackled the Canal Turn at too sharp an angle and unseated his rider.

Kellsboro' Jack, who had been a distant third behind *Golden Miller* at Cheltenham, was now leading a long-strung-out field, closely pursued by *Pelorus Jack*, the gelding who, without a rider, had put two-thirds of the runners out of the 1932 National. The two 'Jacks' came side by side to the last fence, but there *Pelorus Jack* blundered and fell; and *Kellsboro' Jack* maintained his pace over the flat to hold off the challenge of *Really True*, a 66-1 chance, and the fast finishing *Slater*.

It was an outstanding performance for a seven year old not lightly handicapped on 11st 9lb; and an especially well-deserved triumph for his professional jockey Dudley Williams, who had arguably been unlucky when finishing a close-up third on *Sir Lindsay* in 1930, and who had come third again on *Shaun Goilin* in 1932.

Remarkably, for the first time in National history, as many as 19 runners had completed the course, beating the previous record of 16 set in 1909. This year, as then, the finishers included two remounts. That record would stand for another seven years. But *Kellsboro' Jack*'s winning time – breaking by more than four seconds a speed record (*Cloister*'s) that had stood for 40 years – would be surpassed one year later when *Golden Miller* returned to show his true class.

Meanwhile, Mrs Ambrose Clark was so thankful for the success of her £1 gelding that she had vowed never again to subject him to such a stern test. Consequently, *Kellsboro' Jack* joined the select group of winners who have never been beaten over the National course.

In time, however, Mrs Ambrose was persuaded by trainer Anthony to let her horse at least race over less demanding jumps at Liverpool. He came back to compete in the Champion Chase of 1936 and 1937, each time winning in impressive style. Moreover, ridden by Danny Morgan, he finished in the frame in three consecutive Cheltenham Gold Cups, 1934-36, and won the 1935 Scottish Grand National.

With his reputation enhanced, *Kellsboro' Jack* was now retired to the Clarks' estate at Cooperstown in New York State; and following his death from old age he was buried atop one of the Adirondack foothills, below a headstone alongside that of Mr Clark's *Sorley Boy,* who had won the 1936 Welsh Grand National.

See also: Williams, Dudley; Anthony, Ivor.

KEMPTON, John

Trainer of the 1967 Grand National shock winner, *Foinavon* – such a 100-1 no-hoper that John Kempton was not even at Aintree to see his horse run. Instead he was at Worcester that day, winning a novice hurdle on *Three Dons*, also trained at his small yard at Compton in Berkshire. Like *Foinavon*'s owner, Mr Cyril Watkins, he only saw his greatest triumph on TV.

Kempton (born November 13, 1938) originally aimed to become a veterinary surgeon but had to abandon his studies in Epsom through lack of funds. For a while he worked as a blacksmith, then turned to race-riding and set up as a trainer on a shoestring. His greatest success ensued when two of his owners asked him to find a low-priced horse that might be able to run in the National. In 1965, at the Doncaster Sales, he secured *Foinavon* for 2,000 guineas.

Foinavon had not won for two seasons and had fallen four times in succession in Ireland. Now Kempton sharpened up his jumping by sending him out regularly with the Old Berkshire Hunt and putting him over a big, purpose-built spruce fence. He also successfully raced him in a bitless bridle, an unusual ploy which he had previously adopted to bring about much improved form in *Seas End,* the rank outsider on which he had pulled up in the Grand Nationals of 1962 and 1963.

Although *Foinavon* had finished a creditable fourth in the King George VI Chase on Boxing Day, his prospects for the National were dismissed by virtue of his poor showing – seventh and last under Kempton – in the 1967 Cheltenham Gold Cup. With

some regret, the trainer now ruled himself out for the Aintree ride, largely because he would be putting up 10lb overweight. Instead, after unsuccessfully approaching three other jockeys, he booked John Buckingham, a 26 year old rider without experience in the race.

Avoiding the extraordinary pile-up caused by a riderless horse at the small 23rd fence, *Foinavon* came from the rear to win by 15 lengths. But it was regarded as such a fluke that he carried only 5lb more when he returned for the 1968 National and went off at 66-1. This time, he was brought down at the Water.

As with rider John Buckingham, *Foinavon*'s victory represented the high point of Kempton's career. Unusually for a trainer, he liked to ride his horses in races, and once he had stopped riding in 1970 his enthusiasm for training rapidly waned. After he had quit training, he did return briefly to racing as assistant trainer to David Barons in Devon, but then finally made a new career in sailing, establishing a yacht-chartering business in Salcombe, schooling his customers in navigation and sub-aqua diving, and later running a cruise boat to deliver divers around the west coast.

See also: Foinavon; Buckingham, John.

KENDALL, Joseph

Winning jockey on seven year old *Jealousy*, the 5-1 second favourite, in the 1861 Grand National. Having failed to finish on the mare in the 1859 National, Joe Kendall only retained the ride by a stroke of good fortune. The great George Stevens had turned down 13 offers in favour of riding the much-fancied *Jealousy*, but he was then claimed by a retainer to ride another horse who was withdrawn at the last minute.

Kendall had also failed to complete the course when making his National debut in 1856 on *The Potter*, a 10-1 chance; and again in 1857 on *Omar Pasha*. He finally succeeded in getting round at the fourth attempt, in 1860, when he was on the top-weighted *Brunette*, the seventh of seven finishers in the race won by hot favourite *Anatis*. One year later *Anatis* was again the clear favourite while *Brunette* reopposed on 22lb better terms. But Kendall shrewdly deserted the latter to ride *Jealousy* who was correctly regarded by connections as a 'good thing' on a mere 9st 12lb.

In 1863 Kendall resumed the winning partnership

K

for what was to be his sixth and final appearance in the National. *Jealousy* was now the 3-1 favourite but, with an extra 26lb on her back, she was outpaced from the second Becher's onwards and came home the sixth of six finishers. Appropriately, the winner – Lord Coventry's *Emblem* – was ridden by George Stevens, gaining the second of his record five National victories.

See also: Jealousy.

KILMORE

As a relative latecomer – one badly under-rated – Irish-bred *Kilmore* adapted to the challenges of Aintree with extraordinary swiftness and aplomb. On his 1961 Grand National debut, as an 11 year old, he finished a close-up fifth at 33-1. One year later, still unfancied, he came back to win decisively from a field that included three former winners, plus *Wyndburgh*, twice runner-up. And in 1963, with an extra 10lb to carry, he finished a creditable fifth out of 47 starters.

Sired by *Zalophus*, *Kilmore* was out of *Brown Image*, a mare descended from the supremely popular *Brown Jack* who, most unusually, had made his mark by winning the Champion Hurdle before becoming a giant of the Flat, six times winner of the Alexandra Stakes. In Ireland, under several different trainers, Kilmore scored 11 wins in 54 starts over hurdles and fences, but without ever looking more than an honest, workaday performer. Then, in 1960, he moved to England, having been bought for £3,000 on behalf of film producer Nat Cohen, a partner with Stuart Levy in Anglo-Amalgamated Films, the company which had launched the 'Carry on' movies in 1958.

The man responsible for this inspired purchase was Captain Ryan Price. Though renowned primarily as a trainer of hurdlers, he had picked out *Kilmore* as a likely Grand National type. And within a few months of the gelding's arrival at his Findon (Sussex) yard, he had the ten-year-old sufficiently well-tuned to finish fifth in the National behind the winning grey, *Nicolaus Silver*.

His rider that day was Fred Winter, who had won on *Sundew* in 1957. Much impressed with his mount's safe jumping and stamina, Fred saw him as a great prospect for his winning of a second National in 1962. His high hopes, however, were hardly supported by *Kilmore*'s subsequent form. In November, *Kilmore* fell in the Becher Chase at Aintree, and he fell at Lingfield only ten days before the National. Having failed to win any of his five previous races, he now went off equal 12th in the betting on 28-1. The clear favourite was a hugely promising newcomer, *Frenchman's Cove*, seven-year-old son of the 1946 Derby winner *Airborne*.

This National provided a classic example of atrociously heavy ground favouring the older, more experienced horses. The well-supported *Springbok*, an eight year old, fell at the first. The young favourite was brought down at the 19th. Meanwhile, Winter, taking his usual route towards the inside, sat still and patient on his sure stayer, delaying his challenge until the final mile. At the last fence, *Kilmore* touched down in the lead, and thereafter pulled steadily ahead from two other 12 year olds – *Wyndburgh* and former winner *Mr What* – to win by ten lengths and another ten back to the third.

He was never to win again. However, in the 1963 National, with an extra 10lb, the same combination did well to finish sixth despite having been knocked by a horse falling at the Water Jump; and in 1964 Winter loyally stayed with the 14 year old only to be a faller at the fence before the second Becher's. The veteran chaser was then retired to Findon where he lived on for another 17 years.

See also: Winter, Frederick; Price, Ryan.

KING, Jeffery

Born July 6, 1941, Jeff King is arguably the best National Hunt rider never to have been champion jockey and among the greatest never to have won the Grand National. In 2002, when asked to name the six best jumps jockeys of the modern era, seven times champion John Francome named King as the third best – after Tony McCoy and Richard Dunwoody. Yet King, famed especially for his strength in a finish, was unsuccessful in 15 National rides. His best result was in 1969 when coming home third with *Rondetto*, a 13 year old on whom he had fallen at the 26th in 1965 and at the 23rd in 1968.

Altogether, between 1960 and 1981, King won 710 races, including the 1966 King George VI Chase (*Dormant*), the 1967 Hennessy Cognac Gold Cup (*Rondetto*) and the 1976 Whitbread Gold Cup (*Otter Way*). His near-record number of appearances in the Grand National began in 1964 with a non-finishing ride on Mr Jim Joel's *Beau Normand* and continued until 1980 with breaks only in 1967 and 1979.

Loyally he stayed with *Rondetto* as a 14 year old, riding him for a fourth time in 1970 when they came down with seven others at the first open ditch. He fell on *The Laird* (1971) and *Fortina's Palace* (1972), and when in 1973 he fell on the well-supported *Ashville*, a runner-up at the Cheltenham Festival, it was the third time in four years that he had come to grief at the third. However, he finished fourth on Lord Chelsea's *Money Market* in 1975, ninth on 13 year old *Spanish Steps* (1976), and sixth on Lord Vestey's *What A Buck* (1977).

Eleven times he failed to complete the course, but that was often riding relative no-hopers – most notably Japan's seven year old *Fujino-o*, a top-weighted 100-1 shot in 1966 and Lord Chelsea's *Roman Holiday*, a 66-1 chance, in 1974. His last appearance was in 1980 when he fell on Mr Raymond Guest's *Casamayor*, a 50-1 shot. Soon after he began a long career as a trainer.

KINSKY, Prince Karel Andreas

In 1883, as an Austro-Hungarian nobleman – then styled as Count 'Charles' Kinsky – Prince Karel became the first foreigner (excluding the Irish) to ride in the Grand National, winning on his debut with his own chestnut mare, six year old *Zoedone*. His challenge was inspired by the example set the previous year by Lord Manners, who had triumphed first time as an owner-rider.

Like Lord Manners, Kinsky was a prominent huntsman, having been born in 1858 into a Bohemian family with large estates and a stable sufficient to warrant having their own Master of Horse, an English ex-cavalry officer named Rowland Reynolds. His mother, a princess of Liechtenstein, employed Reynolds as riding instructor to her eight children, and it was he who filled Kinsky's boyhood head with the romance of the National.

The count first witnessed the race in 1878 when, as a soldier, he accompanied Empress Elizabeth of Austria on a hunting trip to England. Three years later he moved to London as a diplomat for the Austro-Hungarian Empire, and continued to pursue his passion for hunting. Then, in 1882, the 24 year old Count won £1000 at Newmarket with the Cesarewitch success of *Corrie Roy*. That same day, on the spur of the moment, he approached owner Mr Edward Clayton with an offer for his five year old mare *Zoedone* who had been the third of three finishers in the National

won by Lord Manners on *Seaman*. His offer – 800 guineas with a further 200 guineas if the horse won at Aintree – was accepted, and the mare was sent to Upton to be trained by Mr W.H.P. Jenkins, formerly a successful jump jockey.

Kinsky personally schooled his mare at Upton, rode her to a 20 lengths victory in the Great Sandown Steeplechase, and two months later they lined up for the 1883 National. There were only ten starters – the smallest of all National fields – with Tommy Beasley on the 3-1 favourite *Zitella*. Nonetheless, it was a quality field; also, following much criticism, many fences had been restored to their original size.

Faced with heavy going, Kinsky was advised by Clayton and Jenkins to ride *Zoedone* as though he were out hunting and to rely on her main strength: stamina. He did so to the letter, delaying his challenge until the second Becher's and holding a clear lead from Valentine's onwards. The six year old mare went through the second last fence, but otherwise gave her backers no worries, going on to win by ten lengths from the outsider *Black Prince*.

The story goes that professional jockey Joe Adams, who had pulled up on *Athlacca*, afterwards groused: 'What the hell are we coming to? Last year it was a bloomin' lord won the National, this year it's a furring count and next year it'll be an old woman most likely.' To which, reportedly, Count Kinsky replied: 'Yes, Jimmy, and I hope this old woman will be yourself.'

Taking a 16lb hike in the weights, *Zoedone* was again well ridden by the count to finish fifth in the 1884 National. But the following year evidence strongly suggested that skulduggery – not weight – was the mare's undoing. When Kinsky was about to mount up in the paddock, a smear of blood showed where his white sleeve had brushed the horse's muzzle. Investigation uncovered a minute puncture mark near a nostril.

Had she been 'got at'? Nothing was proved, but certainly the mare – backed down to 5-1 second favouritism – ran as though she had been drugged. She moved listlessly going down and fell at the single hurdle which, in those days, was jumped as a formality on the way to the start. Kinsky remounted, determined to give backers a run for their money. Alas, *Zoedone* lumbered awkwardly in the rear, struggling around until finally collapsing in a heap at the fence before Becher's second time around. The race

K

was won by the favourite, *Roquefort*.

Eight years old, the mare never raced again. The count – later to succeed his father Prince Ferdinand as head of the Kinsky dynasty – also never appeared at Aintree again. However, behind the scenes, he remained a prominent figure in racing, being elected a member of the National Hunt Committee, and becoming an honorary member of the Jockey Club and the French Steeplechase Society.

He also enjoyed a close, much-publicised friendship with the former Jennie Jerome, American-born wife of Lord Randolph Churchill and mother of Sir Winston Churchill. Kinsky was besotted with her. For her part, the promiscuous Lady Randolph Churchill later stated that she would not have seen so much of the count if it had not been for so many unfounded rumours that they were having an affair. But historical evidence indicates that his passion was fully reciprocated and that at one time she hoped to marry him.

And then, all at once, Prince Kinsky's hugely enjoyable lifestyle turned into a nightmare as Europe was torn apart by the madness of the First World War. His people were at war with a country he truly loved. Faced with a most difficult choice, he deliberately avoided fighting against Britain by volunteering for service with the cavalry on the Russian front. He survived the conflict but not its aftermath which saw his family estates swallowed up by the newly created Czechoslovakia. A totally dejected figure, suffering badly from shell-shock, he died in his devastated homeland in 1919.

See also: Zoedone; Foul Play; Jenkins, W.H.P.

KIRKLAND

An exceptionally safe jumper, *Kirkland* made a well-ordered progression to victory in the Grand National. Having won the 1902 Grand Sefton at Aintree, he first ran in the premier handicap chase as a seven year old: in 1903 when he finished strongly to gain fourth place, just a head behind the ageing *Manifesto*. The following year, in a race of many fallers, he was runner-up by eight lengths to the giant *Moifaa*. And he improved once again in 1905 to win by three lengths from *Napper Tandy*.

It was hugely popular success in Liverpool since *Kirkland* was owned by a local industrialist, Frank Bibby, and ridden, as always, by the popular local jockey, Frank 'Tich' Mason. Indeed, so highly valued was this racing partnership that, for fear of a pre-National injury, Mason had been paid £300 not to ride in the two weeks prior to the race.

Bred by an Irish clergyman, the Rev. E. Clifford, Kirkland was sired in Co. Limerick by the Australian stallion *Kirkham* out of the mare *Perizonius*. After showing promising form as a four year old he was bought by the wealthy Mr Bibby and schooled at Lawrenny Park, near Tenby in Pembrokeshire. Though the licence holder was a Mr E. Thomas, the training was primarily conducted by Mr Lort Phillips who had a share in the horse.

As a five year old, *Kirkland* was a prolific winner of chases. Thereafter he was much less successful, but he had showed such a liking for Aintree that, despite an injury scare one week before the 1905 National, he went off the 6-1 second favourite. Ahead of him in the betting was King Edward's VII's *Moifaa*, seeking a second successive victory. But *Moifaa*, burdened with top weight, fell at the second Becher's; and again *Kirkland*'s secure jumping was to prove a key factor in a National which saw 20 of the 27 starters fail to complete the course. Held up on the first circuit, he was produced late to take the lead two fences out; and then, led home by the riderless *Ascetic's Silver*, stayed on strongly for victory.

After a two-year break, *Kirkland* made one last appearance at Aintree, in the 1908 National. Such was his lasting reputation that, despite carrying top weight, the 12 year old gelding was made the 13-2 favourite. For the first time he was a faller, though only at the last fence, and, remounted by Mason, he came home the seventh out of just eight finishers.

See also: Mason, Frank; Bibby, Frank.

KNIGHT, Henrietta Catherine

The sister-in-law of Lord Vestey, chairman of Cheltenham racecourse, Henrietta Knight is arguably the greatest National Hunt lady trainer since Jenny Pitman. Unlike the 'Queen of Aintree', however, she is most famed for her achievements at Cheltenham. In 2002 she sent out *Best Mate* to win a highly competitive Gold Cup. One year later, her champion chaser became the first horse to win back-to-back Gold Cups since *L'Escargot* 32 years before, and then, in 2004, the first to score a hat-trick of Gold Cups since the mighty *Arkle* in 1966.

Born in London on December 15, 1946, Knight is the older daughter of a former Coldstream Guards major-turned-farmer, and she was a schoolmistress (teaching biology) and a selector for the 1988 Olympic eventing team before taking out a full training licence in 1989. She established her base at West Lockinge, near Wantage, Oxfordshire, and six years later her marriage to former champion jump jockey Terry Biddlecombe founded a celebrated training partnership.

Together 'Hen' and Terry would divide the yard and 'compete' to see who had the most winners. But it was essentially working in harness that they had many notable successes including the 1997 Stayers' Hurdle at Cheltenham with Lord Vestey's *Karshi*; the 1998 Grand Annual Chase and the 2000 Champion Chase with *Edredon Bleu*; the 2000 Royal and SunAlliance Chase with *Lord Noelie*; and the 2002 King George VI Chase with *Best Mate*. After his second successive Cheltenham Gold Cup *Best Mate* was widely rated as the best-ever chaser since the might *Arkle*.

Knight's runners in the Grand National have been relatively few – not surprisingly so since she had no liking for such a perilous race. Discouragingly, in 1997, her first challenger, *Full Of Oats*, had fallen with Jim Culloty at the first fence. Six years passed before she was represented again – this time with three strong entries: *Maximize*, owned by her sister Lady Vestey, and *Chives* and *Southern Star*, two of three runners owned by the leisure empire magnate Trevor Hemmings.

Chives, an eight year old high in the handicap under 11st 5lb, was most strongly supported since he had carried 7lb more when finishing runner-up to *Mini Sensation* in the Coral Welsh National, and had finished an eye-catching seventh in the Cheltenham Gold Cup. Going off at 10-1, he was well beaten when he blundered the 11th and was pulled up at the next, having broken a blood vessel. *Maximize* was also well fancied since he had never fallen and had recently been fourth in the William Hill Handicap Chase at the Cheltenham Festival. But now he was one of five fallers at the 19th; and Henrietta's third string, *Southern Star*, was the last of 14 finishers.

At this stage Knight planned to slim down her training operation, concentrating on high quality with perhaps 25 or 30 horses rather than nearly 80. The quality certainly showed in the 2003-4 season when she again saddled the King George VI winner – this time, most unexpectedly, with *Edredon Bleu* at 25-1 – and went on to her historic Gold Cup hat-trick with *Best Mate*. Victory in the 2004 National would have made her the first trainer to saddle the Gold Cup and National winner in the same season since Fred Rimell scored with *Royal Frolic* and *Rag Trade* in 1976. Her only runner, however, was the unfancied *Southern Star* who soon dropped behind and was pulled up before the 18th.

At the end of 2004 Knight was presented with the Jumps Trainer of the Year award. The following March *Best Mate* suffered a broken a blood vessel, so ending his bid to emulate *Golden Miller*'s unique feat of four Cheltenham Gold Cups. There was never a question a of entering him for the Grand National as an alternative. Knight explained: 'He's become public property and I think there would be an outcry if we ever entered him. If he was hurt at Aintree, it wouldn't do the sport any good.'
See also: Biddlecombe, Terence.

KNIGHT, Steven Charles
Steve Knight came relatively late to the hurly-burly of the Grand National – in 1986 when, at the age of 31, he took the ride on *Tracys Special*, a 150-1 outsider from the virus-stricken Andy Turnell stable. After they had fallen at Valentine's first time round, he remarked: 'I met it a bit wrong. Never mind, we will be back to win it next year.' Remarkably, he was half right. He did win in 1987, but most unexpectedly on a different and older gelding: Mr Jim Joel's 11 year old *Maori Venture*. It was just reward for his years of loyalty to the Turnell family through good times and bad.

Born February 4, 1955, Knight had started his jockey career as an apprentice with Richard Hannon, riding his first winner at the age of 16. He soon proved too heavy to ride on the Flat, joined trainer Bob Turnell's yard near Marlborough, Wiltshire, and was still a conditional jockey when he scored his first big-race success: the 1975 Whitbread Gold Cup on *April Seventh*. Thereafter progress was slow, and five years passed before he had other notable victories: winning the Sun Alliance Chase (on *Lacson*) and the County Handicap Hurdle (*Prince of Bermuda*) at the Cheltenham Festival.

In 1982 Knight became the stable's first jockey in place of Andy Turnell who had turned to training following his father's death. Though wins were still few and far between, he remained with the stable as it struggled to survive after being re-established at East Hendred in Oxfordshire. The yard's revival

K

finally came with the arrival of *Maori Venture* on whom Knight twice won Newbury's Mandarin Chase, and was reinforced by the success of *Tawbridge*, winner of five successive novice chases in 1986-87. Though the former was a somewhat dodgy jumper and had failed to get round in the Irish Grand National, Steve still saw him as a stronger prospect for Aintree than the out-of-form *Tracys Special*. Under pressure from jockey and trainer, owner Jim Joel agreed to risk him over the big fences. The opposition in a 40-strong field included two former winners, *Corbiere* and *West Tip*, and the hugely-fancied grey *Dark Ivy*.

True to expectation, *Maori Venture* blundered over a number of fences. But each time he survived a clumsy landing – unlike, most tragically, *Dark Ivy* who, sandwiched between horses, fell fatally at Becher's. Making only his second appearance in the race, Knight patiently held a mid-field position, then timed his late challenge to perfection, advancing on the leading pack at the second Becher's and then outpacing *The Tsarevich* on the run-in after they had overhauled the long-time leader *Lean Ar Aghaidh*. The win, by five lengths, was in the then third fastest time on record. Stablemate *Tracys Special* finished sixth.

The victorious *Maori Venture* was immediately retired by his 92 year old owner who also announced that his winner would be left in his will to the successful jockey.

Knight had only one more ride in the National – in 1988 when *Tracys Special* never handled the soft ground and, after breaking a blood vessel, had to be pulled up at the 21st fence. Then, early in the following season, he too retired from racing.

See also: Maori Venture; Turnell, Andrew.

L

LADY RIDERS

Fourteen women have ridden in the Grand National, and in a total of 17 attempts just four have completed the course: Geraldine Rees, the last of eight finishers on *Cheers* (1982); Rosemary Henderson, fifth on her *Fiddlers Pike* (1994); Carrie Ford, fifth on *Forest Gunner* (2005); and Nina Carberry, ninth on *Forest Gunner* (2006). Women were not allowed to ride in the race until 1976 and only three have taken part in the past 17 years. Their overall record:

1977 Charlotte Brew – *Barony Fort* (200-1) refused 27th
1979 Jenny Hembrow – *Sandwilian* (100-1) fell first
1980 Jenny Hembrow – *Sandwilian* (100-1) pulled up 19th
1981 Linda Sheedy – *Deiopea* (100-1) refused 19th
1982 Geraldine Rees – *Cheers* (66-1) eighth (last); Charlotte Brew – *Martinstown* (100-1) unseated third
1983 Geraldine Rees – *Midday Welcome* (500-1) fell first; Joy Carrier – *King Spruce* (28-1) unseated sixth
1984 Valerie Alder – *Bush Guide* (33-1) fell eighth
1987 Jacqui Oliver – *Eamons Owen* (200-1) unseated 15th
1988 Gee Armytage – *Gee-A* (33-1) pulled up 22nd; Venetia Williams – *Marcolo* (2001) fell sixth; Penny Ffitch-Heyes – *Hettinger* (200-1) fell first
1989 Tarnya Davis – *Numerate* (100-1) pulled up 21st
1994 Rosemary Henderson – *Fiddlers Pike* (100-1) fifth
2005 Carrie Ford – *Forest Gunner* (8-1) fifth
2006 Nina Carberry – *Forest Gunner* (33-1) ninth

Remarkably it was not until late 1971 that the Jockey Club finally yielded to pressure and agreed that women could ride under Rules in Britain – and then only in amateur races on the Flat. The following May, the first all-women jockeys' race, with a 21-strong field, was won by the 50-1 shot *Scorched Earth*, ridden at Kempton Park by Meriel Tufnell. The victorious lady went on to become champion woman rider in Britain and Europe over the next few seasons. But it was not until 1975, the year of her retirement from the saddle, that women gained permission to ride against professionals.

Throughout this period of change the idea of lady riders being allowed to compete in National Hunt racing was strongly resisted – regardless of the fact that women so often risked life and limb over 30 hairy obstacles across country in eventing. Moreover, the Jockey Club remained opposed despite the fact that, way back in 1927, when consulted, it had not disapproved of a woman riding for the first time in Czechoslovakia's supremely demanding Velka Pardubicka marathon chase. (The lady rider, Lata Brandisova, was three times placed in the race, finally won in 1937, and competed over fences for 20 years before a bad fall finally ended her career).

However, in January, 1976, the Sex Discrimination Act came into effect. The following month Diana Thorne (later Mrs Nicky Henderson) became the first lady to ride a winner under National Hunt Rules. And, most importantly, on April 1 of that year, Charlotte Brew from Coggeshall, Essex, became the first woman to complete one circuit of the National course. By finishing fourth and last in the Greenall Whitley Fox Hunters' Chase, her horse *Barony Fort* had qualified for the Grand National proper.

Thus, on April 2, 1977, history was made. As the first woman ever to ride in the National, 21 year old Miss Brew set off on her own *Barony Fort*, priced at 200-1, and successfully cleared 26 of the 30 fences before her 12 year old mount finally refused at the fourth last. It was a noble effort that would have won her huge attention but for one major distraction: *Red Rum* achieving a unique third victory.

There was still much fierce opposition – from *Red Rum*'s trainer Ginger McCain among others – to women riding in the National; and it was greatly fuelled in 1979 when Jenny Hembrow, a former champion point-to-point rider, suffered an extremely heavy, first fence fall on *Sandwilan*. One year later she pulled up at the 19th with the same horse, again a 100-1 outsider. In 1981 mother of twins Linda Sheedy also reached the 19th where the mare *Deiopea* (100-1) refused. Then, in 1982, when Charlotte was again in the line-up (unseated by her mother's *Martinstown* at the third) Geraldine Rees became the first woman to complete the race, coming in the last of eight finishers on *Cheers*, priced at 66-1, with 5-1 on offer for getting round.

L

The first year to see two women riding in the National was 1982. And it happened again in 1983 when Mrs Rees followed up her historic finish with a first fence fall on *Midday Welcome*, a 500-1 no-hoper. With her in the 41-strong field was the first American woman to enter the fray: Mrs Joy Carrier on her husband's *King Spruce* who had won last year's Irish National. She had outstanding credentials, having twice won over the timbers of the Maryland Hunt Cup; and it was an indication of lady riders being taken more seriously that *King Spruce* went off as short as 28-1. He fell at the first Becher's.

Valerie Alder was five years old when her father, John, finished ninth on his *Tant Pis* in the 1965 Grand National. Nineteen years later she achieved her ambition of taking part in the race. She rode her own eight year old *Bush Guide*, a faller at the Canal Turn. The following year, 1985, Mrs Carrier was hoping to be the one lady rider in the race. But in 1984 – the year in which Mrs Ann Ferris became the first lady jockey to ride the winner (*Bentom Boy*) of the Irish Grand National, with her sister Rosemary finishing third – a 40-runner limit had been put on the field at Aintree. *King Spruce*, trained by Bob Champion, was No 41 and eliminated.

In 1986 Caroline Beasley, riding *Eliogarty* in the Fox Hunters' Chase, became the first lady to win a race over one circuit of the Grand National course. The following year there was the prospect for the first time of a brother and sister riding in the National. Gee Armytage was a late booking to ride *The Ellier* after Mark Dwyer had broken his left wrist on the Friday, and so she would join her brother Marcus who was riding *Brown Veil*, trained by their father. But Gee had injured her knee in a fall on the Thursday, and now she was judged unfit to ride. Frank Berry took over on *The Ellier* and finished seventh. Marcus pulled up at the 23rd. But there was still a lady rider: Jacqui Oliver on 12 year old *Eamons Owen*. A 200-1 shot, he ran well before unseating his rider when hitting the top of The Chair.

The 1988 National saw the first and only triple challenge by lady riders: Gee Armytage on *Gee-A*, named after his owner-trainer G.A. Hubbard, 33-1; Venetia Williams on *Marcolo*, 200-1; and Penny Ffitch-Heyes on *Hettinger*, also 200-1, trained by her father. Odds of 12-1 against *Hettinger* completing the course attracted one bet of £1,000. But these were stingy odds about a horse who had the worst jumping record in the 40-runner line-up, having

fallen or unseated his rider five times that season. More realistically, bookmakers City Index sponsored the horse to the tune of £100 for every fence jumped, the proceeds to go to Ian Botham's appeal for the Leukaemia Fund. There were no proceeds. *Hettinger* fell at the first.

The 24 year old rider described it as 'the biggest disappointment of my life. I would love to do it again on something that jumps'. Fortunately, however, she was not on *Hettinger* when the bay gelding reappeared in the 1989 National. Instead a man, Ray Goldstein, took the ride; and the horse went off at even longer odds of 300-1. This time bookmakers Victor Chandler were donating £200 to Leukaemia Research if the pair made it over the first fence and a further £100 for each fence cleared. The partnership collected £600 by jumping five fences cleanly but then they came down in a pile-up at Becher's which saw five horses fall, two of them fatally. Not for the first time Goldstein suffered severe concussion after a ride on the unpredictable *Hettinger*.

Marcolo, ambitiously backed by a punter from Chorley to win £300,000, was a safer jumper. Also he had a lady jockey who was a formidable and successful point-to-point rider. But after safely negotiating five fences, the gelding crashed out at Becher's. Miss Williams, destined to become an outstanding National Hunt trainer, was briefly detained in hospital with a whiplash injury to the neck. (A couple of weeks later she was destined to have two months in hospital after an horrific neck-breaking fall in a hurdle race at Worcester).

In contrast, Gee Armytage, 22-year-old daughter of East Ilsley trainer Roddy Armytage, had a most promising ride on *Gee-A*. Following an appearance on the Terry Wogan show, she had become the 'housewives' choice', backed to win millions of pounds. On the day, *Gee-A* cut out the early pace, briefly disputed the lead, and was still going well when sadly he had to be pulled up after Becher's on the second circuit. At that point, Miss Armytage had strained a muscle in her back. Otherwise, so she judged, they would certainly have completed the course and very possibly run into a place.

This minor injury fuelled the prejudice of Colonel Blimps who still contended that women were not physically strong enough to compete in the National. But more reasonable was the view expressed by the intrepid Miss Armytage before the race: 'It is only a matter of time before a woman rides the winner of the National. It's all about having the right horse and that all-important slice of luck in the running.' She herself indicated that she lacked nothing in the fitness and resolution necessary to win a National when she ran the London Marathon in a most respectable three hours 17 minutes.

In 1989, however, only one lady rider secured a place in the line-up: Tarnya Davis on *Numerate*, a last-minute purchase owned and trained by her father, Peter Davis. Having been placed in his five previous races, the bay gelding was quoted at a stingy 6-1 to complete the course. Yet he was a 100-1 chance in the overall betting and, though jumping well enough, he was exhausted on the sticky ground and had to be pulled up at the 21st. Miss Davis's interest in the National would later be renewed via her marriage to trainer Oliver Sherwood.

In 1990 Miss Armytage was in hospital after breaking bones in a fall. Otherwise she could have taken the ride on *Gee-A* who finished 18th on the day that her brother Marcus won the race in record time on *Mr Frisk*. Three years later, the next lady rider to join the National line-up was 22 year old Judy Davies who, as a 7lb claimer, had to seek special permission from the Jockey Club following a 1991 clamp-down on inexperienced jockeys taking part. Starting as an amateur with trainer Bill Preece before turning professional, she had ridden 11 winners, including two over fences. She had just had her first taste of Aintree's formidable fence when riding in the 1993 John Hughes Chase. Now, two days later, she was to make her National debut on the 300-1 outsider *Formula One*, owned by her father and trained by John Edwards.

On the eve of the race she said that her plan was 'to jump off middle to outer and keep out of the way as much as possible because my fella doesn't like being surrounded by other horses'. But she never did jump off. At the second attempt to start the race, *Formula One* moved forward in the split second before the tape went up and it caught her mount under his neck. Other horses became entangled, left at the start while 30 set off in a race declared void.

Prejudice against lady riders continued. That year, for example, Steve Smith Eccles wrote in his autobiography, *The Last of the Cavaliers*: 'Bluntly, I have never yet seen a girl jump jockey who is any better than a third-rate man. In general, they are more of a nuisance than a virtue and, because they will never compete on my terms, I would prefer if they were not riding at all.'

Yet one year later the 1994 National saw a truly extraordinary challenge by a lady rider: Rosemary Henderson, aged 51. National jockeys were required to have ridden a minimum of 15 winners under Rules. But Mrs Henderson, a vet's wife, was granted special dispensation by the Jockey Club because of her wide experience in point-to-points where she had been successful 39 times.

The oldest rider in the race, she was popularly dubbed 'the Galloping Granny', though, in reality, she had no children. Her horse, 13 year old *Fiddlers Pike* – on whom she had won the Warwick National and the John Hughes Grand National Trial at Chepstow in the previous season – was also the oldest in a 36-strong field: a bay gelding which she owned and trained and regarded as a family pet. Seen at his best in hunter chases, *Fiddlers Pike* was dismissed as 'too old to be taken seriously', and he went off at 100-1.

Standing upright in her irons, amateur Mrs Henderson controlled her no-hoper brilliantly, neatly finessing all the fences and making such persistent late progress on the heavy ground that she finished to tumultuous applause as the fifth of only six riders to complete the course. In the process she landed a family bet of £50 at 8-1 that she would complete – a modest reward for her supreme effort.

Only the second lady rider ever to finish in the Grand National, Mrs Henderson had set a new standard for her sex. Subsequently, however, there were fewer opportunities for lady riders. At the time of the 1999 National, Britain had 214 licensed professional jump jockeys. Only four were women and only one, Sophia Mitchell, had ridden the 15 winners on British courses necessary to qualify for the National. She had ridden 39 winners, including one on the Flat, since turning professional four years earlier. But being only 5ft 1in and a mere 7st 12oz, she had little hope of ever getting a National ride. As she expressed it: 'Many trainers still believe we are not strong enough for riding over fences. I totally disagree. After all, women are among the best all over the world in other equine events like eventing and show-jumping'.

The reluctance of trainers to engage a lady rider in the National was underlined that year when Mr Ray Woodcock, a Halifax punter, had his last chance of pulling off an incredible treble. A decade earlier he had staked a £400 bet, in doubles and one treble,

L

that before the end of the 20th century Cliff Richard would receive a knighthood, a British heavyweight boxer would win a world title, and a woman would ride a National winner. He gained £11,000 with the success of Richard and Lennox Lewis. The 1999 National offered him his last hope of winning a further £128,000.

Unfortunately, there was no sign of a lady rider appearing in the race. Hoping to have a least a run for his money, the punter offered a £50,000 share of his winnings to any trainer or owner prepared to engage a lady jockey for their runner. There were no takers.

Indeed, a whole decade passed before another lady challenger came forward. In 2005 *Forest Gunner* was allotted a place in the handicap proper. The 11 year old, a £4,000 bargain buy, was trained in Cheshire by Richard Ford; and his wife, Carrie, had already won with him over the National fences, in the 2004 Fox Hunters' Chase, just ten weeks after giving birth to a daughter. ('Jumping those fences was easier than childbirth,' she quipped).

Forest Gunner had subsequently won over the same fences when ridden by Peter Buchanan in the Grand Sefton, and in February, 2005, the combination had won the £120,000 Red Square Vodka Gold Cup Chase over an extended three and a half miles at Haydock. But Buchanan was now to be claimed to ride *Strong Resolve* in the National. Consequently, 32 year old Mrs Ford proposed to come out of retirement to take over in the big race which she had first attended as a child in the year that Rees became the first woman to complete the course.

She lacked nothing in experience, having ridden her first point-to-point at the age of 16, and having had 99 rides against professional jockeys. She had won five races out of six on *Forest Gunner*, and since retiring she had maintained her fitness, every day riding out at least four lots, swimming 50 lengths and running two miles or more. And one thing was for certain: she would have no trouble making the weights. Just 5ft 3in tall, she normally weighed under nine stone.

For the first time the possibility of a lady riding the National winner was taken very seriously indeed. Ginger McCain was virtually alone in completely dismissing such an outcome and a number of pundits actually made her their first choice to win the richest-ever National, with a first prize of £406,000. Incredibly, *Forest Gunner* went off as the

8-1 second favourite and bookmakers claimed that his winning would cost them all of £100 million.

Astutely, Mrs Ford turned professional before the race so that, if winning, she would receive an extra £37,000 in riding percentages. For weeks she endured unrelenting media pressure and in the race she did nothing wrong, avoiding trouble and making steady progress from the Canal Turn second time around. Stamina was always the one doubt, and in the end *Forest Gunner* just did not quite stay and was out-paced from two out. But still he finished well enough to take the £17,500 prize for fifth place – five places ahead of last year's winner *Amberleigh House* whose trainer McCain had threatened to bare his bum if a lady rode the winner.

The real potential of lady riders was further established in 2006 when 21-year-old Nina Carberry took over the ride on *Forest Gunner*. Here, as never before, was a lady rider supremely qualified to aspire to Grand National success. On pedigree alone she had outstanding claims: a maternal grandfather (Dan Moore) who had failed by a debatable head to win the 1938 National on *Royal Danieli* and who had trained the 1975 winner, *L'Escargot*; a father (Tom Carberry) who had ridden that 1938 winner; and a brother (Paul) who had won in 1999 on *Bobbyjo*, trained by their father.

More importantly, while growing up with five brothers, Nina had developed into a truly outstanding horsewoman, as evinced in 2005 when she became the first woman to win a professional race at the Cheltenham Festival since Gee Armytage in 1987. Following her later successes over jumps, the 1996 National-winning rider Mick Fitzgerald observed, 'She doesn't ride like a girl'; and even the all-conquering A.P. McCoy recognised that 'for a girl she's exceptional.'

Sadly, Nina's credentials for National success were not matched by her mount in 2006. *Forest Gunner* was now 12 years old, past his best and with an extra 3lb to carry. Nevertheless he was still in contention until four out whereupon he began to fade; and in bringing him home, the last of nine finishers, Nina at least outscored her famous brother Paul who had fallen on *Sir OJ* at the second Becher's. Given the right horse, here surely was a lady rider equipped to make Velvet Brown a reality.

Will a lady rider ever win the Grand National? Not only male chauvinists have dismissed the possibility. As long ago as 1990 Mercy Rimell wrote in

Reflections on Racing: 'I still don't approve of women jockeys – except in point-to-points and hunter chases, of course. Really they're not the right make or shape for it. I don't approve of women riding in open professional races under Rules. They are not strong enough. Most women are not as strong as men.'

But how can the possibility be so confidently dismissed in this age of the superwoman? Until it happened, in 2005, no one would have believed that a woman (Dame Ellen MacArthur) would be sufficiently strong, mentally and physically, to sail round the world in the fastest-ever single-handed time. Equally, there was a time when no one would have imagined women conquering Mt. Everest, rowing solo across the Atlantic, swimming infinitely faster than Johnny 'Tarzan' Weissmuller, winner of five Olympic gold medals and holder of 67 world records, and running marathons in faster times than the immortal Emil Zatopek.

Furthermore, there are plenty of examples of women competing on equal terms with men – and beating them – over the most demanding and hazardous of all fences in three-day eventing. Most famously, in 2003, it was a woman – the extraordinary Pippa Funnell – who became the first person to win eventing's Grand Slam: Kentucky, Badminton and Burghley.

It is only the continuance of prejudice that keeps the odds against a lady riding the National winner. At a time when women are asserting themselves more than ever before in sporting activities National Hunt racing is the one sport where their numbers have declined. Gee Armytage has explained: 'I think it all went wrong through a crop of serious injuries. Venetia Williams broke her neck. I broke my back and Sharron Murgatroyd and Jessica Charles-Jones ended up in wheelchairs. That had a huge impact, not least because it frightened the owners and trainers to death. I hope our time will come again but, these days, any girl who rides well must turn the negative of being a woman into a positive by really projecting herself.'

In 2002 there were four women in the top ten National Hunt trainers but only one woman in the leading 100 jump jockeys: the amateur Polly Gundry in 84th place. Lady jump jockeys had become such an endangered species that the idea of introducing a weight allowance for women was mooted. On the other hand, a different picture was

emerging in Ireland. There, in 2006, for the first time, female riders (Nina Carberry and Katie Walsh) took first and second place in the amateur jump jockeys' championship. Thus it now seems a distinct possibility that one day a woman will be given the chance to ride a truly outstanding chaser in the National. And in all probability she will be Irish.
See also: Brew, Charlotte; Rees, Geraldine.

LADY TRAINERS

Though a number of women had previously been training by way of licences held by their head lads, it was not until 1966 that, following a court action, the Jockey Club finally yielded to pressure and granted training licences to women. That year Norah Wilmot became the first lady to be officially credited as trainer of a winner under Rules.

The ability of lady trainers in National Hunt racing was most forcefully conveyed by Jenny Pitman who, beginning in 1975, saddled her first of almost 800 winners. Her successes included two Cheltenham Gold Cups (1984 and 1991), three Welsh Nationals, a Scottish and Irish National, and the King George VI Chase. But, most famously, she became associated with the Aintree Grand National. In 1983 she was the first of her sex to send out the winner (*Corbiere*) of the National. She repeated that achievement with *Royal Athlete* (1995), and saddled *Esha Ness*, the first home in the void National of 1993.

So far no other woman has trained a National winner. However, following Pitman's trail-breaking success, a number of lady trainers have become major players in National Hunt racing, among them: Mary Reveley, whose 2,000-plus victories include some on the Flat, most notably the Cesarewitch twice and the Cambridgeshire; Venetia Williams whose many winners include *Teeton Mill* (Hennessy Cognac Gold Cup and King George VI Chase), *Jocks Cross* (Welsh National) and *Lady Rebecca* (three successive Cleeve Hurdles at Cheltenham); and, not least, Henrietta Knight, responsible for *Best Mate*, winner of a hat-trick of Cheltenham Gold Cups.
See also: Pitman, Jenny; Knight, Henrietta.

LAMB, The

The most distinctive of Grand National winners, *The Lamb* ranks among the all-time greats in the history of the race. He was the first grey – one of only two

L

– to win the National; the only grey to win the race twice; and the smallest horse (standing no more than 15 hands two inches) to triumph over Aintree's towering fences.

His extraordinary life began in 1862 when a Mr Henchy, a farmer in Co. Limerick, had a mare covered by *Zouave*, a stallion bred by his Irish neighbour. The unnamed mare was by *Arthur*, remounted runner-up in the 1840 National; and the neighbouring farmer was a Mr Courtenay, owner of *Matthew*, the first Irish winner of the National in 1847.

The outcome was a foal so pretty and gentle that Mr Henchy's son called him *The Lamb*. For three years he was treated strictly as a pet, then sold for £30 to a Dublin veterinary surgeon, Joe Doyle, who wanted a little pony to provide outdoor activity for his consumptive daughter. Doyle, however, soon recognised that the grey had jumping potential. In 1867 he successfully prepared the five year old to win the Punchestown Kildare Hunt Plate for a £285 prize. Then, following three disappointing runs, he leased him to Lord Poulett in whose colours he was initially well beaten in a Croydon chase by Lord Coventry's *Chimney Sweep*.

Earlier, when he was being offered for sale at £30, the grey had been rejected as 'not fit to carry a man's boot' by Edward Studd, the owner who had bought the 1866 National winner, *Salamander* for a mere £35. Yet now, as a six year old, he was being prepared for the 1868 National. To his great advantage, he had both an outstanding trainer, Ben Land Snr, and a brilliant amateur rider, George Matthew Ede ('Mr Edwards').

The Lamb was already noted for his spring-heeled agility. Now Land built up his body strength to such visual effect that, despite his diminutive size and the unfavourably heavy going at Aintree, the young grey was sent off at 9-1, third in the betting. The favourite was *Chimney Sweep* and the 28-strong field included the 1865 winner *Alcibiade* and runner-up (by a head) *Hall Court*, now ridden by Ben Land Jnr., who had twice finished second in the National.

Tragically, for the first time, the race claimed a fatal casualty without a fence being jumped, the victim being the favourite who shattered a pastern when he trod on one of the large stones that marked the route across the Melling Road. Meanwhile, *The Lamb* held his position close behind the leaders, and he was second, only a half-length off *Pearl Diver*, as they came to the Water. At this point, the grey was threateningly sandwiched between two riderless horses. Ede reacted with typically cool, quick initiative. He gave one loose horse a slap with his whip, then switched hands to hit the other before timing the Water Jump to perfection.

By the last, the race had become a straight duel between *The Lamb* and *Pearl Diver*, and the decisive factor was the superior riding skill of Ede. Only a few weeks before he had suffered severe lacerations after an horrendous fall in a hurdle race. Now he found remarkable resources of strength to power home the gallant grey to a two lengths victory, with *Alcibiade* a further ten lengths back in third.

Owing to a wasting disease in his hindquarters, *The Lamb*'s return to the National was delayed until 1871. Now aged nine, the grey was weighted with an additional 12lb and was without the services of his winning rider, Ede having suffered a fatal fall in Aintree's Sefton Chase the year before. *The Lamb* was also without his winning trainer; by now Ben Land had chosen to devote his energies to the Flat. But Lord Poulett had a worthy replacement jockey in Chris Green, who had ridden two National winners and one runner-up.

To anyone with faith in superstitions, it would seem that *The Lamb*'s second victory was pre-ordained. Firstly, some three months before the National, Lord Poulett had a dream in which he saw his little grey win by four lengths with the Cheltenham amateur Tommy Pickernell in the saddle. His Lordship promptly booked Pickernell, a veteran of ten Nationals, for the ride.

Secondly, if the popular story is to be believed, hordes of racegoers, detraining at Liverpool railway station on the first day of the Aintree meeting, were given a useful omen when they saw a lamb running down the track after escaping from a wagon in a siding. Not surprisingly, *The Lamb* went off at 11-2, second favourite behind his old rival *Pearl Diver*, and one place ahead of *The Colonel* who was seeking a third successive National win.

Nonetheless, backers of the grey were to experience plenty of unnerving moments There was confusion when a group of picnickers had to scramble for cover after failing to clear the course at the start. Early on, the field was threatened by another grey, 100-1 outsider *Scots Grey*, who was continually swerving, in the process knocking two rivals out of the race. In addition, *The Lamb* was seen to be

274

L

labouring when he ran over a ploughed section of the course. The worst moment came on approaching the Canal Turn the second time around. There, directly in front of *The Lamb*, were two fallen horses. But the fears of backers were unfounded. The little grey jumped clear over both of them. Again, he lost ground when encountering the plough, but thereafter he made relentless progress and, coming to the last, he had only *Despatch* to beat. He kept the lead throughout the run-in to win by two lengths and in the remarkably fast time (for the going) of 9min 35.75sec. Ironically, the runner-up was owned by Mr Studd.

Later that year Lord Poulett's lease on *The Lamb* expired, and the grey reverted to Joe Doyle who sold him to a German, Baron Oppenheim, for the princely sum of 1,200 guineas. However, when the horse came out for a third National in 1872, he was to be burdened with 12st 7lb, an impossible weight for so small a chaser to carry. Nevertheless, he jumped superbly, briefly shared the lead as late as the penultimate fence, and ran on with lion-hearted courage to finish a most worthy fourth. Years later, after competing in 18 Grand Nationals, Pickernell would name *The Lamb* as the best horse that he ever rode.

Three times the grey had run well in the National on his first outing of the season. Already he had done enough to merit an early retirement. But now Baron Oppenheim chose to race him again and again. Only two weeks after his testing Aintree run he was unplaced while trying to carry 12st 10lb. He won his next race by a huge margin, and was then entered for the Grosser Preis von Baden-Baden, a chase of nearly three miles over formidable fences. On that September day, ridden by Count Nicholas Esterhazy, *The Lamb* was far out in front and looking a certain winner. Then, suddenly, he ran into an exceptionally soggy patch of ground, meeting such resistance that he broke a foreleg and had to be destroyed.
See also: Land, Ben Snr; Poulett; Lord; Ede, George Matthew; Pickernell, Thomas; Dreams.

LAMPLUGH, Harry
A combination of favourable circumstances conspired in 1862 to help Harry Lamplugh win the Grand National at his eighth and final attempt. Firstly, a change of ownership enabled him to take the ride on the entire *Huntsman*, a 3-1 favourite

who, with different jockeys, had finished third by only a short neck and one length in 1859 and had been beaten by just half a length in 1860. Secondly, nine year old *Huntsman* had been generously dropped 8lb in the weights following those near-misses. And thirdly, he now had only 12 rivals – the smallest National field for 21 years.

It was nonetheless a highly deserved success. Son of a Yorkshire jump jockey, Lamplugh had started his racing career in France at the age of 17 and had proved himself a sufficiently fine horseman to be recruited as trainer-jockey to the leading French owner Baron C. de la Motte at Chantilly. But initially, as a 'foreigner', his National rides were on long-shots. On his 1853 debut he fell on *The Dwarf*, a rank outsider. The following year his race ended in a refusal by 40-1 chance *Timothy*; and in 1855 he finished fourth on Mr John Elmore's *Janus* at 33-1.

But then, for the first time, French horses challenged for the National. Two were entered – *Jean Du Quesne* and *Franc Picard*. Both, being owned by Baron de la Motte, were prepared by Lamplugh who also elected to ride the former. That year *Jean Du Quesne* was made the 9-2 favourite and he was looking a likely winner when well clear after the Canal Turn second time round. But now he faded fast and failed to finish. One year later Lamplugh brought him home in sixth place. Then, in 1859, he gave him a tremendous ride, catching *Half Caste*, the six year old second favourite, halfway up the long run-in and matching him stride for stride all the way to the line, only to be beaten by 'a short neck'.

Twice more Lamplugh competed at Aintree, failing to finish on *Franc Picard* in 1861 and then happily ending his National career in triumph on *Huntsman*, whom he had bought and trained on behalf of his patron, Viscount de Namur. Coming home four lengths ahead of *Bridegroom*, ridden by *Huntsman*'s former jockey Ben Land Jnr, the Yorkshireman had delivered the first French-owned winner. Furthermore, five years later, he was to saddle the only other National winner to be trained in France: *Cortolvin*, ridden by John Page.
See also: Huntsman; Cortolvin.

LAND, Benjamin Snr
Formerly an amateur steeplechase jockey and Norfolk farmer, Benjamin Land – popularly known as 'Old Ben' – was an outstanding trainer-owner of the mid-19th century whose dream of owning a Grand

275

L

National winner was only thwarted as a result of his reckless gambling.

Land had his first National runner in 1853 when his outsider, *The General*, finished sixth. Two years later his *Needwood* failed to finish. By now, however, he believed that he had an outstanding prospect in a bay gelding called *Emigrant*. Unfortunately he then suffered a losing run at cards while attending the Shrewsbury races. His losses were so heavy that he agreed to sell *Emigrant* for £590 to bookmaker George Hodgman with the promise of a further £100 if the horse won at the local meeting.

Emigrant duly won at Shrewsbury, finished sixth in the 1856 National and won the race the following year – a success doubly galling for Land since his new big hope, six year old *Weathercock*, put in a storming finish only to be outpaced as they neared the winning post. *Weathercock*, the three lengths runner-up, was subsequently sold to a French nobleman, Vicomte Talon, and he was again the National runner-up in 1858.

In 1859 Land again had a strong National contender: six year old *Huntsman*, ridden by his son, Ben Land Jnr. They finished third, beaten only by a short neck and one length by *Half Caste* and *Jean Du Quesne* respectively. But once more financial pressures caused 'Old Ben' to sell a potential champion prematurely. For new owners, *Huntsman* was half a length runner-up in the 1860 National and the winner in 1862 when Land Jnr was on the runner-up *Bridegroom*.

As a trainer, however, 'Old Ben' finally achieved his dream of National glory in supreme style. In 1868 he was responsible for transforming a pretty little pony (Lord Poulett's *The Lamb*) into an outstanding chaser. Moreover, as a coach, he had played a major role in the development of the winning jockey, George ('Mr Edwards') Ede. *The Lamb* won again in 1871 but by then Land was no longer the grey's trainer, having chosen to concentrate on the Flat.
See also: Emigrant; Land, Ben Jnr.

LAND, Ben Jnr

Just as his father failed in his dream of owning a Grand National winner, so his son was to be cruelly denied in his lifelong ambition to win the race as a jockey. Nine times he tried, achieving two seconds and one third place.

His challenges began in 1858 when his mount, *Little Tom*, was a faller. The following year, on his father's *Huntsman*, he put in a storming late burst to finish third by only a short neck and one length. Arguably, young Land was too impatient in his ambition – as indicated in 1860 when he took an early lead on *Goldsmith*, despite having *Huntsman* there as his pacemaker. The former failed to finish while the pacemaker came home second. Two years later, on *Bridegroom*, Land finished four lengths second to the third-time-lucky *Huntsman*.

In 1864, Ben was riding *Arbury*, a 40-1 shot despite having finished second to *Emblem* the previous year. Leading over the first Becher's, they again finished second, three lengths behind the victorious *Emblematic* (a full sister of *Emblem*), with the third horse a distance away. Again, in 1865, on *Merrimac*, Ben was the first over Becher's and then opened up a 20 lengths lead. But *Merrimac* ended up a distant fifth behind the winning *Alcibiade*.

In 1866 Land gained the ride on *Alcibiade*. The winner, however, had been raised 12lb to 12st 2lb, a colossal burden for a six year old. For once Ben played a waiting game, only to suffer a fall just as he was moving into contention at the second Becher's. Three years later, when Land Snr celebrated his training triumph with *The Lamb*, young Ben was on *Hall Court*, who had been beaten only by a head in the 1865 National. They were the seventh of seven finishers. It was the last time Ben was to complete the course. His final ride came in 1870 when he had to pull up *The Elk* after leading briefly at the Water. *See also:* Huntsman.

LAST SUSPECT

Shock winner of the Grand National in 1985 when he only took part after much pleading by jockey Hywel Davies and came from some eight lengths back at the last to snatch victory by one and a half lengths from *Mr Snugfit*, with former winner *Corbiere* a further three lengths back in third. His owner was Anne, Duchess of Westminster whose reluctance to let her horses run in the National was exemplified by her persistent refusal to risk the supreme *Arkle* at Aintree.

A brown gelding, by *Above Suspicion* out of *Last Link*, Last Suspect was bred by the Countess of Mount Charles. His credentials were excellent breeding-wise: a sire who had been a regular winner on the Flat, a dam who had won the Irish Grand National. Disappointingly, however, he had earned a reputation for being a moody, unreliable character, a tail-swisher who too often lost interest and pulled himself up in chases, as indeed he had done at Warwick in his last prep race for Aintree. Following that discouraging performance, both owner and trainer Captain Tim Forster were agreed that he should be withdrawn from the National.

Davies, hearing the news with only a few hours to spare, needed all his Welsh powers of eloquence to make them change their minds. He first tackled Captain Forster; then, at the trainer's suggestion, telephoned the owner directly. He recognised that the horse could be sulky and was possibly lacking in speed. But, as he fairly argued, he had never fallen in a race, had never unseated a jockey, and had proved himself a sound jumper lacking nothing in stamina.

Originally trained by Jim Dreaper in Co. Dublin, *Last Suspect* was first raced in bumpers as a five year old. Bought by the Duchess of Westminster, he was moved three years later to the Oxfordshire stables of Captain Forster who had already turned out two Grand National winners: *Well To Do* (1972) and *Ben Nevis* (1980).

Renowned for his pessimism, the trainer had no expectation of a third success when he saddled the gelding, a 50-1 shot, making his National debut. The opposition included last year's winner *Hallo Dandy*; *Greasepaint*, two times runner-up; the hugely promising *West Tip*; and the big market mover *Mr Snugfit* who, on current winning form, was thrown in at the weights. Moreover, Davies was putting up 3lb overweight.

The race began, as it was to end, with a shock. *Hallo Dandy* fell with three others at the first fence. On the second circuit, *West Tip* was looking all over the winner when he came to grief on landing over the second Becher's. Meanwhile, *Mr Snugfit* was making rapid progress, passing *Last Suspect* and *Greasepaint* and landing in the lead at the last from top-weighted *Corbiere*. Then, on the testing run-in, *Last Suspect* responded to the whip, suddenly finding hidden reserves to close the gap with every stride. He overhauled the tiring *Corbiere* and finally *Mr Snugfit* less than a hundred yards out.

Last Suspect was now retired, but then his well-being prompted the owner to change her mind. It seemed a wise decision; when he returned for the 1986 National, his record for the season was two wins in two marathon races. And still he had never

fallen. But he was now 12 years old, had 11 more pounds to carry, compared with an extra seven for *Mr Snugfit*, the 13-2 favourite. This time he was never in contention, showed his old reluctance to race and was pulled up when labouring at the start of the second circuit. His retirement was final.
See also: Davies, Hywel; Forster, Captain Tim.

LAWRENCE, John Geoffrey Tristam
See: Oaksey, Lord.

LEADBETTER, John
Trainer of ten year old *Rubstic* who became Scotland's first Grand National winner in 1979 when coming home one and a half lengths ahead of *Zongalero*. It was the first time that John Leadbetter had had a runner in the National; and, similarly both horse and rider (Maurice Barnes) were appearing in the race for the first time.

Born December 20, 1943, Leadbetter operated a small yard in the little hamlet of Denholm in Roxburghshire; and he was the third trainer to have *Rubstic* in his care. Bought as a yearling for 500 guineas and owned by former British Lions rugby international John Douglas, the gelding had first been raced over hurdles by another Roxburghshire trainer, Mr C.H. Bell of Hawick. Then, as a four year old, he was moved across the border to the Cumbrian yard of Gordon Richards, who introduced him to long-distance chases.

Later, on being returned to Scotland, he was turned out by Leadbetter to win the Durham National Chase in successive years and to twice finish runner-up in the Scottish National over an extended four miles. Curiously, the trainer's success at Aintree followed immediately after Richards' 1978 win with *Lucius*. Subsequently, Leadbetter entered *Rubstic* in two more Grand Nationals – in 1980 when he fell for the first time in his career, and in 1981 when he finished seventh. He remains the only Scottish-based trainer to have turned out a winner of the Aintree National.
See also: Rubstic; Scotland.

LEADER, Harvey
Trainer of the 1926 Grand National winner *Jack Horner*, Harvey 'Jack' Leader was the fourth son of 'old Tom Leader' who had saddled the 1874 Derby winner *George Frederick*. Born into a racing family which had settled at Newmarket in 1888, he was

L

only 12 years old when riding his first winner. Then – like his brothers Tom, Fred and Colledge – he turned to training and, within two years, had a major success with the victory of *Caligua* in the 1920 St Leger.

Though 'Jack' prepared a National winner for the American polo player Charles Schwartz, he was most noted for his winners on the Flat. He won the 1929 Lincoln with the 100-1 shot *Elton*, three Cambridgeshire Handicaps, and a combined total of 33 races with his most popular runners, *Diomedes* and *Shalfleet*. Following the early deaths of his brothers Fred and Colledge in the 1930s, he was responsible for maintaining the family racing tradition together with his nephew, Ted Leader. He died in January, 1972, aged 78, having retired from training only two months earlier.
See also: Jack Horner.

LEADER, 'Ted' Thomas Edward

Of all the Leaders, so renowned as trainers, Ted was the one who concentrated primarily on a career as a rider. Born in 1903, he became one of the best jump jockeys of the 1920s, and he rode in 12 successive Grand Nationals between 1922 and 1933. Four times he completed the course and three of those rides were on *Sprig*, the chestnut trained by his father Tom. The combination finished fourth in 1925 and 1926, then triumphed in 1927, by one length from the 100-1 outsider *Bovril II*, with *Bright's Boy* a further length back in third.

On his 1922 National debut, 19-year-old Ted had become virtually tailed off on his mount, 66-1 shot *Taffytus*, as the field began the second circuit. But subsequently there were so many fallers that he persevered with the ride and came home the third of only five finishers. In the next two Nationals he fell on *Taffytus*.

In 1926, the year he won the jockeys' championship, Ted could have been on the National winner, *Jack Horner*, who was trained by his uncle, Harvey 'Jack' Leader. American owner Charles Schwartz had offered him a huge sum to take the ride, but he turned it down out of loyalty to Mrs M. Partridge, the owner of *Sprig*. His loyalty was justly rewarded the following year when – despite the fact that *Sprig*, again the favourite, had been raised 11lb in the weights – he won the National at the sixth attempt.

In 1928, when *Sprig* was raised to a top weight of 12st 7lb, he was one of 40 of 42 starters who failed to complete the course in the chaotic race won by 100-1 *Tipperary Tim*. Subsequently Ted failed to finish on *Mount Etna* (1929), *Sandy Hook* (1930), *Swift Rowland* (1931) and *Ottawa* (1932). Elsewhere, he scored many notable victories, including two Cheltenham Gold Cups (on *Ballinode*, 1925, and *Golden Miller*, 1932) and the Champion Hurdle (on *Insurance*, 1932).

Ted's Gold Cup victory on *Golden Miller* – the first of five in succession for the wonder horse – was unique in that he rode into the unsaddling enclosure with winners of both the Grand National and the Gold Cup. At the finish he had thoughtfully grabbed the reins of the loose-running *Grakle*, who had triumphed at Aintree the previous year. For his foresight he was later presented by a grateful trainer, Tom Coulthwaite, with a silver cigarette case inscribed, 'Actions speak louder than words'.

His last National ride, however, was a difficult and hugely disappointing one: on *Golden Miller*, a six year old making his Aintree debut after five successive wins, including a recent repeat success in the Gold Cup. In all his latest wins, *Golden Miller* had been ridden by champion jockey Billy Stott. But now, surprisingly, Ted was asked to take over despite an earlier falling-out with owner Dorothy Paget. According to an unconfirmed rumour, Miss Paget was now miffed because Stott had allegedly expressed doubts about *Golden Miller*'s ability to get round the Aintree course. Whatever the truth, *Golden Miller* was certainly a most difficult ride at this time, and arguably he was going to the National too soon. Indeed, as Ted later explained, he had vowed never to ride the horse again, and he had only agreed after trainer Basil Briscoe had begged this one special favour.

In that 1933 National *Golden Miller*, the 9-1 favourite, jumped too boldly and erratically, and Leader did well to survive as far as the Canal Turn second time around. There, he was finally thrown. 'For a parting present, he gave me a nasty kick in the back. That was the last time I rode him.' After that experience, Ted declared that his mount would 'never make an Aintree horse'.

The following year, after Leader had retired from the saddle, the brilliant *Golden Miller* won at Aintree in record time to complete his historic Gold Cup/Grand National double. Yet, in essence, Ted was right in his judgment. Again and again, the chaser, so supreme at Cheltenham, was to show his

L

aversion to the Aintree fences. Meanwhile, having won almost every major National Hunt race, Ted now began a long and successful career as a trainer. He lived on until 1983.

See also: Paget, Dorothy; Briscoe, Basil; Stott, William; Golden Miller.

LEADER, Tom

Trainer of two Grand National winners – *Sprig* (1927) and *Gregalach* (1929) – Tom Leader was the eldest of five sons of Tom Leader Snr, who, before moving to Newmarket, had trained in Wroughton, Wiltshire, and was responsible for the 1874 Derby winner, *George Frederick*. Three of his brothers – Colledge, Fred and Jack – also became trainers (mainly for the Flat), and one of his three sisters, Ethel, married the trainer Jack Jarvis.

Though Tom alone specialised in National Hunt, it was brother Harvey 'Jack' Leader, based at Exning in Suffolk, who first trained a National winner: *Jack Horner* (1926). One year later, when Tom followed his example with *Sprig*, the 8-1 favourite, he had the added satisfaction of seeing his own son, Ted, riding the winner.

In 1929, Tom had no fewer than five National runners in the record 66-strong field, and the least fancied of them was the seven year old *Gregalach*, one of eight 100-1 shots. Australian Robert Everett took the mount while son Ted elected to ride *Mount Etna* rather than *Sprig*, now a heavily weighted 12 year old. Early in the race *Mount Etna* was knocked over in a mid-air collision. *Sprig*, too, was a faller. Meanwhile, to the trainer's surprise and delight, *Gregalach* went on to win by six lengths.

See also: Sprig; Gregalach.

LEE, Graham Martin

Following the 2004 victory of 12 year old *Amberleigh House*, attention focused primarily on trainer Donald 'Ginger' McCain who had equalled Fred Rimell's all-time record of saddling four Grand National winners. However, no less worthy of merit was the remarkably mature riding of 28 year old Graham Lee who had made only two appearances in the race, finishing third on his debut and now winning with a brilliantly timed late challenge.

Just two weeks later he sealed his new-won fame by winning the 28-runner Scottish Grand National on top-weighted *Grey Abbey*. The ten year old grey was burdened with 11st 12lb, the biggest weight

carried to victory since *Red Rum* won at Ayr in 1974. Yet Lee became the first jockey to score the Aintree-Scottish double since Brian Fletcher in 1974; and for good measure he went on to score an Ayr double for trainer Howard Johnson by winning a juvenile novices' hurdle on *Dalaram*.

Rarely had a jump jockey advanced his career so suddenly and spectacularly after years of relative obscurity. Irish-born (December 16, 1975), Lee had no racing background but was drawn to the sport as a result of growing up in the shadow of Galway racecourse. Initially he faced the problem of needing more weight rather than less. He was just 5ft 6in tall as a teenager and, after a vain bid to make his mark as a Flat jockey, he adopted a high-protein diet to build himself up for National Hunt racing with a weight around 9st 10lb.

A lifelong non-smoker and teetotaller, he rode his first winner (*Blushing Pearl*) at Navan in 1992; and two years later, having crossed the Irish Sea, he opened his British racing account with a win at Edinburgh on the Mary Reveley-trained *Firm Price*. But almost a full decade elapsed before he achieved any notable victories, his progress impeded by a leg-smashing fall at Sedgefield in 1996.

Depressingly, from mid-July, 2003, he went ten weeks without a single winner. Then, seemingly out of the blue, winners came in a veritable avalanche, beginning with a four-timer at Wetherby that included the valuable Charlie Hall Chase on a 40-1 chance, *Ballybough Rasher*; and he went on to achieve no fewer than 94 wins from 625 rides, earning prize money of £1,356,423 and taking him to third place in the jockeys' championship.

The key factor in his dream-like advance was his association with Howard Johnson, whose yard had been greatly boosted by the big-spending of his principal owner, Graham Wylie. It led to winning rides on such class hurdlers as *Inglis Drever* and *Royal Rosa*; also to major chase wins in 2004 for owner Trevor Hemmings on *Southern Star* (Tote Classic Chase) and *Hunters Tweed* (Ladbroke Trophy Chase).

Above all, of course, his new high-profile owed much to his partnership with *Amberleigh House* which had begun in 2003. At the time it seemed that the 11 year old gelding had missed his chance of Grand National glory. In the quagmire of the 2001 National, when ridden by Warren Marston, he had been unluckily knocked over by the riderless

L

Paddy's Return, causing a pile-up at the Canal Turn. Then, despite winning the 2001 Becher Chase, again with Marston, he had been given insufficient weight to make the line-up for the 2002 National.

As it happened, however, Lee's link-up with *Amberleigh House* was most fortuitously timed. Under Tony Dobbin, the gelding had finished runner-up in the 2002 Becher Chase, then fourth in a handicap hurdle at Bangor. In March, 2003, with Marston, he was a distant 15th in a Haydock chase; and at that point Lee had the good fortune to take over, finishing third on *Amberleigh House* when he ran at Bangor in his last prep-race for the National.

Two weeks later Lee had his memorable introduction to the National, with *Amberleigh House* taking third place, beaten for finishing speed by *Monty's Pass* and *Supreme Glory*. Afterwards he said, 'Three out I honestly thought we were going to win and he gave a most unbelievable ride. In the end he didn't quite get home. His stamina was running out like the sand from an egg-timer.' One year later exactly the reverse applied when, with Lee timing his challenge to perfection, the 12 year old closed on the tiring, long-time leader *Hedgehunter* (a faller at the last) and snatched victory by three lengths from *Clan Royal*.

In 2004-05 Lee again won the Charlie Hall Chase, this time on *Grey Abbey*; and immediately afterwards he was reunited with *Amberleigh House*, finishing an encouraging fourth in a warm-up chase over an extended two and a half miles. They went on to Aintree in November and, as usual, *Amberleigh House* ran well in the Becher Chase, albeit to finish fifth on a top weight of 11st 10lb, conceding 24lb to the winner *Silver Birch*.

That month Lee was lying fourth in the jockeys' table with 62 winners when he had the set back of a long lay off, having broken his right arm after falling in a chase at Doncaster and being kicked by another horse as he lay on the ground. He needed to have a six-inch metal plate inserted in his forearm to help speed recovery. But in late January he was back riding as strongly as ever, and at Cheltenham, on Pillar Property Chase day, he won the showpiece race on *Grey Abbey* and followed up with a 50-1 success in the juvenile hurdle on four year old *Akilak*.

Soon after, once again, he was hit by injury, this time fracturing his left collarbone in a fall from *Kew Jumper* in a novice chase at Wincanton. But he recovered just in time to enjoy a fantastic Chel-tenham Festival. He had never ridden a winner at jump racing's showpiece meeting. Now he won the first day opener, the Supreme Novices' Hurdle, on *Arcalis* at 20-1; the second day opener, the 20-runner Royal and SunAlliance Novices' Hurdle, on *No Refuge*; and the third day main event, Ladbrokes World Hurdle, on *Inglis Drever*. Sharing his astonishing treble were trainer Howard Johnson and owners Andrea and Graham Wylie.

Ten days before the 2005 National, Lee was spared having to make a difficult choice when top-weighted *Grey Abbey* was withdrawn after unsatisfactory schooling over Aintree-type fences. It meant that for the third time in three Nationals he would be with *Amberleigh House* on whom he had finished third and first. On the opening day of the Aintree meeting he duly won the valuable Betfair Bowl Chase on *Grey Abbey*. But in the National, age and weight were against *Amberleigh House* and the 13 year old, never in contention, finished tenth. For Lee, however, there was to be huge consolation as, despite ten weeks off with injury, he went on to complete 100 winners in a season for the first time.

In February, 2006, he was back on marathon-winning form, steering *Philson Run* to victory in the Eider Handicap Chase over four miles one furlong, at Newcastle; and two days later he completed a century of winners for the second successive season, this time almost two months earlier. But realistically he had no chance in the Grand National, having stayed loyal to *Amberleigh House* in a race that had never been won by a 14 year old. The old campaigner was pulled up before the 21st and then retired.

Later that year, having parted company with Johnson, Lee began a hugely successful association with Ferdy Murphy at West Witton, North Yorkshire. At the Cheltenham Festival he won the Jewson Novices' Handicap Chase on *L'Antartique* and in the Irish National he was a one length second on *Nine De Sivola*. On to Aintree and he easily won the opening Mildmay Novice Chase on *Aces Four*. But disappointingly his high hopes for the National ended when his mount, 8-1 co-favourite *Joes Edge*, was pulled up lame before the 20th.

One week later, on 5-1 favourite *Nine De Sivola*, Lee was beaten only half a length in the Scottish National by Murphy's second string *Hot Weld*. The following Saturday he took over on *Hot Weld* at Sandown, riding him to become the first horse ever to win the Scottish National and the Betfred (formerly Whitbread) Gold Cup in a career – let alone in the same season.

That success was all the more commendable since only four days earlier Lee had suffered a crushing fall at Punchestown, being taken to hospital with a suspected broken elbow. Happily, he was given the all clear and got back to race fitness – aided in no small part by having built up his strength with an intensive long-term training programme with Chris Barnes of Middlesbrough Football Club. He ended the season on a high, with 88 winners and sixth place in the jumps jockeys' championship. *See also:* Amberleigh House.

LE MARE, Noel

The Liverpool businessman who was 86 years old when he completed his threefold ambition in life: to become a millionaire, to marry a beautiful woman and to own the winner of the Grand National. And that third stage was fulfilled not by just any good winner. His success came with the greatest of them all: the legendary, record-breaking *Red Rum*, three times triumphant and twice runner-up in an incredible five-year span.

Born in 1887, the son of a missionary, Noel Le Mare had been fascinated by the National for 67 years – ever since the day when, as a young engineering apprentice, he was sent out by his foreman to ascertain the winner of the 1906 race (*Ascetic's Silver*). Subsequently, he served for seven years in the Merchant Navy, and then for decades he was preoccupied with business, eventually building up a major civil engineering enterprise, the Norwest Construction Company. But the dream of Grand National victory never deserted him.

He was 78 years old when he finally got around to becoming directly involved. His first runner – in his wife's name – was *Ruby Glen*, a moderate bay gelding, brought down in the 1965 National. Four years later, more encouragingly, he saw his eight year old *Furore II* finish ninth. And then, ironically, he was third time lucky – virtually by accident.

Le Mare was regularly driven to Saturday dinner-dances on the seafront by Donald 'Ginger' McCain who was running a taxi service in Southport, Lancashire; and when McCain set up as a small-time trainer he bought two of his horses. Both proved to be less than mediocre. Later the octogenarian gave the trainer a second chance, asking him to find a

horse to run in the 1972 National. McCain duly bought nine year old *Glenkiln* for 1,000 guineas. The bay gelding was entered for the National. But then, through lack of experience, McCain inadvertently had *Glenkiln* withdrawn at the forfeit stage.

To his great relief, his disappointed patron accepted the error philosophically. Moreover Le Mare chose to double his chances of having a runner in the 1973 Grand National by authorising McCain to spend up to 7,000 guineas on another horse. At the Doncaster Sales, cast-off *Red Rum* – already qualified for the National – was secured for a mere 6,000 guineas.

Subsequently, *Glenkiln* put in his greatest performance, winning the Grand National Trial Chase over one circuit of the National course. He beat the powerful *L'Escargot* by 12 lengths, and in so doing qualified for the National. Thus Le Mare was doubly represented in the 1973 race. *Glenkiln*, partnered by newcomer Jonjo O'Neill, was brought down at The Chair, while the revitalised *Red Rum*, under the experienced Brian Fletcher, realised the old man's dream by just three-quarters of a length from the gallant, top-weighted *Crisp*. Le Mare was so overjoyed that he declined to take a penny of the prize money, dividing it among the stable staff with McCain and Fletcher receiving the largest share of £7,000 each. Meanwhile he went on to finish as the season's leading owner, with £34,197 from wins with three horses.

Enjoying glorious twilight years, Le Mare lived on to witness all of 'Rummy's' extraordinary runs and to see his bargain buy become the most celebrated horse in Grand National history, with a *Red Rum* fan club run by his grandson, Mr Michael Burns. Having retired to the Isle of Man, he died in 1979 at the age of 92. *Red Rum*, who had been retired one year earlier, lived on until 1995. *See also:* Red Rum; McCain, Donald.

L'ESCARGOT

A powerful chestnut gelding of extraordinary consistency, the inaptly named *L'Escargot* won on the Flat, starred over hurdles, then excelled over fences to such a degree that he won successive Cheltenham Gold Cups (1970-71) and finished third, second and finally first in the Grand Nationals of 1973, 1974 and 1975 respectively. He is the only horse apart from *Golden Miller* to have won both the Gold Cup and the National, and judged on his peak perform-

L

ances he rates among the greatest steeplechasers of all time.

L'Escargot was ill-named since he was never remotely snail-like in pace, impressing with his speed from the start. Irish-bred – by *Escart III* out of *What A Daisy* – he was bought as a three year old for 3,000 guineas on behalf of Mr Raymond Guest, the millionaire U.S. ambassador to Ireland, and sent to the Fairyhouse yard of Dan Moore, the master trainer who, as the rider of *Royal Danieli*, had been beaten only a head by *Battleship* in the 1938 Grand National. The following year, making his racecourse debut in February, 1967, he landed a major betting coup by easily winning a Navan bumper at 100-7.

After a second win, again ridden by amateur Ben Hanbury, *L'Escargot* was put over hurdles the following season. With Tommy Carberry, now his regular rider, he promptly made his mark at his first Cheltenham Festival by winning the 1968 Gloucester Hurdle, the equivalent of the present-day Supreme Novices' Hurdle. Later hobdayed to eliminate a wind problem, he ran unsuccessfully in the 1969 Champion Hurdle and then began his chasing career.

Having immediately shown considerable promise over fences, he was sent by his American owner to compete in the United States. He won the 1969 Meadowbrook Chase and later returned to Belmont Park to finish third in the Temple Gwathmey Chase. Back in England, he won the W.D. & H.O. Wills Premier Chase at Haydock and – though trainer Moore feared it was premature – Mr Guest insisted on running the seven year old in the 1970 Cheltenham Gold Cup. He went off at 33-1 and, confounding doubts about him getting the trip, he outpaced *French Tan* on the testing run-in to win by a length and a half – a long-priced upset matched only by *Gay Donald's* success in 1955 and not surpassed until *Norton's Coin's* 100-1 shock success in 1990.

L'Escargot ran poorly for most of the following season but then recaptured his best form with perfect timing, registering his first win of the campaign at Cheltenham. Thriving on heavy going, and again ridden by Carberry, he took his second Gold Cup with a comfortable ten lengths beating of *Leap Frog*; and now there was talk of him emulating the great *Arkle's* hat-trick of wins.

Despite favourable soft going, *L'Escargot* could only finish fourth in the 1972 Gold Cup. Mr Guest, however, had another target in mind. His greatest ambition was to have winners of both the Epsom Derby and the Grand National. He had achieved the first stage with *Larkspur* (1962) and *Sir Ivor* (1968). Now, three weeks after Cheltenham, *L'Escargot* was to go off at Aintree as the 17-2 favourite in a 42-strong field.

It was a brief, rain-soaked National debut. Burdened with the top weight of 12st, *L'Escargot* was baulked and knocked over at the third fence. And in the next season he was set the same demanding task: racing in the National just sixteen days after finishing fourth in the Gold Cup, and again on the 12st mark. This time, outpaced on the good going, he finished third, a full 25 lengths behind *Red Rum* and *Crisp* who had both shattered the course record.

Mercifully, in 1974, *L'Escargot* was not tested in the Gold Cup prior to going to Aintree. Now wearing blinkers, he was on 11st 13lb, carrying 1lb less while *Red Rum* was saddled with 23lb more. But the outcome was the same. Taking the lead at the second Becher's, the amazing 'Rummy' was never headed and won by seven lengths from *L'Escargot*, with the long-shot *Charles Dickens* just a short head back in third. That day it seemed that Mr Guest was doomed to failure in his lifelong dream. Next year his best chaser would be 12 years old while the mighty *Red Rum* would be only ten.

Carberry told trainer Moore that he thought *L'Escargot* would never win a National unless he was kept fresh. So, in 1975, his last race before the National was not the Gold Cup but Cheltenham's two-mile Champion Chase. He finished a respectable fifth but the fact remained that he was going on to Aintree with a record of only one race won in the past four seasons. On the other hand, that record, plus his age, could be seen to have worked in his favour. The handicapper had dropped him to 11st 3lb in the weights. *Red Rum*, the 7-2 favourite, was now giving him 11lb; also, for the first time, he had to contend with unfavoured soft ground.

L'Escargot almost dislodged Carberry when making a mess of the seventh fence. But thereafter he was never in trouble as he hunted round behind the leading pack. Again, after the second Becher's, *Red Rum* sought to dominate, but this time he could not shake off *L'Escargot* who was still full of running when they took the last fence together. On the run-in the 12 year old steadily pulled away to beat an exhausted 'Rummy' by 15 lengths.

Having achieved his ambition after 18 years of

trying, Mr Guest promptly announced that his long-serving chaser had run his last race and would spend his retirement in the care of Dan Moore and his wife Joan. But it was not quite a joyous ending. The following autumn *L'Escargot* was so lively that the Moores chose to run him one more time. He was beaten a head in the Kerry National – whereupon a shocked Mr Guest immediately had the old campaigner shipped to Virginia where he lived on for another decade.

See also: Guest, Raymond; Moore, Dan; Carberry, Tommy.

LIBERATOR, The

Rarely has a Grand National winner been punished by the handicapper as severely as *The Liberator*. In the 1879 race, when he was the 5-1 second favourite on his third appearance, the only error made by rider-owner Mr Garrett Moore was to bring the giant gelding home in a canter – a full ten lengths ahead of the runner-up, Lord Marcus Beresford's *Jackal*.

The handicapper reacted predictably, raising the ten year old by 17lb to the top weight of 12st 7lb – and justifiably, as it proved, since in 1880 Moore and *The Liberator* finished two lengths second to five year old *Empress* who was in receipt of two stone. Less reasonably, however, *The Liberator* was kept on that huge weight in 1881 when, after being remounted by Moore, he was the last of nine finishers. And, incredibly, in 1882, the now 13 year old gelding – making his sixth and last National appearance – was lumbered a third time with 12st 7lb. Ridden by Jimmy Adams, he was one of six fallers in a National that saw only three of 12 starters complete the course.

Irish-bred – by *Dan O'Connell* out of *Mary O'Toole* – *The Liberator* raced unsuccessfully on the Flat before proving himself a natural jumper in winning the 1875 Galway Plate. One year later he showed a measure of promise on his National debut, when, as the extreme 50-1 outsider of 19 runners, he led the field before falling at the 21st fence. But soon afterwards he failed to reach his reserve price at the Dublin sales and subsequently he was snapped up for £500 by the renowned trainer John Hubert Moore.

On returning to Aintree, *The Liberator* was ridden by the great 'Mr Thomas' Pickernell, making his 17th and final appearance in the race. He finished third, four lengths and a neck behind *Austerlitz* and

Congress respectively. The following year, however, he missed the National in hugely controversial circumstances: *Austerlitz* and *The Liberator* – both heavily backed – were withdrawn on the morning of the race, so reducing the field to a mere 12 runners.

A *Bell's Life* reporter had the temerity to accuse Mr J.H. Moore of 'unsportman-like' conduct, the suggestion being that he had scratched *The Liberator* to the benefit of *Pride of Kildare*, ridden by his son Garrett. The trainer responded vehemently in a lengthy letter. 'I have not won or lost £20 on the last Liverpool,' he wrote, and he added, 'I care not one pin for popularity among a certain class.'

More confusion surrounded *The Liberator*'s entry for the 1879 National. This time a Mr Plunkett Taaffe applied in the Dublin courts for an injunction to restrain Mr Moore from running the gelding at Aintree on the grounds that he was joint owner. The court ruled against him, accepting that this partnership had been dissolved the previous year. For some reason, however, Mr Moore decided that *The Liberator* should henceforth run in his son's name.

As the designated owner, 'Garry' Moore chose to ride the horse himself. He had competed twice before in the National, finishing eighth on *Scots Grey* in 1872 and most recently third on *Pride of Kildare*. Now it was third time lucky for both horse and rider. But, without doubt, *The Liberator*'s finest achievement in six National runs was to finish runner-up to *Empress* in 1880. No horse had ever come so close to winning with such a top weight, a feat not to be achieved until the success of *Cloister* 13 years later.

See also: Moore, Garrett.

LINDE, Henry Eyre

A farmer in Co. Kildare, formerly a sergeant in the Royal Irish Constabulary, Henry Eyre Linde became the dominant force in Irish racing of the 1880s, raising training methods to a new level of highly disciplined professionalism that made him the most feared plunderer of top honours in England and France. No one worked their horses more rigorously, and he valued Grand National success above all – to such a degree that he built replicas of Aintree's fences at his base at Eyrefield Lodge, the Curragh.

His success was immediate. In 1880, aided by amateur rider Tommy Beasley, he won the National with *Empress*, a five year old mare who was virtually a chasing novice. The next year he won with *Woodbrook*, who, under Tommy, romped home in

L

the extremely heavy going. And in 1882, the Linde-Beasley partnership was only denied a hat-trick of victories by a mere head.

That year Linde sent out *Mohican*, the 100-30 favourite ridden by Harry Beasley, and *Cyrus*, third in the betting at 9-2. Ironically, in the closest of finishes, with only three of 12 runners completing the course, the five year old *Cyrus* was beaten by *Seaman*, a gelding who had been sold after going through all the rigours of Linde's schooling.

In 1881 Linde had won the Liverpool Hunt Chase with *Seaman*, then the four-mile Conyngham Cup at Punchestown and the Grand Hurdle de Paris. But for once he misjudged one of his charges. He thought the six year old had been pushed to the limit and was liable to break down at any time. So, just four months before the National, he had recommended that the owner sell the horse to Lord Manners, who duly sent *Seaman* to trainer Captain James Machell.

In 1886, the Linde-trained *Too Good*, with Harry Beasley, came second in the National. The following year he sent out the 9-2 favourite *Spahi*, but this time he was expecting too much of a six year old who had never raced over fences before. The chestnut entire, so useful on the Flat, fell at the third fence; and, on his return in 1888, he refused.

That year Linde also saddled the joint favourite, *Usna*, who had never been beaten and was hailed as 'the best steeplechase horse that has ever come out of Ireland'. Unfortunately, his outstanding record had earned the seven year old a top weight of 12st 7lb. He jumped brilliantly for Harry Beasley and was leading as they came to the Canal Turn second time around, challenged only by *Frigate* and Harry's brother Willie. But there, on landing first and looking all over the winner, *Usna* dislocated his shoulder and swerved off course.

Though he won many other races in England and France, including two Grand Steeplechases at Auteuil with *Whisper Low* and *Too Good*, Linde failed to gain a third National success. However, in 1889, Tommy Beasley triumphed on *Frigate* who was recognised as the 'best mare ever to win the National'; and it is noteworthy that *Frigate*, like the victorious *Seaman*, had benefited from regular work-outs over Linde's Aintree-style fences at The Curragh.

In the 1890s, after being badly injured in a hunting fall, Linde began to concentrate on training for the Flat. He enjoyed many more successes but sadly

he did not live to see his prodigy Terry Kavanagh win the 1897 National on *Manifesto*. Eight days before the race he died of Bright's disease.
See also: Empress; Woodbrook.

LITTLE, Captain Joseph Lockhart

Popularly known as 'Josey', Captain J.L. Little triumphed in his first Grand National (1848), snatching victory by half a length on board the 12 year old *Chandler*. It was the closest finish yet seen, and ironically the horse he pipped at the post – 6-1 favourite *The Curate* – was ridden by the great Tom Olliver, who had tutored Little in jump-riding skills.

Born in 1821 at Chipstead in Surrey, Little was an officer in the King's Dragoon Guards until, following a bank crash, he was faced with bankruptcy and compelled to transfer to the financially undemanding 81st Regiment of Foot. *Chandler*, owned by his great friend, Captain William Peel, was his salvation. Winning two chases on the old hunter, he collected enough in winning bets to buy a half-share in the gelding; and then, by winning the National, he gained a further £7,000 from the bookies.

'Josey' Little, otherwise known to the ladies as 'The Captivating Captain', rode in two more Nationals – gaining fifth place in 1849 when *Chandler* was top-weighted with 12st 2lb and in 1850 when the 14 year old failed to finish. Three years later he and Tom Olliver joined forces to land a truly remarkable National coup. In 1853, for the first time, the race was won by a 15 year old, the mud-loving *Peter Simple*. Little was the owner, Olliver the rider.

Little went on to become an accomplished rider on the Flat. But, sadly, the charming captain later suffered badly from gout. He subsequently lost the sight of an eye; and he was only 56 when he died in Paris in 1877.
See also: Chandler.

LITTLE CHARLEY

A Cheltenham-trained bay gelding, owned by Christopher Capel of Prestbury House, *Little Charley* won the 1858 National in a snowstorm – by four lengths from *Weathercock*, runner-up for the second successive year, with outsider *Xanthus* 50 yards back in third place. Of the 16 starters, only five (one remounted) finished in a race which was controversially run after a three-day postponement in the face of persistent bad weather.

The ten year old, sired by *Charles XII* out of an unrecorded mare, was succeeding at the fourth attempt. On his 1855 debut, he was knocked over in the blinding rain. The following year he finished fifth at 40-1 and in 1857 he had failed to finish. Now he was trained by William Holman who had finished third on *Sir Peter Laurie* in the 1852 National and was ridden for the first time by William Archer, father of the legendary Fred Archer.

Ironically, *Little Charley* was winning in the one year when his regular rider, T. Burrows, had a different mount, finishing a distant fourth on *Morgan Rattler*. They were reunited for one more challenge in 1859 but failed to finish.

See also: Archer, William; Holman, William.

LITTLE POLVEIR

Twelve year old winner of the 1989 Grand National when making his fourth appearance in the race, having finished ninth in 1986 and unseating his rider in the next two years. Unusually he was a winner out of the handicap proper; and his victory provided a second National triumph for trainer Toby Balding, 20 years after he had successfully saddled another 12 year old, *Highland Wedding*.

For Balding it was the most fortuitous bonus since only six weeks before the race he had bought *Little Polveir*, already with a National entry, on behalf of Mr Edward Harvey who wanted a suitable horse for his son David, an army captain serving in Germany, to ride in the Grand Military Gold Cup at Sandown. Regarded as 'a safe old plodder', the bay gelding duly carried the 6ft 2in tall, 12st 7lb amateur over the extended three miles to finish fourth, 22 lengths behind the winner *Brother Geoffrey*. Four weeks later he was a decisive winner of the 150th anniversary Grand National under a professional rider, Jimmy Frost, who was putting up 3lb overweight on his debut in the race.

Bred in Co. Antrim – by Triumph Hurdle winner *Cantab* out of *Blue Speedwell* – and named after a salmon-fishing pool in Scotland, *Little Polveir* was bought unraced by Ross-on-Wye trainer John Edwards on behalf of Mr Mark Shone. In March, 1983, he made a remarkable debut over fences: at 40-1 winning a three mile novice chase at Chepstow by 20 lengths. Thereafter he showed himself prone to careless jumping mistakes which limited him to only one win over fences in each of his first five seasons up to 1987. The last of these, however, con-

firmed him as an out-and-out stayer: a ten lengths victory over an extended four miles on heavy ground in the Scottish Grand National at Ayr.

In 1986, as a 66-1 chance in his first Aintree National, *Little Polveir* had performed creditably under Colin Brown to finish ninth. But in 1987 he had made a bad error that unseated Brown at The Chair. His third Aintree run, in the 1988 National, was more promising. Ridden by Tom Morgan, he jumped very well and was actually in the lead and still going strong coming to the 26th. But there he took off too soon and landed smack on top of the fence, surrendering the lead to the ultimate winner *Rhyme 'N' Reason*. Being an eleven year old, it seemed that his chance of National success had passed.

Early in February, 1989, *Little Polveir* had finished a distant third in a chase at Bangor; and it was later that month that Mr Harvey began a 2,000-mile, week-long tour in search of a horse for his son. *Little Polveir* was the first of half a dozen that he saw and the one he liked best. Subsequently, it was Toby Balding who successfully made a 15,000-guineas bid on his behalf – and ironically so, since trainer John Edwards had started out as Balding's assistant.

In 1986 Edwards had had three runners in the Grand National. This year he had originally entered no fewer than six horses including *Little Polveir*. Though sad to lose his 12 year old chaser, he now justifiably had higher hopes of National success than ever before. Two of his remaining five entries made it to Aintree. One was *Dixton House*, the 7-1 clear favourite, who had been bred by National-winning jockey Michael Scudamore. This bay gelding was generally regarded as the best handicapped horse in the race and such a respected tipster as Claude Duval recommended that punters 'stick the family mortgage on'. In addition, Edwards was represented by the talented *Bob Tisdall*, ridden by John White, a jockey who had completed in all his five previous National attempts.

How cruel the Grand National fates can be! Handicapped before his latest runaway win in the Ritz Club Handicap Chase at Cheltenham, *Dixton House* was seemingly thrown-in at the weights. But now he fell on landing too steeply over Becher's first time round. As for the not unfancied *Bob Tisdall*, he broke the tape with a false start, missed the break at the re-start, and cleared only one fence before sulkily refusing to jump another.

Meanwhile, in contrast, *Little Polveir* – a late

market mover, cut from 50-1 to 28-1 – was jumping supremely well. All the gelding's wins had been on ground at least good to soft; and now, with the going heavy, Jimmy Frost knew he could safely bide his time. Starting steadily, he kept clear of early fallers, most notably at the first Becher's where an horrendous five-horse pile-up claimed the lives of outsiders *Seeandem* and *Brown Trix*. Then, after the Canal Turn, he began to move up on the leaders. By The Chair he was sharing the lead with *West Tip*, *Mithras* and *Kersil*. Early on the second circuit he was alone in front but with many others still very much in contention.

Coming to the 20th, *Smart Tar* challenged for the lead, but there he blundered Carl Llewellyn out of the saddle. Eight fences later *Little Polveir* still headed affairs. Last year's runner-up *Durham Edition* now looked a major threat, but on the run-in he laboured in the mud and the only danger seemed to be the riderless *Smart Tar*, who ominously carried the leader towards the rails. As it happened, however, the loose horse provided useful company, narrowly beating the winner in a neck-and-neck battle to the line. In the slow time of 10min 6.9sec, *Little Polveir* had won by seven lengths from another 12 year old, *West Tip*, who was in the first four for the fourth time in as many years. Top-weight *The Thinker* was in third place, just half a length behind.

Curiously, John Edwards had seen one of his former horses win while another – *Cerimau*, now in the charge of last year's winning trainer David Elsworth – fell at the first fence. But there was at least some consolation for Mr Shone, who had owned *Little Polveir* in three unsuccessful Grand National bids. He had backed his old campaigner to win at antepost odds of 40-1.

See also: Frost, James; Balding, Toby; Balding, Clare.

LLEWELLYN, Carl

Welsh-born rider of two Grand National winners – *Party Politics* (1992) and *Earth Summit* (1998) – when both mounts were chance rides. He gained the former after stable jockey Andy Adams had broken a leg and Richard Dunwoody, the most recent jockey on *Party Politics*, had been booked for *Brown Windsor*. Similarly, he took over on *Earth Summit* after Tom Jenks had broken a leg.

With typical modesty, Carl Llewellyn would stress the luck factor. 'It's all about being on the right horse on the right day.' To a degree, he was right – as shown in 2002 when he missed a third victory by choosing to ride *Beau* in preference to *Bindaree*. But it is also about exploiting one's good luck to full effect, and this he did brilliantly.

Indeed, by no stretch of the imagination can Llewellyn be dubbed a 'lucky jockey'. In the early years he exemplified the courage and dedication of jump jockeys in his manner of overcoming so many severe injuries. At one time, after smashing his right ankle, he was told he would never race again. He returned to the saddle seven months later only to suffer, on his second comeback ride, the agony of a broken and dislocated elbow. Still, he determined to get back to racing.

Moreover, he had his share of bad luck in the National – most notably in 1993 when he had high hopes of a second triumph on *Party Politics*, who was bidding to become the first horse since *Red Rum* to win successive Nationals. In the view of trainer Nick Gaselee, *Party Politics* was 'a stone better' than he had been in 1992. But this was the year of the infamous false start and in the void race he was pulled up after completing one circuit.

A farmer's son, born in Pembrokeshire on July 29, 1965, Llewellyn dreamed of riding in the National from the time, as a mere seven year old, that he had watched on television the unforgettable 1973 duel between *Red Rum* and *Crisp*. Having devoted most of his boyhood leisure hours to riding his pony on the family farm in west Wales, he graduated to riding in point-to-points, then spent a year as a £5 a week stable amateur working in Stan Mellor's yard. There he became friends with another Welshman, jockey Hywel Davies, and at his suggestion he applied for a job with West Country trainer Jim Old. It launched his career, Old giving him invaluable experience before releasing him four years later to Capt. Tim Forster so that he would have more riding opportunities.

Carl rode his first National Hunt winner in 1986 and in the 1987-88 season he took the conditional jockeys' title with 41 successes. His first Cheltenham Festival victory came on *Smart Tar* in the 1988 Mildmay of Flete Challenge Cup. That same year he made his eagerly sought Grand National debut – on the Ginger McCain-trained *Kumbi*, a huge, clumsy animal rejected by several jockeys because he had fallen three times at Aintree, twice in the National. For the third time *Kumbi* went off as a

100-1 outsider. But Carl was delighted just to be in the race – his enthusiasm undiminished as the 13 year old bay, on ground too soft for his liking, blundered his way as far as Becher's second time around before exiting with a horrific somersaulting fall. It was, said the jockey, 'a brilliant first ride'.

One year later the Welshman returned to the National on *Smart Tar*, a well-backed eight year old regarded as a safe jumper, having fallen only once in 20 chases. The horse was narrowly first past the winning post, unfortunately without his rider. Again Carl had taken a heavy fall. After moving up alongside the eventual winner *Little Polveir*, he had been propelled out of the saddle at the 20th fence.

It was three years before Llewellyn rode in the National again and – much to his surprise – it was a case of third time lucky. Surprise because *Party Politics* had breathing problems and, when passing the stands on the first circuit, was making terrible gurgling noises. 'I didn't think I had a chance and I was very unhappy. But as the race went on he got stronger and stronger.'

By now Carl was riding regularly for Nigel Twiston-Davies and was achieving many big-race wins – the Mackeson Gold Cup on *Tipping Tim*; the SGB Handicap Chase (*Captain Dibble*); the Afga Hurdle (*Mole Board*); the Greenalls Gold Cup (*Party Politics*), the Sun Alliance Novices' Hurdle (*Gaelstrom*), the Long Distance Hurdle (*Sweet Duke*). But the void National of 1993 had dashed his hopes of a second win on *Party Politics*, and in 1994 he was without an Aintree mount.

In 1995, after being hobdayed, *Party Politics* made a remarkable comeback to the National to finish as runner-up. But he was then ridden by Mark Dwyer. Llewellyn, as long-time stable jockey to Nigel Twiston-Davies, was on the more strongly fancied *Young Hustler* on whom he had finished third in the 1994 Cheltenham Gold Cup. He was unseated at the third; and his National ended at the same fence in 1996 when he was reunited with a 12 year old *Party Politics*, now well past his best, though the jockey had regarded him as a sure-fire each-way prospect.

The following year brought a strong reminder of Carl's expertise at Aintree. This time Twiston-Davies had him on *Camelot Knight*, a 100-1 outsider generally dismissed as a no-hoper. In the words of the popular *Sporting Life* tipster Mark Winstanley: 'There is more chance of Anneka Rice finding the Holy Grail than this horse has of finishing in the first dozen. Scrub him off your Oscar Schindler.' Though outpaced early on and hampered at the seventh, *Camelot Knight* made steady headway from the 24th (Canal Turn) – and finished third behind *Lord Gyllene* and *Suny Bay*. Moreover, he had been disadvantaged by the two-day postponement forced by the IRA bomb scare – a delay that brought faster ground than he liked.

One year later Llewellyn went two places better for his boss: winning on *Earth Summit*, the 7-1 favourite who became the first horse to have won the Aintree, Scottish and Welsh Grand Nationals. Here he had one vital piece of good luck: the arrival of rain on the eve of the race. Without it, he acknowledged, *Earth Summit* could not have won. As it was, the heavy ground suited the mudlark perfectly. For a circuit, Carl was content to hack around at the back and keep out of trouble. Then came the powerful slog through boggy conditions. From two out the only threat was *Suny Bay* and that gallant grey was cruelly anchored, *Crisp*-like, under 12st. *Earth Summit*, with a 23lb advantage, stayed on to win by 11 lengths.

Carl was again on *Earth Summit* in the 1999 National, but the gelding's recent form was not encouraging and this time the faster ground was against him. He did well to finish eighth. The following season, at the age of 34, the jockey enjoyed his best ever start, rattling up 41 winners before mid-November, well on the way to a maiden century. But then came a knock-out fall at Ludlow, followed by a statutory layoff. It was a huge disappointment for the National Hunt workaholic, and the reversal of fortune continued in the 2000 Grand National where he crashed out at the first fence on the 100-1 outsider *Senor El Betrutti*.

Llewellyn was especially unlucky the following year when he looked to have an outstanding chance of winning his third National. His mount was the top-weighted *Beau* with whom he had won the Whitbread Cup by a record 42 lengths and who had been targeted for the 2001 Cheltenham Gold Cup until the Festival meeting fell foul of the great foot-and-mouth epidemic. *Beau* led over the first Becher's and was still ahead when, behind him, a fifth of the field was eliminated at the Canal Turn. Only seven of 40 starters remained as *Beau* led the way back on to the second circuit. But then Carl lost his reins, jerked out of his hands as the horse pecked on landing over the 17th. He managed to hook them back to one side with his stick but tried in vain to juggle them back over the horse's head. No longer under his control, *Beau* unseated him at the 20th, leaving only *Red Marauder* and *Smarty* in contention. 'It was my fault,' he said afterwards, 'I should have had longer reins.'

Such was Llewellyn's competitive nature that, even with two Grand National victories under his belt, he described his Aintree ride on *Beau* as 'the worst day of my racing life – because the National is the greatest race to me and winning it again is the main thing I still want to achieve'.

At the start of the second circuit, he had considered himself to be an odds-on favourite to win; and even after being unseated he thought he might still have won if he had been able to remount immediately. As it was, he chased after his mount who was eventually caught by Colin Roberts, a race-reader for BBC-TV stationed at the Canal Turn. There the never-say-die jockey enterprisingly borrowed the journalist's mobile to telephone the trainer. Should he remount? Twiston-Davies told him to make his own decision, and he decided that it was now too late. Three weeks later the partnership went off as a short-priced, top-weighted favourites in a 25-runner Whitbread Gold Cup. Fading only in the final stages, Beau finished fifth.

Still hungry for that third National success, Carl had no thought of retiring; and in 2002, after suffering a broken nose and concussion in a heavy fall at Cheltenham, he was back for a second bid on *Beau*, now dropped 9lb in the weights, and, at 11-1, the best supported of three runners for Twiston-Davies. *Beau* was such a fancied contender that two days before the race he had been purchased by Mr Trevor Hemmings, the owner of the Blackpool Tower, who already had two horses in the National.

No fewer than sixteen of his rivals had been eliminated when *Beau* encouragingly moved into second place approaching the 14th. But there, alas, he stumbled badly on landing and unseated his rider. Desperately, he held on to the reins, being dragged many yards before having to let go. Subsequently, the luckless Llewellyn saw his horse run on to finish first past the post, ahead of his victorious stablemate *Bindaree*. He had chosen the wrong Twiston-Davies runner – ironically the only time in a 40-race career that *Bindaree* was not ridden by him.

Nevertheless, he had enjoyed an excellent season

and was to finish with 109 winners, a total exceeded only by A.P. McCoy and Richard Johnson. Moreover, the victory of *Bindaree* had a vital influence on his career. It prompted Twiston-Davies to abandon his plans to retire – and so, by association, Carl chose to carry on riding. The trainer now bought out his business partner and assistant Peter Scudamore and planned to restructure his big stable with Llewellyn becoming more involved with the training operation.

Over the years Llewellyn, like so many jump jockeys, had suffered an extraordinary catalogue of injuries: a fractured leg, broken collarbones, wrist, arm, jaw, ankle, nose (eight times), dislocated elbow and spells of concussion. But he worked hard at keeping fit (he had once appeared on TV's 'Gladiators') and now, at the age of 37, this most shrewd and amiable jockey was still no less obsessive in his passion for racing and for the greatest steeplechase especially. As he expressed it, 'I would rather win one more National than two Gold Cups'.

In November, 2002, he was reunited with *Bindaree* in Aintree's Becher Chase. This time the National winner fell at the second fence. There were fears that the fall might have dented the gelding's confidence; and indeed, though reasonably weighted on 10st 11lb in the 2003 National, he jumped less fluently, being well to the rear on the first circuit. Creditably, Carl nursed him round, making so much progress than they came home the sixth of 14 finishers.

The following season, with *Bindaree* returned to his best form, Llewellyn rode him to victory over hot favourite *Sir Rembrandt* in the Welsh National. In March, 2004, after a ten-year gap, he scored his seventh Cheltenham Festival win, on *Fundamentalist* in the SunAlliance Novices' Hurdle, and he went on to Aintree with high hopes. But *Bindaree*, one of four co-favourites in the National, was now heavily weighted on 11st 4lb, and after being hampered he unseated his rider at Becher's first time round. It was Llewellyn's 13th Grand National ride.

Remarkably, as he approached his 40th birthday, Carl was enjoying greater success. His winning tally for the 2003-4 season was 65 compared with only 29 the previous year; and he was heading for an even bigger score in 2004-5 when the 70-strong Twiston-Davies stable was in excellent form. The so-called Peter Pan among jockeys rode yet again in the National and this time finished 11th on *Bindaree*

L

who was carrying only 1lb less than before.

On hitting 40, the oldest jockey in the weighing room still refused to consider retirement, even though he was financially secure with ownership of numerous properties in the Swindon area. Indeed, he had his highest hopes for the new season. He said, 'I've got the best batch of horses to ride in Nigel Twiston-Davies's yard that I have ever had in the past 15 years.' And he picked out *Lord Maizey* as a National horse in the making.

As anticipated, the 2005-06 season started brilliantly for the stable with Carl riding an especially impressive winner (*Ollie Magern*) in the Charlie Hall Chase at Wetherby. He was now combining riding with his duties as assistant trainer to Mark Pitman. But still he was enjoying racing too much to think of retirement. A key factor in his longevity was that, unlike so many jump jockeys, he could easily make 10st (the minimum weight any National Hunt horse can carry) without recourse to wasting and dieting.

In the 2006 Grand National, Carl was unseated at the third from 66-1 shot *Baron Windrush*. Immediately afterwards he took over from Mark Pitman as trainer at Lambourn's Weathercock House Stables and saddled his first runner, *Without A Doubt,* for a novices' chase at Market Rasen. But he had still not given up riding and, sensationally, just two weeks later, his first winner as a trainer was *Run For Paddy* whom he rode to victory in the Scottish Grand National at 33-1. Llewellyn had now captured three National titles – English, Welsh and Scottish.

At the turn of the year, he scored his first Cheltenham double as a trainer: *Too Forward* in the £40,000 Unicoin Homes Chase and *Quartano* in a Listed bumper. With some 45 horses in his charge, he was now virtually riding only in National Hunt Flat races, but with such success that at the start of 2008 he was only 25 short of the 1,000 winners mark.

See also: Twiston-Davies, Nigel; Party Politics; Earth Summit; Fixes.

LOFT, William

Amateur rider of *Cure-All*, the shock winner of the 1845 Grand National in which the successful brown gelding was an outsider not even given an official starting price. Mr William Loft was, in fact, also the winning owner – his horse only running in the name of Mr W. Sterling Crawford as a condition of his late entry in place of Mr Crawford's nominated runner who had to be withdrawn through injury.

The son of a Lieutenant-General, Loft was a keen huntsman who farmed his brother's estate at Healing near Grimsby. He had had no expectation of National glory when he bought *Cure-All* from a Northamptonshire farmer at the Horncastle Fair sales in 1843. There the horse was lamed in a fall when being required to demonstrate his jumping prowess. As a result his reserve price of £260 was abandoned. He was knocked down to Mr Loft for a mere £50.

Nursed back to fitness, *Cure-All* initially served as the farmer's mount when following the Brocklesby Hounds. Then he was tried out in a Lincoln steeplechase; and he showed such surprising ability in getting up from a fall to finish a neck second that he was allowed to take his chance in the National. At Aintree, Loft complained that the frozen course was unfit for racing. But he was outvoted by other owners, and ironically the treacherous conditions worked in his favour.

Following the late withdrawal of the favourite, *The Knight Templar*, there were only 15 runners when the race finally got under way at five o'clock; and *Cure-All*'s victory was largely due to his rider's shrewdness in seeking out a narrow strip of better ground on the second circuit. Challenging for the lead at the last, the brown gelding outstayed the grey *Peter Simple*, who was giving him 7lb in his fifth National bid, and he won fairly cosily by two lengths, with *The Exquisite* a further two lengths back, the third of only four finishers.

Having won the National at his first attempt, Loft returned with *Cure-All* in 1846, this time as the officially recorded rider-owner. But his winner had now been raised 13lb to a top weight of 12st 4lb. Moreover, he faced a much stronger field, with a then record number of 22 starters. He soon had to be pulled up and neither horse nor rider appeared in the National again.

See also: Cure-All.

LOOSE HORSES

In the Grand National, above all, 'loose horses' – those running on riderless – have been responsible for sensational results. In 1932 *Pelorus Jack* ran across the 11th fence, putting two-thirds of the runners out of the race which was won by 50-1 shot *Forbra*. Most notoriously, in 1967, *Popham Down*, a 66-1 chance brought down at the first, veered

L

across the low 23rd fence and brought to a standstill the entire field – that is, with the exception of the trailing *Foinavon* who cleared the fence first time and ran on to win by 15 lengths at 100-1.

The next major pile-up occurred in 1979 when two loose horses veered across the course at The Chair, causing nine runners to be put out of the race. After that debacle gaps were left in the inside running rail so that riderless horses had escape routes approaching The Chair. However, as shown the following year, horses cannot be relied upon to take the path of least resistance. That year, ignoring the exits, a free runner stayed on to appear directly in front of race leader *Delmoss* as he came to The Chair. On this occasion, by good fortune, a collision was averted since the renegade jumped the open ditch and fence cleanly without deviating off line.

As the biggest fence, with runners funnelling on approach to the narrow obstacle, The Chair has always been a major hazard in respect of loose horses. Equally dangerous, as dramatically shown in 2001, is the Canal Turn marking a 90-degree change of direction. Here, riderless horses are liable to miss the sharp bend to the left; and indeed, in the early days – before the corner was fenced off – they were even known to gallop straight on into the canal.

Happily, though pilotless horses can cause chaos, they themselves rarely incur serious injury. There have been just two notable exceptions in modern times. In 1963 eight year old *Avenue Neuilly*, having already unseated his rider, David Nicholson, ran on to break a foreleg at the tenth and staggered on to the next fence where he was caught and painlessly put down. Then, in 2006, *Tyneandthyneagain* fell at the first and ran on riderless only to become fatally wedged in the last open ditch on the second circuit.

In 2007 the Charlie Egerton-trained *Graphic Approach*, who had fallen at the second Becher's, had galloped on loose until the second last when he veered off the National course and into a running rail on the hurdle course. There, knocked unconscious, he was treated on the course for several hours and the concluding bumper race was cancelled to allow vets to continue their work. He was transferred to the local veterinary hospital but it was all in vain. He died a month later.

Today there is a gap in the running rail before and after every fence, but still loose horses tend to stay on track – evidence, it is argued, of the fact that they are herd animals who positively enjoy the challenge.

Remarkably, in 2004, the aptly named *Bounce Back* fell at the first Becher's and then, riderless, fell two more times before calling it a day. Moreover, despite the availability of exits, there have been years when the number of loose horses jumping round has outnumbered those with riders.

Indeed, it is not unusual for a horse to complete the course without a rider. In 1905, *Ascetic's Silver* lost his rider at the third fence but went on alone to be first past the finishing post – a feat he more profitably achieved with his rider still on board the following year. Similarly, the moody mare *Sheila's Cottage* was first past the post in successive Nationals – in 1947 after unseating Arthur Thompson at the 12th fence, and in 1948 when she finished with her jockey.

In 1933, when *Kellsboro' Jack* won in a then record time, he was preceded by the riderless *Apostasy*, a 100-1 outsider. In 1938, when *Battleship* beat *Royal Danieli* by a head, the riderless six year old *Takvor Pacha* came between them on the run-in to finish first past the post. Two years later there was some consolation for Hywel Jones when he fell at the 14th on *National Night*. He was easily able to get back to the stands in time to watch the finish; and there he saw his riderless 100-1 outsider pass the post first – just one length ahead of *Bogskar*, ridden by his brother Mervyn. More recently, in 2002, the riderless *Beau* got up at the 14th to harass and then beat his victorious stablemate *Bindaree* to the finishing post.

At times, a loose horse can be a positive advantage to a legitimate challenger. In 1989, for example, *Smart Tar* unseated his rider at the 20th but later provided useful company for *Little Polveir*, engaging him in a neck-and-neck battle to the line which he won by a squeak. For the most part, however, renegade runners are at least a nuisance and sometimes a menace.

In 2001 there were some vociferous critics who suggested that the National should never have been run on such waterlogged ground. But, as events showed, it was loose horses – not the going – that constituted the greatest hazard. With the hock-deep mud reducing speed and cushioning falls, not one horse or rider suffered a noteworthy injury. All the problems were created by riderless horses who did not take advantage of escape routes.

That year, shortly before the National, trainer Ferdy Murphy said that his *Paddy's Return* 'might surprise a few'. How right he was! Having lost Adrian Maguire at the third, the blinkered, riderless *Paddy's Return* stormed his way ahead and then, just behind the leaders, he veered sharply left across the Canal Turn, cannoning into *Amberleigh House* and creating sufficient havoc to eliminate a fifth of the field. A circuit later he was still running strongly; and, back at the Canal Turn, he made another sideways move, almost hitting *Red Marauder* who survived to be the first of only four finishers (two remounted).

The third finisher that year was *Blowing Wind* who had been baulked into the ditch at the 18th fence by a loose horse. His rider, champion Tony McCoy, suffered a similar, but far more devastating blow in 2005 when two loose horses were responsible for carrying him out on *Clan Royal* as he approached the second Becher's. At the time he was leading the field on the horse he judged to be his best ever chance of winning the race.

That year by far the 'loosest' horse was *Lord Atterbury* who, after falling at the first fence, ran off the racecourse and on to the golf course where he collided with the parked car of Ron Barry, the Jockey Club's Inspector of Courses. He then slipped on the roadway, got up and completed a couple of circuits of the motor racing track before being caught.

But he was not quite the loosest horse in Grand National history. That title goes to *Inkerman*, a rank outsider in the 1863 National. Having lost his amateur rider several fences earlier, he ran on to take the lead at Becher's. Then, on coming to the Canal Turn, he chose to leave the course and set off exploring the adjoining countryside. It was not until long after dark that the lost horse was finally discovered, grazing in a field several miles away.

See also: Canal Turn; Blinkered Runners.

LORD GYLLENE

New Zealand-bred winner of the 1997 Grand National after the race had been postponed 49 hours following IRA bomb scares. Relatively untroubled by the rescheduling, the nine year old gelding became the first since *Troytown* (1920) to dominate the race from start to finish, romping home with ears pricked to win by 25 lengths from *Suny Bay*.

By *Ring The Bell* out of the dam *Dentelle*, *Lord Gyllene* had an interesting pedigree. His sire was a winner of 11 races in Australasia, including the New Zealand Derby, and his dam was sired by *Crest of*

The Wave, a horse bred and raced by Queen Elizabeth II. Through the male line he was linked to two Grand National winners of the 1990s. *Ring The Bell's* sire, *Rangong*, had the same sire (*Right Royal V*) as *Politico*, the sire of *Party Politics*, and *Kambalda*, sire of *Miinnehoma*.

In 1995 a videotape of *Lord Gyllene* was seen by Mr (later Sir) Stanley Clarke, a one-time butcher's boy and apprentice plumber, who was now a multi-millionaire property tycoon, chairman of Newcastle and Uttoxeter racecourses, and a Jockey Club member. He specialised in importing New Zealand talent and on this occasion the horse reminded him of the legendary *Red Rum*. As the new owner, Clarke sent *Lord Gyllene* to the amateur rider Steve Brookshaw who, at his suggestion, had only recently taken out a full licence to train at Uffington, near Shrewsbury. The tall, rangy gelding immediately impressed, only once failing to be unplaced over fences and looking a real Aintree prospect when finishing a good second to *The Grey Monk* at Haydock in the 1995-96 season.

But it was on Mr Clarke's Uttoxeter course (left-handed like Aintree) that *Lord Gyllene* really showed his true mettle. There, between December, 1996, and February, 1997, he scored a hat-trick of wins: over three miles, three miles two furlongs, and then – in the Singer and Friedlander Handicap Chase – over four and a quarter miles. In the latter, when making all and finishing strongly to beat the classy *Mudahim* (receiving 7lb) by eight lengths, he was carrying 11st 9lb. Three days later, when the Grand National weights were announced, he was allotted a mere 9st 13lb, 1lb out of the handicap proper!

That form was greatly strengthened when *Mudahim* went on to win the Irish Grand National. Meanwhile, *Lord Gyllene* had enjoyed another fine run at Uttoxeter, finishing seven lengths second to *Seven Towers* (receiving 6lb) in the Midlands National. Again the distance was four and a quarter miles and this time he was carrying 11st 10lb.

In the circumstances, it now seems extraordinary that *Lord Gyllene* was not the clear favourite for the Grand National. But on the morning of the race he was one of five runners vying for 10-1 favouritism. And two days later, following the postponement forced by IRA bomb threats, he went off at 14-1 – behind *Go Ballistic* (7-1), *Suny Bay* (8-1) and *Avro Anson* (12-1).

The doubts about *Lord Gyllene* centred on the

fact that he was only a novice the previous season, short of experience, and yet to race in a field of more than 11. On the other hand, he was a proven stayer on top form and able to act on all types of going. Furthermore, two circumstances worked in his favour. Contrary to expectations, Kim Bailey decided not to withdraw top-weighted *Master Oats* which would automatically have brought about a 15lb rise in the weights, putting *Lord Gyllene* on 11st instead of 10st. Secondly, the postponement was not a problem for *Lord Gyllene* who had less than a two-hour journey home. Others suffered some distress; and a few, most significantly *Suny Bay*, were not helped by the drying ground.

On the Monday, *Lord Gyllene*, ridden for the third time that year by Tony Dobbin, put in an immaculate display of jumping and relentless galloping. The only threat in the race was posed by the riderless *Glemot* who came perilously close to him at the Water Jump. His nearest rival *Suny Bay*, never out of the first three, made a costly blunder four fences from home. But even without that error the result would have been the same. *Lord Gyllene* was irresistible as he powered home, ears pricked and still full of running, to equal the 25 lengths winning margin achieved by *Red Rum* 20 years before.

Mr Clarke likened his impressive winner to a Kiwi rugby player – strong, athletic and tough, and with stamina never in doubt. He saw no reason why his superstar should not win the National again, and this was made his main target. Unfortunately, *Lord Gyllene* now suffered a sequence of injuries that limited him to only two races in the next three years. He was never the same force again.

In the summer of 2000, Clarke sent him to Martin Pipe – much to the surprise of Steve Brookshaw who had understood that, if *Lord Gyllene* was to go back into training, he would be returned to him. The 13 year old was, in fact, entered for the 2001 National, being allotted a mere 9st 6lb. But he was unfit to run and was now retired to Sir Stanley's estate. *See also:* Brookshaw, Stephen; Clarke, Sir Stanley; Abandoned.

LOSERS

See: Unlucky Losers.

LOTTERY

A nine-year-old bay gelding – originally named *Chance* – *Lottery* won the 1839 Liverpool Steeple-chase that is regarded as the first-ever Aintree Grand National. He was a truly outstanding jumper even though his winning time of 14min 53sec (then racing over ploughed fields land with extremely heavy going) is the slowest in the history of the race.

Bred by a Mr Jackson of Riston Grange, near Hull, he was out of *Parthenia* by another horse named *Lottery*, and he opened his account by winning two modest Flat races as a four year old. Two years later, in 1836, he was sent to the Horncastle Horse Fair in Lincolnshire, where he was purchased for £120 by John Elmore, a leading owner-dealer of North London.

Renamed *Lottery*, he now began a formidable partnership with Jem Mason, the foremost jump jockey of the day. Success in minor two-miles chases in 1837 was followed by victories in the Metropolitan Chase and Daventry Chase in 1838, and subsequently *Lottery* was sent to Epsom to be prepared for the National by George Dockeray, the Flat jockey-turned-trainer who had won the 1826 Derby on *Lapdog*.

Seventeen horses competed in the 1839 National. *Lottery* was backed down to 5-1, being strongly challenged for favouritism by Lord McDonald's English mare, *The Nun*, and the main Irish hopes, *Daxon* and *Rust*. In an incident-packed race, Captain Martin Becher, thrown from *Conrad*, famously took a dive into the first brook which has borne his name ever since; outrageously, *Rust* was later going so well that unsporting punters invaded the course and blocked his path until the rest of the field had passed by; and tragically, on the second circuit, at the brook now known as Valentine's, *Dictator* burst a blood vessel and crashed out to become the race's first fatality.

Coming to the last fence in the lead, *Lottery* put paid to all challengers with a prodigious leap, reportedly all of 30 feet. It was the kind of spring-heeled leap that he was often required to perform at home where his owner liked to entertain guests by having him jump over dining tables and chairs set out on the lawn.

Lottery powered on to win by three lengths and the same from *Seventy Four* and *Paulina* respectively, earning his owner the then considerable sum of £1,200. The following year he was made the 4-1 second favourite in a field of 12. He was in second place as they approached the end of the first circuit, but then he hit the Stone Wall and crashed down amid a pile of broken masonry. Three close-up horses – *Columbine*, *The Nun* and *Seventy Four* – promptly joined him in the debris.

At Aintree in 1841, *Lottery* was no longer threatened by the awesome Wall which had been replaced by a 10ft-wide Water Jump. But now he was given an even greater obstacle to overcome: punitively he had been burdened with 13st 4lb under an absurd new ruling which stipulated that all horses should carry 12st – 'except for the winner of the 1840 Cheltenham Steeplechase who will carry an extra 18lb'.

This drastic penalty was imposed out of fear that *Lottery*'s presence would frighten away many challengers – and, more seriously, reduce attendance in the light of a possible 'one-horse race'. Even then, *Lottery* was held in such extraordinarily high public esteem that he started as 5-2 favourite! In reality, he had no sporting chance at the weights and very properly Jem Mason pulled him up on the second circuit. In 1842 the circumstances were duplicated. Again, *Lottery* carried an 18lb penalty; again he was made favourite (this time, 5-1), and again he was pulled up on the second circuit.

Fortunately for *Lottery*, the National was made a handicap in 1843 with a range from 11st to 12st 8lb, so sparing him that unreasonable 13st-plus. This time he completed the course and most tellingly demonstrated his prodigious jumping when he put in a colossal leap to clear both the reintroduced Wall and the two horses that had just fallen there, directly in front of him.

But the great horse, though 4-1 joint second favourite, was now 13 years old, well past his prime; and with a burden of 12st 6lb (the second highest weight in a field of 16) he could manage only seventh place. He had run his last Grand National. The record books show that he had won the race only once, but almost certainly he would have won a second and maybe a third time if he had not been so savagely penalised for winning at Cheltenham in 1840.

One year later, after winning at Windsor, *Lottery* was retired from racing. Today such an outstanding, lion-hearted champion would be paraded at major meetings and invited to open supermarkets. Instead, the first great steeplechaser of the Victorian age began his retirement as the hack of trainer Dockeray and ended his days as a cart-horse on the streets of Neasden.

See also: Elmore, John; Mason, Jem; Dockeray, George.

LOVELY COTTAGE

The 25-1 winner, in 1946, of the first Grand National to be held after a six-year suspension of the race during the Second World War. With an amateur rider, Captain Bobby Petre, recently demobbed from the Scots Guards, the nine year old gelding triumphed by four lengths from a 100-1 shot, *Jack Finlay*, with the 3-1 favourite *Prince Regent* a further three lengths back in third.

It was a second National success for the winner's sire, *Cottage*, who had died four years earlier at the age of 24. *Cottage*, son of *Tracery* out of a mare by *Marco*, had sired the 1939 winner *Workman*; and another of the great stallion's sons (*Sheila's Cottage*) would win the National in 1948.

Lovely Cottage was bred in Co. Cork by Mr M. J. Hyde, the dam being an outstanding point-to-pointer called *The Nun III*. He won three races over fences in 1944, finished third in the 1945 Irish Grand National, and was then put up for sale at £2,000 with the proviso that another £1,000 would be paid if he ever won the Aintree National. The offer was taken up by Mr John Morant of Brockenhurst, Hampshire, who, only four months before the 1946 National, sent the new arrival to trainer Tommy Rayson at Headbourne Worthy, near Winchester.

In 1946 the advantage was with Irish horses who had had the benefit of wartime racing experience. *Lovely Cottage* was one, but another, much more fancied, was Mr J.V. Rank's *Prince Regent* who had won 14 races including the recent Cheltenham Gold Cup. Despite a top weight of 12st 5lb, he was made the hot 3-1 favourite.

At the Anchor Bridge, with two fences remaining, *Prince Regent* seemed to have an unassailable lead. But he was weakening fast, his task having been frequently increased by the need to escape the persistent harassment of loose horses. By the last fence his lead had been cut to four lengths, and on the long run-in he was soon overhauled by *Lovely Cottage* and *Jack Finlay*, who enjoyed respectively a 21lb and 27lb advantage in the weights. Among the punters who cheered the result was a schoolboy who said he had won 'a fortune'. His name: Peter Bromley, a teenager destined to be a radio commentator on 42 Grand Nationals.

Lovely Cottage missed the 1947 National through injury. When he returned to Aintree the following year he was clearly past his best and, with an extra 10lb to carry, he went off at 66-1. Remounted after

L

a fall, he ran on at his own leisurely pace to be the last of 14 finishers in a race won by *Sheila's Cottage*, the first mare to win the National since *Shannon Lass* in 1902.

See also: Rayson, Tommy; Petre, Captain Robert Charles.

LUCIUS

Nine year old winner of the Grand National – by just half a length and a neck – in 1978 when the race was a highly competitive, wide-open affair after the late withdrawal and retirement of the long-time hot favourite *Red Rum*. It was his first and last appearance in the National; and subsequently, being harshly handicapped, he never won a race again.

By *Perhapsburg* out of an Irish mare (*Matches*) who had twice won over fences, *Lucius* was an unbroken three year old when he was bought at the 1972 Doncaster sales for 1,800 guineas by Cumbrian trainer Gordon W. Richards on behalf of Mrs Fiona Whitaker, wife of an Edinburgh chartered accountant. Highly regarded by the trainer, he won two hurdle races in the 1973-74 season and four more in the following season before making his debut over fences.

It was not an especially auspicious beginning. After finishing third and second in chases at Newcastle, *Lucius* fell in a novice chase at Kelso. But even then Richards was talking about him as a real 'Grand National type'. Rightly, he judged that the bay gelding would improve with experience; and, sure enough, *Lucius* followed up with two wins and two narrowly beaten second spots. In the 1976-77 season he was successful in three out of eight races.

Unusually, *Lucius* was subjected to an extremely hard campaign prior to his Grand National bid – no fewer than nine races. He won three of them, but most promising were his two defeats immediately before going to Aintree. He ran well to finish runner-up in the William Hill Yorkshire Chase at Doncaster and was beaten by only three-quarters of a length in the Greenall Whitley Chase at Haydock. As a result, his 40-1 National odds were soon halved and cut to 14-1 by the time of the race.

To his dismay, less than a week before the National, *Lucius*'s regular partner David Goulding suffered a minor racing injury that deprived him of the ride. At the 11th hour, Richards secured a worthy replacement: former champion jockey Bob Davies. On mounting the horse for the first time in the Aintree paddock, Davies was given just one firm in-

struction: to delay taking a lead as long as possible. *Lucius* invariably lost interest when racing alone.

Lucius took a strong hold from the start but fortunately others went off even faster. Three fell at the first, and the early leader, second favourite *Tied Cottage*, crashed out at Becher's. At the Water, *Lucius* was in a group close-up behind *Sebastian V*, the Scottish Grand National winner, and as they came to Becher's second time around he was challenging for the lead.

The bold jumping of *Sebastian V* continued to keep him ahead and, as it happened, *Lucius*'s one minor error – hitting the third last – proved to be to his advantage. Having lost momentum, he was less in danger of taking the lead too soon. Briefly he surrendered second place to *Coolishall*, and at the last at least five horses were positioned well enough to win. Davies delayed his all-out move as long as he dared, pressing hard on the accelerator from the Elbow onwards. In an extraordinarily packed finish, *Lucius* got home by just half a length from *Sebastian V*, with *Drumroan* only a neck back in third. Barely two and a half lengths divided the first five.

Always burdened with top weight, *Lucius* was narrowly beaten in all his subsequent races and hopes of running him in the 1979 National were dashed by a virus infection. The following season he was retired and thereafter was hunted by the Whitakers in Fife. He died peacefully in his sleep at the age of 27.

See also: Richards, Gordon W.; Davies, Bertram Robert.

LUTTEUR III

Only five horses have won the Grand National at the tender age of five. *Lutteur III*, victorious in 1909, was the last do so; and – like *Alcibiade* (1865), the first to achieve that distinction – he was French-bred.

A chestnut gelding, bred by M. Gaston Dreyfus and bought for 610 guineas by M. James Hennessy of the famed brandy-producing family, *Lutteur III* was a complete failure as a juvenile racer on the Flat. However, his trainer, George Batchelor, persuaded the owner to let him keep the horse as his hack. He strengthened up in the next two years but when put into a hurdle race he finished last.

Then, most unexpectedly, he won a steeplechase at Enghien, and he followed up by winning five chases over the tough Auteuil course – a remarkable feat for a four year old. The following year he was sent to Epsom to be prepared for Aintree by Harry Escott, the man who, in 1894, had trained the great *Cloister* in an aborted bid to win the National in successive years.

Sixteen days before the 1909 National *Lutteur III* proved his well-being in breathtaking style: by romping home in the Champion Steeplechase at Hurst Park ahead of older, high-class jumpers who were meeting him on level terms. As a result, his odds shortened to 100-9, making him joint favourite with *Shady Lady* in a National field of 32 runners, the largest number for 59 years.

As at Hurst Park. *Lutteur III* was ridden by 21 year old Georges Parfrement, a French jockey of Yorkshire descent. Having studied the daunting drop fences, the rider decided to change his style by lengthening his stirrup leathers and to concentrate on settling his horse early on, gently familiarising him with the jumps.

Lutteur III was towards the rear of the field as the leaders tackled Becher's. But he was jumping surely, all the while gaining ground, and by the time they approached the Canal Turn on the second circuit he was challenging for the lead. Meanwhile, *Rubio* and *Mattie Magregor* – last year's winner and runner-up respectively – had been eliminated, and *Ascetic's Silver*, the 1906 winner, had broken down. And now, as *Shady Lady* met with serious interference, the French contender was left in the lead, with only eight year old *Judas* an obvious threat.

Though the winning margin was just two lengths, *Lutteur III* was in full command on the run-in and the third horse, *Caubeen*, finished far behind runner-up *Judas*. It was the second National victory by a French-bred horse; and on good going a record 16 horses had completed the course.

Providentially perhaps, *Lutteur III* missed through injury the 1910 National, a chaotic affair in which only five of 25 finished. But conditions were no better when he returned in 1911. He faced unfavoured heavy ground, with rain still falling, and he had been raised 20lb to a top weight of 12st 3lb. Still he was made the hot 7-2 favourite, having recently won the three-mile Open Steeplechase at Hurst Park.

Unfortunately, this National was even more chaotic than the year before. In torrential rain only four of 26 starters completed the course and three of those had been remounted on the way. *Lutteur III*, following a bolder start, made his exit on the first circuit when he landed atop the fence after Becher's.

Due to recurring tendon trouble, *Lutteur III* did not reappear at Aintree until three years later. He was now ten years old and had been raised a further 3lb in the weights. But at least the going was reasonable and this time the 20-strong field included a second French challenger, *Trianon II*. Starting as 10-1 second favourite, and now ridden by jockey Alec Carter, *Lutteur III* galloped and jumped well throughout. But Carter, like most everyone else, underestimated the staying power of an eight year old at the bottom of the handicap: *Sunloch*, a grandson of the 1874 Derby winner, *George Frederick*.

From the start, Bill Smith on *Sunloch* set a blistering pace. They were leading by 20 lengths at Becher's, by an amazing 40 lengths as they approached Becher's the second time around. Soon only five horses were still standing, among them the French pair whose riders fully expected that the tearaway would come back to them. But they had misjudged the pace; and when, after Valentine's, they launched a most determined challenge it was too late. *Sunloch* jumped faultlessly and galloped on relentlessly to win by eight lengths from *Trianon III*, with *Lutteur III*, on his last appearance, another eight lengths back in third. Only four horses finished.

See also: Parfrement, Georges; Escott, Harry; France.

LYALL, Robert

As the winning jockey on nine year old *Grakle* in the 1931 Grand National – a victory that gave his uncle, trainer Tom Coulthwaite, his third success in the race – Bob Lyall went one better than his eldest brother Frank who rode Mr C. Bower Ismay's *Bloodstone*, a 40-1 chance, to finish runner-up by six lengths to *Jerry M* in 1912.

Bob was the youngest of five sons of Lincolnshire trainer J.G. Lyall, all of whom took their turn as jump jockeys. Frank rode in six Nationals, beginning with a fourth place on *Ravenscliffe* (1907) and ending with a fifth place on *Balscadden* (remounted) in 1915. Bob rode in nine Nationals beginning with a sixth place on the rank outsider *Wavetown* (1924) and ending in 1933 with a fall on Lady Lindsay's *Apostasy*, a 100-1 shot who ran on riderless to finish first past the post ahead of the record-breaking *Kellsboro' Jack*.

L

On each of his first four Nationals, *Grakle* had been ridden by different jockeys – falling with Jack Moloney (1927), refusing with Lyall (1928), finishing sixth under Tim Hamey (1929) and falling with Keith Piggott when favourite in 1930. Now, for the fifth bid, trainer Coulthwaite chose to book his nephew again. After all, Lyall was entirely blameless for the failure in 1928 when a pile-up had resulted in only two of 42 runners completing the course.

This time Bob was under orders to show *Grakle* the whip only as an absolutely last resort since, as experience showed, the horse tended to hang in response to the stick. He followed instructions to the letter. Only in the last hundred yards, when locked in a head-to-head duel with *Gregalach*, did he produce the whip. It was just enough to spur *Grakle* home to win by one and a half lengths, and in the then second fastest time in National history.

In 1931 Lyall also had the distinction of riding the great *Golden Miller* at Leicester when he scored the first of his 29 victories. Though he had his last National ride in 1933, it was not the end of his association with the race. In 1935 he returned to Aintree, commentating for the BBC from a soundproof booth attached to Lord Derby's private box.
See also: Grakle.

LYNAM, Desmond Michael OBE

Fronting the BBC television coverage from Aintree, the avuncular Des Lynam became an integral part of the Grand National scene from 1985 onwards when he was first seen there as anchor-man of Grandstand. Previously, however, he had reported from Aintree for radio. It was his favourite sporting assignment, and his fondest National memory came from his pre-television days: the 1981 victory of Bob Champion on *Aldaniti*.

Born on September 17, 1942, in Co. Clare, Lynam began his career in insurance, then turned to journalism in the 1960s. After working as a local radio reporter he joined BBC Radio Sport in 1969, having his first assignments as a boxing commentator. He switched to BBC TV in 1977.

Of all his many Aintree interviews, the most memorable were his lively exchanges with the straight-talking Jenny Pitman. Typical of their friendly banter was the televised chat before the 1995 National (won by Jenny's *Royal Athlete*). Dismissing the claim by animal rights activists that the National is cruel, she stated: 'The horses have everything they want. If I could come back to the world, I would love to come back as a racehorse.'

Lynam: 'But surely you would not want to come back as a gelding?'

Pitman: 'No, but I know a few people for whom it would do a lot of good. Not you, of course, Des. You might lose your sparkle.'

However, in a later presentation of their famous double-act, Des Lynam did lose a touch of his sparkle – visibly taken aback when Jenny remarked that it was high time he made an honest woman of his long-time live-in partner, Rose Diamond. She herself re-married soon after.

In 1986, when presenting Grandstand from Aintree for the second time, Lynam became directly involved with the race, having ten days earlier leased *Another Duke* to run in his name. Ridden by Paul Nicholls, the 13 year old gelding had run well at the 1985 Cheltenham Festival and had recently finished second in a Nottingham hunter chase. His 200-1 odds certainly belied his jumping ability. But this was his first experience of the Aintree fences and he fell at Valentine's first time.

That year the National was won by the horse who most impressed Lynam, the so consistent *West Tip*. Ironically Des was later interviewing Richard Dunwoody alongside *West Tip* at the Motor Show when the horse stood on his foot and broke it!

In 1989 he had a share in *Numerate*, a rank outsider who, ridden by the only lady jockey in the National (Tarnya Davis), was pulled up at the 21st. Seven years later he was again persuaded to get involved in part-ownership of a racehorse. But this time – much to Mrs Pitman's disgust – it was a Flat horse: *Motcombs Club*, bred by Pat Eddery and named after Des's favourite London restaurant, owned by Phil Lawless, the principal shareholder of the horse.

After more than two decades with BBC TV – presenting *Grandstand*, *Match of the Day* and numerous World Cups and Wimbledon – Lynam controversially joined ITV in 1999, concentrating primarily on fronting football programmes. Though no longer involved with the National, he maintained an interest in the race and in 2000 he joined an eight-man syndicate that bought a chestnut chaser, *Out Of The Deep*, for 5,000 guineas. A fellow member was soccer commentator John Motson who had once turned down a share in *Earth Summit*, later a Grand National winner.

LYNN, William

On July 5. 1829, William Lynn, landlord of Liverpool's Waterloo Hotel, introduced Flat racing to Aintree on land he had leased from the Earl of Sefton. Six years later, he staged a hurdles meeting which attracted Captain Martin Becher, the most celebrated cross-country rider of the day. From Becher, Lynn learned of the spectacular success achieved by publican Thomas Coleman in organising the four-mile Great St Albans Steeplechase which started and finished not far from his Turf Hotel. First run in 1830, the St Albans chase had become the premier race of its kind. Now Lynn resolved to organise a similar attraction for Liverpool.

The first Aintree steeplechase was on February 29, 1836; and that same year the enterprising Lynn was responsible for organising the first Waterloo Cup, the great annual classic of hare coursing which was held on the Sefton family estate at Altcar and, until the 1920s, attracted as many spectators as the Grand National itself. The following year, he combined with John Formby, owner of the nearby, now defunct Maghull racecourse, to stage the renewal of the Grand Liverpool Steeplechase.

Some turf historians choose to regard the 1836 Liverpool Steeplechase (won by *The Duke*, ridden by Captain Martin Becher) as the first-ever Grand National. But by popular assent that honour is now awarded to the Grand Liverpool Steeplechase of 1839, the first to attract a large number of contestants. Lynn played the leading part in its promotion, and the enterprise was now supported by an administrative syndicate of notable dignitaries, including the Earls of Derby, Sefton, Eglinton and Wilton, and Lord George Bentinck and Lord Robert Grosvenor.

A few days before the race, however, Lynn resigned from its management 'due to indisposition'. It is surmised that, as a mere publican, he had found himself uncomfortably overshadowed by the aristocratic Aintree executive. Whatever the circumstances, he never again figured prominently in racing circles.

It is recorded that years later he sadly described his Aintree ventures as 'a most unlucky speculation'. He went on: 'I should have been worth at least £30,000 if I had never had anything to do with it. Now I have to begin the world all over again after 30 years industry.' The man primarily responsible for the birth of the world's greatest steeplechase died in 1870, alone and near insolvency.

See also: Aintree.

M

MACHELL, Captain James Octavius

Owner of three Grand National winners, James Machell was one of the most spectacular gamblers in the history of the Turf. Though he was always known as 'Captain', he loved horse racing far more than Army life – so much so that he resigned his commission at the age of 25 because he had been refused leave to attend Doncaster races. He then gambled all his financial resources – plus money borrowed from friends – on backing his horse *Bacchus* in the Prince of Wales's Stakes at Newmarket.

After *Bacchus* had finished first by a neck, Machell's entire future remained in the balance as the stewards considered an objection to the winner. The verdict went in his favour. *Bacchus* had won him £10,000 – enough to enable him to embark on a full-time career as a trainer, dealer and big-time gambler.

Machell the gambler was ice-cool, shrewd, and usually lucky. He was reputed, while attending races at the Curragh, to have won money by making a stationary jump from the floor on to the mantelpiece in Morrison's Hotel, Dublin. And he had originally become a racehorse owner on the profits from a £1,000 bet on himself to win a walking race from Newmarket to London.

But Machell also had genuine skills – as a trainer and as a fine judge of equine potential. Initially, in 1863, he was training horses for two wealthy owners, Lords Lonsdale and Calthorpe. Then, in 1865, he became racing manager to the celebrated Mr Henry Chaplin. That year, most importantly, he was responsible at yearling sales for buying on Chaplin's behalf a little chestnut colt knocked down for 1,000 guineas. They named him *Hermit*.

One year before *Hermit*'s projected Derby run, Machell was staking as much as £1,000 to win £20,000 on the colt. The Duke of Hamilton was much the worse for drink when he overheard that bet being struck. Scornfully, he offered to lay £30,000 to £1,000 – and to do so six times over. Coolly, Machell took the bet – £180,000 to £6,000 against *Hermit* winning the 1867 Derby. Later a sobered-up duke paid him £1,000 just to cancel the bet.

In 1867, Machell almost had a classic success of his own, his colt *Knight of the Garter* coming second in the 2,000 Guineas. Meanwhile both he and Chaplin continued to back *Hermit* who had impressed in a secret trial. But then, nine days before the Derby, another trial run saw *Hermit* break a blood vessel in his nostrils.

It was Machell who persuaded Chaplin not to withdraw his Derby entry, and who helped trainer Old Bloss to nurse the distressed colt back to fitness; Machell who sought out a last minute replacement for their released top jockey and who gave the chosen young man, Johnny Daley, precise instructions on the racing tactics to be employed.

On a bitterly cold Derby Day, *Hermit* looked completely listless; his starting price was 1,000-15. But Daley followed his instructions to the letter and the chestnut outsider won by a neck, earning his astonished owner £140,000 with the wealth of stud fees still to come. *The Times* reported that Machell had won £63,000. It may not have been that much for he was secretive; and, ever calculating, he may well have hedged his early bets. Whatever, he had certainly earned enough to greatly advance his ambitions as an owner. And increasingly it was steeplechasing – and the Grand National especially – that commanded his attention.

Between 1869 and 1891 he ran no fewer than 20 runners in 17 Grand Nationals. He began with *Gardener* who finished a close-up third, won successive Nationals with six year olds – *Disturbance* (1873) and *Reugny* (1874) – and a third National within four years by scoring with five year old *Regal*, a 25-1 shot in 1876.

Five years later *Regal* finished runner-up; and his other contenders included *Defence*, fourth (1874), *Jackal*, fourth (1878), *The Scot*, fifth in 1881, and *Black Prince*, third in 1885.

Most famously, Machell formed a winning partnership with the great amateur jockey John Maunsell Richardson who both rode and trained *Disturbance* and *Reugny* at Limber Magna, his home in Lincolnshire. But on the eve of their second National success, after Richardson had made no secret of *Reugny*'s brilliant form, they quarrelled bitterly. The dual winning trainer-rider was so appalled at Machell's grasping attitude to racing that he retired at his peak from the saddle.

Born in 1838 in Beverley, Yorkshire, the son of a clergyman, Machell became increasingly cantankerous with the passing years – and oddly so since his gambling was eminently successful. After the 1874 National he sold his three runners – *Reugny*, *Disturbance* and *Defence* – at an enormous profit; and two years later he had the 3-1 National favourite, *Chandos (fell)*, and the ultimate winner, *Regal*. With the profits, he was able to buy back his ancestral home at Crackenthorpe in Westmoreland.

In 1882, according to some record books, Machell went on to train a National winner: *Seaman*, owned and ridden by Lord Manners. But that winner had only been in his charge for a few months. The really hard schooling work had already been done by the leading Irish trainer, Henry Linde; moreover, the final preparation was the responsibility of jockey James Jewitt who had succeeded Joe Cannon in charge of Machell's horses.

Curiously, Machell shared the opinion of Linde: that the six year old bay was far too weak for the National, and he was entered only at the insistence of his owner-rider. To their astonishment, Lord Manners, a relatively raw amateur rider, brought *Seaman* home by a head over the Linde-trained *Cyrus*, ridden by the great Tommy Beasley.

Subsequently, as an owner, Machell's best National result was a third place with *Black Prince* in 1885. His last National runner was the five year old *Emperor* – a distant sixth after being remounted in 1890 and then pulled up in the race the following year. The first owner to have had three Grand National winners died in 1902.

See also: Richardson, John Maunsell; Disturbance; Reugny; Regal.

MADDEN, Niall

When 20-year-old Irishman Niall Madden rode *Numbersixvalverde* at Aintree in 2006 he not only triumphed on his Grand National debut but also on his very first appearance as a jockey in Britain. Moreover, he had succeeded at the first attempt in achieving a victory that his father – also Niall – had six times sought in vain.

Madden Snr – nicknamed 'Boots' because his boots were too big for him when he started riding for Edward O'Grady – had made his National debut as an amateur in 1978. That year he fell on the well-backed *So*; and his next two appearances also ended in falls – on *Kilkilwell* (1981) and *Gandy VI* (1982). But thereafter he completed the course three times in succession on the powerful *Attitude Adjuster*, finishing eighth, fifth and 12th in 1987-89.

Born in November, 1985, Madden Jnr – nicknamed 'Slippers' – was inevitably brought up on stories of the Aintree National. He was just 16 years old when, in July, 2002, he rode his first winner in a handicap hurdle at Wexford. Nineteen days later he scored his second win. And aptly – since he had

always dreamed of one day riding in the Grand National – his third win came on J. P. McManus's *Live Our Dreams*.

Even before his Aintree debut Niall had shown himself as skilled a rider as his father, most notably in the 2004-5 season when his 39 wins included a narrow victory on *Numbersixvalverde* in the valuable Thyestes Chase at Gowran Park. It made him Ireland's champion amateur rider and secured him the position of second jockey to the famed trainer Noel Meade.

Two months after the Thyestes victory Ruby Walsh took over the ride when nine year old *Numbersixvalverde*, still a novice chaser, won the Irish National. But when it came to Aintree, he was naturally booked again for his 2005 winner *Hedgehunter*. For 'Slippers' Madden the dream had become reality.

In preparation for his Aintree debut he studied a video of *Bobbyjo's* 1999 victory borrowed from Paul Carberry, and he walked the course with his father who advised him to hunt around towards the rear on the first circuit and then make a serious move through the field. He was to follow those instructions with remarkable self-assurance and precision, taking the lead at the last and, favoured by the rain-softened ground, driving on to win by six lengths from *Hedgehunter*, a 5-1 joint favourite with 18lb more to carry. It took him to a total of just 30 wins for the season compared with 178 scored by the mighty Tony McCoy who was again frustrated in finishing third on joint favourite *Clan Royal*.

In 2007, five days before the Grand National, Madden rode impressively in the Irish version at Fairyhouse, launching a late charge on 33-1 shot *American Jennie* to finish third, just two and three-quarter lengths off the winner *Butler's Cabin*, ridden by McCoy. Meanwhile, before going to Aintree, *Numbersixvalverde* had again been campaigned over hurdles with a final run over fences, finishing a close-up fourth under Niall in the Bobbyjo Chase. At Aintree, however, he needed to defy a 9lb rise in the weights to score the first back-to-back National wins since *Red Rum* in 1974. Madden did well to bring him home in sixth place, albeit by a distance.

See also: Brassil, Martin; Numbersixvalverde.

MAGUIRE, Adrian Edward

A truly outstanding jockey, strong, fearless and hugely competitive, Adrian Maguire had an excel-

M

lent record in the Grand National without ever winning. His introduction to the race came in 1993, when, aged 21, he deputised for the injured Richard Guest on *Romany King* who had been beaten only three-quarters of a length the year before. The nine year old was more mature and extremely well handicapped; and riding with typical determination Maguire passed the 'winning post' in third place behind *Esha Ness* and *Cahervillahow* only to find that the race had been declared void after a false start.

The following year Maguire came to the Melling Road on the second circuit thinking that he would win the National on *Moorcroft Boy*, the 5-1 favourite. His mount jumped the last in front but then markedly weakened and was overhauled by *Miinnehoma* and *Just So* who slogged out the finish in the mud. Later it was found that third placed *Moorcroft Boy* had broken a blood vessel.

While Maguire is one of many great jockeys to have been denied success in the National, he rates highest of all among brilliant horsemen who have failed to win the jockeys' championship. Most famously, having ridden 194 winners, he was denied the title on the final day of the 1993-94 season by Richard Dunwoody who, in January, had trailed him by 42. Then, in 1995, when marginally ahead of Dunwoody, he was robbed of the championship by injuries.

Born on April 29, 1971, one of ten children of a greenkeeper in Kilmessan, Co. Meath, Maguire rode some 200 winners in pony races from the age of nine, was a champion pony race rider at 15, Ireland's champion point-to-point rider at 19, and Britain's champion conditional jockey at 20 with a record 71 wins in his first full season of 1991-92. Known by fellow jockeys as 'Muttley', he had burst on to the jumping scene in 1991 with his winning of the Fulke Walwyn/Kim Muir Chase and the Irish Grand National on the Martin Pipe-trained *Omerta*. One year later, now riding in England for Toby Balding, he fully justified his 'wonder boy' tag by winning the Cheltenham Gold Cup at the first attempt – an astonishing short-head victory on the 25-1 chance, *Cool Ground*. He was still only 20, and in less than five years he would set a record (since beaten by Tony McCoy) for the quickest 500 winners in Britain.

In 1992 a broken collarbone had prevented Maguire riding the well fancied *Cool Ground* (finished tenth) in the Grand National. After his third places, in 1993 (void) and in 1994, he finished 12th

on *Ebony Jane* in 1995. Then, through injury, he cruelly missed three successive Nationals and as many Cheltenham Festivals. His extraordinary run of ill-luck began with a broken arm at Hereford and was followed by many other injuries including fractures of the leg, knee and collarbone. But he kept bouncing back; and nor was he to be discouraged in late 1998 when his so successful partnership with trainer David Nicholson ended in an unfortunate and acrimonious fall-out.

Subsequently, as stable jockey to Irish trainer Ferdy Murphy, Maguire won the Midlands National on *Ackzo* and a second Scottish Grand National, on *Paris Pike* in 2000. In his distinctive long-reined style, he was riding as brilliantly and strongly as ever, but still victory in the Aintree National eluded him. Renewing his bid, he had finished fourth on *Addington Boy* in 1999; and in 2000, back on the 12 year old who had not won a race since 1996, he finished a most creditable fifth at 33-1. He had now ridden over 150 of Aintree's daunting fences without once suffering a fall.

Unfortunately, *Paris Pike*, Maguire's brilliant winner at Ayr, was injured and unable to run at Aintree in 2001. Instead, the jockey rode *Paddy's Return*, the horse who fell at the third and ran on to cause so much mayhem at the Canal Turn. Meanwhile his young nephew, Jason Maguire, riding the long-shot *No Retreat*, got as far as the Water Jump on his National debut.

The following November Maguire celebrated a major milestone in his career: becoming the seventh jump jockey to achieve 1,000 winners in British racing. And in December, on *Florida Pearl*, he had his second success in the King George VI Chase – a victory enhanced for the family just 24 hours later when Jason steered home 20-1 shot *Tremallt* to win the £50,000 Pertemps Asap Handicap Chase at Kempton.

In 2002 Maguire won the Singer and Friedlander National Trial Handicap Chase on *Streamstown*. But then, yet again, he suffered a most grievous injury: breaking vertebrae in his neck at Warwick and needing two major bone graft operations. For three months he would need to wear a 'halo' brace, a cage-like device designed to keep the head perfectly stable while the neck healed. It cost him the ride on *Florida Pearl* in the Cheltenham Gold Cup and again he was kept out of the National. Richard Guest took over the ride on the well-backed *Paris Pike*.

They came to grief with eight others at the first fence.

Determinedly, after such an appalling succession of injuries and family bereavements, this most courageous of jump jockeys battled to regain race fitness but sadly, in the end, he had to bow to the judgment of the Jockey Club's chief medical adviser who explained that he could never be passed fit, that his neck was so weak that one more fall could confine him to a wheelchair, Thus, aged 31, he was prematurely forced to retire and seek a new career as a trainer, beginning with point-to-pointers in Co. Cork and sending out several horses – most notably the star hurdler *Celestial Wave* – to race under Rules. He ended his riding with a total 1,024 winners, at that time sixth in the all-time list of jump jockeys.

In the light of his misfortunes, not least the missing of four Cheltenham Festivals, Maguire's career record was truly extraordinary. His big race winners included: *Sibton Abbey* (1992 Hennessy Cognac Gold Cup), *King Credo* (1993 Tote Gold Trophy), *Barton Bank* (1993 King George VI Chase), *Mysilv* (1994 Triumph Hurdle), *Viking Flagship* (1994 Queen Mother Champion Chase and 1995 Mumm Melling Chase), *Baronet* and *Paris Pike* (Scottish Grand Nationals of 1998 and 2000 respectively), and *Call It A Day* (1998 Whitbread Gold Cup). He also won the Galway Plate twice, the Imperial Cup twice, the Bula Hurdle twice, the Scottish Champion Hurdle, the Greenalls Gold Cup, the Grand Annual Chase and the Cathcart Chase.

MAHER, Matthew
Owner, breeder and trainer of the remarkable Irish mare *Frigate*, three times runner-up in the Grand National and the last horse (in 1889) to win the National without a previous race in the season. Matthew Maher first entered her as a six year old in 1884 when she finished four lengths second to another six year old, *Voluptuary*. The following year, after *Frigate* had finished second again – beaten two lengths by *Roquefort* – he sold her.

Curiously, *Frigate* failed under two subsequent owners – falling at the first fence in the 1886 National and being pulled up by her owner-rider, Mr F.E. Lawrence, in 1887. Maher was then persuaded by jockey Willie Beasley to buy the mare back, and the improvement was almost immediate. Trained by Maher at Ballinkeele, Co. Wexford, she won the Manchester Handicap and then finished second in

the National. One year later, at the sixth attempt, she won the National by one length from *Why Not*. Maher was not to find her like again. His only subsequent contender was the six year old *Schooner* who finished eighth in 1894.
See also: Frigate.

MANGAN, James Joseph
Trainer of *Monty's Pass*, the ten year old winner of the 2003 Grand National who landed a record near-£1 million betting coup for one of his five co-owners, Mr Mike Futter. Operating a 12-horse yard at Conna, near Mallow, Co. Cork, Jimmy Mangan was relatively unknown outside of Ireland before capturing the great Aintree prize at the first attempt. However, he had had connections with two notable chasers. On his farm he had foaled *Dawn Run*, the celebrated winner of the 1986 Cheltenham Gold Cup; and he had been the original trainer of the 2002 Grand National winner *Bindaree*, buying him as a yearling for only Ir2,000 guineas before selling him on one year later.

Born August 28, 1955, 'J.J' was the son of Paddy Mangan who trained on a small scale at the village of Conna and most famously bred *Doorknocker*, the 1956 Champion Hurdle winner. He rode his first winner as a 16 year old in a local point-to-point, and in 1981 he took over the trainer's licence following his father's death. Primarily, however, he was an enterprising horse-trader who raised cattle and kept some 25 broodmares on the family's 150-acre farm. Success as a trainer came only in the late 1990s after he had won a long, life-saving battle to overcome alcoholism.

In his own rustic way, Mangan embodied the spirit of Irish racing – a true horseman whose life revolved around breeding and trading, and all the while dreaming of the discovery that he had an animal of exceptional potential in his care. The dream was realised with *Monty's Pass*. Previously he had had only one notable success: with *Stroll Home*, winner of the 1997 Galway Plate.

In 1999, as with *Bindaree*, Mangan needed to sell *Monty's Pass*. But this time, to his delight and surprise, the new owners asked him to remain the trainer. Originally he ran *Monty's Pass* in point-to-points and hunter chases. His suspicion that he had an outstanding Grand National prospect was confirmed when the gelding finished second over the Aintree fences in the 2002 Topham Trophy and then,

M

in September, won the Guinness Kerry National over three miles at Listowel. Shrewdly, after one more run in a three-mile chase, he put *Monty's Pass* away for the winter and, prior to the Grand National, only ran him in two-mile novices' hurdles.

According to his wife Mary, Jimmy wore a tie for the first time since their wedding day when he attended the 2003 Grand National. The grey-haired trainer was 'very confident' before the race and afterwards he declared, 'Aintree suits *Monty's Pass* so well, he just could be another *Red Rum*.' But whereas *Red Rum* defied a 23lb rise in the weights to win a second successive National, *Monty's Pass* found an extra 17lb too much on his return. He did well to finish fourth, the best of ten runners carrying 11st or more. Finally, in 2005, the 12 year old honourably carried 11st 6lb to complete the course as the 16th of 21 finishers.
See also: Monty's Pass.

MANIFESTO

The greatest horse in Grand National history? In every sport comparisons between champions of different generations can be invidious in the light of changing conditions. Here it can only be said that the supreme National runner of the second half of the 20th century was *Red Rum* and that the greatest seen in the previous half-century was *Manifesto*.

Neither deserves to be placed second to the other. *Red Rum* had an unequalled three wins and was twice runner-up. On the other hand, he was never burdened with more than 12st – unlike *Manifesto* who, facing more formidable fences, achieved one of his two wins carrying 12st 7lb, finished third on three successive occasions – with 12st 13lb, 12st 8lb and 12st 3lb – and was still humping more than 12st when finishing eighth as a 16 year old.

By the fierce *Man o'War* out of *Vae Victis*, *Manifesto* – a superbly proportioned bay with a white star on his forehead – was bred at Navan in Co. Meath by solicitor and farmer Harry Dyas. Wisely, Dyas gave his young bay plenty of time to develop. Though *Manifesto* had won the Irish Champion Steeplechase as a four year old, he was restricted to only four races in the next two years. Meanwhile he matured into a powerfully built six year old who, after winning the valuable 1894 Lancashire Chase, was set to carry 11st 2lb on his 1895 National debut.

Manifesto's huge promise was not immediately fulfilled. After a worthy, weight-giving fourth place

in his first National, his second bid ended at the first fence where he was brought down in a collision with the 100-1 outsider *Redhill*. But then, in 1897, with a new trainer (Willie McAuliffe of East Everleigh, near Marlborough) and reunited with jockey Terry Kavanagh, he proved himself to be a chaser of truly exceptional strength, stamina and jumping ability.

Before the 1897 National Dyas had offered his two entries – *Manifesto* and *Gentle Ida* – for sale at £5,000 the pair. There were no takers. *Gentle Ida* was withdrawn on the eve of the race. Meanwhile, after being heavily backed by his owner, *Manifesto* went off as 6-1 favourite. He romped home unchallenged, 20 lengths clear of rank outsider *Filbert*, with six year old *Ford of Fyne* a head back in third. It was a devastating blow for the bookmakers, and a bonanza for punters who had landed the 'Spring Double' by backing *Manifesto* for the National and *Winkfield's Pride* (also bred in Co. Meath) for the Lincoln two days earlier.

Subsequently *Manifesto* fell in the Lancashire Chase, but his reputation was firmly re-established when he carried 12st 5lb to victory in the three-and a-half-mile Grand International at Sandown, and then opened up his 1898 account by winning a Gatwick chase when conceding 37lb to the runner-up.

As a result, *Manifesto* was strongly fancied to emulate *Abd-El-Kader* and *The Colonel* by achieving a second successive National win. At this point he was sold for £4,000 (then a huge sum) to wealthy financier Mr Joseph Bulteel and sent to Willie Moore who had already trained two National winners – *Why Not* (1894) and *The Soarer* (1896) – at Weyhill in Hampshire.

Sadly, the prospect of back-to-back wins was ruined by a stable lad's simple error. Just over a week before the big race he neglected to secure *Manifesto's* box. The horse later pushed open the unlatched door, wandered out into the yard and then, in the process of leaping a five-foot gate, bruised a fetlock joint and was put out of action for several months. The poor stable lad, fearing the consequences, did a runner and gained stable work elsewhere under an assumed name.

When *Manifesto* finally returned to Aintree in 1899 it was as an 11 year old, burdened with the top weight of 12st 7lb. He had warmed up with two hurdle races and was now to be ridden by the highly experienced George Williamson. But this time he was only second favourite at 5-1. One point ahead of him in the betting was his former stablemate *Gentle Ida*, still owned by Dyas, and now an outstanding mare with a one-stone advantage in the weights.

Again *Manifesto* was to be threatened by human error. As a necessary protection against frost, the Aintree staff had spread hay on either side of the fences. This was to be removed shortly before the race. Unfortunately, they had neglected to clear away all the hay at the Canal Turn. When landing over the jump *Manifesto* slipped on a patch of straw. Williamson lost both of his irons and felt one boot touch the turf as his mount sank to the ground.

Remarkably, horse and rider managed to recover and shortly afterwards their prospects were improved by the fall of *Gentle Ida* at Valentine's. There were still many runners ahead, but *Manifesto* made relentless progress on the second circuit, finally hitting the front near the final turn for home. He held on without difficulty to win by five lengths from *Ford of Fyne,* who was receiving 25lb.

Mr Dyas had insisted that not even *Manifesto* was capable of giving a stone to his *Gentle Ida*. But the new owner, Mr Joseph Bulteel, had had no such doubts. He had plunged heavily on his horse with punts including, it was said, one ante-post bet of £800 at 12-1. He rewarded jockey Williamson with a gift of £2,800.

Now, once again, there were hopes of back-to-back victories. But these diminished when the weights were announced for the first National of the 20th century. The 12 year old *Manifesto* was allotted a seemingly impossible 12st 13lb. Only twice before had runners carried such a weight: the French champion *L'Africaine*, given an absurd 13st 2lb in 1866, and *Peter Simple*, on 13st 1lb in 1843. The former had been pulled up and the latter had finished eighth.

Moreover, *Manifesto* was opposed by *Hidden Mystery*, a six year old who four weeks earlier had beaten him at level weights at Hurst Park. Since *Hidden Mystery* now had a 13lb advantage, he was made the hot 75-20 favourite for the race. Second in the betting – receiving 24lb from *Manifesto* – was another six year old, *Ambush II*, owned by Edward, Prince of Wales.

In fine weather the small field was quickly reduced to 14 at the first fence where 100-1 *Nothing* bolted off course and *Covert Hack* fell. Riderless, the latter remained a constant nuisance and at the end of the first circuit he was responsible for the fall of the favourite. *Barsac*, fifth the previous year, now

led the field until the Canal Turn where he was headed by *Ambush II*. But all the while *Manifesto* was drawing near and, to thunderous cheers, he drew level with the royal horse two fences from home.

Gallantly *Manifesto* matched *Ambush II* stride for stride. But now the weight factor truly told; and near the end Williamson humanely eased up on a champion who had given his all, and thus, by a neck, he surrendered second place to *Barsac*, an eight year old with a colossal 43lb advantage. It was hats off for a royal victory by four lengths, but also a huge ovation for *Manifesto* whose supremely gallant effort reduced grown men to tears.

Arguably, in defeat, *Manifesto* had run his greatest race. He missed the 1901 National, but when he returned to Aintree in 1902 he was still so highly regarded by the handicapper that he was allotted the top weight of 12lb 8lb. It seemed a crippling mark. Only once in the history of the race had a horse over 13 years of age run into a place; and that was almost half a century ago – in 1853 when 15 year old *Peter Simple* was victorious. And he was carrying only 10st 10lb. *Manifesto*, at 14, and after nearly two years without a run, was now conceding three stone to some horses and more than a stone to his nearest rival, *Drumree*.

This year *Manifesto* had a new rider: one Ernie Piggott, grandfather of Lester, who had ridden once before in the National, finishing third on *Elliman* in 1899. There were 21 starters on extremely heavy ground, and predictably the old campaigner was held up towards the rear. Only late on the second circuit did he make his presence felt – with a forward move so impressive that briefly a miraculous victory seemed within his grasp.

On the gruelling run-in, however, it was clearly an impossible dream. He battled all the way to the line but could make no impression on two youngsters, *Shannon Lass* and *Matthew*, with a 35lb and 38lb advantage respectively. They beat him into third place, by three lengths and three; and yet it was *Manifesto* who won the loudest cheers.

Incredibly, *Manifesto* returned for two more Nationals. In 1903 it was the turn of nine year old *Ambush II* to carry the top weight of 12st 7lb. But, at 15, *Manifesto* was given only 4lb less, and for the first time he was way out in the betting at 25-1. Against all the odds, the old boy, reunited with jockey Williamson, ran on into third place after

Ambush II had fallen at the last. Then, in 1904, he made his swansong and with it another piece of history – as the only 16 year old ever to finish in the National. Ridden again by Piggott, he jumped as surely as ever; only pace was lacking as he came home the last of eight finishers in a field of 26.

The greatest compliment to *Manifesto* that year was the fact that the handicapper had seen fit to lumber him with 12st 1lb. At 16, he had given one stone-plus to all other runners except for *Ambush II*. On that last day at Aintree, the old warrior looked so magnificent that leading Flat-jockey Morny Cannon begged permission to sit on him before he ran his last race. The horse – a runner in a record eight Nationals, only once a faller, and with an unparalleled record of two wins, three times third, and once fourth – had long since become a living legend. *See also:* Bulteel, Joseph; Kavanagh, Terry; Williamson, George; Piggott, Ernie; Moore, Willliam.

MANNERS, Herbert John

The most eccentric of trainers who, at the age of 72, was represented in the 1999 Grand National by his 11 year old gelding *Cavalero*. Admitting to being 'a bit of a nutcase', John Manners was renowned as a farmer who ate his porridge in bed every morning, never rose before ten and, as a natural night-owl, had the curious habit of riding out his horses after dark. On one occasion – in late December, 1998 – a prolonged search for *Cavalero* was necessary. His most valuable horse had bolted into the night after his 72 year old rider had dismounted to open a gate on his farmland, and he was eventually found, unharmed, grazing beside a stream.

A truly rustic, brandy-loving character, Manners often fell foul of authorities, first losing his licence in 1958 and being fined for disorderly conduct in 1982 after he had jumped the rails at Cheltenham to run up the hill and cheer home his chaser, *Knight of Love*, who was giving him his first win on the course. Seven years later he lost his licence for three years when he saddled a point-to-point winner who was found to have run without a weight-cloth. He subsequently named the 'worst horse in the yard' *Sambruco* after the three stewards of the disciplinary committee – Sam Vestey, Bruce Hobbs and Robert Waley-Cohen – who had punished him with such a stiff sentence.

Born on April 25, 1926, Manners had only

makeshift stables on his 400-acre farm near Swindon in Wiltshire, and he lacked access to proper gallops. Yet as a permit-holder he developed a number of fine chasers, most notably *Killeshin* bought at Ascot sales for a mere 1,550 guineas. Seemingly a poor prospect, *Killeshin* became with unorthodox training an outstanding hunter chaser, winning his second race at 100-1 and going on to win the 1996 Eider Chase and the Martell Fox Hunters' Chase at Aintree. An out-and-out mud-loving stayer, he was ridden by Sean Curran to finish seventh and sixth (remounted) in the Grand Nationals of 1997 and 1998 respectively.

Like *Killeshin*, the Manners-bred *Cavalero* went to the 1999 Grand National as a winner (at 33-1) of the Martell Fox Hunters', one of his seven successive victories in the previous season. Unfortunately, his saddle slipped and Curran had to pull him up at the 14th fence. One year later, after winning the Christies Foxhunter Chase at Cheltenham, *Cavalero* unluckily ended up as first reserve for the National, having missed the 40-runner cut by one. He was again entered for the National in 2001 but, shortly after being allotted 9st 11lb, he broke his back in a fall at Warwick.

MANNERS, Lord John

A serving officer in the Grenadier Guards, Lord John Manners pulled off the remarkable feat of winning the 1882 Grand National on *Seaman* when riding in only his second race under Rules and on a horse he had bought only a few months before for £2,000. Still more remarkably, he contrived to win by a head in a slogging match with *Cyrus*, ridden by Tommy Beasley, the top amateur rider of the day.

In truth, Lord Manners was not quite the novice that he was portrayed at the time. He was a highly experienced huntsman (later to become Master of the Quorn), and only a few weeks before his triumph at Aintree he had won the Grand Military Gold Cup at Sandown on *Lord Chancellor* whom, like *Seaman*, he had purchased late in 1881.

That year Lord Manners had seen *Seaman*, a five year old bay gelding, win the four-mile Conyngham Cup at Punchestown – just one month after winning the Liverpool Hunt Chase. In the autumn, after *Seaman* had won the Grand Hurdle at Auteuil, he was surprised to find that the horse, regarded by some as unsound, was up for sale on the recommendation of his trainer, the famed Henry Linde.

Some three months before the National, Lord Manners sent his new purchase to Captain James Machell, who left the final preparation to the highly experienced jumps jockey, James Jewitt. Machell himself shared Linde's belief that the small bay was far too weak for the Aintree marathon. But Lord Manners remained adamant: *Seaman* would run and he himself would take the ride.

On extremely heavy going, which saw only three of 12 starters finish, *Seaman* came within a whisker of breaking down. Somehow, huntsman Manners succeeded in powering the distressed horse home; and subsequently the brave winner was retired to serve as his owner's hack. Having achieved his ambition at the first attempt, Lord Manners did not ride in the National again.

See also: Seaman; Linde, Henry Eyre; Kinsky, Count Charles.

MAORI VENTURE

Winner of the 1987 Grand National on his first and last appearance in the race. Previously regarded as an unsafe jumper, the 11 year old chestnut gelding gave his connections only one anxious moment, steadily progressing from the rear to win by five lengths in the then third fastest time on record. It completed a rare big-race double for his 92 year old owner, Mr Jim Joel, who had won the 1967 Epsom Derby with *Royal Palace* and had first attempted to win the National in 1957.

Maori Venture – sired by the grey *St Columbus* out of *Moon Venture* – had been bred by a Welsh publican, Dai 'Maori' Morgan, so nicknamed following his return from a spell of playing rugby in New Zealand. As a five year old he won a Taunton bumper at 50-1, and was later sent by his new owner, Major Jack Rubin, to West Country trainer Jim Old. His first notable success over fences came on New Year's Eve, 1984, in the Mandarin Chase at Newbury.

Following the owner's death, the gelding was bought at the Ascot sales for 17,000 guineas by Marlborough trainer Andrew Turnell on behalf of Mr Joel. Subsequently, *Maori Venture* scored four wins at Lingfield; then, in the build-up to the 1987 National, he showed confusingly mixed form. He finished third in the Hennessy Cognac Gold Cup, had a second success in the Mandarin Chase and finally was a most promising runner-up in Sandown's Grand Military Gold Cup. But he had also been unplaced

in one chase and a clumsy faller in another, so strengthening the belief that he would be unable to cope with the Aintree fences.

Having seen his well-fancied *Door Latch* fall at the first in the 1986 National, Mr Joel had no great expectations of his latest runner who went off 12th in the betting at 28-1. Ridden by Steve Knight, *Maori Venture* was never prominent on the first circuit and his vulnerability showed alarmingly when he tackled Becher's Brook, coming down so steeply that he nosed the turf on landing. Miraculously he survived. In contrast, *Lean Ar Aghaidh*, well ridden by young newcomer Guy Landau, was leading the field with a breathtaking display of prodigious jumping.

Though less spectacular, *Maori Venture* was now jumping with surprising precision and increasing his pace between fences. Untroubled by Becher's second time around, he closed on the leaders, and coming to the last he joined with *The Tsarevich* in challenging the spring-heeled front-runner who was one length to the good. From the Elbow onwards, *Maori Venture* proved the strongest, pulling away to score by five lengths and four from *The Tsarevich* and *Lean Ar Aghaidh* respectively. The 5-1 favourite, last year's winner *West Tip*, was fourth. Tragically, the second favourite, *Dark Ivy*, had suffered a fatal fall at the first Becher's.

News of the success was radioed to Mr Joel who was then in mid-flight, jetting back to England from South Africa. The following day, at victory celebrations, he announced that *Maori Venture* would be retired to the Childwick Stud and left in his will to the winning jockey.

See also: Joel, H.J.; Turnell, Andrew.

MARES

In 160 runnings of the Grand National, only 13 mares have been successful. The roll of honour: *Charity* (1841), *Miss Mowbray* (1852), *Anatis* (1860), *Jealousy* (1861), *Emblem* (1863), *Emblematic* (1864), *Casse Tete* (1872), *Empress* (1880), *Zoedone* (1883), *Frigate* (1889), *Shannon Lass* (1902), *Sheila's Cottage* (1948) and *Nickel Coin* (1951).

To this female honours list, one might add *Maria Day* (1851), beaten by only 'half a neck'; *Minerva* (1856) runner-up by half a length; and *Melleray's Belle* (1930), second by a neck. Other mares to finish honourable runner-ups include *Martha* (1878), *Lady Ellen II* (1894) and *Cooleen* (1937). And in

M

1882 the Duke of Hamilton's *Eau De Vie* had been desperately unlucky to run out with a broken stirrup leather after dominating the race from the first Becher's to the second. Nevertheless, the dismal reality is clear: only three mares have won since the 19th century and not one for more than half a century.

To be just, this is not a clear-cut indication of the inferiority of mares. The poor record can be partly explained by mathematical probability; by the fact that few mares stay in National Hunt training. A filly becomes a mare at the age of five. But if she is well-bred and has shown reasonably promising racing form, the chances are that she will have been retired by the age of four to be mated with a stallion standing at stud.

In modern times, mares appearing in the Grand National have been outnumbered by geldings by more than 50 to 1. Thus, automatically, the chances of a female victory are hugely reduced. In addition, there are reasons for fearing that a mare might be disadvantaged solely by virtue of her sex. The National is run in early spring, at a time when mares begin to come into season every three weeks. This increases their chances of becoming temperamental – 'acting marish' – on the day of the race. Also it raises the possibility of a mare being sexually harassed during the course of the race.

In the 1937 National, for example, Jack Fawcus had a nightmarish ride on Mr J.V. Rank's *Cooleen* as – from the eighth fence (Canal Turn) onwards – the nine year old mare was attacked again and again by the vicious *Drim*, a 100-1 outsider running riderless after his fall at the first fence. Miraculously kept under control by her rider, *Cooleen* was the second of only seven finishers, three lengths behind *Royal Mail* and ten lengths ahead of another mare, *Pucka Belle*, in third place. Arguably, she might have won but for the savage attention of *Drim*; as it was, she came back under a raised weight to finish fourth in the next two Nationals.

As their overall record suggests, mares appeared more often in the Grand National during the 19th century. Two – *Paulina* and *The Nun* – ran in the first Aintree National of 1839 and finished third and fifth respectively, the latter after being remounted. Two years later, Lord Craven's *Charity* became the first mare to win the race after a tremendous tussle with two greys, *Cigar* and *Peter Simple*, who were beaten just one length and half a length. Then, in 1852, the unquoted outsider *Miss Mowbray* held on bravely to resist the challenge of *Maurice Daley* by one length; and, despite an 8lb rise in the weights, she finished runner-up the following year.

Earlier, in 1847, it was alleged that the renowned Irish mare *Brunette* – a 13 year old burdened with a top weight of 12st 6lb – was nobbled so that she could finish no better than sixth. More certainly there was skulduggery in 1854 when *Miss Mowbray* was the 4-1 second favourite to score a second win. The mare had to be withdrawn shortly before the race following the discovery that someone had applied a blister to her near fore-leg.

In 1882 the Duke of Hamilton's mare *Eau De Vie* was 15 lengths in the lead at the Canal Turn and still going strong as she headed the field on safely clearing Becher's for the second time. But in the process a stirrup leather had broken and now, to the horror of amateur rider Dan Thirlwell, she veered off into the crowd, so putting her out of contention. The view that *Eau De Vie* was an unlucky loser was strengthened the following day when she romped home by 15 lengths in the Sefton Chase.

That year another mare, five year old *Zoedone*, finished a distant third. She came back the following year to win the National with a new owner and rider, Austrian diplomat Count Charles Kinsky; and, raised 16lb, she finished fifth in 1884. A year later the mare was the 5-1 second favourite despite a top weight of 11st 11lb, and she was judged so brave and so dangerous that some person or persons unknown felt it necessary to 'get at' the horse on National day.

Zoedone was a major liability for the layers because she had been coupled in many spring doubles with the recent Lincoln Handicap winner *Bendigo*. The threat was too great to be left to chance, and all the evidence suggests that she was nobbled shortly before the race. The winner was *Roquefort*, the 100-30 favourite, two lengths ahead of another mare of exceptional courage: seven year old *Frigate*.

Frigate remains the most consistent mare in Grand National history – seven times a contender and three times finishing second before winning at the sixth attempt in 1889. Her resilience was most notable in 1888 when she was challenged by *Unsa*, the Irish favourite, for the lead. At the Canal Turn, *Unsa* dislocated his shoulder on landing and, in swerving right, almost carried *Frigate* into the canal. Miraculously, *Frigate*'s regular rider, Harry Beasley, got her back into the race and bravely the mare made up a huge amount of lost ground to finish second. The following year she held on gutsily to win by a length from *Why Not*.

In 1894 a five year old mare *Nelly Gray* was rated so highly as to be made 5-1 joint favourite. As it happened, she bolted after taking the lead at Valentine's. Nevertheless, another mare, six year old *Lady Ellen II*, put in a storming finish to come home a length and a half behind *Why Not*, and a head in front of *Wild Man From Borneo* who would win the following year.

When the Irish-bred *Shannon Lass* won in 1902 – receiving a stupendous 35lb from the great, third-placed *Manifesto* – she was the first successful mare in 13 years. It would be 46 years before Aintree saw another. In the meantime the best-performing mares were *Shady Lady*, third (remounted) in 1911; *Melleray's Belle*, fourth of 66 runners in 1929 and beaten only a neck by *Shaun Goilin* in 1930; and *Cooleen*, the unlucky runner-up in 1937, and fourth in 1938 and 1939.

In 1948, a time when male chauvinism was still the accepted norm, a racing correspondent pointed out that while no one would back a woman athlete in a mixed hurdle race, in National Hunt racing it was now necessary to allow for 'the unpredictability of the female'. He wrote out of bitter experience. For that year, on the morning of the Grand National, he had stressed to his readers than no mare had won the race for 46 years.

Then, in the afternoon, a mare promptly proceeded to romp home in the National at 50-1. She was the notoriously ill-tempered *Sheila's Cottage*, a nine year old daughter of *Cottage* who had sired two other National winners – *Workman* (1939) and *Lovely Cottage* (1946). With a finely timed late challenge she prevailed by a length over *First Of The Dandies*; and arguably, if jockey Eddie Reavey on *Zahia* had not accidentally missed out the final fence, mares – both by *Cottage* – would probably have finished first and second.

Since that shock, however, only one mare has triumphed: *Nickel Coin*, way back in 1951. And with all due respect to her greater staying power, it has to be recognised that this isolated female success came in a year when the running of the National was a fiasco. Following the starter's dismal failure to call an obvious 'false start', there was a mad scramble by some 20 stranded runners to make up lost ground.

The ensuing Light Brigade charge saw a dozen fallers at the first fence. At least as many again fell along the way on the first circuit, and finally only three (one remounted) of 36 starters completed the course.

This time the winning mare was 40-1; and in the light of *Nickel Coin*'s proven stamina and good form, the generous odds reflected the prejudice that had arisen following so many failures by mares in the past. And now normal service was resumed. In the next 40 years only three mares would run in the National with a measure of distinction: *Tibretta*, *Miss Hunter* and *Eyecatcher*.

Of these, *Tibretta* was a mare of outstanding jumping ability who, as a 66-1 outsider, finished third behind *Sundew* and *Wyndburgh* in 1957. Though lacking sufficient pace to win, she could handle Aintree's daunting fences quite brilliantly and she came back to finish a well-beaten second in 1958 and the fourth of only four finishers in 1959.

Most unusually that year, a mare – nine year old *Kerstin* – carried top weight (12st) in the National. She was so highly rated because she had been the one-length runner-up in the 1957 Cheltenham Gold Cup and winner of the race by half a length in 1958. Being without a win in the current season, she went off at 25-1 and was one of more than 20 fallers in the race.

Miss Hunter finished third in 1970, a place also gained by *Eyecatcher* in 1976 and 1977. But it was not until 1991 – the year after modifications had blunted the sharpest edges of the Aintree fences – that mares again made any impression in the National. Then came a remarkable change of fortune: mares finishing in a place four years in a row.

In 1991, *Auntie Dot*, a prolific winner over two and a half miles and less, was a surprising third at 50-1, five lengths and eight behind *Seagram* and *Garrison Savannah* respectively, with Martin Dwyer putting up 4lb overweight. The following year she finished 16th but again a mare was in a third place: eight year old *Laura's Beau*, owned by the legendary gambler J.P. McManus and a well-supported 12-1 chance, having won the Midlands National over four miles at Uttoxeter three weeks earlier.

Laura's Beau had not shown the same form prior to the 1993 National. Nevertheless she completed the course, the last of the seven finishers in the race declared void. Next, in 1994, *Ebony Jane*, winner of the 1993 Irish Grand National, was fancied by some

M

tipsters to become the first mare to win in 43 years. But really it was asking too much of this gallant nine year old who was sent to Aintree only five days after finishing third in the Irish National. The 'tough as hell' mare, a 25-1 shot, did extraordinarily well to slog her way through heavy ground to be the fourth of only six finishers.

The following year *Dubacilla*, runner-up in the Cheltenham Gold Cup, was another mare strongly fancied to match the success of *Nickel Coin* in 1951. Trained by David Nicholson, she had plenty of stamina in her pedigree, as proven by her half-brother *Just So* who had finished second in the 1994 National. Jockey Dean Gallagher described her as 'the ideal National horse'; and, true to form, she stayed on well to take fourth place at the short odds of 9-1.

Clearly, prejudice against mares was beginning to weaken. Yet now they were more and more conspicuous by their absence. No mares appeared in the 1996 National and only one in the years 1997, 1998 and 1999. Of these, by far the greatest hope was *Fiddling The Facts* who was seen as an outstanding challenger in 1999 since she had been placed in the Hennessy Cognac Gold Cup and had been runner-up on her last three outings: in the Welsh National, the Singer and Friedlander and the Greenalls Grand National Trial.

An out-and-out stayer of proven class, her form was irresistible; and, following a late plunge, there was the rare novelty of a mare going off as the Grand National 6-1 favourite. Her owner was Jersey-based Mrs Bunny Roberts, whose grandfather had owned and bred the 1926 Derby winner, *Trigo*; and it had taken all of trainer Nicky Henderson's powers of persuasion to gain her permission to enter the mare in the National. But, unfortunately, *Fiddling The Facts* did not get the desired soft going and she had no luck in the running, being one of five fallers at the second Becher's, brought down in the mêlée which ensued following the fatal fall of seven year old *Eudipe*.

Only three mares appeared in the next eight years: *Wicked Crack*, a nine year old from Ireland who led the field in 2002 just as far as the first fence where she was one of nine fallers; *L'Aventure*, a French-bred six year old, who was the 15th of 21 finishers in 2005; and *Liberthine* who finished a distant fifth in 2007. By now, more than ever before, it had become clear that a majority of trainers were not keen to aim mares at the National.

See also: Humour; Foul Play.

MARSHALL, Bryan

The first 20th century jockey to win successive Aintree Grand Nationals – on *Early Mist* (1953) and *Royal Tan* (1954) – Bryan Marshall was an exceptionally gifted and stylish horseman. Indeed, John Hislop, the hugely successful amateur rider and eminent writer, judged him to be 'the best jockey over fences and hurdles I have seen'; and this was also the opinion expressed by radio commentator Peter Bromley after covering his 42nd and last Grand National in 2001.

Born in February, 1916, Marshall was riding from the age of three and still not in his teens when developing his skills out hunting in his native Tipperary. After being apprenticed in England to trainer Atty Persse, he was just 13 years old when he rode his first winner on the Flat. He went on to ride occasionally for Noel Murless, then had his career cut short by the Second World War during which he served with the 5th Royal Inniskilling Dragoon Guards. He was a captain when, in the D-Day Normandy landings of 1944, he was hit in the neck by a sniper's bullet. Luckily, the wound was not serious and he was soon back in action, seeing out the long European campaign.

After demobilisation in 1946, Marshall – by now far overweight for the Flat – made remarkable progress as a jump jockey, almost immediately proving himself to be an outstanding judge of pace and supremely strong in a finish. He had already ridden *Roi d'Egypte* to win the 1942 Cathcart Chase at Cheltenham while on army leave. Now he rode regularly for the renowned Fulke Walwyn, scoring again in the Cathcart on *Leap Ma*n in 1946, winning the 1947 King George VI Chase on *Rowland Roy* and becoming the 1947-48 champion National Hunt jockey with 66 winners.

On his Grand National debut, in 1947, he had finished the eighth of 57 starters on Miss Dorothy Paget's 12 year old *Kilnaglory*. The following year he was sixth on *Rowland Roy*, and in 1949 he was sixth again, on Miss Paget's *Happy Home*. He missed the next National through injury. However, in 1950-51, he had another outstanding season with 58 winners, including a second King George VI victory, on Queen Elizabeth's *Manicou*.

Meanwhile success in the National continued to elude him. In 1951, on seven year old *Land Fort*, he was a victim of the chaos that resulted in only two horses – *Nickel Coin* and *Royal Tan* – finishing without a fall. The following year, in another rough-and-tumble which saw ten fallers at the first, he was on the favourite *Freebooter*. But the 1950 winner was now burdened with maximum weight and, after completing the first circuit in style, he fell under pressure at the Canal Turn.

Everything now changed as Marshall was recruited by the great master of Ballydoyle, Vincent O'Brien. On St Patrick's Day, only 11 days before the 1953 National, he had his first introductory ride on *Early Mist*. The eight year old was not a natural jumper and trainer O'Brien judged that he needed a rider of Bryan's calibre to dictate his point of take-off. After taking him over two fences, the jockey concurred. 'He's a hesitant sort. I agree with you – I'll have to do his thinking for him.' Thus, a trainer's genius and a jockey's supreme skill combined to forge an irresistible challenge.

At Aintree *Early Mist* was given a masterful ride, taking the lead two fences before the second Becher's and thereafter powering away to win by 20 lengths with plenty in hand. One year later Marshall and O'Brien successfully combined again, this time adopting a reverse approach. With *Early Mist* unfit to run, they relied on *Royal Tan*, a ten year old who had finished second in the 1951 National after surrendering the lead with a blunder at the last, and who had fallen at the last when challenging strongly in the 1952 National. From those errors under an amateur rider (the trainer's youngest brother, 'Phonsie' O'Brien), it was now realised that *Royal Tan* jumped best when allowed to take-off at his own discretion.

Only three weeks before the 1954 National meeting Marshall had fractured his jaw in five places when falling at Kempton. Doctors strongly advised him not to ride at Aintree. Yet there he was to score three wins, having his hardest ride in the big one when, coming from behind, *Royal Tan* prevailed by just a neck in a tremendous duel with *Tudor Line* who had a one-stone advantage. It made Marshall the first rider to win consecutive Aintree Grand Nationals since the amateur Ted Wilson in 1885.

It should have been an occasion for great rejoicing. Unhappily, it was marred by events of the previous day when Marshall almost came to blows with Mr Joe Griffin, the owner of both *Early Mist* and *Royal Tan*. That day Marshall had won the £515 Coronation Hurdle on Mr Griffin's *Stroller*. But by now it had come to light that the owner – known in

the canning trade as 'Mincemeat Joe' – was on the verge of bankruptcy.

In the Adelphi Hotel, late in the evening before the National, Marshall had approached Griffin, requesting £500 still owing to him for his victory on *Early Mist*. A row ensued when the owner finally handed over a wad of notes which proved to be £50 short. In the end, the dispute was only settled by the hotel manager being summoned to bring £50 from the safe, and by Griffin then signing a promissory note to pay any further fees that might be the jockey's due.

Incredibly, after staying up until nearly 4 a.m., Bryan went out the following afternoon and rode two winners on Griffin-owned horses: *Galatian* by less than a length in the Liverpool Hurdle, and then *Royal Tan* in the National. Cruelly, however, the successes could not save Griffin from bankruptcy since the rails bookmakers had refused to give him credit facilities.

One year later, when *Early Mist* and *Royal Tan* reappeared in the National, the former (ridden by Marshall) was now owned by Mr John Dunlop, and the latter (ridden by Dave Dick) ran in the colours of the Prince Aly Khan. Under big weights, on heavy going, they finished ninth and 12th respectively. Remarkably, having sent out four runners, O'Brien had his third successive winner: *Quare Times*, ridden by Pat Taaffe.

In 1956, Marshall rode in his ninth and last National. This time he was both the rider and trainer of *Early Mist*. They fell with three others at the very first fence. The following year, having long contended with injuries and increasing weight, Bryan chose to retire from riding and concentrate on a training career. He had ridden 517 National Hunt winners. After making only a modest living as a trainer, he switched with much greater reward to the horse transportation business. He died in October, 1991, aged 75.

See also: Early Mist; Royal Tan; O'Brien, Michael Vincent.

MARYLAND HUNT CUP

Inaugurated in 1894, the Maryland Hunt Cup is the most prestigious steeplechase of the United States. Whereas America's Grand National Steeplechase is a three-mile race taking in 18 timber fences, the Hunt Cup is run at Far Hills in Maryland over four miles with 22 formidable timber fences to clear; and as such it has proved to be a most effective test in preparing American chasers to tackle Aintree's Grand National marathon. Four winners of the Hunt Cup have crossed the Atlantic to face that challenge, two being victorious and one finishing runner-up.

Mr Howard Bruce's ten year old champion *Billy Barton* was the trail-blazer in 1928. At Aintree he went off at 33-1, remarkably generous odds for a chaser who had not only triumphed in the 1926 Hunt Cup but had also won America's Grand National Point-to-Point (twice), the Virginia Gold Cup and the Meadow Brook Cup. From a field of 42 starters he was to be one of only two horses to complete the course in the most chaotic National yet seen.

This was the year when the well-fancied *Easter Hero* landed atop the eighth fence (Canal Turn) creating a pile-up that saw more than two-thirds of the field eliminated. Thereafter *Billy Barton* led all the way until, after the 26th fence, just three runners were still standing. And when his only serious rival, *Great Span*, lost both his saddle and rider at the penultimate fence, he looked an absolutely certain winner.

Only the 100-1 no-hoper *Tipperary Tim* was plodding behind as the American challenger led to the last fence. But there he stumbled on landing and, though his unseated rider, Irishman Tommy Cullinan, quickly remounted, it was too late to catch the slow but sure-footed outsider. One year later, *Billy Barton* challenged again with Cullinan in the saddle. But now he was 10lb higher in the weights and was one of many fallers in a record 66-strong field.

Next came nine year old *Jay Trump* who, after twice winning over the 5ft high Maryland timbers, won the 1965 National by three-quarters of a length. The following year he scored a third victory in the Hunt Cup. Similarly, in 1980, 12 year old *Ben Nevis* was a dual winner of the Hunt Cup before scoring a 20 lengths victory in the Grand National.

In 1990 there were high hopes of a third horse completing the Maryland Hunt Cup-Grand National double. *Uncle Merlin*, trained – like *Ben Nevis* – by Tim Forster, was a strong, nine year old contender, quietly fancied by his usually pessimistic trainer. Sure enough, the American horse jumped superbly well and was leading the field in the fastest-run of all Nationals until he made an error at the second Becher's. There he pitched forward on landing and his rider, Hywel Davies, hung on in vain around the horse's neck.

In 1998, yet another dual Maryland Hunt Cup winner – *Buck Jakes* – was sent to Tim Forster to be prepared for the National. His credentials were hugely impressive. A big (17.2 hands) grey, winner of 11 races in 22 starts over timbers, he had been trained by Charlie Fenwick, the American who had partnered *Ben Nevis*, one of Forster's three National winners. Moreover, he had smashed *Ben Nevis's* course record by winning his first (1995) Maryland Cup in 8min 30.6sec, and he was a dual winner of the American Grand National Steeplechase.

Following the essential, well-proven procedure, *Buck Jakes* was sent over far in advance in order to qualify for a handicap mark by having three runs in Britain. Unfortunately he never really adapted to English conditions, and though he gained an allotted weight of 10st 12lb for the National, this was on the back of an unimpressive record of 4PP. Subsequently – to the horror of ante-post opportunists who had latched on to the 50-1 odds – he was withdrawn from the National and duly retired.

See also: Tipperary Tim; Jay Trump; Ben Nevis; Crompton Smith, Tommy; Fenwick, Charles.

MASON, Frank

Unusually, in the two weeks prior to the 1905 National, Frank Mason was paid £300 not to ride. The connections of nine year old *Kirkland*, the 1904 runner-up, wanted to eliminate any risk of the horse's regular jockey suffering an injury before the race. The precaution was justified. In a race of many fallers, *Kirkland*, the 6-1 second favourite, jumped round securely to win by three lengths from *Napper Tandy*.

Ironically, a similar insurance policy was not taken out for the 1911 National. Otherwise Mason might well have won the great chase a second time. He was then booked to ride *Glenside* who, like *Kirkland*, was owned by Frank Bibby. But shortly before the National, Mason broke a leg in a fall. *Glenside*, ridden by Jack Anthony, won by a clear 20 lengths.

Liverpool-born, in 1879, Mason – always known as 'Tich' – was a hugely popular local jockey, who, on his National debut in 1899, rode the 33-1 chance *Dead Level* into fourth place. Thereafter, almost invariably, his Aintree mounts figured high in the betting. In 1900, he fell on *Covert Hack* at the first fence, but the following year he was fourth on *Levanter*, the first New Zealand contender and the 5-1 favourite.

Altogether he rode in 11 Nationals, achieving one

win, one second place on *Kirkland* (1904), and a third on Mr Bibby's *Caubeen* (1909); and three times he finished fourth. He was champion jockey in Ireland in 1900, six times the British champion in seven years (1901-07). His total of some 750 wins in Britain stood as an all-time record until the post-war emergence of the great Fred Winter. He died in 1969 at the age of 90.

See also: Kirkland

MASON, Jem

In 1839, Jem Mason, the son of a horse jobber, won the Grand Liverpool Steeplechase (arguably the first Aintree Grand National) on *Lottery*, the horse he had earlier partnered to success in the Cheltenham Steeplechase. At the time he was recognised as the foremost professional jump jockey in the land, and equally famed for his sartorial elegance. Indeed, he was so prominent a public figure that a Savile Row tailor judged it worthwhile publicity to make all his clothes free of charge. When riding he always wore clean white kid gloves and boots that were custommade by two different cobblers, one for the legs and one for the feet.

Popularly known as 'Dandy Jem', Mason made his spectacular racecourse debut in 1834 when, despite his mount's refusal at the first, he rode *The Poet* to a shock victory in the great four-mile St Albans Steeplechase which had been instituted four years earlier. He rode *Lottery* to many successes, and yet curiously this first National winner remained so wary of his rider that the jockey made a habit of wearing a coat over his racing colours until he was safely mounted.

In the 1840 National, the combination came to grief when *Lottery* hit the Stone Wall at the halfway stage. For the next two years they had no chance in the race, being anchored with an 18lb penalty. Yet Mason loyally stayed with Mr John Elmore's horse, even in 1842 when he had his own runner (*Sam Weller*) – a faller – in the race. In 1843, when *Lottery*'s allotted weight was lowered from 13st 4lb to 12st 6lb, they competed together for the fifth and last time, finishing seventh.

Mason, now married to the daughter of *Lottery*'s owner, scored many notable victories elsewhere, including a second Cheltenham Steeplechase and the Leamington Grand Annual. But Aintree was no longer a happy hunting-ground for him. In the 1846 National, his six year old mount, 11-2 favourite

Veluti, broke down. The following year, he fell on *Clinker*, and on his eighth and last appearance, in 1851, the stubborn *Rat-Trap* gave hom a most difficult ride before finishing sixth.

The cruellest blow came in 1854 when Mason came out of retirement to ride *Miss Mowbray*, the 1852 winner. This smart mare offered him a real chance of scoring his second National success; and indeed, on the day, heavy betting made *Miss Mowbray* the hot favourite. But then, shortly before the race, she was withdrawn. It had been discovered that some person or persons unknown had nobbled the horse by applying a blister to her near fore-leg.

Mason finally retired from racing in 1857 when he married for a second time and set up as a horse dealer in London. He died in 1866 from cancer of the throat and was buried in Kensal Green cemetery. The most significant of many tributes to him was that of his great friend and long-time rival Tom Olliver: ' I can say without fear of contradiction that he was the finest horseman in England. I have never ridden with him without envying the perfection of his style.'

See also: Lottery.

MASON, Norman Beresford

On the official Grand National roll of honour, Norman Mason, one-time night club bouncer and self-made millionaire, is recorded as being both owner and trainer of *Red Marauder*, shock 33-1 winner of the chaotic, lottery-style National of 2001. But, as he readily acknowledged, the real credit for his horse's preparation belonged to his stable jockey and assistant trainer, Richard Guest.

Born November 13, 1936, the son of a Sunderland master baker, Mason had two main assets that stood him in good stead as an owner-trainer: a shrewd business sense and a long, lucky streak. Both assets became evident in the 1960s when, as a disco bouncer, he tired of throwing out one repeat offender. To his chagrin, the club owner kept re-admitting the recidivist on condition that he again paid an entrance fee. It resolved Mason to set up his own disco and reap the profits.

His ventures into the leisure industry snowballed. He eventually had night clubs, amusement arcades and a string of bingo halls; and his involvement with racing began when he was given a broodmare in lieu of a debt. As an owner, he had horses trained by Gordon Richards and George Moore; and his luck was good from the start. When he asked Richards to buy a certain horse for him at the Doncaster sales the number cloths were mixed up by chance, and the wrong horse was purchased at half the anticipated price. That day, instead of one, he came away with two horses – *Music Be Magic* and *Centre Attraction* – and both turned out to be prolific winners, the former most notably scoring in the 1985 Freebooter Novices' Chase.

Mason set up his own yard on a derelict, hilltop farm at Brancepeth in Co. Durham, and he had his first winner as a permit-holder in 1993. Four years later he was on the verge of quitting racing after his horses had gone down with strangles, two of them dying from the infection. His fortunes turned the following year when he was introduced to Guest. While the jockey (trainer in all but name) personally schooled all the horses in his 28-strong stable, the owner's key contribution was to create a super-efficient training complex on his 370-acre Brancepeth Manor estate. This included a National-style jump built in an indoor school. And for good measure the superstitious Mason had given ten of his racing team the suffix 'Red', after learning that it was regarded as a lucky colour by the Chinese.

From the beginning Mason told Guest that he had two ambitions: to be champion permit-trainer and to win the Grand National. The first was soon achieved, but on his Aintree debut, in the 2000 National, *Red Marauder* crashed out at Becher's first time round. One year later, on the eve of the National, Mason's Guest-ridden *Red Striker* easily won the Aintree opener; and, with favourable heavy ground now assured, the owner rightly warned punters to overlook *Red Marauder* at their peril.

With the subsequent victory by a distance the lucky bingo-boss hit the jackpot: £233,400 as the winning owner and £28,850 as the registered trainer. Through the schooling and race-riding skills of Guest, 'my miracle worker', he then failed only by a whisker to win the title of National Hunt champion owner which went to Sir Robert Odgen on the final afternoon of the season. He was the first permit-holder to win the National since Frank Gilman with *Grittar* in 1982.

In the 2002 National, Mason was represented by *Red Ark*, a first National ride for Kenny Johnson. Guest had not taken the ride because he was unable to make the necessary 10st and instead rode the much fancied *Paris Pike*. It made no differ-

ence. Both horses fell at the first fence.

By now Mason and Guest had shared some 115 winners, with the former enjoying four years as the leading permit-holder. They began to expand the Co. Durham yard, with the emphasis on chasers, and in the spring of 2003 Guest assumed control as the full-time trainer, turning out 15 winners in his first two months. They had four entries for the National that year. *Red Marauder*, now 13, was retired shortly before the race, and *Mr Bossman* was too far out of the handicap to make the line-up. *Red Ark* was pulled up at the 25th and *Red Striker*, a full brother to *Red Marauder*, fell at the 27th.

Two of Mason's four entries for the 2004 National made it into the handicap proper: *Red Striker* and the in-form *Tyneandthyneagain*. But both were withdrawn when they did not get their favoured soft ground. *See also:* Red Marauder; Guest, Richard.

MASTER ROBERT

Briefly, when training the 1920 Grand National winner *Troytown*, Algy Anthony had a young chestnut gelding called *Master Robert* in his charge at the Curragh. He soon rejected the horse as being too slow for racing and returned him to his breeder, Mr Robert McKinley of County Donegal. Subsequently, after a spell as a plough horse, *Master Robert* – by *Moorside II* out of an old mare called *Dodds* – was sold for £50.

The new owner was Mr Harry Fordham, a leading point-to-point rider who lived near Royston in Hertfordshire. There, the horse proved to be so gentle natured that he was regularly ridden out by Fordham's ten year old daughter Betty; and again he was worked as a plough-horse – over fields now occupied by London's Heathrow Airport and near a hotel that bears his name.

He soon strengthened and duly won a point-to-point by such a huge distance that he was immediately purchased by Mr W. Walker, Master of the Hertfordshire Hunt. But a few weeks later Fordham agreed to take him back following Walker's complaint that the horse was 'wrong in his wind'.

Though *Master Robert* undoubtedly suffered from thick-windedness, his potential as a chaser was sufficient to attract the interest of Lord Airlie and Colonel Sidney Green who became joint-owners and sent him to Aubrey Hastings, the trainer of two National winners, *Ascetic's Silver* and *Ally Sloper*. The nine year old gelding then proved his strength and stamina by carrying a hugely overweight Lord Airlie to victory in the 1922 Scottish Military Plate at Perth.

In 1923 *Master Robert* was seen as a Grand National prospect after taking third place in the Liverpool Foxhunters and later returning to Aintree to win the Valentine Chase for amateur riders. But early in 1924 there were serious misgivings about his fitness for the race. The horse had developed navicular disease – inflammation of a bone in his foot that required regular poulticing; and only a week before the National he was pulled up lame after finishing a close second in a three-miler at Wolverhampton.

Consequently, connections had great difficulty in finding a jockey for *Master Robert*. Peter Roberts, who had ridden him in the Valentine Chase, preferred to ride an outsider called *Palm Oil*. Others also turned down the ride, and finally a relatively unfashionable jockey – Robert Trudgill – was engaged.

The omens were certainly not good for *Master Robert*'s National debut. His 29 rivals included three former winners, *Shaun Spadah*, *Music Hall* and *Sergeant Murphy*; also the hugely fancied *Conjuror II*, backed down to 5-2 favouritism following his brilliant second-by-a-head running in the first Cheltenham Gold Cup.

Worse, on the eve of the race, Trudgill had suffered an horrendous fall in the Stanley Steeplechase, one leg being ripped open and needing multiple stitches. To the disapproval of the Aintree doctor, he insisted that he was fit to ride again.

On National day, however, everything was to go *Master Robert*'s way. *Conjuror II* was going superbly well when a loose horse veered across and brought him crashing down at Becher's. More riderless horses played havoc with the field; and one jockey, the unseated Bill O'Neill, enterprisingly got back into the race by grabbing the reins of *Conjuror II* and using him to catch up with his own horse. But he remounted *Libretto* only to fall again.

Meanwhile *Master Robert*, a 25-1 shot, kept out of trouble; and following the fall of *Old Tay Bridge* at the second last, he and *Fly Mask* began to close on the lone leader *Silvo* who was visibly tiring. They passed *Silvo* at the last and fought out the long run-in – *Master Robert* proving the stronger by four lengths, with *Silvo* a further six lengths back in third.

The gritty Trudgill, who staggered off to the weigh-in with blood leaking from his reopened wounds, was justly rewarded with a £2,000 gift from

the grateful owners. And it seems that King George V also made a nice profit, having reportedly picked out the winner in the paddock for his £5 each-way bet. In view of his navicular condition, *Master Robert* was never raced again. And Aubrey Hastings, who had trained his third National winner, died five years later.

See also: Trudgill, Robert; Hastings, Aubrey.

MATTHEW

On the eve of the 1847 Grand National, at a Liverpool theatre, a female magician went into a mesmeric state during which she forecast that tomorrow's big race would be won by a horse called *Matthew*. Her reported prediction resulted in a huge plunge on newcomer *Matthew*, the race's first-ever Irish 'steamer.'

The Irish cognoscenti had already regarded *Matthew*'s allotted weight (10st 6lb) as a positive gift. Now the nine year old gelding – Coolreaghbred, by *Vestriius* out of an unknown dam, and named after a local priest – was backed from long odds down to 4-1, weakening only a few minutes before the off when he inexplicably drifted out to 10-1 to share joint favouritism with last year's runner-up, *Culverthorpe*.

This was the year when the Liverpool and National Steeplechase was officially redesignated as 'The Grand National Handicap Steeplechase' and appropriately it attracted a record number of 26 runners, with weights ranging from 10st 4lb to 12st 6lb. By the second Becher's, when fewer than ten horses were still standing, *Matthew* was trailing the field, a distance behind the leaders. But thereafter, driven hard by Denis Wynne, the light-weight made relentless progress; and after the last fence he closed rapidly on the two front-runners. The result was a pulsating three-horse finish, with *Matthew* prevailing by one length from *St Leger* (conceding 25lb), with former winner *Jerry* another length back in third. The Irish had their first National winner.

Matthew came back with Wynne the following year but the 8-1 second favourite had an extra stone to carry on atrociously heavy ground and he was soon knocked over in a rough race which saw only six of 24 starters finish. He did not appear at Aintree again.

See also: Wynne, Denis.

MAWSON, George

Winning rider on the 40-1 outsider *Playfair* (1888) when both were making their first appearance in the

M

Grand National. For George Mawson, a little known jockey, it was an extraordinarily lucky debut. Again and again, he narrowly avoided fallers and being knocked over by loose horses; and he was almost thrown when *Playfair* bungled his jump two fences before the second Becher's. As his mount nose-dived on landing, Mawson was left hanging desperately on to his horse's neck, and at that point another rider, Arthur Nightingall on *The Badger*, sportingly reached out to help lever him back into the saddle.

More good fortune followed. At this stage the joint favourite, *Usna*, ridden by Harry Beasley, was looking a most likely winner as he led over Becher's, the only danger being *Frigate*, ridden by Harry's brother Willie. But then *Usna* dislocated his shoulder on landing over the Canal Turn and veered off course to the right. In the process he carried *Frigate* almost into the canal; and though Willie got him back on course he had lost an impossible amount of ground.

Remarkably *Frigate* made up the lost ground to gain the lead by the last fence. But the effort cost him dearly. On the long run-in Mawson had no difficulty in powering *Playfair* ahead to win from *Frigate* by ten lengths, with *Ballot Box* a further four lengths back in third. *The Badger* was the last of nine finishers.

Two years later Mawson returned for his second National, finishing a distant fourth on *Brunswick*, a 100-1 chance. He made another six successive appearances: on *Brunswick* (1891), fell; *Jason* (1892), fell; *Golden Gate* (1893), pulled up; *Aesop* (1894), fifth; *Horizon* (1895), fell as second favourite; and *Van Der Berg* (1896), ninth of nine finishers. Ironically, after he had finished fifth on *Aesop*, he was replaced in 1895 by Arthur Nightingall. This time *Aesop*, now the 5-1 favourite, was well to the fore when he fell at the Canal Turn second time around. *See also:* Playfair; Cannon, Tom.

McCAIN, Donald 'Ginger'

Trainer of the greatest of all Grand National horses, three times winner *Red Rum* (1973, 1974, 1977); and when, after a gap of 27 years, he triumphed again with *Amberleigh House* (2004), he equalled Fred Rimell's all-time record of having turned out four National winners.

Born on September 21, 1930, in Southport, Lancashire, only 15 miles from the Aintree racecourse, Donald – always known as Ginger – McCain had his passion for horse racing fired by his grandfather, being taken to his first Grand National in 1940. As a 13 year old school-leaver, his first job was driving a horse-drawn cart to deliver butter and bacon to corner shops. Later, following two years National Service as an Army dispatch rider, he worked as a stable-boy and competed in a few point-to-points.

Now 6ft 3in tall and sturdily built, he had no hope of making a career as a jockey. Instead, he became a car salesman and part-time taxi driver, then a permit-holder with a small, obscure yard sited near a railway line behind his car showroom on Upper Aughton Road, in the Southport suburb of Birkdale. His first winner was *San Lorenzo* in a selling chase at Liverpool's 1952 Christmas meeting.

It was in 1967 that he first saw *Red Rum*, then the dead-heat winner at Aintree of a five furlong Selling Plate for two year olds. At the time, however, he could not remotely match the 300 guineas for which the horse was bought in by his connections. He was at Aintree again, for the 1968 National, when *Red Rum*, under Lester Piggott, ran in the Earl of Sefton's Handicap Stakes, going down by only a short head to a winner with an 18lb advantage. And one year later he was at Aintree to see the five year old finish a most promising second over hurdles.

That year McCain became the holder of a full training licence. He had only one winner in his first season, none in the second. Then, by chance, came the great turning point in his fortunes. A regular passenger in his taxi was Mr Noel Le Mare, a wealthy retired businessman who shared his dream of having a Grand National contender. On behalf of this octogenarian, he bought the nine year old bay gelding *Glenkiln* for 1,000 guineas at the Doncaster sales.

Glenkiln was duly entered for the 1972 National but, by an appalling administrative error, McCain inadvertently had the gelding withdrawn. Providentially, the gentleman-owner accepted the blunder with good grace and, as extra insurance, he instructed the trainer to find a second horse to represent him in the 1973 National. To his amazement, McCain learned that *Red Rum* was on offer in the Doncaster sales. In August, 1972, he acquired the seven year old for 6,000 guineas.

Lacking turf gallops, McCain worked all his horses on nearby Southport Sands, and there, under his fifth trainer, *Red Rum* improved so dramatically that within seven months he would win six of nine races and bring in £29,646 in win and place prize money. And in winning the 1973 National he shattered *Golden Miller*'s course record by almost 19 seconds.

As for the white-faced *Glenkiln*, he had at last made the National line-up. He had won over the big Aintree fences the previous October and he was ridden by a most promising newcomer to the race, one Jonjo O'Neill. But he was a faller in 1973 and would be again in 1974.

That first National success for *Red Rum* was undervalued since he had prevailed by only three-quarters of a length over the magnificent *Crisp* who was giving him a colossal 23lb. But the following year 'Rummy' proved his true greatness by carrying the 12st top weight to achieve the first back-to-back National victories since *Reynoldstown* in 1936; and just three weeks later he came out again to win the Scottish Grand National.

At times critics would say that *Red Rum* was being over-raced. But McCain's masterful handling of his superstar was to be proved again and again. In five years, his extraordinary Aintree specialist would achieve the unrivalled Grand National record of three wins and two second places. There was amazement in 1977 when *Red Rum*, 12 years old, gained his third success by 25 lengths. However, the previous January McCain had said he was very pleased with the 11st 8lb given to *Red Rum* – a tip in itself. And before that historic National he had never doubted that his horse would win if given decent ground.

Two years later the trainer was brought down to earth when turning out two 100-1 long-shots in the National. *Wayward Scot*, owned by McCain and international footballer Emlyn Hughes, fell at the first fence; and *Brown Admiral* unseated his rider at the 21st. His next runners were Topham Trophy winner *Beacon Time* (1983), pulled up by Jonjo O'Neill, and 100-1 shot *Kumbi* (1984), fell at the 19th. In the latter year he saw the National won by a gelding that he himself had first trained seven years before. But that winner, *Hallo Dandy*, was now in the care of northern trainer Gordon Richards.

In 1985 he again turned out *Kumbi*, a faller at the fifth. The following year he had two runners: *Imperial Black* (66-1) and *Dudie*, a 100-1 shot owned by Liverpool-born businessman John Halewood. The former finished 14th. The latter was remounted after unseating Kevin Doolan at the third but then fell at the first Becher's. Doolan explained

that his ambition was not only to win the National but to prove that McCain was not 'a one-horse trainer'.

It was becoming all too easy for cynics to see McCain in that disparaging light. In 1988 he turned out another 100-1 outsider, 13 year old *Kumbi*, who fell at the 22nd. In 1991, after he had sunk his savings into developing a new yard at Cholmondeley, near Malpas, Cheshire, his National runner, *Hotplate* (80-1), was pulled up at the 22nd. The following year the chestnut gelding led approaching Becher's second time around, but faded soon after and was pulled up before two out. Then, in the void National of 1993, his 50-1 runner *Sure Metal* was disputing the lead when he fell at the 20th.

After 23 years, McCain's famed association with *Red Rum* ended in 1995 when the King of Aintree died at the age of 30. In 1996 he again ran *Sure Metal*, but the bay gelding, ridden by his son Donald, was now 13 years old and a 200-1 outsider. Going off like a scalded cat to lead the way over the first fence, he faded on the second circuit to be the last of 17 finishers. Then, in 1999, McCain ran two more outsiders: 13 year old *Commercial Artist* and ex-Irish chaser *Back Bar*, both 200-1. The former was pulled up at the 17th. The latter, under Dean Gallagher, got round in his own time to finish 14th, so landing a handsome profit for connections who had backed him at 12-1 to complete the course.

It seemed that time was running out for Ginger (now more accurately grey) McCain to achieve one last National hurrah. In 2001 he was aged 70 and entering his 50th year as a trainer. Yet he still had 26 horses at work, and that year he saddled two runners in the National: *Hanakham*, a 12 year old once with Martin Pipe, and the 150-1 outsider *Amberleigh House* whom he had bought for £75,000 on behalf of multi-millionaire Halewood. He thought *Hanakham*, a past winner of the Royal and SunAlliance Chase, had a great chance and he publicly scorned his 100-1 price.

Unfortunately, however, this was the year when the National was controversially run in quagmire conditions, with only four completing the course, two of them having been remounted. *Hanakham* fell at the second, and *Amberleigh House* went at the 15th fence, having suffered a deep cut to his off-hind leg on being hit broadsides by the loose *Paddy's Return* who caused a mass pile-up at the Canal Turn.

Since the golden days of *Red Rum*, McCain had

M

had 14 National runners: eight of them fallers, three pulled-up and none finishing better than 14th. Yet remarkably his dream of saddling another National winner burned as bright as ever. And in November, 2001, he showed he had not lost his Aintree touch by turning out *Amberleigh House* to jump 22 of the National fences in winning the valuable Tote Becher Chase at 33-1.

Much to McCain's chagrin, the handicapper allotted ten year old *Amberleigh House* only 9st 6lb for the 2002 National, meaning that 34 withdrawals were needed to guarantee the horse a run. He had expected a higher weight in view of his horse's recently proven form at Aintree and deplored the presence of 'a string of no-hopers' among the record 144 entries for a race limited to 40 starters. He made a plea for a change in the rules of entry so that any horse which had won over the National course should be given 10st. But the Aintree management rejected the idea, reasoning that it would lower the quality of the field, especially if it admitted runners from the Topham Chase, formerly the John Hughes Trophy.

At this stage *Amberleigh House* was as short as 25-1 and the trainer judged that his horse had 'a very good chance and can run a very, very big race indeed'. But after the final declarations, the gelding was left as the fourth of four reserves. McCain was shattered. He complained bitterly that 'some bloody dross and crap' was left in the race; that some horses were being run just to please their owners; and that multiple entries – such as eight Martin Pipe runners – were making a 'mockery of the National.' He had a case.

Beaten by the cut, *Amberleigh House* ran instead over the inadequate trip of the Topham Chase and finished nowhere. Two weeks later he won a chase over an extended three miles at Bangor. Then, in November, the gelding returned to the Becher Chase, this time finishing a gallant second to *Ardent Scout* and one place ahead of *Blowing Wind* who had been third in two Grand Nationals. Furthermore, fallers in the race had included the last National winner *Bindaree* and the much lauded *Moor Lane*. 'He was giving the winner 8lb and he'll be even better with the extra mile in the National,' said McCain

McCain had now seen his last five Grand National runners sent off at 100-1 or more. But the 72 year old trainer was not to be discouraged. In 2003 he entered three horses for the National: *Ackzo*, *Amberleigh House* and *Lambrini Gold*. This time

Amberleigh House made the line-up on 10st 4lb ('It's amazing what the threat of castration can do to a handicapper') and vindicated the trainer's judgment of his potential. Going off unfancied at 33-1, he galloped into contention at the 24th, the Canal Turn, and was going so well three out that for a brief moment McCain thought he might win on the 30th anniversary of *Red Rum*'s first victory.

For luck *Amberleigh House* was carrying a wisp of *Red Rum*'s mane in his headband. Unfortunately, however, he did not quite have *Rummy*'s stamina. Admirably ridden by Graham Lee, a Grand National debutant, he was second coming to the last but could not remotely match the finishing pace of *Monty's Pass*, and in the last few strides he was overhauled by *Supreme Glory*, the 12 lengths runner-up. Modestly McCain observed: 'If he'd had a proper trainer then he'd have won.'

Owner John Halewood was not alone in believing that *Amberleigh House*'s Grand National chance had come just two years too late. But the trainer's faith in the old gelding never wavered. In November his Aintree specialist was beaten only a short head by *Clan Royal* in the Becher Chase, and McCain was bullish when the 12 year old was allotted 10st 7lb, a rise of only 3lb, for the 2004 National. The 12 year old was generally 25-1 ante-post but the trainer suggested that he should 'really be a very short-priced favourite'. He was proved absolutely right. *Amberleigh House* won the £260,940 first prize at 16-1.

On the morning of that National, as was his custom, McCain had laid flowers on the grave of his beloved *Red Rum* near the winning post. Now, after a fairy-tale victory, he returned there to pay his respects. Earlier he had said that if *Amberleigh House* won he would retire and let his 33 year old son and assistant Donald take over. But now, as the family celebrated at their local pub, the Bickerton Poacher, he began to have second thoughts. He could still dream on – now of outscoring the great Rimell with a record fifth National winner.

Next season, he said, *Amberleigh House* would be back for the Becher Chase and the National – 'and I'm sure he'll run bloody well again'. It was asking for another miracle. Not since *Sergeant Murphy* in 1923 had a 13 year old won the National. But who were we mere mortals to question McCain's optimism? Humbly, he said, 'I'm just an old, broken-down taxi-driver who got lucky in the National.' But, as the record proves, he was still a supreme master in preparing and bringing back horses to tackle the great Aintree fences.

As usual, *Amberleigh House* ran well in the Becher, finishing a most respectable fifth under a top weight of 11st 10lb, conceding 24lb to the winner *Silver Birch*. When he was allotted 11st for the 2005 National, McCain was delighted, declaring: 'It's a grand weight, a winning weight.' However, following withdrawals, the weights rose a further 3lb, and it proved too much for the veteran champion. Never dangerous, he finished tenth.

In January, 2006, McCain emerged with another lively National contender as his ten year old *Ebony Light*, on a light weight of 10st 4lb, with Stephen Craine claiming 5lb, was the 33-1 winner of the valuable Peter Marsh Handicap Chase at Haydock. *Kingscliff* (11st 10lb), running in snatches, was nine lengths second. Senior jumps handicapper Phil Smith admitted that he had difficulty in assessing this form and that subsequently *Ebony Light* may have got off lightly in being awarded only 10st 8lb for the National.

McCain could also be well satisfied with the 10st 7lb allotted to *Amberleigh House*, 10lb less than he carried into tenth place in the 2005 National. Though a 14 year old had never won the race, he still insisted that his veteran star would 'take a lot of beating if the ground comes up good'. In contrast, *Ebony Light* would want soft going. And if either horse won – giving the trainer a record fifth triumph in the National – he vowed to hand in his training licence immediately, passing on the reins to his son Donald.

Two weeks before the Grand National, his challenge was further strengthened by the purchase of *Best Mate*'s full brother *Inca Trail* for 110,000 guineas at the Doncaster sales. Like *Amberleigh House*, the ten year old would run in the colours of John Halewood.

Some three hours before the 2006 National, Aintree's managing director Charles Barnett unveiled a plaque halfway up the stairs leading to the Queen Mother Stand. It read: 'Legendary four times Grand National winning trainer Ginger McCain traditionally watches the Grand National from this place.' It would have soon become outdated if Ginger had landed a fifth victory. But this was never threatened. *Ebony Light* fell at the fifth, *Amberleigh House* was pulled up before the 21st, and *Inca Trail* weakened two out to be the distant eighth of nine finishers.

Over the years McCain had had 25 runners in the Grand National, scoring four wins, two seconds and one third place, with five others completing the course. His last runner at Aintree, *Sword of Damascus*, finished fifth in the concluding bumper of the 2006 National meeting. And two weeks later he completed a double at Haydock Park when *Cloudy Lane* won the Red Square Vodka Novices' Hurdle. It gave him more winners for a season than ever before. But now, at 75, the mighty McCain planned to take a back-seat, with son Donald as trainer and himself as assistant.

In his first season on taking over from his father, Donald McCain Jnr made a flying start, not least scoring on his Cheltenham Festival debut with the seven year old novice *Cloudy Lane* (seen as a future Aintree prospect) who won the Kim Muir Challenge Cup. At that stage he had two National entries: *Inca Trail* and *Maurice*. Neither would make the line-up, but meanwhile his hand was greatly strengthened by the arrival of *Idle Talk* who had been bought by Trevor Hemmings and transferred to the McCain yard.

Idle Talk was seen as a natural for the National. He had been runner-up in the Royal and SunAlliance Chase and fourth in the 2006 Scottish National. And when the weights were announced, he was the *Racing Post*'s 'Pricewise' ante-post recommendation at 40-1. True, he had lost his rider (Jason Maguire) at the fifth in the Cheltenham Gold Cup. But this was viewed as a blessing in disguise. Going on riderless to complete the full course, he had not had a hard race. Four weeks later, however, he blundered the third in the National, soon fell behind, and at the 19th unseated his rider for the third time in successive races. *See also:* Red Rum; Amberleigh House; Le Mare, Noel; Fletcher, Brian; Stack, Tommy; Lady Riders; Burials.

McCOY, Anthony Peter MBE

The most successful jump jockey of all time, a status A.P. McCoy achieved on August 27, 2002, when victory on *Mighty Montefalco* in a three-mile hurdle at Uttoxeter brought up his 1,700th winner, so passing the three year old record total of Richard Dunwoody. Still only 28 and supremely fit, he would advance that record with seasonal double-centuries to set a standard that is unlikely ever to be surpassed.

A. P. McCoy was born in Ballymena, Co. Antrim, on May 4, 1974. His father, Peadar McCoy, a joiner who bred several horses (including the 1993 County

M

Hurdle winner, *Thumbs Up*), had him riding ponies from the age of two; and by the age of 12 Tony was cycling 18 miles a day commuting to the Cullybacky stables of Willie Rock for whom he rode a few point-to-pointers. Four years later, at Rock's suggestion, the teenager moved south of the border to sign apprentice forms with the leading Irish trainer Jim Bolger.

Thoughts of a career as a Flat jockey were soon killed as Tony grew apace, especially while recovering from a broken leg. Having ridden six winners on the Flat and seven over hurdles, he shot up to 5ft 11in tall, ballooning from 7st 10lb to 9st 7lb and needing to diet just to continue over jumps. Then came his big break: at Wexford races, in 1994, trainer Toby Balding invited him to join his staff in Hampshire. Thereafter, his rise to fame was meteoric, his record-breaking achievements relentless.

As a 20 year old, in his first season in Britain, he was the champion conditional jockey, breaking Adrian Maguire's record with 74 winning rides and scoring 50 more than his nearest rival. The following season, 1995-6, he was the senior jumps champion with 175 winners. Subsequently, and primarily in partnership with trainer Martin Pipe, he shattered records galore. In 1997 he galloped to the fastest century of winners on record, in the process landing the Champion Hurdle-Cheltenham Gold Cup double on *Make A Stand* and *Mr Mulligan* respectively, and the Scottish Grand National on *Belmont King*. In 1997-8 he amassed 253 winners to smash Peter Scudamore's nine year old record of 221 in a season. In 1999 he became in record time the sixth jump jockey ever to reach the 1,000-winner mark. In 2001-2 he achieved a phenomenal tally of 289 winners from 1,005 rides, in the process breaking his own record for the fastest 200 winners and beating Sir Gordon Richards' 55 year old record (on the Flat) of 269 winners in a single season.

McCoy followed that with 256 winners in 2002-3, and in 2004 he notched up his ninth successive jockeys' championship with 209 wins from 800 rides that had earned more than £2 million in prize money. Eight of those nine titles had been secured in harness with champion trainer Pipe. Altogether their combination had achieved the staggering figures of 1,092 winners from 3,531 rides with 589 seconds and 393 thirds. And then, in April, 2004, just short of his 30th birthday, the most successful jumps jockey of all time made his momentous decision to transfer to Jackdaws Castle, the state-of-the-art yard of trainer Jonjo O'Neill and his fabulously rich landlord, J.P. McManus.

'Everything I have achieved,' said McCoy, 'is down to Martin and his genius.' But no less it was due to his own supreme horsemanship, allied to extraordinary fitness and strength, and unbounded courage, determination and dedication. With Pipe providing so much ammunition, those qualities enabled him to shoot down all the riding records and build up the most impressive CV in National Hunt history. Only one great race prize eluded the champion throughout those nine dominant seasons: the Grand National.

McCoy had had many successes over the National fences. Yet, year after year, he was frustrated in the main Aintree event. His National rides: *Chatam*, 1995 (unseated at the 12th); *Deep Bramble*, 1996 (closing on the leaders when he went lame at the second last with a ruptured near-fore tendon); *Challenger Du Luc* 1998, (one of five fallers at the first); *Eudipe* 1999, (fell fatally at the second Becher's); the 9-1 favourite *Dark Stranger* 2000, (unseated at the third); *Blowing Wind* 2001, (remounted, finished third); *Blowing Wind* 2002, (distant third); *Iris Bleu* 2003 (pulled up lame before the Water Jump); co-favourite *Jurancon II* 2004 (fell at the fourth); *Clan Royal* 2005 (carried out at the second Becher's); *Clan Royal* 2006 (seven and a quarter lengths third); and *L'Ami* 2007 (a far distant tenth).

What made this annual disappointment all the more extraordinary was the fact that McCoy, unlike any jump jockey before him, had multiple choices of Grand National rides. Indeed, in 2001, he had the unique luxury of being able to choose from ten Pipe-trained runners – a quarter of the National field! He opted for *Blowing Wind*, an eight year old who had landed a famous double with the Imperial Cup and the County Hurdle in 1998. At Aintree they parted company when a loose horse charged across them at the 19th. But McCoy remounted and gave chase in the quagmire conditions to be the third of only four finishers. It was the first time he had completed the full National course.

In 2002, this time with the choice of eight Pipe runners, McCoy again opted for *Blowing Wind*. Though the gelding had yet to win beyond two and a half miles, he regarded him highly; and punters took heed, backing him down to 8-1 favouritism, to take an estimated £150 million from the bookies if he won. As it was, the many each-way backers were rewarded. Weakening two out, *Blowing Wind* again finished a well-beaten third.

In 2003 *Blowing Wind* was one of seven Pipe runners, and again proved the best in finishing eighth. This time, however, McCoy had chosen to ride *Iris Bleu* who had been an early faller the previous year. Though much improved and going off joint second favourite, *Iris Bleu* was still only seven years old and carrying a hefty 11st 3lb. Never in contention, he jumped poorly and was pulled up lame before the Water Jump.

The 2004 Grand National meeting started with a win for McCoy on *Tiutchev* in the £87,000 Martell Cognac Cup Chase; and two days later, after winning the £58,000 Maghull Novices' Chase on *Well Chief*, he lined up for his ninth National with the very highest hopes of success. The French-bred *Jurancon II* was one of four co-favourites; and the handicapper had confessed that he would have given the gelding an extra stone if he had had the evidence of his latest win in a major trial at Haydock.

'I seriously, genuinely believe this one had got the right sort of credentials,' said McCoy. But, as with the ill-fated *Eudipe* and *Iris Bleu*, he was on a seven year old – and so young a contender had not won the National since *Bogskar* 64 years ago. It was the same old story: McCoy's National jinx struck early, with a fall at the fourth fence.

Ironically, Martin Pipe's one Grand National winner – *Miinnehoma* (ridden by Richard Dunwoody in 1994) – had come in the year before McCoy had joined his all-powerful stable. Since then 40 of Pipe's 53 National runners had failed to get round and only four had been placed. Ladbrokes at this point rated the perennial champion jockey as an 8-11 chance never to win the race and evens to win it before he retired.

But, in 2004, as McCoy joined the supremely wealthy J.P. McManus-Jonjo O'Neill set-up at Jackdaws Castle, that evens bet began to look mighty tempting. For, despite his phenomenal achievements, McCoy was still dissatisfied, as hungry as ever for his first National win. As he once harshly expressed it, 'I suppose some people may regard me as a failure unless I win a National – I might even do so myself'. To which remark Carl Llewellyn, twice a National winner, tellingly added: 'And then he'll consider himself a failure if he

doesn't win two Nationals'. Quite simply, National Hunt racing had never known a harder self-taskmaster than the grimly determined A.P. McCoy.

Unfortunately, in the 2004-05 season, virus-hit Jackdaws Castle had to close down for many weeks. Yet McCoy continued to ride the most winners and the stable recovered in time to give him high hopes in the National on *Clan Royal*. He started the Aintree meeting with three seconds and a chase winner (J.P. McManus's *Fota Island*), trained by Mouse Morris; followed up on the Friday with another win for McManus on *Like-A-Butterfly*, trained by Christy Roche; and on National day he won a handicap hurdle on *Genghis*.

All now seemed set fair for what he rated his best-ever chance of riding the National winner. *Clan Royal* had been a somewhat unlucky runner-up the previous year. He had won both the Topham and Becher chases over the Aintree fences, and he was most fairly weighted on 10st 11lb. But yet again his National hoodoo struck. They were about six lengths in the lead coming to the 22nd (Becher's) when *Clan Royal* was unavoidably carried out by a loose horse, with McCoy being unceremoniously dumped into the plastic side-rails.

It would be presumptuous to suggest this this incident cost McCoy his first, so elusive National victory. His saddle had slipped and the breast girth had long since broken; also the winning *Hedgehunter* finished in a seemingly irresistible style. But, without doubt, this misfortune devastated McCoy more than any of his previous disappointments in the National. In the changing rooms, he was inconsolable, despairingly burying his face in his hands. His National record was now two thirds and eight non-fnishes in ten attempts.

Even though he was no longer based with Pipe and had been limited in his rides for the O'Neill stable, he now clinched his tenth successive jockeys' championship and once again – on the last day of the season – reached his double century of winners. The impression remained, however, that he would have happily exchanged that title for a National victory on *Clan Royal*. As he said, 'When you get a horse that loves Aintree like he does, you wonder if you'll ever get as good a chance again.'

Nevertheless, his hopes soared anew when the weights for the 2006 National were announced. Surprisingly, *Clan Royal* was allotted a mere 10st 8lb, 3lb less than the previous year. His handicap

M

mark had been artfully protected by running him over hurdles, and now he became the hot ante-post favourite, ahead of *Hedgehunter* who has been raised 9lb.

Meanwhile, in contrast to his winless experience of the previous year, McCoy enjoyed better fortune at the Cheltenham Festival. On the opening day, riding *Straw Bear*, he was only narrowly beaten by Ruby Walsh on *Noland* in the Supreme Novices' Hurdle; and then he won the Champion Hurdle on *Brave Inca* and went on to boost his tally to three wins.

Now, in seeking his most elusive prize, he decided on a new approach. As he explained to the *Daily Telegraph*'s Jim White: 'Every year I thought I was on a horse that had a chance (in the National). And every year I didn't. So this year, I'm going with a different attitude. I'm not going there thinking it's in the bag. I'll just see what happens. See if a change of mental strategy makes the slightest difference.'

Subsequently, he was in great form at the Grand National meeting. He started with two hurdle wins and on the third day he won the Maghull Novices' Chase on *Foreman* and a 21-runner hurdle race on *Refinement*. But that day he was denied a hat-trick as yet again his National dream ended in disappointment. As planned, he held up *Clan Royal* early on, making steady headway after the 15th and, despite blundering the 19th, was well in contention coming to the last. But thereafter *Clan Royal* was outpaced on the run-in, finishing a length and a quarter behind runner-up *Hedgehunter*, the other 5-1 joint favourite, and with a ten-inch gash under his chest that required 12 stitches.

For the fifth time McCoy was the meeting's champion rider, and he ended the season with 178 wins from 828 rides, so securing the jockeys' championship for the 11th time. But he remained discontented, haunted by the fact that he had failed in 11 attempts to win the Grand National.

Though a broken right wrist put Tony out of action for eight weeks early in the 2006-07 season, he immediately bounced back to top form, reaching the 2,500-winner career milestone in late September. Two months later he took the first major jump prize of the season: the Paddy Power Gold Cup at Cheltenham on 16-1 chance *Exotic Dancer*. He had his share of disappointments: a first fence fall on *Clan Royal* in the Becher Chase, and at the Festival finishing runner-up in the Gold Cup (on *Exotic*

Dancer) and in the Grand Annual (*Hasty Prince*). But then, after a single Cheltenham success (the Brit Insurance Novices' Hurdle on *Wichita Lineman*) he enjoyed his greatest prize of the season: the Irish National on *Butler's Cabin*.

Three days later, as usual, he began the Grand National meeting in style, winning the Betfair Bowl on *Exotic Dancer*, the Top Novice Hurdle on *Blythe Knight* (his 180th winner of the season), and then the Betfair.com Handicap Chase on *Reveillez*. But yet again he was doomed to fail in the National itself.

The previous month McCoy had suffered a loss with the fatal injury of his intended National ride, *Far From Trouble*. Trained by Christy Roche, the eight year old had won the Galway Plate and had proven his stamina with a hugely promising third in the 2006 National Hunt Chase over four miles one furlong. On a favourable weight of 10st 10lb, he had looked to have a massive chance at Aintree.

'He didn't get the chance to show how good he was,' said a saddened McCoy. Now, instead, the champion jockey was to ride *L'Ami*, trained by Francois Doumen. Burdened with a massive 11st 8lb, the French-bred gelding ran prominently early on but made mistakes on the second circuit, weakened three out and was tailed off to finish a remote tenth. For the 12th consecutive time McCoy ended the season as champion jockey. And for the 12th time he had been thwarted in the Grand National. *See also:* Pipe, Martin; O'Neill, Jonjo.

McCRIRICK, John

Channel 4's betting guru since 1983; a famously loud egocentric, always sporting odd headgear and chunky jewellery, and addicted to giant Lusitania cigars. As such, John McCririck is the most colourful character seen in racing since the early 20th century when Abyssinian-born Peter Carl McKay adopted the name of Ras 'Prince' Monolulu to sell his tips ('I gotta horse') while dressed in garish baggy trousers and ostrich-feather head-dress, and flourishing a huge umbrella.

This clown prince of televised racing established his media presence with all the subtlety of a rampaging rogue elephant. To many viewers he came as a breath, or rather whirlwind, of fresh air, sweeping through the once stuffy corridors of racing reportage; to others as an overblown windbag, all too loud in both manner and dress. His ostentation, however, remained an irrelevance. What mattered was that he profoundly understood the psyche and needs of regular punters – 'fellow sufferers' as he calls them. Fearless and extraordinarily energetic for a man of his bulk, he is the punter's champion supreme, ever alert to the interests of the ordinary betting man and constantly battling on his behalf for a fairer deal.

Born April 17, 1940, in Surrey, and educated (three O-levels) at Harrow where he operated as an amateur bookmaker, McCririck worked as a shop assistant in Boots, a commis chef and waiter at London's Dorchester Hotel, a failed course bookie, a *Sporting Life* journalist and a sub-editor on BBC Grandstand before finally hitting the jackpot as a larger-than-life television personality with ITV. Integral to his success has been the support – as business manager, chauffeuse and cordon bleu cook – of his long-suffering wife Jenny whom he always calls 'The Booby', explaining that a booby is a 'silly South American bird that squawks a lot'.

While Channel 4 has never been involved with Grand National coverage, and although McCririck would doubtless deny it, he has in his time had an influence on market moves in the National – most especially in 1994 when he was so bullish about the chances of the favourite *Master Oats* (a faller). For weeks he extolled the merits of this challenger and one week before the race he gave his fancy the full TV-hype treatment. The price about the horse shortened dramatically, and by the morning of the National *Master Oats* – 40-1 when the weights were announced – had become a solid 8-1 joint favourite.

McCririck himself would never claim to be a smart tipster or punter, but he has had his big winning moments, not least in backing *Zafonic* to win the 1993 2,000 Guineas, and two years later supporting *Pennekamp* to beat *Celtic Swing* in the 2,000 Guineas and *Harayir* to beat *Aqaarid* in the 1,000 Guineas. And he had a truly sweet success in 1996 when Coral gave him a £250 charity free bet on the National in a head-to-head contest with his Harrow contemporary and TV arch-rival Julian Wilson.

McCririck commented: 'Wilson used to beat me mercilessly at school. Because of those thrashings, he made me what I am today. Now – at long last – it's my turn to give him a beating. *Rough Quest* will win today's National. There's no way that any other horse in the race can give weight away to him.'

In turn, Wilson countered: 'McCririck couldn't tip a baby out of a pram! His choice of *Rough Quest*

is a typically unintelligent selection … *Son Of War* is my confident selection.' *Son Of War* unseated his rider at the 24th. *Rough Quest* (7-1) became the first favourite to win since *Grittar* in 1982.
See also: Tipsters.

McDONOUGH, Alan and William

An Irish amateur, arguably the most skilled of all riders in early Grand Nationals despite the fact that he never won the race. Alan McDonough finished fifth on *The Nun* in the first strongly contested National of 1839. The following year he was leading the field on the second circuit when his horse (*Arthur*) slipped and somersaulted over Valentine's Brook. Miraculously, he became the first National rider to remount and finish in a place: second, only four lengths behind the winning *Jerry*. In 1841, on *Cigar*, he finished second again, this time beaten only one length by *Charity*.

Born in Co. Galway, Alan McDonough began winning races at the age of 16 and by his early 20s had become a legendary figure in Irish racing before going on to plunder events in England. In 1837 he was one of four riders involved in the second Liverpool Steeplechase to be held at Aintree, finishing runner-up on *The Disowned* to the Welsh-born amateur Henry Potts on *The Duke*.

This was a time of intense rivalry – not entirely sporting – between English and Irish racing supporters. In the 1837 Grand Steeplechase, Irish fans lost a veritable fortune in backing their hot favourite, *Dan O'Connell*. But they were rewarded the following year when – contrary to some published reports – the race was won by *Sir William*. As the *Liverpool Chronicle* observed, the Irish chestnut was given a brilliant ride by his owner, Alan McDonough, to win by 'about 40 yards'.

It is recorded that *Sir William* was 'a handsome savage that nobody could do anything with except his owner.' His successes came to be resented by some English racegoers – to such an extent that on one occasion, at Dunchurch in Warwickshire, a certain Mr Ball invaded the course on horseback and deliberately knocked over *Sir William*. The story goes that a mounted Army officer, one Captain Lamb, pursued the offender for about a mile, finally catching him and giving him the 'father and mother of a thrashing'. But it was small consolation for McDonough. His fall had left him with a broken collarbone and several fractured ribs.

M

While recuperating McDonough – possibly out of financial need arising from gambling losses – sold *Sir William* for £350 to the shrewd operator John Elmore who then resold the chestnut for £1,000 to Lord Cranstoun. Subsequently, the new owner matched his horse for a £1,000 stake against Lord Sheffield's *Jerry*. However, in the run-up to the four-mile race, *Sir William* proved so difficult to control that McDonough had to be summoned at the 11th hour from Co. Galway. He had no trouble winning since *Jerry* duly refused at the first fence.

In the 1839 Grand National, McDonough was joined by his brother William, a leading huntsman with the Galway Blazers. Alan was on Lord McDonald's mare *The Nun* who for a while led the betting at 6-1; Willie on *Rust*, the next best at 7-1. But through bad organisation the start was delayed for two hours. In the interim punters were discouraged by *The Nun*'s portly appearance and by the off Mr Elmore's eye-catching *Lottery* had been promoted to 5-1 favouritism.

Poor Willie McDonough, though initially going well, had no chance on *Rust*. Outrageously, when he took the option of racing wide of the flagged course, a group of self-interested punters, deliberately blocked his path, holding him up until all his rivals has passed by. After a vain attempt to recover lost ground *Rust* had to be pulled up. Meanwhile his brother Alan, having remounted after a fall, brought *The Nun* home in fifth place behind the winning favourite.

One year later, when Alan again remounted, this time finishing second on *Arthur*, the winner ironically was *Jerry* whom he had beaten on *Sir William* the previous year. Having been on the runner-up again in 1841, he made three more National appearances – on *Nimrod* (1844) fell; *Mameluke* (1846), fell after an early collision; and *Brunette* (1847) who finished sixth.

His last National ride was on a truly outstanding mare who had long been a dominant force in Irish steeplechases. Unfortunately she was 13 years old when making her Aintree debut and had suffered a throat infection on arrival in Liverpool. Moreover, she was joint-top in the weights with 12st 6lb and in a National with a record number of 27 runners. Starting slowly, *Brunette* made spectacular progress to join the leaders on the second circuit, but then faded. She was conceding two stone to the winner.

In the same race, brother William was riding

Saucepan, also anchored on 12st 6lb. It was his seventh National and for the seventh time he failed to finish. However, in fairness, it should be noted that he had been well in contention on *Lancet* in 1846 when, unbelievably, a spectator on horseback rode on to the course and knocked him out of the saddle. The great consolation for the McDonoughs was that – after so much skulduggery – their last Grand National saw the first Irish winner in *Matthew*.

McMANUS, John Patrick

The biggest owner in National Hunt racing and the undisputed king of modern punters. Limerick-born, in March 1951, J.P. McManus became hooked on racing at the age of nine when he had a few shillings on *Merryman II*, the 13-2 winner of the 1960 Grand National. Seventeen years later he was staking £50,000 at 3-1 on the Derby winner *The Minstrel* and putting on another £50,000 when the price went out to 7-2. Then, moving on to Royal Ascot, he contrived to make a modest profit despite having reportedly lost over £70,000 on the Coronation Stakes and the King Edward VII Stakes.

According to the *Sunday Times* Rich List, McManus was worth an estimated £561 million in 2007 and had made £252 million playing the foreign exchange markets. But it was gambling on horses that had laid the foundation of his fortune. Starting out as a £10 a week construction worker, driving a JCB digger owned by his father, he left the family's plant hire business at the age of 20 to set up as an on-course bookmaker.

It was not long before he saw more prospects in becoming a punter. Prospering as a gambler (most notably winning £250,000 with a single bet on his *Mister Donovan* in the 1982 Sun Alliance Hurdle at Cheltenham), he progressed in racing as an owner and breeder, and then moved into foreign exchange trading, becoming a multi-millionaire tax exile.

He remains a legendary figure in the betting ring. In 1990 he landed one of his biggest coups with £25,000 on *Trapper John*, an 8-1 winner at Cheltenham. Then, most famously, he became associated with the great hurdler *Istabraq*. In 1997 it was reported that after losing £100,000 on a race at the Cheltenham Festival he got out of trouble by staking £180,000 on his best hurdler at 6-5; and the following year he reputedly had a £130,000 stake on the horse at Aintree.

Istabraq, winner of a hat-trick of Champion

Hurdles (1998-2000), plus the 1997 SunAlliance Hurdle, was certainly his greatest money-spinner, bought for a mere 38,000 guineas. In contrast, there were later guesstimates that he had forked out £500,000 for the 2000 King George VI winner *First Gold* and £300,000 for the staying hurdler *Baracouda*, both trained by Francois Doumen.

J.P.'s first Grand National bid could not have been more short-lived, his *Deep Gale* falling along with nine others at the first fence in 1982. Ten years passed before he began to regularly enter the fray. In 1992 his mare *Laura's Beau* finished third behind *Party Politics* just three weeks after she had won the four-mile Midlands National at Uttoxeter. The following year, when the race was declared void, the mare was the seventh of seven finishers; and in 1994, as a 40-1 chance, she was a faller.

In 1996 his next National challenger, nine year old *Wylde Hide*, was just in touch with the leaders when he unseated his rider at the second Canal Turn. In 1997 his quietly fancied *Time For A Run* had to be withdrawn after injuring himself in his final prep gallop, and his hopes again rested on *Wylde Hide*, who this time unseated his rider (Charlie Swan) at the second Becher's. One year later, under Ken Whelan, his *Gimme Five* exceeded expectations by finishing fifth at 25-1.

Although McManus was the champion jumps owner for the first time in 1999, he was without a National runner that year. Then, in 2000, *Lucky Town*, owned by his wife Noreen and trained by Enda Bolger, was the subject of huge gambles. Having been a good staying-on third in Cheltenham's cross-country chase, he was backed to win £250,000 in one bet alone in a north London shop, and there was an unconfirmed report that J.P. had staked £15,000 each-way at 33-1. He went off in the Grand National at 20-1 and finished eighth. J.P.'s next National contender, in 2002, was *Spot Thedifference*, one of four horses brought down at the 27th fence.

By now McManus, based in Geneva and Barbados, was ranked eighth in an Irish Top 100 Rich List with an estimated worth of £255 million, ahead of his business partner, breeding tycoon John Magnier, 20th. He had reputedly cut his big gambles, describing betting as 'a young man's game'. Yet his involvement in racing was greater than ever. He had 60 horses in the care of a dozen trainers; and most notably he had begun to expand his racing operations with the purchase of Jackdaws Castle, formerly

the Cotswold base of David Nicholson. Here he financed the creation of a state-of-the-art training centre under the control of Jonjo O'Neill.

In January, 2003, the champion two-mile chaser *Flagship Uberalles*, bought for a guesstimated £400,000, was added to his formidable string that included *Like-A-Butterfly*, *Le Coudray*, and *Baracouda* who was to be so impressive in winning the Bonusprint Stayers' Hurdle at the Cheltenham Festival. In addition, he had three powerful entries for the Grand National: *Youlneverwalkalone*, *First Gold*, and ten year old *Mini Sensation*. The latter had been runner-up in the 2002 Midlands National and now, on the build-up to Aintree, he won the Welsh National and the Singer and Friedlander National Trial Handicap Chase.

Both *First Gold* and *Mini Sensation* were eventually withdrawn from the National. The former ran instead on the opening day of the Aintree meeting, winning the £87,000 Martell Cognac Cup Chase. The following day McManus won the £26,000 Martell Cognac Handicap Chase with *Master Tern*, had the first (*Clan Royal*) and the second (*Macs Gildoran*) in the £30,600 Topham Chase; and won the final handicap hurdle with *Patriot Games* at 16-1. Meanwhile there was an ever-mounting plunge on his one Grand National contender, *Youlneverwalkalone*, who was backed down to 8-1 joint second favouritism.

But again the McManus bandwagon came to an abrupt halt in the National. *Youlneverwalkalone*, trained by Christy Roche and ridden by Conor O'Dwyer, started slowly, soon went lame, and was pulled up at 12th. He was found to have fractured his off-fore cannonbone, an injury requiring surgery. J.P. had now had eight runners in the National but had still not bettered his second challenge with *Laura's Beau* in 1992.

Otherwise, however, the Irishman had the Midas touch in all his endeavours. Having studs in Limerick and England, and more than 100 horses in training, he could be expected to be a major Grand National player for many years to come. And he looked to have a potentially major National contender in November, 2003, when his *Clan Royal* won the Tote Becher Chase, adding to his April win in the Topham Chase – both races being over the National fences.

Grand National day, 2004, started well for McManus with his six year old *Puck Out* winning the Martell Cordon Bleu Handicap Hurdle at 10-1. He had four challengers for the big one: top-weighted *Le Coudray, Risk Accessor, Spot Thedifference* and *Clan Royal*. Though he had backed *Le Coudray* each-way at 40-1, *Clan Royal* was clearly his main hope. Nicely weighted on 10st 5lb, he went off as one of four co-favourites and ran brilliantly until blundering the 26th where rider Liam Cooper lost his whip. After the last he squandered valuable ground in wander-ing to the left and finally went down by three lengths to collect £132,000 for second place. *SpotThedifference* finished a distant fifth at 50-1 while *Risk Accessor* had lost his rider at the first Becher's, the fence that also claimed *Le Coudray* second time around.

In May, 2004, McManus shattered the previous National Hunt sales record when he paid 530,000 guineas for the Aintree novice hurdle winner *Garde Champetre*; and the new season began with the sensational transfer of nine times champion jockey A .P. McCoy to Jackdaws Castle, clear evidence, if any were needed, of McManus's determination – with some 250 horses in training – to be the dominant as well as the biggest owner in National Hunt racing.

Unfortunately he was dogged with misfortune in the winter of 2004-5, not least with viruses crippling his Jackdaws Castle operation. By his standards, he had a disappointing Cheltenham Festival, and now he looked for better luck in the Grand National for which he had entered no fewer than 19 horses – far and away a record for a single owner. Six made it to the line-up.

On the first day of the Aintree meeting he won the Red Rum Handicap Chase with *Fota Island*, trained by Mouse Morris, and on the second day the Mildmay Novice Chase with *Like-A-Butterfly*, trained by Roche. Both winners were ridden by Tony McCoy who was booked for *Clan Royal*, the most strongly fancied of his runners in the National.

Briefly McManus had high hopes of victory as *Clan Royal* took the lead at the 15th (The Chair) and stretched it to six lengths approaching the 22nd (Becher's). But there, by the cruellest ill-luck, his main challenger was carried out by a loose horse. With six runners he achieved no better than a seventh place with his recently purchased *Innox*, trained by Doumen. Two others completed the course: *Spot TheDifference* (18th) and *Shamawan*, the last of 21 finishers at 200-1. *Risk Accessor* unseated his rider

at the second and *Le Coudray* was pulled up before the 21st.

In 2006 McManus came out in fighting mode, having vowed to reclaim money lost at last year's Cheltenham Festival. This time, on the Festival's opening day, he had two runners-up: *Straw Bear* in the Supreme Novices' Hurdle and *Spot TheDifference* in the Cross Country Handicap Chase. Then, on the third day, he struck gold with his grey *Reveillez* whom he backed at 6-1 to win the Jewson Novices Handicap Chase.

Meanwhile, his hopes of Grand National success soared to new heights as *Clan Royal* – given a generous weight – shortened to 5-1 favouritism, a starting price that would be shared by *Hedgehunter* following his excellent run in the Cheltenham Gold Cup. Initially, McManus backed any one of his runners to win at 6-1; and on the eve of the National, he was 4-1 to win with one of his four contenders.

At Aintree he won the Top Novice Hurdle with his brilliant *Straw Bear*, and on National day he enjoyed success with *Foreman* in the valuable Maghull Novices' Chase. But again he was frustrated in the big one. His well-backed *Innox* (10-1) fell at the first; and 13 year old *First Gold* unseated his rider at the 23rd, subsequently being retired to join *Baracouda* and *Istabraq* at his owner's Martinstown Stud, in Co. Limerick. In consolation, valuable prize money was picked up by *Clan Royal* in third place and by *Risk Accessor*, a surprising fifth at 66-1; and he finished the season as Britain's champion owner with £1,060,965 and a record of 66 wins from 463 runners, while in Ireland he topped the owners' list for the 11th consecutive year.

In 2007 McManus was the owner with the most Grand National entries (nine), one more than Trevor Hemmings; and he had a cracking lead-up to Aintree. At Cheltenham he won the Cross Country Handicap Chase with his *Heads Onthe Ground* (beating *Silver Birch*), the Foxhunter Chase with *Drombeag* and the four-mile National Hunt Chase with 33-1 *Butler's Cabin*. Then, five days before the National, he landed the Irish version with *Butler's Cabin*, so picking up a 100,000-euro bonus for having a winner at Cheltenham and in the Irish National in the same year.

At Aintree he won the John Smith's Handicap Hurdle with his 25-1 shot *Two Miles West* and the Betfair.com Handicap Chase with his *Reveillez*. But in the National his two runners, heavily weighted

L'Ami and veteran *Clan Royal* finished a far distant tenth and 11th respectively. For the 12th consecutive year he topped the owners list in Ireland, earning well over one million euros in prize money. But he would surely have gladly swapped his season's 57 winners for victory in the Grand National – a success, he said, that he would value more than winning the Cheltenham Gold Cup.
See also: O'Neill, Jonjo.

McMORROW, Michael Leo Aloysius

Irish-born rider of *Russian Hero*, the shock 66-1 winner of the 1949 National. Making his second appearance at Aintree (he had finished 13th on 14 year old *Schubert*, also a 66-1 chance, in 1948), Leo McMorrow rode a superbly well-measured race to confound the critics who judged his mount to be weak on both stamina and jumping ability.

It was the first high-profile triumph for a jockey who had known so many lean times. Beginning in 1937, McMorrow had struggled as a young amateur jockey for three years before having his first winning ride. Subsequently his wartime successes included two wins on the novice *Caughoo* who was destined to be the 100-1 winner of the 57-runner Grand National in 1947. But these wins were few and far between, and this pattern continued even after he had turned professional in 1944. In desperation, he decided to see if he could fare better riding in England.

In Northants he made a reasonable start, riding for trainer Cliff Beechener. Then, after another spell in the doldrums, he had a rare stroke of good luck: the departure of Dick Francis to ride for Lord Bicester gave him the opportunity to join the stables of trainer George Owen at Malpas, Cheshire. And among the chasers there was *Russian Hero*.

It was on *Russian Hero*, a 20-1 chance, that McMorrow had his first winning ride for Owen – scoring by a head in a two-mile chase at Worcester in October, 1948. The combination notched up two more wins, but then there were three failures, including two falls, on the build-up to Aintree. The nine year old was seen as a most dodgy jumper who had no form beyond three miles – so lowly regarded that his breeder-owner Fernie Williamson was able to get 300-1 ante-post odds to a £10 stake for the National.

In this National no fewer than 31 of 43 starters were fallers. Amazingly, *Russian Hero* was among the few who jumped safely, being patiently ridden on the first circuit, making relentless progress on the second, closing on the leaders after the Canal Turn, and taking a clear lead at the last. Ironically, his main challenger was Lord Bicester's *Roimond*, ridden by Francis, who had once helped *Russian Hero* to recover from a life-threatening bout of colic.

Unfortunately for Francis, making his National debut, *Roimond* was top-weighted with 11st 12lb. Conceding 18lb to *Russian Hero* was beyond him; and on the run-in he was easily outpaced, going down by eight lengths, with *Royal Mount* one length back in third. Lord Mildmay's *Cromwell*, the 6-1 favourite, was the fourth of 11 finishers, two of whom had been remounted.

McMorrow, who ended that season with just 12 wins, never knew such glory again. He partnered *Russian Hero* in three more Nationals, each time failing to complete the course. In 1950, raised 10lb in the weights, they fell at the first. In 1951, when only three completed the course, they were baulked by loose horses and brought down on leading at the Chair; and in 1952, back as 50-1 long-shots, they again came down (with nine others) at the first. Indeed, following his first time National success, *Russian Hero* never won another race.

As a freelance jockey, McMorrow competed in four more Aintree Nationals, his other rides being long-shot *Uncle Barney* (seventh and 13th in 1954 and 1955 respectively), and *Merry Windsor* (1956) and *Morrcator* (1957), both fallers. Subsequently, he had a spell riding in the United States, then turned to working as an assistant trainer. Tragically, in Pennsylvania in 1973, he was killed in a motoring accident.
See also: Russian Hero; Owen, George.

MELLING ROAD

The road that intersects the Grand National course, crossing it between the start and the first fence (also the 17th), and again between the 12th (also the 28th) and the 13th (also the 29th). The latter intersection is known as the Anchor Bridge Crossing and, having passed this point, horses are said 'to come back on to the racecourse'. When the course is scheduled for racing this wide road is covered with a sand-based all-weather surface on which horses can gallop safely. The Melling Road is then closed off by big level-crossing style gates which are swung back across the course on non-racing days.

M

MELLON, Paul

Born on June 11, 1907 in Pittsburg, Pennsylvania, and christened in St. George's Chapel at Windsor Castle, Paul Mellon was the son of horse-loving Nora McMullen, an English brewer's daughter, and billionaire Andrew W. Mellon, a banker and industrial magnate who, in the 1920s, became the third biggest money-earner in the United States (surpassed only by John D. Rockefeller and Henry Ford) and who subsequently served as Secretary of the Treasury under three successive presidents and then as U.S. ambassador to Britain (1931-33). Paul himself was renowned as a philanthropist (giving away more than $600 million), an art connoisseur, bibliophile and – not least – as a racehorse owner.

Andrew Mellon once said, 'Every man wants to connect his life with something he thinks eternal'. In making that connection, his son was rewarded with unparalleled success on the Flat – as the only person to have bred and owned winners of the Kentucky Derby, the Epsom Derby and the Prix de l'Arc de Triomphe; and above all, as breeder and owner of the extraordinary *Mill Reef* who – trained by Ian Balding at Kingsclere, Berkshire – took English racing by storm in 1970 and 1971. Yet initially it was jump racing that had attracted him, and the Grand National most especially.

In 1929, while up at Clare College, Cambridge, Mellon had been introduced by friends to fox-hunting; and in 1934 his first chaser, *Drinmore Lad*, began to win races in America. Shipped over to England to be trained by Ivor Anthony and Mrs Aubrey Hastings, *Drinmore Lad* dead-heated with an off-form *Golden Miller* at Gatwick and subsequently became the ante-post joint favourite for the 1936 Grand National, along with the legendary *Miller*. But a leg injury prevented the chaser from running, and when Mellon renewed his National challenge after the war it was only with moderate jumper *Caddie II*, a long-priced faller in 1948 and 1949.

In 1965, Mr Mellon entered *Red Tide*, a very useful eight year old, again only to see Johnnie Haine fall from his runner early on the first circuit. Four years later, his famous black and gold cross colours were carried with some distinction by his well-supported *The Beeches*, ridden by old campaigner Bill Rees. The handsome grey gelding finished fourth but was sold before returning to Aintree where he fell in 1970. The American, already an honorary member of the Jockey Club, was now concentrating on the Flat with spectacular success. He became one of only five men to be honoured by the U.S. National Museum of Racing as 'Exemplar of the sport'; and he was 86 years old when he finally achieved his last great ambition on the Flat: winning the 1993 Kentucky Derby with *Sea Hero*, his third U.S. Classic victory following his Belmont Stakes wins with *Quadrangle* (1964) and *Arts And Letters* (1969).

Yet even now the aged Anglophile, an honorary knight of the realm, had not given up hope of winning the Grand National. In 1995 his colours were carried at Aintree for the fifth time: by eight year old *Crystal Spirit* who had been bred at Kingsclere out of his American broodmare, *Crown Treasure*, and sired by *Kris*, a champion miler. His full brother was the 1981 Derby runner-up *Glint of Gold*, by the great *Mill Reef*.

Balding recalled that they were looking for speed when they sent *Crown Treasure* to *Kris*. Now, eight years later, they were asking *Crystal Spirit* to get nearly four and a half miles. The bay gelding, a winner that year of two-and-a-half-mile chases at Cheltenham and Ascot, did get the distance under Jamie Osborne. But after a prominent run over the first circuit he was well outpaced and finished 14th. It was Mellon's last throw of the dice in the event that he called 'the most exciting game of chance ever invented'. Remarkably, when he died in February, 1999, aged 91, the Kingsclere yard was still occupied by trainer Ian Balding who had enjoyed Mellon's patronage for 63 years.

Among the American's multi-million-pound bequests were £2.5 million to the BHB's Rehabilitation of Racehorses Fund; £1.5 million to the Apprentice School Charitable Trust of the British Racing School; £600,000 to the Royal Veterinary College, and £300,000 to the Animal Health Trust at Newmarket.

See also: Balding, Ian; United States.

MELLOR, Stan

Champion jump jockey in three successive seasons (1959-62), Stan Mellor became in 1971 the first to have ridden a 1,000 winners in Britain. He retired at the end of the following season with a then record total of 1,035 winners, his successes including the Whitbread Gold Cup on *Frenchman's Cove* (1962), the King George VI Chase on *Frenchman's Cove*

(1964) and *Titus Oates* (1969), the Two-Mile Champion Chase on *Sandy Abbot* (1963) and, most sensationally, the Hennessy Cognac Gold Cup on 25-1 chance *Stalbridge Colonist* (1963), beating the mighty *Arkle* by half a length.

Yet he rode in 13 Grand Nationals without success and nine times failed to complete the course. As a jockey, his best result was a second place on *Badanloch* in 1960. As a trainer, he twice saddled a third-placed runner and might well have turned out a National winner if his classy *Royal Mail* had not been hit so hard by the handicapper.

Born on April 10, 1937, Mellor rode his first winners in the 1953-54 season; and he made a promising National debut in 1956 when finishing sixth on *Martinique*, a 40-1 chance. His next rides – *Never Say When* (1958) and the outsider *The Crofter* (1959) – were both fallers. Then, in 1960, he was on his first well-regarded National challenger, Lord Leverhulme's nine year old *Badanloch*. Strongly in contention on the second circuit, they had only one serious rival coming to the last open ditch. But this was the clear favourite, *Merryman II*, who accelerated dramatically to win by 15 lengths from *Badanloch*, with *Clear Profit* a 12 twelve lengths back in third.

After finishing eighth on *Badanloch* in the 1961 National, Mellor ended the season with his best ever total of 118 winners. Then, as champion jockey, he reappeared at Aintree on the 7-1 favourite, *Frenchman's Cove*, son of the Derby winner *Airborne*. Unhappily, however, the course was a veritable quagmire and the weakening seven year old was brought down on the second circuit. But compensation was close at hand. The partnership won the Whitbread Gold Cup and, two years later, the King George VI Chase.

Stan missed the Nationals of 1963 and 1964. (In 1963, riding in the inaugural Schweppes Gold Trophy, he had suffered his worst-ever fall, fracturing his jaw and skull in 14 places.) When he returned to Aintree in 1965 it was on *Ayala*, the 66-1 National winner of two years before. But the chestnut gelding was now well past his best and he fell at the first. The jockey's subsequent National rides were: *Vultrix*, pulled up, 1966; *The Fossa*, a victim of the mass pileup at the Foinavon, 1967; *French Kilt*, 14th, 1968; *Game Purston*, pulled up, 1969; *The Beeches*, fell, 1970; and *Lord Jim*, fell, 1971.

Following his retirement from the saddle

Mellor became a highly successful Lambourn-based trainer; and though he never scored in the National he saddled some notable challengers after a discouraging start. In 1974 his 100-1 runner, Mr W.H. Whitbread's *Beau Bob*, was a faller. The following year, still 100-1, he was going really well when he nose-dived fatally over the second Becher's.

In 1976 he sent out seven year old *Ceol-Na-Mara* to finish fifth. In 1979 his *Alpenstock*, a 100-1 outsider, was one of seven to be brought down in a pileup at The Chair; and in 1980, on desperate ground, his New Zealand-bred *Royal Stuart*, ridden by Philip Blacker, was the last of four finishers. The following year the consistent *Royal Stuart* was fancied to improve on that place, only to blunder the 20th fence and then, at the next, unseat Hywel Davies who was unluckily riding with broken leathers. But this time Mellor had two other contenders: *Pacify* and *Royal Mail*, runner-up in the 1979 Cheltenham Gold Cup. While the former was a faller, the latter, carrying top weight, looked the only threat to *Aldaniti* coming to the penultimate fence. Unfortunately he clouted the fence, almost unseating Blacker, and thereafter weakened, being pushed back into third place by the fast-finishing *Spartan Missile*.

In 1982 Mellor again had three runners. *Cold Spell* was one of ten casualties at the first; *Royal Stuart* was later brought down; and *Royal Mail*, again harshly burdened with top weight, was a faller at the first Becher's. The latter, now 13 years old, again failed to survive Becher's in 1983, and it was not until 1987 that Mellor once more saddled a truly memorable National challenger in *Lean Ar Aghaidh*. Ridden by Guy Landau, a 20 year old newcomer to the race, the great chestnut made breathtaking leaps to lead for much of the way before finishing third behind *Maori Venture* and *The Tsarevich*. One year later they returned and, with an extra stone to carry, finished ninth. *Lean Ar Aghaidh* did, however, manage to win a race over the National fences when he returned in 1990 to land the Fox Hunters, again in breathtaking style.

Elsewhere Mellor saddled a number of big-race winners, most notably *Pollardstown* (1979 Triumph Hurdle), *Royal Mail* (1980 Whitbread Gold Cup), *Saxon Farm* (1983 Triumph Hurdle) and *Lean Ar Aghaidh* (1987 Whitbread Gold Cup). He retired in 2001 after 49 years in racing, though not making a complete break since he sometimes conducted coaching courses for jockeys.

M

MERRYMAN II

On March 26, 1960, when making his Grand National debut, *Merryman II* became the first Scottish-bred winner of the race, and the first winner to have his triumph captured on television. Popularly, at 13-2, he was the first clear favourite to win the National since *Sprig* 33 years before; and the third winner of the race for trainer Neville Crump. Remarkably, too, he was ridden by a 22 year old jockey (Gerry Scott) who was strapped up from neck to waist after breaking his collarbone 12 days earlier.

According to a well-recorded story, *Merryman II* owed his existence to a sudden impulse on the part of the Marquess of Linlithgow, a former Viceroy of India, now retired to his estate at Hopetown, Midlothian. Over breakfast, one spring morning in 1949, the old man amazed his family by expressing an interest in horse racing. Looking up from *The Times*, he remarked that, while he lacked the financial resources to breed a Derby winner, it would give him 'the greatest satisfaction' to breed a Grand National winner.

The marquess's daughter, Lady Joan Hope, recalled that she almost spilled her porridge in surprise. Nevertheless, she helped to turn his dream to reality. A few days later an old friend of the family gifted them an unruly young half-bred mare named *Maid Marion*; and after riding her to hounds for a while, Lady Joan had her covered by *Carnival Boy*, a well-bred stallion owned by the Duke of Northumberland. The result was *Merryman II*.

As it happened, the marquess never saw his National hope run. He died early in 1952, and soon after Lady Joan moved abroad following her marriage to an Army officer. Her elder brother, who succeeded to the title, eventually sold *Merryman II* to Miss Winfred Wallace of Edinburgh, a well-known horsewoman who had previously owned his half-brother, *Robin Hood*. As she was a close friend of the family, the price was a mere £470. Miss Wallace hunted the horse regularly as a five year old, successfully rode him in three point-to-point races; and then, in April, 1958, she entered him for his first race under National Hunt Rules. The race was the Buccleuch Hunters' Chase at Kelso and he won by 20 lengths.

The following February, leading trainer Captain Neville Crump saw *Merryman II* run well to be narrowly beaten in a hunter chase at Leicester. Much impressed, he persuaded Miss Wallace to send him to his stable at Middleham, Yorkshire – a move which had, in fact, already been recommended to

the owner by her friend Peter O'Sullevan. The immediate aim was the Fox Hunters' Chase at Aintree in March. He won comfortably, and one month later, ridden by Scott, confirmed his standing as a first-class chaser with a 12-length victory in the Scottish National.

Merryman II had four races in the build-up for his 1960 Grand National debut. There were no wins; nonetheless, his form was solid and, with his proven ability over the big Aintree fences, he was made favourite in the field of only 26 runners. Next in the betting was *Wyndburgh*, second by only one and a half lengths the previous year, but now raised 9lb in the weights.

On fast going, *Wyndburgh* was a surprising faller at Becher's, and second time round that obstacle also claimed *Mr What*, the 1958 winner, and several others. Meanwhile, *Merryman II*, a big powerful bay gelding who needed to be held up, had survived a blunder at the seventh, and thereafter had been jumping brilliantly, gaining lengths at every fence. After the second Becher's he was challenging *Tea Fiend* and Lord Leverhulme's *Badanloch* for the lead. The former soon weakened, and at the last open ditch *Merryman II* stormed ahead, never threatened as he ran on to win by 15 lengths from *Badanloch*, with *Clear Profit* a further 12 lengths back in third. He was the last horse to triumph over Aintree's formidable, upright fences before they were made to look less daunting by the introduction of a sloping apron on the take-off side.

Crump, who had now turned out three Grand National winners in 12 years, rated *Merryman II* the best Liverpool horse he had trained; and that judgment was justified one year later when the bay gelding returned to Aintree with a new jockey (Derek Ancil replacing the injured Scott) and an extra stone to carry. His cause was not aided at the start where he received a hefty kick on the stifle from Lady Leigh's *Jimuru*. Nevertheless, he made steady progress and, at the second Becher's, landed in the lead, fractionally ahead of *Nicolaus Silver*. From the second last, however, the huge concession of 25lb proved too great. The light-weighted grey triumphed by five lengths, with *O'Malley Point* only a neck behind *Merryman II* in third place.

Scotland's finest National contender made one more appearance in the race: in 1962 when, as an 11 year old, he was harshly the top weight of 32 starters. Ridden by Dave Dick, he finished 13th, so maintaining his unblemished jumping record over the Aintree fences. Now retired, he died suddenly in 1966 at a meet of the North Northumberland Hounds.

See also: Crump, Neville; Scott, Gerald; O'Sullevan, Sir Peter.

MIDLANDS GRAND NATIONAL

In 1997 *Lord Gyllene* finished seven lengths runner-up when carrying 11st 10lb in the Midlands Grand National Handicap Chase. Twenty-three days later, under a mere 10st, he romped home by 25 lengths in the Aintree Grand National. Notably, too, the mare *Laura's Beau* won the Midlands in 1992 and three weeks later finished third at Aintree.

In general, however, the Midlands National – being held in March, so soon before the most famous steeplechase – has not been an especially valuable guide to the form of a horse going on to Aintree. The last winner to score at Aintree was *Rag Trade*, who, after his 1957 Midlands success, won the Welsh Grand National and then beat *Red Rum* by two lengths at Liverpool.

Run over four and a quarter miles at Uttoxeter, the Midlands is the longest but least prestigious of the Aintree imitations. In 1999 *Young Kenny* and *Call It A Day* finished first and second respectively. But when the former went to Aintree the following year he was burdened with a 12st top weight and fell at the tenth. The latter finished sixth.

In March, 2003, the Midlands prize fund was raised from £80,000 to £100,000 – more than half going to the winner with prizes down to sixth place. Third-placed *Jurancon II*, a six year old, went off as one of four co-favourites in the Aintree National. But he fell under champion Tony McCoy at the fourth. One year later, *Akarus*, second in the 2003 Midlands, fell at Aintree's sixth fence, while *The Bunny Boiler*, the Midlands winner of the previous year, finished a distant tenth.

MIINNEHOMA

Winner of the 1994 Grand National when, in a 36-strong field, he was one of no fewer than five horses trained by Martin Pipe, and the choice of his champion stable jockey Richard Dunwoody for whom it was a second victory in the race. Eleven year old *Miinnehoma* was making his National debut just 23 days after finishing a poor seventh in the Cheltenham Gold Cup and he owed his 16-1 starting price largely to heavy local support arising from his ownership by the madcap Liverpool-born comedian Freddie Starr.

Bred in Co. Wexford – by *Kambalda* out of the mare *Mrs Cairns* – *Miinnehoma* was bought at the 1988 Doncaster Sales for 35,000 guineas and initially trained by Owen Brennan at Newark. On his first outing he won a two-mile bumper on heavy ground at Uttoxeter; and the following season – now with Martin Pipe – he won four races over hurdles. A full season passed before he reappeared on the racetrack. Then came an impressive start as a chaser: three races won over three miles or more, including the 1992 Sun Alliance Chase at the Cheltenham Festival.

After promising so much, *Miinnehoma* lost his way in the 1992-93 season, jumping less surely and going without a single success. Again he benefited from a long rest, coming back in March, 1994, to win over two and a half miles at Newbury. That same month he finished far behind *The Fellow* in the Cheltenham Gold Cup, and some forecasters judged that he had little hope of reversing that form with the winner at Aintree.

Miinnehoma, however, went to the National with the advantage of having been lightly raced. On the other hand, *The Fellow*, after twice being a Gold Cup runner-up, had won at Cheltenham on his favoured fast ground and now he was to confront heavy going under a weight of 11st 4lb exceeded only by that of the Czech no-hoper *Quirinus*. The hot 5-1 favourite was mud-loving *Moorcoft Boy*, reported to be in '200 per cent condition' by trainer David Nicholson. There was also a wealth of support for *Master Oats,* who had beaten *Moorcroft Boy* by 15 lengths in the Greenalls at Kempton, and for the well-handicapped *Double Silk* who had humped 12st over the National fences to win the 1993 Fox Hunters.

In his early races, most notably the Sun Alliance Chase, *Miinnehoma* had been ridden by Peter Scudamore who retired shortly after the void 1993 National. Now, as Scu's successor, Dunwoody inherited the ride. Having already won on the gelding at Newbury, he judged that it was best not have him in front for very long. Thus, after getting off to a flying start, he tried to restrain his mount for much of the first circuit. Jumping perfectly, however, his mount travelled so smoothly on the heavy ground that – contrary to plan – he was in the lead by the 17th. Soon he lost interest and the jockey needed to work hard to urge him on.

Fortunately the Irish mare *Ebony Jane* took over the lead at the 21st; and though *Miinnehoma* pecked badly on landing over Becher's second time round, he quickly recovered and was running freely again. Briefly he was ahead at the Canal Turn, then was again passed by *Ebony Jane*. Two out, the mare began to fade, and there *Miinnehoma* was joined and overhauled by *Moorcroft Boy*, ridden by Dunwoody's great rival Adrian Maguire. *Moorcroft Boy* led over the final fence, but the Pipe horse still had plenty in reserve and took command at the Elbow. A new threat now emerged as the long-shot *Just So*, a renowned mudlark, drew alongside. *Miinnehoma*, however, responded to the challenge, holding on in a pulsating finish to win by one and a half lengths with *Moorcroft Boy* a further 20 lengths back in third. Only six horses finished.

After an eight-month break, *Miinnehoma* was raced over two and a half miles at Haydock, beating *General Pershing* by 20 lengths. Then, in the Cheltenham Gold Cup, he was a well-beaten third behind *Master Oats* and the mare *Dubacilla*. This duplicated his successful preparation for the 1994 National. Pipe judged that he was 'as well as he was last year, and may be even better'. But he was now 12 years old and 10lb higher in the handicap, second behind *Master Oats*, the top-weighted 5-1 favourite. At Aintree, on ground faster than he liked, he was never travelling well and was pulled up by Dunwoody after the 21st fence. In May, 1996, he was retired to the Berkshire home of his owner.

See also: Dunwoody, Richard; Pipe, Martin.

MILDMAY, Lord Anthony

Following the death of Lord Mildmay in 1950 a *Times* leading article declared: 'There never was a harder rider, a better loser or a more popular winner.' It was a fitting tribute to a truly great gentleman of the world of steeplechasing. Sadly, however, this most honourable of sportsmen was destined to be best remembered as the 'Prince of Losers', as the unluckiest of all Grand National riders since fate robbed him of victory not just once, but twice.

Anthony Mildmay first appeared on the National scene in 1933 as a gangling (6ft 2in tall) 24 year old amateur on board the 100-1 outsider *Youtell*, owned by his fellow Old Etonian friend Mr Peter Cazalet, who was also riding in the race. Mildmay failed to get beyond the first fence, being left on the turf nursing a broken nose. He was unseated again – at the

second Becher's – when he returned on *Master Orange* in 1935, another 100-1 shot.

Once again, in 1936, Mildmay was on a 100-1 outsider: an enormous, tubed entire called *Davy Jones*. This seven year old chestnut had been bought for a mere £650 by the rider's father, Lord Mildmay of Flete, with the National especially in mind. But there was nothing to recommend the ex-selling plater on current form, and no surprise when this long-striding, hard-pulling type blazed a trail from the start. Other riders believed he was setting too strong a pace and would surely blow up.

Davy Jones, however, showed no signs of flagging. He led over the first fence and was still ahead when the field came to Becher's the second time around. *Reynoldstown*, last year's winner ridden by Fulke Walwyn, was now only a length behind. But he lost ground with a succession of jumping errors, and as they came to the penultimate fence the runaway leader, still going easily, looked all over the winner.

Then it happened. *Davy Jones* pecked on landing, and the strain was enough to break open the buckle of his brand-new reins which had not been knotted because of the horse's very long neck. Now, with the reins hanging loose on either side, Mildmay had no means of steering beyond giving his horse a tap of the whip on one side of his head. The race leader was completely out of control and, at the final fence, his luckless rider could do nothing to stop him veering left and running off the course. It presented the race to *Reynoldstown* who, unopposed, duly cruised home to win by 12 lengths from *Ego*, a 50-1 chance. By luck, he had become the first horse to win successive Grand Nationals since *The Colonel* in 1870.

The following season Mildmay shared the amateur riding championship with 21 wins, but 12 years passed before he was seen in the National again. In the meantime he had succeeded to his father's title and had served with distinction in the Welsh Guards and the Guards Armoured Division. After his wartime service he became the leading amateur rider in steeplechasing for five successive seasons (1946-50), and at the same time he formed a successful partnership with Cazalet, who was now a prominent trainer at Fairlawne in Kent.

In 1948, they believed they had a worthy National contender in seven year old *Cromwell*, a 33-1 chance owned and ridden by Lord Mildmay. This time, in contrast to his last appearance, Mildmay chose to play a waiting game, not making serious headway until they entered the second circuit. He was well placed to challenge after Becher's. And then, once again, fate cruelly turned against him.

The previous year, in a terrible fall on the aptly-named *Fatal Rock* at Folkestone, Mildmay had broken his neck – an injury that had left him liable to sudden attacks of paralysing neck cramps. Now such an attack, crippling his weakened neck muscles, struck him at a critical time. Suddenly, to the dismay of so many racegoers, he was seen to be riding with his head slumped forward. Unable to lift his head, he was riding half-blind over the last mile. In the circumstances, Mildmay worked wonders to come from behind to take third place, seven lengths and six lengths behind *Sheila's Cottage* and *First Of The Dandies* respectively. Again, he was judged to be a most unlucky loser.

Cromwell was so impressive that day that, with an extra 6lb, he was made 6-1 favourite for the 1949 National, This time there were no excuses. Again facing 42 rivals, *Cromwell* and Mildmay were beaten on merit, finishing in fourth place behind the 66-1 winner *Russian Hero*.

Later in the season, Lord Mildmay was directly responsible for the revival of royal interest in National Hunt racing. At his suggestion, Queen Elizabeth became the owner of her first chaser, so beginning a distinguished association with the sport that she would cherish (later as Queen Mother) until beyond her centenary year. Mildmay and Cazalet were entrusted with the task of selecting her first jumper and they opted for *Monaveen*, an Irish-bred eight year old who had run well before falling on the second circuit in the 1949 National.

Owned jointly by the Queen and her elder daughter, *Monaveen* was raced in the colours of Princess Elizabeth, winning three races in succession on his build-up for the 1950 National. At Aintree he came home the fifth of only seven finishers in a field of 49. Among the many fallers was Lord Mildmay on *Cromwell*, down at the ditch after Valentine's. And another unseated jockey was one Dick Francis, later to become the most spectacular of National losers, on the Queen Mother's Cazalet-trained *Devon Loch*.

But never was a rider so cruelly dogged by ill-fortune as the gallant Lord Mildmay. Just two months after appearing in his sixth National, the last of the great Corinthian riders met an untimely death by drowning off a private beach near his home at Mothecombe in south Devon. He was a strong and regular swimmer, and so very possibly his old neck injury contributed to the tragedy. He was 41 years old, at the time of his death the leading amateur rider, and a member of the National Hunt Committee and the Jockey Club. Subsequently, his friend John Hislop described him as 'the foremost figure in steeplechasing today and the very personification of its true spirit'.

The noble lord had ridden eight winners at the Cheltenham Festival and now he was commemorated at the meeting by the Mildmay of Flete Challenge Cup, a handicap chase over two miles and four and a half furlongs. In 2006 it was renamed the Racing Post Plate. He had also been remembered by the Anthony Mildmay/Peter Cazalet Memorial Handicap Chase at Sandown, a popular National trial in January, until 2005 when it took on its sponsor's name; and by one of three courses at Aintree – a mile-and-a-half long – that bears his name.

See also: Cazalet, Peter; Royal Runners; Monaveen.

MISS MOWBRAY

Arguably, the bay mare *Miss Mowbray* is the most extreme outsider to have won the Grand National. In 1852, when she triumphed by one length over *Maurice Daley*, *Royal Blue* (a faller) was the first National runner to be officially priced at 100-1, while *Miss Mowbray* and the runner-up were not even quoted in the betting.

On this occasion, *Miss Mowbray* was regarded as a 'no hoper' despite having been prepared by George Dockeray, trainer of the first National winner, *Lottery*, and despite having already won two major races, the Warwickshire Hunt Cup and the Leamington Open Steeplechase. She was running at Aintree for the first time. Also it was the first National for her rider, the amateur Alec Goodman. But their late challenge was timed to perfection, taking the lead at the last and holding on well to resist the fast-finishing runner-up.

It was not the first time that *Miss Mowbray* had been badly underrated. The mare – bred in Bedfordshire by *Lancastrian* out of the hunter *Norma* – was originally trained at Newmarket for the Flat and soon judged to be worthless. Described as only a 'rat of a thing', too slightly built for chasing, she attracted no offers when put up for sale. Eventually she was sold for 100 guineas but within a few days the disappointed buyer decided she was unsound and successfully demanded his money back. Finally

M

she was bought by the well-known owner, Mr T.F. Mason, after he had ridden her at a hunt.

In complete contrast to her National debut, *Miss Mowbray* went off as a 5-1 favourite on her return to Aintree in 1853 – this despite being 8lb higher in the weights and without her winning rider who had been booked for Mr Mason's more favoured runner, *Oscar*, the 6-1 joint second favourite. Riding the mare was Mr Frank Gordon, a renowned huntsman who was making his first – and last – appearance in the National.

Goodman and Gordon were side by side as they came to the last. But with them was the great Tom Olliver who took the lead on landing and drove on over the slushy ground to win with the 15 year old *Peter Simple*, by three lengths from *Miss Mowbray*, with *Oscar* another three lengths behind. It was *Peter Simple*'s second National success, and Olliver's third after a nine-year gap.

In view of her first and second place record, plus the fact that the famed Jem Mason was coming out of retirement to ride her, *Miss Mowbray* was the most heavily backed entry for the 1854 National. But one hour before the off, much to the disgust of vociferous punters, the mare was withdrawn following the discovery that she had been nobbled by someone applying a blister to her near fore-leg.

The mare was back the following year, this time as the 4-1 second favourite and ridden by Sam Darling. There was driving rain and heavy going, and sadly, just when moving up to challenge the leaders, *Miss Mowbray* slipped on landing, nose-diving so hard that both her neck and back were broken.

See also: Foul Play; Goodman, Alec.

MOIFAA

On appearance alone, *Moifaa* ranks alongside *Tipperary Tim* as the most extraordinary of all Grand National winners. He was a huge (over 17 hands), ungainly brown gelding, with withers rising like a camel's hump, and an overall aspect that prompted the distinguished owner, Lord Marcus Beresford, to call him 'a starved elephant – the ugliest devil you ever saw.'

But for many decades *Moifaa*'s legendary status rested on much more than his remarkable conformation. It was commonly recorded that he had been shipwrecked on his 12,000-mile journey from New Zealand to compete in the 1904 National; that he was given up for dead, then later discovered by fisherman who chanced to find him on a deserted shore.

Unfortunately, details of this romantic tale were always suspiciously vague. The primary source was a history of the Grand National, written by D.H. Monroe and published in New York in 1931. He wrote: 'There is a sort of Robinson Crusoe tale current in America with regard to *Moifaa* which seems to be unknown in England but it makes a splendid legend.

According to this story, *Moifaa* was ship-wrecked off the Irish coast ... Some fishermen, however, while about their business on an early morning a few days later, discovered the horse parading back and forth on the strand of a small island on which he had taken refuge and ferried him ashore ... In view of this story there is humour in the fact that *Moifaa*'s sire was a horse called *Natator* (swimmer)'.

This version of events was perpetuated in *National Velvet*, the best-selling children's novel by Enid Bagnold (1935) and in the hugely successful Hollywood film of the book (1944). Since then conflicting accounts have appeared in print. The most colourful 800-word version – published in May, 1969, in the now defunct British magazine W*eekend* – detailed how *Moifaa* was in a special stall fitted to the deck of a ship when he was swept into the sea during a fierce storm – off Cape Town!

'Passengers and crew took to the lifeboats and were eventually rescued. But *Moifaa* was written off as drowned. At dawn some days after the wreck, a fisherman was casting his nets off the shingly beach of a tiny deserted island when he heard a plaintive whinny. It was *Moifaa*, alive – but only just. He was barely breathing, his tongue was black and swollen, his coat caked with salt and his eyes bloodshot. He had somehow escaped from his stall and had either swum, or been swept, 100 miles from where he had been washed overboard'.

This extraordinary version would have us believe that the fisherman – reading reports of a New Zealand racehorse being drowned – sent a description of the horse to the English racing authorities; that subsequently *Moifaa*'s owner, Spencer Gollan, went out to see for himself and was so shocked by the horse's condition that he declared that he would never race again. 'But once in England, *Moifaa* began a gallant fight back to health. He improved sufficiently to be given gentle work on the flat and over low fences, and eventually Gollan decided to run him in a few minor events.'

The change of scene to Cape Town was especially puzzling. For years to come the popular story – accepted even by the highly respected Aintree historian, Mr Reg Green – was that '*Moifaa* was on his way to England early in 1904 when his ship capsized off the south coast of Ireland. The crew took to the lifeboats, leaving *Moifaa* to fend for himself. He jumped into the sea and came ashore on a spit of sand on the mainland, where he survived for three weeks before being discovered by Irish fishermen. A few weeks later, *Moifaa* went on to win the National at 25-1'.

However, in the absence of contemporary reports, *Moifaa*'s sensational shipwreck saga was always to be viewed with a large measure of caution. And finally, in 2004, it befell the leading racing journalist Brough Scott to separate fact from fiction. Following research in New Zealand, he reported in the *Racing Post* that *Moifaa* had never been shipwrecked, although another Kiwi import, *Kia Ora* (sic), 'had indeed been shipwrecked off Cape Town and was to run in the same National and thus spawn *Moifaa*'s 'swimming' story'.

Further research has identified the ship as the *S.S. Thermopylae* which was abandoned after striking a reef at Table Bay. Two horses, *Chesney* and *Kiora*, were left on board. Subsequently, a police officer swam out to the half-submerged ship and managed to free *Chesney*. There was no trace of *Kiora* who was presumed to have drowned. But ten hours later some locals found him on the shore at Mouille Point, exhausted but unharmed. In the 1904 National nine year old *Kiora* was to be an early faller while *Moifaa*, the winner, was wrongly identified as the shipwreck survivor.

No matter. The known facts behind the racing triumph of *Moifaa* are enough in themselves to establish him as one of the most colourful of all National victors. At the same time, contrary to many reports, he was not the most improbable of National winners. His appearance belied his proven ability. In New Zealand, he had won 11 of 16 races, including, as a five year old, a £500 three-and-a-half mile chase in which he carried 13 stone and conceded at least three stone to his rivals.

New Zealand bred – by *Natator* out of *Denbigh* – *Moifaa* had been sold for a mere £50 as a two year old. After his great winning run in 1901 under the ownership of the famed trainer-rider Alfred Ellingham, he was bought for £500 by Mr Spencer Gollan, a wealthy sheep farmer and bloodstock breeder who was also New Zealand's greatest all-round sportsman. From the beginning, Gollan's target was the

Grand National, a race never won by a New Zealand horse, the best so far having been *Levanter* who finished fifth at 50-1 in 1900, and then fourth as 5-1 favourite in 1901.

In England, *Moifaa* was sent to Epsom to be trained by Australian-born Mr 'Jim' Hickey, who had ridden Mr Gollan's *Norton*, a faller in the 1897 National. Privately, he showed brilliant form when being galloped four miles over fences. But this was not revealed in his three minor races in the build-up to Aintree. Instead he became the subject of derisive comments about his exceptional ugliness which showed to most striking effect on National day when he paraded alongside *Manifesto*, still magnificent-looking in his 17th year.

In the preliminaries, the eight year old gelding towered over all the other 25 runners, including King Edward VII's *Ambush II*, the 1900 winner, and now 7-2 favourite despite being burdened with the top weight of 12st 6lb – almost two stone more than the giant *Moifaa*. And his enormous power showed from the start as Arthur Birch, a relatively inexperienced jockey, needed all his strength to control the hard-pulling 'elephant'.

Moifaa's inordinate size, however, soon proved to be a positive advantage. There was a faller at the first jump; two more, including the favourite, at the third; and another two at the fourth. But while five more went down at the fifth, *Moifaa*'s bulky strength carried him through rather than over the thorn fence. This left him in the lead, and he was still ahead at the end of the first circuit with half the field already eliminated. Well-supported *Detail* was closing as they approached the second Becher's, but his challenge ended at the Canal Turn where he was brought down by the riderless *Ambush II*.

Moifaa was jumping brilliantly now and he was never in danger as he powered home to win by eight lengths from *Kirkland*, with only six others completing the course and the fallers including the aforementioned *Kiora*. It was the first time that the National had been won by a horse from the Colonies, and jockey Birch had won at the second attempt, having failed to finish three years before.

King Edward VII was so impressed by this performance that early in 1905 – after the death of *Ambush II* in training – he instructed Lord Marcus Beresford to negotiate the purchase of *Moifaa* as his Grand National replacement. Lord Beresford, who now described *Moifaa* as 'a great machine', duly

M

obliged at a cost of 2,000 guineas; and the king's new contender was made the 4-1 favourite with last year's runner-up, *Kirkland*, next at 6-1.

Moifaa now had a more experienced rider: Bill Dollery, who had won the 1893 National on *Cloister*. However, he had been raised 19lb in the weights, compared with *Kirkland*'s 9lb extra, and the difference told. The New Zealand giant fell at the second Becher's while *Kirkland* finished strongly, winning by three lengths from *Napper Tandy*. He never raced again. He was retired to work as a hunter; in addition he served as the king's ceremonial horse at the annual 'Trooping of the Colour'.

On May 21, 1910, following the death of Edward VII, the king's body was borne on a gun carriage through the hushed streets of London in a great procession, witnessed by an estimated 500,000 and joined by eight kings and more than 50 dukes, princes and princesses. Legend has it that one mourner, Kaiser Wilhelm II, complained about the order of precedence – because, behind the coffin, he found himself preceded by two animals: *Caesar*, the late king's fox terrier, led by a servant, and, bearing an empty saddle, the immaculately groomed *Moifaa*.

Sadly, however, this story has also been demolished by Brough Scott's research. Though *Moifaa* did figure in the funeral procession, it seems that he was ridden by General Brocklehurst to whom he had been gifted in 1906 to serve as his hack. In the circumstances, little credence can be given to another popularly recorded story: that *Moifaa* made his last public appearance on June 23, 1911 – being ridden in the coronation procession of King George V by Lord Kitchener who, ironically, was to drown at sea.

While *Moifaa* lived on to enjoy long retirement, those connected with his success were less fortunate. His rider, crippled by a fall at Gatwick, died in 1911, aged 36; and his trainer died in the same year, aged 41, in a mental asylum. As for *Moifaa*'s celebrated ex-owner, Spencer Gollan, he died in 1934, aged 74, having been run over by a London bus.

See also: Birch, Arthur; Gollan, Spencer; New Zealand.

MOLONEY, Jack

One of the unluckiest of all jockeys to ride in the Grand National. In his nine appearances between 1927 and 1939, Moloney three times finished runner-up, gained a fourth and fifth place, and in his last pre-war bid for glory was knocked over when colliding at the 28th fence with the eventual winner.

As a young Irish rider, Jack came to prominence in 1927 when riding *Grakle*, a difficult, headstrong five year old, in the Cheltenham Gold Cup. They finished two lengths second to *Thrown In*. Seventeen days later he rode *Grakle* in his first National and, like *Thrown In*, the horse was an early faller.

In the chaotic *Tipperary Tim* National of 1928 Moloney, on *Darracq*, was one of 40 of 42 riders who failed to complete the course. The following year, when a record 66 horses started, he was on the 9-1 favourite, *Easter Hero*, recent winner of the Cheltenham Gold Cup. This time he looked an almost certain winner as the brilliant chestnut, defying a top weight of 12st 7lb, led most of the way, out-jumping and outpacing all others. But then, near Valentine's second time around, *Easter Hero* spread a plate and began to falter. Bravely he ran on in pain, only to be overtaken after the second last by *Gregalach*, who had a 17lb advantage. He finished six lengths behind the 100-1 winner, with *Richmond II* a distant third.

Two years later, Maloney's fortunes took an ironic twist. This time he was on *Gregalach*, now a 25-1 shot, no longer strongly fancied after his fall in the 1930 National and yet again carrying 12st. Jack gave him a magnificent ride and took the last fence only a length behind the race leader. That leader was his former mount, *Grakle*, and with a 7lb advantage he just got up to win by one and a half lengths, in a time only two-fifths of a second outside the 38 year old course record.

In 1933 Moloney was fourth on the American-owned *Delaneige*. They returned together the following year, and again Jack had only one rival coming to the last. Unfortunately, that rival was the incomparable *Golden Miller*, and though *Delaneige* touched down alongside him he was outpaced on the run-in. For the third time, the cool, soft-spoken Irishman had finished second.

After a three-year break, he returned to Aintree, finishing fifth on *Delachance*. Then, in the 1939 National, he made a remarkable challenge on *Black Hawk*, a 40-1 chance, only to have his hopes dashed two fences out when he fell after a collision with *Workman*, who went on to win. Remarkably, eight years later, the veteran jockey came back one more time to ride a 66-1 outsider. His tenth and last National ended in a fall on *First Of The Dandies*, who was to finish one length second under Jimmy Brogan the following year.

MOLONY, Martin

Though he never completed the Aintree Grand National course, Martin Molony (born July 20, 1925) rates among the greatest riders of the post-Second World War era. His versatility was unequalled. Outstanding on the Flat, he won all the Irish Classics, plus the Irish Cesarewitch twice, and he was placed at Epsom in the Derby and the Oaks. At the same time, untroubled by weight problems, he proved no less brilliant over the jumps – winning three Irish Grand Nationals (1944, 1946 and 1950) and the 1951 Cheltenham Gold Cup on 12 year old *Silver Fame* before his riding career was prematurely ended by a skull-fracturing fall at Thurles. He was then only 26.

Martin's brilliant career was further limited by his refusal to follow the example of his elder brother Tim by leaving his native Ireland to take up a permanent position with a leading English stable. He was Irish champion jump jockey six years in succession in the immediate post-war years. But he appeared in only three Aintree Nationals. In 1946 and 1947 he had no chance on the long-shot, *E.P.*, first time pulled up and then a 100-1 faller. His one big hope came in 1948 when he was booked to the ride Lord Bicester's unbeaten *Silver Fame*, the 9-1 favourite. But the so promising nine year old, a half-brother to the 1940 winner, *Bogskar*, was never at his best at Aintree. As was to be his habit, he got no further than Becher's. One year later, Molony was due to ride Lord Bicester's *Roimond* in the National. But a few days before the race he was injured in a fall. Dick Francis, making his National debut, took over the ride and finished second.

Meanwhile, at Cheltenham, Martin had the misfortune to be competing against the irresistible combination of Aubrey Brabazon and Vincent O'Brien's *Cottage Rake*, winner of three successive Gold Cups. In 1948, on Miss Dorothy Paget's *Happy Home*, he finished second to them, by just one and a half lengths; and he was second to them again in 1950 on Lord Bicester's *Finnure*.

Then came his triumphant swansong. In 1951, waterlogged ground resulted in a postponement that saw the Gold Cup held 18 days after the Grand National. Molony was on the course specialist *Silver Fame*, and, in a neck-and-neck duel all the way up the hill, he found extraordinary reserves of strength to get his mount home in the very last stride – the winner by just a short head from Mr J. V.

Rank's *Greenogue*. It was the first time a 12 year old had won the Gold Cup. Then, sadly, only a few months later, came Martin's career-ending fall. He had ridden 179 winners in Ireland, Britain and the U.S.A.; and his 1950 Irish record of 94 jump winners in one year was to stand for 42 years before being broken by Charlie Swan.

Nearly half a century after his retirement from the saddle Martin was one of many famous riders and trainers attending a dinner at Dublin's Fitzpatrick Castle Hotel in celebration of Ireland's Cheltenham Gold Cup heroes. In his speech he nominated *Silver Fame* as 'the greatest I ever rode'. Years earlier, with equal authority, his late brother Tim had named Martin as 'the greatest jockey of them all'.

An Irishman of immense character and courage, Martin had a wife to match. Having suffered from muscular atrophy for many years, the wheelchair-bound Julia Molony was 63 when, in 2002, she undertook a sponsored skydive as part of her campaign to raise £1 million for five charities.

MOLONY, Tim

Like his younger brother Martin, Tim Molony stands out as one of the greatest of jockeys never to win the Grand National. Also, like his brother, he was renowned for his strength in a driving finish – a skill similarly developed by riding in many amateur Flat races before turning professional in 1939. In four successive seasons (1949-52) Tim was champion National Hunt jockey and he clinched the title a fifth time in 1955. Altogether, he won some 900 races (726 in Britain), including a record four successive Champion Hurdles (1951-54) and Vincent O'Brien's fourth Cheltenham Gold Cup on *Knock Hard* in 1953. Over Liverpool's big fences, he had many victories, among them two wins in the Grand Sefton Chase – on *Wot No Sun* and *Key Royal*.

Born in 1919, Tim rode in days before agents were employed, and he set the fashion for jockeys to ring up trainers for rides – ringing so often that for a while he was nicknamed 'telephone Tim'. But, as later shown by the fortunes of Peter Scudamore, John Francome and Tony McCoy, his years of domination as a jump jockey were no guarantee of success in the Aintree National. Tim had no fewer than 11 shots at the coveted prize. In the first nine he only once completed the course and that was after remounting *Bricett* to finish ninth in 1949. In 1951 he was on the 8-1 clear favourite, Mr J.H. Whitney's

M

Arctic Gold who had won his last three races. But after leading over Becher's the six year old was a faller in a chaotic race that saw only three finishers. In 1954 he was on *Dominick's Bar*, one of four horses to perish in the race. His last two rides were his best: fifth on *Key Royal* (1956) and sixth on *Goosander* (1957).

Through all these years, unlike most other riders, Tim was remarkably free of serious injuries. His contemporary, Dick Francis, described him as being 'made of india-rubber' – hence his nickname of The Rubber Man. But when, in 1958, he did finally suffer a broken leg in a fall, it marked the end of his career. Two years later he started training.

In 1967 he produced a lively contender for the National in seven year old *Rutherfords*, who took an early lead and was still at the head of affairs coming to the 23rd fence. But there he was knocked sideways as the riderless *Popham Down* swerved across the face of the fence, causing the biggest pile-up of all time. With only the trailing *Foinavon* clearing the small obstacle first time, *Rutherfords* eventually finished 16th.

Though unrealised at the time, that Aintree meeting was full of irony for Tim. On the day before the National, he had saddled a two year old who was hard-ridden to dead-heat in a five-furlong selling race. The horse, whom he had bought for 400 guineas at yearling sales, subsequently changed hands as a three year old and was moved out of his Melton Mowbray yard. His name was *Red Rum*.

Subequently, Tim was especially successful with the sprinter *Geopelia*. But it was not until late in his 20 year career as a trainer that he had his most notable success: *Carpet General*, winner of the William Hill Gold Cup. He died in 1989 at the age of 70. Named after him is Haydock's Tim Molony Memorial Handicap Chase, an extended three and a half mile race which has been won by numerous future winners of the Grand National.

MONAVEEN

The first Grand National runner (in 1950) to be owned by Queen Elizabeth, later the Queen Mother. To be precise, the royal ownership was shared by the Queen and her elder daughter, the then Princess Elizabeth, in whose name he ran at Aintree. But it was the former who remained dedicated to National Hunt racing while her daughter favoured the Flat.

Monaveen was chosen on behalf of the Queen by Lord Mildmay and his long-term friend, trainer Peter Cazalet. Irish-bred, with a pedigree that included the 1920 Derby winner, *Spion Kop*, he had made an undistinguished start to his career – being used to pull a milk float as a three year old and then, after falling in three English races, being sold for £35. He only began to show racing potential when, as a seven year old, he was fitted with a hood to aid concentration.

Having won two chases in the autumn of 1948, *Monaveen*, under the ownership of Mr D. Hawlesley, was entered for the 1949 Grand National. But he fell in his next race, with his jockey suffering a broken arm. The replacement rider was then injured on the eve of the National, and at the last minute Cazalet's stable jockey, Tony Grantham, was recruited to ride the gelding for the first time. The result was a most impressive showing over the first circuit, followed by a fall at the 19th, the open ditch.

Two months later *Monaveen* won a race at Folkestone, and he ran well in another in June. At that stage he was selected for royal ownership, making his first appearance in the colours of Princess Elizabeth in a three-horse race at Fontwell Park in October. He won with Grantham back in the saddle. And next, watched by the princess at Liverpool, he finished a close-up second to the brilliant *Freebooter* in the Grand Sefton Chase.

Those places were reversed when they met again in the newly instituted Queen Elizabeth Steeplechase at Hurst Park. Moreover, *Monaveen* won that three mile handicap comfortably and went on to a hat-trick of victories, so raising great hopes for his reappearance in the National. He was joint third in the betting, behind *Freebooter* and Lord Bicester's *Roimond*; and. on a warm spring day, the royals turned out in force to watch him run – the King and Queen, the two princesses, and the Duchess of Kent.

Ridden by Grantham, *Monaveen* jumped well throughout and, in a race plagued with falls, was the fifth of only seven finishers in a field of 49 starters, none of whom could match the pace of the Aintree specialist, *Freebooter*. Sadly, however, tragic events were close at hand. Two months after riding in the 1950 National, Lord Mildmay met his death by drowning. And then, back at Hurst Park for another Queen Elizabeth Chase, *Monaveen* fell at the water jump, broke a leg and had to be put down immediately.

See also: Royal Runners.

MONT TREMBLANT

Though beaten 20 lengths by *Early Mist* (receiving 17lb) in the 1953 Grand National, *Mont Tremblant* stands out as one of the great losers. As a six year old novice, the imposing French-bred chestnut gelding with a white blaze had won the 1952 Cheltenham Gold Cup by ten lengths. At Aintree, three weeks after being unplaced in the 1953 Gold Cup, he was burdened with 12st 5lb. For a seven year old this was an incredible top-weight, surpassed only by the 12st 7lb allotted the 1910 runner-up *Jerry M*, and 3lb more than the weight carried to victory by the great *Golden Miller* in 1934. Trained by Fulke Walwyn, *Mont Tremblant* – by *Gris Perle* out of *Paltoquette* – was the seventh and last of Dorothy Paget's Gold Cup winners. Unfortunately he lacked the sturdiness of her *Golden Miller* and, being prone to injury, failed to maintain his early brilliance. He did not compete in the National again and was unplaced in his third Gold Cup. However, at Cheltenham, he did score a famous victory in the 1955 Mildmay of Flete. *See also:* Paget, Dorothy; Walwyn, Fluke; Dick, Dave.

MONTY'S PASS

Winner by a comfortable 12 lengths of the 2003 Grand National which was judged to be of the very highest quality with no fewer than 35 of the 40 runners in the handicap proper. Always in the first six and jumping superbly, ten year old *Monty's Pass* went to the front two out and, under Barry Geraghty, galloped unchallenged past the Elbow to romp home for the third all-Irish success in five years.

By *Montelimar* (USA) out of *Friars Pass*, *Monty's Pass* was bought and trained by Jimmy Mangan, the same Co. Cork horse-trader who had originally bought as a yearling the 2002 Grand National winner *Bindaree* before selling him on a year later. This time, after selling on to a five-man syndicate, he remained as trainer, first running *Monty's Pass* in point-to-points and then hunter chases. Between 1999 and 2001, the gelding won six races over fences and was placed in many more. But it was not until 2002 that he showed he had matured into a chaser of real class. That year he ran well when a staying-on fifth in the Mildmay of Flete at Cheltenham; showed his ability to handle the big Aintree fences when runner-up in the Topham Chase; and then, in September, had his first major success – victory by two lengths in the Guinness

Kerry National over three miles at Listowel.

Reportedly, that Kerry win netted more than £200,000 for Mr Mike Futter, the big-punting head of the Dee Racing Syndicate that owned *Monty's Pass*. Now a far more ambitious coup was to be plotted. After one more run over fences in mid-October, the spectacular jumper was put away for the winter, and on his return in March he was tuned up for the Grand National in the now popular Irish fashion, with two spins over a mere two miles in novices' hurdles.

The one doubt about *Monty's Pass* – one not shared by the bullish Mangan – was his ability to stay four and a half miles. Before going to Aintree he had never won beyond three. But there was huge stable confidence behind him, especially with good ground for the National and the sun shining brilliantly. According to the trainer, having his first ever runner in the National, the horse was always at his best with sun on his back; and so it proved as he emerged to dominate what had previously seemed to be a highly competitive race. Jumping brilliantly throughout, he disputed the lead from the 15th and looked all over the winner when the front-running *Gunner Welburn* tired on approach to the second last. His winning time was an excellent 9min 21.70sec.

Monty's Pass won so impressively that trainer Mangan remarked: 'Aintree suits him so well, he could be another *Red Rum*.' But *Red Rum* had begun winning the National as an eight year old. *Monty's Pass* was ten years old and, now being fully exposed, was never again likely to start on 10st 7lb, receiving weight from 17 other runners. Indeed, when he had first run of the next season – again in the Kerry National – he had no chance in a race where he was giving 35lb to the first two horses home. And for the 2004 National he was raised a massive 17lb in the weights.

Magnan reported him to be 'in great shape', but part-owner Futter judged him to have a hopeless task at the weights and, sure enough, with dead ground also counting against him, he was well outpaced from the 22nd fence onwards. Nonetheless, he stayed on commendably to finish in fourth place at 20-1.

In January, 2005, on the day he was again entered for the National, *Monty's Pass* trailed home seventh and last in a two and a half mile chase at Thurles. Rider Geraghty was not too despondent, stressing that it was far too inadequate trip for the 12 year old. But again the weights were against him in the National. Burdened with 11st 6lb, only 4lb less than the

M

year before, the 12 year old weakened five out and came home the 16th of 21 finishers.
See also: Mangan, James; Geraghty, Barry; Gambles.

MOORE, Arthur

Son of the great Irish jockey-turned-trainer Dan Moore, Arthur's earliest memory of the Grand National was 1958 when, as an eight year old, he had one shilling each-way on the winning *Mr What* at 18-1. Following in his father's footsteps, he was to have four rides in the race – the first in 1970 when, aged 20, he rode *All Glory*, a 50-1 chance who fell at the 19th. The next year he won the Irish National on *King's Sprite*. But at Aintree his mount, *Smooth Dealer*, refused; and in 1972 he had to pull up on *Miss Hunter*. Finally, in 1973, he completed the course, finishing 12th on a 100-1 outsider, *The Pooka*.

Again, like his father, Arthur became one of Ireland's foremost jumps trainers. Notably, in 1989, he sent out *Feroda* to win on consecutive days at the Aintree Grand National meeting. But his few National runners were mostly long-shot no-hopers until 1996 when he had three entries – *Wylde Hide*, *Feathered Gale* and *Scribbler*. Only *Wylde Hide*, owned by the famed gambler J. P. McManus, made it to the line-up. A strongly supported 12-1 chance, he was hampered and unseated his rider when chasing the leading group at the Canal Turn second time around.

In 1997 Moore seemed to have an excellent chance of turning out the first Irish-trained Grand National winner since his father had scored with *L'Escargot* 22 years before. He was triple-handed, with *Wylde Hide*, *Feathered Gale* and *Back Bar*. Unfortunately, his great hope, the mud-loving *Wylde Hide*, was disadvantaged by the IRA bomb scare that led to a 49-hour postponement of the race. In the interim the drying ground counted against him. After making many mistakes he unseated Charlie Swan at the second Becher's.

Conversely, *Feathered Gale*, the 1996 Irish National winner, was supposedly helped by the faster ground. But he jumped poorly and was well tailed off when pulled up four out. Meanwhile the outsider *Back Bar* had fallen at the 17th. The following year Moore was without a National runner, both *Wylde Hide* and *Back Bar* having been withdrawn. But at least he was overjoyed on the day to see his *Jeffell* battle his way back to snatch victory by a head in the Martell Red Rum Chase.

In the 2002 National, Arthur ran *Lyreen Wonder*, a 40-1 chance ridden by newcomer Barry Cash, a second cousin of Walter Swinburn. The nine year old was making steady headway when being hampered and unseating his rider at the 20th. Moore's National tally was now ten runners without one completing the course. However, on the previous day, he had won the Martell Cognac Melling Chase with *Native Upmanship*; and he repeated that Aintree success in 2003 when the race was worth £87,000. Afterwards, as was his custom, he put his trilby on the horse in the winner's enclosure – just as his father had done on the same spot after the 1975 National won by *L'Escargot*.

In 2005 Moore had two runners in the National but still his curious record of non-finishers was maintained. His well-backed, French-bred *Marcus Du Berlais*, recent winner of the Leopardstown Chase, was always trailing and finally unseated Cash at the second Becher's. In contrast, his big outsider, 150-1 chance *Glenelly Gale*, led the field for most of the first circuit, only to weaken in the late stages, being pulled up after the 27th.

In 2006 he saddled 13 year old *Native Upmanship*, a 100-1 shot who was left at the start and finally refused at the 27th. The following year he was without a runner in the National and, at the end of a relatively quiet season in Ireland, he was back placing his trilby between the ears of a winner as his smart *Mansony* scored in the Kerrygold Champion Chase at Punchestown.

MOORE, Daniel

Never was a training triumph more deserved and more appropriate than in 1975 when Dan Moore saddled 12 year old *L'Escargot* who went on to win the Grand National after finishing third and second in the two previous years. It crowned the career of an Irishman who had been eminently associated with the race for 37 years, beginning with his extraordinary Aintree debut as a jockey.

In 1938, in his first National, Moore had a brilliant ride on seven year old *Royal Danieli*, sharing the lead at the first Becher's, striking the front at the tenth, and clearing the last two lengths ahead of his sole rival, the diminutive *Battleship*. Very gradually, on the long run-in, the gap was closed; and when they finished, divided by the width of the track, it was seemingly impossible to separate them. But then, after agonising minutes, the judges

338

declared *Battleship* the winner – by a head!

Until his dying day, Dan would remain convinced that he was in front at the line and that he had been robbed at a time when the photo-finish had not yet been introduced. He returned to ride *Royal Danieli* in two more Nationals, but now the big Irish gelding had been raised 10lb in the weights, each time being the most severely handicapped on 11st 13lb. In 1939 he fell heavily after a misjudged take-off at the first Becher's. In 1940, when 4-1 favourite, he led over Becher's, and was in strong contention for another circuit only to crash out at the second last.

With the Second World War restricting his riding to Ireland, it was 1948 when Dan had his next and final ride in the National, finishing 12th on the 33-1 chance, *Revelry*. Thereafter, his involvement was as a trainer, most notably preparing National contenders owned by Mr Raymond Guest, the millionaire U.S. ambassador to Ireland.

Though National success eluded him through two decades, he proved himself an outstanding trainer with an uncanny knack of spotting potential chasers. During the war he had brought a three year old which he later sold to Mrs Lurline Brotherton for some 3,000 guineas. The horse, named *Freebooter* and trained by Bobby Renton, won the 1950 Grand National. Then in 1964, the National was won by 12 year old *Team Spirit*, a diminutive chaser who, as a four year old, had been bought by the shrewd Moore at Ballsbridge Sales for a mere 250 guineas.

In 1960 he himself had had high hopes of National success with *Team Spirit* who initially had been hunted by his wife and able assistant, Joan. The brave little jumper was the 9-1 third favourite, having won the Mildmay Memorial Chase at Sandown and the four-mile National Trial at Hurst Park. But he was brought down at the second Becher's. Subsequently, he finished ninth in the 1961 National, and he fell at the 19th fence in 1962.

By this time *Team Spirit* had passed into new ownership and following a two-year spell without winning he was sent to Fulke Walwyn to be trained in England. Lower in the weights, and ridden as always by Willie Robinson, he finished fourth in the 1963 National and, without a penalty, triumphed at the fifth attempt as a 12 year old. Moore, it seemed, had missed his best chance of winning the National; and subsequently, without making any impression, he sent out a number of challengers owned by Raymond Guest, among them *Flying Wild*,

Packed Home, Cnoc Dubh and *Smooth Dealer*.

But by now, at last, Dan had a veritable wonder horse in his charge. For eight rewarding years Mr Guest's extraordinarily consistent *L'Escargot* was to be campaigned successfully – on the Flat, over hurdles and fences. Ridden by his son-in-law, Tommy Carberry, the ill-named 'snail' twice won the Cheltenham Gold Cup (1970 and 1971) before going on to National glory.

In 1978 Moore seemingly had another formidable Grand National challenger in *Tied Cottage* who had most encouragingly finished the 20-1 runner-up to *Davy Lad* in the 1977 Gold Cup. At Aintree he was made the 9-1 second favourite and this headstrong front-runner instantly grabbed the lead, though jumping increasingly to the left as he took the first five fences. In the circumstances, Carberry now made a rare and crucial error in taking him to the right side of the track to tackle Becher's where the drop was smallest. On approach, from about 30 yards out, *Tied Cottage* began pulling more and more left until, with a clear lead, he took the fence almost sideways on. Inevitably, he crumbled to the ground on landing.

Happily, *Tied Cottage* survived unscathed; and, ridden by amateur-owner Anthony Robinson, who had made a comeback after a long battle against cancer, he went on to a well overdue victory in the 1979 Irish National. But for trainer and owner more heartaches were to follow. In the next Gold Cup he unluckily fell when narrowly leading *Alverton* at the last. Then came the cruellest cut of all: in 1980, given a brilliant ride by Carberry, the 12 year old gelding led the Gold Cup field from start to finish and was eight lengths clear at the post, only to be later disqualified following a positive drug test.

Dan adored the Cheltenham Festival and had had 14 winners there. But his involvement with the meeting could not have ended in more tragic circumstances. At the time of the Festival, he was in the grip of a terminal illness. And it was three weeks later – during the Grand National meeting – that the Moores learned that *Tied Cottage* had lost the race on a technicality, having digested feed which, entirely inadvertently, had become contaminated by soya beans that had travelled in a cargo hold containing traces of cocoa. It was generally agreed that the traces of theobromine in his urine were so minute that they could never have affected his racing performance.

Within a few months of what had seemed a famous victory, both owner and trainer died. However, the Moores' long connection with the Grand National was to be carried on for decades to come – by Dan's son Arthur and by his maternal grandson, Paul Carberry, winner of the 1999 National on *Bobbyjo*. *See also:* L'Escargot; Moore, Arthur; Guest, Raymond.

MOORE, Garrett

The son of a celebrated Irish sportsman – John Hubert Moore of Jockey Hall, The Curragh – 'Garry' Moore made his Grand National debut in 1872, finishing eighth on *Scots Grey*. Six years later he returned to take third place on the mare *Pride of Kildare*, and the following year he won comfortably on *The Liberator*, a gelding – rejected at auction in 1876 – which his father had shrewdly purchased for £500.

Like his younger brother Willie, Garrett was a supremely stylish amateur rider – 6ft tall and needing to waste all of 10lb to make the 11st 4lb on *The Liberator*. Officially, in 1879, he was the winning rider and owner. However, his ownership was the outcome of a recent ugly dispute between his father and a Mr Plunkett Taaffe. By way of a court injunction, the latter had sought to restrain John Moore from running *The Liberator* in the National on the grounds that he was a co-owner. The Dublin court ruled against him, accepting that the partnership had been dissolved; and subsequently Mr Moore chose to run the horse in his son's name.

It was not the first time John Moore had figured in a National controversy. In 1878 fierce criticism had followed the withdrawal of his heavily backed *The Liberator* on the morning of the race, the suggestion being that, as trainer of two scheduled runners, he was seeking to improve the chances of his other entry, *Pride of Kildare*, ridden by his son Garry. With the additional late withdrawal of the 1877 winner *Austerlitz*, the field was now reduced to just a dozen runners, the smallest number since 1841. The race was won by *Shifnal* who, as favourite, had finished sixth the previous year.

In 1879 *The Liberator* was making its third appearance in the National. On his 1876 Aintree debut he had led the field before falling at the 21st; and in 1877, under the new ownership of J.H. Moore, he had been brought home a close-up third by the great Thomas Pickernell, who was having his 17th and last National ride. Now, with 'Mr Thomas' forced to

retire by injuries, Garrett took over on a day when nine of the 18 starters were ridden by amateurs, four of them from one Irish family, the brothers Beasley. His mount went off the 5-1 second favourite behind Captain James Machell's 1876 winner *Regal*, a stingy 5-2 chance.

Patiently ridden, but always handily placed, *The Liberator* moved up on the leaders from the second Becher's, struck the front after the second last, and then pulled away to win by ten lengths from Lord Marcus Beresford's *Jackal*. Garrett's only error was to win too far. As a result, his mount was set to carry an extra 17lb on his return in 1880, putting him on a top weight of 12st 7lb, a weight that had never been carried to National victory. Remarkably, Garry brought him home in second place, just two lengths behind *Empress* who was receiving a full two stone.

The handicapper was unrelenting. In 1881, as a 12 year old, *The Liberator* remained on the same top weight. Yet he went off as short as 6-1, third in the betting; and he led over the first and was still leading when he came down at Valentine's. There, lying on the turf, Garry suffered a severe shoulder injury on being kicked by *Cross Question*. Yet, with gritty determination, he remounted *The Liberator*, and astonishingly they made up considerable ground, completing the course as the last of nine finishers. It was Moore's fifth and last National ride. Finally beaten by rising weight, he quit the saddle to enjoy a long career as a trainer.

See also: The Liberator.

MOORE, William

The younger brother of Garrett, Willie Moore was first involved with the Grand National as an owner – a somewhat unhappy occasion in 1882 since his new charge, former winner *The Liberator*, was now 13 years old and making his sixth Aintree appearance under the prohibitive top weight of 12st 7lb. Ridden by Jimmy Adams, *The Liberator* was a faller in a race which saw only three of 12 starters finish.

Two years later Willie made his National debut as a rider, failing to finish on the six year old *Idea*; and one year later he was a faller on the five year old *Ben More*. Altogether he rode in seven Nationals and completed the course in just two – fourth on *Chancellor* (1887) and third on *M.P.* (1890). In 1888, the year that *Chancellor* was joint favourite, he failed to finish; and on his last appearance, in 1891, he fell on 25-1 shot *Veil*.

M

It was as a trainer – based at Weyhill, near Andover, Hampshire – that Moore left his indelible mark on the race. He trained three winners: *Why Not* (1894), successful at his fifth attempt; *The Soarer* (1896), victorious on his debut; and the great *Manifesto* (1899) when he achieved his second National victory with top weight of 12st 7lb and went on to finish third three times and finally eighth at the age of 16.

Years later Willie was to be succeeded at Weyhill by his nephew, Frank Hartigan, a versatile, highly successful trainer who would saddle the 1930 National winner, *Shaun Goilin*, and *Old Tay Bridge*, the runner-up in 1925 and 1926.
See also: Why Not; Soarer, The; Manifesto.

MR FRISK

The fastest-ever winner of the Grand National, breaking through the nine-minute barrier in 1990 and shattering by 14.1sec. the record of 9min 1.9sec set by *Red Rum* in 1973. Given the advantage of unusually fast ground, baked hard by weeks of sunshine and wind, he led from the second Becher's onwards. Thereafter, under his amateur rider, Marcus Armytage, he had only one challenger, the remarkably consistent 12 year old *Durham Edition* who was beaten by only three-quarters of a length, with *Rinus* 20 lengths back in third.

Bred by North Yorkshire farmer Mr Ralph Dalton, *Mr Frisk* – by *Bivouac* out of the mare *Jenny Frisk* – won four point-to-points before being sent to the 1986 Doncaster sales. Knowing the temperamental nature of the sire, trainer Kim Bailey was not inclined to make a bid. But his then wife, Tracey, liked the horse; and at her urgings he secured the seven year old gelding for 15,500 guineas. Subsequently Tracey was to play a key role in preparing the horse for his races, leading him off the reins rather than riding because he was prone to back problems and excitable.

Mr Dalton had assured the trainer that *Mr Frisk* went best on fast ground, and so Bailey chose to sell the chestnut gelding on to Mrs Lois Duffey, an American lady who usually visited England in the autumn, a time when there was a good chance of fast going. Mrs Duffey, a daughter of Walter Salmon, who had bred the 1938 Grand National winner *Battleship*, duly came over from Maryland and saw her horse have his first race at Devon and Exeter. That day the trainer feared the worst, so disappointing had 'Friskers' been on the gallops. To his utter

amazement, the novice jumper led from start to finish over three miles to win by 15 lengths. More incredibly, in his first season, he went on to win seven of his nine races.

The following season, when introduced to handicap races, *Mr Frisk* won only two chases. But he started the 1988-89 season well, winning the Punch Bowl Amateur Chase at Ascot, finishing third in the Hennessy Cognac Gold Cup, and winning the Sheila's Cottage Chase at Doncaster for the second successive year. Then, most significantly, he narrowly won the Anthony Mildmay-Peter Cazalet Memorial Chase at Sandown – a success that made him well regarded for the Grand National three months later.

Mrs Duffey was strongly opposed to risking her chaser over the National course. Finally, she agreed to having him entered while making it clear that she was likely to have him withdrawn at a later stage. She was not encouraged when *Mr Frisk* was allotted 10st 11lb, a weight exceeded only by that given to *The Thinker*, a former Cheltenham Gold Cup winner, and *Bonanza Boy*, the runaway Welsh National winner. And at the 11th hour, on seeing the heavy ground at Aintree, she was adamant. *Mr Frisk* would not run.

In the 1989-90 season, *Mr Frisk* again won the Punch Bowl and again finished third in the Hennessy, both with Marcus Armytage in the saddle. Subsequently, Kim Bailey took a gamble in entering him for the National in advance of gaining the owner's approval. Happily, two factors helped to persuade Mrs Duffey to let her horse run. *Mr Frisk* had been allocated the reasonable weight of 10st 6lb. Also, major modifications had been made to the Grand National course – most importantly, the filling in of the ditch on the landing side of Becher's where two horses had fallen fatally the previous year.

In his final Grand National prep-race, the three-mile Kim Muir Chase at Cheltenham, *Mr Frisk* finished fourth under top weight. Twenty-five days later, to the delight of connections, there was prevailing fast ground at Aintree. *The Thinker* had been withdrawn overnight; and the ground was against two well-backed contenders, *Bonanza Boy* and *Call Collect*. But it greatly favoured *Brown Windsor*, the eight year old who last season, as a novice, had won the Whitbread Gold Cup against more experienced handicappers. He went off the 7-1 favourite, with *Mr Frisk* on 16-1.

From the second fence onwards, it was another American-owned horse, *Uncle Merlin*, who took up

M

the running. Jumping superbly, the Maryland Hunt Cup winner set a furious pace and held off *Mr Frisk* and others throughout the first circuit. Coming to Becher's for the second time he was three lengths clear but there, surprisingly, he made his first mistake. He hit the top, pitched forward on landing, and jockey Hywel Davies was hanging round his neck before finally slipping sideways out of the saddle. Left six lengths in the lead, *Mr Frisk* was never headed despite a spirited late challenge from *Durham Edition*, runner-up for the second time.

With a winning time of 8min 47.8sec, *Mr Frisk* had shattered *Red Rum*'s course record and he underlined his class three weeks later by becoming the first chaser to complete the Grand National-Whitbread Gold Cup double in the same year. Indeed, Bailey rated his win at Sandown – by a record eight lengths margin – even more highly than his record-breaking run at Aintree. 'To me that was the performance of his life. He loved every single moment. He was never headed and took those railway fences with such panache it was extraordinary.'

The following season, as a 12 year old, *Mr Frisk* had fitness problems; and with good to soft going at Aintree and an extra stone to carry he was poor value at 25-1 for his National reappearance. Though prominent early on, he had to be pulled up by Armytage before the second Becher's. He did not run at Aintree again. Ironically, the horse who had raced unscathed over the fearsome National course had to be put down in September, 2000, after fracturing his off-hind when slipping on a road near Lambourn. He was aged 21. With watering of firmish ground at Aintree now the order of the day, his Grand National winning time is likely to stand forever.

See also: Bailey, Kim; Armytage, Marcus.

MR WHAT

The last horse to win the Grand National while still a novice – in 1958 when he scored by 30 lengths, the largest winning margin since the freak success of *Tipperary Tim* three decades before. His rider was the English jockey Arthur Freeman (booked only one week before the race) but otherwise it was strictly an Irish triumph – by an eight year old, Irish-bred, -owned and -trained, and racing outside of Ireland for the first time.

Most especially, it was a triumph for trainer Tom Taaffe who had bought *Mr What* (by *Grand Inquisitor* out of *Duchess of Pedulas*) as an unraced

five year old for £500. Early in 1956, in only his second race, *Mr What* won a highly competitive maiden hurdle at Navan and was sold to Dublin businessman Mr D. J. Coughlan. Then, still trained by Taaffe, he won four races over fences and finished second to *Roddy Owen* in the prestigious Leopardstown Chase.

Next came his Aintree debut and the key to his success was the extremely heavy going. *Mr What* was a mudlark and, after being hunted round the first circuit, grew in strength while all his rivals visibly weakened. After the Canal Turn he drew steadily away from the rest of the field. His only real mistake came when he hit the last fence hard. He stumbled on landing, but no matter; he already had a commanding lead which he maintained comfortably throughout the long run-in.

Mr What – so named because his breeder, Mrs Arthur O'Neill, did not know what to call him – was the first National winner for many years to have started the season as a novice chaser. Though he never won another steeplechase in more than 30 attempts, this should not detract from his considerable ability to jump and to stay. In truth, he was the victim of his own success; the handicapper would be unrelenting on a horse who had won by so far. In 1959, he was raised 17lb for his National return, and this time the good ground was not in his favour. Even so he went off the 6-1 clear favourite. Now ridden by 'Tosse' Taaffe, the trainer's son, he stayed on in the wake of many fallers, running creditably to gain third place, one and a half lengths and eight lengths behind *Oxo* and *Wyndburgh* respectively. Only four of 34 starters finished.

Remarkably, the handicapper raised *Mr What* yet again for the 1960 National – only 2lb, but enough to put him on top weight in the small field of 26 runners. Though reunited with Freeman, he faced a hopeless task on still faster ground and was a faller at the second Becher's. One year later, dropped only 2lb in the weight, he finished 11th with former winning jockey Dave Dick in the saddle.

In the 1962 National, *Mr What*, under new ownership, at last had the rain-sodden ground he loved; also he had been dropped a full stone in the weights. It made all the difference. He was a strong contender until the last fence, only to be well outpaced on the run-in – third again, this time behind two other 12 year olds, *Kilmore* and *Wyndburgh*.

Like the victorious *Kilmore*, *Mr What*, now trained by ex-jockey Jack Dowdeswell, came back in 1963. It was his sixth and last National, and as a 66-1 outsider he was brought down four fences from home – a disappointing debut for a young rider who would make many more appearances before winning the race 12 years later: one Tommy Carberry. *See also:* Taaffe, Thomas J; Freeman, Arthur.

MULLINS, William

Born on September 5, 1956 into one of Ireland's most celebrated racing dynasties, trainer Willie Mullins had dreamed of winning the Grand National ever since watching the race on television as a nine year old. Nearly four decades later he finally achieved that ambition with the 14-length victory of *Hedgehunter* in 2005. His four previous contenders had all failed to complete the course.

As a jockey, Willie won the Irish amateur championship six times. His successes in England included the 1983 Fox Hunters' Chase at Aintree and four Cheltenham Festival bumpers. But he only rode in the Aintree National twice. In 1983 he was on 12 year old *The Lady's Master*, a 200-1 outsider who ran out. The following year he fell at the sixth on another long-shot, 100-1 *Hazy Down*. Meanwhile his father, the legendary Paddy Mullins, was enjoying his greatest period as trainer, crowning it with *Dawn Run*'s unforgettable winning of the 1986 Cheltenham Gold Cup.

Although Willie started training in 1988, he continued to ride until 1996 when he scored his last big win: on *Wither Or Which* in the Cheltenham Champion bumper. He had already had many training successses in Ireland, but it was not until 2000 that he saddled his first runner in the National. It proved a most discouraging start. His opening bid was with *Micko's Dream*, a well-fancied 14-1 chance who, only eight years old, had already won nine chases and more than Ir£100,000. The big-punting owners were 24 Irish prison officials who travelled to Aintree en masse and promised to parade their horse at Portlaoise jail if he won. Alas, *Micko's Dream* fell with Jason Titley at the first fence, the only consolation for Mullins being the fact that the race was won by *Papillon*, ridden by one of his stable's regular jockeys, Ruby Walsh.

Mullins, now Ireland's champion jumps trainer, was back in 2002 to enjoy his first wins at the Aintree meeting. On the opening day his greatest star *Florida Pearl* – winner of three Irish Hennessys, the 2001 King George VI Chase and Cheltenham's

Royal and SunAlliance Chase and Champion Bumper – won the Martell Cup Chase with Barry Geraghty to take his earnings to more than £700,000. The next day he turned out *Its Time For A Win* to win the Topham Chase under Walsh.

He had resisted the temptation to run *Florida Pearl* (allotted top weight of 11st 12lb) in the National. Now his hopes rested on another superstar, *Alexander Banquet*, who, despite being plagued by injuries, had a distinguished CV – a winner of eight of the first nine of his 17 races, and having taken the Irish Hennessy on his penultimate start before finishing sixth in the Cheltenham Gold Cup.

Unfortunately, the going was not as testing as he would have liked and, burdened with the second highest weight of 11st 11lb, he blundered and unseated Geraghty at the first Becher's. When he returned two years later he had indifferent seasonal form and, as an unfancied 50-1 chance, he fell at the 18th.

At that point, however, Mullins still had high hopes of having his first National winner. His *Hedgehunter*, an eight year old who had never fallen, was running as strongly as any under David Casey, and looking at least certain of a place – until, at the final fence, lying a close-up third, he fell from exhaustion.

In 2005, with *Rule Supreme*, the trainer won his sixth Hennessy Cognac Gold Cup in seven years. Meanwhile he had shrewdly confined *Hedgehunter* to five runs over hurdles, so protecting his handicap mark. Only after he had been allotted the same National weight as before did he give him a run (a winning one) over fences. One week before going to Aintree *Hedgehunter* had a minor infection. Mullins chose to keep it a secret, even from both owner and jockey; and it was so well kept that the nine year old gelding went off the 7-1 clear favourite. He duly won comfortably, with Walsh only having to push him hard on nearing the Elbow.

It was an especially timely triumph since the great Paddy Mullins, aged 86, had only just retired, handing over the licence at his Co. Kilkenny yard to his youngest son Tom. His all-round successes in a career spanning more than half a century included four Irish Grand Nationals, a Cheltenham Gold Cup and Champion Hurdle, a 1973 Champion Stakes at Newmarket, and remarkably an Irish Oaks, scored in 2003 when he was 84 years old.

In 2006, Willie again had *Hedgehunter* supremely fine-tuned, and just three weeks after his brilliant second-placed run in the Cheltenham Gold Cup

M

the ten year old went off as 5-1 joint favourite in the National. Just as the trainer feared, overnight rain and a later shower tipped the scales against *Hedgehunter* in his bid on top weight to score an historic back-to-back win. Nonetheless, in finishing runner-up to *Numbersixvalverde* who had an 18lb, advantage, he proved himself one of the Aintree greats.

Two weeks later, Willie had a leading contender *Our Ben* in the Irish Grand National. But, like *Hedgehunter*, his seven year old novice was lumbered with 11st 12lb top weight; and this time, ironically, it was drying ground that counted against him and he had to be pulled up.

Willie had long ago established himself as an outstanding trainer, not only in Ireland and at Aintree but also at Cheltenham where his many wins included a remarkable five bumpers. Moreover, the great family tradition was already assured of being carried on for generations to come. All of Paddy's five offspring – Willie, Tom, George. Tony and Sandra – were involved in racing; and remarkably, in the 2007 Totesport Trophy Handicap Hurdle at Newbury, no fewer than five members of the Mullins clan had runners: the four brothers together with their cousin Seamus Mullins who was training some decent chasers in Wiltshire.

That season both Willie and brother Tony had a winner at the Cheltenham Festival. Earlier the former has suffered a terrible loss with the fatality of his Gold Cup hope *Missed That*. But he had the first two in the valuable Thyestes Chase – *Homer Wells* and *Livingstonebramble* – and both were entered for the Grand National, along with *Bothar Na*, *Hedgehunter*, *Joueur d'Estruval* and *Our Ben*.

Four made it to the line-up. *Hedgehunter*, anchored on a top weight of 11st 12lb, finished a distant ninth. *Bothar Na* was pulled up before two out, *Homer Wells* before the second Becher's; and 100-1 shot *Livingstonebramble* unseated his rider at the sixth. Nevertheless, Willie went on to finish the season second to Noel Meade in the Irish jumps trainers' table with 79 winners and prize money of more than 1.5 million euros.
See also: Hedgehunter; Walsh, Ruby.

MUSIC HALL

Nine year old winner of the 1922 Grand National in which half the 32-strong field was eliminated by Becher's Brook and only two of five finishers got round without being remounted. For jockey Lewis Rees it was a National victory following immediately after that of his younger brother Fred on *Shaun Spadah*. And it represented an auspicious start to the training career of Owen Anthony, brother of Jack Anthony, who had ridden to his third National success just two years before.

Sired in County Kildare – by the Northumberland Plate winner *Cliftonhall* out of *Molly – Music Hall* came to Aintree with excellent credentials. As a seven year old, he had won seven races including the 1920 Scottish Grand National. Subsequently he had been sold to Manchester cotton broker Hugh Kershaw, and a few weeks before facing his first Grand National he had won a four-mile handicap chase at Hurst Park.

As in the previous year this was a chaotic National with both the favourite *Southampton* and *Shaun Spadah* falling at the first fence, and only half a dozen runners still standing as the leaders approached the second Valentine's. Here the three main survivors – *Music Hall*, *Drifter* and *A Double Escape* – came perilously close together in a virtual barging match. Though Rees lost an iron, he was luckier than his rivals. *Drifter* split a pastern and *A Double Escape* was so shaken that he fell at the next fence. The former ran on in considerable pain and gamely challenged for the lead at the last. But the handicap was too great, and *Music Hall* plodded on to a twelve lengths victory – the first to have succeeded at Aintree after winning the Scottish National.

Following his National success *Music Hall* finished a good second in the Lancashire Steeplechase at Manchester, then broke down when dominating the field in the Grand Steeplechase de Paris at Auteuil. On his return to Aintree in 1924 he was ridden by the masterful Jack Anthony. But he was now anchored on a top weight of 12st 7lb and soon had to be pulled up. Well past his best, he ran in his third and last National in 1925 when, reunited with Rees, he was a 66-1 outsider, retired after an early refusal.
See also: Rees, Lewis; Anthony, Owen.

MY PRINCE
See also: Sires

344

NATIONAL HUNT COMMITTEE

The formation in 1866 of the National Hunt Committee represented a major milestone in the history of the Grand National. In earlier years the National had somewhat fallen into disrepute, and steeplechasing in general was very much regarded as the poor, rather unsavoury relation of racing on the Flat. Now, with the approval of the Jockey Club, a 14-strong committee took responsibility for regulating steeplechasing; and over the next decade they would greatly improve the image of the sport by way of newly formulated rules and controls strictly enforced by stewards.

Most of the founder members were highly respected figures in racing who had at one time served as members of the Jockey Club; and a number of them had strong connections with the Grand National. They included Mr B.J. Angell and Captain Henry Coventry, owner and rider respectively of the 1865 winner *Alcibiade*; Lord Coventry, owner of winners *Emblem* (1863) and *Emblematic* (1864); Lord Poulett who would win the National with *The Lamb* (1868 and 1871); and Captain J.L. Little who rode the 1848 winner *Chandler* and owned the 1853 winner *Peter Simple*.

On its centenary in 1966 the National Hunt Committee merged with the Jockey Club, the two bodies being fully amalgamated three years later. Then, in June, 1993, their activities were taken over by the British Horseracing Board (BHB), the newly formed governing authority of British racing. In turn, the BHB was succeeded in 2007 by the British Horseracing Authority.

See also: Angell, Benjamin John.

NATIONAL VELVET

National Velvet, Enid Bagnold's 1935 children's novel, was the first best-selling fictional work to focus on the Grand National, its plot revolving around the experiences of Velvet Brown, the 14 year old daughter of an English butcher who wins a piebald gelding with a one shilling raffle ticket and who, within a year, achieves her dream of riding him to victory (overruled after an objection) in the greatest steeplechase on earth.

However, it is the 1944 Hollywood film of the book that has had the most significant impact. Starring a juvenile Elizabeth Taylor, it aroused dreams of glory in many lady riders, including Charlotte Brew who, in 1977, at the age of 21, became the first woman to ride in the National. Not least, it had an inspirational effect on a child viewer called Jennifer Harvey. Years later, as Jenny Pitman, the celebrated trainer of two National winners, she would still watch the film on its many television repeats.

While the book is well-researched in describing the scene at Aintree, the film deviates from the story-line in many respects and is much less accurate in its details of the race. The movie commentator announces that 'there are horses from England, Ireland, France, Spain – and half a dozen other countries'. The starter declares it to be 'a five-mile race' and, whereas Miss Bagnold's National is run in rain on heavy going, the film has the runners going at an absurdly frantic pace, with hooves thundering over rock-hard Californian ground and the leaders finishing like six-furlong sprinters.

Understandably, the film, unlike the book, does not have Velvet Brown confronting naked jockeys in the Aintree changing room. On one important detail, however, both versions concur: Velvet falls to the ground after passing the winning post on *The Piebald* and an objection is immediately lodged under Rule 144 which states that a rider must not dismount before reaching the unsaddling enclosure. The declared winner (in the book) is *Tim's Chance*; in the film, *Ebony Star*.

The Piebald (shortened to *The Pie* in the film) was 'played' by a high-spirited gelding named *King Charles*, a grandson of the great *Man o' War*. Liz Taylor, who had been riding ponies since the age of three, rode him in many sequences with Australian jockey Snowy Baker doubling for her over the big jumps. MGM presented *King Charles* to Liz for her 13th birthday. Many years later Miss Taylor owned several racehorses but there was never a chance of her making a bid for the Grand National. As John Gosden, once employed as her trainer, said: 'She never wanted her horses to run in case they injured themselves' – and that was just on the Flat.

NEWEY, Alfred

In 1905, on the first of his nine Grand National rides, Alfred Newey rode the 100-1 outsider *Buckaway II* into third place, one of only seven of 27 starters to finish. The following year he fell on the same gelding, but then, in 1907, he bounced back spectacularly to win in extraordinary style on the seven year old newcomer *Eremon*.

Everything seemed to be against Newey that day.

N

By the third fence a broken stirrup leather had resulted in him surrendering the lead, and he rode the rest of the race without one of his irons. Eventually, when renewing his challenge at Becher's, he found his mount being continually harried by a riderless horse, Prince Hatzfeldt's six year old *Rathvale*. In desperation, at the Canal Turn, he used his whip to keep the rogue horse at bay.

On the second circuit, after bringing down another runner at the Water, *Rathvale* continued to veer erratically across *Eremon*'s path; and again and again Newey found the need to lash out with his whip. While he successfully kept out of trouble, four horses came to grief at the Canal Turn, leaving *Eremon* with a substantial lead. By Valentine's he was 20 lengths ahead of the field and, though visibly tiring, he held on to win by six lengths from *Tom West*, with *Patlander*, an unquoted outsider, a neck back in third.

Ten days later, after *Eremon* had carried an extra 12lb to a comfortable victory in the Lancashire Chase, Newey had high hopes that the improving seven year old might carry him to a second Aintree success. Those hopes were dashed several weeks later when *Eremon* suffered a fatal injury after bolting on the gallops.

Alf Newey, a short-legged little man from Worcestershire, was to ride in six more Nationals, but he would only once more complete the course. His best chance of a second win appeared to be in 1911 when he took over the ride on Mr Frank Bibby's useful *Caubeen* who had finished third of 32 starters in 1909 and who had been unluckily knocked over in 1910. *Caubeen* was now joint second with *Rathnally* in the betting, behind a favourite, former winner *Lutteur III*, who was anchored on a top weight of 12st 3lb.

Again, however, *Caubeen* was unlucky in running. With a mass of fallers behind them, he and *Rathnally* were vying for the lead when they collided and fell in going for the same gap in the 23rd fence. It left the race at the mercy of Mr Bibby's less fancied runner, the one-eyed *Glenside*, who laboured home in quagmire conditions to win by 20 lengths from the remounted *Rathnally* and two other finishers, also remounted.

One year later Newey again made a most promising challenge on *Caubeen*. They led round the first circuit and for much of the second. But the 11 year old now faded badly and had to be pulled up before the 28th. In 1913 Alf fell on the six year old *Wavelet*.

Then, on his return in 1915, he rode a masterful race on Mr Bower Ismay's *Jacobus*, making a spirited late challenge to bring the 25-1 shot home in second place, beaten two lengths by *Ally Sloper*, with *Father Confessor* eight lengths back in third.

There were no more Aintree Nationals during the First World War. In 1922, 17 years after his third-placed debut, Newey came back for one more ride, taking an early fall on *Grey Dawn* in a chaotic race that saw only three of 32 starters completing the course without a fall.

See also: Eremon.

NEW ZEALAND

The first New Zealand horse to make any impression in the Grand National was *Levanter*, fifth at 50-1 in 1900 and fourth as 5-1 favourite in 1901. Three years later came the first Kiwi victory, scored by the giant *Moifaa*, a 25-1 winner owned by Spencer Gollan, the celebrated sportsman who had previously challenged with his chestnut gelding *Norton*, a faller in 1897.

It was not until 1991 that a New Zealand-bred horse triumphed again at Aintree. That year's Grand National saw the appearance of three Kiwi imports. *Mister Christian*, a 100-1 chance, was in touch on the first circuit but then faded fast before being pulled up at the 21st. *Bumbles Folly*, a 150-1 no-hoper, was also pulled up. But the third Kiwi was the brilliant *Seagram*, a small, tough gelding brought to England as a three year old by Devon trainer David Barons. With a sustained finishing burst, the 12-1 shot overhauled the Cheltenham Gold Cup winner *Garrison Savannah* 100 yards out to win by five lengths.

Six years later *Lord Gyllene* became the third New Zealander to win the National – in his case leading the field from start to finish when the race was postponed for 49 hours following an IRA bomb scare. In winning by 25 lengths, this relentless galloper jumped immaculately and exemplified the toughness and stamina of the Kiwi breed. Other Kiwi-bred chasers to make their mark in Britain include *Royal Mail*, the 1981 Whitbread Gold Cup winner, and *Playschool*, winner of the Hennessy and the Welsh National in 1987.

With a population of only 3.5 million, New Zealand supports a staggering 54 racecourses; and it has a major breeding industry, exporting horses to countries in the southern hemisphere and regularly sending out raiders to Australia, much as Ireland does to Britain. Its premier jump race is the Great Northern Steeplechase run in June over four miles and 25 fences at Auckland's Ellerslie track. Women jockeys – notably Michelle Hopkins and Tracy Egan – have been successful there over jumps.

See also: Moifaa; Gollan, Spencer; Seagram; Lord Gyllene; Barons, David; Clarke, Sir Stanley.

NICHOLLS, Paul

Based at Ditcheat, near Shepton Mallet in Somerset, Paul Nicholls emerged in the late 1990s as the only trainer capable of challenging the mighty juggernaut of the Martin Pipe stable, being runner-up to his great rival in the jump trainers' championship every year from 1999 to 2005. It was a measure of his extraordinary strike-rate that in 2003 he had 153 winners from 583 runners and prize money of £2,164,314. Pipe (190 winners) had netted £2,578,930 but he had competed in 350 more races and had sent out 78 more runners. Similarly, in 2004, Nicholls's winnings of £2,191,809 from 650 runners compared more than favourably with Pipe's return of £2,407,356 from a staggering 1,069 runners.

In 2005 Pipe became champion trainer for the 15th time with £2,827,073 from 1,168 runners compared with Nicholls' £2,754,204 from only 709 runners. Then, in 2005-06, Pipe's final season, Nicholls at last took the title for the first time; and when he retained it the following year it was with prize money approaching an unprecedented £3 million – more than £1 million ahead of his nearest rivals, Jonjo O'Neill and David Pipe.

In view of his truly outstanding record as a jumps trainer, it is extraordinary that Nicholls, against all odds, has gained the unenviable distinction of being the trainer most frustrated in his tilts at the Grand National. Between 1992 and 2007 he had 37 runners in the race with only seven completing the course. Until 2005 none had even finished in a place. At that stage his best result in nine Nationals was a fifth place in 2003 when Montifault, under Joe Tizzard, finished in that position at 33-1.

In 2005, however, Nicholls at last had a horse in the National frame: Royal Auclair. Under newcomer Christian Williams and carrying a mighty 11st 10lb, this 40-1 chance ran brilliantly to finish runner-up to Hedgehunter and to hold off by a head third-placed Simply Gifted, who had an 18lb advantage in the weights.

Nicholls' Grand National CV now reads: 1992, Just So (sixth); 1996, Vicompt De Valmont (tenth), Deep Bramble (pu. before two out), Brackenfield (ur. 19th); 1997, Straight Talk (fell 14th); 1998, What A Hand (fell first), Court Melody (fell sixth), General Crack (pu. 11th); 1999, Strong Chairman (15th), Double Thriller (fell first); 2000, Earthmover (fell fourth), Torduff Express (fell 13th), Flaked Oats, (fell 20th), Escartefigue (ur. 30th); 2001, Earthmover (fell fourth); 2002, Murt's Man (pu. before 17th), Ad Hoc (bd. 27th); 2003, Montifault (fifth), Ad Hoc (fell 19th), Shotgun Willy (pu. 21st), Fadalko (ur. sixth), Torduff Express (fell 27th); 2004, Exit To Wave (pu. before the ninth); 2005, Royal Auclair (second), Heros Collonges (eighth), L'Aventure (15th) and Ad Hoc (fell 22nd); 2006, Royal Auclair (fell first), Cornish Rebel and Le Roi Miguel (pu. before 19th), Silver Birch (fell 15th), Le Duc (ur. eighth) and Heros Collonges (ur. 15th); 2007, Le Duc (ur. sixth), Eurotrek (pu. before 22nd), Thisthatandtother (pu. before the last), and Royal Auclair (fell ninth).

In other major races Nicholls has triumphed with many outstanding jumpers, among them Belmont King (1997 Scottish National), See More Business (1999 Cheltenham Gold Cup and the King George VI Chase of 1997 and 1999), Call Equiname (1999 Queen Mother Champion Chase), Flagship Uberalles (1999 Arkle Chase), Ad Hoc (2001, Whitbread Gold Cup), Strong Flow (2003 Hennessy Cognac Gold Cup) and Kauto Star (2007 King George and Cheltenham Gold Cup), plus such popular stars as Earthmover, Fadalko and Double Thriller.

Bristol born, on April 17, 1962, the son and grandson of a policeman, Nicholls progressed as a schoolboy via gymkhana, hunting and point-to-pointing, rode as an amateur for Les Kennard, then worked for Josh Gifford. He made his mark as a professional jump jockey in the 1980s, riding primarily for West Country trainer David Barons. In that decade he rode 130 winners under Rules – most notably Broadheath (1986 Hennessy) and Playschool (1987 Hennessy, Welsh National and Irish Gold Cup). He rode in two Grand Nationals without getting round. But that was hardly surprising. In 1985 he was on Roman Bistro, a 150-1 chance; the following year on 13 year old Another Duke, a 200-1 no-hoper leased by Des Lynam.

His one truly great regret as a jockey was failing to win the 1988 Cheltenham Gold Cup when he was on the favourite *Playschool*. That day the tough New Zealand-bred gelding ran like a drunken sailor, so hopelessly out of sorts that he had to be pulled up three fences from home. He was never the same horse again; and, though he had passed dope tests, connections remained convinced that he must have been nobbled in some way.

Nicholls' riding career – long threatened by weight problems, peaking at 12st 4lb in the summer of 1989 – was finally cut short by injury, his retirement from the saddle being on medical advice after he had twice broken a leg. He then had two years as assistant trainer to David Barons and in 1991 played a major part in the preparation of Grand National winner *Seagram*. The following year, only a few months after taking out a training licence, he had his own first National runner: *Just So*. It was an encouraging start – the renowned mudlark finishing sixth at 50-1. Two years later, revelling in the heavy going, *Just So* was to be the 20-1 runner-up in the National, just one length and a quarter behind Pipe-trained *Miinnehoma*. But by then the gelding was with a different stable.

Nicholls was now making remarkable progress in building up a high quality training centre at the Manor Farm Stables owned by dairy farmer Paul Barber. In 1994, however, he suffered a most serious blow when his outstanding prospect, *See More Indians*, had to be destroyed after injuring himself while out at grass. *Deep Bramble*, a hugely promising chaser by *Deep Run*, was bought by owner Barber as a replacement; and his subsequent wins made him a strong fancy for the National. But again the trainer was unlucky. *Deep Bramble* never made it to Aintree, having torn neck and shoulder muscles in the Cheltenham Gold Cup.

It was not until 1996 that Nicholls was represented in the National for a second time. This year he had three runners. Most disappointingly his strongly supported *Deep Bramble*, ridden by the great A. P. McCoy, was looking a major threat when he broke down and had to be pulled up before the second-last fence. He had ruptured a near-fore tendon. And worse misfortune followed in 1997. The two-day postponement of the National in the face of IRA bomb threats caused the trainer to withdraw *Belmont King* in the light of the drying ground. Then, cruellest of all, he sent *Straight Talk* back to Liverpool only to see him suffer a fatal fall at the 14th. The one consolation was that *Belmont King* went on to win the Scottish National.

Two years later, however, Nicholls' hopes of a Grand National winner were sky high again. He had two runners: *Strong Chairman* and *Double Thriller*. The latter, an imposing, nine year old giant (17.2 hands), was all the rage from the moment that the weights were announced; and incredibly he became as short as 7-2 after finishing fourth in the Cheltenham Gold Cup.

The situation was hugely dramatic. At the Cheltenham Festival, Paul had sent out the winners of the Gold Cup, the Queen Mother Champion Chase and the Arkle Chase to establish a useful lead over his arch-rival Pipe in the trainers' championship. Now, if *Double Thriller* won at Aintree, he would secure the title he so richly deserved and at the same time become the first trainer since Fred Rimell in 1976 to saddle winners of the Gold Cup and Grand National in the same season.

The disappointment could not have been greater. *Double Thriller* went off the 7-1 joint second favourite under Joe Tizzard and, though wearing a cross noseband to help him settle, he crashed out at the first fence. *Strong Chairman* finished 15th at 50-1. The Grand National hoodoo continued in 2000 when Paul's four runners all failed to finish; and 2002 brought another major disappointment as *Ad Hoc* was unluckily brought down at the 27th when looking a very possible winner.

Then, in 2003, Nicholls seemingly had his finest chance of a Grand National victory – so fine, in fact, that he was made 5-2 favourite to be the winning trainer. His five runners – only one less than Martin Pipe – included *Ad Hoc*, the long-time market leader, and *Shotgun Willy*, backed down to 7-1 favouritism on the day. Both had National-winning riders: Paul Carberry and Ruby Walsh respectively. The day started well for the trainer as he sent out the first and second in the Martell Maghull Novices' Chase. Yet still he was denied success in the big one.

Again, in 2004, Nicholls was engaged in a seesaw, neck-and-neck duel with Pipe in the trainers' championship. At Cheltenham he snatched the lead with a treble, winning the Grand Annual Handicap Chase with *St. Pirran*, the County Handicap Hurdle with *Sporazene*, and, most emotionally, the Foxhunter Chase with 13 year old *Earthmover*, remarkably revitalised to repeat his victory of six years before. He also made his mark at the Grand National meeting, briefly heading his rival when his *Garde Champetre* won the Martell Makro Novices Hurdle.

But he ended up £68,000 in arrears after Pipe had collected for *Lord Atterbury*'s third place in the National. As usual, it was an uneven contest. Pipe had had seven runners in the National while Nicholls had only one, *Exit To Wave*, a 50-1 shot who had not won a race since early 2001.

At the last big jumps meeting of the season, Paul sent out Sandown specialist *Cenkos* to win the Queen Elizabeth Celebration Chase, but Pipe had already sealed his 14th trainers' title with *Korelo*'s winning of a handicap hurdle, and then for good measure he had won the £87,000 Betfred (formerly Whitbread) Gold Cup with *Puntal*, one of his seven runners in the race. Nicholls, in contrast, had only two runners, his 33-1 shot *Royal Auclair* being beaten by just a short head.

The year 2004 ended with hopes of Grand National success revived anew following the hugely impressive run of seven year old *Silver Birch* in the Welsh National, a winning hot favourite under Ruby Walsh. He had already won the Becher Chase over the big Aintree fences and at this stage he was made favourite – one of seven Nicholls entries – for the National. Alas, he had to be withdrawn with a slight leg injury.

Nevertheless, four of Nicholls' entries made it to the National line-up, and this time he not only equalled Pipe's number of runners but he also had the satisfaction of at last outscoring his great rival in the race. With *Royal Auclair* he took the second-place £154,000 prize while Pipe had to settle for a mere £35,000 for *It Takes Time*'s fourth place.

In their annual duel for the trainers' championship Nicholls had now reduced Pipe's lead to £53,000. One week later he narrowly missed the chance to close the gap by £43,448 when his *Cornish Rebel* was beaten a short head in the Scottish National, but at least on the following day a string of lesser wins had left him only £23,792 adrift of the champion trainer. Finally, on the last day of the season, the battle was decided at Sandown where Pipe's *Well Chief* outstayed Nicholls' *Azertyuiop* in the Celebration Chase and both trainers failed with their bids to win the Betfred Gold Cup. Nicholls had now been runner-up to Pipe in seven successive seasons.

In the 2005-06 season the tide turned at last. Nicholls set the pace, reaching 100 winners by January. He sent out the first three home in the Welsh National and, following an unprecedented six-timer at one meeting (Wincanton), he pulled £436,000

clear of Pipe in the title race. That lead stretched to more than £700,000 at the Cheltenham Festival where Pipe was winless for the first time since 1988 and Nicholls, the leading trainer of the meeting, enjoyed three successes: the £57,020 Supreme Novices' Hurdle with *Noland*; the Royal and SunAlliance Chase (*Star De Mohaison*); and the County Hurdle (*Desert Quest*).

For the Grand National he had ten entries compared with Pipe's staggering 22. Six made it to the Aintree line-up, chasers of such high quality that he was 7-2 to train the winner. Remarkably, however, not one of his six completed the course, the biggest shock being the first fence fall of last year's runner-up *Royal Auclair*. During the meeting he was also saddened by news that *Playschool* had died, aged 28, of a heart attack. Nicholls rated him as one of the best he ever rode, if not the best.

The Somerset trainer had now had 33 runners in the Grand National with only one making the frame. And two weeks after Aintree, for the second successive season, he missed having a second Scottish Grand National winner by a short head. Nonetheless, this was a time for celebration as he finally acknowledged that he could not be caught in the race for the trainers' title. His dream was realised at last, his record for the season being prize money of £2,455,466 with 148 wins from 651 runners. Though he had by far the most runners (880), 15 times champion trainer Pipe was narowly pipped on the final day of his swansong season by Philip Hobbs who took second place in the table.

With 125 horses in his care at Ditcheat, Nicholls was again the dominant force in 2006-7, first peaking on the weekend of November 18-19 when he turned out six winners, including a wonderfully exciting prospect in *Kauto Star* who, by taking the Betfair Chase at Haydock, had the chance of a £1 million bonus if he also won the King George and Cheltenham Gold Cup. *Kauto Star* duly obliged and, having also won Aintree's Old Roan Chase and the Tingle Creek Chase, was rightly hailed officially as the best chaser in Britain and Ireland.

Besides winning the Gold Cup Nicholls also scored at the Cheltenham Festival with the brilliant *Denman* (Royal and SunAlliance Chase), *Taranis* (Ryanair Chase) and *Andreas* (Grand Annual). Now it was all systems go for the National. For the first time he was the trainer with the biggest individual stable entry (eight) compared with David Pipe's six. Also for the first time he had laid out one horse (*Eurotrek*) exclusively for the big race.

But *Eurotrek*, who was so impressive in winning the Becher Chase the previous November, was now second highest in the weights with 11st 8lb and he would be tailed off when pulled up before the second Becher's, having been effectively put out of the race by his stable companion *Royal Auclair* who fell in his path at the first Valentine's. Nicholls' other two runners – *Thisthatandtother* and *Le Duc* – also failed to finish.

The huge irony was the fact that the 2007 National had been won by *Silver Birch* who, when trained by Nicholls, had won the Welsh National and the Becher Chase, had been ante-post favourite for the 2005 National before being withdrawn with a leg injury, and had then fallen in the 2006 National. Subsequently sold for 20,000 guineas, *Silver Birch* had triumphed for a rookie trainer (Gordon Elliott) who had never sent out a winner in his native Ireland.

Ever gracious in defeat, Nicholls joked that 'at least I can say I bought a National winner'and he duly telephoned his congratulations to Elliott. He then gained quick compensation as the six year old grey *Neptune Collonges* surprised him by winning the £250,000 Guinness Gold Cup at the Punchestown Festival. And already he was assured of comfortably retaining his champion trainer's title with all-time record prize money.

Supported by such wealthy owners as Paul Barber, Andy Stewart, John Hales, Clive Smith and, not least, Trevor Hemmings, Nicholls remains a truly outstanding trainer with a stable of such strength in depth that he is now likely to dominate National Hunt racing for years to come.

See also: Pipe, Martin Charles; Silver Birch.

NICHOLSON, David

Arguably the greatest National Hunt trainer never to have a winner in the Grand National, David Nicholson, always known as 'The Duke', turned out no fewer than 16 Cheltenham Festival winners and his many big race triumphs included two Mackeson Gold Cups, the Cheltenham Gold Cup, the King George VI Chase, two Scottish Grand Nationals and two Triumph Hurdles. Yet, in 11 attempts at the Aintree National, he had to settle for gaining a place three times – third with *Moorcroft Boy* (1994) and *Call It A Day* (1999), and a fourth place with *Dubacilla* (1995).

Similarly, as a jockey, he had scored many big-race wins, including three successive Welsh Grand Nationals (*Limonali*, 1959, *Clover Bud*, 1960, and *Limonali* 1961), the Schweppes Gold Trophy (*Elan*, 1965), the Imperial Cup (*Farmer's Boy*, 1960), the Whitbread Gold Cup (*Mill House*, 1967), the Cathcart Chase (*Hoodwinked*, 1962) and the Champion Chase (*Tantalum*, 1971); and yet, riding in no fewer than 13 Aintree Nationals, he never finished better than fifth.

Remarkably, the Grand National had also proved no less a bogey race for his father, Herbert (Frenchie) Nicholson, both as jockey and trainer. The many wins of Nicholson Snr included the 1936 Champion Hurdle on *Victor Norman* and the 1942 Cheltenham Gold Cup on Lord Sefton's *Medoc II*, four years after he had been runner-up on the great *Golden Miller* who was then seeking an incredible sixth successive win in the race. But at Aintree he rode in six successive Nationals (1935-40) and fell in all of them. As a trainer he did somewhat better – most notably with Lord Sefton's *Irish Lizard* who finished third in the 1953 and 1954 Nationals.

Born at Epsom on March 19, 1939, David was steeped in racing from childhood, being the son of a leading jumps jockey and Diana, daughter of Cheltenham trainer William Holman. Educated at Haileybury College, he was apprenticed to his father as a teenager and he could not have had a finer tutor. Frenchie Nicholson, joint champion jumps jockey in 1945, became a renowned teacher of young jockeys. His pupils included Michael Dickinson, Paul Cook, Walter Swinburn and Pat Eddery. 'They came on bicycles and left in Rolls-Royce's,' as he neatly expressed it.

Though plagued by asthma attacks from early childhood, David so persistently begged his father to let him ride competitively that he made his debut as a jockey (in a Newmarket Apprentice Plate) when only 12 years old and weighing a mere 4st 7lb. In April, 1955, he rode his first winner, *Fairval* (for his father) over hurdles at Chepstow. Two years later, as a teenager with only four previous rides over fences, he made his Grand National debut, falling at Becher's on Lord Sefton's *Irish Lizard*, who was now 14 years old and a rank outsider. In 1959 and 1960, again riding for his father, he failed to get round on Miss Dorothy Paget's *Cannobie Lee*; and he was a faller again in 1961 on *Vivant*, a 100-1 outsider. Subsequently, in a total of 13 attempts, he was to complete the course only three times – tenth on *Clover Bud*, a 100-1 chance, in 1962; fifth on the seven year old *Vultrix* (1965); and ninth on *Rough Silk* (1972).

In 1963 he was on a rank outsider, *Avenue Neuilly*, who lost him at the tenth and ran on riderless only to suffer another, this time fatal, fall. Then, in 1964, he was on *Ayala*, the shock 66-1 winner of the previous year. But the chestnut gelding, now half a stone up in the weights, fell at The Chair. Three years later, Nicholson appeared to have his best chance on *Bassnet*, the 10-1 second favourite. This time his mount crashed out at the first fence and he was left to look on in wonder as the riderless *Popham Down*, another first fence casualty, went on to bring the field to a standstill at the 23rd, allowing *Foinavon* to win at 100-1. His next National rides were *Bassnet* (brought down, 1968) and *Hove* (fell, 1969).

His last National appearance was on *Highland Seal*, well-supported in 1973 since the previous month he had beaten *Red Rum* by five lengths in the Haydock Park National Trial Chase. But now the tables were to be well and truly turned. Hopelessly outpaced, *Highland Seal* had to be pulled-up on the first circuit; and, staying in the saddle, Nicholson was still at the side of Becher's when Richard Pitman came round again on *Crisp* with a seemingly unassailable lead. Pitman, doomed to be beaten three-quarters of a length by Brian Fletcher and *Red Rum*, would forever remember ruefully how The Duke shouted out, 'Richard, you are 33 lengths clear. Kick on and you'll win.'

The following year Nicholson quit race-riding with a career total of 583 wins over jumps in Britain. By then he had already begun training, having his first winner – *Arctic Coral* at Warwick – in January, 1969. Thereafter – based at Cotswold House, Condicote, Gloucestershire, and from 1992 at Jackdaws Castle, also in the Cotswolds – he was responsible for dozens of outstanding horses, among them *Charter Party* (1988 Cheltenham Gold Cup winner), *Barton Bank* (1993 King George VI Chase), and *Viking Flagship* (1994 and 1995 Queen Mother Champion Chase).

He was the champion trainer for the seasons ending in 1994 and 1995 – the only trainer to interrupt Martin Pipe's sequence of 15 titles. Between 1988 and 1999 he was also the leading trainer at Aintree. Yet his strike-rate there rested largely on victories over hurdles and in a few non-handicap chases. Suc-

cess in the Grand National was to elude him through three decades – albeit narrowly in the 1990s.

His early National challengers were mostly unfancied runners: *Nom de Guerre* (1972, fell); *Go-Pontinental* (1974, fell); *What A Buck* (1977, sixth); *No Gypsy* (1979, bd); *Flitgrove* (1979, pu); *Oakprime* (1983, pu); *Burnt Oak* (1984, pu) and *Jacko* (1984, last but one of 23 finishers). Then, in 1990 and 1991, Nicholson ran *Bigsun* with top jockey Richard Dunwoody on board. Both years the bay gelding was well supported, going off at 15-1 and 9-1 respectively. He finished sixth on his first appearance but the following year was disappointingly pulled up at the 24th.

In 1993 The Duke was strongly represented by *Givus A Buck*, winner of the Ritz Club Chase at Cheltenham. But this was the void National, and to no avail the gelding was the fifth of seven finishers. However, the following year Nicholson had his greatest hope of National success in the wonderfully honest chaser *Moorcroft Boy*, to be ridden by the wunderkind of jump jockeys, Adrian Maguire. Everything seemed in his favour – not least the heavy going. He was a proven out-and-out stayer, this season having won over four miles in the mud at Cheltenham and in the Warwick National, and then finishing second in the Greenalls National Trial. Running from 9lb out of the handicap proper, he was pronounced to be in '200 per cent condition' by his trainer, and he duly went off the 5-1 favourite.

Unfortunately for Nicholson and Maguire, the 36-strong field included two other horses who thrived even more in the bog-like conditions. *Moorcroft Boy* took a two-length lead at the final fence and was still narrowly ahead coming to The Elbow. Then be began to flag badly, giving way to the dour stayers *Miinnehoma* and *Just So*. The former won by a length and quarter with only six runners completing the course. *Moorcroft Boy* was 20 lengths behind in third place.

Eighteen months later The Duke was to bring *Moorcroft Boy* back from a serious neck injury suffered in the Becher Chase to win the Scottish National. Meanwhile, in 1995, he had another well- fancied Grand National contender in *Dubacilla*, a 9-1 chance even though a mare had not won the race for 44 years. But this gallant mare was going to Aintree only 23 days after a hard race in finishing second in the Cheltenham Gold Cup; and now, under Dean Gallagher, she came from behind to finish a creditable fourth.

Sensationally, in 1997, Nicholson started the Grand National meeting with a 196-1 treble and, after turning out six of the first 15 winners, he again had high hopes of success in the big race with *Turning Trix*. The ten year old was a long way out of the handicap on 8st 12lb, but the trainer regarded him as an ideal National type, one capable of making all the running. However, the gelding was badly hampered at the 11th and finished a distant 13th. The Duke at least showed good judgment in one respect, When the weights were announced that year, he had chosen *Lord Gyllene*, then 20-1, for his £100 charity bet, and so he made the Stable Lads' Welfare Trust £2,000 richer.

In 1998 he kept up his great record at Aintree, saddling the progressive *Escartefigue* to win the Martell Cup impressively. But of his three entries for the National only one, eight year old *Banjo*, made it to the line-up, and he was one of five fallers at the first. His ante-post £100 Stable Lads' selection (*General Wolfe* at 33-1) was a non-runner.

For his last Grand National challenge, in 1999, The Duke entered no fewer than five horses: *Escartefigue, Go Ballistic, Baronet, Call It A Day* (all in the handicap proper) and *King Lucifer*. Go Ballistic, the one-length runner-up in the Cheltenham Gold Cup at 66-1, became the ante-post second favourite for the National but then it was decided to switch him and seven year old *Escartefigue* to the Martell Cup, two days earlier. Initially, the trainer had regarded *King Lucifer* as his best hope, staking £100 each-way at 50-1 for his charity bet. But this gelding was also to be withdrawn.

This still left 60 year old Nicholson with two highly rated chances of ending his long association with the National in a blaze of glory. The grey *Baronet*, attractively weighted on 10st 2lb, was owned by Mrs Pat Thompson who had won with *Party Politics* in 1992. He was last year's Scottish National winner and had since shown great fighting qualities when winning over four miles and a furlong at Cheltenham. Still better were the prospects of *Call It A Day*, allotted 10st, a first National runner for owner Mrs Jane Lane whose many smart chasers had included *Mighty Mac*. This nine year old had won the Whitbread Gold Cup, had finished second in the Midlands National and third in the Irish National. He stayed the trip, went on any ground and, not least, he had the advantage of Richard Dunwoody on board.

Never before had the The Duke gone to Aintree with such a strong double hand. But, alas, it was to be a swansong without a fairy-tale ending. *Baronet*, under Richard Johnson, did the splits on landing over the fourth fence. *Call It A Day* went so well that going to the last Dunwoody thought that he might win in his final National. But thereafter his 7-1 chance tired and was well outpaced by *Bobbyjo* and *Blue Charm*. Nicholson retired the following November. In his final week as a trainer he saw his tough chaser *Spendid* beaten three-quarters of a length by *Ever Blessed* in the Hennessy Cognac Gold Cup. It left him just one short of a career total of 1,500 winners.

In March, 2002, Nicholson was appointed the British Horseracing Board's bloodstock representative, serving as a roving ambassador to promote British-bred horses at home and abroad. He died four years later, aged 67. Earlier, when asked how he would wish to be remembered, he replied with typical bluntness: 'As a good tutor of jockeys, a good schooler of horses and a hard bastard.' More properly, he is now remembered as a truly legendary figure of National Hunt racing.

NICKEL COIN

Winner – on her first and last appearance in the race – of the shambolic 1951 Grand National when only three of 36 starters (one remounted) completed the course largely as a result of an undeclared false start. That year, inexcusably, the starter Mr Leslie Firth raised the tape for the off while some 20 runners were still milling around and preparing to take their place in the line-up. More amazingly, no false-start flag was raised, and the result was a mad stampede as horses left at the start went flat out to catch the leaders. Twelve – one third of the field – fell or were brought down at the first fence, and by the end of the first circuit only five were still standing.

These circumstances, however, should not be allowed to detract greatly from the merits of *Nickel Coin*'s performance. True, she was an unfancied 40-1 shot, but that was partly due to sex discrimination. In the past 62 years only two mares – *Shannon Lass* (1902) and *Sheila's Cottage* (1948) – had triumphed in the Grand National. She was, nevertheless, a sound jumper with unlimited stamina, and she had won six races before making her National debut as a nine year old.

Bred in Hampshire by Mr Richard Corbett, *Nickel*

Coin had been sired, out of *Viscum*, by *Pay Up*, winner of the 1936 2,000 Guineas and then fourth to *Mahmoud* in the Derby. When foaled, she was so weak that she could not stand and the vet recommended having her put down. As Jack O'Donoghue, her future trainer, liked to recall, a housemaid threatened to quit if the foal was not spared, and undertook to bottle-feed her. 'The old housemaid kept her in the back kitchen by the fire and the foal used to sleep there on a mattress until she gained in strength.'

At Newmarket yearling sales *Nickel Coin* was bought by Surrey farmer Mr Jeffrey Royle for a mere 50 guineas in the hope that, on her breeding, she might make a good broodmare. But then he found her to be so fragile and nervous that he sold her as a three year old to a Welshman. The new owner, a Mr Williams, named her after a local American-owned metal company, and then wrought a remarkable transformation, working her as a hunter and later as show-jumper.

His aim was to run *Nickel Coin* in point-to-points but she was found not to be fast enough. And so, when she was a seven year old, Mr Royle was able to buy her back for £300 – courtesy of his son Frank who, on demob, used part of his army gratuity to purchase the mare. After a winning spell as a show-jumper, *Nickel Coin* was sent for National Hunt training to O'Donoghue, based near Reigate in Surrey. In 1950 Dick Francis rode the mare in a four-mile chase at Cheltenham and, though they were unplaced, he declared on dismounting: 'If ever there's a mare who'll win the National, it's this one. She's clever, she stays and she jumps. I'd give anything to ride her.' But Francis was claimed for Lord Bicester's *Finnure* (a first fence faller) in the 1951 National. At Aintree, *Nickel Coin* was to be ridden by Johnnie Bullock, an ex-paratrooper and prisoner-of-war who was making his second appearance. In 1950, he had been on 66-1 shot *Cavaliero*, one of four fallers at Becher's first time round.

Remarkably, *Nickel Coin* had raced a dozen times in this season, winning the Manifesto Chase at Lingfield on the way to Aintree. There she was ridden patiently by Bullock who kept his mount out of trouble while chaos reigned all around. Most notably, at the second fence, the 1950 winner *Freebooter* was brought down by Sir Arthur Pilkington's 13 year old *Gallery*; and the front-running favourite, Mr 'Jock' Hay Whitney's *Arctic Gold*, was one of five fallers

at the Canal Turn. Two more – race leader *Russian Hero*, the 1949 winner, and his stablemate *Dog Watch* – went at The Chair on being hampered by loose horses; and now only five of 36 starters were still in the running.

Coming back to the Canal Turn just two horses remained in contention: *Nickel Coin* and *Royal Tan*, a seven year old trained by Vincent O'Brien – his first ever National runner – and ridden by his youngest brother, Mr Alphonsus 'Phonsie' O'Brien. The pair stayed locked together over the Melling Road, the latter having a slight lead and, despite a 12lb disadvantage in the weights, looking marginally the stronger as they approached the last. In only seven years as a trainer, Vincent O'Brien had achieved wonders – winning three successive Cheltenham Gold Cups with *Cottage Rake* and three successive Champion Hurdles with *Hatton's Grace*. Now, some observers argue, he was only deprived of the great National prize by the over-eager riding of his amateur brother. Certainly, *Royal Tan* made a fatal blunder in taking the last fence at speed; and, as 'Phonsie' briefly lost control, *Nickel Coin* snatched the lead and thereafter pulled away strongly to win by six lengths with *Derrinstown*, a 66-1 chance remounted after being brought down at Becher's, coming home a distant third of three finishers.

Having won the National at the first attempt, *Nickel Coin* never raced again. After a spell of hunting she was retired to stud and bred three foals with only one, *King's Nickel* by *Kingsmead*, being raced with a modicum of success.

See also: O'Donoghue, Jack; Bullock, John.

NICOLAUS SILVER

Since the beloved *Desert Orchid* was never allowed to take his chance at Aintree, the 1961 winner *Nicolaus Silver* takes pride of place, alongside *The Lamb*, as the most handsome horse to grace the Grand National. Like the only other grey to win the great steeplechase, he was a veritable show-horse in his striking good looks; also exceptionally well balanced and a wonderfully precise jumper.

In Ireland, however, the young *Nicolaus Silver* was badly underrated. Tipperary-foaled in 1952 – by the bay *Nicolaus* out of the grey *Rays of Montrose* – he was generally judged to be no more than a moderate chaser. And that opinion was shared by one Bobby Beasley (later to ride him to National victory) on seeing him perform in a three-mile chase at Naas in 1960. But the grey's detractors had only seen him race on unfavourably soft or heavy ground. A few wiser observers recognised him as a horse of real potential.

In November, 1960, eight year old *Nicolaus Silver* came on the Dublin market as a result of the sudden death of his trainer, Dan Kirwan. Aware that the grey was already qualified for the Grand National, two parties keenly led the bidding at the Ballsbridge sales: Ivor Herbert, accompanied by the would-be owner, film producer Frank Launder; and Fred Rimell, accompanied by Mr Jeremy Vaughan whose abiding ambition was to go one better than his father who had owned *First Of The Dandies*, the one-length runner-up in the 1948 National. Fred won the neck-and-neck battle with the final bid of £2,600.

After moving to the Rimells' Kinnersley stables in Worcesterhire, *Nicolaus Silver* failed to impress his professional riders, Tim Brookshaw and newly recruited Bobby Beasley. However, he did win his final pre-National race (the amateur riders' Kim Muir Memorial Challenge Cup at Cheltenham, under Bill Tellwright), and Rimell judged that he still had plenty to work on. In the final weeks he brought about such a huge improvement that he sent a telegram to the owner, then in Spain, advising him that his horse had 'a very, very good chance'. Over the years Fred would turn out four National winners. Of them all, he later reflected, *Nicolaus Silver* was the one that filled him with most confidence beforehand.

Nevertheless, he had grave anxieties in the week before the National. Rumours of a massive doping plot were rife; and as a precaution another grey, *High Spot*, was substituted in the box bearing *Nicolaus Silver*'s name. It was not proven that the decoy horse was nobbled, but certainly *High Spot* was never again to be judged fit enough to race. Then, on the eve of the National, there was another scare when *Nicolaus Silver* was 'pricked' in the process of being fitted with racing plates. Overnight, successfully, he had his injured foot in a poultice to draw out the abscess.

Happily, in the race itself, the grey gave rider Beasley only one anxious moment: at Becher's second time round when he pecked precariously on landing. Otherwise, he jumped immaculately. For most of the way last year's winner, *Merryman II*, narrowly had his measure. But from the second last,

the grey's huge (25lb) advantage in the weights, proved decisive. He steadily pulled away on the run-in to win by five lengths.

Besides gaining huge satisfaction in out-doing his father, Mr Vaughan had made a positive killing. That year the value to the winning owner had been greatly increased – from £13,134 to £20,020. Also, heeding the trainer's judgment, he had backed his grey from 40-1 down to the starting price of 28-1. Bookies were only too willing to lay the odds against a grey winning the National for the first time in nine decades. Curiously, by extraordinary chance, Jeremy Vaughan would years later take for his third wife one Miss Noreen Begley, the grand-daughter of Joe Doyle, owner of the only other grey (*The Lamb*) to have won the Grand National!

The key to *Nicolaus Silver* was the ground. With his beautiful, fluent action, he was essentially a top-of-the-ground horse that needed the going to be at least good. The Rimells judged him to be a stone better horse on good or faster ground. Most unusually, it was firm at Aintree in 1961, and then there was similar going in the Whitbread Gold Cup when he was a most creditable second to *Pas Seul*, the 1960 Cheltenham Gold Cup winner. Returning to Aintree, he dominated the Grand Sefton Chase, and the following February he comfortably won the 1962 Great Yorkshire Chase. But when he reappeared in the National with an extra 9lb to carry, the heavy conditions were hopelessly against him. He plodded home, the seventh of 17 finishers.

In 1963, when making his third and last National appearance, the 11 year old *Nicolaus Silver* was past his best. Also he had a new owner, Mr Bernard Sunley, having being sold out of necessity by Mr Vaughan, whose winning streak had taken a dramatic U-turn. As usual, the much-loved grey jumped with admirable precision but finished in tenth place. Subsequently turned out for hunting, his life ended – like that of his famous predecessor, *The Lamb* – as the result of breaking a leg.

See also: Rimell, Fred; Beasley, Bobby.

NIGHTINGALL, Arthur

The most successful member of a family whose active association with the Grand National spanned almost half a century. While his father, John, made his mark on the race as a winning owner (*Shifnal*, 1878) and trainer (*Ilex*, 1890), Arthur Nightingall was outstanding as a jockey – one of only five riders to win three Nationals: on *Ilex* (1890), *Why Not* (1894) and *Grudon* (1901). His consistency was extraordinary. In ten of his 15 Nationals he finished in at least fifth place. Besides his three wins, he was once runner-up, four times third and once fourth.

In contrast, his brother Willie only once completed the course in six National rides. Four times he rode against Arthur at Aintree, but only in 1888 did he surpass him, finishing third on *Ballot Box*, six places ahead of his brother on *The Badger*. Even then it was Arthur who commanded the higher praise – for his sportsmanship in reaching out to pull George Mawson back into the saddle after he had been almost thrown from *Playfair* on hitting the 20th fence. *Playfair* went on to win at 40-1.

Nightingall's marathon involvement with the National began at the age of 18 with a fifth place on *The Badger* in 1886. He was the last of nine finishers on *The Badger* in 1888, and third on *M.P.* in 1889. His first success, in 1890, was the most satisfying. He had been responsible for recognising the potential of *Ilex* after riding the four year old chestnut in a seller. On his recommendation, the horse was purchased by George Masterman, and subsequently trained at Epsom by Arthur's father. Two years later, as 4-1 favourite, *Ilex* won that National by a comfortable 12 lengths.

After that victory Nightingall took third place in three successive Nationals with *Ilex* (1891 and 1892) and *Why Not* (1893). The following year he triumphed again by his masterly riding of 13 year old *Why Not* in a pulsating three-way finish while conceding more than two stone to *Lady Ellen II* and 18lb to *Wild Man From Borneo*. Having conserved the old horse's stamina by hugging the inside rail, Arthur regained the lead on the run-in and held on to beat those two rivals by a length and a half and a head respectively.

In 1895, Nightingall led round the first circuit on the 5-1 favourite *Aesop*, only to fall – for the first time in nine National rides – at the Canal Turn second time around. In 1896 he achieved an honourable fifth place on *Why Not*, now 15 years old; and in 1898 he fell at the Water Jump on a former winner, *The Soarer*. Two years went by and it seemed that Arthur's greatest Aintree days were over. Instead, in the new century, he came back riding as strongly as ever. In 1901, despite all riders petitioning for an abandonment, the National was run in a blinding snowstorm over a course already blanketed in snow.

To his advantage, Nightingall virtually knew his way round blindfolded; and now, riding 11 year old *Grudon*, sixth the previous year, he led the field from start to finish, coming home four lengths ahead of *Drumcree*.

Arthur followed up with a fourth place on 25-1 chance *Detail* in 1902, and, on the same horse, he finished second to *Drumcree* in 1903. He was 36 years old when he had his last National ride, experiencing a rare fall as *Detail* was knocked over in the 1904 race won by the giant *Moifaa*. Like his father, he went on to become a successful trainer, and he died in 1944.

See also: Ilex; Why Not; Grudon.

NIGHTINGALL, John

Unlike his famous son Arthur, John Nightingall rode in four Grand Nationals without ever completing the course. But years later, when the race had only 12 starters, its second smallest field, he was a successful owner-trainer with *Shifnal* (1878); and in 1890 he again saddled the winner, six year old *Ilex*.

Nightingall's early experiences of the race could hardly have been more discouraging. His first ride, rank outsider *Spring* (1859), was a faller; his second, *The Conductor* (1861), also a 40-1 shot, had to be destroyed after a dreadful fall at Valentine's. Then, in 1862, he was involved in the most horrific accident of all. He was on *Playman* when the gelding plunged headlong into the gorse fence preceding the Water and in the process brought down *Willoughby* and *O'Connell*. The young Irish jockey James Wynne was thrown from the latter and then suffered fatal injuries as *Playman* rolled over him.

One year later Nightingall had his last National ride, failing to finish on *Light Of Other Days*. Thereafter, he was to enjoy much happier involvement as an owner and Epsom-based trainer. In 1870 he gained fourth place in the National with his *Surney*, and he went one place better in 1876 when seven year old *Shifnal*, a 25-1 chance, finished a close-up third behind *Regal* and *Congress*.

Shifnal, an entire, was under new ownership when he finished sixth in 1877. But Nightingall shrewdly bought him back the following year and trained him to win by a couple of lengths from *Martha* at 7-1. Tommy Beasley, the rider of the runner-up, lodged an objection on the grounds of foul riding by Jack Jones, but this was swiftly overruled.

In 1889 Nightingall worked wonders to sharpen up *Ilex*, a five year old whose only success had been in a two-mile selling hunters' chase at Leicester. In December the chestnut gelding showed huge improvement in finishing second in the Great Sandown Chase and, given a light weight of 10st 5lb, he was backed down to 4-1 favouritism in the National. His comfortable 12 lengths victory was all the more rewarding for the trainer since it was first of three winning rides by his son, Arthur.

Subsequently, Nightingall turned out *Ilex* to win the 1890 Lancashire Chase at Manchester and, following a huge rise in the weights, to finish third in the Nationals of 1891 and 1892.
See also: Shifnal; Ilex; Nightingall, Arthur.

NORMAN, Timothy
In March, 1966, just one day before he was due to have his first Grand National ride, 21 year old Tim Norman was lucky to survive a car crash near Aintree racecourse. He needed to be cut out of the wreckage and then to have numerous facial stitches. Yet he still passed a fitness test, allowing him to make his National debut on eight year old *Anglo*, a 50-1 chance, also making its first appearance in the race.

There were 47 runners and, beyond belief, the young jockey had an untroubled ride, with the minimum-weighted *Anglo* pulling away from all rivals after the second last to win by 20 lengths from the hot 11-4 favourite *Freddie* who was giving him 21lb.

Norman was 16 years old when, in 1960, he began riding as an amateur jump jockey. He turned professional three years later, that season having his biggest success to that point in winning the three-mile George Duller Handicap Hurdle at Cheltenham on the 25-1 chance *Do Or Die*. Subsequently he joined Fred Winter's Uplands yard where, like the American Tommy Crompton Smith, winner of the 1965 National on *Jay Trump*, he benefited hugely from the experience of a trainer who had twice ridden the winner in the Aintree marathon.

His first ride on *Anglo* was a winning one – in the Fairlawne Chase at Windsor in December, 1965. Winter was sufficiently impressed to have him keep the ride on the busy build-up to Aintree. The partnership followed up with two second places in chases and, just two weeks before the National, they finished fourth at Kempton. Being 8lb of the handicap, *Anglo* was seen as a no-hoper. His surprising success

brought back-to-back victories for Winter in only his second season as a trainer.

The following month Norman enhanced his new-founded reputation with a fine ride on *Kilburn* to win the Welsh Grand National at Chepstow. But now the fickleness of Fate brought about a change of fortune. His riding career was frequently to be interrupted by injuries, and after his winning debut he was destined never to complete the National course again.

In 1967, when *Anglo* reappeared in the Grand National, he was under new ownership, and to be ridden by Bobby Beasley, the winning jockey on *Nicolaus Silver* six years earlier. Norman was on the equally well-backed *Kilburn*. But both horses failed to get round in the notorious Foinavon race which saw chaos created by the riderless *Popham Down*. In 1968, Norman's mount, *Ford Ord*, was the only first fence faller; and he did not ride in the race again until five years later when, on his farewell appearance, he had to pull up on the outsider *Rough Silk*. after being hampered by two loose horses at the 19th. Norman subsequently retired to begin a successful career as a housing developer in Marlborough, Wiltshire.
See also: Anglo.

NORWAY
Jump racing operates on minimal scale in Norway, there being only one racecourse, Ovrevoll, close to Oslo airport. Its so-called Norwegian Grand National is run over a mere two miles five furlongs and the season is so limited that six wins are usually sufficient to secure the jockeys' championship. However, in September, 1999, trainer Rune Haugen entertained Aintree ambitions after his chaser *Trinitro* had made all under British jockey Robert Bellamy to win the Norwegian National. In 2000 *Trinitro*, owned and ridden out by beekeeping expert Ms. Liv Saether Myskja, became the first Grand National runner to be trained in Scandinavia. He was the second National ride for Bellamy, who had last appeared in 1992 on *New Halen* (refused at the 19th); and he was considered to have no chance, being described as Norway's equivalent of Britain's ski-jumper Eddie 'The Eagle'.

True enough, he went off as a 100-1 outsider and crashed out at the first fence. However, he got up to clear every fence without his jockey, encouraging connections to declare that he would be back next year. Alas, though winning three Nationals in Scandinavia, *Trinitro* broke down several times and was not to appear at Aintree again.

NUMBERSIXVALVERDE

Winner of the 2006 Grand National, *Numbersixvalverde* – named after the address of his owner's villa in Portugal – triumphed on his first appearance at Aintree and in only his second season as a chaser. Like *Bobbyjo* (1999) he won a year after winning the Irish National; and, for lovers of sporting trivia, he was the first winner with 17 letters since *Wild Man From Borneo* in 1895.

An Irish-bred brown gelding – by *Broken Hearted* out of *Queens Tricks* – *Numbersixvalverde* was bought by trainer Martin Brassil on behalf of his main patron, property developer Bernard Carroll. Trained at Dunmurray in Co. Kildare, he was not an immediate hit, failing to win a bumper from four attempts prior to breaking his maiden as a six year old on his third run over hurdles.

It was two years before he won again. But he had stamina in abundance and, beginning the 2004-05 season in novice company, he won his first handicap chase in December and followed up one month later with a narrow success over *Kymandjen* in the three-mile Thyestes Chase at Gowran Park on heavy ground. Next, in mid-February, he finished third in a novice chase at Navan, after which Brassil shrewdly rested him to protect his handicap mark for the Irish National. It enabled him to run off the 10st minimum at Fairyhouse and, under Ruby Walsh, he won by three-quarters of a length from the Ted Walsh-trained *Jack High*.

Having won the Irish National when still a novice, *Numbersixvalverde* had seven runs before being sent to Aintree, never finishing better than third. But only three of those seven were over fences; and at least, in January, 2006, he had shown that he retained all his staying ability when a running-on fourth in the valuable Pierse Leopardstown Chase over three miles.

Once again Brassil had protected his handicap mark by employing the now favoured Irish ploy of racing his challenger mainly over hurdles before the framing of the National weights. Subsequently, his chaser's last tune-up race before Aintree was over hurdles and an inadequate two miles three furlongs. He finished third and at this stage had a record of just four wins from 31 starts.

Four weeks later, however, *Numbersixvalderde* went off as a well-backed 11-1 chance in what was recognised as the best-ever Grand National in terms of quality, with all 40 runners in the handicap proper and headed by *Hedgehunter* and *Royal Auclair*, last year's winner and runner-up. The former, was 5-1 joint favourite following his brilliant second-placed run in the Cheltenham Gold Cup.

With Ruby Walsh again booked for *Hedgehunter*, *Numbersixvalverde* was reunited with Niall Madden, a 20 year old Irishman making his National debut in his first season as a professional jockey. Throughout the first circuit, as planned, he was held up towards the rear; and he had his share of luck in the running, most notably when avoiding *It Takes Time* who almost fell in front of him at the first Becher's. Then, from the 17th onwards, he made relentless progress, always in contention after the second Becher's and being in a group of six leading to the penultimate fence.

Coming to the last, he made his surging move, staying on strongly on the rain-softened ground to assert his 18lb advantage over *Hedgehunter* and win by six lengths. A further one and a quarter lengths back was the other 5-1 joint favourite *Clan Royal*, who just snatched third place from *Nil Desperandum*.

Numbersixvalverde had run in only ten chases before winning at Aintree – the fewest since *Miinnehoma* in 1994. His four previous wins had all been on soft or heavy ground, and a key factor in his success was the overnight rain which crucially counted against the brilliant, top-weighted *Hedgehunter*.

In 2006-07 he was again restricted to hurdles until the National weights had been allotted. But inevitably he was raised 9lb for his previous win and this time, again ridden by Madden, he weakened four out to finish a creditable sixth, albeit more than 40 lengths off the winner. In 2008 he missed the National, having failed to recover from an injury. *See also:* Brassil, Martin; Madden, Niall.

O

OAKSEY, Lord OBE

Born March 21, 1929 (one day before *Gregalach* won the 66-runner Grand National at 100-1), educated at Eton, New College Oxford and Yale Law School, and becoming best-known as a TV racing commentator, Lord Oaksey (formerly John Geoffrey Tristam Lawrence) was a leading amateur jockey for two decades, winning the amateurs' jumps title in 1958 and 1971. In the former year he had his first big-race wins – the Imperial Cup on *Flaming East* and the Whitbread and Hennessy Gold Cups on *Taxidermist*. Subsequently he rode in 11 Grand Nationals, his last as a spritely 46 year old; and he missed victory by only three-quarters of a length in 1963 when his *Carrickbeg* was caught on the line by the 66-1 outsider *Ayala*.

To any journalist with experience of covering major sports and meeting tight deadlines, it is a source of amazement that for years this extraordinarily versatile gentleman was able to combine successfully regular National Hunt riding with his duties as racing correspondent to the *Daily Telegraph*, *Sunday Telegraph* and the *Horse and Hound*. His exceptional self-discipline showed most notably in 1963 when, finishing totally exhausted by his near-miss in the National, he still managed to meet his Sunday paper deadline. Within minutes of weighing in he had dashed off to file a moving and remarkably detailed 1,000-word report on the race.

Lord Oaksey's earliest memory of the Grand National was a happy one – as a seven year old, already a seasoned rider in pony hunter trials, who drew the 1937 winner *Royal Mail* in a sixpenny sweepstake. Twenty four years later, when riding as John Lawrence, he became directly and doubly involved with the race. That year, 1961, there was the novelty of three Russian horses being entered for the greatest steeplechase, and Lawrence was dispatched to Moscow to interview their riders, including the Russian champion, Vladimir Prokhov. Three weeks later he met Prokhov again – on the landing side of Becher's. Both had been deposited in the brook. While Lawrence's *Taxidermist* galloped off alone, *Reljef*, the well-disciplined Ukranian mount of the Russian, waited patiently alongside his rider. Though Lawrence advised him by shouting 'nyet, nyet', Prokhov remounted and rode on as far as the Water.

It was fitting that *Taxidermist* should have been Lawrence's first ride in the National. The beloved 'Taxi' was his favourite, a Fulke Walwyn-trained

bay gelding that had given him victory in the Whitbread and Hennessy Gold Cups, the former after an unforgettable duel with *Mandarin*. But he was past his best in 1961, as reflected in his 40-1 starting price. One year later, on his reappearance, he was half those odds; and, jumping beautifully, the ten year old was well placed at The Chair, ahead of the eventual winner *Kilmore*. But frost, followed by torrential rain, had made the ground bottomless; and, hating the mud, he had to be pulled up after the 25th.

In 1963 Lawrence had his third National ride and his greatest chance of winning: on seven year old *Carrickbeg*, a 20-1 shot whom he owned in partnership with another leading amateur rider, Mr Gay Kindersley. At the time John was riding at the top of his form, with victories in the previous week at Sandown on *Rosie's Cousin* and *Solimyth*, and at Newbury on *Most Unusual*. His mount, hampered by a spread plate, had been a recent faller at Cheltenham. However, in 1962 he had won the Kim Muir at Cheltenham and been runner-up in the Whitbread Gold Cup; and on his best 1963 Leopardstown Chase form, he was lightly handicapped.

The National's 47-runner field was a strong one, including three former winners, *Kilmore*, *Nicolaus Silver* and *Mr What*. However, when the leaders reached the Elbow, none was going better than *Carrickbeg*, the youngest horse in the race. He had a two lengths lead and looked all over the winner, destined to make his rider the first amateur to triumph since Captain Bobby Petre on *Lovely Cottage* in 1946. But though he jumped the last nearly a length ahead of *Ayala*, he was near the end of his tether, weakening markedly in the last 100 yards and being caught about 20 yards from the post to go down by a mere three-quarters of a length.

Lawrence accepted such an agonisingly close defeat with typically good grace. Under his psuedonym of 'Marlbrough', he began his *Daily Telegraph* report: 'In almost every way the 1963 Grand National was a superbly satisfactory race, won, as all great prizes should be, fair and square by the best horse on the day. Looking back on the ride of a lifetime, defeat, bitter though it was, now seems a small thing to bear. My most indelible memory will always be of that moment, halfway up the run-in when, with the post in sight, *Carrickbeg* felt – as he must have looked – the winner. It was not to be, but many better men than I have ridden for years without coming so close and I have no regrets.'

Lawrence speculated that he himself was to blame: that maybe at Anchor Bridge, with the third last safely crossed, he had asked his horse to go too soon, that perhaps he should have given him more time to recover after hitting the fence four from home and then having to swerve round the fallen tearaway leader, *Out And About*. 'It is, of course, impertinence to compare *Carrickbeg* with *Devon Loch* – but his collapse, though less visible, was, when it came, 50 yards from the line, almost as abrupt and absolute … One moment he was galloping smoothly, the next we might have been struggling through quicksand.'

Self-deprecatingly, many years later, he would recall: 'I thought my close finish on *Carrickbeg* was my finest hour. Yet in 1975 I was coming out of the Piccadilly Circus tube station when I encountered a grubby man who said: 'I know you, you're the bugger who got tired before his 'orse.' It was true that he had been near total exhaustion towards the end. The fact remains that he would surely have won if he had not lost at least five lengths in having to deviate to avoid the prostrate *Out And About*.

Lawrence had four more National rides in the 1960s, all on long-shots: *Crobeg* (1964, ninth), *Solimyth* (1966, pu), *Norther* (1967, pu) and *Master Marcus* (1968, fell). In 1971, he finished ninth on *Regimental*, a 66-1 chance; and that season, for the second time, he became the leading amateur under National Hunt Rules. The following year he inherited the peerage that had been bestowed on his late father, previously the Hon. Geoffrey Lawrence, presiding judge at the Nuremberg Trials of Nazi war criminals.

Making his first National appearance as Lord Oaksey, John came home seventh on *Proud Tarquin* in 1973, the first winning year of the new wonder called *Red Rum*. His last two National rides were on the champion two-miler *Royal Relief* who was the only casualty at the first fence in 1974, and a faller at the seventh the following year.

Having quit the saddle after riding more than 200 winners, the ever-young Lord Oaksey now steadily increased his activities: joining the Channel Four Racing team in 1986 (ever after to be addressed by John McCririck as 'My Noble Lord'), becoming a columnist for the *Racing Post* in 1988, serving for a while as a Director of Harlech Television (HTV) and then, in 1992, taking on a new role as President of the burgeoning Elite Racing Club. In addition, he

had continued to serve as a Justice of Peace; and, as always he remained most energetic in his work as president of the Injured Jockeys' Fund which he had co-founded in 1964.

As a journalist and author, Lord Oaksey wrote many splendid pieces on the National. None, however, was more important than his moving article in the *Daily Telegraph* following the failure of the 1983 'Save the National' public appeal, on whose behalf he had travelled to the United States and, at 54, had even run in the London Marathon, finishing in a most creditable sub-four-hour time.

Crucially, that article, deploring the possible demise of the National, spurred one reader into action. Ivan Straker, a long-time Aintree devotee and at that time chairman of Seagram (UK), promptly contacted the president of the Canadian distillers, and in consequence the company negotiated the deal that saved the race from extinction.

See also: Ayala; Buckley, Pat; Russia; Age (seven year olds); Injuries.

OBJECTIONS

In 1875 an objection was lodged against the Grand National winner (*Pathfinder*) on the grounds of 'insufficient description' of the horse. It was dismissed as being 'frivolous' and the stewards ordered an objection charge of £5 to be forfeited. Similarly, three years later, the stewards were quick to over-rule an objection to the winner (*Shifnal*) lodged by Tommy Beasley, rider of the two lengths runner-up, on the grounds of foul riding by winning jockey Jack Jones.

In 1891 Captain Roddy Owen, rider of runner-up *Cloister*, lodged an objection to the winner on the grounds that Harry Beasley on *Come Away* had jostled *Cloister* in denying him a clear run through on the rails. It was over ruled by the stewards who judged that Beasley had not infringed the rules by holding his position on the rails. To the relief of the majority of punters, *Come Away*, the 4-1 favourite, was confirmed as the winner by half a length.

See also: Stewards' Enquiries.

O'BRIEN, Michael Vincent

In terms of achievements in both National Hunt and Flat racing, Vincent O'Brien stands unchallenged as the greatest trainer of all time – a fact justly confirmed in 2003 when *Racing Post* readers voted him the supreme figure in the history of the Turf. His amazing record on the Flat alone made him a living

O

legend. He turned out winners of 44 Classics and 25 Royal Ascot races; and his successes included six Epsom Derbys, six Irish Derbys, nine Irish St Legers, five Irish 2,000 Guineas, four English 2,000 Guineas, two Oaks, one French Derby, three Prix de l'Arc de Triomphes, the Breeders' Cup Mile, the Washington International, and the Triple Crown with *Nijinsky*. But first he dominated the jumps; to such a degree that he saddled winners of all major English and Irish hurdles and steeplechases, including 23 at the Cheltenham Festival – and, incredibly, three consecutive Grand Nationals.

Born on April 9, 1917 in Churchtown, Co. Cork, O'Brien was 26 years old when, following the death of his father, he took over a small stable and saddled his first winner as a licensed trainer at Limerick Junction. Incredibly, within eight years of that beginning, he had become the first trainer to have three consecutive winners of both the Cheltenham Gold Cup and the Champion Hurdle. He then turned his attention to the Aintree Grand National with devastating effect.

In the 1951 National, when only three horses finished, O'Brien had to settle for second place after his seven year old chestnut *Royal Tan* (also second in the Irish National) had blundered away his narrow lead at the last. Again, in 1952, *Royal Tan* was challenging strongly when he bungled the last, this time falling. But then the wizard of Ballydoyle (Cashel, Co. Tipperary) got serious. He looked for an outstanding professional jockey to take over from his youngest brother, Alphonsus 'Phonsie' O'Brien, a capable but rather over-eager amateur rider.

Success was immediate. In 1953 – only three weeks after winning a fourth Cheltenham Gold Cup with *Knock Hard* – O'Brien had his first National winner: *Early Mist*, a big chestnut which he had purchased for 5,300 guineas – outbidding Lord Bicester – at the dispersal sale of horses owned by the late Mr J.V. Rank. In 1954, using the same jockey, Bryan Marshall, he won the National again – his *Royal Tan* prevailing by a neck from *Tudor Line*, with Mrs M.V. O'Brien's *Churchtown* back in fourth after breaking a blood vessel.

Finally, in 1955, the great hat-trick specialist became the only trainer to saddle three consecutive winners of the Grand National. That year he had four representatives. Big weights and quagmire conditions counted against *Early Mist* and *Royal Tan* who finished ninth and 12th respectively. His *Oriental Way* was a faller. But his *Quare Times*, a safe jumper strong on stamina, thrived on the bottomless going and, with Pat Taaffe up, he won comfortably on his Aintree debut by 12 lengths.

In 1956 O'Brien did well to get *Royal Tan* fit enough to finish third in the National when he was 12 years old and carrying the second top weight. He had proved his mastery of National Hunt racing; and three years later he chose to concentrate on Flat racing. Altogether he was to win 13 trainers' championships in Ireland, plus four in Britain – over jumps in the 1952-53 and 1953-54 seasons and on the Flat in 1966 and 1977. On his retirement in 1994, after a training career spanning 51 years, he handed over to his son Charles. Subsequently, he and his wife divided each year between their homes in Tipperary and Perth, Australia.

What was the secret of his success? O'Brien had an extraordinary eye for spotting potential, a talent most tellingly demonstrated when he picked out as a yearling the great *Nijinsky*, 1970 Triple Crown winner. As a National trainer he favoured the rigorous approach of Henry Eyre Linde, schooling his Aintree challengers twice every week. He also successfully introduced the new pre-National tactic – one much later followed by the Irish trainers of winners *Bobbyjo*, *Papillon* and *Monty's Pass* – of getting his chasers into a rhythm with prep races over hurdles. Not least he was a shrewd judge of how they should be ridden; and at the same time he always recognised his good fortune in having secured such strong jump jockeys as Martin and Tim Molony, Aubrey Brabazon, and not least Bryan Marshall and Pat Taaffe.

See also: Early Mist; Royal Tan; Quare Times.

O'DONOGHUE, Jack

Trainer of *Nickel Coin* who, in 1951, became the third and last mare to win the Grand National in the 20th century. To be sure, the nine year old had much luck in the running as one of only two horses to complete the course without falling. Yet Jack O'Donoghue, who had a mere ten shillings each-way on his 40-1 winner, insisted that he was not greatly surprised since the mare had beaten many of her 35 rivals earlier in the season. Furthermore, he had noted a curious concourse of favourable omens. He had been born on the 29th, had moved to England in 1929, and now lived in a Surrey cottage with the number 29. 'And *Nickel Coin*'s number on the card for the National was … 29.'

O

Born on July 29, 1907, in Fermoy, Co. Cork, O'Donoghue was a point-to-point rider before being apprenticed to trainer Jack Lombard. On settling in Surrey, he continued to ride in point-to-points and work as a bloodstock agent. Then, shortly after the Second World War, he took out a training licence and established his base at Priory Stables, Reigate, where he was to operate for half a century. Starting with *Arbitration*, at Fontwell in 1946, he had winners on the Flat, over hurdles and fences; and, in addition to *Nickel Coin*, his early successes included the ex-hunter *Air Wedding* on whom, in 1953, Fred Winter became the first jump jockey to ride 100 winners in a season. By the late 1950s Jack had become especially noted for his rare ability to calm and get the best out of difficult, highly strung horses; and because of this gift he was to be sent several temperamental animals from the stable of trainer Peter Cazalet. One of these was *Gay Record* who was eventually to give the Queen Mother her 100th victory under National Hunt Rules. In all, *Gay Record* would win nine races (the last as a 14 year old veteran) and be placed in 22 others.

In the mid-1960s O'Donoghue's stable included as many as six of the Queen Mother's 20 jumpers, plus the Queen's *National Emblem*. Though he never again had a strong Grand National challenger (his next best runner was the Czech-owned and -ridden *L'Empereur* who finished sixth at 100-1 in 1965) Jack was still saddling winners long after turning 80. Indeed, he was the oldest trainer in Britain when he sent out three year old *Hello Mister* to win the 1994 Portland Handicap. It was his biggest Flat win; and the following season, again under apprentice Pat Mc-Cabe, *Hello Mister* became the first horse in 59 years to win the race in successive years.

While *Nickel Coin* was his most famous winner, it was a measure of O'Donoghue's love of animals that he always remained equally proud of his success with *Little Record* who won numerous donkey championships. The soft-spoken, good-natured Irishman finally retired in January 1996. He died two years later, aged 91.
See also: Nickel Coin.

OGDEN, Sir Robert

Rarely has one owner been more strongly represented in the Grand National than Sir Robert Ogden in 2002. That year his colours were carried by three leading contenders, all of them with jockeys who had previously ridden a winner of the race. Top-weighted *Marlborough*, under Mick Fitzgerald, was one of nine fallers at the first. But his grey *Kingsmark* gave Ruby Walsh a brilliant ride, outpaced only after the third last to finish fourth at 16-1. And his Whitbread Gold Cup winner *Ad Hoc*, under Paul Carberry, though most unluckily brought down at the 27th, showed such huge promise that one year later he would be the long-term ante-post favourite to win the race.

In 2003, however, Sir Robert's much-fancied *Kingsmark* had to be withdrawn from the National when found to have heat in a tendon. His remaining runners, *Fadalko* and *Ad Hoc*, both burdened with more than 11st, disappointed – the former unseating his rider at the sixth fence, and strongly supported *Ad Hoc* falling at the 19th. It was a pattern of dashed hopes that for a number of years fairly paralleled the National fortunes of another leading owner, Mr Trevor Hemmings.

Like Hemmings, Sir Robert was a self-made multi-millionaire. Born January 15, 1936, the eldest of six children, he had left school at 15 to work on a farm. Then, after National Service in the RAF, he started up the business that founded his fortune: clearing slag-heap sites and providing quarrying materials for building roads to isolated farmsteads. He later moved into property, becoming an early investor in London's Docklands; and in 2001 he was knighted for services to charity. Five years later he sold his coal-washing and processing business for £24.5 million and was subsequently judged in the *Sunday Times* Rich List to be 'easily worth £135 million'.

Excluding the void race of 1993, when his *On The Other Hand* finished sixth under Neale Doughty, Sir Robert first had a strong National challenger in 1997 when his *Buckboard Bounce*, trained by Gordon Richards and ridden by Paul Carberry, finished fourth at 40-1. That same year he became Britain's leading owner over jumps for the first time. Although he was without a runner in the next four Nationals, he was again champion owner in the 1999-2000 season, and in 2000-01 when he narrowly outpointed Norman Mason, owner of the National winner, *Red Marauder*.

Employing a much-shuffled pack of top trainers, he had some 45 horses in training in 2003. But National success remained elusive. In 2004 his four National entries were *Kingsmark*, *Ad Hoc*, *Iris*

O

Royal and *Fadalko*. Only *Kingsmark* appeared in the line-up. Under a big weight and, without his favoured soft ground, he did well enough to get round, the ninth of 11 finishers. In 2005 *Ad Hoc* fell at Becher's second time round.

In 2006 Sir Robert enjoyed success at the Cheltenham Festival, winning the Arkle Challenge Trophy Chase with his French-bred *Voy Por Ustedes*; and the Royal and SunAlliance Chase with *Star De Mohaison*. But his one runner in the National was a 100-1 long-shot, *Iris Royal*, pulled up before the 17th. The following season his leading winners included *Star De Mohaison*, *Opera Mundi* and *Ungaro*, and most notably the brilliant *Exotic Dancer*, who won the Paddy Power Gold Cup, the Boylesports.com Gold Cup and the Letheby and Christopher Chase, and was runner-up in the King George VI Chase and the Cheltenham Gold Cup. Discouragingly, however, *Exotic Dancer* was allotted joint top weight of 11st 12lb for the National and so he was switched successfully to Aintree's valuable Betfair Bowl Chase over three miles one furlong.

OLD JOE

Seven year old winner of the 1886 Grand National when having his first run over the Aintree jumps. Ridden by Tommy Skelton, third on *Black Prince* the previous year, *Old Joe* out-speeded all his rivals on the run-in to win by a comfortable six lengths from *Too Good*. Skelton's win on a 25-1 shot ended seven years of dominance by amateur riders and for the third year in a row Harry Beasley was on the runner-up. *Gamecock*, next year's winner, was third.

Cumberland-bred – by *Barefoot* out of *Spot* – *Old Joe* was originally sold to huntsman-farmer Joe Graham for £30 and later passed on to a Mr A.J. Douglas who named him after the vendor. The bay gelding was subsequently trained by George Mulcaster at Burgh-by-Sands, Carlisle, and was so frequently run that as a five year old he won two minor races on the same day.

Old Joe had scored in two of his three races prior to making his National debut. However, his prospects at Aintree seemed fairly remote – not least because he had bruised a foot in the previous month, the poultices having been removed only a week ago. Moreover, there were 23 runners, the largest field for 13 years, and they included *Roquefort*, the 1885 winner; *Frigate*, the runner-up of the past two years; and *Too Good*, trained by the redoubtable Henry

Linde, seeking his elusive third National success. *Coronet*, a precocious five year old, was the hot 3-1 favourite.

Frigate went at the first fence and as the field set out on the second circuit the favourite took up the running, his backers greatly encouraged by the departure of top-weighted *Roquefort* before reaching the second Becher's. Approaching the penultimate fence, *Coronet* still headed affairs, but now he was visibly tiring with four other contenders snapping on his heels. At this point, *Old Joe* jumped into the lead and thereafter steadily pulled away, comfortably resisting the brave late challenge of *Too Good* who was at a 17lb disadvantage.

The ecstatic winning owner, who had hit the bookies hard, gave all of the prize money (£1,380) to jockey Skelton and a further £1,000 to trainer Mulcaster. Later, in a fit of wild ambition, he had his bay gelding entered for the Cesarewitch in which he finished far down the field. As for *Old Joe*'s chances of a repeat success in the National, they were ruled out by the handicapper. With an extra stone to carry, and no longer partnered by Skelton, he failed to get round on his reappearances in 1887 and 1888. He was then retired with a career total of 13 races won.

See also: Skelton, Tom.

OLIVER, James Kenneth Murray OBE

Though denied success in the Grand National, Ken Oliver was the most successful of all Scottish-based trainers, being responsible for almost 1,000 winners under Rules, including five successes in the Scottish National, and three times turning out the runner-up in the big one at Aintree: *Wyndburgh* (1959 and 1962) and *Moidore's Token* (1968).

Born on February 1, 1914 at Hassendean Bank, Minto, near Hawick, Oliver became a passionate foxhunter and a prominent point-to-point rider in the 1930s; and, despite being invalided home after wartime service in North Africa and Sicily, he fought back to riding fitness, having his greatest race success on his own mare, *Sanvina*, in the 1950 Scottish Grand National at Bogside. His first winner as both rider and trainer was *Stockwhip* over hurdles at Rothbury in 1953; and he was still a permit-holder when he saddled *Wyndburgh*, beaten only one and a half lengths by *Oxo* in 1959.

Wyndburgh had already finished second and fourth, in the 1957 and 1958 Grand Nationals respectively, on the latter occasion as the 6-1 favourite. He was then owned and trained by Miss Rhona Wilkinson, and just over a month after that second run Rhona became the divorced Oliver's second wife. Together they made a formidable training partnership, with Ken taking out a full licence in 1960.

If the seven year old *Wyndburgh* had not been beaten by *Sundew* in 1957, Miss Wilkinson – not Jenny Pitman (1983) – would have been the first woman to train a Grand National winner. Similarly (a more reasonable might-have-been), Oliver – not Frank Gilman (1982) – would surely have become the first permit holder to saddle the National winner if *Wyndburgh*'s stirrup iron had not broken well over a mile from home in 1959.

Combining training with farming and working for the family's long-established livestock auctioneering firm, Oliver was to enliven the racing scene for nearly half a century. From the 1970s onwards he was popularly known as 'The Benign Bishop', so named after his champion chaser who was transferred to him after the singer Dorothy Squires had attired the fun-loving trainer in ecclesiastical garb at a post-racing party.

In winning terms, he was most famously associated with the Scottish Grand National, having won as a jockey, and five times as a trainer – with *Pappageno's Cottage* (1963), *The Spaniard* (1970), *Young Ash Leaf* (1971), *Fighting Fit* (1979) and *Cockle Strand* (1982). Remarkably, *The Spaniard* had won nine consecutive races and was still a novice when taking the National at Ayr; and when *Cockle Strand* won, Oliver was also responsible for the half-length runner-up *Three To One*.

Three To One was raced in five consecutive Aintree Grand Nationals, finishing fourth on his second attempt in 1981 but falling in all the others. *Pappageno's Cottage* finished tenth in 1964. Non-finishers included *Rambling Jack* (1982), *Fort Vulgan* (1977), *Tregarron* (1976), *Craigbrock* (1971) – and *Moidore's Token* who, after his second place in 1968, returned as a 12 year old, now sweating up badly before the start and being pulled up lame at the 21st.

Elsewhere Oliver's many successes included the 1979 Hennessy Cognac Gold Cup (*Fighting Fit*), the Greenall Whitley Chase, won three times in four years (1972-75) and the 1968 Liverpool Handicap Hurdle (*Drumikill*), plus Cheltenham Festival wins

with *Happy Arthur* (1963), *Fort Rouge* (1965), *Arctic Sunset* (1966) *Roaring Twenties* (1966), *The Spaniard* (1968) and *Tom Morgan* (1977). In 1968, with stable jockey Barry Brogan in the saddle, he achieved the rare feat of turning out five winners from five runners on one card at Wolverhampton. Famous near-misses were with *Drumikill* (second in the 1969 Champion Hurdle), *Flyingbolt* (runner-up in the 1969 King George VI Chase) and the mare *Young Ash Leaf*, beaten one length in the Whitbread Gold Cup only a week after winning the Scottish National.

Beyond training, Oliver was responsible with his great friend and rival Willie Stephenson for resurrecting the Doncaster Bloodstock Sales in 1962 and was founder chairman of the National Trainers' Federation and a director of the Royal Highland and Agricultural Society of Scotland. Not least he was renowned for his abundant *joie de vivre* as epitomised by his motto, 'win or lose, we'll have the booze'.

Ken died in 1999, aged 85, the oldest licence-holder in Britain. His widow took over the reins at Hassendean Bank, finally deciding not to renew her licence at the end of 2006.

See also: Wyndburgh.

OLIVER, Michael Edward

Trainer of the 1986 Grand National winner and great Aintree specialist *West Tip* – a bay gelding that miraculously survived a collision with a lorry (leaving a triangular foot-long gaping wound that needed 80 stitches in his hindquarters). *West Tip* went on to make seven consecutive Aintree appearances, the first of them being a second behind *Baron Blakeney* on the Mildmay course, followed by his six National efforts which included his victory and as two fourth places under 11st 7lb, then gaining a second place in 1989 and finally finishing tenth as a 13 year old.

Born on March 7, 1950, the son of a Worcestershire farmer and racehorse owner, Michael Oliver, was just past his sixth birthday when the Grand National was won by *E.S.B.*, a chaser his father had owned until a few years earlier. However, it was not until he was nine years old that he began to take a special interest in the race – his enthusiasm initially being sparked off by a £1 winning bet on *Oxo*, ridden by his then favourite jockey Michael Scudamore.

Oliver began riding at an early age and can re-

O

member his first point-to-point at Upton-on-Severn aged four. Race-riding appealed to him but after a schooling session at the late John Sheddon's within a week of his first ride, he decided to turn his skills to training itself. He was called 'Mellow Yellow' by his twin brother!

At the age of 17, as soon as he obtained his driving licence, Michael together with his great friend John Weston (who was subsequently to ride many winners for him) began making annual trips to Ireland. On his second visit, having come of age at 18, he fortuitously received a legacy of £2,000 left to him by an uncle in 1952. His passion was always the breeding of National Hunt horses and he returned with four horses, all by *Master Owen*, the sire of *Master H* who would be his first Grand National runner. One of the quartet was *Past Master*, who would go on to become the best handicap hurdler of his year including carrying 12 stone to victory at Haydock in the Wills Hurdle.

By 1973, Michael had already trained more than 20 point-to-point winners but because he had never been an assistant trainer, the Jockey Club were reluctant to grant him a trainer's licence. Given a very restrictive permit, Oliver succeeded in saddling his first winner under Rules with *Straight William* in a chase at Fakenham. The following year, on obtaining his trainer's licence at last, he started out with 14 boxes in his yard at Droitwich, Worcestershire; and, by way of his advanced schooling methods, he quickly gained a reputation for turning out remarkably sure-footed jumpers.

In his intensive schooling programme, jumpers were not only put over conventional fences and hurdles but also over such varied obstacles as tyres, painted oil-drums and coloured poles. Thus, they became well equipped to adapt to changing circumstances and surprises when they came to make their public appearances.

Oliver's training skills were first noticed by his handling of *Master H*, a supremely reliable jumper who was placed to win 18 of his 29 races. After a stunning weight-defying performance in the Worcester Royal Porcelain Chase at Worcester, he was installed as favourite for the National with *Red Rum* in 1978.

Unfortunately, however, all the careful preparation of *Master H* counted for nothing on the day. As Oliver recalls, 'He was so athletic, and jumped like a cat. He twisted in the air as he cleared the sharp bend at the Canal Turn.' In the process his saddle slipped sideways and his jockey, Reg Crank, had no alternative other than to pull him up. (He did not run, as reported by some journalists, in a hunting saddle! Nor has Oliver had a saddle slip ever before or since.) Tragically, there was to be no second chance for *Master H*. The following December, he had to be put down after breaking a shoulder when falling in the King George VI Chase at Kempton when holding third position at the last.

Oliver's next National entry, Peter Luff's *Three Gems*, had to be withdrawn on the eve of the 1979 race. Two years later he saddled *So*, formerly an Irish-trained chaser who had fallen at the tenth when ridden by amateur Niall Madden and trained by Edward O'Grady and fancied for the 1978 National. Now, as a 12 year old, *So* was a 40-1 chance to be ridden by John Francome who, having been given a tempter of £500, proceeded to hunt his way around the back of the field. Jumping superbly, apart from a mistake at the Water Jump, he finished tenth.

It was the following year, 1982, that Oliver took charge of a five year old gelding on behalf of Peter Luff. The newcomer, which he had cannily snapped up in Ireland for a mere £1,700, was *West Tip*. But then, before he had even seen a racecourse, it seemed that the bay was doomed after suffering such an appalling injury in a road accident.

The trainer was all for having the horse put out of his agony. But his wife, Sarah, argued in favour of trying to save him; and, against all odds, *West Tip* recovered – thanks to the surgical skills of Peter Thorne (brother of John Thorne, rider of the 1981 National runner-up *Spartan Missile*) and not least to the patient care of Sarah Oliver in the difficult weeks that followed. In December 1982, he made a winning racecourse debut over hurdles at Warwick only 12 weeks after the accident and the following season took equally well to fences.

In 1985 Oliver had two National runners: *Bashful Lad*, a 50-1 chance ridden by Graham McCourt, and *West Tip* who was the 13-2 joint favourite and was the mount of Richard Dunwoody, also making his debut in the race. The former was one of four horses, including the 1984 winner *Hallo Dandy*, to exit at the first fence.

In contrast, *West Tip* gave Dunwoody a dream ride round the first circuit and none was going better when, on approaching the second Becher's, he got in too close, crumbled on landing and was then hit from behind by a loose horse. His race was over but he had done more than enough to prompt his rider to predict – correctly as it proved – that they would return next year and win.

Of all the horses that have been in his charge, Oliver now nominates *Von Trappe*, an easy winner of the 1985 Coral Cup, as his classiest. But he acknowledges that there has been none to rival his *West Tip* as a natural jumper with exceptional courage and determination.

The scarred bay, ever popular at Aintree, was finally retired at the age of 14 after running at the Cheltenham Festival for a record ninth consecutive year. And two years later Oliver chose to retire from training to concentrate full-time on his business as a bloodstock agent. Today he continues to put his great breeding expertise to good use in buying and selling on horses; and meanwhile Sarah remains very much involved with racing as Chief Executive of the Amateur Jockeys Association of Great Britain. *See also:* West Tip; E.S.B.

OLLIVER, Tom

Arguably the greatest cross-country rider of the 19th century, Tom Olliver had an extraordinary record in the Grand National: 1839 (*Seventy Four*, three lengths second); 1840 (*Seventy Four*, fell); 1841 (*Oliver Twist*, fell); 1842 (*Gay Lad*, first); 1843 (*Vanguard*, first); 1844 (*Wiverton*, fell); 1845 (*Vanguard*, fell); 1846 (*Carlow*, fell); 1847 (*St Leger*, one length second); 1848 (*The Curate*, half a length second); 1849 (*Prince George*, third); 1850 (*Columbine*, failed to finish); 1851 (*Tipperary Boy*, tenth); 1852 (*Agis*, refused); 1853 (*Peter Simple*, first); 1854 (*Maurice Daley*, failed to finish); 1855 (*Bastion*, failed to finish); 1858 (*Escape*, knocked-over); 1859 (*Claudius*, failed to finish).

Thus, his National riding career spanned two decades, and he set a record by riding in the race 17 consecutive times and 19 times in all. Second to Jem Mason on *Lottery* in 1839, he went on to become the first jockey to win two Nationals, the first to have won three, and the first of seven jockeys to have ridden successive winners. Three times he was beaten only by a relative whisker. Moreover, the many riders to benefit from his tutelage included three jockeys – Captain J.L. Little, George Stevens and Tommy Pickernell – who went on to National glory.

Growing up in near poverty ('I was born and bred

hopelessly insolvent'), Sussex-born Olliver developed his horsemanship when riding a few winners on the Flat for his uncle-trainer. But he remained almost penniless and, after briefly migrating to Ireland, he reputedly returned to England with only three halfpence to his name. Thereafter he proved himself to be a genius in handling horses and a total incompetent at handling money.

His skill was to make him the most famous rider in the land, always known affectionately as 'Black Tom' because he had a swarthy appearance and black hair inherited from his Spanish-gypsy ancestors. On the other hand, his one great failing frequently landed him in the debtors' prison, though providentially never at Grand National time. (Popular legend has it that he was once visited in prison by some cavalry offices who asked him how they could be of service to him – to which he replied, 'Send me a damned good wall jumper.')

An instinctive hedonist, Olliver squandered much of his money on women and booze. But, most of all, his financial difficulties were the result of his unfailing generosity and good nature; he was an easy touch for anyone with a hard luck story. With typical wit, he explained that he had changed his given name of Oliver by adding an 'L' because that was the symbol for pound sterling – 'and it's as well to have an extra £ in hand'.

All Olliver's National victories were distinguished by his strength in a driving finish, each time powering his mount ahead on the run-in to win by a comfortable three or fourth lengths. His third success, 11 years after his first win, was the most extraordinary. He was riding the 15 year old veteran *Peter Simple* and as they led into the first Becher's they were struck into by a loose horse. It resulted in the old bay gelding being carried so far out to the left that he was in real danger of running outside the flag marking the inside limit of the course. At that moment, by happy chance, another runner, *Sir Peter Laurie* squeezed through on his inside, giving *Peter Simple* a hefty bump that put him back on the right line. Otherwise there was no luck about this victory. Thriving on the heavy going, *Peter Simple* pulled away from the last, and he still remains the only over-13 year old to win the National.

On retiring from the saddle, Olliver became landlord of 'The Star' at Leamington, but soon switched to a career as a trainer based at Wroughton, near Swindon in Wiltshire. The most famous horse to be

O

trained by Olliver was *George Frederick*, the 9-1 winner of the 1874 Derby. Sadly, 'Black Tom' died shortly before that Classic triumph, and the name of Tom Leader, his head-lad, went into the record books as the trainer.

See also: Grand National; Gay Lad; Vanguard; Peter Simple (bay); Mason, Jem.

OLYMPIANS

Two riders have competed in both the Olympic Games and the Grand National. The first was Henry Morton 'Harry' Llewellyn who was born (July 18, 1911) into the Welsh gentry and became a successful amateur steeplechase jockey, scoring 60 chase victories. Faced with an ever-increasing weight problem, he was on the verge of giving up chasing in 1935 when he was so impressed by the potential of a chestnut gelding owned by his father that he decided to make his Grand National debut.

The nine year old gelding was named *Ego* and, having wasted from 14st down to 10st 7lb, Llewellyn rode him into second place in the 1936 National, 12 lengths adrift of *Reynoldstown* who, under amateur Fulke Walwyn, was giving the 50-1 runner-up 22lb and winning for the second year in succession. The following year *Ego* was raised only 1lb in the weights and went off the 10-1 second favourite behind the great *Golden Miller*. Again the Welshman rode into a place, albeit a well-beaten fourth.

Following distinguished wartime service, rising to the rank of Lieut.-Colonel, Harry Llewellyn rode his bay gelding *Foxhunter* at the 1948 Olympic Games in London where he won a team bronze medal. Four years later, at the Helsinki Games, they jumped an immaculate last round to gain Britain's first ever show-jumping gold medal and – in this final event – Britain's only gold of the 1952 Games. *Foxhunter* was also the only horse to score a hat-trick in the King George V Gold Cup, and he starred in 12 winning Nations Cup teams. Altogether, between 1947 and 1953, Llewellyn won 140 international show-jumping classes.

The second Olympian to appear in the National was Eddie Harty who rode for Ireland as a member of the three-day event team in the 1960 Rome Olympics. Nine years later, as a professional jockey substituting for injured Owen McNally, he rode *Highland Wedding* to victory at Aintree. His younger brother, John Harty, achieved a similar double – riding for Ireland in the 1964 Tokyo Olympics and much later winning the 1980 Irish Grand National on *Daletta*.

See also: Harty, Edward.

O'NEILL, John Joe ('Jonjo')

National Hunt racing has never known a more popular jockey than irrepressible Jonjo O'Neill whose Irish good humour and courage never flagged in the face of horrendous injuries and – immediately after his retirement from the saddle – the challenge of a fight against lymphatic cancer. He was twice champion jumps jockey, in 1977-78 and 1979-80, and rode 885 winners over jumps in Britain, his victories including two Champion Hurdles and two Cheltenham Gold Cups. Yet, remarkably, he rode in eight Grand Nationals without ever completing the course.

His first attempt was in 1973 when he parted company with *Glenkiln* at The Chair while stablemate *Red Rum* fought out his famous winning duel with *Crisp*. His other National rides comprised: *Meridian II* (1976), *Sir Garnet* (1977), *Rag Trade* (1978), *Alverton* (1979), *Another Dolly* (1980), *Again The Same* (1982) and *Beacon Time* (1983). The longest of all these rides was on *Sir Garnet*, being carried as far as The Chair second time around before being knocked out of the saddle by another horse. Twice he had been on the favourite. The first, a former winner, was *Rag Trade*, who was now 12 years old and needed to be pulled up. The other, most tragically, was *Alverton*. Running only 16 days after his Cheltenham Gold Cup triumph, he looked all over the winner on the second circuit until he surprisingly crashed into Becher's and broke his neck in the fall.

Born on April 13, 1952 in Castletownroche, Co. Cork, and formally named John Joe, Jonjo began riding – like John Francome – at the age of six and bareback (on his father's hunter). At 16, he was apprenticed to Michael Connolly at The Curragh, and by the age of 18 had chalked up Flat, hurdles and steeplechase wins. In 1972, he moved to Cumbria to join the Greystoke stable of Gordon Richards; and six years later, having turned freelance, he completed his most prolific season, setting a record for the fastest 100 winners, beating the record set by Fred Winter in 1953 by more than a month and reaching a record tally of 149 victories (for 42 different owners) that was to stand until 1989 when

Peter Scudamore achieved a then astonishing 221. The following year, 1979, *Alverton* gave him his first Cheltenham Gold Cup, while on the Flat he won the York Tote-Ebor in a photo-finish on the remarkable *Sea Pigeon,* who was carrying a record 10st to victory.

Altogether he was to win 15 races on *Sea Pigeon,* including the 1980 Champion Hurdle. Four years later, on the mare *Dawn Run,* he won that race again. Then, on March 13, 1986, came his most famous victory of all: an unforgettable triumph on *Dawn Run* who became the first horse to add victory in the Cheltenham Gold Cup to success in the Champion Hurdle. That day, having stormed back from a seemingly hopeless position at the final fence, horse and rider returned to the most rapturous reception to be witnessed in steeplechasing history.

At the 1987 Cheltenham Festival Princess Anne unveiled a half-size bronze of *Dawn Run* with O'Neill in the saddle. At the time he was six months into the battle with cancer that had hit him just as he was setting up as a trainer. Hard times lay ahead but in the end he emerged triumphant, making his mark as a trainer in Cumbria. His successes included a Royal Ascot winner (*Gipsy Fiddler* in the 1990 Windsor Castle Stakes); and three Cheltenham Festival winners – *Danny Connors* (1991 Coral Golden Hurdle Final), *Front Line* (1995 National Hunt Chase) and *Master Tern* (2000 County Hurdle), all in the colours of the famed Irish owner-gambler J.P. McManus.

Notably, in December, 1999, O'Neill brought back the injury-plagued *Legal Right* to win the £80,000 Tripleprint Gold Cup at Cheltenham by 22 lengths, and one year later the Tote Silver Cup at Ascot. Then, in the summer of 2001, Jonjo left his Ivy House stables near Penrith to move south to Gloucestershire, taking over Jackdaws Castle, formerly the famous training base of David Nicholson. Purchased by McManus, this yard was now to be redeveloped at a cost of millions as a state-of-the-art training centre with 100 boxes. Here the trainer got off to a tremendous start, with 50 winners in the autumn, only to have progress halted by a bout of coughing. But his long-term prospects were excellent; and valuably, in 2002, he was added to the roster of trainers employed by Sir Robert Ogden, the champion jumps owner of the previous season.

That year he entered four horses in the National, none making it to the line-up. But there were consolations aplenty. At the Aintree meeting he had four winners: a 577-1 double with the hurdlers *Sudden Shock* and *Quazar*, a hugely impressive success with his chaser *Carbury Cross*; and on National day with his hurdler *Intersky Falcon* showing astonishing improvement to win by 15 lengths. Jonjo wound up his first season at Jackdaws Castle with a remarkable total of 113 winners and nearly £1million in prize money. He was fourth in the trainers' championship; and he had become the first man to have both ridden and trained 100 winners in a season. At the age of 50 he could look forward to a very bright future indeed.

In the 2002-03 season, his many winners included the hurdler *Mighty Montefalco* who gave Tony McCoy his 1,700th victory to become the most successful jump jockey of all time. He approached the Cheltenham Festival with a tremendously strong hand that included the most exciting novice hurdler, *Rhinestone Cowboy*, and *Keen Leader*, a brilliant novice chaser entered for the Gold Cup. Although his most fancied runners were beaten, he had three winners: *Sudden Shock*, the 25-1 shock winner of the National Hunt Novices' Chase; and hurdlers *Spectroscope* and *Inching Closer.*

At this stage O'Neill had never had a Grand National runner in 16 years as a trainer. Now he had five horses entered and two were outstanding: *Carbury Cross* and *Mini Sensation*. The former, carrying the famous yellow and black colours of Anne, Duchess of Westminster, owner of *Arkle* and the 1985 National winner *Last Suspect*, was the biggest market mover in 149 entries, being slashed by Coral from 33-1 to 16-1 third favourite. The latter also became strongly fancied, having finished runner-up in the 2002 Midlands National, and then winning the 2003 Welsh National on bottomless ground, and the Singer and Friedlander National Trial Chase at Uttoxeter over three and a half miles.

As it happened, only *Carbury Cross* made it to the National. O'Neill's first runner in the race got round in his own time to finish a remote seventh. It was, nevertheless, a memorable meeting for the trainer. He saddled four winners, starting with a 148-1 treble on the Friday – winners *Master Tern* (Martell Cognac Handicap Chase), *Clan Royal* (the £40,600 Topham Chase) and *Iris's Gift* (Sefton Novices' Hurdle) – and ending with *Classic Native* taking the Martell Champion Standard National Hunt Flat Race at 25-1. At the end of the season he was third in the trainers' championship with 114 wins and £1,517,365 in prize money from 546 runners.

O

In November, 2003, the McManus-owned *Clan Royal* looked to be a potentially major National contender when he scored his second victory over the big Aintree fences in winning the Becher Chase by a short head from *Amberleigh House*. Thus, after the 2004 Cheltenham Festival, at which he won the Stayers' Hurdle with *Iris's Gift*, Jonjo moved on to Liverpool with the highest hopes. He had two of the four co-favourites for the National: *Clan Royal*, set to carry a most sporting 10st 5lb, and *Joss Naylor*.

The Grand National meeting started well for O'Neill. He took the opening hurdle with *Iris's Gift* and on the Saturday he won the £87,000 Martell Cognac Aintree Hurdle with *Rhinestone Cowboy*. One hour later triumph in the National seemed imminent as *Clan Royal* was driven into the lead approaching two out. But Liam Cooper had lost his whip when they clouted the 26th fence and now *Clan Royal* was to wander off-line on the run-in, losing vital ground in going down by three lengths to the strong-finishing *Amberleigh House*. Again Jonjo finished third in the trainers' championship, this time with prize money of £1,543,697 from 102 wins.

The new season opened with the promise of still better things to come following the sensational transfer of champion jockey A. P. McCoy to Jackdaws Castle. By December, 2004, O'Neill had had 90 winners, 70 of them ridden by McCoy. But then the yard was hit so badly with sickness from three different virus strains that it had to be closed down for nearly two months. Nevertheless, in late January, the trainer had the biggest individual entry for the Grand National: 14 entries, one more than the usually dominant Martin Pipe.

Four made it to the line-up and their fortunes were remarkably mixed. *Native Emperor*, a 100-1 chance, unseated his rider at the ninth. *Shamawan*, the 200-1 outsider, was the last of 21 finishers. But against all expectations, *Simply Gifted*, ridden by Brian Harding, finished third at 66-1, beaten only a head by runner-up *Royal Auclair*, and so collecting prize money of £77,000. Meanwhile, the stable's No. 1 hope – joint second favourite *Clan Royal* with McCoy aboard – suffered the cruellest fate, being carried out by a loose horse when approaching second Becher's in the lead.

In 2006 O'Neill had seven Grand National entries, headed by *Clan Royal*; and, to his delight, his main challenger was surprisingly allotted a mere 10st 8lb, 3lb less than in 2005. The senior jumps handicapper

Phil Smith explained that he had given him the same rating of 140 because the horse had left the race too far out for him to judge where he might have finished. Nonetheless, it seemed generous for a contender who had been runner-up in the National on 10st 5lb and it sealed *Clan Royal*'s long-held position as the market leader, now cut to as short as 6-1.

At the Cheltenham Festival Jonjo had one winner: the unbeaten hurdler *Black Jack Ketchum* who was immediately quoted at 4-1 for the 2007 Ladbrokes World Hurdle. Meanwhile, in the Gold Cup, a brilliant performance saw runner-up *Hedgehunter* head the National betting; and on the day he and *Clan Royal* went off as joint 5-1 favourites and finished second and third respectively. Creditably, Jonjo's only other runner, *Risk Assessor*, came home fifth at 66-1, and O'Neill ended the season fourth in the trainers' championship with prize money of £1,226,280 and 105 wins.

The following season, when he reached his fastest century of winners, he was runner-up for the trainer's title, not least thanks to two horses: the extraordinary *Exotic Dancer*, winner of four major races besides being runner-up in the King George VI Chase and the Cheltenham Gold Cup, and *Butler's Cabin* who picked up a 100,000 euro bonus for winning at the Cheltenham Festival and in the Irish National in the same year.

Unfortunately, *Exotic Dancer* was hit with a massive, top weight of 11st 12lb for the Grand National and so, instead, he had a winning run in Aintree's valuable Betfair Bowl Chase. O'Neill also turned out *Two Miles West*, the 25-1 winner of the John Smith's Handicap Hurdle, and *Albertas Run*, successful in the 22-runner Listed Handicap Hurdle. But only one of his four National entries made it to the line-up: *Clan Royal*, now 12 years old and past his brilliant best. Never prominent, he trailed home a far distant 11th of 12 finishers.

See also: McManus, John Patrick.

OSBORNE, Joseph

Trainer and owner of *Abd-El-Kader*, the diminutive bay gelding who, in 1851, by just 'half a neck' from the mare *Maria Day*, became the first horse to win the Grand National twice. Born in 1810, Joseph Osborne of Dardistown Castle, Co. Meath, remained a familiar, white-bearded figure in racing circles until the turn of the century. He was a noted gambler; also the editor of *The Horsebreeders' Handbook* and a regular contributor to *Bell's Life*, a forerunner of *The Sporting Life*. In view of his unsurpassed experience and expertise, it is noteworthy that, in 1896, the octogenarian expressed the view that perhaps the best horse to have won the Grand National was *Salamander*, the seven year old who triumphed in 1866 as a 40-1 long-shot.

See also: Abd-El-Kader; Gambles.

O'SULLEVAN, Sir Peter OBE, CBE

Like *Red Rum*, the greatest of all Grand National horses, Sir Peter O'Sullevan, the greatest of all horse racing commentators, is immortalised in bronze at Aintree racecourse – his bust, overlooking the paddock, having being unveiled by the Princess Royal on April 5, 1997, the day he was due to deliver his 50th and last commentary on the National. As a result of the IRA bomb scare, it was to be another 49 hours before the 'Voice of Racing' was heard calling the horses in the 150th running of the race.

Born on March 3, 1918, in Kenmare, Co. Kerry, educated at Charterhouse and then in Switzerland where the fine air was better for his acute asthma, O'Sullevan first heard a radio commentary of the National in 1927 and 20 years later he made his National debut as a commentator, calling the horses under the most difficult circumstances – a huge field of 57 runners disappearing into the heavy rain and mist with *Caughoo*, one of many 100-1 outsiders, emerging as the winner.

In 1950 he became a racing correspondent for the *Daily Express*, a role he would fulfil for 36 years; and he switched from radio to television in 1960 when it was still in black and white. That year brought the first televised Grand National, and he could not have had a more passionate interest in the race. The winner he called home was *Merryman II*, owned by his friend Miss Winifred Wallace and ridden by another friend, Gerry Scott. O'Sullevan had advised the owner to send the former hunter chaser to trainer Neville Crump. Moreover, three months before the race, a bookmaker had agreed to lay him £1,000 to £28 on *Merryman II* to win – odds near 35-1 compared to the starting price of 13-2.

However, on a strictly impersonal level, the National that most stuck in his mind was the 1973 epic, ending with the heart-stirring duel between *Red Rum* and *Crisp*. He rated the losing run of *Crisp*, conceding 23lb, as the greatest steeplechase performance he had ever witnessed.

O'Sullevan, knighted in June, 1997, remained the 'Voice of Racing' for half a century until his retirement in his 80th year after calling home the winner (*Suny Bay*) of the 1997 Hennessy Cognac Gold Cup. In all those years he missed calling only one National – in 1952 when Aintree owner Mirabel Topham chose to bring in her own makeshift broadcasting team. Sir Peter's mastery of his craft was never shown to greater effect than in 1993 when, amid all the confusion of the falsely started void National, he maintained a remarkably astute commentary.

He was no less astute as an owner of horses – most notably the sprinter *Be Friendly* (winner of the Prix de l'Abbaye, King's Stand Stakes and Ayr Gold Cup) and *Attivo* (Triumph Hurdle, Chester Cup and Northumberland Plate). Much less well-known was his sterling work on behalf of racing charities. Among the many beneficiaries of his Peter O'Sullevan Trust are the Brooke Hospital for Animals, the International League for Protection of Horses, Racing Welfare and the Thoroughbred Rehabilitation Centre.

OUTSIDERS

Since the 1860s, when it became the custom to price up the majority of Grand National runners, only five rank outsiders have won the race: *Caughoo* (1947) and *Foinavon* (1967) at 100-1; and *Rubio* (1908), *Russian Hero* (1949) and *Ayala* (1963), all at 66-1. Although *Tipperary Tim* (1928) and *Gregalach* (1929) won at 100-1, they were opposed by several contenders on 200-1.

Many rank outsiders have been placed in the National. Two – *Magpie* (1886) and *Melleray's Belle* (1929) – finished fourth at 200-1. Five horses have been runner-up at 100-1: *Hall Court* (1869), *Pan* (1890), *Filbert* (1897), one-eyed *Bovril III* (1927) and *Jack Finlay* (1946).

Other placed 100-1 outsiders were *Scarrington* (1871), *Buckaway II* (1905), *Annandale* (1931) and *Camelot Knight* (1997), all finishing third; and *Brunswick* (1890), *Lazy Boots* (1935), *Housewarmer* (1946), *Uncle Barney* (1952) and *Gay Navarree* (1962), all fourth. In 2007 *Philson Run* finished fourth at 100-1 but the rank outsider that year was non-finisher *Sonevafushi* (150-1) with three others on 125-1.

See also: Starting Prices; Miss Mowbray.

OVERWEIGHT

The extra poundage carried by a racehorse if its jockey weighs out at a weight higher than that allot-

O

ted to the runner by the handicapper. Conceivably, it might just have made a crucial difference in the 1983 Grand National when amateur rider Colin Magnier put up 1lb overweight on *Greasepaint*, who was beaten three-quarters of a length by *Corbiere*. In 1991 Mark Dwyer put up 4lb overweight when finishing third on the mare *Auntie Dot* at 50-1. But in this case he was well beaten, eight lengths behind *Garrison Savannah* who, in turn, was five lengths behind the victorious *Seagram*.

In 1989 Jimmy Frost put up 3lb overweight on *Little Polveir* and yet still scored a convincing seven lengths win. Most remarkably, Arthur Freeman put up 6lb overweight when winning by 30 lengths on *Mr What* in 1958.

OWEN, Captain Edward Roderick

'Roddy' Owen made his Grand National debut on his own *Kilworth* (a faller in 1885) and subsequently made no impression on *Ballot Box* (a faller, 1887), *Gamecock* (seventh, 1888) and *Kilworth*, now owned by Lord Dudley (refused, 1889). Yet, on his final two appearances, this fiercely competitive Army officer finished runner-up on *Cloister* in 1891 and crowned his amateur riding career with victory on *Father O'Flynn* in 1892.

At his fifth attempt in 1891, he saw victory within his grasp as he came to the last on Lord Dudley's *Cloister* and pressed hard on the heels of the lone leader, *Come Away*. But in his eagerness Owen made a fatal mistake; he chose to go for a non-existent gap between his rival and the rails. Harry Beasley, on the favourite, twice refused to yield his ground, and crucially *Cloister* lost momentum in having to switch to the outside. He was beaten by just half a length.

Owen found defeat a pill too bitter to swallow. He lodged an objection to the winner on the grounds of his rider having 'taken my ground on the run-in'. Subsequently he was confronted by a menacing group of Irishmen, all of whom had backed their favourite *Come Away*. Amateur rider George Lambton, who witnessed the scene, later recalled: 'I can see him (Owen) now, with his back to the wall, cool as a cucumber, saying: 'All right, but wait till it's settled, then I'll fight every one of you, single-handed or the whole lot of you together.'

Owen's bravado was never put the test, the Irish mood turning to rejoicing when the objection was overruled. But the captain was still spoiling for a fight. Now he spoke of seeking out Beasley and giv-

ing him a jolly good thrashing. Fortunately, he was calmed by *Cloister*'s trainer, Richard Marsh, who quipped: 'I don't think I should if I were you. You might come off second best again!'

In truth, given the chance, Owen would have been just as obdurate as Beasley in holding his position on that run to the line. His ruthlessness had already been demonstrated in this 1891 National when *Why Not*, ridden by his friend Charlie Cunningham, had looked the likely winner coming to the second last. Though there had been plenty of room, Owen on *Cloister* had crowded *Why Not*, causing a fall in which Cunningham was so badly injured that his amateur career in racing was ended.

Racing apart, however, Owen was quite a charmer: a dedicated officer in the Lancashire Fusiliers who was renowned for his fearlessness and wit. It is recorded that he was once censured by a general for neglecting his military duties in favour of racing. 'I haven't see much of you lately, Captain Owen', said the general. To which the captain cheekily replied: 'My loss, general – not yours.'

Unlike the unfortunate Cunningham, Welsh-born Owen, amateur winner of some 250 lesser races, was to have one last, successful tilt at the National. In 1892 he secured the ride on *Father O'Flynn*, a small, seven year old bay owned by Mr Gordon Wilson, a subaltern (later colonel) in the Household Cavalry and a fellow Old Etonian. The mount, winner with Owen of his past two races, was a 20-1 chance. The clear 11-2 favourite was *Cloister*, now under new ownership and with a new rider, amateur Mr J.C. Dormer.

Raised 10lb in the weights, *Cloister* made most of the running on the second circuit and was left well in the lead when *Midshipmite* fell at the fence after Valentine's. It seemed to be all over. But all the while *Father O'Flynn* was closing on the favourite and when they came to the run-in the concession of nearly two stone proved too much for *Cloister*. Owen's challenger swept by and relentlessly pulled away to win by a full 20 lengths.

A few days later, his ambition fulfilled, the 36 year old captain went to the War Office in London and applied for active service overseas. He would not ride in England again. Military service took him to the Gold Coast, Uganda, India and finally to Anglo-Egyptian Sudan. There, just four years after achieving his cherished dream at Aintree, Owen died of cholera contracted while taking part with

370

distinction in the Dongola Expedition against the Mahdi. More than half a century on, a bay named after him would win the 1959 Cheltenham Gold Cup – ironically ridden by Harry Beasley's grandson. *See also:* Cloister; Father O'Flynn.

OWEN, George

As jockey and then trainer, George Owen had an involvement with the Grand National spanning more than 30 years, beginning in 1930 when he was a faller on *Theorem*, a 100-1 shot. Five years later his mount – Sir Geoffrey Congreve's *Lazy Boots*, another 100-1 outsider – was the fourth of only six finishers; and in 1940, in his seventh and last National, he was sixth on *The Professor II*. His greatest success, however, was away from Aintree: as the first northern-based jockey to win the Cheltenham Gold Cup – on *Brendan's Cottage* in 1939.

A fractured skull ended Owen's riding career. After the Second World War, he set up as a trainer at Malpas in Cheshire, and there he provided the first rides for an amateur novice named Dick Francis. He finally gained a place on the National roll of honour by preparing *Russian Hero*, the shock 66-1 winner under Irishman Leo McMorrow in 1949. It was a victory that confounded the critics who had judged the gelding to be lacking in both jumping ability and stamina. And ironically, Francis, who had ridden *Russian Hero* several times before, was on the second placed horse, Lord Bicester's *Roimond*.

Although *Russian Hero* never won a race again, Owen continued to be a much respected trainer of National contenders. Most notably, in 1960, when the race was first televised, he had the thrill of seeing his two runners leading the field over Valentine's second time around. But this was the year of *Merryman II*, a favourite winning impressively by 15 lengths. Lord Leverhulme's *Badanlock*, trained by Owen and ridden by Stan Mellor, came second, and Owen was also responsible for the fourth-placed *Tea Fiend*. *See also:* Russian Hero; Francis, Richard.

OWNERS

Most winning owners

3 wins – Captain Henry Machell with *Disturbance* (1873), *Reugny* (1874), *Regal* (1876)

3 wins – Sir Charles Assheton-Smith (formerly Charles Duff) with *Cloister* (1893), *Jerry M* (1912), *Covercoat* (1913)

2 wins – Mr Stanley Howard with *Eremon* (1907), *Jenkinstown* (1910)

Owners who rode their own horses to victory

Capt. J.L. Little – *Chandler* (1848)
Mr F.G. Hobson – *Austerlitz* (1877)
Mr Garrett Moore – *The Liberator* (1879)
Lord Manners – *Seaman* (1882)
Prince Charles Kinsky – *Zoedone* (1883)

Oldest winning owner

Mr Jim Joel who was 92 years old when his *Maori Venture* won in 1987. He lived on until the age of 97. Two winning owners lived to celebrate their 100th birthday: Frank Douglas-Pennant, fifth Lord Penrhyn, who won with *Rubio* in 1908; and Mary Stephenson (later LeBlond), the American owner of 1965 winner *Jay Trump*.

Youngest winning owner

Mr Bryan Burrough, 23 years old when his *Corbiere* won in 1983.

Lady winning owners

Lady Nelson – *Ally Sloper* (1915)
Mrs Hugh Peel – *Poethlyn* (1919)
Mrs M. Partridge – *Sprig* (1927)
Mrs M.A. Gemmell – *Gregalach* (1929)
Mrs F. Ambrose Clark – *Kellsboro' Jack* (1933)
Miss Dorothy Paget – *Golden Miller* (1934)
Mrs Marion Scott – *Battleship* (1938)
Mrs Lurline Brotherton – *Freebooter* (1950)
Mrs Cecily Welman – *Quare Times* (1955)
Mrs Leonard Carver – *E.S.B.* (1956)
Mrs Geoffrey Kohn – *Sundew* (1957)
Miss Winifred Wallace – *Merryman II* (1960)
Mrs Mary Stephenson – *Jay Trump* (1965)
Mrs D.A. Whitaker – *Lucius* (1978)
Anne, Duchess of Westminster – *Last Suspect* (1985)
Miss Juliet Reed – *Rhyme 'N' Reason* (1988)
Mrs Harry Duffey – *Mr Frisk* (1990)
Mrs Pat Thompson – *Party Politics* (1992)
Mrs J. Maxwell Moran – *Papillon* (2000)

In 1999 six runners were owned by women, among them *Baronet*, racing in the colours of Mrs Pat Thompson who had won with *Party Politics*, a gift from her husband only two days before the 1992 National. *Baronet* fell at the fourth. The three placed

O

horses – *Blue Charm* (runner-up), *Call It A Day* (third) and *Addington Boy* (forth) – were all lady-owned.

OXO

Eight year old winner of the 1959 Grand National at his first attempt, bringing victory for jockey Michael Scudamore on his seventh appearance in the race and a rare big-race double for trainer Willie Stephenson who, eight years earlier, had saddled *Arctic Prince* to win the Epsom Derby.

Bred in Dorset (by *Bobsleigh* out of *Patum*) and originally sold as a yearling for 400 guineas, *Oxo* was an inspired purchase by Stephenson who, at the Newmarket Sales in 1957, had made a successful bid of 3,200 guineas for the point-to-pointer on behalf of Mr J.E. Bigg. The sturdy bay gelding took quickly to fences, winning his second ever chase just three months later. The following season, his Aintree build-up – two wins and a good second place – was so impressive that he was made the 8-1 second favourite for his National debut, behind *Mr What* who had been raised 17lb for winning the previous year by 30 lengths.

Early on, Scudamore held up *Oxo* towards the rear, avoiding the mayhem at Becher's where at least six horses fell. They progressed through the field towards the end of the first circuit, and when *Surprise Packet*, the front-runner from the start, fell with three others at Becher's second time round, *Oxo* had only one rival in the lead: the so reliable *Wyndburgh* who had finished second in 1957 and fourth in 1958.

Now came an arguably decisive mishap. As *Wyndburgh* landed steeply over Becher's, one of his stirrups broke. For the sake of balance, jockey Tim Brookshaw slipped his foot out of the one secure iron and, squeezing with his legs, urged his mount on under a considerable handicap. Neck-and-neck the two leaders duelled over the next six fences. *Oxo* then opened up a lead of three or four lengths, but stumbled over the last, and on the run-in the stirrup-less Brookshaw worked wonders to finish fast on *Wyndburgh*. But the winning post came too soon; *Oxo* prevailed by just one and a half lengths with *Mr What* a further eight lengths back in third. Only four of 34 starters finished.

Oxo made one more National appearance – in 1961. But he was no longer the force of old and, with an extra 9lb on his back, he needed to be pulled up by Scudamore after the second Becher's. He was campaigned for three more seasons without winning a single race and was then hunted by his owner.
See also: Stephenson, William A; Scudamore, Michael.

PAGE, John

Having made an impressive Grand National debut – ten lengths runner-up on Lord Poulett's fast finishing *Cortolvin* in 1866 – Johnny Page went on to ride in ten successive Nationals, winning on *Cortolvin* (1867) and *Casse Tete* (1872), and achieving a third place on *La Veine* (1875) and a fourth place on *Pearl Diver* (1871). His five lengths success on *Cortolvin*, a 16-1 shot, made a small fortune for the new owner, the Duke of Hamilton. It was also notable for the fact that it was the first time since the race became a handicap that a horse had carried as much as 11st 13lb to victory.

Warwickshire-born Page was one of the most stylish jockeys of his time, a supreme judge of pace, and so strong in a driving finish that he was nicknamed 'The Pusher'. Following his first National success, he failed to complete in 1868 on the Duke of Hamilton's *Garus*. The next year he was strongly fancied to win on *Fortunatus*, the hot 7-2 favourite in a 22-strong field, but the six year old completely ran out of steam when leading three out and had to be pulled up. Similarly, in 1870, the jockey was frustrated as his mount, *Pearl Diver*, carrying a huge top weight of 12st 7lb, came to the end of his tether when in third place at the penultimate fence and failed to finish.

Though *Pearl Diver* was dropped 16lb for the 1871 National, Page could bring him home no better than fourth behind the record-breaking grey, *The Lamb*. In 1872, however, *The Lamb* was saddled with a prohibitive 12st 7lb while Page had a mount on the minimum 10st: the seven year old mare *Casse Tete* on whom he had achieved a most promising third place in Croydon's Great Metropolitan Chase. Having failed to finish in the two previous Nationals, *Casse Tete* now went off at 20-1.

The going was on the firm side, the pace suicidally fast, and Page wisely chose to bide his time on the first circuit, only coming into prominence at the Canal Turn second time around. By the penultimate fence, his main rivals were *The Lamb* and *Harvester*. But the former now flagged under his enormous weight and the latter was pulled up lame after a bad landing over the last. *Casse Tete* ran on unchallenged to score by a comfortable six lengths.

The following year Page's ride came to an early close when *Casse Tete*'s bridle broke; and he again failed to finish in 1874 on the Duke of Hamilton's six year old *Fantome*. Finally, in 1875 he appeared on the book to have a great chance of ending his National career in triumph. He was on Baron Finot's *La Veine*, the 6-1 favourite. But, realistically, it was another case of a French challenger being harshly handicapped: a mare merely five years old and allotted 11st 12lb. In the circumstances, 'Pusher' Page worked wonders to bring the youngster home in third place – beaten only half a length and three lengths by *Pathfinder* and *Dainty* who were receiving 15lb and 12lb respectively.
See also: Cortolvin; Casse Tete.

PAGET, The Hon. Dorothy Wyndham

Of the 19 women who have owned Grand National winners, the Hon. Dorothy Paget, daughter of the first and last Lord Queensborough, was by far the most extraordinary: a supreme eccentric who, after inheriting a fortune at the age of 21, plunged into horse racing on a hugely extravagant scale, at one time having more than 50 horses in training. Her successful horses included *Golden Miller*, winner of the 1934 Grand National and five consecutive Cheltenham Gold Cups; Gold Cup winners *Roman Hackle* (1940) and *Mont Tremblant* (1952); Derby winner *Straight Deal* (1943); and Champion Hurdler winners *Insurance* (1932 and 1933), *Solford* (1940) and *Distel* (1946).

Between 1945 and 1959, Miss Paget owned 359 winners over jumps in Britain – a total surpassed in the post-war era only by Arthur Stephenson (465) and the Queen Mother (445). Owning statistics were not maintained until 1939, but if they had been available earlier they would probably show her to be the most winning National Hunt owner of all time.

It was estimated that Miss Paget spent nearly £3 million as an owner. She was also an inveterate gambler, one so reckless that she is reputed to have once staked £160,000 (successfully) on a 1-8 shot. Like almost anyone who bets on a regular, indiscriminate basis, she had many more losers than winners. In one year alone she lost as much as £50,000. But then profit was never her primary concern. It was the frisson of betting that appealed. In its pursuit she would drive trainers to despair with her interminable conferences, bullying manner and late night telephone calls (she slept mostly during the daylight hours, dining at 7 a.m. and breakfasting at 8.30 p.m.); and frequently she sought jockey changes, with Dave Dick the only one to gain her long-time favour.

Born in 1905 and educated at Heathfield School,

P

Ascot, Dorothy emerged as a strangely individualistic young woman. At the age of 19, having been trained as a singer, she chose to give her first public performance before an audience of 500 prisoners at Wormwood Scrubs. When attending a French finishing school she established a colony near Paris for displaced Russian aristocrats. Then, after inheriting a fortune, she plunged into the world of motor racing, setting up at great expense a team of Bentleys. Her cars never won a major race, and so she turned to racing horses.

While her fortune came from her mother's side, her love of the Turf was inherited from her father who had won the 2,000 Guineas of 1922 with his horse *St Louis*. In the 1930s, she became the foremost buyer of bloodstock, often incurring huge losses. She paid 6,000 guineas for *Tuppence* who, after failing in the 1933 Derby, was sold for £300; 15,000 guineas for the yearling *Colonel Payne*, sold ten years later for 250 guineas.

Her first outstanding investment was made in 1931, when she was gambling at a chemin-de-fer party in London. There, responding to an offer from trainer Basil Briscoe, she picked up a pair of horses for £12,000. One, named *Insurance*, became the first to win the Champion Hurdle twice (1932 and 1933). The other was the phenomenal *Golden Miller*.

In 1932, after *Golden Miller* had been given a preliminary gallop at Cheltenham, both trainer Briscoe and jockey Ted Leader agreed that it would be unwise to risk the five year old on the prevailing firm ground. But Miss Paget – accompanied as usual by her pack of female secretaries – was adamant. She already had her money down and so he would run in the Gold Cup. For once her overruling was vindicated. A winner at 13-2, 'the Miller' would never be so generously priced again.

Miss Paget's passion for steeplechasing was heightened by rivalry with her cousin, American millionaire 'Jock' Hay Whitney, who had run second placed *Easter Hero* in the 1929 Grand National and third placed *Sir Lindsay* in 1930. Like him, she yearned to win the National above all else; and, while he had so many near misses, she realised her ambition in 1934 with *Golden Miller*'s record-breaking run.

Altogether Miss Paget ran horses in 13 Nationals. After *Golden Miller*'s fifth and final appearance, her great hope was eight year old *Kilstar*, the 8-1 favourite in 1939. Ridden by American-born George Archibald, he finished third, and was then a distant 12th in 1940, the year in which Miss Paget won both the Cheltenham Gold Cup and the Champion Hurdle with horses trained by Owen Anthony.

In 1943 she finally realised her great Flat racing dream when her *Straight Deal* won the Epsom Derby by a head. She was the leading owner of that wartime season; and in the same year she won the Irish National with *Golden Jack*. Then, with the 1946 resumption of the Aintree National after the Second World War, she made a triple challenge. Two of her runners – *Dunshaughlin* and *Astrometer* – were fallers, while the complete outsider of the trio, 100-1 shot *Housewarmer*, finished fourth.

The following year her contenders – *Housewarmer* and *Kilnaglory* – came sixth and eight respectively; and in 1948 and 1949 her *Happy Home* was fourth and sixth. At that stage, it seemed that her involvement in the National was coming to an end. She was unrepresented in both 1950 and 1951.

But the persistent Miss Paget was to return to Aintree with two more strong contenders. In 1952 she ran *Legal Joy*, a nine year old trained by Fulke Walwyn and ridden by Michael Scudamore. He finished runner-up by five lengths to the favourite *Teal*, with *Wot No Sun* a distant third. Then, in Coronation year, she was represented by seven year old *Mont Tremblant*, her 1952 Cheltenham Gold Cup winner, now harshly burdened with a top weight of 12st 5lb, a full stone more than any of the other 30 runners. Ridden by Dave Dick, destined to win the 1956 National on *E.S.B.*, he came home second by 20 lengths to *Early Mist,* who was initiating a hat-trick of National wins for training genius Vincent O'Brien.

For the second successive year Miss Paget had ended up the bridesmaid. And, sadly, her involvement with the National was to end on a tragic note one year later when *Legal Joy*, under Dave Dick, suffered a fatal fall. She herself died in her sleep in February 1960, after several years of poor health not unrelated to a prodigious appetite which at one time raised her weight to more than 20st. She was only 54.

See also: Golden Miller; Briscoe, Basil; Wilson, Gerry; Leader, Ted; Whitney, John Hay; Adelphi, The.

PAPILLON

The Ted Walsh-trained winner of the Grand National in 2000 when he was the subject of a multi-million-

374

pound gamble, being backed down on the morning of the race from 33-1 to 10-1 joint second favouritism. His victory, by one and a half lengths from *Mely Moss*, marked a winning debut in the race for 20 year old Ruby Walsh; and, following the success one year before of Tommy and Paul Carberry, trainer and rider of *Bobbyjo* respectively, it represented another triumph for an Irish father-and-son combination.

Papillon – by *Lafontaine* out of *Glens Princess* – had been bought in 1995 by Ted Walsh on behalf of a long-time American friend of the family, Mrs Betty Moran, well known in the States as a breeder and as owner of *Crème Fraiche*, the 1985 Belmont Stakes winner. At 5,300 guineas he quickly proved to be a fantastic bargain, taking well to fences from the start and, as a mere five year old, picking up some £7,000 from wins at Punchestown and Fairyhouse. Early the following year, he more than doubled his earnings by winning over an extended three miles at Fairyhouse and thus, as an improving novice, a good jumper and a dual course winner, he was made favourite for the 1997 Irish Grand National.

It was a bridge too far. No six year old had won this National for 12 years and now, under Charlie Swan, having his 11th ride in the race, he finished fourth behind a winner, *Mudahim*, much more suited by give underfoot. One year later, when he returned following a disappointing effort in Cheltenham's Fulke Walwyn/Kim Muir Handicap Chase, he was an unfancied 20-1 chance, burdened with the 12st top weight. Yet, brilliantly ridden by Ruby, then an 18 year old amateur, he went down by a mere half a length, beaten by eight year old *Bobbyjo* who had an 11lb advantage.

In February, 1999, *Papillon* was a remote fourth behind *Florida Pearl* in the Hennessy Cognac Gold Cup. Shortly afterwards, he was allotted 10st 11b. for the Grand National, making him the only Irish-trained entry in the handicap proper. However, it was then decided that he should instead have a third go at the Irish version. Subsequently he showed that he had the speed to remain in contention for a long way in the Queen Mother Champion Chase. But 19 days later, carrying 12st top weight, he was unplaced for the first time in the Irish National.

Thereafter *Papillon* continued to disappoint over fences, running up a total of seven races without once being placed. But this was largely because he

was lugging big weights in soft ground. He could be a different proposition on good going; and now, 20 days before the first Grand National of the new millennium, trainer Walsh shrewdly followed the example of the great Vincent O'Brien when turning out three successive winners of the Aintree National and of Carberry when sharpening up *Bobbyjo* to win a year ago. As a confidence-booster, he put the bay gelding in a hurdle race over two and a half miles at Leopardstown; and, given good ground at last, he finished third, with *Bobbyjo* (receiving 23lb) ten lengths back in fifth.

Ostensibly, the 2000 Grand National was the most open in living memory since – uniquely in modern times – 33 of 40 runners were in the handicap proper. Most unusually, too, the field included six who were among the first seven past the winning post in 1999: *Bobbyjo, Call It A Day, Addington Boy, Feels Like Gold, Brave Highlander* and *Kendal Cavalier*. Only the runner-up *Blue Charm* was missing. Furthermore, the return challengers included *Merry People*, the 200-1 shocker who had come from nowhere to challenge for the lead only to fall – for the first time in his life – at the penultimate fence. This year he was 40-1.

But in reality, as so many tipsters rightly judged, *Papillon* had much more than most in his favour. He had his necessary good ground, and he was very well in at the weights – carrying 8lb less than *Bobbyjo*, and being 19lb better off for a half-length beating in the 1998 Irish Grand National. Moreover, he had never failed to finish in 27 races over fences.

The one big nagging doubt about *Papillon*'s chances was his quirkiness. He had a habit of running in snatches and sometimes, unpredictably, he would suddenly decide he had had enough in a race. At Aintree, however, he was on his best behaviour, starting steadily and moving comfortably behind the leaders. Meanwhile five had fallen at the first and the favourite, *Dark Stranger*, had gone at the third. *Star Traveller*, the joint second favourite, jumped to the front at the Canal Turn first time round and was to hold the position until the 20th fence.

Unlike *Papillon*, who moved up to lead from five fences out, *Star Traveller* was not jumping cleanly and rider Richard Johnson, bidding for a Gold Cup-National double, finally pulled him up at the 27th while still well in contention. He had suffered a tendon injury in his near-fore. Ten were still in with a chance at this point but most of them were visibly tiring and soon it had become a two-horse race, between *Papillon* and *Mely Moss* who had made relentless late progress under Norman Williamson.

Mely Moss, having his first race for 346 days, was briefly left in the lead when Ruby had to fractionally check round a loose horse two out. But *Papillon* was marginally ahead over the last and, though he started to idle at the Elbow, he then rallied under pressure and held on strongly to win. Runner-up *Mely Moss* was some 12 lengths ahead of third placed *Niki Dee*, with 50-1 shot *Brave Highlander* seven lengths back in fourth.

With tough foot-and-mouth restrictions cancelling all racing in Ireland for six weeks, *Papillon* had a very limited preparation for the 2001 National: only two outings at just over two miles, finishing first and second. However, when the weights were announced, he was the immediate market mover, having been lowered 2lb to a mark of 10st 10lb. Ladbrokes promptly cut him from 16-1 to 10-1 antepost favouritism. But, following withdrawals, he was to be raised a further 9lb, headed in the weights only by *Beau*, and on a rainy race-day he was totally unsuited by the extremely heavy ground. Remounted by Ruby after being brought down by a loose horse at the 19th, he did extraordinarily well to finish a distant fourth and last.

In 2002 Ruby Walsh thought that *Papillon* was well handicapped for a third tilt at the National. For 51 weeks his training had been geared to that aim, but then, with his price as short as 14-1, he had to be withdrawn with a strained knee ligament. Surprisingly he was again included in the National entries for 2003 despite the fact that he was now 12 years old and had not run for ten months. He was allotted 10st 11lb, a pound more than he had carried as a ten year old. Trainer Walsh pronounced him physically perfect: 'It's a question of how he is mentally, so we will give him a run in a month and find out.' But the result was a disappointing outing over hurdles and, one month before the National, Ireland's much-loved butterfly was retired.
See also: Betting; Walsh, Ted and Ruby.

PARFREMENT, Georges

The first Frenchman to ride a Grand National winner: five year old *Lutteur III* (1909). In making a winning Aintree debut, Georges Parfrement greatly profited from the advice of Lewes trainer Harry Escott who had ridden in four Nationals, being beaten only one and a half lengths on *Cathal* in 1895. Also he made a detailed study of the course beforehand, and after viewing the great drop fences, he wisely decided to lengthen his stirrup leathers.

With 32 horses in the line-up, this race shared with the 1850 National the distinction of having the then largest field in the history of the steeplechase. The starters included the 1908 winner *Rubio*, now raised 18lb in the weights, and the 1906 winner *Ascetic's Silver*, anchored on a prohibitive 12st 7lb; also two past runners-up, *Tom West* and *Mattie MacGregor*. But on the strength of a recent impressive win, under Parfrement in Hurst Park's Champion Chase, *Lutteur III* was backed down to 100-9 joint favouritism with the mare *Shady Lady*.

In a National run in perfect conditions, Parfrement initially held his horse up in the rear. Then, after race leader *Rubio* had fallen at the Water, he began to make relentless progress on the second circuit, taking the lead at the 26th fence and staying on to win cosily by two lengths from *Judas*, with *Caubeen* a distant third.

Supremely stylish and strong, Parfrement was the leading jockey in France, and he had many successes on both sides of the Channel. These included three victories in France's premier jump race, the Grand Steeplechase de Paris, and two wins in the Grand International Chase at Sandown. He rode in three more Nationals: in 1911 when *Lutteur III*, raised 20lb in the weights, exited after landing atop the fence after Becher's; in 1915, when he fell on Lord Lonsdale's *Lord Marcus*; and in 1923 when he pulled up on *Libretto*.

In that last year he scored a five length success on *North Waltham* in the Imperial Cup at Sandown. Shortly afterwards he fell fatally in a race at Enghien. *See also:* Lutteur III; Escott, Harry.

PARTY POLITICS

A giant of a horse (over 17 hands) who, in 1992, won the Grand National at the first attempt, and who remarkably came back three years later to finish second in a fast-run race despite having had a tube fitted in his throat to aid breathing. In the view of his trainer Nick Gaselee, *Party Politics* was a stone better horse in 1993 when he was bidding to become the first to win the National twice since *Red Rum* in 1974. But that was the year of the void race and he was pulled up after completing one circuit.

A brown gelding – by American-bred *Politico* out

of the mare *Spin Again – Party Politics* was bred by Buckinghamshire farmer David Stoddart and sent to the Upper Lambourn yard of Gaselee who put him over fences as a five year old. His potential was quickly declared: wins in two chases at Warwick in his first season (1989-90), then three good wins in the next season on ground both good to firm and soft. Moreover, he was only seven years old when he ran an excellent race to finish second in the Hennessy, behind *Chatam* and ahead of the so genuine *Docklands Express*.

With regular jockey Andy Adams injured, Richard Dunwoody rode *Party Politics* at the start of his 1992 campaign, finishing fifth at Sandown, and fifth again in his final pre-National race at Haydock. In the latter he was beaten ten lengths by *Cool Ground* who went on to win the Cheltenham Gold Cup from *The Fellow* and *Docklands Express*. *Cool Ground* now became the ante-post favourite for the National but, exactly like *Garrison Savannah*, beaten into second place the year before, he would be carrying 11st 1lb after the exertion of winning the Gold Cup by a head.

Party Politics, on 10st 7lb, clearly had a good chance; and thus, only days before the National, he changed hands for a reputed near-£80,000 – bought by Mr David Thompson as a gift to his wife, Patricia. Dunwoody had been booked to ride the strongly fancied *Brown Windsor* and, with Adams still injured, the ride on the biggest horse in the race went to Welshman Carl Llewellyn. They set off well backed at 14-1, with not a few punters regarding the next week's General Election as a tip in itself.

Patiently ridden, *Party Politics* had just one uneasy moment on the first circuit – at Becher's where Llewellyn did well to steer him narrowly clear of the knocked-over second favourite, *Brown Windsor*. Thereafter, he steadily improved his position, moving into the lead after Valentine's and quickening away after three out. With only the rallying *Romany King* providing a threat on the run-in, he stayed on strongly to win by two and a half lengths. With prize money of just under £100,000, the Thompsons, owners of the successful Cheveley Park Stud in Newmarket, had made a very sound investment indeed.

After a seven-month break, *Party Politics* was pulled up in chases at Newbury and Cheltenham, in the latter after breaking a blood vessel. But one month later, reunited with Llewellyn and having been tubed to aid his breathing, he came back to winning form over an extended three and a half miles at Haydock. Though given an extra 9lb in the weights, he was made 7-1 favourite to score a second National victory and was regarded by connections as being at the peak of his form. All to no avail because of a bungled start.

The following season, due to various ailments, *Party Politics* had only one run, winning over three miles at Chepstow in December. Having cracked a pedal bone, he was withdrawn from the National; and it was not until a year later that he began his comeback, finishing a four lengths second to *Master Oats* in the Rehearsal Chase at Chepstow. Four weeks later, at Newbury over three miles six furlongs, he was again beaten by *Master Oats* – this time 45 lengths adrift in third place. Then, in February, he was pulled up before five out in the Greenalls Chase at Haydock.

It was hardly an encouraging record for his return to Aintree in 1995. But there were extenuating circumstances. His last two runs had been on unsuitable heavy ground, and in his final pre-National race he had spread a plate. Now he was thriving in spring sunshine; and though *Master Oats* was all the rage following his 15 lengths win in the Cheltenham Gold Cup, the fact remained that *Party Politics* was 24lb better off for his four lengths beating at Chepstow. He had to carry 10st 2lb, 5lb less than the weight he had carried to victory three years ago. And his rider was 31 year old Mark Dwyer who had twice been successful in the Gold Cup.

With the going on the fast side of good, the tubed giant was again patiently ridden round the first circuit. He progressed rapidly after the 24th (Canal Turn), overhauled the fading *Master Oats* and briefly loomed up as the only threat to the runaway leader *Royal Athlete*. But while *Party Politics* put in a remarkably strong finish, there was no catching Jenny Pitman's 12 year old who, at 40-1, won by seven lengths in the third fastest time in the 149 runnings of the race.

When the weights were declared for the 1996 National, *Party Politics*, still on 10st 2lb, was seen as great value at ante-post odds of 33-1, even though he was unraced since that second place at Aintree. Subsequently, he was given just one prep race, in the Greenalls National Trial at Haydock. He hated the deep going there but at least he completed most of the course before being pulled up in the home straight, and so he still attracted support for this third-and-a-half appearance in the National. After all, he had been pulled up in that same Haydock race before his great run behind *Royal Athlete*.

Such was the appeal of this brilliant jumper that, by National day, his odds of 33-1 ante-post had shortened to 10-1, with *Rough Quest* the 7-1 clear favourite following his fine run as runner-up in the Cheltenham Gold Cup. Llewellyn, back on board, was convinced after a pre race work-out that his former winner had retained his ability. But it was not so. Uncharacteristically, and without interference, *Party Politics* blundered and fell at the third. It was time for retirement.

See also: Gaselee, Nick; Llewellyn, Carl; Tubing.

PATHFINDER

After one circuit of the 1875 Grand National, eight year old *Pathfinder* was labouring so much over ploughed land that his rider, Tommy Pickernell, had half a mind to pull him up. He decided to carry on, just to give the owners a fair run for their money. Meanwhile, more and more horses were falling or being pulled up on the heavy going; and by the second last, a surprised 'Mr Thomas' saw that he had only the mare *Dainty* to beat.

They met the last together and after a neck-and-neck struggle over the long run-in *Pathfinder* prevailed by just half a length with another mare, the 6-1 French favourite *La Veine*, three lengths back in third. An unfancied regular hunter, priced at 100-6, had given 'Mr Thomas' his third and final National win.

Pathfinder – by *Mogador* out of an unrecorded dam – was bred by Mr John Cowley who lived near Rugby, and was originally named *The Knight*. Never highly regarded, he frequently changed hands – first sold to a local farmer who passed him on to his neighbour, Mr George Darby, for £100. Next he was owned by Mr John Coupland, Master of the Quorn. Primarily ridden to hounds, he had his first notable race win in 1874 when 'Mr Thomas' scored on him in the Leicestershire Hunt Steeplechase. Soon afterwards he became the property of Mr Herbert Bird in partnership with the Marquess of Huntly, popularly known as the 'Cock of the North'.

On the lead up to his successful debut at Aintree the lightly raced *Pathfinder* had shown no great form, and he produced nothing special thereafter. He made just one more National appearance, in 1876.

Raised a mere 3lb for his victory, and now ridden by his Epsom trainer W. Reeves, he was never in real contention and failed to complete the course.

See also: Pickernell, Thomas.

PAYNE, Nigel

Appointed Press Officer at Aintree in 1976, Nigel Payne, then marketing director at Ladbrokes, played a key role in his company's invaluable seven-year management of the Grand National and went on to be involved in promoting the great steeplechase for more than two decades. That period of service took in the nightmarish years of 1993, when the race was declared void, and 1997 when the course had to be evacuated following IRA bomb scares. Then, in 1998, at the age of 51, he was rewarded with his happiest National of all.

His job was not as straightforward or as predictable as it might have seemed. On the night of the 'void' National, Charles Barnett, managing director, Lord Daresbury, chairman, David Hillyard of Racecourse Holdings Trust and Nigel were due to meet to discuss how to play the debacle with the press the next day. They wanted to keep the discussions internal but could not shake off the Jockey Club's head of security, Roger Buffham. It fell to Nigel to give him the slip and he did so by telling him they would convene later at the Grosvenor Hotel, Chester. They did, in fact, meet in Lord Daresbury's dining room.

He also has a most unusual memento from the National. Before *Aldaniti*'s victory Josh Gifford told Payne he would quit smoking if the horse won. In the winner's enclosure afterwards, Gifford handed Payne a half smoked packet of Benson & Hedges. Payne smoked the remaining cigarettes but, to this day, still has the packet.

Back in 1992 Payne had been responsible for putting together a six-man syndicate that bought a four year old gelding for 5,800 guineas. Famously, his close friend, soccer commentator John Motson, declined to join the syndicate. A big mistake. The gelding, named *Earth Summit*, was to become the only horse to win the Scottish, Welsh and Aintree Nationals, and would scoop a career total of £372,565 in prize money. He won the 1998 Grand National as 7-1 favourite, and five years earlier Payne had backed him at 33-1 – £100 each-way to win the race by and including the year 2000.

Shortly before that Grand National victory, Payne's account of the postponed 1997 National was

P

published under the title, *Everyone Must Leave.*
Subsequently he combined with syndicate co-member Bob Sims to write *Gold Digger: The Story of Earth Summit Triple National Winner*, with the proceeds being divided between two charities, The Thoroughbred Rehabilitation Centre and Riding For The Disabled. He retired from his role as PR consultant to Aintree in 2007. He is now chief executive of the Horseracing Sponsors' Association.
See also: Earth Summit.

PETER SIMPLE (Grey)

A grey entire, not to be confused with his later namesake, the bay gelding who won the 1849 and 1853 Grand Nationals. This *Peter Simple* was an outstandingly consistent performer in his own right, but unfortunately circumstances conspired to prevent him from achieving a richly deserved victory and having to settle for one second place and two thirds.

Peter Simple – by *Arbutus* out of an unrecorded dam – made his Aintree debut in the third National of 1841 when there were only 11 starters and he was a 6-1 chance, headed in the betting by the first winner *Lottery* and another grey, *Cigar*. Coming to the last, the two greys led neck and neck, but then the mare *Charity* produced an amazing burst on the run-in to snatch victory by one length from *Cigar* with *Peter Simple* just a half length back in third.

The following year *Peter Simple* again finished third, this time well beaten, being 19 lengths and two behind *Gay Lad* and *Seventy Four* respectively. But, in truth, such a losing margin falsely reflected on his competitiveness. He might well have done considerably better but for being baulked late in the race by some unruly spectators. Their intrusion on to the course caused him to throw his amateur rider (a Mr Hunter) out of the saddle. Remounted, the grey fought back to be the third of only five finishers.

In the 1843 National, the first to be run as a handicap, *Peter Simple* had the misfortune to be allotted the second biggest burden in the history of the race: a top weight of 13st 1lb which included an extra 5lb for having won a race since the date of declaration. Yet such was his strong seasonal form that he was still made 3-1 favourite. Pulling hard, as always, the grey held the lead as they set out on the second circuit. But he was headed after Becher's and then faded to finish the eighth of nine to complete the course.

In 1844, *Peter Simple* again carried top weight

(12st 12lb), but now he was not even quoted in the betting, and he fell without ever being in real contention. Then, in 1845, the handicapper at last gave him a sporting chance, dropping him a full stone in the weights. This time he found only one too good, being beaten two lengths by the outsider *Cure-All* to whom he was conceding 7lb. Finally, in 1846, the sixth and last National appearance of the gallant grey ended in a fall.

PETER SIMPLE (Bay)

Winning the Grand National (1849) on his first appearance, the bay gelding *Peter Simple* profited from a false start, stealing an early lead while starter Lord Sefton, drowned by the roar of the crowd, shouted in vain to recall the 24-strong field. There were numerous fallers, three of them fatally. Meanwhile, 11 year old *Peter Simple*, a 20-1 shot recognised as an excellent jumper but a sadly slow galloper, appeared to be the only runner who was not in the least troubled by the extremely heavy going. Leading almost throughout, he won by three lengths from *The Knight of Gwynne*, with the 5-1 favourite *Prince George*, ridden by the famed Tom Olliver, a distance back in third. Only six finished.

Professional jockey Tom Cunningham, also winning on his National debut, was so impressed with *Peter Simple* that he purchased him for their second challenge. Punters were equally hopeful and made the gelding 5-1 favourite. But this National had a record 32 starters and *Peter Simple*, at the age of 12, had been raised 16lb to a top weight of 12st 2lb. He was conceding more than two stone to 18 of his rivals and a massive three stone-plus to three others. In the circumstances, he did well enough to lead after the first circuit, but then faded and failed to finish.

It was almost an action replay in 1851, though this time *Peter Simple*, dropped 9lb in the weights, was not even quoted in the betting and was narrowly headed at the end of the first circuit. Again, in 1852, when ridden by his new owner, Mr G.S. Davenport, he did not figure in the betting, and for the first time he was a faller. Ostensibly, at the age of 14, his days of stardom were over.

Yet the old horse returned for his fifth National in 1853, again with a new owner (Capt. J.L. Little) and this time he was fifth in the betting at 9-1. Three factors contributed to his return to favour. He was now on only 10st 10lb. For the first time since his

379

P

1849 victory he had favourably heavy ground; and not least he was to be ridden by the renowned Olliver. Thriving in the slushy conditions, the mudlark made relentless progress as others faded on the second circuit. He had the narrowest of leads over the last, then bravely hung on to win by three lengths from *Miss Mowbray*, the 5-1 favourite and last year's winner. Only five others finished.

Olliver, previously the only rider to have won two Nationals, now had a third success. It was a second win for owner Little who, coached by Olliver, had ridden *Chandler* to victory in 1848. *Peter Simple* had become the second horse to score a National double and, most remarkably, the first and only one ever to win at the ripe old age of 15.

Rather sadly, under new ownership, the gallant veteran was brought back for a sixth successive National in 1854. The good ground was against him, and cruelly and absurdly the 16 year old was burdened with top weight of 12st, three stone more than two of his rivals. Yet, such was his fame that he was fifth in the betting at 12-1. Inevitably he failed to finish and was duly retired as a living National legend.
See also: Cunningham,Thomas; Olliver, Tom.

PETRE, Captain Robert Charles

The hugely popular winner of the 1946 Grand National on *Lovely Cottage* – not least because he was a recently demobbed Scots Guards officer achieving victory in the first National after the end of the Second World War. It was only his second ride in the race and appropriately he was emulating the feat of another serviceman, Flight Sergeant Mervyn Jones, who had won the only wartime National on *Bogskar* (1940) and had lost his life in action two years later.

Like his great friend, Frank Furlong, winner of the 1935 National on *Reynoldstown*, Old Harrovian Bobby Petre had begun his education at the small preparatory school of St. Neots, Eversley, in Hampshire. Both went on to Sandhurst where they met another horse-mad officer cadet, one Fulke Walwyn. All three were to make their mark as jump riders, Walwyn leading the way as champion amateur rider in 1933 and 1934. Two years later he replaced Furlong on *Reynoldstown* and emulated the National victory of his 9th Lancers fellow officer.

Now Petre took his turn to be the National Hunt star, becoming the leading amateur rider of the 1937-38 season. In 1939 his National debut on *St*

George II ended in a refusal after they had been baulked at the 21st, and his friend Walwyn was a faller on *Dunhill Castle*. One year later Petre, Walwyn and Furlong, all serving officers, were spectators at the last National before the end of the Second World War.

Petre, now a captain in the Scots Guards, did have one wartime ride – winning a handicap chase at Cheltenham while on leave in November, 1940. Otherwise military service kept him out of the saddle for six years. He served in the disastrous Norwegian campaign of 1940, and from 1943 onwards soldiered in Italy. Then, early in 1946, his return to race-riding ended in a fall at Wincanton – ironically on a nine year old gelding called *Lovely Cottage*. Two months later, however, the same combination won a chase at Taunton, and in April they moved on to Aintree. Capt. Petre was one of only four amateur riders in the 34-strong National and his mount was a 25-1 chance.

All the rage was the red-hot, 3-1 favourite *Prince Regent*, who came to Aintree with 14 victories behind him, including the recent Cheltenham Gold Cup. He had the advantage over English chasers of having raced regularly in Ireland during the war. Conversely, on a handicap weight of 12st 5lb, he was conceding 21lb or more to 31 of his rivals; and at the age of 11 he was facing the Aintree fences for the first time.

The field also included *Bogskar* and *MacMoffat* who had fought out the finish in the last Grand National. But that was six years ago. Now they were 13 and 14 respectively; and both would fall in the race. Meanwhile, Petre gave the nine year old *Lovely Cottage* an immaculate ride, judging his challenge to perfection. At the second last he was some 20 lengths behind the leaders but then steadily overhauled them to win by four lengths from *Jack Finlay*, a 100-1 outsider, with the gallant *Prince Regent*, who had led over the last, a further three lengths back in third.

Captain Petre, now a professional rider, appeared in only one more National: in 1947 on Lord Bicester's promising eight year old *Silver Fame*. His ride ended in a fall three fences from home. One year later *Silver Fame* (a faller at Becher's) went off as the National favourite. But Petre was not the rider. He had turned to training at Tunworth, Hampshire; also he had suffered a freak accident. While overseeing a beach workout of his horses at Bognor

Regis he had slipped on a breakwater, sustaining a fracture so bad that his leg had to be amputated.

The indefatigable Petre soon returned to riding out with his horses. But then he was dealt another cruel blow after one of his horses had failed a dope test at a race meeting. The trainer was not in attendance at the time and there was no evidence that he was in any way involved in the doping. However, under Jockey Club rules, he was automatically held responsible and deprived of his licence. Thereafter he would only attend the National as a keen spectator and, in 1985, as one of the National winning jockeys, each receiving a trophy from the Princess Royal. He lived on until his 85th year in 1996.
See also: Lovely Cottage; Prince Regent; Rayson, Tommy.

PICKERNELL, Thomas

Shaded only by Tom Olliver as the most persistent of all Grand National jockeys, the astonishing Tommy Pickernell – always choosing to compete under the pseudonym of 'Mr Thomas' – rode in no fewer than 17 Nationals in 19 years (1859-1877). Moreover, he did not willingly retire at the age of 43 but only after an horrendous fall at Sandown had left him blind in one eye and with his jaw broken in three places.

After finishing fifth on his debut, he won the National at his second attempt – on *Anatis* (1860); again on *The Lamb* (1871), and a third time on *Pathfinder* (1875) when he was 41 years old. In addition, he was third on *Shangarry* (1867) and *The Liberator* (1877) and fourth on *The Lamb* (1872).

Cheltenham born, in 1834, Pickernell was most profitably tutored by two masters of Aintree, the great Tom Olliver and William Holman. But he never expected to ride in the National since, under family pressure, he emigrated to Tasmania to pursue a career as a sheep farmer. There he took up steeplechasing to such effect that he was presented with a signed petition requesting that he should cease 'taking the bread from the mouths of professional jockeys'.

Bored with sheep farming, Tommy returned to England and remained the scourge of professional riders with countless wins on the Flat as well as over the jumps. Cheltenham owner Christopher Capel, who had won at Aintree the previous year with *Little Charley*, gave him his first National ride in 1859, on the nine year old mare *Anatis*, a 25-1 chance. The following year, *Anatis* was the 7-2 hot favourite. But

she needed most careful handling; owing to weakness in the forelegs, she had not been risked over a single jump in the past 12 months. 'Mr Thomas' nursed her round to perfection, going only flat-out on the run-in when they prevailed by just half a length from *Huntsman*.

Twice more Pickernell rode *Anatis* in the National. In 1861, raised 8lb in the weights, she was brought down by a faller, and in 1862 the 12 year old mare – harshly burdened with a further 8lb – had to be pulled up. Tommy missed the next two Nationals, and then in six rides he only once completed the course – taking third place on *Shangarry* in 1867. His other rides: *Tommy Lumpkin*, pulled up, 1865; *Milltown*, failed to finish, 1866; *Daisy*, pulled up, 1868; *The Nun*, fell, 1869; and *Hall Court*, failed to finish, 1870.

After this barren spell his second winning ride came about in bizarre circumstances, bordering on the supernatural. Some four months before the 1871 National he received a letter from Lord Poulett which read:

'My dear Tommy, Let me know for certain whether you can ride for me at Liverpool on The Lamb. I dreamt twice last night I saw the race run. The first dream he was last and finished among the carriages. The second dream, I should think an hour afterwards, I saw the Liverpool run. He won by four lengths and you rode him and I stood close to the winning post at the turn. I saw the cerise and blue sleeves and you, as plain as I write this. Now let me know as soon as you can and say nothing to anyone.'

Reality only fractionally failed to match the dream. Three years after his first National win, and now 12lb up in the weights, Lord Poulett's little grey triumphed by just two lengths, not four. At the Canal Turn, Tommy jumped *The Lamb* clear over fallen horses, and they won in a new record time of 9min 37.75sec.

In 1872, *The Lamb* again put in a miraculous leap to sail over fallen horses and was a contender right up to the penultimate fence. But then he surrendered the lead and finally finished fourth, beaten only by his huge handicap weight of 12st 7lb. The following year Tommy fell at the 23rd on another Lord Poulett grey, six year old *Broadlea*, and in 1874 he failed to finish on *Eurotas*, also a six year old.

One year later, as was his custom, Tommy took a 'wee dram' before setting off in the National. This time, however, he perhaps over-indulged since he subsequently revealed that he had needed to ask a fellow jockey which way to face at the start. In any event, the booze did not harm his riding.

His mount was the unfancied *Pathfinder*. Approaching the second Becher's, the bay gelding was struggling so much on the heavy ground that 'Mr Thomas' wondered whether he should pull him up. He decided against it, solely to give the owners a run for their money. Then, to his surprise, *Pathfinder* seemed to find a second wind. He ran on strongly to the last obstacle, and fought neck-and-neck with *Dainty* over the run-in to snatch victory by a mere half-length.

Disappointingly, in 1876, 'Mr Thomas' had to pull up on *Defence*, a joint second favourite who had been placed fourth two years before. But in the next National he made his experience tell to the full in managing to steer *Liberator*, a 25-1 shot, into third place. Though he never suspected it at the time, he had ridden in his last National. And sadly he was ill-prepared for his forced retirement.

The National Hunt Committee recognised his unrivalled experience by appointing him their first Inspector of Courses. Nonetheless, in later years, the great jockey – commonly styled as 'one of the first gentlemen jockeys of the Turf' – fell on such hard times that friends needed to organise collections to rescue him from extreme poverty. He died, aged 78, in 1912.

See also: Anatis; The Lamb; Pathfinder; Huntsman.

PIGGOTT, Ernest

Three times National Hunt champion jockey and twice winner of the Aintree Grand National, Ernie Piggott founded one great horse-racing dynasty and joined forces with another when he married Margaret Cannon, who was a descendant of Sam Day, three times winning rider in the Derby, and a sister of famed jockeys Mornington and Kempton Cannon.

Ernie, grandfather of the supreme Lester, was born in 1878 and served his apprenticeship at Danebury, near Stockbridge, Hampshire, where his father-in-law Tom Cannon, winner of 13 Classics, including the 1882 Derby on *Shotover*, had trained the 1888 National winner *Playfair*. He made his National debut in 1899, finishing in third place on *Elliman* in the race won by the mighty *Manifesto*. Three years later, when he next appeared, he again came third, this time on *Manifesto*, who arguably produced his greatest run that day as a top-weighted 14 year old racing on unfavourable heavy ground.

In 1903 Mr J.G. Bulteel's *Manifesto* was reunited with his winning rider George Williamson, while Ernie was on the owner's seven year old, *Dearslayer*. Both were 25-1 chances. The younger horse, however, was a faller. *Manifesto* again finished third; and one year later – with Ernie back on board – he was the eighth of eight finishers at the grand old age of 16.

Riding mostly in Belgium and France, Ernie missed the next four Grand Nationals; and in 1908 he had declared himself unavailable to ride the six year old *Mattie Macgregor* who subsequently finished second. In 1909, his mount, *The Lurcher*, was a faller. Two years later he was the National Hunt champion jockey, but it was not until 1912 that he had a strongly fancied National ride: Sir Charles Assheton-Smith's *Jerry M* who had finished second two years before.

Jerry M was again carrying top weight, but Ernie had already ridden the bay gelding to victory at Hurst Park and now his mount was the 4-1 joint favourite. At Aintree, as instructed, he delayed his challenge as long as possible, then timed it to perfection, seizing the lead on the run-in and winning by six lengths.

The following year Piggott was booked for Sir Charles's seven year old *Covertcoat* in the National. But shortly before the race a broken hand cost him the ride. Under replacement Percy Woodland, *Covertcoat* romped home to win by a distance. Next, in 1914, Ernie was on seven year old *Jacobus* (a faller); and ironically, in 1915, he was on *Distaff* (pulled up) while *Jacobus*, under Alfred Newey, finished runner-up by just two lengths.

During the First World War, when substitute 'Nationals' were held over an infinitely easier Gatwick course, the most impressive winner was *Poethlyn*, an eight year old successful under Piggott in 1918. They were reunited in the restored 1919 Aintree National and, despite being given top weight, *Poethlyn* went off as the 11-4 favourite.

When *Poethlyn* scored by eight lengths he was the shortest-priced winner in National history. Ernie had gained his second success in the race, and he had now ridden two of only four horses that had carried 12st 7lb to victory. There were reasonable hopes that he might achieve a third win the following year. Again *Poethlyn* was a short-priced favourite (3-1) and carrying the same weight. But this time he and Ernie fell at the first fence.

Piggott's last National ride, in 1921, also ended in a fall – on *Old Tay Bridge* who would finish runner-up in the Nationals of 1925 and 1926. Altogether he had appeared in the race 11 times spread over a 22 year period. Subsequently, he established himself as a trainer at Letcombe Regis, near Wantage; and later, after his retirement, he moved to Oxford. He died in 1967, aged 88, having lived to see his son Keith train a Grand National winner (*Ayala*, 1963) and his extraordinary grandson score the first three of nine Derby wins, plus three victories in the Oaks and two in the St Leger.

See also: Jerry M; Poethlyn.

PIGGOTT, Keith

Son of dual Grand National winner, Ernie Piggott, and father of the incomparable Lester, Keith had no memory of his own, unusual debut in the National. It happened in 1928 when, riding *Trump Card*, the second favourite, he fell at the fence after Becher's first time round. The fall itself was hardly noteworthy since this was the year of *Tipperary Tim* when only two of 42 starters completed the course. What was unusual was the fact that the following morning Keith started getting himself ready to go to Aintree for the National. He had suffered such a lingering concussion that he did not realise the race had already been run.

As Lester recalls in his autobiography, this was one of his father's favourite stories. 'He had to go to the local cinema and watch the newsreel film to find out what had happened.' The following year it was turn of Keith's younger brother, Victor, to be a faller (on *Kilbrain*) in his first – and only – National.

On his return to Aintree in 1930, Keith was again thrown from his mount, the favourite *Grakle*. He would later recall that he should have won but for falling off three fences from home – because the horse was going 'too well' at the time. One year later – to his ever-lasting regret – he was prevented by a broken thigh from riding *Grakle* again in the National. Instead, Bob Lyall took the ride – and won by one and a half lengths!

Born in 1904 in Stockbridge, Hampshire, Keith began riding during the First World War, as a teenage apprentice on the Flat. He had his first win, at Newbury, on his 15th birthday. Being sturdily built and 5ft 7in tall, he soon lost the battle with the scales and was forced to turn to National Hunt racing. In a career lasting nearly 30 years he won almost 500 races, including the 1939 Champion Hurdle on *African Sister*, trained by his uncle, Charlie Piggott. But in five attempts (his other rides were *Slater*, 1934, *Blaze*, 1936, and *Buckthorn*, 1937) he was destined never to finish in the National.

A huge consolation, however, came in 1963 when, as a trainer, he saw the National narrowly won by his first runner at Liverpool: the 66-1 chance, *Ayala*. Keith had originally bought the horse in 1960 for just 250 guineas. Three years later, when this big chestnut triumphed, Piggott was the co-owner with Mr. P.B. ('Teasy Weasy') Raymond. And he crowned that season by becoming the champion National Hunt trainer.

Like his father before him, Keith united two horse-racing dynasties, his wife Iris being a great granddaughter of J. Rickaby, who trained the 1855 Derby winner *Wild Dayrell*; the daughter of the Classic-winning jockey Fred Rickaby; and the sister of yet another Fred, who won five Classics before his tragic death in the First World War when only 24 years old. An accomplished horsewoman in her own right, Iris twice rode the winner of the four-and-a-half-mile Northumberland Town Plate. Their son Lester was born in 1935 and taught to ride from the age of two.

In the Second World War, Keith served in the Royal Observer Corps, and in 1945 he established himself as a trainer at the South Bank yard in Lambourn. Three years later he saw 12 year old Lester have his first ride in public. His son would go on to ride in his first Derby at 15, finish second in the Derby at 16, and win the premier Classic at 18. Incidentally, in 1967, Lester won a Flat race at Aintree on an unknown two year old – by the name of *Red Rum*.

The year before, Keith had chosen to retire from training at the age of 62. Subsequently he sold South Bank to Barry Hills, and moved to Kintbury, between Newbury and Hungerford. He died, aged 89, in 1993, one year before his extraordinary son rode the last of his 4,493 Flat winners in Britain.

See also: Ayala.

P

PILE-UPS

The worst Grand National pile-up occurred in 1967 when 20 runners were put out of the race as the riderless *Popham Down* veered across the front of the low 23rd fence. It brought to a standstill the entire field with the exception of *Foinavon* who came from behind and ran on to win at 100-1. However, 18 horses eventually completed the course. Not so in 1928, when *Easter Hero* landed atop the fence at the Canal Turn first time round. It caused some 18 of 42 starters to fall or to be pulled up. And only two completed: *Tipperary Tim*, the 100-1 winner, and *Billy Barton*, remounted.

The 1979 National saw the greatest confusion since *Foinvaon's* year as two loose horses ran across the course at The Chair and ended the race for nine runners. Ten years later a five-horse pile-up at the first Becher's tragically claimed the lives of two outsiders. Then, in 2001, when the race was run in quagmire conditions, a loose horse (*Paddy's Return*) veered sharply down the eighth fence at the Canal Turn and within seconds eight runners were eliminated.

See also: Fallers; Loose Horses; Foinavon; Tipperary Tim; Little Polveir; Red Marauder.

PIONEER

Though he was a half-brother to the 1843 winner, *Vanguard*, the six year old bay gelding *Pioneer* surprised everyone, including his own connections, when winning the 1846 Grand National by three lengths and three from *Culverthorpe* and *Switcher* respectively. That year everything had seemed to be against him. It was his first Aintree appearance, and the National had a then record number of 22 starters, including the previous winner *Cure-All*. He was a rank outsider, not even quoted in the betting. His owner, a Mr Adams, had openly declared that the horse was not worth a bet; and he had a virtually unknown rider, W. Taylor.

Furthermore, *Pioneer* – by *Advance* out of an unidentified mare – seemed unreasonably high in the weights on 11st 12lb, and he had absolutely nothing to commend him on appearance. He was a miserable-looking specimen with a long shaggy coat and protruding bones; a veritable forerunner of the ugly *Tipperary Tim*, who would be the first 100-1 winner in 1928.

As usual, the hard-pulling grey *Peter Simple*, making his sixth National appearance, soon headed the field; and he continued to set a fast pace until his fall early on the second circuit. Meanwhile, two well-fancied 10-1 chances had been unluckily eliminated. Mr Alan McDonough on *Mameluke* was unseated in a collision; and outrageously his brother William McDonough was going well on *Lancet* when he was knocked out of the saddle by a mounted spectator who had ridden on to the course.

All the while *Pioneer* was plodding along towards the rear of the field. Only after the halfway stage did he begin to make a forward move and he was still well behind as *Culverthorpe* led the way over the second Becher's, closely followed by *Switcher*, *Firefly* and *Veluti*. Huge cheers now welcomed the advance of *Veluti*, the 11-2 favourite ridden by the famed Jem Mason, but they turned to groans as the six year old broke down at the penultimate fence. It seemed that *Culverthorpe* had only to stay on his feet to win.

Culverthorpe was still looking a sure winner as he led over the last. But then, seemingly out of nowhere, *Pioneer* came into the reckoning with a relentless late surge that steadily closed the gap and finally carried him to a comfortable three lengths win. Only four others completed the course.

Although it was a sensationally well-timed challenge, it could be argued that *Pioneer* would never have won but for a blunder by officials. Owing to faulty flagging in marking out the course, the race had been run over a record distance of roughly five miles, making it an unprecedented test of stamina. Possibly the handicapper took this freak circumstance into consideration when framing the weights for the 1847 National. For remarkably – despite the fact that he had gone on to win the prestigious Leamington Grand Annual Chase – *Pioneer* was now the first National winner to reappear without a single extra pound on his back.

This time, with a new jockey (Captain William Peel), who had reportedly purchased the horse for £1,000), *Pioneer* was fourth equal in the betting at 15-1. He came home a creditable fourth in a close-run finish. Finally, on his last appearance in 1848, he was going well when he was unluckily brought down. But there was ample compensation for his rider. The National was narrowly won by 12 year old *Chandler*, a one-time cart-horse that Captain Peel had bought for a mere 20 guineas and who was now co-owned and ridden by his brother officer, Captain 'Josey' Little.

PIPE, David

Following in father's footsteps can sometimes be an awesome prospect, and not least when you are the son of Martin Pipe, Britain's most successful ever jumps trainer. David Pipe, however, could scarcely have been better prepared for the challenge when, in May, 2006, he succeeded the 15 times champion National Hunt trainer as master of the great Pond House Racing Stables at Nicholashayne, near Wellington, on the Somerset-Devon border.

On leaving boarding school in Taunton, young Pipe had been tutored in riding by Jimmy Frost. He rode in his first point-to-point race on February 8, 1992, the day after his 19th birthday, and over the next five seasons he rode 22 winners between the flags, plus two under Rules, one being *Bonanza Boy* in the Ludlow Gold Cup. But he was always fighting a losing battle with the scales, and when he surrendered his 6ft 4in frame swiftly ballooned up to a natural 14st.

Most valuably David now had brief spells working with Michael Dickinson in the United States, Criquette Head-Maarek in France and Joey Ramsden in South Africa. Then, based at Purchas Farm, only a mile from his father's Pond House operation, he began to train point-to-pointers, sending 164 winners over six seasons with one, *Well Armed*, scoring 15 times.

In 2003 Pipe Jnr had an outstanding hunter-chaser in his charge: *Lord Atterbury*, a seven year old who hacked up in the novices' amateur chase over the Mildmay fences at Aintree and then comfortably won over four miles one furlong in Cheltenham's Amateur Hunt Chase. The following year, having won a three-mile point-to-point under 12st 7lb, the chestnut was entered by David for the Grand National.

On being allotted a mere 9st 12lb, *Lord Atterbury* was not unfancied. Indeed, it was suggested that an impressive run in the Christie's Foxhunter Chase at the Cheltenham Festival could see him catapult to the head of the market. But the reverse occurred. Jumping badly, the eight year old put in such a dismal performance that he drifted from 20-1 out to 40-1 for the National.

Nevertheless, *Lord Atterbury* was now transferred to Martin Pipe to give him extra ammunition in his neck-and-neck battle with Paul Nicholls for the trainers' championship. Pipe Snr had six other runners, including one of four co-favourites, *Jurancon*

II, ridden by champion Tony McCoy. Yet only one of his seven completed the course: *Lord Atterbury*. Though he bulldozed through a number of fences, his stamina was never in doubt and he kept going under Mark Bradburne to finish third, just five lengths off the winner, *Amberleigh House*.

Thus, it could be said that David – albeit unofficially – had bettered his famous father's start in the National. Pipe Snr had sent out 15 runners before getting one (winner *Miinnehoma*) in the frame. Pipe Jnr, at the first attempt, had trained one to finish third – a place that most importantly contributed £66,000 towards the prize money amassed by his father in pursuit of a 14th trainers' championship.

David now worked as his father's assistant prior to taking over the reins at Pond House at the end of the 2005-6 season. Ten days later, on May 9, 2006, in a novice chase at Kelso, *Standin Obligation* – Martin Pipe's last winner as a trainer – became David's first winner. The following October, Pipe Jnr had his biggest success so far, winning Wetherby's Charlie Hall Chase with *Our Vic*; and in December he scored a treble at Ascot, including the £100,000 Ladbroke Handicap Hurdle with *Acambo*. By mid-February, 2007, he had become the first British trainer to reach a century of winners in his first season.

Following the trend set by his father, 34-year-old David Pipe had six entries for the 2007 Grand National. But then, at the Cheltenham Festival, he suffered the devastating loss of his strongest prospect, the eight year old French import *Little Brick* who had been backed to win £1 million at Aintree. In the end only two of his six made the line-up: *Puntal* who finished a distant eighth under Tom Scudamore, and *Celtic Son*, pulled up before the second Becher's.

Nonetheless, Pipe Jnr had enjoyed a spectacular first season in charge at Pond House. At its end he was third in the trainers' championship with prize money of more than £1.6 million. And not least among his 134 winners was *Gaspara* who, by winning the Imperial Cup Handicap Hurdle at Sandown and going on the following week to win at the Cheltenham Festival, qualified for a £75,000 bonus. *Gaspara*'s lucky owner? None other than the irrepressible Martin Pipe.

See also: Pipe, Martin Charles

PIPE, Martin Charles CBE

The son of a successful Somerset bookmaker, Martin Pipe became Britain's most prolific trainer

P

of all time in 2000 when he passed – and subsequently far outstripped – Arthur Stephenson's record total of 2,988 winners, Flat and jumps combined. He was the National Hunt's champion trainer for the first time in the 1988-9 season with 208 winners, so dwarfing the previous record of 120 achieved by Michael Dickinson in 1982-3. Thereafter, he proceeded to re-write the record books, again and again gaining the most wins in a jump season (peaking at 243 in 1999-2000) and the most prize money in a season (best, £2,827,073 in 2004-5), and along the way scoring the fastest century of winners (November 3, 2001), the fastest double century (February 23, 2000), and the most trainers' championships (15). When he finally retired in 2006, after 32 years as a trainer, he had a staggering total of 4,180 winners in Britain – 3,927 of which came over the jumps.

Such was his extraordinary supremacy that between 1989 and 2005 only David Nicholson (in 1994 and 1995) interrupted his sequence of 15 trainers' titles; and throughout these years his first stable jockey – in turn, Peter Scudamore, Richard Dunwoody and Tony McCoy – was virtually guaranteed the jockeys' championship if he could survive the incredible pace and pressures of taking so many rides all over the country.

Pipe not merely dominated National Hunt racing for nearly two decades. He revolutionised the sport by setting new standards with his supremely scientific approach in the pursuit of equine fitness. He led the way in exploiting to the full such innovations as equine swimming pools, uphill all-weather gallops and treadmills; pioneered his own style of interval training; even set up his own laboratory for regular blood-testing of horses and analysis of their metabolism.

Training on an unprecedented scale, he combined quality with quantity, scoring on the Flat with six wins at Royal Ascot and success in the Cesarewitch (twice), Northumberland Plate, the Sagaro Stakes and Doncaster Cup, and more especially saddling winners of such major jump races as the Champion Hurdle and the Hennessy, Mackeson and Whitbread Gold Cups. He set a new benchmark with 32 winners at the Cheltenham Festival; and when he won the Aintree Grand National with *Miinnehoma* in 1994 he completed a full set of the major Nationals, having previously won the Welsh National (five times) and Irish and Scottish Nationals in 1991 and

1993 respectively. The one big jumps prize to elude him was the Cheltenham Gold Cup. Over the years he had 31 runners in the race, coming closest with *Rushing Wild*, the runner-up in 1993.

Born on May 29, 1945, Pipe had his first job in a betting office where he swept the floors and chalked up the prices. He later became manager of a betting shop at Butlin's in Minehead. Though he had never mounted a horse until the age of 18, he briefly rode in point-to-points and as an amateur under Rules; and in the process he gained just one winner (*Weather Permitting* in a point-to-point at Bishopsleigh, Devon) and a smashed thigh at Taunton in December, 1972, when he fell off a horse named *Lorac* (his wife's Christian name spelt backwards).

Martin's success as a trainer was entirely made possible by the considerable business acumen of his father, David Pipe, who chose to sell his 35 betting offices in the West Country and devote himself to building up superb training facilities at Pond House, a converted pig farm at Nicholashayne, Somerset. Instead of taking over the bookmaking business as expected, the son found himself gaining experience, initially in point-to-points, as a trainer. In May, 1975, he had his first winner, *Hit Parade*, ridden by Len Lungo in a Taunton selling hurdle; and in 1981 his first big-race success, *Baron Blakeney*, 66-1 winner of the Triumph Hurdle.

In 1981 he also had his first Grand National runner: *Three Of Diamonds*, a 100-1 outsider owned by his long-time business colleague, ex-table tennis star Chester Barnes. The chestnut gelding fell at the 24th fence and, one year later, still a 100-1 chance, was the distant seventh of the eight finishers. Pipe had only two National runners (both fallers) in the next six years. But, from 1989 onwards, he was always at least double-handed and eventually he was to resort to multiple challenges, incredibly entering as many as 17 horses in 1994. Five made it to the 36-strong line-up, among them the 16-1 winner *Miinnehoma*, ridden by Richard Dunwoody.

Most amazingly, in 2001, Pipe had ten runners – a quarter of the Grand National field. This constituted a world record for the most horses run by a trainer in one race, surpassing his recent total of nine out of 18 runners in a conditional jockeys' handicap at Taunton which he won with his 25-1 shot *Big Wheel*. Jokingly, he talked of going better than Michael Dickinson who, in 1983, had the first five home in the Cheltenham Gold Cup. But this

National was run in quagmire conditions and only one of his ten (*Blowing Wind*) completed the course, the distant third of four finishers after being re-mounted.

No trainer comes remotely near Pipe's record of having had 81 runners in the Grand National, and that total is excluding his five in the void race of 1993. Only Jenny Pitman ever rivalled his multiple challenges – in 1995 when she outscored his four with six runners, including the winner *Royal Athlete*. In the circumstances, the outcome of his challenges seems somewhat modest: one winner, one runner-up, three placed third.

To be sure, his contenders had their share of bad luck; and in 1996 his gallant *Encore Un Peu*, running 9lb out of the handicap, was only declared the runner-up – beaten a length and a quarter by the favourite *Rough Quest* – after a stewards' enquiry. Nevertheless, by 2004, he had had 52 non-finishers out of 72 starters, with 33 failing to complete the first circuit. Controversially, his scattergun approach involved entering an unusual number of six and seven year olds, and among these, in 2002, was a six year old (*Majed*) who had never raced over fences in Britain. As a result, Ginger McCain was one trainer who felt that Pipe's multiple entries, including no-hopers, was 'making a mockery of the National' by keeping out more worthy would-be challengers.

In March, 2002, Martin Pipe passed the 200 winners mark in one season for the eighth time in 14 years, and he became the first trainer in National Hunt history to have reaped £2 million prize money in one season. But at Pond House these milestones brought no rejoicing. The family was now in deep mourning for the supreme driving-force behind the growth of Britain's winningmost training centre: David Pipe Snr, who had passed away after a long illness at the age of 78.

Nevertheless the great Pipe juggernaut rolled on, albeit facing an ever-increasing challenge for supremacy from the Somerset stable of trainer Paul Nicholls. And by now there were signs of a new generation coming to the fore. Martin's only son, David, was running a 20-strong stable of point-to-pointers close by his father's stables, so gaining experience in preparation to take over the full licence when the Pond House maestro finally decided to stand down.

Martin Pipe had seven runners in the 2004 National. His leading contender, the seven year old

French-bred *Jurancon II*, fell at the fourth, and four more of his runners went at the first Becher's. Of the seven only *Lord Atterbury*, primarily trained by David, completed the course to finish third. That place – following Pipe's win with *Tiutchev* in Aintree's £87,000 Martell Cognac Cup – earned him another, vital £66.000 in his seesaw battle with Nicholls for the trainers' title which he finally took for a 14th season with prize money of £2,407,356 from a staggering 1,069 runners, 175 of them winners. He ended the season in style, winning the last big jump race, the £150,000 Betfred (formerly Whitbread) Gold Cup with one of his seven runners, *Puntal*. It was his third success in Sandown's showcase.

For once, in 2005, Pipe did not lead the trainers with entries for the National, his 13 nominees being surpassed by 14 from Jonjo O'Neill who had now taken over the services of champion jockey McCoy. On the day, however, he had four runners in the line-up, a number matched by Nicholls and O'Neill. All three trainers were in the prize money, Nicholls scoring best with runner-up *Royal Auclair* (£154,000), followed by O'Neill with third-placed *Simply Gifted* (£77,000) and Pipe with fourth-placed *It Takes Time* (£35,000).

Once again Pipe and Nicholls were locked in a titanic duel for the trainers' championship. Nicholls now missed a great chance to close the gap when his *Cornish Rebel* was beaten only by a head in the Scottish National. The battle continued right down to the wire with Pipe clinching his 15th title in the past 17 seasons with *Well Chief*'s Celebration Chase win at the last-day meeting at Sandown.

Going into 2006, Nicholls at last had a sizeable lead in the title race. When it came to the National, Pipe hit new heights with no fewer than 22 entries compared with Nicholls' high quality ten. But there was every probability that he would need to win the race to have any chance of retaining his trainers' title. And that chance diminished further following Pipe's dismal showing at the Cheltenham Festival. With 34 winners, he was second only to Fulke Walwyn as the Festival's most successful trainer, but now – despite having 38 runners – he had no winner for the first time since 1988. Nicholls, in contrast, had three wins, stretching his lead to more than £700,000.

An unusual barren period for Pipe finally ended on the first day of the Grand National meeting when

P

he took the valuable Betfair Bowl Chase with *Celestial Gold*. But he had no success with his five runners in the National. Only one completed the course: *Puntal* finishing sixth on his first outing in 484 days.

It was the end of an era. At long last Pipe's domination of the trainers' championship was over. He ended the season third in the table – behind Paul Nicholls and Philip Hobbs – and now announced his retirement and the passing over of the reins to his son David. Besides being 15 times champion trainer (on money earned), he had 20 times been the leading trainer in terms of races won.

Pipe's overall Grand National record

1981: *Three Of Diamonds*, fell 24th
1982: *Three Of Diamonds*, seventh; **1986**: *Ballinacurra Lad*, fell five out; **1988**, *Strands of Gold*, fell 22nd
1989, *Bonanza Boy*, eighth; *The Thirsty Farmer*, 11th
1990: *Bonanza Boy*, 16th; *Star's Delight*, pu. 13th; *Torside*, pu. sixth; *Huntworth*, ur. 15th
1991: *Bonanza Boy*, fifth; *Huntworth*, pu. 24th
1992: *Huntworth*, pu. 17th; *Omerta*, pu. seventh; *Bonanza Boy*, ref. 19th
1994: *Miinnehoma*, won; *Roc de Prince*, sixth; *Run For Free*, brought down 17th; *Paco's Boy*, pu. 17th; *Riverside Boy*, ref 18th
1995: *Riverside Boy*, eighth; *Chatam*, fell 12th; *Errant Knight* ur. first; *Miinnehoma* pu. 21st
1996: *Encore Un Peu*, second; *Riverside Boy*, 12th; *Chatam*, pu. fifth; **1997**: *Evangelica* 17th; *Mugoni Beach*, pu. 21st
1998: *Challenger du Luc*, fell first; *Diwali Dancer*, fell first; *Damas*, ref. 11th; *Pond House*, pu. 15th; *Decyborg*, pu. 27th
1999: *St Mellion Fairway*, ninth; *Eudipe*, fell fatally 22nd; *Tamarindo*, fell sixth; *Cyborgo*, pu. 19th
2000: *Dark Stranger*, ur. third; *Art Prince*, fell first; *Royal Predica*, fell first
2001: *Blowing Wind*, third; *Art Prince*, fell first; *Tresor De Mai*, fell second; *Khaki Crazy*, fell third; *Exit Swinger*, fell sixth; *Northern Starlight*, ur. sixth; *Strong Tel*, fell sixth; *Dark Stranger*, ref. eighth; *You're Agoodun*, bd. eighth; *Moondigua*, ur. 15th
2002: *Blowing Wind*, third; *You're Agoodun*, seventh; *Royal Predica*, eighth; *Carryonharry*, fell first; *Iris Bleu*, fell fifth; *Gun 'n Roses*, fell seventh; *Manx Magic*, fell fatally 20th; *Majed*, fell 22nd
2003: *Blowing Wind*, eighth; *Majed*, 12th; *Royal Predica*, 13th; *Burlu*, fell 22nd; *You're Agoodun*, ur. 19th; *Polar Champ*, ur. eighth; *Iris Bleu*, pu. 15th
2004: *Lord Atterbury*, third; *Jurancon II*, fell fourth; *Puntal*, ur. 19th; *Montreal*, *Akarus*, *Blowing Wind*, *Bounce Back*, all exited at the first Becher's
2005: *It Takes Time*, fourth; *Iznogoud*, 12th; *Polar Red*, 13th; *Lord Atterbury*, fell first.
2006: *Puntal*, sixth; *It Takes Time*, pu. after 3 out; *Iznogoud*, pu. before 27th; *Therealbandit*, pu. before 27th; *Whispered Secret*. ur. first.
See also: Miinnehoma; Dunwoody, Richard; McCoy, Anthony; Nicholls, Paul.

PITMAN, Jennifer Susan OBE

The undisputed 'Queen of Aintree', Jenny Pitman was the first woman to train a Grand National winner (*Corbiere*, 1983), a feat she repeated with the victory of *Royal Athlete* in 1995. She also saddled *Esha Ness* who was first past the post in 1993 when the race was declared void; and her family connection with the race was further enhanced by the achievements of her first husband, Richard Pitman, and their son Mark, the former finishing second on *Crisp* in 1973, the latter riding the 1991 runner-up *Garrison Savannah* and training the 2001 runner-up *Smarty*.

A mercurial lady of great character and resilience, Mrs Pitman became renowned for her toughness and volatility, but no less for her warmth and compassion and her ready wit and plain-speaking (she once presented a *Sun* reporter with a mounted toilet roll inscribed, 'For writing so much crap about me'). Above all, she was a trainer who fell totally in love with her horses, valuing their safe return far more than any victory.

Born on June 11, 1946, nee Jennifer Harvey, the fourth of seven children of a Leicestershire stockman, she grew up on the humblest of farms, the family home having neither electricity nor running water. But she was just 14 months old when she was first put on a pony; and when she was 15 George Harvey, who trained a couple of point-to-pointers, gave his daughter her first ride in a race on *Dan Archer*. (Her father had an astute eye for equine potential and years later would play a valuable role in Jenny's career, accompanying her to sales and on shopping expeditions around Britain and Ireland).

In 1965, while still in her teens, she married jockey Richard Pitman; and subsequently they began taking in a few liveries and then building up a successful point-to-point yard. Richard was to have plenty of big-race wins in the early 1970s while Jenny worked relentlessly to combine bringing up two sons with running the yard. But eventually the marriage began to flounder, and following the break-up Jenny's life became so precarious that she considered taking a job in a shoe shop. When she happened to mention this to the great Fred Winter he so fiercely disapproved that she resolved to soldier on as a trainer. Operating on a shoestring, she moved into the rundown, 16th century Weathercock House in Upper Lambourn, Berkshire; and – by dint of her great industry, determination and talent – she would eventually transform a derelict yard into a first-class training complex.

Overcoming many setbacks along the way, Jenny had her first winner under Rules in 1975 and truly made her mark when saddling *Watafella* to win the 1977 Midlands National. But that year – when *Red Rum* scored his extraordinary third triumph – no attention was paid to her first runner in the Grand National. This was *The Songwriter*, a 200-1 rank outsider, owned by Mr P.R. Callander who had written hits for Cliff Richard and Tony Christie. Knocked about by riderless horses, he was pulled up by Bryan Smart at Becher's second time around.

The following year *The Songwriter* finished eighth at 50-1, and in 1979 her runner, *Artistic Prince*, was a major challenger until falling at the 26th. Then, in the 1980-81 season, Mrs Pitman gained more prominence as she turned out *Bueche Giorod* to win six races, including the Massey Ferguson Gold Cup; and thereafter she made relentless progress to prove herself the supreme lady trainer of long-distance chasers.

In 1982 she won the Welsh National with *Corbiere* who went on to triumph in the 1983 Grand National, winning by three-quarters of a length from *Greasepaint* who had an 11lb advantage. And in 1984 she followed up by also becoming the first woman to saddle the winner of the Cheltenham Gold Cup. This was a truly a stupendous training feat, the winner being her beloved *Burrough Hill Lad* who had overcome so many injury problems. The great-

est of her chasers, he had already won the Welsh National (1983) and would go on to win a Hennessy Cognac Gold Cup and a King George VI Chase. No less remarkably, Mrs Pitman brought back *Corbiere* to finish third in the Grand Nationals of both 1984 and 1985; and in 1986 she took her third Welsh National with *Stearsby*.

In 1988 *Burrough Hill Lad* was entered for the Seagram Grand National and for once, unusually, Jenny Pitman was content with the judgment of senior handicapper Christopher Mordaunt, who had allotted her 12 year old superstar the second highest weight of 11st 9lb. Unfortunately *The Lad* did not make it to Aintree; and instead she had to rely on *Smith's Man*, a 50-1 chance, who was pulled up at the third fence. One year later she ran *Team Challenge* who finished ninth and *Gainsay* – a first National ride for her son Mark – who fell at the 19th.

Mrs Pitman worked wonders again in 1991 when she nursed back the injured *Garrison Savannah* to gain her second Cheltenham Gold Cup victory, this time with her son in the saddle. Moreover, despite an interrupted work schedule, 'Gary' came out three weeks later to make a magnificent bid to emulate *Golden Miller*'s unique achievement of winning the Gold Cup and National in the same year. He led over the last, only to be outpaced on the run-in by *Seagram*.

In 1993 Mrs Pitman was absolutely enraged by the Grand National's bungled starting procedure and stormed into the weighing room, searching for the Aintree stewards to demand that the race be stopped. She had two strongly fancied runners: *Garrison Savannah* and *Royal Athlete*, so closely matched that her son had had difficulty in opting to ride the former. But ironically in this void National, it was her third string, *Esha Ness*, who finished first to no purpose while *Royal Athlete* fell at the tenth and 'Gary' was pulled up after one circuit. Moreover, *Esha Ness* had registered the second fastest time (9min 1.4sec) in National history.

The following year she had only one runner: *Garrison Savannah*. Though faced with unfavourably heavy ground, he led halfway but then, after being unluckily hampered, refused at the 17th. In sharp contrast, Mrs Pitman had a record number of six runners in the 35-strong field of the 1995 Grand National. Among them – somewhat reluctantly – was *Royal Athlete*. She had wanted to run the 12 year old in the Scottish National and only sent him to Liverpool under pressure from the owners. For once the First Lady of Aintree was awry in her judgment. Going off at 40-1, *Royal Athlete* triumphed in commanding style. Of her other starters, only *Garrison Savannah* completed the course, finishing ninth at 16-1.

Royal Athlete's success was all the more special for Mrs Pitman because he had been beset with leg troubles and had injured himself so badly in the Hennessy Cognac Gold Cup that there had been doubts whether he would ever race again. To have nursed him back to fitness was a huge achievement; and now, to crown a most memorable season, she followed up with *Willsford*'s victory in the Scottish Grand National.

At Aintree in 1996, *Superior Finish* under Richard Dunwoody made a storming late charge to snatch third place in the National. Next came a truly momentous year for Mrs Pitman. In March, 1997, *Mudahim*, her recent Racing Post Chase winner, captured the Jameson Irish Grand National in a photo-finish. It meant that she had now joined Martin Pipe as the only trainer to have won all of the big four Grand Nationals. In the summer she married her long-time partner and assistant David Stait; and in the New Year Honours List she was awarded an OBE.

In other respects, however, this was a year of horror and heartbreak. The horror came when she needed to have a cyst removed from her throat and evidence of thyroid cancer was detected. Later she would need surgery to take away the thyroid and two lymph modes, followed by radioactive treatment. The heartbreak came at the Grand National where she was twice reduced to tears – firstly on the Saturday when, with the race postponed 49 hours following IRA bomb scares, she initially refused to leave her horses; and again on the Monday when her horse, *Smith's Band*, ridden by Dunwoody and in strong contention, had a heart attack on falling at the 20th fence.

Happily, on Christmas Eve, 1998, Jenny got the all clear from the cancer specialists. She then chose the Cheltenham Festival to announce her impending retirement; and subsequently her last Grand National appearance as a trainer was a hugely emotional affair. At a ceremony held in her honour, she was presented with a diamond-set brooch and admitted to the exclusive Grand National Club which has around 100 members, all having life member-

ship of the course; and there was the inevitable television interview by Des Lynam. That day her last National contender, *Nahthen Lad*, finished 11th, but most appropriately she won the closing bumper with *King Of The Castle*.

Mrs Pitman's final winner under Rules was *Scarlet Emperor* at Huntington in late May, 1999. It brought her career total to 797, with all the major jump prizes won. The following December, most deservedly, she was presented with the Helen Rollason Award for Inspiration which celebrates the achievements of women who have overcome adversity and proved an exceptional commitment to sport, and who, by their actions and strength of character, have influenced and inspired others.

Even now, however, retirement brought no release from the nervous pressures of the Grand National. In 2001 she was in tears after seeing Timmy Murphy come home second on *Smarty*, one of only two finishers not to have fallen. Before her son Mark had taken over at the Weathercock House yard, she herself had originally trained *Smarty*, winning four chases with him. Then a major rupture of a fore-leg tendon had kept the so promising chaser out of action for 21 months.

In 2002 Mrs Pitman, now living in the Berkshire village of Kintbury, followed the example of her former jockey John Francome and successfully turned to writing novels. Later she also took up training greyhounds. But emotionally, through the activities of Mark, her involvement with racing would remain strong. And above all, her name would always be associated with the Grand National in which, excluding her trio in the void race of 1993, she had sent out 39 runners, scoring two firsts, one second and three thirds.

Her overall National record

1977: *The Songwriter* (pu. 22nd) **1978**: *The Songwriter* (eighth); **1979**: *Artistic Prince* (fell 26th); **1981**: *Lord Gulliver* (fell 13th); **1982**: *Artistic Prince* (fell first) and *Monty Python* (ref. 22nd); **1983**: *Corbiere* (won), *Monty Python* (ref. 15th) and *Artistic Prince* (ref. 20th); **1984**: *Corbiere* (3rd); **1985**: *Corbiere* (third); **1986**: *Corbiere* (fell fourth); **1987**: *Smith's Man* (11th) and *Corbiere* (12th); **1988**: *Smith's Man* (pu. third); **1989**: *Team Challenge* (ninth) and *Gainsay* (fell 19th); **1990**: *Team Challenge* (11th), *Mick's Star* (19th), *Gainsay* (fell 14th); **1991**: *Garrison Savannah* (second), *Golden*

Freeze (17th), *Abba Lad* (pu. 17th), *Team Challenge* (ref. 19th); **1992**: *Willsford* (20th), *Team Challenge* (21st); **1994**: *Garrison Savannah* (bd. 17th); **1995**: *Royal Athlete* (won), *Garrison Savannah* (ninth), *Lusty Light* (fell first), *Superior Finish* (ur. tenth), *Esha Ness* (fell 12th), *Do Be Brief* (fell 20th); **1996**: *Superior Finish* (third), *Lusty Light* (16th); **1997**: *Nahthen Lad* (ninth), *Smith's Band* (fell 20th); **1998**: *Nahthen Lad* (pu.11th); **1999**: *Nahthen Lad* (11th).

See also: Corbiere; Royal Athlete; Garrison Savannah; Esha Ness; Pitman, Richard; Pitman, Mark; Lynam, Desmond; National Velvet.

PITMAN, Mark Andrew

It is difficult to imagine anyone having a more emotional introduction to the Grand National than that experienced by Mark Pitman. At the impressionable age of seven, he watched on TV in his aunt's sitting-room the agonising finish of the 1973 race in which his father, on *Crisp*, failed by three-quarters of a length to give 23lb and a beating to an eight year old newcomer called *Red Rum*. Years later he recalled, 'I was absolutely gutted. I cried like a baby and locked myself in a bedroom for six hours after the race.'

The elder son of Richard and Jenny Pitman, Mark was born on August 1, 1966, the Monday following England's World Cup soccer triumph. At the age of ten he and his younger brother, Paul, moved with their mother to Weathercock House, Upper Lambourn, into a home then without electricity and with derelict stables. While his brother was to become an accountant, Mark chose to emulate his father's career as a jump jockey. As a teenager he gained valuable experience with trainer David Nicholson, and later with Martin Pipe. He made his riding debut in 1983, finished second in the conditional jockeys' championship of 1986-87, and turned professional in 1988.

His career truly took off when riding for his mother. In December, 1988, he scored a one-day treble at Cheltenham that included a win on *Garrison Savannah* in the three-mile Coral Hurdle. The following April brought his first Grand National ride: on *Gainsay*, a 25-1 chance, trained by his mother and owned by Errol Brown, lead singer of the pop group Hot Chocolate. His mount jumped well and was still in touch at the 19th when he fell after being hampered by *Gala's Image*.

Back at Aintree for the 1990 National, an out-of-form *Gainsay*, now 66-1, fell at the 14th. Earlier that year, however, Pitman had suffered a far bigger disappointment. Riding *Toby Tobias* in the Cheltenham Gold Cup, he had finished four lengths ahead of the odds-on *Desert Orchid* only to be beaten three-quarters of a length by the 100-1 shot *Norton's Coin*. It revived memories of his father's short-head defeat on *Pendil* in 1973. Nonetheless, it was an outstanding first Gold Cup ride. He finished the season with his best-ever total of 57 wins; and the following year, serving as his mother's chief jockey, he came back to score his greatest triumph: riding *Garrison Savannah* to a short-head Gold Cup victory over *The Fellow*. ('When I won I felt like I'd died and got to heaven)'.

Less than two hours later, Mrs Pitman's elation turned to extreme anxiety as Mark failed to get to his feet after falling in the County Hurdle and was stretchered off to hospital with a fractured pelvis. However, such was his dedication that he was already asking whether he would be fit in time to ride in the National three weeks later. And remarkably he made it, getting the leg-up on *Garrison Savannah* who was bidding to become the only horse to emulate the National-Gold Cup double of *Golden Miller* in 1934.

His hopes were never higher. 'Gary' was the 7-1 joint second favourite, behind *Bonanza Boy*, and to form students he was a handicap 'snip', carrying just 11st 1lb, the weights having been set before his Cheltenham triumph. And, sure enough, for much of the race he travelled like a good thing, leading the way over the last and being eight lengths clear of his nearest rival, *Seagram*, as they came to the Elbow.

Now the nightmare of the 1973 National came back to haunt him as, just like his father before him, he was to have victory snatched from his grasp on the punishing run-in. Suddenly, at the Elbow, the race leader began to falter. As Mark later recalled: 'It was as if somebody reached into a car and took the engine out. In three strides he went from galloping to going up and down on the spot. *Seagram* came past us as if we were standing still and won by five lengths. I was so glad it wasn't a slogging battle over the last 150 yards. I looked into Gary's eyes when we came in and saw that the old horse had given everything.'

Two years later, when *Garrison Savannah* returned to Aintree, he had been raised to the second highest weight of 11st 8lb. As a result, Pitman had deliberated a full week on whether to ride him or

P

Royal Athlete who had 18lb less to carry. Finally he opted for the former. But it was of no consequence since this was the National declared void after a botched-up start. *Royal Athlete*, under Ben de Haan, fell at the tenth. 'Gary' was pulled up after one circuit while Mrs Pitman's third string *Esha Ness* ran on to be first to complete the course.

In 1995 Jenny Pitman had a record six horses in the National, but this year Mark was at Aintree as assistant to his mother. On the morning of the race he walked the course with jockey Jason Titley and gave the Aintree newcomer detailed instructions on how *Royal Athlete* needed to be ridden with extreme delicacy. To their delight, the 12 year old never put a foot wrong and romped home to win by seven lengths at 40-1.

Two years later Mark set out as a trainer in his own right, occupying the Saxon House stables, not far from his mother's famous Weathercock House premises. His first runner, *Sailin Minstrel*, won at Worcester in July. Then, in his first full season with a trainer's licence, he looked forward to having his first Grand National runner: 12 year old *Superior Finish*, who had been third for his mother in 1996. But he lost the battle to get the 12 year old race-fit in time for the 1998 race.

By the time of the 1999 Cheltenham Festival, where he turned out a 50-1 bumper winner, *Monsignor*, Mark had some 50 horses in his care and badly needed larger premises. Providentially, his mother chose this time to announce her impending retirement, so enabling him to move back to the Weathercock Stables with his wife Natasha. Eventually all 80 boxes there were occupied; and in November, at the first attempt, he turned out the winner of the Hennessy Cognac Gold Cup at Newbury: *Ever Blessed*, ridden by Timmy Murphy.

Back at Cheltenham in 2000 Mark again scored with the classy *Monsignor*, this time winning the Royal and SunAlliance Novices' Hurdle. And in 2001, with 70 horses in training, he prepared to follow in his mother's famous footsteps by turning out his first Grand National entries. One week before the race, to his huge disappointment, one of his two intended runners, 20-1 shot *Browjoshy*, was found to be lame in a hind leg. Nonetheless, he made a hugely encouraging debut, sending out *Smarty*, a 16-1 chance ridden by Timmy Murphy.

Faced with unsuitably heavy ground, the eight year old – schooled over two replica National fences

at Lambourn – did extraordinarily well to finish second, one of only two horses to complete the course without being remounted. It was yet another highly emotional moment for Mark's mother, who, seeing just two horses – *Smarty* and *Red Marauder* – running towards the second last, buried her head between her knees and began crying.

In the 2001-02 season Mark had 80 horses in his yard. But he experienced a dismal winter, all too often his best prospects being put out with injury or sickness. He entered six for the National but only *Smarty*, who had finished second to *Amberleigh House* on his return to Aintree in the Becher Chase, made it to the line-up. Most disappointingly, *Browjoshy*, who was 'going like a rocket at home' and all season had been aimed at the National, missed the cut by just one.

Like Ginger McCain, trainer of *Amberleigh House*, Pitman was bitterly critical of a 'fundamentally flawed' balloting system which decided the pecking order of horses sharing the same weight when the handicap was framed, but made no allowance for subsequent changes in their ratings. Thus *Browjoshy* and *Amberleigh House* were placed by random ballot below horses inferior on current ratings.

Meanwhile *Smarty* had had two runs over hurdles to tune him up for Aintree. Pitman judged him to be a stone better there, but the nine year old, ridden by Tom Scudamore, was badly hampered at the first and was pulled up at the ninth with his blinkers and bridle displaced. Again Aintree had proved an unhappy hunting-ground for Mark. He had now had all of his 19 runners at the Grand National meeting beaten. And he did not have another runner in the National until 2004 when *Smarty* narrowly made the cut, only to finish a remote sixth of 11 finishers at 100-1.

Immediately after the 2006 Grand National meeting, 39 year old Pitman handed over the reins at Weathercock House Stables to his relatively new assistant Carl Llewellyn who would combine training with race-riding on a reduced scale. He would, he said, continue to be involved with the yard but would now give more time to his family commitments in Spain.

See also: Garrison Savannah; Llewellyn, Carl; Pitman, Jennifer.

PITMAN, Richard
Although he had his share of big-race wins – among them, two King George VI Chases (1972-73) on

Pendil; the Champion Hurdle (1974) on *Lanzarote*; and the Hennessy Cognac Gold Cup (1972) on *Charlie Potheen* – Richard Pitman stands out as the jockey who has suffered the most heartbreaking near-misses. Twice he was destined to finish runner-up in both the Grand National and the Cheltenham Gold Cup; and two of those four disappointments came in the most dramatic circumstances, just 16 days apart, in March, 1973.

Born on January 21, 1943, Richard began his family's long and distinguished association with the National in 1967 when he rode 13 year old *Dorimont*, one of 14 100-1 outsiders in the 44-strong field. Having fallen at the third, he was a mere spectator when the great pile-up at the 23rd allowed *Foinavon* to win. The following year he finished on *Manifest*, a 66-1 chance, being narrowly beaten into 11th place by his great rival Eddie Harty, Fred Winter's stable jockey, on the 100-1 outsider *Steel Bridge*.

In 1969, it was Richard who had the ride on 11 year old *Steel Bridge*, now a 50-1 shot. Leading over Becher's, his mount stayed on tremendously well to be only three lengths behind the leader at the last. But on the run-in they could make no impression on the strongly supported *Highland Wedding* and finished second, 12 lengths behind a winner ridden by the jockey (Harty) who continually frustrated Pitman's racing hopes.

Now, with the dawn of the 1970s, Pitman was beginning the five-year purple patch of his riding career. In 1970 he won the Whitbread Gold Cup on *Royal Toss* at 20-1; and in 1972 he was united with two absolutely outstanding steeplechasers: *Pendil*, at one stage the winner of 19 out of 21 chases, and the mighty *Crisp*, sent over from Australia.

In 1971 *Crisp* had won Cheltenham's two-mile Champion Chase by a staggering 25 lengths. The following year he was favourite to win the Gold Cup and, with soft going, Winter decided that he should be held up to get the three and a quarter mile trip. Richard rode accordingly, but too late it was discovered that the powerful front-runner hated restraining tactics. From two out he faded to finish a well-beaten fifth.

Three weeks later Pitman returned to the Grand National after a two-year gap to ride *Lime Street*, a popular choice with local punters because he carried the name of Liverpool's main railway station. At the fourth fence *Lime Street* suddenly dug in his hooves and catapulted the jockey out of the saddle. But no

matter. Richard could look forward to great opportunities in the season ahead. On *Pendil*, he ended the year with a five lengths victory over *The Dikler* in the King George VI Chase; and the most accurate of jumpers went on to Cheltenham, having been unbeaten in 11 chases.

Though tackling a new distance, *Pendil* looked a near certainty to win the Gold Cup. He went off as 4-6 favourite and odds-on backers felt confident as he cleared the penultimate fence and drew several lengths clear. But there Richard seemingly erred in choosing to steady his mount as they approached the last. Shortening his stride, *Pendil* fiddled the last while his nearest rival *The Dikler* gained ground with a huge final leap. On the run-in, Pitman worked frantically to galvanise *Pendil* into maximum effort but crucially momentum had been lost. Flying at the finish, *The Dikler*, brilliantly ridden by Ron Barry, snatched victory by a short head and in course record time.

Sixteen days later Pitman had high hopes of better fortune in the Grand National. *Crisp* was so highly regarded that he carried the joint top weight of 12st and shared 9-1 favouritism with another newcomer, *Red Rum*. This time, following the Gold Cup experience, they would not make the mistake of trying to hold up a chaser who loved to bowl along in front.

In consequence, *Crisp* now gave Richard the most exhilarating ride he had ever known, soaring over the great fences with almost contemptuous ease to lead by some 25 lengths at the 19th, and by 15 at the last. But then, as *Crisp* began to lose his smooth action, Richard made what he subsequently judged to be a disastrous error. He picked up his stick to give his tiring horse a wake-up flick, and as he took his right hand off the reins *Crisp* drifted to the left. It was only a brief deviation off-line but arguably fatal, costing him perhaps three lengths as *Red Rum* closed the gap on the long run-in to snatch victory in his last few strides by just three-quarters of a length. Both horses had shattered the course record by more than 18 seconds.

Since *Crisp* had been conceding 23lb to *Red Rum*, he was popularly regarded as the greatest horse to run in the National without winning. Similarly, *Pendil*, also ridden by Richard, was to be rated – after *Flyingbolt* – as the greatest chaser never to have won the Cheltenham Gold Cup.

Following his near-misses at Cheltenham and Aintree, Richard at least had the consolation of end-

P

ing the 1972-73 season with his best-ever total of 84 winners, and he also ended 1973 on a high note, riding *Pendil* to a second victory in the King George VI Chase. The following March the great chaser again went to the Gold Cup with an unbeaten seasonal record behind him, and again he was the odds-on favourite. Coming to the third last he was positively cruising, Richard taking care not to the strike the front too soon. But then, as the leaders tackled that downhill fence, the 100-1 outsider *Sir Ken* crashed to the ground; and *Pendil*, with no means of escape, was brought down.

Sixteen days later Richard had his sixth and final Grand National ride, on nine year old *Francophile*. Though never in contention, the 16-1 shot got as far as the 28th before refusing, so enabling his jockey to collect £150 on a bet against him completing one circuit. Pitman ended the season with 79 winners, and the following year he made one last bid to win the Cheltenham Gold Cup. Faced with hock-deep mud, he did remarkably well on *Soothsayer* to finish runner-up again, six lengths behind the mudlark *Ten Up* and half a length ahead of John Francome on the more fancied *Bula*.

It was Pitman's final season. Having ridden 470 winners over jumps, he retired in 1975 to begin a much longer second career as a racing presenter for BBC television. Remarkably, for all his major disappointments and many injuries (including ten broken noses, five collarbones, fractures of ribs, an arm, a leg and an ankle) the 5ft 5in tall ex-jockey remained a bright and breezy character; and, never one to duck a challenge, he returned twice more to Aintree – in 1978 and 1979 – to tackle the National course for television purposes. On the second occasion he rode *Barony Fort* while Captain Mark Phillips was on the Queen's three-day eventer *Columbus*. Phillips completed the circuit but Richard, stubbornly driving his reluctant mount at the tricky third fence, ended up rolling on the turf. As ever, he saw the funny side of his mixed fortunes.

He was to enjoy covering many more Nationals, though not so much in 1991 when he relived the anguish of his 1973 defeat as he watched his son Mark leading over the last on *Garrison Savannah* only to be overhauled on the run-in by the fast-finishing *Seagram*. Proudly he saw the family tradition carried on not only by his son as a successful jockey-turned trainer, but also by Tara Pitman, one of two daughters by his second marriage. In 2002 she won an amateurs' charity race at Ascot and was riding out for trainer John Hills at Uplands, where her father had been employed by Fred Winter 38 years before.

See also: Crisp; Pitman, Jenny and Mark.

PLACES

In general, for betting purposes, the first four horses are judged to be 'placed' – thus rewarding each-way punters – when there are 16 or more starters in a handicap race. On this basis the horses which have most often finished in a place are:

> *Manifesto* (six times) – 1895 (fourth), 1897 (first), 1899 (first) 1900 (third), 1902 (third), 1903 (third)
> *Red Rum* (five times) – 1973 (first), 1974 (first), 1975 (second), 1976 (second), 1977 (first)
> *Frigate* (four times) – 1884 (second), 1885 (second), 1888 (second), 1889 (first)
> *Wyndburgh* (four times) – 1957 (second), 1958 (fourth), 1959 (second), 1962 (first)
> *West Tip* (four times) – 1986 (first), 1987 (fourth), 1988 (fourth), 1989 (second)

PLAYFAIR

Shock winner of the 1888 Grand National on his first and last appearance in the race. Trained by the great Flat jockey, Tom Cannon, and ridden by a little known jockey, George Mawson, seven year old *Playfair* won at 40-1 and, unusually, with the sporting assistance of an opposing rider.

At the fence after the second Becher's, *Playfair* managed to wriggle over after straddling the obstacle but nose-dived so sharply on landing that Mawson, a newcomer to the race, was propelled forward and left hanging desperately to the horse's neck. At that point, the nearest rider, Arthur Nightingall on *The Badger*, generously reached out to lever the desperate jockey back into the saddle.

Mawson then had another lucky break. Two Beasley brothers – Harry on the seven year old *Usna* and William on the well-supported *Frigate* – were leading as they came to the Canal Turn. But there, *Usna*, the Irish joint favourite, dislocated his shoulder on landing and, veering off the course, carried *Frigate* far out to the right, almost into the canal.

Given a masterly ride, *Frigate* contrived to make up a mass of lost ground and regain the lead at the last. But the recovering effort had used up all her reserves of energy and she could not resist the challenge of *Playfair* who strode on to beat her by ten lengths, with *Ballot Box* a further four lengths back in third. *The Badger* was the last of nine finishers.

A black gelding – by *Ripponden* out of an unrecorded mare – *Playfair* had a humble background, having been bought as a five year old after winning an obscure Farmers' Hunt race. He won similar races for his new owner, Mr Hedworth Barclay, and was then bought by Mr E.W. Baird, a subaltern (later to become a Brigadier-General) in the tenth Hussars. Baird rode him in numerous hunters' races, both over fences and on the Flat, and he also took the ride when the gelding, on his last outing before making his successful Aintree debut, won a hunters' hurdle race at Kempton Park. Following his National victory *Playfair* made only one more racecourse appearance – at Sandown where he ran out in the Grand International Chase.

See also: Cannon, Tom; Mawson, George.

POETHLYN

In 1919 nine year old *Poethlyn*, as 11-4 favourite, became the shortest-priced winner in Grand National history. Only one horse has completed the course at shorter odds: *Regal* who (remounted) finished sixth in 1879 as 5-2 favourite.

In fact, the bay gelding – by *Rydal Head* out of *Fine Champagne* – was the shortest-priced winner in more ways than one. As a frail-looking foal, bred by Major and Mrs Hugh Peel in Wales, he had been sold to a Shrewsbury publican for a mere £7. Two years later, after *Poethlyn* had developed well, the Peels had second thoughts. They bought him back for £50, and he rewarded them by winning his first chase at Blackpool when four years old.

Trained by Harry Escott at Lewes, *Poethlyn* won all of his four chases in 1918, and those successes included the last of the wartime substitute 'Nationals' held at Gatwick where he scored impressively under Ernie Piggott. That race, over four miles 856 yards, was no real test of jumping ability. Nevertheless, when the Aintree Grand National, was revived in 1919, he was so highly regarded that the handicapper lumbered him with the top weight of 12st 7lb, three stone more than the second favourite, *Charlbury*.

The revived race had 22 runners, including two past National winners, *Ally Sloper* and *Sunloch*, plus *Vermouth*, winner of the 1916 Gatwick substitute.

But, like *Charlbury*, all these struggled on the extremely heavy going and failed to get round. Meanwhile, apart from dropping his hind legs in the Water, *Poethlyn* galloped and jumped strongly throughout, leaping into the lead at the second Becher's. The principal threat at that stage was the 66-1 outsider *All White*, ridden by a last minute substitute jockey, Tommy Williams. But then, approaching the Canal Turn, Williams was seized with stomach cramps, and he pulled up temporarily to be sick – the consequence, it was later said, of having recently snacked on seafood at the racecourse.

Poethlyn powered on to win by a comfortable eight lengths from *Ballyboggan*, with *Pollen* a further six lengths back in third. Williams, who later insisted that he had the winner 'stone-cold' before his stomach upset, brought *All White* home to be the fifth of seven finishers.

It was a second National victory for Piggott and for trainer Escott who had the added satisfaction of seeing his son Anthony make a third-place debut on *Pollen*. Also, for only the second time, the National had a winning woman owner: Mrs Hugh Peel, following immediately from Lady Nelson's 1915 success with *Ally Sloper*.

Poethlyn was only the fourth horse to carry 12st 7lb to victory in the National – a feat never equalled since. But arguably he was not in the same class as his famous predecessors: *Cloister* (1893), *Manifesto* (1899) and *Jerry M* (1912). To be sure, he was a strong, reliable jumper, a fact underlined when, a few weeks after his National win, he ran away with the Lancashire Steeplechase under 12st 9lb. However, the Aintree fences had not been rebuilt to their full height by the time of the post-war renewal; and certainly Piggott did not rate his second winner as highly as *Jerry M* whom he judged to be the best jumper he had ever known.

Poethlyn ran only once more in the National – in 1920 when, again carrying top weight, he was made 3-1 favourite on the strength of his record of 11 successive chase victories. But this time, on heavy going and in torrential rain, he and Piggott came down at the very first fence. He was retired immediately afterwards.

See also: Piggott, Ernest; Escott, Harry.

PONTIN, Sir Frederick William

Horse racing was the principal pastime of Sir Fred Pontin, the Walthamstow-born entrepreneur who, in the 1960s, built up a chain of holiday camps to rival the empire of the pioneering Billy Butlin. He advertised his business by giving his horses such names as *Go Pontin*, *Go Pontinental* and *Pontigo*. But it was his simply named *Specify*, a 28-1 chance, that gave him his greatest reward: winning the 1971 Grand National by a neck from *Black Secret*.

Five years after that Aintree triumph, Pontin was knighted for his work on behalf of the Variety Club of Great Britain; and three years later his Pontin's Holdings was taken over by Coral, the bookmakers, for £56 million. Still wheeler-dealing well into his eighties, Sir Fred died in 2000 at the age of 93. Curiously, horse racing – with the Grand National as a main target – also became a major preoccupation of Trevor Hemmings, the self-made multi-millionaire who led a management buyout of Pontins holiday camps in 1987.

See also: Specify; Hemmings, Trevor.

POPHAM DOWN

The ten year old and 66-1 chance who, having been knocked down at the first fence in 1967, went on without his rider (M.C. Gifford) to successfully negotiate another 21 fences before causing the worst pile-up in National history.

See also: Foinavon.

POSTPONEMENTS

In 1855 severe frost caused the Grand National to be postponed from the Wednesday to the following week. Similarly, in 1858, heavy snowfalls resulted in the race being transferred from Wednesday to Saturday. In the latter case, it was then run amid snow flurries and a gale – conditions which many felt merited cancellation; and only five of 16 starters were able to finish.

In 1901, racing conditions again looked impossible: a fierce blizzard was raging and Aintree was already blanketed in snow. The majority of riders signed a petition in favour of a postponement, but the stewards rejected it. The only concession they would make to the weather was to dispense with the parade. It took 16 minutes to get the 24 runners off at the start. Fifteen failed to complete the course and one was destroyed after breaking a leg.

In 1997 the National was abandoned for 49 hours following an IRA bomb scare. Officially this was counted as 'a postponement', and therefore bets for the Saturday remained valid for the Monday race.

However, all the major firms gave punters the option to cancel bets that had been placed after 10 a.m. on the Thursday.

See also: Abandoned.

POTTS, Henry

In 1937, when the Liverpool Racecourse Executive incorrectly celebrated the Centenary Year of the Grand National, they were awarding to Mr Henry Potts the distinction of being the first of many amateurs ('gentleman riders') to win the world's most famous steeplechase. On March 1, 1837, when there were only four runners in the Grand Liverpool Steeplechase at Aintree, he had won on *The Duke* by 'about 30 yards' and in an estimated time of 15 minutes.

We now know that the first Liverpool Steeplechase was held at Aintree in 1836 and that the 1839 chase was the first to be worthy of the title 'grand'. Nevertheless, the 1837 event was recognised as the first Grand National by Mr T.H. Bird when he wrote his history, *A Hundred Grand Nationals*, in 1937. That year he interviewed Potts' granddaughter. The lady, Miss Gwladys C. R. Ash, told him: 'It has always been handed down to us that our grandfather won the first Grand National, and his family was proud of the fact ... but he always said he was a bit ashamed of himself, because he rode unknown to his parents.'

Mr Potts' shame in not telling his parents reflects the low esteem in which steeplechasing was held at the time. It was regarded as somewhat unseemly for persons of high social standing to compete against professionals, hence the use of pseudonyms by some amateur riders in later Grand Nationals.

Consequently, Mr Potts never rode in the great Aintree steeplechase again; and he only did so in 1837 as an 11th hour replacement for the celebrated professional jump jockey Captain Martin Becher. The captain had given up the ride on *The Duke* because he could not reach Aintree in time, having been involved in a race at St Albans the previous day.

In 1836, Becher had won the first Liverpool Grand Steeplechase (then a selling race) on *The Duke*, owned at that time by Mr W. Sirdefield, proprietor of the George Inn at Great Crosby. Thus, under Potts in 1837, the eight year old chestnut gelding became the first dual winner of the Liverpool Steeplechase.

Remarkably, considering this was not yet a handicap race, *The Duke* went off at the generous odds of 6-1 on his return, compared with *Dan O'Connell* 5-4 and *The Disowned* 3-1. *Zanga* was the 12-1 outsider of four. Reputedly, Irish supporters lost a small fortune in backing the favourite who finished a far distant third under his excessively heavy owner, Mr J.F. Knaresborough.

Born near Mold, in Denbighshire, in 1810, Henry Potts hailed from wealthy, landowning gentry, and, though strictly an amateur, he was recognised as an outstanding horseman. While he did not reappear in the 1838 Liverpool Steeplechase (Becher was reunited with *The Duke* and finished third), he did compete twice at that meeting. Riding his own mare, *The Countess*, in a race over three miles, he was in the lead, looking a certain winner when they fell. Potts remounted and finished fifth. Later that same day they raced again, being placed in a hurdle race.

Potts gave up steeplechasing following his marriage and moved to Chester, thereafter regularly riding with the Cheshire hounds. He died six days before the running of the 1884 Grand National.

POULETT, Lord

A godson of King William IV, Lord Poulett was the most distinguished amateur sportsman of his day: joint founder of the Hampshire Cricket Club, master of the Hambledon Hounds, a keen yachtsman and a useful rider on the Flat and over the jumps. In 1866 he became a founder member of the Grand National Hunt Committee, formed to administer and govern jump racing in Britain; and that same year he made a most determined bid to win the premier steeplechase.

Lord Poulett entered three runners for the 1866 Grand National: *Cortolvin*, 8-1 second favourite; *Reporter*, an unquoted outsider; and *Ace of Hearts*, a 30-1 chance ridden by the renowned amateur, George ('Mr Edwards') Ede. Only *Cortolvin*, ridden by newcomer John Page, finished – second by ten lengths to Mr Edward Studd's *Salamander*.

One year later Page won the National on *Cortolvin*, but it brought no joy for Lord Poulet who had bred the horse in Ireland. Despite that second place at Aintree, he had judged the horse to be not genuine and had sold him to the Duke of Hamilton. Seemingly a shrewder judge, the duke had plunged hugely on his 16-1 shot, so extricating himself from financial difficulties.

That year, Lord Poulett's runner, *Genievre* finished a distant tenth behind *Cortolvin*. But no matter. The following year, Poulett came back with a vengeance, gaining his first National win with an extraordinarily small grey called *The Lamb*, ridden by 'Mr Edwards'. This time his judgment of horse flesh had been vindicated. Following an inspired search in Ireland, he had bought the *The Lamb* from Dublin veterinary surgeon Joseph Doyle, even though the grey had previously been rejected by his old rival, Mr Studd, as 'not strong enough to carry a man's boots'.

Wisely, Lord Poulett rested his 'little wonder' after that demanding Aintree run. And in the next two years he limited himself to running his five year old *Cristal* (pulled up in 1870). Then he brought back *The Lamb* to win again, this time recruiting 'Mr Thomas' Pickernell for the ride, having seen him win on the grey in a dream. Leading in his dual winner, the proud owner was severely jostled by the jubilant crowd – and simultaneously relieved of his pocket watch by some light-fingered punter. It was nonetheless the most cherished moment of his racing years.

See also: The Lamb; Pickernell, Thomas; Dreams.

POWELL, Mr A

So inadequate were the records and reports of the early Aintree steeplechases that the winning rider of Lord Craven's *Charity* in the 1841 Grand National is simply identified as 'Mr. Powell'. According to Mr T.H. Bird, writing in his 1937 history, *A Hundred Grand Nationals*, this was Mr A. Powell who 'first appeared in the preliminary steeplechase of 1836 at Liverpool, when he rode the favourite, *Laurie Todd*, and was disputing the lead with *The Duke* when someone, probably one of *The Duke*'s backers, suddenly shut in his face a gate through which he was riding, and he and the horse came down'.

Confusingly, however, several Powells were riding in steeplechases at this time, and it may well be that the unlucky jockey in 1836 was the more colourfully named rider, Horatio Nelson Powell. However, histories generally agree that Mr A. Powell was a highly experienced cross-country rider, almost certainly the one who rode in the 1839 National, on *Railroad*, the sixth of seven finishers. As Mr Bird described him: 'This Mr Powell was a very 'tough customer', a good deal of a swashbuckler, who in his greenhorn days went from his home

P

in Gloucestershire to a steeplechase meeting in Norfolk, to 'show the natives how to ride'.

In the 1840 National, Powell was on the 3-1 favourite, Lord McDonald's *The Nun*. He remounted after a fall but had to pull her up a 100 yards later. Then, after his victory in 1841, he was booked to ride the second favourite at Aintree: Lord Mostyn's *Seventy Four* who, under the great Tom Olliver, had been the runner-up to *Lottery* in the 1839 National. Though well in the lead after the second Becher's, *Seventy Four* tired on the run-in, finally being worn down by *Gay Lad*, on whom Olliver won by four lengths.

Altogether it would seem that this Powell appeared in nine Nationals, other rides simply attributed to 'Powell' being *Charity*, 1844, fell; *Peter Swift*, 1845, failed to finish; *Brenda*, 1846, fell; *Variety*, 1848, failed to finish; and *The Curate*, 1849, fell. Another Powell (H. N.) rode *Culverthorpe* who finished fifth in 1847.

See also: Charity.

POWELL, Brendan Gerard

Winning rider of *Rhyme 'N' Reason* in the 1988 Grand National – an astonishing achievement on two counts. After surviving a belly-flopping slide on landing over Becher's first time, Brendan Powell took his mount from last to first. In addition, he was making only his second appearance in the race, having one year earlier broken his arm when falling on *Glenrue*, a 33-1 chance, at the third fence. After that painful debut he had declared: 'I didn't care a jot about breaking my arm because I had achieved my chief ambition to take part in the National.'

Unusually for a jumps jockey, this amiable, modest and quiet-natured Irishman (born on October 14, 1960) was a lifelong teetotaller, so lean and light that he could ride at a minimum weight without need of extreme dieting and saunas. Following his first ride as a 14 year old amateur in Ireland he had many years of partnering second-rate horses and struggling to make a reasonable living. By his own admission, he was not a stylish rider, but he lacked nothing in perseverance and finally it was rewarded.

Having ridden his first winner, at Windsor in 1982, he gained valuable experience as a 7lb claimer employed by Stan Mellor; and, no longer a conditional jockey, he made marked progress in 1986 and 1987, finishing the seasons with 45 and 48 winners respectively. Then, riding for trainer David

Elsworth, his career really took off – most notably through his new partnership with *Rhyme 'N' Reason*. Together they won a three-mile handicap chase at Lingfield. In December, 1987, they were beaten only a length by *Playschool* in the Welsh National, and they began the New Year with victory in the Anthony Mildmay-Peter Cazalet Memorial Chase at Sandown.

In February, Powell won his first £10.000 race: the Tote Gold Trophy on *Jamesmead*. Then came more successes with the so busy *Rhyme 'N' Reason*: three-mile wins in the Fairlawne Chase at Windsor and in the valuable Racing Post Handicap Chase at Kempton where the gelding finished ahead of such noted chasers as *Lean Ar Aghaidh*, *Mr Frisk* and *The Tsarevich*. At the Cheltenham Festival, Brendan won the Cathcart on *Private Views*. The only disappointment in this long-extended purple patch was a fall four out on *Rhyme 'N' Reason* in the Cheltenham Gold Cup.

But neither trainer nor jockey were discouraged by this fall since the nine year old, running strongly at the time, had jumped the fence brilliantly merely to slip on landing. They went on to the Grand National with confidence sky high. Their so consistent chaser, a winner already of 13 races, was the 10-1 second joint favourite, along with *Lean Ar Aghaidh* who, similarly, was carrying the second highest weight of 11st behind the evergreen *West Tip* on 11st 7lb.

In 1987 Brendan's parents had travelled to Aintree to see him ride in his first Grand National. Mrs Sheila Powell then came close to collapse on seeing her son stretchered away to hospital after breaking an arm in falling at the third. Therefore, she stayed at home in 1988. But her husband went to Aintree and he backed their son to win. Meanwhile, following the slithering fall at Cheltenham, Brendan had insisted on the horse being fitted with a neck strap. 'At most jumps,' he would explain afterwards, 'I was just clinging onto it, as I had no contact with his mouth whatsoever'.

Sacred Path, the heavily backed favourite, was one of three fallers at the first fence. Then, at the first Becher's, it seemed that *Rhyme 'N' Reason* would make an early exit, too. He belly-flopped and skidded along on landing, with Powell miraculously managing to stay in the saddle. Somehow the horse succeeded in scrambling to his feet, but at that stage he was plum last of 33 runners still standing and his rider thought that all chance of winning was gone.

Brendan's only aim now was survival. But, as at Cheltenham, his mount seemed to grow stronger the further he went. When *Little Polveir* fell at the 26th, Powell found himself leading the field sooner than he would have wished. Thus, it was a blessing in disguise when his mount faltered at the second last, allowing *Durham Edition* to pull ahead. Given a lead up to the run-in, *Rhyme 'N' Reason*, noted for his finishing speed, stormed back in the last 200 yards to win by four lengths.

Subsequently, Brendan was called before the stewards who inquired into his use of the whip from the second last fence. They accepted his explanation after viewing the film of the race and taking evidence from the vet. The fact was that the flap had broken off his whip with the first smack on the run-in. 'Without the flap,' he said, 'it was like slapping him with a twig.'

Brendan's great winning streak continued so strongly that between April and the end of the season he was to ride 30 winners. And such was the upturn in his fortunes that by the time of the 1989 Grand National he had passed 50 winners in a season for the first time. He now had the ride on the well-supported *Stearsby*, recent winner of a Nottingham chase by 20 lengths. They were up with the leaders at Valentine's when *Stearsby* suddenly slammed on the brakes to dump his rider at the 11th. But consolation was soon forthcoming, with victory on *Roll-A-Joint* in the Scottish National.

The following year, in the Aintree National, he finished 14th on the seven year old *Ghofar*. Then, at the time of the 1991 National, he was out for the rest of the season, having undergone an operation for a perforated stomach following a kick when *Beau Rou* fell at Liverpool. In 1992 he broke a leg, and as soon as it healed he broke it again. Briefly he feared that he might have to retire. But at that stage his career was given a fresh kick-start when a chance winning ride at Hereford introduced him to Dorset trainer Bob Buckler.

Better bookings followed. However, it was not until 1995 that he would have another Grand National ride and then it was to be on the longest-priced of five Jenny Pitman entries: *Do Be Brief*. They fell at the 20th while Mrs Pitman's *Royal Athlete* went on to win at 40-1.

Again there was a long gap between his National rides. In 1998 he had been hoping to ride *St Mellion Fairway* at Aintree. But then Andrew Thornton, recent winner of the Cheltenham Gold Cup on *Cool Dawn*, became available through the late withdrawal of *Superior Finish*. He took the ride, finishing fourth on *St Mellion Fairway* while the luckless Powell was condemned to the obscurity of riding at Hereford.

At the 1999 Cheltenham Festival, Powell had a sensational success, riding the 50-1 bumper winner *Monsignor*. However, he went on to Aintree with little hope of success. He was on *Mudahim* who had won the Irish National in his prime but was now 13 years old, well past his best. They parted company at the first Becher's. Then again, exactly as one decade before, there was quick consolation in the Scottish National, this time with victory on *Young Kenny* – an eight year old who, with wins also in the Greenalls and Midlands National, was seen as an outstanding candidate for Grand National honours.

Early in the following November it seemed certain that Brendan's riding days were over. He had suffered terrible chest injuries and numerous broken ribs when falling from *Rathgibbon* at Newton Abbot. One lung had collapsed, the other had filled with blood, and he was left fighting for his life during ten days in intensive care at Torbay Hospital. His weight plummeted to seven stone.

On leaving hospital, the gritty Irishman reluctantly determined to give up smoking. But even now – having previously survived broken legs, a ruptured spleen and a twice-broken thigh – he was not prepared to concede that, at 39, it was time he retired from the saddle. With such a great prospect as *Young Kenny*, he still dreamed of glory in the Cheltenham Gold Cup – and another Grand National win.

In Brendan's absence, Norman Williamson won three times on *Monsignor*. No matter. There was still the Grand National and *Young Kenny*; and his hopes were high as the nine year old, trained by Peter Beaumont and ridden by Russ Garritty, sealed his position at the head of the market by winning the National Trial Chase at Uttoxeter on his penultimate start before going to Aintree.

Six weeks before the 2000 Grand National, however, the omens were less good as *Young Kenny*, reunited with Powell, finished a distant fourth over an extended three and a half miles at Haydock. And meanwhile that performance at Uttoxeter had been sufficient to see him lumbered with the 12st top weight for Aintree. Powell was the senior jockey in the race and on ground faster than ideal his mount fell at the tenth. It was Brendan's seventh and last ride in the race, and soon afterwards his hope of one final famous victory on *Young Kenny* ended when he had to pull up early on the second circuit of the Whitbread Gold Cup.

Powell hated having to retire. But it was now inevitable. In a 20 year career he had ridden 648 winners around the world, including some on the Flat in Jersey; and at the time of his retirement only Richard Dunwoody had taken more rides. He numbered *Rhyme 'N' Reason* and *Dublin Flyer* (1995 Mackeson Gold Cup) among his finest memories.

In the summer of 2000 Powell started his new career as a trainer, ably supported by his wife Rachel who ten years earlier had looked after Grand National winner *Mr Frisk*. Together they worked tirelessly to develop derelict stables at Twyford near Winchester. Making slow but steady progress, they had an extraordinary 23,300-1 treble at Fontwell Park in January, 2005, and their 50-box yard now included a hugely promising jumper *Colonel Frank*, winner of three successive chases.

Powell sent out some 250 winners in his seven years at Twyford. Then, when the lease ran out in 2007, he moved to Lambourn, renting Newlands, the yard formerly occupied by trainer Brian Meehan. He now had more than 90 horses in his care and his clients included two of the foremost jumping owners, J. P. McManus and David Johnson.

See also: Rhyme 'N' Reason; Elsworth, David.

POWER, James Joseph

Irish-born rider of *Freebooter*, the 10-1 joint favourite who impressively won the 1950 Grand National by 15 lengths from *Wot No Sun*. The success owed much to Jimmy Power's acrobatic agility in recovering after his mount had made one near-disastrous error at The Chair. There, *Freebooter*, normally the safest of jumpers, took off too soon and hit the obstacle square on, pitching the jockey out of the saddle. Clinging desperately on to his horse's neck, Power contrived to regain his seat and, after giving *Freebooter* time to recover, steadily made up lost ground. *Freebooter* was left in the lead when his only serious rival *Cloncarrig* nose-dived over the second last. As the winning jockey said afterwards, 'I was never more relieved to see a horse fall.' Thereafter, he was able to dominate the race unchallenged.

Like *Freebooter*, his regular mount, Jimmy Power came from Co. Waterford. Born on November

ber 8, 1922, he was a professional rider in Ireland during the Second World War, switched to racing in England in 1947, and first demonstrated his fine horsemanship at Aintree when riding *Clyduffe*, a 14 year old no-hoper, in the 1949 National. That year he made a most extraordinary recovery after his old horse had slumped to his knees on landing over Becher's first time. Moreover, he nursed his 66-1 chance home – the tenth of 11 finishers.

The following season Power had the good fortune to be booked by a leading trainer, Ripon-based Bobby Renton. He impressed when winning at Wetherby on Mrs Lurline Brotherton's *Chimay*; and as a result, in October, he was given the leg-up at Nottingham on Mrs Brotherton's prize chaser *Freebooter* who, seven months earlier, had won Aintree's Champion Chase under Tim Molony. They finished well, in third place behind *Knight Of The Deep* and the 1949 Grand National winner *Russian Hero*.

Next they tackled one circuit of the National fences, impressively carrying 12st 4lb to victory in the Grand Sefton, winning by eight lengths from the royal star *Monaveen*. The placings were reversed in the prestigious Queen Elizabeth Chase run at Hurst Park on December 31. But now the New Year brought Power's most successful run, his wins including the Great Yorkshire Chase on *Freebooter* and Cheltenham's County Hurdle on *Blue Raleigh*, and culminating with his Grand National triumph.

To win the National by 15 lengths was remarkable enough, but all the more so this year when there were 49 starters, including *Russian Hero*, Lord Bicester's hugely fancied *Roimond*, and *Freebooter*'s old rival *Monaveen*. On this occasion *Freebooter* was conceding 12lb to *Monaveen* who, as the first royal contender for 42 years, was running in the presence of King George VI, Queen Elizabeth and the royal princesses.

As it happened, only seven runners were to complete the course. *Russian Hero* went at the first. *Roimond*, last year's runner-up and now joint favourite, fell with Dick Francis at the seventh. Due to the brilliant horsemanship of Tony Grantham, *Monaveen* miraculously survived a blunder at the 14th but faded in the later stages to finish a distant fifth.

Jimmy Power was to enjoy more triumphs at Aintree – winning the Grand Sefton on *Freebooter* for a second time in 1951, and the 1956 Topham Trophy on *John Jacques*. But for injury he would also have been on *Freebooter* in 1953 when, with

George Slack deputising, he waltzed away with the Becher Chase.

As his record proved, *Freebooter* was a true Aintree specialist. However, on his return for the 1951 National, not even Power's masterful riding could prevent the top-weighted Liverpool favourite being brought down at the second fence in the chaos that followed an undeclared false start. And one year later he suffered the same fate, unluckily being brought down on Lady Joicey's *Cardinal Error*, a 33-1 chance.

Elsewhere Power had big-race successes, most notably riding the giant *Limber Hill*, trained by Billy Dutton who was famed for his extraordinary win on 100-1 *Tipperary Tim* in the 1928 Grand National. Together they impressively won the 1955 King George VI Chase and the 1956 Cheltenham Gold Cup. Meanwhile, however, Jimmy had suffered a huge disappointment in the National. In 1953 he was on the Renton-trained 7-1 favourite *Little Yid* who was prominent throughout the first circuit but then rapidly tired and finally refused towards the finish.

Power had six more National rides. His 1954 bid on Lord Leverhulme's 66-1 outsider *Royal Stuart* ended in a refusal. In 1955 he fell on another outsider, *Sun Clasp*; and in 1956 he was on the well-supported *Pippykin* who also failed to finish. The following year, more encouragingly, he made a bold challenge on *The Crofter*, another 66-1 outsider. They were well placed going to the last, only to be well outpaced on the run-in and to finish fifth.

Disappointingly *The Crofter* was a faller when they returned in 1958 and the following year Power was on a 100-1 no hoper, *Sundawn III*, who was brought down at the first Becher's. It was the 36 year old Irishman's tenth and last National ride. On retirement he turned to farming in Yorkshire, though until his late 60s he continued to ride out at the Malton yard of Pat Rohan, son-in-law of Billy Dutton.

In 2006 Jimmy was invited back to Cheltenham for the 50th anniversary of his Gold Cup win on *Limber Hill*. And by now, following the death of Bruce Hobbs, he had become, at 83, the oldest surviving National-winning jockey.
See also: Freebooter.

POWER, Robert

Triumphant rider of *Silver Birch* in the 2007 National when, as a substitute jockey having only his second ride in the race, he fought out a furious three-way finish to snatch victory by three-quarters of a length from *McKelvey*, with *Slim Pickings* close-up in third.

'It's unreal,' he said immediately afterwards. 'I never thought that this was a dream that could come true.' Yet there was never a hint of self-doubt in the manner of his winning. Aged 25, Robbie Power gave *Silver Birch* a masterful ride – settling the 10 year old into an easy rhythm on the run-up to the first Becher's, then steadily advancing from mid-field and timing his all-out challenge to perfection.

He had one anxious moment: when narrowly avoiding *Bewleys Berry* who had fallen directly in front of them at the second Becher's. Thereafter he made relentless progress, taking the lead at the last and just holding on in a battle to the line so fiercely contested that both Power and Barry Geraghty (on *Slim Pickings*) were banned for excessive use of the whip. It was Ireland's sixth victory in nine years.

Two years earlier, on his National debut, Power had gained valuable experience of the Aintree fences, albeit getting round in his own time to be the 18th of 21 finishers on the veteran, so reliable, cross-country specialist *Spot Thedifference*, trained by Enda Bolger. And not least he had long enjoyed the benefit of expert guidance from his father, the legendary Irish showjumper Con Power.

On the day of his son's triumph, Power Snr was in Fontainebleau, attending a major pony show jumping show in a coaching capacity. His parting advice, as Robbie recalled, was: 'Don't be worried about the fences. It's the same as any other chase. Ride the exact same way you would to an ordinary fence – just slip your reins a bit over Becher's.'

From early childhood Robbie had been coached by his father and fed on the romance of the Grand National – especially learning about the 1947 success of *Caughoo*, the 100-1 winner that had been bred by his grandfather Patrick Power. Like his father he was soon excelling in the show-jumping world, earning a silver medal at the European Junior Championships in 2000. One year later he switched to race-riding.

His first major wins came in 2003. Riding for Paddy Mullins, he partnered *Nearly A Moose* to victory in the Galway Plate; and that same year he won the Midlands National on *Intelligent* for Jessica Harrington. In 2004 he was the leading 'claimer' in Ireland, and later he became a regular partner of the star chaser *Newmill*. Then, to his huge disappoint-

P

ment, a broken foot cost him the winning ride on *Newmill* in the 2006 Champion Chase at the Cheltenham Festival.

The following year, however, his fortunes were reversed. At Cheltenham, *Silver Birch* finished second in the Cross-Country Chase under Jason Maguire, his regular partner and the closest friend of the horse's rookie trainer Gordon Elliott. But when it came to the National Maguire was committed to *Idle Talk*, trained by Donald McCain. Robbie picked up the spare ride and so realised his 'impossible dream'.

He then crowned his glorious season by riding what one commentator judged to be 'a sensational race that bettered even his Aintree effort'. In the valuable ACC Bank Champion Hurdle at the Punchestown Festival, he drove home 20-1 shot *Silent Oscar* to snatch victory by a neck from the 7-4 favourite *Macs Joy*, ridden by Barry Geraghty. It gave trainer Harry Rogers the biggest win of his career and landed a 120,000 euro jackpot for owner Patrick Convery.

See also: Elliott, Gordon; Silver Birch.

PRICE, Captain Henry Ryan MC

Having served with distinction in the 6th Commandos (North Staffordshire) during the Second World War, Captain Ryan Price rapidly emerged as an outstanding trainer of the post-war era, becoming champion National Hunt trainer for the first of five times in 1954-55. Though he had major successes on the Flat and in chases, he was initially renowned as a brilliant trainer of hurdlers, his many wins including three Champion Hurdles, with *Clair Soleil* (1955), *Fare Time* (1959) and *Eborneezer* (1961). But then, continuing his formidable partnership with jockey Fred Winter, he proved himself no less adept at preparing chasers.

Initially, the partnership was unlucky in the National. In 1959 they had a strong contender in *Done Up* who had recently proved his stamina by winning over four miles at Hurst Park. But he was badly hampered and brought down in a terrible pile-up at the first Becher's. The following year they were equally hopeful with *Dandy Scot*, a 10-1 chance. Unfortunately, the wonderfully consistent ten year old had over-impressed the handicapper by winning four of his last five chases. Like the second favourite *Wyndburgh*, a surprise faller at the first Becher's, he was burdened with a hefty 11st 7lb top weight and

he fell at the Canal Turn.

Two years later, however, Price had his just reward as Winter rode *Kilmore* to a decisive ten lengths victory over luckless *Wyndburgh*, runner-up for the third time. Moreover, but for a fall-out with the racing authorities, he would almost certainly have been the trainer of a second National winner in 1966; and, but for the *Foinavon* fiasco, he would very probably have had a third winner in 1967.

Born in 1912, Price was a brilliant horseman in his own right, having ridden more than a hundred point-to-point winners before taking up training in 1937 on behalf of Lord Nunburnholme. Most valuably he had a keen eye for spotting horses with potential. He was the first to recognise *Kilmore* as a likely Aintree type, buying the ten year old for £3,000 on behalf of his patron, Nat Cohen. In Ireland the gelding had been judged to be no more than a reliable but moderate chaser. Yet within only a few months of moving to Price's yard – the Findon (Sussex) base at which Robert Gore had prepared successive National winners, *Jerry M* (1912) and *Covertcoat* (1913) – *Kilmore* finished a creditable fifth in the National. And one year later he was the winner.

Price was no less inspired in his 2,500 guineas purchase of another Irish-bred gelding, this time on behalf of Mr Cohen's business partner, Stuart Levy. The horse – formerly called *Flag of Convenience* and now renamed *Anglo* – had been a flop on the Flat. Under Price's tutelage, he soon won over hurdles and a season later scored four successive wins in novice chases. But he was never to run for the trainer in the National.

In February, 1964, amid huge controversy, Price was disqualified from training for the rest of the season because of his handling of *Rosyth* who, despite dismal seasonal form, came out to win a second successive Schweppes Gold Trophy at 10-1. As he himself put it, he was disqualified because 'it is a crime to improve a horse and a far bigger crime to win too many races'. Since Ryan's training licence was suspended for the rest of the season, *Anglo* was sent to his great friend Winter who was just setting up as a trainer at Lambourn. Two years later the eight year old chestnut won the National at 50-1. At the dawn of his training career Winter had now turned out two Grand National winners in a row.

Meanwhile the reinstated Price had turned out *Vulcano* (pulled up in the 1965 National); and in 1996, when *Anglo* won, he was represented by

Vulcano and a hugely promising nine year old chestnut, *What A Myth*, who, having a seasonal score of five wins out of five and soft going to his liking, was made the 11-2 second favourite. The former finished ninth under John Gifford; the latter disappointingly fell with Paul Kelleway in a six-horse pile-up at the second Becher's.

The following year Price was triple-handed and never with stronger hopes of winning another National. *What A Myth* was back after finishing a good third in the Cheltenham Gold Cup, though now with 12st top weight; and *Vulcano* returned for a third run, now as an unfancied 40-1 chance. In contrast, there was huge stable confidence behind *Honey End*, a ten year old brown gelding with six wins for the season behind him. Ridden by leading jockey Gifford, he went off the 15-2 favourite.

Unfortunately, however, this was the year of the infamous *Popham Down*, the year when that leading, riderless horse veered across the course at the 23rd fence, causing a pile-up that brought almost the entire field to a standstill. Far back enough to avoid the chaos, *Foinavon* came through to grab a huge lead and win at 100-1. Despite having to be taken back some 50 yards before clearing the 23rd, *Honey End* came home second, 15 lengths behind the freak winner. *Vulcano* failed to finish.

At least Price had the consolation of ending that season as champion trainer for the fifth time and with his biggest haul of winners (73). But once again he was now to fall foul of the authorities, and again his troubles followed success in 'The Schweppes'. *Hill House*, in 1967 his fourth winner of the race, not only showed a remarkable improvement in form but also tested positive for the steroid cortisol. After a long-drawn-out brouhaha, the trainer was finally exonerated by evidence that *Hill House* generated his own cortisol.

In 1968 the versatile Price won his third Cesarewitch with *Major Rose*. He was again unsuccessful in the National with three runners: *What A Myth*, fell; *Regal John*, refused; and *Master of Art*, fell. But the following year he crowned his training career by revitalising the 12 year old *What A Myth* to win the Cheltenham Gold Cup. Then, for the last time, triple-handed as usual, he went on to Aintree. He had one class runner, *Bassnet*, ridden by Gifford into fifth place. The others had no real chance: *Peccard* and *Terossian*, non-finishers ridden by American amateurs, brothers George and Paul Sloan respectively.

Thereafter Price began to concentrate on training for the Flat and most notably turned out two Classic winners: *Ginevra* (1972 Oaks) and *Bruni* (1975 St Leger). Other successes included the *Sandford Lad* (1973 Nunthorpe Stakes), *Giacometti* (1974 Champion Stakes) and *Sir Montagu* (1976 Ebor Handicap); and remarkably, in 1974, he kept *Giacometti* so fine-tuned that he also finished third in the Derby in between being runner-up in the 2,000 Guineas and the St Leger.

Ryan Price retired late in 1982 with a career total of nearly 2,000 winners and died four years later on his 74th birthday.

See also: Kilmore; Anglo; Gifford, Josh.

PRINCE REGENT

A son of *My Prince*, who sired three Grand National winners – *Gregalach* (1929), *Reynoldstown* (1935 and 1936) and *Royal Mail* (1937) – *Prince Regent* is rivalled only by *Crisp* for the distinction of being rated the greatest steeplechaser to run in the National without ever winning.

As many an Irishman will contend, Adolf Hitler was responsible for the failure of this magnificent chaser to capture the Aintree prize. Bought as a two year old by millionaire Mr J.V. Rank, then trained by Tom Dreaper, *Prince Regent* had his racing career restricted to Ireland for five seasons by the Second World War. He had his first win, as a six year old over hurdles, in May, 1941. The following year he ran up a string of steeplechase successes that included the Irish Grand National, in which he was carrying 12st 7lb and conceding 12lb to Miss Dorothy Paget's second-placed *Golden Jack*. Thereafter he twice finished runner-up in the Irish National when giving away up to three stone in the weights.

Unfortunately, *Prince Regent* had to miss the 1945 Cheltenham Gold Cup due to a warble, just behind his withers, that prevented him carrying a saddle. But one year later he promptly showed his class by winning the Gold Cup by five lengths. It brought his career tally to 14 wins; and three weeks later he made his Aintree debut in the first post-war National. He went off the 3-1 favourite despite having been lumbered with a top weight of 12st 5lb, which meant giving two-stone-plus to most of his 33 rivals.

Significantly, *Prince Regent* had been denied previous experience over Aintree's tall, sturdy fences –

and this, together with the prevailing heavy ground, told against him. As an 11 year old, arguably past his best, he now learned painfully that he could not brush through the obstacles as in Ireland. Ridden by Tim Hyde, he blundered over the fourth fence and Valentine's, then stood back at the open ditch, scraping over the fence so narrowly that he came to a momentary halt on landing.

Nevertheless, the great bay gelding was back in contention by the Water Jump, and after stumbling over the 17th fence, he made relentless progress. This time he took Valentine's cleanly, then powered into the lead. All the while, however, he was pestered by loose horses, and again and again he needed to raise his pace to shake them off. He was still leading at the last. But on the 495-yard run-in he had no more reserves of energy and was overtaken by *Lovely Cottage* and *Jack Finlay* to whom he was giving 25lb and 31lb respectively. He finished third, seven lengths behind the winner.

When *Prince Regent* returned one year later he was harshly burdened with an extra 2lb so that he was now conceding more than two stone to 38 of his 56 rivals and at least 19lb to all others. Yet, such was his reputation, that the 12 year old was again made the favourite, this time 8-1, heading the second largest field in National history. With very testing conditions also against him, he did remarkably well to finish fourth, 30 lengths behind the 100-1 winner *Caughoo* (received 35lb).

Finally, in the 1948 National, still lumbered with top weight (12st 2lb), the veteran *Prince Regent* was carried out by a loose horse at the fence after Becher's second time around. His career record was 21 wins in 49 races, and these included two successes over the National fences – in the 1946 Champion Chase and the 1947 Becher Chase.

See also: Sires; Rank J.V.; Hyde, Timothy; Lovely Cottage; Caughoo; Dempsey, Edward; Dreaper, Thomas William.

PRIZE MONEY
In 2005 the prize money for the Grand National was raised to a record £700,000, with £406,000 for the winner, £154,000 going to the runner-up, £77,000 to the third finisher, £35,000 to the fourth, £17,500 to the fifth and £10,500 to the sixth. This was marginally decreased in 2006 and 2007. It was raised again in 2008 to £800,000. However, the Aintree management has long been discussing plans to raise

prize money much higher in a bid to establish the National as the richest race of its kind in the world – the aim being to make it worth £1 million by the year 2010.

How times have changed since the first National of 1839 when the race was a sweepstake with the winner taking the entry fees of 20 sovereigns, plus 100 sovereigns added. The following year this was increased to 150 sovereigns added, with the second horse to receive 30 sovereigns, and the third saving his stake. Curiously, in 1842, the organisers offered no added money for the winner and no prize for the second who only saved his stake. The entry fee, however, was increased to 23 sovereigns.

Thereafter the rewards steadily mounted – 1,000 guineas added in the early 1880s rising to 3,000 sovereigns in 1907, by which time a share of the stakes had been extended to the fourth placed horse. The £5,000 mark was reached in 1914, but then the added money dropped back to £4,000 in the depression years of the 1930s.

In 1940 the £5,000 added money was restored, only falling to back to £4,000 for the first National after the Second World War. This rose to £6,000 in the 1953 Coronation year and took its biggest leap so far in 1958 when it was made up of £7,000 from the organisers, Messrs Topham, and an extra £5,000 given by the Irish Hospital Sweepstakes. The next major increase came in 1961 when Messrs Schweppes Limited matched the contribution from the Irish Sweepstakes, so giving a total of £17,000 added. The value to the winning owner was now £20,020; and for the first time there were cash rewards for jockeys, trainers and stable staff involved with the four placed horses.

Sponsorship now saw the added money rise to £30,000 in 1972, £50,000 in 1975, £60,000 in 1980, £70,000 in 1986, £80,000 in 1987. By 1992 when sponsorship by Seagram Ltd was passed on to its subsidiary company, Martell, the National was worth £125,000, with prize money for the three-day Aintree meeting peaking at £516,000. One decade later the Grand National prize money would be raised by £100,000 to £600,000 with a 17 per cent increase boosting the total reward for the three-day meeting to a record £1,930,000.

Then, in November, 2004, Scottish and Newcastle, the brewer, took over sponsorship and raised prize money for the first John Smith's Grand National to £700,000, roughly one million euros. At the same time, the three-day Aintree meeting had its total prize fund increased by ten per cent.

The National now offered twice as much prize money as the Cheltenham Gold Cup. However, despite all the increases, it remains infinitely less rewarding than the world's richest Flat race, the Dubai World Cup, worth some $6 million in prize money; and well behind other leading Flat races including the Japan Cup, the Breeders' Cup Classic, the Hong Kong Cup, the Breeders' Cup Turf and Europe's richest horse race, the Epsom Derby.

PSEUDONYMS

In the mid-19th century it was a measure of steeplechasing's somewhat unsavoury image that it became the custom for amateur riders of relatively high social standing to shield their identity by adopting pseudonyms when 'racing across country' against professionals. The first amateur of distinction to do so in the Grand National was Old Etonian George

Matthew Ede who chose to appear as 'Mr Edwards' in 1858 when making his Aintree debut and finishing runner-up on *Weathercock*, a 25-1 long-shot. Under that name he rode in eight Nationals and won on *The Lamb* in 1868.

The most notable amateur to use a pseudonym was Thomas Pickernell who, starting in 1859, rode in 17 Grand Nationals under the name of 'Mr Thomas'. In 1860, when 'Mr Thomas' scored the first of his three National victories, sixth place in the race was taken by *Bridegroom*, ridden by a 'Mr Ekard' – an anagram concealing the true surname of the rider, a certain Rev. Edward Drake.

The most aristocratic of amateurs to ride in the National under an assumed name was Viscount Melgund who made his debut in 1874, riding Captain James Machell's *Defence*, a 33-1 chance, into fourth place. Appearing as 'Mr Rolly' – his nickname as an Eton schoolboy – he rode in three more Nationals, each time ending in a fall.

Q

QUARE TIMES

Winner of the 1955 Grand National – on his first and last appearance in the race – by a comfortable 12 lengths, so giving trainer Vincent O'Brien an unprecedented third successive victory following his wins with *Early Mist* and *Royal Tan*.

Bred in Ireland by Mr P.P Sweeney of Thurles, *Quare Times* – by *Artist's Son* out of *Lavenco* – was sold as a yearling for 300 guineas and later re-sold to Mrs Cecily Welman. Remaining at Ballydoyle with O'Brien, he was unraced before the age of six and first showed considerable potential as an eight year old when winning the 1954 National Hunt Chase at Cheltenham. The following year he was one of four horses sent to the National by the greatest of Irish trainers.

Hopes of an O'Brien hat-trick were greatly diminished when the trainer saw the Aintree course. It was so badly waterlogged that the stewards had decided to eliminate the Water Jump where the ground was at its most desperate. Certainly, the quagmire conditions were totally unsuitable for *Early Mist*, the 9-1 second favourite, and for *Royal Tan*. Moreover, both were severely handicapped, the only runners in the 30-strong field to carry more than 12st.

Of the others in the O'Brien quartet, *Oriental Way* was not considered good enough, and it was unknown how well the free-running *Quare Times* would handle the ground. But there were three factors in the latter's favour. He was a good jumper, an out-and-out stayer, and he had the perfect partner in powerful Pat Taaffe.

As instructed, Taaffe set off on the outside which offered a better chance of avoiding fallers and loose horses. To be sure, *Quare Times* was perilously close by when *E.S.B.* nose-dived over Becher's, bringing down *Roman Fire* in the process. But thereafter he steered clear of all trouble, making steady progress on the second circuit and, with his proven stamina, dominating from the Canal Turn onwards.

Very briefly, at the last open ditch, *Quare Times* was challenged for the lead by *Carey's Cottage*, ridden by Pat's younger brother 'Tosse' Taaffe and trained by their father. But it didn't last. Jumping immaculately throughout, *Quare Times* powered ahead on the run-in to win easily from *Tudor Line*, runner-up for the second year in a row. *Carey's Cottage*, a further four lengths back, came third.

It was a triumph for the rigorous training methods of O'Brien who, in turn, gave great credit to the rider. 'Pat suited him ideally, as he rode short and sat up his neck.' Subsequently *Quare Times* was paraded through Mullingar, the hometown of his owner, Mrs Cecily Welman. He was never sound enough to run in the National again. However, as a jumper, he ranked among the best of the post-war era; and soon after his Aintree triumph he proved his versatility by winning a two-miler over hurdles at Leopardstown. He then won only one more race before being retired.

See also: O'Brien, Vincent; Taaffe, Pat.

RACE DAY

Originally the Aintree Grand National was run on a Tuesday and was later moved to Friday. The switch to a Saturday came in 1947 at the suggestion of Prime Minister Clement Attlee who advised racecourse chief Mrs Mirabel Topham that the change would be to the advantage of British industry in the post-war recovery period.

In 1957, for the last time, the National reverted to the traditional Friday. It was somehow imagined that this move might boost falling attendances. But the experiment – not helped by inclement weather – brought no improvement and was not repeated. Thereafter Saturday remained the norm, although in 1997, after the Saturday meeting had been abandoned in the face of an IRA bomb scare, the race was run on the following Monday.

RAG TRADE

As winner of the 1976 Grand National, ten year old *Rag Trade* thwarted by just two lengths *Red Rum*'s bid for an unprecedented third victory; landed a record fourth success for trainer Fred Rimell following his wins with *E.S.B.* (1956), *Nicolaus Silver* (1961) and *Gay Trip* (1970); and gave owner Mr P.B. Raymond a second triumph following his win with *Ayala* (1963).

A chestnut gelding – by *Menelek* out of *The Rage* – *Rag Trade* was bred in Ireland by Mr Ian Williams, son of Evan who had won the 1937 National on *Royal Mail*. Initially trained in Northumberland by George Fairbairn, he had won only two races by February, 1975, when he was sent to the Doncaster sales. There, as a nine year old, he was bought for the surprisingly large sum of 18,000 guineas by the celebrated hairstylist popularly known as Mr 'Teasy Weasy' Raymond.

Immediately he was sent to Epsom trainer Arthur Pitt to be prepared for the National just two months away; and there he was to be ridden by the most fast-improving jump jockey in the land, 22 year old John Francome, making his second appearance in the race. Reasonably well supported at 18-1, he trailed in the last of ten finishers in a 31-strong field.

Three weeks later *Rag Trade* showed himself to be a highly progressive chaser by comfortably winning the Midlands Grand National at Uttoxeter. Nevertheless Mr Raymond chose to have him switched in the summer to the Kinnersley (Worcestershire) yard of Fred Rimell. After five races,

including a latest success in the Welsh Grand National, the gelding returned to Aintree to be ridden by the Rimells' stable jockey John Burke.

A crowd approaching 50,000, the largest for years, turned out for the 1976 National. *Barona* headed the market on 7-1, but overwhelmingly attention was focused on the top-weighted, second favourite *Red Rum*, seeking a third win after finishing first, first and second in the previous three years, and now back with fastish ground in his favour. *Rag Trade*, who had crashed through several fences when winning the Welsh National, was seventh in the betting, backed down from 20s to 14-1.

Well placed throughout the second circuit, *Rag Trade* was one of five horses bunched in the lead coming to the penultimate fence. Then, as *Red Rum* hit the front on landing over the last, a deafening roar hailed the prospect of a record third win. But *Rag Trade* was only fractionally behind, and now on the flat he accelerated to gain a four-length advantage. Bravely 'Rummy' rallied over the final furlong but his extra 12lb in the handicap was always against him. He went down by two lengths with the mare *Eyecatcher* eight lengths back in third.

Rag Trade was an unusual Grand National winner in that he was so disparaged by his connections. Francome had declared him to be 'the most horrible horse I've ever ridden' and had said that he would not care to ride him again. Mercy Rimell described him as 'a great big common horse who looked like a Suffolk Punch'. Unlike other National winners trained by her husband, he was a long-striding horse, clumsy in his jumping but – as shown when winning at Aintree – powerful enough to blunder his way through fences.

Though the publicity conscious Mr Raymond was always named as the owner, *Rag Trade* was, in fact, also part-owned by a Mr Bill Lawrie and Mr Herbert Keen. Following the National win, however, the partnership broke up and – in the wake of injury problems – the gelding missed the 1977 race won by *Red Rum* and, amid some acrimony, was returned by Raymond to his original trainer.

When *Rag Trade* came back for his third Grand National in 1978, he was the well-supported 8-1 favourite, not least because he was to be ridden by Jonjo O'Neill who, two months earlier, had completed the fastest 100 winners in a National Hunt season. But by now he was 12 years old, had dodgy legs and was carrying 5lb more than in his winning prime.

R

Always struggling, he was pulled up lame before the second Becher's, and was subsequently found to have broken down so badly that he had to be put down.
See also: Burke, John; Rimell, Fred; Raymond, P.B.

RANK, James Voase

Together with Lord Bicester and American millionaire Mr 'Jock' Hay Whitney, Mr J.V. Rank, flourmilling tycoon and elder brother of film magnate Lord (J. Arthur) Rank, stands out as one of the most persistent of owners to seek Grand National glory in vain. And arguably he was the unluckiest of that frustrated triumvirate.

Spanning two decades, Rank had 14 runners in the National and would have had many more but for the interruption of the Second World War. He had horses finishing second (once), third (twice) and fourth (three times). Only by freakish bad luck did success elude him. Indeed, he was unlucky in all of his three sporting ambitions: to win the National, the Derby and coursing's classic, the Waterloo Cup. He had a runner-up in all three: *Cooleen* in the 1937 National; *Scottish Union* in the 1938 Derby; and his greyhound *Joker's Resort* in the 1935 Waterloo Cup.

Curiously, in marked contrast, he enjoyed extraordinary success when challenging for the Scottish National, winning three times with his *Southern Hero* (1934, 1936 and 1939) and with his *Young Mischief* in 1938.

Rank's great Aintree quest began with the failure of *Southern Hero* in the Nationals of 1933 and 1934. In the latter year he established his training yard at Druid's Lodge (bought from Percy Cunliffe) on Salisbury Plain, and in 1935 he installed Noel Cannon there as his trainer.

Already Rank had been shrewd enough to take a special interest in young chasers by *My Prince*, the sire of the 1929 National winner, *Gregalach*; and thus he had sent two expert friends to look at a promising gelding called *Reynoldsown*, owned by Major Noel Furlong. His advisers reported back that the horse was not worth an offer. Their dismal judgment was cruelly exposed when *Reynoldstown* won the National in 1935, and again in 1936 when Mr Rank's *Bachelor Prince* finished third to the first horse to win successive Nationals since 1870.

There was no *Reynoldstown* to contend with in 1937. Nonetheless salt was rubbed into Mr Rank's wounds as another son of *My Prince* triumphed. Worse, Mr Rank's nine year old mare, *Cooleen* – a 33-1 chance beaten three lengths by *Royal Mail* – could be counted as an unlucky loser, having been continually harassed in the race by the savage attentions of a riderless outsider called *Drim*.

In 1938, again ridden by Jack Fawcus, *Cooleen* went off the 8-1 joint favourite. She finished well back in fourth, with Mr Rank's other runner, *Bachelor Prince*, in tenth place. And curiously they occupied exactly the same finishing positions in the 1939 National.

Meanwhile, resolved not to make the same mistake twice, Rank had sent a representative to the 1936 Dublin sales with specific instructions to buy any decent looking yearling by *My Prince*. This time he hit the jackpot with the purchase of *Prince Regent* who, following the outbreak of war, was returned to Ireland to be trained by Tom Dreaper. Alas, fate was once more against the flour-milling millionaire. *Prince Regent* became the champion chaser in Ireland and, with English racing restored in 1946, he immediately won the Cheltenham Gold Cup. But the war had denied him experience over the Aintree fences, and it counted against him when he was sent on to the National as an 11 year old. Giving at least 21lb to 31 of his 33 rivals, and being hampered by loose horses, he finished third.

In 1947, again on top weight, *Prince Regent* finished fourth of 57 starters in the National, with Mr Rank's other runner, *Brick Bat*, a distant 11th; and the following year the great champion was carried out by a loose horse. It was no consolation to the owner to find that his horse was now recognised as one of the all-time greats who had never won the National.

In 1950 and 1951 the only contender in Mr Rank's familiar quartered colours of blue and primrose was *Shagreen*, his 1949 Irish National winner whom he had bred from his excellent stayer, *Cooleen*. The gelding won the 1950 Grand Sefton Chase and many other races. But he was a faller in both his Aintree Nationals. Next Mr Rank had high hopes for his most promising seven year old, *Early Mist*. Sadly, however, the luckless owner did not live to see him make his National debut in 1952. He died in January of that year, aged 70.

Ridden by Pat Taaffe on a misty day, *Early Mist* was one of ten fallers at the first fence. Then, most ironically, there came one final twist of fate. Having run in Mrs Rank's name, *Early Mist* was now sold in a dispersal sale, being bought for 5,300 guineas by

Vincent O'Brien on behalf of Mr Joe Griffin. The big chestnut promptly won the 1953 National by a most comfortable 20 lengths!

There was further irony in the fact that the long-frustrated Lord Bicester had been the underbidder when *Early Mist* came up for sale. As O'Brien commented later: 'How ironical that I should win the 1953 National at the first attempt for a new owner, after Mr. Rank and Lord Bicester had spent many years and thousands of pounds, with this one object in view.'

See also: Cooleen; Prince Regent; Dreaper, Tom.

RATINGS

The weights to be carried by horses in the Grand National are primarily determined by the official ratings (0 to 175) maintained in respect of all National Hunt horses by the British Horseracing Authority which, in 2007, succeeded the British Horseracing Board (BHB) as the governing body of British racing.

Throughout the season the ratings, which are applied to all handicap races, are revised weekly to take into account the latest performances. But, significantly, these revisions do not affect the National weights once they have been framed in February, roughly two months before the race.

The higher the rating the higher will be the weight allotted, with each single point rise in the rating being the equivalent of a 1lb rise in the weights. However, the Grand National is exceptional in that the official handicapper may not rely on the ratings alone but may, at his discretion, choose to give extra weight to a horse that has shown especially good form over the National fences.

In 1960, as a means of excluding horses palpably not strong enough for such a marathon test, the BHB introduced a minimum rating of 120 for National qualifiers. But this was reduced to 110 in 1997 since the previous year had seen a National with only 27 starters, the smallest field since 1960. As a result, many more horses were entered; and since 1999, when only 32 ran, there has been no danger of the National failing to achieve its safety limit of 40 runners.

Moreover, in recent years the National has attracted horses of such quality that there has been a steady rise in the rating required to gain a place in the line-up. In 2005 no qualifiers had a rating below 134. In 2007 the 119 entries included 17 horses rated at 150 or above and only six rated 110-120. Phil

Smith, the senior jumps handicapper, concluded: 'It's not worth entering any more if your horse is rated 120 or 125 and I think most owners and trainers have recognised that.'

Interestingly, the past ten Nationals have had winners in an official rating range of 136 to 147, whereas the previous ten winners were rated between 146 and 155, statistics now strongly favouring those in the middle range of the weights.

See also: Handicapping; Weights.

RAYMOND, P.B.

While such devotees of the Turf as Whitney, Courage, Rank and Bicester spent decades in vain pursuit of one Grand National winner, Mr P.B. Raymond – without any real affinity for the sport – owned only two Grand National runners and won with both of them: *Ayala* (1963) and *Rag Trade* (1976).

Born in 1912, Raymondo Pietro Carlo, the son of a barber, Raymond first worked in his father's shop, making false moustaches from clippings on the floor. Frustrated in his ambition to become an actor, he briefly tried wrestling at £5 a bout; then, at the age of 26, he opened his first hairdressing salon in Mayfair. A hugely flamboyant character, with a pencil-line moustache, bouffant hairstyle and a gift for self-publicity, he soon became hairstylist to the rich and famous. His clientele included the Duchess of Windsor and movie stars Vivien Leigh, Valerie Hobson and Googie Withers; and his business mushroomed, comprising at its peak a chain of 34 hairdressing salons. The media dubbed him indelibly 'Mr Teasy Weasy'.

In 1963, just one year after suffering a heart attack, Raymond had his first National winner courtesy of trainer Keith Piggott who had sold him a half-share in his 250-guineas purchase of *Ayala*. But he was not there to witness his first-time success, his flight to Aintree having been cancelled because of bad weather.

Thirteen years later his *Rag Trade* triumphed by two lengths over the immortal *Red Rum*. But he did not celebrate his second National victory. Indeed, the Rimells, who trained his winner, regarded him as 'a very difficult man' and certainly as the most unappreciative and ungenerous of their owners. Subsequently, after *Rag Trade* had been plagued with injuries, Raymond chose to switch his winner to another trainer.

R

However, for many years Raymond had to contend with extreme ill-health. In 1971 he had suffered from cancer of the mouth, requiring surgery that left him with severely impaired speech; and three years after his second National success he experienced an appalling family tragedy when his pregnant daughter, his son-in-law and two grandsons were killed in a motorway crash. He himself lived on until the age of 80.

See also: Ayala; Rag Trade; Rimell, Fred.

READ, David

Veteran rider of the seven year old mare *Shannon Lass*, 20-1 winner of the 1902 Grand National, by three lengths from *Matthew*, with the mighty *Manifesto* (aged 14 and conceding 35lb to the winner) a further three lengths back in third place. It was only his second appearance in the race, having previously ridden *Corner*, the 200-1 rank outsider who was the 11th of 11 finishers in 1899. After his victory, David Read had only two more National rides: on *Aunt May* (1903) and *Biology* (1904). Both were fallers.

See also: Shannon Lass.

RED ALLIGATOR

Comfortable winner of the 1968 Grand National, replicating the 20 lengths victory of his half-brother, *Anglo*, two years before, and providing the first of three National-winning rides for his jockey, 20 year old Brian Fletcher. Remarkably, the nine year old gelding went off on the minimum 10st weight despite having finished third on his previous appearance in the race.

Like *Anglo*, *Red Alligator* was bred by Mr William Kennedy, a farmer near Downpatrick in Northern Ireland. Sired by the stallion *Magic Red,* he was out of *Miss Alligator* who had finished sixth in the 1949 Oaks and had yet been sold for only 70 guineas at the Dublin sales of 1952. Thus *Miss Alligator* became only the second mare to produce two Grand National winners, the first being *Miss Batty*, dam of *Emblem* (1863) and *Emblematic* (1864).

Curiously, Mr Kennedy made no great profit from breeding two National winners. He had sold *Anglo* for £140 as a foal. Then he let *Red Alligator* go at yearling sales for 340 guineas. Subsequently, the handsome chestnut won only one hurdle race in 27 outings, but a marked improvement came when he

was switched to new stables by his owner, Mr John Manners, a butcher and farmer of Co. Durham.

Trained by Denys Smith, a neighbour of Mr Manners in Bishop Auckland, *Red Alligator* soon proved to be a sound jumper and most resolute stayer in steeplechases. His resolution was there for all to see in the 1967 National when, after the mass débâcle at the 23rd, he was put back three times at the fence, and then gave chase so well under young Fletcher that they finished third behind the runaway leader *Foinavon* and the favourite *Honey End*.

Following that promising National debut, *Red Alligator* was joint third in the betting in 1968, the clear favourite in a 45-strong field being Mr Gregory Peck's *Different Class*. Ridden patiently on the first circuit, he gave Fletcher only one anxious moment: when they had to jump clear of the prostrate *Polaris Missile*, one of six fallers at Becher's. Thereafter he moved steadily through the field to take the lead from *Different Class* at the last open ditch and then, from the penultimate fence onwards, drawing remorselessly away from all others. Twenty lengths back at the finish was the Scottish hope *Moidore's Token*, a neck ahead of the favourite.

In all *Red Alligator* won 11 chases but, saddled with an extra 13lb, he was never again the same force in the National. As the 13-2 clear favourite he was a faller in 1969; and on his final appearance in 1970 he was a casualty at the last open ditch.

See also: Fletcher, Brian; Smith, Denys.

RED MARAUDER

Sensational 33-1 winner by a distance of the 2001 Grand National when the race controversially went ahead on hock-deep ground and – evoking memories of *Tipperary Tim* in 1928 – only four of 40 runners completed the course, and two of those having been remounted. His rider, Richard Guest, subsequently acknowledged him to be 'probably the worst jumper ever to win a National'. Indeed, prior to the race, he came under the scrutiny of the Jockey Club's safety panel and only won acceptance on a casting vote.

Red Marauder – by *Gunner B* out of *Cover Your Money* – was bred by David and Anne Jenks of the Hartshill Stud in Chedworth, Gloucestershire, and bought as a yearling by millionaire businessman Mr Norman Mason on the recommendation of Tom Robson, trainer of the 1964 Champion Hurdler *Magic Court*. Like so many progeny of *Gunner B* he quickly emerged as a smart hurdler – the 33-1 winner of his first race, a juvenile hurdle at Hexham, and one month later of a novices' hurdle at Ayr.

But Mason's dominant ambition was to win the National; and it was hoped that *Red Marauder* would make up into a useful chaser since, even though *Gunner B* was noted for producing useful hurdlers, there was plenty of stamina on his dam's side. Her sire, *Precipice Wood*, had won the Ascot Gold Cup and had produced the Cheltenham Gold Cup winner *Forgive 'N Forget*. Moreover, *Cover Your Money*'s grand-dam was a half-sister to *Tiberetta* who had been second and third in the National, and dam of *Spanish Steps*, three times in the National frame.

In October, 1994, as a four year old, *Red Marauder* finished third in a handicap hurdle. Then, having broken down with bad legs, it was more than three years before he was turned out again – this time for a winning chasing debut at Hexham. Ten months later, with a new regular rider, assistant trainer Richard Guest, he began a run of three successive wins, including, in November, 1998, Ascot's valuable First National Bank Gold Cup. Yet again, however, there was a long break with leg trouble.

Fifteen months later he came back to win a handicap chase at Wetherby and was entered for the 2000 Grand National only after Guest had inadvertently missed the Cheltenham Gold Cup's entry deadline. With a record of five wins in six chases, all on softish ground, he was well supported at 18-1. However, the horse had never won over much more than two and a half miles, and on his one attempt at three miles – in the Racing Post Chase at Kempton – he had finished a distant sixth. There were doubts about his stamina; also the drying ground at Aintree was judged to be against him. Jockey Guest bullishly predicted that he would win, but with a high handicap weight of 11st 2lb and the ground on the fast side of good, the ten year old made three consecutive mistakes, the last ending in a fall at the first Becher's. That same month he went on to the Irish National and finished a far distant tenth.

In September, at Market Rasen, *Red Marauder* scored his first win over three miles, but in February he ended his build-up for the 2001 National with a first fence fall at Haydock. Guest acknowledged that he was not a natural jumper. On the other hand, he was hugely encouraged by the persistent rain at Aintree, and all the more so when, on the eve of the

National, he rode *Red Striker* – a full brother to *Red Marauder* – to a comfortable win in a novices' handicap chase.

Ostensibly the 2001 National was all the more competitive since the Cheltenham Festival had been abandoned in the face of the foot-and-mouth epidemic. But this year it was being run controversially in quagmire conditions; and luck-in-the-running was to be everything. *Red Marauder*, so patiently ridden, certainly had his ample share. Ten horses failed to get beyond the first four fences. Then at the Canal Turn, eight more were eliminated in a pile-up caused largely by a loose horse, the blinkered *Paddy's Return*, who veered sharply down the fence behind the leaders. Only narrowly missing the mayhem, *Red Marauder* successfully climbed through the fence.

Proven mudlark *Edmond*, the 10-1 joint favourite, fell at The Chair, and when top-weighted *Beau* led the field back on the second circuit only seven runners remained. Now the unluckiest rider was Carl Llewellyn, seeking his third National win. He lost his reins on *Beau* at the 17th and was unseated three fences later. Shortly after, Timmy Murphy on *Smarty* turned to Guest and said, 'You know there's only two of us left.'

Sensibly, both riders erred on the side of caution rather than indulging in an immediate all-out duel. Meanwhile, far behind them, two horses were remounted at the 19th. Their riders, Tony McCoy (*Blowing Wind*) and Ruby Walsh (*Papillon*), agreed not to race until they had safely cleared the last.

For the second time, at the Canal Turn, *Red Marauder* had a narrow escape when avoiding a collision with the ubiquitous *Paddy's Return*. Two fences later, *Smarty* jumped the better. But his only rival stayed on well, got back in front two out and, though climbing through the last fences, steadily pulled away on the long slog home.

Though he finished distances ahead of *Smarty*, *Blowing Wind* and *Papillon*, his winning time of 11min 0.1sec was the slowest since *Zoedone*'s 11min 39sec in 1883 when the race was partly run over ploughed fields. He had made about ten jumping errors on his clumsy way to victory, but as his rider stressed: 'He just didn't want to go down.'

Following his victory *Red Marauder* had a recurring tendon ailment and faced a battle to regain fitness for the 2002 National. He was duly entered and allotted 10st 9lb in the weights. But then, after a pleasing workout, a scan revealed 'bruising in his

R

leg and a little heat'. Still without a run since his Aintree win, he was put away for the season in the hope that he might come back as a 13 year old to run in the Hennessy Cognac Gold Cup and then the National of 2003. But in November he was a last minute withdrawal from the Hennessy due to unsuitable ground and one week later he was scratched from a chase at Warwick because of coughing.

It was not until February, 2003, that he had his first run since winning the 2001 National. In a handicap hurdle at Newcastle he stayed on to be fourth under a sympathetic ride by Guest, now his official trainer – a reappearance so encouraging that Ladbrokes promptly halved his National odds to 25-1. But the veteran chaser continued to be beset with problems and two days before the National he was withdrawn and retired. He had won nine of 21 outings including the 1998 First National Bank Gold Cup at Ascot and the 2000 John Smith's Handicap Chase at Wetherby.

See also: Guest, Richard; Mason, Norman.

RED RUM

The undisputed King of Aintree; as a three- time winner, the most successful horse in the entire history of the Grand National. In 1973, on his big-race debut as an eight year old, he won in record-breaking time by three-quarters of a length. The following year he became the first since *Reynoldstown* (1936) to carry 12st to victory and score back-to-back wins. He followed up with two second places, both under top weight; then returned as a 12 year old to achieve his unprecedented treble, astonishingly by 25 lengths. Thus, in five Nationals, he had cleared 150 fences without ever threatening to fall.

Such are the bare facts relating to five years in the life of a supreme Aintree specialist who, in retirement, enjoyed a celebrity rivalled only by the glamorous *Desert Orchid*. Recognised as a veritable national treasure, he spawned a souvenir industry; opened countless fetes, supermarkets and betting shops; had a walk-on part in BBC TV's 'Sports Personality of the Year' programme; was memorialised with a life-sized bronze statue at Aintree, and finally, at the age of 30, laid to rest alongside the Grand National winning post.

But it is the background to the success story of *Red Rum* that is most astounding in the light of his achievements. The greatest runner in the world's most famous steeplechase was sired by a top-class miler (*Quorum*) out of a so-called 'mad mare' (*Mared*), who was almost impossibly difficult to ride. Gaining his name from the last three letters of the names of his dam and sire, he fetched a mere 400 guineas from a sole bidder in yearling sales; started his racing career in a five-furlong sprint; failed to win any of his 14 races in the 1969-70 season; and, having suffered from the dreaded pedalostitis bone disease, was put up as a virtual 'cast-off' in the Doncaster sales, where he finally passed into the hands of a former taxi-driver with whom he would develop into a living legend.

Bred at Rossenarra Stud in Co. Kilkenny, Ireland, by Martin McKenery, *Red Rum* was bought as a yearling for 400 guineas, being first owned by Mr Maurice Kingsley, a Manchester manufacturer and major punter who had previously prospered with the 1950s triple Champion Hurdle winner *Sir Ken*. Most appropriately he made his racecourse debut at Aintree – in a two-year old selling plate which was run over five furlongs on the day before the chaotic Foinavon Grand National of 1967. Well backed by his owner, and trained by former champion jump jockey Tim Molony, he dead-heated with the filly *Curlicue*.

Already gelded, and having been hard ridden on the Flat (twice placed with Lester Piggott in the saddle), *Red Rum* next passed into the ownership of Mrs Lurline Brotherton who had won the 1950 Grand National with her *Freebooter*. Her trainer was still the indefatigable Bobby Renton, and at his Yorkshire stable *Red Rum*'s introduction to jumping began.

Following Renton's retirement in 1971, his assistant Tommy Stack took over the stable. But Stack soon quit training to concentrate on riding, and was succeeded by Anthony Gillam. Thus, *Red Rum* had three different trainers in as many years. He had started jumping well enough, winning three times over hurdles and five times over fences. But then came a long losing run and foot problems. In August, 1972, despite an excellent performance when finishing a close-up fifth in the Scottish Grand National, he was sent to the Doncaster sales.

Donald 'Ginger' McCain, a car dealer and part-time Southport taxi-driver, had not long begun training when he first saw *Red Rum* run in the 1967 seller at Aintree. He was quite taken with the two year old but did not attend the subsequent auction for lack of funds. Now, five years later, he bought the over-raced gelding for 6,000 guineas on behalf of his octogenarian patron Mr Noel Le Mare.

Just two days later, *Red Rum* was exercised for the first time on Southport's sands, and then, to McCain's absolute horror, his prize purchase immediately showed clear signs of lameness. Despairingly, the trainer had him pulled out of the string and gently walked in the sea while the rest of his string continued on the 'gallops'.

Then came what seemed like a miracle. When 'Rummy' eventually stepped back on to the beach there was no hint of lameness. Only months later did McCain learn of *Red Rum*'s past history of pedalostitis in the off-fore hoof. But soon this became of no concern. Clearly benefiting from daily walks in the brine, he was never again to suffer from lameness with the one exception that briefly followed his first Grand National win.

Meanwhile, though based in most unprepossessing stables (set behind a humble car showroom in urban Birkdale) a revitalised *Red Rum* made magnificent progress: winning five successive chases within seven weeks, the last over three miles three furlongs when he was ridden for the first time by Brian Fletcher. In the New Year, on the build-up for the 1973 Grand National, he finished third, second and fourth in races. But that was on unfavourable soft ground. The omens for Aintree were excellent – provided that he got at least good going.

The connections' prayers for good ground were answered, and accordingly *Red Rum*'s betting odds shortened dramatically. By the off he had become 9-1 joint favourite, along with the outstanding Australian chaser *Crisp*, in a 38-strong field that also included the dual Cheltenham Gold Cup winner *L'Escargot* and *Black Secret* who had previously finished second and third in the National. In addition McCain was saddling another runner for Mr Le Mare: ten year old *Glenkiln*, a live 33-1 chance ridden by Jonjo O'Neill, making his National debut.

From the first Becher's onwards, the giant *Crisp* turned the race into a procession: three lengths in the lead at the Canal Turn, ten lengths at the Anchor Bridge, 15 at The Chair, some 25 lengths by the 19th. Then, coming to Becher's second time around, Fletcher – a past winner on *Red Alligator* (1968) – began his relentless effort to close the gap of some 100 yards.

At the last, Richard Pitman on *Crisp* was still some 15 lengths ahead. But now, on the testing long run-in, the huge weight differential cruelly took its toll. Caught in his dying strides, the brave Aussie champion went down by just three-quarters of a length to *Red Rum*, both horses having shattered *Golden Miller*'s 39 year old record time by more than 19 seconds. The third, *L'Escargot*, was 25 lengths away.

Not unreasonably, the gallant *Crisp* was viewed as the true hero of that National – a worthy favourite who had jumped and raced magnificently, only to be 'robbed' by a colossal 23lb disadvantage in the weights. The greatness of *Red Rum* had yet to be fully appreciated. Indeed, those who viewed him as a 'lucky winner' felt their case was strengthened in the autumn, when, after three successive wins, *Red Rum* was rematched against *Crisp* at Doncaster. This time, at level weights, *Crisp* won by eight lengths.

Red Rum ended a hugely profitable year being beaten a short head by *Red Candle* in a thrilling Hennessy Gold Cup. Then, in February, he had the first of two preparatory races for another Grand National. Impressively, he won by eight lengths over an extended three miles at Catterick when giving two and a half stone to four of his rivals. But next, at Haydock, he ran on alone after jockey Fletcher had been knocked out of the plate.

Unharmed, and thriving on his regular seaside gallops. *Red Rum* returned to Aintree with 12st top weight and went off at 11-1, third in the betting behind a 7-1 favourite (*Scout*) carrying two stone less, and *L'Escargot* on 11st 13lb. On the first circuit he was patiently ridden behind the leading pack, neatly side-stepping fallers at the Canal Turn and maintaining his position behind the leading pack. Then, as one year before, Fletcher made his move at the 19th; and this time from the second Becher's onwards *Red Rum* took control. Never headed thereafter, he came home a comfortable seven lengths winner from *L'Escargot*, with *Charles Dickens* a short head back in third.

Red Rum had now firmly established himself among the Grand National's 'all-time greats' and he reinforced his new-founded reputation when, only three weeks later, he won the four-mile Scottish Grand National by four lengths from *Proud Tarquin*. On this occasion, with a top weight of 11st 13lb, he was conceding at least 15lb to other runners and a mighty 29lb to the bottom weights.

In 1975, after winning the Haydock Park National Trial Chase, *Red Rum* was a disappointing fourth in Haydock's Greenall Whitley Chase. Nevertheless, at Aintree, he was backed down to 7-2 favouritism – extraordinary odds considering that no horse had ever won three successive Grand Nationals. Furthermore, again on top weight, he was now giving 11lb instead of 1lb to the so consistent *L'Escargot*; and for the first time at Aintree he was facing hated soft ground.

The going was the key factor. Never at ease on the soft, 'Rummy' laboured towards the rear in the early stages and after one circuit Fletcher was thinking that he might have to pull him up. But *Red Rum* rallied, to such good effect that he took a short lead after Valentine's and he held it as far as the penultimate fence. But *L'Escargot* was always close up and moving more easily. They were level at the last but at that stage Fletcher knew that the great game was lost. On the run-in, the 12 year old chestnut gelding pulled away to win on his swansong by 15 lengths. And two weeks later *Red Rum* was unplaced in his bid to win another Scottish National.

At this stage *Red Rum*'s remarkable Grand National record – two wins and one second place – had been a triumph for four men: trainer McCain, jockey Fletcher, head lad Jackie Grainger and stable lad Billy Ellison. But sadly this quartet was to be broken up as McCain fell out in turn with the others – Fletcher being replaced by Tommy Stack, Grainger being sacked, and Ellison going after briefly being promoted to head lad. Thereafter, for many years, 'Rummy' was in the most capable care of stable lad Billy Beardwood.

In the 1976 Grand National, *Red Rum* was carrying top weight for the third successive year and he went off the 10-1 second favourite, behind the Scottish National winner *Barona*. But this time there were some hard-nosed critics who judged he was 'over the hill'. After all, since the 1975 Grand National he had gone eight races without a win, and in following the same path to Aintree he had finished sixth and fifth in the Haydock chases. Moreover, he had parted company with his regular rider, a three times National winner.

Reunited with Stack, his one-time trainer and jockey, *Red Rum* was never prominent on the first circuit. But thereafter, running wide to avoid fallers, he progressed steadily until, at the penultimate fence, he was one of five leading contenders jumping almost in unison. At the last a terrific leap enabled him to touch down marginally ahead of *Rag*

Trade and *Eyecatcher*; and briefly a record-breaking third win seemed a real possibility.

That dream faded when *Rag Trade*, with a 12lb advantage, was spurred into a four length lead. But this time *Red Rum* was not to be hopelessly outpaced on the run-in. He fought back magnificently only to have the winning post come too soon. He went down to *Rag Trade* by two lengths. A further eight lengths back was *Eyecatcher*, ridden by Fletcher who was gaining a place for the fourth successive year.

Again, in 1977, *Red Rum* arrived at Aintree with a seasonal record that hardly inspired confidence. Since the last National his only success in eight outings had come in a three-horse chase at Carlisle. He was now 12 years old, top weight in a 42-strong field; and, though joint second in the betting at 9-1, he was opposed by a 15-2 favourite (*Andy Pandy*) who had already beaten him twice that season, and by the well-supported Cheltenham Gold Cup winner *Davy Lad*.

But this was Aintree, fortunately bathed in ground-drying sunshine after two days of rain; and as they prepared for the line-up *Red Rum* was strutting around imperially, as if he owned the place. And justifiably so. For now he was about to prove himself the nonpareil of the world's toughest steeplechase, jumping immaculately while all around him others were struggling to cope with the fences. Seven went at the first, four (including *Davy Lad*) at the third, another two at the fourth.

The shape of the race was totally deceptive. At Becher's first time, more fallers left *Boom Docker*, a 66-1 chance, at the head of affairs; and the tearaway proceeded to open up a lead of perhaps 40 lengths before calling it a day at the 17th. His refusal enabled *Andy Pandy* to strike the front, and in turn the favourite established a 12 length lead. But then, having previously jumped impressively, he fell on landing over the second Becher's. Suddenly, Tommy Stack found himself leading earlier than he would have wished.

But no matter. *Red Rum* was in prime form. He raised the pace from the Canal Turn onwards and by the second last only one serious challenger remained: *Churchtown Boy* who, only two days earlier, had won the Topham Trophy over two miles six furlongs of the National course. Now, receiving 22lb, he was just two lengths behind. That gap widened dramatically, however, after *Churchtown*

Boy had bungled his jump. From that moment – to the ecstasy of the huge crowd – there was only one horse in it. *Red Rum* pulled away in majestic style to win his third Grand National by the truly remarkable margin of 25 lengths. *Eyecatcher* was a further six lengths back in third, with only seven others finishing, two of them having being remounted.

Red Rum had become the first horse in 138 years to win three Grand Nationals. And incredibly, as a 13 year old in 1978, he was the ante-post favourite to win the race a fourth time. This despite the fact that, in the intervening year, he had had six races without a win and, most recently, had been tailed off in the Haydock National Trial and had finished sixth in Haydock's Greenall Whitley Chase.

'Rummy' was always a different proposition at Aintree and his lively pre-race form on the gallops encouraged the belief that he was entirely capable of winning a fourth National. But then, on the eve of the great day, he was found to have a hairline fracture of a small foot bone. Britain's best-loved horse would never be risked on a racecourse again.

The next day he appeared at Aintree – but only to lead the pre-race parade of the 37 Grand National runners. It was an honour that would annually be accorded the Aintree King for another 15 years. Throughout that period he also travelled the length and breadth of the country making public appearances, and enjoying such celebrity that a Japanese-American businessman, Rocky Aoki, made an offer (rejected) of one million dollars to buy him to promote the opening of his chain of restaurants. He appeared on various TV shows, was guest of honour at the switching-on of the Blackpool illuminations, and was immortalised at Aintree by a bronze statue unveiled by the Princess Royal and sculpted by Philip Blacker, who had finished fourth behind *Red Rum* on *Spanish Steps* in 1973, and fourth and third in the Nationals of 1980 and 1981 respectively.

To mark *Red Rum*'s 30th birthday on May 2, 1997, Aintree staged a special evening meeting with five races named in his honour. Its 'King' paraded around the paddock, posed for photographs, nibbled at a huge 30-candled cake. Five months later, his great heart began to give out. His distress could not be prolonged and McCain gave him one last polo-mint (his favourite reward) before bidding him a fond farewell. The celebrity of his beloved chaser would never fade. Indeed, in the next millennium he would be chosen to feature on stamps issued by the Isle of Man Post Office. And in 2007 a poll of nearly 2,000 people found *Red Rum* to be the most famous horse of all time, gaining 45 per cent of the vote, followed by the fictional *Black Beauty* (33), *Shergar* (23) and *Desert Orchid* (16).

Just how great was *Red Rum*? Ridden by 24 different jockeys, including Lester Piggott, his overall record is not so extraordinary: 110 starts, 27 wins and second or third in 37 others. His wins comprised three of 24 over hurdles, 21 of 76 chases, and three of ten Flat races. But most unusually he won over distances ranging from five furlongs to four and a half miles; and, displaying a wonderful economy of effort in his perfectly measured jumping, he never once fell in his 100 races over jumps.

To be sure, he is not to be rated alongside the truly great steeplechasers who proved their excellence in such weight-for-age classic chases as the Cheltenham Gold Cup and the King George VI. But in common with *Arkle*, the greatest of them all, he had exceptional intelligence and was proud, courageous and good-natured. And on one racecourse, Aintree, his spiritual home, he was quite simply a handicapper nonpareil.

See also: McCain, Donald; Molony Tim; Renton, Robert; Fletcher, Brian; Stack, Tommy; Le Mare, Noel; Crisp.

REES, Frederick Brychan

Winning rider (by a distance) in the 1921 Grand National when *Shaun Spadah* was the first of four finishers and the only horse in a field of 35 to complete the course without falling. Having no equal in a driving finish, F. B. 'Dick' Rees was the foremost jump jockey of the 1920s. He rode in 11 Nationals, finishing fifth on his Aintree debut, first on his second appearance, and two years later – following the victory of his elder brother Lewis on *Music Hall* – being the runner-up on 12 year old *Shaun Spadah*.

Born in 1894 in Tenby, South Wales, the son of a Pembrokeshire vet who rode in point-to-points, Rees began riding out for a stable close by Bangor racecourse. In the First World War, he saw action serving in the infantry and finally with the Royal Flying Corps. Then, on demob, he turned to race-riding as an amateur; and he was such a natural horseman that he quickly established himself as the outstanding National Hunt rider. Turning professional in 1920, he won the jockeys' championship five times between 1920 and 1927; became

R

in 1924 the first jump jockey to ride 100 winners in a year; and won every major jump race in Britain. His successes included three Cheltenham Gold Cups, on *Red Splash* (1924), *Patron Saint* (1928) and *Easter Hero* (1929); the Champion Hurdle on *Royal Falcon* (1929); and the 1925 Grand Steeplechase de Paris on *Silvo*.

Rees was still an amateur when, like his elder brother, he made his National debut in 1920. On *Neurotic*, he was the fifth of five finishers. One year later, returning as a professional, he was to be personally congratulated by King George V on his victory. In the next three Nationals he loyally stuck with a severely handicapped *Shaun Spadah*. They fell at the first fence in 1922 but the following year, though still on top weight, he gave the bay gelding a copybook ride to be beaten only three lengths by *Sergeant Murphy* who had an 18lb advantage. In 1924, they were the seventh of eight finishers.

Rees never repeated his early National success, but then more often than not he was on heavily weighted horses. In 1925 he came fifth, riding *Silvo* who had been raised to 12st 7lb after his third place the previous year. And *Silvo* was carrying the same top weight when he and Rees fell in 1926. Two years later Rees appeared to have a real chance on *Master Billie*. In 1927 they had fallen at the last open ditch; now the nine year old gelding was the 5-1 favourite carrying only 10st 8lb. But this was the most extraordinary National of all, the year when only two of 42 runners finished, with *Tipperary Tim* winning from the remounted *Billy Barton*.

In 1929, Rees fell on seven year old *Lloydie*; and his last National ride, in 1931, was arguably his unluckiest. He was again on the 5-1 favourite, this time *Easter Hero*, the brilliant horse who had been largely responsible for the great pile-up in 1928 and who, despite spreading a plate, had finished second to *Gregalach* in the 66-strong field of 1929. Having won the past two Cheltenham Gold Cups, *Easter Hero* was again on 12st 7lb.

Coming to the second Becher's, *Easter Hero* was in striking distance of the leaders when a riderless horse brought down Miss Dorothy Paget's *Solanum*. The six year old sprawled directly in front of *Easter Hero* and there was no way that Rees could avoid a crashing fall. Though greatly disappointed, the jockey at least reacted with more restraint than on the other occasion that he had been unseated from the great chaser. Famously it had happened in the

Grand Steeplechase de Paris, at the water jump directly in front of the stands. Reportedly, on getting to his feet, the cheeky champion gave a V-sign to the crowd and then, amid great cheers, proceeded to relieve himself in the water!

A great character, courageous soldier and truly brilliant horseman, Fred Rees retired in the 1930s and tragically died in 1951 at the age of 57. *See also:* Shaun Spadah; Rees, Lewis Bilby.

REES, Geraldine
The first woman to complete the course in the Grand National. Her historic accomplishment – the last of eight finishers on the bay gelding *Cheers* – came five years after the first attempt by a lady rider (Charlotte Brew) and was achieved despite intense media pressure and plenty of criticism from sexist fuddy-duddies who continued to argue that women were ill-equipped to tackle Aintree's most formidable fences.

In reality, Hampshire-born Geraldine Rees was very well equipped. The 26 year old daughter of Captain James Wilson, who trained at Sollom near Preston, she had tackled daunting obstacles in three-day eventing, representing her country in the 1973 Junior European Championships and as a senior jumping round the most testing courses at Badminton and Burghley. She had also been the leading female National Hunt rider, albeit with most of her experience over hurdles.

Geraldine had a dream-like debut in National Hunt racing. In 1977, with just two point-to-point races behind her, she picked up a spare ride – on an outsider, *Twidale*, in a novice hurdle at Carlisle – and led the field from start to finish. Then she went on to complete an amazing hat-trick. Of course, it could not last. Plenty of falls and failures followed; and when she eventually had her first ride in a novice chase it ended with a first fence fall and a broken thumb. But that didn't stop her coming back three days later to take third place in a race at Cartmel; and after a brief break with injury she again bounced back, this time riding three winners.

In 1981, having ridden in Aintree's Red Rum Novices' Handicap Chase, Geraldine set her sights on tackling the National fences. She was set to ride *Gordon's Lad* who, like the great Rummy, had been trained on the Southport sands. But two weeks before the 1982 National her chaser went lame. Frantically, the family sought to buy a replacement holding an entry for the race. Just one candidate was found: ten year old *Cheers* who, ridden by Peter Scudamore, had been the last of 12 finishers in the 1981 National.

More disappointment followed when – only eight days before the National – they were the underbidders at Doncaster Sales. *Cheers* went for £8,000 to trainer Charles Mackenzie, bidding on behalf of his wife and Mrs Susan Shally. But then, on the Monday, came great news: the new owners had agreed that Geraldine should take the ride. She had just five days to prepare.

In 1982, for the first time, two women were riding in the National. Charlotte Brew, who had reached the 26th fence in 1977, was on her mother's *Martinstown*, a 100-1 chance. *Cheers* was priced at 66-1, the first lady-ridden runner to be shorter than 100-1. The bookies were offering 5-1 against Geraldine completing the course, and the odds had been as short as 4-1 when her husband, Henry Rees, bet £120 on her reaching the finishing post.

The early omens were not good. *Cheers* – as nervous as his rider – reared up in the paddock, played up when going down to the start, and had to be turned and taken well back before being the last to join the line-up. Happily they avoided the first fence mêlée where the fallers included last year's winner, *Aldaniti*. But two fences later *Coolishall* jumped across them, colliding with *Cheers* in mid-air and unseating Ron Barry in the process. Miraculously, unlike her only lady rival, Geraldine survived the third – possibly aided by the fact that she had rubbed resin into the seat of her breeches before the race.

Always jumping cleanly, *Cheers* was well placed throughout the first circuit, then rapidly began to lose ground. When loose horses swerved across the second Becher's, greatly reducing the field, only six horses were ahead of him and just one behind. But the leaders were now almost out of sight and soon *Cheers* was relegated to last by the improving *Three of Diamonds*. From this point on, Geraldine was aware of the deafening roar as crowds urged her on to complete the course. In ordinary circumstances, being so far behind, *Cheers* might have been pulled up. But on this day, trailing in last was almost akin to winning. By finishing, a lady rider, wearing pearl earrings and long, blonde hair piled up under a crash helmet, had done better than such hardened professionals as John Francome, Jonjo O'Neill, Phil

Tuck and Ben de Haan, and former winners Bob Champion and Bob Davies.

After her famous finish, totally exhausted both physically and mentally, Geraldine was quickly brought down to earth. Fresh from the first of many television interviews, she was legged up for the next race and fell at the first hurdle. Three and a half weeks later she rode *Cheers* again, in a chase at Southwell, and pulled him up at the fourth last. Sadly, the gelding went lame soon afterwards and had to be put down. In 1983 Geraldine again aimed to ride *Gordon's Lad* in the National. Again he was not fit in time; and again a late substitute – 12 year old *Midday Welcome* – was found. This time there was a complete reversal of fortune. The brown gelding, a 500-1 no-hoper, came down at the first. Mrs Rees now had far fewer riding opportunities as her father began to concentrate on training for the Flat. In 1987 she sustained a broken pelvis in a fall at Ayr: and subsequently she became a trainer in her own right.

See also: Lady Riders.

REES, Lewis Bilby

Though he could not match his younger brother's strike-rate over jumps, Lewis Rees was a brilliant rider in his own right. In 1922, one year after brother Fred had won the Grand National on *Shaun Spadah*, he emulated that feat – winning by 12 lengths on the nine year old *Music Hall*.

That year half of the 32-strong field had been eliminated before the first Becher's. By the second Valentine's only a handful remained, and here three leaders rose perilously close together: *Music Hall*, *Drifter* and *A Double Escape*. In the barging match, Rees lost an iron. But his rivals fared even worse. *Drifter* split his coronet, the lowest part of a horse's pastern, while *A Double Escape* was so badly shaken that he crashed out at the next fence.

The triple clash was arguably decisive. In pain, the disadvantaged *Drifter* courageously ran on to clear the last a mere half-length behind *Music Hall*. But inevitably he weakened on the run-in and Rees could bring his mount home unchallenged. *A Double Escape* was remounted to become the last of five finishers.

Altogether, Lewis rode in eight Aintree Nationals, mostly on long-priced outsiders; and his win on *Music Hall* was the only time he completed the course. But his many successes elsewhere included

R

a win on *Brown Jack* in the 1928 Champion Hurdle – one year before his celebrated brother won the race on *Royal Falcon*.

The family's association with the National was renewed in 1957 when Lewis's son, Bill Rees, had his first of 11 rides in the race. His best results were finishing fourth on *Scottish Flight II* in 1961, and fourth again, on Mr Paul Mellon's *The Beeches*, in 1969. He also had the distinction of twice riding in the Royal colours of the Queen Mother – on *Laffy*, a faller in 1964, and on *The Rip*, seventh in 1965. *See also:* Music Hall; Lewis, Frederick Brychan.

REFUSALS

Refusals – the result of horses declining to jump a fence – are relatively commonplace in the Grand National as horses, out of sheer exhaustion or fear of the most daunting jumps, may decide they have had enough. But refusals, unlike falls and loose running horses, are not a major cause of carnage. In 1967, for example, when *Foinavon* profited from the pile-up caused by the riderless *Popham Down*, only three of the 26 non-finishers were recorded as having 're-fused'. In 1928, when just two of 42 starters completed the course, only five refusals were recorded. Remarkably, too, there were only two refusals in 1929 and 1947 when the National had its biggest fields – 66 and 57 respectively.

REGAL

A magnificent looking chestnut entire was all the rage before the 1876 Grand National. His name was *Chandos*, and he had finished fourth in the Derby three years before. Like *Reugny*, the 1874 National winner, he was a six year old who had been bought from Lord Aylesford by the master gambler Captain James Machell. And he was made the overwhelming 3-1 favourite in a 19-strong field.

But Machell had another runner: the five year old *Regal*, a black gelding by *Saunterer* out of the 1865 Oaks winner *Regalia*. Remarkably he was a 25-1 chance despite his long distance credentials, which most notably included a win over four miles in the 1875 Great Sandown Chase. *Chandos*, in contrast, had only shown his brilliance over hurdles.

Both *Chandos* and *Regal* were well poised to challenge the leaders by the second Becher's. But already the inferior jumping of the former had shown as he almost nosed the ground on landing. Now, despite fine handling by jockey James Jewitt, he crashed out at the fence after Valentine's, while *Regal* moved up to join *Shifnal* and *Congress* at the last.

Throughout the second half of the long run-in, the race was a titanic duel between young *Regal* and ten year old *Congress*; and, in arguably the most thrilling of finishes, *Regal* – ridden by his trainer Joe Cannon – prevailed by just a neck with three lengths back to Lord Marcus Beresford's *Chimney Sweep*. It gave Machell his third National winner in four years.

The ever shrewd Machell promptly bought *Congress* in time to win Aintree's Grand Sefton Chase and then sold him, along with *Regal*, to Lord Lonsdale. It proved a smart move. Punished with top weight of 12st 7lb, and now ridden by Cannon, *Congress* finished second again in the next National. *Regal*, raised almost a stone and ridden by Jewitt, was a faller.

When Machell re-purchased *Regal* to enter him in the 1879 National, punters took it as a clear sign, backing him so heavily that he was made the short-est-priced of all favourites: an absurd 5-2. But he was never a serious threat and made numerous jumping errors before falling on the second circuit and being remounted by Jewitt to finish a well-beaten sixth.

Again *Regal* changed hands, carrying the colours of Lord Aylesford in the 1880 National. He had been dropped only 1lb in the weights, but he was reunited with Cannon, and so again he was made favourite, this time at 5-1 in a field of only 14 runners that included two other past winners, *Shifnal* and *The Liberator*. He fell at the second fence, one of only four runners to fail to finish.

Confusingly, Machell now chose to buy him back again; and the gamble almost came off. On his fifth appearance in the race, with Jewitt again in the saddle, *Regal* finished four lengths second to *Woodbrook*, with the third horse far behind. Three years later, in 1884, Machell entered *Regal* for yet one more National. He was now 13 years old but the handicapper had no respect for old age. A 50-1 shot, he was carrying 3lb more than when winning as a five year old and, though he took the lead late on the first circuit, he broke down on the second. *See also:* Machell, Captain James; Cannon, Joe.

REMOUNTS

In 1979 American amateur rider Charlie Fenwick remounted *Ben Nevis* after falling in a pile-up at The

Chair, then wisely pulled up at the next fence. But one year later, when *Ben Nevis* reappeared, trainer Tim Forster was so pessimistic that his unusual parting instruction to the jockey was 'Keep remounting'. On this occasion it was unnecessary. The 40-1 chance romped home to win by 20 lengths.

The general view is that remounting is a procedure only to be considered in exceptional circumstances. According to an old jockeys' saying: 'There are fools, bloody fools – and jockeys who remount'. Indeed, countless horses have been remounted during the rough-and-tumble of the Grand National and not one has gone on to win.

Nevertheless, some remounts have made amazing recoveries – the standard being set in the second National of 1840 when *Arthur*, challenging for the lead, slipped at the second Becher's and turned a complete somersault. His rider, Alan McDonough, staggered to his feet and somehow managed to remount and give chase to the leaders. He produced such a storming late run that he finished four lengths second to *Jerry*, and ahead of two other finishers who had not been remounted.

In 1911, when only four runners completed the course, all three finishers behind *Glenside* had been remounted. The runner-up, *Rathnally*, finished so strongly that, with another 50 yards or so, he would have been the first remounted horse to win the National.

It was exactly the same in 1921 when *Shaun Spadah* won from three remounted finishers. That year saw both a courageous and a foolish display of remounting. Coming to the penultimate fence, *The Bore*, 9-1 favourite, had looked the likely winner before falling. Heroically, his rider-owner, Mr Harry Atherton Brown, climbed back into the saddle with a broken collarbone and, with his right arm hanging limp at his side, he rode on to gain a distant second place. Conversely, there were no plaudits for Captain G.H. Bennet when he finished fourth on *Turkey Buzzard*. Afterwards an outraged owner, Mrs H.M. Hollins, attacked him with her umbrella for having remounted her horse three times after falling.

In the same race 13 year old *Bonnie Charlie* fell no fewer than four times before his American rider, Mr Morgan Blair, accepted defeat. In this case, however, there were no repercussions; he was riding his own horse. Meanwhile, the experience on *Turkey Buzzard* did nothing to reduce the stubbornness of Captain Bennet. The following year, on *A Double*

Escape, he again remounted his horse to become the fifth of five finishers.

In 1924 jockey Bill O'Neill adopted a most original method of remounting. Having fallen at Becher's on *Libretto*, he caught another loose horse – the hot favourite *Conjuror II* – and rode him to catch up with his original mount at the Canal Turn. But it was to little avail since the remounted *Libretto* soon fell again.

In 1928, for the first time, a horse (the American champion *Billy Barton*) finished both second and last after being remounted as late as the final fence. Under jockey Tommy Cullinan, he came home a distance behind *Tipperary Tim*.

More remarkable, however, was the athletic achievement of jockey Alan Power in 1951 when starter Leslie Firth let the field go with more than half the runners facing the wrong way. The result was a mad scramble to make up lost ground, with 12 horses coming to grief at the first fence. Only two completed the course without falling. The persistent Power finished a distant third and last after remounting the 66-1 Irish contender *Derrinstown* no less than three times.

In the infamous 1967 National, when all but *Foinavon* were brought to a standstill by the mass pile-up at the 23rd, a record six of 18 finishers had been remounted. Among them was *Red Alligator* who recovered to finish third before winning the following year.

Most spectacular was the recovery in 1982 of the grey *Loving Words* after unluckily being brought down when two horses fell in his path at the fourth last. Four horses were a 100 yards or more ahead of him. Yet Richard Hoare remounted him almost immediately and pushed him out to overhaul *Delmoss* in the last strides to grab third place, albeit 15 lengths and a distance behind *Grittar* and *Hard Outlook*.

By the turn of the century there was added incentive for remounting in the light of hugely increased prize money for placed horses – rewards steadily rising to reach, in 2005, £406,000 for the winner, £154,000 for the runner-up, £77,000 for the third finisher, £35,000 (fourth), £17,000 (fifth) and £10,500 (sixth). At the same time, however, jockeys needed to beware of facing disciplinary action under the rules concerning proper riding. They could face such action if it was felt that that they had attempted to complete the course on an exhausted horse that

R

should have been pulled up. And they were now required by Instruction H18 to 'dismount as soon as possible from any lame horse'.

Remounting was never more worthwhile than in 2001 when extremely heavy ground and the pile-up caused by *Paddy's Return* resulted in the course being littered with fallers. Indeed, after Carl Llewellyn had been unseated from *Beau* at the 20th fence, only two horses were left standing: *Red Marauder* and *Smarty*. Thus, *Blowing Wind* (Tony McCoy) and *Papillon* (Ruby Walsh) were both remounted at the 19th fence and gently steered round to be well rewarded for finishing third and fourth respectively. Meanwhile, after *Beau* had been caught by an official, Llewellyn enterprisingly borrowed the man's mobile and called Nigel Twiston-Davies to ask whether he should remount. The trainer told to him do whatever he wanted, and on this occasion he duly decided against remounting.

In 2002 *The Times* racing journalist Mr Alan Lee advocated a ban on remounting in steeplechases; and indeed, such a ruling would certainly have been welcome in the bad old days of reckless amateur riders. Nowadays, however, jockeys can hopefully be credited with a more human and commonsense approach – only remounting when their horse has not suffered a serious fall and, in their judgment, is not too exhausted or distressed to soldier on.

That said, early in 2005 a racing incident sparked off stronger calls for a remounting ban, the argument being that jockeys, however caring, are not qualified to judge whether a horse is fit to continue; and that this can only be determined by a vet's examination.

Remounted finishers on record are
1839, *The Nun* (fifth); **1840**, *Arthur* (second); **1841**, *Goblin* (seventh); **1842**, *Peter Simple* (third); **1858**, *Conrad* (fifth); **1879**, *Regal* (sixth); **1881**, *The Liberator* (ninth); **1890**, *Why Not* (fifth) and *Emperor* (sixth); **1906**, *Gladiator* (seventh) and *Phil May* (ninth); **1907**, *Buckaway II* (seventh); **1908**, *Kirkland* (seventh); **1909**, *Red Hall* (15th) and *Count Rufus* (16th); **1911**, *Rathnally* (second), *Shady Girl* (third) and *Fool-Hardy* (forth); **1913**, *Carsey* (third); **1915**, *Balcadden* (fifth); **1921**, *The Bore* (second), *All White* (third) and *Turkey Buzzard* (fourth); **1922**, *Sergeant Murphy* (fourth) and *A Double Escape* (fifth); **1925**, *Sergeant Murphy* (tenth); **1926**, *Ben Cruchan* (13th); **1927**, *White Park* (sixth); **1928**, *Billy Barton* (second;) **1929**,

Camperdown (tenth); **1932**, *Annandale* (seventh) and *Sea Soldier* (eighth); **1933**, *Merriment IV* and *Ballybrack* (position unrecorded); **1936**, *Comedian* (tenth); **1937**, *Don Bradman* (seventh); **1939**, *Under Bid* (11th); **1947**, *Halcyon Hours* (tenth), *Martin M* (12th) and *Rowland Roy* (15th); **1948**, *Lovely Cottage* (14th); **1949**, *Perfect Night* (11th); **1951**, *Derrinstown* (third); **1952**, *Sergeant Kelly* (tenth); **1968**, *Highlandie* (15th); **1971**, *Limeburner* (12th) and *Common Entrance* (13th); **1977**, *Hidden Value* (tenth) and *Saucy Belle* (11th); **1982**, *Loving Words* (third); **1998**, *Killeshin* (sixth); **1999**, *Merry People* (16th) **2001**, *Blowing Wind* (third) and *Papillon* (fourth); **2002**, *Mely Moss* (11th).

RENTON, Robert

A clergyman's son, Yorkshire-born Bobby Renton established himself as one of the outstanding National Hunt trainers of the post-Second World War period. Aintree jumpers were his speciality. He turned out winners of all the major steeplechases there – including, most notably, the brilliant *Freebooter*, winner of the 1950 Grand National by 15 lengths.

Freebooter – bought by Renton for £3,000 on behalf of Mrs Lurline Brotherton – was rated by the Ripon-based trainer as the best horse he ever had in his care. He proved his liking for Aintree by winning the 1949 Champion Chase and, that same year, by carrying 12st 4lb to victory in the Grand Sefton. But in 1951, all hope of a repeat National win was lost when, in the chaos of an undeclared false start, *Freebooter* was brought down at the second fence.

Renton was so skilled in preparing horses for Aintree's big fences that it seemed only a matter of time before he had a second National winner. But fate decreed otherwise. In 1954, he made the fatal error of choosing to run his great hope *Tudor Line* without a 'pricker', the small brush that was usually fitted on the side of his bridle to dissuade him from jumping to the right. At the last *Tudor Line* jumped to the right and crucially lost ground that cost him the race – beaten a neck by *Royal Tan*, trained by another great Aintree specialist, Vincent O'Brien. One year later, with an extra 10lb on his back, *Tudor Line* was to be second again. The trainer's other runners, *Little Yid* and *No Response*, both failed to finish.

In 1954 Renton had bought a five year old grey gelding, *Glorious Twelfth*, for millionaire Jim Joel, who wanted to own a horse with Grand National potential. In the 1955-56 season, *Glorious Twelfth* won the Champion Novices' Chase at Manchester and the Tantivy Chase at Hurst Park. Then, in 1957, as Joel's first National runner, he finished fourth under 'Jumbo' Wilkinson. It was a most promising Aintree debut for the eight year old. Unfortunately it was promise unfulfilled. The grey refused at the 11th in 1958 and, carrying 10lb less, was brought down on his last appearance in 1959. Recognising that *Glorious Twelfth* was past his best, Joel made a present of him to the trainer.

In 1962 Renton challenged unsuccessfully with *Siracusa*, tenth, and *Ernest*, 12th. The following year he sought to give Mrs Brotherton a second National winner as he saddled the well-supported *Dagmar Gittell* who had been fourth in the Mackeson Gold Cup. Like *Freebooter*, the eight year old had proved himself over the Aintree fences, winning several races at Liverpool, including the Topham Trophy of the previous year. But there were doubts about his stamina and so it proved as he was soon outpaced and later pulled up by Johnny East.

Without ever knowing it at the time, Renton did eventually have a horse better than *Freebooter* in his stable. A huge disappointment, this novice jumper was raced 14 times in the 1969-70 season. He had six different jockeys, ran usually on hated soft going, and was finally tried in blinkers – all to no avail. When the octogenarian trainer retired in 1971, the stable was passed on to his assistant trainer and jockey, Tommy Stack. The failed horse was included. His name was *Red Rum*.

See also: Freebooter; Red Rum.

RESERVES

A reserve system for the Grand National has been available since 1997 but it was not put into operation until 2000. That year, for the first time, the four horses who came closest to making the 40-runner cut-off at Thursday's final declaration stage were named as reserves. A reserve can only run if one of the 40 declared is withdrawn by 9.30 a.m. on the eve of the National. On this occasion, the opportunity did not arise. However, in 2001 *Merry People* sneaked into the race as the first reserve following the late withdrawal of *Inn At The Top* because of the heavy ground. He unseated his rider at the seventh.

In 2004, there were only 39 runners because, faced with unsuitable ground, *Tyneandthyneagain* was not withdrawn until the morning of the race.

Consequently, it was suggested that, to make absolutely sure of having the maximum field of 40 runners, a reserve should be allowed to join the line-up if a vacancy occurs on Grand National day. However, this idea was dismissed by the Aintree management. They explained, 'The difficulty is that we need to get the list of runners out all over the world and changing the field on the day of the race is not practical. The race is so widely bet on that people need to know the field as soon as possible.'

REUGNY

When *Reugny*, a chestnut entire, won the 1874 Grand National, it completed back-to-back victories for the owner (Captain James Machell) and for the trainer and rider (John Maunsell Richardson); and, by coincidence – just as in 1873 with *Disturbance* – their winner was a six year old winning by six lengths.

Like so many French-bred horses, *Reugny* – by *Minos* out of *Reine Blanche* – was put over jumps at a very early age. Under the ownership of Lord Aylesford, he was only four years old when being successfully raced over hurdles and in three steeplechases. The following year, ridden by Joe Cannon, he had an undistinguished National debut: a 40-1 chance who failed to finish.

Subsequently, *Reugny* was bought by the shrewd, big-time gambler, Captain Machell, and put into training by Richardson at Limber Magna in Lincolnshire. Showing huge improvement, he was duly entered for the 1874 National in which Machell would also be represented by *Disturbance* and *Defence*. Since no National winner had ever carried more than 11st 13lb the former seemingly had no chance on a colossal 12st 9lb, and the latter was a well exposed eight year old.

Richardson openly acknowledged that *Reugny* was by far the best of his three contenders and consequently his friends readily plunged in with big bets. Machell, who had delayed getting on, was horrified to see his horse backed down to 5-1 favouritism – and so enraged that he virtually accused his trainer of having abused his position of trust. Richardson, in turn, was so disgusted by the unfounded suggestion that he resolved, after the National, to never ride in another race.

As when winning the National the year before, Richardson held up his horse on the first circuit, only making a determined forward move after the second Becher's. The mare *Columbine* headed the field at that stage but faded on approaching the second last, leaving the way for Lord Marcus Beresford's ex-cavalry charger *Chimney Sweep* to open up a seemingly unassailable six lengths lead. On the run-in, however, jockey Jack Jones resorted to the whip in vain. *Chimney Sweep* had nothing more to give and, despite having blundered over the last, *Reugny* strongly outpaced him to the finish.

Having been sold by Machell, *Reugny* appeared in only one more National – in 1877 when he was brought back as a nine year old, carrying 8lb more than his winning weight. Never in serious contention, he was pulled up by his amateur rider Ted Wilson. He was never to win another race while Wilson was destined to win successive Nationals in the next decade.

See also: Richardson, John Maunsell; Machell, Captain James.

REYNOLDSTOWN

Winner, at the first attempt, of the 1935 National in record-breaking time; and one year later becoming the first horse since *The Colonel* (1870) to win the race twice in succession. He was subsequently retired with the unique 100 per cent Grand National record of two runs and two wins.

It was in 1932 that trainer Major Noel Furlong returned to his native Ireland in the hope of finding a potential National winner to be ridden by his son, Frank. The horse he chose – bought for £1,500 – was a jet-black five year old, named *Reynoldstown* after his birthplace north of Dublin. The gelding, out of *Fromage*, was by *My Prince*, who had sired both the winner (*Gregalach*) and runner-up (*Easter Hero*) of the 1929 National.

Luck as well as good judgment was on the major's side. *Reynoldstown* had already been offered to that most persistent of all National-challenging owners, 'Jock' Hay Whitney. But the American millionaire had been unable to get over to Ireland in time to view the horse. Furlong's good fortune, however, was not immediately evident. *Reynoldstown* proved to be highly temperamental. In December, 1932, he was unimpressive in two novice steeplechases, falling in one of them, and falling again the following March when ridden by Frank at Cheltenham. On the other hand, in 1933, he was unbeaten in long-distance hurdle races.

Reynoldstown's promise was sufficient to attract the interest of another millionaire seeking a potential

Grand National winner: Mr J.V. Rank, the flour-milling tycoon. On the understanding that Furlong might be prepared to sell, he sent two expert friends to look the horse over. They reported back that he was 'a long-backed, narrow gutted brute' and not worth an offer. Curiously, one of them also insisted that the gelding's colour was an ominous sign.

In 1935, the eight year old *Reynoldstown* made his National debut as Major Furlong's second string, his more fancied entry being *Really True*, the runner-up in 1933. The former had scored three victories that season under Frank Furlong, but he had fallen in the recent Grand National Trial at Gatwick and so went off at 22-1. Leading the market was *Golden Miller*, the shortest-ever price favourite at 2-1 following his fourth successive Cheltenham Gold Cup victory.

With 'The Miller' unseating his rider on the first circuit, the race developed into a duel between *Reynoldstown* and Mr Whitney's *Thomond II*, the second favourite. They forged ahead after the second Becher's, but when they came to the long run-in the latter was doubtless feeling the effects of his hard battle with *Golden Miller* at Cheltenham only 15 days earlier. He now began to fade, conceding second place to *Blue Prince* while the long-striding *Reynoldstown* held on to win by three lengths.

Reynoldstown, carrying 11st 4lb, had a winning time of 9min 20.2sec. Arguably this was a new National record since the previous year, *Golden Miller*, on 12st 2lb, had clocked a then record time of 9min 20.4sec or 9min 20.2sec, depending on which of two timekeepers was believed.

In 1936 *Reynoldstown* returned with an extra 12lb and with a new rider, Mr Fulke Walwyn, who replaced his great friend and former fellow Army officer Frank Furlong (now overweight). At 10-1 he was fourth in the betting – behind *Avenger*, *Golden Miller* and *Castle Irwell*. Again 'The Miller' failed on the first circuit, having being brought down at the first fence and remounted in vain. Then, at the modest 17th fence, *Avenger*, the 100-30 favourite, tragically broke his neck in a crashing fall. The runaway leader was the tubed *Davy Jones*, a 100-1 outsider, and he was still going strong when *Reynoldstown* came within a length of him at the second Becher's.

Thereafter, *Davy Jones* looked all over the winner as he jumped more cleanly than his rival and still led at the penultimate fence. But then, by the remotest of chances, the buckle of his bridle snapped open. Anthony Mildmay had no means of steering, and his horse, so full of running, veered off the course at the final jump. *Reynoldstown*, striding on to win by a full 12 lengths, was regarded as one of the luckiest of all National victors.

In normal circumstances, Major Furlong would have sought a hat-trick of National wins with his powerfully built gelding. But in 1937 he refused to enter him, in protest at the newly introduced handicap range. The weights, formerly ranging from 12st 7lb to 10st 7 lb, were now to extend over 35lb, with a new minimum weight of 10st. *Golden Miller* was the luckless favourite who had to make that huge concession to some of his rivals.

There was, nevertheless, a hat-trick of a kind. For the third year in succession the National was won by a son of *My Prince*, the winner being *Royal Mail*, an all-black half-brother to *Reynoldstown*, who now began a long, well-earned retirement at Marston St Lawrence, near Banbury. The dual National winner was 24 when he had to be put down after cutting his foot on a broken bottle and developing tetanus. He was buried near the stables, and there, in 1985, he was to be joined by another old National campaigner, *Well To Do*, the 1972 winner.
See also: Furlong, Noel; Furlong, Frank; Walwyn, Fulke.

RHYME 'N' REASON

Winner of the 1988 Grand National when making his first and last appearance in the race. Ridden by Irishman Brendan Powell, who had broken an arm on his National debut the previous year, *Rhyme 'N' Reason* went to Aintree only three weeks after falling in the Cheltenham Gold Cup, and in a remarkable recovery he triumphed by four lengths despite having trailed the field after a belly-flop slide on landing over the first Becher's.

Bred in Downpatrick, Co. Down, *Rhyme 'N' Reason* had a promising pedigree, having been sired by the powerful French-bred stallion *Kemal* out of *Smooth Lady*, an unraced half-sister of the 1984 Grand National winner *Hallo Dandy*. Starting out with two wins in Irish bumpers, he was bought as a four year old by the eminent trainer Michael Dickinson on behalf of Miss Juliet E. Reed, and he began the 1983-84 season with a hat-trick of wins in three-mile novice hurdles. Then, as Dickinson chose to switch to the Flat and later move to the United

States, the bay gelding continued to make remarkable progress under a new trainer, David Murray-Smith. In only his second season he won four chases and the first of these was the Irish Grand National – won at the age of six!

Talk of *Rhyme 'N' Reason* being a potential 'wonder horse' soon faded, however, as he went through the next two seasons without a single win. Judged an unreliable jumper, he was now sent to the Whitsbury, Hampshire, yard of David Elsworth, a trainer renowned especially for his success with Flat handicappers. Almost at once he recaptured his form of old, and on the build-up to the 1988 Grand National he won four of eight chases, finished runner-up in two and third in another. His two seconds were notable enough: beaten a length by *Playschool* in the Coral Welsh Grand National, and behind Cheltenham Gold Cup winner *Charter Party* and a neck ahead of *Desert Orchid* at Sandown. The only blot on his record was his last pre-Aintree run. In the Gold Cup, when making rapid progress, he fell at the 19th fence.

That one error, four fences out, was not a fall in the full sense of the word – merely a skidding slip when losing his footing on landing. It was enough, however, to deny him favouritism in the National. Though he had otherwise outstanding form and was well-handicapped on 11st, he went off behind the late market leader, *Sacred Path*, and on the same 10-1 mark as *Lean Ar Aghaidh*, whom he had beaten in the Racing Post Handicap Chase at Kempton.

The tragic death of *Forgive 'N Forget* in the Gold Cup had made Juliet Reed hesitate about putting her favourite horse over Aintree's fences. But finally she agreed with the trainer that this was the right year to let *Rhyme 'N' Reason* take his chance. Elsworth himself was brimful of confidence. 'I've no doubt that if he negotiates the obstacles he will win!' And he put his money where his mouth was, backing the horse at twice the starting price.

A tearaway start saw three fallers at the first fence: two outsiders and the heavily backed *Sacred Path*. Cautiously, Brendan Powell took *Rhyme 'N' Reason* down the outside towards the rear; and doubts about the gelding's jumping seemed well-founded as he slithered on his belly when landing awkwardly over Becher's. Brilliantly, Powell managed to stay in control and set off again. Now plum last and looking completely out of the race, they gradually worked their way back into the reckoning;

R

and with four runners being eliminated at the second Becher's, they moved into second place behind *Little Polveir*, closely followed by *Durham Edition*, old *West Tip* and *Monanore*.

When *Little Polveir* landed on top of the 26th fence, unseating his rider, *Rhyme 'N' Reason* was left in the lead. But he stalled badly at the second last and now *Durham Edition* looked all over the winner as he powered ahead for a three lengths lead at the final fence. *Rhyme 'N' Reason*, however, was an out-and-out stayer renowned for his finishing speed. Two years before, on *Young Driver*, the luckless Chris Grant had been passed on the run-in to go down by two lengths to *West Tip*. Similarly, he suffered the same frustration as *Rhyme 'N' Reason*, responding to vigorous use of the whip (the subject of a stewards' enquiry), steadily closed the gap, then pulled ahead to win by four lengths. *Monanore*, a further 15 lengths back, was third, and the gallant, top-weighted *West Tip* was fourth.

In the owner's enclosure, Miss Reed had been jumping up and down so excitedly that she lost the contents of her handbag. But later, to her dismay, she would find that the near-fall at Becher's was not without unfortunate consequences for *Rhyme 'N' Reason*. He had suffered a fractured hock that swelled up so alarmingly that the vet thought he might need to be put down. Surprisingly, he responded well to intensive treatment; and, though he would never race again, was able to enjoy retirement at the Woodhaven Stud in Hampshire owned by Miss Reed in partnership with financier John Moreton. *See also:* Powell, Brendan; Elsworth, David; Stewards' Inquiries.

RICHARDS, Gordon W.

Though he was named after the greatest Flat jockey of the time, it was in National Hunt racing and as a trainer that Gordon Richards emerged as a legendary figure of the Turf. With the elusive exception of the Cheltenham Gold Cup, he captured all the major chasing honours including the King George VI Chase three times and the Grand National twice, with *Lucius* (1978) and *Hallo Dandy* (1984).

Born on September 7, 1930, in Bath, the eldest of ten children of a timber-dealer, Richards truly learned his trade in the school of hard knocks. Having ridden a cart-pony bareback since the age of four, he was 11 years old when packed off in wartime to serve as a stable apprentice in Poole.

Moving on to join trainer J.C. Waugh at Chilton, near Didcot, he was 13 when he made his racing debut at Salisbury and promptly earned himself a whipping for having, against orders, revealed his horse's true potential.

Gordon Richards was now given the initial 'W' by Jack Waugh in response to a Clerk of the Scales who demanded that his jockey be distinguished from the champion rider on the Flat. The distinction was soon unnecessary. At 15, the boy had become too heavy for the Flat, and he transferred to the National Hunt Wroughton (Wiltshire) yard of Ivor Anthony, the man who had trained two Cheltenham Gold Cup winners, and two Grand National winners: *Kellsboro' Jack* (1933) and *Royal Mail* (1937).

There 'GWR' gained invaluable experience, learning not only from Anthony but also from stable jockey Danny Morgan who had won the 1938 Cheltenham Gold Cup on *Morse Code*, plus three Scottish Nationals and three Champion Chases. But the learning curve was then cut short by National Service in the 'Glorious Glosters' with whom the tough teenage recruit earned a number of medals – not in the Korean War, which he narrowly missed, but in the boxing ring.

On demob in 1950, Gordon became stable jockey to Johnny Marshall, based near Alnwick in Northumberland. He had only a moderate race-riding career, coming nearest to a major victory when finishing runner-up on *Merry Windsor* in the 1957 Scottish National. Two years later that career ended in a fall on *Sea View* in a chase at Perth. He was left with a crushed vertebrae at the base of his spine.

In 1954 Gordon had married Jean Charlton, a landowner's daughter. Now, with two small children to support, they scraped a living by running a livery stable and horse-dealing business. But always he had dreamed of becoming a trainer and eventually that dream turned to reality when he was invited to train jumpers owned by Northumbrian farmer Adam Pringle. Looking over Mr Pringle's horses, Richards judged that only one – an unbroken gelding called *Playlord* – was a promising sort. And that one horse laid the foundation of a new career that was to net him almost 2,000 winners in the next 34 years.

Sadly, the owner died shortly before *Playlord* made his debut over hurdles. Given first offer by his widow, Richards bought the gelding for £1,400 loaned by his wife's aunt, and later he sold a half-share for £1,500. The gamble quickly paid off with a hat-trick of hurdle wins, successes that led to Richards gaining new patrons. Meanwhile his finances were greatly boosted by fees he received for providing horses for a scene in the movie *Becket* that was filmed near his stables on Bamburgh beach, Northumberland.

With that windfall Richards was able to move to Cumbria and take over from Tommy Robson as master of the well-established Castle Stables at Greystoke, near Penrith. There, in 1967, *Playford* was first put over fences, and subsequently he won eight chases partnered by Ron Barry. He gave Richards his first major success with an easy victory in the 1969 Great Yorkshire Chase, and two months later he would arguably have won the Cheltenham Gold Cup but for quagmire conditions which saw him finish third. The following month, on firm ground, he won the Scottish National at 9-1. But then, in the Hennessy Gold Cup, he was brought down hard by a faller directly in his path. He was never the same horse again and was only nine years old when he had to be put down following a heavy fall at Doncaster.

Nonetheless, *Playford* had set Richards firmly on his way. The number of his horses in training grew apace, most notably with the addition of six year old *Titus Oates* whom Richards bought at the 1968 Ascot sales for £14,750 guineas. This purchase, on behalf of Mr Philip Cussins, constituted a world record fee for a jumper; and the great gamble paid off. *Titus Oates* won 17 chases including the 1969 King George VI Chase and the 1971 Whitbread Gold Cup.

By now Richards was proving his versatility as a dual purpose trainer. At one time in the 1970s he had as many as 70 Flat horses in his yard. But it was over hurdles and fences that he won his major honours; and in the 1975-76 season he had 105 winners to finish third in the National Hunt trainers' table.

Meanwhile, he had made an inauspicious start to his bids for Grand National success. In 1972 he had the ante-post favourite *Red Sweeney*, but two days before the race the chestnut had to be withdrawn with a bruised foot. Instead he was represented by *Gyleburn*, a 20-1 chance who fell at the first. In 1974, he ran *Straight Vulcan* who was well placed until falling at the 18th, and in 1977 his runner, *Sir Garnet*, unseated Jonjo O'Neill at the Canal Turn second time around.

Not least of Gordon's talents was his keen eye for spotting chasing potential at the sales. At the 1972 Doncaster sales he picked out an unbroken three year old whom he bought for a mere 1,800 guineas on behalf of Mrs Fiona Whitaker. Early on, he spoke of the bay gelding as 'a Grand National type', and so it proved in 1978 when *Lucius* gave the master of Greystoke his first National winner. With Bob Davies as the late replacement jockey, the nine year old won in the closest of finishes, by half a length and a neck. Richards' other runner, *Tamalin*, bellyflopped on landing over Becher's but miraculously recovered to finish 12th.

Cruelly, that triumph was followed by a year of disaster. The stable was hit by a virus; an infection caused *Lucius* to miss a return to the National. Then came the saddest blow in Gordon's life: his wife and most industrious aide died of a heart attack. In 1980 Richards had hopes of achieving a second National win with his nine-year-old grey *Man Alive*. But luck remained against him. On the morning of the race he saw the quagmire conditions and knew his top-weighted runner had no chance. He was promptly withdrawn and it was not until 1982 that Gordon (now remarried) was again represented in the National.

That year he had two runners: *Man Alive* and *Current Gold*. It was two years since the former had won the Mackeson; now, past his peak, he dumped Andy Turnell at the first. The latter, with Neale Doughty, finished a distant fifth. But then, in 1983, the Greystoke trainer was hugely encouraged by the performance of his nine year old *Hallo Dandy* who finished fourth in the National at 60-1 – this on soft ground that he hated. Given good going, he could surely win. Richards brought *Hallo Dandy* to a perfectly timed peak for his 1984 return. The going was good, and remarkably the great hope of Greystoke had been raised only 1lb in the weights. Under Doughty, he duly won by four lengths at 13-1.

Subsequently, Gordon made nine attempts to achieve a third Grand National victory; all were doomed to fail, some unluckily, one tragically. *Hallo Dandy*, with an added 10lb, returned in 1985, only to fall under Graham Bradley at the first. In 1986, reunited with Doughty, he finished 12th. One year later, the stable was thought to have an outstanding chance with the grey gelding *Dark Ivy*. He went off as the 11-2 second favourite and was rated by Phil Tuck as the best horse he ever rode in the National. Sadly, however, when being sandwiched at Becher's, he fell and broke his neck.

R

After a three-year gap, Richards had another outstanding challenger: nine year old *Rinus*, a 13-1 chance. But he had his best form on the soft and now unusually fast going denied the trainer a deserved third success. Under Doughty, who was completing the course for the seventh time in seven Nationals, *Rinus* finished third – some 20 lengths behind the record-breaking *Mr Frisk* and *Durham Edition*, both of them firm-ground specialists. The following year, *Rinus*, a well-supported 7-1, unseated his rider at the 20th.

Again, in 1992, Greystoke had a fancied runner: *Twin Oaks*, the 9-1 third favourite. But, as Richards rightly judged, the 12 year old had been hit too hard by the handicapper. Under the top weight of 11st 7lb, he finished fifth. The following year, the trainer felt he was not without a chance in running the relative long-shot *On The Other Hand*, winner of the Grand Military Gold Cup. Unfortunately, this was the farcical void National. Under Doughty, who got round for the ninth time, the gelding came home the sixth of seven finishers.

Through all these years of National frustration, Richards had winners aplenty elsewhere. Backed by wealthy patrons, he concentrated exclusively on National Hunt racing, and he had such great money-spinners as *The Man Himself*, *Another City*, *Music Be Magic*, *The Langholm Dyer*, *Little Bay*, *Jim Thorpe*, *Randolph Place*, *Carrick Hill Lad* and *Gallateen*. He had a second Scottish National with *Four Trix* (1990). In his best-ever season (1990-91) he had 118 winners, 80 of them in chases; and he topped the century mark in 1992-93 when he was the leading northern trainer and fourth in the national championship.

In 1993, at the dispersal sale following the death of his great friend and northern rival W.A. Stephenson, Richards went to 68,000 guineas to buy a big-footed grey on behalf of Mr John Hales. The gelding had won over hurdles and Gordon saw him as a potentially great chaser. And so it proved; *One Man* won the 1994 Hennessy Cognac Gold Cup, then the King George VI Chase twice (1995, 1996).

In 1995 Richards was represented in the Grand National by *General Pershing* who fell under David Bridgwater at the fifth. In 1997 he had his 19th and last runner in the race: *Buckboard Bounce*. The 11 year old had had a rushed preparation over hurdles following a layoff with a leg problem, and Paul Carberry did well to bring him home in fourth place at

40-1. Ironically, as a result of contractual obligations, Richards' stable jockey Tony Dobbin was free to ride *Lord Gyllene* – the winner.

One year later, Gordon became gravely ill with lung cancer but, being a stubborn workaholic, he bravely soldiered on, being rewarded with *Unguided Missile*'s victory in the William Hill National Hunt Chase and *One Man*'s winning of the Queen Mother Champion Chase at Cheltenham.

Originally, Richards had nine entries for the 1998 Grand National, most notably *The Grey Monk*, *Addington Boy* and *Buckboard Bounce*. None made it to the line-up and, far worse, the eve of the National was a nightmare with the loss of the brilliant *One Man*, put down after breaking a hind leg in the Mumm Melling Chase at Aintree. The trainer's favourite horse had won 20 of his 25 races.

Tough, straight-talking, and widely known as 'The Boss', Richards died the following September, three weeks after celebrating his 68th birthday. Remarkably, his irrepressible mother, Gladys, was alive to lead the many mourners; and the funeral cortege through the village of Greystoke was headed by *Better Times Ahead*, Gordon's last winner of the season, ridden by his most long-serving jockey Ron Barry. Two years later a permanent memorial – in the form of a bronze bust – was unveiled close to the Carlisle paddock where so many of his stable stars had paraded, once including five winners on the same card.

See also: Lucius; Hallo Dandy; Barry, Ron; O'Neill, Jonjo; Doughty, Neale; Dobbin, Tony.

RICHARDS, Nicky

Born on February 25, 1956, Nicky Richards, son of the great Gordon, had begun race-riding at the age of 15, winning on his first outing on the Flat and in 1972 completing a unique treble – as the only jockey ever to have won on his debut on the Flat, over hurdles and over fences. The following year he had become the leading amateur on the Flat and in 1974 he might have been the National Hunt amateur champion but for an injury that was to end his riding career. Thereafter he assisted his father in preparing many big-race winners.

Following the death of his father, he took over the training of some 50 horses at Greystoke and he scored with his first runner, successful at Carlisle in October, 1998. Unfortunately that winner, *Better Times Ahead*, was not appropriately named. As a trainer, Nicky encountered many early difficulties – not least a first year blighted by a virus at the yard. However, in 1999, his first Grand National runner, *Feels Like Gold* (cut from 150-1 to 50-1) did remarkably well under Brian Harding to finish fifth from far out of the handicap; and in November he showed his liking for Aintree by leading from start to finish in winning the Tote Becher Chase by 11 lengths. However, when he returned to the National in 2000 it was as a 12 year old with an extra half-stone on his back. He finished 14th at 28-1.

More hard times came in 2001 with the devastating foot-and-mouth epidemic that saw pyres burning all around the Greystoke base. Nicky's National runner, the veteran *Feels Like Gold*, had not raced for 20 weeks before going to Aintree, and there he was one of the casualties in the pile-up at the Canal Turn. But subsequently the tide turned, with 36 winners being turned out in the 2002-3 season and the promise of better things to come from his 60-strong Cumbrian yard. Though he was again without a runner in the National, Richards made a sensational start to the 2005 Aintree meeting, taking the three hurdle races of the first day with the wins of *Monet's Garden*, *Faasel* and *Turpin Green*, all ridden by Tony Dobbin. He finished the season with 50 winners and began the new season with a stronger hand than ever before.

In 2006 Richards had two entries for the National: *Big-And-Bold* and *Direct Access*. Only the latter made it to the line-up and was pulled up by Tony Dobbin before the 19th. In 2007 he again had two National entries: *Ransboro* and *Turpin Green*. The former, on 9st 12lb, had no hope of making the cut. The latter, on 11st 1lb, was withdrawn after finishing third in the Cheltenham Gold Cup; instead he ran in Aintree's Betfair Bowl Chase, finishing a disappointing fifth. The following day, Friday the 13th, Richards had better luck with *Monet's Garden* winning the Melling Chase.
See also: Richards, Gordon.

RICHARDSON, John Maunsell

It is entirely conceivable that J. M. Richardson would have become one of the greatest of all Grand National riders if it had not been for one sordid little incident prompted by that deadliest of sins in the racing game: Greed.

It happened in March, 1874, when Richardson, an outstanding amateur horseman and all-round athlete, was due to ride in the National on the 5-1 favourite *Reugny*, a French-bred six year old owned by Captain James Machell, trainer, dealer and big-time gambler. Just one year earlier Richardson had won the National for the same owner on *Disturbance*.

The incident arose from Machell's discovery that friends of Richardson had taken the best value about *Reugny*, betting heavily enough to help force the price down. Now, unable to get better than 5-1 odds, the owner lost control and accused his rider of robbing him of a favourable investment. In reality, however, Machell had only himself to blame. After working the captain's horses at his Lincolnshire home, Limber Magna, Richardson had advised the owner well in advance to back *Reugny* in the National. For once the shrewd Machell had dithered and delayed too long.

Richardson was now so offended that he threatened to quit the ride on *Reugny*. Finally he agreed to honour his commitment – just this one time. But after that he wanted no further part in the shabby, money-grabbing business. It would be his last ride in the National and, indeed, in any other race.

That year, on *Reugny*, Richardson – so lithe and agile that he was nicknamed 'The Cat' – travelled mainly in the rear, nursing round a young horse who was not certain to stay. Not until halfway round the second circuit did he make his move, steadily gaining ground on the tiring leaders until, approaching the last, only Lord Marcus Beresford's *Chimney Sweep* remained ahead.

Unlike *Reugny*, *Chimney Sweep* took the final obstacle cleanly and looked all over the winner. But then Richardson saw that the leader was not responding to the whip. Encouraged, he kept hard at work throughout the run-in, passing the leg weary rival and going on to win by six lengths, with the outsider *Merlin* a further four lengths back in third. Two other Machell-owned horses – also trained by Richardson – were among the finishers: *Defence*, fourth, and top-weighted *Disturbance*, sixth.

Uninfluenced by the glory of victory, 28 year old Richardson stood by his word. He never raced again. And thus he retired from the scene with the extraordinary record of two successive wins in only four National appearances. Moreover, he had trained both winners after buying them at a bargain price on Machell's behalf. His only failures had been on his 1871 debut when falling on Machell's *Magnum Bonum*, a 50-1 long-shot, and the following year

R

when Lord Eglinton's *Schiedam* was brought down.

One can only conjecture what Richardson might have achieved if he had continued his gold-plated partnership with Machell. The fact is that Machell, without his No 1 rider and trainer, was represented in many more Nationals, winning with *Regal* (1876) and later having horses placed second, third and fourth. In any event, Richardson stands out in Grand National history as a great gentleman rider and one of only eight to achieve successive National victories. Lincolnshire-born in 1846, he was educated at Harrow and Cambridge. At the former he gained his nickname 'The Cat', excelling on the track and at fencing, cricket and racquets. At the latter he gained his cricket blue, three times playing in the Varsity match.

He began riding in steeplechases while still at Cambridge and following his graduation he won the 1870 National Chase at Cottenham on *Schiedam*. Two years later he rode 56 winners to become the champion amateur rider. Though he quit racing at an early age he was to ride as a huntsman for many more years, having succeeded the late Lord Yarborough as Master of the Brocklesby hounds. And such was his cat-like agility that in all his years of riding he never suffered more than one broken collarbone in falling.

Having later married Lord Yarborough's widow, Richardson turned to politics and, in 1894, was elected the Conservative MP for the Brigg division of Lincolnshire. Though, after two National victories, he never raced again, he did, in fact, return to Aintree – in 1876 as the owner of *Zero*, a six year old to be ridden by his great Old Etonian friend, Viscount Melgund, who chose to compete under the pseudonym of 'Mr Rolly'.

That day Captain Machell was doubly represented – by *Chandos*, the 3-1 favourite, and *Regal*, a 25-1 shot – and he would win with the latter by a neck. Meanwhile, Richardson's last involvement with the National had ended in alarming circumstances. When *Zero* fell at the 27th fence 'Mr Rolly' lay severely injured and initially doctors, including specialist Sir James Paget, judged that he had broken his neck. Happily they were mistaken. Lord Melgund fully recovered, went on to win many major races. including the Paris Steeplechase on his Richardson-trained *Miss Hungerford*; and afterwards, as the Earl of Minto, he became Viceroy of India.

See also: Machell, Captain James; Disturbance; Reugny.

RIDERLESS HORSES
See: Loose horses.

RIMELL, Frederick
One of the all-time greats of National Hunt racing, Fred Rimell won four jump jockeys' championships (including one shared), then rose to still greater heights as a trainer, his many big-race successes including a record number of four Grand National winners: *E.S.B.* (1956), *Nicolaus Silver* (1961), *Gay Trip* (1970) and *Rag Trade* (1976). Yet, ironically, his first direct involvement in the National, in 1936, could not have been more discouraging. At the age of 23, he was riding *Avenger*, the 100-30 favourite trained by his father, and challenging for the lead when the brilliant seven year old blundered into the relatively low 17th fence and was instantly killed by his neck-breaking fall.

Fortunately, Fred was already far too enamoured with the racing game to be disheartened by that tragic National debut. Born in 1913, the son of a dedicated trainer, he thrived on the hunting, shooting and fishing environment in which he grew up. Aged 12, he was apprenticed to his father Tom, and he rode his first winner on the Flat at Chepstow: a horse called *Rolie*, owned by his grandfather. At 18, he went to the 1932 Grand National but, being judged too inexperienced to ride in the race, it was only to help his father saddle up *Forbra*, the 50-1 winner.

Then came the most happily fortuitous event of his life. Riding somewhat recklessly with the Croome Hunt, Fred was thrown at a jump and landed in a large brook. To his rescue came a young girl whom he had first met at a Sunday tennis party: Mercy Cockburn, an accomplished horsewoman who had successfully ridden international class show-ponies from the age of seven and point-to-point winners since she was only 14. He climbed up behind her and together they rode on to join in the chase. He had literally fallen in love.

In 1937, when 17 year old Mercy married Fred, it was the beginning of one of the longest and most successful husband-and-wife partnerships in the history of the Turf; also the cementing of the Rimell dynasty, with the family's great riding tradition being carried on by their children, and no less impressively by their grandchildren.

Initially, Fred seemed likely to become most renowned as a jockey. As a professional rider he won 34 races on the Flat; then, forced by rising weight to make a switch, he quickly made his mark over the jumps. In the 1938-39 season he became the champion National Hunt rider with 61 wins, so following his brother-in-law, Gerry Wilson, who had been champion for the six previous seasons. He retained the title in the war-truncated 1939-40 season.

Most noted for his power in a tight finish, Fred twice rode five winners in one day – at Windsor and at Cheltenham. The National, however, continued to be his bogey race. He was a faller on *Delachance* (1937), *Teme Willow* (1939) and *Black Hawk* (1940). Indeed, his best result in five rides was finishing 12th on *Provocative* in 1938. That ride was noteworthy for the fact that Fred had generously reached out to yank Bruce Hobbs back into the saddle after the young jockey had lost his balance on landing over the seventh fence. Bruce, of course, went on to win the National on little *Battleship*.

After a wartime break, limited racing was resumed in the 1944-45 season. Fred, who had been driving RAF lorries, came back to win the Champion Hurdle on *Brains Trust* and to share the jockey championship with Herbert 'Frenchie' Nicholson, both on just 15 winners; and in 1945-46, for the third time, he won the championship outright. But then his riding career was abruptly ended by a fall on *Coloured School Boy* in the 1947 Cheltenham Gold Cup. For the second time Fred had fractured his neck and this time he was eight months in plaster.

He never rode again and his everlasting regret was that he had never ridden a winner of the Cheltenham Gold Cup or a single winner at Liverpool, either on the Flat or over the jumps. But just as one brilliant career ended, so an even more brilliant career began to blossom. He had started training in 1945 and now, with the indispensable support of Mercy as his working partner, he built up at Kinnersley, Worcestershire, one of the most successful stables in England.

He went on to win almost every major race in the National Hunt calendar, including four Grand Nationals; two Cheltenham Gold Cups (with *Woodland Venture*, 1967, and *Royal Frolic*, 1976); two Champion Hurdles (*Comedy of Errors*, 1973 and 1975); the Triumph Hurdle three times (*Coral Diver*, 1969, *Zarib*, 1972, and *Connaught Ranger*, 1978); four Welsh Grand Nationals (*Creeola II*, 1957, *Glenn*, 1968, *French Excuse*, 1970, and *Rag Trade*, 1976); four Mackeson Gold Cups (*Jupiter Boy*, 1968, *Gay Trip*, 1969, and 1971, *Chatham*, 1970); the Scottish

Grand National (*The Fossa*, 1967); the Two-Mile Champion Chase (*Another Dolly*, 1980); the Whitbread Gold Cup (*Andy Pandy*, 1977); and three Irish Sweeps Hurdles. Four times champion jockey, he now became five times champion trainer, gaining the title in 1951, 1961, 1969, 1970 and 1976.

In the 1956 National the sensational fall of *Devon Loch* commanded so much attention that Fred's skilled preparation of the 'lucky' *E.S.B.* did not fully get the recognition it deserved. Though an outstanding jumper, the big brown gelding had not proven his ability to get the trip, and yet he achieved the fourth fastest time in the history of the race – a worthy winner in his own right.

One key to the Rimells' success was their shrewd judgment of a horse's potential. Thus, in November, 1960, at the Ballsbridge sales, they successfully bid £2,600 on behalf of Mr Jeremy Vaughan for an eight year old grey called *Nicolaus Silver*. The gelding's former trainer said they had paid too much. Yet, after only one win under their care, he triumphed in the 1961 National by five lengths from the previous year's winner, *Merryman II*. He was the first grey to win the event for 90 years, and only the second ever.

But, above all, Fred's success was achieved by his supremely thorough training methods. Besides exploiting to the full the outstanding facilities of Kinnersley, with its rolling hills and gallops of every conceivable kind, he would transport his horses for work on racecourse and beach, and was also a great believer in 'loose schooling' – standing in the centre of an enclosed oval and, like a circus trainer, cracking a hunting crop to send a riderless horse over jumps.

The value of his painstaking schooling (varied but never too rigorous) was well illustrated when he sent out *Gay Trip* – another shrewd Rimell buy – to win the 1970 National by 20 lengths. The little eight year old, burdened with top weight at Aintree, had never won beyond two and a half miles before. But here his immaculate jumping outclassed all the others.

The following year, having been raised 9lb in the weights, *Gay Trip* fell at the first fence. Yet the trainer had him back in 1972 to finish two lengths second to *Well To Do* in a 42-strong field. His other runner, *The Pantheon*, was a faller. Subsequently he ran *Rouge Autumn*, fifth at 40-1, and *Sunny Lad*, 15th, in 1973; *Rough House*, fell, *Rouge Autumn*, seventh, and *Sunny Lad* 16th, in 1974; and fallers *Rough House* and *Junior Partner* in 1975.

R

Then, in 1976, Fred worked wonders again, taking over the training of *Rag Trade*, tenth in the previous year's National, and getting the big, clumsy gelding to peak fitness with perfect timing to win by two lengths from the incomparable *Red Rum*. Thereafter, he sent out four challengers for each of the next three Nationals.

In 1977 he had high hopes of a fifth victory with the 15-2 favourite *Andy Pandy* and, true to expectation, the eight year old bay gelding opened up a 12 lengths lead coming to Becher's for the second time. But there he stumbled and fell on landing – one costly error that was largely forgotten in the euphoria that greeted *Red Rum*'s historic third victory. Rimell took fourth place with his 40-1 chance, the big, powerful *The Pilgarlic*. His *Brown Admiral* was a faller, as was his 100-1 shot *Royal Thrust*. After falling on the latter Colin Tinkler grabbed another loose outsider, *Duffle Coat*, to get a ride back to the weighing room. The horse promptly bolted with him and, on reaching the unsaddling enclosure, threw up his head so violently that he left the rider with a bloody nose.

In 1978 Fred's four runners were all 33-1 chances, and again *The Pilgarlic* proved the best, finishing fifth. His others were *Mickley Seabright*, sixth; *Brown Admiral*, tenth; and *Double Negative*, fell. That same year a fire destroyed the Rimells' office with all their records and many trophies, and it was rumoured that Fred was about to retire. Instead he came back to achieve another impressive run of victories including the £20,085 Royal Doulton Hurdle in which 20-1 *Royal Gaye* beat the famous trio of *Sea Pigeon*, *Night Nurse* and *Monksfield*. But he could not improve on his record four National victories.

In 1979 he sent out yet another quartet, this time taking fourth place with *The Pilgarlic* and sixth place with his ten year old Gold Cup winner *Royal Frolic*, anchored on top weight of 11st 10lb. *Geoffrey Secundus* was brought down in a seven-horse pile-up at The Chair and his outsider *Double Negative* was an early faller.

Yet again, in 1980, he was four-handed, and his best hope seemed to be *Another Dolly*, recent winner (following a disqualification) of the two-mile Queen Mother Champion Chase at Cheltenham. He went off at 12-1, despite atrociously heavy ground being clearly against him, and he fell at the first Becher's, continuing Jonjo O'Neill's unlucky run in the National. Once more it was left to *The Pilgarlic* to do the Rimells proud; and amazingly the 12 year old came home the third of only four finishers, so giving him a National sequence of fourth, fifth, fourth and third.

One year later the most triumphant of all National trainers died, but the Rimell legend lived on as Mercy took over the Kinnersley yard and carried on successfully until her retirement in 1989. In that period the remarkable lady sent out a total of 232 winners, including *Gaye Brief* who gained the yard's third Champion Hurdle in 1983, and *Gala's Image* who won the Arkle Trophy; and finally *Three Counties*, winner of the 1989 Christie's Foxhunter at Cheltenham. Her last Grand National runners were *Pilot Officer* who fell at The Chair in 1983 and refused in 1984; *Ten Cherries*, an 11th fence faller in 1986; *Eton Rouge*, an 80-1 chance, pulled up four fences from home in 1988; and finally *Gala's Image* who finished seventh in 1989 on ground far too soft for his liking.

The family's racing interests were now carried on by Mercy's daughter Scarlett and her husband Robin Knipe, a prominent amateur rider until a broken back at 32 had ended his career. They bred the 1995 Cheltenham Gold Cup winner *Master Oats* at their Cobhall Court Stud near Hereford and, though they had quit training after the 1985-86 season, they renewed their permit 15 years later, encouraged by the promise of their resilient mare *Ardstown* who had finished in the money in 16 successive point-to-points and hunter chases.

Then yet another generation of Rimells came to the fore. Kate, grand-daughter of Fred and Mercy, won the 1989 Foxhunter Chase on *Three Counties*; and her brother Mark, though lacking the dedication to succeed as a jockey in his twenties, subsequently made a major breakthrough in his second season (2004-05) as a trainer, most notably scoring with *Oneway*, winner of five successive chases, and *Crossbow Creek*, bred and owned by his mother Mary, who won the 2005 Lanzarote Hurdle at Kempton Park.

But amazingly it was the evergreen Mercy Rimell, now a great-grandmother, who would now revive the family connection with the Grand National. In 2007, when approaching her 88th birthday, she was the breeder and owner of a lively National contender: eight year old *Simon*, who, on his last outing, had stayed on impressively to win by ten lengths the three-mile £100,000 Racing Post Chase.

She considered him to be an ideal National type. 'He is only a little horse, barely 16 hands. But a short-striding horse is better suited to the National than the bigger, galloping type of horse. Three of our four National winners were around 16 hands. It means you can be nimble at the fences, put yourself right more easily. A lot would say it's nonsense, but at least it's my theory.'

At first Mercy was inclined to wait another year before making a National challenge with *Simon* who was in the same family as her champion hurdler *Gaye Brief*. But in the end, bearing in mind that 'another year and I might not be here', she was persuaded to run by trainer John Spearing who operated at the same Kinnersley stables from which the Rimells had sent out four National winners.

Unfortunately, on the day, *Simon* did not get his favoured soft going. He travelled and jumped supremely well under Andrew Thornton and was well in contention at the second Becher's. But three fences later, for the first time in 19 races, he made his one mistake and fell. The dream of another Rimell triumph was over – at least for another year.

Arguably the canny Mercy had been right in thinking of waiting until 2008. And, despite *Simon's* uncharacteristic fall, she basically still held the same view of the great race. 'The Nationals we won were proper Nationals, not with these modified fences. Any horse that jumps a park course now should, in my opinion, jump around Aintree.'
See also: E.S.B.; Nicolaus Silver; Gay Trip; Rag Trade; Rimell, Tom; Biddlecombe, Terry.

RIMELL, Tom

Born into a family of hop-growing farmers in the Vale of Evesham, Tom Rimell was 14 years old when he ran off to Newmarket to seek stable work. Subsequently he became head lad to trainer Fred Butters and in one season helped to turn out no fewer than 48 two year old winners on the Flat. Then, setting up on his own, he made his base at Kinnersley near Severn Stoke in Worcestershire, taking over the magnificent yard which, created by the Earl of Coventry, had produced two Grand National winners: *Emblem* (1863) and *Emblematic* (1864).

Tom's own involvement with the National was a curious mixture of triumph and tragedy. Triumph came by happy chance in 1932 when he was aiming the seven year old *Forbra* at Aintree's Stanley Steeplechase. Unexpectedly, *Forbra* now won a chase

at Taunton and, under the current rules, made himself ineligible for any future novice chases. With nowhere else to go, it was decided to run *Forbra* in the National one year earlier than originally planned. He won at 50-1.

The tragedy came in 1936 when Tom was challenging for the National with another seven year old: Mrs Hilda Mundy's *Avenger*, fourth in the 1935 Cheltenham Gold Cup and subsequently the brilliant winner of the National Hunt Handicap Chase. Tom rated him 'the best jumper I've ever trained'. The horse was to be ridden by the trainer's 23 year old son Fred, and so outstanding was his form that he went off as the 100-30 favourite, ahead of the renowned *Golden Miller*.

Avenger was lying second at the Water Jump, then crashed into the relatively small (4ft 6in) 17th fence and died on landing. It would be 20 years before the Rimells had happier memories of Aintree with the fortuitous victory of *E.S.B.*, the first of four National winners to be trained at Kinnersley by Tom's brilliant son.
See also: Rimell, Fred; Fobra; Hamey, Tim.

ROBINSON, George William

Winning jockey in the 1964 Grand National when riding 12 year old *Team Spirit* for the fifth successive year. Having finished fourth the previous year, they now caught *Purple Silk* on the run-in to triumph by just half a length, with *Peacetown* a further six lengths back in third. The win was all the sweeter because it was so unexpected. Years later he recalled: 'Even when my fellow was staying on at the Elbow, I remember thinking, 'well at least I'll be second'. And when he got to the finish, he felt as though he could have gone round again.'

Irish-born (August 5, 1934), Willie Robinson was a hugely talented rider, so versatile that in 1958, when he made his Aintree National debut on *Longmead* (a second fence faller), he went on to finish second in the Epsom Derby on the 100-1 outsider *Paddy's Point*. It was only two years since he had turned professional, and already he had achieved a major jumps victory, the 1957 Irish Grand National on *Kilballyown*.

Now retained by trainer Dan Moore in Co. Meath, Robinson immediately struck up a winning partnership with eight year old *Team Spirit*. In the 1960 Grand National, however, the diminutive gelding, third in the betting at 9-1, fell at the second

431

R

Becher's. The following year, when the upright fences had been modified, they finished ninth.

Meanwhile, Robinson had firmly established himself as an outstanding jump jockey. He had finished third on *Zonda* in the 1960 Cheltenham Gold Cup. And one year later, when Fred Winter suffered a broken collarbone, he took over on the great Fulke Walwyn-trained *Mandarin* to win the Hennessy Cognac Gold Cup. In 1962, again riding for Walwyn, he won the Champion Hurdle on *Anzio*, while Winter, back on *Mandarin*, rode to glory in the Cheltenham Gold Cup.

That year, for a third time, Willie had ridden *Team Spirit* in the National, only to be unseated at the 19th fence. But now came a significant coinciding of events. *Team Spirit* was sent to trainer Walwyn's Lambourn stables, and Robinson became Walwyn's first jockey as Winter's illustrious riding career drew towards a close.

In 1963, when the mighty (over 17 hands) *Mill House* was switched to the Walwyn stable, Robinson gained the plum ride, winning the most prestigious Cheltenham race by 12 lengths, a second Hennessy, and the King George VI Chase. In the 47-runner Grand National he rode *Team Spirit* into fourth place and eight months later they won the Grand Sefton at Aintree.

In 1964, *Mill House* was odds-on to win a second successive Gold Cup, There were only four runners but they included a new wonder horse, the incomparable *Arkle*. Finishing five lengths in arrears, Willie was hugely disappointed. Two weeks later, however, he had an ample consolation. On the eve of the Grand National he won the Coronation Hurdle on *Dionysus III*. The following day he won the Liverpool Hurdle on *Sempervivum* – and then, coming from behind on *Team Spirit*, snatched victory in the National itself.

At Cheltenham, the following year, Robinson again showed his great strength in a driving finish when spurring home *Kirriemuir* to win the Champion Hurdle at 50-1. In the Gold Cup, however, he and *Mill House* – now in decline – were no match for Pat Taaffe and the still-improving *Arkle*. Sixteen days later, riding in the Grand National for trainer Keith Piggott, he was well placed on seven year old *Leedsy* when they fell at the 18th.

Robinson rode in three more Grand Nationals. In 1966 he was a faller at Becher's on *Popham Down* and in 1968 was the last of 17 finishers with *Quintin*

Bay. His tenth and final appearance came in 1970 when, aged 36, he was on *The Fossa*, The bay had finished fourth in 1966, fifth in 1968, and 11th in 1969. But now he was an over-the-hill 13 year old and he refused at Becher's on the second circuit. Willie retired shortly afterwards and returned to Ireland. He could look back on a truly outstanding career, his many successes including three Hennessy Gold Cups and two Champion Hurdles, with just one main regret – that he had been denied back-to-back Cheltenham Gold Cups by that greatest of all chasers: the extraordinary *Arkle*.

In his 70th year Robinson was still operating as an owner-breeder in Ireland, and that year, on the day of the 2004 Grand National, he saw the opening race, the two-mile Martell Cordon Bleu Handicap Hurdle, won by J.P. McManus's *Puck Out*, a horse he had bred to be a sprinter.

See also: Team Spirit.

ROIMOND

A chestnut gelding – by *Roidore* out of *Ellamond* – Lord Bicester's eight year old *Roimond* earned his place among the Grand National's great runners-up in 1949 when, under a top weight of 11st 12lb, he was outstayed from the last fence by *Russian Hero* (receiving 18lb) who prevailed by eight lengths. It was the first of seven Grand National rides for unlucky Dick Francis.

That same season *Roimond*, trained by George Beeby, had finished second in the King George VI Chase. His misfortune was to be severely handicapped in five successive Nationals (1948-52). Though he fell in four of those races he never carried less than the 11st 7lb allotted for his Aintree debut. In 1950 he was a joint 10-1 favourite burdened with 12st 1lb, and he was dropped only 1lb on each of his subsequent appearances. Francis, his regular jockey, described him as a moody sort. He wrote: 'Sometimes he tackled the job with a will to win, and on those occasions he was magnificent, but on other days he would set off in a race as if he were utterly bored by it all.'

See also: Bicester, Lord; Francis, Dick; Russian Hero.

ROQUEFORT

Winner of the 1885 Grand National as 100-30 favourite, giving leading amateur rider Ted Wilson his second victory in succession and trainer Arthur

R

Yates the first of his two National winners. One year earlier, on his Aintree debut as a five year old, *Roquefort* had finished third, ten lengths behind the victorious *Voluptuary*. Shrewdly, the winning jockey had recognised his potential; and, by persuading his friend Mr Arthur Cooper to buy the young gelding at auction for 1,275 guineas, secured the ride for the future.

Bred in 1879, *Roquefort* – by *Winslow* out of *Cream Cheese* – first ran as a four year old in military races and the following season was bought by Captain Bobby Fisher of the 10th Hussars. After his third place in the National he was only put up for sale because Fisher anticipated a long layoff from riding after breaking his leg in a fall.

Trained by Yates at Bishops Sutton, Hants, *Roquefort* was recognised as an extremely difficult ride: invariably hard-pulling and liable, given the opportunity, to veer off the course. But on a good day he was an outstanding jumper with great finishing pace, and Wilson was the one rider who could ride him effectively. Raised 9lb for his National reappearance, he was judged to have just two main rivals, both mares: *Frigate*, the 1884 runner-up, and Count Charles Kinsky's *Zoedone*, the 1883 winner.

Disgracefully, as it happened, *Zoedone* was never allowed to compete. Having been heavily backed in spring doubles with the Lincoln Handicap winner *Bendigo*, her success would have been disastrous for the layers; and all the evidence suggests that she was 'nobbled' shortly before the race. Blood from a tiny puncture near her nostril indicated that she had been injected with some malignant substance and she performed accordingly: falling at a hurdle in the preliminary canter, then struggling from the start and trailing the field when she finally fell at the second Becher's. She would never race again.

Frigate, in contrast, had many great racing days ahead; and this year, just as in the 1884 National, she was strongly in contention under Harry Beasley coming to the last, only to be outpaced on the run-in by her Wilson-ridden rival. *Roquefort* held on to win by two lengths and reportedly landed an enormous bet for Mr Cooper.

The cost of that victory for *Roquefort* was an extra 17lb to carry on his return in the 1886. Though on a top weight of 12st 3lb, he went off as the 5-1 second favourite, took an early lead from the start, and was still well to the fore when, on the way to the second Becher's, he over-jumped and fell heavily.

In the circumstances, it was extraordinary that the eight year old – now under new ownership – should be raised a further 5lb for his fourth appearance in 1887. No horse had ever finished in a place, let alone win the National, on 12st 8lb. Nevertheless *Roquefort* was again the second favourite and he looked a very possible winner as the leaders rounded the final turn. But then, as *Savoyard* hung towards him, he swerved through the rails and cut himself badly while his rider took a very heavy fall.

Two years later, again with a new owner but still ridden by Wilson, *Roquefort* came back as the 6-1 favourite, closely followed in the betting by the remarkably consistent *Frigate*. Now on 12st, he made steady progress on the second circuit and was lying third when he fell two fences out. Meanwhile, *Frigate* was moving up fast to snatch the lead at the last. Four times the bridesmaid at Aintree, she was to triumph at her sixth attempt.

In 1891 it was *Roquefort* who lined up for his sixth National, and for the fifth time he was running under new ownership. The latest buyer was none other than Arthur Yates, his long-time trainer, but nonetheless the 12 year old – like former winners *Voluptuary* and *Gamecock* – was regarded as too old to be a serious challenger. He went off at 40-1. Initially, it seemed that the brown gelding had been badly overpriced. Prominent from the start, he shared the lead with *Cloister* and *Gamecock* at the end of the first circuit. But thereafter he laboured, his position only aided by so many horses falling or being pulled up. In this, his final National, he came home a distant fourth behind three seven year olds while 12 year old *Gamecock* was the last of six finishers at 66-1.

See also: Wilson, Edward; Yates, Arthur; Foul Play.

ROUGH QUEST
Successful 7-1 favourite in the 1996 Grand National, coming home a length and a quarter ahead of *Encore Un Peu* but only being declared the winner after a stewards' enquiry. Having taken the lead halfway up the run-in, the ten year old had displayed his old tendency to hang left under pressure and came perilously close to his rival. Nonetheless, he won convincingly, and David Bridgwater, rider of the runner-up, told the stewards that his chance had in no way been affected.

Bred in Ireland by Mr Michael Healy, *Rough Quest* was by *Crash Course* out of *Our Quest*. Having appeared only in National Hunt Flat races, he

433

R

came into the joint ownership of Andrew Wates and his mother Phyllis, Lady Wates. Director of the family's Croydon-based building group, Mr Wates was a former top amateur rider and permit-holder who had won the 1970 Fox Hunters' at Aintree and who had put up 12lb overweight when riding *Champion Prince*, a 66-1 chance, as far as the Water Jump in the 1968 Grand National. His family had also owned *Hard Outlook*, the 1982 runner-up, and *Sommelier*, the fifth in 1986.

Initially trained by Tim Etherington, *Rough Quest* disappointed over hurdles, then showed considerable promise as a novice chaser with wins in 1991 and 1992. But it was three years before he won again. In the meantime, he had a new trainer: Irishman Terry Casey who arrived at the Wates's Henfold House Stables near Dorking, Surrey, to take over from Etherington who was returning to Yorkshire to succeed his father at their Malton stables.

After more disappointing runs in 1994, *Rough Quest* was diagnosed as suffering from a muscle enzyme disorder which caused lactic acid to build up in his hindquarters. A special feeding regime was introduced: a diet strong on carbohydrates and vitamin E at the expense of the usual high-protein feed. This, with a new exercise schedule, brought about a major upturn in his form. He won the Ritz Club Handicap Chase at the 1995 Cheltenham Festival and one month later a Grade 2 handicap chase at Punchestown.

In the 1995-96 season he twice fell in races. But in between he finished a useful second in the Hennessy Cognac Gold Cup. Then, just three weeks after narrowly winning the Racing Post Chase at Kempton, he finished a four lengths second to *Imperial Call* in the Cheltenham Gold Cup. Suddenly the ten year old, due to race off a 19lb higher mark in future handicaps, looked incredibly well weighted with 10st 7lb for the Grand National. He attracted huge support accordingly. But then, three days after the Gold Cup, it was reported that he would be withdrawn from Aintree and aimed at the later Irish National instead.

Happily for ante-post backers both owner and trainer had second thoughts two days later. After riding *Rough Quest* in his workouts, Casey felt the bay gelding was moving and jumping better than ever, and entirely capable of racing just 16 days after Cheltenham. Even so, the National's clear favourite was not without his detractors. Some argued that he

had a shaky jumping record, having fallen four times in just 14 starts including his one time over National fences in the 1994 John Hughes Trophy. There were doubts about his stamina since he was unproven beyond three miles two furlongs; and some even argued that he was ungenuine when it came to a hard-fought finish.

Jockey Mick Fitzgerald, however, was brimful of confidence. Most importantly, he was familiar with *Rough Quest's* tendency to idle once he hit the front. Accordingly, he held him up on the first circuit and only made a forward move after the 19th fence when they began to pick off rivals with ease. Lying five lengths second at the last, he finally took the lead from the Elbow and held on from *Encore Un Peu*, receiving 7lb, with *Superior Finish* a further 16 lengths back in third. His winning time of 9min 8sec was the second fastest in the history of the race.

Beset with training problems, *Rough Quest* ran only twice in the 1996-97 season, starting with an impressive win in a Folkestone hurdle over a trip two miles shorter than his Aintree triumph. He missed the National through injury, but he came back strongly to finish third in the King George VI Chase and he was going well in the 1998 Cheltenham Gold Cup until falling six out – his first fall since the John Hughes Trophy almost four years earlier.

Though now 12 years old and raised to 11st 4lb, he was still well fancied for a second National win with Fitzgerald in 1998; and apart from a mistake at the second Becher's he jumped superbly. But in the clinging mud he ran out of steam after Valentine's and was pulled up at the penultimate fence. In the following season, when aged 13, *Rough Quest* won a hunter chase at Newbury, and in the last of his four races he fell at Aintree in the Martell Fox Hunters' Chase. He was now retired, having won more than £370.000 in prize money.

See also: Casey, William Terence; Fitzgerald, Michael Anthony; Stewards' Enquiry.

ROWLANDS, Fothergill

Although he only twice rode in the Grand National and never completed the course, Fothergill Rowlands, popularly known as 'Fogo', was a leading amateur rider for many years and, more importantly, a key figure in the mid-19th century development of steeplechasing which, prior to his intervention, had fallen into disrepute through lack of a standard set of rules and a strong central authority to enforce them.

In 1859, Rowlands failed in his attempt to stage a new, well-ordered steeplechase for farmers and huntsmen at Market Harborough. But the following year he was wholly successful in this: organising a Grand National Hunt Steeplechase funded by 12 different hunts. The conditions were £10 for each entry with £500 added, and the race over four miles was restricted to amateur jockeys and to horses, all carrying 12st, which had never won previously.

It marked the birth of the National Hunt Chase which, with almost unchanged conditions, is still run each year at the Cheltenham Festival. More significantly, it established a new standard for jump racing, being efficiently organised and strictly controlled in accordance with rules that became known as 'the Harborough Act'. Six years later the name of his pioneering race was taken up as the title of the newly-formed, 14-strong body that took responsibility for regulating steeplechasing: the Grand National Hunt Steeplechase Committee, later shortened to the National Hunt Committee.

The son of a Monmouthshire doctor, 'Fogo' Rowlands took over his father's medical practice but later abandoned it to concentrate on National Hunt riding as an amateur. Initially he had horses with the great Tom Olliver, then started to train them himself. As a jump jockey he enjoyed great success, primarily on the horses of his friend Lord Strathmore. But strangely he was in the evening of his career when he first rode in the Grand National.

In 1861, having already managed to stake £100 at 50-1 odds on his winning the race, he bought *Brunette*, the seventh of seven finishers in the National of the previous year. But, despite having been dropped a full stone in the weights, the mare went off at 33-1 and had to be pulled up towards the end of the first circuit.

Rowlands tried once more, in 1863, this time on his *Medora* with whom he had achieved major chase successes. Having outstanding form, his mount was allotted a top weight of 12st and made third choice in the market. At the end of the first circuit, *Medora* was lying six lengths second, but he was jumping clumsily and again the sporting doctor had to pull up.

ROYAL ATHLETE

One of six Jenny Pitman-trained runners in the 35-strong field of the 1995 Grand National, *Royal Athlete* most unusually won as a 12 year old making his first (and last) appearance in the race, and with a rider (Jason Titley) also having his first experience of the great steeplechase. Unusually, too, he was a long-priced winner for the 'Queen of Aintree' – unfancied at 40-1 (66-1 in the morning) because he had a long history of leg problems and no wins since suffering an injury so severe that it was feared he would never race again.

Bred in Ireland, *Royal Athlete* – out of the mare *Darjoy* – was a son of the French-bred stallion *Roselier* who now has an outstanding record as a sire of Grand National stars. Costing Ir10,500 guineas at Ballsbridge sales, he was one of four unbroken three year olds bought in Ireland by Mrs Pitman on an inspired shopping spree in the autumn of 1986. (Her other brilliant buys were *Garrison Savannah*, *Esha Ness* and *Willsford*.)

Nicknamed 'Alfie' in the Lambourn yard, *Royal Athlete* first raced in 1987, finishing third in a bumper. His owner, a gambling man, was eager to have him raced early the following season. But Mrs Pitman was opposed to training him on artificial surfaces in the summer for fear of aggravating his leg problems. As a result, on the owner's instructions, she sadly entered the chestnut gelding in the Ascot sales. By good fortune, he did not get to the sales but remained with the trainer after a private deal had been struck. Mrs Pitman's clients, Wokingham (Berkshire) car dealers Gary and Libby Johnson, bought him for £1,500.

It hardly seemed a bargain. The delicate *Royal Athlete* needed such gentle handling that he had been off the racecourse for almost two years when, in the 1988-89 season, he appeared well down the field in a novice hurdle at Newbury. But he went on to win two novice hurdles, and the following season he proved himself a major prospect endowed with both speed and stamina. Having won the Long Walk Hurdle at Ascot, he quickly adapted to fences, winning five chases including Aintree's Mumm Club Chase and, most remarkably, Ascot's Reynoldstown Novices' Chase in which he lost some 20 lengths with a blunder at the fourth last and yet stormed back to win by 15 lengths.

Royal Athlete had now completed a five-month spell in which he had scored six wins in eight outings, collecting over £74,300 made up of prize money and a £10,000 bonus for the Aintree result. But then it was all despair again, with the return of his old leg problems. The champion novice chaser of

1989-90 was now kept off the course for two seasons. Returning in December, 1992, he scored only a single win that season – in a mere minor hurdle race at Windsor. However, he did put in one magnificent run over fences: at Cheltenham, as a 66-1 Gold Cup outsider, he powered up the hill to finish a most creditable third, nine lengths behind the winner, *Jodami*.

Again, so much promise turned to bitter disappointment. Going on to Aintree, he was regarded as a handicap good thing on a mere 10st 4lb, and he was the most strongly fancied of Mrs Pitman's three runners. But this was the void Grand National. He fell at the tenth while stablemate *Esha Ness* went on to be first past the post to no purpose. The following November, *Royal Athlete* returned to form with a chase win at Cheltenham; then two weeks later came disaster. In the Hennessy Cognac Gold Cup at Newbury, he crashed out at the 13th fence, hitting the birch so hard that one leg was ripped open. The gaping wound required more than 30 stitches. It seemed likely that his racing career was over.

'Alfie's' eventual recovery was due entirely to the extraordinarily dedicated care he received at Mrs Pitman's yard: nine months of careful nursing with his wound initially being cleaned and re-dressed twice every day. Finally, in January, 1995, 14 months after his horrendous fall, he returned to racing, taking third place over hurdles at Haydock. In February he was sixth in the Agfa Diamond Chase at Sandown and second in a four-runner chase at Windsor. In March he was put over hurdles at Doncaster, prior to a Cheltenham Gold Cup bid two weeks later.

On Gold Cup day he was withdrawn with a vet's certificate. But two days later he was perfectly sound and the Grand National now seemed an obvious target. But not to Jenny Pitman. For once she made a rare error of judgment in being much keener to go to the Scottish National ('I rated him a stone-bonking certainty for Ayr'). In the end, however, she bowed to the wishes of the Johnson brothers. At Aintree, she would have six runners with her highest hopes being for *Garrison Savannah*, the choice of her stable jockey Warren Marston. Unable to pick and choose, she entrusted *Royal Athlete* to a young Irish rider with limited experience in England: 24 year old Jason Titley.

Royal Athlete, fourth in the weights on 10st 6lb, was now 12 years old; and in his last race he had been beaten 37 lengths over hurdles – hardly form to attract punters' support. The hot 5-1 favourite was Gold Cup winner *Master Oats*, with short prices also for *Dubacilla* and *Miinnehoma*, second and third respectively at Cheltenham.

On the Saturday morning Titley walked the course with the trainer's son and assistant Mark Pitman who told him, 'Alfie is such a difficult ride. You have to imagine his reins are like a thread of cotton, you need so light a contact on his neck. That way he'll jump.' As it was, *Royal Athlete* jumped like a stag, giving his rider a reassuringly good feel after a small fright at the first fence where seven of his 34 rivals were eliminated. Thriving on the good ground, he was allowed to run freely, tracking the leaders on the inside round the first circuit and taking the lead at the first fence second time around.

Thereafter *Royal Athlete* looked in command. *Master Oats* produced a strong run to draw level at the 19th and together, after the Canal Turn, they began to draw away from the rest of the field. But the favourite, at an 18lb disadvantage, faded under pressure approaching the last, leaving only the tubed *Party Politics* as a possible threat. On the run-in, 'Alfie' sprinted away to win comfortably, by seven lengths from *Party Politics*, followed a further six lengths back by *Over The Deel*, a 100-1 outsider, and the fast-finishing mare *Dubacilla*.

Clearing the 30 obstacles with almost disdainful ease, Mrs Pitman's second Grand National winner had completed the course in the third fastest time in 149 runnings. For a 12 year old, he had relatively few miles on the clock – just 33 races in his sporadic career; and so he was entered for the 1996 National, being allotted 10st 13lb in the weights. But frost and snow had played havoc with his preparation and, lacking a preliminary run, he was withdrawn and then retired. The rest of his days were spent at the Gloucestershire stables of former trainer John Chugg, a long-time friend of Mrs Pitman. For years he was hunted and entered in dressage and showjumping events, and was hacked out every day until his death at the age of 20.

See also: Pitman, Jenny; Titley, Jason.

ROYAL BLUE

In 1852, ridden by George Stevens, a 19 year old newcomer destined to achieve five Grand National wins, *Royal Blue* was the first runner in the race to be officially quoted at the then record odds of 100-1. Carrying a bottom weight of 9st, he was a faller and did not appear at Aintree again.

ROYAL MAIL

Eight year old winner of the 1937 Grand National, making his first appearance in the race the greatest success for the Welsh – his owner (Mr Hugh Lloyd Thomas), trainer (Owen Anthony) and rider (Evan Williams) all being sons of Cymru. After back-to-back National victories, *Reynoldstown* was not appearing again. And now it was his half-brother who dominated the race – the all-black *Royal Mail*, out of the mare *Flying May*, being another son of the great *My Prince*, who had already sired two National winners, *Gregalach* (1929) and *Reynoldstown*.

Bought as an unbroken three year old by Mr Hubert Hartigan, *Royal Mail* had soon been re-sold to Mr Lloyd Thomas, a keen amateur rider who was to serve as assistant secretary to the Prince of Wales, later King Edward VIII. Three months before the 1937 National, the King had announced his abdication and now it was his uncrowned brother, George VI, who, together with Queen Elizabeth, attended the so-called centenary race.

Golden Miller, five times winner of the Cheltenham Gold Cup, was the 8-1 favourite. But, again on 12st 7lb, he was now all the more heavily penalised by a 7lb reduction in the minimum weight. Moreover, he was conceding 8lb to *Royal Mail*, who had already beaten him by two lengths over the National fences in the Becher Chase.

As in the previous year *Golden Miller* refused to run beyond the open ditch at the 11th fence, and in a race of many fallers *Royal Mail* took the lead early on the second circuit. Foot perfect, he was never headed thereafter and was threatened only by *Cooleen*, a mare who suffered from being continually harassed by a loose horse. Showing superior speed on the run-in, *Royal Mail* won by three lengths from *Cooleen*, with another mare, *Pucka Belle*, a further ten lengths back in third. Only seven of 37 starters finished.

Owner Mr Lloyd Thomas planned to take over the ride on *Royal Mail* in the 1938 National. He had often ridden his black gelding in races and now he trained purposefully for his second appearance in the National (he had fallen on his own *Destiny Bay* in 1934). But tragically, only a month before the great race, he was killed in a steeplechase fall at Derby. Evan Williams again took the ride, albeit on behalf of a new owner, Mrs C. Evans.

Royal Mail went off fourth in the betting, the joint favourites being *Blue Shirt* and last year's runner-up *Cooleen*. But, raised 8lb, he now struggled on top weight and had to be pulled up. Surprisingly, the handicapper was no less severe when the former winner returned in 1939. Again on the peak mark of 12st 7lb, and this time ridden by Danny Morgan, he was the ninth of 11 finishers. It was his last National. Thirty three years later the race would be won by *Well To Do,* who had been bred by the widow of the ill-fated Mr Lloyd Thomas.
See also: Williams, Evan; Anthony, Owen.

ROYAL RUNNERS

Edward, Prince of Wales (the future King Edward VII) was the first member of the royal family to show a genuine interest in the Grand National. He began to attend the race in the 1870s, much encouraged by his friend and racing adviser Lord Marcus Beresford who had strongly challenged with his brown gelding *Chimney Sweep* (runner-up in 1874 and fourth in 1876 and 1877). In 1879 the heir apparent became involved by way of his half-share in 11 year old *Jackal* who, under the registered ownership of Beresford, finished runner-up to *The Liberator*.

The first Grand National runner to carry the royal colours was *The Scot*, son of the 1865 Derby winner *Blair Athol*. He had finished fifth in 1881 and had fallen in 1882. Yet, in 1884, when the eight year old reappeared under the ownership of the Prince of Wales, he attracted instant support, being backed down to 6-1 favouritism.

Ridden by the hugely experienced Jack Jones, who had won on *Shifnal* (1878) and had finished second on *Chimney Sweep* and *Jackal, The Scot* was the fastest away, leading over the first fence and jumping brilliantly around the first circuit. But then, while still well placed, the royal favourite made a complete hash of Becher's second time around, crashing into it head-on.

Four years later the Prince tried again, with *Magic* (eighth); then in 1889 with *Magic* (fifth) and *Hettie* (a faller). After his *Hettie* had failed again in 1890, he went through a whole decade confining his racing interest to the Flat. Then he celebrated the dawn of a new century in spectacular style: winning the 1900 National with *Ambush II*, his recently purchased six year old; and following up with the Triple Crown triumph of his *Diamond Jubilee* in the 2,000 Guineas, Derby and St. Leger.

In August, 1901, following the death of Queen Victoria in January, the prince was crowned King

R

Edward VII. Thus, when *Ambush II* reappeared at Aintree in 1903, he became the first National contender ever to represent a reigning monarch. Though raised 18lb to the maximum 12st 7lb, he looked likely to score a second victory until falling at the very last fence.

After such a near miss, the king attended the National again in 1904, only to see his *Ambush II*, now the top-weighted 7-2 favourite, fall at the third. The shock winner was the New Zealand giant *Moifaa*, who had been likened to 'a starved elephant' by Lord Marcus Beresford.

Early in 1905 *Ambush II* was being prepared for yet another tilt at the National when he died after breaking a blood vessel in training. Eager to be represented at Aintree, the king instructed Beresford to buy a replacement quickly. The choice, ironically, was to be the big *Moifaa*, bought for 2,000 guineas. Now carrying the royal colours, he went off as 4-1 favourite despite having been raised 19lb in the weights. It was too great a burden. He fell at Becher's second time round and never raced again.

The king's last Grand National challenger was the bay gelding *Flaxman* in 1908. Though the eight year old was an unfancied 33-1 chance, he moved well on the heavy going and remained in strong contention throughout the first circuit. But then, most unluckily, his rider, Algy Anthony, broke a stirrup leather; and hopes of a second royal victory finally ended when *Flaxman* blundered badly at the Canal Turn. Anthony did well to bring him home in fourth place.

Edward VII's successor, King George V, did not share his father's passion for racing, and it was not until 1950 that the royal colours were again seen at the National. That year they were carried by *Monaveen*, owned jointly by Queen Elizabeth and Princess Elizabeth, and entered in the name of the latter. For the first time there was a mass royal turnout – the race being attended by the King and Queen, both their daughters, and the Duchess of Kent.

It was during a dinner party at Windsor Castle, following the victory of King George VI's *Avila* in the 1949 Coronation Stakes at Ascot, that Lord Mildmay, the champion amateur rider, had suggested that the Queen might enjoy having a horse in National Hunt racing. Subsequently, his friend and trainer Peter Cazalet bought *Monaveen* for £1,000 on her behalf. The eight year old, who had once pulled a milk float in Navan, had run well in the 1949 National before falling at the 19th.

At Fontwell Park, on October 10, *Monaveen* became the first horse to run for a Queen of England since *Star* ran for Queen Anne in 1714. He showed excellent form, winning on that initial outing, finishing second to *Freebooter* over National fences in the Grand Sefton Chase, and beating the likes of *Freebooter*, *Wot No Sun* and *Roimond* to win the three-mile Queen Elizabeth Chase at Hurst Park.

It was a most promising run-up to the 1950 Grand National, and on a glorious spring day at Aintree the royals saw their tough, bold jumper come home a respectable fifth to *Freebooter*, only seven of 49 starters having completed the course. Two months later, however, they were saddened by the news of Lord Mildmay's death by drowning. Then, on his reappearance in the Queen Elizabeth Chase, *Monaveen* fell at the water jump and, with a badly broken leg, had to be put down. He was buried near the winning post.

Happily, at the end of the year, the Queen had her first big success with the victory of *Manicou* in the King George VI Chase at Kempton Park. The entire was the first horse to carry her new colours – blue, buff stripes, blue sleeves, black cap with gold tassel – which had been originally worn by her great-uncle Lord Strathmore who had ridden without finishing in the Grand Nationals of 1847 and 1848.

Increasingly, following the 1953 Coronation, Elizabeth as Queen Mother was to emerge as a dedicated supporter of National Hunt racing, with the new Queen becoming a passionate follower of the Flat. The Queen was to have winners of every domestic Classic apart from the Derby. Meanwhile, over half a century, her mother had spectacular successes with her chasers though, by a strange twist of fate, triumph in the Grand National would elude her.

After the appearance of *Monaveen*, it was five years before the Queen Mother had another National challenger: the French-bred *M'As-Tu-Vu*, an eight year old ridden by Arthur Freeman. A 22-1 chance, he ran prominently over the first circuit, then tired rapidly and fell. The following year, 1956, she had two runners: *M'As-Tu-Vu*, now 40-1, and the more strongly fancied *Devon Loch*, ridden by Dick Francis. The former fell at the 19th. The latter powered ahead from the last, with a mighty cheer anticipating the first royal winner of the National for 56 years.

The rest is well-known history. Far in the lead, with the winning post no more than 50 yards ahead,

Devon Loch inexplicably belly-flopped on the ground as though sprawling over some invisible fence; and all at once a stunned silence fell over the vast Aintree crowd. With unfailing dignity, the Queen Mother concealed her greatest disappointment in racing as she proceeded to console a shattered and bewildered Dick Francis and to warmly congratulate Dave Dick and Mrs Leonard Carver, the surprised jockey and owner respectively of the winning *E.S.B.*

A few days later, the Queen Mother wrote to trainer Peter Cazalet: 'We will not be done in by this and we will just keep on trying.' However, it was to be another eight years before she had her next runner in the National. Her eight year old *Laffy*, a classy French import ridden by Bill Rees, went off as one of four joint favourites but fell at the fourth. The following year she was at Aintree to see one of her best-loved horses – ten year old *The Rip* – run in the 1965 National. The Queen Mother had a special affection for *The Rip*. Bred by the landlord of The Red Cat at Wootton Marshes in Norfolk, he was out of a 50-guinea, unruly mare who had been sent to be covered by the Queen Mother's retired champion chaser, *Manicou*. She had admired him as a most striking foal, and when he was a yearling – then named *Spoilt Union* – she bought him for 400 guineas.

Re-named *The Rip*, he was slow to mature and scored only once over hurdles. But eventually he developed into a powerful chaser and over eight seasons he was to win 13 races and be placed in 16. In his one National he went off as the 9-1 second favourite, and was close up with the leaders as far as the second Becher's. But thereafter he was thoroughly outpaced and came home a distant seventh of 14 finishers out of a 47-strong field.

Over the years the Queen Mother had many outstanding jumpers; and five times she had more winners in a season than any other owner. In May, 1994, trainer Nicky Henderson saddled her 400th winner, *Nearco Bay* at Uttoxeter. In December, 2001, at the age of 101, she was at Sandown to see her *First Love* romp home in a novice hurdle; and the following March, also at Sandown, the same horse became the last of her 461 winners. In Britain she had had 445 winners over jumps, a post-war owners' record surpassed only by Arthur Stephenson's 465. But there had been no royal runners in the Grand National for the past 36 years – a surprising gap since, from 1973

to 1990, Her Majesty's principal trainer had been the great Fulke Walwyn who had won the 1936 National on *Reynoldstown* and had turned out the 1964 winner, *Team Spirit*.

In 2002, following the Queen Mother's death, Queen Elizabeth decided to honour her mother's memory and love of the National Hunt by racing her best young jumpers. And when, in February, 2003, *First Love* won a novice chase at Folkestone he became the first horse to win over fences in the sovereign's colours since *Ambush II*'s success in the 1900 Grand National.

Though so many years have passed without a royal Grand National runner, members of the royal family still take an interest in the race. The Queen herself is known to like a flutter, and at least once she has organised a National sweepstake for her family and staff at Windsor Castle. In 1996 this 'sweep' had a £10 stake for each of the 27 runners drawn out of a hat. The Queen reportedly drew *Into The Red* who finished 15th at 33-1. The £270 pot went to Prince Edward who had *Rough Quest*.
See also: Devon Loch; Francis, Dick; Cazalet, Peter; Mildmay, Lord; Walwyn. Fulke.

ROYAL TAN

Winner by a neck of the 1954 Grand National, so giving a second successive victory for all parties concerned: trainer Vincent O'Brien, jockey Bryan Marshall and owner Mr Joe Griffin. An outstanding Aintree specialist, the chestnut gelding ran in six Nationals, finishing first, second, third and 12th, and lying third at the last when (in 1952) he had his only fall in the race.

Bred in Tipperary – by *Tartan* out of *Princess of Birds* – *Royal Tan* was sent by his second owner, Mrs M.H. Keogh, to Cashel-based Mr O'Brien who, within only eight years of taking out a training licence, had saddled *Cottage Rake* to win three successive Cheltenham Gold Cups and *Hatton's Grace* to win three successive Champion Hurdles. Again the Irish wizard worked wonders, getting the blaze-faced, chestnut gelding proficient enough to finish – with only a 12-day interval – second in both the Irish and Aintree Grand Nationals as a seven year old.

On that Aintree debut in 1951, *Royal Tan* was actually in the lead when he approached the final fence; and, after the chaos largely due to an undeclared false start, he had only to hold off the challenge of the mare *Nickel Coin* to win. But then,

R

urged on by an over-eager amateur jockey (the trainer's youngest brother Alphonsus 'Phonsie' O'Brien, also in his first Aintree Grand National), the young gelding blundered badly at the last. His rider lost control long enough for the plodding *Nickel Coin* to take the lead and, with a 12lb advantage, hold on to win by six lengths, with the re-mounted *Derrinstown* a distant third and last.

Raised 7lb in the weights, *Royal Tan* returned to Aintree in 1952 with a new owner, Mr Griffin, a young Dublin businessman who had prospered in the post-war canning trade. But he did not have a new rider, and once again under 'Phonsie' he blundered at the last. This time, when lying third and closing fast on *Teal* and *Legal Joy,* he crashed to the ground.

Injury kept *Royal Tan* out of the 1953 National which was won comfortably by his stablemate *Early Mist*, ridden by professional Bryan Marshall. The following year, after *Early Mist* had broken down, Marshall was invited over to Ireland to ride *Royal Tan* in a pre-Aintree gallop over fences with Mrs Vincent O'Brien's *Churchtown*. That day, heeding advice from 'Phonsie' who had learned from his mistakes, he found that the chestnut – quite unlike *Early Mist* – jumped best when left to take off at his own discretion.

There were only 29 starters in the 1954 National, the smallest field for 19 years. Nevertheless, confusion reigned at the first where *Royal Tan*, the 8-1 joint second favourite, was almost brought down by *Alberoni*, one of three fallers. Three more went at the second, and by Becher's only 20 runners remained. Two fences later, at the Canal Turn, *Royal Tan* was last but one in the field, and he only began to make significant progress when they approached Becher's the second time around.

At Valentine's *Royal Tan* jumped into a narrow lead from *Tudor Line* and *Churchtown*; and from two fences out, after the latter had broken a blood vessel, it became a two-horse race. Though *Tudor Line*, with a full stone advantage, led at the second last, tiredness caused him to jump to the right. It cost him crucial ground there, and again at the last where, given his head, *Royal Tan* for once sailed over cleanly and into a three lengths lead. Remarkably, *Tudor Line* now rallied under the forceful riding of George Slack, gaining ground with every stride. But it was just too late. In the closest finish for 16 years *Royal Tan* prevailed by a neck, with

Irish Lizard, the favourite, ten lengths back in third, and *Churchtown* fourth.

It was *Royal Tan*'s first win for more than two years, and when he came back for a fourth National in 1955 he was not fancied for a repeat success, having been raised 11lb to a top weight of 12st 4lb. Indeed, he was 11th in the betting at 28-1. In contrast, *Early Mist*, only 1lb lighter, was the 9-1 second favourite.

Financial difficulties had compelled Mr Griffin to sell both of his Grand National winners – *Royal Tan* to Prince Aly Khan and *Early Mist* to Mr John Dunlop. Both, however, were still trained by Vincent O'Brien who was four-handed in the race, his other runners being *Quare Times* and *Oriental Way*. For his hat-trick bid, Bryan Marshall reverted to *Early Mist*, with Dave Dick taking over on *Royal Tan*.

On heavy ground – so waterlogged that the Water Jump was eliminated – weight told decisively against *Early Mist* and *Royal Tan*. They finished ninth and 12th respectively, while *Quare Times*, on 11st, stormed home under Pat Taaffe to win by 12 lengths, with *Tudor Line* again the runner-up.

The 1956 National will always be remembered as the year of the great loser, the race being handed to Dave Dick on *E.S.B.* after the mysterious collapse of the Queen Mother's *Devon Loch*. Nonetheless, *Royal Tan*, though well-beaten, merits a special mention. As a 12 year old, giving weight to all except *Early Mist* (a faller), he made up many lengths from the Anchor Bridge to pass *Eagle's Lodge* and take third place. Then, in 1957, in his sixth and final Grand National, he was unluckily carried out by a loose horse.

See also: O'Brien, Vincent; Marshall, Bryan.

RUBIO

The romance of the Grand National was supremely exemplified by the victory of ten year old *Rubio* in 1908. He was the first American-bred winner. At Newmarket yearling sales he had been bought for a mere 15 guineas. After breaking down, early in his racing career, he had been put between shafts and used to pull a hotel bus. And in the National he went off as a 66-1 rank outsider.

Rubio – by *Star Ruby* out of *La Toquera* – began his chequered life in Sacramento, California: at the Rancho del Paso Stud operated by the American millionaire, James Ben Ali Haggin. However, his sire – bought for 1,000 guineas by Mr Haggin – was

Cheshire-bred, a half-brother to the immortal *Sceptre*, winner of four of the five English Classics in 1902.

In 1899, Haggin took a huge – and financially un-rewarding – gamble; he sent 87 yearlings to the Newmarket sales. Few of them fetched a decent price and among those cheaply sold was *Rubio*, bought for 15 guineas by Septimus Clarke, a Northamptonshire farmer and dealer. Subsequently, as a four year old, *Rubio* was sold for 95 guineas to Major Frank Douglas-Pennant of Whittlebury, Northants.

One year later, at Leicester Repository sales, *Rubio* failed to reach his reserve of 60 guineas. But he had shown unusual pace as a hunter, and so Dou-glas-Pennant sent him to be trained by Bernard Blet-soe, owner of 1901 National winner *Grudon*. A hat-trick of minor race wins soon followed.

At that stage, *Rubio* broke down badly, and, on the recommendation of a vet, he was lent to the pro-prietor of a hotel (now called the Saracens Head) at Towcester. The idea was to strengthen the horse by having him pull the hotel bus which transported guests to and from the local railway station. He per-formed this task every day for two months, then started to work out with his owner's hunters.

By late 1906 *Rubio* was back in training, and the following year he raced with mixed fortunes, falling at Gatwick but finishing runner-up at Hurst Park and, most significantly, winning well at Towcester when carrying 12st. On being entered for the 1908 National he was allotted only 10st 5lb.

Rubio was now being trained at Stockbridge in Hampshire by Mr Fred Withington, and it was planned that stable jockey William Bissill should take the ride in the National. But the stable had a more fancied National contender, *Mattie Macgregor*, and when Ernie Piggott became unavailable as her rider, Bissill was given a choice of rides. After a four-mile trial gallop involving the pair Bissill opted for the six year old mare.

That day Withington remarked to a friend, 'Bissill has chosen the wrong horse.'

He was right, and the jockey who profited from the error was the relatively inexperienced Henry Bryan Bletsoe, son of *Rubio*'s former trainer. It was his first ever ride in the National.

There was no betting interest in the American-bred *Rubio*, nor in two other horses, *Chorus* and *Prophet III*, which, though English-bred, were

American-owned – by Mr Foxhall Keene, a major pioneer of steeplechasing in the United States. All three went off at 66-1, the favourite being 12 year old *Kirkland*, the 1905 winner, who was returning after a three-year absence with a top weight of 11st 12lb.

Though the weather was fine and warm, the going was heavy and none of the 24 starters moved on it more confidently than *Rubio*. He hit the first fence hard, but otherwise was never in trouble. He led at the end of the first circuit and by the time they ap-proached the last fence he had only one serious rival – ironically the young *Mattie Macgregor*, a 25-1 chance.

At the last *Rubio* jumped much the stronger and powered away to win by ten lengths from the mare, with *The Lawyer III* six lengths back in third, ahead of King Edward VII's *Flaxman*. *Kirkland* had fallen at the last but was remounted to finish seventh of eight finishers. Meanwhile, Withington had made National history, as the first trainer to provide both winner and runner-up.

Bill Bissill did not repeat his error of judgment in 1909. This time he rode *Rubio* while Bletsoe was on *Young Buck*, a 100-1 rank outsider. But *Rubio* was now 18lb up in the weights; and on good going and in a field of 32 (equalling the record of 1850). Going off at 20-1, he led the way for almost all of the first circuit, then broke down at the Water Jump and fell. The following year *Rubio* was retired from racing. Major Douglas-Pennant would not have another National contender, but decades later, after inheriting the title of Lord Penrhyn, he would set a record of his own – as the first peer to become a centenarian. *See also:* Withington, Fred.

RUBSTIC

Winner of the 1979 Grand National, by one and a half lengths from *Zongalero*, when he was appearing in the race for the first time. He came to Aintree with a most promising record: proven stamina and jump-ing ability, and a record of having never fallen in a race. Yet he went off as one of eight horses priced at 25-1 – relatively unfancied not least because the National had never been won by a horse trained in Scotland.

Sired by *I Say*, who had finished third in the 1965 Epsom Derby, *Rubstic* was out of an unraced mare, *Leuze*, and had cost a mere 500 guineas as a year-ling. Owned by the former British Lions rugby international John Douglas, he was originally trained by Charles Bell at Hawick in Roxburghshire, then sent across the border to the Cumbrian yard of Gordon W. Richards who twice turned him out to win over fences.

Rubstic now returned to Scotland, switched from the burgeoning Richards stable to the relatively small Denholm yard of John Leadbetter in Roxburghshire. His subsequent successes included two wins in the three-and-a-half-mile Durham National Chase at Sedgefield. More significantly, he was also twice runner-up in the Scottish National run over an extended four miles.

Like *Rubstic*, his rider, 28 year old Maurice Barnes, was having his first experience of the Grand National in 1979. However, he had the benefit of guidance from his father, Tommy Barnes, who, on his first and last ride in the race, had finished second on *Wyndburgh* in 1962. Now, also on his debut, he was to go one better. Strongly in contention from Becher's onwards, *Rubstic* was challenging *Zongalero* and *Wagner* for the lead as they approached the Chair, with the favourite and Cheltenham Gold Cup winner *Alverton* close behind.

The leaders steered clear of two riderless horses ahead of them. But the pack hunting behind them was not so fortunate. The loose runners veered across the course at The Chair and in the ensuing chaos nine contenders were put out of the race. As a hugely reduced field entered the second circuit, the race seemed to be at the mercy of Jonjo O'Neill on the lightly handicapped favourite. But then, having looked so full of running, *Alverton* completely misjudged his jump at Becher's and crashed fatally to the ground.

At the last fence, three horses were jointly in the lead: *Rubstic*, *Zongalero*, and *Rough and Tumble* who had made steady progress under John Francome. Briefly *Rough and Tumble* had a fractional advantage but on the long run-in *Rubstic*'s superior stamina prevailed, enabling him to win the hard slog to the finishing post by one and a half lengths. The runner-up, *Zongalero*, was ridden by Bob Davies who had been a half-length winner on *Lucius* the year before. *Rough and Tumble* was five lengths back in third, narrowly ahead of *The Pilgarlic*. Only seven of 34 starters completed the course.

For *Zongalero* that close finish completed a most frustrating treble: a runner-up hat-trick, having also been second in the Mackeson Gold Cup and the Massey-Ferguson Gold Cup. He went on to end the season without a single win.

Raised 11lb in the weights, Scotland's first Grand National winner returned in 1980 and, having won his two pre-Aintree races, he was made the 8-1 favourite. He went off smartly at the start and, on heavy going, he was closing on the leader *Delmoss* as he approached The Chair. But there he mistimed his jump and, for the first time in his racing career, crumbled to the ground. When he appeared in the 1981 National as a 12 year old *Rubstic* was still so highly regarded that he was third in the betting at 11-1. He finished seventh in a 39-strong field.

See also: Barnes, Maurice; Leadbetter, John.

RULES OF ENTRY

The Grand National rules of entry have been greatly modified over the years, primarily for the purpose of raising the quality of contenders and achieving a greater degree of safety. Today the race is restricted to horses above the age of five and with a BHA rating of at least 110. A horse not qualified for a rating in Great Britain or Ireland may also be eligible at the handicapper's discretion provided that he is satisfied that the horse would merit a minimum rating of 110 and that the horse has run at least three times in chases run under Rules.

In recent years – primarily in response to criticism following three fatalities in the 1998 National – further safety precautions have been introduced. The participation of all the declared runners is now subject to their passing a pre-race veterinary inspection. Furthermore, it has become mandatory for all horses who have not run at least six times over fences in Britain to be discussed by the Jockey Club's Entry Review Panel.

Indeed, after the second forfeit stage in March, the panel can recommend voiding the entry of any horse considered unsuitably equipped for the perils of the National. In 2006 this five-man panel, seeking to ensure the welfare of horses and riders, was chaired by Chris Collins who rode 50-1 shot *Mr Jones* into third place in the 1965 National.

Though the rules of entry are regarded as excellent in principle, they have incurred some criticism in practice – most especially in 2002 when a record entry of 144 produced no fewer than 16 horses that had not run six times over fences in Britain. These included a six year old handicap hurdler, Martin Pipe's *Majed*, who had never raced over fences in

Britain and was still a novice despite seven attempts at Auteuil as a four year old trained in France. Yet, controversially, the weights allotted allowed *Majed* and several other lesser lights to get into the race while winners of such prestigious races as the Tote Becher Chase, the Grand Yorkshire Chase and the Foxhunters' Chase were excluded.

Overall, however, the entry rules have achieved their aim of far greater safety; and the same applies to rules governing the eligibility of jockeys. From 1990 onwards they not only had to pass a medical examination before being allowed to ride but also they should have ridden 'not less than 15 winners in steeplechases or hurdles'. This threshold was introduced after the 1989 National in which the 300-1 outsider *Brown Trix*, ridden by a 52 year old amateur, had suffered an especially distressing end – slithering helplessly into the ditch after falling at Becher's Brook.

Until 2002, it was possible to apply for special dispensation from the 15-winner rule. Thus, without the qualification, amateur Joe Tizzard was granted permission to ride *Straight Talk* in 1997. But thereafter the rule was strictly applied. In 2003, Martin Pipe approached the Jockey Club in vain when seeking special permission to use his 18 year old amateur Jamie Moore who, in the week before the National, had a career total of ten winners. The request was declined. However, in this instance, aided by the all-powerful resources of the Pipe stable, the jockey was able to ride two trebles to qualify with four days to spare! At Aintree he finished 13th on *Royal Predica*.

Less fortunate, in 2004, was Old Etonian Tom Greenall, 19 year old son of Aintree chairman Lord Daresbury. He was denied a National ride when, under the misapprehension that bumper winners counted, he fell two short of the 15 winners minimum. However, he qualified the following year to ride long-shot *Glenelly Gale*, and led the field for much of the first circuit, finally pulling up before three out.

In 2006 amateur Sam Waley-Cohen, 23, had high hopes of riding the Nicky Henderson-trained *Liberthine* in the National. After all, a year earlier, he had completed one circuit of the course on that mare in the Topham Chase. He had ridden her to victory over professionals in the 2005 Mildmay of Flete Chase at the Cheltenham Festival; and he had won Aintree's 2005 Fox Hunters on *Katarino*. But, to his dismay, he learned that no exceptions were to be made under the 15-winner rule. He had ridden only six winners under Rules.

The rigidity of this ruling was seriously brought into question as – immediately prior to the big race – Sam proceeded to win twice over the National fences in two days, hosing up on *Katarino* in the 30-runner Foxhunters' and the next day winning the 29-runner Topham Chase on *Liberthine*. Thus, in the autumn of 2006, the rule was slightly relaxed; the Licensing Committee would consider on an individual basis applicants who had ridden ten or more winners over fences.

Consequently, in March, 2007, Waley-Cohen was granted special permission to ride in the National since by now he had taken his record under Rules to 13 wins over fences. It was on his 25th birthday that he set out on the 40-1 shot *Liberthine*; and he enjoyed an unforgettable ride, prominent from the first Becher's and being left in front when coming to it second time around. The only mare in the race finally weakened from two out, but nonetheless finished a most creditable fifth.

See also: Ratings; Handicapping; Entries.

RUNNERS-UP

Of all Grand National runners-up the highest rated must be ten year old *Crisp*, beaten three-quarters of a length by *Red Rum* in 1973 when conceding 23lb to the winner, with both first and second breaking the course record.

Other outstanding runners-up include: *Congress*, a neck second to *Regal* in 1876 and one year later four lengths runner-up to *Austerlitz* (receiving 27lb); *Wyndburgh*, one and a half lengths second to *Oxo* in 1959 when, from the second Becher's, Tim Brookshaw was riding with a broken stirrup iron; *Freddie*, down by three-quarters of a length to *Jay Trump* in 1965, and second again the following year to *Anglo* (receiving 21lb), both races having a 47-strong field; *Greasepaint*, three-quarters of a length second in 1983 to *Corbiere* (receiving 11lb) and four lengths second in 1984 to *Hallo Dandy* (receiving 14lb); *Durham Edition*, beaten three-quarters of a length by *Mr Frisk* (1990), with *Rinus* 20 lengths back in third, in the fastest-ever Grand National; *What's Up Boys* (2002), beaten one and three-quarters of a length when giving 16lb to winner *Bindaree*, with another 27 lengths back to third-placed favourite *Blowing Wind*.

R

The record for being runner-up in the National is three times, jointly held by *Frigate* (1884, 1885 and 1888) and *Wyndburgh* (1957, 1959 and 1962). The latter is the only horse to be runner-up three times without ever winning the race.

Sixteen horses have twice finished runner-up: *Seventy Four* (1839, 1842); *The Knight Of Gwynne* (1849, 1850); *Weathercock* (1857, 1858); *Arbury* (1863, 1864); *Hall Court* (1865, 1869); *Congress*, 1876, 1877); *Cloister* (1891, 1892); *Cathal* (1895, 1898); *Old Tay Bridge* (1925, 1926); *MacMoffat* (1939, 1940); *Tudor Line* (1954, 1 955); *Freddie* (1965, 1966); *Red Rum* (1975, 1976); *Greasepaint* (1983. 1984); *Durham Edition* (1988, 1990); and *Suny Bay* (1997, 1998).

Closest runners-up

Hall Court (1865), a head to *Alcibiade*
Cyrus (1882), a head to *Seaman*
Royal Danieli (1938), a head to *Battleship*.
Jean De Quesne (1859), a short neck to *Half Caste*
The Doctor (1870), a neck to *The Colonel*
Congress (1876), a neck to *Regal*.
Melleray's Belle (1930), a neck to *Shaun Goilin* (conceding 21lb)
Tudor Line (1954), a neck to *Royal Tan* (conceding 14lb)
Black Secret (1971), a neck to *Specify*

Most remote runners-up

Aesop (1893) by 40 lengths to *Cloister* (conceding 31lb)
The Bore (1921), a distance (remounted) to *Shaun Spadah*
Billy Barton (1928), a distance (remounted) to *Tipperary Tim*. Two finished
Irish Mail (1913), a distance to *Covertail*. Three finished
Tiberetta (1958), 30 lengths to *Mr What*
Smarty (2001), a distance to *Red Marauder*. Four finished, two remounted

Runners-up carrying the biggest weight of 12st 7lb

Congress (1877), 11 years old. Beaten four lengths by five year old *Austerlitz* (receiving 27lb)
The Liberator (1880), 11 years old. Beaten two lengths by five year old *Empress* (receiving two stone)

Jerry M (1910) 7 years old. Beaten three lengths by nine year old *Jenkinstown* (receiving 30lb)
Shaun Spadah (1923), 12 years old. Beaten three lengths by 13 year old *Sergeant Murphy* (receiving 18lb)
Easter Hero (1929), nine years old. Beaten six lengths by seven year old *Gregalach* (receiving 17lb) with a record field of 66 runners

Runner-up with the lowest weight

Maurice Daley (1852) with 9st 6lb (including 2lb overweight). Beaten one length by *Miss Mowbray* (conceding 12lb)

Jockeys who have ridden the most runners-up (three)

Tom Olliver – *Seventy Four* (1839), St Leger (1847), *The Curate* (1848)
Harry Beasley – *Frigate* (1884 and 1885), *Too Good* (1886)
Jack Moloney – *Easter Hero* (1929), *Gregalach* (1931), *Delaneige* (1934)
George Slack – *Tudor Line* (1954 and 1955), *Tiberetta* (1958)
Chris Grant – *Young Driver* (1986), *Durham Edition* (1988 and 1990)

RUSSIA

In 1956, an unusual Grand National guest of Aintree supremo Mrs Miriam Topham was the former Russian Premier, Georgi Malenkov. Possibly, on his return home, he was responsible for arousing interest in the race. In any event, in 1961 a small thaw in the Cold War was signalled by the surprising news that Russia – or, to be precise, the then Soviet Union – had for the first time entered horses for the National. There were to be three challengers: *Epigraf II*, *Reljef* and *Grifel*. Unfortunately, however, they had no experience of jumping fences as formidable as those at Aintree; and they had never raced in Britain. Therefore, the handicapper, without any yardstick for assessment, automatically lumbered them with top weight of 12st.

Following this news, journalist-amateur jockey John Lawrence (later Lord Oaksey) was sent to Moscow to interview the Red Army riders, including the Russian champion, Vladimir Prakhov. Three weeks later they met again – in Becher's Brook. Both had been dumped there in a five-horse pile-up.

Lawrence's mount, *Taxidermist*, duly galloped on alone, but *Grifel*, a well-disciplined Ukranian horse, most correctly stood by his fallen rider. 'Nyet, nyet', shouted the experienced Lawrence. But Prakhov chose to ignore him. Aided and urged on by a Russian team official who had invaded the course, he remounted and set off in vain pursuit of the field, finally pulling up with one circuit completed.

Since the unfit *Epigraf II* had been a late withdrawal, there was only one other Russian runner, the ungainly looking seven year old *Reljef*. He unseated his rider, Boris Ponomarenko, at Valentine's first time round. It was a gallant bid on the part of the Russians but one unlikely ever to be repeated – at least not without preliminary races to guide the handicapper. As it was, they were hopelessly outclassed, and absurdly giving almost two full stone to the winner, *Nicolaus Silver*.

RUSSIAN HERO

Shock 66-1 winner of the 1949 Grand National, by eight lengths from Lord Bicester's top-weighted *Roimond*. It was the nine year old gelding's first run in the race. He had failed (falling twice) in his last three races; and on three subsequent Aintree appearances he would fail to get round the course. Indeed, after his one great triumph, he never won a race again – anywhere.

Russian Hero – by *Peter The Great* out of *Logique* – was bred, reared and owned by Mr Fernie Williamson, a tenant farmer of the Duke of Westminster. He was sent to be trained at Malpas in Cheshire by George Owen, an ex-jockey who had ridden in eight Grand Nationals, with a best fourth place on *Lady Boots* in 1935. And he went to his first National – only at the owner's insistence – with a reputation for being an unreliable jumper and lacking in stamina.

There were 43 starters, with more than half of them – including the 1947 winner *Caughoo* – going off as 66-1 outsiders. The 6-1 favourite was eight year old *Cromwell*, seen as an unlucky loser the previous year when he finished third after his owner-rider Lord Mildmay had been seized with crippling cramp in his neck. Miss Dorothy Paget's

Happy Home, fourth in 1948, was second in the betting.

Though many fell on the first circuit, at least a dozen horses were still in contention when they came to Becher's second time around. They were headed by *Royal Mount*, closely followed by *Roimond*, the first National ride for Dick Francis. All the while *Russian Hero* was making relentless progress, and when *Royal Mount* began to tire after Valentine's the outsider joined battle with *Roimond*, taking a clear lead at the last and then, with an 18lb advantage, outpacing him over the run-in. *Royal Mount* was nine lengths back in third, with *Cromwell* fourth.

It was a huge coup for owner Williamson who had placed £10 on his horse at ante-post odds of 300-1; a brilliantly judged ride by the winner's Irish jockey, Leo McMorrow; and an extraordinary reversal of form on the part of a gelding who had never before shown such sure-footed jumping or an ability to last out more than three miles.

Though regularly partnered by McMorrow, *Russian Hero* never raced so smartly again. In the 1950 National, with an extra 10lb to carry, he fell at the first when contending for the lead. In 1951 he did well to avoid the chaos at the first two fences and was leading at the 14th, only to be brought down at The Chair in a race which saw only three finishers. In 1952, his last National, he was a 50-1 chance and one of ten horses to fall at the first.

See also: Owen, George; McMorrow, Michael Leo Aloysius; Francis, Richard; Gambles.

RUTTLE, Jack

Trainer (at Celbridge, Co. Dublin), of nine year old *Workman*, who in 1939 became the first Irish-bred and -trained horse to win the Grand National since *Troytown* (1920). One year before *Workman* had finished third in his first National under jockey Jim Brogan. On Ruttle's initiative, Tim Hyde, a jockey more renowned for his exploits in the show-jumping ring, was persuaded to take over the ride for his reappearance at Aintree. With a perfectly timed challenge, Hyde brought *Workman* home to win by three lengths from the great Scottish hope, *MacMoffat*. *See also:* Workman.

S

SALAMANDER

During his lifetime, Mr Edward Studd, a wealthy retired indigo planter, was always to be remembered as the man who rejected the Grand National's greatest grey (*The Lamb*) as 'not strong enough to carry a man's boots'. Yet, curiously, that same gentleman had earlier proved himself to be a remarkably shrewd judge of equine potential – by buying *Salamander*, a much-despised gelding who had originally been sold as a three year old for a mere £35.

Salamander – by *Fire-eater* out of *Rosalba* – had been bred by Mr J. Bourchier of Bagotstown, Bruff, Co. Limerick. He let the horse go for a song because he had a slightly crooked leg; and, in turn, the new owner, horse-dealer John Hartigan of Limerick, sold the gelding as part of a £450 three-horse 'job lot'. Mr Studd trusted in his own judgement in buying horses, and this time on his scouting mission he had picked out one of the greatest bargains in Grand National history.

By 1866, *Salamander* had developed at his Rutland base into a strikingly handsome seven year old, with his early deformity no longer in obvious evidence. Moreover, he had revealed blistering form on the gallops – a fact that Mr Studd, as owner and trainer, took pains not to advertise. For his National entry, he booked 45 year old Mr Alec Goodman, the brilliant amateur who, in 1852, had made a winning National debut on the outsider *Miss Mowbray*. But he did not allow the jockey to try out the horse before going to Aintree; and on the day of the race he backed his unfancied runner to win £40,000.

On this, his one and only appearance in the National, *Salamander* went off as a 40-1 outsider, largely because he was up against the great French jumper, *L'Africaine*, who earlier in the season had given him a stone and a 40 lengths beating at Warwick. This time, however, *L'Africaine*, on a colossal 13st 2lb, was giving him 37lb.

Following a heavy snowstorm, it was to be a race of many fallers – primarily as the result of a second fence pile-up. *L'Africaine* was one of many eliminated there; and on the second circuit, *Alcibiade* and *Hall Court*, last year's first and second, fell at Valentine's and Becher's respectively. But it made no difference to the outcome. *Salamander* was now producing a devastating turn of foot, pulling away from the others with consummate ease to win comfortably by ten lengths from Lord Poulett's *Cortolvin*. Only three more of the 30 starters completed the course.

Salamander's superiority was so marked that some sore losers, hearing that Mr Studd had laid a big stake on his horse, suggested that – to lengthen his odds – the gelding had been deliberately given his head in running down the racecourse before the start. Certainly the huge crowd, estimated at 30,000, did not give the winner the ovation that he so richly deserved. But if there were any doubts about his true merits these were dispelled one week later when he won the Warwick Grand Annual Chase at a canter.

Salamander now seemed destined to become one of the all-time greats of jump racing. But then came tragedy. He was running away with a minor race at Crewkerne in Somerset when he stumbled over a relatively small fence, broke his back and had to be destroyed. The following year the National was won by the horse he had beaten so easily – *Cortolvin*, now owned by the Duke of Hamilton. Lord Poulett, who had rashly sold him, gained quick consolation with the success of *The Lamb* in 1868, and again in 1871. Interestingly, nearly 30 years later, Mr Joseph Osborne, the doyen of racing correspondents, and the owner-trainer of *Abd-El-Kader*, the first winner of successive Nationals (1850-51), wrote that, in his view, *Salamander* was arguably the best horse ever to have won the National.

See also: Goodman, Alec.

SANFORD, Stephen

Stephen (Laddie') Sanford became the first American owner of a Grand National winner in 1923 when 13 year old *Sergeant Murphy* triumphed by four lengths over Sir Malcom McAlpine's past winner *Shaun Spadah*, a 12 year old conceding 18lb to the winner. His success set off a veritable avalanche of National challengers owned by wealthy Americans and he himself sent out no fewer than 14 runners between 1922 and 1931.

While *Sergeant Murphy* was the last of his advanced age to win the National, Sanford was a young Cambridge undergraduate who had been gifted the chestnut gelding by his father, carpet tycoon John Sanford. Bought for £1,200 from bookmaker Martin Benson, the gift-horse was intended to serve him for hunting with the Leicesterhire packs. But *Sergeant Murphy*, who had finished sixth and fourth in the Nationals of 1919 and 1920 respectively, proved too much of a handful for his new owner and was therefore returned to training at Newmarket by George Blackwell.

At the 1922 National, young Sanford saw his 12 year old fall at the Canal Turn first time round and then, on being remounted, storm back to be the fourth of five finishers. One year later he found himself being presented as the winning owner to King George V. The polo-playing American had truly caught the National 'bug'.

Supported by his millionaire father, he proceeded to buy more strong challengers, starting with *Drifter* who had been runner-up and then fifth in the Nationals of 1922 and 1923. But a second success eluded him. In 1924 *Drifter* finished fourth at 40-1, one place ahead of *Sergeant Murphy*; and the following year they were ninth and tenth respectively. Then, in 1926, the American was represented by the well-backed *Mount Etna* (a faller) and by *Bright's Boy* who came third, just four lengths off the winning *Jack Horner*.

Sandford's hopes were highest in 1927 when Jack Anthony took the lead on *Bright's Boy* at the final open ditch. But his eight year old, on a top weight of 12st 7lb, was marginally outpaced on the run to the last fence and again came home third, this time only two lengths behind the winning favourite, *Sprig*. His other runner, 66-1 shot *Marsin*, was a faller. In 1928 – the year when only two of 42 starters completed the course – *Bright's Boy* again carried top weight and he fell at the seventh fence, just before the field was decimated by a pile-up at the Canal Turn.

The American had four more runners in the National: *Mount Etna* and *Bright's Boy* in 1929, and *Sandy Hook* in 1930 and 1931. All failed to complete the course.

See also: Sergeant Murphy; Americans; United States.

SASSOON, Captain Reginald Ellice

Riding in five successive Grand Nationals (1927-31), Reginald Sassoon only once completed the course – his best result coming at his first attempt when, on eight year old *Ballystockart*, a 100-1 shot, he was the seventh of seven finishers in a field of 37.

Nevertheless, he merits special mention – as one of the most courageous of all amateurs to compete at Aintree.

A member of the great banking and merchant firm of Sassoon, Reggie first proved his courage in the trenches of the First World War. Despite seriously defective eyesight, he succeeded in joining the Irish Guards in 1914. One year later, he could have

settled for light duties after being wounded at Loos. Instead, he returned as soon as possible to his regiment and for his heroism in action he was awarded the Military Cross.

Horse riding was then the main recreation of Guards officers, and after the war Sassoon saw steeplechasing as an irresistible challenge. He was not a natural horseman and he needed to wear spectacles when he took up the sport. Yet every winter, as a businessman based in India, and later in China, he would return to England to compete under National Hunt rules.

At one point he had five bad falls in six weeks; in turn, he suffered concussion, head injuries, bruised ribs and finally a dislocated shoulder. Friends urged him to quit before he killed himself. But nothing could discourage him. He truly loved the sport, and in 1925, at Fontwell Park, he at last rode a winner.

Sassoon was now building up a string of horses with Percy Woodland at Cholderton in Wiltshire, and after further successes he set his sights on the National. Three times he rode in the race on his *Ballystockart*, failing to finish on his second and third appearances. Then, in 1930, he was a faller on the promising *Newsboy* which he had bought for 3,000 guineas.

His last National ride was in 1931 on six year old *Pixie*, a 100-1 outsider. It ended with a refusal. But later that year Reggie at last had an Aintree success, winning the Valentine Chase on *West Indies*. The mare, which he had bought for £5,000, was a brilliant young chaser; and though many regarded her as too speedy and headstrong to cope with the National fences, the captain resolved to run her in the great race in 1932. But two months before the National, *West Indies* – with another rider – fell and broke her back in a Newbury race.

That same year Sassoon's devotion to steeplechasing was recognised by his election to membership of the National Hunt Committee. But he never lived to serve on the sport's governing body. At Lingfield, his favourite horse, *Clear Note*, fell heavily and rolled over his rider. The brave captain died five days later from multiple injuries. He was 39, a true Corinthian whose courage and passion for 'chasing was infinitely greater than his riding skill.

SAUNDERS, ('Dick') Charles Richard

The oldest winning rider in the history of the Grand National. As though that distinction, achieved at the age of 48, was not enough, the amateur Dick Saunders won on *Grittar* in 1982 by a comfortable 15 lengths and on his first and only appearance in the race. He announced his retirement from the saddle immediately after his spectacular National debut, but he went on to play a major role in racing for another two decades.

Ostensibly, it is astonishing that an amateur rider without any previous Grand National experience should have triumphed in a 39-strong field against such notable professionals as John Francome, Peter Scudamore, Jonjo O'Neill, Neale Doughty, Andrew Turnell, Phil Tuck, Ben de Haan, and former winners Bob Champion and Bob Davies. But the bare facts are deceptive. In reality, though he had not ridden before in the race, and had only ever seen it on television, he was very familiar with its fences, having seven times ridden in the Liverpool Fox Hunters' Chase.

Born in 1933 at Harlestone, the son of a Northamptonshire farmer, Dick Saunders progressed as a rider by way of Pony Club events, hunting and point-to-points. His graduation to National Hunt racing was long delayed by his need to concentrate on developing his own farming enterprise, eventually extending to some 3,000 acres. Meanwhile he rode regularly with the Pytchley Hunt and for many years he was hugely successful riding point-to-pointers and hunter chasers for Leicestershire farmer Frank Gilman.

Saunders was 32 when he rode his first winner under National Hunt rules, and three years later, in 1969, he was expecting to make his Grand National debut on *Steel Bridge* on whom he had won a chase at Punchestown. But connections changed their mind about having the horse ridden by a jockey putting up 7lb overweight. Instead, Richard Pitman took the ride and finished second at 50-1.

Saunders first rode *Grittar* in a point-to-point in 1979; and, in 1981, following one of many injuries sustained in riding falls, he was reunited with the horse who had been ridden in the meantime by his daughter Caroline. Almost immediately the partnership clicked. After one unplaced run, they won four successive races including the Foxhunter Chases at both Cheltenham and Liverpool; and, significantly, the latter chase over one circuit of the National course was won by 20 lengths. The following season, in their last outing before the Grand National, Dick brought *Grittar* home a respectable sixth in the Cheltenham Gold Cup.

As a most reliable jumper with proven stamina, *Grittar* was obviously an excellent prospect for the National; and in the circumstances it seemed logical that a leading professional would be engaged for the ride. (An obvious choice would have been champion jockey John Francome who, in February, had ridden *Grittar* into second place in the Whitbread Trial Handicap Chase at Ascot). But Frank Gilman, as owner-trainer, would not hear of it. He had faith in Saunders' fine horsemanship; also no one was more familiar with his nine year old chaser. Remarkably, too, punters were not to be put off by the selection of an elderly amateur. On the day they made *Grittar* the 7-1 clear favourite in a 39-strong field.

Dick duly rode his first National to perfection. He had planned to take the shortest, inside route and to ensure a good pace that would exploit *Grittar*'s stamina. But initially the latter strategy was unnecessary as the perpetual front-runner *Delmoss*, also on the inside, led a mad stampede that saw no fewer than ten horses eliminated at the first fence. Always well to the fore, he tracked the tearaway leader who finally began to fade at the 18th. Then, at the second Becher's, *Grittar* jumped into the lead and was never headed thereafter, drawing steadily away on the long run-in to win by 15 lengths from *Hard Outlook*, a 50-1 chance, with the remounted grey *Loving Words* a distance back in third.

Saunders was only the fourth winning amateur in the National since the Second World War; also the first serving member of the Jockey Club and the first current Master of Foxhounds to have won the race. Furthermore, he was the only amateur in the 20th century to have triumphed on his first and last attempt – a feat previously achieved by just one rider: Lord Manners on *Seaman* in 1882. Having retired from race-riding, he now became more active as a Jockey Club official, busying himself as a steward and later as chairman of the licensing committee. More immediately, however, he worked on behalf of the Jockey Club's public appeal to save the Grand National, joining Lord Oaksey, Fred Winter and campaign organiser Lord Vestey on a fund-seeking trip to the United States.

In 1996, Saunders was one of the officials involved when Mick Fitzgerald survived a stewards' inquiry after finishing first on *Rough Quest* – ironically so because the winner was the first favourite to win the National since *Grittar* in 1982 and was trained by Terry Casey, who had ridden *Grittar* in all his hurdle races when head lad to Frank Gilman. At Aintree, he became chairman of the stewards and a member of the Grand National review panel. In the former capacity, he was responsible for giving the traditional pre-race address, stressing the need to take a steady approach to the first fence and warning that a rider could face disciplinary action if attempting to complete the course on a tired horse who should have been pulled up. He served as chairman of the Burghley Horse Trials, as a show judge and coordinator of the Royal International Horse Show; and still maintained his involvement with hunting and point-to-pointing, and did sterling work as a trustee of the Injured Jockeys' Fund.

Moreover, with his valuable support, daughter Caroline, as Mrs Bailey, became a leading trainer of pointers and hunter chasers. She had her own triumphs at Aintree, most notably at the 2001 Grand National meeting when she saddled the first and second in the Martell Fox Hunters' Chase. She also had winners of Foxhunters' at Cheltenham, Stratford and Punchestown; and her outstanding hunter chaser, *Gunner Welburn*, became a leading contender for 2003 Grand National after being transferred from her point-to-point yard to Andrew Balding.

Sadly, her father would not live to see that race. In 2002 he died from cancer at his Northamptonshire farm, aged 68.

See also: Grittar; Gilman, Frank.

SCOTLAND

In the 1929 Grand National, when a record 66 contenders took part, the Scottish-owned *Melleray's Belle* finished fourth at 200-1, and one year later the brave mare, now 20-1, was beaten only a neck by *Shaun Goilin*. But it was not until 1979 that Scotland had its one and only National success: *Rubstic*, trained by John Leadbetter at Denholm in Roxburghshire, and ridden by the unsung jockey Maurice Barnes. A winner by one and a half lengths from *Zongalero*, the ten year old gelding had proven stamina and a record of having never fallen in a race. But in the light of previous Scottish failures he started at generous odds of 25-1.

Hopes of a Scottish winner had previously soared in 1939 when Captain L. Scott Briggs' *MacMoffat*, another 25-1 chance, put in a tremendously strong finish to take second place, three lengths behind *Workman*. The gelding was only seven years old and was well backed to go one better in 1940. That year,

carrying an extra 7lb, he looked all over the winner at the second last where the fall of the favourite, *Royal Danieli*, left him with a clear lead. But he was harassed by a loose horse to the last and then beaten for pace on the run-in by *Bogskar*. Having finished runner-up in successive years, *MacMoffat* was now laid up by the suspension of racing for the Second World War. When he finally came back to the National, in 1946, he was 14 years old, well past his best, and a 50-1 faller.

The most deserving of all Scottish challengers first appeared as a seven year old in 1957. *Wyndburgh* was bred, trained and owned by Miss Rhona Wilkinson, soon to become the wife of Hawick trainer Kenneth Oliver. This gallant little gelding ran in six Grand Nationals, achieving the remarkable record of three times runner-up, once fourth, once sixth and once falling. He finished second to *Sundew* on his Aintree debut and two years later was an unlucky loser when, under the handicap of a broken stirrup iron, he was beaten only one and a half lengths by *Oxo*. No less remarkably, he was runner-up on his last appearance as a 12 year old in 1962.

In 1965 Scottish hopes were again sky-high. The outstanding contender was eight year old *Freddie*, bred, owned and trained by Reg Tweedie at his farm in Berwickshire. Having won the 1964 Cheltenham Foxhunters' and his two latest races, he was made the 7-2 favourite for the National. He was allotted the top weight of 11st 10lb in a field of 47.

Once again it was the handicapper who denied a Scottish victory. A 5lb disadvantage proved crucial as *Freddie*, given a masterful ride by Pat McCarron, was beaten just three-quarters of a length by the great American chaser, *Jay Trump*, twice winner of the Maryland Hunt Cup.

Freddie was so impressive in defeat that in 1966 he went off at 11-4, the shortest price favourite since *Golden Miller* started at 2-1 in 1935. Again he finished runner-up in a field of 47 – albeit by 20 lengths. But then he was conceding no less than a stone and a half to the winner, *Anglo*. Incredibly, the handicapper now raised *Freddie* a further 6lb for the 1967 National. This time, as the third favourite, he finished 17th in the race which saw the mass pile-up created by riderless *Popham Down*.

In 1968 Scotland again had a strong contender in 11 year old *Moidore's Token*, trained – like the unlucky *Wyndburgh* – by the Olivers. The bay gelding was the second of 17 finishers but had been

S

beaten a full 20 lengths by *Red Alligator*. The following year he was pulled up on the second circuit. The winner, twelve year old *Highland Wedding*, had been bred at Prestwick, Ayrshire, but he was trained in England and owned by an American and a Canadian.

In 1986 a second Scottish victory briefly seemed possible when *Young Driver*, a 66-1 chance, was leading the National field at the last with only one rival in a challenging position. An ex-Irish chaser, *Young Driver* was a first National runner for Scottish trainer John Wilson and favourably weighted in the light of his recent head second to *Hallo Dandy* at Ayr. Now, ridden by Chris Grant, he again found one too good for him as Richard Dunwoody produced *West Tip* with a perfectly timed challenge to win by two lengths, with third placed *Classified* a further 20 lengths back in third. At the age of nine *Young Driver* had reached the peak of his career. Subsequently he faded into obscurity, only to be brought back to the National in 1990 with a new owner and trainer. He was now 13 years old and, not over-generously priced at 150-1, he was pulled up at the eighth.

In 1999 Scotland produced a surprising runner-up in the National: the consistent but lowly rated *Blue Charm*, a 25-1 chance trained in Cupar, Fife, by Sue Bradburne and named after a salmon fly used by local fishermen on the River Tay. He was 16lb out of the handicap proper but he had twice won around Aintree's Mildmay course and now, under veteran Lorcan Wyer, replacing the trainer's injured son Mark, he led over the final fence only to be outpaced on the flat by *Bobbyjo*, the ten lengths winner.

Subsequently, the biggest hope of a Scottish-trained winner came in 2005 when *Strong Resolve* was a hugely fancied contender, backed down to 9-1. But this striking grey, trained by Lucinda Russell near Kinross, weakened after the first circuit and came home the 17th of 21 finishers. Since only two per cent of British racehorses are trained in Scotland, the prospects of a second National winner coming from north of the border remain fairly remote.
See also: Rubstic; Leadbetter, John; Barnes, Maurice; Wyndburgh; Oliver, James Kenneth; Unlucky Losers; Runners-Up.

SCOTT, Gerald

Under restrictions imposed by present-day medical surveillance, Gerry Scott would almost certainly not have enjoyed a winning ride in the 1960 Grand National. But they were not so rigid then and the 22 year old, northern-based jockey was determined to compete in the toughest steeplechase despite having broken his collarbone in two places only twelve days before the race. His mount, after all, was the 13-2 clear favourite: *Merryman II*, on whom he had won the 1959 Scottish National by twelve lengths.

While trainer Neville Crump had a replacement jockey standing by, Scott had himself strapped up from neck to waist and duly declared that he was fit to ride. He had, in fact, been examined by a panel of three doctors. But he never showed his agony as they manipulated his shoulder and arm, and gained permission to ride by two votes with one against. Then, still making light of his physical handicap, he gave *Merryman II* a copybook ride, taking the lead at the final ditch and steadily pulling away to win by 15 lengths. It was only his second experience of the National. And his victory was the last one achieved before the fences were modified.

Born on January 5, 1938 at Saltburn, when it was still in Yorkshire, Scott grew up in the dales where his parents ran riding schools and were involved with point-to-points and show-jumping. He was only 16 when, in 1954, he left Barnard Castle School to become an apprentice jockey to the renowned Neville Crump. Two years later he rode his first winner, gradually maturing as a rider, aided in no small part by advice from stable jockeys Johnny East and Arthur Thompson of dual Grand National-winning fame; and, above all, by the encouragement of a boss who was his greatest hero.

Scott's introduction to the Grand National came in 1959 when he picked up a spare ride on *Surprise Packet*, a 100-1 outsider. Remarkably they made the running from the start, held the lead as far as Becher's where they were briefly joined by *Tibretta*, then stayed in front again until, arriving at Becher's the second time round, they came to grief in a four-horse pile-up that left *Oxo* and *Wyndburgh* to fight out the finish. Then followed his famous partnership with *Merryman II*. He rode the tough bay gelding just three times – and won three times. They took the 1959 Scottish National and the following year the Aintree National (the first to be televised) and a prestigious chase at Wetherby on Boxing Day.

Ironically, Gerry's greatest day in racing was followed two days later by his worst. On the Monday after winning the National he was paired with four favourites at Worcester. Two were pulled up, the next fell, and he was not fit to ride the last one which duly won with David Nicholson deputising. It was just one of many instances of injury interrupting his career. Most disappointingly, in 1961, injury forced him to give way to the experienced Derek Ancil and so lose a serious chance of winning successive Grand Nationals. With an extra stone to carry, and conceding 25lb to the winner, *Merryman II* finished five lengths second to *Nicolaus Silver*.

In 1962, with typical fortitude, Scott rode *Springbok* in the Hennessy Cognac Gold Cup with a broken wrist encased in plaster – and he still managed to win in a photo-finish with stablemate *Rough Tweed* (David Nicholson). But that year he was again too badly injured to ride in the National. This time, under Dave Dick, *Merryman II* finished 13th while the well-fancied *Springbok* fell at the first fence. But in 1963, when *Springbok* was the 10-1 favourite, Gerry took the ride and finished fifth in a 47-strong field. The following year they came home in sixth place.

Scott next appeared in 1966, on the well-supported, eight year old *Forest Prince*. They were leading as the field approached the second last, but then began to fade and finished third, 25 lengths and five behind *Anglo* and *Freddie* respectively. Two years later, in his sixth and final National, Gerry pulled up after the 25th on the 50-1 shot, *Phemius*.

During his career, which brought him some 200 winners, the courageous, unassuming Scott was plagued by injuries – among them, eleven fractures of bones in his legs, a dislocated hip, a broken collarbone ten times. He had nine screws inserted in his lower limbs. Yet it was a freak, skull-cracking fall from a horse on the road at Middleham – not the racecourse – that finally ended his career in 1971 after 18 years with the great Captain Crump. He was in a coma for ten days with a severe haemorrhage; and this time the doctors were adamant that he could never ride again.

Scott's accident had occurred when his horse reared over backwards on being suddenly confronted with a bread van coming round a corner. Philosophically he later recalled that at least some good came out his fall just two days later. 'Thanks to Lord Cadogan, an owner of ours, the Jockey Club made it compulsory for lads to wear skull-caps when riding out'.

It did not end his involvement with the greatest steeplechase. From 1973 onwards he served as an official race starter. He assisted Keith Brown who had the misfortune of starring in the fiasco of the 1993 National; and in 1996, when he was the deputy senior starter and longest-serving starter in Britain, he pressed down the lever which sent up the tapes at Aintree, so making him the only man to have both won and started a Grand National. In 2003, on the eve of his 65th birthday, he was due to officiate at his last meeting at Haydock, where the Farewell to Gerry Mares' Only Flat Race was to be run in his honour. And that was the first year in almost half a century that he was not directly involved in the Grand National.

See also: Merryman II; Crump, Neville.

SCOTTISH NATIONAL HANDICAP CHASE

Held at Ayr every April, the Scottish National is run over four miles one furlong on a left-handed oval circuit – a marathon test of stamina without the so demanding jumps of Aintree. Originally a three-mile chase known as the West of Scotland Grand National, it was first run in 1867 at Bogside in Ayrshire, the birthplace of steeplechasing in Scotland. It was named the Scottish Grand National in 1880, and so remained until 1978 when 'Grand' was dropped from the title. Following the closure of the Bogside course, it was transferred to Ayr in 1966.

In 1922 *Music Hall* became the first Scottish winner to go on to victory – two years later – at Aintree; and the feat was immediately emulated by *Sergeant Murphy* in 1923, the year after his success at Bogside. In reverse, *Kellsboro' Jack* won at Bogside in 1935, two years after winning at Aintree.

In modern times three Scottish Nationals winners – *Merryman II* (1959), *Little Polveir* (1987) and *Earth Summit* (1996) – have achieved Grand National victory one or two years later. And *Sebastian V* failed to do so by only half a length when finishing runner-up to *Lucius* in 1978. But only the great *Red Rum* has pulled off the double in the same year. Just three weeks after his second successive Aintree victory, carrying 12st top weight, the extraordinary 'Rummy' successfully carried 11st 10lb at Ayr, giving 20lb and a four lengths beating to the Lord Oaksey-ridden *Proud Tarquin*.

Conversely, such famed Aintree National winners as *Aldaniti*, *Corbiere*, *West Tip* and *Rubstic* (twice Scottish runner-up) have suffered defeat at Ayr. And the unluckiest of all was Scotland's own *Freddie* – beaten by half a length in the 1964 Scottish National and then by three-quarters of a length in the 1965 Grand National. The winner of that 1964 race, receiving 22lb, was the infamous *Popham Down* who three years later would be responsible for the mass pile-up that resulted in *Foinavon* winning the Grand National at 100-1.

In 1986 the Scottish victory of *Hardy Lad* was the highlight of the 29-year training career of Jumbo Wilkinson who, as a leading northern jump jockey, had ridden in eight Grand Nationals, finishing fourth on *Glorious Twelfth* (1957) and third on *Clear Profit* (1960), and only once failing to complete the course.

In 1999 *Young Kenny*, trained by Peter Beaumont, became the first favourite to win the £70,000 Scottish National since *Red Rum* 25 years before. Carrying top weight of 11st 10lb, he won comfortably; and, as an eight year old who had already claimed the Midlands National and the Greenalls, he was seen as a big hope for the 2000 Grand National. But that year he was lumbered with the top weight of 12st and, well-backed at 14-1, he fell at the tenth.

Meanwhile trainer Ferdy Murphy had long been telling people that he would win the 2000 Scottish National with *Paris Pike*. Sure enough, his eight year old novice fully justified 5-1 joint favouritism, giving a second victory for Adrian Maguire who had previously won on *Baronet* (1998). But when, after missing a season with a leg injury, the well-backed *Paris Pike* finally made it to Aintree in 2002 he was one of nine starters to depart at the first fence.

In 2001 the first three home in the Scotttish National were *Gingembre*, *Ad Hoc* and *Supreme Glory*. Only *Ad Hoc* made it to Aintree in 2002, where he was brought down at the 27th. But all three were in the line-up for the 2003 Grand National. Two failed to finish while *Supreme Glory* came home second to *Monty's Pass* at 40-1. The 7-1 favourite that year was *Shotgun Willy* who had been beaten only half a length by *Take Control* in the 2002 Scottish National. But now, under a big weight of 11st 9lb, he was pulled up at the second Becher's.

The most successful trainer in respect of the Aintree and Scottish Nationals is Neville Crump. He turned out three winners of the former and five of the latter.

See also: Oliver, James Kenneth.

SCUDAMORE, Michael

The winning jockey of the 1959 Grand National (on *Oxo* by one and a half lengths from *Wyndburgh*),

following a second place on *Legal Joy* (1952) and a third place on *Irish Lizard* (1954). Michael Scudamore went on to establish a 20th century record of 16 consecutive National appearances – a run only cut short by a career-ending fall in a minor hurdle race in November, 1966.

Born on July 17, 1932, the son of a Herefordshire farmer and a prominent point-to-point rider, Michael 'Scu' made his public riding debut in the late 1940s when his father, Geoffrey, fetched him off the stand at Hereford to take a spare ride in a hunter chase. At that time you did not need a licence to compete. He began his jump jockey career in 1950, and the following year, while still an amateur, he was one of a distinguished quartet – with Fred Winter, Dave Dick and his great friend Pat Taaffe – who made their Grand National debut. All four would win the race before the decade was out.

In 1951, Scudamore was an unlucky victim of the chaos ensuing from an undeclared false start. On *East A'Calling*, a 50-1 chance, he was brought down at the first fence – one of the 12 fallers there in a race that saw only three of 36 starters finish. In 1952, a 47-strong field met with similar mayhem, ten falling at the first. This time, however, Michael (now a 19 year old professional) kept out of trouble. Coming to the last on Miss Dorothy Paget's *Legal Joy*, he shared the lead with *Teal*, only to be outpaced on the run-in, coming home five lengths second, with Dave Dick on *Wot No Sun* a distant third.

In the 1953 National, Scudamore was on seven year old *Ordnance*, one of many of his rides for trainer Fred Rimell. They blazed the trail from the start, narrowly heading *Early Mist* at Becher's and then opening up a ten length lead. But *Ordnance* blundered and fell at the 20th fence as *Early Mist* renewed his challenge and powered on to win by 20 lengths.

One year later, for the only time in 16 Nationals, Scudamore was on the favourite: Lord Sefton's *Irish Lizard*, who had finished third the previous year. This time he delayed his challenge, moving up fast in the late stages. But there was no catching the leaders on the run-in. Only a neck separated *Royal Tan* and *Tudor Line* at the finish. *Irish Lizard*, ten lengths back, was again third.

In the 1956-57 season, Scudamore was second in the jockeys' championship to Fred Winter. He won the King George V1 Chase on *Rose Park* and the Cheltenham Gold Cup on *Linwell*; and he crowned the year with victory on *Creeola II* in the Welsh National. Yet his fortunes in the Grand National remained hugely disappointing: 11th place on old *Irish Lizard* (1955), falls on *Much Obliged* (1956 and 1957) and on *Valiant Spirit* (1958). Meanwhile his fellow debutants – Messrs Taaffe, Winter and Dick – had scored one win apiece.

Now at last it was his turn. The mount for his ninth National ride was eight year old *Oxo*, an ex-point-to-pointer trained by the remarkably versatile Willie Stephenson who had turned out an Epsom Derby winner (*Arctic Prince*, 1951) and the winner of three consecutive Champion Hurdles (*Sir Ken*, 1952-54). *Oxo* was made the 8-1 second favourite, behind last year's winner *Mr What*.

Moving up through the field on the second circuit, *Oxo* and *Wyndburgh* came to dispute the lead from the second Becher's onwards. Close friends, the two jockeys – Scudamore and Tim Brookshaw – were talking to one another along the way. But now Brookshaw suffered a fatal handicap: his off-side stirrup iron broke and, freeing his foot from the one good iron, he rode on determinedly in great discomfort. Almost certainly it cost him the race. *Oxo* – brilliantly controlled by Scudamore after hitting the last fence hard – held off a brave, late challenge by just one and a half lengths. For the second time in three years *Wyndburgh* was the National runner-up.

One year later it was Scudamore who took the ride on *Wyndburgh*, now the 8-1 second favourite. But the so consistent brown gelding had been raised 9lb to 11st 7lb, and he fell at the first Becher's, thus failing for the first time in four appearances to make the frame. Similarly, when Michael was reunited with *Oxo* in 1961 there was an extra 9lb to carry. The former National winner was pulled up on the second circuit.

Scudamore had five more National rides but none favoured with good fortune. He pulled up at the 26th on *Chavara*, a 50-1 chance, in 1962; finished 19th on 12 year old *O'Malley Point* in 1963. Then came his best chance, on the joint favourite *Time*. At the second Becher's he engineered a truly extraordinary recovery after *Time* had nose-dived on landing, but unluckily the bay was baulked and brought down when still in contention four fences from home.

The following year Scudamore fell on *Bold Biri*, a 100-1 outsider owned, like *Oxo*, by Mr J.E. Bigg. Finally, in 1966, he was up with the leaders and going really well when his mount, *Greek Scholar*,

was one of six horses involved in a pile-up at the second Becher's. In 1967 *Greek Scholar* was to finish fourth in the National – but without the same rider. Five months earlier, after 16 years of riding without breaking a bone in his body, Michael had suffered an horrendous fall when the Rimell-trained hurdler *Snakestone* slipped on a bend at Wolverhampton. He was left with a punctured lung, a broken jaw and cheekbone, a cracked skull and – most seriously – permanently damaged vision in his left eye.

That season he had both trained and ridden horses in Norway; and, one week before his career-ending fall, his last winning ride had been on the Queen Mother's 14 year old *Gay Record*. Now, by necessity, he turned exclusively to training; and at the same time, to great effect, he helped to develop the riding skills of his son, Peter. As a trainer for more than 30 years, his successes have included *Fortina's Palace*, winner of the 1970 Cheltenham Grand Annual Steeplechase, and *Bruslee*, winner of the 1974 Mackeson Gold Cup.

In the 1972 National *Fortina's Palace* was a faller. However, two years later Scudamore was double-handed and while his long-shot *Estoile* was a faller his other runner, 50-1 shot *Charles Dickens*, ridden by Andy Turnell, exceeded all expectation, being beaten only a short neck by *L'Escargot*, the runner-up to *Red Rum*. He then challenged with *Spittin' Image*, a faller in 1975, eighth in 1976, and a faller again in 1977.

In 1992, on behalf of Peter Scudamore Bloodstock Ltd, he had in his charge an unnamed three year old destined, as *Earth Summit*, to win the National in 1998. And that year, remarkably, he rode a winner for the first time in 32 years. The occasion was a charity race at Wincanton in aid of the Injured Jockeys' Fund, and at the age of 66, on *Barneys Bell*, he finished ahead of his son Peter and grandson Tom. Three years later, when, Tom appeared in his first Grand National, the oldest of the Scudamores was still riding out every day at the stables of Nigel Twiston-Davies; and subsequently, eight years after retiring, and now into his seventies, he was back training winners, many ridden by his elder grandson.

In 2005, almost 40 years after his last National ride, Michael Scu was once again involved with the race. He was due to have two runners, *Astonville* and *Turnium*, but the latter was withdrawn on the eve of the race. The former, a 100-1 shot, was pulled up lame before the 13th.

S

In 2007 his one National entry, *Espoir Du Bocage*, had no hope of making the cut. However, shortly before the National weights were announced, he sent out *Heltornic*, ridden by grandson Tom, to win the Red Square Vodka Gold Cup, in the process beating no fewer than ten horses entered in the National. Among his other successes that year was winning a novice handicap chase at Kempton with *Lady of Scarvagh* at 50-1.

Meanwhile Michael had been joined by his younger grandson and namesake, serving as an assistant, eventually taking over the training licence in 2008. A relative latecomer to racing, Michael Jnr was 22 years old when he began riding point -to-point in 2006 and then made his amateur Flat-racing debut, having reduced from 13st 7lb in his rugger days in Gloucester Academy to a trim 10st 11lb.

See also: Scudamore, Peter; Scudamore, Tom; Oxo.

SCUDAMORE, Peter Michael

Born (June 13, 1958) in Hereford, Peter Scudamore rode his first winner under Rules in August, 1978; and by the time of his retirement, 15 years later, he had eclipsed all other riders in National Hunt history with a then career record of 1,678 winners (792 of them in association with trainer Martin Pipe), eight jockeys' championships, and at that time an unprecedented 221 wins in a single season (1988-89). His victories included three Welsh Nationals and a Scottish National, the Hennessy Cognac Gold Cup twice, the Champion Hurdle twice, the Mackeson Gold Cup, the Grand Annual Chase and the Queen Mother Champion Chase. Yet, like his great archrival John Francome, he was destined never to win the Grand National.

'Scu', as he became popularly known, had a grandfather (Geoffrey) who was a prominent point-to-point rider, and a father (Michael) and godfather (Pat Taaffe) who were both giants of jump racing and winning Grand National jockeys. He was riding almost as soon as he could walk; and, though his mother Mary was always urging him to 'get a proper job', he was so set on a riding career that he once packed his bags to leave home after being told that he could not take a very dodgy ride in a point-to-point.

Initially he worked for Willie Stephenson, trainer of *Oxo* on whom his father had won the 1959 Grand National. He made his debut in the race in 1981, the year of Bob Champion's emotional victory on *Aldaniti*. Never a serious threat on 20-1 chance *Cheers*, he was the last of 12 finishers in a 39-strong field. His subsequent National rides were: 1982, *Tragus* (sixth); 1983, *Fortina's Express* (pu); 1984, *Burnt Oak* (pu); 1985, *Corbiere* (third); 1986, *Broomy Bank* (sixth); 1987, *Plundering* (16th); 1988, *Strands Of Gold* (fell); 1989, *Bonanza Boy*, (eighth); 1990, *Bonanza Boy* (16th); 1991, *Bonanza Boy* (fifth); 1992, *Docklands Express* (fourth); and 1993, *Captain Dibble* (pu) in the void National.

Thus he rode in 13 consecutive Nationals and, though never finishing better than third, was only once a faller. His greatest chance of emulating his father came in 1985 when the injury of Ben de Haan enabled him to take over the ride on *Corbiere* who had won in 1983 and finished third in 1984. Two days earlier, in the Topham Trophy, Peter had taken a heavy fall on *Burnt Oak* at the fence before Becher's, breaking his nose and badly bruising the calf muscle of his left leg. With typical gutsiness, he concealed his pain as he sought to prove that he was still fit to ride.

Though carrying top weight, *Corbiere* was looking a likely winner with only two fences to go. At that point, Peter heard a voice shout out, 'Keep going, Scu, you'll win!' It was John Burke, standing by the rail after pulling up on *Lucky Vane* first time round. But seconds later *Corbiere* was being challenged by *Mr Snugfit*, who had a 24lb advantage, and then, on the run-in, came a storming finish by *Last Suspect*, a 50-1 chance with a 19lb advantage. The weight differences were decisive. *Corbiere* finished third again – four and a half lengths behind *Last Suspect* and three lengths behind *Mr Snugfit*.

Scudamore had high hopes again in 1988 when, on the Martin Pipe-trained *Strands Of Gold*, he enjoyed a great ride over the first circuit. Still full of running, the little bay took the lead at the fence before Becher's second tine round. But then, taking the steepest route tight to the inside wing, allowing little room to correct himself if wrong, the horse hit Becher's hard and fell. In a rare show of temper, 'Scu' hurled his helmet and stick to the ground. It was the first time in eight Nationals that he had ended up on the floor and no horse had been travelling better at the time.

His 13th and last bid to win the National was equally frustrating in its way. Though having the choice of several Pipe runners, he opted to ride the heavily backed *Captain Dibble* for Nigel Twiston-

Davies. Together they had won the 1992 Scottish National. Now, at Aintree, they went well for one circuit, but to no purpose in a race declared void. Four days later, making his last ride a winning one (on *Sweet Duke* at Ascot), he retired while still champion jockey, and soon after embarked on a new career as a racing journalist, TV commentator and assistant to trainer Twiston-Davies.

The following week the first winner he ever saddled as assistant trainer was a future Grand National winner, *Earth Summit*, then a five year old losing his maiden tag in a novices' hurdle at Chepstow. And, ironically, one year after his retirement from riding, his successor as Pipe's stable jockey, Richard Dunwoody, won the Grand National on *Miinnehoma*, the horse Scudamore had ridden to victory in Cheltenham's 1992 Sun Alliance Chase.

Of all the Nationals involving Scudamore as a commentator, none was more emotionally distracting than that of 2002. He saw his 19 year old son Tom pull up after the Canal Turn on the Mark Pitman-trained *Smarty*. Also, as assistant to Twiston-Davies, he was disappointed to see the yard's *Frantic Tan* depart at the fifth and the stable's leading fancy, *Beau*, unseat his rider at the 14th. But then, to his wildly demonstrative delight, came the dramatic, three-quarters-of-a-length win by *Bindaree*, another horse he had helped to train. Son Tom would probably have ridden the horse but for his agreement to ride *Smarty*. It was a victory of unsuspected consequences. It resulted in trainer Twiston-Davies abandoning his thoughts of retiring. Instead, he chose to buy out Peter's half-share in their 80-acre Naunton training establishment and restructure his operations.

Peter left Naunton with some of the horses, including *The Villager*, and in 2002, while continuing as a BBC racing pundit and columnist for the *Daily Mail*, he bought a farm in Herefordshire and began operating a new training establishment in harness with his father and sons.

See also: Scudamore, Michael; Scudamore, Tom.

SCUDAMORE, Tom

In 2001, as a BBC television commentator, Peter Scudamore nervously watched his son, Tom, make his Grand National debut on *Northern Starlight*. At 18, Tom was the youngest rider in the race, just one year older than Bruce Hobbs, the youngest-ever National-winning rider. The third generation of Scud-amores to ride in the race went out at the first Becher's.

Born May, 1982, and coached early on by his father, Tom was riding winners in the 1999-2000 season while still only 17 and studying for his A-levels at Cheltenham College. He rode at point-to-points for David Pipe, son of champion trainer Martin Pipe; and, directly on leaving school he was employed by the latter. Notably, and not least because his grandfather Michael was watching, he won the 2000 Tote Bookmakers Handicap Hurdle on *Maid Equal*; and that season he became the champion amateur rider under Rules.

Having ridden 52 winners as an amateur, Tom turned professional in his 20th year, and he continued to be attached to Martin Pipe's Somerset stable and, through his father, to have close links with the yard of Nigel Twiston-Davies. In 2002 he was again the youngest jockey in the National. Four days before the race, after stable jockey Jamie Goldstein had broken his left leg, he had been asked by his father if he wanted to ride *Bindaree*. But Tom stayed loyal to Mark Pitman's *Smarty*, who had finished second at Aintree the previous year. As it happened, super-sub Jim Culloty won on *Bindaree*. *Smarty* was badly hampered at the first and was pulled up at Valentine's with his blinkers and bridle displaced.

In 2003 champion jockey Tony McCoy had the pick of seven Pipe runners in the National, opting for *Iris Bleu*, the 8-1 joint second favourite. But it was Tom who had the best ride for Pipe, finishing eighth on *Blowing Wind*, who had been third in the two previous years. The following year he had a disappointing ride on *Shardam*, trained by Twiston-Davies. The seven year old pecked on landing over the first, then blundered the third, unseating his rider who was taken to hospital with a suspected broken wrist. In 2005 he finished 12th on a Pipe outsider, 125-1 shot *Iznogoud*.

By this time McCoy had left to join trainer Jonjo O'Neill and Pipe had duly replaced Scudamore with Jamie Moore. Tom began to ride more often for his father. In the past, he acknowledged, he had been trying too hard to win rather than riding a horse according to its merits. Now came signs of improvement with a more relaxed approach. In November, 2005, he rode 17 winners including ten in one week. On Boxing Day, the bad fall of Richard Johnson presented him with the late spare ride on *Monkerhostin*

S

in the King George VI Chase and they were beaten only a neck by *Kicking King*. And the following month, riding for Pipe, he had his biggest win to date: the £100,000 Ladbroke Hurdle at Sandown on the 25-1 chance *Desert Air*. But again he had no real chance in the National, being back on the 200-1 outsider *Iznogoud* who had to be pulled up before the 27th.

In 2007 there was a huge family triumph when he won the valuable Red Square Vodka Gold Cup on *Heltornic*, trained by his grandfather and with his young brother Michael the head groom. On the following Saturdays he won the four mile one furlong. Eider Chase at Newcastle on *Nil Desperandum*, hailed as an outstanding National contender, and the VC Casino.com Gold Cup Chase at Newbury on *Madison Du Berlais*.

Then cruelly his fortunes were suddenly reversed. At the Cheltenham Festival he was unluckily brought down when going well on *Heltornic* in the William Hill Trophy Handicap Chase, and one day after the Festival his strong hopes of a winning Grand National ride were sadly diminished as he had to pull up in the Midlands National on the fatally injured *Nil Desperandum*.

In late March it was announced that Tom was to be made No 1 stable jockey to David Pipe, so recalling the great Martin Pipe-Peter Scudamore years. But the young Pipe only had two long-shots in the National. Tom completed the course, albeit a far distant eighth on 80-1 chance *Puntal*, while the other Pipe runner, *Celtic Son*, was pulled up before the second Becher's.

See also: Scudamore, Peter.

SEAGRAM

By coincidence, the most aptly named winner of the 1991 Seagram-sponsored Grand National – by five lengths from *Garrison Savannah*, the recent short-head winner of the Cheltenham Gold Cup. Like *Moifaa*, 87 years before, he was New Zealand-bred and winning on the first of his two appearances in the race.

Seagram was bought as a three year old for 80,000 New Zealand dollars (c. £3,600) by Kingsbridge (Devon) trainer David Barons on the recommendation of Kiwi trainer Kenny Brown. Barons looked for toughness and staying-power, and this relatively small chestnut hopefully had both, being by the English-bred *Balak*, a winner of 33 of his 74 races, and the unraced *Llanah*, a dam from a family noted for stamina.

Initially running in the colours of a Liverpool-based haulage company (Maincrest Ltd), he was named by their managing director who was doing some work for Seagram at the time and thought the company might wish to buy him if he developed into a National prospect. He won one race over hurdles in each of his first three seasons, 1983-86. But by now Maincrest had lost interest and Barons bought him back.

Seagram scored his first success over fences in April, 1987, winning on firm ground at Hereford. But then he broke down badly. During an 18-month layoff both his forelegs needed to be treated with carbon-fibre tendon implants, and for a while it was doubtful that he would ever race again. But happily he recovered completely to win four chases over three miles or more in the 1988-89 season. In the meantime he passed into the joint ownership of trainer Barons and Sir Eric Parker in whose colours he subsequently ran.

Three wins followed in the 1989-90 season, including Kempton's Charisma Gold Cup. In addition he finished third to *Desert Orchid* in the Racing Post Chase and second to *Bigsun* in Cheltenham's Ritz Club Handicap Chase. Then, in his build-up to the National, he showed his great potential with a win over four miles at Cheltenham on New Year's Day and victory in the Ritz Club in March. Three weeks later he went to Aintree, well supported at 12-1. But *Garrison Savannah*, the 7-1 second favourite behind *Bonanza Boy*, was regarded by form students as the handicap 'good thing', the weights having been set before his Gold Cup success. He was on just 11st 1lb, 9lb more than *Seagram*.

Always to the fore, *Garrison Savannah* – trained by the masterful Jenny Pitman and ridden by her son Mark – seemed almost certain to emulate *Golden Miller*'s unique Gold Cup-National double as he took the lead at the 23rd fence and began to pull away. Meanwhile *Seagram* had been patiently ridden by 25 year old Nigel Hawke, making his first appearance in the race. Having survived one solitary blunder at the 12th, they had made steady headway on the second circuit, closing on the leaders by Valentine's; and when 'Gary' landed smoothly over the last fence, they were in second place – roughly eight lengths behind.

Now came the long run-in and, as so often in the

past, it proved the critical test. As they approached the Elbow, the leader suddenly began to falter. While he had nothing more to give, *Seagram* found an extra gear, surging past to lead over the last 100 yards and to win by five lengths, with the mare *Auntie Dot* a further eight lengths back in third.

For the drinks firm Seagram, the result was a welcome publicity bonus – albeit with a touch of irony. Twice the UK company chairman, Major Ivan Straker, had been given the chance to buy the horse. Twice he had declined. Now it befell him to present the trophy to the winning owner Sir Eric Parker.

Seagram went on to come close to winning the Whitbread Gold Cup. But one year later, when he returned to Aintree as a 12 year old, it was with a prohibitive extra 12lb to carry, making him the second highest in the weights. Moreover, his seasonal form was poor: unplaced in six outings, unseating Hawke at Haydock in February and being pulled up when not jumping well at Cheltenham in March. Not surprisingly, he started at long odds of 33-1, never went well, and was tailed off before three out. A horse of great courage rather than class, he was retired and died of colic in 1997, aged 17.

See also: Barons, David; Hawke, Nigel; Straker, Ivan.

SEAMAN

Winner of the 1882 Grand National, on his first and only appearance at Aintree, six year old *Seaman* snatched victory by a head from his half-brother *Cyrus* in one of the most exciting finishes ever seen. Most remarkably, in duelling with a rival 11lb better off and ridden by hat-trick-seeking Tommy Beasley, *Seaman* was powered home by Lord John Manners, a Grenadier Guards officer who had had minimal experience of riding in chases.

The circumstances behind his victory could not have been more ironic. Only a few months earlier Lord Manners had bought *Seaman* for £2,000 following an extraordinary misjudgment on the part of Henry Linde, the Irish wizard who had trained the past two National winners and who was now seeking a third success with two challengers, *Cyrus* and the short-priced favourite *Mohican*.

Seaman – a bay son of *Xenophon* out of *Lena Rivers* – had been hard-trained by Linde to score three notable wins in 1881: the four-mile Conyngham Cup at Punchestown, the Liverpool Hunt Chase and the Grande Hurdle at Auteuil. But thereafter the

famed trainer concluded that the small horse had reached his peak and was liable to break down at any time. Consequently he encouraged the owner to sell.

Lord Manners promptly sent *Seaman* to Captain James Machell to be prepared for the National. As it happened, Machell shared Linde's misgivings about the gelding's strength for such a stern test; also he declared that he had had insufficient time to get him fully fit. But the new owner insisted that he should run, and with himself as the rider. Moreover, his hefty win bets were largely responsible for the bay's odds being cut to 10-1.

With a snow blizzard raging, the race was run in quagmire conditions that saw only three of 12 starters complete the course. Of those that failed to finish none was more unlucky than the Duke of Hamilton's *Eau De Vie*. The seven year old mare had opened up a 15 lengths lead by the Canal Turn and was still well in command on clearing Becher's second time around. But there a stirrup leather suddenly broke and rider Dan Thirlwell was unable to prevent her veering off the course. One day later she underlined her well-being by comfortably winning Aintree's Sefton Chase, but it was small consolation; and in the following year's National, raised 16lb in the weights, she would be the last of seven finishers.

When *Eau De Vie* ran out after Becher's another mare, *Zoedone*, was left in the lead. But she began to fade two fences out, and by the last it had become a strictly two-horse contest between the two sons of *Xenophon*, *Cyrus* and *Seaman*. At that stage it seemed that the latter was indeed too weak for the test. He was clearly distressed, on the verge of breaking down completely. Yet, against all the odds, Manners somehow managed to drive him on and snatch victory from the outstanding amateur rider of the day.

Seaman would never race again. Having earned a very early retirement, he saw out his remaining years as a hack for Lord Manners, who was Master of the Quorn, and as a pet for his children.

See also: Linde, Henry Eyre; Manners, Lord John.

SECURITY

In the early years of the Grand National security measures were virtually non-existant, with responsibility for crowd control falling on a totally inadequate racecourse staff. Without police on special duty, Aintree attracted plenty of pickpockets and prostitutes. Brawls were commonplace and

S

invasions of the course during running were readily achieved.

Over the years security was steadily increased, most notably developing into a huge police operation following the abandonment of the 1993 National after a breakdown of the starting procedure. It was increased still further in 1996 when there were some 400 police and over 500 security guards on duty, with the number of closed circuit TV cameras rising to 18 so that every part of the racecourse and all enclosures could be monitored. Since then it has also been customary to have a police helicopter flying overhead with a video downlink to keep an eye on any potential threat. And, on the night before the race, all the fences have a one-man guard and a security light backed up by patrolling personnel with guard dogs.

In 1997 security was raised to a new level – 500 policemen on duty following heightened fears of a major animal rights protest and in the light of Thursday's IRA terrorist campaign against the motorway network. It was then put to its greatest test when bomb scares forced the Grand National to be postponed for 49 hours. By mistakes valuable lessons were learned. Not least, procedures for evacuating the course in an orderly fashion had been shown to be woefully weak, a problem exacerbated as loudspeaker announcements were obliterated by the roar of the police helicopter hovering over the main crowds.

In 1998 security was increased still further – not least because, on the Thursday, police had intercepted a massive car bomb bound for England: nearly 1,000lb of home-made explosives, together with detonators, timing devices and Semtex boosters, found in a BMW about to board a Holyhead-bound ferry at Dun Laoghaire, Dublin. Subsequently racegoers were subjected to multiple searches by 500 police officers and 800 security staff on duty. Only authorised motorists were allowed into the main car parks. Officers with dogs searched each vehicle and the car park in the centre of the course was closed.

In 1999 security was again tighter than ever with a record number of 900 security personnel on duty in addition to the police. For this meeting Aintree had spent £630,000 on security that included the erection of 60 electronic airport-style scanning arches through which racegoers passed after having their bags searched.

The following year, 15 days before the National,

the staff was evacuated while the Army Bomb Disposal Unit was called in to investigate an unaccounted-for object which was eventually found to be harmless.

Added precautions were again necessary in 2001 following the great outbreak of foot-and-mouth disease. This year racegoers had to walk through disinfected foot-baths before they were asked to empty their pockets, and pass through a security scanner and have their bags checked. And security has remained even tighter still since the 9/11 terrorist attacks in the U.S.

However, security has been found wanting in one respect: the guarding of horses. This was exposed in 2006 when a tabloid newspaper reporter, posing as a stable lad, walked through three checkpoints and gained access to the leading contender, *Hedgehunter*. He subsequently claimed that he had gained entry without a pass and while carrying on his person eight tranquilliser pills (the 'stopping' drug ACP) which have been effectively used to dope racehorses.

To ensure there was no repeat in 2007, many more stable guards were on duty, with staff wearing high-visibility identification holders displaying their details. As usual, there were airport-style checks, including bag searches and metal-detecting scanners; and again police used Spotterscope, a high-zoom camera operated from a helicopter and capable of identifying a person's face at more than 800ft.

SEFTON, the Earls of

In 1829, as head of the Molyneux family with vast ancestral estates in Lancashire, the second Earl of Sefton leased for horse-racing the land at Aintree that ten years later would become the traditional home of the Grand National. In 1836 he saw the first steeplechase to be run at Aintree, but sadly he died one year before the 1839 Grand Liverpool Steeplechase, now popularly recognised as the first Grand National.

His eldest son was a key figure in advancing the new enterprise. As Viscount Molyneux, he had laid the foundation stone of an Aintree grandstand in 1829, and in 1836 he had served as umpire and starter for the first steeplechase held over the course. Two years later, as the third earl, he was among the peers who formed a syndicate to promote racing at Aintree and make plans for holding the Grand Liverpool Chase there.

S

It was the new Lord Sefton who, after several false starts, dropped the flag to set off 17 runners in the Aintree Grand Liverpool Chase of 1839. Top-hatted, he acted as starter for many Nationals to follow. Yet, while remaining the chief administrator, he did not actually have a runner in the race until 1850. His horse, *Little Fanny*, failed to finish, as did his next runner, 50-1 outsider *Shillibeer*, in 1854.

The family's first really determined effort to win the National came in 1862 when Lord Sefton took over ownership of *Xanthus*, a renowned front-runner of uncertain age who had been third in 1858, a faller in 1859, then third and fifth in 1860 and 1861 respectively. This time he finished fourth in a small field of 13.

Successive earls of Sefton maintained the family connection with Aintree racing and none more so than Hugh William Osbert Molyneux, the 7th earl. Born in December, 1898, educated at Harrow, he served in the Royal Horse Guards and became a life-long supporter of both Flat and National Hunt racing, acting as a local steward at various courses and sitting on many committees as a member of the National Hunt Committee and the Jockey Club.

A prominent racehorse owner in his own right, this Lord Sefton never won a Classic race but had many major wins, most notably the 1942 Cheltenham Gold Cup with his French-bred *Medoc II*, trained by Reg Hobbs and ridden by H. 'Frenchie' Nicholson. His most successful chaser was *Irish Lizard*, trained by Nicholson and the winner of 14 races.

As a one-time Lord Mayor of Liverpool (1944-45) Lord Sefton would have been an especially popular Grand National-winning owner. But it was not to be. Six times he bid for the prize with his honest, long-serving *Irish Lizard* and was dogged by bad luck from the start. In 1951, when both horse and rider (Pat Taaffe) made their National debut, they were brought down in the first fence pile-up that followed a mad stampede arising from the undeclared false start. One year later, *Irish Lizard* was again brought down at the first, one of ten horses to be eliminated there.

In 1953, only two days after winning the Topham Trophy Chase over one circuit of the National course, *Irish Lizard* came out again for the big one. This time he finished third at 33-1 – albeit well beaten and not helped by the fact that his jockey, Bob Turnell, was putting up 5lb over-weight. Then,

in 1954, when raised only 1lb and ridden by Michael Scudamore, he went off as the 15-2 favourite and finished third again. The following year *Irish Lizard* finished 11th; and he was a faller two years later when, at the ripe old age of 14, he was trundled out yet again as a 66-1 rank outsider.

Throughout these years Lord Sefton was a leading figure behind the Grand National, and as the long-time Senior Steward he would annually address National jockeys assembled in the weighing room, emphasising the folly of going off too fast in the charge to the first fence. Many times he welcomed members of the royal family to Aintree and in 1956 he was with the Queen Mother when she saw the collapse of her *Devon Loch*.

Eight years later he became involved in a bitter battle to save the race he so greatly loved. In 1949 he had sold Aintree racecourse to the lessees, Topham's Ltd., in the belief that its future operation was in safe hands. But on July 1, 1964, to his horror, the company's chairman, Mrs Mirabel Topham, announced that she was selling the racecourse to Capital and Counties Property Ltd. for building development.

Lord Sefton promptly sought an injunction from the High Court to restrain such action. He contended that a clause in the sale precluded the land from being used for any purpose other than racing and agriculture. Judgment was given in his favour, but this was reversed on appeal to the House of Lords. For years thereafter the future of the Grand National remained uncertain, and sadly the noble lord did not live to see the matter conclusively resolved. He died on April 13, 1972, and being without heir the title died with him.

See also: Topham, Mirabel.

SERGEANT MURPHY
Winner of the 1923 Grand National, *Sergeant Murphy* rates as one of the truly great stalwarts of the race. Victorious at the age of 13, he remains the oldest winner since the 19th century; and remarkably he came back to finish fifth in 1924 and tenth (remounted) on his farewell appearance as a 15 year old. He was the first National winner to be American-owned; also the second horse (following *Music Hall*, 1922) to succeed at Aintree after winning the Scottish National.

A chestnut gelding, bred in Co. Meath, by *General Symons* out of *Rose Graft*, he made his Aintree National debut in 1919, one year after

459

running in the last wartime substitute staged at Gatwick and won by *Poethlyn*. Though he was the sixth of only seven finishers, it was not a particularly auspicious debut since the winner, again *Poethlyn*, was now giving him two stone in the weights.

In 1920, with a new jockey and new owner, *Sergeant Murphy* was the fourth of five finishers – again showing himself to be a sound jumper, strong on stamina rather than pace. He did not compete in the 1921 National which was won by his regular rival *Shaun Spadah*. Instead, he was sold by bookmaker Martin Benson to be used as a hunter. The buyer, American carpet tycoon John Sanford, was spending £1,200 on a present for his son Stephen, a Cambridge undergraduate.

Stephen ('Laddie') Sanford aimed to ride *Sergeant Murphy* with the Leicestershire hounds. But, as it happened, he found the gelding too headstrong to handle, and so he sent him back to Newmarket to be trained by George Blackwell, most renowned as a trainer for the Flat, and especially as the man who had prepared the 1903 Triple Crown winner, *Rock Sand*.

Returned to Aintree for the third time, even the safe-jumping *Sergeant Murphy* could not avoid the chaos of the 1922 National which saw half the field down by the first Becher's. He himself was leading when he came down two fences later. But this game gelding was never to fail to finish in six Grand Nationals. Remounted, the 12 year old fought back to gain fourth place, with only five of 32 runners completing the course; and subsequently he proved his well-being by winning the Scottish Grand National with his new rider, Captain G.H. 'Tuppy' Bennet.

Captain Bennet, a veterinary surgeon, was arguably the most fiercely competitive of all amateur riders: the man who had stubbornly remounted *Turkey Buzzard* three times to take fourth place in the 1921 National, and who had got back in the saddle to finish fifth on *A Double Escape* in 1922. Happily, no such desperate recovery was needed in 1923 when the 13 year old went off as a respected 100-6 chance.

Throughout the first circuit, *Sergeant Murphy* was foot-perfect and up with the leaders, while numerous rivals, vaguely identifiable in the fog, floundered in his wake. He jumped into the lead at the second Becher's and thereafter held off all challengers to win by three lengths from the gallant *Shaun Spadah*, who was giving him 18lb. Young

Sanford had become the National's first American winning owner.

Heady with success, and given generous parental support, 'Laddie' Sanford bought more National contenders. None, however, served him as well as *Sergeant Murphy*. In 1924, the old soldier was leading as they came to the Water Jump, but he stumbled on landing and was finally relegated to fifth place. In 1925, for the second time, he completed the course after being remounted. In a 33-strong field, he was the last of ten finishers – nonetheless a truly remarkable performance for a 15 year old harshly burdened with 11st 7lb.

Captain Bennet was no longer his rider. Tragically, he had died in the year of his National triumph, receiving a fatal kick after falling in a post-Christmas chase at Wolverhampton. Three years later, old *Sergeant Murphy* – sadly denied the retirement he so richly deserved – was also lost on the racecourse, put down after breaking a leg at Bogside in the West of Scotland Handicap Chase, worth just £197.

See also: Bennet, Geoffrey Harbord; Blackwell, George; Sanford, Stephen.

SHANNON LASS

Winner of the 1902 Grand National on her one and only appearance in the race. Irish-bred – by *Butterscotch* out of *Mazurka* – *Shannon Lass* finished third in a Limerick chase when only a three year old, and subsequently twice changed hands, latterly being bought by English bookmaker Ambrose Gorham who had her prepared for Aintree by his private trainer, James Hackett, at Telscombe near Brighton.

Ridden by David Read, a veteran jockey having only his second National ride, the seven year old *Shannon Lass* went off at 20-1 for a race run on heavy going which saw one joint favourite, the Duke of Westminster's *Drumree*, brought down at the fourth, and the other, Lord Coventry's *Inquisitor*, fall on the second circuit.

Coming to the last fence, six year old *Detail*, carrying a feather-weight 9st 9lb, looked a major threat under Arthur Nightingall who was bidding for his fourth National victory and his second in succession. But there the newcomer blundered away his chance; and though the great *Manifesto*, now 14, made a spirited late effort under Ernie Piggott, two horses dominated the gruelling run-in, with the speedier *Shannon Lass* outpacing the six year old, 50-1 long-shot *Matthew* to win by three lengths. *Manifesto*, conceding 35lb to the winner, was a further three lengths behind in third.

This was the first National victory by a mare since *Frigate* 13 years before, and it would be another 46 years before a mare (*Sheila's Cottage*) was successful again. *Shannon Lass* had now won eight steeplechases for owner Gorham who donated much of his National winnings to the restoration of Telscombe's church. But, soon retired to serve as a broodmare at stud, she never won another race.

See also: Read, David; Mares.

SHAUN GOILIN

Winner of the 1930 Grand National, ten year old *Shaun Goilin* triumphed by just a neck and one and a half lengths from *Melleray's Belle* and *Sir Lindsay* respectively in the tightest of finishes for nearly half a century. The finish was all the more unusual since – with only six runners completing the course – American-owned horses came home third, fourth and fifth.

Shaun Goilin was a 'bastard' chestnut, his dam, *Golden Day*, having been served late one evening by an unknown, unbroken, three year old colt after straying from her paddock in Co. Limerick. Subsequently he was purchased for only 22 guineas and raced as a four year old on the Flat in Ireland. But he won only one race before suffering a leg injury so serious that there was talk of putting him down.

Happily he responded to treatment and was then sold on to Mr W.H. Midwood, a Liverpool cotton broker and Master of the Cheshire hounds. Ironically, Mr Midwood was to realise his lifelong ambition with a relatively cheap buy after spending a small fortune on five previous National challenges, most notably in 1924 with his third-placed *Silvo*, a bay gelding that had cost him 10,500 guineas, at least ten times the sum he paid for *Shaun Goilin*.

Trained at Weyhill, Hampshire, by Frank Hartigan, *Shaun Goilin* was a late developer, who did not show his true potential until, as a nine year old, he impressively won the 1929 Grand Sefton at Aintree. On the strength of that showing and two other pre-National wins – plus the fact that he was to be ridden by Irishman Tommy Cullinan (recent winner of the Cheltenham Gold Cup on *Easter Hero* and the Champion Hurdle on *Brown Tony*) – the pale chestnut went off as second favourite for the 1930 National. Among his 40 rivals were four American-

owned challengers headed by millionaire 'Jock' Hay Whitney's *Sir Lindsay*; the favourite *Grakle*, ridden by Keith Piggott; and last year's 100-1 winner, *Gregalach*, now top-weighted on 12st.

This year, for the first and only time in National history, two greys – *Glangesia* and *Gate Book* – led the field from the start, and they were still showing the way when they took Becher's almost in unison. *Gate Book* fell at the 12th but Mr R.K Mellon's attractive grey continued to make all going as far as Becher's second time around. There, *May King* figured in one of the most spectacular falls ever seen – sprawling sideways over the fence and then landing beside jockey Gordon Goswell in the ditch beyond. Miraculously, both horse and rider escaped unharmed. Meanwhile, a handful of runners were closing the gap behind the tiring *Glangesia*, and by two fences from home the race was a three-way battle, between the mare *Melleray's Belle, Sir Lindsay* and *Shaun Goilin*.

At the last *Melleray's Belle* was leading by a length from *Sir Lindsay*. But the great American hope hit the fence hard and his rider, Dudley Williams, lost both his irons as the horse pecked on landing. Cullinan, always close up in third on *Shaun Goilin*, seized his chance; and on the long run-in they wore down the leaders to squeeze home by the narrowest margin since *Seaman's* victory by a head from *Cyrus* in 1882. That year, however, the third horse was a long way back. This time the third horse, *Sir Lindsay*, was a mere one and a half lengths behind, and arguably might have secured a much-sought-after American victory if his rider had not been severely handicapped by the loss of his irons.

Having won at the first attempt, *Shaun Goilin* returned for three more Nationals, performing honourably on each occasion under a big weight. In 1931, when raised 11lb and reportedly hampered by an enlarged knee joint, he finished sixth at 33-1. In 1932, still on 12st 4lb, he was third at 40-1 while two other former winners, *Gregalach* and *Grakle*, failed to get round; and in 1933, as a 13 year old on 12st 1lb, and now ridden by amateur Peter Cazalet, he maintained his record of having always completed the course.

See also: Hartigan, Frank.

SHAUN SPADAH

Ten year old winner by a distance of the 1921 Grand National when, with a then record number of 35 starters, he was one of only four finishers and the only one to complete the course without falling. He was bred in Co. Meath by an Irishman (Mr P. McKenna), owned by a Scot (Mr Malcolm McAlpine), trained at Lewes by an Englishman (George Poole) and ridden by a young Welshman (Fred Rees) who would become the greatest National Hunt jockey of his day.

Shaun Spadah – lowly bred by *Easter Prize* out of *Rusialka* – was bought as a yearling by Irishman Dick Cleary, and in 1913, as a two year old, he was sent to The Curragh to be trained by Algy Anthony. Remarkably, Anthony – the man who was to prepare the 1920 National winner, *Troytown* – rushed to judgment and rejected the young bay as having insufficient speed for racing. However, on his return, the horse strengthened with hunting, and in 1915, after winning his first race at Downpatrick, he changed hands three times before finally coming into the ownership of Mr (later Sir) Malcolm McAlpine.

In the 1918 wartime substitute National at Gatwick, *Shaun Spadah* had been soundly beaten by *Poethlyn*, and on that evidence he was an unfancied 33-1 shot on his 1919 debut in the Aintree National. In accordance with the betting, he failed to finish while *Poethlyn*, the top-weighted 11-4 favourite, romped home to become the shortest-priced winner of the event and only the fourth horse to carry 12st 7lb to victory.

Two years later, when *Shaun Spadah* reappeared at Aintree, a sizeable increase in prize money had led to the largest number of runners yet seen; and the big field, combined with very heavy going, contributed to an exceptional casualty rate. Half the field was eliminated by the Canal Turn, and by the end of the first circuit only four horses remained in serious contention: *Turkey Buzzard*, *Shaun Spadah*, *All White* and the 9-1 favourite, *The Bore*, who had finished third the previous year.

Early on the second circuit both *Turkey Buzzard* and *All White* fell, and of the two left standing *The Bore* looked the more likely winner as they duelled their way to the penultimate fence. But there the bay gelding crashed to the ground, leaving *Shaun Spadah* in the clear, and needing only to stay on his feet to win by a distance. Defying the agony of a broken collarbone, amateur rider-owner Harry Atherton Brown heroically remounted *The Bore* to bring him home in second place. *All White* was remounted to finish a distant third; and *Turkey Buzzard* came in

fourth after being remounted three times.

The finish was an action replay of the 1911 National which *Glenside* had won from three remounted horses. This time, however, a record number of runners had come to grief – 33 falling and one refusing.

It was a similar story in 1922 – another unusually large field (33) with only five finishers, two of them remounted. This time, however, *Shaun Spadah* was carrying top weight of 12st 3lb. He fell at the first fence, leaving Fred Rees plenty of time to watch the victorious ride by his elder brother, Lewis, on *Music Hall*.

In the circumstances, the handicapper seemed to act most harshly in raising *Shaun Spadah* to the maximum 12st 7lb for the 1923 National. Punters certainly thought so. Now 12 years old, he went off at 20-1. Nevertheless, given a masterly ride by Fred Rees, he finished runner-up – beaten only three lengths by his old rival, *Sergeant Murphy*. One year later, on his swansong, he finished seventh, conceding weight to all those ahead of him. He was retired with the excellent record of 19 races won, including Kempton's Coventry Chase and Aintree's Becher Chase.

See also: Rees, Frederick Brychan; Sergeant Murphy.

SHEILA'S COTTAGE

Shock winner of the 1948 Grand National in a storming finish that saw her grab the lead on the run-in to hold on for a one-length victory over *First Of The Dandies*. She was the first mare to win since *Shannon Lass* in 1902, the first of three National winners to be saddled by the brilliant trainer Neville Crump, and the first of two to be ridden by Arthur Thompson.

Bred by Mrs P. Daly in Co. Limerick, *Sheila's Cottage* had a most promising pedigree, having been sired by *Cottage* who had already fathered two National winners: *Workman* (1939) and *Lovely Cottage* (1946). Unfortunately, from her dam *Sheila II*, she had inherited a vile temperament that made her the most difficult of rides; and as a result she changed hands several times before being purchased for 350 guineas by Sir Hervey Bruce, a Catterick-based officer in the Royal Scots Greys.

In 1946 Sir Hervey sent *Sheila's Cottage* to Middleham in Yorkshire to be trained by former cavalry officer Neville Crump, and there it was found that stable jockey Arthur Thompson was the only rider capable of controlling the moody madam who was prone to bite and to kick. He twice rode her to victory in chases at Haydock, but then, as a 40-1 chance in the 1947 National, she was brought down at the 12th fence. She got up to be first past the post without her rider.

Next she was as headstrong as ever in the Scottish National, then run at Bogside on the Ayrshire coast. Having unseated Thompson when going well three out, she proceeded to run into the sea, swimming an inlet, and finally being collected at midnight from Irvine police station. Undeterred, Sir Hervey proceeded to back his mare heavily to win a chase at Cheltenham. She finished third and on New Year's Day a discouraged owner sold the eight year old for 3,500 guineas to John Procter, a trawler-owner and Lincolnshire farmer and hotelier.

Still trained by Crump and ridden by Thompson, *Sheila's Cottage* was raised 6lb for her 1948 Grand National challenge. Three weeks before the race she was found to be lame, and a fortnight later it was still uncertain whether she would run. But then the rains came and it was decided to risk her on the softened ground. This time she went off at the longer odds of 50-1.

It was a National packed with shocks and hard luck stories. Lord Bicester's *Silver Fame*, the favourite in a 43-strong field, was brought down at the first Becher's, and two more dangerous contenders were removed on the second circuit when *Lough Conn*, last year's runner-up, burst a blood vessel, and *Prince Regent* was carried out by a riderless horse. After Becher's second time around, seven year old *Cromwell*, close behind the leading *First Of The Dandies*, looked full of running. But, as in 1936, his owner-rider, Lord Mildmay, was struck by misfortune just as victory seemed within his grasp. This time he was seized by recurrent cramp in his injury-weakened neck muscles and, unable to hold up his head, rode on virtually blind.

Two fences from home, the most likely-looking winner was a 100-1 outsider: the blinkered mare *Zahia*, another daughter of *Cottage*. There, running on strongly, she drew level with *First Of The Dandies*, and threatened to pull well away. But, again, misfortune struck. Astonishingly, jockey Eddie Reavey misread his route (the course was not yet dolled off) and went so wide that he missed out the last fence – a heartbreaking blow for owner

F. N. Gee who had backed his mare £100 each-way.

Suddenly, with *Cromwell* and *Zahia* out of the reckoning, *Sheila's Cottage* was the closest challenger to the *First Of The Dandies*, who had a clear lead at the last but was beginning to labour. Thompson made his move with clinical precision, drawing level with the leader some 50 yards from home and gradually nosing ahead to win by one length, with *Cromwell*, the unluckiest of losers, a further six lengths back in third.

Sheila's Cottage maintained her ill-tempered reputation to the end. Two days after winning the National, when receiving a friendly pat from Thompson, she turned nasty and bit off the top joint of one of the jockey's fingers. She was never raced again. Retired to stud, the mare was eventually gifted to her rider and, on her passing, she was laid to rest in his garden in Wexford, Ireland.

See also: Crump, Neville; Thompson, Arthur Patrick.

SHIFNAL

Nine year old winner of the 1878 Grand National which, following the controversial late withdrawal of heavily backed *Austerlitz*, with 'heat in a leg', had only 12 runners, the least number since the 11-strong field of 1841. It was third time lucky for *Shifnal*, a brown entire – by *Saccharometer* out of *Countess Amy* – that had originally been bought out of a selling race at Alexandra Park by Epsom trainer John Nightingall.

In the 1876 National, when ridden by Robert l'Anson, *Shifnal* had headed the field at the end of the first circuit and coming to the last had shared the lead with *Regal* and *Congress*. But midway on the run-in he was overhauled by both and finished third, a neck and three lengths off his rivals. The following year, starting as favourite with the same rider and a new owner (Sir M. Crofton), he was never a threat and finished sixth.

Shrewdly, trainer Nightingall bought back the entire who was to be dropped 7lb for his third National challenge. He also booked a jockey, John Jones, with a most consistent record in the race: four rides (1874-77), finishing second, fifth, fourth, and fourth again.

Following the withdrawal of last year's winner *Austerlitz*, there was a late plunge on five year old *His Lordship*, backed down to 9-2 favouritism. But it was *Shifnal* who led over the first fence, where his

S

cause was greatly aided by the departure of the favourite, brought down by a faller. For most of the first circuit he held the lead, though all the while strongly pressed by *Martha* under the brilliant young Tommy Beasley who was having the second of his 12 rides in a race that he would win three times.

Early on the second circuit *Martha* took over the lead and was still ahead on clearing the last. Yet she markedly weakened on the run-in and Jones, seeing his chance, galvanised his mount into a renewed effort. In the end they won rather cosily, by two lengths with the well-backed *Pride of Kildare* a further ten lengths adrift in third place.

Two years later *Shifnal* returned to Aintree but, with an extra 13lb on his back, he was never a serious contender, finishing ninth of only 14 starters. He was subsequently retired, having won nine chases for his owner-trainer.

See also: Nightingall, John; Jones, John.

SILVER BIRCH

Surprise 33-1 winner of the National in 2007 when, by squeezing home three-quarters of a length ahead of the fast-finishing *McKelvey*, he gave the Irish their sixth success in nine years. Remarkably, he had been turned out by a rookie trainer (Gordon Elliott) who had not yet had a single winner in his native Ireland; had a trainer, an owner (Brian Walsh) and a jockey (Robbie Power) who were all still in their twenties; and had only been bought 11 months earlier as 'a fun horse for cross-country races'.

Most pointedly, it was noted that, by a curious twist of fate, *Silver Birch*, sold for a mere 20,000 guineas at last year's Doncaster Spring Sales, had previously been in the care of champion trainer Paul Nicholls who over 15 years had sent out 37 runners in search of National glory, his best result being a second place with 40-1 shot *Royal Auclair* in 2005. This year all of his four contenders had failed to finish.

Silver Birch – by *Clearly Bust* out of *All Gone* – was a five year old when he scored his first win in a two and a half mile novice hurdle at Chepstow; and two months later he proved his stamina by winning a chase over more than three miles one furlong on heavy going at Plumpton. Then, late in 2004, he proclaimed himself an outstanding National prospect. Eighteen days after winning by a neck at Newton Abbot, he jumped well and stayed on resolutely to beat *Just In Debt* a length in the Becher Chase over the National fences; and the following month he com-

pleted a hat-trick of victories under Ruby Walsh by succeeding National hero *Bindaree* as winner of the Welsh version.

The reaction was immediate. *Silver Birch* was made 14-1 ante-post favourite for the Grand National; and in February, when he was allotted 10st 9lb for Aintree, only *Clan Royal* narrowly headed him in the betting. Then Nicholls' great hope for National success was lost; one month before the race *Silver Birch* was ruled out with heat in a leg. Instead the trainer would saddle the National runner-up.

It was a dramatically changed picture when *Silver Birch* finally made it to the National in 2006. Inexplicably out of form, he had been pulled up in his two previous races, and now he went off at 40-1. To be sure, he was a shade unlucky to fall at The Chair where he was hampered. But it seemed that his chance had gone and his owners, Des Nichols and Paul Barber, were now agreed that the nine year old should be sold.

The buyer, in May, 2006, was 25 year old Brian Walsh, who ran Rheindross Stud at Kilcock in Co. Kildare; and 20,000 guineas was a small price to be paid by a man who, one month earlier, had forked out £220,000 for Aintree bumper winner *Rhacophorus* – at the time a record for a jumps mare in training.

Purchased essentially for cross-country racing, *Silver Birch* was now ridden out with the Ward Union Hunt and later given a run in a men's open point-to-point. In the process, trainer Elliott eventually had him back galloping and jumping with all his confidence and enthusiasm of old. In December, under Jason Maguire, he ran in the three miles seven furlong cross-country chase at Cheltenham; and though he finished eighth, he had only weakened coming to the last, being beaten just eight lengths by course specialist *Spot Thedifference*. Three months later he returned and, with exactly the same ground conditions, he achieved a significantly faster time to finish second to *Heads Onthe Ground*.

There had been thoughts of saving *Silver Birch* for the La Touche race at Punchestown in late April and then perhaps heading for the marathon Pardubicka in the Czech Republic. But now the National was an obvious choice. There, on 10st 6lb, he would be carrying 6lb less than on his previous appearance. But with Maguire already committed to Donald McCain's *Idle Talk*, he would have a substitute rider, Robbie Power, having only his second ride in the race.

The main concern – and reason for his weakness in the betting – was that the Aintree going might be too fast for *Silver Birch* whose six wins under Rules had all been on soft or heavy ground. But, as it happened, a week of watering produced a perfectly 'good' surface, with sufficient give to allay any fears on the part of his connections. As for 25 year old Power, he was to give his mount the coolest of rides, settling him in mid-field during the charge down to the first Becher's and keeping in contact with the leaders from the 12th fence onwards.

Apart from pecking on landing over the second Becher's, *Silver Birch* never put a foot wrong, maintaining a lovely rhythm throughout, moving into second place after three out, putting in a mighty leap at the last to take the lead from *Slim Pickings* and just holding off the late challenge of *McKelvey* at the finish.

The victory represented a tremendous training feat on the part of Gordon Elliott and was hugely profitable for owner Walsh who had backed his relatively cheap buy. Inevitably, much was made of the fact that the supreme jumps trainer, Paul Nicholls, had missed out on his chance of having his first National winner. But, in reality, if *Silver Birch* had remained in his yard, it seems that he would never have enjoyed success in Aintree's great showpiece.

Regarding the owners' decision to send *Silver Birch* to the sales, Nicholls explained: 'I said he'd make a good hunter chaser or point-to-pointer. He wasn't qualified for those races in Britain for another year, but he was in Ireland, and what a great job Gordon Elliott has done. If *Silver Birch* had stayed at Ditcheat he'd have never won a National because we wouldn't have brought him back through the point-to-point, cross-country route; we'd have run him in a handicap chase somewhere, got put up 10lb and never have been well enough handicapped to land a National.'

In 2008, Silver Birch was ruled out of the National with tendon injuries and, at the age of 11, any chance of a second Aintree success had now surely passed him by.

See also: Elliott, Gordon; Power, Robert; Nicholls, Paul.

SIRES

Of all the great sires of steeplechasers, the greatest in terms of the Grand National is *My Prince*. He sired the winners of four Nationals: *Gregalach* (1929) out of *St Germaine*; *Reynoldstown* (1935 and 1936) out of *Fromage*; and *Royal Mail* (1937) out of *Flying May*. In addition he fathered three outstanding horses that were placed in the National: *Easter Hero* (second in 1929), *Thomond II* (third in 1934 and 1935) and *Prince Regent* (third in 1946 and fourth in 1947).

Though they never won the National, the most brilliant sons of *My Prince* were *Easter Hero* (out of *Easter Week*) and *Prince Regent* (out of *Nemaea*). The former was twice winner of the Cheltenham Gold Cup and was carrying 12st 7lb top weight when finishing second in a 66-strong National field to his half-brother *Gregalach*. The latter might well have won the National but for the race's five-year suspension in the Second World War. In 1946, when he finally had his chance, he was 11 years old. That year *Prince Regent* won the Cheltenham Gold Cup and at Aintree finished third to younger horses (*Lovely Cottage* and *Jack Finlay*), to whom he was conceding 25lb and 31lb respectively. In 1947, as the top-weighted favourite, he came fourth.

My Prince was a half-brother to *Hurry On*, winner of the 1916 St Leger. Yet he himself had only a modest Flat-racing record, his best distance being around a mile, and in 1915 he failed to reach his 100 guineas reserve price at auction. Subsequently he was bought by the British Bloodstock Agency, sold on to the Irish Board of Agriculture for £200, then placed as a stallion with Mr A. H. Maxwell at Lusk, near Dublin.

Another giant among sires of steeplechasers is *Cottage*, son of *Tracery* out of a mare by *Marco*, the grand-sire of *My Prince*. He, too, was an indifferent racehorse, winning only one minor event on the Flat. Yet he sired three Grand National winners: *Workman* (1939), *Lovely Cottage* (1946) and the mare *Sheila's Cottage* (1948), plus *Cottage Rake*, three times winner of the Cheltenham Gold Cup. Moreover, in 1948, he might well have had a different National winner if his daughter, *Zahia*, a 100-1 chance, had not accidentally missed out the final fence.

Similarly, *Ascetic*, son of the 1867 Epsom Derby winner *Hermit*, was a relative failure on the racecourse, running mainly as a sprinter and never beyond a mile and a half. Yet he was the pre-eminent sire of chasers in the late 19th century and early 20th century. Irrespective of the quality of mares he covered, he was consistently responsible for outstanding

S

jumpers; and among them were three Grand National winners: the great *Cloister* (1893), *Drumcree* (1903) and *Ascetic's Silver* (1906). Furthermore, he had winners of the Irish, Welsh and Scottish Nationals; and two of his grandsons – *Troytown* (1920) and *Sergeant Murphy* (1923) – were successful at Aintree.

In more recent times, the outstanding sire has been *Roselier*, responsible for 17 Grand National runners, among them: winners *Royal Athlete* and *Bindaree*, dual runner-up *Suny Bay*, *Moorcroft Boy* (third), *Ebony Jane* (fourth) and *Kingsmark* (fourth), and seven more who completed the course. His other notable staying chasers included *Kendal Cavalier* and *Carvill's Hill* (Welsh National winners), *Baronet* (Scottish National) and *Seven Towers* (Midlands National).

The prolific *Vulgan* sired three Grand National winners: *Team Spirit* (1964), the lucky *Foinavon* (1967) and *Gay Trip* (1970). *Menelek* sired two winners, *Hallo Dandy* and *Rag Trade*; and *Crash Course* scored with winner *Rough Quest*, runner-up *Romany King*, and *Esha Ness*, first home in the void National of 1993.

Remarkably, within a five-year period, three Grand National winners – *Party Politics* (1992), *Miinnehoma* (1994) and *Lord Gyllene* (1997) – were linked through the male line. New Zealand-bred *Lord Gyllene* was a son of *Ring The Bell* whose sire was *Rangong*. In turn, *Rangong* had the same sire – *Right Royal V* – as *Politico*, sire of *Party Politics*, and *Kambalda*, sire of *Miinnehoma*.

See also: Breeding.

SKELTON, Tommy

After seven successive Grand National wins by amateur riders, professional jockey Tommy Skelton ended the run in 1886 by driving home *Old Joe*, a 25-1 chance, to win by a comfortable six lengths. A delighted owner, Mr A. J. Douglas, who had made a killing with a big bet at long odds, presented the jockey with the prize money of £1,380.

With the winner set to carry an extra stone on his reappearances in 1887 and 1888, the successful jockey chose not to ride him again. His decision was fully justified. In those years *Old Joe* failed to get round. Meanwhile, in 1887, Skelton followed up his victory with a second place on *Savoyard*, beaten three lengths on the run-in by *Gamecock*. And in 1888 he came home fourth on Lord Rodney's seven year old *Ringlet*.

Altogether, Skelton rode in six successive Nationals and achieved the rare distinction of finishing in a place on each of his first four appearances. On his 1885 Aintree debut, he had been third on Captain Machell's *Black Prince*, a 33-1 chance. His last two National rides were on *Voluptuary*, the one-time Derby runner who had triumphed at Aintree five years earlier. On both occasions the old campaigner was a faller.

See also: Old Joe.

SMITH, Denys

Trainer – in Bishop Auckland, Co. Durham – of the 1968 Grand National winner, *Red Alligator*, who was owned by his neighbour, butcher and farmer John Manners. Prior to being switched to his yard, the chestnut gelding had won only one hurdle race in 27 outings. Under Denys Smith, he developed into a most reliable jumper, especially strong on stamina.

In the trainer's view, *Red Alligator* was unlucky not to have won more than one Grand National. On his 1967 Aintree debut the eight year old chestnut gelding was caught in the great pile-up that brought all the field except *Foinavon* to a standstill. It took him three attempts to clear the 23rd fence but he still managed to finish third. And that year Denys Smith also saddled the fourth-placed *Greek Scholar*. Then, in 1969, *Red Alligator*, the 13-2 favourite with an extra 13lb to carry, was only cantering when he unluckily tripped over a faller and unseated his rider, Brian Fletcher, at the 19th.

Born in 1924, Smith was initially training and driving trotting horses, then became a permit-holder turning out his first winner (*Owens Mark*) at Sedgefield in 1958. Taking out a full licence three years later, he went on to become the champion jumps trainer of 1967-68 with 55 winners and one of the most successful of all dual-purpose trainers with a career total of some 1,700 winners, divided almost evenly between the Flat and National Hunt. His versatility showed most strongly when, in successive years, he saddled the Grand National winner and then the 1969 Lincoln winner, *Foggy Bell*.

Although *Red Alligator*'s success was the highlight of his career, it was also a time of sadness following the death, only two days earlier, of his father-in-law Bert Richardson, the man who had encouraged him to become a trainer. In turn, Smith encouraged the progress of several leading young riders, most notably Brian Fletcher who served as his apprentice, being given his first National ride at the age of 19 and going on to become a triple winning rider in the race – with *Red Alligator* and then with *Red Rum* (1973 and 1974). Smith retired in October, 2002, when, at 78, he was one of the oldest and longest-serving trainers.

See also: Red Alligator; Fletcher, Brian.

SMITH, 'Tommy' Crompton Jnr

Winning amateur jockey in 1965 when eight year old *Jay Trump* became the first Grand National victor to be American-bred, -owned and -ridden. Born into a family of racing and hunting fanatics, Tommy was only six months old when his father, a dairy farmer, had him strapped in a basket saddle to join in a hunt. And from early childhood he was being told of the glorious excitement of the English Grand National by a grandfather, Harry Worcester Smith, who had once shipped his hounds across the Atlantic so that he might experience hunting in Ireland.

Harry, a millionaire Massachusetts mill-owner, had retired early to devote his energies to hunting and steeplechasing, and to his paramount ambition: to produce the first all-American Grand National winner. Sparing no expense, he came over on the Lusitania in 1912 with his son Crompton, plus 17 horses and seven handlers. The plan was to establish a stable in Ireland where they would train horses for the 1913 National and select the best to be ridden by Crompton.

To Harry's voluble disgust, that cherished dream ended when his son, a fine cross-country horseman, had to abandon riding jumpers after a serious leg-breaking fall while hunting. No other American rider was readily available and the cantankerous Harry would not countenance using an English or Irish jockey. The dream came alive again when his grandson was born, but the old man died, aged 80 in 1945, before the boy had emerged as an outstanding rider in steeplechases.

The first racecourse Tommy ever saw was the Aintree Grand National circuit as depicted on a large, illustrated map that hung over the drawing-room fireplace in the family home at Middleburg, Virginia. And such was his subsequent passion for racing that he quit college to concentrate on riding as an amateur. He soon made his mark as a jump jockey, being only 21 when he first won the Maryland Hunt Cup. But it was as a talent-spotter that he had his most remarkable success. In 1960 he was asked by Mrs Mary Stephenson, a leading huntswoman in Ohio, to find

her a horse likely to make an outstanding steeplechaser. His inspired choice – picked up for a mere $2,000 out of a seller – was *Jay Trump*, a much-raced three year old who had consistently failed on the Flat and had once suffered an accident requiring 29 stitches in his off-foreleg.

Trained and ridden by Tommy, *Jay Trump* went on to win 11 races, including the premier American steeplechase, the Maryland Hunt Cup, twice. Then, eight months in advance, he was sent to England to be prepared for the 1965 National by a fledgling trainer, Fred Winter. Tommy followed four months later to benefit, like *Jay Trump*, from the experience of a master jockey-turned-trainer who had twice won the National.

Smith and *Jay Trump* won three of five races in the build-up for the National. Then, most crucially, the American literally lived with the bay gelding when he needed to be isolated as a coughing epidemic swept through Lambourn in Berkshire. Against the odds, *Jay Trump* escaped infection and went to Aintree fifth in the betting behind *Freddie*, Scotland's 7-2 hot favourite.

Following Winter's instructions precisely, Tommy cruised patiently round the first circuit, keeping to the inside and so avoiding a five-horse pile-up at Becher's. On the second circuit, they steadily moved up through the field and from the second last they were engaged in an all-out duel with Pat McCarron and *Freddie*. Tommy's only error was to resort to the whip when leading by a length on the run-in. One crack was enough to make the bay gelding swish his tail resentfully. At once the American realised his mistake and thereafter rode out with hands and heels to prevail by just three-quarters of a length from a favourite with a 5lb disadvantage.

Three months later, *Jay Trump* was leading at the last in France's premier chase, the Grand Steeplechase de Paris at Auteuil. But Tommy had needed to waste excessively, losing 16lb to make the weight, and now he lacked the strength to power his horse home to victory. They finished third, beaten by just two and a half lengths by the winner *Hyeres III*.

Back in the States, their brilliant partnership triumphed yet again, with a third victory in the four-mile Maryland Hunt Cup. The nine year old *Jay Trump* was then promptly retired, and within a year Tommy's own racing career had ground to a halt. Briefly he turned to training, then quit the sport in

S

favour of a full-time job in education.
See also: Jay Trump; Winter, Fred; Maryland Hunt
Cup; Americans; United States.

SMITH, William

When Cheltenham-based Bill Smith made his Grand
National debut in 1913 he was a little-known jockey
of minimal experience over fences, and so there was
some surprise when he grabbed the lead on 25-1
shot *Blow Pipe* at Becher's Brook and impressively
pulled further ahead of the field. But it was a false
dawn. Soon after clearing Valentine's *Blow Pipe*
began to fade and then fell.

One year later Smith adopted the same front-running tactics on eight year old *Sunloch*. By the first
Becher's he had established a lead of a full 20
lengths, and early on the second circuit he had extended it to an extraordinary 40 lengths. Again he
had seemingly set a suicidal pace that could not possibly be sustained. And certainly this was the judgment of his nearest rivals, Charles Hawkins and Alec
Carter, the riders of French challengers *Trianon III*
and *Lutteur III* respectively.

But when they finally made their charge they
found that it was all too late. Though *Sunloch* stumbled over the last, Smith held him together to win
by eight lengths. He had virtually 'stolen' the race.

A key factor was *Sunloch*'s light weight of 9st
7lb. He was receiving a full three stone from the
favourite *Covertcoat* who had won the 1913 National by a distance, and only a pound less from the
joint second favourite *Lutteur III*, the 1909 winner.
Nonetheless he was given a faultless ride by Smith
who, in the last prep race for Aintree, a two-miler at
Derby, had brought him home first by a distance.

Smith went on to become champion jump jockey
in the following season. But this remained his one
great ride at Aintree. In 1915, in his third and last
National there, he failed to finish on *Thowl Pin*; and
then the racecourse was taken over for three years
by the War Office. However, Smith did have a most
memorable ride in the 1917 substitute National
staged at Gatwick. Yet again he set much of the
pace, and this time he was desperately unlucky. He
had the race at his mercy on American-bred
Limerock when, like *Devon Loch* 39 years later, his
mount collapsed only yards from the winning post.
Most probably he had slipped on a patch of ground
made treacherous by a recent snowfall.
See also: Sunloch.

SMITH ECCLES, Steve

In his chequered riding career, Steve Smith Eccles
had his share of major victories, most notably scoring three Champion Hurdle victories (1985-87)
when riding *See You Then* for trainer Nicky Henderson. He was a most accomplished jockey, belying
his reputation as the clown prince of steeplechasing.
However, his involvement with the Grand National
is more noted for humourous incidents than for racing achievements.

Born on June 9, 1955, the son of a Derbyshire
miner, Smith Eccles had no riding experience beyond
sitting on a pit pony when, at 15, he started out as a
stable lad with Newmarket trainer Harry Thomson
Jones. Apprenticed to ride in 1972, he had his first
winner, *Ballysilly*, in a novice hurdle at Market
Rasen in November, 1974; and three years later he
began a hugely successful partnership with the two-
mile champion chaser *Tingle Creek*. Then, in 1978,
came his first Cheltenham Festival victory. Defiantly
riding with a cracked collarbone strapped up, he triumphed on *Sweet Joe* in the Sun Alliance Chase.

In 1979 Steve had high hopes of making a spectacular Grand National debut riding *Zongalero* for
Henderson. Alas, eight days before the race, he fell
head first in a Devon handicap hurdle. He tried to
make light of his injuries but the next day, being
compelled by pain to see a specialist, he learned that
he had a broken neck – one vertebra fractured and
two others displaced. He was out for the season.
Meanwhile Bob Davies took over on *Zongalero*, a
20-1 chance who finished runner-up, beaten just one
and a half lengths by *Rubstic*.

One year later Smith Eccles was back on
Zongalero for his first National ride. But the bay
gelding had been raised 8lb; and, more significantly,
knowing what to expect, he was now a most reluctant
jumper. He struggled over the 19th where there were
seven fallers, and refused at the next. Subsequently
Steve fell on *Zongalero* at the second Becher's in
1981, and fell on 50-1 shot *Sun Lion* in 1982.

In 1983 he was leading the field on *Keengaddy*
after the first Becher's but was carried wide at the
Canal Turn, losing much ground and then falling at
Valentine's. Thereafter, Steve's best chance in ten
National appearances came in 1986 when he rode
Classified who had been fifth the previous year
under John White. They led after the secon Becher's
only to finish a well-beaten third at 22-1.

As a freelance, Steve achieved remarkable consistency; in 1989-90, for example, he rode 56 winners with a strike-rate of one in four. He began the following season with nine successive wins, just failing to set an all-time record when he was beaten at Plumpton on an odds-on favourite before scoring by 20 lengths on *Spofforth* to reach 10 wins in 11 rides. Altogether he rode 868 winners in England; and on *Zongalero*, the perpetual bridesmaid, he finished second in Mackeson, the Massey Ferguson and the Hennessy.

Thus, his overall National record does him scant justice: *Zongalero* (1980) refused; *Zongalero* (1981) fell; *Sun Lion* (1982) fell; *Keengaddy* (1983) fell; *Hill of Slane* (1984) 11th; *Hill of Slane* (1985) fell; *Classified* (1986) third; *Classified* (1987), unseated from the 9-1 third favourite when his saddle slipped; *Conclusive* (1990) fell; *Bonanza Boy* (1992) unseated at the 19th.

See also: Humour.

SOARER, The

Winner of the 1896 Grand National which had a 28-strong field, the largest for 23 years. A seven year old, Irish-bred bay gelding (by S*kylark* out of *Idalia*) *The Soarer* was making his first appearance in the race – as was his amateur rider, Captain David Campbell – and he won at 40-1 by a length and a half from former winner *Father O'Flynn*.

It was very much a personal triumph for Campbell who, while serving in Ireland with the 9th Lancers, had bought the horse unbroken and had first ridden him as a four year old, finishing runner-up in the Irish Grand Military Chase. He regularly took him out on the gallops for trainer Willie Moore, and he rode him in all of his 12 races (seven won) as a five year old.

In contrast, in 1895, *The Soarer* ran unsuccessfully in eight chases before ending a bleak year with a Boxing Day win over three and a half miles at Kempton Park. Following two more defeats early in 1896, Mr Campbell sold the gelding for £600 – but only on condition that he rode him some two months later in the National and that, if successful, would be allowed to retain the Cup and half of the £1,975 stake. The new owner was William Hall Walker, son of a former Mayor of Liverpool, later to become a colonel in the First World War, a Member of Parliament, and then Lord Wavertree, a leading breeder of thoroughbreds.

Having been defeated in ten of his previous 11 outings, and having fallen in his last pre-Aintree race at Hurst Park, *The Soarer* was disregarded in the betting – except, that is, by owner Hall Walker who risked £50 at the long odds. Equally unfavoured by the punters was *Father O'Flynn*, making his fourth appearance since winning the National by 20 lengths in 1892. He, too, was 40-1.

The shocks soon came. Most notably, the great *Manifesto* fell at the first, and last year's winner *Wild Man From Borneo* went down at the fourth. Meanwhile *The Soarer* was always handily placed, and he snatched the lead two fences from home, thereafter just holding on to resist the challenge of the fast-finishing *Father O'Flynn* who was 13lb worse off in the weights. For the first time a serving cavalry officer had ridden the National winner.

The Soarer reappeared in 1897 but, raised 19lb, he never jumped securely and crashed out at the first Valentine's, leaving Campbell, on special leave from India, nursing a broken collarbone. There was no concession by the handicapper the following year when he was ridden by Arthur Nightingall, twice a National winning jockey. Still prone to over-jumping, he crashed out at the Water Jump. It was his third and last National and he was never to win another race.

See also: Campbell, Captain D.G.M.; Wavertree, Lord.

SOVIET UNION
See: Russia.

SPAIN

For many years Spanish involvement with the Grand National was limited to the seven appearances between 1952 and 1976 of the extraordinary, accident-prone Duque of Alberquerque whose best effort was an eighth place in 1974. In 1990 a fellow countryman took up the challenge: champion amateur jockey and young veterinary student José Simo, riding *Gallic Prince* in the colours of Iberian Airlines. Trained by Philip Hobbs, the 11 year old gelding was a proven stayer, having won a year earlier at Uttoxeter over four and a half miles. But he was now a full stone out of the handicap and regarded as a no-hoper. To his great credit, faced with unfavourable fast going, Simo safely brought his mount home in 13th position. One year later he challenged on the outsider *Southernair* and was unseated at the seventh.

See also: Alberquerque, Duque de.

S

SPECIFY

Nine year old winner of the 1971 Grand National which saw one of the most competitive finishes in modern times, the last fence being jumped by five leading horses almost in unison. *Specify* speared through a fortuitous gap at the Elbow to take the inside rail; then, superbly ridden by John Cook, driving all out with hands and heels, he grabbed victory on the line – by a neck from *Black Secret*, with *Astbury* two and a half lengths back in third.

Specify – a brown gelding by *Specific* out of *Ora Lamae* – was bred in Norwich by Mr Alan Parker and bought for £300 as a foal by former royal jockey Arthur Freeman, who had won the 1958 National on *Mr What*. Like former National winners *Jay Trump* and *Anglo*, he was hard-raced without distinction as a two year old. Then, after an unimpressive first season over hurdles, he was passed on to a succession of different owner-trainers.

He improved as a four year old to win three successive minor events. Then, at six, his future looked in serious doubt as he broke a bone in his head when falling in the Schweppes Gold Trophy Hurdle. But he came back to prove himself a most consistent jumper, and after winning a Windsor chase in February, 1970, he changed hands for the fifth time. The buyer, for £12,000, was holiday camp supremo F. W. (later Sir Fred) Pontin who, combining business with pleasure, would later give his horses such names as *Go Pontin*, *Go Pontinental* and *Pontingo*. Now he wanted to have a runner in the forthcoming Grand National; and at Aintree, ridden by Cook, *Specify* ran well before being brought down at the second Becher's.

Stabled with trainer John Sutcliffe at Epsom, *Specify* returned for the 1971 National without a seasonal win behind him and he was 14th in the betting at 28-1. Nevertheless, owner, trainer and jockey were hoping to bring off an unprecedented double, having two months earlier won the Schweppes Gold Trophy with 33-1 outsider *Cala Mesquida*.

Never prominent in the early stages, *Specify* jumped securely in the wake of many fallers, five of them, including the favourite *Gay Trip*, going at the first fence. By Valentine's, however, he was well placed behind the tearaway leaders and held his position while many more fell by the wayside. At the last fence he was lying fifth in a group so bunched up that any one of five looked a possible winner; and

his final challenge over the last 50 yards was then timed to perfection.

When *Specify* returned one year later it was again without any impressive form behind him; and this time without jockey Cook whose career had been ended by a serious leg-breaking fall. However, he had a most able rider in Irishman Barry Brogan who had been runner-up in the 1968 National on *Moidore's Token*; and, unusually for a former winner, still relatively young, he had been dropped 2lb in the weights and was 11th in the betting at 22-1. Starting strongly, he remained in contention as far as the second Becher's and came home in the torrential rain the sixth of only nine finishers. This time *Black Secret* (third) and *Astbury* (fifth) were ahead of him. He was never to win another race.

See also: Cook, John; Freeman, Arthur.

SPECK, William

Of all unlucky riders in Grand National history, there have been few more tragic figures than the courageous little jockey Billy Speck who was six times runner-up in the jockeys' championship between 1926 and 1933 without ever winning the title.

In his first three Nationals he failed to finish – on *Donegal* (1930), *Drim* (1931) and *Dusty Foot* (1932). Then, in 1933, he was united with an outstanding chaser: Mr J.H. Whitney's seven year old chestnut gelding *Thomond II*. But, unluckily, *Thomond II*'s emergence coincided with that of a horse-in-a-million, the six year old *Golden Miller*.

In the 1933 Cheltenham Gold Cup, Speck spurred his horse into a useful lead on the second circuit, but his great friend Billy Stott was merely biding his time on *Golden Miller*. *Thomond II* was beaten ten lengths. One year later, when 'the Miller' won the Gold Cup again, *Thomond II* did not compete, being aimed exclusively at the National. At Aintree, however, he was burdened with 12st 4lb, 2lb more than his great rival, and he was pegged back into third place behind *Golden Miller* and *Delaneige*, in receipt of 12lb. Though he had finished ten lengths adrift, Billy suggested that he might have won but for losing precious ground when baulked by *Gregalach* being pulled up after the Canal Turn.

In 1935 came the unforgettable Cheltenham Gold Cup in which *Golden Miller* and *Thomond II* were locked in a titanic battle to the winning post, the former prevailing by just three-quarters of a length. Over drinks afterwards, Billy Speck remarked to winning jockey Gerry Wilson: 'When we are old and grey, sitting back and enjoying a drink, we can tell them how we did ride at least one great horse race, one day in our lives.' Never, as it sadly happened, were more ironic words spoken.

Fifteen days later battle was resumed at Aintree, with *Golden Miller* going off in the National as 2-1 favourite, followed by *Thomond II* on 9-2. This time, however, *Thomond II* had an 8lb advantage in the weights, and his prospects seemed to soar when the triple Gold Cup winner unseated his rider two fences after Valentine's. At the last *Thomond II* rose in unison with *Reynoldstown*. But then, on the run-in, he faded behind *Reynoldstown* and *Blue Prince*. Again Billy was relegated to third in the National.

At the time it was the widely held view that Speck would have won the National on *Thomond II* if the gelding had not had such a desperately hard race only 15 days before. Indeed, Mr Whitney had been strongly advised not to run his horse in the Gold Cup when there was so much in his favour for a National challenge.

Billy could reflect that, at 31, he could look forward to more Grand National chances. But it was not be. Tragically, only a few weeks later, he broke his back when being thrown from the difficult *Gwelo* in the first race of the Cheltenham spring meeting. He died six days later, a loss mourned by hundreds who followed his cortège past the racecourse on its way to the churchyard of his home village Bishops Cleeve.

See also: Whitney, John 'Jock' Hay.

SPONSORSHIP

Commercial sponsorship of races in England began with the Whitbread Gold Cup in 1957. One year later the Grand National had its first sponsor with the Irish Hospital Sweepstakes contributing £5,000 towards the prize money. In 1961 and 1962 there was an additional £5,000 from Schweppes Limited, so enabling cash rewards to be given to jockeys, trainers and stable staff involved with the four placed horses. Then, in 1963, when Schweppes chose to finance their own valuable Gold Trophy Handicap Hurdle at the Aintree meeting, their National sponsorship was taken over by Messrs Vaux Limited who matched the £5,000 from the Irish Sweepstakes.

In 1965 it was announced that Aintree would have to be sold because of financial difficulties, and thereafter each year the Grand National was billed as being potentially the last. But it was not until 1972 that the race again had the support of a sponsor, Messrs BP Limited, to the tune of £10,000. Subsequently, this was replaced by £20,000 from the Walton Group of Liverpool in 1974; £40,000 from *The News of the World* (1975-77), *The Sun* (1978) and the Colt Car Company (1979); £50,000 from *The Sun* (1980-81); and £51,000 from *The Sun* (1982-83).

In December, 1975, the National had only been saved by the intervention of the bookmaking giants Ladbrokes who had negotiated a seven-year tenancy deal with Bill Davies, the property developer. On its expiry the situation again became critical following the failure of a public appeal to save the National. But then, in 1984, came salvation in the form of Seagram Distillers, the Canadian whisky giants. Prompted by Mr Ivan Straker, a dedicated Aintree supporter, then chairman of Seagram (UK), the company saved the great race at the 11th hour by putting up the millions that enabled the racecourse to come under the control of the Jockey Club and be run by subsidiary Racecourse Holdings Trust and now known as Jockey Club Racecourses. In addition Seagram sponsored the National to the tune of £51,000 in 1984-85, rising to £55,000 in 1986.

Over eight Seagram years, facilities at Aintree were much improved; and most appropriately, in 1991, the Grand National was won by a horse named *Seagram*. The following year, sponsorship of the National meeting was taken over by Martell Cognac, a subsidiary of Seagram Distillers. A later renewal of the agreement ensured that the world's most famous steeplechase would be known as the Martell Grand National until 2004.

In October, 1996, Martell's Grand National backing won the International Sponsorship of Sport Award at the inaugural convention in Geneva. Their 13 years of support, greatly raising the profile of the race, closed with a cash injection of over £2 million for the 2004 National meeting, taking their total financial backing to around £10 million for race sponsorship and a further £15 million in promotional back-up. Then, in November, 2004, Scottish and Newcastle, the brewer, signed a three-year contract to sponsor the three-day meeting; and 2005 saw the first John Smith's Grand National, with its prize money raised to £700,000, the million mark in terms of euros. Subsequently, John Smith's extended the contract for a further three years, taking its sponsorhip up to 2010.

See also: Straker, Major Ivan.

SPRIG

In 1927, for the first time, millions of Britons could share in the excitement of the Grand National by way of the wireless and the BBC's initial broadcast of the event. And commentator Meyrick Good of *The Sporting Life* could not have called home a more popular winner. Not just because *Sprig*, winner by one length, was the 8-1 favourite, but more because his victory could be viewed as a fitting memorial to the sacrifice of so many who had fallen in the First World War.

Ten years earlier, when home on leave from the trenches, Captain Richard Partridge had bred a chestnut colt by *Marco* out of *Spry*. He named the foal *Sprig* and dreamed of one day riding him in the National when the great conflict was over. But cruelly fate intervened, the captain being killed in action when the 1918 Armistice was only a few weeks away. Nonetheless, his mother determined to keep that dream alive. Eventually she sent *Sprig* to the Newmarket trainer Tom Leader.

Ridden by the trainer's son, Ted Leader, *Sprig* was an eight year old when he finished a respectable fourth in the 1925 National. He so impressed as a 33-1 long-shot that he was promoted to 5-1 favouritism the following year. Again he finished fourth.

In 1927, *Sprig* was raised substantially in the weights, to 12st 4lb. But, as in the past two years, Ted Leader maintained his support of Mrs Partridge's dream, again turning down big money offers to take other rides. (In 1926 he had passed over a huge sum in rejecting the chance to ride *Jack Horner*, the horse that won the National for American Charlie Schwartz.

This year the National was run on heavy going with a new record number of 37 starters. The fallers came fast and furious, the pattern being set by *Thrown In*, the Cheltenham Gold Cup winner, who crashed out at the first fence. By Becher's second time round, the field had been cut by two thirds. Here a 100-1 outsider, *Bovril III*, narrowly led from *Keep Cool* and *Master Billie*, with *Sprig* and three others in close order behind.

Sprig made his move at the Canal Turn, putting in such an enormous leap that it carried him from fifth place into a marginal lead. But two horses, *Bright's Boy* (top-weighted) and *Bovril III*, were staying with him; and the former moved ahead at the final open ditch only to be overhauled by *Sprig* as they came to the last fence. Now, on the long run-in *Bovril III*'s huge weight advantage showed as he put in a storming finish to join in a triple dash for the line. In a pulsating finish, the winning post came just in time for *Sprig*. He finished one length ahead of *Bovril III* (20lb better off) with *Bright's Boy*, ridden by the renowned Jack Anthony, only a further length behind.

It was an extraordinary performance by *Bovril III*, a one-eyed no-hoper who had raced wide throughout under his owner Mr G.W. Pennington (later Sir William Pennington-Ramsden). But the overwhelming ovation was for *Sprig* and Mrs M. Partridge, the third woman to lead in a National winner.

Again ridden by Ted Leader, *Sprig* came back with maximum weight in 1928; and again there was a record field. *Sprig* fell at the fifth fence – at least avoiding the biggest pile-up in steeplechasing history which would see 20 horses eliminated at the Canal Turn. Following that disaster, caused by *Easter Hero*, only two of 42 starters completed the course: *Tipperary Tim*, the 100-1 winner, and the re-mounted *Billy Barton*.

Unbelievably in the light of that chaos, no fewer than 66 horses were allowed to compete in the 1929 National. *Sprig*, now a 12 year old on the top weight of 12st 5lb, was a 50-1 chance, and understandably Leader deserted him in favour of Stephen Sanford's *Mount Etna*. His replacement was the experienced Anthony Escott, son of the celebrated trainer, who ten years earlier had finished third on *Pollen*, the first of his six National rides.

Both *Sprig* and *Mount Etna* were to fall in a race which saw 56 runners failing to finish. And again there was a shock result: victory for another 100-1 outsider, *Gregalach*, the least favoured of five runners trained by Tom Leader. On retirement, *Sprig* had won 11 chases, including the 1924 Stanley Chase at Aintree and the 1926 National Hunt Handicap Chase at Cheltenham.

See also: Leader, Tom and Ted.

SPRING DOUBLE, The

A long-established wager in which bets on the Lincoln Handicap, at the start of the Flat season, are

coupled with the Grand National that usually follows a week later. No trainer has saddled the winner of both races in the same year, but Dermot Weld came close in 1984 when he won the Lincoln with *Saving Mercy* at 14-1 and saddled *Greasepaint*, the 9-1 favourite and four-length runner-up in the National. Ivor Anthony trained the winner of both races, but in different years – with *Royal Mail* (the 1937 National) and *Quartier Maitre* (the 1940 Lincoln).
See also: Betting.

STACK, Thomas Brendan

The Irish-born jockey who made Grand National history in 1977 when he rode 12 year old *Red Rum* to his unparalleled third success, and by an extraordinary 25 lengths winning margin. In this, the penultimate season of his 13-year riding career, Tommy Stack was to finish champion National Hunt jockey for the second time and with his best-ever total of 97 winners.

It was a hugely deserved reward for a most popular and knowledgeable rider who, at one time, seemed to have missed his chance of National glory. In 1972 he had been the first jockey to ride *Red Rum* for trainer Ginger McCain, winning the three-mile Windermere Handicap Steeplechase at Carlisle. But, being retained by another stable, he was not always available. Seeking a regular rider, McCain had eventually turned to Brian Fletcher who would partner *Red Rum* in 28 races, including the Grand Nationals of 1973, 1974 and 1975 in which he finished first, first and second respectively.

Born on November 15, 1945, a Co. Kerry farmer's son, Stack started out as an insurance clerk in Dublin before quitting to work at the yard run by the father of his school friend (later top jockey) Barry Brogan. Then, at the age of 19, he joined the staff of Yorkshire trainer Bobby Renton in the hope of pursuing a riding career. He scored his first win (on *New Money* at Wetherby) in October, 1965, making sufficient progress to turn professional two years later and to achieve 50 winners in the 1970-71 season. Curiously, the last winner he rode that season for Renton was a six year old gelding, named *Red Rum*, who the following year would be sent to the Doncaster sales.

At this point, on the retirement of 83 year old Renton, Stack took over the Ripon stable as both trainer and jockey, and briefly he had *Red Rum* in his charge. But soon, having chosen to concentrate on riding, he left to become first jockey to the pro-

lific trainer W. A. Stephenson. In the 1974-5 season he was to capture the National Hunt jockey championship with 82 winners, and he would take the title again in 1976-77 with 97 winners.

Until that year he had made no impression in the Grand National. In 1971, on his debut in the race, he had finished 11th on a 66-1 chance, *Final Move*. The following year, his mount *Saggart's Choice* was a faller at the first fence. Next, in 1974, he had a major disappointment when finishing 11th on eight year old *Scout*, the 7-1 clear favourite who was on the minimum weight despite three successive wins. That year, on 12st top weight, *Red Rum* scored his second successive victory.

Stack fared no better in his title-winning year of 1975. His mount *Clear Cut*, a 20-1 chance, was a faller, while *Red Rum* again ran impressively to finish second on soft going that he hated. But then, by a chance twist of fate, his hopes of National success were suddenly revived. Following a disagreement, McCain had chosen to part company with *Red Rum's* regular rider. Ron Barry took over on 'Rummy' in the Hennessy Cognac Gold Cup. But subsequently he was tied to another stable; and so McCain returned to his old friend, Tommy Stack.

In the 1976 National, Tommy rode a finely judged race but once again, though battling well to the finishing line, *Red Rum* found one too good for him at the weights. He finished two lengths second to *Rag Trade*, receiving 12lb; and eight lengths back in third was *Eyecatcher*, ridden by *Red Rum's* former jockey, Brian Fletcher.

That day it seemed that a third National win for *Red Rum* was now a forlorn hope. But one year later McCain was more confident than ever that his superstar could win – even though he was 12 years old, again on top weight, and facing a favourite, *Andy Pandy*, who had twice beaten *Red Rum* that season and looked thrown in at the weights. And so it proved. When *Andy Pandy*, 12 lengths ahead, fell at the second Becher's, Stack found himself in the lead sooner than he would have wished. But thereafter they were never headed.

Subsequently, Stack made many public appearances with the most celebrated horse in the land, and most memorable of all was *Red Rum's* walk-on role in the BBC's 'Sports Review of the Year' programme staged at the New London Theatre. Tommy, confined to a wheelchair following a pelvis-breaking fall in the parade ring at Hexham, was unable to

S

attend in person. Instead he appeared on a huge TV screen to be interviewed by Frank Bough. As he spoke, 'Rummy' cocked his ears and looked knowingly towards the screen – a recognition of his partner that brought huge applause. 'See,' quipped his jockey, 'he is far more intelligent than me.'

After that great 1976-77 season, in which he had also won the Schweppes Gold Trophy Handicap Hurdle on *True Lad* and Cheltenham's Grand Annual Challenge Cup on *Tom Morgan*, Tommy's fought back from his injury to return in March, 1978, riding as determinedly as ever – and just in time to be reunited with *Red Rum* in the Greenall Whitley Breweries Steeplechase at Haydock.

For *Red Rum*, a 33-1 outsider finishing sixth, this was just a last tune-up for a sixth tilt at the National. But later he was found to have a stress fracture of a small bone in the foot. Withdrawn, on the eve of the National, 13 year old 'Rummy' had run his last race. Instead, in his seventh National, Stack was on *Hidden Value*, a faller at the second fence.

Tommy soon had the consolation of a major prize: the Whitbread Gold Cup, won on *Strombolus*. But then, after five unplaced rides at Hexham, and feeling the effects of his injuries more and more, he decided to call it a day. He was 32 and had wisely prepared for his retirement, investing in a livery stable to be run with the help of his wife Liz. He had a career total of 606 winners.

In 1988 he took out a full trainer's licence in Ireland and quickly made his mark, winning the inaugural Cartier Million at Phoenix Park with *Colwyn Bay*. In 1994 he captured his first English Classic – the 1,000 Guineas with *Las Meninas*; and in 1998 he won the Irish 1,000 Guineas with *Tarascon*.

Then, at Christmas, 1999, his life was suddenly in peril when he was struck down by a savage form of meningitis. For 13 days he lay unconscious on a life-support machine, and he remained in a Cork hospital for two months. It led to deafness and impaired balance but, as before, his toughness of spirit prevailed. Fighting back to resume business as usual and ably assisted by his son, Fozzie, he has since trained many more big-race winners as master of Thomastown Castle in Tipperary, his notable horses including *Kings Mill*, *Title Roll*, *Kostrama* and *Runyon*. *See also:* Red Rum; McCain, Donald.

STALBRIDGE, Lord

Owner and trainer of *Bogskar*, the seven year old winner of the 1940 Grand National who, like the runner-up *MacMoffat*, was prevented by the war from returning to Aintree until six years later when both were fallers.

A former officer in the 14th Hussars, and a holder of the Military Cross, Lord Stalbridge first challenged for the National in 1926 with *Thrown In*, a chestnut he had bought one year earlier as an entire. Now gelded, and trained by Owen Anthony at the owner's Pounds Farm stables at Eastbury, Berkshire, the ten year old finished seventh at 33-1, a creditable performance since he was ridden by Lord Stalbridge's son, the Hon Hugh Grosvenor, an amateur with minimal experience over fences.

In 1927, when appearing in only his ninth steeplechase, Mr Grosvenor rode *Thrown In* to a surprise victory in the Cheltenham Gold Cup, winning by two lengths from five year old *Grakle*, destined to win the National in 1931. As a result, his father's *Thrown In* was third in the betting for the 1927 National, behind *Sprig* (the winner) and *Grakle*. He fell at the first fence and tragically Mr Grosvenor never raced again. Having taken up a military post in Australia, he was killed one year later in an air crash.

Lord Stalbridge contested the National again in 1931 when his *Trump Card*, a 13 year old outsider, failed to finish. Then, two years after his triumph with *Bogskar*, he experienced further grief with the news that Flight-Sergeant Mervyn Jones, his National winning jockey, had failed to return from a wartime flying mission. Meanwhile, however, he had bred and personally trained another very useful chaser: *Red Rower*, who finished third in the 1941 Cheltenham Gold Cup. One year later *Red Rower* comfortably won the Grand Annual from Lord Sefton's *Medoc II* and was made favourite for the Gold Cup. Though the placings were now reversed, with *Medoc II* prevailing by eight lengths, *Red Rower* came back to win when the next Gold Cup was held in 1945.

Lord Stalbridge, a steward of the National Hunt Committee, was last represented in the National in 1947 when *Bogskar*, making his third and final appearance, was 14 years old and a 100-1 outsider. As in the year before he was a faller. Two years later, on Christmas Eve, his owner died at the age of 69. Among his lasting legacies to racing is Wincanton racecourse, which he helped to save from liquidation and have moved to its present location in 1925. *See also:* Bogskar; Jones, Mervyn Anthony.

STARTING PRICES
Horses with the shortest starting prices in the Grand National are:

2-1 – *Golden Miller* (1935), ur at the 11th.

5-2 – *Lottery* (1841), pu; *Regal* (1879), sixth, remounted; *Conjuror II* (1924), ko.

11-4 – *Poethlyn* (1919) won; *Freddie* (1966) second.

3-1 – *The Nun* (1840), fell; *Peter Simple* (1843) eighth; *Trout* (1855), fell; *Huntsman* (1862) Won; *Jealousy* (1863) sixth; *Chandos* (1876), fell; *Zitella* (1883) fifth; *Coronet* (1886) sixth; *Poethlyn* (1920), fell.

100-30 – *The Brewer* (1859), fell; *Despatch* (1872), third; *Mohican* (1882), fell; *Roquefort* (1885) Won; *Avenger* (1936), fell.

7-2 – *Anatis* (1860) won: *Fortunatus* (1869), pu; *The Colonel* (1870) won; *Ambush II* (1904), fell; *John M.P.* (1906), fell; *Lutteur III* (1911), fell; *Freddie* (1965) second; *Red Rum* (1975), second.

Poethlyn, carrying a top weight of 12st 7lb, became the shortest priced winner in 1919, one year after winning the 1918 wartime substitute National at Gatwick. The following year he was a faller at 3-1.

Horses with the longest starting prices
500-1 – *Midday Welcome* and *Never Tamper* (1983); *Mount Oliver, Late Night Extra* and *Doubleuagain* (1986); *Cranlome, Gala Prince, Valencio, Lucky Rew, Le Bambino, Brit* and *Spartan Orient* (1987); and *Tarqogans Best* (1993 void).

300-1 – *Sydney Quinn* and *Tower Moss* (1983); *Brown Trix, Hettinger, Kersil, Mearlin* and *Smartside* (1989); *Quirinus* (1993 void).

Of these outsiders, only three completed the course: *Cranlome*, 14th, *Gala Prince*, 20th, and *Brit*, 21st. Remarkably, early morning prices on Grand National day, 1987, offered five horses – *Cranlome, Gala Prince, Lucky Rew, Le Bambino* and *Spartan Orient* – at 1,000-1. And again, in 1989, three horses – *Brown Trix, Kersil* and *Smartside* – were available early at 1,000-1.

The longest-priced winners are four 100-1 shots: *Tipperary Tim* (1928), *Gregalach* (1929), *Caughoo* (1947) and *Foinavon* (1967). The first runner to go off at 100-1 was *Royal Blue* (1852), a faller under George Stevens who would go on to become the most successful National jockey of all time. In the 57-strong National of 1947 a record number of 26 horses would start at 100-1.

In 1886 the National had its first 200-1 outsiders: *Fontenoy* (refused) and *Magpie* who finished a most creditable fourth behind three other seven year olds. But it was not until nearly a century later that starting prices really took off. In 1983 the field of 41 runners included three 200-1 chances, two priced at 300-1, and, most sensationally, two priced at 500-1.

The upward trend continued. In 1986 three contenders were priced at 500-1 and the following year no fewer than 17 of 40 runners started at 100-1 or more and these included a record seven in the 500-1 bracket. Such was the good judgment of the layers that only four of the 17 completed the course, the best being *Big Brown Bear*, 13th at 200-1, with *Cranlome* 14th at 500-1.

Since the *Foinavon* fiasco of 1967 no winner has had a starting price of more than 50-1. In the 1990s – disregarding *Esha Ness* who was first home at 50-1 in the void National of 1993 – only one of nine winners (*Royal Athlete*, 40-1) started longer than 16-1. So far this century there have been three: *Red Marauder* (33-1), *Bindaree* (20-1) and *Silver Birch* (33-1).
See also: Favourites; Outsiders.

STEEPLECHASING
The sport of steeplechasing was born in Ireland in 1752 when a Mr Edmund Blake challenged a Mr Cornelius O'Callaghan to a cross-country race from St John's Church in Buttevant, Co. Cork, to St Mary's Church in Doneraile some four and a half miles away. Racing from steeple to steeple, they had to jump a number of stone walls, ditches and hedges. Forty years later a similar event was held in England. But it was not until 1811 that the first English steeplechase over a course especially laid out with obstacles was held at Bedford; and 1830 before the first British steeplechase meeting was formally staged at St Albans by Thomas (Tommy) Coleman, keeper of an inn which he renamed the Turf Hotel. In 1836 Aintree had its first Grand Liverpool Steeplechase, arguably the inaugural Grand National. But it was not until 1839 that this annual event, now with 17 starters, was held on a scale worthy of that distinction.
See also: Grand National.

S

STEPHENSON, William Arthur

Incredibly, the name of W.A. Stephenson does not appear on Aintree's Grand National Roll of Honour – neither as an owner nor as a trainer. Incredibly, because no one in National Hunt history has been so successful in both capacities. As an owner, he enjoyed 465 wins over jumps between 1946 and 1992 – a post-war record approached only by the Queen Mother's 445. As a trainer, he turned out 2,644 winners over jumps and 344 on the Flat – an all-time record until the advent of the relentless Martin Pipe juggernaut.

Stephenson's jumps successes included the 1987 Cheltenham Gold Cup with *The Thinker*; the Scottish Grand National (twice); the Welsh and Midlands Grand Nationals; the Mackeson Gold Cup; the Melling Chase and the Topham-John Hughes Memorial Trophy. Yet, curiously, in a career spanning more than four decades, he never became champion National Hunt trainer, and most unluckily, unlike his great northern rival Gordon Richards, he never scored in the Aintree Grand National, having to settle for two second places and two thirds.

Most especially he was unlucky not to win the race with *Durham Edition*, an outstanding Aintree specialist who ran in four successive Nationals, finishing four lengths second in 1988; fifth in 1989; three-quarters of a length runner-up to the record-breaking *Mr Frisk* in 1990; and sixth in 1991. He was unlucky, too, with *The Thinker* whose Aintree debut was delayed by injury until 1989. Then, under top weight of 11st 10lb and ridden by Simon Sherwood, he made up an amazing amount of ground from the 28th fence to finish an heroic third behind *Little Polveir* and *West Tip* to whom he was conceding 24lb and 13lb respectively.

Arthur Stephenson, or 'W.A.' as he was always known in racing circles, was born in 1920 and had his first win in 1946 when he trained and rode *T.O.D.* to victory at Rothbury. As a trainer, he became renowned for his unbounded energy, his retiring nature (he avoided the Press like the plague) and his modesty. He was, so he claimed, primarily 'a horse-dealing farmer', and indeed for 14 years he operated as a permit-holder, training only for himself. 'Little fish are sweet' was his favourite saying, and his modus operandi was largely to produce novice winners and sell them profitably, often to his patrons. Thus, while being ten times the leading trainer and three times the top owner in his number

of wins, he was never champion trainer or owner in terms of prize money.

Based near Bishop Auckland, Co. Durham, he followed his first big winner – *Kinmont Wullie* (1961 Scottish National) – by turning out *Cocky Consort* to finish a good third at 50-1 in the 1962 Cheltenham Gold Cup and *Mr Jones* to win the 1962 Becher Chase. The following year he won the Ludlow Gold Cup and the National Hunt Chase with *Time*. But while he was regularly to top 100 winners in a season, National success continued to elude him.

He made an impressive enough start in 1961 when he saddled *O'Malley Point* who made a late spurt under the highly experienced Paddy Farrell to be beaten only a neck in third place behind *Merryman II*, the five lengths runner-up to *Nicolaus Silver*. In 1963 his *Mr Jones*, ridden by Farrell, was a faller at Aintree. But the following year Stephenson was most strongly represented by *Time*, one of his many winners to be owned by the clothing store magnate John Cheatle. The bay gelding, ridden by Michael Scudamore, went off as one of four co-favourites, only to be brought down by a loose horse four fences from home. Stephenson's other runners, *Supersweet* and *Sea Knight*, finished 12th and 15th respectively.

Then, in 1965, the trainer again gained third place – this time in a 47-strong field with *Mr Jones*, a 50-1 chance now ridden by his new owner Christopher Collins who would go on to become champion amateur jockey in the next two seasons. His other runner, *Ronald's Boy*, one of 20 100-1 outsiders, was a faller; and his long-shots, *Major Hitch* and *Supersweet*, also failed to finish in 1966.

The 1967 National was, of course, a farce with the mass pile-up that saw only one horse and rider clear the 23rd fence at the first attempt. However, Stephenson's *Kirtle-Lad* did get over – albeit without his rider. Paddy Broderick caught up with him on the landing side, remounted and briefly had hopes of closing on the lucky *Foinavon*. His was the one challenger in with a chance until, maddeningly, he refused at the Canal Turn.

Seemingly, after running non-finishers *Kirtle-Lad* (1968), *Battledore* (1970 and 1971) and *Rigton Avenue* (1972) 'W.A' had his best-ever chance of a National victory in 1974. That year he turned out *Scout*, the 7-1 favourite ridden by Tommy Stack; and this so promising eight year old bay gelding, winner of his last three races, was on the minimum weight, receiving 27lb and a full two stone respectively from the horses second and third in the betting. But, as it proved, that pair were truly exceptional: top-weighted *Red Rum* who would defy a 23lb rise to win by seven lengths, and future winner *L'Escargot* who would be the runner-up.

Disappointingly, though not for Ladbrokes who stood to lose £1 million if he won, *Scout* was never in serious contention and was the 11th of 17 finishers. The trainer's other starters, S*tephen's Society* and *Karacola*, failed to finish. Next, in 1979, he sent out the unfancied *Wagner* who was given a masterful ride by Ridley Lamb to finish fifth at 50-1; and then, in 1983, he saddled *Fortina's Express* who was to be pulled up by Peter Scudamore.

Four years later Stephenson had his greatest training triumph. Following a snowstorm, *The Thinker* was much favoured by stamina-sapping conditions in the 1987 Cheltenham Gold Cup. The chestnut with the white blaze had thrived in such conditions when winning the 1986 Midlands National and now he overhauled two rivals to win the Gold Cup by a length and a half from *Cybrandian*. Yet 'W.A.' was not there to see it. Instead he had chosen to go to his local Hexham course where he had seven little fish in the pot.

Subsequently, *The Thinker* was well-fancied for the 1987 Grand National but disappointingly was a late withdrawal. That year, as in 1986, Stephenson was represented by *Why Forget* who had been placed in the Scottish National (for the second time) and in the Whitbread Gold Cup of 1985. The brown gelding was an out-and-out stayer but not a fluent jumper. He finished 19th, three places worse than the previous year.

Stable hopes of success were much higher in 1988 when ten year old *Durham Edition* made his National debut. He had been third in the Hennessy Cognac Gold Cup and had recently won by 25 lengths in a three-miler at Market Rasen. Indeed, jumping the last at Aintree, Chris Grant thought he was going to win on the 20-1 chestnut gelding. But, as on *Young Driver* in 1986, he was to have victory snatched away on the run-in, this time by the strong finishing *Rhyme 'N' Reason*. *Durham Edition* was beaten by four lengths, with *Monanore* 15 lengths back in third. W.A.'s other runner, *Sir Jest*, seven times a winner this season, had refused at the 27th.

In 1989, after a lengthy layoff with injury, *The Thinker* finally made it to Aintree; and this year offered Stephenson his greatest hope for success. He had no fewer than four runners in the 40-strong field: *Durham Edition*, the 15-2 second favourite; *The Thinker*, 10-1; *Sir Jest*, 40-1, and *Polar Nomad*, 80-1. As predicted by rider Grant, *Durham Edition* did not quite stay in the soft ground and faded from second to fifth place on the run-in. *Sir Jest* was brought down at the first Becher's and *Polar Nomad* was pulled up at the 23rd. Meanwhile *The Thinker's* splendid third place under top weight, conceding 18lb to winner *Little Polveir*, underlined what might have been if only he could have appeared sooner.

In 1990 Stephenson had three runners in the National: *Sir Jest*, ninth, *Nautical Joke*, unseated rider at the 27th, and the magnificent *Durham Edition* who came closest of all to giving the veteran trainer a long-deserved victory, finishing a close second at 9-1. The following year 'W. A.' was preparing *The Thinker* for a second tilt at the National but tragically he had to be put down after breaking a leg. Once again it was left to *Durham Edition*, now 13 years old, to carry the flag and most honourably he finished sixth, his worst position in four consecutive appearances.

Stephenson's last Grand National runner was *Stay On Tracks*, who finished ninth in 1992. That year the great man died, a formidable trainer until the end. In the million-guinea dispersal sale of horses from his yard were the famous *One Man*, who would win two King George VI Chases and the two-mile Champion Chase, and *Over The Deel* who was to finish third in the 1995 National at 100-1.

See also: Grant, Christopher; Durham Edition.

STEPHENSON, William

When *Oxo* won the 1959 Grand National by one and a half lengths, Willie Stephenson became one of only two trainers (along with the great Vincent O'Brien) to have saddled both National and Epsom Derby winners in the 20th century. Eight years earlier he had turned out *Arctic Prince* to win the Derby by six lengths at 28-1; and he had followed up by taking three successive Champion Hurdles (1952-54) with *Sir Ken*, so emulating O'Brien's feat with *Hatton's Grace* (1949-51).

The son of a Co. Durham farmer, and a cousin of his aforementioned namesake, Stephenson, born on October 9, 1911, started out as a jockey on the Flat, being apprenticed at 14 to the Newmarket trainer, Major Vandy Beatty, and later serving as a chief

S

work rider at the nearby stables of royal trainer Captain Cecil Boyd-Rochfort. Most sensationally, as a 16 year old apprentice, he figured in the extraordinary finish to the 1927 Cambridgeshire, riding *Niantic* (25-1) to dead-heat with *Medal* (20-1). Huge controversy surrounded the result, most onlookers being convinced that the true winner was *Insight II*, officially judged to be a length back in third.

It was nonetheless an astonishing ride by one so young. Other early victories included the Yorkshire Cup and Manchester November Handicap; and it was a measure of the boy's fierce determination that he continued riding into the 1930s when he needed to waste his tall, lean frame down to almost seven stone. A broken leg then interrupted his riding career, and subsequently his battle with the scales was lost during Royal Artillery service in the Second World War.

On demob, Stephenson enterprisingly set up at Royston in Hertfordshire as a dual-purpose trainer; and with astonishing speed he achieved major successes not only as a trainer but also as a gambler. His smartest move of all came in 1950 when, on holiday in Paris, he decided to take in the jumping at Auteuil. There he saw a three year old bay finish third in a race which he thought the horse should have won in a canter. He contacted the owner and snapped up the prospect for about £1,000. Thus he acquired the supreme *Sir Ken* who easily won his first English race, the Lancashire Hurdle at Liverpool in 1951, and was sold on to Manchester businessman Maurice Kingsley. Usually partnered by champion jockey, Tim Molony, *Sir Ken* would be unbeaten for three seasons, winning 16 consecutive hurdle races. In 1954, the year of his third Champion Hurdle success, Stephenson also sent out the Eclipse winner *King of the Tudors* and the Yorkshire Oaks winner *Feevagh*.

Having scored his greatest wins on the Flat and over hurdles, Willie further demonstrated his versatility after buying the six year old point-to-pointer *Oxo* for 3,200 guineas on behalf of his patron, Mr J.E. Bigg. When asked what he planned to do with his new purchase, he simply and firmly replied: 'Win the National.'

Within a year and a half, he had trained the jumping novice to win three chases and then the National at the first attempt. On that great day at Aintree he had remained supremely confident that *Oxo* would win; and victory was all the sweeter since it positively obliterated his gambling losses on the first two days of meeting.

Before him, only two trainers had achieved the National-Derby double: Dick Dawson with *Drogheda* (1898) and Derby winners, *Fifinella* (1916), *Trigo* (1929) and *Blenheim* (1930); and George Blackwell with *Rock Sand* (1903) and *Sergeant Murphy* (1923). Subsequently they would be eclipsed by Vincent O'Brien, who saddled three National and six Derby winners.

Though Stephenson failed in his efforts to turn out a second National winner, he made a very strong bid to win the race in 1963. That year, only a few days before the race, he bought the former hunter chaser *Hawa's Song* from his cousin Robert because, as he said, 'I think he will win'. Encouragingly, the ten year old, trained by Robert's brother Arthur, had recently beaten *Springbok*, the National favourite, at Manchester; and now, in a 47-strong field at Aintree, he was going off as a 28-1 chance on the minimum weight.

Brilliantly ridden by newcomer Paddy Broderick, *Hawa's Song* was the third of 22 finishers, behind *Ayala* and *Carrickbeg*. But for Stephenson the trainer it was an altogether unhappy day. He saddled two other contenders. *Vivant*, again ridden by Rex Hamey, son of the 1932 National winning jockey, was brought down early, so failing for the third time to complete the course. Worst of all, *Avenue Neuilly*, a 66-1 outsider, met with disaster, unseating David Nicholson at the tenth, then running on only to break a foreleg in a later fall.

Stephenson finally retired in 1980, having successfully combined training with farming for 35 years, and having played a key role, with Ken Oliver, in the revival of the Doncaster Bloodstock Sales. Married in 1940 to Barbara 'Bobbie' Nicholson, he had five daughters. He died in November, 1988, aged 77.

See also: Oxo; Scudamore, Michael.

STEVENS, George

Idol of the masses, a genuine legend in his own lifetime, George Stevens remains the most successful Grand National rider of all time: five times victorious – on *Freetrader* (1856), *Emblem* (1863), *Emblematic* (1864) and *The Colonel* (1869 and 1870). Moreover, it was only by a cruel twist of fate that he was deprived of a sixth National winner.

In 1861 Stevens had set his heart on riding a seven year old mare called *Jealousy*, turning down 13 offers of other rides for the privilege. Then, at the

11th hour, one of his retainers insisted that he ride for him. Ironically his horse was withdrawn shortly before the race and Stevens was a frustrated spectator as *Jealousy* came home in first place.

George's record of five wins from 15 National rides is all the more remarkable when one considers that, after making his 1852 National debut as a 19 year old aboard *Royal Blue* (the first 100-1 outsider), he went three years without a mount in the race. Then, given his second chance, he promptly showed his enormous potential by driving home *Freetrader*, a 25-1 shot, to snatch victory by half a length.

Stevens was born to ride – in 1833 in a house on Cleeve Hill, overlooking the natural amphitheatre of Cheltenham racecourse. He ran away from home in his early teens to work as a stable lad and he had his first major win at the age of 18 in the Grand Annual Steeplechase at Wolverhampton. The brilliant career that followed owed nothing to luck beyond his initial good fortune in having the great Tom Olliver as a tutor. The rest was pure skill. Though a lightweight, frail of build, he developed power in his arms and legs, and he possessed an instinctively fine racing brain: a supreme judge of pace and a master of the waiting game, almost always riding from behind in the National and steadily working his way up through the field. In addition, like Lester Piggott on the Flat, he had a gift for choosing mounts of great potential.

Stevens reasoned that by trailing the field on the first circuit he would be less liable to be brought down by falling horses and that he would have more in reserve for a tight finish. His patience was most dramatically exhibited in 1863 when he nursed Lord Coventry's chestnut *Emblem* around four miles of Aintree before launching her attack to such devastating effect that she won by 20 lengths. The following year he scored again, this time on *Emblem's* frail-looking full sister, *Emblematic*, and so equalling Olliver's record of three National wins.

That year Stevens had backed his mount to win £300; in addition Lord Coventry passed on to him the £500 he had won in a bet. The proceeds enabled George to build a home for himself atop Cleeve Hill. And he named it 'Emblem Cottage'.

In 1869, out of several offered mounts, Stevens chose *The Colonel*, a powerfully built six year old entire. And again he successfully played the waiting game, becoming the first jockey to have won four Nationals. It was much less easy the following year.

He was back on *The Colonel*, but this time with an extra 19lb in the weights. Moreover, he now had a rival in the waiting game. George Holman, on second favourite *The Doctor*, chose to trail alongside *The Colonel* at the rear of the field. And when Stevens made his move on the second circuit, Holman went too.

The consequence was a finish that many experts rated the most exciting in steeplechase history as *The Colonel* and *The Doctor* matched each other stride for stride over the long run-in. Employing all his strength and skill, Stevens urged his mount home by a neck, with *Primrose*, unlucky in running, five lengths back in third.

That year, only the mass popularity of Stevens could explain how the heavily handicapped *The Colonel* could have been backed down to 7-2 favouritism. After the race George was being hailed as a genius; and – as always following his victory in the National – the locals celebrated around a bonfire lit on Cleeve Hill. However, not even his most ardent supporters could strongly fancy him in 1871 when he returned for a third ride on *The Colonel*, now burdened with a colossal 12st 8lb. Dropped out as usual in the rear, the twice winner came home in sixth place.

Altogether, Stevens had now ridden in 15 Nationals. Besides his five wins he had twice finished in a place – third on *Emblematic* (1865) and fourth on *Maria Agnes* (1860). His other rides were: *Freetrader* (failed to finish, 1857), *Lough Bawn* (refused, 1858), *Harry* (fell, 1862), *The Doctor* (failed to finish, 1866) and *Tennyson* (eighth, 1867)

Immediately after the 1871 race rumours of his imminent retirement spread like wild fire. With nearly 100 steeplechase victories to his credit, he was expected to distinguish himself as a trainer. But he never had the chance. Just three months later the nation was stunned and saddened to hear that the supreme jump jockey was dead. Remarkably, the master horseman, who had so often negotiated the hazardous fences of Aintree, had lost his life while out riding his hack on Cleeve Hill.

On his way back to Emblem Cottage, after meeting friends at The Rising Sun, his hat had been blown off by a gust of wind. As a nearby lad reached up to hand it back, the horse took fright and bolted down the steep hill. Near its base, the steed stumbled over a drainpipe and Stevens was propelled into the gutter, smashing his head against a boulder. Never recover-

S

ing consciousness, he died the following day of a fractured skill, his life ending where it had begun.

The spot where he fell is marked with a plaque that reads: 'In memory of George Stevens, the rider of five Grand National winners who, after riding 20 years with no serious accident was here killed by a fall from his hack only three months after riding 'The Colonel' in the Grand National of 1871.'
See also: Freetrader; Emblem; Emblematic; Colonel, The.

STEWARDS' ENQUIRIES
To widespread amazement a stewards' enquiry was called after *Rhyme 'N' Reason*, a gelding renowned for his fast finishing, had stormed home to win the 1988 Grand National by a clear four lengths from *Durham Edition*. Brendan Powell, in only his second National, had seemingly given a truly astonishing display of horsemanship, staying in the saddle after the ten year old had made a belly-flop landing over the first Becher's and then advancing from last to first. But the stewards were now questioning his use of the whip from the second last fence to the finish.

They viewed the video of the race, took evidence from the vet, and heard the jockey's explanation. Powell explained that the flap had broken off his whip with the first smack on the run-in and that thereafter it was like slapping him with a twig. On all the evidence they agreed that a caution would suffice. The result remained unaltered.

More sensationally, a lengthy stewards' enquiry followed the finish of the 1996 Grand National which saw *Rough Quest*, the 7-1 favourite, pass the winning post a length and a quarter ahead of *Encore Un Peu*. Halfway up the run-in, after heading the race leader, *Rough Quest* had displayed his old tendency to hang to his left under pressure. Though he drifted into his rival's path the horses never quite touched. But David Bridgwater momentarily reined back on *Encore Un Peu* while Mick Fitzgerald spurred on *Rough Quest* under hands and heels.

The enquiry was conducted by a five-man panel that included Dick Saunders who had won the 1982 National on *Grittar*, a horse previously ridden by Terry Casey, the trainer of *Rough Quest*. After nearly 15 minutes they judged that the result should stand. Jeremy Ker, the stewards' secretary, said that the decision was unanimous and that it would have been the same at any racecourse in Britain. Bridgwater thought that the high profile of the race had been a

factor and that 'had it been Hereford I'd probably have got it'. On the other hand, he accepted defeat with plenty of good humour and acknowledged that if he had been given the race in the stewards' room he would not have felt that he had truly won the Grand National. Remarkably, a regular punter on the outcome of enquiries placed a £70,000-plus bet to win just £3,000 on *Rough Quest* keeping the race.
See also: Objections.

STOTT, William
One of the outstanding jockeys – in company with the likes of John Francome and Peter Scudamore – to be denied success in the Grand National. Billy Stott was the champion National Hunt rider for five successive seasons, 1927-32; and in the following season he rode *Golden Miller* to five wins in five races, including the Cheltenham Gold Cup. With his other victory that year on *Insurance*, he had achieved the Champion Hurdle-Gold Cup double.

A strong, short-legged jockey, born at the dawn of the 20th century and initially successful on the Flat, Stott made his first National appearance in 1929 when in chaotic scenes 66 horses went to the post and only ten completed the course. In the circumstances it was a supremely promising debut – finishing third on six year old *Richmond II*, a 40-1 chance. Yet in four subsequent Nationals he would only once complete the course and that was after he had remounted Lord Glenapp's *Annandale* to finish seventh in 1932.

In the 1932 Cheltenham Gold Cup, won by the five year old *Golden Miller*, Stott had been unlucky to be thrown off *Kingsford*, the second favourite, after the complete outsider *Aruntius* had jumped across his path when in the lead. His rare stroke of good luck came the following year when owner Dorothy Paget, having fallen out with jockey Ted Leader, chose him to take over on *Golden Miller*. However, after winning at Cheltenham, he did not keep the ride for the Grand National.

Why did Miss Paget revert to Leader for *Golden Miller*'s National debut? One explanation was that connections regarded Billy's physique as being too frail for the great Aintree challenger. But another story has it that Stott had made the error of remarking to someone that he doubted *Golden Miller*'s ability to get round at Aintree. Somehow, it seems, this reached the ears of the volatile Miss Paget and she reacted accordingly.

As it happened, *Golden Miller*'s inexperience and high handicap mark did count against him at Aintree. He nearly unseated Leader with his blunder at the second Becher's and he succeeded in doing so when stumbling over the Canal Turn. Meanwhile Billy was still going well on *Pelorus Jack*, and from the last open ditch onwards they were locked with *Kellsboro' Jack* in a battle for the lead. But then, at the last, *Pelorus Jack* misjudged his take-off and fell on landing.

A few days after the National, Stott was badly injured in a car crash. But one year later he was back – and again he fell on *Pelorus Jack*, this time without ever being a major contender. It was his last National. He was popularly known as the 'India rubber ball' because he was short and rounded in build and seemed to bounce off the turf when experiencing a crashing fall. Ostensibly, his many tumbles did him little damage. But arguably they took their toll in an unrealised way. In 1936 the five times champion suffered a fatal heart attack.

See also: Golden Miller.

STRAKER, Major Ivan Charles

A lifelong fan of the Grand National, Ivan Straker, as chairman of Seagram Distillers (UK), was responsible for ensuring the continued existence of the race when, in 1984, he persuaded his company to take on its sponsorship. For eight years the race was to prosper with Seagram backing, years that saw a marked improvement in Aintree's facilities and race programme.

Born on June 17, 1928, and educated at Harrow and RMA Sandhurst, Major Straker served in the Army until 1962. Twenty three years later he was delighted to see the National won by *Last Suspect*, a 50-1 chance trained by his friend Captain Tim Forster, who had been a fellow officer in the 11th Hussars. And the following year, 1986, he himself had a most worthy National contender in *The Tsarevich*.

On his National debut, the bay gelding finished seventh; and one year later he seemed a likely winner when going best of all as the leaders came to the Elbow. But then, on the run-in, *The Tsarevich* was outpaced by *Maori Venture*, a winner by five lengths and in the then third fastest time recorded. In the excitement the 58 year old owner of the runner-up collapsed with a minor transient stroke. Happily, the major recovered completely. Meanwhile, on his last National appearance in 1988, *The Tsarevich* finished seventh, so completing the course for the third successive year.

In 1991, Straker saw the Seagram National have an eponymous winner. Ironically, he had twice been offered *Seagram* to run for the sponsors. But he had declined, judging not unreasonably that the horse's success would afford valuable publicity irrespective of ownership.

By 2000, however, Straker seemingly had another truly outstanding Grand National prospect in his eight year old *Paris Pike*, winner of the Scottish National. That victory had been all the sweeter for the owner since he was a former chairman of Ayr racecourse; and he had high hopes when his gelding finally made it to Aintree in 2002. *Paris Pike* was to be ridden by Richard Guest, the winning jockey of one year before. He had the desired good ground, and with a trainer (Ferdy Murphy) in form, he was backed down to 10-1. Alas, he was one four fallers at the first fence. Subsequently he was pulled up in the Scottish National and he failed to recapture his old zest after falling in his first race of the new season.

See also: Seagram; Sponsorship.

STUDD, Edward

Owner and trainer of *Salamander*, the seven year old gelding who produced a devastating turn of foot in romping home to a ten lengths victory in the 1866 Grand National. As a keen gambler, Edward Studd had taken care not to reveal his runner's brilliant form on the gallops and consequently he was able to make a killing in backing him at 40-1.

Studd was a wealthy retired indigo planter who had returned from the Far East to settle in Rutland. Such was the snobbery in the racing hierarchy at the time that he was regarded as something of an upstart and an unsporting opportunist. In particular he was criticised for his practice of making the rounds of bookmakers to seek the best odds – 'not the sort of thing,' one racing pundit wrote, 'we are accustomed to expect from the landed gentry of England.'

The fact remains that Studd was remarkably adept in scouting far and wide for equine potential and his judgment was generally sound except for his one great blunder in rejecting *The Lamb*, destined to be a dual winner of the National. Before winning with *Salamander*, he had had only one National contender: *The Dwarf*, pulled up in 1865. After the victory he challenged five more times and never had

S

a runner finishing worse than sixth.

In 1867 his six year old *Shangarry*, ridden by the celebrated 'Mr Thomas', was placed third. Then came three bids with *Despatch*, a brown gelding who finished sixth in 1869, second in 1871 and third, as 100-30 favourite, in 1872. Most galling was the defeat of 1871 since *Despatch* went down by two lengths to *The Lamb* with 'Mr Thomas' in the saddle. Studd's last National runner was *Alice Lee*, the fifth of only six finishers in 1873.

See also: Salamander; Lamb, The.

SUCCESSIVE WINNERS

Only four horses have won successive Grand Nationals: *Abd-El-Kader* (1850-51), *The Colonel* (1869-70), *Reynoldstown* (1935-36) and *Red Rum* (1973-74).

Seven jockeys (five professional, two amateur) have ridden the winner in successive years: Tom Olliver (1842-43), George Stevens (1863-64), Mr John Maunsell Richardson (1873-74), Tommy Beasley (1880-81), Mr Ted Wilson (1884-85), Bryan Marshall (1953-54) and Brian Fletcher (1973-74).

Vincent O'Brien (1953-55) is the only trainer to have turned out three successive National winners. Eight other trainers have scored with two successive winners: Edwin Weever (1863-64), R. Roberts (1869-70), John Maunsell Richardson (1873-74), Henry Linde (1880-81), Robert Gore (1912-13), Noel Furlong (1935-36), Fred Winter (1965-66) and Donald 'Ginger' McCain (1973-74).

SUNDEW

As the 20-1 winner of the 1957 Grand National, 11 year old *Sundew* was unusual in two respects. Firstly, he heralded from a small yard in which he was the solitary jumper. Secondly, he came to Aintree with the off-putting record of having twice suffered a crashing fall in the race. Indeed, the form of this giant chestnut (17 and a half hands) had been so uncertain the previous year that his owner (Mrs Geoffrey Kohn) had sent him to the December sales at Newmarket. There, unknowingly to her good fortune, he failed to reach his reserve of £2,500.

Mrs Kohn had originally paid £3,000 for *Sundew* shortly before the 1955 National. But the Irish-bred gelding – by *Sun King* out of *Parsonstown Gem* – looked an unlikely prospect for the big race. Recently he had been beaten in the Leopardstown Chase by *Copp*, who was now the 7-1 favourite at Aintree. Furthermore, the 30-strong line-up included no fewer than four runners trained by Vincent O'Brien who was seeking his third consecutive victory.

In a testing slog through the mud, jockey Pat Doyle gave *Sundew* a most enterprising ride. They miraculously avoided disaster when a riderless horse landed directly in their path at The Chair. They were in the lead at the end of the first circuit, and they were still narrowly ahead of O'Brien's *Quare Times* at the second Becher's. But then, at the last open ditch, the tiring *Sundew* came to grief.

Sundew's prospects looked much brighter before the 1956 National. The previous year, with Fred Winter in the saddle, he had been runner-up in the Welsh Grand National at Chepstow when giving nearly two stone to the winner. He had also beaten the 1955 National winner *Quare Times* in the National Trial at Haydock, and so he went off at Aintree the 8-1 second favourite.

Once again, this time under Winter, *Sundew* jumped brilliantly throughout the first circuit, leading the way over the Water Jump. But then, with *Devon Loch* and *E.S.B.*, almost alongside him, he nose-dived over Becher's, pitching his rider on to the ground. The following November, back at Aintree, he jumped clumsily in the Grand Sefton Chase, and when he came back for his third Grand National bid he was pushed out to 20-1 in the betting.

As the only chaser in the care of trainer Frank Hudson at Henley-in-Arden, Warwickshire, *Sundew* was at least never short of work; and, though not the best of jumpers, he lacked nothing in sheer power and strength. These were his crucial assets in the 1957 National. Left in the lead by the fourth fence fall of front-running *Armorial III*, he survived a clumsy jump at Becher's and stayed ahead by powering through, rather than over, smaller fences. For the third time, he was ahead on entering the second circuit; and this time, largely due to the skilled handling of Winter who took the shortest, inside route, he kept on his *Tipperary Tim*-sized feet, coming home eight lengths ahead of the fast-closing *Wyndburgh*.

The victory brought a prize of nearly £9,000 for Mrs Kohn, who only a few months earlier had been prepared to sell her chaser for £2,500. It was an especially welcome change of fortune since she had seen her *Quite Naturally* fall at the first fence in the 1953 National and, worse, she had given up her half-share in *E.S.B.* before that chaser had won the 1956 race.

But sadly this was *Sundew*'s seventh and last steeplechase success. Against Fred's advice, he ran in the Whitbread Gold Cup at Sandown, where he was pulled up. Then, towards the end of the year, after two unimpressive runs, he was involved in a pile-up at Haydock's water jump. Breaking his back on landing, he had to be put down and was buried on the course where he had met his fatal fall.
See also: Winter, Fred.

SUNLOCH

Seeking a record-breaking fourth Grand National win, and his third victory in succession, Sir Charles Assheton-Smith shrewdly attempted to buy eight year old *Sunloch* to strengthen his 1914 challenge with *Covertcoat*, the top-weighted favourite. But Leicestershire farmer Mr Thomas Tyler, owner and trainer of the bay gelding, declined to make a handsome profit on his original £300 purchase. Though *Sunloch* – an English-bred (by *Sundorne* out of *Gralloch*) grandson of 1874 Derby winner *George Frederick* – had no outstanding chase form over three miles or more, he believed his horse had a serious chance on a bottom weight of 9st 7lb. And he was absolutely right.

As in the previous year, when only three managed to finish, this was a National with a great procession of fallers, only six of 20 starters surviving as far as Valentine's second time around. In 1913, jockey Bill Smith had sought to make the running on *Blow Pipe*. Now he adopted the same tactics on *Sunloch* – but with one important difference. This time his mount was not a faller. Instead he powered into an extraordinary lead – 20 lengths at Becher's, 40 lengths shortly before approaching it again.

Had he gone to fast? This was certainly the early judgment of riders on horses still in contention, most notably those on the two fancied French challengers, *Trianon III* and former winner *Lutteur III*. But now, as they gave chase, they soon realised that they had miscalculated. Though they greatly reduced the gap, there was no catching the sure-jumping leader. *Sunloch* had stolen the race, coming home eight lengths clear from *Trianon III*, with *Lutteur III*, conceding nearly three stone to the winner, a further eight lengths back. Only four runners finished.

Ostensibly, it was a great escape for Tom Tyler who, being heavily in debt, had backed his horse

ante-post at 100-1. However, he was by nature a highly sociable and generous character and he was so lavish in celebrating the victory and making gifts to the jockey and stable staff that not enough of his windfall remained to settle his debts. Consequently, he soon agreed to accept an offer from Sir Charles for the gelding.

As it happened, it was not a great loss. *Sunloch* never shone again, winning only one more race, a very minor affair. Moreover, Sir Charles died a few months after he had made the purchase. Returned to Mr Tyler, *Sunloch* missed the 1915 National and when, after the three lost years of the First World War, he made his second appearance at Aintree, he was a 13 year old, the oldest horse in the race. He was pulled up on the first circuit.
See also: Smith, William.

SUNY BAY

The greatest grey to compete in the Grand National without winning. Runner-up in successive years (1997-98), *Suny Bay* had outstanding credentials on breeding. Out of the moderate jumper *Suny Salome*, he was sired – like National winners *Royal Athlete* (1995) and *Bindaree* (2002) – by the prolific *Roselier*. His grand-sire, *Sunyboy,* was second in the Irish St Leger before developing into a smart three-mile hurdler and his grand-dam was by *Vulcan*, sire of National winners *Team Spirit*, *Foinavon* and *Gay Trip*.

Suny Bay first went to Aintree as an eight year old in 1997. Having won the Greenalls Grand National Trial Chase at Haydock, he was in line for a £100,000 bonus in addition to the £178,000-plus first prize. Unfortunately, this was the year of the IRA bomb scare that caused the race to be postponed 49 hours; and he was not helped by the drying ground in the interim. Trained by Charlie Brooks and ridden by Jamie Osborne, he was beaten 25 lengths by the pillar-to-post winner, *Lord Gyllene*.

One year later, following a decisive win in the Hennessy, *Suny Bay* was again runner-up in the National, this time beaten by virtue of having to carry top weight of 12st on heavy going. Patiently ridden by Graham Bradley, he moved up on the leaders at Becher's second time around only to be outpaced in the later stages by *Earth Summit* who was receiving a massive 23lb. The following December things were put in perspective when the grey faced *Earth Summit* at level weights over three miles at Haydock. He beat him by three and a half lengths with *Lord Gyllene* 50 lengths back in third. *Suny Bay* now had a record of 21 starts, 11 wins, two seconds and £360,330 in prize money. He was the top-rated chaser in Britain.

In 1999 the majestic grey was with Simon Sherwood in his first year of training as Brooks's successor at Uplands in Lambourn. Harshly he had been dropped only 1lb for the National, and with top weight of 11st 13lb he was giving 12lb to his nearest rival. On ground faster than he would have liked, he never looked a contender and finished 13th.

In the build-up to the 2000 Grand National, *Suny Bay* had shown nothing to suggest that he retained his old form. However, the handicapper was this year reintroducing the 'Aintree factor' in assessing entries; and, as a two-time runner-up, he was duly allotted the second highest weight of 11st 12lb. Clearly past his best, he went off at 66-1 and again finished 13th.

See also: Greys.

SUPERSTITION

Jockeys are notorious for observing superstitious practices, their rituals – especially before the Grand National – being too numerous and varied to record in full. However, for persistent observation, Graham Thorner surely takes the prize. After winning the 1972 National on *Well To Do* he chose to wear the same underpants in all his races for years to come; and ultimately they had so disintegrated that he needed to wear a second pair just to keep them on.

In 1982, when the veteran Dick Saunders won the National on *Grittar*, he and his wife Pam made certain that they were wearing exactly the same clothes they had worn when travelling to Aintree for the Fox Hunters' Chase the previous year. John Buckingham, who rode the last 100-1 National winner, *Foinavon*, was far from alone among jockeys in always taking care to wave at magpies. Tony Dobbin, who won on *Lord Gyllene*, aims never to leave the weighing room first. Timmy Murphy always dons his right boot before the left one. And though not generally superstitious, Mick Fitzgerald always regarded seven as his lucky number; and, true enough, *Rough Quest* was No 7 when he won the National.

Owners, trainers and even relations of riders are also prone to superstition. In 1935, when *Reynoldstown* first won the National, owner-trainer Major Noel Furlong had passed a funeral en route to Aintree. The story goes that, when returning to the course one year later, he deliberately kept driving around Liverpool until he had seen a funeral procession again. Clearly it was worthwhile. *Reynoldstown*, raised 12lb in the weights, won again – scoring what was seen as the luckiest of victories because long-time leader *Davy Jones* had run out at the last after the buckle of his reins had broken.

Richard Dunwoody's parents went to see their son ride in his first National in 1985. When he fell on *West Tip* at Becher's Brook they concluded that they had brought him bad luck and never went to the National again. Their absence seemingly worked as Richard went on to establish an outstanding record in the race. By and large if a jockey wins the race he likes to have the same peg in the changing room for the rest of his career.

The owner most renowned for superstition is Jim Lewis but his champion chaser was never to be risked in the hurly-burly of the National. In 2003, when his *Best Mate* was due to run in the Gold Cup, he would not leave his Worcestershire home for Cheltenham until he had found a vehicle registration adding up to his lucky number 25. Eventually he had to visit the local garage to find one. And, in 2004, when *Best Mate* scored his third successive Gold Cup, Lewis had taken care to travel, as always, by the same route (via the village pub); to be carrying his lucky, knitted black cat; and to be wearing his lucky black overcoat with Aston Villa tie and scarf. For her part, trainer Henrietta Knight – as always – wore the same blue suit and pearl necklace.

SWAN, Charles

The greatest Irish-based jump jockey of the modern era to be denied success in the Grand National. Nine times – in consecutive seasons, 1989-90 to 1997-98 – Charlie Swan was Ireland's champion jump jockey. He was the first in his country to ride 150 winners in a season, the first to reach 1,000 winners. He won the 1993 Irish Grand National on *Ebony Jane* and the Whitbread Gold Cup twice, on *Ushers Island* (1994) and *Life Of A Lord* (1996); rode ten winners at the Aintree Grand National meeting and 17 at the Cheltenham Festival, being the leading rider there in 1993 and 1995. Yet in eight attempts at the National – discounting his second on *Cahervillahow* in the 1993 void race – his best finish was fifth place on *Lastofthebrownies* in 1990 when making his debut in the race.

Born on January 20, 1968, Charlie was seven years old when he watched the 1975 Grand National on television and saw his father, amateur rider Captain Donald Swan, crash out at the fourth after leading from the start on his own horse, *Zimulator*, a 100-1 outsider. He cried at the time. But ever after he remained determined to ride in the race one day.

Donald Swan, a London-born British Army officer boldly raising a family near an IRA stronghold in the troublesome 1970s, was equally keen that his son should succeed as a rider. He had him riding a pony at the age of four and, having turned to training, he would get eight year old Charlie to help break in young horses. The boy was only 15 when, at Naas in March, 1983, he rode his winner, *Final Assault*, a two year old maiden trained by his father. He then began a four-year apprenticeship with trainer Kevin Prendergast, riding 57 winners on the Flat and for a while sharing a flat in Kildare with Kieren Fallon.

While still an apprentice on the Flat, Charlie's winners included a Group 3 success at Phoenix Park on *The Beau Sidhe*. But his weight rose too much when resting with a broken leg in 1986 and so he turned to jumping under the tutelage of Dessie Hughes. His introduction to the Cheltenham Festival in 1987 brought no encouragement, ending in an arm-breaking fall, made all the more painful by his ride in an ambulance that crashed into a car. But within three years he had moved into the top rank, most notably riding the Mouse Morris-trained *Trapper John* to victory in the 1990 Stayers' Hurdle. It was his first Cheltenham Festival winner and the first Irish success there for two years.

Since 1980 Swan had studied every Grand National on video, and one decade later he at last fulfilled his dream of riding in the race. His father offered him £100 for every fence he led on the Morris-trained *Lastofthebrownies*. But Charlie's primary ambition was to outscore him by getting beyond the fourth fence. He achieved that and much more – coaxing his 20-1 chance round on unsuitably fast ground to come home fifth. One year later, riding the 100-1 outsider *Mick's Star*, he miraculously stayed on board after landing too steeply over the first, and with blood streaming from his nose he rode on to complete the course in 13th place.

In 1992, at the 11th hour, he picked up a most difficult ride on *Roc de Prince* and nursed the dodgy jumper round to finish 17th. Then, after finishing second in the void National, he failed for the first time to get round in 1994 – being catapulted out of the saddle when the 50-1 shot *Henry Mann* keeled over at the first fence. In 1995 he finished eighth on the 12 year old Martin Pipe-trained *Riverside Boy*, and in 1996 he was seventh on *Life Of A Lord* for top Irish trainer Aidan O'Brien.

One year later Swan thought he had his best ever chance of winning the National. He was on the strongly fancied *Wylde Hide*, the main Irish hope owned by J. P. McManus and trained by Arthur Moore. But that chance was sadly lessened by the IRA bomb scare that caused the race to be postponed for 49 hours. All the while the ground was drying out more, and *Wylde Hide* was best on soft going. In 1996 he had been going well in the National until unseating Francis Woods at the 24th. This time, as an 11-1 chance, he was well out paced, made a bad mistake at the 21st and unseated his rider at the next.

The following year Charlie made his Grand National swansong – riding *Him Of Praise* for trainer Oliver Sherwood. The eight year old was strongly supported, having begun that season with four consecutive wins, including one over an extended four miles. But he could be quirky and now, he stubbornly dug in his heels at the 27th. Swan's disappointment was all the greater since that same day, on desperate ground, he had been beaten a head on the odds-on *Istabraq* in the Martell Aintree Hurdle.

The Grand National remained the race that he most wanted to win. But by now he had begun to combine the roles of jockey and trainer, gradually building up sizeable stables behind the family's ancient country house near the village of Cloughjordan in Co. Tipperary. Though only 30, he no longer had the same appetite for race-riding; and therefore, in September, 1998, he decided to stop riding in steeplechases, so effectively ending any chance of adding to his nine jockeys' championships.

He might have retired altogether except for one huge incentive: continuing his famous partnership over hurdles with the legendary *Istabraq*. In March, 2000, they achieved their third victory in the Smurfit Champion Hurdle at Cheltenham, and but for the foot-and-mouth epidemic that put paid to the 2001 Festival they would almost certainly have scored an unprecedented fourth success.

At Aintree, on the eve of the 2003 Grand National, Swan enjoyed success as both rider and trainer, winning a listed hurdle race with *Patriot Games* at 16-1. The next day, immediately before the National, he had his last ride in public, finishing third on *Like-A-Butterfly* in the Martell Cognac Aintree Hurdle. He dismounted to a huge ovation, so ending a career in which, over jumps and Flat combined, he had achieved 1,312 victories. He had also won more races over jumps in Ireland (1,188) than any other rider.

Over the years Swan's riding record had prompted the suggestion that he was a better rider over hurdles than fences. The fact remains that he was a consummate tactician in both disciplines. Courageous, fiercely competitive, and unrivalled in his judgment of pace and his timing of moves. Indeed, he was rated by master trainer Aidan O'Brien as quite simply 'the best jump jockey in the world'; and, but for his reluctance to leave his native Ireland, he could have been stable jockey to the omnipotent Martin Pipe.

Ever modest, charming and popular, Swan showed his ability over fences most strikingly by his great ride on *Viking Flagship* in the 1995 Queen Mother Champion Chase; and but for the controversial disqualification of *Cahervillahow* in 1991 he would have held the distinction of three Whitbread Gold Cup victories. Now, with a burgeoning stable, and youth on his side, he could have every hope of one day winning the Grand National as a trainer.

SWEEPSTAKES

In its early years the Grand National was run as a sweepstake – that is a race in which the entrance fees, forfeits, subscriptions or other contributions from the owners are divided proportionally among the owners of the winner and placed horses.

Off-course, Grand National sweepstakes are commonly organised at workplaces, even at royal palaces, with participants contributing equally in the hope of gaining a runner in the draw. Usually, all the kitty goes to the holder of the winner.

In 1931, a Grand National lottery known as the Irish Hospital Sweepstakes was introduced. The first winner was a London-based Italian, Emilio Scala, who collected £354,544 when the draw produced his ten-shilling ticket bearing the name of *Grakle*.

TAAFFE, Patrick

First and foremost, Pat Taaffe will forever be linked with the incomparable *Arkle*, having ridden him to 24 of his 27 wins including a hat-trick of Cheltenham Gold Cup victories (1964-66). That supreme bay gelding was, of course, never allowed to take his chance in the Grand National. Nevertheless, soft-spoken, long-legged Pat stands out as one of the most long-serving and talented of all Grand National riders. Seventeen times he rode in the race, first winning by a comfortable 12 lengths on *Quare Times* (1955) and then, in a fairy-tale ending to his career, winning even more decisively on *Gay Trip* (1970).

Born in Rathcoole, Co. Dublin, in 1930, the son of the 1958 Grand National winning trainer, Tom Taaffe, Pat took to the hunting field, point-to-points and the Dublin show ring as a schoolboy, riding his first winner under Rules (*Ballincarona*, a chance bumper ride at Phoenix Park in 1947) as a 16 year old amateur, and just over two years later – now nearly 6ft tall – beginning a long, triumphant career as jockey to the powerful Tom Dreaper stable at Kilsallaghan, Co. Dublin. He turned professional in 1950.

Like Fred Winter, Dave Dick and Michael Scudamore, Pat made his Aintree National debut in 1951, the year of the chaotic, undeclared false start which saw only three of 36 starters get home. On Lord Sefton's *Irish Lizard*, a 50-1 chance, he was brought down, one of 12 fallers at the first fence. The following year, on Mrs J. V. Rank's *Early Mist*, he was again a victim of scrummaging at the first fence where there were ten fallers, including, again, *Irish Lizard*.

The fates seemed to be against Taaffe as *Early Mist* now changed hands, prior to winning the 1953 National. Instead, that year, he had the mount on 13 year old *Overshadow*, who was a creditable fourth of five finishers at 33-1. Then, in 1954, came tragedy. He was an early leader on giant *Coneyburrow*, the joint second favourite, who recovered after blundering at the Water Jump, only to suffer a fatal fall at the final ditch – one of four horses to perish in the race. Pat's younger brother, 'Tosse' Taaffe, was fourth on Mrs M. V. O'Brien's *Churchtown* who was found to have broken a blood vessel.

In 1955, trainer Vincent O'Brien saddled four horses in pursuit of his third consecutive National win. His past winners, *Early Mist* and *Royal Tan*, both on big weights, were unfavoured by the quagmire conditions. But his *Quare Times* was a safe jumper, especially strong on stamina; and Pat gave him a copybook ride, delaying his challenge until after the second Becher's, then outpacing all rivals on the run-in to win easily from *Tudor Line*, with the younger Taaffe back in third place on *Carey's Cottage*. Looking back, years later, O'Brien would always emphasise that he owed much of his Grand National success to the strong riding of two men, Bryan Marshall and Pat Taaffe.

Pat was unable to ride in the 1956 National when brother 'Tosse' finished third on 12 year old *Royal Tan*. In that year he suffered a most horrendous fall at Kilbeggan, only regaining consciousness in a Dublin hospital. His multiple injuries included a badly fractured skull; and yet, quite incredibly, against all expectation, he recovered to return to the saddle.

In the 1957 National, he was brought down on *Icelough*, trained by his father; and in 1958 he was brought down again, this time on the Duchess of Westminster's *Sentina*. Unfortunately, that year, Pat was already committed when *Mr What*, trained by his father, needed a late replacement jockey. Arthur Freeman was booked for the ride and, though putting up 6lb overweight, he duly won by 30 lengths on a young gelding who had previously beaten *Sentina* in the Troytown Chase at Navan.

In 1959 Pat fell at the 13th on the third favourite, *Slippery Serpent*, while his younger brother was the third of four finishers on the favourite *Mr What*. And now his run of unsuccessful rides was to extend to 11 Grand Nationals, the others being: 1960, (*Jonjo*, fell); 1961, (*Jonjo*, seventh); 1962, (*Kerforo*, fell; 1963, (film star Gregory Peck's *Owen's Sedge*, seventh); 1964, (*Pappageno's Cottage*, tenth); 1965, (*Quintin Bay*, pu); 1966, (*Flying Wild*, pu); 1969, (*Rosinver Bay*, ref).

In the meantime, Pat had had his glory years on *Arkle*, their many wins including three Cheltenham Gold Cups, the King George VI Chase, the Irish Grand National, two Hennessy Cognac Gold Cups and the Whitbread Gold Cup. He had also won no fewer than six Irish Grand Nationals and in 1968 he had scored a record fourth Cheltenham Gold Cup victory for Dreaper on *Fort Leney*. But by now his Aintree National career seemed as good as over. It was 1970. At the age of 40 he had already decided that this would be his final year of race-riding.

T

Now came one of those curious twists of fate that have so often brought romance to Grand National history. Terry Biddlecombe, the jovial jockey who had interrupted Pat's run of Gold Cup wins, suffered an injury that left him unable to ride little *Gay Trip* in the National. Terry suggested to trainer Fred Rimell and his wife Mercy that the veteran Pat would be a suitable replacement. They had the same idea – not least because it was at Pat's suggestion that they had originally bought *Gay Trip* for a friend.

In the 1970 National, unusually, all the 28 runners carried less than 11 stone with the exception of eight year old *Gay Trip* on 11st 5lb. With top weight, and having never won beyond two and a half miles, he was seventh in the betting, at 15-1. Pat chose to ride a waiting race, hunting round behind the leaders, taking a narrow lead two fences out, pulling clear at the last, and then powering over the run-in to win by 20 lengths.

Uniquely, the popular Taaffe had won Grand Nationals 15 years apart – the perfect climax to an astonishingly successful riding career which had included a record 25 wins at the Cheltenham Festival and an unequalled number of victories in major National Hunt races. Though he had lost the tips of two fingers in a domestic accident, he was recognised as a superb horseman with 'perfect hands' and as a supreme judge of pace. It was a measure of his consistency that, in nearly 100 Cheltenham rides, he had a 30 per cent winning strike-rate and was placed in 25 per cent of them.

Pat went on to become an excellent trainer, remembered especially for his successes with *Captain Christy*, whose wins included the 1972 Irish Sweeps Hurdle, the 1973 Scottish Champion Hurdle, the 1974 Cheltenham Gold Cup and the King George VI Chase in 1974 and 1975. However, he was unsuccessful with his National challengers: *Beggar's Way*, falling at the first Becher's in 1973, and *Roman Bar* finishing ninth in 1978 after falling in 1977 and 1976.

Tragically, Taaffe's second career was to be cut short by ill-health. He died, aged 62, in July, 1992, a year after undergoing a heart transplant operation. But at least, in his last decade, he had the reward of seeing the family tradition being most capably carried on by his son Tom.
See also: Quare Times; Gay Trip; Arkle; O'Brien, Michael Vincent; Taaffe, Thomas Snr and Jnr

TAAFFE, Thomas Snr

In 1955, Irish trainer Tom Taaffe paid a mere £500 for five year old *Mr What*. Three years later, when the gelding was owned by Dublin businessman Mr D.J. Coughlan, he saddled him to win the Grand National by 30 lengths – the greatest winning distance for three decades. And this was with a jockey (late booking Arthur Freeman) putting up 6lb overweight.

In more than 30 subsequent attempts, mudlark *Mr What* never won a race again. Nevertheless, the trainer worked wonders to get him fit enough to finish third in the 1959 National, for which he had been raised a massive 17lb. On that occasion, *Mr What* was the 6-1 favourite, ridden by the trainer's son, 'Tosse' Taaffe.

As an adventurous teenager Tom Taaffe had spent several years in Australia before returning to set up as a trainer at Rathcoole, Co. Dublin. There he encouraged his sons, Pat and 'Tosse', to ride from infancy, and between them they were to have 25 rides in Aintree Grand Nationals. Both were riding non-finishers in the National won by their father's challenger in 1958.

Though overshadowed by his elder brother, 'Tosse' – so nicknamed to avoid confusion with his father – had the distinction of riding into a place on half of his eight National rides, and three times in succession: fourth on *Churchtown* in 1954, third on *Carey's Cottage*, trained by his father, in 1955, and third on *Royal Tan* in 1956.

Following his last National ride on *Loving Record* (pulled up in 1963) he took over training from his father. He returned *Loving Record* to Aintree in 1965 and 1966, finishing eighth and 12th respectively; and in 1973 he sent out the 100-1 outsider *Culla Hill*, a faller at the first Becher's.
See also: Mr What; Taaffe, Pat.

TAAFFE, Thomas Jnr

At one time Tom Taaffe Jnr considered taking up a career in accountancy rather than becoming a jockey and facing the prospect of endless comparisons with his famous father, Pat. But genetic influences soon overcame that notion. Racing was in his blood; and on leaving school he joined trainer Arthur Moore. He rode his first winner at Phoenix Park in July, 1981, and during his 15 years with Moore he scored more than 400 wins.

Unlike his father, he was denied success in the Grand National. But then he never had such promising rides. Born on June 15, 1963, he first rode in the National as an 18 year old amateur on *Mullacurry*, a faller in 1982. Turning professional, he fell on *Clonthturtin*, a 100-1 outsider in 1984, and his mount *Tubbertelly* refused in 1985. But he finished fifth on *Sommelier*, another 50-1 chance, in 1986, and was third in 1988 on *Monanore* at 33-1. The following year he suffered a severe fall on the 50-1 grey *Sergeant Sprite* in a five-horse pile-up at the first Becher's; and in 1990, taking over from the injured Gee Armytage, he was back on *Monanore*, now 13 years old and a 100-1 no-hoper. They were carried out, scattering photographers in their wake, at the 14th.

At the age of 30 Tom finally tired of the ever more demanding struggle to keep down his weight. In 1995 he took out a training licence and built up a fine stable at Portree Farm overlooking the Co. Kildare town of Straffan, a few miles from where his father had trained. At the same time he displayed a rare talent for trading in horses whose potential he discerned at the sales.

Arguably, his most inspired purchase was *Kicking King* whom he bought for 21,000 guineas as a yearling on behalf of a syndicate that included himself. In January, 2002, on the day that Tom's son (another Pat) was born, *Kicking King* won a bumper at Leopardstown. Subsequently he was second to *Back In Front* in Cheltenham's Supreme Novices' Hurdle, and then, in March, 2004, runner-up behind *Well Chief* in the Arkle.

At the end of that year, after four chase successes in Ireland, *Kicking King*, ridden by Barry Geraghty, fulfilled his huge promise as the winning, six year old favourite in the King George VI Chase at Kempton Park. Yet another Taaffe had truly arrived. As a trainer, Tom had triumphed in the race his father had won as a jockey on *Arkle* and twice as a trainer with *Captain Christy*; and he went on to still greater glory with *Kicking King*'s victory in the 2005 Cheltenham Gold Cup, the race in which his father had four times finished on the winner and four times on the runner-up. For good measure, *Kicking King* ended a great season by hacking up in the Guinness Gold Cup at Punchestown and, on Boxing Day, 2005, again won the King George VI, this time held at Sandown Park during Kempton Park's redevelopment.

In 2006-07 *Kicking King* was ruled out for the season with recurrence of a tendon injury and Taaffe's main front-runner was *Cane Brake*, winner of two of Ireland's biggest three-mile handicap chases. Meanwhile relatively scant attention was focused on his first-ever entry for the Grand National: *Slim Pickings*, an eight year old who had never won beyond three miles and had finished fifth in Cheltenham's Racing Post Plate over two miles five furlongs.

But National-winning jockey Barry Geraghty had schooled him over Aintree-type fences and Taaffe reckoned that 'he might surprise people'. He did – travelling strongly throughout, leading at the 26th, then only being headed after hitting the last. Thereafter he battled hard all the way on the run-in to finish third, just two lengths off the winner, *Silver Birch*. The 'slim pickings' for that place were £74,970.

It had been a bold bid by the trainer who was seeking to match his feat of winning the Cheltenham Gold Cup at the first attempt. Unfortunately Taaffe was not there to see it. He had been stranded in Ireland as his travel arrangements went awry.

TACTICS

What is the best tactical plan for riding in the Grand National? Obviously, this will be partly dictated by the horse's known strengths or weaknesses. Some will idle if they get in front too soon, some may be natural front-runners. According to the state of the going, some may be favoured by a fast pace, others by being held up for a strong finish. On one point, however, experienced jockeys are generally agreed: that in the National it is wise to avoid tracking horses that are dodgy jumpers. It is also generally acknowledged – though all too often disregarded at the time – that it can be disastrous to be caught up in a mad stampede to the first fence where so often bunching has led to falls.

The best route to take in the race? On this, jockeys are by no means agreed. A majority say they want to be on the inside or the outside at the start. Carl Llewellyn, who twice rode the winner, chose to start near the inside on *Party Politics*, but in the case of *Earth Summit* he went on the outside because his horse did not like being crowded. Similarly, Mick Fitzgerald, successful on *Rough Quest*, opted for the least perilous, longest route, running wide to keep out of trouble before closing in at a later stage.

Lord Mildmay, who studied films of the race for many years, chose the inside route. Fred Winter, the only person to win the National twice as both jockey and trainer, also always favoured racing towards the inside. He contended that you should be near the front from the start to avoid trouble and try to be first over the Melling Road. In 1985, when Peter Scudamore finished third on past winner *Corbiere*, he had been given precise instructions by trainer Jenny Pitman about how to ride and what route to take. She, too, favoured the shortest, inside route, though it is generally recognised that this path is not to be recommended for horses of moderate jumping ability and lacking experience of such formidable fences.

On the other hand, many highly respected riders have recommended taking a middle course, certainly in the early stages. Jockey-turned-trainer Jim Dreaper has argued: 'If you are on the inner and something goes wrong, you have only one option – to pull out into all the traffic. You have more chance in the middle, and you lose virtually no ground. The time to move to the inside is after Becher's.'

Similarly Dick Francis has stressed the value of starting in the centre. He argued that down the half-mile stretch going away from the stands the ground slopes very gently from right to left so that drops over fences are greatest near the rails. A horse may easily lose more time making the extra effort in jumping there than he gains by being on the inside. And the centre has two other big advantages. 'If one is in the middle of the course one can go either way to the right or the left to avoid visible trouble ahead, but if one is on the rails, a horse falling or veering leaves no chance of escape. The centre also brings one into the best position for negotiating the bend after Becher's and the sharp left-hand turn at the Canal'.

Most significantly perhaps, Richard Dunwoody favoured a middle route early on. In his autobiography, *Obsessed*, he details his approach before his win on *West Tip* in 1986. 'I mentally rehearsed how I wanted to ride the race: line up in the middle, travel down the middle to Becher's and then track back towards the inner, jump the Canal Turn at a slight angle to save ground, try to get a little daylight before jumping The Chair, get a lead down to Becher's second time round, hold on to him, leave it as late as possible.'

In 1985 Dunwoody and *West Tip* had looked to be heading for victory when, caught out by the drop, they fell at Becher's second time around. Now, following the new race plan in 1986, they came back to win – and to finish in the places the next three years

in a row. And in 1994 the jockey won the National again, on *Miinnehoma*.

However, for all the pro-middle arguments, it is perhaps worth noting the advice of Graham Bradley in regard of The Chair: 'You want to be on the inner or outer in tackling this narrow and biggest (5ft 2in) fence.' And he spoke with some authority, having three times come to grief at that daunting obstacle. As for the formidable Becher's Brook, dual National-winning jockey Carl Llewellyn has warned against taking it straight since the horse's eye may be distracted to the bank and rails ahead. 'The secret is to drift out to the right on the approach and then cut back left at take-off, so the horse is looking at the grass on the course after touching down.'

Though some horses – *Lord Gyllene* being an outstanding example – have virtually made all the running with success, results generally favour the view taken by David Nicholson and many others who have argued that it is best to hunt round the first circuit letting the horse settle and enjoy himself. No rider adopted the prolonged waiting approach more effectively than George Stevens, who five times swooped to conquer in the 19th century; and as recently as 2004 the value of the old adage, 'hunt round on the first and ride a race on the second', was most supremely well demonstrated by the winning run of *Amberleigh House*.

TASKER, John

The winning jockey in the 1854 Grand National when *Bourton* romped ahead on the run-in to win by 15 lengths from *Spring*, with *Crabbs* a further ten lengths back in third. Curiously John Tasker was riding the 4-1 favourite when his previous three National rides had been on outsiders not even quoted in the betting. He had failed to finish on Lord Seaham's *Pegasus* in 1850 and he had fallen in 1852 on *Cogia* who was not priced in a race which saw *Royal Blue* as the first 100-1 runner.

Having pulled up on another outsider, *The Victim* in 1853, Tasker returned to Aintree as a jockey of no repute who had failed to complete the course in three starts. Nevertheless he gave *Bourton* a copybook ride, moving up on the second circuit to take the lead from *Crabbs* approaching the last and then producing a devasting turn of speed on the flat. On his two previous National appearances, with a much lesser weight, *Bourton* had been a faller under the experienced Sam Darling.

One year later winning owner Willliam Moseley again put Tasker up on the National favourite: *Trout* who, having shown consistently good form since his success in the Cheltenham Steeplechase, went off as short as 3-1. They led the way to Becher's and were still well in contention on the second circuit only to fall at the Canal Turn.

It was Tasker's last appearance at Aintree. That same year brought an extraordinary double tragedy. The jockey suffered a fatal fall in a chase at Warwick and some six weeks later, on the same course, his National winner suffered the same fate. Following his National win, *Bourton* had been sold for £50 on the understanding that he would be retired from racing. But the new owner had not honoured the agreement and the bay gelding fell fatally when tackling the water jump at Warwick.
See also: Bourton.

TEAL

On April 5, 1952, Mr Harry Lane's ten year old *Teal* had the unique distinction of winning the Grand National after all radio listeners had been told that he was a first fence faller. It happened because, following an unresolved dispute with the BBC, Aintree boss Mrs Mirabel Topham had brought in her own team of amateur commentators.

By *Bimco* out of *Milton Queen*, *Teal* was originally so lowly rated that Irish breeder Mr Gerald Carroll of Clonmel put him on sale for £2. 10s. No one took up the offer. Later he sold him with another horse to Mr Richard Gough of Tipperary – for £35 the pair. For a similar sum *Teal* was sold again, in England; and eventually, under the ownership of Thornaby-on-Tees hunting farmer Mr Ridley Lamb, he developed into a winning point-to-pointer. Then came success in the United Border Chase at Kelso, a victory so impressive that he was bought in May, 1951, for £3,000 by Mr Harry Lane, a wealthy engineering contractor from South Shields.

In 1952, on his National debut, *Teal* was the most respected of four runners sent out by top trainer Neville Crump – ahead of his *Skyreholme*, *Traveller's Pride*, and *Wot No Sun* who had been runner-up to *Freebooter* in the 1950 National. Following three wins in the current season, he was the 100-7 second favourite and the ride of Arthur Thompson who had brought home Crump's first National winner, *Sheila's Cottage*, in 1948. Owner Lane, a 22-stone, white-capped mountain of a man, had such high ex-

pectations of *Teal* that he financed an Aintree outing for 600 of his employees to share in his triumph. Thompson was even more confident, stating boldly that – barring interference – *Teal* would win.

The previous year a disorderly, undeclared false start had resulted in a mad stampede with 11 fallers at the first fence. This year there was a long delay after horses had prematurely broken the tape. But still, despite warnings, there was a frenetic start, and now ten of 47 runners went down at the first. They included Mrs J.V. Rank's well-supported *Early Mist*, with Pat Taaffe up, and old *Russian Hero*, the 1949 winner. *Teal*, however, got away with starting fast; indeed, he was never to be out of the first two. At the third fence, he led narrowly from *Freebooter*, the favourite, and *Brown Jack III*, ridden by his Spanish owner, the Duque de Alberquerque. Thompson, who always favoured front-running, held on to the lead throughout most of the first circuit. Then, at Becher's the second time, *Teal* pecked badly on landing and was headed by Bryan Marshall on the top-weighted 1950 winner *Freebooter*. Michael Scudamore on Miss Dorothy Paget's *Legal Joy* moved up into third.

As they approached the Canal Turn, *Teal* had edged back in front and now, under pressure, *Freebooter* took off too soon and fell. By the last, *Teal* and *Legal Joy* were leading neck-and-neck, followed by the fast improving *Royal Tan*, last year's runner-up. But then, just as in 1951, *Royal Tan* and rider 'Phonsie' O'Brien made a hash of the final fence – this time ending in a fall. On the long run-in *Teal* outpaced *Legal Joy* to win by five lengths, with his stablemate *Wot No Sun* way back in third place. It landed a massive six-figure gamble for the winning owner.

The following February, in his first race since the National, *Teal* showed hugely impressive form when finishing second to *Knock Hard* in the Great Yorkshire Chase. As a result he became the ante-post favourite for the Coronation year National. But sadly he never made it to Aintree. Three weeks before he fatally suffered a ruptured gut when unplaced behind *Knock Hard* in the Cheltenham Gold Cup – a race which Crump had firmly believed he would win.
See also: Crump, Neville; Thompson Arthur Patrick.

TEAM SPIRIT

Most worthy winner – by just half a length – of the 1964 Grand National, when he was tackling the Aintree course for the fifth successive year. Like

T

Battleship (1938) he was a gutsy, half-pint horse, American-owned; and his success meant that Fulke Walwyn, after saddling two seconds, had at last joined the select group of men to have both ridden and trained a National winner.

Having been sired by *Vulgan* (out of *Lady Walewska*), little *Team Spirit* was a half-brother to *Foinavon*, destined to win the 1967 National at 100-1. He was bred in Co. Kildare and snapped up as a four year old for 250 guineas by that most shrewd Irish judge, jockey-turned-trainer Dan Moore who had been beaten only by a head on *Royal Danieli* in the 1938 National. Initially the gelding was hunted by the trainer's wife, Joan. Then, as with *Freebooter* (1950), Moore was to sell a future National winner at a sizeable profit.

Under the ownership of Mrs D.R. Brand, *Team Spirit* began racing over hurdles in 1957 and first visited England in the 1959-60 season, winning the Mildmay Memorial Chase at Sandown and the four-mile Hurst Park National Trial. On the strength of those successes, the eight year old went off as the 9-1 third favourite on his Aintree National debut. It was an inauspicious start. He tried to refuse at the second Becher's, then crashed on landing, with his jockey Willie Robinson narrowly escaping being trampled by oncoming runners. One year later – after the upright fences had been modified – he got round, finishing ninth. But he was now going through a two-year spell without a single win.

At this point he came under the ownership of a syndicate comprising two Americans, John K. Goodman and Ronald B. Woodward, and an Englishman, Gamble North. In the 1962 National they saw him fall at the 19th fence. But the following year, with a new trainer, Fulke Walwyn, he showed a marked improvement. He won a three-miler in fine style at Cheltenham where Walwyn also had his second successive Gold Cup winner (*Mill House* with Robinson up). Then, most favourably handicapped at Aintree, he came from far behind at the second Becher's to finish fourth, albeit well behind the third-placed *Hawa's Song*.

After four failed attempts, it was being suggested that *Team Spirit*, though always tackling the Aintree fences with remarkable bounce and courage, was perhaps too small to triumph there. He came to the 1964 National as winner of the Grand Sefton Chase, but he was now 12 years old and, at 18-1, 12th in the betting, with four younger horses – *Time*,

Pappageno's Cottage, Flying Wind and the Queen Mother's *Laffy* – sharing favouritism.

As in 1963, the tearaway *Out and About* set a mad pace from the start, this time opening up a huge lead with *Peacetown*. Predictably he began to fade on the second circuit, but at the Canal Turn *Peacetown* still had a substantial lead, while *Team Spirit* was in a group of five steadily beginning to close on him. Most progressive of these was *Purple Silk*, the first to clear the last fence, and increasing his lead to two lengths as he came to the Elbow.

John Kenneally kept the nine year old *Purple Silk* going well throughout the testing run-in and, 50 yards from home, thought he was going to win. But Robinson spurred on *Team Spirit* to even greater effect. The gallant old gelding, only 1lb better in the weights, galloped on relentlessly to snatch victory in the dying strides by just half a length, with *Peacetown* six lengths back in third.

Roy Edwards, rider of the long-time leader *Peacetown*, believed that he would have won but for making one bad mistake four out. By the same token, Kenneally took the view that he would have won but for *Peacetown* leaving *Purple Silk* in front too soon. But undeniably *Team Spirit's* victory was well-deserved, and, like *Battleship* in 1938, the American-owned winner was promptly retired to the United States.

See also: Walwyn, Fulke; Robinson, G. William; Americans; United States.

TELEVISION

In 1948 the BBC televised three National Hunt races from Sandown Park and soon after brought regular coverage from Kempton Park and Ascot. Yet it was not until 1960, after years of failed negotiations, that Aintree supremo Mrs Mirabel Topham finally agreed terms for televising the Grand National. The trail-blazing commentators were Peter O'Sullevan, Clive Graham and Peter Bromley; and the programme was presented by Cliff Michelmore, a late replacement for the appendicitis-striken David Coleman.

In 1955 Mrs Topham had introduced motor-racing to Aintree, with the construction of a racetrack following the National course. This now proved useful in enabling the BBC to have a mobile camera mounted on a motor car tracking the race field. In addition, a huge scaffolding tower was erected so that Peter Bromley, having to conquer his vertigo, could cover the far side of the course.

Following criticism of the 1959 National, when only four horses finished and one was destroyed, Lord Sefton had given the jockeys a pre-race briefing, stressing that the usual cavalry charge to the first fence would be folly on the fast going. Obediently, they went off at a relatively sedate pace and only one horse fell at the first. Nevertheless, the TV cameras captured plenty of spectacular falls. Only eight of 26 starters completed the course and popularly, for the first time since 1927, the race was won by the clear favourite: *Merryman II* at 13-2.

It befell the famous Irish broadcaster Michael O'Hehir, stationed at Becher's, to capture the most chaotic scene of all – in 1967 when the riderless *Popham Down* brought almost the entire field to a standstill at the 23rd fence. His marked Irish brogue rose to a rapid-fire crescendo as he gamely sought to capture the carnage: '*Rutherfords* has been hampered, and so has *Castle Falls*. *Rutherfords* is a faller. *Rondetto* has fallen. *Castle Falls* is down. *Norther* has fallen. *Kirtle-Lad* has fallen. *The Fossa* has fallen. There's a right pile-up ... *Leedsy* has climbed over the fence and left his jockey there ... and with all this mayhem, *Foinavon* has gone off on his own.'

A major advance in coverage came in 1969 when, with Coleman the presenter, the National was televised in colour for the first time. There was one minor hiccup: the masterful O'Hehir, on duty as usual at Becher's, made a rare slip in calling the eventual winner *Highland Wedding* as a faller. Thereafter he moved to B.B.C. Radio and called another 16 Nationals before being succeeded by his son Tony who did 12 radio commentaries and then became a regular member of the TV team.

In 1985, the avuncular Des Lynam successfully began his 13 years conducting the proceedings. However, in 1995 there was a relative slump in viewing figures – down to 11.9 million from an average of 16 million in recent years. In 1996 the figure was lower still, 11.2 million. But remarkably, in 1997, when the National was rescheduled for Monday following IRA bomb threats, the race attracted a record audience of nearly 15.1 million, making it the most-watched sports event on TV that year. Martin Hopkins was then producing the television coverage for the first time, while sadly it marked the farewell commentary of Peter O'Sullevan who, following a radio debut in 1947, was covering his 50th and last Grand National.

In 1998 O'Sullevan (now Sir Peter) was succeeded as the lead commentator by Australian Jim (J.A.) McGrath – 'Hotspur' of the *Daily Telegraph* – who had 24 years experience of covering races. His first year at Aintree had been in 1993 when the race was declared void; and in 1997, the year of the IRA bomb scare, he had been one of the last to leave the course because everyone had forgotten that he was still in a commentary box down at Becher's Brook.

This year, for the first time in Britain, mini-cameras were attached to jockeys' helmets, so presenting a unique view of riding over the Aintree fences. The Jockey Club gave permission for three jockeys to be fitted with recording equipment in three races – the John Hughes Memorial Trophy on Thursday, the Martell Fox Hunters' Chase on Friday and the Grand National. The footage was processed to help create a £220,000 mobile simulator, the Morphis MovieRide Theatre, comprising a gleaming white capsule in which up to 20 viewers could experience the full range of emotions felt by jockeys riding in the Grand National. After a nationwide tour, the virtual reality ride, with a commentary by Carl Llewellyn, became a permanent attraction in the Aintree Visitors' Centre.

The mini-camera, together with a transmitter sewn into a vest worn over the top of the rider's body protector, weighed only just over 2lb. This was included when the jockey weighed out for a race and when weighing in afterwards; and its use came into question in the 1999 National. That year, Sean Curran, the rider of 50-1 chance *Cavalero*, hinted that the extra weight could have contributed to him having to pull up on the run to The Chair. His saddle – extra light to allow for the added two pounds – had begun to slip following an earlier blunder. If it had been heavier, he reasoned, it might not have been such a problem.

In 1999 the National attracted only 10.1 million viewers. However, the standard of coverage was higher than ever, with a record number of 45 cameras catching the action compared with the 16 used when the race first went out live in 1960. The roving infield vehicle now carried two gyroscopic cameras instead of one; also, in addition to helicopter shots, higher camera angles were achieved using a hoist capable of towering to 250ft. Commentary was now shared by McGrath, John Hanmer and Tony O'Hehir.

T

In 2000 the British viewing figure was down to a mere 8.9 million, a drop attributed to the fine weather in the south of England on the afternoon of the race. But, according to the British Audience Research Bureau, it was still the most-watched television sporting event of the year – excluding football, and beating the audiences achieved by the Sydney Olympics, Wimbledon and the Open golf. Also this year was notable for the appearance of Sue Barker and Clare Balding taking over from Des Lynam, who was now working for ITV. Richard Dunwoody conducted interviews with jockeys in the weighing room. Further technical developments were the use of a tracking camera to follow the runners as they approached the Canal Turn and a 'camcat' suspended over the last fences and home straight to follow the climax. But this year the helmet-cams worn by three jockeys were rendered inoperative because, with the weather closing in, the helicopter relaying the picture signal could not fly at the required 1,000 feet.

In 2001 the National was beamed live to 148 countries across the globe, and that year, for the first time, mainland China – with 200 million potential viewers – elected to take live coverage, so swelling the TV audience to an estimated 650 million. In advance, a Chinese TV crew filmed a documentary of the National which attracted an audience of 170 million. On the actual race day, the eight-hour time difference meant Chinese enthusiasts staying up to 11.45 p.m. to view the coverage live.

This year the BBC had 48 cameras around the course – both on and off the track – providing more detailed coverage than ever before. Furthermore, internet users could now watch the action on a BBC website; and in Britain the National was commanding 70 per cent of the total television audience compared with 30 per cent for the Derby.

However, the operation was carried out with unexpected difficulty. The dreadful weather caused technical problems that knocked out the Becher's vantage point manned by O'Hehir. It was left to Hanmer, positioned for the 30th year opposite the third fence, to commentate with the aid of a monitor on the action over 24 of the 30 fences instead of his usual dozen. He could not identify the fallers in a ten-horse pile up at the Canal Turn because TV coverage had switched at that point to a long wirecam overhead shot from a helicopter, making the horses look more like giant ants.

In 2003 the British viewing had fallen to as low as 7.8 million. But it was still seen by an estimated 600 million in more than 80 countries compared with 40 countries when Martell began their sponsorship in 1992. In 2004, the last year of Martell sponsorship, British viewing rose sharply to 10.3 million, ahead of coverage of the Olympic Games and surpassed in sport only by international soccer matches in the Euro Cup. In 2005, the audience peaked at 9.5 million, outscoring by nearly two million the preceding attraction: the royal wedding of Prince Charles and Camilla.

In 2007 the fall back to 7.6 million could be attributed to a week of brilliant April sunshine. Both Aintree and the BBC now recognised that viewing figures could be boosted by running the National 45 minutes later – at 5 p.m., a peak time for live TV sport. But this seemed an unlikely move. As pointed out by Lord Daresbury, chairman of Aintree racecourse, such timing would be too late for the vast majority of viewers in Asia.

See also: Broadcasting; O'Sullevan, Sir Peter; Lynam, Desmond; Bromley, Peter; Balding, Clare Victoria.

TEMPEST, Captain Arthur Cecil

An officer in the 11th Light Dragoons, Captain A.C. Tempest had the unusual and frustrating distinction of riding in four Grand Nationals and twice finishing in the runner-up spot – beaten a head on a 50-1 shot in 1865, and four years later beaten three lengths on a 100-1 outsider.

Born in 1837, this doughty Yorkshireman was 20 years old when he was commissioned and posted to Ireland. There he was tutored by the famed horseman Alan McDonough; and subsequently he would win the Aintree Sefton Chase on his mentor's horse, *Bryan O'Lynn*. Ironically, both Tempest and McDonough suffered from National secondsitis. The latter rode in six Nationals, finishing second in 1840 on *Arthur*, and again in 1841, by just one length, on *Cigar*.

For Tempest his huge disappointments came on the same horse, *Hall Court*. Most unusually, in the 1865 National, he was riding this six year old against a horse that he owned: *Merrimac*, a 33-1 shot ridden by the famed Ben Land Jnr who so far had a record of two seconds and a third place in the race. When *Arbury* fell at the second Becher's, it left *Merrimac* heading the field and he went on to open up a lead of more than 20 lengths.

But *Merrimac* faded so badly in the later stages that Tempest on *Hall Court* was spared any conflict of interests. Two fences out the captain easily over-hauled his own contender and, landing over the last, they held the narrowest of leads from the French-bred five year old *Alcibiade*, ridden by another Army officer, Captain Henry Coventry of the Grenadier Guards. Over the last 200 yards the two distant lead-ers were inseparable, seemingly finishing in a dead-heat. The line judge, however, pronounced *Alcibiade* the winner by a head. Fifty yards back in third place, denied a hat-trick of victories, was George Stevens on the 1864 winner *Emblematic*.

Uniquely, this most exciting of finishes had been fought out between two officers who were both hav-ing their first ride in the National. Having tri-umphed, Coventry never competed in the race again. But Tempest was back the following year, this time deserting *Hall Court* in favour of his own *Merrimac* who had been the fifth of six finishers in 1865. It was almost a repeat performance, *Merrimac* being the last of only five finishers.

Three years later, Tempest was reunited with *Hall Court* who, in the meantime, had fallen in two Na-tionals and had then finished seventh under Ben Land Jnr. He gave the ten year old rank outsider a masterful ride, steadily moving through the field on the second circuit and then putting in a storming fin-ish over the run-in to snatch second place, three lengths behind *The Colonel* who was giving Stevens his fourth National win.

It was the first time that a 100-1 shot had come so close to winning. *Hall Court* returned for two more Nationals, failing to finish in both, even though, on the first occasion, he was ridden by the great 'Mr Thomas' Pickernell. That year, 1870, Captain Tempest made his last National appear-ance, riding his own *Karslake*, a 50-1 chance. He was in the lead at the second Becher's but thereafter his six year old bay gelding rapidly faded and failed to finish.

See also: Hall Court; Coventry, Captain Henry.

THOMAS, Mr
See: Pickernell, Thomas

THOMPSON, Arthur Patrick
Irish-born rider of two Grand Nationals winners: *Sheila's Cottage* (1948) and *Teal* (1952), both trained by Neville Crump at Middleham, Yorkshire.

As Crump's stable jockey, Arthur Thompson had been an automatic choice to ride nine year old *Sheila's Cottage* by virtue of the fact that he was the only one who could control the ill-tempered mare. Their 1948 success greatly advanced the career of the jockey and of a trainer who would go on to sad-dle ten winners of various Nationals – three at Ain-tree, plus five Scottish and two Welsh.

The son of a watchmaker, Thompson's introduc-tion to riding came about by chance when, following the death of his mother, he was sent as a small boy to live with his aunt in the country. There he met a cousin who was a keen amateur rider and, under his influence, he proved himself to be a natural-born horseman. In his early teens he was taken on as an apprentice by Kilkenny trainer John Kirwan, and he made his racing debut in 1931, starting off with a win over hurdles at Mallow.

Having been Ireland's champion apprentice on both the Flat and over jumps, Thompson moved to England in 1936, riding for several different trainers until his career was interrupted by Army service in the Second World War. Joining the Northumberland Fusiliers, he became a 'Desert Rat', seeing long periods of action in the North African campaign be-fore being one of thousands of troops captured by General Rommel's Afrika Korps. Three years as a prisoner-of-war followed. Then, in 1945, as Russian troops closed in on his prison camp in Germany, he managed to escape and commandeer a bicycle that enabled him to ride west to meet up with American forces.

Demobilised, Thompson resumed his race-riding career in November, 1945, now needing to fight hard to reduce his weight from 11 and a half stone. The following year, at Middleham, he began a long and successful partnership with Crump who had just completed wartime Army service as a captain in charge of tank training. And there, almost immedi-ately, he was introduced to the difficult, headstrong mare *Sheila's Cottage*.

In 1947, following two wins on the mare at Hay-dock, Thompson was back on her for his debut in a Grand National that had attracted 57 runners. They fell at the 12th fence, with the fiery madam, a 40-1 chance, getting up to run on riderless and be first past the post. Next, in the Scottish National at Bog-side, *Sheila's Cottage* was looking a likely winner when she unseated the jockey at the third last and bolted off the course.

T

One year later *Sheila's Cottage* came back to Aintree with an extra 6lb to carry and now starting at the longer odds of 50-1. Always handily placed on the first circuit, she moved up after the second Becher's to join three others – *Zahia, Happy Home* and *Cromwell* – in giving chase to the long-time leader *First Of The Dandies*. And now her cause was greatly aided by two crucial misfortunes. The luckless Lord Mildmay was seized with cramp in his previously broken neck and was no longer in full control of his *Cromwell*. And, unbelievably, after drawing level with the leader on *Zahia*, jockey Eddie Reavey misjudged the route and took the bay mare wide of the final fence.

Making a supremely well-timed challenge, Thompson caught up with *First Of The Dandies* some 50 yards from home and pushed on to snatch victory by one length, with the so unlucky *Cromwell* six lengths back in third. Success, however, did nothing to improve the mare's manners. Two days later, the jockey was giving *Sheila's Cottage* a friendly pat when she bit off the top joint of one of his fingers. Subsequently, following her retirement, the moody madam was gifted to Arthur and years later was laid to rest in the back garden of his Co. Wexford home.

In the 1949 Grand National, Thompson had a fine ride on *Astra*, another 50-1 chance, only to be unluckily brought down with just three fences remaining. Two weeks later he won the Scottish National on *Wot No Sun* and he retained the ride at Aintree in 1950. With only seven of 49 starters completing the course, they came home in second place, beaten 15 lengths by the powerful *Freebooter*.

Thompson ended that season with 60 winners and third place in the jockeys' championship. But the tall jockey was still struggling to make the weight on low-handicapped horses, as was shown in the 1951 National when he put up 3lb overweight on Major A.C. Straker's *Partpoint* who had been allotted a mere 10st 5lb. As it happened, he had no chance in this chaotic race which saw only three finishers with the third remounted. *Partpoint* was badly disturbed in the confusion of an undeclared false start; and though he avoided the 12 fallers at the first fence, he never settled and crashed out at the Canal Turn.

In 1952 *Wot No Sun* returned to the National, but this time he was ridden by Dave Dick while Arthur had the pick of Crump's four runners, ten year old Irish-bred *Teal*, who was seeking his fourth win of the season and was now second favourite behind *Freebooter*. There was a long delay after one false start, and again chaos early on, with no fewer than ten horses being eliminated at the first fence. But *Teal* and the top-weighted *Freebooter* successfully steered clear of the trouble and soon forged into the lead.

Coming to Becher's second time around, *Teal* still held a narrow lead. But there he dipped his head perilously on landing, and only Thompson's masterful control averted disaster. The stumble enabled *Freebooter* to move ahead, but only briefly. By the Canal Turn, *Teal* had gained a one-length advantage, and now, under pressure, *Freebooter* over-reached the jump and fell. It resulted in a straight battle between *Teal* and Miss Dorothy Paget's *Legal Joy*, the former prevailing by five lengths, with *Wot No Sun* a bad third.

It was a typical ride by Thompson who favoured aggressive tactics, always keeping well in touch with the leaders and heading the field whenever possible. Altogether he rode in nine Nationals, but following his second victory he was never again on a strong contender. Hopes of a second challenge on *Teal* were sadly ended when the bay gelding suffered a fatal injury in the 1953 Cheltenham Gold Cup. Instead, that year, he rode *Larry Finn*, a 40-1 shot, who was to be brought down at the 11th. Again, in 1954, he was on a 40-1 chance: the 12 year old *Southern Coup* who was the eighth of nine finishers.

Thompson's last National ride was in 1956 on the grey *High Guard*. They were one of four fallers at the first fence. Late that same year the popular jockey judged that he was no longer sufficiently strong to maintain his own high standards. He retired at the age of 40 and died 32 years later at home in his native Co. Wexford.

See also: Sheila's Cottage; Teal; Crump Neville.

THORNE, John

The 1981 Grand National will forever be remembered for the heroic triumph of Bob Champion on *Aldaniti*. But it was also memorable for an extraordinary ride by another man of exceptional courage and determination: Mr John Thorne, a farmer and Master of Foxhounds, who finished the four lengths runner-up on the 8-1 favourite, *Spartan Missile*.

Thorne, the breeder, owner, trainer and amateur rider of *Spartan Missile*, was at that time a 54 year old grandfather, who had shed over two stone to make his first appearance in the National. Setting off towards the rear of the field, his nine year old gelding made steady progress until a blunder at the 18th had seemingly ended his chance. But then, towards the finish, Thorne galvanised his horse to astonishing effect. Suddenly, out of the blue, *Spartan Missile* emerged as a major challenger, third at the last, rapidly overhauling *Royal Mail*, and then gaining on the leader – albeit too late – with every stride.

If *Aldaniti* had failed to resist that late challenge, the Grand National would still have had a fairy-tale ending. Like Champion, Thorne had remarkable fighting qualities. He was only 17 years old in March, 1945, when, serving with the British Sixth Airborne Division in the push across the Rhine, he landed in a glider seven miles behind the German lines. Years later, after breaking his back in a fall, he was advised by doctors never to ride again. But he fought his way back to fitness and, riding his *Polaris Missile*, won the 1966 National Hunt Chase at Cheltenham.

After his wartime service as a Paratroop officer, Thorne had become a farmer in Warwickshire where he built up the highly successful Chesterton Stud, hunted regularly with the Warwickshire hounds and rode as an amateur for 33 seasons. By 1968 he had been pleased to leave the race-riding to his teenage son Nigel, a most promising amateur; and in that year's National Nigel was a faller on *Polaris Missile*, a 66-1 chance. But nine months later Nigel was tragically killed in a motor accident when returning from a race meeting. Though grief-stricken, John now stubbornly resolved to abandon his plan to retire from National Hunt riding.

In March, 1981, he finished fourth in the Cheltenham Gold Cup on *Spartan Missile*, a chestnut gelding by *Spartan General* out of his *Polaris Missile*. Since the horse had also twice won Liverpool's Fox Hunters' Chase (once with Thorne riding without irons from Becher's onwards), he looked an outstanding prospect for the National 16 days later.

As big John once joked: 'I always wanted to swim the Channel and ride in the National. But I was too fat for the National and too thin for the Channel'. But now, in preparation for his National bid, he ruthlessly starved himself to get down from his usual 13st to his lightest in 20 years: 11st 5lb, so putting up just three pounds overweight.

Arguably, *Spartan Missile* might have won the National given more time to recover from his Cheltenham run. In any event, Thorne, always the true gentleman, was totally magnanimous in defeat. He was the first to congratulate Champion on his victory and in the evening entertained him at a dinner he hosted at Warwick's Westgate Hotel. Later he hailed Bob's win as 'the best story this century'.

In 1982 injury prevented *Spartan Missile* returning to Aintree. And tragically, only a few weeks before the National, John Thorne was killed in a Bicester point-to-point fall. In the 1983 National, *Spartan Missile*, now trained by Mrs Thorne's son-in-law Nicky Henderson, unseated his rider (Hywel Davies) at the second Becher's. In 1984, on this third and final appearance, he finished 16th.

THORNER, Graham Edward

The reigning champion jockey who won the 1972 Grand National on the eight year old chestnut gelding *Well To Do*. It was only his second appearance in the race, having previously finished fourth – just four lengths behind the winner – on the 66-1 chance *Bowgeeno* in 1971.

Born on January 27, 1949, the son of a Somerset farmer, Graham Thorner went direct from school to serve his apprenticeship with trainer Captain Tim Forster at Letcombe Bassett near Wantage, Oxfordshire; and he was to remain with him from the age of 15 until his retirement. After riding three winners as a 17 year old, he turned professional in 1967 and steadily progressed to capture the National Hunt jockeys' title with 74 winners in the 1970-71 season.

It was to his absolute delight that *Well To Do* was an 11th hour entry for the 1972 National. He knew the horse better than any other, having first ridden him over hurdles as a five year old and having won four races on him in the previous season. Also the gelding was favourably weighted on a mere 10st 11lb, with such consistent form that a late rush of money saw his odds (33-1 ante-post) cut to 14-1 by the off.

The great danger in the 42-strong field was the dual Cheltenham Gold Cup winner *L'Escargot*, a worthy favourite despite a 12st top weight. As he would prove in the next three Nationals, he was a truly outstanding Aintree specialist. Unhappily, however, this first occasion was to see him baulked and knocked over at the third fence. Many others fell on this day of strong winds and pouring rain, and as the leaders came to the last just four runners,

T

closely bunched, remained in the race with a chance.

Timing his challenge to perfection, Thorner took *Well To Do* into a fractional lead on landing, and they stayed on best of all over the stamina-sapping run-in. Their success was scored at the expense of Terry Biddlecombe who was beaten two lengths as the concession of 22lb on former winner *Gay Trip* proved too great to bear. A further three lengths behind were *Black Secret* and *General Symons*, dead-heated for third place.

Thorner had six more National rides: *Quintus* (12th in 1974); *Land Lark*, a fatal casualty at The Chair (1975); *Black Tudor* (tenth, 1976); *Prince Rock* (fell at the 12th, 1977), *Tamalin* (12th, 1978) and second favourite *Mr Snowman* (fell at the second Becher's, 1979). His 1978 ride was especially noteworthy for the extraordinary recovery he made when *Tamalin*, trained by Gordon Richards, belly-flopped on landing over the second Becher's. Against all odds, he contrived to get his horse back into the race, to such amazing effect that he was close up on the leaders at the third last. The game chaser, previously a Hennessy runner-up, had nothing left to give, but at least the jockey's Houdini act won him a prize. Sponsors *The Sun* presented him with the Ted Dexter Award for the best riding performance in the National.

Shortly afterwards, however, Thorner suffered a most horrendous fall at the first hurdle at Worcester. On landing his mount was immediately knocked over by another horse and Graham was left trapped underneath, his feet still in the stirrup irons. One leg was broken as the horse stood up, and then it was agonisingly twisted as he grabbed the reins to prevent the animal from galloping off. It saved him from being dragged away but in the process the horse fell back on him, and he lost consciousness.

Courageously, Thorner overcame this and other severe injuries. But one year later, having rounded off his career with victory on *Casbah* in the 1979 Grand Annual Challenge Cup Chase at Cheltenham, he retired from the saddle. Elsewhere, most notably, he had scored on *Royal Marshall II*, winner of the 1974 Hennessy Cognac Gold Cup and the 1976 King George VI Chase. And other successses among his 650 wins included the Arkle Challenge Trophy (twice), the 1974 Coral Golden Handicap Hurdle, and the 1977 Mandarin Chase.

Though no longer competing, Thorner still played a part in one more Grand National success. In 1979 the dual Maryland Hunt Cup winner *Ben Nevis* had been sent over to be trained by Captain Forster, and subsequently Graham's advice on riding in the race was to prove invaluable to the American amateur Charlie Fenwick. Brought down on *Ben Nevis* in the 1979, Fenwick rode the 40-1 shot to victory in 1980.

Thorner went on to become a trainer based at Letcombe Regis. Outstanding among his stable stars were *King's Parade*, *Get Out Of Me Way* and *Inish Glora*; and races won included the Great Yorkshire Chase, the Greenham Hurdle and the Philip Cornes Saddle of Gold Final.

See also: Well To Do; Forster, Captain Tim; Superstitions.

TIMES

The first Grand National, run over an ill-defined distance of four miles plus, was won by *Lottery* in 14min 53sec. It remains the slowest winning time on record. The following year that time was reduced by more than two minutes. The time was not taken in 1843 when the race was made a handicap; and for record purposes times should only be counted since 1863 when the course distance was increased by about a quarter of a mile to its present near four and a half miles.

The winning times have been lowered as follows

1840 – *Jerry* 12min 30sec

1845 – *Cure-All* 10min 47sec

1846 – *Pioneer* 10min 46sec (an exceptional time since faults in flag placing produced a course distance of nearly five miles)

1847 – *Matthew* 10min 39sec

1850 – *Abd-El-Kader* 9min 57.5sec

1862 – *Huntsman* 9min 30sec

1933 – *Kellsboro' Jack* 9min 28sec

1934 – *Golden Miller* 9min 20.4sec or 9min 20.2sec (two separate timekeepers failed to agree).

1935 – *Reynoldstown* 9min 20.2sec

1973 – *Red Rum* 9min 1.9sec

1990 – *Mr Frisk* 8min 47.8sec

Since saddling *Mr Frisk* to win in the fastest-ever time, trainer Kim Bailey has suggested that his record will never be beaten since the Aintree authorities will resort to watering rather than ever again having the race run on such fast ground. Though unofficial, it is perhaps noteworthy that Jenny Pitman's *Esha Ness* completed the course in the exceptionally fast time of 9min 1.4sec when finishing first in the void National of 1993. The going was good to firm. Most creditably, in 1996, *Rough Quest* achieved 9min 0.8sec when the going was good.

In the 19th century only 14 winners failed to complete the course in under 11 minutes: the slowest, in order, being *Lottery* (1839), *Discount* (1844), *Gay Lad* (1842), *Charity* (1841), *Jerry* (1840), *Emblematic* (1864), *Woodbrook* (1881), *Zoedone* (1883), *Emblem* (1863), *Alcibiade* (1865), *Regal* (1876), *Little Charley* (1858), *Salamander* (1866) and *The Colonel* (1869).

Since the debacle of 1928, when *Tipperary Tim* was the first of two finishers, only seven winners have failed to break the ten-minute mark: *Caughoo* (1947), *Quare Times* (1955), *Well To Do* (1972), *Ben Nevis* (1980), *Little Polveir* (1989), *Earth Summit* (1998) and *Red Marauder* (2001). *Earth Summit*'s winning time (10min 51.4sec on bottomless ground) was the slowest since *Zoedone*'s 11min 39sec in 1883 when the race was still run partly over ploughed fields. Three years later, when the going was even more desperate, *Red Marauder* (11min 0.1sec) became the first winner since *Zoedone* to record a time of more than 11 minutes.

TIPPERARY TIM

Shortly before the 1928 Grand National, as the horses appeared in the tree-lined paddock, a friend of amateur jockey William Dutton called out: 'Billy boy, you'll only win if all the others fall down.' And so it happened. In the most extraordinary of all Nationals, 41 of 42 starters either fell or were pulled up. The only exception was Dutton's mount, *Tipperary Tim*, who came home a distance ahead of the only other finisher, the remounted *Billy Barton*.

Tipperary Tim was a 100-1 shot who, in the view of all experts, had no business competing with other thoroughbreds. By *Cipango* out of *Last Lot*, he was ugly and misshapen and mean. He had a metal tube in his throat to aid his breathing. And his feet were like flat-irons. Moreover, he had a 'parrot mouth', a malformation of the upper jaw which sets the upper front teeth overhanging the lower jaw, so preventing a horse from grazing and often inducing digestive troubles.

This dark-brown gelding, so ill-tempered, ungainly and over-sized, had never won a notable race

in his ten-year life. His own trainer (Joseph Dodd of Whitchurch, Shropshire) confessed that he had no real turn of speed. As a yearling he had been sold for a mere 50 guineas and then used as a hack on which stableboys ran their errands. However, four things could be said in Tim's favour. He had great stamina. His feet were so big that he had never fallen down. His malformed mouth prevented his teeth from connecting when he tried to bite people. And, like so many giants of National Hunt racing, he was Irish-bred, in Co. Tipperary where he was named after Tim Crowe, a local long-distance runner who had won the Windsor-London marathon.

Tipperary Tim was a gift horse – presented to Lancashire owner Mr C. F. Kenyon by an Irish dealer as compensation for the disappointing form of other horses he had bought on his behalf. At the time, the donor, a Mr McKenna, remarked: 'He is a very promising chaser and he will win the Grand National for you one day.' Sadly, the owner did not live to see any hint of such promise. Following his death in 1923, the gelding was bought on the advice of trainer Dodd for 420 guineas by Mr Kenyon's youngest brother, Harold. Subsequently he won a few minor races but then had to be tubed.

Tipperary Tim was not the complete outsider in the 1929 National. There were five others priced at 200-1. The quality was represented by only a handful of runners, most notably: top-weighted *Sprig* and *Bright's Boy*, who were separated by only two lengths when they had finished first and third respectively the previous year; *Master Billie*, the 5-1 favourite; the six year old French mare *Maguelonne*; and, not least, the great American hope *Billy Barton*, a champion over timber with victories in the Maryland Hunt Cup, the Virginia Gold Cup, and the Meadow Brook Cup.

From the start, predictably, eight year old *Easter Hero* led the cavalry charge to the first fence. He was always a headstrong front-runner and notorious for his bold, erratic jumping. Remarkably, in view of the cracking pace and the extremely heavy going, only one horse (*Scraptoft*) failed at the first. Another victim was claimed at the fourth. Then came the major shock of *Sprig*, with Ted Leader, falling at the fifth.

The catastrophe came at the eighth fence – the Canal Turn. Crazily angled at near 45 degrees, the precocious *Easter Hero* leapt at the five-foot hedge and landed almost sideways on top. There, gasping, the normally elegant chestnut seesawed before

T

slithering back into the ditch and ending up like the wreckage of a windmill.

Hard on his flying heels, unable to avoid collision, were *Grackle* and *Darracq*. They joined him in the ditch to present an insurmountable equine barrier to more than 20 horses close behind. In seconds the scene was a nightmarish tangle of writhing mounts and fallen riders, jockeys scrambling for cover through treacly mud, horses running spare with their stirrup leathers flapping.

So, in one floundering swoop, the Grand National field was reduced by more than two-thirds. With little more than a quarter of the distance covered, the greatest steeplechase had been transformed into a spectacle of farcical confusion. And the Canal Turn pile-up was just the beginning. More astonishing events were to lead to the craziest result in the race's 89-year history.

Only nine horses successfully negotiated the Canal Turn. *Billy Barton* surged strongly into the lead, challenged by *Maguellone*, *May King* and *De Comfort*. And way, way behind all the runners, the sure-footed *Tipperary Tim* plodded on with all the grace of a rampant rhinoceros. He had had no trouble at the Canal Turn. By the time he reached it much of the wreckage had been scrambled away. He had heaved himself over – last, and at leisure.

As the field entered the second lap, Tim was still trailing – running wide, as was Dutton's chosen route throughout. But soon only four others of the 42 starters were left in the hunt. *De Comfort* fell at the fence before Becher's and, though remounted, promptly toppled over again at the next big one. Meanwhile, *Billy Barton* was leading all the way – safely over the Canal Turn a second time, then over Valentine's and two lengths ahead of *Great Span*.

Next, at the plain 26th fence, when very much in contention, both *Maguelonne* and *May King* fell. So it was, everyone agreed, now a straight duel between the American challenger and *Great Span*. *Tipperary Tim*, some six lengths behind, was a gallant but seemingly irrelevant survivor.

Less than a length separated the two leaders as they approached the penultimate fence. Both took off perfectly, almost together. Then came heartbreak for *Great Span*'s rider. The saddle slipped off entirely and 17 year old jockey Bill Payne was dumped ingloriously in the mud.

Now it really was a two-horse race – between *Billy Barton*, the 33-1 chance, and *Tipperary Tim*,

the outsider with artificial breathing apparatus. And how the hundreds of American visitors cheered. If anything at all seemed certain on this mad March afternoon of mishaps it was that their Billy would win. Just one more fence, then the last, long stretch for which he had far superior speed.

Suddenly, to a great 'Oh!' of astonishment from the enclosure, the unbelievable happened. *Billy Barton*, the horse who had triumphed over awesome jumps in the Maryland Hunt Cup, now fumbled his last leap. He hit the 30th, stumbled on landing, and rider Tommy Cullinan slipped to the ground. In a flash he had remounted. But too late. *Tipperary Tim* had closed the gap and now those lost precious seconds gave him all the advantage he required.

Landing as surely as ever on his soup-plate feet, Tim squelched on through the heavy mud. The wheezing through his tubed throat was drowned by the roar of the crowd who, for all their losses, could not ignore such an irresistible, irrational success. *Billy Barton* came in second, and last.

Never before had so few horses finished in the National; never had so many fallen. And it was the first time that a 100-1 shot had won. One man, wild with excitement, fought his way towards the beaming bookmakers, telling the world that he had backed Tim the tortoise at 200-1. Meanwhile, a flabbergasted trainer explained to the Press that the horse had only been entered because 'he never falls down'.

The bookies made enormous profits everywhere except in Tipperary, where other Tims, by no means tiny in number, had sentimentally put their shillings on the winner.

Tipperary Tim became a seven-day wonder, the most talked-about horse in the world. But his victory was strictly regarded as a fluke – a fact reflected when he returned for the 1929 National. He was raised from the minimum weight to only 10st 10lb for his win. Again he was priced at 100-1. And this time, uniquely, he did fall – along with *Billy Barton* and 38 others on a day when 56 of 66 runners failed to complete the course and the race produced another 100-1 winner, *Gregalach*.

Now, only a year after winning a record prize of £11,255, the one-time hack slipped back into obscurity – sold for a trifling £50 at the Royal Dublin Society Horse Show. Ironically, in contrast, the distant, remounted runner-up, *Billy Barton*, was immortalised in bronze, his statue permanently gracing the entrance to America's famous Laurel Park racetrack.

Today, when entry qualifications are far more demanding, it seems most unlikely that there will ever again be another National winner quite like the tubed plodder, *Tipperary Tim*.
See also: Dutton, William Parker.

TIPSTERS

The Grand National tipping game begins every year in February when, nearly two months in advance of the race, the senior jumps handicapper reveals the weights he has framed in respect of all horses entered for the event. On National day it can be difficult enough to find the winner from 40 runners. Yet at this early stage the tipsters are venturing to make a selection from more than 100 entries.

An impossible challenge? By no means. On February 22, 1998, faced with 105 entries, the *Racing Post*'s 'Pricewise' (then Melvyn Collier) nominated *Earth Summit* as the best bet at 25-1. On April 4 his selection won at 7-1. Five years later 'Pricewise' (now Tom Segal) struck again in February, choosing *Monty's Pass*, available at 40-1, from a record entry of 149. Monty won at 16-1. And then, in 2006, 'Pricewise' and several other tipsters selected *Numbersixvalverde* from 148 entries. Available at 25-1, he won at 11-1.

The great attraction for the ante-post punter is that odds on offer in February are likely to be infinitely more inviting than those available as the race day draws near. On the other hand, there is the very high risk that at any time in the next two months he could lose his stake as a result of the backed horse being withdrawn because of injury, illness, loss of form, or perhaps the prospect of unfavourable ground at Aintree.

On the race day itself, racing tipsters have sometimes had extraordinary success with their Grand National predictions. In 1995, for example, Julian Muscat of *The Times* tipped the 40-1 winner *Royal Athlete* while his colleague Gerald Hubbard, *The Times* 'Private Handicapper', chose four from the 35-strong field, with three of them – *Royal Athlete*, *Party Politics* and *Dubacilla* – finishing in the frame. The following year both Hubbard and former champion jockey Peter Scudamore correctly selected *Rough Quest* and *Encore Un Peu* to finish first and second – a most valuable straight forecast.

But it was in 2000 that tipsters had their most spectacular success. On race day *Papillon* at 33-1 was the recommendation of 'Pricewise' and of the *Racing Post*'s Mel Cullinan and Tom Segal, plus its Irish correspondent Tony O'Hehir. Furthermore, *Papillon* won a majority of votes when a poll of racing correspondents was conducted for a BBC TV preview. In consequence, his win at 10-1 was said to have cost the bookies around £10 million.

Unfortunately, however, such tipsters' triumphs can be matched by stories of spectacular failures. John Francome, for example, has often been inspired in his judgments, but on Grand National day, 1996, he declared on Channel 4's 'Morning Line': 'You can scrub him (*Rough Quest*) out. He has not got his ground. He has had a hard race at Cheltenham. He has fallen twice this year and he would need to travel in a horse-box to get the trip.'

One year later that misjudgment was totally eclipsed by the colourful advice given by Mark Winstanley, who told readers of *The Sporting Life* that *Lord Gyllene* 'has as much chance of success as Ginger Spice joining a convent ... This slowcoach has not got the class to win a National and I will be amazed if he reaches a place'. And he went on to write of *Camelot Knight*, 'There is more chance of Anneka Rice finding the Holy Grail than this horse has of finishing in the first dozen.'

Lord Gyllene was never headed and won by 25 lengths while *Camelot Knight* finished third at 100-1. However, to give the entertaining Mr Winstanley his due, he did get second place with his selection of *Suny Bay*; and the following year he boldly selected *St Mellion Fairway* who, subsequently cut from 40-1 to 20-1, finished fourth.

As for amateur tipsters, they have had their spectacular successes. In 1993, for example, an Oxford vicar, presumably with divine guidance, correctly picked the first three horses home in the Grand National. But sadly, through human intervention, this was the National declared void after a disastrous false start.

Remarkably, too, in 2004, it was the front news page of *The Times* rather than the sports pages that gave the best advice. There it was reported that veterinary surgeons of the University of Liverpool, led by Chris Proudman, a senior lecturer in equine surgery, had studied the fate of all 560 horses in the past 15 Grand Nationals. Proudman concluded that the best bets were *Clan Royal* and *Amberleigh*

T

House. They finished second and first respectively.

Reportedly Proudman had now predicted the first three home in the last three Nationals. But the run didn't last. In 2005 he gave as his top three runners: *Forest Gunner* (fifth), and *Double Honour* and *Lord Atterbury* who both failed to complete.

Among the few women tipsters, the most notable has been the Irish nun, Sister Rita Dawson of the Sisters of Charity. Betting on behalf of the St Margaret of Scotland Hospice in Clydebank, she scored a hat-trick of Grand National winners in 2000-02. Inevitably her winning habit at Aintree came to an end. However, she picked four winners at the 2007 Cheltenham Festival and, though she failed with her National selections (*Clan Royal* and *Joes Edge*), at least the hospice gained as Ladbrokes provided her £500 stake-money with the promise of another £500 if she were to lose.

See also: McCririck, John.

TITLEY, Jason

The winning jockey on *Royal Athlete* in 1995 when both horse and rider were appearing in the Grand National for the first time. The 12 year old chestnut gelding, a 40-1 chance, was given a copybook ride, never faltering on his way to victory by seven lengths from former winner *Party Politics* and in the third fastest time (9min 4.10sec) in the history of the race.

Born prematurely on March 2, 1971 – in Scotland when his parents were on holiday – Jason grew up in Shannon, Co. Clare, graduating from pony club events to ride his first winner (*Capincur Lady* at Limerick) at the age of 17. Four years later, the same trainer, John Brassil, provided Jason's first major winner: *How's The Boss*, a 20-1 success in the 1992 Ladbroke Handicap Hurdle. It was the beginning of a purple patch in which the young jockey was to make a winning debut at the Cheltenham Festival on *My View* in the Coral Golden Hurdle Final, win the Jameson Irish Grand National on *Vanton* and the Galway Hurdle on *Natalie's Fancy*. Then, along with his claim, he inexplicably lost his winning form and his riding opportunities began to dry up.

The tide finally turned in 1994 when, having taken up freelancing, the fresh-faced youngster managed to pick up some useful rides in England. He gained an introduction to Aintree when finishing sixth on *Shawiya* in the Martell Hurdle and soon after he was sixth again, on *Into The Red*, in the Scottish Grand National which was won by six year old *Earth Summit*.

But the real breakthrough only arose because Mrs Jenny Pitman needed to find six jockeys for her record number of runners in the 1995 Grand National. Her stable jockey Warren Marston opted for *Garrison Savannah*. Subsequently she booked Rodney Farrant for *Lusty Light*, Peter Niven (*Superior Finish*), John White (*Into The Red*) and Brendan Powell (*Do Be Brief*). Five days before the race she completed her sextet. At Fontwell, Jason learned that he was to have his first Grand National ride on *Royal Athlete*.

Mrs Pitman had never used Jason before but she was familiar with his riding – not least because of the 1994 Scottish National in which she had had three runners including third-placed *Superior Finish*. She chose him because she judged him to be a very sympathetic rider and her main hope now was that he would get her injury-prone 'Alfie' round safely. Favouring a run in the Scottish National, she was only sending *Royal Athlete* to Aintree under pressure from the owners. But, as it happened, he jumped superbly throughout and finished so strongly that 24 year old Jason could afford to stand up in the stirrups and punch the air at least 50 yards from the line.

Very often a victorious Grand National jockey has been brought back to earth with a bump when returning to the scene of his greatest triumph. So it was for Jason. In the 1996 National, riding *Bavard Dieu* for Nick Gaselee of *Party Politics* fame, he was thrown off at the very first fence, broke two ribs and so immediately lost a winning ride on *Stompin* in the Cordon Bleu Handicap Hurdle. It was a double blow since he was on 44 winners and hoping to reach 50 for the season. The following year, riding again for Jenny Pitman as a replacement for the injured Farrant, he finished a distant ninth in the National on *Nahthen Lad*. Then, shortly after, he again turned up trumps for Mrs P, riding *Mudahim* to a photo-finish victory in the Jameson Irish Grand National and so completing the trainer's clean sweep of the big-four Nationals.

For a while Jason now served as first jockey to Henrietta Knight, then chose to settle back in his native land where he continued a successful riding career. It was to be three years before he reappeared in the Grand National. And again he gained a sharp reminder of the vagaries of Aintree fortunes. His mount, eight year old *Micko's Dream*, owned by 24 Irish prison officers and trained by Willie Mullins, was one of five fallers at the first fence. It was his last National. In November, 2001, after pulling up a horse at Thurles, he made a snap decision to retire and take over running of the family pub in Quin, Co. Clare. *See also:* Royal Athlete.

TOPHAMS, The

For 130 years members of the Topham family played a key role in the staging of the Grand National and for 117 of those years they had complete control over the operations of Aintree racecourse. That association began in 1843 when Yorkshire-born Edward William Topham – nicknamed 'The Wizard' for his skill as official handicapper at Chester races – was given the task of assessing the runners for the first National to be run as a handicap. It ended in 1973 when Mrs Mirabel Topham, the widow of Edward's grandson, Ronald, sold Aintree racecourse for £3 million.

In 1843 Edward Topham allotted the 16 runners weights ranging from 11st to 12st 6lb, with the exception of the favourite *Peter Simple* on 12st 8lb, plus a 5lb penalty for his most recent wins. That same year he left his mark on the race – changing its name from 'The Grand Liverpool Steeplechase' to 'The Grand Liverpool and National Handicap Steeplechase', and, most admirably, introducing race-cards which included a map of the course, the names of runners and jockeys, and details of the colours to be worn.

In 1856, having taken over the lease of Aintree (owned by Lord Sefton), Mr Topham became responsible for the management of the racecourse. One of his first innovations was the introduction of a two-day meeting to encompass the National. Subsequently he was responsible for many improvements that would raise the status of the spring meeting; and in 1949, almost exactly one century after he had first leased Aintree, the Topham family would buy the course outright.

By that time Mirabel Dorothy Topham (née Hillier), a former musical-comedy actress, had emerged as the dominant force behind the Grand National. Her power arose as a consequence of her marriage in 1922 to Arthur Ronald Topham, who found himself in charge of Tophams Ltd., lessees of Aintree racecourse, following the death in 1932 of his elder brother. Hard-drinking, quick-tempered and lacking self-discipline, Ronald was totally unsuited for a position of such responsibility; and increasingly he came to rely on his strong-willed wife to run the family business. She became a director of Tophams Ltd in 1935, then chairman in 1937.

Mirabel Topham literally oversaw Aintree racecourse, having taken up residence with Ronald at Paddock Lodge, originally the groundsman's cottage which had been converted and extended into a four-bedroom property. Here also lived her two main pillars of support: her niece Patricia Bidwell-Topham, and later her nephew Jim Bidwell-Topham who was to serve as clerk of the course from 1956 until 1973.

During the Second World War, when Aintree racecourse was requisitioned by the War Department, Mrs Topham waged her own battles, fighting the authorities whenever she thought that the turf of the National circuit was in danger of being damaged by the huge military presence, Then, within two months of the departure of the Army, Mirabel was the great driving force behind the frantic efforts to get Aintree fit for the first post-war National in April 1946.

Her power became absolute in 1949 when Messrs Topham Ltd. purchased Aintree for a reputed £275,000 from the Earl of Sefton who had previously rented out the racecourse. Mirabel was now managing director of the controlling company, and she immediately made her mark by extending the spring meeting to four days and instituting a new chase, the Topham Trophy Steeplechase, to be run over a circuit of the National course.

Over the next quarter of a century, Mrs Topham was responsible for a variety of innovations. She developed the additional Mildmay course, opened in 1953; and in 1955 she introduced motor racing to Aintree with the construction of a three-mile race-track that quickly gained a reputation as one of the best in the world, hosting a European Grand Prix and five British Grands Prix. But, above all, her name was to become inexorably linked with the Grand National.

While expressing concern that only quality chasers should have the chance to run in the race, she was equally resolute in resisting demands that the National course should be made easier. She declared: 'As long as I am in control, it will remain a severe test of both horse and jockey. Other courses have fences which bad jumpers can brush through. That's not steeplechasing. Horses which hit my fences know they have done so. They usually fall.'

A dynamic, forceful and mercurial personality, Mirabel was the key figure in the development of the National as a steeplechase of world-wide renown; also a larger-than-life character (18-stone at her peak) frequently involved in major controversy. Her toughness as a businesswoman first gained prominence in 1952, when a long-drawn-out dispute over the copyright of the Grand National radio commentary led her to break off negotiations with the BBC and bring in her own, less experienced commentators. Fortunately, the dispute was resolved in time for proper coverage in 1953, but then came a long tussle over television rights. This issue was finally resolved in 1960, when – for the first time – the whole nation had the opportunity to watch the most famous steeplechase.

The Grand National, meanwhile, had come to be regarded as a national treasure, an event – on a par with the FA Cup Final – that in the popular view somehow transcended the interests of private enterprise. Thus, in 1964, there was a huge outcry at the news that Mrs Topham was planning to sell Aintree racecourse to Capital and Counties Property Ltd for building development. She referred to the high cost of maintenance and the falling attendances, and said she would like to see the race go to Ascot. But the sale was promptly forestalled by Lord Sefton who sought an injunction from the High Court.

The key argument on behalf of Lord Sefton was his claim that such a sale would contravene a covenant included in the contract of the sale of Aintree racecourse to Tophams Ltd in 1949. This stipulated that the land being sold was to be used only for racing or agriculture during the lifetime of Lord and Lady Sefton.

In court, Lord Sefton stressed that the sole motive behind his action was to safeguard the Grand National. Members of the National Hunt Committee also appeared to express their view that it was neither desirable nor practicable to try to stage the National anywhere but Aintree. The injunction was won but it was not a conclusive victory since, as the court recognised, nothing could compel Tophams Ltd. to go on financing horse racing at Aintree; and indeed the facilities there were to deteriorate markedly during this period of insecurity.

As it happened, the National survived, though in a continuing atmosphere of uncertainty as the legal wrangling went on. In 1967 the dispute went to the House of Lords, and there the peers reversed the High Court's approval of Lord Sefton's injunction and awarded costs in favour of Tophams Ltd. Then followed a variety of efforts to find some way of saving Aintree for racing – negotiations with local councils, talk of forming a consortium of wealthy businessmen to take control, discussions with Lancashire County Council and Liverpool's Corporation. All came to naught.

Finally, in 1973, Mrs Topham's 40-year involvement with the Grand National came to an end with the £3 million sale of Aintree racecourse to Liverpool-born property developer Mr Bill Davies. There was a cynical reaction when she expressed her cherished hope that the greatest race would survive the transition. But it was misjudged. Her wish was to be realised, and she would see seven more Nationals run before her death in 1980 at the age of 88.

During the latter half of her reign at Aintree, public interest in the Grand National had been so intense and possessive that it was not unusual for Mirabel to be harshly portrayed in villainous colours, as a great spoilsport, and as an Iron Lady, long before another Mrs T. took over that title. Yet today her financial demands pale into insignificance compared with the mullti-millions paid out for TV rights. Mrs Topham was, quite simply, a shrewd and highly enterprising businesswoman; ahead of her time in seeking sponsorship of the Grand National, and in recognising the value of TV rights and how television coverage might adversely affect the size of the National attendance.

The last tenuous link between Aintree and the Tophams was broken in 2007 when Mr Nicholas Ryan, the great-great-grandson of Edward Topham, chose to sell Paddock Lodge overlooking the new parade ring and winners' enclosure. It had been continuously occupied by members of the Topham family for almost three-quarters of a century.

See also: Davies, Bill; Sefton, Lord; Aintree; World War II.

TOWNLEY, Captain Thomas Manners

A keen amateur horseman, who four years earlier had been serving in the Crimean War, Captain Thomas Manners Townley had the unusual distinction of riding in only one Grand National and being unluckily beaten by half a length on an entire who would later return to Aintree to win the race by a comfortable four lengths.

Educated at Eton and Trinity College, Cambridge, Townley was encouraged by his father to prepare himself for a clerical career. Instead, he chose to join the 10th Hussars, subsequently being posted to India where he became enamoured with horse racing. Then, after the end of the Crimean War in 1856, he resigned his commission so that he could indulge his passion for race-riding.

His one great chance in the National came in 1860 when he took the ride on seven year old *Huntsman*, who had been third the previous year – by only a short neck and one length – and was now owned by his close friend and former fellow officer, Captain George Warwick 'Jonas' Hunt.

Previously *Huntsman* had been trained and owned by Ben Land Snr and ridden by his son. But now Ben Land Jnr was booked to ride Hunt's much more fancied contender, *Goldsmith*. Raised 6lb for his promising Aintree debut, *Huntsman* was a 33-1 outsider in the 19-strong field since he was supposed to be running as a pacemaker for his stablemate.

As it happened, inexplicably, Ben Land Jnr chose to set his own front-running pace on *Goldsmith*. At the second fence he was leading by some five lengths and still ahead at Becher's. Thereafter he faded and failed to finish. Meanwhile Townley gradually brought *Goldsmith* into contention, moving into fourth place at the end of the first circuit.

But then, as his mount clumsily cleared the second Becher's, Townley lost both stirrup irons, and while he juggled to regain them he lost ground to the leaders, *Xanthus* and the favourite *Anatis*. Subsequently, *Goldsmith* produced a tremendous burst of speed to share the lead with *Anatis* at the last, but there he stumbled on landing, and again his rider lost an iron.

On the run-in *Huntsman* bravely fought back to draw level with *Anatis*, ridden by the great 'Mr Thomas' Pickernell and 12lb better offer in the weights. But Townley could feel his mount weakening and so, in desperation, he shouted out an offer of £1,000 for his rival to surrender the race. Perhaps he would have done better to keep his mind on the business in hand. Ignoring the offer, Pickernell flourished his whip for the first time and drove *Anatis* home to win by half a length. *Xanthus* was a further six lengths back in third.

Five years later Townley hoped to make one more bid for National glory on a useful chaser who, like two former National runners, was named *Jerry*, But

the horse broke down a few days before the race and had to be withdrawn. In contrast, *Huntsman*, curiously dropped 8lb, came back under new ownership in 1862 and won as the 3-1 favourite.
See also: Huntsman.

TRAINERS

In the early years of the Grand National, there were no high-powered, high-profile National Hunt trainers as are so familiar today. Indeed, for the most part, trainers had no profile at all in an age when so many jumpers were owned by members of the landed gentry who had them prepared privately by an uncredited employee or a professional jockey.

An exception was George Dockeray who is credited as the trainer of the first two National winners, *Lottery* (1839) and *Jerry* (1840), and *Miss Mowbray* (1852). But he was merely responsible for their final tuning-up alongside his Flat thoroughbreds at Epsom, and he was primarily renowned for his achievements as a jockey, having won the 1826 Derby on *Lapdog* at 50-1 and the 1829 Oaks on *Green Mantle*.

In 1860 Cheltenham-based Wiliam Holman became the first trainer to have saddled three National winners. And in the following decade Captain James Machell emerged as the dominant owner-trainer, preparing horses for Lords Lonsdale and Calthorpe and becoming racing manager to Mr Henry Chaplin of Derby fame. But while Machell owned three National winners – *Disturbance* (1873), *Reugny* (1874) and *Regal* (1876) – all were trained by the jockeys who rode them to victory.

By now, more and more owners were beginning to turn to so-called 'public trainers', and among these professionals one stood head and shoulders above all others: Henry Eyre Linde, a Co. Kildare farmer who, in the 1880s, became the most famous trainer of steeplechasers in Europe. He sent out *Whisper Low* and *Too Good* to defeat the French in the Grand Steeplechase at Auteuil, saddled two successive Grand National winners and only missed a hat-trick by the narrowest of margins, his five year old *Cyrus* being beaten by a head in 1882. Building replica Aintree fences on his gallops at the Curragh and working his horses more rigorously than almost anyone before, Linde set new standards for training that would be taken up and eventually advanced by all the great trainers who followed.

Amazingly, as it now seems, it was not until 1966

T

that the Jockey Club condescended to grant training licences to women, and then the privilege was only gained following court action by the resolute Florence Nagle and a High Court ruling in her favour. That same year, in August, Miss Norah Wilmot became the first woman to have officially trained a winner in Britain, scoring at Brighton with the Scobie Breasley-ridden *Pat*.

Since then a number of outstanding women trainers have emerged in National Hunt racing, among them Jenny Pitman, Mercy Rimell, Mary Reveley, Venetia Williams and Henrietta Knight. So far only one – Mrs Pitman –has been successful in the Grand National, having saddled the winner in 1983 and 1995. Notably, in 1999, Sue Bradburne, with just 15 horses in her stable in Cupar, Fife, turned out the 25-1 National runner-up, *Blue Charm*.

In 1983, for the first time, no fewer than four women trainers had runners in the National, and Mrs Pitman led the way with three representatives: *Royal Athlete*, *Artistic Prince* and *Monty Python*. In 1995 she became the first trainer to have as many as six runners in the National and triumphed with *Royal Athlete* at 40-1.

The most winning Grand National trainers
Four wins

    Fred Rimell – *E.S.B.* (1956); *Nicolaus Silver* (1961); *Gay Trip* (1970); *Rag Trade* (1976)

    Donald 'Ginger' McCain – *Red Rum* (1973, 1974, 1977); *Amberleigh House* (2004)

Three wins

    George Dockeray – *Lottery* (1839); *Jerry* (1840); *Miss Mowbray* (1852)

    William Holman – *Freetrader* (1876); *Little Charley* (1858); *Anatis* (1860)

    William Moore – *Why Not* (1894); *The Soarer* (1896); *Manifesto* (1899)

    Hon. Aubrey Hastings – *Ascetic Silver* (1906); *Ally Sloper* (1915); *Master Robert* (1924)

    Tom Coulthwaite – *Eremon* (1907); *Jenkinstown* (1910); *Grakle* (1931)

    Vincent O'Brien – *Early Mist* (1953); *Royal Tan* (1954); *Quare Times* (1955)

    Neville Crump – *Sheila's Cottage* (1948); *Teal* (1952); *Merryman II* (1960)

    Tim Forster – *Well To Do* (1972); *Ben Nevis* (1980); *Last Suspect* (1985)

Two wins

    Edwin Weever – *Emblem* (1863); *Emblematic* (1864)

    R. Roberts – *The Colonel* (1869, 1870)

    Chris Green – *Half Caste* (1859); *The Lamb* (1871)

    Harry Lamplugh – *Huntsman* (1862); *Cortolvin* (1867)

    J.M Richardson – *Disturbance* (1873); *Reugny* (1874)

    Henry Eyre Linde – *Empress* (1880); *Woodbrook* (1881)

    John Nightingall – *Shifnal* (1878); *Ilex* (1890)

    Robert Gore – *Jerry M* (1912); *Covertcoat* (1913)

    Tom Leader – *Sprig* (1927); *Gregalach* (1929)

    Noel Furlong – *Reynoldstown* (1935, 1936)

    Fred Winter – *Jay Trump* (1965); *Anglo* (1966)

    Jenny Pitman – *Corbiere* (1983); *Royal Athlete* (1995)

    Nigel Twiston-Davies – *Earth Summit* (1998); *Bindaree* (2002)

Trainers who have won riding their own charges

    Tom Cunningham – *Peter Simple* (1849)

    Tom Olliver – *Peter Simple* (1853)

    Charlie Boyce – *Emigrant* (1857)

    Chris Green – *Half Caste* (1859)

    Harry Lamplugh – *Huntsman* (1862)

    J. M Richardson – *Disturbance* (1873) and *Reugny* (1874)

    Joe Cannon – *Regal* (1876)

    Harry Beasley – *Come Away* (1891)

    Aubrey Hastings – *Ascetic's Silver* (1906)

Winning trainers who had previously ridden to Grand National victory

    Algy Anthony – rode *Ambush* (1900); trained *Troytown* (1920)

    Fulke Walwyn – rode *Reynoldstown* (1936); trained *Team Spirit* (1964)

    Fred Winter – rode *Sundew* (1957) and *Kilmore* (1962); trained *Jay Trump* (1965) and *Anglo* (1966)

    Tommy Carberry – rode *L'Escargot* (1975); trained *Bobbyjo* (1999)

T

Trainers with the most runners in a Grand National

Martin Pipe: ten of 40 in 2001 – best: third place with *Blowing Wind* (remounted, 116-1)

Martin Pipe: eight of 40 in 2002 – best: third place with *Blowing Wind* (8-1)

Martin Pipe: seven of 40 in 2003 – best: eighth with *Blowing Wind* (20-1)

Martin Pipe: seven of 39 in 2004 – best: third place with *Lord Atterbury* (40-1)

Jenny Pitman: six of 35 in 1995 – best: first with *Royal Athlete* (40-1)

Paul Nicholls: six of 40 in 2006 – none finished

Tom Leader: five of 66 in 1929 – best: first with *Gregalach* (100-1)

Martin Pipe: five of 39 in 1993 – void race

Martin Pipe: five of 36 in 1994 – best: first with *Miinnehoma* (16-1)

Martin Pipe: five of 37 in 1998 – none finished

Martin Pipe: five of 40 in 2006 – best: sixth with *Puntal* (66-1)

Paul Nicholls: five of 40 in 2003 – best: fifth with *Montifault* (33-1)

Fulke Walwyn: four of 43 in 1948 – best: fourth place with *Happy Home* (33-1)

W.A. Stephenson: four of 40 in 1989 – best: third place with *The Thinker* (10-1)

Martin Pipe: four of 38 in 1990 – best: 16th with *Bonanza Boy* (16-1)

Martin Pipe: four of 35 in 1995 – best: eighth with *Riverside Boy* (40-1)

Martin Pipe: four of 32 in 1999 – best: ninth with *St. Mellion Fairway* (200-1)

Martin Pipe: four of 40 in 2005 – best: fourth with *It Takes Time* (18-1)

Paul Nicholls: four of 40 in 2000 – none finished

Paul Nicholls: four of 40 in 2005 – best: second with *Royal Auclair* (40-1)

Paul Nicholls: four of 40 in 2007 – none finished

Willie Mullins: four of 40 in 2007 – best: ninth with *Hedgehunter* (9-1)

See also: Champion Trainers; Lady Trainers.

TROYTOWN

A giant (17 hands) Irish gelding who, in 1920, on his first and last appearance in the Grand National, powered home to a comfortable 12 lengths victory. Arguably, this seven year old would have become one of the all-time greats of steeplechasing but for a fatal fall in France the following summer.

Bred in Co. Meath by his owner, Major Thomas Collins-Gerrard, *Troytown* was by *Cyllene*'s son *Zria* out of *Diane*, a mare whose bloodline included the great American stallion *Lexington*. He went to the National with outstanding credentials. One year before, on the eve of the 1919 National, he had dominated the Stanley Steeplechase only to be deprived of victory by his jockey's error in taking the wrong course. Two days later he had won the Champion Chase and he had followed up in the summer with a hugely impressive victory in the Grand Steeplechase de Paris at Auteuil.

Moreover, to his advantage, he had a trainer (Algy Anthony) who had won the 1900 National on *Ambush II*, and a rider (Jack Anthony) who had won the National twice, on *Glenside* (1911) and *Ally Sloper* (1915). He was heavily backed by a huge Irish contingent who rated him unbeatable.

One horse, however, was more strongly fancied in 1920: ten year old *Poethlyn*, who had become the shortest-ever price winner the previous year. Again ridden by Ernie Piggott, and again carrying top weight (12st 7lb), *Poethlyn* came to Aintree with 11 successive victories behind him. He went off as 3-1 favourite, three points shorter than *Troytown* who was second in the weights on 1first 9lb.

Twenty-four runners set off in pouring rain, in a fierce gale, and on already boggy ground. And when *Poethlyn* came down at the very first fence, it rapidly developed into a one-horse race. While 19 contenders fell in his wake, *Troytown* ran on relentlessly, untroubled except at the fourth fence from home where the blinding rain and slippery ground caused him to take off too soon.

It made no difference. *Troytown* was so powerful that he bulldozed his way through the only fence that he failed to jump cleanly. That error lost him the lead to *The Bore*, but it was quickly regained and, never seriously challenged, he romped home by far the freshest of only five finishers. Through no choice of his own, Anthony had found himself leading the field almost from start to finish on a horse who would not be restrained. Having gained his

507

T

third National victory, he likened the experience to having ridden on a steam engine.

That summer, *Troytown* returned to Auteuil for another crack at the Grand Steeplechase. This time he finished third but seemed so unwearied that connections chose to run him again, five days later in the Prix des Drags. There he broke a leg on hitting one of the smaller fences and had to be put down. He was buried in the nearby animals' cemetery at Asnieres.

See also: Anthony, John Randolph.

TRUDGILL, Robert

A number of jockeys declined the offer of a ride on the unfancied *Master Robert* in the 1924 Grand National. They included Peter Roberts, an amateur who had ridden the chestnut gelding to victory at Aintree in the 1923 Valentine Chase and who now preferred to ride *Palm Oil*, a 66-1 outsider. In desperation, the connections turned to Bob Trudgill, a West Country freelance jockey who, nearing the end of a none-too-profitable career, welcomed any ride he could get.

Trudgill had ridden in the National once before, falling in 1922 on the rank outsider *Confessor*. Now, on the eve of the 1924 race, he fell on *Charlie Wise* in the Stanley Steeplechase, incurring a huge gash to a leg that required multiple stitches. Against doctor's advice, he insisted that he was fit to ride the next day.

At the time it seemed a purposeless act of bravado. *Master Robert*, formerly a plough horse sold for £50, suffered from inflammation of a bone in his foot, and only a week before the National he had been pulled up lame at the end of a three-mile chase at Wolverhampton. His 29 rivals included three former winners (*Shaun Spadah*, *Music Hall* and *Sergeant Murphy*). Moreover, according to the betting, there could be just one winner: 12 year old *Conjuror II*. He had been an unlucky third in the 1923 National when ridden by a very inexperienced amateur. Since then he had been beaten by only a head in the inaugural Cheltenham Gold Cup and now, again to be ridden by the top amateur Harry Brown, he went off at Aintree at 5-2, short-priced favouritism which has only been surpassed by the 2-1 about *Golden Miller* in 1938.

But fate was on Trudgill's side. When going well, *Conjuror II* was knocked over by a loose horse at Becher's. Riderless runners were responsible for many more falls and, as one of the few to avoid in-terefence, Trudgill was able to make a late challenge on *Master Robert* to win by four lengths. He then staggered to the weigh-in, with blood oozing from his reopened wounds. It was his one day of glory. His courage was rewarded with a £2,000 gift from the winning owners.

Success, and doubtless a few celebratory drinks, certainly raised Trudgill's spirits. At the ensuing Adelphi Hotel banquet, he disregarded his leg injury and – in a demonstration of his winning ride – he entertained the 1,500 guests by climbing on to the top table, 'galloping' along it and finishing with a jump over Becher's represented by 20 magnums of champagne. But he was to ride in only one more National, pulling up on *Ammonal*, a 66-1 chance, the following year.

See also: Master Robert.

TSAREVICH, The

Five lengths runner-up in the 1987 Grand National, when *Maori Venture* was the first of 22 finishers. Though the white-faced bay gelding failed to win the race, finishing seventh on his two other appearances, 1986 and 1988, Major Ivan Straker's *The Tsarevich* was a brilliant jumper with the distinction of not once falling in his entire career. Trained by Nicky Henderson, he won 15 of his 54 starts and more than £120,000 in prize money. He was 23 years old when he died after suffering a heart attack in 1999.

See also: Straker, Major Ivan.

TUBING

Tubing is a drastic surgical operation performed on a horse with a breathing problem caused by obstruction in the larynx arising from defective vocal cords. It involves inserting a metal tube in the trachea (windpipe) below the larynx so that air can bypass the obstruction; and a horse so treated can be recognised by a small hole at the front of its lower neck. Two tubed horses have won the Grand National: the 100-1 chance *Tipperary Tim* (1928) and the giant *Party Politics* (1992).

TURNELL, Andrew

Trainer of *Maori Venture* who won the 1987 Grand National on his first and last appearance in the race. The victory climaxed a family involvement with the race that had begun four decades earlier when Andrew Turnell's father, Robert, making his Aintree debut in a 57-strong field, rode *Some Chicken*, a 40-1 shot, into fifth place. Between them, father and son rode in no fewer than 20 Grand Nationals. Neither achieved better than third place. Both, however, had successful careers as rider and then trainer.

Born on August 27, 1948, Andy Turnell had his most winners when riding horses trained by his father at Ogbourne Maizey, north of Marlborough in Wiltshire, on behalf of millionaire Jim Joel. Unhappily, his first National ride came in 1967, the year of the Foinavon fiasco. He fell at the first on the 66-1 chance *Meon Valley* and in the process brought down *Popham Down*, the gelding who would run on riderless and bring the field to a standstill 22 fences later.

Noted for his unusually short style of riding, Andy rode in 12 more Nationals, usually on long-priced outsiders. He finished eighth on *Kellsboro' Wood* (1969), fell on *Fort Ord* (1970) and on *Kellsboro' Wood* (1971 and 1972), and pulled up on *Beau Parc* in 1973. Then came his most memorable ride: in 1974 when he finished third – behind *Red Rum* and *L'Escargot* – on the 50-1 shot *Charles Dickens*.

The following year he was on *April Seventh*, trained by his father. The gelding went on to win the Whitbread Gold Cup, and reunited with Andy, to win the Hennessy Cognac Gold Cup. But at Aintree he was unluckily brought down at the first Becher's; and, funnily (though not for everyone), Andy was so desperate as he fell backwards that he grabbed out for the first thing in his reach. It was the silks of Paul Kelleway, and in the process he pulled the rival jockey off his mount *Barona*. Paul was furious, his frustration only reinforced when *Barona* won the Scottish National two weeks later and the following year was a fast-finishing fourth in the Aintree National.

Turnell was eighth that year on *Spittin Image* but failed to finish in his last three Nationals – on *April Seventh* (1978), *Lord Browndodd* (1979) and *Churchtown Boy* (1980). He had been riding with distinction for 17 seasons when, in 1982, he turned to training following his father's death. At the time the future looked bleak. The number of horses in training declined; also he had notice to quit the rented yard near Marlborough. Eventually a move to new premises at East Hendred, Oxfordshire, was made possible with the help of Mr Joel and a few other owners, but then the stable was crippled by a virus infection.

Providentially, the training operation was saved following the arrival of *Maori Venture*, purchased for 17,000 guineas by Andy at the Ascot sales on behalf of Mr Joel. Following his victory in the 1987 Mandarin Chase at Newbury, Andy and his stable jockey Steve Knight persuaded Mr Joel to let him take his chance in the National. His victory exceeded their wildest measure, and for good measure the yard's second string, *Tracys Special*, finished a creditable sixth at 50-1.

The stable continued to flourish with horses such as *Katabatic*, *Cogent* and *Squire Silk*. Turnell's subsequent National runners were *Tracys Special* (pulled up, 1988); *Kittinger* (refused at the 24th, 1992); and *Country Member* (well-supported after winning Sandown's Grand Military Cup but now one of seven to exit at the first in 1995). Then, after a lean spell, Andy made a most surprising decision: he chose to leave his southern base and to switch to training Flat horses in Yorkshire.

There were difficult years ahead; and by 2002 he had just 15 horses in his yard. One of them, however, was the home-bred *Darshaan* colt *Jelani*, owned by his landlords John and Claire Hollowood. That year *Jelani* became his first classic runner in the Vodafone Derby, finishing a most creditable fourth as a rank outsider. In 2005 Andy returned to the region of his roots, taking over Jeff King's Elm Cross House stables near Swindon.

See also: Maori Venture; Joel, H.J.; Turnell, Robert.

TURNELL, Robert

Born on November 18, 1914, Bob Turnell, father of Andrew, came late to the Grand National. Yet he rode seven times in the race between 1947 and 1956, having his greatest disappointment in 1950 when he approached the second last on *Cloncarrig* with only one of 48 other starters in serious contention. There, when marginally in the lead, he hit the top of the fence and fell. Unchallenged, *Freebooter* ran on to win by 15 lengths.

Three years later, when putting up 5lb overweight, Bob finished third on a 33-1 shot, Lord Sefton's *Irish Lizard* – a most creditable performance since the Lizard had run only two days earlier to win the Topham Trophy over one circuit of the National course. His other National rides were: *Some Chicken*, fifth at 40-1 in 1947; *War Risk*, 11th in 1948; *Brighter Sandy*, brought down, 1949;

T

Cloncarrig, fell, 1951; and *Carey's Cottage*, seventh in 1956.

Turnell held a professional jockey's licence for more than 30 years, riding his first winner (on the Flat) as a 15 year old apprentice in 1929. The Second World War interrupted his career and on demob from the army in 1946, though still claiming a weight allowance, he promptly demonstrated his versatile horsemanship in winning the Grand Sefton Chase at Aintree on *War Risk*.

Starting as a trainer in 1954, he was hugely successful, most notably through his long and close association with millionaire Jim Joel for whom he turned out 233 winners. His first major triumph, however, came with *Pas Seul* whom he had bought as a yearling for £600 on behalf of stockbroker John Rogerson. *Pas Seul* won the 1960 Cheltenham Gold Cup and the following year won the Whitbread Gold Cup when giving a massive 21lb to the Grand National winner *Nicolaus Silver*.

Arguably *Pas Seul* would have won another Cheltenham Gold Cup if only – as Turnell claimed – he had not been doped two days before the race by intruders at the Ogbourne Maizey yard, near Marlborough, Wiltshire. As it was, he was beaten only a length and a half by *Saffron Tartan* in 1961, and, as favourite, finished fifth in 1962. Unfortunately, the 11 year old gelding was past his best when sent to Aintree in 1964. Anchored under the top weight of 12st, he crashed out at the 12th fence, while Bob's other runner, *Beau Normand*, three times a winner that season, refused one fence earlier.

For two decades Turnell regularly sent out Grand National challengers and of all his dozens of runners the most persistent was the gallant chestnut *Rondetto*, winner of the 1967 Hennesy Cognac Gold Cup. Though burdened with the second highest weight of 11st 6lb on his Aintree debut in 1965, he was well-backed and was leading with *Peacetown* at the second Becher's, only to tire and fall at the 26th. Meanwhile, Bob's less well-fancied *Red Tide*, owned by Paul Mellon, had unseated Johnnie Haine on the first circuit and, riderless, would crucially interfere with the hot favourite *Freddie*, destined to finish second, just three-quarters of a length behind *Jay Trump*.

Two years later, at the age of 11, *Rondetto* was still higher in the weights and he refused in the fiasco of *Foinavon*'s triumph. In 1968 he fell at the 23rd, scene of last year's pile-up. But then, remarkably, Turnell had him back to such fitness that he re-

turned in 1969 as a 13 year old with his ever-loyal partner Jeff King to put in a tremendous challenge to finish third to *Highland Wedding* and *Steel Bridge*. Bob also saddled fourth-placed *The Beeches* and *Limeburner*, 12th. The following year, as the oldest horse on parade, *Rondetto* was one of eight to exit at the first open ditch; and *Bowjeeno*, Bob's other 22-1 challenger, was an early faller.

In 1971, the National fate of *Pas Seul* was repeated by that of Mr Joel's classy jumper *The Laird* who had been beaten only a neck by *Fort Leney* in the 1968 Cheltenham Gold Cup. Following a hat-trick of wins, the gelding was heavily backed at Aintree. But he was second in the weights under 11st 12lb and he fell at the third. In the same race, Turnell ran *Charter Flight* (pulled up) and *Limeburner*, who led at the 24th fence and was still well in contention when falling at the second last. Remounted by John Buckingham, he finished 12th. His subsequent National runners – *Bullocks Horn* and *Limeburner* (1972) and *April The Seventh* (1975 and 1978) – all failed to finish.

It was Mr Joel's good fortune to live on to the ripe old age of 97 and to have his dream of Grand National victory finally achieved by *Maori Venture* in 1987. Cruelly, by his untimely death at the age at the age of 67 in 1982, Bob missed seeing the triumph he had so richly deserved.

See also: Turnell, Andrew; Joel, H.J.

TWISTON-DAVIES, Nigel Anthony

Trainer of two Grand National winners – *Earth Summit* (1998) and *Bindaree* (2002). By coincidence, both his winners were ridden by substitute jockeys: Carl Llewellyn taking over on *Earth Summit* when Tom Jenks broke a leg, and Jim Culloty being a late recruit for *Bindaree* after Jamie Goldstein had broken his right leg only three days before the big race.

The son of a farmer and breeder, Twiston-Davies was born on May 16, 1957, in Crickhowell, Powys, and grew up in Hertfordshire where his parents had a farm opposite that of Peter Scudamore's family. With Peter he learned to ride at pony school. Then, as an amateur jockey, always battling against weight, he rode for Richard Head, Fred Rimell, Kim Bailey and David Nicholson, winning 17 races over jumps before starting farming and running a few point-to-pointers.

Remarkably, in the light of his later success, he

was a reluctant trainer. In 1981 he began to combine farming with very modest training as a permit-holder at Grange Hill Farm, Naunton, near Cheltenham. His first win came at Hereford in 1982 with *Last Of The Foxes* which he himself owned and rode, but it was not until 1987 that he had a notable success – with his prolific mare *Mrs Muck* in the Ascot Long Distance Hurdle. Two years later he only took out a full licence because his farming had been hit by the agricultural recession. Much of his farmland was sold off to his local patrons, Raymond and Jenny Mould.

He emerged as a major force on the National Hunt scene in 1992 when his big-race winners were *Tipping Tim* (National Hunt Handicap Chase and the Mackeson Gold Cup); *Captain Dibble* (Scottish National and SGB Chase); *Dakyns Boy* (Feltham Novices' Chase); and *Corrouge* (Scottish Champion Hurdle). In 1993, when he was joined by Peter Scudamore as assistant trainer, his many successes included the Great Yorkshire Chase and the Sun Alliance Novices' Chase with *Young Hustler*; the Sun Alliance Novices' Hurdle with *Gaelstrom*; the Long Walk Hurdle with *Sweet Duke*; and the Becher Chase with *Indian Tonic*.

An all-weather gallop had been laid out in 1989 and, like the mighty Martin Pipe, Nigel introduced plenty of interval training, with short canters being all the more necessary because of the hilly terrain above the Gloucesterhire hamlets of Naunton and Guiting Power. Such was the stable's consistency that four times, between 1993 and 1998, Nigel finished a season third in the trainers' prize money table. For a number of years, however, he continued to be frustrated in his efforts to turn out a Grand National winner.

In 1993 he had the leading National contender in eight year old *Captain Dibble*, the chosen mount of Scudamore who had ridden him to victory in the Scottish National and who now had high hopes of Aintree success at the 13th attempt. But, as 'luck' would have it, this was to be the void National and *Captain Dibble* had to be pulled-up after completing one circuit. It would be three years before he ran in the race again, then well past his prime and finishing 11th.

In 1994 Nigel had another strong National challenger: *Young Hustler*, winner the previous year of the Sun Alliance Novices' Chase. He was so hopeful that he reportedly backed him to the tune of £1,000

when the weights were announced and his young chestnut gelding was readily available at 33-1. It looked a good bet when *Young Hustler* finished a creditable third in the Cheltenham Gold Cup. He shortened to 16-1. But it was asking a lot of a mere seven year old to turn out again so soon for the National; in addition, Aintree's heavy ground was against him. Ridden by David Bridgwater, he was in fourth place when unluckily brought down by a loose horse at the 11th.

In 1995 Twiston-Davies had three National runners, headed by *Young Hustler* who was even more strongly fancied. This time he had not had a hard race in the Gold Cup, finishing a distant fifth. His whole season had been well geared to this one race and he was to be ridden by Carl Llewellyn, the winning jockey of 1992 on *Party Politics*. But *Young Hustler*, going off the second favourite at 10-1, was unlucky again, his rider losing his seat at the third fence. Nigel's other runners fared only marginally better: *Dakyns Boy* falling at the tenth, *Camelot Knight* at the 21st.

Remarkably, in 1996, *Young Hustler* had still stronger support. He had not actually fallen in his two previous Nationals and he had since proved his Aintree jumping ability in winning November's Becher Chase under Chris Maude. Now, with the same rider, he went off at 8-1 and, under a top weight of 11st 7lb, did well enough to finish fifth with all those ahead of him receiving a stone or more. Nigel had had four other entries – *Earth Summit*, *Grange Brake*, *Tipping Tim* and *Captain Dibble* – but three were withdrawn while *Captain Dibble* finished 11th at 40-1.

In 1997 Twiston-Davies had three long-priced runners in the 36-strong Grand National: *Grange Brake*, *Dakyns Boy*, and *Camelot Knight* who was 22lb out of the handicap. *Grange Brake* refused at the 27th, but his two 12 year olds performed remarkably well. *Dakyns Boy* finished eighth; and – much to the trainer's surprise – *Camelot Knight*, totally outpaced on the first circuit, ran through the field to finish third at 100-1. One will never know what the latter would have achieved but for the IRA bomb scares which had brought a 49-hour postponement and ground drying out to lessen his prospects.

The following season Nigel endured a dreadful spell, saddling 72 consecutive losers. But the drought ended in December, most notably with the victory of *Earth Summit* in the Welsh National, and

T

he had high hopes for Aintree with two major contenders: *Young Hustler* and *Earth Summit*. Ironically, it was the former, nicely dropped in the weights, who was initially hailed as a great handicap snip on 10st 2lb. But, following the withdrawal of *Young Hustler*, it was the mud-loving latter who became all the rage as the ground turned in his favour. *Earth Summit* had proved his staying and jumping ability as the youngest-ever winner of the 1994 Scottish National, and by his mud-slogging success in the Welsh National. He went off a worthy 7-1 favourite and beat his only threatening rival, *Suny Bay* (conceding 23lb), by 11 lengths.

It was a remarkable training feat on the part of Twiston-Davies, having brought *Earth Summit* back to full fitness after missing a full season with a career-threatening ligament injury. The ten year old had now become the first horse to win the Scottish, Welsh and Aintree Nationals. Yet, following his greatest triumph, the trainer remained as reserved as ever, famously telling Des Lynam: 'I don't do interviews.' That season, for the fourth time, he was third in the trainers' table.

In the 1999 National he again ran *Earth Summit*, plus 13 year old *Camelot Knight*. The former, struggling to recapture his form, and now raised 9lb in the weights, finished eighth. The latter, who had not won for six years, was unluckily brought down at the second Becher's. One year later, Nigel had only one Grand National runner: the old faithful *Camelot Knight* who, at 14, completed the course – albeit finishing 14th at 150-1. Happily, however, the trainer finished the season on a very high note. He had begged owner Sylvia Tainton to let him run her beloved *Beau* in the Whitbread Gold Cup and the seven year old duly became the first horse to win the race by a distance, a performance that immediately saw him made the ante-post favourite for the 2001 National.

Twiston-Davies ended the season with 87 winners, taking fifth place in the trainers' prize money table, his successes in 2000 including the Hennessy Cognac Gold Cup with *King's Road*, the Champion Stayers' Hurdle at Punchestown with *Rubhahunish*, and three major hurdle races with *Mister Morose*. But distressing times lay ahead. The new season brought a run of 45 consecutive losers. Most tragically, in November, there was the death of his very great friend and neighbour Jenny Mould whose colours had been carried on such stalwarts as *Tipping Tim* and *Mister Morose*.

At least, in 2001, Nigel had reason to be hopeful about his Grand National prospects. He had an outstanding contender: *Beau*, who had won the Great Yorkshire Chase as well as the Whitbread. Initially, the eight year old had been aimed at the Cheltenham Gold Cup. With that race lost to the foot-and-mouth epidemic, he was switched to Aintree and top-weighted on 11st 10lb. In quagmire conditions, only seven horses remained when *Beau* led the field on to the second circuit, but unluckily Carl Llewellyn lost his reins as the gelding pecked on landing over the 17th and was unseated three fences later, leaving only *Red Marauder* and *Smarty* in the race.

Nigel's other runner, seven year old *Spanish Main*, had fallen at the first. It marked an abrupt ending to newcomer Jamie Goldstein's hopes of bettering his father Ray who, in 1989, in his one and only National, had been brought down on *Hettinger* at the first Becher's, suffering such bad concussion that he could barely remember the race.

Immediately after that run William Hill made *Beau* their 16-1 favourite for the 2002 Grand National. However, this was the beginning of a sharp downturn in the fortunes of Twiston-Davies. In partnership with Peter Scudamore he had expanded his yard to a 96-box operation. In ten years he had been responsible for almost 700 winners. But now quantity far outweighed the quality, and the 2001-02 season developed into the worst that the trainer had known for a decade. Prior to the Grand National, after a spell of almost four months with only two winners, he became so discouraged by his unrewarding workload that he planned to quit the sport at this season's end.

Nevertheless, in the 2002 National, he had three runners: *Beau*, *Bindaree* and his De Vere Gold Cup winner *Frantic Tan*; and he was unusually bullish about his chances, quoted as saying 'I think I will win this year'. *Beau* was his No 1 hope, set to run in new colours after an 11th hour sale to millionaire businessman Trevor Hemmings, seeking a replacement for his ill-fated star chaser *Young Kenny*. With Llewellyn again in the saddle, he was backed down to 11-1. He was lying second when he unseated his rider at the 14th. *Frantic Tan*, 50-1, had lost Tom Jenks at the fifth. Meanwhile, *Bindaree*, 20-1, made steady progress, taking the lead at the second Becher's and after losing it at the last, storming back magnificently to outpace *What's Up Boys* on the run-in.

Down by the winning post Nigel had watched the thrilling finish with his close friend Philip Hobbs, trainer of *What's Up Boys*. With that victory, he almost doubled his prize money for a season with only 35 winners, finishing seventh in the trainers' championship. More importantly, it was a success that prompted him to abandon his plans to retire from training. Subsequently he bought out Scudamore's half-share in the Naunton training establishment and, with his enthusiasm renewed, planned a major restructuring of his operations.

It was the end of a remarkably long partnership. He and 'Scu' had ridden together as children, had bought land together for training, had made their homes near one another and were part-owners of the local Hollow Bottom pub in the Cotswold village of Guiting Power. But now it was judged that the business was no longer profitable enough to support two families.

Early in 2003 the trainer's operations were briefly shut down after an outbreak of equine herpes that led to the loss of two mares, suffering from paralysed hind legs. Meanwhile he had three Grand National entries: *Bindaree* and out-of-the-handicap *Prancing Blade* and *Whereareyounow*. Only *Bindaree* made it to the Aintree line-up, seeking to be the first back-to-back winner since *Red Rum* in 1974. His early fall the previous November in Aintree's Becher Chase did not augur well. However, after struggling in the initial stages, he made considerable headway to finish a respectable sixth.

The following season *Bindaree* showed his best form of old when winning the Welsh National from the hot favourite *Sir Rembrandt*; and at the Cheltenham Festival his stablemate *Fundamentalist*

won the Royal and SunAlliance Novices' Hurdle. But the trainer's revival did not extend to the National. *Bindaree*, now on 11st 4lb, unseated Llewellyn at the first Becher's, and still more disappointing was the early departure of *Shardam*. Twiston-Davies had predicted that the seven year old, runner-up in the William Hill Handicap Chase at Cheltenham, would win. Instead he lost his rider at the first open ditch.

Twiston-Davies now had a record of 21 National runners, with two wins and one third place. And the new season started brightly for his 70-strong yard and for his first jockey Llewellyn. Enjoying training more than ever before, and with facilities being upgraded, he reached 50 winners more quickly than ever before. But he had only *Bindaree* in the 2005 National and, though he rated his chance 'as good as when he won the race', the 11 year old weakened after the first circuit and was the 11th of 21 finishers. A small consolation came at the end of the day with his *The Cool Guy* winning the National Hunt Flat race at 50-1.

In 2006 he had five Grand National entries: *Baron Windrush*, *Lord Maizey*, *Ollie Magern*, *Red Georgie* and *Shardam*. Only *Baron Windrush* made it to the line-up – a 66-1 chance who blundered and unseated Llewellyn at the third fence. In 2007 he won the Midlands National with *Baron Windrush*, but one month later he had only two long-shots in the Aintree National: *Knowhere*, an unreliable jumper who unseated his rider at the first Canal Turn, and *Naunton Brook*, a 125-1 chance, who was pulled up before the 23rd.

See also: Earth Summit; Bindaree; Scudamore, Peter; Llewellyn, Carl; Culloty, Jim.

U

UNITED STATES

Though the U.S.A. has more than 100 racetracks, and annually stages more thoroughbred races than any other country in the world, jump racing remains essentially a minority sport most famously represented since 1894 by the Maryland Hunt Cup, a four-mile chase over 22 formidable, 5ft-high upright timbers.

Inevitably, it was the major British Flat-races that first stirred the ambition of U.S. owners. In 1881 Pierre Loillard, an American of French descent, won the Epsom Derby with *Iroquois*, while the multimillionaire Wall Street gambler James R. Keene took both the Cesarewitch and the Cambridgeshire with his colt *Foxhall*. In 1901, Keene's great business rival Willliam Collins Whitney won the Derby with *Volodyovski*.

But in later years it was the Grand National that came to grip the imagination of Americans more than any other race held overseas. Trailblazing interest in the race was James Keene's son Foxhall, a key figure in the development of steeplechasing in the U.S. In 1908 he had two English-bred runners at Aintree: *Chorus*, the last of eight finishers, and *Prophet III* who failed to complete the course.

That year, for the first time, the race was won by an American-bred horse, *Rubio*, at 66-1. True, he was essentially a British product, having been sold for 15 guineas as a yearling at Newmarket. But no matter. It was a beginning. In 1911 and 1912 Foxhall Keene unsuccessfully ran *Precentor II*; and in 1920 and 1921 the well-known American sportsman Morgan Blair challenged to no effect as a rider, falling on the rank outsider *Bonnie Charlie*. He fell again in 1922 when riding Keene's long-shot *Masterful*. Then, in 1923, American interest was truly set alight by the victory of 13 year old *Sergeant Murphy*.

Sergeant Murphy, who had been fourth (remounted) the previous year, was American-owned, a £1,200 gift from the carpet tycoon John Sanford to his son Stephen, a Cambridge undergraduate. His victory set off a veritable avalanche of wealthy Americans seeking to capture the prize, usually by buying suitable contenders in England and Ireland, and some years later sending over their own homebred challengers.

Leading the cheque-book cavalry charge with expensive British buys, young 'Laddie' Sanford was to have 12 more runners between 1923 and 1931, his best results being with *Bright's Boy*, third in 1926 and 1927. In the former year, however, another American owner triumphed. Only two weeks before the race the renowned polo player and New York stockbroker Charles Schwartz had brought *Jack Horner* for the then substantial sum of £4,000, with the promise of another £2,000 if the nine year old chestnut won the National. He won at 25-1.

Ironically, Morgan Blair had been a co-owner of *Jack Horner* the previous year when, having backed himself to get round, he finished seventh on the future winner. The persistent Blair went on to challenge with 11 runners between 1927 and 1933 but he never scored more than fifth place.

Meanwhile other Americans had joined in the Aintree gold-rush. Gordon Selfridge, the founder of the Oxford Street store, opened up with *Misconduct*, a faller in 1927, and he fared no better in making five subsequent bids with his *Ruddyman*. Far more promising, in 1928, was the challenge of Mr Howard Bruce's American superstar *Billy Barton*, an all-conquering chaser whose victories included the Maryland Gold Cup and the Virginian Gold Cup. Alas, this was the most chaotic National of all, with only 100-1 shot *Tipperary Tim* staying on his feet. *Billy Barton* (remounted after falling at the last) finished, by a distance, second and last.

Billy Barton, raised 10lb in the weights, fell again in the 1929 National, and the runners of Messrs Blair, Selfridge and Sanford all failed to finish. But now there was a new, most formidable American player: John 'Jock' Hay Whitney, owner of the brilliant Cheltenham Gold Cup winner *Easter Hero*. Most unluckily, having spread a plate, *Easter Hero* finished second (conceding 17lb to the winner) in a National with a record 66 runners. He would prove his greatness by winning a second Gold Cup by 20 lengths, but for Whitney the National remained an unlucky race.

Fate was against him again in 1930 when his well-backed *Sir Lindsay* pecked on landing a length second over the last. Rider Dudley Williams lost his stirrups but still managed to finish third, only one and a half lengths behind the winner *Shaun Goilin*. In fourth place was the American-bred grey Glangesia, sent over from Pennsylvania by another U.S. millionaire, Mr (later General) Richard K. Mellon; and the fifth of six finishers was Mr Blair's *Ballyhanwood*.

Americans were now relentless in bidding for National success. Whitney had 12 more runners between 1930 and 1940, and three times he had to settle for third place. Mellon had four more contenders. In 1932 he was so determined that he had *Glangesia*'s Irish-born amateur rider James E. Ryan accompanied across the Atlantic by an athletic coach who restricted him to a diet of toast and caviar on board the Mauretania. But the grey was a faller, as was Mellon's other runner, *Alike*.

That year U.S. interest was at an all-time high, being further represented by Whitney's *Dusty Foot* (refused); three Blair-owned runners who failed to complete; Selfridge's *Ruddyman* (refused); the favourite *Heartbreak Hill* (sixth), owned by Mrs Charles S. Bird from Pennsylvania; and Mr. A.H. Niblack's American-bred *Sea Soldier*, remounted by his regular U.S. hunt rider, Andy Wilson, to be the last of eight finishers.

One year later, amid wild celebrations, the Stars and Stripes were at last raised again at Aintree with the 1933 record-breaking victory of *Kellsboro' Jack*, albeit Irish-bred and English-trained, but owned by Mrs Florence Ambrose Clark, wife of the American sewing-machine millionaire. Then, in 1936, hopes of an American-bred winner were sky-high as billionaire Paul Mellon, following the example of his cousin, shipped over *Drinmore Lad*, a jumper so useful that he became the joint ante-post favourite with the great *Golden Miller*. Unfortunately, *Drinmore Lad* had to be withdrawn with a leg injury; and Mellon – later a giant among Flat-racing owners with winners of the Kentucky Derby, Epsom Derby and Prix de l'Arc Triomphe – was to be unsuccessful with five National runners, his last being as late as 1995 when *Crystal Spirit* finished 14th.

In 1938 the great U.S. breakthrough finally came with the victory of the diminutive, chestnut entire *Battleship* – American-bred (in Kentucky), American-owned (by Mrs Marion du Pont Scott, wife of the Hollywood film star Randolph Scott), and ridden by Bruce Hobbs, who happened to have been born in the U.S. while his English father was managing horses for Ambrose Clark. It was the first time that a chaser had crossed the Atlantic to conquer – a feat that would be repeated by *Jay Trump* (1965) and *Ben Nevis* (1980), the first winners to be American-ridden.

In 1939 Mrs Scott made another National bid, this time with six year old *War Vessel*, a woefully inexperienced half-brother of *Battleship*. He was an early faller. In 1948, Mr Mellon ran his *Caddie II*, a heavily weighted faller. And in 1951, the in-

domitable 'Jock' Whitney was trying yet again – this time with his chestnut *Arctic Gold*, another six year old, who went off as 8-1 favourite but came to grief in a race that was ruined by an uncalled 'false start' and ended with only three of 36 starters reaching the finish.

It now became apparent that the Second World War had brought to an end the era of massed challenges by American owners. Henceforth, U.S. entries were fewer but generally of a higher quality. In 1963, there was only one American-owned runner in the 47-strong National field: *Owen's Sedge*, a striking grey who had been bought for 7,000 guineas only two months earlier by film star Gregory Peck. The ten year old had impressive winning form; also he had a top veteran trainer in Tom Dreaper and an Aintree wizard, Pat Taaffe, in the saddle. His big handicap, however, was a second top weight of 11st 6lb, and after being baulked by loose horses, he finished a creditable seventh.

In 1964, two strong challengers were American-owned: the grey *Flying Wild*, one of four co-favourites, running in the colours of multi-millionare Raymond Guest; and 12 year old *Team Spirit*, making his fifth successive appearance and now representing a syndicate of owners, Americans Ronald Woodward and John Goodman and Englishman Gamble North The former fell at the first fence; the latter snatched victory by half a length and was promptly retired to the United States.

The following year Mr Paul Mellon's *Red Tide* was a faller. However, another pulsating finish resulted in a genuine American success: the victor by three-quarters of a length being *Jay Trump*, a dual winner of the Maryland Hunt Cup, trained by Fred Winter, but bred in Pennsylvania by Mr Jay Sessenich, owned by Mrs Mary Stephenson of Ohio, and ridden by the leading American rider Tommy Crompton Smith.

In 1966, when Mrs Muriel Topham remained adamant that this year's Aintree Grand National would be the last, there was no lack of foreign challengers. American interest focused on *Flying Wild*, reappearing for Mr Guest, and on *King Pin*, a 100-1 shot ridden by Tim Durant, a 66 year old American seeking to become the oldest rider to win the race. Both were disappointingly pulled up.

In 1967 there was huge interest in the appearance of the bay gelding *Different Class* because he was owned by Gregory Peck who had popularly declared the Grand National to be 'the world's greatest sporting spectacle'. His seven year old was brought down, a victim of the craziest pile-up in National history. However, he impressed sufficiently to be made favourite the following year – and to be allotted the second highest weight of 11st 5lb. In a 45-strong field, he was conceding 19lb to the winner *Red Alligator* and 11lb to runner-up *Moidore's Token* who beat him only by a neck. In 15th place, after being remounted, was 100-1-outsider *Highlandie*, owned and ridden by the irrepressible Durant, at 68 the oldest-ever rider to complete the course.

In 1969 American Thomas McKoy became a winning National owner, in partnership with Canadian Charles Burns following their timely purchase of *Highland Wedding* who was successful on his third appearance in the race. Additional U.S. interest was supplied by Mr Paul Mellon's grey, *The Beeches*, who finished fourth, and by two American amateurs, brothers Paul and George Sloan, who rode 50-1 shots *Terossian* and *Peccard* respectively but failed to complete the first circuit. (Eight years later George Sloan, now head of a chain of health farms in Tennessee, took a year off work to ride in Britain in a bid to become National Hunt champion amateur jockey. Stabling most of his horses with Josh Gifford, he achieved his ambition with 23 wins, but without making a second appearance in the National.)

In 1970 American owners were again prominent. General R.K. Mellon's *Vulture* finished a well-beaten second and Mrs E.W. Wetherill's *Dozo* was fourth. The following year *Vulture* was generously still on 10st, but this time he was a faller; as was Mr Raymond Guest's *Cnoc Dubh*.

It was ironic. Mr Guest, U.S ambassador to Ireland during the 1960s and 1970s, was the one American owner who bestrode the Atlantic like a colossus. His Flat succcesses included the Epsom Derby with *Larkspur* (1962) and *Sir Ivor* (1968), and the Preakness Stakes, Citation Handicap and American Derby with *Tom Rolfe* (1965). Yet, between 1957 and 1974, he was unsucccessful with 11 runners in the Grand National.

However, he did have one truly great chaser in *L'Escargot*, the dual Cheltenham Gold Cup winner of 1970 and 1971. Having finished third and second to *Red Rum* in 1973 and 1974, *L'Escargot* – Irish-bred, -ridden and -trained – finally gave Mr Guest his long-sought Aintree victory, beating the great 'Rummy' by 15 lengths in 1975. It was, of course,

essentially an Irish triumph. In contrast, a true American challenge was to be mounted four years later with the entry of *Ben Nevis*, an 11 year old who, though bred in England and trained for point-to-points, had subsequently been moved by his owner, Redmond C. Stewart, to the United States. There he had duly won all of his 12 races, seven of them over timber and including victories in the Maryland Hunt Cup of 1977 and 1978 – the latter in record time.

In the 1979 National *Ben Nevis* was a victim of the worst pile-up since *Foinavon*'s year. But he came back in 1980 and, though presumed to be seriously disadvantaged by atrociously heavy conditions, he was the first of only four finishers, fully 20 lengths ahead of *Rough and Tumble*, ridden by John Francome. He was a 40-1 winner with an American amateur rider, Baltimore banker Charlie Fenwick.

The most unusual American challenge of this decade came in 1983 with the entry of the Irish-trained *King Spruce*, owned by Mr Rusty Carrier of Unionville, Pennsylvania. It was unusual because the rider was the owner's wife, Joy Carrier, the first American woman to compete in the National. She had outstanding credentials, having been the first of her sex to win the Maryland Hunt Cup in 1980, a feat she had repeated the following year. Moreover, she was on a nine year old that had won the Irish Grand National of the previous season and was now priced as short as 28-1. Unfortunately, though *King Spruce* was without a win in the current season, the handicapper had taken no chances, allotting him a hefty 11st 4lb. The challenge ended with a fall at the first Becher's.

By the turn of the century 11 National winners had been American owned: *Sergeant Murphy* (1923), *Jack Horner* (1926), *Kellsboro' Jack* (1933), *Battleship* (1938), *Team Spirit* (1964), *Jay Trump* (1965), *Highland Wedding* (1969), *L'Escargot* (1975), *Ben Nevis* (1980), *Mr Frisk* (1990) and *Papillon* (2000). But since the triumph of Jay Trump in 1965, challenges by American-bred horses had become very rare indeed. Most notable of the few was Mrs R.V. Chapman's *Uncle Merlin*, a winner of the Maryland Hunt Cup (1989) who had been correctly sent over well in advance to become a handicap qualifier under the expert handling of Captain Tim Forster, trainer of three National winners.

Remarkably, considering that two Maryland Hunt Cup winners had already triumphed at Aintree, *Uncle Merlin* (with a fair seasonal record of 02412) was way out of the handicap for the 1990 National, have been originally allotted a mere 8st 13lb. Ridden by former National-winning jockey Hywel Davies, he took up the running well before the first Becher's, maintained a blistering pace and jumped superbly to lead *Mr Frisk* for 22 fences. He was still in the lead, by three lengths, when his only error resulted in him hitting the top of Becher's second time around and pitching his 'bitterly disappointed' jockey on to the turf.

It was the great hard luck story of the race and a telling reminder of the need to take very seriously the challenge of a horse with Maryland Hunt Cup winning form. As it happened, the 1990 record-breaking winner *Mr Frisk* was owned by 83 year old Mrs Lois Duffey of Maryland, a daughter of Walter Salmon who had bred the 1938 National winner *Battleship*. However, he was English-bred and had always been trained and raced in England. Mrs Duffey died in 2007.

In 1996, the field included an ex-Irish chaser, *Bavard Dieu*, who was owned by a partnership of no fewer than 14 Grand National-mad Americans, including John Goodman, co-owner of the 1964 winner *Team Spirit*. Operating under the banner of Saguaro Stables, they had bought the chestnut gelding the previous year and moved him to the yard of Nick Gaselee, trainer of the 1992 winner *Party Politics*. They all made the journey to Aintree, only to see their 50-1 runner unseat last year's winning jockey Jason Titley at the first fence.

Two years later there was at last good reason to anticipate another American-bred winner. *Buck Jakes*, a dual Maryland Cup winner, was being aimed at the National, and just like *Ben Nevis* and *Uncle Merlin*, the big, ten year old grey was being prepared by Captain Tim Forster. Unfortunately for ante-post punters it was a false dawn. Though *Buck Jakes* qualified for handicapping purposes by having three runs in Britain, it was with a dismal record of 4PP. The handicapper took no chances in allotting him 10st 12lb and he was soon withdrawn.
See also: Americans; Maryland Hunt Cup; Sanford, Stephen; Whitney, John Hay; Mellon, Paul; Guest, Raymond; Jack Horner; Kellsboro' Jack; Battleship; Jay Trump; Ben Nevis; Smith, Tommy Crompton.

UNLUCKY LOSERS

Grand National history is littered with hard luck stories, and the following rate highly as unlucky losers:

1843 – *Dragsman*, ridden by Mr John Crickmere, who finished third (three and a half lengths behind the winning *Vanguard*) after jumping the side-gate near the last fence and bolting off the course.
1846 – *Culverthorpe*, three lengths second to *Pioneer*, being overhauled on the run-in in a year when the course, incorrectly flagged, covered nearly five miles.
1929 – *Easter Hero*, second to 100-1 shot *Gregalach* (receiving 17lb) in a record 66-strong field and after twisting a plate at Valentine's second time round.
1930 – *Sir Lindsay*, third by just one and a half lengths after his rider had lost his stirrups on landing over the last fence.
1936 – *Davy Jones*, a seven year old tubed entire, owned by Lord Mildmay of Flete and ridden by his son Anthony. A 100-1 outsider, he looked a certain winner when leading at the penultimate fence. But then, by the remotest of chances, the buckle of his bridle broke open. Mildmay had no means of steering and at the final fence *Davy Jones* veered off the course, handing over the race to the less fluent *Reynoldstown*.
1937 – *Cooleen*, Mr J.V. Rank's nine year old mare, ridden by Jack Fawcus, who had the misfortune to be continually harassed, sometimes savagely, by a riderless, 100-1 no-hoper called *Drim*. Conceivably, without this unwanted attention, she could have been a 33-1 winner instead of finishing second to *Royal Mail* by only three lengths.
1948 – *Cromwell*, another unlucky ride for (now Lord) Mildmay. His seven year old was running most impressively after clearing Becher's second time around. But then Mildmay was struck by crippling cramp in his injury-weakened neck muscles. With his head slumped down, he rode on virtually blind for another mile and still, amazingly, finished in third place, seven lengths behind the winner. In turn, the mare *Zahia*, a 100-1 chance, was also unlucky – looking a likely winner when, in error, rider Eddie Reavey steered the wrong course and missed out the final fence.
1954 – *Tudor Line*, a 10-1 chance who, though beaten fair and square, would have won the National but for losing crucial ground by jumping to the right at the last two fences. Fatally, trainer Bobby Renton had chosen to leave off the 'pricker', a small brush usually fitted on the right side of his bridle to encourage him to keep straight. *Tudor Line* went down

by a neck to *Royal Tan*; and one year later, carrying an extra 10lb, he was second again – this time beaten by 12 lengths.

1956 – *Devon Loch*, the Queen Mother's ten year old who inexplicably slithered into a pancake landing on the turf when he had a commanding lead with less than 50 yards to the winning post.

1959 – *Wyndburgh*, Scotland's nine year old hope, who would almost certainly have triumphed if one of his rider's stirrup irons had not broken as they landed over the second Becher's. Tim Brookshaw, the leading National Hunt jockey, slipped his other foot free of the iron and performed an extraordinary feat of horsemanship in duelling with race leader *Oxo* all the way to the last. Miraculously, on the run-in, *Wyndburgh* rallied and was closing fast on Michael Scudamore's mount, but the winning post

came just too soon. They went down by a mere one and a half lengths, with the previous year's winner *Mr What* eight lengths back in third. *Wyndburgh* had been second on his National debut in 1957, fourth in 1958, and would be runner-up for a third time in 1962.

1973 – *Crisp*, the super-strong Australian chaser who was 15 lengths clear at the last only to be beaten three-quarters of a length when conceding 23lb to *Red Rum*. Both horses had broken the National course record.

2007 – *McKelvey*, the Welsh hope who was beaten three-quarters of a length by *Silver Birch*. Ridden by 20 year old Tom O'Brien, the leading conditional jump jockey in Britain and nephew of the great Flat trainer Aidan O'Brien, he came home fastest of all despite finishing lame with a tendon injury.

VALENTINE'S

The second of two brooks which, together with a stone wall (later removed), provided the most difficult jumps in the original Grand National. Arguably, at that time, it was more deserving of notoriety than the first brook (Becher's) for it was here, in 1839, that the race saw its first fatality: a horse called *Dictator* who died after falling and bursting a blood vessel.

Following the 90-degree direction change at the Canal Turn, Valentine's is the ninth and 25th obstacle; the first of four fences, all 5ft high, in a straight line on the way to the Melling Road. It borders a 5ft 6in wide brook and, though now recognised as the lesser of the two brook-jumps, it still commands respect since, like Becher's, it presents an inordinate drop on the landing side.

It derives its name from the front-running outsider that finished third in the 1840 National. *Valentine* was ridden and owned by Alan Power, an Irish amateur, who had laid a huge bet that he would be the first to reach the Stone Wall, then sited roughly at the halfway stage. Briefly this bet seemed to be lost as *Valentine*, in the lead, suddenly pulled up at the second brook. At that point, however, he reared up on his hind legs and then incredibly contrived to take off in a twisting leap that somehow carried him over ditch and fence. Power won his bet and *Valentine*, a no-hoper not quoted in the betting, did well to gain third place, eight lengths and four behind *Jerry* and *Arthur* respectively.

VANGUARD

A bay gelding, 12-1 winner by three lengths from *Nimrod* of the first Grand National (1843) to be run as a handicap. *Vanguard*, on 11st 10lb, was the first winner for a leading Flat-race owner (Lord Chesterfield) at a time when steeplechasing was generally despised by the Turf traditionalists. And his superior jumping enabled Tom Olliver to become the first rider to bring home the National winner in successive years.

The 16 runners in 1843 included the in-form grey *Peter Simple*, 3-1 favourite despite his huge top weight of 13st 11lb, and the first National winner, 13 year old *Lottery*, now 4-1 and burdened with 12st 6lb on his fifth and last appearance in the race. From the second Becher's *Dragsman* held the lead and seemed a certain winner coming to the last. But then, inexplicably, he swerved to the right, jumped a gate and bolted away from the course. It enabled *Vanguard* to strike the front and outpace *Nimrod* on the run-in. Remarkably *Dragsman* was brought back on course, eating up lost ground to finish only half a length behind the runner-up.

Vanguard ran in only one more National: in 1845 when he appeared under the ownership of his professional rider. Going off as 4-1 favourite in a 15-strong field, he led for much of way round the first circuit but then struggled under his burden of an extra stone on treacherous ground and had to be pulled up.

For several years Olliver continued to ride *Vanguard* in other races, including a Swindon chase in which he beat the former National winner, *Charity*. It is recorded that he regarded the bay gelding so fondly that, after his death, he continued to sit on him by having a sofa made from his hide. *See also:* Olliver, Tom.

VELKA PARDUBICKA

Held every October outside the industrial town of Pardubice, some 60 miles east of Prague in the Czech Republic, the Velka Pardubicka is arguably the one steeplechase more demanding than the Aintree Grand National. It was first staged in 1874 when the course was laid out by the Bohemian Racing Association, and – suspended only during wartime – it remains the Republic's most valuable race.

The marathon chase is over four miles two and a half furlongs on a flat, cross-country course with 32 obstacles. Unlike the National, however, it has a twisting route with 16 turns and a steep double-bank preceded by one awesome hedge, known as 'Taxis'. The latter – the fourth fence, jumped only once – is almost 6ft high, 6ft wide, and with a broad, deep ditch on the landing side.

Since it takes in several, often rain-soaked, ploughed fields, the race is run at a slower pace than at Aintree, though on good going the winner may get round in about nine minutes. Before the First World War, the race was won 20 times by British jockeys but only one of them – George Williamson, successful in 1890 – was also triumphant in the Grand National, on *Manifesto* (1899). Most sensationally, unlike the National, it was once won by a lady rider – in 1937 by Lata Brandisova, who had previously finished in a place three times.

In 1973 amateur jockey Chris Collins became the first Englishman to enter the Pardubicka for more

V

than half a century and he won in record time on the favourite, *Stephen's Society*. No less famously, in 1995, Upper Lambourn trainer Charlie Mann – having exploited a loophole in the international jockeys' licensing system – triumphed on his *It's A Snip* by one and a quarter lengths. It was an incredible achievement since six years earlier it seemed that a broken neck had ended his riding career.

Following that injury, and after 149 winners, Charlie had been refused a licence by the Jockey Club. Yet he fought back spectacularly as a trainer and most daringly returned to riding. Like his father and grandfather, both winners of the Military Cross, he thrived on danger – to such a degree that he tried hand-gliding, parachuting, race driving, and even took a course in bullfighting. He was the first British trainer of a Pardubicka winner, and for good measure his *It's A Snip* also finished second and third in the race.

Over the years a number of top British and Irish professionals have tackled the challenge and failed. In 1996 Norman Williamson finished second on *Irish Stamp* and judged it to be the hardest nine minutes of his racing life. Richard Dunwoody was then third on *It's A Snip*. Returning in 1998, he was in front on *Risk of Thunder* only to be unseated at the second of two closely sited hedges. Ruby Walsh (on *Superior Finish*) and Paul Carberry (*Irish Stamp*) were other Irish riders who came to grief.

In 1999 *Risk of Thunder*, trained in Co. Limerick by Enda Bolger and part-owned by film star Sean Connery, finished second under Walsh, replacing the injured Dunwoody. The winner, earning a prize of 1.7 million crowns (about £34,000) was *Peruan* who went on to become the event's equivalent of *Red Rum* by winning in 2000 for the third successive year, being a close runner-up in 2001, and even turning out in 2002 when, at the age of 14, he was unplaced.

That year trainer Mann's hopes of a second victory were ruined by extremely heavy ground. Just over an hour before the race he felt compelled to withdraw *Celibate* who had finished sixth that year in the Grand National. The new great hero of the race was a German jockey, Peter Gehm, who became in 2004 the only man to have ridden the winner four years in succession. But in winning again that year on the mare *Registana* not even Gehm could match the celebrity status of Josef Vana, the veteran Czech who rode and trained the runner-up

Retriever. Vana had the unique distinction in modern times of having ridden five Pardubicka winners; and in 2006, aged 53, he rode and trained *Juventus*, the runner-up to Germany's *Decent Fellow* in the 116th Pardubicka.

Ironically, having won possibly the toughest race in the world four times in succession and been a regular rider in Britain, Gehm was paralysed from the waist down as a result of a fall exercising a two year old at home.

See also: Czech Republic.

VESTEY, Lord

In 1982 the future of the Grand National was in the gravest doubt as the seven-year lifeline extended by Ladbrokes came to an end and Liverpool property developer Bill Davies was now asking £7 million for Aintree racecourse. With much fanfare the Jockey Club launched its Aintree Grand National Appeal. But its initial fund-raising efforts were distinctly inept and the following year Lord ('call me Sam') Vestey was the man chosen as chairman to breathe new life into the campaign.

Following hard negotiations with Mr Davies, Lord Vestey saw the appeal target reduced to £4 million, But despite his vigorous efforts, which included a transatlantic trip (accompanied by Lord Oaksey, Fred Winter and Dick Saunders) to launch a separate appeal in the United States, the campaign fell far short of its aim; and ultimately it was only the 11th-hour intervention of the Canadian whisky firm, Seagram, that saved the day, with Mr Davies finally settling for £3.4 million.

Like not a few Jockey Club members, Lord Vestey, owner of a 5,000-acre estate outside Cirencester, Gloucestershire, is an Old Etonian, ex-Army (the Scots Guards) and a multi-millionaire. Born March 19, 1941, he derived his fortune from the family's Liverpool-based domination of the late 19th century meat trade – hence his nickname 'Spam'. He was only three years old when his father was killed in action in Italy and aged 30 when he and his cousin Edmund inherited control of the Vestey empire.

By the late 1980s the family interests were valued at £1.3 billion. In 1995 their main London operating company, Union International, went into receivership, involving £400 million losses, but profits subsequently rose and in 2006 (even though Socialist president Hugo Chavez had seized their vast cattle ranches in Venezuela) the estimated worth of Lord

Vestey and his family remained at £750 million.

In 1981 Lord Vestey married Celia Knight and thus became a brother-in-law of the now famed jumps trainer Henrietta Knight; and in 1990 he became chairman of Cheltenham's Steeplechase Company. However, as a racehorse owner and breeder, he has had rather more success on the Flat. In the 1977 Grand National his *What A Buck* finished sixth at 20-1 and in 1979 his eight year old *Flitgrove*, also a son of *Royal Buck*, was pulled up.

In 2003, appropriately when he was a house guest at Windsor Castle, Vestey had his first Royal Ascot winner, taking the Royal Hunt Cup with *Macadamia* whom he had bred at his Gloucestershire home. That same year Lady Vestey had a well-supported National contender: *Maximize*, trained by her sister. But for the first time in his racing career *Maximize* was a faller – at the 19th under Jim Culloty, the previous year's winning jockey.

VOID NATIONAL

To echo the words of President Franklin D. Roosevelt after Pearl Harbour, April 3, 1993, is 'a date that will live in infamy' in Grand National history. It was the day when the 150th running of the world's greatest steeplechase – witnessed by an estimated 300 million world-wide television audience – was reduced to total farce by the failure of Jockey Club officials to operate their antiquated starting system. Thirty of 39 horses set off following a second false start. In the failure to recall them, 12 completed one circuit before being pulled up, 11 went out on the second circuit, and seven covered the full four and a half miles of the course before learning that the race had been declared null and void. There could be no re-staging of the race. As *The Sporting Life* banner headline proclaimed, British racing had been made the 'Laughing Stock Of The World'.

The embarrassing sequence of events began at 3.25 p.m. when – earlier than usual – the runners were brought on to the racecourse 25 minutes before the designated starting time. Following a parade led by *Red Rum*, they needed to wait ten minutes before lining up for the start, and a few became agitated. Then, at the initial line-up, there was further delay as police cleared away animal rights protesters who had invaded the course in front of the first fence and responded to a hoax telephone call saying that an incendiary device had been planted in the Becher's fence.

At 3.59 p.m., nine minutes late, the bowler-hatted starter, Captain Keith Fyffe Brown, pulled the lever to raise the tape which, suspended between two gantries, stretched 80 yards across the course. Aged 64, he was starting his last National after 20 years as a racecourse official. But now the lightweight tape – exquisitely, if not accurately, described by Mrs Jenny Pitman as '60 yards of knicker elastic' – blew back in the wind and became caught up with several runners and riders. Shouting 'false start', Capt. Brown held his red flag aloft. Accordingly, flagman Ken Evans, positioned about 100 yards down the course, raised his flag to warn the advancing jockeys. All pulled up before the first fence.

At 4.03 p.m. the runners were again lined-up for the start. Again Capt. Brown pulled his lever. This time it was much more chaotic. The tape caught *Formula One*, the mount of Judy Davies, under his head. Other horses became entangled, and when the tape wrapped around the neck of Richard Dunwoody he was almost pulled off *Wont Be Gone Long*. Again Capt Brown shouted 'false start' and raised his red flag. But this time, disastrously, the flag did not unfurl. Thirty horses jumped off and, without seeing any signal ahead from Mr Evans, their riders had them over the first fence and away.

Various efforts were made by officials, trainers and stable lads to wave down runners but few jockeys got the message until late on the first circuit. Twelve horses were pulled up after one circuit and most notably they included two of the market leaders: *Captain Dibble*, ridden by Peter Scudamore for an owner who had travelled over from Belgium, and *Party Politics*, the 7-1 favourite who was rated by his trainer a stone better than when winning in 1962. The seven horses who completed the course were, in finishing order: *Esha Ness* (John White), *Cahervillahow* (Charlie Swan), *Romany King* (Adrian Maguire), *The Committee* (Norman Williamson), *Givus A Buck* (Paul Holley), *On The Other Hand* (Neale Doughty) and *Laura's Beau* (Conor O'Dwyer).

John White, who had ridden the course in the second fastest ever time, covered his face to hide his despair. Shattered, too, by the declaration of a void race was Mr Patrick Bancroft, the owner of *Esha Ness*, who had dreamed for years of having a National star. As for Mrs Pitman, the trainer of 50-1 shot *Esha Ness* and two other runners, she had already stormed off in an effort to confront the stewards. On glimpsing the finish on television, she burst into tears and was consoled by valet John Buckingham, rider of 100-1 *Foinavon* in the 1967 National. Like most racing professionals she was appalled by the incompetence of officials.

That day the unhappy Captain Brown needed a police escort as he departed Aintree. Later, as Mrs Pitman observed, there was an unreasonable move to shift the blame on to Mr Evans, a recall flagman of over ten years' experience and on duty at his third National. But the fault quite obviously lay with the employment of a pitifully archaic starting system that did not function properly. The flimsy, non-elasticated tape had failed to snap upwards as it should have done and, with the advantage of hindsight, it was clear that, after the first false start, Brown should have elected to flag-start the race.

As critics pointed out it was absurd that, in age of such advanced technology, there should have been no radio or mobile telephone link between the starter and the recall flagman. Alternatively, it was suggested, Aintree could have had electronically operated lights on both sides of the rails in front of the first fence, with the starter pressing a button to set them flashing red. Whatever, in fairness to Captain Brown, it may be noted that he had told the Jockey Club one year before that the starting gate was inadequate.

As it was, everyone was a loser one way or another with the exception, perhaps, of the race's history of which this was another colourful chapter. Aintree reimbursed travelling costs, entry fees and jockey riding fees but nothing could compensate for the disappointment after so much pre-race preparation. Naturally, less sympathy extended to the big bookmaking firms who had wasted hundreds of thousands of pounds on advertising and had to pay back an estimated £75 million in stake money. Not least the big loser was the Chancellor of the Exchequer who had been deprived of an estimated £6 million in betting duty.

See also: Abandoned; False Starts; White, John.

VOLUPTUARY

Winner of the 1884 Grand National – an extraordinary success since he was a six year old who had never jumped fences in public before. *Voluptuary* was trained by the brothers William and Ted Wilson at Ilmington, Warwickshire; and, ridden by the latter, he outpaced the mare *Frigate* through the mud of the run-in to win by four lengths. In the process, he earned the distinction of being the only National winner to have previously run in the Epsom Derby.

A son of the 1872 Derby winner *Cremorne*, out of *Miss Evelyn*, *Voluptuary* had been bred and reared at Hampton Court on behalf of Queen Victoria; then sold at auction for £700. Subsequently, carrying the colours of Lord Rosebery in the 1881 Derby, he led round Tattenham Corner before fading and finishing sixth to *Iroquois*. Victories on the Flat came in Chester's Dee Stakes and the Biennial Stakes at Royal Ascot. Then, under the ownership of Mr H. F. Boyd, who had acquired him for a mere 150 guineas at the Newmarket sales, he was given just two runs over hurdles prior to taking on the Aintree fences.

Voluptuary was not the only son of a Derby winner in the 1884 National. The 6-1 clear favourite in the 15-runner line-up was *The Scot*, son of 1864 Derby winner *Blair Athol*, and the first National contender to represent a member of the royal family – Edward, Prince of Wales. Going off at a reckless pace on the heavy ground, his race ended at the second Becher's where he plunged into the fence. Meanwhile *Voluptuary* had steadily moved up through the field and, with a perfectly timed challenge, jumped ahead of *Frigate* at the last.

After his debut victory, *Voluptuary*'s career took a most unusual turn – as the first Grand National winner to get billing in a London theatre production. He was sold to actor Leonard Boyne who – while starring in a melodrama called The Prodigal Daughter – nightly rode him over a mock Water Jump on the revolving stage of the Drury Lane Theatre.

At the end of his theatrical days, *Voluptuary* was returned to Mr Boyd and entered in three more Nationals. He fell in 1889 and, though raised in the weights the following year, was going well until falling at the last open ditch. He made his swansong as a 13 year old in 1891 – now a 66-1 outsider who had to be pulled up.

See also: Wilson, Edward

WALES

The greatest Grand National day for Wales was March 19, 1937, when the race was won by *Royal Mail* who, though stabled at Wroughton in Wiltshire, had a Welsh trainer (Ivor Anthony), a Welsh rider (Evan Williams) and a Welsh owner (Mr M.H. Lloyd Thomas). Previously the most notable Welsh success had been in 1933 when American-owned *Kellsboro' Jack* – trained by Ivor Anthony and ridden by Welshman Dudley Williams – smashed the course record.

Only one Grand National winner has been trained in Wales: *Kirkland*, the nine year old chestnut gelding who won in 1905, having previously finished fourth and then second. He was prepared by part-owner Mr Lort Phillips at Lawrenny Park, near Tenby in Pembrokeshire. However, many Welshmen have figured prominently in Grand National history, most notably the three Anthony brothers Jack, Ivor and Owen. Jack rode three National winners: *Glenside* (1911), *Ally Sloper* (1915) and *Troytown* (1920); the aforementioned Ivor trained two winners, *Kellsboro' Jack* (1933) and *Royal Mail* (1937); and Owen trained winner *Music Hall* (1922) and runner-up *Irish Mail* (1913).

When the brothers Fred and Lewis Rees won the Grand National – on *Shaun Spadah* (1921) and *Music Hall* (1922) respectively – it marked the completion of a hat-trick of victories by Welsh jockeys. The great Fulke Walwyn, who won on *Reynoldstown* in 1936, may have been based in Lambourn, but he was born in Wales and he went on to train the 1964 National winner, *Team Spirit*. Also Welsh-born was Neale Doughty who won on *Hallo Dandy* (1984); and the following year Cardigan-born Hywel Davies scored a shock 50-1 win on *Last Suspect*. Then Carl Llewellyn became the most successful post-war Welsh jockey with two National victories: *Party Politics* (1992) and *Earth Summit* (1998).

The best chance of a second Welsh-trained winner appeared to come in 2005 with the challenge of *Take The Stand*, a classy staying chaser sent out by Peter Bowen. The nine year old had proven stamina, winning over an extended four miles at Uttoxeter and he had finished a five-length runner-up to *Kicking King* in the recent Cheltenham Gold Cup. But at Aintree, after making steady headway, he unseated his rider at The Chair; and one week later he was unplaced in the 21-strong Scottish National, having been set to concede nearly two stone to most other runners.

In 2007 Pembrokeshire-based Bowen again had two strong challengers: eight year old *McKelvey* who had won six of his 19 starts, including a valuable four-mile handicap chase at Uttoxeter the previous summer; and *Ballycassidy* who, one year earlier, had been leading the National field by six lengths when he fell at the 25th. Moreover, his was a stable in form; on the Friday, having just missed the cut for the National, *Dunbrody Millar* had won the Topham Chase under Jamie Moore at 25-1.

Now, once again, *Ballycassidy* was always to the fore in the National, and led from the 17th to the 18th. But four fences later he was hampered at the second Becher's and then he blundered, unseating his rider at the Canal Turn. Meanwhile *McKelvey*, having been held up on the first circuit, was making relentless headway, so much that he was lying third coming to the last. On the long run-in he made up a good six lengths and was finishing strongest of all when he failed by just three-quarters of a length to beat *Silver Birch* to the winning post.

Only when he pulled him up did jockey Tom O'Brien become aware that *McKelvey* had been 'running lame' at the finish. It was found to be a tendon injury. The Welsh could count themselves unlucky not to have welcomed home a Grand National winner for the first time in more than a century.

WALL, The

Originally, the Grand National obstacles included a stone wall, 4ft 8in high, sited towards the end of the first circuit and in front of the stands. In 1840, this hazard – to be jumped only on the first circuit – was bitterly criticised in the Press because *Lottery*, the previous year's winner, had crashed into the stonework, bringing down with him three other horses, including the 3-1 favourite, *The Nun*.

As a result the Stone Wall was replaced in 1841 with an artificial water jump. That year seven of the 11 starters completed the course, only three falling and one being pulled up. But this, it seems, was too tame for the Aintree executive. Two years later, to the dismay of owners and riders alike, the Wall was reintroduced. Again, it was responsible for two horrendous falls amid shattered masonry; and subsequently it was demolished forever. At first it was replaced with a post and rails. Then, in 1847, the Water Jump was brought back.

W

WALSH, Rupert 'Ruby'

Son of the popular Irish trainer Ted Walsh, and named after his grandfather (another successful trainer), Ruby was just nine years old when he walked with his father around the Grand National course prior to the 1989 victory of *Little Polveir*. Eleven years later, aged 20, he returned to make an extraordinary National debut, winning by a length and a half on American-owned *Papillon*, a nine year old gelding trained by his father, and so emulating the father-and-son triumph scored by Tommy and Paul Carberry with *Bobbyjo* the previous year. More remarkably, in his next four National rides he would twice finish in fourth place and score a second, hugely impressive 14 length victory on *Hedgehunter*, the 7-1 favourite of 2005.

Walsh's first National success represented a most gritty reversal of fortune. In September, 1999, he had broken his collarbone and the following month, ten days after his comeback, he had broken a leg in a freak accident while riding in the Czech Republic. In January, while schooling, another fall had re-opened his leg fracture, and he was only just fit in time for the Cheltenham Festival in March. Yet one month later he triumphed in a National which saw 16 fallers.

His second triumph established him as the first jockey to have won the Welsh, Irish and Aintree Nationals in the same season. One week later, riding *Cornish Rebel*, a brother to *Best Mate*, he attempted to complete an unprecedented four-National grand slam in the Scottish version and failed only by a short head to beat *Joes Edge* to the winning post.

Born on May 14, 1979 in Fermoy, Co. Cork, Ruby was inseparable in his youth from his brother Ted, one year younger. Unlike him, however, Ted Jnr was to grow too big to make a jockey. In his late teens he was 6ft 2in tall and 17st, and well suited to become a prominent prop forward with Naas Rugby Club and to serve briefly as a night club bouncer. Meanwhile Ruby (5ft 10in tall) had been discouraged by his father from taking the usual path of point-to-points as an introduction to race-riding. Instead he was encouraged to ride cross-country, tackling the walls and ditches of Co. Limerick. At the same time he was proving his mettle elsewhere, as a tough little rugby scrum-half and Gaelic footballer.

Ruby's progress as a jockey was meteoric. He was twice the leading amateur rider in Ireland while in his teens (the first time when still a schoolboy). In 1998, on *Papillon*, he finished a neck runner-up to *Bobbyjo* in the Irish Grand National. He then marked his first professional season in 1999 by winning the Irish jockeys' championship with 96 victories; and remarkably, he was still only 19 when he rode *Risk of Thunder* into second place in the great marathon test of the Velka Pardubicka.

In his first Aintree National, Ruby was riding the most spectacular late market-mover in the history of the race. A popular choice of tipsters, *Papillon* was backed down on the day from 33-1 to 10-1 joint second favourite, along with *Star Traveller*, and a point behind *Dark Stranger*, the mount of champion jockey Tony McCoy. The good ground was in his favour, and so was his handicap mark. On 10st 12lb, *Papillon* was receiving 8lb from last year's winner *Bobbyjo*, making him 19lb better off at the weights carried when only a neck had divided them in the Irish National.

Riding with remarkable composure and fine judgment of pace, Ruby took the last fence with a half-length lead and then, in a hard-driving finish, narrowly held off the persistent challenge of Norman Wiliamson on *Mely Moss*. Fifteen days later he reinforced his soaring reputation by completing a great double for the Walshes, this time winning the Irish Grand National on *Commanche Court*, and the same partnership rounding off a great season with victory in the £72,000 Punchestown Heineken Gold Cup.

In February, 2001, *Papillon* was the ante-post favourite to win the Grand National again. Then came the great foot-and-mouth outbreak and, with racing curtailed in Ireland, Ruby kept fit with cycling, skiing in Switzerland and riding out regularly for Willie Mullins. He had just three races prior to the National – all at the Aintree meeting – and then the ground turned too heavy for *Papillon*. After being knocked out of the saddle by a loose horse at the 19th, Walsh remounted to complete the course a distant last of four finishers.

Two weeks later, on his first visit to Ayr, Ruby rode a 1,889-1 treble, and the following week he won a 25-runner Whitbread Gold Cup on *Ad Hoc*. In 2002 another magnificent ride saw him finish a close-up second on *Commanche Court* in the most open of Cheltenham Gold Cups. There was a major disappointment as *Papillon*, specially prepared for a third tilt at the National, had to be withdrawn with strained knee ligaments. Instead, Ruby took the ride on Sir Robert Ogden's grey *Kingsmark*; and despite carrying 11st 9lb on unfavourably fast ground he finished fourth, so establishing an enviable record of having ridden in three Grand Nationals and being placed every time. The day before he had won the Topham Chase on *Its Time For A Win*; and two weeks later he rode brilliantly to win the Scottish National on 20-1 chance *Take Control*, just one part of a colossal 5,716-1 four-timer at Ayr.

By now Ruby was recognised among the greatest jump jockeys of his generation, one so tactically brilliant that he might have been a serious challenger to the great A.P. McCoy if he had been riding full-time in Britain. As it was, he made riding in Ireland his first priority, specifically for his father and Willie Mullins, and flew over three or four times a week to take rides in Britain, usually for trainer Paul Nicholls.

In 2003 he had a fantastic Grand National meeting, starting with a 33-1 winning ride on *Le Duc* in the novices' hurdle, and two days later scoring a treble before the big race. For the National itself, he had had a difficult choice between *Shotgun Willy*, runner-up in the 2002 Scottish National, and the long-time market leader *Ad Hoc*. He opted for the former who emerged on the day as the 7-1 favourite. But *Shotgun Willy*, burdened with a hefty 11st 9lb, missed the break and was never in contention before being pulled-up before the 22nd. *Ad Hoc* had fallen two fences earlier.

It was a measure of Ruby's brilliance that, despite being Ireland-based and having far fewer rides than other leading jockeys, he finished fifth in Britain's 2002-03 jockeys' championship with 77 wins and prize money of £1,512,530. And it was typical of the man that, in July of that season, he returned to racing only one week after a fall at Kilbeggan had left him unconscious, with a few teeth loosened and a jaw needing stitches.

In September 2003 he was put out of action for two months after breaking his right hip at Listowel. On crutches he embarked on a race-viewing holiday abroad, taking in the Breeders' Cup in the U.S. and the Melbourne Cup in Australia. Then, on his return to the saddle, he was committed to ride regularly for Nicholls who was locked in a neck-and-neck battle with Martin Pipe for the trainers' championship.

At the 2004 Cheltenham Festival he won the Queen Mother Champion Chase on *Azertyuiop* and the Grand Annual Handicap on *St Pirran*. And on the opening day of the Grand National meeting he aided Nicholls' title challenge by winning the Martell Makro Novices' Hurdle on *Garde Champetre*. But then, on the eve of the National, he broke his left wrist in a fall and so missed the ride on *Exit To Wave* – not a severe loss since the 50-1 shot was well behind when being pulled up before the ninth.

However, high hopes of another Grand National success sprang anew in November, 2004, when Walsh scored a front-running victory in the Becher Chase on the Paul Nicholls-trained *Silver Birch*, a seven year old whom, he said, 'reminded me of *Papilllon*'. One month later they were strengthened further when – in scoring a treble for Nicholls at Chepstow – he rode *Silver Birch* to an impressive victory in the Welsh National that resulted in the gelding being promoted to Grand National favouritism.

Subsequently *Silver Birch* had to be withdrawn from the National. But no matter, Walsh would have the ride on a no less promising contender in *Hedgehunter*; and meanwhile he was in irresistible winning form. At the 2005 Cheltenham Festival he won the new Daily Telegraph Festival Trophy Chase on *Thisthatandtother* and the Champion Bumper on *Missed That*. Then came victory in the Irish National on *Numbersixvalverde*, beating by just three-quarters of a length *Jack High*, trained by his father.

The previous month, after an almost three months layoff with a broken left leg, Irish jockey David Casey had made a glorious comeback, scoring in the Bobbyjo Chase at Fairyhouse with *Hedgehunter*, on whom he had won the 2004 Thyestes Chase, and then winning the Hennessy Cognac Gold Cup at Leopardstown on *Rule Supreme*. But cruelly he now suffered a serious right hip injury and lost any chance of again riding *Hedgehunter* at Aintree where one year before they had fallen when in contention at the last.

Conversely, the fates remained very much on Ruby's side. On the eve of the Grand National he picked up a spare ride to win the Sefton Novices' Hurdle on *Asian Maze*. He followed up with a handicap chase win on *Sleeping Night*, and the next day he triumphed in the big one after *Hedgehunter*'s one serious rival, *Clan Royal*, had been carried out by a loose horse at the second Becher's. It was nonetheless a wholly deserved second Grand National win. He was still only 25 years old; and, despite splitting his time between Ireland and Britain, he now regained the Irish jockeys' title.

Early in 2006 injuries twice forced Ruby to rest for several weeks. But again he returned in irresistible style, starting the Cheltenham Festival with a superb late winning run on *Noland* in the Supreme Novices' Hurdle and following up with an equally brilliant finish to win the William Trophy Handicap Chase on *Dun Doire*. Finally, by finishing on the Gold Cup runner-up *Hedgehunter* and winning the County Handicap Hurdle on *Desert Quest*, he secured the £2,000 prize for the Festival's top jockey.

His winning run continued at the Grand National meeting. On the first day he had two victories, and on National day, in stunning style, he took the Scottish and Newcastle Aintree Hurdle on the mare *Asian Maze*. Then, one hour later, he was mounting *Hedgehunter*, the National 5-1 joint favourite following his brilliant run in the Gold Cup.

Arguably, only overnight rain denied Walsh a third Grand National success. Certainly, the softened going counted against *Hedgehunter*, burdened with a top weight of 11st 12lb, 11lb more than last year. Headed at the last, he was outpaced on the run-in, unable to give 18lb to *Numbersixvalverde* whose four previous wins (including the Irish National with Ruby) had been on soft or heavy.

Two weeks later, for the second successive year, Ruby (on *Ladalko*) was to be beaten a short head in the Scottish Grand National. Nonetheless, of all current jockeys, he had by far the most successful record in National races. And, despite being out of action for 12 weeks with injury, he ended the season with his fourth Irish jockeys' championship, retaining the title with 90 winners, nine clear of Barry Geraghty. His sister Katie finished runner-up to Nina Carberry for Ireland's champion amateur title.

The following season Ruby kicked off with another record – becoming the first jockey to land a hat-trick of Kerry Nationals when winning on 10-1 chance *Bothar Na*. In one month (November) his many wins included a four-timer at Cheltenham, the Betfair Chase on *Kauto Star* at Haydock and a three-timer at Newbury. His extraordinary run (primarily for Paul Nicholls) continued in December with wins on *Kauto Star* in the Tingle Creek Chase and the King George VI; and the following month he reached the fastest 100 winners in Irish jump racing history. At the Cheltenham Festival he won the Royal and SunAlliance Chase (*Denman*), the Ryanair Chase (*Taranis*) and the Gold Cup (*Kauto Star*).

With such a record it was perhaps unsurprising that his National mount, *Hedgehunter*, was backed down to 9-1 despite being burdened with 11st 12lb, a weight not carried to victory since *Red Rum*'s second success 33 years ago. But *Red Rum* had then been a nine year old in his prime. It was too much to ask of 11 year old *Hedgehunter* and Walsh – completing the course for the sixth time in seven Nationals – did well enough to bring him home a distant ninth.

Almost immediately afterwards Ruby returned to jackpot-striking form, riding *Neptune Collognes* to a surprise victory in the £250,000 Guinness Gold Cup at the Punchestown Festival. He ended the 2006-07 season as top jumps jockey in Ireland with 125 wins, 46 more than his nearest rival Davy Russell, and he had ridden another 72 winners in England.

See also: Papillon; Hedgehunter; Walsh, Ted; Nicholls, Paul.

WALSH, Ted

Trainer, journalist and smooth-talking TV racing analyst, Ted Walsh originally made his mark as a jockey. Eleven times he was the Irish champion amateur rider, won more than 600 races on the Flat and over jumps, and partnered four Cheltenham Festival winners, including the 1979 Champion Chase hero *Hilly Way*. In his youth he saw *Nicolaus Silver* win the 1961 Grand National and dreamed that he was the jockey. But he was destined to ride only once in the race – on *Castleruddery*, a 33-1 shot who refused at the fifth in 1975. His great National triumph was to come as a trainer, saddling the first winner of the 21st century, *Papillon*, ridden by his son Ruby.

Born on April 14, 1950, in Fermoy, Co. Cork, the son of a publican and liveryman, Ted retired from riding immediately after winning the 1986 Foxhunter Chase at Cheltenham on *Attitude Adjuster*, a future National contender who finished eighth (1987), fifth (1988) and 12th (1989). He took over the training of horses at the family base in Co. Kildare when his father died on New Year's Day, 1991, and he had his first National runner the following year when the French-bred *Roc De Prince* finished 17th under Charlie Swan.

Quality rather than quantity was the mark of Ted's immense training skill. Operating the small Bushy Park stables at Kill, near Naas, with no more than two dozen horses in his care, he won the 1996

Austrian Derby with *Commanche Court*, then produced the same horse to score his first Cheltenham Festival success in the 1997 Triumph Hurdle. Three years later he achieved an extraordinary double: winning the Martell Grand National with *Papillon* and, just 15 days later, the Irish Grand National with seven year old *Commanche Court*, until then a chasing maiden.

It was essentially a family triumph. Both National winners were trained by Ted; ridden by his 20 year old son Ruby; and ridden out on non-schooldays by his 15 year old daughter Katie. In addition, Ted's wife Helen looked after the accounts, while older daughter Jennifer, acted as Ruby's agent and 19 year old son Ted Jnr helped out in the yard at weekends.

At the end of the season in 2000 he had just one win from three runners in Britain but prize-money of £295,450; and remarkably, his small yard of 20 horses now included three of the best chasers in all Ireland: *Papillon*; *Commanche Court*, winner of the Heineken Gold Cup as well as the Irish Nat-ional; and *Rince Ri* who had been going so well in the Cheltenham Gold Cup when unseating Ruby three out.

In the chaotic 2001 Grand National, *Papillon*, raised 7lb in the weights, was the fourth of four finishers after being remounted at the 19th fence. The following year Ted achieved an outstanding training feat in bringing back *Commanche Court*, a 25-1 chance, to finish strongly, one and three-quarters second to *Best Mate*, in a hugely competitive 18-runner Cheltenham Gold Cup. Typically, the most good-natured Irishman was the first to congratulate connections of the winner, Two weeks later, the 52 year old trainer's hopes of a second Grand National victory were dashed when it became necessary to withdraw *Papillon*, as short as 14-1 for the race, because of a strained knee ligament. He next had two classy National entries in 2004: *Rince Ri* and *Commanche Court*, the former becoming second favourite in the ante-post betting. Both, however, were discouragingly high in the weights and were to be withdrawn.

Though without a runner in the 2005 Aintree National, Walsh finished that season in fine style, turning out *Jack High* to finish a close runner-up to *Numbersixvalverde* in the Irish National and then to be the 16-1 winner of the Betfred (former Whitbread) Gold Cup at Sandown. The following season he had two runners in the Aintree National won by Numbersixvalverde: the well-backed Jack High who

unseated his rider at The Chair, and 13 year old *Rince Ri* who refused at the 27th. In 2007, when the National was held on Ted's 57th birthday, *Jack High* fell at the first Becher's.
See also: Papillon; Walsh, Rupert 'Ruby'.

WALWYN, Fulke Thomas Tyndall
Described by Lord Oaksey as 'the finest trainer of staying chasers' (a view that was significantly shared by the successful Rimells), Fulke Walwyn belongs to that elite group of men who have both ridden and trained a Grand National winner, scoring first as an amateur riding *Reynoldstown* to a 12-length victory in 1936 and, 28 years later, turning out little *Team Spirit* to win on his fifth appearance in the race.

Born in Monmouthshire in 1910, the son of an Army colonel, Walwyn went direct from school (Malvern) to Sandhurst and then served for six years as a cavalry officer in the 9th Lancers. During that period he was three times the leading amateur jumps jockey, and he turned professional on leaving the Army in 1936.

His first Grand National ride was on *Ready Cash*, a faller in 1934. Two years later, still an amateur, he returned to win on *Reynoldstown*, the first horse to triumph at Aintree in successive years since *The Colonel* in 1870. His good fortune on that occasion was twofold. Firstly, he gained the winning ride because his great friend and fellow officer in the 9th Lancers, Frank Furlong, was now overweight. Secondly, he profited when, at the penultimate fence, a broken buckle on the reins of race leader *Davy Jones* made it impossible for Anthony Mildmay to prevent his horse running off the course at the last.

Nonetheless, Walwyn was a fine horseman in his own right. He had needed all his skills to keep aboard the highly strung *Reynoldstown* who made a series of jumping mistakes over the final fences; also he had lost his whip about a half-mile from the finish. Injury deprived him of the ride on fifth-placed *Delachance* in the 1938 National, and the following year, on his last appearance, he was unseated by *Dunhill Castle*.

In 1939, Walwyn was forced to retire from the saddle after he had suffered a second fracture of the skull in a fall at Ludlow that had left him unconscious for a month. Shortly before he had had his last winner when riding for Neville Crump. They were to become lifelong friends, having almost parallel careers as cavalry officers who became great National Hunt trainers. Both now had their new training careers interrupted by the Second World War, though Fulke's efforts to rejoin the Army were rejected on medical grounds; and both would bounce back to achieve spectacular success in National Hunt racing.

In the 1936 National, Dorothy Paget's great *Golden Miller* had shown his extreme dislike of Aintree fences when, having been brought down at the first and remounted, he then persistently refused to tackle Valentine's. But the following autumn Fulke had skillfully steered him round the course to finish second in the Becher Chase; and only injury had killed any chance of him keeping the ride on the Miller. Miss Paget had never forgotten it; and after the Second World War she sent her horses to Walwyn, so giving a tremendous boost to the development of his Saxon House stables at Upper Lambourn. Subsequently he would train more than 350 winners for that most demanding of owners.

In 1946-47, the first full jumping season after the war, Walwyn had 36 horses in his stables, and he immediately made his mark by becoming champion trainer with 60 winners. He was to take that title four more times, in 1948, 1949, 1958 and 1964, proving himself without equal in producing three-mile chasers.

For the 1948 National Fulke sent out four runners, including Miss Paget's two contenders – *Happy Home* (fourth) and *Housewarmer* (a faller). In 1952 he was responsible for her *Legal Joy*, who finished four lengths second to *Teal*, with *Wot No Sun* a bad third. The following year he saddled the second again: Paget's top-weighted *Mont Tremblant*, winner of the 1952 Cheltenham Gold Cup and the first of his three winners of the Racing Post Chase.

Many successes followed elsewhere but it was not until 1964 – his last season as champion trainer – that he finally triumphed in the National. In 1961 and 1962 he had challenged unsuccessfully with *Taxidermist*, his winner of the Whitbread and Hennessy Gold Cups. In 1963 he had saddled *Blonde Warrior* (16th) and *Team Spirit* (fourth). Now, at last, he gained victory by just half a length when Mr J. K. Goodman's *Team Spirit* edged ahead of *Purple Silk* in the last few yards – a triumph all the more creditable for Walwyn since the 12 year old was winning after four previous attempts, the first three under a different trainer.

Ironically, his next challenger would become remembered as a villain rather than a hero of the National. In 1966 *Popham Down*, his second Scottish National winner, was a faller at the first Becher's. The following year, after being brought down at the first, he ran on riderless and, by suddenly swerving across the face of the small 23rd fence, was responsible for causing the biggest pile-up in National history, with only the 100-1 shot *Foinavon* clearing the fence first time.

In 1973, on the death of Peter Cazalet, Fulke took over as the principal trainer of the Queen Mother's horses – a hugely successful association that climaxed most memorably with the 1984 Whitbread Gold Cup when Her Majesty's *Special Cargo* got up to win in a three-way photo, by a short head from *Lettoch* and the same again from *Diamond Edge* (also Walwyn-trained). It was the seventh time that Fulke had turned out the winner of the Whitbread.

Altogether he would train over 2,000 winners, including victors of the Cheltenham Gold Cup four times, the King George VI Chase five times, the Hennessy Gold Cup seven times, and the Scottish National and Champion Hurdle twice. And he achieved a record 40 winners at the Cheltenham Festival. But he was denied a second National success even though he had several well-fancied challengers.

In 1971 his so consistent *Lord Jim* went off as the 9-1 second favourite only to fall at the 11th fence. Two years later he had a strong contender in *Highland Seal* who, in the previous month, had beaten *Red Rum* by five lengths in the Haydock Park National Trial Chase. But this time 'Rummy' scored his famous victory over *Crisp* while *Highland Seal*, trailing far in their wake, was pulled by David Nicholson. Walwyn's other runner, *The Pooka*, finished 12th at 100-1.

In 1975 and 1976 he ran *The Dikler*, his extraordinary, white-faced winner of the Cheltenham Gold Cup, the King George VI Chase and the Whitbread. Though past his best, the giant bay finished fifth and then sixth at the age of 13. In 1977 his *Gay Vulgan* shared second favouritism with *Red Rum*. He had won over four miles at Cheltenham the previous January but now failed the endurance test and had to be pulled up. Then, in 1978, Walwyn ran two 50-1 shots – *Never Rock*, 15th, and *Double Bridal*, fell.

In 1982 the veteran trainer gained fourth place with the powerful, front-running *Delmoss*, a 50-1 shot who came back as a 13 year old in 1983 to finish tenth. That same year he was represented by the second favourite, *Bonum Omen*, who had proved his stamina by winning over marathon trips at Cheltenham and Warwick. But the nine year old mudlark had missed the previous season with injury and now he went out with a refusal. Subsequently, Walwyn ran *Fauloon*, 18th in 1984 and a faller the following year.

Fulke Walwyn was an absolute perfectionist, a stern but fair taskmaster, meticulous in his attention to detail. He retired in 1990 with an unequalled record as a trainer of long distance chasers, and died the following year, aged 80. Meanwhile, his wife Cath had taken over as the principal trainer of the Queen Mother's horses until she herself retired at the end of the 1992-93 season. Peter Walwyn, the great trainer who retired in 1999 after turning out 1,783 winners on the Flat, was Fulke's cousin.

Appallingly, in 2007, only days after the death of her daughter, Cath Walwyn was robbed of her daughter's jewellery, along with many of Fulke's racing trophies, including the Grand National cups presented after his victory as rider of *Reynoldstown*, and as trainer of *Team Spirit*.
See also: Reynoldstown; Team Spirit.

WANDERER

Irish winner of the 1855 Grand National, largely by virtue of his ability to jump securely in treacherous conditions. It was a victory that confounded the winning owner, Mr Dennis. Convinced that his modestly built bay (a 25-1 chance) would fail to stay in the heavy going, he had chosen to bet heavily on *Wanderer*'s much longer-priced stablemate *Boundaway* who failed to finish.

Twenty runners lined up for the 1855 National which had been postponed because of frost from the week before. A *Bell's Life* commentator wrote that 'with very few exceptions, we question if a worse field ever started for the race'. He also described *Wanderer* – Irish-bred by *Verulam* out of *Mrs Stapley* – as 'a rough, undersized, common-looking hunter'.

The 3-1 favourite was *Trout*, winner of the Cheltenham Chase, running in the colours of Mr William Moseley, who had won last year's National with *Bourton*. There was also huge support for *Miss Mowbray*, first in 1852, second in 1853, and then the nobbled hot favourite of the 1854 National. Tragically, however, this popular mare was poised to challenge the leaders at the second Becher's when she slipped on landing and nose-dived so forcefully that she broke her neck and back.

Meanwhile, in the driving rain, *Wanderer* continued to lead the field, and when *Trout* blundered at the Canal Turn, only *Freetrader* and *Maurice Daley* remained possible threats. At this point, jockey J. Hanlon chose to restrain the free-running *Wanderer*. His caution was justified. Side by side, the two rivals were driven into the lead, only to crash through the last fence. As they lost their momentum, *Wanderer* moved smoothly past them to win by two lengths from *Freetrader* with *Maurice Daley* a further four lengths behind. It was *Wanderer*'s first and last National run. *Freetrader* would win the following year, also at 25-1.

WATER JUMP

Situated in front of the stands and tackled only once, the Water Jump is the 16th and last obstacle on the first circuit of the Grand National course, and the only one less than 4ft 6in high. It comprises a 2ft 6in high thorn fence with a 12ft 6in stretch of water, 2ft deep, on the landing side tapering to just a few inches at its lip. In 1852 it was described by Lord Sefton as a 'very large but perfectly fair jump', and more recently it has been judged by Dick Francis to be the easiest of them all.

The artificial water was first introduced to the National in 1841 to replace the dangerous Stone Wall which intersected the course near the halfway stage. In 1843 it was removed as the Wall was tried for one year more. Then, in 1847, the Water Jump returned as a permanent feature, with the exception of 1955 when the course was so seriously waterlogged that it was bypassed for the first time.

The Water Jump has rarely presented serious difficulties for horse and rider. Indeed, it is believed that one of the last horses to fall there was *Ardoons Pride*, a 200-1 outsider ridden by Richard Dunwoody's grandfather, Dick Thrale, in the 66-runner National of 1929. However, with a left-hand turn to follow, it is arguably unwise to get too close to the inside for fear of other horses cutting across to gain ground as they begin the second circuit and the long run, roughly 400 yards, to the 17th fence.

WATKINSON, William

On his Grand National debut in 1921 Tasmanian-born Bill Watkinson fell on the rank outsider

Blazers. At the time no one could have imagined how fast this little-known, underrated Australian would progress as a jump jockey. He was destined to complete the course in four of his next five National rides, finishing second, fifth, ninth, and – on his last appearance – in the winner's enclosure.

Indeed, his record might have been better still but for an unlucky incident when he was riding eight year old *Drifter*, in the 1922 National. In a tussle between the three leaders at the second Valentine's, *Drifter* split a coronet, the lowest part of a horse's pastern. The brown gelding gamely ran on but, painfully handicapped, was beaten 12 lengths by *Music Hall*.

In 1923, with *Drifter* raised 10lb in the weights, Watkinson brought him home fifth to the first American-owned winner, Stephen Sanford's *Sergeant Murphy*. Young Sanford was sufficiently impressed to buy *Drifter* for his 1924 challenge, but he did not retain the Australian for the ride. While *Drifter* finished fourth at 40-1, Watkinson was on the moderate newcomer *Fairy Hill II*, a faller.

One year later, reunited with *Drifter*, he finished ninth, one place ahead of Sanford's other runner, 15 year old *Sergeant Murphy* (remounted). It was his last ride for Sanford; and, ironically, he was now to have his greatest victory riding for another wealthy American: Charlie Schwartz, who, just two weeks before the 1926 National, had bought *Jack Horner* for £4,000 with the guarantee of another £2,000 if the nine year old should win at Aintree.

Seeking his second National win, 'Laddie' Sanford had two strong contenders in 1926: *Mount Etna* and *Bright's Boy*. But the former was a faller and the latter, though taking the lead at the second Valentine's, could not match the finishing speed of the lightly weighted *Jack Horner*. Seventh the previous year, *Jack Horner* now dominated on the run-in to win by three lengths from *Old Tay Bridge*, who, conceding 25lb to the winner, was runner-up for the second successive year. *Bright's Boy* was a further length back in third.

Charlie Schwartz was so overjoyed that he proposed to give his jockey a £4,000 bonus, later amended to four annual gifts of £1,000. Sadly, however, triumph was almost immediately followed by tragedy. Three weeks later Watkinson suffered a fatal fall when riding in a £100 steeplechase at Bogside in Scotland.

See also: Jack Horner.

WAVERTREE, Lord
Early in 1896, Lord Wavertree, then plain Mr William Hall Walker, paid £600 for a seven year old bay gelding called *The Soarer*. The owner, Captain David Campbell of the 9th Lancers, agreed to the sale on condition that he would ride the horse in the forthcoming Grand National – and he duly won that race by a length and a half and at odds of 40-1.

Having staked £50 on *The Soarer* to win at even longer odds, Hall Walker used much of his winnings to expand the Liverpool Art Gallery (later named the Walker Gallery) which his father had helped to found when he was the city's mayor. Subsequently, he established the Tully Stud in Kildare and during the Great War he was to donate the stud to the nation.

Meanwhile his bids for a second National success had met with dismal failure. *The Soarer* fell on his reappearances in 1897 and 1898; and his *Hill Of Bree* failed to get round in 1904 and 1906. However, by association, he had huge successes on the Flat in 1909 when *Minoru* – whom he had bred and briefly owned – won the 2,000 Guineas and the Derby for King Edward VI.

Ten years later, immediately after the First World War, Mr (now Colonel) Hall Walker resumed his National challenges, this time with a five year old brown gelding, incongruously named *All White*. His 1919 bid failed in unprecedented circumstances. An injury to All White's regular jockey Bob Chadwick necessitated a last-minute replacement and the only available rider was the little-knownTommy Williams. The combination was most promisingly well placed when they cleared Becher's second time around. But then, to the amazement of onlookers, the horse was suddenly pulled up for no apparent reason.

Very quickly, however, the reason became clear. Williams was leaning over to bring up some seafood he had consumed at Aintree earlier that afternoon in the belief that he was not required to ride. To his credit, he set off again in pursuit of the now distant leaders and to such good effect that he finished fifth on his 66-1 outsider. For years to come, when recalling the race, he would insist that but for his stomach pains he would have easily coped with *Poethlyn*, the top-weighted winning favourite.

Born on Christmas Day 1856, and educated at Harrow, Hall Walker was now elevated to the House of Lords on completing 20 years as Tory M.P. for Widnes. As Lord Wavertree, he brought back *All*

White to contest six more Nationals, always without success. The only time the horse completed the course again was in 1921 when – after falling and being remounted – he was the third of only four finishers out of 35 starters. On his last run, in 1927, he was a 100-1 outsider (pulled up). Lord Wavertree died six years later, aged 76.

See also: The Soarer; Chadwick, Robert.

WEIGHTS

The greatest weight carried by a Grand National runner is 13st 4lb, the burden allotted to the 1839 winner *Lottery* in 1841 under a one-off ruling whereby the winner of the Cheltenham Steeplechase had to carry an extra 18lb. He was pulled up after Becher's on the second circuit. The lowest weight carried is 8st 4lb allotted to *Conrad* who, in 1858, was the last of five finishers after being remounted.

The highest weight carried by a National winner is 12st 7lb – a feat achieved by *Cloister* (1893), *Manifesto* (1899), *Jerry M* (1912) and *Poethlyn* (1919). Before the Second World War it was usual for the top weight to be 12st 7lb, but subsequently only two horses have been so severely handicapped: *Prince Regent*, fourth in 1947, and *Freebooter* when he failed to finish in 1951 and 1952.

Since 1956 the maximum National weight has been 12st and only one horse has carried that much to victory: *Red Rum* when scoring his second successive success in 1974. Three – *Crisp* (1973), *Red Rum* (1975) and *Suny Bay* (1998) – have finished runner-up under that maximum.

Since the success of *Poethlyn* in 1919, only three horses have won when carrying top weight: *Royal Tan* (1954) on 11st 7lb; *Gay Trip* (1970) on 11st 5lb and lastly *Red Rum* in 1974 and again in 1977 when winning by 25 lengths as a 12 year old on 11st 8lb. Moreover, since *Corbiere* won on 11st 4lb in 1983 only two runners (*Rhyme 'N' Reason*, 1988, and *Hedgehunter*, 2005) have carried as much as 11st to victory.

The lowest weight carried by a National winner is 9st 6lb, under which *Freetrader* won by half a length in 1856. In 1937 the minimum weight to be carried was fixed at 10st, and since then – excluding *Esha Ness* in the void National of 1993 – the race has been won only nine times by horses running off that lowest mark: *Caughoo* (1947), *Ayala* (1963), *Anglo* (1966), *Foinavon* (1967), *Red Alligator* (1968), *Rubstic* (1979), *Little Polveir* (1989, carry-

ing 3lb overweight), *Lord Gyllene* (1997) and *Bobbyjo* (1999).

See also: Handicapping.

WELL TO DO

Nine year old winner of the 1972 Grand National on his first and last appearance in the race, and representing the first of three victories for trainer Captain Tim Forster who, in this instance, was also the owner.

Sired by the French stallion *Phebus* out of the unraced little mare *Princess Puzzlement*, *Well To Do* had an outstanding pedigree that could be traced back to three National winners: *Gregalach*, *Reynoldstown* and *Royal Mail*. He had been bred by Mrs Aline Lloyd Thomas whose late husband Hugh (killed in a riding accident) had owned the 1937 winner *Royal Mail*; and he was bought for £750 as an unbroken three year old by Forster on behalf of Mrs Heather Sumner.

Subsequently the chestnut gelding took over three years to show any racing promise. Then, in mid-1971, after he had won a handicap hurdle and five steeplechases, his owner tragically died of cancer. In her will she bequeathed to Forster any one of her five horses, and he unhesitatingly chose *Well To Do*.

The following season Forster had doubts about running his gift-horse in the National. Indeed, it was with just 15 minutes to spare that the trainer – at the behest of widower Mr John Sumner – sent a telegram to meet the deadline for the final confirmation of entries. That same day the decision looked fully justified as the gelding showed his well-being by finishing in a four-mile chase at Cheltenham ahead of *Black Secret* and *Astbury*, the second and third respectively in the 1971 Grand National.

In the light of that run, plus the booking of champion jockey Graham Thorner, it was not surprising that *Well To Do* became a late springer in the National market, being backed down from 33-1 to joint fourth in the betting at 14-1. The clear favourite in a field of 42 was the top-weighted dual Cheltenham Gold Cup winner *L'Escargot*. But he was knocked over at the third fence, and by Becher's second time around just six horses were left in serious contention: past winners *Gay Trip* and *Specify*, plus *Black Secret*, *Astbury*, *Well To Do* and the 40-1 chance *General Symons*.

Well To Do took the narrowest of leads on landing over the last, and as they came to the Elbow, he was

W

locked in a duel with *Gay Trip*. But arguably *Gay Trip*'s cause had not been helped by jockey Terry Biddlecombe's policy of running wide in search of better ground. Now, on the rain-sodden run-in, a 22lb disadvantage in the weights proved crucial and he was beaten by two lengths, with *Black Secret* and *General Symons* three lengths back for a dead-heated third place.

Almost the entire population of Letcombe Bassett turned out to welcome *Well To Do* back to the Berkshire village where he had been trained. Subsequently he won a three-mile chase at Towcester which had been named after him. But he did not run at Aintree again, and on his retirement he was returned to the home of Mr Sumner at Marston St Lawrence, Northants. He died in 1985, being buried beside the dual National winner *Reynoldstown*.
See also: Forster, Captain Tim; Thorner, Graham.

WELSH NATIONAL

In its early years the Welsh National – first held at Cardiff in 1895 – was run over a mere two and a half miles. But ever since 1949 it has been run at Chepstow over three miles five and a half furlongs; and after being switched back from Easter to February in the 1960s it became recognised as one of the main trials for the Grand National. In 1976 *Rag Trade* became the first winner to go on to glory at Aintree, beating *Red Rum* by two lengths.

Since 1979 the Welsh National has been held at the end of December and only two more winners have followed up with victory in the Grand National: *Corbiere* (1982-83) and *Earth Summit* (1997-98). In 1992 Martin Pipe dominated the race with the first four home – *Run For Free*, *Riverside Boy*, *Miinnehoma* and *Bonanza Boy*. Two went on to Aintree but this was the year of the void National. *Riverside Boy* was pulled up after one circuit; *Bonanza Boy* refused at the 25th. The former won at Chepstow the following December and *Miinnehoma* won the 1994 Grand National.

Overall, provided that they do not encounter markedly different going, horses placed in the Welsh National have a reasonable record in the big one at Aintree. In 2001, for example, the finishing order at Chepstow was *Supreme Glory*, last year's winner *Jocks Cross*, *Bindaree* and *What's Up Boys*. Three months later *Bindaree* and *What's Up Boys* were first and second respectively in the Grand National. Supreme Glory went to Aintree the following year

and finished runner-up at 40-1, with *Gunner Welburn*, third in the 2002 Welsh National, in fourth place.

In 2003 *Bindaree* returned to Chepstow to win the Welsh National from *Sir Rembrandt* and *Hedgehunter*. At Aintree, as one of four co-favourites, he unseated his rider at the first Becher's. However, *Hedgehunter*, another co-favourite, was a long-time leader, running and jumping brilliantly until falling at the last. He would win as 7-1 favourite the following year.

WESTMINSTER, Anne, Duchess of

Owner of *Last Suspect*, the shock 50-1 winner of the 1985 Grand National, and far more famously of *Arkle*, the greatest steeplechaser of all time. Considering that she had so many major National Hunt successes, Anne, Duchess of Westminster had an extraordinarily limited association with the National – one that reflected her reluctance to risk her horses in so hazardous a race. Above all, she staunchly refused to run *Arkle* in the Liverpool marathon, and later offered the classic riposte: 'Anyway, I knew he would win it, so what's the point in running?'

Arkle, bought for 1,150 guineas on her own judgment as an unbroken three-year old, won 27 races including the Cheltenham Gold Cup three times, the Hennessy twice, the Whitbread Gold Cup, King George VI Chase and the Irish Grand National. Her many other big-race winners included the versatile *Ten Up* (1974 Sun Alliance Chase and 1975 Cheltenham Gold Cup), *Ben Stack* (1964 Champion Chase), *Kinloch Brae* (1969 Cathcart Challenge Cup), and *Wandering Light* whose success in the 1998 National Hunt Chase gave her a total of 11 Cheltenham Festival victories, just three less than the record of Dorothy Paget, the leading post-war owner. Yet, in a period of almost four decades, the duchess had just five Grand National runners – including a winner.

Born Anne Winifred Sullivan, on April 13, 1915, the only daughter of a Brigadier-General, she grew up in Co. Cork and by her teens had developed into an outstanding horsewoman, regularly riding to hounds and taking part in horse shows. During the war she was a personnel driver with the First Aid Nursing Yeomanry, and in 1947 she became the fourth wife of the elderly second Duke of Westminster, the richest man in England, who was nicknamed 'Bend 'Or' after the first of his grandfather's four Derby winners.

The duke died in 1953 and two years later the duchess – always known to her friends as Nancy – became increasingly involved on racing, with the great Irish trainer Tom Dreaper taking charge of her horses. Her first major winner was *Sentina* who in 1958 won Cheltenham's National Hunt Handicap Chase. The eight year old gelding went on to take his chance in the Grand National and, under Pat Taaffe, was unluckily brought down at the first Becher's. It did not endear the race to the duchess and 17 years elapsed before she was persuaded to have an entry again. The result was the sensational victory – by one and a half lengths – of her *Last Suspect*, trained by Captain Tim Forster and ridden by Hywel Davies.

The following year *Last Suspect* was brought out of retirement to appear at Aintree again. This time he struggled before being pulled up at the 18th. And again – though she briefly owned (and named) *Foinavon*, the 100-1 winner of the 1967 National – more than a decade passed before the duchess had another National challenger. In 1997 she was represented by *River Mandate* who, never in contention, was pulled up four out. Finally, in 2003 her famous colours of yellow and black were carried by *Carbury Cross* who had won the Martell Handicap Chase at Aintree the year before but had then fallen in the Scottish National. The first Grand National runner to be saddled by Jonjo O'Neill, he finished a never dangerous seventh.

Hugely popular with racegoers, Anne, Duchess of Westminster, was much involved with breeding, having kept up her family's famous Eaton Stud near Chester; also she was a major supporter of charities and a patron of the Riding for the Disabled Association. She died, aged 88, just four months after her last Grand National challenge.

See also: Last Suspect; Arkle; Forster, Captain Tim; Davies, Hywel.

WEST TIP

Distinguished by a huge body scar – the legacy of 80 stitches in his hindquarters that saved him from the knacker's yard after a near-fatal collision with a lorry in 1982 – the bay gelding *West Tip*, regularly ridden by Richard Dunwoody, stands out as one of the most consistent and popular of all Aintree specialists. He ran in six consecutive Grand Nationals, beginning with an eye-catching debut in 1985, and subsequently finished first, fourth, fourth, second and tenth.

Having been sired by *Gala Performance* – out of the unraced mare *Astryl* (who was by the great sire *Vulgan*) – *West Tip* shared his sire with another Aintree specialist, *Greasepaint*, runner-up in the Nationals of 1983 and 1984 as well as Champion Hurdle winner *Monksfield*. Bought as a foal for 850 guineas at the Ballsbridge sales, then resold there as a yearling for 5,400 guineas, he was still unraced under Rules when, in his fifth year, he was snapped up in Ireland by Worcestershire trainer Michael Oliver for a mere £1,700 on behalf of his patron Mr Peter Luff . The new owner simply agreed to the purchase on hearing the horse's name. In fact, the bay's name was a misspelling of West Tipp – the abbreviation of West Tipperary.

He arrived at the Droitwich stables of Michael Oliver in 1982 and he had still to make his racecourse debut when he suffered his appalling accident. It was a misty morning and the string were warming up whilst awaiting the arrival of stable jockey Philip Hobbs from Somerset. *West Tip* was at the tail of the string and spun around when he was overtaken by a speeding lorry. A protruding hook caught his near-side hindquarters and tore into the flesh, leaving a deep, one-foot long triangular gaping hole. It looked horrendous and the first thought was to have him put down. But incredibly he was to recover to full fitness following a three hour operation by Mr Peter Thorne (brother of John of *Spartan Missile* fame) assisted by the trainer's wife Sarah, who subsequently nursed the horse back to his recovery.

The five year old bay finally made his racecourse debut in December, 1982, on his owner's birthday, winning a two-mile novices' hurdle at Warwick, quickly followed by another win at Chepstow. Thereafter, he showed extraordinary consistency, only once finishing out of the first four in his next seven races and most promisingly taking third place in Cheltenham's SunAlliance Novices' Hurdle behind the illustrious *Sabin du Loir* and *Dawn Run*.

In 1983-84, when put over fences, *West Tip* was a natural jumper from the start and Dunwoody, a rising star, rode him to four consecutive victories the following season, including the Mildmay-Cazalet Chase at Sandown and the Ritz Club Handicap Chase at the Cheltenham Festival. Sixteen days later, when both horse and jockey were making their

National debut, *West Tip* went off at 13-2 joint favourite with Greasepaint.

In an unpredictable National, *West Tip* jumped and travelled easily and was looking a very likely winner as he challenged for the lead at the second Becher's. But there he got in too close, stumbled on landing, and fell after being hit by a loose horse from behind. Young Dunwoody was sufficiently impressed with the horse's potential to declare: 'We'll come back next year and win.' And he was right.

In 1986 *West Tip* finished seventh in Cheltenham's Ritz Club Chase. Following the February freeze, he had needed the run. Then, just two weeks before the National, he broke his season's duck by winning a handicap chase at Newbury. His trainer had him peaking at just the right time. He came in for some criticism for running him so close to the National, but he knew his horse well. In spite of being raised 10lb in the weights, *West Tip* went off as the 15-2 second favourite.

Riding patiently to his pre-race plan, Dunwoody took a middle course as far as Becher's before tacking inwards to save ground. Never far off the pace, *West Tip* held a prominent position on the second circuit, moving into sixth place as they came to Becher's again. Two others were close behind, the rest of the field nowhere. As the tempo quickened, only three could maintain the pace: *Classified* ridden by Steve Smith Eccles, *West Tip* and, most especially, *Young Driver* who, under Chris Grant, looked likely to provide another long-priced winner.

Leading by a length at the last, *Young Driver* briefly pulled away on the long run-in but then, as they approached the Elbow, Dunwoody launched his well-timed attack. *West Tip* moved smoothly ahead and, with ears pricked, held on to win by two lengths with *Classified* holding off the late challenge of *Mr Snugfit* to finish a further 20 lengths back in third place. It was a rare example of a horse winning the National after being a casualty in the race the previous year.

For the 1987 Cheltenham Gold Cup, Dunwoody was retained by David Nicholson to ride *Charter Party*. His horse fell at the fifth fence while *West Tip* finished a close fourth under Peter Hobbs, watched by an anxious Dunwoody. But they were reunited for the National, and with yet another 10lb added, *West Tip*, the 5-1 favourite, did well to come fourth, 13 lengths behind the speedy *Maori Venture*.

In 1988 *West Tip*, still on 11st 7lb, again ran cred-itably to finish fourth in the National. More remarkably, in 1989, after finishing fifth in the Gold Cup, he returned to Aintree as a 12 year old to finish second, seven lengths behind *Little Polveir*. Sixteen days later, at Cheltenham, he scored his second hunter chase win under Marcus Armytage (the biggest certainty of all time according to his trainer); and just nine days later Peter Hobbs rode him into fourth place in the Whitbread Gold Cup.

Even now his Aintree days were still not over. In 1990 he returned for one more National and, ridden by Hobbs, finished tenth – an exceptional performance for a 13 year old carrying 10st 11lb. Moreover, the following year he was to set an all-time record by running for a ninth consecutive year at the Cheltenham Festival.

It marked the end of a racing career in which *West Tip* had proved again and again that he possessed exceptional stamina and courage. As Dunwoody noted in his autobiography, *Obsessed*, he was a natural for the Grand National. 'He's aware of what is happening around him; he notices when a horse makes a mistake and if it looks likes falling he will almost shift in mid-air to get out of the way. Sometimes he sees things before I do and fills me full of confidence. He is an intelligent horse who doesn't want to fall.'

Trainer Oliver fondly remembers that *West Tip* was so intelligent that he developed a knack of releasing the catch on the door of his box; and indeed, on one occasion, he actually contrived to join a horse in the neighbouring box. At home he was totally laid back and as slow as a hearse, but he rose to the occasion on the big stages of Cheltenham and Aintree to run his best races there. He was a 'natural jumper' and at the racecourse he invariably showed unbounded determination. *West Tip* died, aged 24, in 2001.

See also: Oliver, Michael; Dunwoody, Richard.

WHITBREAD, Colonel William Henry

Chairman of the centuries-old brewing group, Colonel Bill Whitbread was a lifelong devotee and supporter of National Hunt racing; the benefactor who, in 1957, inaugurated the Whitbread Gold Cup, a three-mile-five-furlong chase to be held at Sandown three weeks after the Grand National. It was a great, trail-blazing milestone in the history of steeplechasing, being the first-ever race to be commercially sponsored and becoming firmly established as the most valuable handicap chase after the National. It was initially won by *Much Obliged* – by a neck from a six year old priced at 20-1: the extraordinary *Mandarin*.

Born on December 22, 1900, Bill Whitbread was an amateur rider in two Grand Nationals. In 1925 he fell on his own horse, *Ben Cruchan*, and the following year, determined to complete the course, he remounted the same horse to come home the 13th of 13 finishers. Between 1956 and 1976, as an owner, he had 12 runners in the National, and the most successful of these was his last representative: ten year old *Barona*, the 7-1 favourite (ahead of *Red Rum*), ridden by Paul Kelleway into fourth place.

Educated at Eton and Corpus Christi College, Cambridge, Whitbread served with distinction in the Second World War, was a member of the National Hunt Committee from 1956-68, thereafter serving as a member of the Jockey Club until his death one month before his 94th birthday. Memorably, the colonel had lived to see *Mr Frisk* become the first horse to win the Grand National and the Whitbread Gold Cup. Sadly, however, the great race no longer bears his name. After 2002, being under new sponsorship, it became the Attheraces Gold Cup, and then, in 2004, the Betfred Gold Cup.

WHITE, John

The jockey who had the heartbreaking disappointment of 'winning' the 1993 Grand National on *Esha Ness* only to learn seconds later that the race had been declared void following a false start. Remarkably, it had never occurred to him that he was racing to no purpose. He explained: 'Coming to The Chair, we were being signalled to go towards the inside of the fence and I thought that some protesters had probably sat down on the other side … I could hear the commentary coming from the stands as we jumped the Water, so I thought the race was on.'

Esha Ness was the first of seven finishers and he had recorded the second fastest time (9min 1.4sec) in the history of the race. White, who buried his face in his hands at the end, had completed the course for the eighth time in nine National appearances. If the result had been recognised as valid he would have collected £20,000 as his share of prize money, plus a Citroen car bonus.

Born on July 29, 1953, John White made his Grand National debut as an amateur in 1984 when he finished 16th on *Spartan Missile*. He was fifth on *Classified* (1985), seventh on *The Tsarevich* (1986), and then came his best effort: five lengths second on *The Tsarevich* to *Maori Venture*, the 1987 winner. One year later, on the same bay gelding, now 12 years old, he finished seventh.

The 1989 Grand National meeting started most auspiciously for White. For the opening race, an extended three miles over hurdles, he picked up a spare ride on the Cheltenham Gold Cup flop *Slalom*, and scraped home in a photo finish. Subsequently, his National mount, *Castle Warden*, was withdrawn because of the heavy ground. But again he enjoyed the luck of the Irish. On the eve of the National, trainer John Edwards decided that he could not take a chance on jockey Philip Fenton who had sustained a neck injury when falling at The Chair in the John Hughes Memorial Handicap Chase. So White picked up the ride on the not unfancied *Bob Tisdall*.

And then his lucky run ended. *Bob Tisdall*, well suited by the heavy conditions, was eager to jump off first time. Unfortunately, the starter called for a fresh line-up. At the second attempt John could not get his horse back into line. They missed the break and then, at the second fence, *Bob Tisdall* stubbornly refused to go on. It was the first time in six attempts that the jockey had failed to complete.

In 1990 White was on a strong Nicky Henderson-trained contender: *Brown Windsor*, the eight year old who had come to prominence the previous year when, as a novice, he had beaten experienced handicappers to win the Whitbread Gold Cup at Sandown. This season he had run consistently well, winning the two-and-a-half-mile Cathcart Chase at Cheltenham and finishing a good neck second to Ghofar in the Hennessy Gold Cup. As a result he went off the 7-1 clear favourite in the National. But *Mr Frisk*, who had finished a close up third in the Hennessy, was now much better off at the weights and won in record time on the fast ground. Well outpaced, *Brown Windsor* finished fourth, 33 lengths behind the winner.

White again completed the course in 1991, finishing 14th on *Ten of Spades*, but in 1994 he fell at the last on an exhausted *Into The Red*. The following year, when Mrs Pitman had no fewer than six runners, he was at last back in the National on *Esha Ness*. But the 12 year old gelding was now well past his best, and he fell at the 12h, with the luckless rider collecting a broken nose and a hoofprint on his forehead.

W

Thereafter he concentrated on training at his father's yard in Co. Wexford. Having completed the National course eight times in 11 appearances, he could count himself unlucky never to have ridden the official winner.

See also: Void National.

WHITNEY, John 'Jock' Hay

Born on August 17, 1904, educated at Yale and New College, Oxford, multi-millionaire John Hay Whitney was the most persistent of American owners seeking Grand National victory – and the unluckiest. Burdened with massive top weight of 12st 7lb, and having twisted a plate at the second Valentine's, the first of his 14 runners, *Easter Hero,* finished second in 1929 when there was a record number of 66 starters. His next runner (*Sir Lindsay,* in 1930) was disadvantaged when rider Dudley Williams lost his stirrups on landing over the last and finished in third place, just one and a half lengths behind the winner. And twice more Whitney took third place, with *Thomond II* in 1934 and 1935.

In 1934, when his *Thomond II* was lumbered with 12st 4lb, the winner was the immortal *Golden Miller,* receiving 2lb and owned by Whitney's cousin, the eccentric Dorothy Paget. Ironically, 'Jock' had been responsible for introducing Miss Paget to jump racing and, just as at Aintree, her *Golden Miller* triumphed at the expense of *Thomond II* in the Cheltenham Gold Cups of 1933 and 1936.

Furthermore, fate had been against Whitney in 1932 when he had the chance to buy a five year old gelding called *Reynoldstown.* As it happened, he was unable to make time to travel to Ireland to view the horse. Instead, the well-bred son of *My Prince* went to Major Noel Furlong for £1,500 and he duly won the Nationals of 1935 and 1936.

Through seven generations 'Jock' Whitney was directly descended from John Whitney, an Englishman who in 1635 had emigrated with his wife and five sons to Watertown, Massachusetts, where he founded one of America's wealthiest dynasties. His grandfather was William C. Whitney, a one-time Secretary of the Navy, who left over 20 million dollars on his death in 1902.

The young Whitney became hooked on jump racing when he went to Oxford in 1924, one year after the Grand National had been won by 13 year old *Sergeant Murphy* owned by the American Cambridge graduate Stephen Sanford. From the start he established himself as a major player by virtue of his £11,000 purchase of two star chasers out of the estate of the late Captain Alfred Lowenstein, the Belgian financier who had mysteriously vanished while flying to Brussels over the North Sea.

One of the two chasers was the Grand Steeplechase de Paris winner *Maguelonne.* The other was *Easter Hero,* a brilliant son of *My Prince,* who had led the field in the 1928 National only to misjudge his jump at the Canal Turn and land on top of the fence, causing a mass pile-up that reduced the field by more than two-thirds. Now, trained by Jack Anthony, he promptly rewarded Whitney by winning the 1929 Cheltenham Gold Cup by 20 lengths.

Going on to Aintree as 9-1 favourite, *Easter Hero* would surely have made history by completing the Gold Cup-National double if only he had not been allotted the maximum weight (conceding 17lb to his winning half-brother *Gregalach*) and had not twisted a plate on the second circuit. He duly proved his greatness the following year by again winning the Gold Cup by 20 lengths, this time from future *National hero Grakle.*

The first dual Gold Cup winner was immediately made the 5-1 ante-post favourite for the 1930 National. But then it was found that he had strained a tendon at Cheltenham. Instead, Whitney had to rely on his *Sir Lindsay* who was an unlucky third. The following year, with an extra stone to carry, *Sir Lindsay* was a faller; and yet again the American owner was frustrated to see *Easter Hero,* the top-weighted 5-1 favourite, brought down as two horses fell directly in his path.

Having retired the great *Easter Hero* to serve as his hunter in Virginia, Whitney had ten more runners before the interruption of the Second World War – in 1932, Dusty Foot (refused);1933, *Dusty Foot* (fell); 1934, *Thomond II* (third), Lone Eagle II (pu); *1935, Thomond II* (third), R*oyal Ransom* (fell); 1936, *Double Crossed* (eighth), *Royal Ransom* (fell), *Rod And Gun* (fell); and 1940, *National Nigh*t (fell).

While Miss Paget had achieved her National ambition with *Golden Miller* in 1934, it seemed that her cousin had now given up the chase. Whitney had wide-ranging business and State commitments; and during the Second World War he served in the U.S. Air Force, rising to the rank of colonel. But then, after a 15-year gap, he returned to Aintree in 1951 with a truly serious contender: *Arctic Gold.* The six year old chestnut gelding had won his previous three races and was now the 8-1 favourite in a 36-strong field that included last year's winner *Freebooter* and the 1949 first and second, *Russian Hero* and *Roimond* respectively.

But this was to be a chaotic National largely because of an undeclared false start that saw a mad stampede to the first fence where 12 runners came to grief. *Arctic Gold* escaped the pile-up and led the way to Becher's, but then, at the Canal Turn, he was one of five fallers in a race that would see only three finishers with the third having been remounted. Clearly, Whitney was just not meant to have any luck in the National.

He never challenged again, even though, from 1957 to 1961, he was resident in London as the American ambassador to Britain. He died in 1982, aged 77.

See also: Easter Hero; Paget, Dorothy.

WHY NOT

Excepting old *Peter Simple* and the extraordinary Manifesto, the Grand National has never known a more enduring campaigner than *Why Not*, a lion-hearted chaser, sired in Co. Meath by *Castlereagh* from a mare named *Twitter*. On his 1889 National debut, the eight year old gelding finished second by just one length after a tremendous duel with *Frigate*, hard-ridden by Tommy Beasley. Raised a full stone, he came fifth the following year (remounted after falling at the fourth); and in 1891, though top-weighted on 12st 4lb; he was looking the likely winner just before falling at the second last. Yet his racing career had barely begun.

Why Not missed the 1892 National. That year, however, he changed hands for the third time; and now, under the ownership of Captain C.H. Fenwick, and trained by Willie Moore at Weyhill, Hampshire, he enjoyed a new lease of life. In 1893, as a 12 year old, he finished third in the National under the expert handling of Arthur Nightingall; and he went on that year to score three successive wins, including the Grand Sefton at Liverpool. His reputation was so great that he was made 5-1 joint favourite for his Aintree return even though the race had never been won by a 13 year old.

With two fences remaining, the 1894 National had developed into a three-way battle between *Why Not*, *Lady Ellen II* and *Wild Man From Borneo*. Briefly *Why Not* lost the lead, but all the while Nightingall shrewdly kept to the inside rail, saving

a few yards that proved critical as all three joined in battle over the run-in. In a breathtaking finish, the veteran *Why Not* prevailed by just a length and a half and a head from the Lady and the Wild Man respectively. He was conceding more than two stone to the former and more than a stone to the latter.

Remarkably, *Why Not* came back for two more Nationals. In 1895, burdened with 12st and ridden by an amateur, he finished fifth at 50-1. And in 1896, when reunited with Nightingall, he came fifth again – only the second 15 year old ever to complete the National course. He was then retired, having competed in seven Nationals and only once failing to finish fifth or better.

See also: Nightingall, Arthur; Moore, William

WIDGER, John

Like his father Thomas before him, John Widger was a highly successful horse-dealer in Co. Waterford. Unlike his brothers Tom and Joseph, he never rode in the Grand National. But six times he was represented in the race as an owner, most notably with *Wild Man From Borneo*, the winner in 1895; six year old *Matthew*, second at 50-1 in 1902; and *The Gunner*, third at 25-1 in 1904.

Widger's shrewdness as a buyer was further exemplified by his purchase of a yearling that he named *Jerry M* after his horse-dealing friend Jerry Mulcair. Subsequently sold at a handsome profit, the horse would develop into a chaser so outstanding that, on his National debut in 1910, he was handicapped with the top weight of 12st 7lb. *Jerry M* finished second and came back two years later to win while still burdened with that daunting weight.

See also: Widger, Joseph.

WIDGER, Joseph

When amateur rider Joseph Widger finished third in the 1894 Grand National he blamed himself for not having run a smarter tactical race on the family's *Wild Man From Borneo*. It was a harsh judgement. He was having his first experience of the race. He was riding a six year old, 40-1 outsider, also new to the National. Moreover, the joint favourite *Why Not* and the mare *Lady Ellen II* had finished ahead by a mere length and a half and head respectively.

Since *Wild Man From Borneo* had been conceding almost a stone to *Lady Ellen II*, Widger was justified in supposing that he could do better next year. And so it proved. Rather kindly, the 'Wild

W

Man' was raised only 2lb for the 1895 National, and this time the jockey timed his challenge to perfection, overhauling the well-backed *Cathal* on the run-in to win neatly by a length and a half.

Born in 1864, the youngest of five sons of a renowned Waterford horse-dealer, Joe Widger learned to ride in his infancy, was only ten when he won his first pony race, and was so passionate about racing that he ducked out of school at the age 14 to cross the Irish Sea and win a steeplechase at Bangor, North Wales. One year later he showed his natural talent by winning a three-mile chase at Cork despite having lost his bridle one mile out.

In 1893, Joe planned to follow in the footsteps of his brother Tom who had first ridden in the National in 1883, finishing fourth on *Downpatrick* and then following up with a fifth place on *Black Prince*. With the support of brother Mike, he bought the Irish-bred *Wild Man From Borneo*. The chestnut gelding was registered as being owned by another brother, John; and his winning of the 1895 National was the highest point in a family association with the race that spanned three decades.

Altogether, Joe competed in seven Nationals. In 1896 he was on Waterford while his brother Tom took over on 'Wild Man' and brother, Mike, was represented by the mare *Miss Baron*. All three horses were fallers. In 1901 he failed to finish on *Sunny Shower*, a 100-1 shot owned by his wife, and in 1903 he fell on brother John's *Matthew*. Finally, in 1904, still riding as an amateur, he was beaten only a neck into third place on John Widger's *The Gunner*. He ended his long involvement with the race as the owner of *Drifter*, who was runner-up in 1922 and fifth in 1923.

Such is the enduring appeal of the Grand National that, one hundred years after his victory on *Wild Man From Borneo*, some 300 descendants of the horse-dealing Widgers joined in Waterford centenary celebrations. Moreover, the family name was again to figure in National history when, in 1999, one Robert Widger rode Fred Sainsbury's *Choisty* in the great race that had been won by his great-grand-uncle, Joe.

In 1998, *Choisty* had fallen at the first Becher's. The following year, as a 200-1 outsider ridden by 19 year old Widger, he was baulked by other fallers and brought down at Becher's second time around. Then, in the 2000 National, the 50-1 Widger-*Choisty* partnership fell at the fourth fence.

In 2001 Robert Widger's hopes were high as he took over the ride on one of three 10-1 co-favourites: *Inis Cara* who had been switched a few days earlier to Venetia Williams' stable. But this was the great mudbath National which saw only four finishers (two remounted). Again Widger's bid ended at the fourth.

See also: Wild Man From Borneo.

WILD MAN FROM BORNEO

Seven year old winner of the 1895 Grand National when, following his most impressive, third-placed debut the previous year, he had been generously raised a mere 2lb by the handicapper. On the run-in *Wild Man From Borneo* overhauled his only serious rival, *Cathal*, to win fairly cosily by a length and a half, with *Van Der Berg* a bad third, narrowly ahead of a useful newcomer called *Manifesto*.

Irish-bred – by *Decider* out of *Wild Duck* – *Wild Man From Borneo* was a chestnut with three white socks. He had been bought as a foal by James J. Maher, a distinguished breeder and trainer, who would later breed the 1913 Grand National winner *Covertcoat* and, most famously on the Flat, a succession of English Classic winners: *Caligua* (1920 St. Leger), *St Louis* (the 2,000 Guineas of 1922), *Manna* (the 2,000 Guineas and Derby of 1925), and *Sandwich* (1931 St Leger).

Maher hunted *Wild Man From Borneo* as a three year old, and two years later, after the gelding had won several chases in Ireland and England, he let him go for £600. The buyers were Mike and Joe Widger, members of a Co. Waterford family of horse-dealers whose one great ambition was to have a National winner. Shrewd judges of equine potential, they had focused on 'Wild Man' after seeing him finish runner-up in two Aintree races run on successive days.

They were quickly rewarded. *Wild Man From Borneo*, registered in the name of their elder brother, John Widger, won two chases; and then, on his 1894 National debut, ridden by Joe, he narrowly led over the last and figured in a dramatic three-way battle to the line, beaten only a head into third place by *Lady Ellen II* who was a length and a half second to *Why Not*.

The Widgers had trained 'Wild Man' for that first National bid. But now, for his return to Aintree, they had him prepared by trainer James Gatland at Alfriston, East Sussex. The brothers Joe and Mike both moved there to help with the workouts. Also in the stable was *Father O'Flynn*, the 20 lengths winner of the 1892 National; and Gatland fancied him more than 'Wild Man' for the 1895 race.

But unlike *Father O'Flynn*, who finished seventh, *Wild Man From Borneo* was thrown in at the weights and able to win with something in hand. Belatedly, the handicapper got the message. On his return in 1896 'Wild Man' was raised more than a stone, the only horse set to carry 12st in a field of 28, the largest number of runners for 23 years. Significantly, Joe Widger deserted him in favour of *Waterford*, and the ride on 'Wild Man' was taken over by his brother Tom who had finished fourth on *Downpatrick* in the 1883 National.

Having won at 10-1, *Wild Man From Borneo* now went off at 40-1. He fell at the fourth fence while *Father O'Flynn*, also 40-1, did much to vindicate Gatland's judgment by finishing a close-up second after being baulked two fences from home.

Though subsequently dropped 9lb in the weights, 'Wild Man' had to be pulled up by Joe Widger in his final National of 1897. By that time, the nine year old gelding had been sold to Miss F. E. Norris (later Mrs Joe Widger) and thus he became the first horse to run in the National for a registered lady owner. *See also:* Widger, Joseph.

WILLIAMS, Dudley

Few professional jockeys in Grand National history have had such dramatically contrasting fortunes as those experienced by Welsh-born Dudley Williams. On his Aintree debut in 1928, riding 100-1 outsider *Rathory*, he was a victim of the great Canal Turn pile-up that preceded victory for no-hoper *Tipperary Tim*, the first of only two finishers. The following year he fell on *Harewood* in the maelstrom of a 66-runner National. On his third appearance in 1930 he was judged to be an unlucky loser on *Sir Lindsay*. And on his sixth and last National ride in 1933 he rode *Kellsboro' Jack* to a record-smashing victory.

Like Ivor Anthony, the trainer of *Kellsboro' Jack*, Williams hailed from Carmarthenshire. When the American-owned seven year old won in a new record time of 9min 28sec, his rider modestly gave all the credit to the bay gelding, a 25-1 shot, whom he described as ' foot-perfect in his jumping and gaining at least a length at every fence.' The fact remained that he had given *Kellsboro' Jack*, a newcomer to the race, a masterful ride; and the

Welshman's swansong success was richly deserved in the light of his earlier bids for glory.

In the 1930 National, riding Mr J.H. Whitney's *Sir Lindsay*, Williams had been only a length off the leader *Melleray's Belle* when he lost his stirrups as the horse pecked on landing over the last. Despite this huge handicap, he finished in third place, only one and a half lengths behind *Shaun Goilin*, the winner by a neck. In 1931 the Welshman fell on Sir Harold Wernher's well-backed Ballasport. The following year he again gained third place, this time on *Shaun Goilin* who was now 12 years old and carrying 11lb more than when winning two years before.

After the success of *Kellsboro' Jack*, neither horse nor rider appeared in the race again. However, Williams was indirectly involved with later Nationals. In 1957, before the first of his two winning rides, champion jockey Fred Winter sought his advice. The Welshman recommended taking a course on the inside – a tactic not favoured by most jockeys since it involved a greater drop over some fences, most notably Becher's. By way of compensation, he reasoned, there was less chance of interference. Winter rode accordingly and, taking the shortest route, won on *Sundew* by eight lengths.
See also: Kellsboro' Jack.

WILLIAMS, Evan

Winner of the 1937 Grand National on *Royal Mail* – a triple Welsh triumph since the rider, owner (Mr H. Lloyd Thomas) and trainer (Ivor Anthony) were Welshmen. Born in 1912, Williams first rode in the National in 1933, as a willowy amateur finishing well down the field on *Chadd's Ford*, a 50-1 shot owned by the American sewing-machine millionaire, Mr F. Ambrose Clark. He was unrelated to the Welshman, Dudley Williams, who won that 1933 race on *Kellsboro' Jack*, running in the colours of Mrs Ambrose Clark.

Three years later, as a professional, Evan Wiliams had his then greatest success – replacing champion jockey Gerry Wilson and riding *Golden Miller* to the gelding's fifth successive Cheltenham Gold Cup victory. Owner Dorothy Paget now sent out *Golden Miller* for another National bid, despite a 7lb lowering of the minimum weight which resulted in her horse conceding a massive 35lb to some rivals. 'The Miller' was brought down at the first fence, and though Evan quickly remounted and gave chase, the great gelding stubbornly refused – as one year before – to go beyond the open ditch after Valentine's.

Irrationally, regardless of his obvious antipathy to the Aintree fences, *Golden Miller* was returned for the 1937 National. Fortunately, as usual, Miss Paget made a jockey change, so that Williams was free to take the ride on *Royal Mail* who that season had already beaten 'the Miller' over the course in the Becher Chase. The eight year old jumped faultlessly throughout to win by three lengths from *Cooleen*.

In 1938 owner Mr Lloyd Thomas was planning to ride *Royal Mail* himself in the National. But one month before the race he was killed in a steeplechase fall at Derby. Williams again took the ride, and this time, being raised 8lb to top weight, *Royal Mail* had to be pulled up. It was Evan's fourth and final National ride. But one more famous victory lay ahead. In 1940, being back in favour with the volatile Miss Paget, he took the ride on her *Roman Hackle*, the even-money favourite for the Cheltenham Gold Cup. They won comfortably, by ten lengths and two from *Black Hawk* and *Royal Mail* respectively.

Williams went on to become a successful Flat race trainer, taking over at the famous Kingsclere stables after the war and winning the inaugural King George VI and Queen Elizabeth Stakes with *Supreme Court* in 1951. Retiring from Kingsclere in 1953, he was later a Master of Foxhounds in Ireland. Among horses he bred was *Taxidermist*, the 1958 Whitbread Gold Cup winner; and his son Ian was responsible for breeding *Rag Trade*, winner of the 1976 Grand National.

Evan died in July, 2001, aged 89. At that time he was the last surviving pre-war Gold Cup winning jockey; and, among jockeys of that era who had won the Grand National, only Bruce Hobbs (*Battleship*, 1938) remained.

See also: Royal Mail.

WILLIAMS, Venetia Mary

In 1988 Venetia Williams became the eighth woman to ride in the Grand National, crashing out at Becher's on the 200-1 shot *Marcolo*. The bay gelding did a complete somersault and his amateur rider was knocked unconscious and subsequently detained in hospital with a whiplash injury to the neck. A couple of weeks later Miss Williams suffered an horrific fall in a novice hurdle at Worcester, this time breaking the so-called 'hangman's bone' in her neck and having to spend three months in traction in hospital.

That paralysing fracture, which could easily have proved fatal, ended Venetia's race-riding career. Yet her involvement with the National was far from over. She was to gain valuable training experience working with Martin Pipe and Barry Hills, and with the legendary Colin Hayes in Australia, and serving eight years as assistant to John Edwards. Then, after setting up on her own in 1995, she rapidly built a reputation as an outstanding National Hunt trainer. Starting with just nine horses, within three years she had more than 60.

Born on May 10, 1960, Venetia gained an early interest in riding and racing from her mother, a successful show-jumping competitor, and from her grandfather, Percival Williams, who rode and bred horses on the Flat. She was once described by one of her owners as a 'racing mix of Margaret Thatcher and Princess Diana'.

Based at Kings Caple, near Hereford, she had barely begun training before she achieved fame by turning out *Teeton Mill*, a hugely improved ex-hunter, formerly trained by Caroline Saunders, to win the 1998 Hennessy Gold Cup. The grey followed up with victory in the King George VI Chase and went off as favourite in the 1999 Cheltenham Gold Cup.

Venetia made amazingly rapid progress, her wins including the 2000 Welsh Grand National (with *Jocks Cross*), the Scottish Champion Hurdle, the Ascot Chase, and Cheltenham's Grand Annual Chase and Cleeve Hurdle (three times with little *Lady Rebecca*). Her success was belied, however, by her Grand National record. In 1997 she had two runners: *Don't Light Up*, a rank outsider who fell at the 13th, and *Celtic Abbey*, a 66-1 chance, who unseated Richard Johnson at The Chair. In 1998 *Celtic Abbey*, under Norman Williamson, fell at the 26th.

Then, in 1999, she had two highly rated National entries: *Teeton Mill* and *General Wolfe*. The former was allotted the 12st top weight but unfortunately he had to be withdrawn after the Cheltenham Gold Cup in which he slipped the tendon of his off-hind hock and needed surgery. The latter had been the 16th of 17 finishers in the 1997 National when trained by Tim Forster. Now, carrying the second highest weight, he came home 12th – the first of her runners to complete the course.

In 2001, on his last National appearance, *General*

Wolfe refused at the eighth. Venetia's more strongly fancied runner was *Inis Cara* who had joined her stable only two days earlier following a disagreement over jockey arrangements between the owners and trainer Michael Hourigan. He had won a £70,000 race at Leopardsown and in November at Clonmel he had finished third to Gold Cup winner *Looks Like Trouble* and a head in front of classy *Florida Pearl*. Now, disappointingly, he fell at the fourth.

Inis Cara was back for the 2002 National, this time being pulled up at the Canal Turn second time around. Williams ended the season eighth in the trainers' championship with prize-money of £581,419 from 55 wins. In both 2003 and 2004 her *Bramblehill Duke* sneaked into the National as a reserve following a late withdrawal. On the first occasion the 11 year old fell at the second fence and on his return, as a 200-1 chance, he unseated his rider at the first Becher's. Nonetheless, Venetia's overall record was steadily improving, and in 2004 she had risen to sixth place in the trainers' championship with prize money of £935,615 from 89 wins.

The following year she scored at the Cheltenham Festival with *Idole First* in the 29-runnner Coral Cup Handicap Hurdle. But it was not until 2007 that she again challenged for the National. This time she had three entries and one was considered a truly outstanding contender: *Nil Desperandum*, a ten year old, formerly trained in Ireland by Frances Crowley, who had finished sixth in the 2005 National and had been a good fourth at 33-1 in 2006.

For the 2007 National, his target all season, *Nil Desperandum* was marginally down in the weights on 10st 6lb, and in February he became a huge antepost favourite when he carried 11st 12lb to an impressive victory in Newcastle's Eider Handicap Chase over four miles one furlong. The following month, at Cheltenham, Venetia won again with *Idole First* (in the Racing Post Plate Chase) and by now *Nil Desperandum* was 10-1 favourite to become the first horse since *Highland Wedding* (1969) to win the Eider and the National in the same year. Then tragedy struck.

After much deliberation, it had been decided not to run *Nil Desperandum* in the Cheltenham Gold Cup but to go instead to the Midlands National held at Uttoxeter the following day. There, heart-rendingly, he was to be pulled up fatally injured. Instead of having the likely favourite, Venetia went to the National with two outsiders: the grey *The Outlier* who, lacking his favoured soft or heavy ground, unseated his rider at the 19th; and 150-1 no-hoper *Sonevafushi* who faded on the second circuit and was pulled up before two out.

WILLIAMSON, George

With the exception of a fall on *Ardcarn* in 1896, consistent George Williamson never finished worse than seventh in eight Grand Nationals. His record: *Hollington* (1892), sixth; *Tit For Tat* (1893), fourth; *Carrollstown* (1894), seventh; *Leybourne* (1895), sixth; *Ardcarn* (1896), fell at the 28th; *Manifesto* (1899), won; *Manifesto* (1900), third; *Manifesto* (1903), third.

His single victory, in 1899, stands out as one of the greatest rides in the history of the race: a five-length triumph on *Manifesto*, carrying a top-weight of 12st 7lb for his second National win. It also earned George the distinction of being the only rider ever to have won both the Grand National and – nine years earlier – its Czech equivalent, the marathon Pardubicka.

At Aintree, the major test of his horsemanship came at the Canal Turn where *Manifesto*, on landing, slipped on a patch of hay laid out as protection against frost. Williamson lost both irons and felt the toe of one boot touch the ground as his mount sank to the ground. But miraculously both horse and rider managed to recover and made steady progress to collar the leaders late on the second circuit. Having made a small fortune from a winning bet, owner Mr J.G. Bulteel rewarded the jockey with a £2,800 bonus.

Manifesto had equalled the record winning weight. Now, one year later, again with Williamson aboard, he set the record weight for a place, finishing third with 12st 13lb. In fact, he could have finished second, but once he knew that his hugely disadvantaged 12 year old could not catch *Ambush II*, Williamson had humanely eased up and was beaten a neck into third place by *Barsac*, a rival in receipt of more than three stone.

George had one more ride in the National – in 1903 when he achieved another third place on *Manifesto*, now 15 years old and still carrying in excess of 12st. In a stirring duel with seven year old *Kirkland*, they snatched third place by a head and earned tumultuous cheers worthy of a National victory.

See also: Manifesto.

W

WILSON, Edward

Mr E.P. 'The Farmer' Wilson epitomised the spirit of keen amateurism that became so prominent a feature of steeplechasing in the 1880s. Seven successive Grand Nationals were won by amateur riders in the years 1879-1885 and Wilson brought that run to a climax by winning Nationals back-to-back – a feat that would not be repeated until Bryan Marshall's double 69 years later. His winners: *Voluptuary*, by four lengths from *Frigate* in 1884, and *Roquefort*, by two lengths from *Frigate* in 1885.

For Ted Wilson it was a triumph for perseverance. Sixteen times he rode in the race, beginning in 1873 with the first of four successive rides on *Congress*. On the fourth attempt, in one of the most thrilling of all finishes, his ten year old mount went down by just a neck to the five year old *Regal*. The following year, 1877, *Congress* again finished second but now, under the new ownership of Lord Lonsdale, he was ridden by Joe Cannon. Wilson, meanwhile, had pulled up on *Reugny*. His next National rides were *Curator*, sixth in 1878; *Bob Ridley*, fifth in 1879; *Fay*, fell in 1882; *Montauban*, sixth in 1883.

It was in his tenth National, in 1884, that he succeeded at last – on *Voluptuary*, a former Derby winner who had never before raced over fences. It was as much a triumph of training as riding; indeed the winner had been trained by Ted and his brother William at the family home in Ilmington, Warwickshire.

One year later Wilson returned to Aintree to ride *Roquefort*, the five year old who had finished third, beaten by ten lengths, to *Voluptuary*. The brown gelding, a headstrong, hard-pulling animal, was recognised as a difficult ride. Nonetheless, after his National debut, he had been bought on Wilson's recommendation by Mr. A. Cooper, and in 1885 he went off as a 100-30 favourite.

Roquefort took the lead approaching the last and thereafter held off the challenge of *Frigate*, hard-ridden by Tommy Beasley, to win by two lengths. Ironically, Beasley – the last rider to win successive Nationals – had now finished second to Wilson two years in a row.

For 'The Farmer' this was to be the peak of his riding career. He rode in five more Nationals, each time ending on the floor. Three of those rides were on *Roquefort* who was harshly punished by the handicapper for his 1885 victory – first raised 17lb in 1886 and then, despite having fallen, put up a further 5lb, in 1887. That latter year, despite a colos-sal top weight of 12st 8lb, he was looking a likely winner as the leaders turned for home. But then he began pulling hard to the right and carried his rider into the rails.

In 1890, following falls on *The Fawn* (1888) and *Roquefort* (1889) Wilson ended his distinguished National career in the royal colours – riding the mare *Hettie* on behalf of Edward, Prince of Wales. They fell in a three-horse pile-up at the Canal Turn on the first circuit.

See also: Voluptuary; Roquefort; Congress.

WILSON, Gerry

Seven times champion jockey between 1933 and 1941, Gerry Wilson first appeared on the Grand National scene in 1929 when there was the largest-ever field of 66 runners. He was the eighth of ten finishers on the 200-1 rank outsider *Delarue*. In 1930 he was again on the outsider *Delarue* (knocked over), and in 1932 and 1933 he fell on *Coup De Chapeau*. Then, in 1934, he appeared for the first time on a well-fancied National mount, and he triumphed on seven year old Golden Miller who won in record-breaking time and became the only horse to achieve the Cheltenham Gold Cup-National double in the same year.

During his spectacular career 'The Miller' had 15 different riders. But it was the tough, sturdy and fiercely determined Wilson who formed the greatest partnership with the gelding. He had been the first jockey to take *Golden Miller* over fences – in 1931 when the four year old was beaten only a short head at Newbury. Together, besides their unique 'double' of 1934, they triumphed in the Gold Cup of 1935 when Wilson also won the Champion Hurdle on *Lion Courage*.

That fourth Gold Cup win in succession for *Golden Miller* was almost immediately followed by controversy and disappointment. Though now lumbered with a top weight of 12st 7lb, the wonder horse was made the shortest-price favourite ever for the National, at one point as short as 6-4. Then, disturbingly, Wilson reported that he had been offered £3,000 to stop the gelding at Aintree. He had rejected the offer but was unwilling to name the person who had made it.

Subsequently, *Golden Miller* was guarded night and day by special security men. Meanwhile, in a fall at Wolverhampton, Wilson suffered severe bruising to an already damaged collarbone. On the big race day he declared himself fit to ride with the aid of pain-killing injections. But double failure followed. In the National, *Golden Miller*, off at 2-1, unseated Wilson at the second fence after Valentine's. Twenty four hours later, running at the insistence of that most demanding owner, Miss Dorothy Paget, 'the Miller' threw Wilson again – this time at the very first fence in the Champion Chase.

It was the end of the famous partnership. Wilson had already fallen out with trainer Basil Briscoe following his suggestion that 'The Miller' had been wrongly prepared for the National. And now, acrimoniously, trainer and owner were parting company. Wilson was replaced by Evan Williams who rode *Golden Miller* to his fifth successive Gold Cup victory, and then, unsuccessfully in the 1936 National.

Born in 1903, Wilson was an outstanding horseman, with skills gained as a boy in the hunting field followed by an apprenticeship on the Flat. He had his best season in 1934-35 when he rode 73 winners. At that time he married Fred Rimell's sister Vera; and curiously it was his brother-in-law who was to deprive Gerry of a seventh successive championship in 1939. That year, following falls on *Milk Punch* (1937) and *Stalbridge Park* (1938), Wilson completed the National course for the first time since his triumph on *Golden Miller*, but he did so only after remounting Lord Derby's *Under Bid* to be the 11th of 11 finishers.

The Second World War put an end to Wilson's National rides, his tenth and last appearance being in 1940 when he fell on 50-1 long-shot *Dunhill Castle*. But he clinched his seventh and last jockeys' crown in the 1940-41 season, took out a licence to train in 1944, and one year later made his mark as the trainer of *Brains Trust*, the Champion Hurdle winner, ridden by his brother-in-law.

One more time he came close to National glory – in 1948 when his *First Of The Dandies* led over the final fence, only to be beaten for speed by *Sheila's Cottage* who prevailed by one length. Subsequently, the outstanding rider of the immediate pre-war period retired to become landlord of a Berkshire pub. He died in 1968 at the age of 65.
See also: Golden Miller; Briscoe, Basil; Paget, Dorothy.

WILSON, Major John Philip
The Grand National was a race perfectly designed for Major 'Jack' Wilson, a gritty Yorkshireman who thrived on daredevil challenges. In the First World War, when serving as a pilot in the Royal Flying Corps, he had made one of the first parachute jumps from a balloon – an experience said to be responsible for his hair turning prematurely white. He took part in the first bombing raids on German airfields and he shot down a Zeppelin over Hull.

As an all-round sportsman, Wilson was best known for having played cricket for Cambridge University and Yorkshire. But he was also a keen amateur rider and huntsman, and in 1923 he made his National debut on *Trentino*, a 66-1 outsider. Severely stunned after being thrown headlong over Becher's, he nevertheless came back two years later, at the age of 36, to ride the lightly weighted *Double Chance*.

Trained by Fred Archer, a nephew of the legendary, 13-times champion jockey, *Double Chance* had been a failure on the Flat and had broken down with strained tendons after being raced over fences. But the nine year old chestnut gelding had since recovered to win five minor races; and now, on the long Aintree run-in, Wilson galvanised him into a devastating late sprint to overhaul the favourite *Old Tay Bridge*, ridden by the triple National winner, Jack Anthony. Having won by four lengths on his Aintree debut, *Double Chance* never ran in the race again. Wilson came back for his third and last National ride in 1926 when he fell at the first fence on *Grecian Wave*.
See also: Double Chance.

WINNERS (Horses)
Only one Grand National contender has achieved as many as three wins: *Red Rum*, successful in 1973, 1974 and 1977. Six horses have scored two wins: *Peter Simple* (1849, 1853); *Abd-El-Kader* (1850, 1851); *The Lamb* (1868, 1871); *The Colonel* (1869, 1870); *Manifesto* (1897, 1899); and *Reynoldstown* (1935, 1936).

WINNERS (Jockeys)
The most Aintree Grand National wins by jockeys:
Five
George Stevens – *The Freetrader* (1856), *Emblem* (1863), *Emblematic* (1864), *The Colonel* (1869), *The Colonel* (1870).
Three
Tom Olliver – Gay *Lad* (1842), *Vanguard* (1843), *Peter Simple* (1853)

W

Mr. Thomas – *Anatis* (1860), *The Lamb* (1871), *Pathfinder* (1875)

Mr T. Beasley – *Empress* (1880), *Woodbrook* (1881), *Frigate* (1889)

Arthur Nightingall – *Ilex* (1890), *Why Not* (1894), *Grudon* (1901)

Mr J.R. Anthony – *Glenside* (1911), *Ally Soper* (1915), *Troytown* (1920)

Brian Fletcher – *Red Alligator* (1968), *Red Rum* (1973), Red Rum (1974)

Two

J. Page – *Cortolvin* (1867), *Casse Tete* (1872)

Mr J. M. Richardson – *Disturbance* (1873), *Reugny* (1874)

Mr E.P. Wilson – *Voluptuary* (1884), *Roquefort* (1885)

Ernie Piggott – *Jerry M* (1912), *Poethlyn* (1919)

A. P. Thompson – *Sheila's Cottage* (1948), *Teal* (1952)

Fred Winter – *Sundew* (1957), *Kilmore* (1962)

Richard Dunwoody – *West Tip* (1986), *Miinnehoma* (1994)

Carl Llewellyn – *Party Politics* (1992), *Earth Summit* (1998)

Ruby Walsh – *Papillon* (2000), *Hedgehunter* (2005)

WINNING MARGINS
See: Finishes.

WINTER, Frederick Thomas CBE

The only person to have won the Grand National twice as both jockey and trainer; also the only man to have both ridden and trained winners of the Grand National, Cheltenham Gold Cup and Champion Hurdle. Born September 20, 1926, Fred Winter was the outstanding jump jockey of the 1950s and the dominant jump trainer of the 1970s; and, in the light of his dual career achievements, plus his reputation as a sportsman of the utmost integrity, he is arguably the greatest figure in the history of National Hunt racing.

Four times he was cchampion jockey, eight times champion trainer. In 17 seasons he rode 4,298 races, won on 923 occasions, finished second 577 times and third 509 times. He won the Grand National on *Sundew* (1957) and *Kilmore* (1962). In his first two seasons as a trainer he won two Grand Nationals, with *Jay Trump* (1965) and *Anglo* (1966); and three times he saddled the National runner-up.

Never was the cliche 'born to racing' more justi-
fied. The son of a first-class jockey and trainer (also Fred), he was born at Andover, Hampshire, in a bungalow named *Cherimoya* after the filly on which his father had won the 1911 Oaks as a 16 year old apprentice. At Ewell Castle School, he was a contemporary of another future National-winning jockey, Dave Dick, who became a lifelong friend.

In 1939, when only 13 years old, he began riding on the Flat, scoring his first win at Salisbury on his father's *Tam O'Shanter* when his rivals included Gordon Richards and Harry Wragg. Subsequently he had many rides for his father and Sir Noel Murless but he struggled to waste down to near 9st, and rising weight limited his career on the Flat. Then came military service. He joined the 6th Battalion Parachute Regiment and, subsequently commissioned, ended his service in Palestine.

Coincidentally, when on Christmas leave in 1947, his first ride in a steeplechase and his first jumping success came on *Carton*, the horse that had given his old school-friend Dave Dick his first win (on the Flat) at Brighton in 1938. Demobbed the following year, he concentrated on National Hunt riding, though early on it seemed that his career would be curtailed by injuries – the worst being a fractured spine that put him out of racing for a year.

He then began his successful 16-year association with trainer Captain Ryan Price, and in 1951 he made his Grand National debut on *Glen Fire*, a 33-1 chance. Other riders wagered that he would not get beyond the first Becher's. But he did better than 11 of his rivals who came down at the first. Narrowly avoiding the chaos largely caused by an undeclared false start, he won his bet by getting as far as the Canal Turn.

Though he was champion jump jockey with a record total of 121 wins in the 1952-53 season, Winter did not appear in the National again until 1955. One year earlier a broken leg had ensured that he was only a spectator at the race. It was nonetheless a key occasion in his life: at Aintree in 1954 he first saw Diana Pearson, the future Mrs Winter.

In the 1955 National, Fred fell at the 11th fence on seven year old *Oriental Way*, at 33-1 the least fancied of four Vincent O'Brien runners. The following year, 24 hours after winning Liverpool's Coronation Hurdle on *Amoureux II*, he was on *Sundew*, the big chestnut whom he had previously ridden into second place in the Welsh Grand National when conceding nearly two stone to the winner. They went off as second favourites and led into the second circuit. But *Sundew*, having jumped brilliantly until that point, nose-dived at the second Becher's, leaving *Devon Loch* and *E.S.B.* to figure in a sensational finish, with the latter prevailing under his closest friend Dave Dick. 'I was cantering at the time,' said Fred.

When *Sundew* came back to win the 1957 National at 20-1, it was largely due to a masterful ride by the champion jockey, who took him on the shortest, inside route and kept control despite a perilously low jump at Becher's and a number of other errors. Having made most of the running, they won comfortably by eight lengths from *Wyndburgh*, who was receiving a stone in weight.

Winter ended the season as champion jockey for a third time. Yet he failed to get round in his next three Nationals – on *Springsilver* (1958), *Done Up* (1959) and *Dandy Scot* (1960); and in 1961, after winning his third Champion Hurdle on *Eborneezer* and his first Cheltenham Gold Cup on *Saffron Tartan*, he was fifth in the National on *Kilmore* who, like former winners, *Jerry M* (1912) and *Covertcoat* (1913), was trained (by Ryan Price) at Findon, Sussex.

At the start of the 1961-62 season Fred accepted a retainer to ride for Fulke Walwyn, who would later judge him to be the greatest jockey he had seen: a rider of extraordinary courage and tremendous strength for a driving finish; and a supreme tactician with unrivalled ability to recognise and quickly seize an opening. At the same time, it was agreed that he should fulfil existing obligations to Ryan Price; and so, after winning the 1962 Cheltenham Gold Cup on the Walwyn-trained *Mandarin*, he reappeared on *Kilmore* in the National.

It was to be Winter's most spectacular year as a rider. At Aintree, boggy ground put stamina at a premium – conditions ideal for *Kilmore*. Playing a waiting game, Fred delayed his challenge until the second last, jumped into the lead at the final fence, then powered ahead to win by ten lengths from *Wyndburgh* (again), with the 1958 winner *Mr What* a further ten lengths back in third. The first three were all 12 year olds. And Winter had become just the third jockey to win the Gold Cup and the National in the same season.

Two and a half months later, back on board *Mandarin*, Winter achieved his most remarkable victory (and arguably the greatest ride of all time):

winning the four-mile 110-yard Grand Steeple-Chase de Paris at Auteuil. Everything seemed against him on that June day. The little French-bred *Mandarin* was facing the tricky, figure-of-eight course for the first time and on unfavourably heavy ground. After a week of wasting and a night's sleep almost completely lost owing to violent stomach cramps, Fred was feeling physically sick. Worse, at the fourth fence, a broken rubber bit left him without brakes or steering – and with 21 fences and over three and a half miles still to go. Yet miraculously, by exerting pressure with his knees and shifting his weight, he contrived to guide the brave chaser round the tortuous course; and, though *Mandarin* injured a leg at the fourth last, he was brought home to win by a short head from *Lumino*. And for good measure, 40 minutes later, Winter won the Grande Course de Haies hurdle race on *Beaver II*.

In the 1963 National Fred reappeared on *Kilmore*, now raised 10lb and not helped by faster ground. There was a 47-strong field, and they did well to finish sixth after *Kilmore* had been kicked by a horse falling at the Water Jump. Loyally, one year later, the jockey stayed with *Kilmore* for what was to be his 11th and last National ride. The former winner, now 14 years old, fell at the 21st, just as a third Winter triumph was beginning to seem possible.

During his racing career, fearless Fred had experienced 319 falls. His innumerable injuries included a cracked skull twice, and a broken back and a broken leg that cost him two whole years of riding. Under today's more stringent medical controls he would certainly not have been allowed to ride as often as he did. His strike record was nonetheless truly outstanding and, unbelievably, he was now to become even more successful as a trainer.

In the summer of 1964 Winter moved into the disused, dilapidated Uplands yard at Upper Lambourn, Berkshire. Starting with only a handful of horses, four of them jumpers from Ryan Price who had temporarily lost his licence, the new trainer would eventually expand Uplands' capacity to 60 boxes and transform it into the foremost National Hunt yard in the land, the home of such giants as *Bula*, *Crisp*, *Midnight Court*, *Pendil*, *Lanzarote*, *Celtic Shot* and *Killiney*.

His progress was phenomenal. Originally his yard was the very humble next-door neighbour of the famed Saxon House from which Fulke Walwyn had sent out *Mandarin* for his great triumphs in 1962 and then *Team Spirit* to win the 1964 Grand National. Yet, in his very first season, Winter trumped all the big stables by his masterful preparation of *Jay Trump*, the first National winner to be American-bred, -owned and -ridden. And no less importantly he passed on his invaluable experience of riding at Aintree to *Jay Trump*'s dedicated amateur rider, Tommy Crompton Smith.

Beginner's luck? That notion was promptly quashed when the Master of Uplands repeated the trick: sending out *Anglo*, a 50-1 shot, to win the 1966 National by 20 lengths. And three years later he had another 50-1 shot in the frame: *Steel Bridge* who, under Richard Pitman and on the minimum weight, was 12 lengths second to *Highland Wedding*. Ironically, the winner was ridden by substitute Eddie Harty who, one year before, had finished tenth on *Steel Bridge*, then 100-1.

Thereafter Winter went from strength to strength, becoming the dominant trainer of the 1970s with 830 winners and seven champion trainer titles. In that decade his triumphs included the King George VI Chase twice with *Pendil* and – by the 1978 success of his long-time first jockey John Francome on *Midnight Court* – the one great prize that had long eluded him as a trainer: the Cheltenham Gold Cup.

Ordinarily, that decade would also have brought Winter a third Grand National winner. Artfully, in 1973, he raced the Australian-bred Crisp in the two-mile Champion Chase at Cheltenham before sending him, 18 days later, over the four and a half miles at Aintree. The strategy worked well enough, as *Crisp* led the National field for four miles 850 yards. Unfortunately, however, this was no ordinary year. Just one horse was able to close on the runaway leader and, with a 23lb advantage, he caught *Crisp* within five strides of the winning post to win by three-quarters of length. It was the cuellest of cruel defeats. But at least a new star had been born: an eight year old called *Red Rum*.

That same year Winter prepared a much less serious challenger: Spanish-bred *Nereo*, a seven year old to be ridden by his 54 year old owner. Early on a stirrup leather broke, but the indomitable Duque de Alberquerque took another eight fences before finally pulling up at the Canal Turn. As 100-1 outsiders, the same combination finished eighth in 1974 and fell in 1976. Then, after being ruled unfit to ride, the multi-injured Duke could only look on as *Nereo* came back to fall at the second Becher's in 1977 and finish 14th in 1978.

One year later, however, Winter had two worthy National challengers in *Rough And Tumble*, a former three-day event horse to be ridden by Francome, and *Lord Browndodd*, with Andy Turnell. Both were proven stayers who had never fallen. They kept that record intact, though the latter had to be pulled up after figuring prominently as far as the second Becher's.

Meanwhile *Rough and Tumble* was staying on as well as any, taking a narrow lead two out and seeming to have every chance of giving his great jockey that elusive National success. But *Rubstic* and *Zongalero* were alongside him at the last and, from the Elbow onwards, they proved the stronger, the former prevailing by just one and a half lengths in the battle to the line. *Rough and Tumble* finished five lengths back in third.

One year later, for a third time, Winter would have to settle for a second place in the National as *Rough and Tumble*, under Francome, laboured home 20 lengths adrift of *Ben Nevis* in conditions so desperate that only four finished. It was nonetheless a gallant effort by a runner-up who had gone 16 months without a win.

Winter had no success with later Grand National runners: *Rolls Rambler* and *Rough and Tumble* (1982), both refused; *Venture To Cognac* (1983), eighth; *Musso* (1985), pulled up; *Plundering* (1986), a faller at the Canal Turn; *Brown Trix* (1987), a 100-1 chance who unseated his rider; *Insure* (1987), the last of 22 finishers; *Insure* (1988), unseated rider at the 23rd. But no matter. The 1980s brought him victories in three Mackeson Gold Cups, the Hennessy Gold Cup and the Sun Alliance Chase, and in 1985 an eighth champion trainer title – a record total that would not be surpassed until 2000 by Martin Pipe. By now he had captured virtually every top prize in the National Hunt racing calendar.

Officially he ended his great training career with the victory of *Celtic Shot* in the 1988 Champion Hurdle. But, in reality, that winner and his last National runner (*Insure*) were prepared by his assistant Charlie Brooks – because, ironically and most cruelly, the champion jockey and trainer, who had survived more than 300 falls, had had retirement forced upon him by a skull fracture and a debilitating stroke incurred in a fall down the stairs in his own house in September, 1987. He died two days

after the 2004 Grand National at the age of 77.
See also: Sundew; Kilmore; Jay Trump; Anglo;
Crisp; Price, Ryan.

WITHINGTON, Fred

The first trainer to prepare both the winner and runner-up in a Grand National. The distinction was achieved in 1908 when the 66-1 outsider *Rubio* triumphed by ten lengths from the six year old Irish mare *Mattie Macgregor*.

Fred Withington, an outstanding amateur horseman, had himself ridden in two Nationals. In 1897 he was beaten by only a head into third place on Major 'Weasel' Orr-Ewing's six year old *Ford of Fyne*, albeit 20 lengths behind the great *Manifesto*. The following year, when *Ford of Fyne* went off the 11-2 favourite, they finished sixth.

In 1906 Withington had only just started to train at Danebury, near Stockbridge in Hampshire, when he was sent *Rubio*, an American-bred chestnut gelding who, as a yearling, had fetched a mere 15 guineas at the Newmarket sales. Originally trained by Bernard Bletsoe, who had won the 1901 National with *Grudon*, the horse had broken down after winning three minor races in 1903 and, as an unorthodox means of strengthening him up, he had since been put into harness, hauling a hotel coach that operated between the local station and the Prospect Arms, Towcester.

Now back in training at Danebury, *Rubio* won two races in 1907 before being entered for the National. At the time, however, Withington was thought to have a stronger contender in *Mattie Macgregor*, a six year old owned by Australian William Cooper, father-in-law of *Rubio*'s owner, Major Frank Douglas-Pennant. Thus, when Ernie Piggott became unavailable, jockey William Bissill welcomed the chance to switch from *Rubio* to the more fancied *Mattie Macgregor*.

The beneficiary was Henry Bletsoe who, as the son of the previous trainer, had ridden *Rubio* back in 1903. Though strongly challenged by *Mattie Macgregor* coming to the last, he was able to power *Rubio* home to a comfortable victory – the first Amnerican-bred winner of the National.

In the 1909 National *Rubio* was a faller and *Mattie Macgregor* refused. It had nonetheless been a spectacular start to Withington's training career, and he went on to become a leading, hugely respected trainer for another 22 years, eventually being elected to the National Hunt Committee and the Jockey Club and becoming the first jumps trainer to serve as a steward.

See also: *Rubio*.

WOODBROOK

Comfortable winner of the 1881 Grand National, never being seriously threatened after he had been presented with the lead at Valentine's, first time round, by the fall of *The Liberator* (remounted) who had won in 1879 and had been runner-up in 1880. Revelling in the boggy conditions, he came home four lengths ahead of former winner *Regal*, with *Thornfield* – joint favourite with *Woodbrook* – a well beaten third. It was a second successive triumph for amateur rider Tommy Beasley and Irish trainer Henry Eyre Linde.

Bred, named and owned by the renowed Irish sportsman Captain (later Colonel) Tom Kirkwood of Woodbrook, near Boyle. Co. Roscommon, *Woodbrook* was a chestnut by *The Lawyer* out of *The Doe* and, through the dam, a grandson of the prolific sire *Touchstone,* who had won the 1834 St. Leger. He was first introduced to the National fences in November, 1879, when, as a five year old, he finished first by four lengths in the Grand Sefton Chase only to be disqualified on a technicality, having been entered with 'an insufficient description'.

Four months later, he made his National debut with Harry Beasley in the saddle. But trainer Linde had a more fancied contender in the mare *Empress*, a five year old who was a stone better off in the weights and ridden by Harry's eldest brother Tommy. *Empress*, running her last race before being retired to stud, duly won by two lengths from *The Liberator* (giving him two stone). *Woodbrook* finished a promising fifth.

Both Beasleys rode in the 1881 National but this time the great Tommy took over on *Woodbrook* with brother Harry on Linde's lesser hope *Fair Wind*. Only 13 lined up for the start in quagmire conditions and *The Liberator*, 6-1 third favourite, led the field until falling at Valentine's. Despite a kick from a passing horse that left him with a badly bruised shoulder, owner-rider Garrett Moore bravely managed to remount. But it was a hopeless cause on a 12 year old star still harshly burdened with a 12st 7lb top weight.

Following that fall *Woodbrook* was never headed and, jumping brilliantly throughout, he went on to win unextended, by four lengths from the 1876 National winner *Regal* who, on the second circuit, had made amazing progress from the rear. *The Liberator* was the last of nine finishers.

A few weeks later, at Sandown, the tables were turned in the Grand International Chase which *Regal* narrowly won from *Torpedo* and *Fair Wind* who had failed to finish at Aintree. But the unplaced *Woodbrook* was then on 12st 7lb, almost a stone worse off with the winner. He would not run in the National again. Having been sold for £1,300 to Herr Oeschlaeger, a German, he suffered a fatal illness at Newmarket the following year.

Herr Oeschlaeger had previously sought National success by buying the 1878 runner-up *Martha* only to see the mare, again ridden by Tommy Beasley, finish third. Following the loss of *Woodbrook* he made one more National bid, with the American-bred, six year old *Idea*, who failed to finish in 1884. In contrast, Woodbrook's original owner, Captain Kirkwood, enjoyed further successes, most notably winning two Ascot Gold Cups with *The White Knight*.

See also: Linde, Henry Eyre.

WOODLAND, Percy

Belief in the power of fate is irresistibly supported by the way chance blessed the spectacularly successful riding career of Percy Woodland. Twice he won the Grand National – and on both occasions he only gained the winning ride as a late replacement for an injured, less fortunate, jockey.

There was, however, no marked element of luck in the actual riding. Woodland, son of a well-known Hendon trainer, was a hugely talented horseman who won his first race at the age of 13. He was equally in demand over the sticks and on the Flat, though some purists disapproved of the way he retained his short-stirrup Flat-racing style when going over the jumps.

Born in 1882, Percy was an 18 year old professional when he rode in the National for the first time, finishing tenth on the 66-1 outsider *Model*. The following year, 1901, when atrocious conditions warranted postponement of the race, he had the misfortune to see his mount, *True Blue*, another 66-1 chance, destroyed after breaking a leg. In his third National, he pulled up on Lord Denman's *Whitehaven*.

Then, in 1903, he surprisingly found himself on *Drumcree*, the 13-2 National favourite, after his regular amateur rider Hugh Nugent, son of trainer Sir Charles Nugent, had been injured in a riding fall. Despite being raised 12lb for having finished second in 1901, and a further 7lb, after finishing seventh in 1902, *Drumcree* won by three lengths; and any suggestion that this was a one-off lucky break for Woodland was quickly dispelled when, the very next day, he went out and rode the winners of the Liverpool Handicap Hurdle and the Champion Chase. That year he was champion jumps jockey with 54 wins.

In the next seven years Percy reappeared in the National only twice – brought down on *Benvenir* (1904) and finishing three lengths second on *Napper Tandy* (1905). But there was good reason for his absences. He was regularly riding in France where he achieved the extraordinary distinction of winning the French Derby twice and the Grand Steeplechase de Paris twice.

In 1911 Woodland returned to Aintree to ride *Jenkinstown*, winner of the National one year before. His mount, raised more than a stone in the weights, had to be pulled up. But two years later fortune favoured Percy again. At the last minute, after Ernie Piggott had broken a hand in a fall, he was recruited to ride *Covertcoat*, a seven year old owned by Sir Charles Assheton-Smith, who had already had two National winners.

This year, though racing conditions were reasonable, there was an inordinate number of casualties; and with two fences remaining only three runners were still standing: *Carsey*, *Covertcoat* and *Irish Mail*. When *Carsey* fell at the last, *Covertcoat* was left all alone, needing only to plod up the run-in to win by a distance from *Irish Mail*, with the remounted *Carsey* another distance behind. Only three of 22 starters had finished.

Having won two Nationals, ten years apart, Woodland rode twice more in the race – in 1914 when *Covertcoat*, the 7-1 favourite, failed to finish with a top weight of 12st 7lb; and finally on second favourite *Charlbury* (pulled up) in 1919 when the race returned to Aintree after a three year suspension during the First World War. He died in 1958.

See also: Drumcree; Covertcoat.

WORKMAN

In late March 1939, less than six months before the outbreak of the Second World War, nine year old

Workman became the first Irish-bred and -trained winner of the Grand National since *Troytown* (1920), and the first of three National winners to have been sired (out of the mare *Cariella*) by *Cottage*, who would also be responsible for *Cottage Rake*, three times winner of the Cheltenham Gold Cup.

Bred by Mr P.J. O'Leary at Charleville, Co. Cork, *Workman* was originally owned by an Irish doctor on whose death he was sold for a mere £26. Subsequently, on the strength of his form shown in point-to-points and a winning race debut over four-and-a-quarter miles in the La Touche Memorial Cup at Punchestown, he was bought as a seven year old by Irish trainer Jack Ruttle on behalf of the Liverpool-born industrialist Sir Alexander Maguire.

The following year, on his National debut in 1938, *Workman*, ridden by Jimmy Brogan, was a major threat until two fences out when he began to fade, ultimately finishing a bad third to *Battleship* and *Royal Danieli*. He subsequently finished a promising fourth at Aintree in the Grand Sefton Chase and won the three-mile Naas Plate on his build-up for a second tilt at the National. Trainer Ruttle recruited Tim Hyde, more renowned for his prowess in show-jumping, to take the ride.

There were 37 runners, the largest field since 1931, and again *Workman* was opposed by *Royal Danieli* who had been beaten by only a head in the 1938 National. But this time *Royal Danieli*, 6lb worse off at the weights, crashed out at Becher's first time around. *At the Water*, the favourite, Miss Dorothy Paget's *Kilstar*, led narrowly from Lord Derby's *Under Bid*. Workman, however, was always in close attendance, and he finally gained the lead after the second Valentine's. Thereafter he was never headed, though at the 28th fence *Black Hawk* came so close that the two horses collided. *Black Hawk* went down; Hyde steadied his mount and held on to resist by three lengths the strong late challenge of the Scottish hope, *MacMoffat*.

Workman was raced for four more seasons in Ireland, but he completely lost his form of old, never winning another race and never appearing in the National again. In contrast, *MacMoffat* came back to finish runner-up again in 1940 and, most remarkably, after a five-year war-enforced break, he returned to run (albeit falling) in the Nationals of 1946 and 1947, the latter at the age of fifteen.
See also: Hyde, Tim; Ruttle, Jack.

WORLD WAR I

On March 16, 1915, when the war was into its eighth month, the Jockey Club announced its decision not to suspend race meetings for the duration. Accordingly, ten days later, the Grand National went ahead as usual, albeit before a relatively small, uniform-dominated crowd. Appropriately, on a day when Prime Minister Lloyd George was promising suffragette Sylvia Pankhurst to pay men's wages to women employed in war work, Lady Nelson became the first woman to own a National winner (*Ally Sloper*) and collect the prize money of £3,515.

Nine months later, however, Aintree racecourse was requisitioned by the Army, and it was to remain unavailable for racing for the next three years. In the interim, a substitute steeplechase was introduced at Gatwick. Initially named 'The Racecourse Association Steeplechase', it was run on March 24, 1916, and had a prize value of 500 sovereigns. The distance was four miles 836 yards, but none of its 29 fences posed a severe test of jumping ability, the highest – the 11th (and 23rd) – being 4ft 10in. There were 21 starters, just one faller, and the race was won by Mr P.F. Heybourne's *Vermouth*, a six year old ridden by Jack Reardon at 100-8. The 9-2 favourite, *Ally Sloper*, finished eighth.

In 1917, the Gatwick substitute race – re-named 'The War National Steeplechase' – went off late after a snowstorm, now abated, had delayed the second race. There were 19 starters, and it was a contest most notable for its bewildering and sensational finish. Eleven were still in contention as the field came to the second last fence. There, three front-runners fought for the lead, and it was *Limerock* who surged ahead from *Ballymacad* and *Chang*. Impressively moving away on the run-in, he had the race at his mercy when – shades of *Devon Loch* so many years later – he suddenly sank to his knees and then rolled over, throwing jockey Bill Smith to one side.

His mysterious collapse handed the race to *Ballymacad*, a ten year old ridden by Edmund Driscoll and trained by Aubrey Hastings. He won by eight lengths from *Chang*, with *Ally Sloper* third; and shortly afterwards the winning owner, Sir George Bullough announced that he would be donating his £1,000 winnings to the St Dunstan's Home for Blinded Soldiers.

Why had *Limerock* fallen on the run-in? One suggestion was that the horse had crossed his legs and tripped himself up. Another, more probable, theory was that he had slipped on a treacherous, snow-softened patch of ground.

There was no such element of bad lack about the third and last Gatwick substitute race in 1918. It had a remarkably high class field which included three future winners of the Grand National: *Poethlyn*, *Shaun Spadah* and *Sergeant Murphy*; and the impressive victor was Mrs Hugh Peel's eight year old *Poethlyn*, ridden by Ernie Piggott.

See also: Gatwick

WORLD WAR II

In January, 1940, the Jockey Club cancelled the English Derby. But remarkably, on April 5th, seven months after the Second World War had begun, the Grand National went ahead on schedule. It was not quite business as usual. The crowds were somewhat diminished, and a great many spectators were in uniform – evidence that more than two million young men (including some of the National jockeys) had been called to arms. Appropriately, the race winner (*Bogskar*) was ridden by a Serviceman: Flight Sergeant Mervyn Jones.

One month later Winston Churchill became the wartime leader. In June came the fall of France. And, in the last four days of August, Liverpool was heavily bombed as the Luftwaffe sent over a nightly average of 150 bombers to blitz Merseyside. The 'phoney war' was well and truly over and once again Aintree racecourse was requisitioned by the War Department. It served as a major depot for military vehicles and a station for Army personnel, housing at its peak some 16,000 troops, primarily Americans preparing for the D-Day invasion of mainland Europe.

Based at Paddock Lodge near the parade ring, the racecourse lessees – Ronald and Mirabel Topham, supported by their nephew Jim Bidwell-Topham and his sister Patricia – did their best to safeguard their family interests. Their main concern was to protect the turf on the two-mile National circuit, but they fought in vain when trying to discourage the military from erecting huge concrete blocks to prevent aircraft from landing on the course. This time there was no possibility of holding wartime substitute Nationals at Gatwick. There, the racecourse had been cleared of fences and redesigned to provide an airfield and underground storage for mustard-gas.

Six years would pass before the Aintree Grand National was held again, a resumption on April 5, 1946, that was due in no small part to reorganisation driven by Mirabel, the former musical comedy actress who had been chairman of Tophams Ltd since 1937. Meanwhile, many men associated with National had lost their lives in the global conflict – among them, four winning riders: Frank Furlong and Bob Everett, flying with the Fleet Air Arm; Flight Sergeant Mervyn Jones (RAF); and Tommy Cullinan, serving with an Anti-Aircraft unit.

WYNDBURGH

In terms of consistent endeavour, *Wyndburgh* was the horse most deserving of a Grand National success. Trained in Scotland, this brave little brown gelding ran in six Nationals, being runner-up three times, once fourth and once sixth, and only once falling. No other contender has a comparable record without winning the race.

In 1957, on his Aintree debut as a seven year old, *Wyndburgh* was owned and trained by Miss Rhona Wilkinson, an accomplished horsewoman who had bred him and ridden him as a hunter and point-to-pointer. That year he came from behind on the second circuit and was still making ground when he finished eight lengths second to *Sundew*, ridden by Fred Winter.

In 1958, with an extra 10lb to carry, he went off the 6-1 favourite, not surprisingly since he had won the Grand Sefton over the National fences and Newcastle's four-mile Eider Chase. But he failed to show the sparkle of his earlier Aintree run and was a distant fourth to *Mr What*. The following year, Miss Wilkinson became Mrs Kenneth Oliver, wife of a Hawick auctioneer who had been a leading amateur rider and was now emerging as the most successful Scotland-based trainer. For the 1959 National they managed to book the leading National Hunt jockey, Tim Brookshaw. Again *Wyndburgh* made relentless progress on the second circuit and was left in the lead with *Oxo* following a pile-up at the second Becher's. But there one of his stirrup irons had broken. Brookshaw slipped his other foot out of the iron, and, though greatly handicapped, maintained a long duel with *Oxo* and was still closing on the leader when he was beaten by a mere one and a half lengths.

Wyndburgh suffered his only fall (at the first Becher's) in 1960, when, carrying his highest weight of 11st 7lb, he was ridden by Michael Scudamore who had won on *Oxo* the previous year. Reunited with Brookshaw in 1961, he finished sixth at 33-1. Then, as a 12 year old, wholly unfancied at 45-1, he made a remarkable comeback. He was contending for the lead with three others at the last and, on the run-in, was outpaced in quagmire conditions only by *Kilmore*, the winner by ten lengths, with *Mr What* a further ten lengths back in third.

For the first time in National history the first three home were 12 year olds; and for the second time the Scottish hope was runner-up to a horse ridden by the brilliant Fred Winter. On this occasion, his swansong, Wyndburgh had been most creditably ridden by a newcomer to the race, Tommy Barnes. Seventeen years later, most fittingly, Tommy's son Maurice – benefiting from his father's experience – was to triumph on his National debut, riding Scotland's first winner, *Rubstic*.

See also: Unlucky Losers; Brookshaw, Tim; Runners-Up; Oliver, James Kenneth Murray.

WYNNE, Denis

The Irish jockey who became a national hero in 1847 when, riding nine year old *Matthew*, he gave his countrymen their first winner of the great Aintree steeplechase that, for the first time, was officially styled 'The Grand National Handicap Steeplechase'.

Renowned for his power in making a late challenge, 'Denny' Wynne made his National debut in 1846, finishing a creditable third on a rank outsider, Lord Howth's five year old *Switcher*. The following year, on Matthew, he was in a record field of 26 runners that included *Jerry*, the 1840 winner; *Pioneer* who had not been raised in the weights for his victory the previous year; and the famous mare *Brunette* who had long been a dominant force in Ireland.

Since *Brunette* was now 13 years old and lumbered with a top weight of 12st 6lb, Irish punters shrewdly chose to plunge on the lightly weighted *Matthew*, backing him down to as short as 4-1 on the day. Inexplicably, however, the brown gelding was a late drifter in the market, going off as 10-1 joint favourite with last year's runner-up Culverthorpe. He was never prominent on the first circuit and, along with *Brunette*, well behind the leaders as they came to the second Becher's. But at that point Wynne began his forward move, up to third place coming to the last, and then galvanizing *Matthew* into a remarkable late surge to snatch victory in his final strides, one length ahead of *St Leger* (conceding 25lb), ridden by the great Tom

Olliver. Former winner *Jerry* was a further length back in third.

The winning combination returned the following year when *Matthew*, raised a full stone in the weights, was brought down by a horse falling directly in his path. In 1849 Wynne finished a distant fourth on five year old *Alfred*, and in 1850 he was unlucky not to register a second National win. His mount was *The Knight of Gwynne* who had been raised 15lb for being runner-up the previous year, and now he was runner-up again, beaten one length by little *Abd-El-Kader* who had a massive 24lb advantage.

After failing to finish on the rank outsider *Fugleman* in the 1851 National, Wynne was booked the following year to ride the hat-trick-seeking *Abd-El-Kader*. But the dual winner was now up a stone and, though leading as far as the Canal Turn, he had to be pulled up at the end of the first circuit. The popular Irishman had five more National rides: on *Currig* (1853), last of seven finishers; *Crabbs* (1854, a well-beaten third; *Little Charley* (1855), knocked over; *Hopeless Star* (1857), pulled up; and *Black Bess* (1858), fell. Ironically his 12th and last National was won by his former mount *Little Charley*, successful at the fourth attempt.

See also: Matthew; Wynne, James.

WYNNE, James

In 1862, riding *O'Connell*, the 33-1 outsider, young James Wynne followed in the footsteps of his famous father with tragic results. On the morning of his first Grand National, he learned that his sister had died in Ireland. Lord de Freyne, owner of *O'Connell*, told him that he need not take the ride and that he would arrange for him to get home as soon as possible. But James declined; he had dreamed so long of competing in the world's greatest steeplechase that his father had won 15 years before.

This year, for only the second time, the National went off with a field of 13. To the superstitious few who saw it as a bad omen, hard realists could counter that with so few runners there was much less chance of bunching and a serious fall. And that risk seemed to have been further diminished when, by the second fence, two refusals had reduced the field to a mere 11.

Yet still disaster struck. It happened towards the end of the first circuit as a handful of horses came to the gorse fence before the Water Jump. A horse named *Playman* plunged into the fence, bringing down two others, *Willoughby* and *O'Connell*. The former got up, with his amateur owner-rider still in the saddle. Meanwhile Wynne remained injured on the ground as the riderless *Playman* rolled over on top of him. James never regained consciousness, dying in the night from internal injuries.

The plain fence at which Wynne suffered his fatal fall was usually taken at great speed. Subsequently, to reduce the pace here, an open ditch was introduced on the approach and the redesigned fence, a formidable 5ft 2in high, became known as The Chair.

YATES, Arthur

Owner, rider and trainer, Arthur Yates of Bishops Sutton, Hampshire, was closely associated with the Grand National for more than three decades, beginning with disaster in 1862, when his riderless *Playman* fell with fatal result upon jockey James Wynne, and ending in triumph in 1893 when he was the trainer of *Cloister*, who set a new course record and was the first winner – by a staggering 40 lengths – to carry the maximum 12st 7lb.

In the 1860s and 1870s, Yates was renowned as a leading amateur rider who scored some 460 wins in England and on the Continent before turning to training on a huge scale at Bishops Sutton. Yet, without success, he had only four rides in the National: on six year old Q.C. (1870), finishing seventh; *Harvester* (1872), pulled up; *Crawler* (1873), fell; and *Furley* (1874), failed to finish.

Arguably, he was unlucky not to have won in 1872 when riding his own *Harvester*, a 25-1 chance burdened with the second highest weight of 12st. As he cleared the penultimate fence, strongly challenging for the lead, the seven year old was looking a likely winner, but there he over-jumped and on landing wrenched off a racing plate and went lame. Yates had to pull him up, so handing over the race to *Casse Tete* who, on a mere 10st, had the lightest weight of nine finishers.

As an owner – following in the footsteps of his great-uncle John Elmore, owner of the first National winner, *Lottery* – Yates was no more successful. His first four runners – *Playman* (1862), *Plum Cake* (1869), *Harvester* (1872) and *Buridan* (1881) – failed to complete the course. But then, as a trainer,

he had spectacular success, turning out nearly 3,000 winners – two of them in the Grand National – and in 1892 setting a long-standing record with 124 winners in a jumps season.

In 1885 Yates saddled *Roquefort*, the six year old National favourite who led over the last and held off *Frigate*, the previous year's runner-up, by two lengths. And six years later, after he had taken over ownership, he brought back the 12 year old Aintree regular to finish fourth at 40-1. The runner-up that year – beaten by only half a length – was Lord Dudley's brilliant young *Cloister*; and it was now Yates's good fortune to be sent the seven year old following a change of ownership.

Under amateur John Dormer, who rode out regularly for Yates, *Cloister* went off favourite in the 1892 National but, at a 28lb disadvantage, he was beaten 20 lengths into second place by *Father O'Flynn*. The following year Yates further improved the most brilliant staying chaser and, after *Dormer* had lost an eye in a fall at Sandown, he gave the ride to his experienced stable jockey Bill Dollery. As 9-2 favourite, *Cloister* won at a canter, scoring what was hailed as the most impressive victory in the history of the race.

For the 1894 National the handicapper hit *Cloister* with a staggering 12st 12lb; and Yates's hopes of a third victory were to be dashed amid great controversy as the wonder horse, made 6-4 favourite, was withdrawn a few days before race, allegedly having been injured in a final gallop at Sandown. Market moves prompted rumours of foul play but nothing was proved.

See also: Roquefort; Cloister; Hobson, Frederick.

Z

ZOEDONE

Winner of the 1883 Grand National when ridden by her new owner, Count 'Charles' Kinsky, who was having his first ride in the race. The six year old *Zoedone* took the lead near the second Becher's and dominated a ten-strong field to win by ten lengths from outsider *Black Prince*. On heavy ground, her winning time of 11min 39sec was by no means the worst in history. But for slowness it has never since been equalled or surpassed.

Zoedone – a chestnut mare by *New Oswestry* out of *Miss Honiton* – initially ran in minor hunters' races for his owner, Mr T. Jackson, an Oswestry farmer. As a four year old she was bought in 1881 for £170 by Mr Edward Clayton, a Rutlandshire owner more renowned for his large stable of flat-race horses. He rode her himself in just one hunters' race before sending her to Aintree for her National debut, with amateur Captain Arthur 'Doggie' Smith in the saddle.

It was Smith's third successive National, having finished ninth on past winner *Shifnal* (1880) and fourth on *New Glasgow* (1881). Now, with a field of only 12 running on heavy ground in a snow blizzard, he most creditably brought the inexperienced *Zoedone* home, albeit a well-beaten third of three finishers.

As a regular huntsman, the London-based Austro-Hungarian diplomat Count Kinsky had been attracted by the handsome chestnut two years earlier. Now, flushed with a 1,000 guineas windfall from Corrie Roy's victory in the Cesarewitch, he immediately approached Mr Clayton with an offer to buy *Zoedone* for £800 with the promise of a further £200 if the mare won the National.

Mr Clayton agreed, and on his part at least there was an understanding that Captain Smith would again ride *Zoedone* in the National. But Kinsky had other ideas. He sent the mare to be trained by Mr W.H. Jenkins at Upton, Warwickshire, undertook much of the schooling himself, and then rode her to victory in the Great Sandown Chase. Two months later, on his Aintree debut, the count rode her to a comfortable victory in the smallest of all National fields.

They returned in 1884 when, with a 16lb hike in the weights, *Zoedone* did well to finish fifth against stronger opposition. But the following year, on her third appearance, she completely lacked her old sparkle. In those days it was customary for all the runners to jump a 'practice hurdle' on their way down to the start. *Zoedone*, the 5-1 second favourite, fell at this trivial obstacle. Remounted, she then started slowly in the race proper and struggled around listlessly before crashing into the fence before Becher's second time around.

Alarmingly, the mare lay motionless on the ground for many minutes, and it was a quarter of an hour before she recovered sufficiently to be led away. All the evidence suggested that the mare – heavily backed in doubles with *Bendigo*, winner of the Lincoln – had been 'poisoned' before the race. (One suggestion was that she had been injected with hartshorn). Whatever the truth, and nothing was ever proved, *Zoedone* never raced again.

See also: Kinsky, Prince Karel Andreas; Foul Play.

BIBLIOGRAPHY

In addition to all British national newspapers, the *London Evening Standard* and especially the *Racing Post* and *The Sporting Life*, the following books have been consulted:

Armytage, Marcus, *Hot Cherry*. Highdown, 2005
Bagnold, Enid, *National Velvet*, William Heinemann Ltd., 1935.
Balding, Ian, *Making The Running: A Racing Life*, Headline Book Publishing, 2004.
Barrett, Norman (editor), *The Daily Telegraph Chronicle of Horse Racing*, Guinness Publishing Ltd. 1995.
Bird, T.H., *A Hundred Grand Nationals*, Country Life Ltd., 1937.
Budden, John, *The Boss: The Life and Times of Gordon W. Richards*, Mainstream, 2000.
Burridge, Richard, *The Grey Horse; The True Story of Desert Orchid*, Pelham Books, 1992.
Campbell, Judith, *Royal Horses*, New English Library, 1983
Champion, Bob & Powell, Jonathan, *Champion's Story: A Great Human Triumph*, Victor Gollancz Ltd.,1981.
Cottrell, John, *The Punters' Guide to the Grand National*, SportsBooks, Ltd., Cheltenham, 2007.
Cranham, Gerry, Pitman, Richard & Oaksey, John, *The Guinness Guide to Steeplechasing*, Guinness Superlatives Ltd, 1979.
Dorman, John, *Racing Champion – Desert Orchid*, The Crowood Press, 1990.
Doust, Dudley, *221 Peter Scudamore's Record Season*, Hodder & Stoughton, 1989.
Ennor, George & Mooney, Bill, *The World Encyclopedia of Horse Racing*, Carlton Books, 2001.
Fitzgerald, Mick, with Evans, Carl, *A Jump Jockey's Life*, Mainstream, 1999.
Francis, Dick, The Sport of Queens, Michael Joseph, 1999
Francome, John, Born Lucky, Pelham Books, 1985.
Frost, Jimmy, with Johnson, Lucy, *Touched By Frost*, Highdown, 2003
Graham, Clive & Curling Bill, *The Grand National: An Illustrated History of the Greatest Steeplechase in the World*, Barrie & Jenkins Ltd., London, 1972.
Green, Reg, *A Race Apart: The History of the Grand National*, Hodder & Stoughton, 1988.
Green, Reg, *The Grand National, Aintree's Official Illustrated History*, Virgin Publishing Ltd., 2000.
Green, Reg, *Kings For A Day, Aintree's Bravest Sons*, Mainstream Publishing, 2002.
Green, Reg, *Over Becher's Brook*, Sport in Word Ltd, Charley, 1997.
Green, Reg, *National Heroes: The Aintree Legend*, Mainstream Publishing. 1997.
Harman, Bob, *The Ultimate Dream: 75 Years of the Tote Cheltenham Gold Cup*, Mainstream Publishing, 2000.
Holland, Anne, *Grand National: An Official Celebration*, Macdonald Queen Anne Press, 1991.
Holland, Anne, *Steeplechasing: A Celebration of 250 Years*, Little, Brown and Co., 2001.
Hughes, John and Watson, Peter, *Long Live The National*, Michael Joseph Ltd., 1983.
Johnson, Richard & Lee, Alan, *Out Of The Shadows*, Greenwater Publishing, 2002.
King, Peter, *The Grand National: Anybody's Race*, Quartet Books Ltd., 1983.
Magee, Sean, *Complete A-Z of Horse Racing*, Channel 4 Books, 2001.
Magee, Sean, *The Channel Four Book Of Racing*, Sidgwick & Jackson, 1989
Mason, Finch, *Heroes and Heroines of the Grand National*, The Bibliographical Press, London, 1911.
McCain, Ginger, *Red Rum: A Racing Legend*, Weidenfeld & Nicolson, 1996.
McCririck, John, *John McCririck's World Of Betting*, Stanley Paul 1992.
McIlvanney, Hugh, *McIlvanney on Horseracing*, Mainstream Publishing, 1995.
Morris, Tony & Randall, *John, Horse Racing: Records, Facts and Champions*, Guinness Publishing Ltd., 1990.
Oaksey, John, *Oaksey On Racing*, The Kingswood Press, 1991.
O'Sullevan, Peter, *Calling The Horses*, Stanley Paul, 1989
Pegg, Norman, *Focus On Racing*, Robert Hale Ltd., 1963.

Penfold, John, *Gallant Spirit, The Authentic History of Liverpool Races and the Grand National*, Portway Press 1999.

Peters, Stewart, *The Grand National, The History of the Aintree Spectacular*, Tempus Publishing, Stroud, 2005.

Peters, Stewart, *Modern Nationals, The Aintree Spectacular*, Tempus Publishing, Stroud, 2002.

Pye, J.K., *A Grand National Commentary*, J.A. Allen & Co. Ltd., 1971.

Rimell, Mercy, *Reflections on Racing*, Penguin Books Ltd., 1990.

Rimmer, Joan, *Aintree's Queen Bee*, SportsBooks Ltd., 2007.

Scudamore, Peter, *The Autobiography Of A Champion*, Headline Book Publishing, 1993

Smith Eccles, Steve with Lee, Alan, *The Last of the Cavaliers*, Pelham Books, London, 1993.

Smith, Sean, *Royal Racing*, BBC Worldwide Ltd., London, 2001

Tyrrel, John, *Chasing Around Britain*, The Crowood Press, Swindon, 1990.

Ward, Andrew, *Horse-Racing's Strangest Races*, Robson Books, 2000.

Wathen, Guy, *Great Horsemen of the World*, David & Charles, 1990.

Welcome, John, Great Racing Disasters, Arthur Barker Ltd., 1985

White, John, *The Racegoers' Encylopaedia*, Collins Willow, 1996.

Williams, Guy St John, *Martin Molony – A Legend In His Lifetime*, Hillgate Publishing, 2000.

Wilson, Julian, *The Great Racehorses*, Queen Anne Press, 1987.

Wilson, Julian, *Some You Win: A Life in Racing*, Collins Willow, 1998.

WINNERS AND PLACED HORSES 1839 -2007

YEAR	HORSE	DISTANCE	OWNER	TRAINER	RIDER	AGE	WT	STARTED	FINISHED	GOING	TIME M/SEC	S.P.
1839	**Lottery**		**Mr John Elmore**	**G.Dockeray**	**J. Mason**	**aged**	**12.0**	**17**	**7**	**hy**	**14.53**	**5-1**
	Seventy Four	4 lengths	Sir George Mostyn	—	T. Olliver	aged	12.0					
	Paulina	3	Mr Theobald		Mr Martin	aged	12.0					
	True Blue		Mr Stephenson		Mr Barker	aged	12.0					
1840	**Jerry**		**Mr Villebois**	**G. Dockeray**	**Mr B. Bretheron**	**aged**	**12.0**	**12**	**4**	**gd**	**12.3**	**12-1**
	Arthur *	4	Mr Barry		Mr A. McDonough	aged	12.0					8-1
	Valentine	4	Mr A. Power		Mr A. Power	aged	12.0					
1841	**Charity**		**Lord Craven**		**Mr Powell**	**aged**	**12.0**	**11**	**7**	**gd**	**13.25**	**14-1**
	Cigar	1	Mr Anderson		Mr A. McDonough	aged	12.0					4-1
	Peter Simple	½	Hon. F.Craven		Walker	aged	12.0					6-1
1842	**Gay Lad**		**Mr John Elmore**		**T. Olliver**	**aged**	**12.0**	**15**	**5**	**gd**	**13.3**	**7-1**
	Seventy Four	4	Lord Mostyn		Powell	aged	12.0					6-1
	Peter Simple *	15	Mr Hunter		Mr Hunter	aged	12.0					6-1
1843	**Vanguard**		**Lord Chesterfield**		**T. Olliver**	**aged**	**11.10**	**16**	**9**	**g/f**	not taken	**12-1**
	Nimrod	3	Mr Mare		Scott	aged	11.0					10-1
	Dragsman	½	Mr Holman		Mr Crickmere	aged	11.3					10-1
	Claude Duval		Col. Hanson		Tomblin	aged	11.7					n.q.
1844	**Discount**		**Mr Quartermaine**		**Mr Crickmere**	**6**	**10.12**	**15**	**9**	**soft**	c. 14.0	**5-1 jtfav**
	The Returned	20	Mr W.Sterling Crawford		Scott	aged	12.0					15-1
	Tom Tug	1	Mr Tilbury		Rackley	aged	10.7					n.q.
1845	**Cure-All**		**Mr W. Sterling Crawford**		**Mr W.J. Loft**	**aged**	**11.5**	**15**	**4**	**soft**	**10.47**	**n.q.**
	Peter Simple	2	Mr Thornton		Frisby	aged	11.12					9-1
	The Exquisite	2	Capt. Boyd		Larry Byrne	aged	11.12					n.q.
1846	**Pioneer**		**Mr Adams**		**W. Taylor**	**6**	**11.12**	**22**	**5**	**gd**	**10.46**	**n.q.**
	Culverthorpe	3	Mr Payne		Rackley	aged	11.4					12-1
	Switcher	3	Lord Howth		D. Wynne	5	12.4					n.q.
	Firefly		Lord Waterford		L. Byrne	aged	12.4					7-1
1847	**Matthew**		**Mr J. Courtenay**	**J. Courtenay**	**D. Wynne**	**9**	**10.6**	**26**	**6**	**gd**	**10.39**	**10-1 jtfav**
	St Leger	1	Mr Watt		T. Olliver	aged	12.3					15-1
	Jerry	1	Mr Moseley		Bradley	aged	11.6					100-8
	Pioneer		Mr O'Higgins		Capt. Peel	7	11.12					15-1

Year	Horse	Dist	Owner	Trainer	Jockey	Age	Weight	Ran		Going	Time	Odds
1848	Chandler		Capt. J.L.Little	T. Eskrett	Capt. J.L. Little	12	11.12	29	4	soft	11.21	12-1
	The Curate	½	Mr Brettle	—	T. Olliver	aged	11.12					6-1fav
	British Yeoman	1½	Mr Elmore	—	Mr Bevill	aged	11.4					n.q.
	Standard Guard		Mr Storey	Mr Storey	Taylor	aged	10.12					100-6
1849	Peter Simple		Mr Mason Jr	T. Cunningham	T. Cunningham	aged	11.0	24	6	soft	10.56	20-1
	The Knight Of Gwynne	3	Capt. D'Arcy	—	Capt D'Arcy	11	11.0					8-1
	Prince George	a dist.	Mr T. Mason	Mr T. Mason	T. Olliver	aged	10.10					5-1fav
	Alfred		Mr Buchanan	—	D. Wynne	5	10.6					12-1
1850	Abd-El-Kader		Mr J. Osborne	J. Osborne	C. Green	8	9.12	32	7	gd	9.57.5	n.q.
	The Knight Of Gwynne	3	Mr J. Fort	—	D. Wynne	aged	11.8					12-1
	Sir John	3	Lord Waterford	—	J. Ryan	aged	11.8					7-1
	Tipperary Boy		Mr Hughes	—	S. Darling	6	10.0					n.q.
1851	Abd-El-Kader		Mr J. Osborne	J. Osborne	T. Abbot	9	10.4	21	10	g/s	9.59	7-1
	Maria Day	½ a neck	Mr C. Higgins	—	J. Frisby	aged	10.5				—	100-6
	Sir John	2	Lord Waterford	—	J. Ryan	aged	11.12					7-1
	Half-And-Half		Mr Oakes	—	R. Sly Jr.	aged	10.8					n.q.
1852	Miss Mowbray		Mr T.F. Mason	G. Dockeray	Mr A. Goodman	aged	10.4	24	7	gd	9.58.5	n.q.
	Maurice Daley	1	Mr Cartwright	—	C. Boyce	aged	9.4					n.q.
	Sir Peter Laurie	5	Capt W. Barnett	—	W. Holman	aged	11.7					30-1
	Chieftain		Mr Atkinson	—	Harrison	aged	10.12					10-1
1853	Peter Simple		Capt. J.L. Little	T. Olliver	T. Olliver	15	10.10	21	7	soft	10.37.5	9-1
	Miss Mowbray	3	Mr T.F. Mason	—	Mr F. Gordon	aged	10.12					5-1fav
	Oscar	3	Mr T.F. Mason	—	Mr A. Goodman	aged	10.2					6-1
	Sir Peter Barnett		Capt W. Barnett	—	W. Holman	aged	11.8					12-1
1854	Bourton		Mr W. Moseley	H. Wadlow	J. Tasker	aged	11.12	20	7	gd	9.59	4-1fav
	Spring	15	Mr Barber	—	W. Archer	6	9.10					20-1
	Crabbs	10	Mr J.R. Henderson	—	D. Wynne	aged	9.2					10-1
	Maley		Mr J.R. Henderson	—	Thrift	aged	9.10					50-1
1855	Wanderer		Mr Dennis	—	J. Hanlon	aged	9.8	20	7	soft	10.25	25-1
	Freetrader	2	Mr W. Barnett	—	Meaney	6	9.4					50-1
	Maurice Daley	4	Mr Cartwright	—	R. James	aged	9.6					20-1
	Janus		Mr Elmore	—	H. Lamplugh	aged	9.10					33-1

Year	Horse	Dist	Owner	Trainer	Jockey	Age	Wt	Ran		Going	Time	SP
1856	**Freetrader**		**Mr W. Barnett**	**W. Holman**	**G. Stevens**	7	9.6	21	6	gd	10.9.5	**25-1**
	Minerva	½	Mr Davenport	—	R. Sly Jr.	6	9.10					25-1
	Minos	4	Mr G. Hobson	—	R. James	aged	9.4					n.q.
	Hopeless Star		Mr Tyler	—	W. White	aged	10.2					25-1
1857	**Emigrant**		**Mr G. Hodgman**	**C. Boyce**	**C. Boyce**	11	9.10	28	8	hy	10.6	**10-1**
	Weathercock	3	Mr B. Land	—	C. Green	6	8.12					25-1
	Treachery	5	Mr T. Hughes	—	Poole	5	9.0					n.q.
	Westminster		Mr T. Hughes	—	Palmer	aged	9.2					n.q.
1858	**Little Charley**		**Mr C. Capel**	**W. Holman**	**W. Archer**	10	10.7	16	5	hy	11.5	**100-6**
	Weathercock	4	Viscount Talon		Mr Edwards	10	10.7					25-1
	Xanthus	50 yards	Mr W.G. Craven	Mr Craven	F. Balchin	aged	11.0					33-1
	Morgan Rattler		Sir E. Hutchinson	—	T. Burrows	aged	10.4					100-6
1859	**Half Caste**		**Mr Willoughby**	**C. Green**	**C. Green**	6	9.7	20	8	gd	10.2	**7-1**
	Jean Du Quesne	a short neck	Count F. de Cunchy	—	H. Lamplugh	aged	9.9					10-1
	Huntsman	1	Mr B. Land	—	B. Land Jr.	6	11.2					100-8
	Midge		Mr J. Garnett	—	D. Meaney	aged	9.4					33-1
1860	**Anatis**		**Mr C. Capel**	**W. Holman**	**Mr Thomas**	10	9.10	19	7	gd	nt	**7-2fav**
	Huntsman	½	Capt. G.W. Hunt		Capt. T.M Townley	7	11.8					33-1
	Xanthus	6	Mr W.G. Craven	Mr W.G. Craven	F. Balchin	aged	10.0					10-1
	Maria Agnes		Mr Golby	—	G. Stevens	6	9.8					10-1
1861	**Jealousy**		**Mr J. Bennett**	**C. Balchin**	**J. Kendall**	7	9.12	24	5	gd	10.14	**5-1**
	The Dane	2	Capt. Christie	—	W. White	5	10.0					33-1
	Old Ben Roe	4	Mr W. Briscoe	—	G. Waddington	aged	10.7					10-1
	Bridegroom		Mr B.J. Angell	—	Mr FitzAdam	aged	10.7					25-1
1862	**Huntsman**		**Viscount de Namur**	**H. Lamplugh**	**H. Lamplugh**	9	11.0	13	5	gd	9.3	**3-1fav**
	Bridegroom	4	Mr B.J. Angell	—	B. Land Jr.	aged	10.13					10-1
	Romeo	20	Mr C. Bennett	—	Mr C. Bennett	aged	8.12					100-8
1863	**Emblem**		**Lord Coventry**	**E. Weever**	**G. Stevens**	7	10.10	16	6	gd	11.2	**4-1**
	Arbury	20	Mr J. Astley	—	Mr A. Goodman	aged	11.2					25-1
	Yaller Girl	2	Mr W. Briscoe	—	Mr Dixon	aged	10.13					20-1
	Fosco		Mr G. Holman	—	Mr G. Holman	aged	9.11					40-1
1864	**Emblematic**		**Lord Coventry**	**E. Weever**	**G. Stevens**	6	10.6	25	5	gd	11.5	**10-1**
	Arbury	3	Mr J. Astley	—	B. Land Jr.	aged	11.12					40-1
	Chester	a dist.	Mr Dalton	—	W. White	aged	10.0					40-1
	Thomastown		Mr T.M. Naghten	—	J. Murphy	aged	12.0					33-1

Year	Horse	Margin	Owner	Trainer	Jockey	Age	Weight	Ran	Fin	Going	Time	Odds
1865	**Alcibiade**		**Mr B.J. Angell**	**Cornell**	**Capt. H. Coventry**	**5**	**11.4**	23	6	hy	11.16	**100-7**
	Hall Court	a head	Capt. J.M. Brown		Capt. A.C. Tempest	6	11.0					50-1
	Emblematic	50 yards	Lord Coventry		G. Stevens	5	11.10					5-1fav
	Mistake		Mr F. Jacobs		Jarvis	5	10.8					n.q.
1866	**Salamander**		**Mr E. Studd**	**J. Walters**	**Mr A. Goodman**	**7**	**10.7**	30	5	hy	11.5	**40-1**
	Cortolvin	10	Lord Poulett		J. Page	7	11.6					8-1
	Creole	4	Mr Welfitt		G. Waddington	aged	10.10					15-1
	Lightheart		Mr A.W. Clayton		E. Jones	aged	11.5					50-1
1867	**Cortolvin**		**Duke of Hamilton**	**H. Lumplugh**	**J. Page**	**8**	**11.13**	23	10	gd	10.42	**100-6**
	Fan	5	Mr Barber		Thorpe	5	10.3					9-1
	Shangarry	4	Mr E. Studd		Mr Thomas'	6	10.13					14-1
	Globule		Mr T.V. Morgan		G. Holman	aged	11.7					14-1
1868	**The Lamb**		**Lord Poulett**	**Ben Land**	**Mr Edwards**	**6**	**10.7**	21	7	hy	10.3	**10-1**
	Pearl Diver	2	Mr E. Brayley		Tomlinson	aged	10.12					9-1
	Alcibiade	10	Mr B.J. Angell		Col. G.W. Knox	8	11.10					16-1
	Captain Crosstree		Mr R. Herbert		W. Reeves	aged	10.5					33-1
1869	**The Colonel**		**Mr J. Weyman**	**R. Roberts**	**G. Stevens**	**6**	**10.7**	22	9	gd	11	**13-1**
	Hall Court	3	Capt. J.M. Brown		Capt. A.C. Tempest	10	10.12					100-1
	Gardener	1	Capt. J. Machell		Ryan	7	10.7					66-1
	Alcibiade		Mr B.J. Angell		Col. G.W. Knox	9	11.2					20-1
1870	**The Colonel**		**Mr M. Evans**	**R. Roberts**	**G. Stevens**	**7**	**11.12**	23	8	gd	10.10	**4-1fav**
	The Doctor	a neck	Mr V. St.John		G. Holman	9	11.7					5-1
	Primrose	5	Mr W.R.Brockton		Mr W.R. Brockton	6	10.12					10-1
	Surney		Mr J.Nightingall		R. I'Anson	aged	10.4					100-8
1871	**The Lamb**		**Lord Poulett**	**C. Green**	**Mr Thomas**	**9**	**11.5**	25	8	gd	9.35.75	**5-1**
	Despatch	2	Mr E. Studd		G. Waddington	8	10.0					10-1
	Scarrington	4	Mr T. Wilkinson		Cranshaw	8	11.4					100-1
	Pearl Diver	a neck	Mr E. Brayley		J. Page	aged	11.5					4-1fav
1872	**Casse Tete**		**Mr E. Brayley**	**A. Cowley**	**J. Page**	**7**	**10.0**	25	9	f	10.14.5	**20-1**
	Scarrington	6	Mr T. Wilkinson		R. I'Anson	9	11.2					100-6
	Despatch	6	Mr E. Studd		G. Waddington	aged	10.4					100-30fav
	The Lamb	2	Baron Oppenheim		Mr Thomas	10	12.7					100-8
1873	**Disturbance**		**Capt. J. Machell**	**Mr J.M. Richardson**	**Mr J.M Richardson**	**6**	**11.11**	28	6	gd	nt	**20-1**
	Ryshworth	6	Mr H. Chaplin		Boxall	7	11.8					8-1
	Columbine	10	Mr W.H.P. Jenkins		Harding	aged	10.9					50-1
	Master Mowbray	a bad fourth	Mr J. Goodliff		G. Holman	aged	10.7					12-1

Year	Horse	Dist	Owner	Trainer	Jockey	Age	Wt			Going	Time	SP
1874	**Reugny**		**Capt. J. Machell**	**J.M. Richardson**	**Mr J.M. Richardson**	**6**	**10.12**	22	8	gd	10.4	**5-1fav**
	Chimney Sweep	6	Lord Marcus Beresford	—	J. Jones	7	10.2					25-1
	Merlin	4	Capt. Thorold	—	J. Adams	aged	10.7					40-1
	Defence	4	Capt. J. Machell	—	Mr Rolly	8	11.13					33-1
1875	**Pathfinder**		**Mr H. Bird**	**W. Reeves**	**Mr Thomas**	**8**	**10.11**	19	8	hy	10.22	**100-6**
	Dainty	½	Mr S. Davis	—	Mr Hathaway	9	11.0					25-1
	La Veine	3	Baron Finot	—	J. Page	5	11.12					6-1fav
	Jackal	a head	Mr H.Baltazzi	—	R. Marsh	5	11.11					7-1
1876	**Regal**		**Capt. J. Machell**	**J. Cannon**	**J. Cannon**	**5**	**11.3**	19	7	gd	11.14	**25-1**
	Congress	a neck	Mr Gomm	—	Mr E.P. Wilson	10	11.8					25-1
	Shifnal	3	Mr J. Nightingall	—	R. I'Anson	7	10.13					25-1
	Chimney Sweep	3	Lord Marcus Beresford	—	J. Jones	9	10.8					25-1
1877	**Austerlitz**		**Mr F.G. Hobson**	**R. l'Anson**	**Mr F.G. Hobson**	**5**	**10.8**	17	7	gd	10.1	**15-1**
	Congress	4	Lord Lonsdale	—	J. Cannon	11	12.7					20-1
	The Liberator	a neck	Mr G. Moore	—	Mr Thomas	8	10.12					25-1
	Chimney Sweep	4	Lord Marcus Beresford	—	J. Jones	10	10.13					7-1
1878	**Shifnal**		**Mr J. Nightingall**	**J. Nightingall**	**J. Jones**	**9**	**10.12**	12	7	gd	10.23	**100-15**
	Martha	2	Capt. A.Crofton	—	Mr T. Beasley	7	10.9					20-1
	Pride of Kildare	10	Capt. Bates	—	Mr G. Moore	7	11.7					6-1
1879	**The Liberator**		**Mr G. Moore**	**J.H. Moore**	**Mr G. Moore**	**10**	**11.4**	18	10	gd	10.12	**5-1**
	Jackal	10	Lord Marcus Beresford	—	J. Jones	11	11.0					1000-65
	Martha	2	Mr Oeschlaeger	—	Mr T. Beasley	8	10.13					50-1
	Wild Monarch	½	Marquis de St. Sauveur	—	Andrews	8	11.7					20-1
1880	**Empress**		**Mr P. Ducrot**	**H.E. Linde**	**Mr T. Beasley**	**5**	**10.7**	14	10	gd	10.2	**8-1**
	The Liberator	2	Mr G. Moore	—	Mr G. Moore	11	12.7					11-2
	Downpatrick	a head	Col. Lloyd	—	P. Gavin	6	10.7					100-15
1881	**Woodbrook**		**Capt.T.Y.L. Kirkwood**	**H.E. Linde**	**Mr T. Beasley**	**7**	**11.3**	13	9	hy	11.5	**11-2jtfav**
	Regal	4	Capt. J. Machell	—	J. Jewitt	10	11.12					11-1
	Thornfield	a bad third	Mr Leopold de Rothschild	—	R. Marsh	5	10.9					11-2jtfav
1882	**Seaman**		**Lord Manners**	**J. Jewitt**	**Lord Manners**	**6**	**11.6**	12	3	hy	10.42.2/5	**10-1**
	Cyrus	a head	Mr J. Gubbins	—	Mr T. Beasley	5	10.9					9-2
	Zoedone	a bad third	Mr E.C. Clayton	—	Capt. A.J. Smith	5	10.0					25-1
1883	**Zoedone**		**Count C. Kinsky**	**W.H.P. Jenkins**	**Count C. Kinsky**	**6**	**11.0**	10	7	hy	11.39	**100-8**
	Black Prince	10	Mr P. George	—	D. Canavan	8	10.4					33-1
	Mohican	6	Major Bunbury	—	Mr H. Beasley	6	12.1					9-1

1884	**Voluptuary**		**Mr H.F. Boyd**	**Mr E.P. & W. Wilson**	**Mr E. P. Wilson**	**6**	**10.5**	**15**	**6**	**hy**	**10.5**	**10-1**
	Frigate	4	Mr M.A. Maher	—	Mr H. Beasley	6	11.3					10-1
	Roquefort	6	Capt. Fisher-Childe	—	J. Childs	5	10.5					10-1
1885	**Roquefort**		**Mr A. Cooper**	**A. Yates**	**Mr E.P. Wilson**	**6**	**11.0**	**19**	**9**	**gd**		**100-30 fav**
	Frigate	2	Mr M.A. Maher	—	Mr H. Beasley	7	11.10					7-1
	Black Prince	4	Capt. J. Machell	—	T. Skelton	10	10.5					33-1
	Redpath	2	Mr Zigomala	—	Mr A. Coventry	10	10.5					20-1
1886	**Old Joe**		**Mr A.J. Douglas**	**G. Mulcaster**	**T. Skelton**	**7**	**10.9**	**23**	**8**	**gd**	**10.14 3/5**	**25-1**
	Too Good	6	Count Erdody	—	Mr H. Beasley	7	11.12					7-1
	Gamecock	5	Mr E. Jay	—	W. E. Stephens	7	10.12					50-1
	Magpie	4	Mr E. Woodland	—	Mr W. Woodland	7	10.5					200-1
1887	**Gamecock**		**Mr E. Jay**	**J. Gordon**	**W. Daniels**	**8**	**11.0**	**16**	**6**	**gd**	**10.10 1/5**	**20 1**
	Savoyard	3	Baron W. Schoder	—	T. Skelton	9	10.13					100-14
	Johnny Longtail	a bad third	Lord Wolverton	—	J. Childs	9	10.6					40-1
	Chancellor		Capt. Foster	—	Mr W.H. Moore	7	10.12					20 1
1888	**Playfair**		**Mr E.W. Baird**	**T. Cannon**	**G. Mawson**	**7**	**10.7**	**20**	**9**	**gd**	**10.12**	**40-1**
	Frigate	10	Mr M.A. Maher	—	Mr W. Beasley	10	11.2					100-9
	Ballot Box	4	Mr P. Nickalls	—	W. Nightingall	9	12.4					25 1
	Ringlet	1	Lord Rodney	—	T. Skelton	7	11.11					100-9
1889	**Frigate**		**Mr M.A. Maher**	**Mr M.A. Maher**	**Mr T. Beasley**	**11**	**11.4**	**20**	**10**	**gd**	**10.1 1/5**	**8 1**
	Why Not	1	Mr D. Jardine	—	Mr C.J. Cunningham	8	11.5					100-9
	M.P.	a bad third	Mr J. Rutherford	—	A. Nightingall	8	10.9					20 1
	Bellona		Mr Abington	—	Mr C. W. Waller	7	11.2					20 1
1890	**Ilex**		**Mr G. Masterman**	**J. Nightingall**	**A. Nightingall**	**6**	**10.5**	**16**	**6**	**gd**	**10.41 1/5**	**4-1fav**
	Pan	12	Mr E. Woodland	—	W. Halsey	7	10.5					100-1
	M.P.	a bad third	Mr J. Rutherford	—	Mr W.H. Moore	9	11.5					8-1
	Brunswick		Mr Lancashire	—	G. Mawson	6	10.4					100-1
1891	**Come Away**		**Mr W.G. Jameson**	**H. Beasley**	**Mr H. Beasley**	**7**	**11.12**	**21**	**6**	**gd**	**9. 58**	**4-1fav**
	Cloister	½	Lord Dudley	—	Capt. E.R. Owen	7	11.7					20-1
	Ilex	a bad third	Mr G. Masterman	—	A. Nightingall	7	12.3					5-1
	Roquefort		Mr A. Yates	—	F. Guy	12	11.13					40-1
1892	**Father O'Flynn**		**Mr G.C. Wilson**	**G.C. Wilson**	**Capt. E.T. Owen**	**7**	**10.5**	**25**	**11**	**gd**	**9.48 1/5**	**20 -1**
	Cloister	20	Mr C.G. Duff	—	Mr J.C. Dormer	8	12.3					11-2
	Ilex	2	Mr G. Masterman	—	A. Nightingall	8	12.7					20-1
	Ardcarn		Major Kirkwood	—	T. Kavanagh	5	10.10					10-1

1893	**Cloister**		**Mr C.G. Duff**	**Arthur Yates**	**W. Dollery**	**9**	**12.7**	**15**	**8**	**f**	**$9.32\frac{2}{5}$**	**9-2 fav**
	Aesop	40	Capt. Michael Hughes	—	A.H. Barker	7	10.4					100-12
	Why Not	a bad third	Capt. C.H. Fenwick	—	A. Nightingall	12	11.12					5-1
1894	**Why Not**		**Capt C.H. Fenwick**	**W. H. Moore**	**A. Nightingall**	**13**	**11.13**	**14**	**9**	**gd**	**$9.45\frac{2}{5}$**	**5-1 jtfav**
	Lady Ellen II	1½	Mr J. McKinlay		T. Kavanagh	6	9.10					25-1
	Wild Man From Borneo	a head	Mr John Widger	—	Mr Joseph Widger	6	10.9					40-1
1895	**Wild Man From Borneo**		**Mr John Widger**	**James Gatland**	**Mr Joseph Widger**	**7**	**10.11**	**19**	**11**	**hy**	**10.32**	**10-1**
	Cathal	1½	Mr F.B. Atkinson	—	H. Escott	6	10.9					100-8
	Van Der Berg	a bad third	Major A. Crawley	—	W.A. Dollery	9	9.13					25-1
	Manifesto		Mr H.M. Dyas	—	T. Kavanagh	7	11.2					100-8
1896	**The Soarer**		**Mr W. Hall-Walker**	**W.H. Moore**	**Mr D.G.M. Campbell**	**7**	**9.13**	**28**	**9**	**gd**	**$10.11\frac{1}{5}$**	**40-1**
	Father O'Flynn	1½	Mr C. Grenfell	—	Mr C. Grenfell	11	10.12					40-1
	Biscuit	1½	Mr W.C. Keeping	—	E. Matthews	8	10.0					25 1
	Barcalwhey		Capt. A.E. Whitaker	—	C. Hogan	6	9.8					1000-30
1897	**Manifesto**		**Mr H.M. Dyas**	**W. McAuliffe**	**T. Kavanagh**	**9**	**11.3**	**28**	**10**	**gd**	**9. 49**	**6-1fav**
	Filbert	20	Mr G.R. Powell	—	Mr C. Beatty	7	9.7					100-1
	Ford Of Fyne	a head	Major J.A. Orr-Ewing	—	Mr F. Withington	6	10.7					25-1
	Prince Albert		Mr J.S. Forbes	—	Mr G.S. Davies	9	10.8					25-1
1898	**Drogheda**		**Mr C.G.M Adams**	**Mr E. Woods**	**J. Gourley**	**6**	**10.12**	**25**	**10**	**hy**	**$9.43\frac{3}{5}$**	**25-1**
	Cathal	3	Mr R. Ward	—	Mr Reginald Ward	9	11.5					7-1
	Gauntlet	4	Mr F. D. Leyland	—	W. Taylor	7	10.13					100-12
	Filbert		Mr G. R. Powell	—	Mr C. Beatty	8	9.12					25-1
1899	**Manifesto**		**Mr J.G. Bulteel**	**W.H. Moore**	**G. Williamson**	**11**	**12.7**	**19**	**11**	**gd**	**$9.49\frac{4}{5}$**	**5-1**
	Ford Of Fyne	5	Major J.A. Orr-Ewing	—	E. Matthews	8	10.10					40-1
	Elliman	2	Mr Audley Blyth	—	E. Piggott	8	10.1					20-1
	Dead Level		Mr J.C. Dormer	—	F. Mason	7	10.6					33-1
1900	**Ambush II**		**The Prince of Wales**	**Algy Anthony**	**A. Anthony**	**6**	**11.3**	**16**	**11**	**gd**	**$10.1\frac{2}{5}$**	**4-1**
	Barsac	4	Mr C.A. Brown	—	W. Halsey	8	9.12					25-1
	Manifesto	a neck	Mr J.G. Bulteel	—	G. Williamson	12	12.13					6-1
	Breemount's Pride		Mr G. Edwardes	—	Mr G.S. Davies	7	11.7					20-1
1901	**Grudon**		**Mr B. Bletsoe**	**B. Bletsoe**	**A. Nightingall**	**11**	**10.0**	**24**	**9**	**hy**	**$9.47\frac{4}{5}$**	**9-1**
	Drumcree	4	Mr O.J. Williams	—	Mr H. Nugent	7	9.12					10-1
	Buffalo Bill	6	Mr J.E. Rogerson	—	H. Taylor	7	9.7					33-1
	Levanter		Mr J.D. Edwards	—	F. Mason	aged	9.10					5-1fav

1902	**Shannon Lass**		**Mr A. Gorham**	**James Hackett**	**D. Read**	**7**	**10.1**	**21**	**11**	**hy**	**10. 3$\frac{3}{5}$**	**20-1**
	Matthew	3	Mr John Widger	—	W. Morgan	6	9.12					50-1
	Manifesto	3	Mr J.G. Bulteel	—	E. Piggott	14	12.8					100-6
	Detail		Mr White-Heather	—	A. Nightingall	6	9.9.					25-1
1903	**Drumcree**		**Mr J.S. Morrison**	**Sir Charles Nugent**	**P. Woodland**	**9**	**11.3**	**23**	**7**	**gd**	**10. 9$\frac{2}{5}$**	**13-2fav**
	Detail	3	Mr White-Heather	—	A. Nightingall	7	9.13					100-14
	Manifesto	20	Mr J.G. Bulteel	—	G. Williamson	15	12.3					25 1
	Kirkland	a head	Mr F. Bibby	—	F. Mason	7	10.8					100-8
1904	**Moifaa**		**Mr Spencer Gollan**	**W. Hickey**	**A. Birch**	**8**	**10.7**	**26**	**8**	**gd**	**9. 58$\frac{3}{5}$**	**25-1**
	Kirkland	8	Mr F. Bibby	—	F. Mason	8	10.10					100-7
	The Gunner	a neck	Mr John Widger	—	Mr J. W. Widger	7	10.4					25-1
	Shaun Aboo		Major J.D. Edwards	—	A. Waddington	6	10.1					n.q.
1905	**Kirkland**		**Mr F. Bibby**	**Lort Phillips**	**F. Mason**	**9**	**11.5**	**27**	**7**	**gd**	**9. 48$\frac{4}{5}$**	**6-1**
	Napper Tandy	3	Capt. McLaren	—	P. Woodland	8	10.0					25-1
	Buckaway II	4	Mr P.E. Speakman	—	A. Newey	7	9.11					100-1
	Ranunculus		Mr T. Nolan	—	C. Hollebone	7	9.12					7-1
1906	**Ascetic's Silver**		**Prince Hatzfeldt**	**Aubrey Hastings**	**Mr A. Hastings**	**9**	**10.9**	**23**	**9**	**gd**	**9. 34$\frac{4}{5}$**	**20-1**
	Red Lad	10	Mr E. M. Lucas	—	C. Kelly	6	10.2					33-1
	Aunt May	2	Mr B.W. Parr	—	Mr H.S. Persse	10	11.2					25 1
	Crautacaun		Mr J. Wynford Philipps	—	Ivor Anthony	8	10.6					100-6
1907	**Eremon**		**Mr S. Howard**	**Tom Coulthwaite**	**A. Newey**	**7**	**10.1**	**23**	**8**	**gd**	**9. 47$\frac{1}{2}$**	**8-1**
	Tome West	6	Mr H. Hardy	—	H. Murphy	8	9.12					100-6
	Patlander	a neck	Mr W. Nelson	—	J. Lynn	11	10.7					n.q.
	Ravensciffe		Mr R.J. Hannam	—	F. Lyall	9	10.9					100-7
1908	**Rubio**		**Major F. Douglas-Pennant**	**Fred Withington**	**H.B. Bletsoe**	**10**	**10.5**	**24**	**8**	**hy**	**10. 33$\frac{1}{5}$**	**66-1**
	Mattie MacGregor	10	Mr W.C. Cooper	—	W. Bissill	6	10.6					25-1
	The Lawyer III	6	Mr P. Whitaker	—	Mr P. Whitaker	11	10.3					100-7
	Flaxman		H.M. King Edward VII	A. Anthony		8	9.12					33-1
1909	**Lutteur III**		**M. James Hennessy**	**H. Escott**	**G. Parfrement**	**5**	**10.11**	**32**	**16**	**gd**	**9. 53$\frac{1}{5}$**	**100-9 jt.fav**
	Judas	2	Mr B.W. Parr	—	R. Chadwick	8	10.10					33-1
	Caubeen	a bad third	Mr F. Bibby	—	F. Mason	8	11.7					20-1
	Tom West		Mr H. Hardy	—	H. Murphy	10	10.9					100-6
1910	**Jenkinstown**		**Mr Stanley Howard**	**Tom Coulthwaite**	**R. Chadwick**	**9**	**10.5**	**25**	**5**	**gd**	**10. 44$\frac{1}{5}$**	**100-8**
	Jerry M	3	Mr C.G. Assheton-Smith	—	E. Driscoll	7	12.7					6-1fav
	Odor	3	Mr R.H. Hall	—	Mr R.H. Hall	9	9.8					n.q.
	Carsey		Prince Hatzfeldt	—	E.R. Morgan Jnr	7	10.7					100-8

1911	**Glenside**		**Mr F. Bibby**	**Capt. R.H. Collis**	**Mr J.R. Anthony**	**9**	**10.3**	**26**	**4**	**hy**	**10.35**	**20 1**
	Rathnally*	20	Mr O.H. Jones	—	R. Chadwick	6	11.0					8-1
	Shady Girl*	3	Mr P. Nelke	—	G. Clancy	10	10.5					33-1
	Fool-Hardy*		Mr W. Macneill	—	Mr W. Macneill	10	9.7					50-1
1912	**Jerry M**		**Sir C. Assheton-Smith**	**Robert Gore**	**E. Piggott**	**9**	**12.7**	**24**	**7**	**gd**		**4-1 jtfav**
	Bloodstone	6	Mr C. Bower Ismay	—	F. Lyall	10	11.6					40-1
	Axle Pin	4	Lord Derby	—	Ivor Anthony	8	10.4					20 1
	Carsey		Mr C.H. Wildenburg	—	Mr H.W. Tyrwhitt-Drake	9	10.13					100-8
1913	**Covertcoat**		**Sir C. Assheton-Smith**	**Robert Gore**	**P. Woodland**	**7**	**11.6**	**22**	**3**	**gd**	**10. 19**	**100-9**
	Irish Mail	a dist.	Mr W.T. Drake	—	Mr Owen Anthony	6	11.4					25-1
	Carsey*	a dist.	Mr C.H. Wildenburg	—	Mr H.W. Tyrwhitt-Drake	10	12.0					100-9
1914	**Sunloch**		**Mr T. Tyler**	**Tom Tyler**	**W.J. Smith**	**8**	**9.7**	**20**	**4**	**gd**	**9. 58⅘**	**100-6**
	Trianon III	8	Mr H de Mumm	—	C. Hawkins	9	11.9					100-8
	Lutteur III	8	M. James Hennessy	—	A. Carter	10	12.6					10-1
	Rory O'Moore		Mr P. Whitaker	—	Mr P. Whitaker	13	11.8					20-1
1915	**Ally Soper**		**Lady Nelson**	**Aubrey Hastings**	**Mr J.R. Anthony**	**6**	**10.6**	**20**	**5**	**gd**	**9. 47⅘**	**100-8**
	Jacobus	2	Mr C. Bower Ismay	—	A. Newey	8	11.0					25-1
	Father Confessor	8	or Lord Suffolk	—	A. Aylin	6	9.10					10-1
	Alfred Noble		Mr T.H. Barnard	—	T. Hulme	11	10.12					25-1
1916-18 WARTIME SUBSTITUTE NATIONALS HELD AT GATWICK												
1919	**Poethlyn**		**Mrs Hugh Peel**	**Harry Escott**	**E. Piggott**	**9**	**12.7**	**22**	**7**	**gd**	**10.8⅖**	**11-4 fav**
	Ballyboggan	8	Mr E.W. Hope-Johnstone	—	W. Head	8	11.10					9-1
	Pollen	6	Mr J.L. Dugdale	—	A. Escott	10	11.4					100-7
	Loch Allen		Mr V. Stewart	—	J. Kelly	8	10.0					33-1
1920	**Troytown**		**Major T.G.C. Gerrard**	**Algy Anthony**	**Mr J.R. Anthony**	**7**	**11.9**	**24**	**5**	**hy**	**10. 20⅖**	**6-1**
	The Turk II	12	Mr C.L. Willcox	—	R. Burford	10	9.8					n.q.
	The Bore	6	Mr H.A. Brown	—	Mr H.A. Brown	9	10.1					28 1
	Sergeant Murphy		Mr M.H. Benson	—	W. Smith	10	10.1					100-7
1921	**Shaun Spadah**		**Mr T.M. McAlpine**	**George Poole**	**F.B. Rees**	**10**	**11.7**	**35**	**4**	**hy**	**10. 26**	**100-9**
	The Bore*	a dist.	Mr H.A. Brown	—	Mr H.A. Brown	10	11.8					9-1fav
	All White*	a bad third	Lord Wavertree	—	R. Chadwick	7	10. 13					30-1
	Turkey Buzzard*		Mrs H.M. Hollins	—	Capt. G.H. Bennet	8	12.2					100-9
1922	**Music Hall**		**Mr H. Kershaw**	**Owen Anthony**	**L.B. Rees**	**9**	**11.8**	**32**	**5**	**gd**	**9. 55⅘**	**100-9**
	Drifter	12	Mr Joseph Widger	—	W. Watkinson	8	10.0					18-1
	Taffytus	6	Mr J.C. Bulteel	—	T.E. Leader	9	11.0					66-1
	Sergeant Murphy*		Mr S. Sanford	—	C. Hawkins	12	11.0					100-6

Year	Horse	Dist	Owner	Trainer	Jockey	Age	Weight	Ran	Pos	Going	Time	Odds
1923	**Sergeant Murphy**		**Mr S. Sanford**	**George Blackwell**	**Capt. G.H. Bennet**	13	11.3	28	7	gd	9.36	100-6
	Shaun Spadah	3	Sir M. McAlpine	—	F.B. Rees	12	12.7					20-1
	Conjuror II	6	Major C Dewhurst	—	Mr C.P. Dewhurst	11	11.0					100-6
	Punt Gun		Mrs J. Putnam	—	M. Tighe	10	11.1					20 1
1924	**Master Robert**		**Lord Airlie**	**Aubrey Hastings**	**R. Trudgill**	11	10.5	30	8	gd	9.4	25 1
	Fly Mask	4	Mr T.K. Laidlaw		J. Moylan	10	10.12					100-7
	Silvo	6	Mr W.H. Midwood		G. Goswell	8	12.2					100-7
	Drifter		Mr S.Sanford		G. Calder	10	10.5					40-1
1925	**Double Chance**		**Mr D. Goold**	**Fred Archer**	**Major J.P. Wilson**	9	10.9	33	10	gd	9.42 1/5	100-9
	Old Tay Bridge	4	Mrs W.H. Dixon		J.R. Anthony	11	11.12					9-1fav
	Fly Mask	6	Mr T.K. Laidlaw		E. Doyle	11	11.11					10-1
	Sprig		Mrs M. Partridge		T.E. Leader	8	11.2					33-1
1926	**Jack Horner**		**Mr A.C. Schwartz**	**Harvey Leader**	**W. Watkinson**	9	10.5	30	13	gd	9.36	25-1
	Old Tay Bridge	3	Mrs W.H. Dixon		J. R. Anthony	12	12.2					8-1
	Bright's Boy	1	Mr S. Sanford		E. Doyle	7	11.8					25-1
	Sprig		Mrs M. Partridge		T. E. Leader	9	11.7					5-1fav
1927	**Sprig**		**Mrs M. Partridge**	**Tom Leader**	**T. E. Leader**	10	12.4	37	7	hy	10.20 1/5	8-1fav
	Bovril III	1	Mr G.W. Pennington		Mr G.W. Pennington	9	10.12					100-1
	Bright's Boy	1	Mr S. Sanford		J.R. Anthony	8	12.7					100-7
	Drinmond		Mr G. Balding		Mr J.B. Balding	10	11.2					66-1
1928	**Tipperary Tim**		**Mr H.S. Kenyon**	**Joseph Dodd**	**Mr W.P. Dutton**	10	10.0	42	2	hy	10.23 1/5	100-1
	Billy Barton *	a dist.	Mr Howard Bruce		T.B. Cullinan	10	10.11					33-1
1929	**Gregalach**		**Mrs M.A.Gemmell**	**Tom Leader**	**R. Everett**	7	11.4	66	10	gd	9.47 1/5	100-1
	Easter Hero	6	Mr H.H. Whitney		J. Moloney	9	12.7					9-1fav
	Richmond II	a bad third	Mr R. McAlpine		W. Stott	6	10.6					40-1
	Melleray's Belle		Mr W. Wilson		J. Mason	10	10.2					200-1
1930	**Shaun Goilin**		**Mr W.H. Midwood**	**Frank Hartigan**	**T. Cullinan**	10	11.7	41	6	gd	9.40 1/5	100-8
	Melleray's Belle	a neck	Mr W. Wilson		J. Mason	11	10.0					20-1
	Sir Lindsay	1 1/2	Mr J.H. Whitney		D. Williams	9	10.6					100-7
	Glangesia		Mr R.K. Mellon		J. Browne	10	10.4					33-1
1931	**Grakle**		**Mr C.R. Taylor**	**Tom Coulthwaite**	**R. Lyall**	9	11.7	43	9	gd	9.32 1/5	100-6
	Gregalach	1 1/2	Mrs M.A.Gemmell		J. Moloney	9	12.0					25-1
	Annandale	10	Lady Glenapp		T. Morgan	9	10.7					100-1
	Rhyticere		Mr V. Emanuel		L. Niaudot	aged	10.12					50-1

566

1932	**Forbra**		**Mr W. Parsonage**	**T.R. Rimell**	**J. Hamey**	**7**	**10.7**	**36**	**8**	**gd**	**9. 44$\frac{3}{5}$**	**50-1**
	Egremont	3	Mrs Ireland	—	Mr E.C. Paget	8	10.7					33-1
	Shaun Goilin	a bad third	Mr W.H. Midwood	—	D. Williams	12	12.4					40-1
	Near East		Mr H. B. Brandt	—	T. McCarthy	7	10.10					50-1
1933	**Kellsboro' Jack**		**Mrs F. Ambrose Clark**	**Ivor Anthony**	**D. Williams**	**7**	**11.9**	**34**	**19**	**g/f**	**9. 28**	**25 1**
	Really True	3	Major Noel Furlong	—	Mr F. Furlong	9	10. 12					66-1
	Slater	a neck	Mr G.S.L. Whitelaw	—	Mr M. Barry	8	10.7					50-1
	Delaneige		Mr J.B. Snow	—	J. Moloney	8	11.3					20-1
1934	**Golden Miller**		**Miss Dorothy Paget**	**Basil Briscoe**	**G. Wilson**	**7**	**12.2**	**30**	**8**	**g/f**	**9. 20$\frac{2}{5}$**	**8-1**
	Delaneige	5	Mr J.B. Snow	—	J. Moloney	9	11.6					100-7
	Thomond II	5	Mr J.H. Whitney	—	W. Speck	8	12.4					18-1
	Forbra		Mr W. Parsonage	—	G. Hardy	9	11.7					100-8
1935	**Reynoldstown**		**Major Noel Furlong**	**Major Noel Furlong**	**Mr F. Furlong**	**8**	**11.4**	**27**	**6**	**g/f**	**9. 20$\frac{1}{5}$**	**22-1**
	Blue Prince	3	Lady Lindsay	—	W. Parvin	7	10.7					40-1
	Thomond II	8	Mr J.H. Whitney	—	W. Speck	9	11.13					9-2
	Lazy Boots		Sir Geoffrey Congreve	—	G. Owen	9	10.7					100-1
1936	**Reynoldstown**		**Major Noel Furlong**	**Major Noel Furlong**	**Mr F. Walwyn**	**9**	**12.2**	**35**	**10**	**gd**	**9. 37$\frac{4}{5}$**	**10-1**
	Ego	12	Sir David Llewellyn	—	Mr H. Llewellyn	9	10.8					50-1
	Bachelor Prince	6	Mr J.V. Rank	—	J. Fawcus	9	10.9					66-1
	Crown Prince		Mr R. Strutt	—	Mr R. Strutt	11	10.7					66-1
1937	**Royal Mail**		**Mr H. Lloyd Thomas**	**Ivor Anthony**	**E. Williams**	**8**	**11.13**	**33**	**7**	**s**	**9. 59$\frac{4}{5}$**	**100-6**
	Cooleen	3	Mr J.V. Rank	—	J. Fawcus	9	11.4					33-1
	Pucka Belle	10	Mr E.W.W. Bailey	—	Mr E.W.W. Bailey	11	10.7					100-6
	Ego		Sir David Llewellyn	—	Mr H. Llewellyn	10	10.9					10-1
1938	**Battleship**		**Mrs Marion Scott**	**Reg Hobbs**	**B. Hobbs**	**11**	**11.6**	**36**	**13**	**g/f**	**9. 27**	**40-1**
	Royal Danieli	a head	Mr H.C. McNally	—	D. Moore	7	11.3					18-1
	Workman	a bad third	Sir Alexander Maguire	—	J. Brogan	8	10.2					28-1
	Cooleen		Mr J.V. Rank	—	J. Fawcus	10	11.8					8-1 jtfav
1939	**Workman**		**Sir Alexander Maguire**	**Jack Ruttle**	**T. Hyde**	**9**	**10.6**	**37**	**11**	**gd**	**9. 42$\frac{1}{5}$**	**100-8**
	MacMoffat	3	Capt.L. Scott Briggs	—	I. Alder	7	10.3					25-1
	Kilstar	15	Miss Dorothy Paget	—	G. Archibald	8	10.3					8-1fav
	Cooleen		Mr J.V. Rank	—	J. Fawcus	11	11.8					22-1
1940	**Bogskar**		**Lord Stalbridge**	**Lord Stalbridge**	**M.A. Jones**	**7**	**10.4**	**30**	**17**	**g/f**	**9. 20$\frac{3}{5}$**	**25-1**
	MacMoffat	4	Capt L. Scott Briggs	—	I. Alder	8	10.10					8-1
	Gold Arrow	6	Mr J.R. Neill	—	P. Lay	8	10.3					50-1
	Symaethis		Mr T. Westhead	—	M. Feakes	8	10.7					100-6

1941-1945 WAR YEARS NO RACE

1946	**Lovely Cottage**		**Mr. J. Morant**	**Tommy Rayson**	**Capt. R. Petre**	**9**	**10.8**	**34**	**6**	**gd**	**9. 38⅕**	**25-1**
	Jack Finlay	4	Mr L.S. Elwell	—	W. Kidney	7	10.2					100-1
	Prince Regent	3	Mr J.V. Rank	—	T. Hyde	11	12.5					3-1fav
	Housewarmer		Miss Dorothy Paget	—	A. Brabazon	9	10.2					100-1
1947	**Caughoo**		**Mr J.J. McDowell**	**Herbert McDowell**	**E. Dempsey**	**8**	**10.0**	**57**	**21**	**hy**	**10. 3⅕**	**100-1**
	Lough Conn	20	Mrs M. Rowe	—	D. McCann	11	10.1					33-1
	Kami	4	Sir Allan Gordon Smith	—	Mr J. Hislop	10	10.13					33-1
	Prince Regent		Mr J.V. Rank	—	T. Hyde	12	12.7					8-1fav
1948	**Sheila's Cottage**		**Mr J. Procter**	**Neville Crump**	**A.P. Thompson**	**9**	**10.7**	**43**	**14**	**g/f**	**9. 25⅗**	**50-1**
	First Of The Dandies	1	Major D.J. Vaughan	—	J. Brogan	11	10.4					25-1
	Cromwell	6	Lord Mildmay	—	Lord Mildmay	7	10.11					33-1
	Happy Home		Miss D. Paget	—	G. Kelly	9	11.10					33-1
1949	**Russian Hero**		**Mr W.F. Williamson**	**George Owen**	**L. McMorrow**	**9**	**10.8**	**43**	**11**	**g/f**	**9. 24⅕**	**66-1**
	Roimond	8	Lord Bicester	—	R. Francis	8	11.12					22 1
	Royal Mount	1	Mrs May Harvey	—	P.J. Doyle	10	10.12					18 1
	Cromwell		Lord Mildmay	—	Lord Mildmay	8	11.3					6-1fav
1950	**Freebooter**		**Mrs L. Brotherton**	**Robert Renton**	**J. Power**	**9**	**11.11**	**49**	**7**	**g/f**	**9. 24⅕**	**10-1jtfav**
	Wot No Sun	15	Major T.D. Wilson	—	A.P. Thompson	8	11.8					100-7
	Acthon Major	10	Mrs J.S. Gorman	—	R.J. O'Ryan	10	11.2					33-1
	Rowland Roy		Mr A.G. Boley	—	R. Black	11	11.7					40-1
1951	**Nickel Coin**		**Mr J. Royle**	**Jack O'Donaghue**	**J.A. Bullock**	**9**	**10.1**	**36**	**3**	**s**	**9. 48⅘**	**40-1**
	Royal Tan	6	Mrs M.H. Keogh	—	Mr A.S. O'Brien	7	10.13					22-1
	Derringtown *	a bad third	Mr P. Digney	—	A. Power	11	10.0					66-1
1952	**Teal**		**Mr H. Lane**	**Neville Crump**	**A. P. Thompson**	**10**	**10.12**	**47**	**10**	**g/f**	**9. 21½**	**100-7**
	Legal Joy	5	Mrs D. Paget	—	M. Scudamore	9	10.4					100-6
	Wot No Sun	a bad third	Major T.D. Wilson	—	D.V. Dick	10	11.7					33-1
	Uncle Barney		Mr L. Michaelson	—	J. Boddy	9	10.4					100-1
1953	**Early Mist**		**Mr J.H. Griffin**	**Vincent O'Brien**	B. Marshall	8	11.2	31	5	gd	9. 22⅘	20-1
	Mont Tremblant	20	Miss D. Paget	—	D.V. Dick	7	12.5					18-1
	Irish Lizard	4	Lord Sefton	—	R. Turnell	10	10.6					33-1
	Overshadow		Mrs J.A. Wood	—	P. Taaffe	13	10.4					33-1

1954	**Royal Tan**		**Mr J.H. Griffin**	**Vincent O'Brien**	**B. Marshall**	**1.**	**11.7**	**29**	**9**	**s**	**9. 32 4/5**	**8-1**
	Tudor Line	a neck	Mrs E. Truelove	—	G. Slack	9	10.7					10-1
	Irish Lizard	10	Lord Sefton	—	M. Scudamore	11	10.5					15-2 fav
	Churchtown		Mrs M.V. O'Brien	—	T. Taaffe	9	10.3					10-1
1955	**Quare Times**		**Mrs W.H.E. Welman**	**Vincent O'Brien**	**P. Taaffe**	**9**	**11. 0**	**30**	**13**	**hy**	**10. 19 1/5**	**100-9**
	Tudor Line	12	Mrs E. Truelove	—	G. Slack	10	11.3					10-1
	Carey's Cottage	4	Mrs D.J. Coughlan	—	T. Taaffe	8	10.11					20-1
	Gigolo		Mrs M.Milne Green	—	R. Curran	10	11.3					100-6
1956	**E.S.B.**		**Mrs L. Carver**	**Fred Rimell**	**D.V. Dick**	**10**	**11.3**	**29**	**9**	**gd**	**9. 21 1/5**	**100-7**
	Gentle Moya	10	Mr J.J. Straker	—	G. Milburn	10	10.2					22-1
	Royal Tan	10	Prince Aly Khan	—	T. Taaffe	12	12.1					28-1
	Eagle Lodge		Mr N.A. Mardon	—	A. Oughton	7	10.1					66-1
1957	**Sundew**		**Mrs G. Kohn**	**Frank Hudson**	**F.T. Winter**	**11**	**11. 7**	**35**	**11**	**g/s**	**9. 42 2/5**	**20-1**
	Wyndburgh	8	Miss R.M.P. Wilkinson	—	M. Batchelor	7	10.7					25-1
	Tiberetta	6	Mr E. R. Courage	—	A. Oughton	9	10.0					66-1
	Glorious Twelfth		Mr H.J. Joel	—	R. Wilkinson	8	11.1					100-8
1958	**Mr What**		**Mr D.J.Coughlan**	**Tom Taaffe**	**A. Freeman**	**8**	**10.6**	**31**	**7**	**hy**	**9.59 4/5**	**18-1**
	Tiberetta	30	Mr E.R. Courage	—	G. Stack	10	10.6					28-1
	Green Drill	15	Lord Cadogan	—	G. Milburn	8	10.10					28-1
	Wyndburgh		Miss R.M.P. Wilkinson	—	M. Batchelor	6	11.3					6-1fav
1959	**Oxo**		**Mr J.E. Bigg**	**Willie Stephenson**	**M.Scudamore**	**8**	**10.13**	**34**	**4**	**gd**	**9.37 4/5**	**8-1**
	Wyndburgh	1½	Mrs J.K.M. Oliver	—	T. Brookshaw	9	10.12					10-1
	Mr What	8	Mr D.J.Coughlan	—	T. Taaffe	9	11.9					6-1fav
	Tiberetta		Mr E.R. Courage	—	A. Oughton	11	10.9					20 1
1960	**Merryman II**		**Miss W.H.S. Wallace**	**Neville Crump**	**G. Scott**	**9**	**10.12**	**26**	**8**	**gd**	**9.26 1/5**	**13-2fav**
	Badanloch	15	Lord Leverhulme	—	S. Mellor	9	10.9					100-7
	Clear Profit	12	Mr B. Sunley	—	B. Wilkinson	10	10.1					20-1
	Tea Friend		Mr J.D. Pickering	—	P.G. Madden	11	10.0					33-1
1961	**Nicolaus Silver**		**Mr C. Vaughan**	**Fred Rimell**	**H.R. Beasley**	**9**	**10.1**	**35**	**14**	**f**	**9 22 3/5**	**28-1**
	Merryman II	5	Miss W.H.S. Wallace	—	D. Ancil	10	11.12					8-1
	O'Malley Point	a neck	Mr A. Elliott	—	P.A. Farrell	10	11.4					100-6
	Scottish Flight II		Mrs A.T. Hodgson	—	W. Rees	9	10.6					100-6
1962	**Kilmore**		**Mr N. Cohen**	**Ryan Price**	**F.T. Winter**	**12**	**10.4**	**32**	**17**	**hy**	**9.50**	**28-1**
	Wyndburgh	10	Mrs J.K.M. Oliver	—	T.A. Barnes	12	10.9					45-1
	Mr What	10	Mr G.V. Keeling	—	J. Lehane	12	10.9					22-1
	Gay Navarree		Mr J.F. Hoey	—	Mr A. Cameron	10	10.0					100-1

1963	**Ayala**		**Mr P.B. Raymond**	**Keith Piggott**	**P. Buckley**	**9**	**10.0**	**47**	**22**	**s**	**9.35 4/5**	**66-1**
	Carrickbeg	3/4	Mr G. Kindersley	—	Mr J. Lawrence	7	10.3					20-1
	Hawa's Song	5	Mr W. Stephenson	—	P. Broderick	10	10.0					28-1
	Team Spirit		Mr R.B. Woodard	—	G.W. Robinson	11	10.3					13-1
1964	**Team Spirit**		**Mr J.K. Goodman**	**Fulke Walwyn**	**G.W. Robinson**	**12**	**10.3**	**33**	**15**	**s**	**9.46 4/5**	**18-1**
	Purple Silk	1/2	Mr T. Beattie	—	J. Kenneally	9	10.4					100-6
	Peacetown	6	Mrs F. Williams	—	R. Edwards	10	10.1					40-1
	Eternal		Lt. Col, R. Fenwick-Palmer		Mr S. Davenport	13	10.2					66-1
1965	**Jay Trump**		**Mrs M. Stephenson**	**Fred Winter**	**Mr T.C. Smith**	**8**	**11.5**	**47**	**14**	**gd**	**9.30 3/5**	**100-6**
	Freddie	3/4	Mr R.R. Tweedie	—	P. McCarron	8	11.10					7-2fav
	Mr Jones	20	Mr C.D. Collins	—	Mr C.D. Collins	10	11.5					50-1
	Rainbow Battle		Mr W. Shand-Kydd	—	G. Milburn	9	10.13					50-1
1966	**Anglo**		**Mr S. Levy**	**Fred Winter**	**T. Norman**	**8**	**10.0**	**47**	**12**	**gd**	**9.52 4/5**	**50-1**
	Freddie	20	Mr R.R. Tweedie	—	P. McCarron	9	11.7					11-4fav
	Forest Prince	5	Mrs D. Thompson	—	G. Scott	8	10.8					100-7
	The Fossa		Mr R. Greatbach	—	T.W. Biddlecombe	9	10.8					20-1
1967	**Foinavon**		**Mr C.P.T. Watkins**	**John Kempton**	**J. Buckingham**	**9**	**10.0**	**44**	**18**	**gd**	**9.49 3/5**	**100-1**
	Honey End	15	Mr C. Pugh	—	J. Gifford	10	10.4					15-2fav
	Red Alligator	3	Mr J. Manners	—	B. Fletcher	8	10.0					30-1
	Greek Scholar		Mr J. Thornton Jnr.	—	T.W. Biddlecombe	8	10.9					20-1
1968	**Red Alligator**		**Mr J. Manners**	**Denys Smith**	**B. Fletcher**	**9**	**10.0**	**45**	**17**	**gd**	**9.28 4/5**	**100-7**
	Moidore's Token	20	Miss P. Harrower	—	B. Brogan	11	10.8					100-6
	Different Class	a neck	Mr Gregory Peck	—	D. Mould	8	11.5					17-2fav
	Rutherfords		Mr J. Bonnier	—	P. Buckley	8	10.6					100-9
1969	**Highland Wedding**		**Mr T.H. McCoy Jnr**	**Toby Balding**	**E. P. Harty**	**12**	**10.4**	**30**	**14**	**gd**	**9.30 4/5**	**100-9**
	Steel Bridge	12	Mr J.L. Drabble	—	R. Pitman	11	10.0					50-1
	Rondetto	1	Mr A.B. Mitchell	—	J. King	13	10.6					25-1
	The Beeches		Mr Paul Mellon	—	W. Rees	9	10.1					100-6
1970	**Gay Trip**		**Mr A.J. Chambers**	**Fred Rimell**	**P. Taaffe**	**8**	**11.5**	**28**	**7**	**g/f**	**9.38**	**15-1**
	Vulture	20	General R.K. Mellon	—	S. Barker	8	10.0					15-1
	Miss Hunter	1/2	Mrs W. Macauley	—	F. Shortt	9	10.0					33-1
	Dozo		Mrs E.W. Wetherill	—	E.P. Harty	9	10.4					100-8
1971	**Specify**		**Mr F.W. Pontin**	**John Sutcliffe**	**J. Cook**	**9**	**10.13**	**38**	**13**	**g/f**	**9. 34 1/5**	**28-1**
	Black Secret	a neck	Mrs J. Watney	—	Mr J. Dreaper	7	11.5					20-1
	Astbury	2 1/2	Mr B.P. Jenks	—	J. Bourke	8	10.0					33-1
	Bowgeeno		Mr V.T. Holt	—	G. Thorner	11	10.5					66-1

Year	Horse	Dist	Owner	Trainer	Jockey	Age	Weight	Ran	Fin	Going	Time	SP
1972	**Well To Do**		**Capt. T. Forster**	**Capt. Tim Forster**	**G. Thorner**	9	10.1	42	9	s	10.8⅘	**14-1**
	Gay Trip	2	Mr A.J. Chambers	—	T.W. Biddlecombe	10	11.9					12-1
	Black Secret**	3	Mrs J. Watney	—	S. Barker	8	11.2					14-1
	General Symons**		Mrs E.N. Newman	—	P. Kiely	9	10.0					40-1
	Astbury		Mr B.P. Jenks	—	J. Bourke	9	10.0					25-1
1973	**Red Rum**		**Mr N.H. Le Mare**	**Donald McCain**	**B. Fletcher**	8	10.5	38	8	f	9.19	**9-1jtfav**
	Crisp	¾	Sir Chester Manifold	—	R. Pitman	10	12.0					9-1jtfav
	L'Escargot	25	Mr R.R. Guest	—	T. Carberry	10	12.0					11-1
	Spanish Steps		Mr E.R. Courage	—	P. Blacker	10	11.13					16-1
1974	**Red Rum**		**Mr N.H. Le Mare**	**Donald McCain**	**B. Fletcher**	9	12.0	42	17	gd	9.20.3	**11-1**
	L'Escargot	7	Mr R.R. Guest	—	T. Carberry	11	11.13					17-2
	Charles Dickens	a short head	Lt. Col. P. Bengough	—	A. Turnell	10	10.0					50-1
	Spanish Steps		Mr E.R. Courage	—	W. Smith	11	11.9					15-1
1975	**L'Escargot**		**Mr R.R. Guest**	**Dan Moore**	**T. Carberry**	12	11.3	31	10	gd	9.31.1	**13-2**
	Red Rum	15	Mr N.H. Le Mare	—	B. Fletcher	10	12.0					7-2fav
	Spanish Steps	8	Mr E.R. Courage	—	W. Smith	12	10.3					20-1
	Money Market		Lord Chelsea	—	J. King	8	10.13					14-1
1976	**Rag Trade**		**Mr P.B. Raymond**	**Fred Rimell**	**J. Burke**	10	10.12	32	16	f	9.20.9	**14-1**
	Red Rum	2	Mr N.H. Le Mare	—	T. Stack	11	11.10					10-1
	Eyecatcher	8	Mr J.R. Bosley	—	B. Fletcher	10	10.7					28-1
	Barona		Mr W.H. Whitbread	—	P. Kelleway	10	10.6					7-1fav
1977	**Red Rum**		**Mr N.H. Le Mare**	**Donald McCain**	**T. Stack**	12	11.8	42	11	gd	9.30.3	**9-1**
	Churchtown Boy	25	Mssrs B. Arnold & J. Watkins		M. Blackshaw	10	10.0					20-1
	Eyecatcher	6	Mr J.R. Bosley	—	C. Read	11	10.1					18-1
	The Pilgarlic		Mrs G. Poole & Mr A. Poole									
1978	**Lucius**		**Mrs D.A. Whitaker**	**Gordon W. Richards**	**B.R. Davies**	9	10.9	37	15	f	9.33.9	**14-1**
	Sebastian V	½	Mr R.M.C. Jeffreys	—	R. Lamb	10	10.1					25-1
	Drumroan	a neck	Mrs G. St John Nolan	—	G. Newman	10	10.0					50-1
	Coolishall	2	Mr & Mrs P.W. Harris	—	M. O'Halloran	9	10.0					16-1
1979	**Rubstic**		**Mr J. Douglas**	**John Leadbetter**	**M. Barnes**	10	10.0	34	7	gd	9.52.9	**25-1**
	Zongalero	1½	Mr D. Montagu & Sir James Goldsmith		B.R. Davies	9	10.5					20-1
	Rough And Tumble	5	Mr L. Dormer	—	J. Francome	9	10.7					14-1

Year	Dist	Horse	Owner	Trainer	Jockey	Age	Wt	Ran	Fin	Going	Time	SP
		The Pilgarlic	Mrs G. Poole & Mr A. Poole	—	R.R. Evans	11	10.1					16-1
1980		**Ben Nevis**	**Mr R.C. Stewart Jnr**	**Capt. Tim Forster**	**Mr C. Fenwick**	12	10.12	30	4	hy	10.17.4	**40-1**
	20	Rough And Tumble	Mr L. Dormer	—	J. Francome	10	10.11					11-1
	10	The Pilgarlic	Mrs G. Poole & Mr A. Poole	—	R. Hyett	12	10.4					33-1
		Royal Stuart	Mr and Mrs J. Murray Begg	—	P. Blacker	9	10.10					20-1
1981		**Aldaniti**	**Mr S.N. J. Embiricos**	**Josh Gifford**	**R. Champion**	11	10.13	39	12	gd	9. 47.2	**10-1**
	4	Spartan Missile	Mr M. J. Thorne	—	Mr M.J. Thorne	9	11.5					8-1fav
	2	Royal Mail	Mr and Mrs J. Murray Begg	—	P. Blacker	11	11.7					16-1
		Three To One	Mr J.C. Manners & Mrs J.K.M. Oliver	—	Mr T.G. Dun	10	10.3					33-1
1982		**Grittar**	**Mr F.H. Gilman**	**Frank Gilman**	**Mr C. Saunders**	9	11.5	39	8	gd	9.12.6	**7-1fav**
	15	Hard Outlook	Lady Wates	—	A. Webber	11	10.1					50-1
	a dist.	Loving Words*	Mr A. Netley	—	R. Hoare	9	10.11					16-1
		Delmoss	Mr J. Goodman	—	W. Smith	12	10.3					50-1
1983		**Corbiere**	**Mr B.R.H. Burrough**	**Mrs Jenny Pitman**	**B. De Haan**	8	11.4	41	10	s	9, 47.4	**13-1**
	¾	Greasepaint	Mrs N. Todd	—	Mr C. Magnier	8	10.7					14-1
	20	Yer Man	Mr N. Keane	—	T.V. O'Connell	8	10.0					80-1
		Hallo Dandy	Mr R. Shaw	—	N. Doughty	8	10.1					60-1
1984		**Hallo Dandy**	**Mr R. Shaw**	**Gordon W. Richards**	**N. Doughty**	10	10.2	40	23	gd	9, 21.4	**13-1**
	4	Greasepaint	Mr M.J. Smurfit	—	T. Carmody	9	11.2					9-1fav
	1½	Corbiere	Mr B.R.H. Burrough	—	B De Haan	9	12.0					16-1
		Lucky Vane	Miss B. Swire	—	J. Burke	9	10.12					12-1
1985		**Last Suspect**	**Anne, Duchess of Westminster**	**Capt. Tim Forster**	**H. Davies**	11	10.5	40	11	g/s	9, 42.7	**50-1**
	1½	Mr Snugfit	Mr A. Greenwood	—	P. Tuck	8	10.0					12-1
	3	Corbiere	Mr B.R.H. Burrough	—	P. Scudamore	10	11.10					9-1
		Greasepaint	Mr M.J. Smurfit	—	T. Carmody	10	10.13					13-2 jtfav
1986		**West Tip**	**Mr P. Luff**	**Michael Oliver**	**R. Dunwoody**	9	10.11	40	17	g/s	9, 33	**15-2**
	2	Young Driver	Mr J.B. Russell	—	C. Grant	9	10.0					66-1
	20½	Classified	Cheveley Park Stud	—	S. Smith Eccles	10	10.3					22-1
	1½	Mr Snugfi	Mr T.P. Ramsden	—	P. Tuck	9	10.7					13-2fav

Year	Horse	Dist	Owner	Trainer	Jockey	Age	Wt (st.lb)	Ran	Fin	Going	Time	SP
1987	Maori Venture		Mr H.J. Joel	Andrew Turnell	S.C. Knight	11	10.13	40	22	gd	9.19.3	28-1
	The Tsarevich	5	Major I.C. Straker		J. White	11	10.5					20-1
	Lean Ar Aghaidh	4	Mrs W. Tulloch		G. Landau	10	10.0					14-1
	West Tip		Mr P. Luff		R. Dunwoody	10	11.7					5-1 fav
1988	Rhyme 'N' Reason		Miss Juliet E. Reed	David Elsworth	B. Powell	9	11.0	40	9	g/s	9.53.5	10-1
	Durham Edition	4	Mr R. Oxley		C. Grant	10	10.9					20-1
	Monanore	15	Full Circle Thoroughbreds D Pic		T.J. Taaffe	11	10.4					33-1
	West Tip	8	Mr P Luff		R. Dunwoody	11	11.7					11-1
1989	Little Polveir		Mr E. Harvey	Toby Balding	J. Frost	12	10.3	40	14	hy	10.6.9	28-1
	West Tip	7	Mr P. Luff		R. Dunwoody	12	10.11					12-1
	The Thinker	1½	T. McDonagh Ltd		S. Sherwood	11	11.10					10-1
	Lastofthebrownies	6	Mrs A. Daly		T. Carmody	9	10.0					16-1
1990	Mr Frisk		Mrs H.J.Duffey	Kim Bailey	Mr M. Armytage	11	10.6	38	20	f	8.47.8	16-1
	Durham Edition	¾	Mr R. Oxkey		C. Grant	12	10.9					9-1
	Rinus	20	Mr A. Proos		N. Doughty	9	10.4					13-1
	Brown Windsor	12	Mr W. Shand Kydd		J. White	8	10.10					7-1fav
1991	Seagram		Sir Eric Parker & Mr D.H. Barons	David Barons	N. Hawke	11	10.6	40	17	g/s	9.29.9	12-1
	Garrison Savannah	5	Autofour Engineering		M. Pitman	8	11.1					7-1
	Auntie Dot	8	Mrs R. Wilson		M. Dwyer	10	10.4					50-1
	Over The Road		Mr J. Upson		R. Supple	10	10.0					50-1
1992	Party Politics		Mrs D. Thompson	Nick Gaselee	C. Llewellyn	8	10.7	40	22	g/s	9.6.4	14-1
	Romany King	2½	Mr. L. Garrett		R. Guest	8	10.3					16-1
	Laura's Beau	15	Mr J. McManus		C. O'Dwyer	8	10.0					12-1
	Docklands Express	8	Mr R. Baines		P. Scudamore	10	11.2					15-2
1993 RACE VOID	Esha Ness		Mr P. Bancroft	Mrs Jenny Pitman	J. White	10	10.0	39	7	g/f	9.1.4	50-1
	Cahervillahow		Mrs M. Valentine		C. Swan	9	10.11					25 1
	Romany King		Mr U. Schwarzenbach		A. Maguire	9	10.7					15-2
	The Committee		Corcrain Enterprises Ltd		N. Williamson	10	10.0					25-1
1994	Miinnehoma		Mr Freddie Starr	Martin Pipe	R. Dunwoody	11	10.8	36	6	hy	10.18.8	16-1
	Just So	1¼	Mr H. Cole		S. Burrough	11	10.3					20-1
	Moorcroft Boy	20	Mr K. Manley		A. Maguire	9	10.0					5-1 fav.
	Ebony Jane		Mr J. Lynch		L. Cusack	9	10.1					25-1

Year	Horse	Dist.	Owner	Trainer	Jockey	Age	Wt	Ran	Fin	Going	Time	SP
1995	**Royal Athlete**		**Gary & Libby Johnson**	**Mrs Jenny Pitman**	**J.F. Titley**	12	10.6	35	15	gd	9.4.1	**40-1**
	Party Politics	7	Mrs D. Thompson		M. Dwyer	11	10.2					16-1
	Over The Deel	6	Mr G. Tobitt		Mr C. Bonner	9	10.0					100-1
	Dubacilla	½	Mr H. Cole		D. Gallagher	9	11.0					9-1
1996	**Rough Quest**		**Mr A.T.A. Wates**	**Terry Casey**	**M.A. Fitzgerald**	10	10.7	27	17	gd	9.0.8	**7-1fav**
	Encore Un Peu	1¼	Mr V. Nally		D. Bridgwater	9	10.0					14-1
	Superior Finish	16	Mr P. McGrane		R. Dunwoody	10	10.3					9-1
	Sir Peter Lely	a short head	J. Doyle Ltd.		Mr C. Bonner	9	10.0					33-1
1997	**Lord Gyllene**		**Sir Stanley Clarke**	**Steve Brookshaw**	**A. Dobbin**	9	10.0	36	17	gd	9.5.9	**14-1**
	Suny Bay	25	Uplands Bloodstock		J. Osborne	8	10.3					8-1
	Camelot Knight	2	Mr M. Gates		C. Llewellyn	11	10.0					100-1
	Buckboard Bounce	1¼	Sir Robert Ogden		P. Carberry	11	10.1					40-1
1998	**Earth Summit**		**Summit Partners Two**	**Nigel Twiston-Davies**	**C. Llewellyn**	10	10.5	37	6	hy	10.51.5	**7-1fav**
	Suny Bay	11	Uplands Bloodstock		G. Bradley	9	12.0					11-1
	Samlee	a dist.	White Lion Partnership		R. Dunwoody	9	10.1					8-1
	St Mellion	1¼	St. Mellion Estates Ltd		A. Thornton	9	10.1					20-1
	Fairway											
1999	**Bobbyjo**		**Mr. R. Burke**	**Thomas Carberry**	**P. Carberry**	9	10.0	32	18	gd	9.14.1	**10-1**
	Blue Charm	10	Mrs S. Bradburne		L. Wyer	9	10.0					25-1
	Call It A Day	a neck	Mr D. Nicholson		R. Dunwoody	9	10.2					25-1
	Addington Boy	1¼	Mr F. Murphy		A. Maguire	11	10.7					7-1jtfav
2000	**Papillon**		**Mrs J. Maxwell Moran**	**Ted Walsh**	**R. Walsh**	9	10.12	40	17	gd	9.9.7	**10-1**
	Mely Moss	1¼	Mr D. Mercer		N. Williamson	9	10.1					25-1
	Nikki Dee	12	Mr G. Dilger		R. Supple	10	10.13					25-1
	Brave Highlander	7	Mr S. Embiricos		P. Hide	12	10.0					50-1
2001	**Red Marauder**		**Mr N. Mason**	**Norman Mason**	**R. Guest**	10	10.11	40	4	hy	11.0.1	**33-1**
	Smarty	a dist.	Mrs T. Brown		T.J. Murphy	8	10.0					16-1
	Blowing Wind *	a dist.	Mr P. Deal		A.P. McCoy	8	10.9					16-1
	Papillon*		Mrs J. Maxwell Moran		R. Walsh	10	11.5					14-1
2002	**Bindaree**		**Mr H. Mould**	**Nigel Twiston-Davies**	**J.Culloty**	8	10.4	40	11	gd	9.9	**20-1**
	What's Up Boys	1¼	R.J.B. Partners		R. Johnson	8	11.6					10-1
	Blowing Wind	27	Mr P. Deal		A.P. McCoy	9	10.6					8-1fav
	Kingsmark	9	Sir Robert Ogden		R. Walsh	9	11.9					16-1

Year	Horse	Owner	Trainer	Jockey	Age	Wt	Ran		Going	Time	SP
2003	**Monty's Pass**	**Dee Racing Syndicate**	**James J.Mangan**	**B.J. Geraghty**	**10**	**10.7**	**40**	**14**	**gd**	**9.21.7**	**16 1**
	Supreme Glory 12	Mr C. Moorsom	—	L. Aspell	10	10.2					40-1
	Amberleigh House 2	Halewood International Ltd	—	G. Lee	11	10.4					33-1
	Gunner Welburn 14	Mr W. Ritson and Mr D. Hall	—	B. Fenton	11	10.2					16-1
2004	**Amberleigh House**	**Halewood International Ltd**	**Donald McCain**	**G. Lee**	**12**	**10.10**	**39**	**11**	**gd**	**9.20.30**	**16 1**
	Clan Royal 3	J.P. McManus	—	L. Cooper	9	10.5					10-1
	Lord Atterbury 2	Mr D. Johnson	—	M. Bradburne	8	10.1					40-1
	Monty's Pass 29	Dee Racing Syndicate	—	B.J. Geraghty	1	11.10					20-1
2005	**Hedgehunter**	**Mr Trevor Hemmings**	**Willie Mullins**	**R. Walsh**	**9**	**11.1**	**40**	**21**	**g/s**	**9. 20.8**	**7-1fav**
	Royal Auclair 14	Mr C. Smith	—	C. Williams	8	11.10					40-1
	Simply Gifted a head	Mr S. Hammond	—	B. Harding	10	10.6					66-1
	It Takes Time 4	Mr D. Johnson	—	T. J. Murphy	11	10.11					18-1
2006	**Numbersix-** **valverde**	**Mr O. Carroll**	**Martin Brassil**	**N.P. Madden**	**10**	**10.8**	**40**	**9**	**g/s**	**9. 41**	**11-1**
	Hedgehunter 6	Mr Trevor Hemmings	—	R. Walsh	10	11.12					5-1jtfav
	Clan Roya 1¼	Mr J.P. McManus	—	A.P. McCoy	11	10.10					5-1jtfav
	Nil Desperandum a short head	Mr M.L. Shone	—	T.P. Treacy	9	10.7					33-1
2007	**Silver Birch**	**Mr B. Walsh**	**Gordon Elliott**	**R.M. Power**	**10**	**10.6**	**40**	**12**	**gd**	**9.13.6**	**33-1**
	McKelvey ¾	Mr N. Elliott	—	T.J. O'Brien	8	10.4					12-1
	Slim Pickings 1¼	Doubtful Five Syndicate	—	B.J. Geraghty	8	10.8					33-1
	Philson Run 15	Gale Force One	—	D. Jacob	11	10.5					100-1

aged = a horse over six years old but of unspecified age

* = remounted

** = dead heat third